The Earlier Letters *of* John Stuart Mill 1812-1848

Edited by

FRANCIS E. MINEKA
The Class of 1916 Professor of English
Cornell University

With an Introduction by

F. A. Hayek, F.B.A.
University of Freiburg i.B.

UNIVERSITY OF TORONTO PRESS
ROUTLEDGE & KEGAN PAUL

London: Routledge & Kegan Paul
Reprinted 1964 in the U.S.A.
Reprinted in paperback 2015

ISBN 978-0-8020-5123-3 (cloth)
ISBN 978-1-4426-3148-9 (paper)

The profile of John Stuart Mill is reproduced from the medallion by Alphonse Legros presented to the Manchester City Art Gallery by the artist.

COLLECTED WORKS OF JOHN STUART MILL

VOLUMES XII – XIII

The Earlier Letters of John Stuart Mill 1812-1848

Edited by FRANCIS E. MINEKA

THESE VOLUMES of Mill's letters have been awaited eagerly by all scholars in the field of nineteenth-century studies. They inaugurate most auspiciously the edition of the Collected Works of John Stuart Mill planned and directed by an editorial committee appointed from the Faculty of Arts and Science of the University of Toronto and from the University of Toronto Press.

In this collection of 537 letters and excerpts of letters are included all the personal letters available. It contains 238 hitherto unpublished letters and 72 letters with previously unpublished passages. Letters previously published have been recollated whenever possible. All are meticulously edited and annotated.

The letters of these two volumes provide invaluable material for a study of Mill before the publication in 1848 of the *Principles of Political Economy,* when he became a widely recognized public figure and his correspondence took on more of a public character. By 1848, too, were virtually completed most of the correspondences with the friends and intimates of his youth and early manhood: Carlyle, John Sterling, J. P. Nichol, Gustave d'Eichthal, Auguste Comte, Alexis de Tocqueville, Robert Barclay Fox, W. J. Fox, John and Sarah Austin. These series of letters constitute the best supplement to the most interesting and moving sections of Mill's *Autobiography,* for they reveal many sides of his intellectual and emotional development during the formative and most productive years of his life.

FRANCIS E. MINEKA is The Class of 1916 Professor of English, Cornell University. Before joining the Cornell faculty, he had taught chiefly at Hamilton College and the University of Texas. At Cornell he has served as Chairman of the Department of English (1948-57) and as Dean of the College of Arts and Sciences (1957-62). He is the author of *The Dissidence of Dissent: The Monthly Repository, 1806–1838* (1944), a co-editor of *Masters of British Literature* (1958), and has contributed to various professional journals. He was awarded Guggenheim and Fulbright fellowships for 1962–63 to collect and edit the later (1849–73) letters of Mill, eventually to be published in the Collected Works.

The Collected Edition of the works of John Stuart Mill has been planned and is being directed by an editorial committee appointed from the Faculty of Arts and Science of the University of Toronto, and from the University of Toronto Press. The primary aim of the edition is to present fully collated texts of those works which exist in a number of versions, both printed and manuscript, and to provide accurate texts of works previously unpublished or which have become relatively inaccessible.

TO THE MEMBERS OF

THE CORNELL UNIVERSITY CLASS OF 1916

Preface

CREDIT FOR THE CONCEPTION of this edition belongs to Professor F. A. Hayek, who while a member of the faculty of the London School of Economics nearly twenty years ago began an organized effort to assemble the widely scattered early letters of John Stuart Mill. At that time the only collected edition of Mill's correspondence was the one edited by Hugh S. R. Elliot which was published in 1910. It contained 268 letters, largely from the last twenty-five years of Mill's life; only fifty-two of the letters were from the period covered by the present edition. A considerable number of the early letters had been published elsewhere, but in no one place could one find the correspondence for the period of Mill's life to which approximately three-fourths of his *Autobiography* is devoted.

Professor Hayek's decision to assemble as complete a collection as possible through the year 1848 was wholly sound. In that year, with the publication of *Principles of Political Economy*, Mill became a widely recognized public figure, and his correspondence thereafter often took on much more of a public character as his advice and his opinions were sought by correspondents from all over the civilized world. By 1848, also, were virtually completed most of the correspondences with the friends and intimates of his youth and early manhood, with Thomas Carlyle, John Sterling, J. P. Nichol, Robert Barclay Fox, W. J. Fox, Gustave d'Eichthal, Auguste Comte, Alexis de Tocqueville, and John and Sarah Austin. These series of letters constitute the best supplement to the most interesting and moving sections of Mill's *Autobiography*, for they reveal many sides of Mill's intellectual and emotional development during the formative and most productive years of his life.

These were the years of which he later said, in commenting on his early reaction against orthodox Benthamism, "I found the fabric of my old and taught opinions giving way in many fresh places, and I never allowed it to fall to pieces, but was incessantly occupied in weaving it anew." The new strands in the fabric were by no means wholly of British origin, though Mill acknowledged the importance of Wordsworth, Coleridge, and Carlyle in the reshaping of many of his views. The imported strands came in part from Germany (usually somewhat transmuted in the writings of Carlyle, Coleridge, and Coleridge's disciple, John Sterling), but more significantly from France. Most important were the strands emanating from the Saint-

Simonians (as seen in the correspondence with D'Eichthal) and from the positivism of Comte and the critical views of democracy held by Tocqueville.

Mill was not engaged solely in reweaving the fabric of his opinions during these years, however; he was also busily engaged in trying to influence the opinions of others. For five years he edited a radical quarterly, the *London and Westminster Review*, and during that same time he worked behind the scenes to force the Radicals in Parliament into concerted action. The letters between 1835 and 1840 present the best picture available of his activities as an editor and of his hopes and frustrations as a thwarted politician.

Little will be found in the present edition, however, to throw more light upon one of the major influences in Mill's life between 1831 and 1848—that of Mrs. Taylor. I have included the two letters of this period by Mill to Mrs. Taylor which Professor Hayek first published in his *John Stuart Mill and Harriet Taylor: Their Friendship and Subsequent Marriage* (1951), but no additional letters to Mrs. Taylor before 1849 have been found.

The 534 letters and excerpts of letters published herein comprise all the personal letters that I have been able to find, except that I have excluded a small number of undated and undatable short notes of little significance. No effort has been made to include the letters written for publication in newspapers, which are listed in the *Bibliography of the Published Writings of John Stuart Mill* edited by Ney MacMinn, J. R. Hainds, and James McNab McCrimmon (1945), nor to include official letters written by Mill in carrying out his duties at the East India Company.

All fifty-two of the letters before 1849 published by Elliot, including eighteen to Carlyle, eighteen to John Sterling, and six to Edward Lytton Bulwer, have been re-collated wherever possible and for the first time annotated. Included also are some other series of Mill's early letters that had been published before the appearance of Elliot's edition: twenty to Gustave d'Eichthal, edited by Eugène d'Eichthal; twelve to John Pringle Nichol, edited by William Knight; twenty-one to John Robertson, edited by Mrs. G. D. M. Towers; forty-four to Auguste Comte, edited by Lucien Lévy-Bruhl; fifteen to Robert Barclay Fox, edited by H. N. Pym; nine to Macvey Napier edited by the latter's son; and eighteen letters and excerpts from letters, largely to Mill's family, included by Alexander Bain in his life of Mill.

Several other series were published after Elliot's edition appeared: thirteen letters to W. J. Fox in Richard Garnett's life of Fox; nine to George Henry Lewes in Anna T. Kitchel's *George Lewes and George Eliot*; and fourteen to Alexis de Tocqueville edited by J.-P. Mayer in his collected edition of Tocqueville's work. All have been re-collated wherever the originals have been available.

Mill's letters to John Pringle Nichol have not been found, and the text of these is that published by William Knight. The text of the letters to Tocqueville is reproduced from J.-P. Mayer's edition of the works of Tocqueville and has not been re-collated, though additional annotation has been provided. Even very brief published excerpts from otherwise unlocated letters have been included, in the hope that they may provide clues to the eventual finding of the originals.

It has been possible to add a good many as yet unpublished letters to the various series published by Elliot and others—notably letters to Carlyle, D'Eichthal, R. B. Fox, W. J. Fox, and Napier. A number of additional series, of which hitherto either none or only a scattered few had been published, appear in print for the first time: letters to Edwin Chadwick, Albany Fonblanque, John and Sarah Austin, Joseph Blanco White, William Tait, Aristide Guilbert, Henry S. Chapman, John Mitchel Kemble, Henry Cole, and Sir John F. W. Herschel. In all, this edition contains 238 hitherto unpublished letters and 72 letters which have previously unpublished passages.

While Professor Hayek was chiefly responsible for the assembling of the letters, the work of editing and annotating has been mine. The method I have followed in preparing the text has been to reproduce the original as closely as possible, and I have rarely yielded to the temptation to insert a bracketed *sic*. I have silently transferred in a relatively small number of letters dates and addresses from the end to the heading of the letter. In rare instances only has punctuation been inserted and then the insertion has been noted. Mill's letters in French are presented as they were written; errors have not been corrected and obsolete spellings have not been modernized. The text of his letters to Comte has been collated with the originals in the Library of the Johns Hopkins University; the text of Lévy-Bruhl's edition differs in paragraphing, punctuation, and spelling from that of the original letters, though in other respects it is very accurate.

The first note to each letter provides the following information: the location of the manuscript when it is known (some transcribed by Professor Hayek as early as 1943 cannot now be located); addresses and postmarks where they have been available; the place of publication of previously published letters. If no printed source is indicated, the letter, to the best of my knowledge, has hitherto been unpublished. Except for several letters published in full by Michael Packe in his biography of Mill, no mention has been made of excerpts published by him, since he had full access to Professor Hayek's collection. The editor has located over sixty additional letters since the publication of Mr. Packe's biography.

A good deal of effort has been expended upon dating as accurately as possible letters not dated by Mill. Sometimes it has been possible to do such dating by means of external evidence that is corroborative of details in the letter (e.g., Letters 11 and 382); at other times I have had to depend solely on internal evidence. In some instances previously published letters (e.g., Letters 47 and 96) were incorrectly dated, and corrections have had to be made.

Recipients of letters and names of persons mentioned have normally been identified only on the occasion of their first appearance in the letters. To avoid the necessity of an over-abundance of cross-references, an extensive name and subject index is provided. The page reference set in bold type after an indexed name indicates the location of the identifying note. Authors of books mentioned in the letters usually have not been otherwise identified.

While I have made some successful efforts to enlarge Professor Hayek's original collection, I am by no means assured that additional early letters may not yet make their appearance. In fact, I hope that the publication of this edition will bring to light many more. Efforts to trace many once in the possession, for instance, of Alexander Bain, the first biographer of Mill, have proved thus far unavailing. I should appreciate receiving information of any uncollected Mill letters, since I am planning, in collaboration with Professor Dwight N. Lindley of Hamilton College, an edition of the later (1849–1873) letters. If additional early letters come out of hiding, it may be possible to include them in an appendix to the later letters.

There remains the pleasant task of acknowledging generous help from many persons and institutions. Professor Hayek in his Introduction to this edition has acknowledged some of his indebtednesses during the period when he was collecting the letters. Since he has turned over to me all his extensive correspondence relating to the collecting, it is incumbent upon me to acknowledge on his behalf—and my own—major contributions during that period by the following persons: W. H. Browning, W. C. Dickinson, the late Mrs. Vera Eichelbaum, Miss Philippa G. Fawcett, J. L. Harlan, the late Norman E. Himes, the late Lord Keynes, J. A. La Nauze, Ney MacMinn, J. M. McCrimmon, Emery Neff, A. M. Carr Saunders, Hill Shine, the Right Rev. Charles L. Street, Jacob Viner, and Gordon Waterfield. In addition many individuals, too numerous to mention here, generously answered queries and offered useful suggestions.

My own debts incurred since I took over in 1953 the task of editing the letters have likewise been many. In efforts to enlarge Professor Hayek's collection I have been aided by H. L. Beales, Joseph Hamburger, Peter M. Jackson, Cecil Lang, J.-P. Mayer, Anna J. Mill, James M. Osborn, John M.

Robson, Henry Siegel, Jack Stillinger, and William E. S. Thomas. Alice Kaminsky, Dwight N. Lindley, Emily Morrison, and Robert Scholes have provided me at various times with valuable research and editorial assistance. Among my colleagues at Cornell I have received generous help in spotting allusions and tracing quotations from M. H. Abrams, Robert M. Adams, Harry Caplan, David Davis, J.-J. Demorest, Ephim G. Fogel, and Gordon Kirkwood, and from a former colleague, Luitpold Wallach. Professor John M. Robson of the University of Toronto by his critical reading of the manuscript at a late stage gave me the benefit of his extensive knowledge of Mill, thereby considerably improving the edition. A former graduate student of mine, Dr. Eileen Curran, collated some letters for me and supplied useful information from her detailed knowledge of the history of English periodicals. George H. Healey and Felix Reichmann of the Cornell University Library staff have been unfailingly helpful. Mertie Decker and Eleanor Rosica have typed what must have seemed to them endless numbers of pages of manuscript. Among British librarians I have been chiefly indebted to Mr. G. Woledge and Mr. C. G. Allen of the British Library of Political and Economic Science of the London School of Economics, to Mr. A. N. L. Munby of the Library of King's College, Cambridge, and to J. S. Ritchie of the National Library of Scotland. J.-P. Mayer and his publishers (the Librairie Gallimard) have granted me permission to reprint the letters of Mill in the copyrighted edition of the works of Alexis de Tocqueville. Indebtedness to the many libraries which possess the originals of these letters is recorded in the notes to the letters, but I should like to express here in particular my thanks to the four libraries which have by far the largest holdings: those of The Johns Hopkins University, the London School of Economics, the National Library of Scotland, and Yale University. I acknowledge also with gratitude a Faculty Research Grant from Cornell University and funds for travel and research from the endowment provided by the Cornell Class of 1916 for the Professorship which I have the honour to hold.

Professor Hayek at the close of his Introduction implies that in this project the fun was all his, but the hard work, mine. I can only say that I have deeply appreciated the opportunity he gave me to do the work. I have had fun too.

FRANCIS E. MINEKA

Cornell University
September 1, 1962

The hope expressed in the foregoing Preface that more of Mill's earlier letters can still be located has been in small part fulfilled by the addition of three letters that have come to light while this edition was in process.

Since pagination was already completed at this point, the three letters have been added at the end of the second volume (Volume XIII of the Collected Works) and assigned numbers appropriate to their place in the sequence. References to these additional letters have been included in the Index.

F.E.M.

May 15, 1963

Contents

Contents

Introduction

BY F. A. HAYEK

JOHN STUART MILL has not been altogether fortunate in the manner in which his memory was served by those most concerned and best authorized to honour it. It is true that his stepdaughter, heir, and literary executor, Helen Taylor, promptly published the *Autobiography*, which chiefly determined the picture posterity formed of Mill, and that the only other manuscript ready for publication was also rapidly printed. But during the next forty years, while Mill's fame persisted undiminished, little was done either to make his literary work more readily accessible or his other activities better known. There are few figures of comparable standing whose works have had to wait nearly a hundred years for a collected edition in English to be published. Nor, while his reputation was at its height, did any significant information become available that would have enabled another hand to round off the somewhat angular and fragmentary picture Mill had given of himself. He had been quite aware that his more public activities would be of interest to later generations and had begun to mark some of the copies of his letters which he had kept as suitable for publication. But Helen Taylor appears increasingly to have been more concerned to prevent others from encroaching upon her proprietary rights than to push on with her own plans for publication. It was only when the material so jealously guarded by her finally passed to one of Mrs. Mill's granddaughters, Mary Taylor, that an outsider was called in to publish some of the more readily accessible correspondence. Again, however, Mary Taylor reserved to herself part of the task which she was hardly qualified to carry out and in fact did not bring to completion. When at last after her death the papers in her possession became generally accessible, interest in Mill seems to have been at a low point and those papers were allowed to be widely dispersed. Nothing illustrates better the temporary eclipse of his fame than that some of the institutions which then acquired important parts of these papers did not trouble to catalogue them for another fifteen years.

It would seem that at least in his native country, during the period between the two great wars, Mill was regarded as one of those outmoded figures of the recent past whose ideas have ceased to be interesting because they have become commonplace. Most of the battles he fought had been won and to many of those who knew his name he probably appeared as a somewhat dim figure whose *On Liberty* they had been made to read at school but whose "Victorian" outlook had lost most of its appeal. There was, perhaps, also some suspicion that his reputation had been somewhat exaggerated and that he had not been a great original genius but rather an honest, hardworking, and lucid expositor of ideas that other and greater minds had originated. He even came to be regarded, very unjustly, as the last of the "orthodox" tradition in economics and politics. In fact, however, few men have done more to create the intellectual climate in which most of what he stood for was finally taken for granted.

The gradual but steady revival of the interest in John Stuart Mill in the course of the last twenty years is based on a truer understanding of the significance of his work.[1] Though nothing could be more misleading than to represent him as a "typical" Victorian or a "typical" Englishman (he certainly was neither), he was one of the most representative figures of the changes of thought that were germinating during his lifetime. During the forty years after his death he governed liberal thought as did no other man, and as late as 1914 he was still the chief source of inspiration of the progressive part of the intellectuals of the West—of the men whose dream of an indefinitely peaceful progress and expansion of Western civilization was shattered by the cataclysms of war and revolution. But even to that development Mill had unquestionably contributed by his sympathies for the rising aspirations of national self-determination and of socialism. His reputation declined with the confidence in the steady advance of civilization in which he had believed, and for a time the kind of minds who had believed in him were attracted by more revolutionary thinkers.

It must probably still be admitted that it is not so much for the originality of his thinking as for its influence on a world now past that Mill is chiefly of importance today. We may still discover that he is a better guide to many of our present problems than is generally appreciated. But there can be no question that his influence is such that to the historian of thought all information we have about Mill's activities, his contacts, and about the channels through which ideas reached him and through which he acted upon others is nearly as important as his published work. This is particularly true of a man like Mill who strove to keep his mind open to new ideas but upon whom accident and personal idiosyncrasies nevertheless acted to decide in some measure what would and what would not enter his system of thought.

The present volume contains some of the most important sources of

1. This new interest is by no means confined to the Western world. A bibliography of John Stuart Mill, published in *Keizai Ronshu, The Economic Review of Kansai University* (Osaka), VI, no. 7 (Nov., 1956), lists, in addition to about 350 works about Mill in European languages, over 180 in the Japanese language alone!

information we have on all the different spheres of Mill's activities. The work on the collection of these letters started about the same time as the new interest in Mill began to make itself felt but for reasons presently to be explained, publication has been long delayed. Some of the early results of these efforts have however already been used in various contributions to our knowledge of Mill which have appeared during this period, particularly in Mr. Michael Packe's vivid *Life of John Stuart Mill* (1954). The following brief account of the circumstances which led to the present edition may be found useful.

Although more than fifty years ago there were published two volumes of *Letters of John Stuart Mill*, edited by Hugh S. R. Elliot, these were in the main confined to the last twenty-five years of Mill's life. Of the earlier and most productive period the edition contained only three series of letters which happened to have been returned to Mill or his heirs. Many more belonging to this period have been published in some thirty different places, while an even larger number of unpublished letters was found to be dispersed among many private and public collections.

This unsatisfactory state of affairs, of which every student of nineteenth-century ideas must soon become aware, induced me nearly twenty years ago to attempt to bring together the main body of Mill's early correspondence as a supplement to the existing collection. This soon proved a much bigger task than I had anticipated and a task, moreover, which in one sense I had started too late and in another sense too early. Eighteen or even thirteen years earlier I should still have found together all or at least part of Mill's own papers which in the meantime had been dispersed; and as it soon appeared, much important information had been destroyed by fire during the bombing of London only a few months before I started my work. On the other hand, wartime conditions in England made inaccessible for the next five years some of the material that had to be examined. In the circumstances I carried the task of collection as far as was then possible, but had in the late forties to postpone its completion, first temporarily and then, consequent upon my move from London to Chicago, indefinitely. By then I had completed the editing of one rather special set of Mill's letters which, for reasons explained in the Introduction to the edition published in 1951 (*John Stuart Mill and Harriet Taylor: Their Friendship and Subsequent Marriage* [London and Chicago, 1951]) seemed to demand separate treatment. That experience taught me that if I was not for years to abandon all my other work I could not adequately perform the same task for the complete collection. I was therefore only too grateful when not long after, an expert in the field, Professor Francis E. Mineka of Cornell University, agreed to assume responsibility for that arduous task.

The editing of the present volume is entirely his and in the course of this work he has also been able to add to the collection of transcripts I had assembled over sixty additional hitherto unpublished letters by Mill.

It may be useful if, before commenting on the character of the present volumes, I give a brief account of the fate of the books and papers which were in Mill's possession at the time of his death, so far as this became known in the course of the search for his letters. Mill died on May 7, 1873, at Avignon, where for the preceding fifteen years he had spent much of his time in the house he had bought to be near his wife's grave.[2] His step-daughter and sole heir, Helen Taylor, continued to live there most of the time for another thirty years, jealously guarding her exclusive rights to all of Mill's literary remains and steadfastly refusing requests for permission to publish any of his letters. The draft of a letter of hers written not long after Mill's death (on the back of a letter addressed to her, dated July 30, 1873) shows that she was then contemplating publication of some of his letters:

> I have all my dear stepfather's letters, preserved, looked through from time to time by himself, arranged in order by myself, and left by him in my hands with directions, verbal and written, to deal with them according to my judgement. When the more pressing task of the publication of his MSS. is completed, I shall, if I live, occupy myself with his correspondence, if I do not live it will be for my literary Executors to decide what to do with it.[3]

It seems that by "all [her] dear stepfather's letters" she meant no more than the drafts he had begun to keep from about 1848 or 1849. But she did make some efforts to recover from the heirs of his correspondents sets of earlier letters in exchange for those written to him and it was probably in this manner that the letters to Sterling and Bulwer included in the Elliot edition came to be among the Mill papers.

Nothing came of Helen Taylor's plans for publication and the Mill papers rested at the Avignon cottage until 1904, when Helen Taylor's niece Mary Taylor (the younger daughter of Mrs. Mill's son Algernon) succeeded in persuading the old lady, who at seventy-three appears to have been somewhat peculiar and senile, to return to England. Early in 1905 a friend of Mary Taylor's (Mary Ann Trimble, who earlier had spent some time at Avignon with Mary Taylor) returned to Avignon and, with the assistance of a married couple who had accompanied her from England

2. As I am revising this Introduction for publication (January, 1962) I learn that last autumn this house, visited by so many admirers of John Stuart Mill, was torn down, the operations actually beginning while a committee formed to assure its preservation and conversion into a museum was holding its first meeting!

3. The Mill-Taylor Collection, British Library of Political and Economic Science (London School of Economics), vol. 53.

(according to a diary Mary Taylor kept at the time) did there "the work of three months in three weeks. Half a ton of letters to be sorted, all manner of rubbish to be separated from useful things, books to be dusted and selected from, arrangements to be made for sale, and 18 boxes to be packed."[4]

A considerable part of Mill's library and at least some of his papers were disposed of at a sale held at Avignon from May 21 to 28, 1905.[5] Some of the manuscripts were acquired by a local bookseller, Romanille, from whom at least one bound volume was bought by an American scholar,[6] while a London clergyman bought a manuscript entitled "On Social Freedom" which he published (reputedly with the consent of Helen Taylor, who had died a few months before it appeared) as a posthumous work of Mill in the *Oxford and Cambridge Review* of June, 1907, and which was republished in book form under Mill's name as late as 1941, though it now appears that it was not a work by Mill but a manuscript sent to Mill for his opinion by one of his admirers.[7]

On their return to England Helen Taylor had been taken by her niece to Devon, where she died at Torquay on January 29, 1907. As she appears, in the words of the younger woman, long before that time to have "lost her memory to a great extent," all business, even the signing of legal documents, was conducted on her behalf by Mary Taylor. One of the first steps taken by the latter soon after the return to England was, on the advice of John Morley, to give that part of Mill's and Helen Taylor's library which had been stored in London to Somerville College (one of the women's colleges at Oxford). Miss Taylor retained a few books and Somerville College was to be entitled to dispose of what it did not want and in the course of 1906 actually sold some of the books.[8]

4. *Ibid.*, vol. 58.

5. The manuscripts mentioned in the two following notes which are known to derive from this sale bear a printed label inside the front cover which states "De la bibliothèque de / John Stuart Mill / Vendue à Avignon / les 21, 23, 24, 26, 27, 28 Mai 1905." Some at least of the books are reported to have been bought by the poet Paul Mariéton and to have been left by him to the library at Avignon (see Jules Véran, "Le Souvenir de Stuart Mill à Avignon," *Revue des deux mondes*, septembre 1937), but attempts by several persons to find them there have failed.

6. This volume of manuscripts of various minor published works by Mill was bought by Professor George Herbert Palmer of Harvard University and given by him to the library of his University where it is now preserved in the Houghton Library, classed as "MS Eng 1105."

7. See the article by Jules Véran cited in note 5 above, and, for the evidence showing that the manuscript is not by Mill, J. C. Rees, *Mill and His Early Critics* (Leicester: University College, 1956).

8. There was also a story current in London twenty years ago that some of Mill's books had been given at some time to Morley College (a workingmen's college in the South of London); but though the library of that institution escaped when the main building was destroyed by bombs, no such books can be traced now, and unless they

It seems that shortly after Helen Taylor's death Mary Taylor placed the collection of Mill's correspondence in the hand of Mr. Hugh S. R. Elliot. Little is known about him or the authority he was given and the fragments of information we have about the proceedings are somewhat puzzling. There is extant an account by Mr. Elliot of his relations to Mary Taylor[9] from which the following passages may be quoted:

As to the private letters of Mill to his wife & daughter, we hesitated for a very long time about them; but Miss Taylor, who is a lady of very peculiar ideas and habits, did not wish them to be published. She has it in her mind to bring out another volume in a few years' time, consisting exclusively of Mill's letters to his wife, daughter, and sisters; but wants to delay this until the last of Mill's sisters[10] is dead. Whether it will ever be done I cannot say. She guards the letters very jealously; and it was only after much pressure and persuasion that I was allowed to see them at all.

As to her published introduction, following mine in the book, it was entirely an afterthought. In the study of the private letters, I formed a very unfavourable opinion both of Mrs. Mill and of Miss Helen Taylor. It appeared to me that they were both selfish and somewhat conceited women, and that Mill (who must have been a very poor judge of character) was largely deceived with regard to them. Of course I could not state my views openly in a book which is published by Miss Mary Taylor at her own expense. But in my original introduction, I found it impossible to allude to the women without unconsciously conveying into my language some suggestion of what I thought. To this Miss Mary Taylor took the strongest possible exception. I reconsidered the whole matter, but found myself unable to speak any more favourably of them than I had done. For some days Miss Taylor declined even to see me, and we were completely at a deadlock; but at last it was agreed that I should omit all mention of Mill's private life and that Miss Taylor should herself write a second introduction (for which I took no responsibility) and say what she liked. I did not greatly care for her contribution, but it was a necessary compromise. Myself, however, I entertain no sort of doubt that Miss Taylor is right in her main belief that there was no "guilty" intrigue. . . .

There is, on the other hand, an account which the late Sir Frederick R. Chapman gave twenty-five years ago in a letter to an American scholar:

Miss Mary [Taylor] mentioned another fact that seemed very strange to me. She had placed the whole of the copies of Mr. Mill's correspondence at the disposal of Mr. Elliot when assisting him in the preparation of the published letters. When he had made his selection he induced her to destroy the rest save only what she termed the "intimate letters" which she intended to embody in another book. I understand that the book has never appeared.

---

were among a quantity of books stored in the destroyed main building the story is probably incorrect. On the whole it seems that all the books, except "a box" returned to Mary Taylor, stored in the Pantechnicon in 1905, were given to Somerville College, which still has the original list.

9. In a letter by Hugh Elliot to Lord Courtney, dated May 8, 1910. MS at London School of Economics.

10. Mrs. Mary Colman, who died on January 15, 1913.

Assuming that she has told me the actual facts I should say that her weakness is as remarkable as Mr. Elliot's meaningless advice or request to destroy the balance of the letters which must have been very numerous.[11]

Though Sir Frederick's recollection was no doubt correct, there is every reason to doubt Miss Taylor's account of the events and it is by no means certain that any destruction of letters did take place at that time (whatever may have happened at Avignon in 1905). Not only most of the letters which Mr. Elliot published but so many others are known to have been preserved that I am on the whole inclined to think that nothing was destroyed then.

Mary Taylor appears to have proceeded with her plan of preparing a further volume of family letters and it seems that by the beginning of 1918 she had, with the assistance of Miss Elizabeth Lee (sister of Sir Sidney Lee and author of the article on Helen Taylor in the *Dictionary of National Biography*), completed a typescript and was negotiating through a literary agent (Mr. A. P. Watts) with Messrs. Longmans, Green & Co. concerning publication. Since the files of all parties involved (the literary agent, the publishers, Miss Mary Taylor's solicitors and, at least in part, her literary executors) were destoyed by fire during the London "Blitz" in December, 1940, it is now impossible to say with certainty why it was not published. But some letters of Mary Taylor together with the recollections of one of the partners of the literary agents (Mr. C. A. Watts, who in his old age still distinctly remembered the "irresponsible Miss Mary Taylor") show that after a period of irresolution Miss Taylor suffered a "nervous breakdown," accompanied by insomnia and illusions. After certification she was in March, 1918, taken to an institution in London where she died on November 6, 1918.

In her will Mary Taylor had left all copyrights and letters and correspondence referring to John Stuart Mill and Helen Taylor to the National Provincial Bank Ltd. as residuary legatees and literary executors who were to be free to use this material in any way they saw fit. An inventory of her possessions mentions among the contents of "a gunpowder proof safe," a collection of "Public Letters to and from J. S. Mill A to Z," and a packet of private letters. The former together with various other manuscript material the Bank decided, on the report of a Mr. P. W. Sergeant who had been asked to value them, to sell by auction, while it was thought that "the intimate letters relating to the family quarrel . . . could not be offered for sale publicly."

11. A letter by Sir Frederick R. Chapman to Professor J. M. McCrimmon, now of the University of Illinois, Urbana, Illinois, dated July 26, 1935. I wish to thank Professor McCrimmon for letting me have the text of this letter and permitting me to reprint it. The episode is briefly discussed on p. vi of Professor McCrimmon's doctoral dissertation in Northwestern University Library.

A first sale was accordingly held at Sotheby's of London on March 29, 1922, which produced a gross amount of £276.19.–. Of this, however, £200 were paid on behalf of the Trustees of the Carlyle House Memorial Trust for a set of seventy-seven letters by Thomas Carlyle to Mill (which in the following year were published by Mr. Alexander Carlyle in *Letters of Thomas Carlyle to John Stuart Mill, John Sterling and Robert Browning* [London: T. Fisher Unwin, 1923]). The twenty-one lots of Mill manuscripts proper seem all to have been bought by various London booksellers and altogether to have fetched no more than £76.19.–. They appear to have contained numerous notebooks, mostly botanical, and miscellaneous correspondence. Most of the Mill manuscripts now in various American libraries derive from this sale.[12] Quantitatively the largest part (although much of it of a kind not readily salable otherwise) was in 1926 sold by one of the booksellers to the Library of the London School of Economics, where it constitutes the nucleus of the Mill-Taylor Collection, since much enriched by many additions.

Because of the loss of part of the relevant files of the National Provincial Bank, we do not know why the sale of a large part of the papers was postponed for five years. But on June 27, 1927, Sotheby's sold another fourteen lots described as "The Property of Miss Mary Taylor, dec.," containing mostly letters to Mill, but also one lot containing "upwards of 132 autograph letters to his wife on literary work and travel." It seems that both the material now at Yale University Library and that acquired by Lord Keynes and now at King's College, Cambridge, derive from this sale. The National Provincial Bank apparently retained only the small collection of correspondence exchanged between Mill and his brothers and sisters and a few family documents and portraits, all of which were in 1943 presented by the Bank to the London School of Economics for inclusion in the Mill-Taylor Collection.

Although it seemed appropriate to use this occasion to give an account of what happened to Mill's own books and papers, the material deriving from them could in fact make little contribution to the present edition. This is intended to cover the period up to 1849, which, because Mill did not then keep copies of his letters, is so little represented in Elliot's edition of his letters, which was based on his papers. In so far as the present collection was to go beyond bringing together the considerable number of earlier letters that had been published in a great variety of places and a few unpublished ones known to be preserved in libraries, the main effort had to be directed towards tracing descendants of Mill's correspondents in the

12. See the annotated catalogues of this and the second sale in the British Museum Library.

hope that some of their papers might be preserved. This indeed absorbed the greater part of the time I was able to devote to the project, yet the results were not great. Even in England, where in general family papers are preserved perhaps longer than anywhere else, two wars have led to the destruction of much of the extraordinary quantity of manuscript material which had accumulated by 1914. It was not so much destruction by enemy action as the appeal for old paper for salvage and the insistence of air-raid wardens that lofts should be cleared of all inflammable matter which caused most of the loss. In more than one instance it seemed at least likely that what I was searching for had only a short while before left the place where it had rested undisturbed for two or three generations. I should add that wherever I succeeded in tracing descendants of Mill's correspondents, my inquiries were invariably met with the greatest courtesy and helpfulness. I can of course not claim that I have exhausted even all the likely leads and no doubt in the course of time further letters by Mill will turn up by accident. But while I do not feel that further systematic search in England would be likely to produce much, there may well be such opportunities on the Continent and particularly in France which, during the greater part of the time I was engaged on this work, was inaccessible to me. If, for instance, good fortune had somewhere preserved the letters which for some years after his visit to France as a boy Mill wrote to his "first friend" Antoine Jérôme Balard,[13] later a distinguished chemist, these would probably tell us more about his early development than any document which might still be found in England.

There are various obligations I have incurred in the work on the material now published in this volume and which I wish to acknowledge in this place. All the work I did on the collection was done while I held a professorship at the London School of Economics and Political Science and I have received all sorts of assistance from the Economic Research Division of that institution, including the provision of assistance and of some funds for various incidental expenditures. Dr. Ruth Borchardt and Miss Dorothy Salter (now Mrs. F. H. Hahn) in succession helped me for long periods of the work. I must also especially mention the Library of the London School of Economics, or the British Library of Political and Economic Science as it is officially called, which as custodian of the Mill-Taylor Collection not only has provided much of the material of this book but also has often helped by buying at my suggestion documents to which I otherwise might not have obtained access. It was in these circumstances very generous of the authorities of the School to give first to me and then

13. Cf. the reference to Balard in Mill's letter to Auguste Comte dated August 12, 1842—Letter 367 in the present collection.

to Professor Mineka permission to use the material collected in any way we thought best. Of the many others who in various ways have helped I ought to single out the National Provincial Bank Ltd. which, after so many years conscientiously watching over the interests of Mill's heirs, finally decided to hand over to the uses of scholarship what the bombs had spared of the papers of the late Mary Taylor.

The chief credit for the appearance of this edition, however, belongs of course to the editor. Only those who have tried their hands at this kind of task at least on a small scale will appreciate the amount of painstaking care and ingenuity that has to be devoted to an edition of the size of the present one before the reader can use it with the implicit trust and ease which a good editor's work assures. I am the more indebted to Professor Mineka because he was prepared to take over the more burdensome part of the task I had half-playfully commenced. The tracing of unpublished manuscripts is the kind of detective work which most people will enjoy doing as a recreation in their spare time. But while the pleasure of the hunt was largely mine, the solid hard work to which the reader owes this edition is entirely Professor Mineka's.

F.A.H.

University of Chicago
January, 1962

Abbreviations and Short Titles

A. Carlyle: *Letters of Thomas Carlyle to John Stuart Mill, John Sterling and Robert Browning*, ed. Alexander Carlyle, New York, 1923

Arsenal: Bibliothèque de l'Arsenal, Paris

Autobiog.: *Autobiography of John Stuart Mill*, published for the first time without alterations or omissions from the original manuscript in the possession of Columbia University, with a Preface by John Jacob Coss, New York, 1924

BFR: *The British and Foreign Review, or European Quarterly Journal*, 1835–44

Bain, *JSM*: Alexander Bain, *John Stuart Mill: A Criticism: With Personal Recollections*, London, 1882

Bain, *James Mill*: Alexander Bain, *James Mill: A Biography*, London, 1882

Brit. Mus.: British Museum, London

Caroline Fox, Journals. *See* Pym

Cosmopolis: "Letters of John Stuart Mill to Gustave d'Eichthal," ed. Eugène d'Eichthal, in *Cosmopolis*, VI (April-May, 1897), 21–38, 348–66, and IX (Feb.-March, 1898), 368–81, 780–90

D'Eichthal Corresp.: John Stuart Mill, *Correspondance inédite avec Gustave d'Eichthal, 1828–1842, 1864–1871*, éd. Eugène d'Eichthal, Paris, 1898 (same as preceding, but translated into French)

Dissertations: John Stuart Mill, *Dissertations and Discussions: Political, Philosophical, and Historical*, 4 vols., London, 1859–75

ER: *The Edinburgh Review*, 1802–1929

Early Draft: *The Early Draft of John Stuart Mill's Autobiography*, ed. Jack Stillinger, Urbana, 1961

Elliot: *The Letters of John Stuart Mill*, ed. Hugh S. R. Elliot, 2 vols., London, 1910

FQR: *The Foreign Quarterly Review*, 1827–46

Fawcett: Mrs. [Millicent] Fawcett, *Life of the Right Hon. Sir William Molesworth*, London, 1901

Fraser's: *Fraser's Magazine for Town and Country*, 1830–82

Garnett: Richard Garnett, *The Life of W. J. Fox . . .*, concluded by Edward Garnett, London, 1910

Hayek: F. A. Hayek, *John Stuart Mill and Harriet Taylor: Their Friendship and Subsequent Marriage*, London and Chicago, 1951

JSM: John Stuart Mill

Johns Hopkins: The Johns Hopkins University Library

Kew: Archives of the Royal Botanic Gardens, Kew

King's: Keynes Collection, King's College Library, Cambridge University

Kitchel: Anna T. Kitchel, *George Lewes and George Eliot: A Review of Records*, New York, 1933

Knight: "Unpublished Letters from John Stuart Mill to Professor Nichol," ed. William Knight, in *Fortnightly Review*, LXVII (May, 1897), 660–78

LSE: The British Library of Political and Economic Science, at the London School of Economics and Political Science

LWR: *London and Westminster Review*, 1836–40

Leeds: Brotherton Library, University of Leeds

Lévy-Bruhl: *Lettres inédites de John Stuart Mill à Auguste Comte, publiées avec les réponses de Comte*, éd. L. Lévy-Bruhl, Paris, 1899

Lindley: Dwight N. Lindley, "The Saint-Simonians, Carlyle, and Mill," unpublished Columbia University dissertation, 1958 (available from University Microfilms, Ann Arbor, Mich.)

Logic: John Stuart Mill, *A System of Logic, Ratiocinative and Inductive; Being a Connected View of the Principles of Evidence and the Methods of Scientific Investigation*, 2 vols., London, 1843

MR: *The Monthly Repository*, 1806–38

MacMinn, *Bibliog.*: *Bibliography of the Published Writings of John Stuart Mill*, ed. Ney MacMinn, J. R. Hainds, and James McNab McCrimmon, Evanston, Ill., 1945

Mayer: Alexis de Tocqueville, *Œuvres, papiers et correspondances*, édition définitive publiée sous la direction de J.-P. Mayer, Paris, 1951– , tome VI, *Correspondance anglaise*, éd. J.-P. Mayer et Gustave Rudler, Paris, 1954

Mineka, *The Dissidence of Dissent*: Francis E. Mineka, *The Dissidence of Dissent: The Monthly Repository, 1806–38*, Chapel Hill, N.C., 1944

Morrison: *Catalogue of the Collection of Autograph Letters and Historical Documents Formed between 1865 and 1882 by Alfred Morrison*, compiled and annotated under the direction of A. W. Thibaudeau, 6 vols., London, 1883–92, IV

NLS: The National Library of Scotland, Edinburgh

Napier Corresp.: *Selections from the Correspondence of the late Macvey Napier, Esq.*, ed. by his son, Macvey Napier, London, 1879

Packe: Michael St. John Packe, *Life of John Stuart Mill*, London, 1954

Pankhurst: Richard K. P. Pankhurst, *The Saint Simonians, Mill and Carlyle*, London, [1957]

Pym: *Memories of Old Friends, Being Extracts from the Journals and Letters of Caroline Fox, from 1835 to 1871*, ed. H. N. Pym, 2nd ed., 2 vols., London, 1882

QR: *The Quarterly Review*, 1809–

Tait's: *Tait's Edinburgh Magazine*, 1832–61

Thom: *The Life of the Rev. Joseph Blanco White, Written by Himself; with Portions of his Correspondence*, ed. John Hamilton Thom, 3 vols., London, 1845

Towers: C. M. D. [Robertson] Towers, "John Stuart Mill and the London and Westminster Review," *Atlantic Monthly*, LXIX (Jan., 1892), 58–74

Tuell, *John Sterling*: Anne Kimball Tuell, *John Sterling: A Representative Victorian*, New York, 1941

UCL: Library of University College, the University of London

WR: *Westminster Review*, 1824–1914

Yale: Yale University Library

THE EARLIER LETTERS OF JOHN STUART MILL

1812–1837

My dear Sir,

121

Mr. Walker is ~~a~~ very intimate friend of mine, who lives at
No. 31 in Berkeley Square. I have engaged him, as ~~soon as~~ he is soon coming here
to go to your house, and get for me
the 3d. and 4th. volumes of Hooke's
Roman history. But I am ~~going over~~ recapitulating
the 1st. and 2d. volumes, having
finished them all except a few pages
of the 2d. I will be glad if you
will let him have the 3d. and 4th.
volumes. I am yours sincerely

Newington Green. John Stuart Mill.
Tuesday 1812.

Letter 1, to Jeremy Bentham, from MS in the British Museum

. . . 1812–1830 . . .

1. TO JEREMY BENTHAM[1]

[July 28, 1812][2]

MY DEAR SIR,

Mr. Walker[3] is a very intimate friend of mine, who lives at No. 31 in Berkeley Square. I have engaged him, as he is soon coming here, first to go to your house, and get for me the 3.^{d} and 4.th volumes of Hooke's Roman history.[4] But I am recapitulating[5] the 1.st and 2.^{d} volumes, having finished them all except a few pages of the 2.^{d}. I will be glad if you will let him have the 3.^{d} and 4.th volumes.

I am yours sincerely

JOHN STUART MILL.

Newington Green,
Tuesday 1812.

1. *Addressed*: Jeremy Bentham Esq. / Queen Square Place / Westminster. The holograph of this letter (Brit. Mus. Add. MSS 33,544, f. 621) is believed to be the earliest extant in the handwriting of John Stuart Mill.

Jeremy Bentham (1748 NS–1832). The intimate connection between James Mill and the great Utilitarian philosopher began about 1808, when JSM was two years old. In 1810 Bentham, in order to maintain a closer collaboration with the elder Mill, gave him as a residence the house once John Milton's, which Bentham owned and which adjoined Bentham's home known as Queen Square Place. A few months' trial of the house proved it to be so little habitable that Mill was obliged to move his family. Until 1814 they lived at Newington Green, when Bentham at last secured Mill as a neighbour by leasing No. 1 Queen Square and renting it to him at a reduced rate. Bentham, who had also been a child prodigy, interested himself in JSM's education. Beginning in 1809 the Mill family often paid extended summer visits to Bentham at his summer homes, first at Barrow Green House, Oxted, and later at Ford Abbey. (See Letters 2 and 3.) Shortly before JSM wrote this letter his father had evidently mentioned to Bentham his forebodings of what his own untimely death might mean to his son's education. Bentham, in a letter to James Mill dated July 25, 1812, promised, "if you will appoint me Guardian of Mr. John Stewart [*sic*] Mill, I will in the event of his father's being disposed of elsewhere, take him to Q.S.P. [Queen Square Place] and there or elsewhere, by whipping or otherwise, do what soever . . . necessary and proper, for teaching him to make all proper distinctions, such as between the Devil and the Holy Ghost, and how to make Codes and Encyclopedias and whatsoever else may be proper to be made, so long as I remain an inhabitant of this vale of tears . . ." (MS at Yale). A portion of James Mill's acceptance of the offer, printed in Bain, *James Mill*, pp. 119–20, expresses the hope that "we may perhaps leave him [JSM] a successor worthy of both of us."

2. A note on the verso in another (probably Bentham's) hand says 29 July 1812, but Tuesday of that week fell on July 28.

3. For this note, and notes 4 and 5, see next page.

2. TO AN UNIDENTIFIED FRIEND OF THE FAMILY[1]

September 13, 1814

I have arrived at Ford Abbey without any accident, and am now safely settled there. We are all in good health, except that I have been ill of slight fever for several days, but am now perfectly recovered.

It is time to give you a description of the Abbey.[2] There is a little hall and a long cloister, which are reckoned very fine architecture, from the door, and likewise two beautiful rooms, a dining-parlour and a breakfast-parlour adorned with fine drawings within one door; on another side is a large hall, adorned with a gilt ceiling; and beyond it two other rooms, a dining and drawing-room, of which the former contains various kinds of musical instruments, and the other is hung with beautiful tapestry.

To this house there are many staircases. The first of them has little remarkable up it, but that three rooms are hung with tapestry, of which one contains a velvet bed, and is therefore called the velvet room. The looking-glass belonging to this room is decorated with nun's lace.

Up another staircase is a large saloon, hung with admirable tapestry, as

---

3. Unidentified.

4. Nathaniel Hooke, *The Roman History, from the Building of Rome to the Ruin of the Commonwealth* (4 vols., London, 1738–71, and later editions). By a happy coincidence JSM's essay based on Hooke's history has been preserved. A friend of the family copied it out in a manuscript now in the possession of the British Museum (Add. MSS 33,230). The six-year-old JSM did more, however, than merely recapitulate uncritically Hooke's history, as this footnote reveals: "Plutarch (vi[vide] p. 273, 301) calls this man Publicola. But Hooke (vi p. 255) and Dionysius Halicarnassus (chronology of the Consuls (pp. 766–7) calls him Poplicola. It is always spelt Ποπλικολας (Poplicola) in Greek not Πυβλικολας (Publicola). Therefore that is the reason of its being Poplicola in Dionysius not Publicola, as in Plutarch. Livy also calls him Poplicola. I know not the reason of its being Poplicola in Hooke and Livy. It is also spelt Ποπλιος (Poplius) in Greek, not Πυβλιος (Publius). It must doubtless be a mistake in Langhorne's Plutarch."

5. Substituted for "going over," which has been crossed out.

* * * *

1. Published in Bain, *JSM*, pp. 4–5. MS not located. The portion in brackets is Bain's summary. Bain says, "The event which gave rise to the letter was the migration of the whole family (in July) to Bentham's newly acquired residence, Ford Abbey, in Somersetshire." The first paragraph would seem to suggest a somewhat earlier date than Bain gives. On July 30 James Mill wrote Francis Place from Ford Abbey: "Mrs. Mill & the children arrived in safety on Monday evening. . . . John has had a pretty sharp indisposition for the last two days; occasioned by something in disorder in the digestive system, which a sudden change in times & modes of dieting has probably occasioned. Today he is better; but he has had so much fever, as to be already weakened" (Brit. Mus. Add. MSS 37,949, f. 18).

2. This was the first year of Bentham's occupancy of Ford Abbey. The Mill family spent substantial portions of the following three years with him there. For other accounts of the building, see Bain, *James Mill*, pp. 129–36; *Works of Jeremy Bentham*, ed. J. Bowring (Edinburgh and London, 1838–43), X, 478–80; and C. M. Atkinson, *Jeremy Bentham* (London, 1905), p. 163.

also a small library. From this saloon issues a long range of rooms, of which one is fitted up in the Chinese style, and another is hung with silk. There is a little further on a room, which, it is said, was once a nursery; though the old farmer Glyde, who lives hard by, called out his sons to hear the novelty of a child crying in the Abbey! which had not happened for the whole time he had lived here, being near thirty years. Down a staircase from here is a long range of bedrooms, generally called the Monks' Walk. From it is a staircase leading into the cloisters. The rest of the house is not worth mentioning. If I was to mention the whole it would tire you exceedingly, as this house is in reality so large that the eight rooms on one floor of the wing which we inhabit, which make not one-quarter of even that floor of the whole house, are as many as all the rooms in your house, and considerably larger.

I have been to the parish church which is at Thornecomb. Mr. Hume[3] has been here a great while. Mr. Koe[4] came the other day, and Admiral Chietekoff[5] is expected. Willie[6] and I have had rides in Mr. Hume's curricle.

[He goes on to say—] What has been omitted here will be found in a journal which I am writing of this and last year's journeys. [He then incontinently plunges again into descriptive particulars about the fish-ponds, the river Axe, the deer-parks, the walks, and Bentham's improvements.]

3. TO MRS. HARRIET BURROW[1]

Ford Abbey, Oct. 27th 1817

DEAR GRANDMOTHER,

I write to you now, as both my Sisters are writing, and there is not likely to be another parcel going to town for a great while.

I have very little news to tell you: Willie has informed you of the accident which has happened to James's[2] eye. Willie, Harriet,[3] and Clara,[4] have

3. Joseph Hume (1777–1855), radical MP 1818–55, was a lifelong friend of James Mill from the time of their schooldays at Montrose Academy in Scotland.

4. John Herbert Koe (1783–1860), barrister, and later judge of county courts, had been for some time an amanuensis of Bentham.

5. Paul Vasilievitch Tchitchagof (or Chichagov) (1767–1849), Russian admiral, was a friend of Bentham and his brother, Sir Samuel, who had spent a number of years in Russia.

6. Wilhelmina Forbes Mill (1808–1861), JSM's eldest sister.

* * * *

1. MS at LSE. *Addressed*: Mrs. Burrow. Published in Packe, p. 35.

Mrs. Burrow, JSM's maternal grandmother, was of a Yorkshire family. After the death of her husband she continued to administer his private asylum for the insane at Hoxton.

2. James Bentham Mill (1814–1862), JSM's brother.

3. Harriet Isabella Mill (1812–*ca.* 1897).

4. Clara Esther Mill (1810–1886).

begun music: and you learn from Willie's and Clara's letters, this also. Willie and Clara are ready to begin the first lesson: Harriet has not finished the treble notes.

The rainy weather has at length set in here, after an exceedingly dry autumn. I am however very glad to say, that no rain now can do any injury to the crop, which is almost all in.

We are still learning to write. How much Willie and Clara have improved you will know by reading their letters.

I hope that all my aunts and uncles are very well. I did not know that I had a new little cousin, till Willie saw it in the paper. I believe my Mother has written to you a very long letter: and I suppose that she has told you all the little news that we have: so that I have very little to tell you: moreover, I had only two days notice to write four letters: or else I would probably have written more.

We are all in very good health, except little Jane,[5] who has got a little cough. I had lately the tooth-ache very bad. I hope that you are also in very good health.

Since we were here, there has been a groping in the pond for eels. Mr. Bragg's two sons went into the mud, (after almost all the water had been let out) and groped with their hands for eels. Those caught were, many of them, very large ones. A number of trout, caught in the river, were afterwards put in that pond.

All of us send our love to you and all our other relations, and our good friends. I am,

Your affectionate Grandson

JOHN STUART MILL

4. TO SIR SAMUEL BENTHAM[1]

Acton Place, Hoxton, July 30, 1819

MY DEAR SIR,

It is so long since I last had the pleasure of seeing you that I have almost forgotten when it was, but I believe it was in the year 1814, the first year we were at Ford Abbey. I am very much obliged to you for your inquiries with respect to my progress in my studies; and as nearly as I can remember I will endeavour to give an account of them from that year.

5. Jane Stuart Mill (1816?–1883).

* * * *

1. Published in Bain, *JSM*, pp. 6–9. MS not located. A copy of the first three paragraphs, in an unidentified hand, is at Johns Hopkins. On June 17, 1820, Jeremy Bentham in a letter to David Ricardo discussing the importance of securing James Mill's assistance in establishing a "Chrestomathic" school in Bentham's garden, cited

In the year 1814, I read Thucydides, and Anacreon, and I *believe* the Electra of Sophocles, the Phœnissæ of Euripides, and the Plutus and the Clouds of Aristophanes. I also read the Philippics of Demosthenes.

The Latin which I read was only the Oration of Cicero for the Poet Archias, and the (first or last) part of his pleading against Verres. And in Mathematics, I was then reading Euclid; I also began Euler's Algebra, Bonnycastle's principally for the sake of the examples to perform. I read likewise some of West's Geometry.

Æt. 9.—The Greek which I read in the year 1815 was, I think, Homer's Odyssey. Theocritus, some of Pindar, and the two Orations of Æschines, and Demosthenes on the Crown. In Latin I read the six first books, I believe, of Ovid's Metamorphoses, the five first books of Livy, the Bucolics, and the six first books of the Æneid of Virgil, and part of Cicero's Orations. In Mathematics, after finishing the first six books, with the eleventh and twelfth of Euclid, and the Geometry of West, I studied Simpson's Conic Sections and also West's Conic Sections, Mensuration and Spherics; and in Algebra, Kersey's Algebra, and Newton's Universal Arithmetic, in which I performed all the problems without the book, and most of them without any help from the book.

Æt. 10.—In the year 1816 I read the following Greek: Part of Polybius, all Xenophon's Hellenics, The Ajax and the Philoctetes of Sophocles, the Medea of Euripides, and the Frogs of Aristophanes, and great part of the Anthologia Græca. In Latin I read all Horace, except the Book of Epodes; and in Mathematics I read Stewart's Propositiones Geometricæ, Playfair's

---

this "letter, which I believe you [Ricardo] saw, and which though I have never told him [James Mill], I intend to trumpet forth in print" as proof of James Mill's skill as an educator. "The letter in question is one written by John Mill in answer to one from my Brother to me, concerning the progress made by him in his studies." (*The Works and Correspondence of David Ricardo*, ed. Piero Sraffa [11 vols., Cambridge, 1951–55], VIII, 198.) There is no evidence that the letter was printed before Bain published it. Bain records that the letter was given to J. A. Roebuck in 1827 by Jeremy Bentham's amanuensis, and that it was endorsed in Bentham's handwriting:

1819 John Mill
July to Acton
30 S B place
J Ms and Sisters
Studies since 1814
15 years old
24 May 1821

Sir Samuel Bentham (1757–1831), younger brother of Jeremy, naval architect and engineer, rose to the rank of brigadier general in the service of Russia; in England, was Inspector General of Navy Works, 1795–1807, and Commissioner of the Navy, 1807–12. After retirement he bought an estate in the south of France. This letter may have served to pave the way for Sir Samuel's invitation to JSM to come to France for an extended residence in 1820–21. Its account of his studies should be compared with that in his *Autobiography*.

Trigonometry at the end of his Euclid, and an article on geometry in the *Edinburgh Encyclopædia*. I also studied Simpson's Algebra.

Æt. 11.—In the year 1817 I read Thucydides a second time, and I likewise read a great many Orations of Demosthenes and all Aristotle's Rhetoric, of which I made a synoptic table. In Latin I read all Lucretius, except the last book, and Cicero's Letters to Atticus, his Topica, and his treatise, De Partitione Oratoria. I read in Conic Sections an article in the *Encyclopædia Britannica* (in other branches of the mathematics I studied Euler's Analysis of Infinities and began Fluxions, on which I read an article in the *Encyclopædia Britannica*), and Simpson's Fluxions. In the application of mathematics I read Keill's Astronomy and Robinson's Mechanical Philosophy.

Æt. 12.—Last year I read some more of Demosthenes, and the four first Books of Aristotle's Organon, all which I tabulated in the same manner as his Rhetoric.

In Latin, I read all the works of Tacitus, except the dialogue concerning oratory, and great part of Juvenal, and began Quintilian. In Mathematics and their application, I read Emerson's Optics, and a Treatise on Trigonometry by Professor Wallace, of the Military College, near Bagshot, intended for the use of the cadets. I likewise re-solved several problems in various branches of mathematics; and began an article on Fluxions in the *Edinburgh Encyclopædia*.

Æt. 13.—This year I read Plato's dialogues called Gorgias and Protagoras, and his Republic, of which I made an abstract. I am still reading Quintilian and the article on Fluxions, and am performing without book the problems in Simpson's Select Exercises.

Last year I began to learn logic. I have read several Latin books of Logic: those of Smith, Brerewood, and Du Trieu,[2] and part of Burgersdicius, as far as I have gone in Aristotle. I have also read Hobbes' Logic.

I am now learning political economy. I have made a kind of treatise from what my father has explained to me on that subject,[3] and I am now reading Mr. Ricardo's work[4] and writing an abstract of it. I have learnt

2. Seven years later JSM and the friends associated with him in the study club that met at George Grote's home in Threadneedle Street reprinted Du Trieu's work (see *Autobiog.*, p. 85): Philippus Du Trieu, *Manuductio ad Logicam; sive Dialectica Studiosae Juventuti ad Logicam Praeparandae. Ab Editione Oxoniensi anni 1662 Recusa.* Londini, typis B. M'Millan, 1826. A copy of this rare reprint is at the University of Chicago; another is at Somerville College, Oxford.

3. JSM's first instruction in the subject was given to him by his father during their walks (*Autobiog.*, p. 19): "He expounded each day a portion of the subject, and I gave him next day a written account of it, which he made me rewrite over and over again until it was clear, precise, and tolerably complete. . . . The written outline of it which resulted from my daily *compte rendu* served him afterwards as notes from which to write his Elements of Political Economy."

4. David Ricardo, *Principles of Political Economy and Taxation* (London, 1817);

a little natural philosophy, and, having had an opportunity of attending a course of lectures on chemistry, delivered by Mr. Phillips, at the Royal Military College, Bagshot,[5] I have applied myself particularly to that science, and have read the last edition of Dr. Thomson's system of chemistry.

What English I have read since the year 1814 I cannot tell you, for I cannot remember so long ago. But I recollect that since that time I have read Ferguson's Roman and Mitford's Grecian History. I have also read a great deal of Livy by myself. I have sometimes tried my hand at writing history. I had carried a history of the United Provinces from their revolt from Spain, in the reign of Phillip II., to the accession of the Stadtholder, William III., to the throne of England.

I had likewise begun to write a history of the Roman Government, which I had carried down to the Licinian Laws. I should have begun to learn French before this time, but that my father has for a long time had it in contemplation to go to the Continent, there to reside for some time.[6] But as we are hindered from going by my father's late appointment in the East India House,[7] I shall begin to learn French as soon as my sisters have made progress enough in Latin to learn with me.

James Mill played a major part in the production of this work, for it was undertaken by his reluctant friend only after Mill's persistent insistence.

Ricardo seems to have been genuinely interested in JSM's development, invited the boy to his home, and on the very day (Sept. 5, 1823) when he was stricken with his fatal illness addressed to James Mill an extended criticism of a paper by JSM on the measure of value (*Works of David Ricardo*, IX, 385–87).

5. For an account of this experience and of the impression made by JSM at the College, see his father's letter to Ricardo, Oct. 26, 1818 (*Works of David Ricardo*, VII, 313–14). Ricardo in reply commented on JSM's retired education and noted the boy's "need of that collision which is obtained only in society, and by which a knowledge of the world and its manners is best acquired" (*ibid.*, p. 326).

6. That James Mill had talked with his friends about moving his family to France as early as the autumn of 1814 may be seen in a letter from Edward Wakefield to Francis Place, Nov. 27, 1814 (Brit. Mus. Add. MSS 35,152, ff. 114–15). On Sept. 6, 1815, James Mill wrote to Francis Place to encourage the latter to join him in moving to the Continent: "I foresee nothing there which would make it uncomfortable for us to reside as soon as we please. Assure yourself that the French people will soon be very quiet & contented slaves, & the despotism of the Bourbons a quiet, gentle despotism. There I may live cheap—my children will acquire a familiarity with the language & with the manners & character of a new people. When they have enough of this we shall remove into Germany, till the same effects are accomplished, & after that if we please, we may go to Italy. We shall then return accomplished people, and, men & women of us, I hope, able to do something for the cause of mankind. We shall, at any rate, have plenty of knowledge; the habit of living upon little; & a passion for the improvement of the condition of mankind" (Brit. Mus. Add. MSS 35,152, ff. 160–64).

7. He was appointed on May 12, 1819, as Assistant to the Examiner of India Correspondence at a salary of £800. Rising by fairly rapid steps, he became head of the office, with the rank of Examiner, on Dec. 1, 1830. JSM was appointed a junior clerk in the office on May 21, 1823.

I have now and then attempted to write Poetry. The last production of that kind at which I tried my hand was a tragedy. I have now another in view in which I hope to correct the fault of this.

I believe my sister Willie was reading Cornelius Nepos when you saw her. She has since that time read some of Cæsar; almost all Phædrus, all the Catiline and part of the Jugurtha of Sallust, and two plays of Terence; she has read the first, and part of the second book of Lucretius, and is now reading the Eclogues of Virgil.

Clara has begun Latin also. After going through the grammar, she read some of Cornelius Nepos and Cæsar, almost as much as Willie of Sallust, and is now reading Ovid. They are both now tolerably good arithmeticians; they have gone as far as the extraction of the cube root. They are reading the Roman Antiquities and the Greek Mythology, and are translating English into Latin from Mair's Introduction to Latin Syntax.

This is to the best of my remembrance a true account of my own and my sisters' progress since the year 1814.

I hope Lady Bentham, and George,[8] and the young ladies are in good health.

Your obedient, humble servant,

JOHN STUART MILL.

To Sir Saml. Bentham.

5. TO SARAH AUSTIN[1]

Montpellier[2] 17 Janv. 1821

MADAME

Je n'ai reçu que depuis deux jours la lettre dont vous avez bien voulu m'honorer. Croyez, Madame, à ma réconnaissance de tout ce qu'elle contient: réconnaissance qui aurait été grande, si vous aviez écrit sous de

8. George Bentham (1800–1884), son of Sir Samuel, became one of the most distinguished of nineteenth-century botanists.

* * * *

1. *Addressed*: A / Madame Austin. MS at King's.

Sarah Austin, née Taylor (1793–1867), translator and miscellaneous writer. She married John Austin (1790–1859), later known as a writer on jurisprudence, in 1819. Their first home was in Queen Square, in close proximity to the homes of Jeremy Bentham and James Mill. JSM quickly grew fond of the Austins, and they were close friends for many years. JSM studied German with Mrs. Austin, and in 1821–22 Roman law with her husband. As a young man JSM often greeted her in his letters as "Dear Mütterlein," but in later life he criticized her severely (*The Early Draft of John Stuart Mill's Autobiography*, ed. Jack Stillinger [Urbana, 1961], pp. 147–48).

2. JSM was the guest of Sir Samuel Bentham and family from June, 1820, to June,

meilleures auspices: jugez donc combien elle doit l'être dans le cas actuel. J'avoue que je ne suis point digne de cet *effort* que vous avez fait pour m'écrire: puisque deux ou trois lignes à la fin d'une lettre à mon père sont tout ce que vous avez eu de ma part, depuis que j'ai quitté l'Angleterre. Je vous prie de vouloir bien pardonner ma negligence, et recevoir cette lettre en expiation de ma faute. Puisque vous lisez toutes mes lettres à mon père, il est inutile que je vous raconte la manière dont je m'occupe ici: la lettre qui accompagne celle-ci vous donnera tous les renseignemens là dessus que vous pouvez désirer. Il ne me reste donc plus qu'à vous remercier des bons conseils que vous me donnez: ne doutez pas qu'ils ne produisent tout l'effet que vous souhaitez.

Le cours publics que je suis dans ce moment ne termineront pas encore de quelque temps. Le professeur de Logique[3] ne fait guère que d'entrer dans son sujet: le professeur de Zoologie[4] n'a fait encore que douze leçons. Il est cependant probable que si les cours durent encore longtems, je n'en attende pas la fin: Je partirai d'ici au milieu du mois prochain, pour retourner à Paris. J'aurai donc l'honneur de vous revoir avant qu'il soit longtems: J'espère que nous aurons l'occasion de causer ensemble sur toutes les choses dont vous parlez, et sur beaucoup d'autres dont je n'ai pas la place ni le tems de vous entretenir momentanément. Ce sera alors que j'aurai l'honneur de vous assurer moi même de ma reconnaissance, non seulement de l'interêt que vous prenez à tout ce qui m'arrive, mais de la bonté avec laquelle vous vous êtes donner la peine de soigner l'éducation de mes sœurs: Je ne sais si elles sentent toute l'étendue de cette bonté, mais je vous assure que je la sens, et que je ne manquerai pas de vous en remercier, à mon retour, de vive voix. — Je suis très fâché que vous ne jouissiez pas d'une santé pareille à mes vœux: J'espère qu'elle vous sera

---

1821, first at Sir Samuel's *château* in the valley of the Garonne, then at an apartment in Toulouse. In the fall, after an extended tour of the Pyrenees, the Benthams took him to a new estate which they had purchased near Montpellier. For about six months JSM attended courses in the Faculté des Sciences in the local university. A manuscript letter-journal addressed to his father and covering approximately the first six months of his stay in France is in the British Museum (Add. MSS 31,909). Professor Anna Jean Mill has recently published most of this journal as well as portions of a contemporary notebook of JSM which is in her possession: *John Mill's Boyhood Visit to France* (Toronto, 1960).

3. One M. Gergonne, "a very accomplished representative of the eighteenth century metaphysics" (JSM, *Autobiog.*, chap. II). Identified by Professor Mill as Joseph Diez Gergonne (1771–1859), professor of astronomy and Dean of the Academy at Montpellier. An exercise book containing JSM's notes on Gergonne's lectures on logic is at LSE. Professor Mill prints the text of the notes on the 19th lecture (*John Mill's Boyhood Visit to France*, pp. 110–15). Another notebook, entitled by JSM, "Traite de Logique / redigé d'après le cours de Philosophie / de M. Gergonne / Doyen de la Faculté des Sciences / de l'Academie de Montpellier / avec des Notes / par J. Mill," is in the Pierpont Morgan Library.

4. Professor Mill identifies him as Jean Michel Provençal.

bientôt rendue. Veuillez bien, assurez M^r votre époux de mes sentimens de réconnaissance pour lui; et croyez, Madame, que je serai toujours,

Votre serviteur très obligé

Pardonnez mon *embrouillomanie.* J. S. MILL

6. TO JAMES MILL[1]

[Paris]
25 Avril 1821

MON CHER PÈRE,

Je vous écris cette lettre de Paris, où je suis arrivé hier, après un heureux voyage. Vous voyez que mon départ a été un peu retardé, presque de jour en jour, mais je n'ai pas la place de vous donner des détails: ce sera pour la prochaine lettre que je ne tarderai pas à vous envoyez. Il y a long tems que je ne vous ai rien ecrit. Ce n'est pas qu'il me manquait de la matière, mais il y a bien près d'un mois que je devais partir incessamment de Montpellier, par consequent pour diminuer le post, je n'ai pas voulu pas ecrire avant mon arrivée ici. J'aurai encore de quoi remplir deux longues lettres pour ramener le journal à la date de la présente. Je vous les enverrai de suite.

J'apprends par vos deux lettres à M. Say,[2] qu'il a eu l'extreme complaisance de me communiquer, qu'il est décidé que j'irai passer quelque tems à Caen. Je suis bien convaincu que vous avez formé cette determination après avoir bien pesé le pour et le contre: et c'est certainement vous êtes le plus capable d'en juger. Cependant malgré le respect que je dois à M. Lowe,[3] et les bontés qu'il a pour moi, je ne vous cache pas que je suis fâché d'aller chez lui en revenant de chez M. Bentham, et cela principalement parceque je vois bien que cela fait de la peine à toute la famille. Ne croyez pas qu'ils soient guidés par l'amour propre, mais leur plus grand desir était toujours que je revinsse chez vous aussitôt que je les eusse quittés pourque vous puissiez juger des instructions qu'ils ont eu la bonté de me donner, et savoir si leurs idées cadrent avec les vôtres. Ce n'est pas le sentiment d'un seul d'entre eux mais de toute la famille; et je ne puis que me féliciter qu'ils n'aient pas su d'abord que je devais aller

1. Original not located. Text from copy contained in unpublished letter of Jeremy Bentham to Sir Samuel Bentham, in Brit. Mus., Add. MSS 33,545, f. 516.

2. Jean Baptiste Say (1767–1832), prominent French economist. In 1814 Say had visited England and through James Mill had been introduced to Ricardo and Bentham. JSM was a guest in Say's home for a time in 1820. (See *Works of David Ricardo,* VI, xxv.)

3. Joseph Lowe, a Scottish friend of James Mill and a writer on statistical subjects, who had emigrated to Caen in 1814.

ailleurs que chez vous après les avoir quittés: car s'ils l'avaient su je suis persuadé qu'ils ne se seraient jamais donnés tant de peine pour mon instruction—Je ne puis plus ecrire; croyez que je serai toujours

votre dévoué et obéissant fils

J. S. Mill

7. TO JAMES MILL[1]

[Norwich]
[Autumn, 1822][2]

[The letter begins with a short account of his studies. He read Blackstone (with Mr. Austin) three or four hours daily, and a portion of Bentham's "Introduction" (I suppose the "Morals and Legislation") in the evening.] I have found time to write the defence of Pericles[3] in answer to the accusation which you have with you. I have also found some time to practise the delivery of the accusation, according to your directions. [Then follows an account of a visit of ten days with the Austins to the town of Yarmouth, with a description of the place itself. The larger part of the letter is on the politics of Norwich, where "the Cause" (Liberal) prospers ill, being still worse at Yarmouth. He has seen of Radicals many; of clear-headed men not one. The best is Sir Thomas Beever,[4] whom he wishes to be induced to come to London and see his father and Mr. Grote.[5] At Yarmouth he has dined with Radical Palmer,[6] who had opened the borough to the Whigs; not much better than a mere Radical.] I have been much entertained by a sermon of Mr. Madge,[7] admirable as against

1. Published in Bain, *JSM*, pp. 27–28. MS not located. The portions in brackets are Bain's summary.

2. According to Bain, the letter was undated, but written while on a visit to Norwich with the Austins. The approximate date, however, can be inferred from the reference to the composition of the defence of Pericles here and in the succeeding letter.

3. In his *Autobiog.* (pp. 50–51) JSM records that after he wrote his first argumentative essay in the summer of 1822 his father recommended that his next exercise in composition should be of the oratorical kind: "Availing myself of my familiarity with Greek history and ideas and with the Athenian orators, I wrote two speeches, one an accusation, the other a defence of Pericles, on a supposed impeachment for not marching out to fight the Lacedemonians on their invasion of Attica."

4. A mis-spelling of the name of Sir Thomas Branthwayt Beevor (1798–1879), a Norfolk squire who became a supporter of William Cobbett.

5. See Letter 8, n. 1.

6. Presumably Nathaniel Palmer (1779–1854), solicitor. The *Examiner* for Jan. 20 and May 19, 1822, in reports of Norfolk County meetings on Jan. 12 and May 11, 1822, respectively, summarized portions of the remarks by Mr. N. Palmer of Yarmouth, attacking the Tory ministry.

7. Rev. Thomas Madge (1786–1870), co-pastor of Octagon Chapel (Unitarian), Norwich, 1811–25; minister of Essex Street Chapel, Strand, London, 1825–60.

Calvinists and Catholics, but the weakness of which as against anybody else, I think he himself must have felt. [The concluding part of the letter should have been a postscript—]

I wish I had nothing else to tell you, but I must inform you that I have lost my watch. It was lost while I was out of doors, but it is impossible that it should have been stolen from my pocket. It must therefore be my own fault. The loss itself (though I am conscious that I must remain without a watch till I can buy one for myself) is to me not great—much less so than my carelessness deserves. It must, however, vex you—and deservedly, from the bad sign which it affords of me.

8. TO MR. AND MRS. GEORGE GROTE[1]

Q[ueen] S[quare] 14 Novr. 1822

MY DEAR SIR AND MADAM,

I crave pardon for addressing you jointly. It is a liberty for which, like a true lawyer, I have two reasons, a technical and a rational one. My technical reason (for confirmation of which vide Blackstone) is that *baron* and *feme* are one person in law. My utilitarian reason is that to do otherwise might imply that I failed of rendering to one of you, the tribute of gratitude which your friendship so justly deserves at my hands.

I have little news to tell you, save that which regards the Util. Soc.[2] On this subject my father still preserves the most profound silence. (I am sure that I shall often remind you of the pleasure with which I anticipate its meetings, by the life-and-death style in which I speak and write about it). The unsettled state of mind in which Alfred[3] has been, and is still kept, from the uncertainty of his destination, has prevented him from giving any attention to the thing: and I have great fears that in the event of his being able to enter into it at all he will still have too little time to *read* and to study hard on Utilitarian subjects. Still I have great hopes of him, but I

1. MS in the possession of Mr. E. F. Buxton, Fairbridge, Tonhill, Kent, in 1944. George Grote (1794–1871), banker, MP (1832–41), and historian of Greece, was introduced to James Mill by David Ricardo in 1819 and soon became an intimate of the Bentham-Mill circle. He and his wife Harriet (née Lewin) frequently entertained many of the Benthamite group in their home over the banking establishment in Threadneedle Street. Except for some later periods of estrangement from Mrs. Grote, JSM was a lifelong associate of the couple.

2. The Utilitarian Society, the first of the study and discussion groups with which JSM was associated (*Autobiog.*, p. 56). The Society at first consisted of only three members, Richard Doane, W. G. Prescott, and JSM. Later members included Eyton Tooke, William Ellis, George J. Graham, and J. A. Roebuck.

3. Identification uncertain. Possibly Alfred Say, son of the French economist, J. B. Say.

have greater hopes of R. Doane,[4] who as I see, is very much in earnest about the thing, who has read my father's Pol. Ec.[5] with great attention as a preparative. He has also made considerable progress in writing his introductory essay; and I will venture to prophecy, from what I know of him by his conversation and by the application which he shows, nothwithstanding his want of encouragement, that he will be an active and useful member, and will profit by the Society, as well as that he will be a source of profit to all the other members.—I have not seen Mr. W. Prescott[6] since I saw you last, but it is unnecessary that I should see him till Alfred's fate is decided. As for myself, I have not only completed Jug True,[7] but have commenced writing for the Util. Rev.[8] and I hope that, on your return, the Defence of Pericles,[9] which is now undergoing a transmutation from a highly illegible to a tolerably legible state, will undo all the impression which the accusation may have made on your mind. (A propos, pardon this scrawl).

You who interest yourself so strongly in favour of M. Berchet,[10] will be delighted with Santa Rosa:[11] who grows every day in the good opinion of all the Utilitarians who see him. I hope to see him play a conspicuous *role* in your society: both for his own sake, and for yours.

ERRATUM in your letter. For *STERN MORALIST* read *DESPONDING PHILANTHROPIST*. It is the more appropriate appellation. The other I do not think at all correct.

Yours ever

J. S. MILL

4. Richard Doane, then an amanuensis to Jeremy Bentham. It was he who secured permission for the Society to meet in Bentham's house. Doane was called to the bar of the Inner Temple in 1830, and practised in the courts until his death on Feb. 8, 1848.

5. *Elements of Political Economy* (London, 1821).

6. William George Prescott (1800–1865), then junior partner in the banking firm of Grote, Prescott, & Co.

7. The reference is obscure, but may be to his lost "reply to Paley's Natural Theology" (*Early Draft*, ed. Stillinger, p. 79). Bentham and his friends often denominated Christianity as Jug (shortened form of Juggernaut).

8. Possibly the plans for the Society included the establishment of such a review, but the reference is more probably to the long-projected Benthamite organ which eventually materialized in Jan., 1824, as the *Westminster Review*.

9. See preceding letter, n. 3.

10. Probably Giovanni Berchet, Italian poet and patriot then a refugee in England, rather than Ambrogio Berchet, likewise an Italian refugee. See M. C. W. Wicks, *The Italian Exiles in London, 1816–1848* (Manchester, 1937).

11. Santorre Annibale de Rossi de Pomarolo, Count of Santarosa (1783–1825), Italian patriot, who had arrived in London in early Oct., 1822, after having been denied further refuge in France. Santarosa was an especial favourite of Sarah Austin. See *ibid.*, and Gordon Waterfield, *Lucie Duff Gordon* (London, 1937), p. 36.

9. TO EDWIN CHADWICK[1]

Saturday
afternoon
[February 19, 1827]

DEAR CHADWICK

As Graham[2] is unable to walk tomorrow we had better perhaps postpone our walk to next Sunday.

Very truly yours
J. S. MILL

10. TO EDWIN CHADWICK[1]

E.I.H. [East India House]
Monday
[March 26, 1827]

DEAR CHADWICK

If you have any influence with Thwaites,[2] you will oblige me greatly by exercising it in favour of a gentleman of the name of Taylor[3] who is about to appear for the first time as a public singer, at the Concert at Covent Garden or Drury Lane (I forget which) on Wednesday. I could tell you much about Mr Taylor which would interest you very strongly in his behalf, but this I reserve till I see you. I believe his qualifications to be of a very high order, but he does not ask to be praised, he is only anxious that if he

1. *Addressed*: Edwin Chadwick Esq / 9 Lyon's Inn. *Postmark*: 8 MORN 8 / 19 FE / 1827. MS at UCL.

Edwin (later Sir Edwin) Chadwick (1800–1890), sanitary reformer. At this time, a law student and journalist; secretary to Jeremy Bentham, 1831–32; member of various Poor Law, factory, and sanitary commissions. A lifelong friend and correspondent of JSM.

2George John Graham (1801–1888), a member of JSM's Utilitarian Society; in 1838 became Registrar General of Births and Deaths.

* * * *

1. *Addressed*: Edwin Chadwick Esq. / 9 Lyon's Inn. *Postmark*: 2.A.NOON / MR26 / 1827 and T.P. / Lombard St. Paper watermarked *1818*. MS at UCL.

2. The proprietor of the *Morning Herald*, for whom Chadwick had worked as a reporter.

3. Edward Taylor (1784–1863), after having failed in business, was at this time embarking upon a career in music, in which he achieved distinction. From 1837 to 1863 he was Gresham Professor of Music, Gresham College, London. His performance on March 28, 1827, at Covent Garden was favourably reviewed in the *Morning Chronicle* on March 29. JSM had probably become acquainted with the Taylor family of Norwich through John Austin and his wife Sarah (Taylor) Austin.

should sink, he may sink quietly, without being treated with severity or with ridicule.

Very truly yours

J. S. MILL

I should say perhaps that I write to you not at his request but at that of his relations who are my very particular f[riends].[4]

J.S.M.

11. TO EDWIN CHADWICK[1]

Thursday
½ past four
[April 12, 1827]

DEAR CHADWICK

Being engaged to breakfast with McCulloch[2] tomorrow, I cannot walk before breakfast—but if the weather should be sufficiently fine to tempt you out I shall hope to meet with you *chez* Graham at eleven: Elliott[3] has been informed.

I hope you are not the "young law student of Lyon's Inn" whose *chère amie* tried to throw herself into the Thames yesterday?

yours most truly

J. S. MILL

P.S. What is the reason that you lawyers always have pens with nibs an inch wide?

12. TO EDWIN CHADWICK[1]

Saturday
2 o'clock
[1827?]

DEAR CHADWICK

Graham is *absolutely* engaged tomorrow, & I am *conditionally* so. I have therefore agreed with Grant[2] not to walk tomorrow unless Elliott comes,

4. Corner torn off.

* * * *

1. *Addressed*: Edwin Chadwick Esq. MS at UCL. Published in S. E. Finer, *The Life and Times of Sir Edwin Chadwick* (London, 1952), p. 11, but dated 1824. The date is established by the event recorded in the second paragraph. *The Times* on April 12, 1827, p. 3, reported the attempted suicide of one Mary Ann Jones, who had been "cohabiting with a young law student of Lyon's Inn."

2. John Ramsay McCulloch (1789–1864), economist.

3. Thomas Frederick Elliot (1808–1880), nephew of the first Earl of Minto, and later Permanent Assistant Under-Secretary for the Colonies, 1849–68.

* * * *

1. *Addressed*: Edwin Chadwick Esq. / 9 Lyon's Inn. MS at UCL.

2. Horace Grant (1800–1859), a colleague of JSM in the Examiner's office at the India House, 1826–45.

which I understand is not probable—But if you think he will come, pray come yourself and I shall be ready to join you.

Very truly yours

J. S. MILL

13. TO JEREMY BENTHAM[1]

[*ca.* April 24, 1827]

I certainly did not understand you to have expressed any desire that my name should be in the title page. Nevertheless, if you positively require it, I am willing that it should be so,[2] rather than that you should imagine I had taken less pains with the work under the idea of its being (so far as I am concerned) anonymous. But I confess I should greatly prefer that my name should be omitted. That the work should be benefited by it is out of the question. I myself might be benefited inasmuch as it would prove that you thought me worthy to be the editor of a work of yours. But on

1. MS at Yale. Draft of letter on sheet used first to cover letter of another person addressed to "J. Bentham Esq. / 2 Queen Square Place / Westminster" and then to cover a note addressed "John S. Mill Esq." It is endorsed in JSM's hand "Notes from Mr. Bentham respecting the publication of my name as editor of his Rationale of Evidence" and has a label attached, "Notes from Mr. Bentham 1827 to 1830. No. 1." Published in part in Packe, p. 73.

Yale also has three letters by Bentham on this matter, to one of which this is evidently an answer.

Q.S.P. 18 Apr. 1827

Dear John

It is matter of no small surprise to me to see the title page without your name to it. Nothing could be more clearly understood between us than that it should be there. I do not say that the word title page was used on that occasion—but such was the meaning. If what you have done has been written under a different impression, so much the worse for me—and if the book be good for any thing, for the [world?] at large.

J.B.

J. S. Mill Esq.

Q.S.P. 24 / Apr. 1827

My dear John

Your name is of far too great importance to the work to be omitted in the title page to it.

J.B.

J. S. Mill Esq.

My substituted title I suppose you have. / If you have not you will let me know.

2. Bentham accepted JSM's reluctantly given consent:

Q.S.P. 24 Apr. / 1827

Dear John

Amen.

If you know not what that means send to the Booksellers for a Hebrew Dictionary.

J.B.

J. S. Mill Esq.

P.S. Name at the end of the Preface

the other hand very little of the labour which I have bestowed upon the book appears on the face of it, or can be known to any one who was not acquainted with the MS.[3] If my name were annexed to it people would think that I wished to make a parade either of your good opinion [of][4] me, or of the few notes which I have added.[5] The notes are not of sufficient value to make it of any consequence to the public to know who wrote them—I should be very sorry to be suspected of wishing to obtain a reputation at a cheap rate by appearing before the public under the shelter of your name.

14. TO EDWIN CHADWICK[1]

[1827?]

DEAR CHADWICK

Tooke[2] cannot come this evening—therefore I must beg you to defer your visit till further notice—Tuesday & Friday next he is disengaged, therefore I hope you will also keep yourself at liberty for one of those days—I cannot yet answer for myself.

Yours ever

J. S. MILL

15. TO EDWIN CHADWICK[1]

Tuesday
[1827?]

DEAR CHADWICK

Tooke will be with me tonight.

Yours ever

J. S. MILL

3. JSM had begun in late 1824 or early 1825 preparing the *Rationale of Judicial Evidence* for publication. "Mr. Bentham had begun the treatise three times, at considerable intervals, each time in a different manner, and each time without reference to the preceding. . . . These three masses of manuscript it was my business to condense into a single treatise." (*Autobiog.*, p. 80.) He had also to make Bentham's involved style readable, and to supply "any *lacunae* which he had left." The work was published in 1827 in five volumes, with a Preface signed John S. Mill. For JSM's later attitude to this work, see Letter 226, esp. n. 2.
4. Page torn.
5. The word "added" is crossed out but the word substituted for it, which may have been "appended," is mostly torn away.

* * * *

1. *Addressed*: Edwin Chadwick Esq. / 9 Lyon's Inn. Paper watermarked 1825. MS at UCL.
2. William Eyton Tooke (1808–1830), son of the economist Thomas Tooke (1774–1858) and one of JSM's closest friends. His suicide in 1830 (see Letter 29) deeply affected JSM.

* * * *

1. *Watermark*: 18[25?]. Paper appears identical with that of preceding letter. MS at UCL.

16. TO ARTHUR AYLMER[1]

[Nov. 27, 1827]

London Debating Society

SIR

The half yearly subscription[2] for September last being now due, you are requested to forward it, with all arrears of former subscriptions, to my address.

I am, Sir
Your most ob^{t}. Servt.

J. S. MILL, Treasurer

1 Queen Square
Westminster

17. TO EDWIN CHADWICK[1]

E.I.H.
Friday
[Dec. 22, 182(7?)]

DEAR CHADWICK

I am requested by Mr. & Mrs. George Grote to beg the favour of your company at dinner this day se'nnight at six—62 Threadneedle Street. You will meet Graham and Roebuck,[2] & probably myself.

Very truly yours

J. S. MILL

1. *Addressed*: Arthur Aylmer Esq / 41 Great Russel [*sic*] Street / Bloomsbury. *Postmarks*: ??? / ??? / 1827; 2ANOON2 / 27NO / 1827; ?ANOON? / 28[?]NO / 1827; and ??? / 27 NO / ??? On outside in another hand: "Turn Over" "Gone away not known where / T Redbourn / R T [?] Summers [?]" MS at LSE; a page of JSM's "Speech on the Church" (published in *Autobiography by JSM, with an Appendix of Hitherto Unpublished Speeches*, ed. Harold J. Laski [London, 1924], pp. 310–25) is written on verso. Actually a form letter in another hand; JSM filled in "September," his signature and address, and wrote the address on the outside.

Aylmer has not been identified.

Early Draft, ed. Stillinger (pp. 112–15) contains a somewhat fuller account of the founding and early years of the London Debating Society than does *Autobiog.*

2. Ten shillings.

* * * *

1. *Addressed*: Edwin Chadwick Esq. / 9 Lyon's Inn. *Postmark*: 2A. NOON / DE 22 182[7?]. MS at UCL.

2. John Arthur Roebuck (1801–1879), politician. At this time a law student, he had first been introduced to JSM at the India House by Thomas Love Peacock about 1824. For some years Roebuck, George John Graham, and JSM (the "Trijackia" they called themselves) were very close friends. The cause of the ultimate break between JSM and Roebuck in the 1830's was probably Roebuck's disapproval of JSM's attachment to Mrs. John Taylor.

18. TO W. H. FERRELL[1]

[Jan. 14, 1828]

London Debating Society

SIR,

I have the honour to recal [*sic*] your attention to my last half yearly circular, and to request that your arrears of Subscription, amounting to £1 may be discharged at your earliest convenience.

I have the honour to be,

Your obedient Servant

J. S. MILL, Treasurer.

1 Queen Square
Westminster

19. TO CHARLES COMTE[1]

Londres, 25 janvier 1828.

MON CHER MONSIEUR COMTE

Je m'occupe depuis quelque temps d'une critique de la Vie de Bonaparte par Sir Walter Scott,[2] et surtout des deux premiers volumes, contenant une esquisse historique de la révolution française. Je ne me dissimule pas combien la tâche que je me suis imposée est au dessus de mes forces; mais on est ici dans une si crasse ignorance sur la révolution, et tous, jusqu'aux individus les plus instruits, ont des idées tellement ridicules sur la nature de cette crise politique, qu'avec mon peu de lumières et de connaissance des faits j'ai crû pouvoir faire quelque chose pour dessiller les yeux de mes compatriotes. C'est pour avoir des renseignemens un peux moins imparfaits sur quelques-uns des évènements les plus remarquables de la révolu-

1. *Addressed*: W. H. Ferrell Esq / 22 Hatton Garden. *Postmarks*: 12 NOON 12 / 14 JA / 1828 and 10FNOON10 / JA 15 / 1828. On outside in another hand: "Gone away not known where—G [?]. Ellis / E. Midzoth" [?] obscured by postmark. MS at LSE; the last page of JSM's "Speech on the Church" is written across the outside of the letter; across the letter itself is written: "write to Bowring." Like Letters 16, 21, and 23, this is a form letter; JSM filled in the amount of arrears ("£1"), his signature and address, and wrote the address on the outside.

Ferrell has not been identified.

* * * *

1. *Addressed*: A Monsieur / Monsieur Comte / Rue Richer / à Paris / France. *Postmarks*: Angleterre, and Janvier / 28 / 1828. MS at LSE.

François Charles Louis Comte (1782–1837), liberal political writer, son-in-law of the economist J. B. Say.

2. Published as "Scott's Life of Napoleon," *WR*, IX (April, 1828), 251–313.

tion, que j'ose vous prier de vouloir bien m'indiquer les preuves sur lesquelles s'appuient trois faits, énoncés comme certains dans votre Histoire de la Garde Nationale.[3]

1° L'intention qu'eut la cour, dans les jours antérieurs à l'époque de 14 juillet, de faire le procès des chefs du parti populaire.

2° L'intention qu'elle eut de faire la contre-révolution, en-fesant partir le roi de Versailles pour aller à Metz, à l'époque du repas des gardes du corps dans les premiers jours d'octobre 1789.

3° Les assurances solennelles faites par le roi à M. de Lafayette, avant le voyage de Varennes, qu'aucun projet d'évasion n'était entré dans sa tête.

Les preuves que j'ai pu recueillir sur ces trois faits ont bien assez de poids pour que moi en me[. . . ?][4] particulier je n'en doute nullement. Cependant elles ne montent pas audessus d'une grande probabilité, et il faut quelque chose de plus que des probabilités, pour satisfaire à un public aussi prévenu que le nôtre. Vous me ferez donc, Monsieur, le plus grand plaisir, en m'indiquant les moyens de parvenir à une certitude plus parfaite à l'égard de ces circonstances.

D'ailleurs, comme il est probable que vous ayez lû l'ouvrage de Sir Walter Scott, je n'ai pas besoin de vous dire combien d'obligation je vous aurais de toute indication que vous voulûssiez bien me donner relativement aux erreurs de ce livre. Elles sont si nombreuses, qu'il est impossible de les relever toutes; mais, d'autant qu'on connaît un plus grand nombre, on est à portée de faire une meilleure choix, pour démontrer l'infidélité de cet ouvrage prétendu historique, et le faire tomber dans le decrédit absolu qu'il mérite.

Pour vous épargner pourtant une peine inutile, je dois vous dire que je sais déjà à peu près tout ce qu'on peut apprendre en lisant la plupart des Mémoires sur la Révolution, ainsi que les ouvrages historiques de Mignet,[5] Toulongeon,[6] et autres. Dans le cas donc où vous eussiez la bonté de me donner quelques renseignemens, il n'est pas besoin de vous occuper de ces matières-la.

Mon père me charge de le rappeler à votre souvenir, et de vous prier de servir d'interprète à ses sentimens auprès de Mme votre épouse, ainsi que de M. et Mme Say, et de leur aimable famille. Veuillez bien agréer le témoignage de mon respect et de mon amitié.

J. S. MILL

3. *Histoire de la Garde nationale de Paris* . . . (Paris, 1827).

4. MS torn.

5. F. A. M. Mignet, *Histoire de la Révolution française de 1789 à 1814* (Paris, 1824; London, 1826). JSM had reviewed it with high praise in *WR*, V (April, 1826), 385–98.

6. François Emmanuel, vicomte de Toulongeon, *Histoire de France depuis la Révolution de 1789* . . . (Paris, 1801–10).

20. TO JOHN BOWRING[1]

10th March 1828.

MY DEAR SIR

Your letter, which I received this morning, is a more good-natured one than I fear mine was. I am much obliged to you for not being offended at my *taking huff* as I did, and I will now tell you exactly what I think of Mr George Bentham's book[2]—and what I am ready to say of it, if you think that it would be more satisfactory to Mr Bentham[3] than an entire omission.

I do not think that Mr. G. B's book affords any proof of want of talent—far from it—but many of haste, and want of due deliberation. This mistake was, as it seems to me, that of supposing that he was qualified to write on such a subject as Logic after two or three months' study, or that so young a logician was capable of maintaining so high a ground as that of a critic upon Whately.[4] The consequences of his mistake have been twofold: first of all, he has produced nothing but minute criticism, which even when most just, is particularly annoying to the person criticized when so much stress appears to be laid upon it. This minute criticism is often just, sometimes very acute, but frequently, also, if I am not mistaken, altogether groundless. Instead of this, a good critic on Whately should have laid down as a standard of comparison, the best existing or the best conceivable *exposition of the science*, & examined how far Whately's book possesses the properties which should belong to *that*. In the second place, Mr George Bentham seems not to be aware, that Dr Whately is a far greater master of the science than *he* is, & that the public will think the disproportion still greater than it is. It would therefore have been wiser in him not to have assumed the tone of undisputed & indisputable superiority over Whately, which marks the greater part of his critique. To be entitled to do this, a writer should not only *be* superior, but *prove* himself to be superior, in knowledge of the subject, to the author whom he criticizes. He should let people see that if he differs from Whately, it is not because W. knows more than he but because he knows more than W.

1. *Addressed*: John Bowring Esq. / 4 Highbury Park. *Postmark*: EVEN. 4 / MAR 10 / 1828. MS at LSE. Published with one omission in Packe, p. 65.

John Bowring (1792–1872), linguist, writer, and later statesman, had been editor of the *Westminster Review* since its inception in 1824. He was a close associate of Jeremy Bentham and became his literary executor.

2. George Bentham published *An Outline of a New System of Logic* in 1827.

3. Jeremy Bentham, George's uncle.

4. Richard Whately (1787–1863), then Principal of St. Alban's Hall, Oxford, and later (1831) made Archbishop of Dublin, had published his *Elements of Logic* in 1826.

I have put this more strongly, and enlarged upon it more fully, to you, than I should in the W. R.[5] But I should think it wrong, in noticing the book, not to say something of this sort.

Very truly yours,

J. S. MILL

21. TO BENJAMIN KEEN[1]

[April 23, 1828]

London Debating Society

SIR

The half yearly subscription for March last being now due, you are requested to forward it, with all arrears of former subscriptions, to my address.

Arrears £2
Subscr^{n} 10/

I am, Sir
You most ob^{t}. Servt.

J. S. MILL, Treasurer

1 Queen Square
Westminster

22. TO CHARLES COMTE[1]

Londres
27 juin
1828

MON CHER M. COMTE

Vous me ferez plaisir en voulant bien accepter quelques exemplaires de ma critique de Walter Scott,[2] dont M. Bodin[3] a la bonté de se charger. Je vous prie d'en garder autant que vous voudrez, et de placer les autres

5. No such review by JSM appeared in the *Westminster*.

* * * *

1. *Addressed*: Benjamin Keen Esq. / 1 Pump Court / Temple. *Postmarks*: 7. NIGHT.7/23.AP/1828 and 10.F.NOON.10/AP.25/1828. *Endorsed*: [Neither direction nor signature is legible] / T. Forth. MS at LSE; written on the verso of a page of the debating speech published by Laski as "Notes of my Speech against Sterling" (*Autobiog*. ed. Harold J. Laski, pp. 300–309). A form letter in another hand, except for details filled in by JSM, as in Letters 16 and 18.

Keen has not been identified.

* * * *

1. *Addressed*: A Monsieur / Monsieur Comte. MS at LSE.
2. See Letter 19, n. 2.
3. Possibly Félix Bodin (1795–1837), journalist and historian.

comme vous le trouverez bon. Je vous engage seulement à en faire part à M. Say, et de lui en donner un ou deux, s'il veut bien me faire l'honneur de les accepter.—Comme il est très probable que j'écrive encore quelques articles de revue, sur la révolution française et sur l'ancien régime, je désirerais beaucoup que ceux qui pourraient avoir les moyens et la bonne volonté de me faire parvenir des renseignemens utiles là dessus, pûssent juger au moyen de cette brochure, quelles sont ceux qui me manquent. Au reste, je ne vois guère que [?] moi en angleterre qui rendent justice à la révolution.

Agréez, Monsieur, l'expression de mes sentimens respectueux.

J. S. MILL

J'ai lieu de vous remercier très sincerement, de m'avoir fait faire la connaissance de M. Victor Jacquemont.[4] Il me paraît très estimable à tous les égards.

23. TO ARCHIBALD THOMSON[1]

[Nov. 26, 1828]

London Debating Society

SIR

The half-yearly subscription for September last being now due, you are requested to forward it, with all arrears of former subscriptions, to my address.

Arrears 10/ I am, Sir,
Subscr^{n} 10/ Your most ob^{t}. Servt.

J. S. MILL, Treasurer

The same to Mr Alfred Thomson (£1.)
1 Queen Square
Westminster

23A. TO THOMAS COATES (*see* page 742)

4. Victor Jacquemont (1801–1832), naturalist and traveller. Presumably JSM met him in London, where he consulted with British authorities and the East India Company before sailing for India in the summer of 1828.

* * * *

1. *Addressed*: Archibald Thomson Esq. / 17 Mitre Court Buildings / Temple. *Postmarks*: ?? ??? ?? / 26 NO / 1828 and ??VEN / NO 27 / 1828 and T.P. / B^{d}Way We?^{r}. *Endorsed*: Gone abroad. [Two illegible signatures]. MS at LSE; written on the verso of a page of the debating speech published as "Notes of my Speech against Sterling" (*Autobiog*., ed. Harold J. Laski, pp. 300–309). A form letter in another hand, except for details filled in by JSM, as in Letters 16, 18, and 21.

Neither Thomson has been identified.

24. TO GUSTAVE D'EICHTHAL[1]

London, 11th March, 1829

MY DEAR FRIEND,

I have been so much occupied of late that I have not had leisure even to think of writing to you, and if your brother[2] had not afforded me the present opportunity, I should probably have deferred that pleasure some time longer. I hope that you will receive the Statements and Reports of the Council of the London University[3] along with this letter, the Warden[4] having promised to send them to me in time to be given to your brother before his departure. If he should omit to do so, which I trust he will not, I will take the earliest subsequent opportunity of sending them to you. I am glad to hear that you are busily engaged in writing on the subject of England, and am not surprised to learn that you find a great number of unexpected difficulties in giving an account of the state of society here.[5] As there is nobody even in England who is by any means qualified to treat so immense a subject with any thing like completeness, it would be very wrong in you to be discouraged by finding that there is a great deal that you do not know—it is sufficient if you know, as I am satisfied you do, very much on the subject of England which is known to few, perhaps to none of your countrymen. It would have been a good thing for the interest of your book, if you had been here at this moment: you would have seen, what you did not see when you were here, a state of great political excitement. The excitement does not reach the labouring classes, but it pervades all the rest of the community to such a degree that, as I am credibly informed, it has to a great degree put a stop to buying and selling, at least

1. *Addressed*: A Monsieur / M. Gustave d'Eichthal / à Paris. Draft (incomplete) at LSE. MS at Arsenal. Published, with minor errors, in *Cosmopolis*, VI, 22–25, and in *D'Eichthal Corresp.*

Gustave d'Eichthal (1804–1886), son of a rich Jewish banking family, first became acquainted with the writings of Henri Saint-Simon through his mathematics teacher, Auguste Comte. D'Eichthal on a visit to England first saw JSM on May 30, 1828, when he accompanied Eyton Tooke to a meeting of the London Debating Society at which JSM spoke. D'Eichthal became a close friend of JSM, his chief contact with the Saint-Simonians, and a lifelong correspondent.

2. Adolphe d'Eichthal, younger brother of Gustave.

3. The first report of the council of the recently established University had been made on Oct. 30, 1826. Other early reports and statements by the Council are listed in H. H. Bellot, *University College, London, 1826–1926* (London, 1929), App. I, pp. 429–30.

4. Leonard Horner (1785–1864), geologist and educator, was Warden of London University, 1827–31.

5. D'Eichthal's projected book on England was never completed. His son, Eugène d'Eichthal, later published some of the notes he had taken for the book: "Condition de la classe ouvrière en Angleterre (1828)," in *Revue historique*, LXXIX (May, 1902), 63–95.

on a large scale, as no one can think of any thing except the Catholic question. Since the debate in the House of Commons, and the majority of 188 in favour of the question, nobody doubts the success of the bill;[6] and it is very gratifying, and most creditable to our ministers, that they have not clogged the measure with any objectionable or ungracious provisoes or restrictions. The most disgraceful artifices have been employed by the Duke of Cumberland[7] and Lord Eldon[8] in order to work upon the mind of the King; & it is a fact which you may rely upon, that the Duke of Wellington, the Lord Chancellor,[9] and Mr Peel,[10] left Windsor on Wednesday last *out of office*, their resignations having been accepted, & the Anti-Catholics had already begun to arrange a ministry when the King grew alarmed and sent off an express to beg the Duke of Wellington still to consider himself in office. It is of the greatest importance that the probable effect of this measure should be known in France. Its effect in Ireland will be a trifle compared to its effect in England. It forms an era in civilization. It is one of those great events, which periodically occur, by which the institutions of a country are brought into harmony with the better part of the mind of that country—by which that which previously existed in the minds only, of the more intelligent portion only of the community, becomes the law of the land, and by consequence raises the whole of the community to its own level. The greatest advance in the national mind, until thus adopted by the government and incorporated in the institutions of the country, is the advance only of the leading minds, of those who already were furthest in advance: It does not bring forward the whole nation, but widens the distance between the advanced posts and the rear. Much as we have improved in the last 20 years, it is only a part of us that has improved, there remained millions of men in a state of the same brutal ignorance and obstinate prejudice in which they were half a century ago. But this measure will bring forward the rear-guard of civilization: it will give a new direction to the opinions of those who never think for themselves, & who on that account can never be changed unless you change their masters & guides. The intelligent classes lead the government, & the government leads the

6. This was a division on the first reading of the Catholic Emancipation bill in the early morning hours of Saturday, March 6. Final passage of the bill in the House of Commons came on March 30, and in the House of Lords on April 10; royal assent was granted on April 13, 1829.

7. Ernest Augustus, Duke of Cumberland (1771–1851), fifth son of George III, had long been strongly opposed to any relaxation of the Catholic penal laws.

8. John Scott, first Earl of Eldon (1751–1838), jurist, was twice Lord Chancellor.

9. John Singleton Copley, Baron Lyndhurst (1772–1863), had succeeded Eldon as Lord Chancellor in 1827.

10. Sir Robert Peel (1788–1850), long an opponent of Catholic Emancipation, but convinced that the country was determined to have it, in March 1829 introduced the bill for granting the measure.

stupid classes.—Besides all this, the alteration of so important and so old a law as that which excludes Catholics from political privileges, has given a shake to men's minds which has loosened all old prejudices, and will render them far more accessible to new ideas and to rational innovations on all other parts of our institutions: our ministry, moreover, having been so reviled and attacked by the Tory & high church party that it never can act in concert with them again, must now throw itself wholly on the liberals for support. As for the Tory party, it is broken; it is entirely gone. It placed all on this stake, & it has lost it. What would not in itself have taken much from their power, will now utterly destroy it, because, as they had mustered all their strength to resist this question, it is their decisive overthrow. Ten or twelve years ago, Lord Sidmouth[11] said to an acquaintance of mine, that the King's government had not strength to do any thing which the clergy opposed. That idea is now at an end; the clergy have opposed this with all their might, & as they have failed, the influence of the church, its moral influence at least, is gone. The Church has no hold on the affections of the people: All its influence rested upon the opinion of its power: It is now seen to have very little power; and the effect of this discovery will be so great that I really begin to think that I shall see the downfall of the church in my time. I have said nothing to you on any subject except the Catholic question, but it is so much the most important event now happening that I could hardly have chosen a topic likely to be more interesting to you. By the way, it is now certain that our ministers are disposed to carry freedom of trade even further than their predecessors: I hope that you will do the same. Believe me,

Yours ever

J. S. MILL.

25. TO JOHN STERLING[1]

India House
Wednesday
[April 15, 1829]

DEAR STERLING

I have given a greater number of perusals to your note than I believe I ever gave to any epistle before. I should not however have troubled you with any answer to it, if you had not seemed to take sufficient interest in

11. Henry Addington, first Viscount Sidmouth (1757–1844), Tory politician.

* * * *

1. Published in Elliot, I, 1–3. MS at King's. The date has been pencilled in in a different hand. Paper bears 1827 watermark.

John Sterling (1806–1844), son of Edward Sterling (1773–1847), the "Thunderer" of *The Times*, though a writer of some merit, is best known as the subject of Thomas

what concerns me, to lead me to believe that I might talk to you upon a subject so entirely personal as the state of my own mind without your considering it a bore or an intrusion. I was unwilling that you should leave the London Debating Society without my telling you how much I should regret that circumstance if it were to deprive me of the chance not only of retaining such portion as I already possess, but of acquiring a still greater portion of your intimacy—which I value highly for this reason among many others, that it appears to me peculiarly adapted to the wants of my own mind; since I know no person who possesses more, of what I have not, than yourself, nor is this inconsistent with my believing you to be deficient in some of the very few things which I have. But though I feared that this loss to myself would, or at least might, be the *consequence* of your resignation I never imputed that resignation to any other *cause* than those which you have stated, and which are, in good truth, cause sufficient. I am now chiefly anxious to explain to you, more clearly than I fear I did, what I meant when I spoke to you of the comparative loneliness of my probable future lot. Do not suppose me to mean that I am conscious at present of any tendency to misanthropy—although among the very various states of mind, some of them extremely painful ones, through which I have passed during the last three years, something distantly approximating to misanthropy was *one*.[2] At present I believe that my sympathies with society, which were never strong, are, on the whole, stronger than they

---

Carlyle's finest biography. After leaving Cambridge in 1827, he was associated with his college friend, Frederick Denison Maurice, in the editing of the *Athenæum*, July-Dec., 1828. Disciples of S. T. Coleridge, he and Maurice joined the London Debating Society "as a second Liberal and even Radical party, on totally different grounds from Benthamism and vehemently opposed to it" (JSM, *Autobiog.*, p. 90). In two debates devoted to discussing the respective merits of Wordsworth and Byron, JSM allied himself for the first time with Sterling and the Coleridge-Wordsworthians. (See Karl Britton, "J. S. Mill: A Debating Speech on Wordsworth, 1829," *Cambridge Review*, LXXIX [March 8, 1958], 418–23.) This was the beginning of the intimate friendship with Sterling, to whom JSM later said he had been more attached than he had ever been to any other man (*Autobiog.*, p. 108). Sterling likewise testified to the value of the friendship: in a letter to his son, July 29, 1844, he wrote, "My intimacy with him [JSM] has been one of the great fortunes of my life,—though hardly—I suppose were ever two creatures more unlike than he & I" (Tuell, *John Sterling*, p. 69).

The occasion of this letter was Sterling's resignation from the London Debating Society. In the first draft of his *Autobiography* (see *Early Draft*, ed. Stillinger, p. 133) JSM attributed Sterling's resignation to an especially sharp exchange between the two of them in a debate involving their political philosophy. The resignation was followed, however, by the development of an even closer personal friendship than had previously existed. The earliest extant letter of Sterling to JSM, March 31, 1830 (King's), is concerned with seeking JSM's advice on assisting the Spanish rebels.

2. This seems to be the only reference in an extant letter to JSM's soul-crisis, which had its onset in the winter of 1826–27 and which is discussed in *Autobiog.*, chap. v. Similar later disturbances, however, are mentioned in letters to Carlyle, e.g. Letter 72.

ever were. By loneliness I mean the absence of that feeling which has accompanied me through the greater part of my life, that which one fellow traveller, or one fellow soldier has towards another—the feeling of being engaged in the pursuit of a common object, and of mutually cheering one another on, and helping one another in an arduous undertaking. This, which after all is one of the strongest ties of individual sympathy, is at present, so far as I am concerned, suspended at least, if not entirely broken off. There is now no human being (with whom I can associate on terms of equality) who acknowledges a common object with me, or with whom I can cooperate even in any practical undertaking without the feeling, that I am only using a man whose purposes are different, as an instrument for the furtherance of my own. *Idem sentire de republicâ*, was thought by one of the best men who ever lived to be the strongest bond of friendship:[3] for *republicâ* I would read "all the great objects of life," where the parties concerned have at heart any great objects at all. I do not see how there can be otherwise that *idem velle, idem nolle*, which is necessary to perfect friendship.[4] Being excluded therefore from this, I am resolved hereafter to avoid all occasions for debate, since they cannot now strengthen my sympathies with those who agree with me, & are sure to weaken them with those who differ.—Yours faithfully

J. S. MILL

26. TO GUSTAVE D'EICHTHAL[1]

London, 15th May 1829

MY DEAR D'EICHTHAL,

Many thanks to you for your interesting letter, which has been read not only by Tooke[2] and myself but by several others of our friends with very great pleasure. Before I say more, I will answer the question which

3. The thought of the quotation is characteristically Ciceronian, though it has not been possible to find in Cicero's writings a statement worded precisely in JSM's phrasing. Cf. Cicero, *De Amicitia*, iv, 15; *De Officiis*, I, xvi, 51; and *Oratio Pro Cnæo Plancio*, ii, 5.

4. Cf. *Idem velle atque nolle, ea demum firma amicitia est* ("An identity of likes and dislikes is after all the only basis of friendship"), Sallust, *Bellum Catilinae*, xx, 15. Cf. also this passage: "A question was started, how far people who disagree in a capital point can live in friendship together. Johnson said they might. Goldsmith said they could not, as they had not the same *idem velle atque idem nolle*—the same likings and the same aversions." (James Boswell, *Life of Samuel Johnson*, ed. J. W. Croker [London, 1839], III, 218.)

* * * *

1. *Addressed*: A Monsieur / M. Gustave d'Eichthal. MS at Arsenal. Published in part in *Cosmopolis*, VI, 25–28, and in *D'Eichthal Corresp.*, pp. 7–12.

2. Eyton Tooke also corresponded with D'Eichthal; some of his letters are in *D'Eichthal Corresp.*

your brother has just put to me in your name. The Parliamentary accounts of the expenses of management, amounts of deposit, and other information relating to Saving Banks are not at all mixed up with those of Benefit Societies. They are quite separate.—Nothing of much importance or interest has taken place here since the settlement of the Catholic question,[3] except the discussion respecting the duties on Silk,[4] which shews that our ministry is disposed not only to persevere in the measures of their predecessors with respect to free trade, but to carry the principle still further. It is much to be feared that they will not take the opportunity which the present state of our relations with Portugal affords, for abrogating the Methuen treaty,[5] by which we are bound to admit the Portugal wines at a lower duty than those of other countries. If we were free from this engagement, it might be hoped that your ministry would consent to lower the duties on some of our manufactures, on condition of our lowering those on your wines. But I suppose the stupid affairs of Russia & Turkey would prevent any discussions between the two Governments on commercial policy at present.[6]—I am glad to hear that you have made so much progress in your work on England.[7] I am however inclined to think from your letter to Tooke, that there is some danger of your praising this country beyond its due. You were very naturally struck with the superiority of the English to the French in all those qualities by which a nation is enabled to turn its productive and commercial resources to the best account. But this superiority is closely connected with the very worst point in our national character, the disposition to sacrifice every thing to accumulation, & that exclusive & engrossing selfishness which accompanies it. I am well aware how much of this is owing to our political institutions, under which every thing is accessible to wealth and scarcely any thing to poverty. But I fear that the commercial spirit, amidst all its good effects, is almost sure to bring with it wherever it prevails, a certain amount of this evil; because that which necessarily occupies every man's time & thoughts for the greater part of his life, naturally acquires an ascendency over his mind disproportionate to its real importance; & when the pursuit of wealth, in a degree

3. See Letter 24, n. 6.

4. An extensive debate on the subject had taken place in the House of Commons on April 13 and 14.

5. English policy was in opposition to the reactionary King Miguel I, who had usurped the throne of Portugal. His young niece Maria, the legitimate Queen, was at this time in England. The Methuen Treaty had been in force since 1703. By it and a similar arrangement with Spain, Portuguese and Spanish wines had long been admitted into England at a much lower duty than French wines.

6. England and France were both deeply concerned in the Russo-Turkish War of 1828–29, and later this year both participated in a settlement of it which also guaranteed the independence of Greece.

7. See Letter 24, n. 5.

greater than is required for comfortable subsistence,—an occupation which concerns only a man himself & his family,—becomes the main object of his life, it almost invariably happens that his sympathies & his feelings of interest become incapable of going much beyond himself & his family. You must have observed even while you were here, although mixing as you did, with the best class of Englishmen, how difficult it is to interest them in any thing which has not some bearing upon what they call their advancement in life. In all countries you find men in middle life in a great degree selfish & worldly, but there are few countries besides this where even the young men are many of them avowedly so. In France or Germany the laughable aberrations of sentiment & enthusiasm are common, the odious ones of coldness & selfishness rare. In this country the reverse is the case. Here, it requires great tact & knowledge of society to enable a man to appear deeply in earnest on any subject without exposing himself to be laughed at—& the etiquette of what is called good society is to appear profoundly insensible to every impression, external or internal. You say that you dread to think what a great nation we shall be, now when we have got rid of bigotry. I do not myself think that bigotry was, or is, our worst point. It is indifference, moral insensibility, which we have need to get rid of. I wish that I saw the least chance of our improving in this respect, without either a political revolution, or such a change in our national education as it would, I fear, require a revolution to bring about. You are far ahead of us in France. You have only to teach men what is right, & they will do it: they are uninformed, but they are not prejudiced, & are desirous & eager to learn. Here, the grand difficulty is to make them desire to learn. They have such an opinion of their own wisdom that they do not think they *can* learn; & they have too little regard for other people to care much whether they learn or no, in things which only interest the nation in general, or mankind at large. Our middle class moreover have but one object in life, to ape their superiors; for whom they have an open-mouthed & besotted admiration, attaching itself to the bad more than to the good points, being those they can most easily comprehend & imitate. It is true that those who wish to do good, are here enabled, by that *esprit d'association* which you so much admire, to effect more, in proportion to their numbers, than they do in France. It is a great fault in your nation to surround themselves as you say with an atmosphere of personal vanity, which makes them desire to get all the honour of every thing to themselves, & not to call in the cooperation of others lest they should be compelled to share the credit with them. The fault of your public men certainly is, a desire for display. Here there is not so much anxiety of that kind. Applause which "leads to nothing", is less valued. But the applause which has exchangeable value, that which produces its worth in pounds sterling, or in substantial power, the applause of the ruling classes, is as highly esteemed & as anxiously sought after here as elsewhere. We are it is true improving rapidly; chiefly however in throwing off prejudices. We no longer think our institutions the best possible; but we commit gross blunders in every attempt we make to mend them. Still it is something to have a fair field open. Sound ideas and good sense applied to public affairs, have, I believe, considerably more chance of being listened to & exercising influence at the present moment than at any time in the last hundred years. But where are they to be found? There are no men of talents among us. Our writers & our orators are, almost to a man, *des gens mediocres*. I do not know whether yours are any better; probably not; but they will be. We have at any rate not one member of either house of parliament who approaches within twenty degrees of M. de Broglie.[8]—Tooke desires me to ask you, whether you can recommend to him any French works adapted for the instruction of the people on the elements of the sciences of politics & morals. It seems that the Society for the Diffusion of Useful (or rather Useless) Knowledge[9] has appointed a Translation Committee, of which Tooke is likely to be one of the most active members. I suppose that if there be any such works they must be very recent, I am almost sure there are none prior to the present century.—He also wishes to know whether you can point out any works which it would be worth while for him to read, for his own instruction, on French Administration, & on the science of Administration in general—a science so little studied here that we are indebted to France both for the name & the very idea.—Of course the *thing* goes on here as well as every where else, but it has been so little thought of or studied scientifically that the very word itself is not yet naturalized in our island. Tooke also wishes to know whether a collection of the works of St Simon[10] & his school, just sufficient to give him an idea of their general views &

8. Achille Léonce Victor Charles, duc de Broglie (1785–1870), liberal statesman.

9. The Society, which Thomas Love Peacock nicknamed the "Steam Intellect Society," had been founded in 1826 under the leadership of Henry Brougham to publish in inexpensive editions works on science, history, economics, ethics, and philosophy. For a good brief account of the Society's activities, see R. K. Webb, *The British Working Class Reader, 1790–1848* (London, 1955), pp. 66–73.

10. Claude Henri de Rouvroy, comte de Saint-Simon (1760–1825), founder of the school of French socialist thought which was to be the subject of many of JSM's letters during the next three years. For studies of his connections with the movement, see Emery Neff, *Carlyle and Mill* (New York, 1926); Richard K. P. Pankhurst, *The Saint Simonians, Mill and Carlyle* (London, [1957]); and the unpublished Columbia University doctoral dissertation by Dwight N. Lindley, "The Saint-Simonians, Carlyle, and Mill" (1958), available from University Microfilms, Ann Arbor, Mich. The best modern study of Saint-Simon is Frank E. Manuel's *The New World of Henri Saint-Simon* (Cambridge, Mass., 1956).

principles, would be voluminous or expensive. I am only now about to begin to read the work of M. Comte[11] which you so strongly recommended to me. When I have read it, I shall be extremely desirous of having some discussion with you on the principles of the Producteur party, especially that respecting "l'hérédité de la proprieté," on which subject their doctrine as you express it seems to me a great heresy, but of course I cannot tell what I should think of it until I know with what qualifications & reservations they receive it. I myself think, with Mr Bentham, that property ought to escheat to the state in preference to collateral heirs, where there is no testamentary disposition. You will probably have perceived from our debates that the proposition of introducing some system of Poor Rates into Ireland is about to be seriously entertained by our Government.[12] The progress of opinion on this subject within a few years has been very striking. I am inclined to think that the discussions on this subject will be extremely instructive, & well worthy of attentive consideration from your statesmen.

Believe me yours faithfully

J. S. MILL.

27. TO GUSTAVE D'EICHTHAL[1]

London 8th October 1829

MY DEAR D'EICHTHAL

I can hardly expect forgiveness for having allowed so long an interval to elapse without writing to you, especially after you so warmly invited me, not only to write, but to correspond and discuss with you on some of the subjects on which it is of most importance that you, and I, and all men, should think rightly. The truth is however that it was long before I found time to read the books which you were so kind as to leave with me, and since that time I have been too much occupied with other things to be

11. Auguste Comte (1798–1857), pioneer sociologist and founder of positivism, with whom JSM conducted an extensive correspondence between 1841 and 1847 (see Letters 334 ff.), though the two never met. In 1828 D'Eichthal had sent JSM a copy of *Système de politique positive*, which Comte had written while still a disciple of Saint-Simon and which formed the *Troisième cahier du Catéchisme des Industriels* (1823).

12. The question had been discussed in the House of Commons on May 7, and on May 14 Lord Darnley presented a petition in the House of Lords for the extension of the English Poor Laws to Ireland in a modified form.

* * * *

1. *Addressed*: A Monsieur / M. Gustave d'Eichthal / à Paris. MS at Arsenal. Published, with minor errors, in *Cosmopolis*, VI, 28–32, and in *D'Eichthal Corresp.*, pp. 13–21.

able to write to you at all. I have not yet been able to read any of the articles of the Producteur.[2] I cannot therefore give you my opinion so fully as I may perhaps hereafter, on the doctrines of the St Simon school. As far however as I can judge at present, if I were ever to become a proselyte of that school, it would rather be on the grounds of your last letter to me, than of any of the books I have read. In your letter I do not know that there is much in which I disagree though there are some things. I cannot say as much for the books. When I read the "Opinions Littéraires, Philosophiques et Industrielles"[3] which I took up with some expectations, I was perfectly astonished at the shallowness of it. It appeared to me the production of men who had neither read nor thought, but hastily put down the first crudities that would occur to a boy who had just left school. When, however, I read Comte's "Traité de Politique Positive,"[4] I was no longer surprised at the high opinion which I had heard you express of the book, & the writer, and was even seduced by the plausibility of his manner into forming a higher opinion of the doctrines which he delivers than on reflexion they appear to me at all entitled to. I find the same fault with his philosophy, that he does with the philosophy of the eighteenth century [;] it is only the *partie critique* which appears to me sound, the *partie organique* appears to me liable to a hundred objections. It abounds indeed, with many very acute remarks though all of them of a kind which the progress of events is suggesting at this moment to all minds, which are *au niveau du siècle* throughout Europe: but it is a great mistake, a very common one too, which this sect seem to be in great danger of falling into to suppose that a few striking and original observations, are sufficient to form the foundation of a *science positive.* M. Comte is an exceedingly clear and methodical writer, most agreeable in stile, and concatenates so well, that one is apt to mistake the perfect coherence and logical consistency of his system, for truth.[5] This power of systematising, of tracing a principle to its remotest consequences, and that power of clear and consecutive exposition which generally accompanies it, seem to me to be the characteristic excellencies of all the good French writers; and are nearly connected with their characteristic defect, which seems to me to be this: They are so well satisfied with the clearness with which their con-

2. A periodical (Oct., 1825–Dec., 1826) established after the death of Saint-Simon by his disciples, edited for the first six months as a weekly by a M. Cerclet and thereafter as a monthly by Barthélemy Prosper Enfantin.

3. By various writers, including Saint-Simon, Léon Halévy, Dr. Joseph Bailly, and Charles Duveyrier, Paris, 1825.

4. Evidently Comte's *Système de politique positive.* See Letter 26, n. 11.

5. This passage should be read in the light of Macaulay's slashing criticism of James Mill in three successive numbers (March, June, and Oct., 1829) of the *Edinburgh Review*, a criticism which is also reflected in JSM's *Logic*, VI, vii and viii. See also *Autobiog.*, pp. 110–13.

clusions flow from their premisses, that they do not stop to compare the conclusions themselves with the fact though it is only when they will stand this comparison that we can be assured the premisses have included all which is essential to the question. They deduce politics like mathematics from a set of axioms & definitions, forgetting that in mathematics there is no danger of partial views: a proposition is either true or it is not, & if it is true, we may safely apply it to every case which the proposition comprehends in its terms: but in politics & the social science, this is so far from being the case, that error seldom arises from our assuming premisses which are not true, but generally from our overlooking other truths which limit, & modify the effect of the former. It appears to me therefore that most French philosophers are chargeable with the fault which Cousin imputes to Condillac,[6] of insisting upon only seeing *one* thing when there are many, or seeing a thing only on one side, only in one point of view when there are many others equally essential to a just estimate of it. If I were to point out all the instances in which this fault is observable in Comte's book, I must go through every page, for it pervades his whole book; & as it seems to me, it is this fault which alone enables him to give his ideas that compact & systematic form by which they are rendered in appearance something like a *science positive*. To begin with the very first and fundamental principle of the whole system, that government and the social union exist for the purpose of concentrating and directing all the forces of society to some one end. He cannot mean that government should exist for more than one purpose, or that this one purpose should be the direction of the united force of society to more than one end. What a foundation for a system of political science this is! Government exists for all purposes whatever that are for man's good: and the highest & most important of these purposes is the improvement of man himself as a moral and intelligent being, which is an end not included in M. Comte's category at all. The united forces of society never were, nor can be, directed to one single end, nor is there, so far as I can perceive, any reason for desiring that they should. Men do not come into the world to fulfil one single end, and there is no single end which if fulfilled even in the most complete manner would make them happy. Then again when M. Comte comes to enquire what this end is, it must be either the dominion of man over man, which is conquest, or the dominion of man over nature, which is production: the first was the end of society in the ancient world & in the feudal ages, (not true in the least)—this is gone by, therefore the other must be the end of society now: why so, pray? Are conquest & production, the only two

6. The closest approximation to this criticism of Condillac that the present editor has been able to find is in the third lecture of Victor Cousin's *Cours de l'histoire de la philosophie: Histoire de la philosophie du XVIIIe siècle* (2 vols., Paris, 1829).

conceivable purposes that human beings can combine for! This is one of a thousand things which shew that the St Simon philosophy could only originate in France. If M. Comte were a native of England, where this idol "production" has been set up and worshipped with incessant devotion for a century back, & if he had seen how the disproportionate importance attached to it lies at the root of all our worst national vices, corrupts the measures of our statesmen, the doctrines of our philosophers & hardens the minds of our people so as to make it almost hopeless to inspire them with any elevation either of intellect or of soul, he would have seen that a philosophy which makes production expressly the one end of the social union, would render the only great social evil, of which there is much danger in the present state of civilisation, irremediable. It leads too, to the grand practical conclusion of the St Simon school, that the business of government must be placed in the hands of the principal *industriels*, the *pouvoir temporel* at least, & the *pouvoir spirituel* in the *savans* & *artistes*: I do not know how it may be in France, but I know that in England these three are the very classes of persons you would pick out as the most remarkable for a narrow & bigotted understanding, & a sordid & contracted disposition as respects all things wider than their business or families. I have a thousand things more to say on this subject, but I must pass to another. There is according to M. Comte only one law of the development of human civilisation. You who have been in England can say whether this is true. Is it not clear that these two nations, England & France, are examples of the *advance of civilisation* by two different roads, & that neither of them has, nor probably ever will, pass through the state which the other is in? It is the lower animals which have only one law, that of their instinct. The order of the developement of man's faculties, is as various as the situations in which he is placed. It is melancholy to observe how a man like M. Comte has had all his views of history warped & distorted by the necessity of proving that civilisation has but one law, & that a law of progressive advancement; how it blinds him to all the merits of the Greeks & Romans (& the demerits of the middle ages) because there was improvement in some things at such periods, he thinks there must have been so in all: why not allow that while mankind advanced in some things, they went back in others? There is positively no place for England in M. Comte's system: he has given a list of all the states which the social system can be in, and England is in none of them. Notwithstanding all this there are many excellent & new remarks in M. Comte's book: & if people could be contented to take part & leave the rest, these doctrines would probably receive the proper corrections & modifications & would be very valuable. But if the proselytes of Saint Simon insist upon forming a sect, which is a character above all to be avoided by independent thinkers [,] & imagine themselves under a necessity, if they belong to the sect, to take all its dogmas without exception or qualification, they will not only do no good but I fear immense mischief. Substituting one fragment of the truth for another is not what is wanted, but combining them together so as to obtain as large a portion as possible of the whole. I have not even left myself space to tell you with how much pleasure I have read your pamphlet, which has made almost an entire convert of me, and the few sheets which your brother shewed me of your work on England.[7] I shall however write to you again by your friend, I hope I may now say *our* friend, M. Victor Lanjuinais,[8] whom I hope I shall see more of when he returns from Scotland; what I have seen of him I like extremely. Meanwhile believe me

Yours faithfully

J. S. MILL.

28. TO GUSTAVE D'EICHTHAL[1]

India House
London
7th November 1829

MY DEAR D'EICHTHAL,

As I am several letters in your debt, I take advantage of the departure of our friend M. Lanjuinais[2] to pay one instalment. To my great regret I have seen but little of M. Lanjuinais during his residence here, having been prevented first by his absence from town, then by my own, afterwards by his again, and finally by his departure before the expected period. However he permits us to hope that we shall see him again for a short time in the early part of next summer.—One object which I have in writing to you at present is to inform you of a project which we have formed and which there is some prospect though but a doubtful one of our being able to realize, of starting a morning newspaper, of which Chadwick should be the editor, and almost all your friends in this country frequent writers.[3] The prospects of success would be very encouraging. You know in how low a state the newspaper press of this country is. In France the best thinkers & writers of the nation, write in the journals & direct public

7. See Letter 24, n. 5.
8. Victor Lanjuinais (1802–1869), economist and liberal politician.

* * * *

1. *Addressed*: A Monsieur / M. Gustave d'Eichthal / à Paris. MS at Arsenal. Published, with errors and omissions, in *Cosmopolis*, VI, 32–38, and in *D'Eichthal Corresp.*, pp. 22–34. D'Eichthal's answer appears in the latter volume, pp. 39–68.
2. See preceding letter, n. 8.
3. Nothing came of this projected newspaper.

opinion; but our daily & weekly writers are the lowest hacks of literature, which when it is a trade, is the vilest & most degrading of all trades, because more of affectation & hypocrisy, & more subservience to the baser feelings of others, are necessary for carrying it on, than for any other trade, from that of a brothelkeeper upwards. We are not in so low a state here, as not to have in some measure found this out; & there is consequently rather a general sense of the needfulness of some newspaper conducted by men really in earnest about public objects, & really forming their opinions from some previous knowledge & not from the mere appearances of the moment, or the convenience of party advocacy. The old ties of party and the attachment to established opinions have at the same time been so greatly weakened among all the reading classes, that the times are very favourable for starting new opinions, and especially any which hold out sufficient hopes of extensive good, to enlist in their behalf that enthusiasm and *dévouement*, which are now wandering about the world seeking an object worthy of them. We possess moreover the means of rendering this paper the best as a mere vehicle of intelligence; as a mere newspaper in short, which yet exists; & have therefore no doubt of its success provided we can raise the money which of course is doubtful, but of which we have considerable hopes. As this newspaper will pay very particular attention to French affairs, and will endeavour, as one of its grand objects to make its readers understand not only French politics but the whole social state of France, including all that is doing in the world of literature & philosophy by that active and important member of the European community, & in short to explain the character of that general movement which is taking place in the human mind all over the Continent of Europe but especially in France, we shall be very anxious to have a first rate correspondent at Paris, capable of supplying, (along with the general news of the day in politics, literature & philosophy) sound & enlarged views on all these subjects. I imagine there is scarcely any person except yourself who, with the other necessary qualifications, possesses that knowledge of England, which a Frenchman writing for Englishmen would need, & I am speaking the sentiments of all my expected *collaborateurs* when I request, that if we succeed in realizing our scheme, you will undertake this department of it. We should wish to have regular letters as often as you could find time to write them, similar to those in the Times, which, though by no means first rate, have done great good here. Of course we should not wish you to undertake so great a portion of our labour without participating in our reward (the pecuniary part of it I mean) either in the shape of a regular engagement, or of a proportion of the profits in case of success, according to your own preference, and to the amount of capital which we can succeed in raising, to commence our operations. If by ill fortune you should not be disposed to undertake what I have proposed to you, I beg that you will consider whether there is any other person whom you could recommend to us for the same purpose, or with whom you could divide the task. In the mean time, as it is best that a scheme of this sort should be known to as few persons as possible until it is certain of being prosecuted, it will be desirable that you should not speak of it more than may be necessary for obtaining what we want.—I have not left myself room to say much to you on the Saint Simon school, & indeed, having been out of town, I have not yet had an opportunity of reading any of the articles of the Producteur.[4] I am chiefly anxious at present to tell you of the things which I approve and admire in this school, as I am rather afraid that my former letter may have left an impression on your mind, that I do not think so highly of them as I actually do. In the first place then I highly approve and commend one of the leading principles of their system, which they have established to conviction, the necessity of a *Pouvoir Spirituel*. They have held out as the ultimate end towards which we are advancing & which we shall one day attain, a state in which the body of the people, i.e. the uninstructed, shall entertain the same feelings of deference & submission to the authority of the instructed, in morals and politics, as they at present do in the physical sciences. This, I am persuaded, is the only wholesome state of the human mind; & the knowledge that we ought to look to it as the ultimate end, has a great tendency to protect us from many errors which the philosophers of the 18th century fell into, & which all will be liable to who suppose that the diffusion of knowledge among the labouring classes & the consequent improvement of their intellects is to be the grand instrument of the regeneration of mankind. Before, however, this state can be attained or even aimed at it is necessary that several great steps should be taken in the improvement of the social organisation; & principally that the great social sinister interests should be removed, since while these exist, those, who would otherwise be the instructed classes, have no motive to obtain real instruction in politics & morals, & are subjected to biasses from which the students of the physical sciences are exempt. They can drive a trade in the ignorance and prejudices of others; they either write for the classes who have sinister interests, and minister to their selfishness and malevolence, or else, addressing themselves to the common people, they find in the well grounded discontent of the people against their institutions sufficient materials for acquiring popularity without either instructing their intellects, or cultivating right habits of feeling and judging in their minds. I object altogether to the means which the St Simonists propose for organizing the *pouvoir spirituel*. It appears to me that you cannot organise it at all. What is the *pouvoir spirituel* but the

4. See preceding letter, n. 2.

insensible influence of mind over mind? The instruments of this are private communication, the pulpit, & the press. If you attempt to collect together the instructed, you must have somebody to chuse them, & determine who they are: in what respect, then, will this differ from an elective national assembly, with a qualification for eligibility, not a qualification of property but of education?—The second great service which in my opinion the St Simonists have rendered, is not by having been the first to notice (for all persons of course have adverted to it more or less) but having illustrated more copiously than had been done before, and having paid more attention & attached more importance than other philosophers to the fact, that institutions which if we consider them in themselves, we can hardly help thinking it impossible should ever have produced any thing but the most unqualified mischief (the Catholic church for example) may yet, at a particular stage in the progress of the human mind, have not only been highly useful but absolutely indispensable; the only means by which the human mind could have been brought forward to an ulterior stage of improvement. A due attention to this great truth, which is the result of enlarged views of the history of mankind, is also thereby a necessary condition to those views. Without it, there is no possibility of viewing or judging past times with candour, or trying them by any standard but that of the present. And yet, he who does not do this, will judge the present as ill as the past. For surely at every *present* epoch there are many things which would be good for that epoch, though not good for the being Man, at every epoch, nor perhaps at any other than that one: & whoever does not make this distinction must be a bad practical philosopher even for his own age, yet he will not make the distinction for the present who does not make it for the past. Every age contains countries, every country contains men, who are in every possible state of civilisation, from the lowest of all, to the highest which mankind have reached in that age, or in that country. Yet one hardly meets with a single man who does not habitually think & talk as if whatever was good or bad for one portion of these countries or of these individuals was good or bad for all the other portions. It is very unlikely that any person who is imbued with the spirit of the St Simon school, should fall into this error. They have, and their system tends to produce even as it appears to me in excess, that eclecticism, and comprehensive liberality, which, as it widens the range both of our ideas and of our feelings, is far more pardonable & less mischievous even when most *exagéré*, than the opposite fault. They have that spirit which is most opposed to the spirit of criticism and disceptation; that which induces us, not to combat but to pass over & disregard the errors in what is presented to us, in order to seize and appropriate to ourselves that portion or fragment (however diminutive) of truth, which there must necessarily be at the bottom of every error, which is not a mere fallacy in ratiocination. As the great danger to mankind is not from seeing what is not, but from overlooking what is; since clever & intelligent men hardly ever err from the former cause, but no powers of mind are any protection against the evils arising from imperfect and partial views of what is real; since not errors but half truths are the bane of human improvement, it seems to follow that the proper mode of philosophizing & discussing for a person who pursues the good of mankind & not the gratification of his own vanity, should be the direct opposite of the *philosophie critique* of the last century: it should consist, not in attacking men's wrong opinions, but in giving them that knowledge which will enable them to form right ones that will push off the wrong ones, as the new leaves push off the withered ones of the last year. The great instrument of improvement in men, is to supply them with the other half of the truth, one side of which only they have ever seen: to turn round to them the white side of the shield, of which they seeing only the black side, have cut other men's throats & risked their own to prove that the shield is black. It is not sufficiently considered by many zealots for even right opinions, that you have done little or nothing for a man when you have merely given him an opinion. An opinion suggests hardly anything to an uninformed mind; it may become a watchword, but can never be a moving & influencing and living principle within him. Words, or any thing which can be stated in words, benefit none but those minds to whom the words suggest an ample store of correct and clear ideas, & sound & accurate knowledge previously acquired concerning the things which are meant by the words. It is therefore of little use altering men's opinions, & it is often very mischievous to unsettle them, until you have brought their minds to that higher state of cultivation, of which better opinions are the natural & almost spontaneous growth. But merely in order to do this, we must not attack their opinions *en masse*, but fix our attention on what is good in those opinions, & endeavour to lead them on from this & through this to something better. This is practical eclecticism. Without intending it I have been illustrating at great length one of the most valuable parts of the St Simon philosophy, though not at all peculiar to it, the distinction between the *partie critique* & the *partie organique* of any philosophy & between the critical, & the organical, epochs of the human mind. I am inclined to think that one idea connected with this matter, did really originate with them, viz. that a principle may be valuable & in a certain sense even true *comme principe critique* which *comme principe organique* or even as a simple logical proposition is false. The logical explanation of this I take to be, that a proposition, though false as a whole, may comprehend as part of itself, may logically include the negation of some prevailing error. I think that the St Simonists have also great merit in having pointed out as the first step in the investigation of practical political truths, to ascertain what is the state into which, in the natural order of the advancement of civilisation the nation in question will next come; in order that it may be the grand object of our endeavours, to facilitate the transition to this state. Keeping this in view, it will often follow, that we must uphold or even establish institutions which are liable to produce great evils, evils which in other states of society might be without alloy; provided that these institutions have, at the same time, a tendency to counteract other mischievous tendencies, which happen to be more prevailing or more to be apprehended in that age, by which of course must always be meant, in that state of the human mind. On this subject I should differ from the St Simonists, chiefly in this respect; they seem to think that the mind of man, by a sort of fatality or necessity, grows & unfolds its different faculties always in one particular order, like the body; & that therefore we must be always either standing still, or advancing, or retrograding; whereas I am satisfied, that better consideration would shew, that different nations, indeed different minds, may & do advance to improvement by different roads; that nations, & men, nearly in an equally advanced stage of civilization, may yet be very different in character, & that changes may take place in a man or a nation, which are neither steps forward nor backward, but steps to one side. Here ends, I believe, all that I have to say at present on the St Simon school.—Tooke has shewn me all your letters; in the last there are two things which pleased me extremely. One is your remark that analysis & synthesis have directly opposite meanings in mathematics from what they have in philosophy: this, which is not only a just but a profound observation, also occurred to Dugald Stewart,[5] the second volume of whose Philosophy of the Mind contains that with many other excellent remarks on similar subjects. The other is, your observation that there is no incompatibility between the morality of enlightened self-interest & that of *dévoûement*: neither of these phrases comprises the *principle* of morals, but they express two kinds of impulses, both of which might, & do to a certain extent, lead men to virtue, & which it is desirable to put forward alternately as incentives to it, according to the age, the nation, or even the individual, whom you are addressing.

I hope soon to hear from you after having merited that pleasure by these two long letters. For the present believe me

Yours most sincerely

J. S. MILL.

5. Dugald Stewart (1753–1828), Scottish philosopher. His *Elements of the Philosophy of the Human Mind* appeared in three volumes between 1792 and 1827.

29. TO GUSTAVE D'EICHTHAL[1]

London, 9th February 1830

MY DEAR GUSTAVE

I had for several weeks been on the point of writing to you a long letter on the great subject which you have so deeply at heart, and had just for the first time obtained an interval of leisure for that purpose, when the horrible event took place which has deprived me of one whom I had counted upon as a friend and companion through my whole life.[2] I could not mix up the first intelligence of our loss with an abstract philosophical discussion. Poor Mr Tooke[3] was anxious that you should be informed of it, and wished me to communicate it to you, but I anxiously hoped that you might learn it first through some other channel. I am deeply indebted to you, my dear Gustave, for your expressions of sympathy in my own affliction.[4] There is no ground for the apprehensions which you express of my being overcome and crushed by this unexpected blow. Many who knew him and loved him less than I did, have felt the immediate shock much more forcibly. It is not the intensity, but the durability of such grief, which bears hard upon me, and I feel it most in the enervation, & almost extinction, for the present, of all my activity, and all my concern for mankind or for my duties. It seems to me as if I had never cared for any one but him, and had never laboured but for his sympathy and approbation. Yet though I should detest myself if I ever ceased to think and feel as I now do concerning his loss, I know that this effect of it will not last. The more affectionately I cherish his memory, the more ardently shall I pursue those great objects in which he took so deep an interest. I should care little for life or for mankind, but for the thought that there are among them a few men like him, & that all have in them the capacity of becoming at least an approximation to what he was. There are yet two or three living, but for whom I should no longer value existence: for though there have been a few, very few, who had sufficient native energy and firmness to pursue cheerfully the good of posterity, without being

1. *Addressed*: A Monsieur / Monsieur Gustave d'Eichthal / Place des Victoires No 5 / à Paris. *Postmarks*: Fevrier/15/1830/ and F/11–4. MS at Arsenal. Published, with minor errors and omissions, in *Cosmopolis*, VI, 348–55, and in *D'Eichthal Corresp.*, pp. 117–30. The latter work also includes the last letter of Eyton Tooke to D'Eichthal (pp. 90–110) and D'Eichthal's letter of Feb. 3 to JSM on Tooke's death (pp. 111–16).

2. Eyton Tooke committed suicide on Jan. 27, 1830. For a notice of the inquest, see *Examiner*, Jan. 31, 1830, p. 76. Henry Solly in *These Eighty Years* (London, 1893), I, 134–38, attributes Tooke's derangement to what Tooke mistakenly thought was an unrequited love for Solly's sister. See also, however, Letter 117.

3. Thomas Tooke, the father of Eyton.

4. In D'Eichthal's letter of Feb. 3, 1830, to JSM. See n. 1 above.

upheld by the aid and encouragement of some in their own generation, I am so far removed from that state of mind that I can just understand it sufficiently to believe it possible. But as I have said before, those who made life valuable to me are not all gone, and though scarcely any of them were equal to Eyton and none superior to him in purity and singleness of mind combined with warmth and kindliness of affection, yet I cannot entirely droop or relax in my exertions while they survive, and remain unchanged towards me, and progressively improving in the developement of their intellectual and moral capabilities. I know too, that our loss will be an additional bond of connexion to me with those who loved him and who pursue the great objects of his life. The time however when I shall feel this effect of it has not yet arrived.

While I write this, I have received your note enclosing Eyton's last letter to you:[5] the expression of his last thoughts and feelings on the great interests of humanity. It was kind in you to send it, particularly now when the last relic of our friend must be so valuable to you. I had however seen it already, as he shewed it to me before he sent it off. I accept gratefully your offer of sending a reply to it, addressed to me; but I do so, only because I should be interested by any thing which you would write on those topics; for though I fundamentally agreed with him, his objections to the St Simonian philosophy are not exactly those on which I should mainly insist, nor are stated in the exact terms or manner in which I should urge them. I am not about to make this letter a controversial one, for this event has so scattered my thoughts that I have been able to carry on no continued train of reflexion since it occurred. Besides, I have a great dislike to controversy, and am persuaded that discussion, *as* discussion, seldom did any good. This may shew you how completely I am cured of those *habitudes critiques*, which, you seem to suppose, are the only obstacle to my adopting the entire doctrine of your school. The *esprit critique* is almost the only one which prevails among the best and most instructed men of this country as well as of France; and it will be one of the objects of my philosophical and practical labours, (as it would have been one of those of poor Eyton if he had happily lived to pursue his designs), to contribute to the formation of a better spirit. This is a debt which I owe partly though not entirely to the St Simonian school: I had much changed from what I was, before I read any of their publications; but it was their works which gave order and system to the ideas which I had already imbibed from intercourse with others, and derived from my own reflexions. A part of the objection I have to controversy, is that it keeps up the *esprit critique*. I am averse to any mode of eradicating error, but by establishing and inculcating (when that is practicable) the opposite truth; a truth of some

5. Evidently Tooke's letter of Jan. 19, 1830. See n. 1.

kind inconsistent with that moral or intellectual state of mind from which the errors arise. It is only thus that we can at once maintain the good that already exists, and produce more. And I object to placing myself in the situation of an advocate for or against a cause. I will read the books of those from whom I differ, I will consider patiently and mature in my own mind the ideas which they suggest, I will make up my own opinion, and set it forth with the reasons. When I see any person going wrong, I will try to find out the fragment of truth which is misleading him, & will analyse and expound that; I will suggest to his own mind not inculcate in him as from mine the idea which I think will save him. And when this is done, or at least if it were universally done, no one's offended *amour propre* would make him cling to his errors; no one would connect, with the adoption of truth, the idea of defeat; and no one would feel impelled by the ardour of debate & the desire of triumph, to reject, as almost all now do whatever of truth there really is in the opinions of those whose ultimate conclusion differs from theirs. In short, I do not insist upon making others give up their own point of view & adopt mine, but I endeavour myself to unite whatever is not optical illusion in both. When by this means I shall have clearly embraced in my own view the entire truth, & shall be able to represent to others that whole, of which they have before seen a part, I shall have great confidence in their ultimate adoption of it. Truth will then have no enemy but the *esprit critique*, which makes men unwilling to look for truth in the midst of error; & I am unwilling to strengthen this spirit by maintaining any opinions in the spirit of argumentation and debate. This being the system which I have determined to act upon, I shall of course apply it to my intercourse with you. I will read every thing which you may be so kind as to send me, whether from yourself or from the results of the united labours of your school. All that I have read of their works is of a character to make me wish to be acquainted with all their other speculations. If the result of the perusal of these works should be, my entire conversion, which I regard as extremely unlikely, I shall at once confess it; if I desire further explanations, I shall solicit them from your kindness, and I will always state to you my reasons for differing where I do differ. But on no account will I discuss with you. And therefore I do not feel that I should be justified in encouraging the project which you give me some hints that you have formed, of coming to England with a view to my complete initiation in the St Simonian doctrine. As a friend whom I extremely value, and who shared with me the friendship of him whom we have lost, it would give me great pleasure to see you, and to converse with you; and I am both touched and flattered that you should think me of so much importance either to yourself or to society, as to think of undertaking a journey with the sole view of bringing me over to opinions identical with your own. But I am well convinced that if this be ever accomplished, it will not be the effect of any sudden or rapid conviction produced by a few days or weeks of verbal discussion, but the result of time and my own reflexions aided by those works, & those suggestions, which I hope you will continue to furnish me with, from time to time. I should therefore decline all verbal controversy even if you were here. It would only risk the weakening or altering our present feelings towards each other, as we should probably find each other much more intractable than we expect, and as almost every man shews himself in dispute worse than he really is & appears unreasonably wedded to his opinions when called upon to defend them on a sudden, & is apt to put forward other arguments than those which have really made an impression on his own mind.

I no longer adhere to the objections I formerly urged against the St Simonian school, as some of the points which I objected to, appeared from a perusal of the Producteur (every word of which I have read with as great care and interest as any book I ever saw) never to have been held by them in the sense in which I thought them objectionable, & as you informed me in your answer[6] to my two letters that the other points had been given up. I was much pleased to find that although you are a sect, you are an improving sect, and that your creeds are not made up never to be altered. Of all the improvements in your doctrine, mentioned in your letter, I fully approve: but I still retain all my objections to your practical views, to your *organisation*, which appears to me impracticable, & not desirable if practicable, like that of Mr Owen.[7] You know, however, that I have not yet read or heard the reasons which you can adduce and my mind therefore remains open to conviction. But your proposal that when I am convinced of the soundness of your views I should correspond and cooperate with your society induces me to state to you at once the reasons which would prevent me from doing so even if I were convinced that the whole body of your doctrine is true. It appears to me utterly hopeless and chimerical to suppose that the regeneration of mankind can ever be wrought by means of working on their opinions. I think that mankind, and I am sure that my own countrymen, are in a state of mind which renders them incapable of receiving a true *doctrine générale*, or of understanding it in a true sense if they did receive it. In France it is perhaps possible that they might receive it, but not in the sense in which it is meant, nor would it produce, even admitting its truth, the good effects which you

6. D'Eichthal's letter of Nov. 23, 1829 (*D'Eichthal Corresp.*, pp. 39–68) rather than his letter of Dec. 1, 1829 (*ibid.*, pp. 69–89).

7. Robert Owen (1771–1858), wealthy manufacturer and pioneer socialist, sponsor of various communal experiments in both England and America, author of *A New View of Society* (1813–14). For JSM's account of his and his friends' debates with Owenites in 1825, see *Autobiog.*, pp. 86–88.

anticipate from it. I can conceive a whole people professing St Simonism, and acting precisely as they do now, just as there have been & are many entire nations professing Christianity, & whose conduct is yet utterly selfish and worldly, and in defiance of the whole scheme of Christian ethics. In England, on the other hand, the very idea of beginning a reformation in men's minds by preaching to them a comprehensive doctrine, is a notion which never would enter into the head of any person who has lived long enough in England to know the people. Englishmen habitually distrust the most obvious truths, if the person who advances them is suspected of having any general views. To produce any effect on their minds, you must carefully conceal the fact of your having any system or body of opinions, and must instruct them on insulated points, & endeavour to form their habits of thought by your mode of treating single and practical questions. When you have gained a high reputation with them for knowledge of facts, & skill and judgment in the appreciation of details, you may then venture on enlarged views; but even then, very cautiously and guardedly. A journal which should start by a systematic exposition of far-sighted views and extended principles, would not have twenty subscribers. I conceive therefore that your school, in their method of proceeding, by declaring themselves the apostles of a new doctrine, and seeking to inculcate that doctrine first, and to produce all other kinds of good as consequences of that, are violating the first & greatest rule of their own philosophy, which is, that we ought to consider what is the stage through which, in the progress of civilization, our country has next to pass, and to endeavour to facilitate the transition & render it safe & healthy. I am convinced that my own country & I suspect that France must pass through several states before it arrives at St Simonism, even if that doctrine is true; & that although we ought to arrive if we can at a general system of social philosophy, and to keep it always in our own view, we ought not to address it to the public, who are by no means ripe for its reception, but to avail ourselves of the good which is in them, to educate their minds by accustoming them to think rightly on those subjects on which they already think, to communicate to them all the truths which they are prepared for, and (in England at least where the philosophie critique has never yet got the better of the doctrine théologique et féodale) to endeavour to alter those parts of our social institutions and policy which at present oppose improvement, degrade and brutalize the intellects and morality of the people, & by giving all the ascendency to mere wealth, which the possession of political power confers, prevents the growth of a *pouvoir spirituel* capable of commanding the faith of the majority, who must and do believe on authority. You are also I am convinced mistaken in supposing that the religious feelings which prevail here, are of a character with which St Simonism would at all be capable of allying itself. But of this I must write hereafter, and it shall be soon. Excuse the very imperfect exposition of my sentiments which I have given. Mr Tooke I understand is somewhat recovered from the dreadful shock, Mrs Tooke is still very ill. I have seen neither since it occurred.

Yours affectionately

J. S. MILL.

On reading this letter again today (10th. February) I think I can express my meaning better by saying that I conceive your error to be this: you imagine that you can accomplish the perfection of mankind by teaching them St Simonism, whereas it appears to me that their adoption of St Simonism, if that doctrine be true, will be the natural result and effect of a high state of moral and intellectual culture previously received: that it should not be presented to the minds of any who have not already attained a high degree of improvement, since if presented to any others it will either be rejected by them, or received only as Christianity is at present received by the majority, that is, in such a manner as to be perfectly inefficacious.

I have a thousand other things to write, and your future letters shall be answered without any repetition of this unseemly delay.

J.S.M.

30. TO GUSTAVE D'EICHTHAL[1]

March 6, 1830

MY DEAR GUSTAVE

I take the opportunity of a friend who is going to Paris, for fulfilling the intentions of our deceased friend as expressed in his last letter to you, by sending you the enclosed pamphlet of Dr Channing,[2] the American preacher. I quite agree in his admiration of it, and I conceive that it expresses very clearly and forcibly the great vice of your system as well as that of Mr Owen, and many others *qui courent le monde aujourd'hui.* I hope you will read it and tell me what you think of it.

I have read and forwarded the letter to Mr Burns.[3] The report which it

1. MS at Arsenal.

2. William Ellery Channing (1780–1842), Unitarian clergyman and writer. One may conclude from Tooke's remarks in his last letter to D'Eichthal, Jan. 19, 1830 (*D'Eichthal Corresp.*, p. 106), that the pamphlet must have been the reprint of a *Christian Examiner* article of Channing's: *Remarks on the Disposition which now prevails to form Associations, and to accomplish all objects by organized masses* (London: Edward Rainford, 1830). Collected editions of Channing's works usually reprint it with the title: "Remarks on Associations." It contains interesting anticipations of some of JSM's views in *On Liberty*, particularly on the values of individuality and the dangers of the tyranny of society.

3. William Burns, author of *The New Era of Christianity; or, its influence on the moral regeneration of society* (London, 1831). See Pankhurst, p. 43.

contains of the proceedings at one of your meetings would have convinced me if I were not already satisfied, of the unfitness of your scheme for *this* country at least. It would be impossible to induce any one here to look at it with a serious face. I wonder how you have hitherto escaped the jokers and epigrammatists of the Parisian *salons.*

Pray be so good as to make my remembrances to Adolphe. I will write to him as soon as I have time & I hope he will write to me.

Yours in great haste

J. S. MILL.

31. TO HENRY COLE[1]

India House. 26 May. 1830.

MY DEAR COLE

As I know that you are acquainted with Dr Hooker,[2] which is an honour I have not attained to, I should be obliged to you if you would do me the favour to communicate to him the accompanying notes which I made in looking over his excellent British Flora[3] just published. I request you however to do so only in case you should think on reading them, that there is any thing in them which might possibly be interesting to Dr Hooker.

The only points which I myself think of any consequence, are those which relate to *Œnanthe aprifolia* & *Vicia sativa*, & you would not be far wrong if you were to suppose that most of the remainder are put down chiefly to make up a number. However it is possible that some of the Stations mentioned may be unknown to Dr Hooker.

As I am very favourably situated for observing the plants of Surrey, which have hardly been observed at all since Ray's[4] time if we except those in the immediate vicinity of London, which are figured in Curtis's Flora

1. MS at Kew.

For earlier evidence of what became JSM's lifelong interest in botany see *John Mill's Boyhood Visit to France*, ed. Anna Jean Mill. Over the years he contributed many notes to the *Phytologist* (see MacMinn, *Bibliog.*). A number of his notebooks containing botanical observations are in the Mill-Taylor Collection of LSE.

Henry (later Sir Henry) Cole (1808–1882), official and editor, was later a member of many commissions dealing with public exhibitions. He first became acquainted with JSM in the London Debating Society and in the summer of 1832 accompanied him on a walking tour.

2. Sir William Jackson Hooker (1785–1865), botanist and director of Kew Gardens.

3. *The British Flora* (London, 1830).

4. John Ray (1627–1705), sometimes called the father of natural history in England.

Londinensis[5] and many of which appear to have become extinct in the situations where Curtis found them I may possibly be able hereafter to make other communications of a nature similar to this, if the present one should prove to be of any use. I have explored some parts of the County very fully, and almost every part of it more or less, but I expect to make many more discoveries before I have done.

Pray excuse my troubling you in this matter, and believe me

Yours ever,
JOHN S. MILL

32. TO SARAH AUSTIN[1]

7th August 1830

DEAR MRS AUSTIN

At your request I put into writing what I said to you the other night on the subject of Mr Austin's lectures.[2] What appears to me of most importance is that he should not spend time in endeavouring to make the lectures which have been already delivered, better than they are. They stand greatly in need of curtailment, but I do not believe that there is a single member of the class who would wish them to be changed in any other respect. There is only one opinion expressed in the lectures which I have heard controverted at all; & the manner of exposition has excited the admiration of every body. The only fault found is, that the different points are over explained; that they are dwelt upon longer & repeated oftener, than is necessary to a complete understanding of them. I am certain that all which the class would desire in respect to the earlier lectures is that they should be *very* much abridged & perhaps many of the historical details dispensed with altogether: not because those details are not con-

5. William Curtis (1746–1799), botanist and entomologist. An edition in five volumes of his *Flora Londinensis*, enlarged by G. Graves and W. J. Hooker, is dated London, 1777–1828.

* * * *

1. *Addressed*: Mrs John Austin / 26 Park Road. Sealed by a red seal, bearing the letters JSM. MS in the possession of Mr. Gordon Waterfield.

2. When the University of London opened in 1828, John Austin, who had been appointed in 1827 to the chair of jurisprudence and the law of nations, was unable because of ill health to lecture in the first session. He began his lectures in the fall of 1829 to a large class of able students. Though an eloquent, profound, and original lecturer, he did not continue to attract students, because of his passion for accuracy and elaboration. In Nov., 1830, so few students registered that he postponed beginning the course until Jan., 1831, when eight students enrolled. He persevered for two more years but gave up lecturing after June, 1833, though he did not resign his chair until Jan., 1835. See Bellot, *University College*, pp. 96–102. Eventually JSM contributed part of his notes on Austin's lectures to fill a lacuna in the MS when they were published in full.

sidered useful & interesting, but because it is impossible to do every thing, and because there are other things which they are much more anxious to know.—Though the class were extremely delighted with the course as far as it went, they certainly were very much disappointed that Mr Austin did not get through a greater portion of the subject; & they anticipate with great pleasure the completion of it in the lectures on which he has obtained for them the privilege of attendance, at the conclusion of the next year's course. The only thing which in my opinion could at all endanger the permanent success & utility of the professorship, would be his not being able to include a view of all the essential parts of the science in his next series of lectures. Now the present class very well know that next to his health, the great cause of his getting through so little was his being obliged to prepare his lectures as he went on, not having them ready written. If he spends any time in improving his present lectures, more than is necessary for sufficiently shortening them, he will be in precisely the same difficulty, with the remainder of his subject, as he was this year with the whole of it. On the contrary, if he contents himself with using the scissors abundantly, & sets about the preparation of the subsequent lectures immediately, he will be several months in advance, & will be able, without that fatigue & harassing excitement which destroy his health, to prepare the lectures carefully, include a large portion of the subject in each, & avoid repetition & over explanation.

I would not recommend his continuing the Tables at present, as those which are printed embrace the entire field of law, & it is of so much more importance that he should complete his course of lectures next year.

From the very high opinion which has been expressed of the last course by those to whom I have lent my notes, I have considerable hopes that the class next year will be satisfactory in respect of numbers. But I should not be at all discouraged even if the number was small—because it is only a *complete course*, which can do much to spread the reputation of the lecturer. If he should be able to complete the subject next year, I have not the least doubt that he will have a numerous class the year after.

I deem it however of the greatest importance with a view to his class next year, that he should deliver an interesting introductory lecture. I know his well grounded aversion to vague generalities, & I know as certainly as he does, that it is impossible to teach any thing that is worth knowing of a whole science, in a short general view. But it is not necessary that an introductory lecture should be an abridged view of the science. The best introductory lectures extant are not so: Brown's[3] introductory lecture to

3. Thomas Brown (1778–1820), professor of moral philosophy at Edinburgh and a highly popular lecturer. The reference here is to his *Lectures on the Philosophy of the Human Mind* (4 vols., Edinburgh, 1820).

his course of metaphysics for example. The proper notion of an introductory lecture seems to be that it should resemble the preface to a book, which gives the reasons for writing the book & the reasons for reading it. Especially on the moral sciences, whose rank as sciences or whose scientific character itself is not generally recognized, there seems to be an ample field for remarks of a most useful description in opening a course of lectures. He might explain, what is meant by general jurisprudence: in what respect a course of jurisprudence differs from a course of lectures on the law of any particular country, & also from lectures on the science or art of legislation: the grounds of the opinion, that there really is a science of general jurisprudence, & that it is worth studying: proof of the perverting & confusing effect of the study of law as it is commonly pursued, without being accompanied by the study of jurisprudence: examples of the erroneous notions usually formed as to what jurisprudence is, & the silly talk of Blackstone,[4] & others of our lawyers, when they erect the technical maxims of their own law into principles of jurisprudence. All these topics, with a hundred others of the same kind, which will occur to Mr Austin himself, would afford ample materials for a highly useful introductory lecture, & one which need not be chargeable with vagueness or generality. I am satisfied, & so are several others of the class, that if his introductory lecture of last year had treated of these topics, in the manner in which we all know he would have treated them if at all, his class would have been twice as numerous as it was. I am quite convinced that if he delivers a lecture of this kind next year, he will have a numerous class, & that if he does not, he will have a comparatively small one.

But if he will not write such a lecture as this, let him not think of writing another but deliver the first lecture of the course itself as his introductory lecture. The general remark last year in his class room after the close of his lecture on Law in general, was, that it was very unfortunate that he had not delivered that very lecture instead of his introductory one.

Yours affectionately J. S. MILL.

P.S. The one opinion which, as I mentioned in the letter, has been controverted, is this: that every right of action must be founded on an injury. Excuse bad penmanship, as I write unavoidably in haste.

4. Sir William Blackstone (1723–1780), judge, first professor of English law at Oxford, author of the famous and influential *Commentaries on the Laws of England* (4 vols., Oxford, 1765–69).

JSM is here in the Benthamite tradition in criticizing Blackstone; Bentham's first sizable book, *A Fragment on Government* (1776), was an attack on the *Commentaries.*

33. TO JAMES MILL[1]

[Paris]
[Aug. 13, 1830]

I have had some conversation with M. Say,[2] and a great deal with Adolphe d'Eichthal and Victor Lanjuinais, and I have been a very assiduous reader of all the newspapers since I arrived. . . . At present, if I were to look only at the cowardice and imbecility of the existing generation of public men, with scarcely a single exception, I should expect very little good; but when I consider the spirit and intelligence of the young men and of the people, the immense influence of the journals, and the strength of the public voice, I am encouraged to hope that as there has been an excellent revolution without leaders, leaders will not be required in order to establish a good government. [He then goes on to give a detailed account of how the revolution was accomplished—the flinching of the generals of the army, the cowardice and meanness of Dupin[3] above everybody. He has the lowest opinion of the ministry, not a Radical among them except Dupont de l'Eure;[4] all mere place-hunters. Thiers,[5] at the meeting for organizing the resistance, showed great weakness and pusillanimity. (I heard him long afterwards say he detested Thiers.) Of the new measures he praises most the lowering of the age-qualification to the Chamber from 40 to 30: he

1. Published in part in Bain, *JSM*, pp. 41–42. MS not located. The portion in brackets is Bain's summary.

JSM seems to have arrived in Paris during the week of Aug. 8; he remained until the first week of Sept. The Revolution had arisen swiftly after the publication on July 26 of reactionary ordinances which violated the Charter of 1815 by suppressing the liberty of the press, dissolving the recently elected chambers, and proclaiming a new electoral law. By July 30 the Revolution was in effect completed when Charles X revoked the new ordinances. On July 31 the Duke of Orleans, Louis Philippe, was proclaimed Lieutenant General of the kingdom, and on Aug. 2 Charles abdicated. Louis Philippe was formally offered the throne on Aug. 7, and took the oath of office as King of the French on Aug. 9.

2. Probably Jean Baptiste Say rather than his son Horace Emile Say (1794–1860), also an economist.

3. André Marie Jean Jacques Dupin (1783–1865), called Dupin aîné, a cautious participant in the overthrow of Charles X, was too much attached to the cause of Louis Philippe to suit the republicans.

4. Jacques Charles Dupont (de l'Eure) (1767–1855), liberal statesman, member of the Chamber of Deputies from 1817 to 1848. He was appointed Minister of Justice by the new government, but after struggling in vain against the reactionary tendencies of the new dynasty, resigned his post before the end of the year.

5. Louis Adolphe Thiers (1797–1877), historian and statesman, then virtually at the beginning of his long political career, which culminated in the Presidency, 1871–73. In Jan., 1830, with Armand Carrel and François Mignet he had founded the *National* newspaper, which supported the liberal opposition to Charles X's government. He favoured constitutional monarchy rather than a republic, however, and played a major role in publicizing and advancing the claims of Louis Philippe to the throne.

has seen no one that attaches due importance to this change.] I am going to the Chamber of Deputies to-morrow with Mr. Austin, and next week, I am to be introduced to the Society of "Aide-toi,"[6] where I am to be brought in contact with almost all the best of the young men, and there are few besides that I should at all care to be acquainted with. . . . I have heard an immense number of the most affecting instances of the virtue and good sense of the common people.

34. TO JAMES MILL[1]

[Paris]
August 20th, 1830.

I have mixed very much among the people since I arrived, and have taken every opportunity which I could find or make of conversing with persons of all classes. The result so far exceeds all my previous expectations of good, that I can scarcely trust it without further experience. The fact with which I have been most struck in the French people, is the extraordinary simplicity of character which seems to pervade them all, especially the working classes. I have conversed with many who have taken part in the three days' contest, not to mention the wives and families of some of them, and I have invariably found that their sole anxiety was to convince me that they had acted right, or rather there seemed to be no design to make any particular impression upon me, but they appeared to come out with what was uppermost in their own minds, and that was the morality and lawfulness of their resistance. I have not perceived the slightest tinge of *fanfaronnade* or vanity in their language or in their sentiments. I have not heard one word of self-applause, nor boasting about the heroism or *dévouement* of the people of Paris, nor any credit taken to themselves for

6. *Aide-toi, le ciel t'aidera*, a political society formed during the Restoration to combat reaction and foster liberal ideas. Among its members were Barrot, Béranger, Carrel, Duchâtel, Guizot, Lafayette father and son, and J. B. Say. See also Letter 36.

* * * *

1. Published, but with no identification of authorship, in the *Examiner*, Aug. 29, 1830, p. 547, as one of three letters on the "State of the Public Mind and of Affairs at Paris." A prefatory note was appended: "We have been favoured with copies of the following letters from two gentlemen, whose knowledge, ability, and exalted principles, induce us to attach great value to all their opinions and statements. The importance of the subject matters treated in the letters, and the close insight they give us of the state of affairs at Paris, have induced us to insert them entire, though we thus somewhat transgress the space usually allotted for political disquisition."

The two gentlemen were undoubtedly John Arthur Roebuck and JSM. Evidence for this identification may be found in the present editor's article, "JSM: Letters on the French Revolution of 1830," *Victorian Studies*, I (Dec., 1957), 137–54. The MS has not been located.

having preserved order or avoided excesses; it does not seem to occur to them at all that they have done any thing extraordinary. They had but one idea, that of fighting for their legal rights, and the observance of the legal rights of others followed as an immediate corollary. The inconceivable purity and singleness of purpose, almost amounting to *naïveté*, which they all shew in speaking of these events, has given me a greater love for them than I thought myself capable of feeling for so large a collection of human beings, and the more exhilarating views which it opens of human nature will have a beneficial effect on the whole of my future life. Though I mention particularly their language and conduct with respect to politics, I have seen the same simplicity of character in their every day intercourse, and I could relate various traits of it, but I will not, because none of them separately prove much, though their number, and the total absence of all indications of a contrary nature, constitute a strong body of evidence.

Another most striking circumstance, is the total absence of acrimony with which they speak of the authors of the attempt to establish despotism. This speaks wonderfully in favour of their character as a people, even if it should lead them, as I fear it will, to a culpable leniency in their treatment of these great offenders. The feeling of satisfaction at having got rid of men whom they despised, appears to have superseded all personal feelings of hostility against the individuals, and the struggle bore in their minds so exclusively the character of self-defence, that the ulterior purpose of executing vengeance upon their enemies hardly occurred to them. The conduct of the manufacturing population of the faubourgs has been exemplary. Attempts were made to excite disturbances among them, with a view to the destruction of machinery and the exclusion of foreign artizans. A large body of them assembled and marched to the Prefecture of Police with a petition on these two subjects. The *prefect*, M. Girod (de l'Ain)[2] came out and agreed [argued?] the matter quietly with them, in a short and pithy speech, upon which they very peaceably marched back. The next day, however, the *attroupemens* were rather more numerous and considerable, and I know from several quarters, that the government were seriously alarmed; they arrested some of the instigators, some of whom proved to be criminals returned from the galleys, and three were printers of an ultra-Catholic and royalist journal. But the next day all was quiet, and people who had been much alarmed the day before, confessed that there was no danger. It is very curious to see proclamations stuck about the streets, from all sorts of obscure individuals, sometimes of the humblest class, on all subjects which came uppermost. On this occasion there

2. Louis Gaspard Amédée Girod (de l'Ain) (1781–1847), Orleanist politician, under the new government Prefect of Police in Paris from Aug. 1 to Nov., 1830. His speech to the workers referred to was made on Aug. 16.

appeared several excellent placards from common workmen, explaining to their fellow-labourers the interest which they had in maintaining the security of property, and the advantage they ultimately derive from all improvements in the productive power of labour. I will try to procure one or two of these placards and take them to England with me, though I fear it will be rather difficult to get them. Among other curious placards which are stuck up, there is an exculpatory one from the charcoal-carriers (*charbonniers*). A deputation of these people had waited upon Charles the Tenth a few days before the *coup d'etat* on the occasion of a *fête*, and it had been reported that one of them had used some expressions of encouragement to him, which gave great offence to the remainder of the people. The charbonniers finding themselves in consequence slighted and looked shy upon by the other classes of the people, put forth this proclamation, signed by several of them in behalf of the rest, saying, that they had gone to the Tuileries because they could not help it, as they would have been thrown out of employment and reduced to starvation if they had not, but that none of their number had used any such expressions as those described [ascribed?] to them, and that they had fought like the others on the 28th and 29th. This vindication, which I have seen numbers of men in ragged coats spelling out as they best could on the walls, did not, it seems, produce the desired effect; consequently the charbonniers assembled, hoisted an enormous tri-coloured flag, and proceeded to the Prefecture of Police, where the eternal M. Girod de l'Ain came out and was harangued by them; heard their justification of themselves, and their complaint against the sort of stigma which had been thrown upon them; told them that he believed their story, and hoped that nobody would thereafter say any thing to their disadvantage, so thereupon they marched back. I have seen as much of my former friends at Paris as their time would allow, and have made a number of new acquaintances; this, however, is a very bad time for making the acquaintance of any of the known men, as they are for the most part employed, or are soon likely to be employed on public duties. I have, however, been able to compare a multitude of testimonies on the recent and present state of affairs, and have found that what I have hitherto told you is perfectly correct in the gross, though incorrect in many of the details. Thus, I have now reason to believe that what I told you respecting the good conduct of Lafitte[3] during the revolution was at least exaggerated and that he was scarcely an exception to the general apathy and cowardice

3. Jacques Laffitte (1767–1844), financier and statesman. His house in Paris had been virtual headquarters of the moderates who gained control of the Revolution. Although one of the leaders in the movement to place the Duke of Orleans on the throne, he was within a year bitterly regretting that action. On Nov. 3, 1830, he became President of the Council of Ministers but in March, 1831, he was ignominiously ousted.

of the monied classes. On the other hand, it is not true that none of the Deputies took part in the fight. There are about fifteen or sixteen, all members of the *extrême gauche*, whom, as I am assured by ——— of the Society *Aide-toi* the Society can perfectly count upon as the devoted friends of the people (and this I already begin to see in their Parliamentary conduct). Of these, as many as were at Paris, took a share from the first in the whole business, and ran the same risk with the others. You will not be surprised to hear that Lafayette[4] and his son are among these fifteen or sixteen, but Benjamin Constant[5] is not, nor Lafitte, nor Casimir Perier,[6] nor almost any one whom you probably knew by name. Though the *libéraux* in the Chamber of Deputies are generally so little to be relied upon (and those in the Upper House are in general much worse), I have the greatest confidence in the force of circumstances and of public opinion. The cry is becoming general for the dissolution of the Chamber, and there are already signs, that in order to prolong their political existence, they will consent to make a number of the required concessions. Within the last day or two the newspapers have assumed a much more decided tone than before in favour of important alterations in the constitution, and in particular a considerable extension of the elective franchise. There are about 100 resignations or annullations of election, and a law is now passing through the Chamber, compelling all who accept places to vacate their seats, as in England. This law is retrospective to the beginning of the present session, and it is said that many place-holders will lose their seats. These elections are expected to strengthen exceedingly the bands of the *côté gauche*. The

4. The aged Lafayette (he was seventy-three), who assumed command of the National Guard, was the one leader of the liberal forces who by his tremendous prestige and popularity might have been able to establish a republic. Though his sympathies were republican, he was gradually persuaded to accept as then safer for France what he hoped would be a "popular throne, in the name of the national sovereignty, surrounded by republican institutions." His public acceptance of Louis Philippe on the balcony of the Hotel de Ville on July 31 ended the hopes of the republicans and clinched the throne for Louis Philippe. In the following Dec., Lafayette, having served his purpose for the King, was ousted from the command of the National Guard. His son, Georges Washington Motier de Lafayette (1779–1849), a member of the Chamber of Deputies, had been away from Paris during the "Three Days" of the Revolution, but returned on Aug. 1.

5. Benjamin Constant de Rebecque (1767–1830), influential writer and liberal politician. Lafayette had written him on July 26: "A terrific game is being played here. Our heads are at stake. Bring yours along." Although in failing health, Constant drove at once to Paris and participated in the deliberations of the leading deputies. In August he was appointed President of the Legislative Committee of the Council of State. Louis Philippe gave him 200,000 francs to pay his debts.

6. Casimir Périer (1772–1832), financier and statesman, a moderate liberal who had at first tried to mediate between the liberals and the throne, had been a member of the provisory commission of five during the Revolution, and had only reluctantly accepted Charles X's dethronement and Louis Philippe's elevation. He succeeded Laffitte as head of the ministry in March, 1831.

Society *Aide-toi*, which contributed so greatly to the success of the two last general elections, will apply itself with the same rigour, and with a great increase of power, to the management of the approaching partial one. My next letter[7] will relate chiefly to this Society, which is one of the most powerful and best organized political bodies that ever existed, and the leading members of which will most certainly, in a few years, direct the destinies of France. They are quite eager to place me *au courant* of all their proceedings, and to give me all kinds of information concerning France, and I shall endeavour to keep up a correspondence with some of them when I return to England, as I think it may be of considerable use. I had almost forgotten to tell you that one of the things most talked of here, is a proposition for reading [sending?] a deputation to thank the people of England for their subscriptions. I believe that an exaggerated notion of the amount of the money subscribed had much to do with this scheme, and that it is not likely to be realized immediately, if at all. If the deputation goes, * * * will probably be a member of it.

I have not told you a tenth part of what I have to say. I shall write again in a day or two.

35. TO JAMES MILL[1]

Paris, Aug. 21, 1830

Affairs are now in so strange and critical a situation, that I have determined to write you a letter to-day, in spite of my having sent you a hasty, long epistle yesterday. I hope the matter it will contain will prove a sufficient apology.

The Chamber of Deputies is now an Assemblée Constituante, possessing, in fact, the power of working any reform, no matter how extensive. No outward force opposes itself, or can oppose itself, to its determinations, on any ground derived from right springing from existing or past institutions. It has elected a monarch: it has suppressed the religion of the state; it has declared every peer created by Charles to be no longer a peer. Its power, in short, is illimitable, provided it act in accordance with the will of the people. The fear is not, that it will hazard too much, that it will exceed the people's wishes, but that it will fall far short of what the people most vehemently desire. It seems the universal opinion, that both in ability and intention it is unfit for its situation—that it is no fair representation of the French nation—that it is calculated seriously to retard improvement, and in

7. Letter 36 not 35.

* * * *

1. Printed, like the preceding letter (see n. 1), in the *Examiner*, Aug. 29, 1830, pp. 547–48. MS not located.

great measure for the present moment to nullify, in a beneficial sense, the effects of the present revolution. Elected under circumstances widely different from the present, its intended mission was of a different character from that which has now devolved on it. Under Charles the electors and the vast body of the people had identical interests; the popular candidates were then those who combated Charles: under Philippe the electors and the people have widely different interests; they who were popular candidates have lost that character, and since the courage of the Parisian workmen has routed the old enemy, and placed them at the head of affairs, they have begun to play the master, and to attempt the subjugation of the very class to whom they owe even their very existence. This is practised after various forms and under various names; all their proceedings being replete with deeply instructive lessons for those who are accustomed to abuse the people.

When the workmen of Paris, after three days' fighting, had driven out Charles and dispersed his army, they were absolute masters of the city. In the midst of their highest excitation, in the moment of victory, surrounded by their dead and wounded brothers, fathers, aye, and children and wives and mothers—these men, these ignorant, despised, and long-abused people shrunk from all unnecessary carnage—the moment resistance ceased, that moment they abstained from assault—they took equal care of the soldier who had opposed and of the citizen who had aided them. Surrounded by every temptation that perfect licence could offer, not one excess was committed. Vast treasures passed through their hands untouched, and signal punishment was immediately the lot of any one who for one instant departed from the strictest honesty and decorum. (One man was shot by his comrades for stealing a melon.) These men were actually starving, and yet they would take no recompense. Having effected their glorious object, they calmly retired to their homes and resumed their accustomed avocations. The *educated* and the *rich* now came upon the stage. The hour of danger was passed, one government was overthrown, another was to be framed. Compare the conduct of this party with that of the people, the mob, who had fought during the ever memorable three days.

No sooner was it ascertained that all danger was really past, than a hungry crowd appeared, eager for place and careless of public interests. The old generals and courtiers of Napoleon, the abettors and fautors of Charles, the rich bourgeois, all appeared in the character of place-hunting courtiers of Philippe. A spectacle more disgusting can hardly be imagined. The scoundrels who had been the willing instruments of despotism under Charles, and Louis, and Napoleon, now came to be on the watch for the good things that were to be anew distributed in consequence of the popular victory. The Chamber of Deputies was, in fact, now to be the distributor. In the first place the crown was given to the Duke of Orleans: this was perhaps a matter politically wise, or at least necessary. Then came the Ministers. You know the choice. Sebastiani,[2] who has never done, and is incapable of doing any thing good: Gérard,[3] whose first act has been to create himself a Marshal of France: Dupin, who has lost all public confidence by his cowardice and base servility: Guizot,[4] a favourer of the new Aristocracy: Louis,[5] who is universally disliked, perhaps I might say despised: in short, not one person, Dupont excepted, has been chosen who has the confidence and good will of the people. Now come the acts of those persons. First, a constant striving to shield the instruments of the late Government from punishment. The magistrature continued. The very men who had opposed the liberty of the press; who had condemned and severely punished every writer who was bold enough to attack the Ministry of Charles; who to their utmost had striven to maintain his abominable despotism; these men are continued in their situations. Next, in the moment when a new Government was to be framed, a mere juridical law, viz. relating to punishment, is introduced, solely to preserve the late Ministers from death. Then comes the series of operations carried on to maintain power in their own hands. The first grand instrument to this end is delay; this, in the first days of their sitting, was so palpable, that it roused the indignation of the young men who surrounded the door of the Chamber, and gave a healthy movement to this corrupt body, by the salutary influence of fear. There was shown an unwillingness to propose explicit and formal guarantees; these, however, they were obliged to propose. The King, better than they, met them more than half way; he was more willing to offer than they to propose guarantees. The law of election next occupied their attention. It is curious to see how this has been dealt with. When we first arrived, every journal, with perhaps the single exception of the *Courier*,

2. Count François Horace Bastien Sebastiani (1772–1851), Minister of the Navy in the new government, and later Minister of Foreign Affairs. Like Périer, he had been reluctant to make the break with King Charles.

3. Count Etienne Maurice Gérard (1773–1855) had been one of Napoleon's favourite generals and was long an opponent of the Bourbons. He co-operated closely with Lafayette during the Three Days. Despite JSM's statement he seems not to have been made a marshal until the following year.

4. François Pierre Guillaume Guizot (1787–1874), historian and statesman. Though a former president of the Society Aide-toi and a leader of the liberal opposition to the government of Charles X, he sought a middle way between absolutism and democracy. On July 27 he had been called upon to draft the protest of the deputies against the ordinances which had provoked the Revolution. He has been called the champion of "a monarchy limited by a limited number of bourgeois." From Aug. to Nov., 1830, he was Minister of the Interior in the new government and thereafter held various posts; from Oct., 1840, to the fall of Louis Philippe in the Revolution of 1848, he was the master spirit of the government. JSM later came to regard Guizot as a great thinker and writer (see Letters 282 and 304).

5. Baron Joseph Dominique Louis (1755–1837) held the portfolio of finance until Nov., 1830.

endeavoured to stultify the people, and convince them that no necessity for change existed. This would not do, the public were too wise, so, gradually, step by step, and as slowly as possible, the journals have turned round, and now the lowering the suffrage is almost universally proposed; but the Chamber has done nothing more than abolish the double vote and make the age required in the elector 25, in the elected 30. The qualification has not been touched, neither as regards the deputy nor the electors. They have been exceedingly busy, however, in changing the prefects, the mayors, and all the place-holders in the departments. Their friends have now come in, and the situation of deputy has at length become a profitable appointment. But as for regulating the internal government in a way to secure peace and safety to the citizens, they seem never to dream of the necessity of such a thing. Every thing really important is formally put off to the next session, and matters by which humbug may have influence are taken into consideration. They now pretend to be occupied with the accusation of the Ministers. They have instituted a committee, which committee yesterday moved for new powers, and obtained them; but they have so completely mystified their very plain duty, that I can by no means understand what they are driving at. One thing is plain, they are doing every thing to create delay, in the hope that the public indignation will subside.

During all these sad delays the country is really without a Government, and here we cannot but compare the conduct of the people and the Deputies, and offer homage to the former. Without a Government, the country is nevertheless perfectly quiet: since the revolution not a single murder or robbery has taken place in Paris. Again, the poor starving workmen assembled some days since, and went in a body to the Prefect, beseeching him to exclude all the foreign workmen. The Prefect made them an excellent speech, pointing out to them the error under which they lay, and the poor fellows immediately returned, and quietly dispersed. Are not these speaking examples of true devotion to the cause of good government; as splendid as the conduct of the Deputies is base? I know no more important matter for investigation than would be now the state of the popular mind at Paris, and the causes which produced it. There appears among the victors of the three days no personal feeling, nothing but a desire to manifest to the world the justice of their cause, to prove that they have been actuated by no sinister interests, but were led on solely first to defend themselves, and then to rid themselves of an evil which was no longer supportable. The same spirit which then directed still continues to influence them. No riot, no attempt at pillage, no vain glory has been manifested by them. They calmly await the requisite reform of their Government, despairing indeed of much good from the present Chamber, but looking forward with hope to the next. So far from the journals being now in advance of the people, it is plain that the people are impelling the journals forward. They have now to make a great advance, or others will arise, and being *au niveau* of the people, will completely ruin the existing papers. It is strange to see how little of true knowledge those now in existence contain. They all can declaim well, but I have often heard more real sense, and really applicable knowledge, in one conversation, than has been contained in all the journals that have appeared since I arrived here. A new and very different set of instructors is now evidently required by the people.

36. TO JAMES MILL[1]

[Paris]
27 August 1830
finished on the 28th

I have been exceedingly fortunate during my stay here, in having been brought into contact with a much greater number of persons such as I most desired to know, than I could possibly have had reason to expect at a time when all persons of any note are so much occupied. I am even much inclined to believe that I know more of the views and expectations professed by the different coteries than many of the men themselves, as it seems to me that most people at Paris associate chiefly with the men, and read the journals, of their own precise *nuance d'opinion.* But I consider myself particularly fortunate in having formed an acquaintance with M. Tanneguy Duchâtel,[2] and with the principal members of the society Aide-toi.

I have had some most interesting conversations with M. Duchatel whose correspondence with Mr. Wilmot Horton[3] you probably remember. I knew him by reputation as one of the most enlightened men in France, and particularly as one of those who had profited most by the writings of the English political economists. I found that this was perfectly true. He seems to me to unite in an extraordinary degree the best qualities of a young Frenchman (for he seems to be under thirty) with the acquirements of an instructed Englishman, and especially with a knowledge of details and a habit of reflection on important practical questions, which few Frenchmen possess, the events of the last fifteen years having called into exercise few

1. *Addressed*:James Mill Esq. / East India House / London / Angleterre /. *Postmarks*: 28 / AOUT / 1830 and AU 31 / 1830. MS in the Charles A. Brown Collection in the University of Rochester Library, Rochester, N.Y. First published in *Victorian Studies*, I (Dec., 1957), 137–54.

2. Charles Marie Tanneguy, comte Duchâtel (1803–1867), one of the founders of the *Globe*, later held various ministerial posts.

3. Sir Robert John Wilmot-Horton (1784–1841) had published in four series *An Inquiry into the Causes and Remedies of Pauperism* (London, 1830), the third series of which contained a correspondence with Duchâtel.

valuable qualities except those of a party pamphleteer, or at most a writer on the first principles of government. Most of the men with whom I converse seem to be well aware of this deficiency, or at least, readily admit it when stated. If there were many young men like Duchâtel, you would soon see a great difference in the character of their newspapers and of their parliamentary debates. At present any one of twenty men whom one could name in England could write every day the leading articles of all their newspapers as rapidly as his pen could move. But now when all the great questions of legislation, education, & social improvement in general will be brought on the tapis successively, the men who are already prepared to discuss these subjects *avec connaissance de cause* will soon occupy almost exclusively the ear of the public, & will also, if things go on smoothly, obtain the greatest influence in the government. Duchâtel is already appointed a *conseiller d'état*. What he told me about the present state of politics I will tell you another time. The information he gave me concerning the state of the labouring classes, the division of property, the restraints on population, & the state of education I have not time to put on paper just now, but I believe that Roebuck has written a long letter to Mr. Grote[4] on the subject, which he has probably shewn to you. I shall see M. Duchâtel as often as I can while I remain here, & shall endeavour to obtain his permission to correspond with him. He made very particular enquiries respecting you and your occupations.

The society *Aide toi et le Ciel t'aidera* is composed of men probably much less instructed than M. Duchâtel, but far more democratic in their opinions and more capable of taking a leading part in turbulent times by their qualifications as men of action. They are all young men, & most of them have been engaged in active hostility to the government from very early youth; several who belonged to the society have even suffered capital punishment for having engaged in some of the numerous conspiracies which have existed at different periods since the restoration. M. Odilon-Barrot,[5] the most distinguished *avocat* in the Courts at Paris, was president of the society for some time, & is still a member, but being now préfet of Paris he of course can take no part in their proceedings. The present organisation of the society was, I believe, formed for the purpose of facilitating anti-royalist elections under the Villèle ministry:[6] they had, and

4. George Grote had been in Paris in the spring of 1830 and had been introduced to the Lafayette circle. On July 29 he opened a credit with his banker at Paris (Jacques Laffitte) for £500 for the use of the committee directing the revolutionary cause at the Hôtel de Ville (see Mrs. Grote, *The Personal Life of George Grote* [London, 1873], pp. 63–65).

5. Camille Hyacinth Odilon Barrot (1791–1873), liberal politician, had joined the National Guard and taken active part in the Revolution. He served also on the committee appointed to usher the deposed King out of the country.

6. The reactionary ministry of Jean Baptiste Seraphin Joseph, comte de Villèle (1773–1854), lasted from 1822 to 1827.

have, correspondents all over France, and without some such association these elections certainly would not have taken the turn they did, especially as all the liberal newspapers were then tied up by the censorship. The success of the last elections was also in a great degree owing to the efforts of the society; & they were the first persons who gave the signal for the late revolution, in which the little concert & organisation which existed was wholly their work. They are in constant communication with Lafayette, & with a very small number of deputies, the few whom they believe to have a real wish for the establishment of a popular government in France, the purpose for which they now remain united, & in the pursuit of which they are willing, & believe themselves able, to overturn the present ministry if it refuses the concessions which they consider necessary. I have no doubt that when the exertions of these people become more visible than they have been hitherto, they will be called the republican party: but it certainly is not true that they wish to establish a republic. If it had depended upon them, they would have made the duke of Orleans king, but after making considerable alterations in the constitution: and they appear now to regret extremely that when they had arms in their hands, when the people looked to them as their leaders & would have obeyed them before the *hommes du lendemain* had made their appearance, they did not proceed to the Hotel de Ville with Lafayette and Audry de Puyraveau[7] & declare Lafayette lieutenant general of the kingdom & themselves a provisional government, by a proclamation signed by Lafayette & countersigned by their president: who being in correspondence with every considerable town would have been followed by the leading liberals all over France, all of whom are in the habit of receiving *L'Empulsion* from the society. The society is not wholly composed of men of the same shade of opinion but the committee takes care to have a majority always on its side; the members of the committee are agreed on the following points: that as an ultimate end, universal suffrage should be aimed at: that however in the present stage of education among the people, not above one third of whom can write (M. Duchâtel told me that some members even of the departmental colleges could not write their names) they ought to be satisfied with a considerable extension of the suffrage; that the whole people might however either now, or in a very little time, be admitted to chuse a body of electors, that there should be no hereditary peerage, & no conditions of eligibility except the age of 25. They are extremely dissatisfied with the conduct of the ministry. They say, that the men who have profited by the revolution are afraid of the men who made the revolution, & for that very reason. In consequence, the ministers have no confidence in what the society, who know more about

7. Pierre François Audry de Puyraveau (1773–1852), industrialist and politician, who actively supported Lafayette in the Revolution. On July 28 he contributed muskets to the revolting workers.

the state of the country than anyone else, tell them respecting the general dissatisfaction they are exciting in the departments by some of the appointments which they have made & by their efforts to keep down *l'élan révolutionnaire* all over the country. The situation of the ministers is certainly difficult, but they have the folly to be guided in their appointments not by the wishes of the district itself but by the recommendation of the deputy, who nine times out of ten is a man who dreads the popular feeling, & who is so little of the same mind with the public that he has not the slightest chance of being reelected. The members of the society appear to be apprehensive that in consequence of the pusillanimity of the ministry the royalists may be able to raise disturbances in some of the provinces: but from what I can learn, this appears to me very improbable. You may judge of the degree of influence which the society is supposed to have among the people, by the circumstance that Lafayette, a few days ago when there was some danger of violent proceedings on the part of some bodies of workmen, sent to request that the society would issue an address to the labouring classes. Lafayette is in constant communication with the society, & several of the leading members are on his staff. I am to be presented to him by the president of the society next Tuesday, which is the day on which he receives company. I find in all those people the most friendly inclinations towards England: which I am glad to know as I am convinced that I shall hear the contrary asserted in many quarters at home, in the progress of events. They also seem to have a much better comprehension of English politics than is common in France: they understand the vices of our government, they see through the Whigs, & at the same time they, or at least those of them who have been in England, know enough of the state of feeling in English society to be aware of the mischief that might arise from their fraternising with any party among us, and especially from their connecting themselves with the disreputable part of our radicals. I think that I have myself been of some use in putting them on their guard against Sir Thomas Beevor and Cobbett,[8] against Bowring[9] and people of that kind. If you see Mr.

8. Following a dinner on Aug. 16 at the London Tavern to honour the people of Paris for their part in the Revolution, Beevor and James Paul Cobbett (1803–1881), son of William Cobbett (1763–1835), the well-known radical writer and politician, were sent to Paris as "Ambassadors of the Reformers of England" to present an "Address to the brave people of Paris." The presentation was made on Aug. 23 at the Hôtel de Ville with Lafayette and a deputation of the National Guard in attendance (see *The Times*, Aug. 27, 1830, p. 2). Beevor's and James Cobbett's speeches were later printed in *Cobbett's Weekly Political Register,* Sept. 11, 1830, pp. 342–45. Cobbett radicals and Benthamite radicals were always scornful of each other.

9. John Bowring on Aug. 28 also made a presentation of English addresses to the people of Paris at the Hôtel de Ville in the presence of Lafayette and the Prefect of Paris. Bowring, however, represented a different group of English reformers from Cobbett's followers. Bowring bore an address from a dinner on Aug. 17 (one night

Murray[10] of The Times, pray tell him that his visit to Lafayette has evidently been of great use. It is probable that two or three members of the society will (as individuals) come to England shortly. If they do, we must exert ourselves to the utmost to make their stay there useful & agreeable and to make them as much our friends as we possibly can, since the occasions will be innumerable when they will need such information & such advice as we & our friends can alone give them among Englishmen advice which they are at present very well disposed to receive from us as they know how hearty we are in their cause.

Lanjuinais will probably come—I am very anxious that he should be acquainted with you.

J.S.M.

37. TO WILLIAM JACKSON HOOKER[1]

East India House.
12th October
1830.

DEAR SIR,

Pray accept my most sincere thanks for the very interesting and handsome present of specimens which you have been so obliging as to confer upon me.

I will take an early opportunity of sending to you specimens of the few plants, which I was so fortunate as to find that I had had greater opportunities than yourself of observing. I shall also avail myself of your permission to communicate to you any observations which I may hereafter be able to make, that are likely to be at all interesting to you. I had not the slightest idea when I made the former ones, that they could be of any value to any one except myself.

I have gathered for you some specimens of what I imagine to be the Atriplex erecta; it is certainly the only Atriplex to be found in the station mentioned by Smith,[2] and it has not the characters of any other English

---

after Cobbett's dinner) at the London Tavern, at which were present such men as Henry Warburton, MP, Joseph Hume, MP, George Grote, and James Silk Buckingham. *The Times* reported this dinner at length on Aug. 18, p. 5. Bowring, though an intimate of Jeremy Bentham, was never highly regarded by either James or John Mill.

10. James Murray (d. 1835), Foreign Director of *The Times.*

* * * *

1. MS at Kew.

2. Sir James Edward Smith (1759–1828), founder of the Linnean Society and author of *English Botany* (36 vols., 1790–1814), and *English Flora* (4 vols., 1824–28).

Atriplex. The valves of the calyx of the fruit are in many instances very thickly set with projecting sharp points, but these points do not amount to prickles, being composed of the same herbaceous substance with the calyx itself; and moreover the calyx has not unfrequently, though in a slight degree, the appearance of the leaves of the ice-plant, which must arise from a number of small shining glands, easily rubbed off by the touch. I do not know whether the specimens will preserve this character when dry, therefore I mention it now, having examined the plant more minutely than I ever did before. I have not Smith's work by me at this instant, else I would consult it to see whether his Atriplex erecta possesses the last mentioned character.

I will endeavour to collect Fungi for you, indeed I have already picked up some, but I am afraid I shall not be able to effect much this autumn.

Believe me
most sincerely yours
J. S. MILL

• • • 1831 • • •

38. TO WILLIAM JACKSON HOOKER[1]

India House.
26th January 1831.

My dear Sir,

I owe you many apologies for having so long delayed forwarding to you the small parcel of specimens which is all I have to offer in return for all those which you were so good as to send me. The fact is that I have been so completely engrossed by other occupations that I have not been able, till now, to perform the annual duty of looking over my herbarium.

The specimens I now send are, I regret to say, not in general very good ones, but they are the best I have; I will endeavour to procure better ones next summer. I began collecting fungi so late, & had so little time to hunt for them, that I am able to send only two or three I am afraid very common ones.

You will find however specimens such as they are of all the plants which you expressed a wish to see, except one, as to which I must plead guilty to having misinformed you, the Thalictrum majus. How I came to commit this blunder I cannot conceive, as the plant is entered both in my herbarium and in my catalogue as Thalictrum flavum. In compensation I send you a plant which, I believe I did not mention before: the Lilium martagon, a plant new to the British flora, but certainly wild, & as far as it is possible to judge, indigenous.

It fills, as I imagine, nearly the whole of an extremely thick & close coppice wood, near Headley in Surrey. I first saw it about four years ago, when the coppice or rather a part of it was cut down, & the ground was seen to be covered with this plant; but as it never flowered I did not know what it was, though I wondered at it a good deal; but in June this year (I believe shortly after I wrote the notes on your Flora[2] to which I owe the privilege of corresponding with you) I discovered in another corner of the wood, a considerable number of full grown plants all of them on the point of flowering, two of which I gathered & now send to you. They are badly preserved, but there is no doubt of the identity of the plant, & as little of its being completely wild: If it ever escaped from a garden, it

1. MS at Kew.

2. See Letter 31.

must have been at a very remote period, for there is no garden near, & the immense abundance of the plant in this coppice proves that if not indigenous, it is as completely naturalized as a plant can possibly be.

If chance, or your zeal for science, should ever bring you into the neighbourhood of Dorking[3] (the most beautiful probably in the S. of England) it would be a great pleasure to me to shew you this spot, as well as the habitats of various other rare plants in that neighbourhood.

I have not been able to learn anything more respecting the Verbascum ferrugineum in the vicinity of Hampton Court & the Moulseys [*sic*], as I am no longer residing in that neighbourhood, but I will endeavour to revisit the spot. It certainly is not indigenous there, but it appeared to me to be completely naturalized. From your sending me the Rhynchospora alba, I conclude that it may not be known to you that the boggy or rather the wet parts of Cobham common in Surrey are covered with it. Accept once more my best thanks for your letter & its accompaniments & believe me

Most truly yours

J. S. MILL.

P.S. I send but one specimen of the Lycopodium from Esher Common, having lost the other.

39. TO GUSTAVE D'EICHTHAL[1]

India House
March 1st
1831

MY DEAR GUSTAVE

I write to you merely a few lines to shew that I am not inclined to neglect my absent friends. Adolphe will tell you every thing which I could say in a letter, and much more.

3. JSM's acquaintance with this area dated back at least to the summer of 1822, when his father took a summer residence at Dorking, where, Bain notes (*James Mill*, p. 204), "the family stayed six months in the year; he remaining there throughout his six weeks' holiday, and going down from Friday to Monday, during the rest of the time. To the end of his life, he [James Mill] kept up this arrangement, shifting his quarters from year to year; but finally settling in the small rural village of Mickleham, on the Dorking road, not far from Leatherhead and Epsom."

* * * *

1. *Addressed*: Monsieur / Gustave d'Eichthal. Published in *Cosmopolis*, VI, 355–56, and in *D'Eichthal Corresp.*, pp. 147–48. MS at Arsenal.

Your two friends, M. Janski and M. Bontemps,[2] have not had more success in converting me to St Simonism than Duverryer [*sic*][3] and you; but if you are sufficiently catholic, in the original & correct sense of the word, to rejoice at any progress which does not bring any proselytes within your pale, I think you will be pleased with two or three articles of mine in the Examiner, headed "The Spirit of the Age",[4] which Adolphe is so kind as to take charge of for you.

Your doctrine begins to be talked of, & to excite some curiosity here—I have been the means of making it known to some persons, at their request: & in short, although I am not a St Simonist nor at all likely to become one, *je tiens bureau de St Simonisme chez moi.*

Pray commend me to Duveyrier; and to your two chiefs,[5] even; if their *haute mission* has not prevented them from retaining any trace of me in their remembrance.

tout à vous

J. S. MILL

Je vous félicite de l'acquisition de Globe.[6]

40. TO SARAH AUSTIN[1]

[Spring or summer 1831]

How I wish I were by your side, and could speak to you instead of writing. You may lay down your anxiety, my dear Mütterlein, I hope never to resume it.

In the first place, the shutting up the University for a year is a cock-

2. Members of the Saint-Simonian hierarchy of seventy-eight persons organized in Paris by Le Père Enfantin in 1831. They were listed in the division of labour "Sans fonctions." Cf. H. R. D'Allemagne, *Les Saints-Simoniens, 1827–37* (Paris, 1930), p. 106.
3. Charles Duveyrier (1803–1866), one of the leading writers among the Saint-Simonians. Early the following year he visited London with D'Eichthal to promote the Saint-Simonian cause in England. See Letter 47, n. 1.
4. Three of the series of five essays under this title had thus far appeared, in the *Examiner* for Jan. 9, Jan. 23, and Feb. 6. The whole series has been republished in *The Spirit of the Age*, ed. F. A. Hayek (Chicago, 1942).
5. Saint Amand Bazard (1791–1832) and Barthélemy Prosper Enfantin (1796–1864), at this time *pères suprèmes* of the Saint-Simonian order. Later this year Bazard resigned because of his violent disagreement with Enfantin's advanced views on the relation of the sexes.
6. Beginning on Jan. 18, 1831, its title had become *Le Globe: Journal de la Doctrine du Saint-Simon.*

* * * *

1. MS in the possession of Mr. Gordon Waterfield.

and-bull story.[2] Romilly[3] tells me that it was talked of by one or two of the members of council among themselves, but never was proposed to the Council, & R. is firmly persuaded it never will be proposed, & would have no chance of being carried.

Romilly is in better spirits about the University than he has long been. He says that he and my father and Mr Wm Tooke[4] met together yesterday & looked over papers &c. &c. to see what could be done to reduce the expense, & the result was such as to convince Romilly that by the end of next year the receipts will exceed the disbursements.

So much for the University. Then Romilly tells me that it is now certain or nearly certain that a Professorship of Jurisprudence will be endowed by subscription for three years.[5] I do not know whether I ought to have told you this as long as there could be even the slightest doubt: but I do not think there can be the slightest, from the manner in which he spoke of it, and besides I could not help telling you. However let us keep our joy to ourselves for the present. I never could bring myself to believe that we should lose you, and now I am sure we shall not.

Now you must write me a joyful note to make amends for your sorrowful one.

Ihre Söhnchen,

J. S. M.

41. TO GUSTAVE D'EICHTHAL[1]

27 August 1831.

My dear Gustave

I suppose it is of no use writing to you about any thing except what relates to the doctrine of St Simon. With respect to the translating of the St Simonian books, I think the time has hardly come for it—indeed my

2. Financial difficulties and internal dissension had caused much trouble in the session of 1830–31 of the recently founded London University. On March 26, 1831, the Warden, Leonard Horner, had resigned as of the end of the term. For the best account of this period in the history of the University, see chap. vi of H. H. Bellot, *University College, London, 1826–1926* (London, 1929).

3. Probably John, later first Baron Romilly (1802–1874), who, though not a member of the Council of the University, was appointed in April, 1831, member of a committee to consider the future management of the University. See *ibid.*, p. 209.

4. James Mill and William Tooke (1777–1863), later president of the Society of Arts, were members of the first Council of the University.

5. This was a matter of some concern for John Austin, since his receipts from students' fees were small. See Letter 32. An endowment of his chair of £200 per annum for three years was raised later in 1831. Cf. Bellot, *University College*, p. 99, and Letter 43, the penultimate paragraph.

* * * *

1. *Addressed*: Monsieur / Gustave d'Eichthal / à Paris. MS at Arsenal.

own opinion is that to have any chance of making converts in this country it would be advisable not to translate the existing books, but to write new ones better adapted to the state of the English mind. However I was told some time ago by Mr Owen, that some of his friends were translating your works.[2] Whether they understand them sufficiently to be able to translate them in the proper manner, I do not know—but I suspect not.

I do not know to what merits of my own, as respects the doctrine of St Simon, I am indebted for regularly receiving the Globe—but I beg you to make my acknowledgments to your chiefs, and to accept them yourself, for the great pleasure which it has afforded me. I read it regularly and have derived great advantage from it, and though there is as little chance as ever of my becoming one of you, I do not differ from you nearly so much as I did.

I am much obliged to you for introducing me to the acquaintance of Mr Silsey,[3] and I hope you will confer on me a similar favour whenever any of your friends comes to this place.

Pray make my affectionate remembrances to Adolphe and all friends. Is there any chance that Lanjuinais will come here in the approaching vacation?

Yours most truly

J. S. MILL.

42. TO THOMAS CARLYLE[1]

[Oct. 7, 1831][2]

MY DEAR SIR

When I wrote to you this morning that I was about to dine with a Frenchman who was an intimate friend of mine I was not aware that both the brother and the uncle of that friend were known to you, the first (M.

2. Lindley, p. 195, points out that apparently only two contemporaneous translations of Saint-Simonian books into English were made: one a translation by Thomas Carlyle of Saint-Simon's *Nouveau Christianisme* which Carlyle never published; the other a translation of the same work by James E. Smith, a Universalist minister and Owenite, published in 1834 by B. D. Cousins with the title *New Christianity*.

3. Unidentified.

* * * *

1. *Addressed*: Thomas Carlyle / 4 Ampton St. / Mecklenburg Sqe. By permission of the Harvard College Library.

2. The letter is undated, but JSM and Adolphe d'Eichthal called on Carlyle on Monday, Oct. 10, 1831. See *Two Notebooks of Thomas Carlyle*, ed. C. E. Norton (New York, 1898), p. 205. The National Library of Scotland has an unpublished letter by Carlyle, dated the previous Wednesday night (Oct. 5), inviting JSM to meet Mrs. Carlyle, recently arrived from Scotland, for coffee at half-past six on Friday evening. JSM had met Carlyle for the first time on Sept. 2, 1831.

Gustave d'Eichthal) in correspondence with you, and the uncle[3] a friend of your brother. My friend is extremely desirous of making your acquaintance, and as he leaves town for Edinburgh on Tuesday, Monday next is the only day on which I could have an opportunity of introducing him to you. If it is quite convenient and agreeable to you, it would be a great pleasure both to me and to him if you would permit us to call upon you on that evening. I think I may promise that you will like him.

He is acquainted with no person at Edinburgh, and if when you see him you should be disposed to give him any introductions there, I am sure they will be well bestowed and properly appreciated.

Believe me
Yours most truly
J. S. MILL

Friday
evening.

43. TO JOHN STERLING[1]

From the 20th of October to the
22d. India House. 1831.

DEAR STERLING

You must have wondered at not hearing from me sooner; and not without good reason. It is true that I have not heard from you *non plus*, so that we seem to have been equally neglectful of one another. But, 1. very probably a letter from you is now on its way here. 2. *Your* silence ought only to be counted from your arrival,[2] and *mine* from your setting out. 3. I have had only my ordinary occupations, while you have had all the trouble of settling in a new place, of commencing an entirely new mode of life and kind of occupation, and when this was just done, you were turned out by a vile hurricane & obliged to begin the whole thing over again.[3] 4. A letter from home is still more precious than even the most

3. The Baron d'Eichthal, with whom Dr. John Carlyle spent nearly a year in Munich, 1827–28.

* * * *

1. MS at King's. Published with minor variants in Elliot.

2. Sterling had arrived at St. Vincent in the West Indies in the early summer of 1831 to take up duties as superintendent of a sugar plantation, Colonarie, an estate belonging to the Coningham family, and the chief source of his mother's income. See Tuell, *John Sterling*, p. 111.

3. For an account of the hurricane of Aug. 11, 1831, see Sterling's letter to his mother of Aug. 28, 1831, printed in Thomas Carlyle, *Life of John Sterling* (London, 1851), chap. XII, pp. 102–10.

interesting letter from abroad. 5. Though you have not written to *me,* you have to others, & I have seen part of what you wrote: now when a man is a great way off, his letter to one of his friends may be taken *mutatis mutandis* as a letter to all, but that cannot be said of *their* letters to him.—You see I have stated the case against myself as strongly as I can, in order to leave you nothing to add to it. As I have no excuse to make which will not leave my case worse than it is already, I can only make you the best reparation in my power by writing you an exceedingly long letter this time. I suppose it is right to assume that you must desire *en premier lieu* to hear about public affairs, now when they are in so ticklish a state: but really I can tell you little more than you will learn from the newspapers. The rejection of the Reform Bill by the large majority of 41 in the House of Lords,[4] has given an immense impulse to the *mouvement* in this country. All chance that the Bill when passed should prove a healing measure is at an end. The House of Lords is now as *much* detested as ever the House of Commons was. Nothing less than the creation of from 60 to 100 liberal Peers, to change the character of the House, can now give it any chance of remaining in existence. It is said that they flinch, and will pass the Bill without any new creation, but that will not now save them. They will come into collision with the Reformed House on some other point, & will certainly go to the wall. You may consider the fate of the Church as sealed. Only two Bishops voted for the Bill; about five more staid away, the rest voted against it.[5] The hierarchy being thus, as a body, hostile to it, while the temporal Peers were almost equally divided, the first brunt of public indignation has fallen upon the Prelacy. Every voice is raised against allowing them to continue in the House of Lords, and if I do not express my conviction that they will be excluded from it before this day five years, it is only because I doubt whether the House itself will last so long. I cannot say I regret either the approaching downfall of the Peers or that of the Church. I certainly think it desirable that there should be a conservative branch of the legislature; and that there should be a national clergy or clerisy, like that of which Coleridge traces the outline, in his work on Church & State.[6] If therefore I thought that the present Peerage & Clergy would ever consent to become the peerage of a government constituted on anti-jobbing principles, & the clergy of a non-sectarian church, I should

4. On the second reading, Oct. 8, 1831.

5. The *Examiner* for Oct. 9 (p. 650) reported: "About the Reverend Bench 'there can be no mistake.' Only one Bishop, Dr. Maltby, voted as present, with the proxy of the venerable Bishop of Norwich. Twelve Bishops present, and nine Proxies, were against the Bill."

6. Samuel Taylor Coleridge, *On the Constitution of the Church and State, according to the idea of each; with aids towards a right judgment on the late Catholic Bill* (London, 1830).

pray for their continuance. But they never will. Can a Peerage so ignorant as ours is proved to be by its recent vote, of the spirit of the age, & the feelings of the people, ever be able to fulfil with judgment the ends of a *checking* body, which are, to yield to all steady impulses of opinion, which are likely to be permanent, & to resist those which are in their nature temporary & changeable? And as for the clergy, who does not see that they are mainly divisible into two great categories, the worldly-minded, & the sectarians? I know that you will not agree with me, but I think that Coleridge would, in thinking that a national clergy ought to be so constituted as to include all who are capable of producing a beneficial effect on their age & country as teachers of the knowledge which fits people to perform their duties & exercise their rights, and as exhorters to the right performance & exercise of them: now I contend that such persons are to be found among all denominations of Christians, nay even among those who are not Christians at all: provided (which I deem an essential condition in the present stage of human progressiveness) they abstain from either directly attacking, or indirectly undermining Christianity, & even adopt (as far as without hypocrisy they can) those means of addressing the feelings & the conscience, to which a connexion with Christianity has given potency. An infidel who attempts to subvert or weaken the belief of mankind in Christianity, ought not in my opinion to form a part of the national *clerisy*; not because he may not be performing a conscientious duty in so doing, but because it is to me a proof that he misunderstands the wants & tendencies of his age, & that the effect of his exertions would probably be to make men worse instead of better by shaking the only firm convictions & feelings of duty which they have, without having even a remote chance of furnishing them with any effectual substitute. Accordingly in France, where Christianity has lost its hold on men's minds, my reasoning would not apply. There, I believe that a Christian would be positively less fit than a St Simonian (for example), to form part of a national church. These then are my ideas of a church establishment; ideas which I shall promulgate to the public in some shape or other when I shall see a good opportunity for their being attended to. But I feel certain that no church, not founded on this comprehensive principle, can, or ought to stand. I believe that if any class of Christians, Socinians for example, or even Deists, or Atheists, were excluded you could not select your clergy from the remainder of mankind without including persons less fit in every respect than some whom you would exclude. Besides, you would then retain that encouragement to hypocrisy, that holding out of worldly motives first to the adoption & next to the obstinate retention of particular creeds, which has disgusted so many high-minded men with church establishments: which has made them to be considered as obstacles to improvement, as the creation of a class with an interest adverse to the progressiveness of the species. In the present age of transition, everything must be subordinate to *freedom of inquiry*: if your opinions, or mine, are right, they will in time be unanimously adopted by the instructed classes, and *then* it will be time to found the national creed upon the assumption of their truth.— But what chance is there that the Church as at present constituted, will consent to undergo, even by the most insensible steps, this transformation? and that, too, at a time when insensible steps will not suffice. If they would, the recent elevation of Whately to the archbishopric of Dublin & of Maltby[7] to the bishopric of Chichester, would greatly encourage me; the former because I think him one of the fittest men in the country to hold a high station in a national church such as I conceive it should be; the latter for the very reason which makes others disapprove of it, his want of orthodoxy. But all this might do while the people were attached to the Church. At present they are hostile to it: hostile consequently, to all church establishments, because they know of none better than this: & they would be more likely to accept an entirely new one, than one which they considered to be a transformation of this. Why is it almost the natural course of things in politics, that destruction must precede renovation? It is because reform is delayed till the whole attachment of the public to the *entire* of the institution is gone, & then they feel a distrust of anything which looks like patching up the old edifice. So I believe it to be both with Church & State at this moment. You have no doubt seen in the English papers, the speeches at public meetings and the various Resolutions which have been agreed to. These are generally very strong; but they were, in every case, the weakest which there was the least chance that the people would have adopted. Almost everywhere, if any person came forward & proposed stronger Resolutions, they were carried by acclamation, much to the dissatisfaction of those who called the meeting & prepared the proceedings. I am convinced that we are indebted for the preservation of tranquillity solely to the organisation of the people in Political Unions. All the other Unions look to the Birmingham one, & that looks to its half dozen leaders, who consequently act under a most intense consciousness of moral responsibility & are very careful neither to do nor say anything without the most careful deliberation. I conversed the other day with a Warwickshire magistrate who told me that the meeting of 150,000 men a few days previous would have done *any* thing without exception which their leaders might have proposed. They would have passed any resolutions, marched to any place, or burnt any man's house. The agricultural people are as determined as the manufacturers. The West is as *exalté* as the North. Colonel Napier

7. Edward Maltby (1770–1859), then Bishop of Chichester, later, 1836–56, Bishop of Durham, voted for the Reform Bill. See n. 5 above.

made a speech at the Devizes meeting the other day[8] for the express purpose (as I hear) of letting the men in the North perceive, that the West is ready to join in any popular movement if necessary; & since that speech (which the leaders in vain attempted to prevent him from delivering) he has received numbers of letters from all parts of the country, saying that they all look to him as their leader, & are ready to place themselves under his command. If the ministers flinch or the Peers remain obstinate, I am firmly convinced that in six months a national convention chosen by universal suffrage, will be sitting in London. Should this happen, I have not made up my mind what would be best to do: I incline to think it would be best to lie by and let the tempest blow over, if one could but get a shilling a day to live upon meanwhile: for until the whole of the existing institutions of society are levelled with the ground, there will be nothing for a wise man to do which the most pig-headed fool cannot do much better than he. A Turgot,[9] even, could not do in the present state of England what Turgot himself failed of doing in France—mend the old system. If it goes all at once, let us wait till it is gone: if it goes piece by piece, why, let the blockheads who will compose the first Parliament after the bill passes, do what a blockhead can do, viz. overthrow, & the ground will be cleared, & the passion of destruction sated, & a coalition prepared between the wisest radicals & the wisest anti-radicals, between all the wiser men who agree in their general views & differ only in their estimate of the present condition of this country.—You will perhaps think from this long prosing rambling talk about politics, that they occupy much of my attention: but in fact I am myself often surprised, how little I really care about them. The time is not yet come when a calm & impartial person can intermeddle with advantage in the questions & contests of the day. I never write in the Examiner now except on France, which nobody else that I know of seems to know any thing about; & now & then on some insulated question of political economy. The only thing which I can usefully do at present, & which I am doing more & more every day, is to work out *principles*: which are of use for all times, though to be applied cautiously & circumspectly to any: principles of morals, government, law, education, above all self-education. I am here much more in my element: the only thing that I believe I am really fit for, is the investigation of abstract truth, & the more abstract the better. If there is any science which I am capable

8. Sir William Francis Patrick Napier (1785–1860), later General, historian of the Peninsular War. The King on Oct. 9 in indignation at Napier's speech sent Earl Grey a copy of the *Globe* for Oct. 7 which contained a report of it. The King favoured dismissal of Napier from the army, but Grey dissuaded His Majesty from such a step. See Charles Grey, 2d Earl Grey, *The Reform Act, 1832; the Correspondence of the late Earl Grey with His Majesty King William IV . . .* , ed. Henry Earl Grey (2 vols., London, 1867), I, 368.

9. Anne Robert Jacques Turgot, baron de l'Aulne (1727–1781), statesman and economist, Comptroller General (1774–76) under Louis XVI.

of promoting, I think it is the science of science itself, the science of investigation—of method. I once heard Maurice[10] say (& like many things which have dropped from him, its truth did not strike me at first but it has been a source of endless reflexions since) that almost all differences of opinion when analysed, were differences of method. But if so, he who can throw most light upon the subject of method, will do most to forward that alliance among the most advanced intellects & characters of the age, which is the only definite object I ever have in literature or philosophy so far as I have any *general* object at all. *Argal*, I have put down upon paper a great many of my ideas on logic, & shall in time bring forth a treatise: but whether it will see the light until the Treaty of Westphalia is signed at the close of another cycle of reformation & antagonism, no one can tell except Messrs. Drummond,[11] M'Niel,[12] Irving,[13] & others, who possess the hidden key to the Interpretation of the Prophecies. I have just put the finishing hand to my part of a work on Political Economy, which Graham & I are writing jointly:[14] our object is to clear up some points which have been left doubtful, to correct some which we consider to be wrong, & to shew what the science is & how it should be studied. I have written five essays; four on detached questions & one on the science itself. Graham is to write five more on the same subjects: we are then to compare notes, throw our ideas into a common stock, talk over all disputed points till we agree (which between us two, we know by experience to be by no means an indefinite postponement) & then one of us is to write a book out of the materials. Graham is to add a sixth essay on a very important part of the subject which is above my reach, & which I am only to criticize when it is done. I am now resting upon my oars. Yesterday I completed my task, & having reached a sort of landing-place (vide the Friend)[15] I have asked

10. Frederick Denison Maurice (1805–1872), liberal divine; for JSM's assessment of him, see *Autobiog.*, chap. v.

11. Henry Drummond (1786–1860), politician and joint founder of the Irvingite Church, built a church at Albury; in 1834 visited Scotland as an apostle and was ordained as angel for Scotland.

12. Rev. Hugh M'Neil (1795–1879), rector at Albury, closely associated with the Irvingites at this time; later (1868–75), Dean of Ripon.

13. Rev. Edward Irving (1792–1834), founder of the Irvingite or Catholic Apostolic Church, friend of Carlyle. He and his followers specialized in prophecy and the gift of tongues.

14. This project arose from the discussions of the study group that met at Grote's house in Threadneedle Street. (See JSM, *Autobiog.*, pp. 83–86.) The plan for a joint publication with Graham did not materialize. JSM's essays appeared years later under the title *Essays on Some Unsettled Questions of Political Economy* (1844). See Letters 86, 424, 425, 427.

15. S. T. Coleridge, *The Friend. A literary, moral, and political weekly paper*, 28 nos. (Penrith, 1809–10); collected edition, with alterations and additions (3 vols., London, 1818). The preface to the latter edition, after describing the general introduction, concludes, "three several collections of essays, in some degree miscellaneous and called Landing-Places . . . complete the work."

myself what recreation I could offer myself by way of reward for past & encouragement to future exertions; & nothing better has yet occurred to me, than writing to you. The next thing I shall do will be to complete my speculations on Logic: very likely I shall not get to the end of the subject yet, viewed as I understand it; but I shall at least gather in another harvest of ideas, & then let the ground lie fallow a while longer.[16] After this I shall probably put down upon paper a vast quantity of miscellaneous ideas which are wrought out to a certain extent in my head, but which it would be quite premature to publish for a long while to come. I have nothing in view for the public just now, except (when the Reform Bill shall have past) to resume my series of papers headed the Spirit of the Age;[17] and to write an article or two for the Jurist (now about to be revived) on some abstract questions of general legislation.[18] When I shall have completed all this, then if the East India Company is abolished and funded property confiscated, I shall perhaps scrape together the means of paying my passage to St Vincent's & see whether you will employ me to teach your niggers political economy. I take it for granted that if a Reformed Parliament should begin taking measures for the emancipation of the slaves, you will all join the United States, who being lovers of liberty, will I trust go to war with Republican England to restore you & the other colonists, to the inalienable rights of freemen.

I have done nothing in this letter but talk to you about the world in general and about myself. I must now talk to you about other people, and particularly about several new acquaintances of mine that I had not made or had only just begun to make when you left this white world. First of all, I went this summer to the Lakes,[19] where I saw much splendid scenery, and also saw a great deal both of Wordsworth and Southey;[20] and I must tell you what I think of them both. In the case of Wordsworth, I was particularly struck by several things. One was, the extensive range of his

16. He did not publish his *Logic* until 1843.

17. See Letter 39, n. 4.

18. No article of his seems to have appeared in the *Jurist* until Feb., 1833: "Corporation and Church Property," reprinted in his *Dissertations*, I, 28–67, with the title "The Right and Wrong of State Interference with Corporation and Church Property."

19. His MS journal of this holiday, "Tour of the Lakes," extending from July 19 to Aug. 15, 1831, is in the Bodleian Library. Anna J. Mill has published excerpts: "John Stuart Mill's Visit to Wordsworth, 1831," *Modern Language Rev.*, XLIV (1949), 341–50.

20. JSM had met Southey at a breakfast party given by Henry Taylor on Nov. 14, 1830. Others in the party included Edward Strutt, Charles Villiers, Thomas Frederick Elliot, and Charles Greville. See *The Greville Memoirs*, ed. Lytton Strachey and Roger Fulford (8 vols., London, 1938), II, 57–58. JSM had breakfast with Wordsworth and the same group on Feb. 27, 1831 (*ibid.*, p. 122). Anna J. Mill, "JSM's Visit to Wordsworth," thinks that JSM may have met Wordsworth even earlier at Henry Taylor's.

thoughts and the largeness & expansiveness of his feelings. This does not appear in his writings, especially his poetry, where the contemplative part of his mind is the only part of it that appears: & one would be tempted to infer from the peculiar character of his poetry, that real life & the active pursuits of men (except of farmers & other country people) did not interest him. The fact however is that these very subjects occupy the greater part of his thoughts, & he talks on no subject more instructively than on states of society & forms of government. Those who best know him, seem to be most impressed with the catholic character of his ability. I have been told that Lockhart[21] has said of him that he would have been an admirable country attorney. Now a man who could have been either Wordsworth or a country attorney, could certainly have been anything else which circumstances had led him to desire to be. The next thing that struck me was the extreme comprehensiveness and philosophic spirit which is in him. By these expressions I mean the direct antithesis of what the Germans most expressively call onesidedness. Wordsworth seems always to know the pros and the cons of every question; & when you think he strikes the balance wrong, it is only because you think he estimates erroneously some matter of fact. Hence all my differences with him, or with any other philosophic Tory, would be differences of matter-of-fact or detail, while my differences with the radicals & utilitarians are differences of principle: for *these see* generally only one side of the subject, & in order to convince them, you must put some entirely new idea into their heads, whereas Wordsworth has all the ideas there already, & you have only to discuss with him concerning the "how much," the more or less of weight which is to be attached to a certain cause or effect, as compared with others: thus the difference with him turns upon a question of varying or fluctuating quantities, where what is *plus* in one age or country is *minus* in another & the whole question is one of observation & testimony & of the value of particular articles of evidence. I need hardly say to you that if one's own conclusions & his were at variance on every question which a minister or a Parliament could to-morrow be called upon to solve, his is nevertheless the mind with which one would be really in communion: our principles would be the same, and we should be like two travellers pursuing the same course on the opposite banks of a river.—Then when you get Wordsworth on the subjects which are peculiarly his, such as the theory of his own art—if it be proper to call poetry an art, (that is, if art is to be defined the expression or embodying in words or forms, of the highest & most refined parts of nature) no one can converse with him without feeling that he has advanced that great subject beyond any other man, being probably the first

21. John Gibson Lockhart (1794–1854), son-in-law and biographer of Sir Walter Scott.

person who ever combined, with such eminent success in the practice of the art, such high powers of generalization & habits of meditation on its principles. Besides all this, he seems to me the best talker I ever heard (& I have heard several first-rate ones); & there is a benignity & kindliness about his whole demeanour which confirms what his poetry would lead one to expect, along with a perfect simplicity of character which is delightful in any one, but most of all in a person of first-rate intellect. You see I am somewhat enthusiastic on the subject of Wordsworth, having found him still more admirable & delightful a person on a nearer view than I had figured to myself from his writings; which is so seldom the case that it is impossible to see it without having one's faith in man greatly increased & being made greatly happier in consequence. I also was very much pleased with Wordsworth's family—at least the female part of it. I am convinced that the proper place to see him is in his own kingdom—I call the whole of that mountain region his kingdom, as it will certainly be as much thought of hereafter by the people of Natchitoches or of Swan River, as Mænalus and the Cephissus, or Baiae and Soracte by ourselves, and this from the fortuitous circumstance that he was born there & lived there. I believe it was not there that you were acquainted with him, & therefore I am not telling you an old story in talking about the little palace or pavilion which he occupies in this poetic region, & which is perhaps the most delightful residence in point of situation in the whole country. The different views from it are a sort of abstract or abridgment of the whole Westmoreland side of the mountains, & every spot visible from it has been immortalised in his poems. I was much pleased with the universality of his relish for all good poetry however dissimilar to his own: & with the freedom & unaffected simplicity with which every person about him seemed to be in the habit of discussing & attacking any passage or poem in his own works which did not please them.—I also saw a great deal of Southey, who is a very different kind of man, very inferior to Wordsworth in the higher powers of intellect, & entirely destitute of his philosophic spirit, but a remarkably pleasing & likeable man. I never could understand him till lately; that is, I never could reconcile the tone of such of his writings as I had read, with what his friends said of him: I could only get rid of the notion of his being insincere, by supposing him to be extremely fretful and irritable: but when I came to read his Colloquies,[22] in which he has put forth much more than in any other work, of the natural man, as distinguished from the writer aiming at a particular effect, I found there a kind of connecting link between the two parts of his character, & formed very much the same notion of him which I now have after seeing & conversing with him. He seems to me to be a

22. Robert Southey, *Sir Thomas More; or, Colloquies on the Progress and Prospects of Society* (2 vols., London, 1829).

man of gentle feelings & bitter opinions. His opinions make him think a great many things abominable which are not so; against which accordingly he thinks it would be right, & suitable to the fitness of things, to express great indignation: but if he really feels this indignation, it is only by a voluntary act of the imagination that he conjures it up, by representing the thing to his own mind in colours suited to that passion: now, when he knows an individual & feels disposed to like him, although that individual may be placed in one of the condemned categories, he does not conjure up this phantom & feels therefore no principle of repugnance, nor excites any. No one can hold a greater number of the opinions & few have more of the qualities, which he condemns, than some whom he has known intimately & befriended for many years: at the same time he would discuss their faults & weaknesses or vices with the greatest possible freedom in talking about them. It seems to me that Southey is altogether out of place in the existing order of society: his attachment to old institutions & his condemnation of the practices of those who administer them, cut him off from sympathy & communion with both halves of mankind. Had he lived before radicalism & infidelity became prevalent, he would have been the steady advocate of the moral & physical improvement of the poorer classes & denouncer of the selfishness & supineness of those who ought to have considered the welfare of those classes as confided to their care. Possibly the essential one-sidedness of his mind might then have rendered him a democrat: but now the evils which he expects from increase of the power wielded by the democratic spirit such as it now is, have rendered him an aristocrat in principle without inducing him to make the slightest compromise with aristocratic vices and weaknesses. Consequently he is not liked by the Tories, while the Whigs and radicals abhor him. And after all, a man cannot complain of being misinterpreted, who always puts the worst interpretation upon the words and deeds of other people. As far as I have yet seen, speculative Toryism and practical Toryism are direct contraries. Practical Toryism simply means, being *in*, and availing yourself of your comfortable position *inside* the vehicle without minding the poor devils who are freezing *outside*. To be a Tory means either to be a place-hunter and jobber or else to think that (as Turgot expressed it) tout va bien, parce que tout va bien pour eux; to be one qui ayant leur lit bien fait, ne veulent pas qu'on le remue. Such Toryism is essentially incompatible with any large and generous aspirations; nor could any one who had such aspirations ever have any power of realizing them under our system, whatever might be his attachment to the forms of the Constitution, because the inert mass of our sluggish and enervated higher classes can be moved by nothing that does not come from without, & with a vengeance; they cannot be led, but must be driven: the clamours of the "fierce democracy" can alone stir their feeble and lazy minds, & awaken them from the sleep of indifference. What can you do when there is no faith in human improvement, & every glaring, disgusting evil which they cannot deny is set down as the inevitable price we pay for social order, & irremediable by human efforts? "It is all very true, but what can we do?" is the ready answer of everybody who can possibly avoid doing something; & you can say nothing in reply but this, "Then if you can do nothing for that society which has hitherto made nobody the happier unless it be yourselves, the rest of mankind must try what they can do to improve their own lot without your assistance, & then perhaps you may not like their manner of proceeding." If there were but a few dozens of persons safe (whom you & I could select) to be missionaries of the great truths in which alone there is any well-being for mankind individually or collectively, I should not care though a revolution were to exterminate every person in Great Britain & Ireland who has £500 a year. Many very amiable persons would perish, but what is the world the better for such amiable persons.[23] But among the missionaries whom I would reserve, a large proportion would consist of speculative Tories: for it is an ideal Toryism, an ideal King, Lords, & Commons, that they venerate; it is old England as opposed to the new, but it is old England as she might be, not as she is. It seems to me that the Toryism of Wordsworth, of Coleridge (if he can be called a Tory) of Southey even, & of many others whom I could mention, is *tout bonnement* a reverence for *government* in the abstract: it means, that they are duly sensible that it is good for man to be ruled; to submit both his body & mind to the guidance of a higher intelligence & virtue. It is therefore the direct antithesis of liberalism, which is for making every man his own guide & sovereign master, & letting him think for himself & do exactly as he judges best for himself, giving other men leave to persuade him if they can by evidence, but forbidding him to give way to authority; and still less allowing them to constrain him more than the existence & tolerable security of every man's person and property renders indispensably necessary. It is difficult to conceive a more thorough ignorance of man's nature, & of what is necessary for his happiness or what degree of happiness & virtue he is capable of attaining than this system implies. But I cannot help regretting that the men who are best capable of struggling against these narrow views & mischievous heresies should chain themselves, full of life & vigour as they are, to the inanimate corpses of dead political & religious systems, never more to be revived. The same ends require altered means; we have no new principles, but we want new machines constructed on the old principles; those we had before are worn out. Instead of cutting a safe channel for the

23. The following sentence has been crossed out in the MS: "I should only regret the women, whose proper sphere is that of the private virtues."

stream of events, these people would dam it up till it breaks down every thing & spreads devastation over a whole region.

Another acquaintance which I have recently made is that of Mr. Carlyle,[24] whom I believe you are also acquainted with.[25] I have long had a very keen relish for his articles in the Edinburgh & Foreign Reviews, which I formerly thought to be such consummate nonsense; and I think he improves upon a nearer acquaintance. He does not seem to me so entirely the reflexion or shadow of the great German writers as I was inclined to consider him; although undoubtedly his mind has derived from their inspiration whatever breath of life is in it. He seems to me as a man who has had his eyes unsealed, and who now looks round him & sees the aspects of things with his own eyes, but by the light supplied by others; not the pure light of day, but another light compounded of the same simple rays but in different proportions. He has by far the largest & widest liberality & tolerance (not in the sense which Coleridge justly disavows,[26] but in the good sense) that I have met with in any one; & he differs from most men who see as much as he does into the defects of the age, by a circumstance greatly to his advantage in my estimation, that he looks for a safe landing *before* and not *behind*: he sees that if we could replace things as they once were, we should only retard the final issue, as we should in all human probability go on just as we then did, & arrive again at the very place where we now stand. Carlyle intends staying in town all the winter: he has brought his wife to town (whom I have not seen enough of yet to be able to judge of her at all): his object was to treat with booksellers about a work which he wishes to publish,[27] but he has given up this for the present, finding that no bookseller will publish anything but a political pamphlet in the present state of excitement. In fact literature is suspended; men neither read nor write. Accordingly Carlyle means to employ his stay here in improving his knowledge of what is going on in the world, at least in this part of it, I mean in that part of the world of ideas and feelings which corresponds to London. He is a great hunter-out of acquaintances; he hunted me out, or rather hunted out the author of certain papers in the Examiner[28] (the first, as he said, which he had ever

24. See Letter 42, n. 2.

25. Carlyle in his *Life of John Sterling*, Part I, chap. XII, and Part II, chap. II, says that though he had learned of Sterling from JSM and the Austins in 1831 he first met him in Feb., 1835.

26. Cf. Coleridge, *The Friend* (London, 1818), I, 158–63, and *Aids to Reflection* (London, 1825), pp. 101–3.

27. *Sartor Resartus.* Carlyle eventually had to "slit [it] up into strips, and send it forth in the Periodical way" (*Letters of Thomas Carlyle, 1826–1836*, ed. C. E. Norton [London, 1889], p. 368). It first appeared in *Fraser's* from Nov., 1833, to Aug., 1834.

28. The essays in JSM's "The Spirit of the Age" series.

seen in a newspaper, hinting that the age was not the best of all possible ages): & his acquaintance is the only substantial good I have yet derived from writing those papers, & a much greater one than I expected when I wrote them. He has also, through me, sought the acquaintance of Fonblanque[29] (of the Examiner) whom I found him to be an admirer of, and who though as little of a mystic as most men, reads his writings with pleasure. I expect great good from Fonblanque; he is fashioned for the work of the day, as befits one who works for the day, but he is one of those on whom one may most completely rely for being ready to turn over a new leaf when the old one is read through.

I have to add yet another new acquaintance to all these, and one who is by no means the least remarkable among them; I mean Stephen,[30] the Counsel to the Colonial Office, son of the Master in Chancery. I have only yet seen him two or three times, but I hope to see much more of him, especially as I have now gone to live in his immediate neighbourhood, at Kensington.[31] I have hardly met with any person who seems to me to take such just views of the age and of futurity as he does; to be so free from any exaggeration or one-sidedness, and to combine the speculative & the practical in so just a proportion. He cannot fail hereafter to exercise a great influence over the destinies of his country, not so much perhaps by what he does, as by what he makes other persons do. He is at this moment the directing spirit not only of the Colonial Office but of several other departments of the government: under great restraints & disadvantages of course, from the unteachable quality of those placed over him & their dread of anything like a principle, arising from their consciousness of inability to comprehend in one view all that is involved in it & all the consequences to which it leads. Stephen is reputed a saint: I do not know in what sense he is one, though I know that he carries the observance of the Sabbath to the extent of puritanism. But if all the English evangelicals were like him, I think I should attend their Exeter Hall[32] meetings myself, and subscribe to their societies. I will write to you at greater length about Stephen when I have seen more of him.

29. Albany Fonblanque (1793–1872), radical journalist, editor of the *Examiner*, 1830–47.

30. James (later Sir James) Stephen (1789–1859), Colonial Under-Secretary, father of Leslie and Fitzjames Stephen. In the last week of Sept., 1831, Stephen had accompanied JSM, Henry Taylor, and Frederick Elliot on a visit to Coleridge at Highgate (see *Correspondence of Henry Taylor*, ed. Edward Dowden [London, 1888], p. 39).

31. James Mill had moved his family from Queen Square to Vicarage Place, Church Street, Kensington, in the spring of 1831.

32. A large building erected in the Strand in the year of this letter for the activities of dissenting religious and charitable societies. With a hall seating five thousand, it was for many years the meeting place for various large dissenting religious groups.

As for our common friends and acquaintances here, I have but little to tell you concerning them. Mrs. Austin will of course write to you. I do not know whether the subscription for endowing the Jurisprudence chair is yet full,[33] but no doubt is entertained that it will be so. Mr. Austin is still engaged in bringing out his first eight lectures, which are soon to appear. He is in good health & spirits upon the whole. I have not seen or heard anything about Maurice; I hope our separation is not to be everlasting. Wilson[34] has very recently returned from Germany, where he has spent about a year. I have seen very little of Charles Buller;[35] you are probably aware that he is not in this Parliament, but he is sure of being returned for Liskeard when the Bill passes. The greatest change that has occurred in any one since I saw you is in Roebuck; he has pulled off his strait jacket, and now moves freely: his mental powers are no longer enslaved by fixed forms of words, and phrases strung together syllogistically with the false appearance of Euclidean demonstration. His intellect has greatly expanded, & the asperities of his character are much softened: and though there still remains, & possibly may always remain, much in his mental character which you and I would greatly object to, I have now no doubt of his being a useful, powerful, and constantly improving member of the only Church which has now any real existence, namely that of writers and orators.

The Colonization scheme[36] is going on prosperously. They have formed a plan for a new colony, to be settled on their principles on the coast of Southern Australia near the place where the newly discovered navigable river discharges itself into the sea. They are endeavouring to form a Land-Company to settle the country, & have the promise of an excellent Charter from Government when the company is formed. The Colonial Office I believe to be heartily with them at present. Our friend Graham has gone into the scheme with his usual vigour, & is now one of their leading minds: he wrote their last two pamphlets. Wakefield[37] now moves openly in the thing, though it is not declared publicly that he was the originator of it; but there is no reason now for keeping his connexion with it altogether a secret, as he has made himself very advantageously known to the public

33. See Letter 40, n. 5.

34. Probably John Wilson, a London friend of JSM, later an assistant factory commissioner and an editor of the *Globe* newspaper.

35. Charles Buller (1806–1848), liberal politician; pupil of Carlyle, 1822–25; MP for West Looe, Cornwall, 1830–31; MP for Liskeard, 1832–48; secretary to Governor General of Canada, 1838; Judge-Advocate General, 1846.

36. Both Sterling and Mill had associated themselves as early as 1830 with the Colonization Society, of which the moving spirit was Edward Gibbon Wakefield. The plan for the colonization of South Australia was an outgrowth of the Society's work.

37. Edward Gibbon Wakefield (1796–1862), colonial statesman. Wakefield had abducted an heiress in 1826; he was imprisoned from 1826 to 1829 and his marriage cancelled by Parliament.

by, really, a most remarkable book on the punishment of death, founded on the observations he made while in Newgate.[38] You are aware that our old enemy, Wilmot Horton,[39] has gone to Ceylon as governor, so that he no longer stands in the way of a rational scheme of colonization.—The St Simonists are making immense progress in France, & are doing great good there: France has nobody comparable to them on the whole. They talk of sending missionaries *here*; that will do them no good, I think.—This letter I hope will call forth an equally long one from you. I beg to be duly remembered to Mrs. John Sterling.

Yours faithfully

J. S. Mill

44. TO GUSTAVE D'EICHTHAL[1]

30th November
1831

My dear D'Eichthal

I know you too well to write to you on any subject except that of the great, and truly apostolic work in which you are engaged, and to which, though I am very far indeed from entirely agreeing with you, I have for some time been accustomed to look, as the greatest enterprise now in progress, for the regeneration of society.

I am greatly indebted to you and your associates, for being thought worthy to receive the Globe. If I did not sympathize with you in any other respect, it would still be a noble spectacle to see a body of men standing erect and fronting the world as you do. But the daily reading of the Globe, combined with various other causes, has brought me much nearer to many of your opinions than I was before; and I regard you as decidedly *à la tête de la civilisation.*

I am now inclined to think that your social organisation, under some modification or other, which experience, no doubt, will one day suggest to yourselves, is likely to be the final and permanent condition of the human race. I chiefly differ from you in thinking that it will require many, or at least several, ages, to bring mankind into a state in which they will

38. *Facts relating to the Punishment of Death in the Metropolis* (London, 1831).

39. Sir Robert John Wilmot-Horton. A controversy stirred up by him had resulted in the temporary dissolution of the Colonization Society. Two extant letters by Sterling to JSM relate to this controversy: see Tuell, *John Sterling*, pp. 95–97.

* * * *

1. MS at Arsenal. Published in *Cosmopolis*, VI, 356–58, and *D'Eichthal Corresp.*, pp. 149–52. The slightly variant version of it published by Elliot, I, 19–21, is based upon a copy made by D'Eichthal on May 14, 1870, and sent to JSM; this copy is now at Johns Hopkins.

be capable of it; & that in the mean time they are only capable of approximating to it by that gradual series of changes which are so admirably indicated and discussed in the writings of your body, and every one of which independently of what it may afterwards lead to, has the advantage of being in itself a great positive good. Your system, therefore, even supposing it to be impracticable, differs from every other system which has ever proposed to itself an unattainable end, in this, that many, indeed almost all attainable good lies on the road to it.

You, I am aware, think that all who adopt your system, prove thereby that they are capable of performing all which it would require of them if it became universal. I think not. But since you think so, it was your duty to commence, as you have done, the experiment of realizing it on such a scale as is permitted to you. I watch the experiment; and watch it with all the solicitude and anxiety of one, all whose hopes of the very rapid and early improvement of human society are wrapt up in its success.

If men of such ardent and generous enthusiasm, such strong and penetrating intellects, and such extensive views, are found unable to act up to their own conceptions of duty, what hope is there for the rest of mankind? If the Saint-Simonian society holds together without schism & heresy, and continues to propagate its faith and extend its numbers, at the rate it has done for the last two years—if this shall continue for a few years more, then I shall see something like a gleam of light through the darkness. But if not—then what is done will not be of no avail; I shall not despair, nor ought you. But it will be a grievous downfal[l] to our hopes.

Write to me sometimes, my dear friend. Be not afraid that your labour will be lost. I have never yet read a single article in the Globe which has not wrought something within me; which I have not been in some measure the better for. And if the hour were yet come for England—if it were not as vain to seek a hearing for any "vues organiques" in England now, as it would have been for your master St Simon in the height of the revolution—I know not that I should not renounce every thing, and become, not one of you, but as you.

But our 10 août, our 20 juin, and perhaps our 18 Brumaire,[2] are yet to come and which of us will be left standing when the hurricane has blown over, Heaven only knows.

Yours ever

J. S. MILL.

2. Significant dates in the history of the French Revolution: Aug. 10, 1792, the uprising of the Jacobins which led to the establishment of the revolutionary Commune of Paris, the subsequent September massacres and the overthrow of the monarchy; June 20, 1789, the Oath of the Tennis Court, whereby the deputies of the new National Assembly swore that they would not separate until they had established a constitution for France; Nov. 9, 1799 (18 Brumaire), beginning of the *coup d'état* which placed Napoleon Bonaparte in power.

45. TO GUSTAVE D'EICHTHAL[1]

London
6th December 1831.

MY DEAR D'EICHTHAL,

Ever since your note was given to me by M. Arlès,[2] I have been turning over in my mind your ideas concerning the dissemination of your principles in this country, and considering to what persons the Globe might be sent with prospect of advantage. I should not recommend its being sent either to the leading newspapers or to the leading members of parliament. It would not be read, or it would be read just enough to be altogether misunderstood. I have however thought of a few persons to whom it would be useful. Some of these I know to be in some measure prepared to receive many of your opinions favorably. Others will make your doctrine known by attacking it. Now since you have been violently attacked already by Southey, in so widely circulated a work as the Quarterly Review,[3] & mentioned in several newspapers of large circulation, as a set of dreamers and visionaries, it is desirable that you should be attacked a great deal more, & by a great variety of persons, in order that being attacked on all sides, your doctrine may have all its sides laid bare and divulged. Each person in pointing out the things which *he* dislikes, will shew to some other person that there are things which *he* would like. While you are only attacked as anarchists & levellers, you will excite no attention here, but when you come to be represented by A as anarchists; by B as absolutists; by C as levellers; by D as hierarchs; by E as infidels; by F as mystical religionists; by G as sentimentalists; by H as metaphysicians & political economists; & so forth; the public will see that an absurdity which has so many different faces, cannot be quite an absurdity; or at least, that it is an absurdity unlike others, & worth studying.

Among the young members of parliament (as for the old ones, they are hopeless) I only know two to whom there would be the least use in sending the Globe; & of them I am not sure. One is Mr T. Hyde Villiers,[4] the same who originated in parliament the proposition for equalizing the duties on French & on other foreign wines. He has now a place in the govern-

1. MS at Arsenal. Published in *Cosmopolis,* VI, 358–61, and in *D'Eichthal Corresp.,* pp. 153–59.

2. Presumably François Barthélemy Arlès–Du Four (1797–1872), a leader of the Saint-Simonians at Lyon, later a successful industrialist. Originally, his name was Arlès.

3. A review of *Doctrine de Saint Simon., Exposition* (2nd ed., Paris, 1830), *QR,* XLV (July, 1831), 407–50.

4. Thomas Hyde Villiers (1801–1832), politician and close friend of JSM, who wrote a brief eulogy of him upon his untimely death. See Letter 64, n. 18.

ment; he is secretary to the India Board, & his address is there. (N.B. Do not confound the India *Board* with the India *House.*) His brother[5] is now at Paris as one of the commissioners to negociate about free trade.

The other member of parliament to whom I allude is Mr Edward Lytton Bulwer[6] (his address is 36, Hertford Street, May-fair.) He is the author of several literary productions which have been very successful; & he is now the editor of the New Monthly Magazine, a periodical publication of considerable sale, very frivolous until lately, but which under his management has become very much the reverse. If you ever see it, you will remark in it *des vues d'avenir* which are exceedingly rare in this country.

It is not worth while to send the Globe to any of our daily newspapers; but if you send it to Mr Sterling[7] (South Place, Knightsbridge) who is one of the principal writers in the Times, there is some chance of its being of use. I know that he has read particular articles in the Globe, & has been much pleased with them. It may be of use to send it to two of our best provincial papers, if you can do so conveniently, the "Scotsman", an Edinburgh paper, and the "Brighton Guardian." The former, with some prejudices, is the most "progressif" of all our newspapers, scarcely excepting the Examiner. The Brighton paper is remarkable for a certain force and boldness of speculation, though the writer is sadly *abroad.*

Your should certainly send the Globe to Colonel T. Perronet Thompson,[8] the principal proprietor of the Westminster Review. He is partially acquainted with your doctrine, & likes some things in it, but dislikes others: I believe he has some notion of writing in his review about you. I am satisfied no one can do so without going egregiously wrong, unless he be a regular reader of the Globe. If your packets are sent to the Westminster Review office, Wellington Street, Strand, they will reach him.

If you like to send the Globe to Southey, his address is Robert Southey Esq. Keswick, Cumberland. Your brother will be able to advise you about sending it to Professor Wilson[9] of Edinburgh, the principal writer in Blackwood's Magazine, the great organ of our Tories. If you do, he will be sure to write about you; he will compliment you, and attack you, and will say a great deal about you which the public will not hear from any

5. George William Frederick Villiers (1800–1870), later fourth Earl of Clarendon and fourth Baron Hyde, diplomat and foreign minister.

6. Edward George Earle Lytton Bulwer, later Bulwer-Lytton, and subsequently first Baron Lytton (1803–1873), novelist and politician.

7. Edward Sterling, father of JSM's friend John Sterling.

8. Thomas Perronet Thompson (1783–1869), general, politician, and writer, especially on economics, and from 1829 to 1836 proprietor and editor of the *Westminster Review.* Some months after this letter, Thompson attacked the Saint-Simonians: "Saint-Simonism," *WR*, XVI (April, 1832), 279–321.

9. John Wilson (1785–1854), the "Christopher North" of *Blackwood's Magazine* and professor of moral philosophy at Edinburgh University.

one else, and which will excite their curiosity; he did all this for our utilitarian school of the old Westminster Review. But it will be matter of accident & humour whether he treats you as well-meaning men or impostors.

One of the most "progressif" men in this country is Dr Whately, lately appointed Archbishop of Dublin; which is in itself equivalent to a revolution in the Church. He is well entitled to receive the Globe. So is the Reverend J. Blanco White,[10] (Oriel College, Oxford), a Spanish Catholic priest, of considerable abilities, now a clergyman of the Church of England. He is acquainted at least with Comte's book, & by this time (I have no doubt) with your subsequent publications, & is on the whole well disposed towards you. Any impression made upon these two men will spread far and wide.

You should send the Globe to Mr Stephen (James Stephen Esq. Kensington Gore) Council to the Colonial office; one of the ablest men connected with our Government, & a very important man in it, whoever happens to be minister. Although an Evangelical Christian, that is, a sort of Puritan and connected with Puritans, he is one of the most *progressif* men we have, & I have heard him speak of your master Saint Simon with considerable praise. I think it would be of great use to send him the Globe, & that it will interest him greatly if he has time to read it.

Mr Empson,[11] (Harcourt Buildings, Inner Temple) Law Professor at the East India College, and one of the principal writers in the Edinburgh Review, is a very proper person to receive the Globe.

I believe you already send it to the Rev. W. J. Fox,[12] the enlightened and eloquent Unitarian preacher. If you do not, you should commence doing so without delay.

Perhaps the Reverend Dr Arnold,[13] Head Master of Rugby School near Birmingham, would be a proper person. He is one of the most enlightened and liberal of our clergy; but I am not sufficiently acquainted with his turn of mind to be able to judge in what manner your doctrines would affect him.

When I can think of any other fit persons, I will write to you again.

I will thank you not to shew this letter to any person except Adolphe, and M. Enfantin or such other of your associates as it may specially concern, as I should be sorry that any of the persons I have mentioned should know that I had written to you any particulars concerning them.

10. Joseph Blanco White (1775–1841), theological writer. For some of JSM's later correspondence with him see Letters 121, 122, and others.

11. William Empson (1791–1852), later editor of the *Edinburgh Review*, 1847–52.

12. See Letter 49, n. 1.

13. Thomas Arnold (1795–1842), educator and historian, father of Matthew Arnold.

From what M. Arlès has told me concerning the late change in your society, I am inclined to think that it is a beneficial one; but I regret exceedingly to learn that it has detached M. Bazard & several others altogether from your body. I suppose I shall learn from the Globe such particulars as I am not yet acquainted with. If not, I beg you to write to me, as there is nothing which I am more anxious to be apprised of, than the *internal* history of your society.

Yours faithfully

J. S. Mill.

• • • 1832 • • •

46. TO GUSTAVE D'EICHTHAL[1]

Wednesday
25 Jan^{y}. [1832]

My dear Gustave

I will answer your questions one by one.

1. I do not think that M. Lemire[2] could *at first* support himself here by giving lessons in French. I think that in two or three months he might be able to do so, if his friends and yours exert themselves. I am sorry to say that *my* exertions are pre-engaged in behalf of another.

2. I shall have great pleasure in dining with you tomorrow to meet Mr Crellin.[3] I will come to you straight from the India House.

3. I will endeavour to obtain for you or Duveyrier an admission to the London Institution.[4]

4. Most of those who receive the Globe in this country have received it only a short time, and several of them are likely to be prejudiced against you at first. Perronet Thompson, for instance, is thinking of writing *against* you, in the Westminster Review,[5] of which he is one of the chief proprietors. Stephen, and Hyde Villiers, are men in office, whose whole time is occupied; and though you should, I think, throw yourself in their way if an opportunity offers, I do not think it would answer any good purpose to call upon them. Most men in this country have a strong prejudice against any attempt to *talk them over* as the vulgar say; to talk to them with the view of effecting any particular change in their general habits of thinking.

Of all whom you mention I think Bulwer and Empson are the only two with whom there would be any use in your having a personal interview

1. MS at Arsenal.

D'Eichthal and Duveyrier were in London at this time as missionaries for the Saint-Simonian cause.

2. Unidentified, except that he is listed as one who, along with JSM and others, made some corrections in a speech delivered by Duveyrier in London about this time. See H. R. D'Allemagne, *Les Saint-Simoniens, 1827–37* (Paris, 1930), p. 155.

3. Unidentified.

4. The London Institution, for the advancement of literature and the diffusion of useful knowledge, founded in 1805. See *A Catalogue of the Library of the London Institution* (4 vols., London, 1835–43).

5. See preceding letter, n. 8.

for the present. I will give you an introduction to Bulwer whenever you please. Empson I should like to speak to on the subject before you make any attempt to see him; besides, he is seldom to be found at home except by appointment. But I could easily contrive that you should see him—& probably Perronet Thompson also.

Yours affectionately

J. S. MILL.

47. TO GUSTAVE D'EICHTHAL[1]

India House
Saturday
[Jan. 28, 1832]

MY DEAR GUSTAVE

Mr Grote desires me to say that he will have great pleasure in cashing any bill of yours, whether signed by yourself or Duveyrier. I am also desired by him & by Mrs Grote to say that they hope very much to see you, & when you return from your journey to Paris they will ask you to fix a day for visiting them at Dulwich & not returning till the next day. Grote & I had much conversation respecting the St Simonian doctrine during the evening: he has a tolerably accurate knowledge of its general features, & I think you would not lose your time in conversing with him.

Would it be inconvenient to you to take with you to Paris some numbers of the Examiner for Marchais[2] & for M. de Lasteyrie?[3]

1. *Addressed*: G. d'Eichthal Esq. / 38 Great Coram Street / Brunswick Square. *Postmark*: EVE / JA 28 [?] / 1832 [?] / Leadenhall St. MS at Arsenal. Published in part in *Cosmopolis*, VI, p. 355, and in *D'Eichthal Corresp.*, p. 146, but dated in both as of Jan., 1831. The postmark is not easily decipherable but other evidence establishes Jan. 28, 1832, as the correct date for this letter and Jan. 30 for the next letter. There is no evidence that D'Eichthal and Duveyrier were in London in Jan., 1831; for evidence that they were there in Jan., 1832, however, see *Two Notebooks of Thomas Carlyle*, ed. C. E. Norton (New York, 1898), p. 248, and Lindley, p. 8, n. 11. Furthermore, the "tomorrow's Examiner" was clearly the number for Sunday, Jan. 29, 1832, in which JSM published (p. 73) a few paragraphs favourable to the Saint-Simonians.

2. André Louis Augustin Marchais (1800–1857), politician. He had been a founder of the Society *Aide-toi*, many of whose members JSM had met in Paris in Aug., 1830.

3. Either Ferdinand Charles Léon, comte de Lasteyrie-Dusaillant (1810–1879), politician and archaeologist, or his father, Charles Philibert, comte de Lasteyrie-Dusaillant (1759–1849), industrialist, philanthropist, publicist, and writer on agriculture.

I will give you a copy of tomorrow's Examiner (which contains some mention of St Simonism) for le père Michel Chevalier.[4]

The missing numbers of the Globe have not yet reached me, but I suppose I shall find them here on Monday morning.

You will oblige me by making my best acknowledgments to le père Enfantin, if he retains any recollection of me, for the great pleasure and profit which I have derived and am continually deriving from his words and deeds.

Yours faithfully
J. S. MILL.

48. TO GUSTAVE D'EICHTHAL[1]

India House
Monday
[Jan. 30, 1832][2]

MY DEAR GUSTAVE

I send you a copy of the Examiner which contains my notice of the St Simonians. It is very incorrectly printed. This copy is for Chevalier; if you wish for one for yourself in addition, I will procure it for you.

I would ask you to take with you a few numbers of the Examiner for Marchais & for M. de Lasteyrie, if I had any means of sending them to you soon enough.

A friend of mine whom I hope you will soon be acquainted with, has had some conversation with Mr Sterling respecting St Simonism, and represents him as so hostile to it, that I think there would be no use whatever in my mentioning the subject to him or in your attempting to see him. Indeed from all I hear of the opinions & feelings which your doctrine is exciting in those who have but recently received the Globe, I expect that for a considerable time much obloquy will fall not only upon the St Simonians, but even on all who venture to hint the possibility of their being other than madmen or rogues. My saying as much for them in the Examiner as I have done, est déjà un acte de courage.

Yours faithfully
J. S. MILL.

4. Michel Chevalier (1806–1879), economist, editor of the *Globe*; later, author of *Lettres sur l'Amérique du Nord* (Paris, 1836). Strictly speaking, only Bazard and Enfantin were accorded the title *Père* in the Saint-Simonian hierarchy.

* * * *

1. MS at Arsenal.
2. See preceding letter, n. 1.

49. TO WILLIAM JOHNSON FOX[1]

India House
April 3^{d}. 1832.

MY DEAR SIR,

I am sorry that you should think of apologizing for a proposal by which I ought to be, and am, very much flattered. There was no brusquerie on your side to be apologized for, but much dullness and incapacity of speaking intelligibly on mine: as is usual when I am taken unexpectedly and have anything to say on the spur of the moment. I learn every day by fresh instances, that only when I have a pen in my hand can I make language and manner the true image of my thoughts. This is not only a fault in itself, but an index to many other faults.

What I would say now, and would have said at the moment, but for my habitual unreadiness, is, that nothing would be more agreeable to me than to be allowed to insert in the Monthly Repository anything I might write which might be so fortunate as to be deemed fit for it; but that I would avoid, as I always do, any literary engagement, wishing to write nothing for its own sake, but always because I am led to write it by the course of my habitual pursuits, and in execution of the general purposes of my life. Most persons, if I were to say this to them, would set me down as a perfect monster of affectation and self-conceit; yet it is only putting into words what all persons ought at all times to have in their minds, as the guiding principle of their conduct. If it were my vocation, as it is probably yours, to instruct the general public, by preaching, public speaking, and popular writing, I should devote myself to it; and there is scarcely any person with whom I should be so proud to cooperate as with yourself. But this is not what I am fittest for; nor do I find that time renders me fitter for it, but rather the contrary. Times and circumstances may come in which I should probably think it my duty, however unfit, to buckle to the task, and make it, for the time, the principal aim of my life. But at present many things, far less conspicuously useful, but yet not unworthy that some one should make them his chief object of intellectual pursuit, must continue to hold the first place in my thoughts. And no one can do anything well,

1. *Addressed*: Rev. W. J. Fox / Upper Clapton. MS at King's. Published, with minor errors, in Garnett, pp. 100–101.

William Johnson Fox (1786–1864), preacher, writer, and politician. After serving for a time as co-editor of the Unitarian magazine, the *Monthly Repository*, Fox in 1831 purchased it and soon converted it into a liberal, secular periodical. For a study of JSM's relations with Fox and the *Monthly Repository*, see Mineka, *The Dissidence of Dissent*, pp. 271–83. Before the time of this letter JSM through Fox had become acquainted with the latter's parishioner, Mrs. John Taylor (years later, JSM's wife), who also wrote for the *Monthly Repository* (see *ibid.*, p. 423).

in this earthly pilgrimage of ours, in doing which he steps out of his way and delays his journey.

I will not, therefore, make any promise, nor should I feel justified in leading you to reckon upon my offering anything to the Monthly Repository. But what I do not *undertake*, it by no means follows that I shall not *do*; and I was even thinking at the very time when your note reached me, of writing something which might possibly suit the design of the Repository. At all events, whenever I do write anything of the kind, I can find no mode of disposing of it that would be more pleasing to me than by giving it to the world under your auspices.[2]

With many thanks for the extremely delicate and flattering tenour of your note

Believe me

Most truly yours

J. S. MILL

50. TO JOHN STERLING[1]

London
24th May 1832.

MY DEAR STERLING The manner in which time passes over our heads without our perceiving it is quite frightful. It is now seven months since I wrote to you, and if I had not referred to a memorandum-book to learn the fact, I should not have thought it was three. Absence! All persons, some few excepted, are sufficiently prone to neglect the absent, not because they forget them, but because there is always something to be done for things or persons near at hand, which, it seems at the moment, will less bear to be put off. But I think this is peculiarly a fault of mine. I neglect almost every person whose daily life is not intermixed with my own. However this may be, accept my confession, and believe that, notwithstanding all appearances, you are as much and as often in my thoughts as when you were in England.—It seems to me that there is a very great significance in letter-writing, and that it differs from daily intercourse as the dramatic

2. The first result of this carefully guarded promise of help appeared in the Oct. number (pp. 649–59) for 1832: an essay "On Genius," with the signature which JSM at first adopted in the *Monthly Repository* of "Antiquus," but afterwards discarded for "A." The only reprint of the essay is in *Four Dialogues of Plato,* trans. J. S. Mill, ed. Ruth Borchardt (London, 1946), pp. 28–40.

* * * *

1. *Addressed*: John Sterling Esq. / St Vincent's. *Postmark*: N / MY24 / 1832. MS at King's. Published, with minor variants, in Elliot, I, 21–26. In reply to an unpublished brief letter by Sterling of early 1832, received by JSM in early March; MS at King's.

differs from the epic or narrative. It is the life of man, and above all the chief part of his life, his inner life, not gradually unfolded without break or sudden transition, those changes which *take place* insensibly being also *manifested* insensibly; but exhibited in a series of detached scenes, taken at considerable intervals from one another, shewing the completed change of position or feeling, without the process by which it was effected; affording a glimpse or partial view of the mighty river of life at some few points, and leaving the imagination to trace to itself such figure or scheme as it can of the course of the stream in that far larger portion of space where it winds its way through thickets or impenetrable forests and is invisible: this alone being known to us, that whatever may have been its course through the wilderness, it has had *some* course, & that a continuous one, & which might by human opportunity have been watched and discovered, though to us, too probably, destined to be for ever unknown. What wonder therefore if when seen at these distant intervals, the stream sometimes seems to run east, sometimes west, and its general direction remains as mysterious as that of the Niger? Yet if such glimpses are numerous, some general tendency shall predominate even in the few furlongs of water-way which they may chance to disclose, and it shall not remain doubtful towards what sea, in the long run, the waters tend to discharge themselves.

I had no idea when I began this letter, that I should yield to the habit of moralizing and poetizing which has grown upon me. But I meant to say something very simple. When you wrote to me, you promised a longer letter, which was to give me some notion of a slave colony; and glad shall I be to receive it; but after all, *that* will be, in itself, no more valuable to me, than any other information on the same subject from any person with equal opportunities and deserving of equal reliance: but what I can have only from you, and what would be far more valuable to me, whether resulting from a letter respecting slave colonies or from anything else, would be a knowledge of *you*, namely of what has passed and is passing in your own mind, and how far your views of the world and feelings towards it, and all that constitutes your individuality as a human being, are or are not the same, are or are not changed. That is the knowledge which it is the most proper object of letters, between friends, to communicate; otherwise if their separation is prolonged, they cannot help becoming more or less strangers to one another.

As for myself, I doubt not but that I have much to tell you of this kind which you, and even myself eventually, might read with interest. For I know that there never pass seven months of my existence without change, and that not inconsiderable or unimportant: and I really do not recollect what my last letter to you[2] was about (except that part of it was about Words-

2. Letter 43.

worth and Southey) or what was my state of mind when I wrote it; only I remember that I must have had much to say, since my epistle amounted to a quarto volume. It is not of much use to write to you about politics. You of course know from the newspapers and from your other friends through what a sea of troubles "the Bill"[3] has at last been navigated in safety to within sight of land. You know the utter prostration or rather annihilation of the Tory party; how all the vitality has gone out of them; they having most unwisely chosen to make this the decisive, the final struggle; which accordingly it is. One unspeakable blessing I now believe that we shall owe to the events of the last ten days; to whatever consummation the spirit which is now in the ascendant, may conduct us, there is now a probability that we shall accomplish it through other means than anarchy & civil war. The irresistible strength of a unanimous people has been put forth, and has triumphed without bloodshed: it having therefore been proved, once for all, that the people can carry their point by pacific means, the natural and habitual reluctance of mankind to suffer and to inflict wounds and death, yet remains and may yet remain in its pristine strength, being no longer liable to be gradually worn away by the perpetual recurrence of the thought & feeling that these are the necessary though bitter means to some ardently desired end. What will come next it is quite vain to attempt to anticipate. Much grievous disappointment—some consequent moral and intellectual good, some evil;—some oversetting of evil and wrong; as yet little setting up of right; but above all a clear field to work in and a consequent duty on all whose vocation is not different, to address themselves to the work.

With regard to our common acquaintances, most of what I have to tell is, I think, favorable; many, and some from whom it was scarcely to be expected, have become "sadder and wiser men."[4] By sadder, I do not mean gloomier, or more desponding: nor even less susceptible of enjoyment, or even gaiety; but I mean that they look upon all things with far deeper and more serious feelings, and are far more alive to those points in human affairs, which excite an interest bordering on melancholy. Their earnestness, if not greater, is of a more solemn kind, and certainly far more unmixed with dreams of personal distinction or other reward. This is also, in a measure, the case with myself; except that, so far as respects the last point, the change had taken place long before. I have long since renounced any hankering for being happier than I am; and only since then have I enjoyed anything which can be called well-being. How few are they who have discovered the wisdom of the precept, Take no thought of the morrow;

3. On June 7 the Reform Bill became law.

4. Cf. Coleridge: "A sadder and a wiser man / He rose the morrow morn" (*Rime of the Ancient Mariner*).

when considered as all the sayings of Christ should be, not as laws laid down with strict logical precision for regulating the details of our conduct; since such must be, like all other maxims of prudence, *variable*: but as the bodying forth in words of the *spirit* of all morality, right self-culture, the principles of which cannot change, since man's nature changes not, though surrounding circumstances do. I do not mean by using the word self-culture, to prejudge any thing as to whether such culture can come from man himself, or must come directly from God: all I mean is that it is culture of the man's self, of his feelings and will, fitting him to look abroad and see how he is to act, not imposing upon him by express definition, a prescribed mode of action; which it is clear to me that many of the precepts of the Gospel, were never intended to do, being manifestly unsuited to that end: witness that which I have just cited; or the great one of doing to all men as you desire that they should do to you; or of turning the left cheek &c. which last the Quakers have made themselves ridiculous by attempting to act upon a very little more literally than other people. All these would be vicious as moral statutes, binding the tribunal, but they are excellent as instruction to the judge in the *forum conscientiae*, in what spirit he is to look at the evidence; what posture he must assume in order that he may see clearly the moral bearings of the thing which he is looking at.

I have not seen, nor scarcely heard, of Maurice, since you left England. Can you tell me anything of him? Trench[5] I have seen, and had some correspondence with. He seems to me to take a most gloomy view of the prospects of mankind—gloomier even than yours, in your letter to Mrs Austin who (par parenthèse) has not been very well lately, but is recovering. Carlyle passed the whole of a long winter in London; & rose in my opinion, more than I know how to express, from a nearer acquaintance. I do not think that you estimate him half highly enough; but neither did I, when I last saw you.

It was worthy of your kindness to think not only of your friend, but of your friend's friends, and to pick up sea-shells for them on the other side of the globe because we had once done so together at Looe.[6] It is one of the things which so few persons would have thought of besides yourself.

I hope and believe that I shall not again allow so long an interval to

5. Richard Chenevix Trench (1807–1886), later (1863) Archbishop of Dublin, had become acquainted with Sterling at Cambridge, where both were members of the "Apostles"; he had taken part in the expedition of Torrijos to Spain in 1830.

6. Sterling had written: "I have gathered some of the common little shells here for your young friends. Perhaps you remember our labours on their behalf along the shore at Looe." This must have occurred during their visit to Cornwall together in the summer of 1829, when they first became close friends (see Tuell, *John Sterling*, p. 70).

elapse without writing to you. I had great compunction in not writing to you when we learned the melancholy fate of poor Torrijos[7]—and I should have done so, but that I am little fitted for comforting the afflicted, and I knew not in that case, of any comfort to administer. It was chiefly with reference to you, and to Madame Torrijos, that it seemed to me there was ground for sorrow; though the extinction of such a man, even when there was little more for him to do or to enjoy, seemed like the violent blotting out of a star from heaven.

With many kind remembrances to Mrs Sterling, believe me, affectionately yours,

J. S. MILL

51. TO THOMAS CARLYLE[1]

India House
29th May
1832.

MY DEAR FRIEND,

To be moderate, I will only thank you twice: once for writing, and once for being the first to write. The good-natured excuse which you make for my silence will not serve me: I always felt that I ought to write first, and not you; but it always seemed that there would be some better time for writing than the present one. In particular, I have had an unusual number of letters to write since I saw you: and to me it appears a very weighty matter to write a letter: there is scarcely anything that we do, which requires a more complete possession of our faculties, in their greatest freshness and vigour; and all the more so, because if it is elaborate it is good for little. Besides, I knew that I was corresponding with you, in some

7. General José Maria Torrijos (1791–1831), Spanish patriot, was captured while attempting a liberating invasion of his native country, and was executed Dec. 11, 1831. Sterling's cousin, Robert Boyd, was among those who shared the fate of Torrijos. For Sterling's connections with the Torrijos affair, see Carlyle, *Life of John Sterling*, Part I, chaps. IX, X, XIII. Sterling's letter had been written immediately after receiving news of the death of Torrijos: "I thought I had made up my mind—but this horrible fate of such a man and one whom I have known as well as you and I know each other—has overpowered me completely."

* * * *

1. *Addressed*: Thomas Carlyle Esq / Craigenputtock / Dumfries / N.B.[?]. *Postmarks*: FREE / 29MY29 / 1832; and DUMFRIES / 31 MAY 1832. Franked by E. Strutt. MS at NLS. Published, with minor errors and omissions, in Elliot, I, 26–32. Carlyle and his wife, after spending the winter of 1831–32 in London, had left London for Scotland on March 25. His first letter to JSM after the return to Craigenputtock, dated May 18, 1832, is published in A. Carlyle, pp. 4–7, as is his answer of June 16, pp. 8–11.

measure, through the Examiner.[2] All this is not intended as an excuse, but a confession; that you may see what paltry reasons sufficed with me for putting off the discharge of a duty. But it is very idle to complain of my own faults, instead of mending them; as every man can, if he will; and as I trust I yet shall, all the less slowly from having known you.

I believe I have fulfilled most of your parting injunctions; some of them, however, less soon than I might and ought. For several weeks after your departure, I waited for some time when it would be quite convenient to call upon poor Glen:[3] till finding that no such moment arrived, I did at last what I might have done at first, disregarded convenience and did the thing out of hand: and the great joy which it seemed to give him, satisfied me not that I had done right, for I was thinking much more of you than of him; but that you had done right in instigating me to call upon him. Since that time we have seen each other frequently: and I have cultivated his acquaintance the more, because he has so few persons in London besides me who are at all able to help or encourage him. I have been much struck by the exact manner in which every opinion that you have ever expressed to me about him has been proved true by what I have since seen of him; Mrs Carlyle's opinion in so far as it differed from yours, was, I am satisfied, entirely groundless. I am somewhat doubtful however, how far he is capable of deriving much advantage of an intellectual kind from the intercourse of others: his mind seems to be always in his own thoughts and in them only; & these not matured but extemporaneous: it seems almost time thrown away to give out thoughts to him; he seems never to lay hold of them. But if any one could teach him to make a proper use of his own materials, it would be doing to him an unspeakable service, & to others much good through his means. I do not see my way clearly to being able to assist him in this respect, but I see that our intercourse affords some sort of satisfaction to him, and therefore, probably does him some kind of good: what, and how much, will doubtless in time be made manifest. He talks of writing to you, and I am sure that it would make him extremely happy to hear from you: what he saw of you has evidently made a very deep impression upon him.—I have also called upon Fraser:[4] only once, however; but in his case there was not the same strong inducement: I have no doubt that we shall see more of each other.

2. From the autumn of 1830 through 1834 JSM contributed almost every week. See MacMinn, *Bibliog.*, pp. 11–42. Most of his writings were unsigned but Carlyle was often able to recognize JSM's style.

3. William Glen (d. 1852), a native of the Craigenputtock region, had met Carlyle through Dr. John Carlyle. He had recently come to London to study law. Though gifted and well educated, he soon gave evidence of the mental disturbance which ended his career.

4. Probably William Fraser (*ca.* 1805–1852), editor of the short-lived *Foreign Review* (1828–30), rather than James Fraser (d. 1841), publisher of *Fraser's Magazine.*

Your parting gift, the paper on Biography and on Johnson,[5] has been more precious to me than I well know how to state. I have read it over and over till I could almost repeat it by heart; and have derived from it more edification and more comfort, than from all else that I have read for years past. I have moreover lent it to various persons, whom I thought likely to reap the same benefit from it, and have in no instance been disappointed: among others, to some in whom it has created, or increased, a most earnest desire to see and know you, and who are most worthy that this desire should be gratified; as I trust it one day will be, if possible through my means, unless an iron Necessity, insuperable by the free will of man, should hereafter, as heretofore, prevent.

Thanks for what you tell me respecting your recent occupations. I look forward with very delightful anticipations to your review of the Corn Law Rhymer,[6] and to your paper on Göthe:[7] it was a disappointment to me that the former did not appear in the last Edinburgh, though I knew it was scarcely possible. Taylor[8] tells me that Southey is writing an article[9] on the same subject, & is in communication with the author, who is a real working man, named Reuben Elliott.[10] I have seen no review of his poems as yet, except in the Monthly Repository, the Unitarian periodical, edited by Mr Fox, whom I conjecture to be the author of this particular paper.[11] The tone of it is very good, and there are very few persons who could have written it, but I think it misses the most striking aspect under which the poems can be looked at; viz. as works which will go down to posterity as one of the principal memorials of this age; from which a large portion of its character will be known, which is registered in little else of a permanent nature: being chiefly those melancholy features in the position of the working class towards the other classes and towards the world altogether, which have impressed upon so earnest and so loving a heart, a character of almost unrelieved gloom, bitterness, and resentment. The poet

5. Carlyle's review of J. W. Croker's edition of Boswell's *Life of Johnson* was published in two parts: "Biography," *Fraser's*, V (April, 1832), 253–60; and "Boswell's Life of Johnson," *ibid.* (May, 1832), 359–413.

6. "Corn Law Rhymes," *ER*, LV (July, 1832), 338–61. See n. 10 below.

7. "Goethe's Works," *FQR*, X (Aug., 1832), 1–44.

8. Henry Taylor (1800–1886), poet, dramatist, and member of the Colonial Office. Cf. Letter 43, n. 20 and 30.

9. No such article seems to have been published; in his review of the poetry of the servant-girl Mary Colling, however, Southey praised the genius of the Corn Law Rhymer but condemned his poetry "for the spirit of ferocious jacobinism which it breathes" (*QR*, XLVII [March, 1832], 92).

10. JSM was mistaken both as to the name and the occupation of the Corn Law Rhymer. He was Ebenezer Elliott (1781–1849), proprietor of his own business in the iron trade at Sheffield.

11. The article has been identified as by W. J. Fox: "The Poor and Their Poetry," *MR*, VI (1832), 189–201.

just shews enough of his natural character to render the portraiture of the artificial one which is superinduced upon it more deeply impressive. I am convinced that these poems, having, as they have, sufficient intrinsic merit to live, will hereafter be a text for annotations, explanations, and commentaries without end, & that future historians, (when such, worthy of the name, shall arise) will build largely upon it.

With respect to Göthe, there was a short obituary notice of him in the Examiner,[12] which you would not like. I could have kept it out if I would have undertaken to write something myself, at the instant; but as I knew my own ignorance, and would not write at haphazard, the matter was put into the hands of those who thought they knew, & in reality did know, more, but yet (as seems pretty obvious) not enough. The article was made up of two fragments written by two different persons. So rare in this country is any, even the most common-place, knowledge of Germany, that none of the other papers gave any observations at all on the extinction of the greatest man then living in Europe: and Bulwer in his next number, that is in the small print, drafted his notice almost entirely from that in the Examiner. How yours in the next number,[13] will square with it, he probably cares as little, as I dare say you do.

As you see the Examiner, you are acquainted with the greater part of what I have been busy about, since you left us. To the papers signed A.B.[14] you must add every thing which has been written about France, except the notices of the cholera, and a review of a trumpery pamphlet. If you should happen to see the second number of Tait's Magazine, you will see in it an article of mine,[15] on a book which I have also reviewed in the Examiner[16] by our acquaintance Cornewall Lewis. If you have not seen it and will let me know how I may best send you a copy, I will do so, though unless it interest you as being mine, it scarcely will otherwise. On the whole, the opinions I have put forth in these different articles are, I think, rather not inconsistent with yours, than exactly corresponding to them; & are expressed so coldly and unimpressively that I can scarcely bear to look back upon such poor stuff. I have not yet come up even with my friends the St Simonians; & it would be saying very little even if I had.

12. "Goethe," *Examiner*, April 8, 1832, p. 235.

13. "Death of Goethe," *New Monthly Mag.*, XXXIV (June, 1832), 507–12.

14. A review article in two parts: "An Outline of Sematology, or An Essay toward Establishing a New Theory of Grammar, Logic, and Rhetoric," *Examiner*, March 25, 1832, pp. 194–95, and April 1, 1832, pp. 211–12.

15. "Use and Abuse of Political Terms," *Tait's*, I (May, 1832), 164–72. See also Letter 95. *Tait's Edinburgh Magazine*, a literary and politically radical monthly, continued publication until 1861.

16. "Remarks on the Use and Abuse of some Political Terms. By George Cornewall Lewis . . . ," *Examiner*, April 22, 1832, pp. 259–60.

Lewis (1806–1863), statesman and author, later (1852–55) editor of the *Edinburgh Review.*

A propos of the St Simonians, they have been obliged to give up the Globe and everything else which they had in hand. The immediate causes of their stoppage are certain legal obstructions which have been thrown in their way by some of the seceding members, & a demand of 130000 francs by the Government (very insidiously allowed to reach that amount before it was brought forward) for arrears of stamps, & penalties for infraction of the stamp laws. In the later numbers of the Globe, there was, I think, on the whole some evidence of improvement in their views and feelings—Enfantin and about fifty more, among whom are our two friends d'Eichthal and Duveyrier, have now retired to a place called Ménilmontant at a short distance out of Paris, where they are all living together, and are employed, as they assert, in training themselves to preach to the world by their example, which, they are beginning to find out, is after all the most impressive and in every way profitable aspect of the life even of those whose vocation it is to be the Speakers of the Word. This is decidedly *un progrès*, as they would say; & if you believe them, their present state, like every thing else which has happened to them or to any son of Adam, is for the best; that is, for the greatest ultimate success of the St Simonian faith. It is difficult to conjecture how far this optimism of theirs is itself a *faith*, or a mere trick of self-deluding vanity, determined to put the best face upon every thing both to themselves and others. I do not know many of the particulars of their life at Ménilmontant; but it appears that one feature of it is to do without domestic servants, which they consider a vestige of slavery: & they take their turns to perform all menial offices for one another. I do not know how they reconcile this with their maxim, *à chacun selon sa capacité*, but I suppose they have some salve or other for it. Their adoration for Enfantin seems to be on the increase rather than on the wane; & it is well to reverence the best man they know, but I wish they had a better still.

With regard to politics, their aspect of things has somewhat changed since you wrote, and the momentary check sustained by radicalism has been converted into a triumph, far more complete than could have been achieved otherwise. The Tory party, at least the *present* Tory party, is now utterly annihilated. Peace be with it. All its elevated character had long gone out of it, and instead of a Falkland[17] it had but a Croker,[18] instead of a Johnson[19] nothing better than a Philpotts.[20] Wellington himself found that if he meant to be minister he must be a Whig; and the rest of his

17. Lucius Cary, second Viscount Falkland (1610?–1643).

18. John Wilson Croker (1780–1857), politician and essayist, a leading contributor to the *Quarterly Review*.

19. Dr. Samuel Johnson.

20. Henry Philpotts (1778–1869), Bishop of Exeter, defender of the Peterloo massacre of 1819 and opponent of the Reform Bill.

party though in the main Whigs already, did not chuse that particular phasis of Whiggery & determined to be nothing at all; & truly they had no very great step to make into absolute non-entity. There is now nothing definite and determinate in politics except radicalism; & we shall have nothing but radicals and whigs for a long time to come, until society shall have worked itself into some new shape, not to be exactly foreseen and described now.

Mrs. Austin has been very far from well of late, but is nearly recovered. She often talks of Mrs Carlyle and you. Austin began lecturing immediately after your departure, and part of my occupation since you went away has been in attending his lectures.[21] Buller is now here and in good health: he has written a very pleasant article in the Foreign Quarterly Review on Prince Pückler's book,[22] which I think you would like to read.

On the very day on which you went away, Taylor wrote to me to propose that we should call upon you together. He is very well, and as usual, very busy governing the West Indies: a difficult work, of which he more than all other persons is the workman.

I am in no immediate want of the three little volumes; therefore they may wait any convenient opportunity.

I do not think I have any more facts to tell you; and I have filled my letter with nothing else. Another time I shall not wait for such an accumulation of what, after all, is very secondary material for a letter—especially between you and me, so little of whose conversation used ever to turn upon mere incidents. Make my heartiest remembrances to Mrs Carlyle and believe me

Most truly yours (and hers)

J. S. MILL

52. TO GUSTAVE D'EICHTHAL AND CHARLES DUVEYRIER[1]

30th May 1832
India House

MY DEAR D'EICHTHAL AND DUVEYRIER

Nothing but the pressure of a variety of occupations has hindered me for so long a period from writing to you; not to tell you anything, for I

21. See Letter 32, n. 2.

22. "Letters of a German Prince" [Pückler-Muskau], *FQR*, IX (May, 1832), 290–312.

* * * *

1. *Addressed*: Monsieur / M. Gustave d'Eichthal / Rue Monsigny / No. 6/ à Paris. *Postmarks*: 3/JUIN / 1832; [illegible] 32; and ANGLETERRE. Published in part in *Cosmopolis*, VI, 361–63, and in *D'Eichthal Corresp.*, pp. 160–63. MS at Arsenal.

have nothing to tell; but to ask for news of you and all that you do, as I no longer have regular intelligence of you through the Globe.[2]

I am unable to be with you on the first of June, as I had previously engaged myself to pass the short vacation which this house allows me, in a different place and in a different manner.[3] And I should prefer visiting Paris, and you, at any other time. To attend such a summons as that which was issued in the last number of the Globe, to those who have placed their *avenir* in St Simon, would be to associate and identify myself with the St Simonians: now this would be an act of religious *dévouement*, and highly meritorious, in any person who was completely associated with you *par les sentiments*; but in me, it would be nothing of the kind; and would even give a false idea of the feelings I entertain towards your society. I did not go to Weimar to attend the funeral of Göthe, nor to Birmingham to join the Political Union, nor to Warsaw to encourage the Poles; yet my sympathies were with all three, just as they are with you.

For the same & various other reasons, I did not, as Duveyrier suggested, write a series of letters on St Simonism for the Morning Chronicle. St Simonism is all in all to you, St Simonians; but to me it is only *one* among a variety of interesting and important features in the time we live in, & there are other subjects & other occupations which have as great a claim upon me as it has, in themselves, & a much greater from being, just now, more in season. St Simonism therefore must wait its time, & you may rely that it shall have justice done to it, as far as that is possible from my point of view, on the first favorable opportunity.

I have been extremely pleased with the later numbers of the Globe. The seceders from your society certainly had excellent *remplaçans*: Cavel, Delaporte, and Lagarmitte[4] are anything but ordinary men. Now when I have mentioned names, I beg that when you write, you will send me the names of all the St Simonians who have retired to Ménilmontant or who remain in the Rue Monsigny. I shall treasure up their names, and should like much to be acquainted with them all. Tell me all you can about each of them in particular.

Tell me also what are your pursuits, your thoughts & projects, where you now are. I have some knowledge of the mere exterior of your lives from

2. The *Globe* had ceased publication with the number of April 20, 1832. See preceding letter.

3. JSM's journal of his walking tour with Henry Cole, July 19 to Aug. 6, 1832, through Hampshire, West Sussex, the Isle of Wight, and ending in the New Forest, is at Mount Holyoke College.

4. (Henri?) Cavel and (Michel?) Delaporte were assistant editors of the *Globe*. Henri Lagarmitte (1807–1834), journalist, was listed among the members of the third grade of Saint-Simonians (see D'Allemagne, *Les Saint-Simoniens*, pp. 118, 266, and 271).

Duveyrier's letter to Mrs Crellin, but I want to know what you are meditating, what are your studies, & *travaux d'élaboration*, now that you are not propagating your ideas among the public. This temporary secession might be for you the occasion of *un grand progrès*. I suppose that a St Simonian can learn only from his own thoughts or those of other St Simonians; but I who am not a St Simonian, though I greatly admire the St Simonians, & think that they are in many respects far ahead of all Europe, am yet firmly convinced that you have yet much to learn, in political economy from the English economists (inferior as they are to you in many points) and in the philosophy of history, literature and the arts, from the Germans. Certainly I think you have far surpassed all these people in some things, but have fallen far short of them in others: & that a more diligent study of them would change some of your opinions, and suggest to you many positive thoughts of great value, which would bring down some of your generalities & abstractions into detail.

I did as d'Eichthal wished in regard to Father Enfantin's parting address: after ascertaining that Black[5] would print it, I translated it for him & it appeared in the Morning Chronicle[6] (it was however very incorrectly printed). With regard to the delay in my letter which appeared in the Globe,[7] you are, I suppose, aware that Desprat[8] kept it for a fortnight or three weeks, in expectation of an opportunity. It was very well translated, though with some omissions & abbreviations which made it rather more St Simonian than I intended.

I wrote two letters to Adolphe d'Eichthal[9] during our *crise politique*, which contained all I had to say on that subject. I shall write to him a longer letter very shortly, & request him to shew it to Gustave.

All your friends here, whom I know, are very well. I have seen Mrs Crellin twice; *elle est très intéressante*. Write soon & often, now you have leisure. Ever yours

J. S. MILL.

5. John Black (1783–1855), journalist, editor of the *Morning Chronicle*, 1817–43. For JSM's tribute to Black, see *Autobiog.*, chap. IV.

6. "Saint Simonianism—Parting Address to the Public," signed Enfantin, *Morning Chronicle*, April 27, 1832, p. 1; reprinted in Pankhurst, pp. 84–87.

7. For April 18, 1832, p. 433. The letter was published in English as an article entitled "Comparison of the Tendencies of French and English Intellect," *MR*, NS VIII (Nov., 1833), 800–804. See Hill Shine, "JSM and an Open Letter on the Saint-Simonian Society in 1832," *Journal of the History of Ideas*, VI (Jan., 1945), 102–8.

8. Etienne Desprat, according to Pankhurst (p. 72), a former member of the Spanish Cortes, who had been delegated to represent the Saint-Simonians in England until the return of D'Eichthal and Duveyrier.

9. These letters have not been located.

53. TO GUSTAVE D'EICHTHAL[1]

June 29th
1832

MY DEAR GUSTAVE

The object of my present letter is not to tell you news, for I have none to tell; nor to discuss, for I have not time. It is merely to thank you for your letter; to say how glad I always am to hear from you, and how much I wish that the exalted destiny which you still believe to await you, may be realized; to send you two numbers of the Examiner in continuation of those which I hope you have already received through Desprat; & to beg you to ask of Duveyrier the two following questions;

1st. What he did with the ticket to the library of the London Institution:[2] William Prescott to whom it belongs, has asked me for it.

2dly. Whether he has done with my Examiners for 1831 and the beginning of 1832.

The gentleman who takes this letter will bring any thing back. He will be at Paris for a week or two, and his address is, Mr Rowland Mackenzie,[3] chez M. Roy, Route de Choisy, Barrière d'Italie.

Many remembrances to Duveyrier, and to all friends. In your letter you say that you send me the list of the inhabitants of your retreat at Ménilmontant, but it has not reached me.

Believe me
Most truly yours
J. S. MILL.

54. TO THOMAS CARLYLE[1]

London, 17th July 1832

MY DEAR FRIEND

Many thanks for your little note.[2] I hope this letter will find all your perplexities at an end, and the paper on Göthe[3] proceeding smoothly, or perhaps long since finished and sent off. I recognise in your account of

1. *Addressed*: M. Gustave d'Eichthal. MS at Arsenal.
2. See Letter 46, n. 4.
3. Unidentified.

* * * *

1. *Addressed*: Thomas Carlyle Esq / Craigenputtock / Dumfries. *Postmarks*: FREE / 19 JY 19 / 1832, and DUMFRIES / 21 JUL 1832. Franked by E. Strutt. MS at NLS. Published, with minor variants, in Elliot, I, 32–36. Answer by Carlyle is dated Aug. 28, 1832, published in A. Carlyle, pp. 11–16.
2. Of June 16, 1832. Published in A. Carlyle, pp. 8-11.
3. See Letter 51, n. 7.

what was passing in your mind, a very perfect picture of what I often experience in mine; especially if I attempt to give a *general* view of any great subject, when I feel bound not merely to say *something* true, but to omit nothing which is material to the truth. I also participate in what you call your superstition, about never turning back when one has begun. Were it not that imperfect and dim light is yet better than total darkness, there would be little encouragement to attempt enlightening either oneself or the world. But the real encouragement is, that he who does the best he can, always does some good, even when in his direct aim he totally fails. For although the task which we undertake is, to speak a certain portion of precious Truth, and instead of speaking any Truth at all, it is possible our light may be nothing but a *feu follet*, and we may leave ourselves and others no wiser than we found them; still, that any one sincere mind, doing all it can to gain insight into a thing, and endeavouring to declare truthfully all it sees, declares *this* (be it what it may), is itself a truth; no inconsiderable one; which at least it depends upon ourselves to be fully assured of, and which is often not less, sometimes perhaps more, profitable to the hearer or reader, than much sounder doctrine delivered without intensity of conviction. And this is one eternal and inestimable preeminence (even in the productions of pure Intellect) which the doings of an honest heart possess over those men of the strongest and most cultivated powers of mind when directed to any other end in preference to, or even in conjunction with, Truth. He who paints a thing as he actually saw it, though it were only by an optical illusion, teaches us, if nothing else, at least the nature of Sight, and of *spectra* and phantasms: but if somebody has not seen, or even believed that he saw, anything at all, but has merely thrown together objects and colours at random or to gain some point, it is all false and hollow, and nobody is the wiser or better, or ever can be so, from what has been done, but may be greatly the more ignorant, more confused, and worse.

I have read your little paper on Göthe in Bulwer's Magazine.[4] There was little in it which I had not already heard from your lips, otherwise there are passages which would if they had been entirely new to me, have excited me to much thought, and may therefore do that service to any other mind which is prepared for them. I do not myself, as yet, sufficiently know Göthe, to feel certain that he is the great High Priest and Pontiff you describe him; I know him as yet only as one of the wisest men, and men of greatest genius, whom the world has yet produced; but if *he* be not all that you say he is, certainly no other man has arisen in our times, who can even for a moment be suspected of being so. In him alone, of all the celebrated men of this and the last age, does a more familiar knowl-

4. See Letter 51, n. 13.

edge, and the growth of our own faculties, discover more and more to be admired and less and less to be rejected or even doubted of. Who shall succeed him? or when shall he find even an *unworthy* successor. There is need that the "march of mind" should raise up new spiritual notabilities; for it seems as though all the old ones with one accord were departing out of the world together. In a few days or weeks the world has lost the three greatest men in it, in their several departments; Göthe, Bentham, and Cuvier;[5] & during the same period what a mortality among those second-rate great men, who are generally in their own time much more celebrated than the first, because they take pains to be so; such men as Casimir Périer, or Mackintosh,[6] or Sir William Grant,[7] or General Lamarque,[8] or the last of Scotch judges, John Clerk of Eldin,[9] or even (to descend low indeed) Charles Butler.[10] And here is Sir Walter Scott about to follow.[11] I sometimes think that instead of mountains and valleys, the domain of Intellect is about to become a dead flat, nothing greatly above the general level, nothing very far below it. It is curious that this particular time, in which there are fewer great intellects above ground and in their vigour, than can be remembered for many ages back, should be the precise time at which every body is cackling about the progress of intelligence and the spread of knowledge. I do believe that intelligence and knowledge are less valued just now, except for purposes of money-making, than at any other period since the Norman Conquest, or possibly since the invasion of the Romans. I mean, in our own country. But even in Germany, the great men seem to have died out, though much of their spirit remains after them, and is, we will hope, permanently fixed in the national character.

I have not been idle since my last letter, but have rather read, than either meditated or written: all that I have written you must have seen in the Examiner; it consists of sundry papers on French politics and two long articles on Pledges,[12] which are in very bad odour with some of our

5. Goethe had died on March 22; baron Georges Cuvier, the celebrated French naturalist, on May 13; and Jeremy Bentham on June 6.

6. Sir James Mackintosh (1765–1832), philosopher and historian. In 1835 James Mill published his critical *Fragment on Mackintosh.*

7. Sir William Grant (1752–1832), Master of the Rolls, advocate of reform of criminal law.

8. Maximilien Lamarque (1770–1832), French general and orator.

9. John Clerk, Lord Eldin (1757–1832).

10. Charles Butler (1750–1832), prominent Roman Catholic lawyer and writer.

11. Sir Walter Scott died Sept. 21, 1832.

12. For a list of Mill's contributions to the *Examiner* in this period, see MacMinn, *Bibliog.*, pp. 18, 21–22. The two articles entitled "Pledges" appeared in the numbers of July 1 and 15, pp. 417–18, 449–51. JSM years later confessed that the articles had been ill-timed and that they had cost the *Examiner* two hundred subscribers (*The Early Draft of John Stuart Mill's Autobiography,* ed. Jack Stillinger [Urbana, 1961], p. 144, n. 424).

radicals. It is a proof of the honest and brave character of Fonblanque, that he wished to have these articles: every thing he ever prints that does not chime in with common-place radicalism, costs him money; his paper is in a perpetual alternation of slowly working its way upwards by its liveliness and ability and then tumbling plump down all at once by some act of honesty. I do not know that this has happened in the present case, but I have little doubt of it.

I am about to make a short ramble in the country just now,[13] after which I shall return to work, and I hope with more solid and valuable results than I have hitherto done: that so I may produce something worthy of the title you give me, and in which I rejoice, that of one of your scholars. You also call me one of your teachers; but if I am this, it is as yet only in the sense in which a schoolmaster might speak of his teachers, meaning those who teach under him. I certainly could not now write, and perhaps shall never be able to write, any thing from which any person can derive so much edification as I, and several others, have derived in particular from your paper on Johnson.[14] My vocation, as far as I yet see, lies in a humbler sphere; I am rather fitted to be a logical expounder than an artist. You I look upon as an artist, and perhaps the only genuine one now living in this country: the highest destiny of all, lies in that direction; for it is the artist alone in whose hands Truth becomes impressive, and a living principle of action. Yet it is something not inconsiderable (in an age in which the understanding is more cultivated and developed than any of the other faculties, & is the only faculty which men do not habitually distrust) if one could address them through the understanding, & ostensibly with little besides mere logical apparatus, yet in a spirit higher than was ever inspired by mere logic, and in such sort that their understandings shall at least have to be *reconciled* to those truths, which even then will not be *felt* until they shall have been breathed upon by the breath of the artist. For, as far as I have observed, the majority even of those who are capable of receiving Truth into their minds, must have the logical side of it turned *first* towards them; then it must be quite turned round before them, that they may see it to be the same Truth in its poetic that it is in its metaphysical aspect. Now this is what I seem to myself qualified for, if for any thing, or at least capable of qualifying myself for; and it is thus that I may be, and therefore ought to be, not useless as an auxiliary even to you, though I am sensible that I can never give back to you the value of what I receive from you.

I have no news worth telling you; scarcely any news of any kind. Mrs.

13. See Letter 52, n. 3.
14. See Letter 51, n. 5.

Austin is quite recovered. Charles Buller is now in Cornwall; he was a little indisposed when he set out, but is now I trust in good health. Pray make my most friendly remembrances to Mrs. Carlyle, and let me hear from you in due season.

Yours ever faithfully,

J. S. MILL.

Glen bids me tell you that he has heard from your brother,[15] who is at Naples, very well, and comfortable. I told Glen that you had made affectionate mention of him in your letter, at which he seemed much gratified.[16]

55. TO HARRIET TAYLOR[1]

[Aug., 1832?]

Benie soit la main qui a tracé ces caractères! Elle m'a écrit—il suffit; bien que je ne me dissimule pas que c'est pour me dire un éternel adieu.

Cette adieu, qu'elle ne croie pas que je l'accepte jamais. Sa route et la mienne sont séparées, elle l'a dit: mais elles peuvent, elles doivent, se rencontrer. A quelqu'époque, dans quelqu'endroit, que ce puisse être, elle me trouvera toujours ce que j'ai été, ce que je suis encore.

Elle sera obéie: mes lettres n'iront plus troubler sa tranquillité, ou verser une goutte de plus dans la coupe de ses chagrins. Elle sera obéie, par les motifs qu'elle donne,—elle le serait quand même elle se serait bornée à me communiquer ses volontés. Lui obéir est pour moi une nécessité.

Elle ne refusera pas, j'espère, l'offrande de ces petites fleurs, que j'ai apportées pour elle du fond de la Nouvelle-Forêt. Donnez-les lui s'il le faut, de votre part.

15. Dr. John Carlyle (1801–1879), physician, and translator of Dante.
16. This postscript appears in the margin of the last page.

* * * *

1. MS at LSE. No salutation or signature. Published in Hayek, p. 38, and, translated, in Packe, p. 139, but dated as of late July, 1832. The approximate date has been inferred from the reference to the New Forest in the last paragraph. Since the walking tour of JSM had begun on July 19 and concluded in the New Forest on Aug. 6 (see Letter 52, n. 3), the Aug. date seems more likely.

JSM's acquaintance with Mrs. John Taylor had begun in 1830, probably in July, in the Taylor home at a dinner party at which W. J. Fox, J. A. Roebuck, and Harriet Martineau were also present. Friendship between JSM and Mrs. Taylor developed into love, but at the time of this letter she had evidently tried to break off the relationship, telling him that they must not meet again.

56. TO JOHN TAYLOR[1]

Saturday [Sept. 1, 1832]
I.H.

MY DEAR SIR

Two acquaintances of mine, MM. Jules Bastide[2] and Hippolyte Dussard,[3] distinguished members of the republican party in France, have been compelled to fly their country for a time in consequence of the affair of the fifth & sixth of June. They were not conspirators, for there was no conspiracy, but when they found the troops and the people at blows, they took the side of the people. Now I am extremely desirous to render their stay here as little disagreeable as possible, and to enable them to profit by it, and to return with a knowledge of England and with those favourable sentiments towards our English *hommes du mouvement* which it is of so much importance that they and their friends should entertain. I am particularly desirous of bringing them in contact with the better members of the Political Union, that they may not suppose our men of action to be all of them like the Revells and the Murphys whom they saw and heard on Wednesday last.[4] Yourself and Mr. Fox are [the][5] persons I should most wish them to see. But I do not like to give them a letter of introduction to you without first ascertaining whether it would be agreeable to yourself. Will you therefore oblige me with a line to say, if possible, that you will allow me to tell them to call upon you, or otherwise to say that you would rather not. I have not mentioned the matter to them, nor shall I do so until I have the pleasure of hearing from you.

Ever truly yours
J. S. MILL

1. *Addressed*: John Taylor Esq. / 4 Christopher Street / Finsbury Square. *Postmark*: SP 1 1832. MS at Yale. Published in Hayek, pp. 38–39.
John Taylor (1796–1849), wholesale druggist, husband of Harriet Taylor, with whom JSM had fallen in love. Taylor was actively interested in the Radical cause.
2. Jules Bastide (1800–1879), publicist and politician, had fled to England after being condemned to death for the part he had taken in riots in Paris on June 5 at the time of the funeral of General Lamarque. He was in exile in England for two years.
3. Hippolyte Dussard (1798–1876), economist. As Hayek points out, JSM had probably met him and Bastide in Paris in 1830.
4. The *Examiner* for Sept. 2, 1832, p. 568, reports the meeting of Wednesday, Aug. 29, of the National Political Union, to discuss the condition of Ireland. Major Revell presided, a Mr. Murphy made a fiery attack on Henry Brougham for the government's Irish policy, and the meeting passed a resolution of sympathy "with the People of Ireland in their efforts to throw off the galling and oppressive imposts of Tithes and Church-cess."
5. Part covered by seal.

57. TO SARAH AUSTIN[1]

13th September, 1832

MY DEAR MUTTERLEIN

How could you so far misunderstand me as to suppose that it could be a question with me whether I would sacrifice two days to you? I thought that it would be sacrificing two days *of* you. That was one reason among others why I wished you to be consulted.

The letter I have received this morning from Polvellen, & which informs me of the cause which will unfortunately keep you there for some time longer,[2] decides the question, & I shall not set out from this place till Thursday next. I do not expect to be at Devonport before Saturday, as I shall probably take Bath in my way & bring on Roebuck along with me.

But remember that whatever may happen, I stay at Polvellen no longer than you do. So you must either stay there to the end of my time or be punished for suspecting me by knowing that you carry me off prematurely.

The letters which accompany this have been here (one of them at least) some time in expectation of some opportunity for conveying them. But I believe there was no urgency. I have sent to Tait's Magazine (for the number which will appear on the 1st of next month) a notice of Mr. Austin's book,[3] which though it is but short you will I think be pleased with—& what I value much more, you will be pleased with me for writing it.

Affectionately yours

J. S. MILL

58. TO THOMAS CARLYLE[1]

India House
17th September 1832

MY DEAR CARLYLE

You did me but justice in supposing that I had for some time been in hopes of a letter from you before I received your last.[2] When it arrived, it found me in a state of as impatient expectation as one *should* be in

1. MS in the possession of Mr. Gordon Waterfield.
2. Evidently the illness of John Austin; see next letter.
3. "Austin's Lectures on Jurisprudence," *Tait's*, II (Dec., 1832), 343–48. A review of John Austin's *The Province of Jurisprudence Determined* (London, 1832).

* * * *

1. *Addressed* (in another hand): Thos. Carlyle Esq / Craigenputtock /Dumfries. *Postmarks*: FREE / 17 SE 17 / 1832, and DUMFRIES / 19 SEP 1832. Franked by T. Hyde Villiers. MS at NLS. Carlyle's answer of Oct. 16 is in A. Carlyle, pp. 16–23.
2. Of Aug. 28. Published in A. Carlyle, pp. 11–16.

for an event which does not depend upon oneself. I plead guilty to having neglected the biographical department, having nothing to relate which seemed important to myself, and forgetting that all news is important to those who can *see* nothing and have few opportunities even of hearing. To begin therefore with myself, not only as the person whom I see oftenest and with whom I am most intimate, but as almost the only person (known to you) whom I have seen for the last two months, all others having long been absent from this Babylon, or at least Babel, of ours.—Your letter found me still in London, where I still am, but where I hope to be no longer after Thursday next. I had not promised to pass more than a fortnight of my holydays with the Bullers, & not wishing to lose entirely the benefit of the long summer days, I made a walking tour for a previous fortnight about the end of July, & then returned to allow others to be absent; and have been kept in town ever since. During this interval of from five to six weeks, I have worked if not harder, yet with more obvious fruits than I have done during any period of equal length for years past, having begun and finished three several papers on subjects extremely various. The first & longest is a political and moral dissertation on the rights and duties of the state with regard to endowments for public purposes,[3] or what you call in Scotland mortifications, including the estates of ecclesiastical & other corporations, universities, &c. This will appear in the Jurist, a quarterly journal or review of Legislation & Jurisprudence, carried on by several friends of mine, radical-utilitarians of a better than the ordinary sort, of whom I think sufficiently well to be able to cooperate with them in their own field of usefulness, though perhaps they would not always join me in mine. The second & shortest of my three articles, I have sent to Tait; it is a short review of Mr Austin's book on Jurisprudence,[4] & was chiefly intended as a recommendation of that work, though there is besides, some "doctrinal matter" as Napier[5] I suppose would call it, & a good deal of critical matter. Finally, I have written a rambling kind of article,[6] in which many, I will not say great, but big things are said on a small occasion, namely in the form of strictures on a well-meaning but flimsy article which recently appeared in the Monthly Repository. Touching this Monthly Repository[7] let me here say two or three words, as you probably do not know what it is. Till lately it was conducted by a Committee of Unitarian ministers & was a sectarian publication, the "Evangelical Magazine" of

3. See Letter 43, n. 18.
4. See preceding letter, n. 3.
5. Macvey Napier (1776–1847), editor of the *Edinburgh Review*, 1829–47; earlier, editor of the supplement to the sixth edition of the *Encyclopædia Britannica* (to which James Mill contributed).
6. "On Genius," *MR*, VI (Oct., 1832), 649–59.
7. See Letter 49, n. 1.

the Unitarians. Not long since, it was placed under the editorship, & soon after became the property of Mr. Fox, the same who has figured in the Political Union in London, and who, though no Göthe or Jean-Paul, is fit for better things than to be either a Unitarian preacher or a radical orator. Since the M.R. has been under his management, it has gradually divested itself of its sectarian character, and is much improved in all respects, though the editor & his writers are very far from seeing to the bottom of things yet. They are but Unitarians & liberals, unsectarianized, & with a larger & more tolerant spirit than common. Into my first parcel of books I will put some numbers of this periodical, which will, I think, like Bulwer's,[8] acquaint you with a new phasis of mind: at least I know nothing that is exactly like it, & among the persons whom Mr Fox most frequents I have met with several men & women who are decidedly *characters*, realizing an idea of their own & free from halfness of all sorts. I am not sure, indeed that much of this individuality appears in the Monthly Repository. When you next come to town I think you would like to know some of these people, as they also would to know you, for they are mostly great admirers of your writings, which however I am very doubtful whether they would find so much to their liking if they understood them thoroughly. As for this article of mine, those who best know me will see more character in it than in anything I have ever published; other people will never guess it to be mine. *You*, I hope, will find all the three articles *true*, the only praise I covet, & certainly rarer than any other in our times. But in this last you will find many things which I never saw, or never saw clearly till they were shewn to me by you, nor even for some time after. I think that the M.R. is read by persons with open improvable minds, & that ideas thrown among them will find soil in which to germinate; especially as they read their *own* magazines for doctrine, & others only for amusement. You see I adhere to my system, which is to be as particular in the choice of my vehicles, as you are indiscriminate, & I think we are both right. Do not buy any of these things; I will send them to you, with the exception perhaps of the no. of Tait, which in order to send I must first buy, & which would be a sorry half-crown's worth either to you or me; and which moreover will not like claret improve by travelling, nor be taken in gratis as ballast.

Every man's work is the chief part of his life, and since my return to town it has been the whole of mine, except some little reading, which is also in some sort work. Among things read "during the period under review," as we at this house say in our despatches, are to be numbered your two articles on the Corn Law Rhymer and on Göthe.[9] The former I

8. The *New Monthly Magazine.*
9. See Letter 51, notes 6 and 7.

found *true*: the latter I believe to be so, rather on your authority & from such knowledge as I myself have of Göthe than from what is said of him in the article: it does not, I think, carry so much of its own evidence with it as might have been *wished*: whether more might have been *done* is a question on which I can only express a doubt. In the meantime, I think I can perceive that your writings are making some way; awakening, though but partially, some minds. At least I find more people than before, or certainly more than I knew of, who do not dismiss them at once as "mysticism", "raving", &c. &c. &c.

The Austins are still at Polvellen, where Mr. Austin has had two successive attacks of illness, from the last of which he had not completely recovered when I last heard. Mrs Austin was busy translating Falk's memoir of Göthe;[10] & Charles Buller was writing an article for the Foreign Quarterly, on I know not what subject, which he had delayed beginning till they were obliged to shut him up for some hours a day for the express purpose: so at least says Mrs Buller. I have seen Glen but twice since I came to town, once for a moment only. He did *not*, it seems, write anything about Fanny Kemble. The paper therefore to which you allude must be the work of *Diabolus*.[11] I think he (Glennus not Diabolus) seemed less uneasy in mind than formerly; this might be accidental: in other respects he is much the same. It always seems to please him much when he hears that you continue to take interest in him.

You will have learnt from an article of mine in the Examiner,[12] the only one I have written for the last two months, that our friends the St Simonians have been tried. Enfantin, Chevalier & Duveyrier have been sentenced to a year's imprisonment & a fine: Barrault[13] & Rodrigues[14] only to a trifling fine. They were convicted on the charge of forming a society for the discussion of political & religious subjects without leave of the government, & also on a charge of preaching immoral doctrines, a charge founded on the theory of *la femme libre*.[15] There were other charges on which they were

10. *Characteristics of Goethe, From the German of Falk, von Müller, . . .* (London, 1833).

11. Carlyle in his letter of Aug. 28, indirectly quoting his brother: "Did he [Glen] not *write* something about Fanny Kemble? I said: *Aut Glennus aut Diabolus.*" Frances Anne Kemble (1809–1893) was then at the height of her fame as an actress.

12. An untitled article, *Examiner*, Sept. 9, 1832, p. 585.

13. Emile Barrault (1799–1868), publicist, travelled in the East, 1833–35, to propagate the new faith.

14. Olinde Rodrigues (1794–1851), economist and financier, early follower of Saint-Simon, remained a faithful Saint-Simonian until, like Bazard, he quarrelled with Enfantin over Enfantin's dogma on women.

15. Even after the breakup of the Saint-Simonian establishment at Ménilmontant, a group of disciples travelled to Constantinople and the East *pour chercher la femme-Messie.*

acquitted. Duveyrier is said to have made a very striking defence: Enfantin's seems to have made little impression except that of the ludicrous. There was much in the conduct of them all, which really one cannot help suspecting of quackery. In the witness-box, none of them would take the oath without Enfantin's permission: this he refused, on the ground that the name of God is not mentioned in the form of the oath. In defending himself, he several times made a long pause *pour attendre des inspirations*, & he gave strange looks at various people, to shew as he said the power of a look. The St Simonians all wear beards, and a peculiar costume, & marched to the place of trial in a body, singing if I recollect right, a succession of hymns, written and set to music by themselves. Enfantin claimed to have two women as his counsel, one of whom was Cecile Fournel,[16] who you may remember *protested* so vehemently against the immorality of his doctrines, but who has since, with her husband,[17] returned into the bosom of his church. When one remembers Irving, one believes that all this *may* be sincere. Yet surely there is an *admixture* of charlatanerie in it, I mean on the part of the Supreme Father.

Adolphe d'Eichthal has been here; I saw him for a few minutes only: he has had the cholera, & looked in very indifferent health.

Now as to books. I have not either Dumont or Babbage,[18] but I expect to have the former very soon; when I do I will send it. My own collection of books is a very strange one: it consists partly of books collected when I was writing on some particular subject; these are chiefly on the French Revolution, & French political history from Louis 14th downwards: & partly of books which I bought because they were *not* to be found in my father's library: which accounts for my having scarcely any *standard* English or French prose books. I am richest in the minor & the very recent French writers. I have most of the standard German & Italian books; the former you do not want, nor probably the latter. I have various classics, chiefly the poets, as my father cares less about them. For the same reason, I have many of the later English poets, whom my father despises. I am rich in no other department nor can I give any general idea of my other books.

16. In the Saint-Simonian hierarchy, in the "Degré des femmes," she had held the position of "Chef de service," and was in charge of the department for the conversion of women. Her testimony in the trial—a letter to the court—is in D'Allemagne, *Les Saint-Simoniens*, p. 300.

17. Marie Jérôme Henri Fournel (1799–1876), engineer, had given up his position as director of the works at Le Creusot to join the movement. He later wrote a biography of Saint-Simon.

18. Carlyle had requested "Dumont's *Mirabeau* and Babbage's two Books." The first of these would have been Etienne Dumont, *Recollections of Mirabeau* (London, 1832). One of the two books by Charles Babbage must have been his *On the Economy of Machinery and Manufactures*, which reached three editions in the year of its publication, 1832. The other book was probably Babbage's *Reflections on the Decline of Science in England and on Some of its Causes* (London, 1830).

I have not yet received the books you took with you, but as I have not particularly wanted them I have not enquired at Longman's,[19] & I will give them a fortnight's grace till I return. I have not yet hit upon any arrangement that would do, for sending you the Examiner, but I hope to find the means when I return to town. The only copy I have of my own, I keep for reference, and cannot well do without: the only inconvenience of sending it, would be that it must be sent back, but that is a sufficiently considerable one to induce me to seek for some other expedient before I resort to this, which may remain in reserve, as a last resort.

Fonblanque is better, but not yet strong or well. He is at present in the country. He goes on writing with his usual fertility, but I think he feels himself a little at fault in the altered situation of politics, & it is creditable to him that he is conscious of it. If coincidence were proof of causation, I should say that the pledge-mania had been abated by the tone which his paper has taken respecting it. What may be true is, that the Examiner has furnished arguments to those who were not disposed to give pledges, & has shewn that a person may refuse them without being a Tory & all that is wicked, a tax-eater & what not. I finish this letter in the presence of my friend John Wilson, who offers to be the bearer of it as far as Edinburgh, but as he is not going nearer to you I prefer availing myself of a Government frank which I can generally have for the asking. With best remembrances to Mrs Carlyle, believe me

Yours ever faithfully

J. S. MILL.

59. TO WILLIAM JOHNSON FOX[1]

India House
18 October
1832.

MY DEAR SIR

My friend André Marchais, who pays me the compliment of making me the depository and instrument of all the plans he forms for bringing about a good understanding between the patriotic party in France and the best of the English radicals, has suggested something which appears to me

19. The bookseller's, who arranged for transportation of packages of books.

* * * *

1. *Addressed*: Rev. W. J. Fox / 1 Stamford Grove / Upper Clapton. *Postmarks*: 7 NIGHT 7 / OC 18 / 1832, and 8 MORN 8 / OC 19 / 1832. The MS for the portion of the letter published by Garnett, pp. 101–2, is now at King's; the MS of the hitherto unpublished portion is at Yale.

highly important and to which, if you think well of it, you have it in your power to be mainly instrumental.

You are aware of the virulent and unceasing persecution which Louis-Philippe keeps up against the liberal press, insomuch that the Tribune has been prosecuted between sixty & seventy times. Out of the first sixty prosecutions, resulted even against this violent paper only five verdicts: but though the prosecutors succeed only in one case out of twelve, the Court imposes such heavy fines that the liberal press cannot long exist under such oppression and the editors are almost always in prison. An association has therefore been formed at Paris, of which my excellent friend Marchais is the secretary, for the purpose generally of promoting the liberty of the press, and specially of raising subscriptions to pay the fines. You will find the prospectus of the Association in the third page of the enclosed *Courrier* Français.

Now those among the French patriots who know enough of the English radicals to desire their cooperation & sympathy are anxious to obtain subscribers in England for this association, and above all they wish that the Political Unions should bear some public testimony of sympathy and fraternity on this important occasion. No one can do more than you can to bring both these things about, and no one can judge more soundly what would be the best mode of doing it.

The more you see & converse with French people, the more importance you will attach to things of this kind. Every such mark of sympathy produces a great momentary effect; but they require to be, again & again, repeated: for so few Frenchmen ever come here, that they do not learn, except from such public occurrences, that the English people, all but the Tories,[2] esteem, and wish well to, the French. Bastide, for example, came over as he confesses, full of prejudice against the English, but is already quite an altered man & is most eager to convince those of his countrymen who have never been here, that the English are not as many Frenchmen think, aristocrats at heart even to a man, & full of jealousy & selfish animosity against France.

I am anxious to say many things to you about this & other matters connected with it, & particularly to engage most earnestly your good offices in favour of Dussard & Bastide; to give the one all the consolations possible in his exile, & the other every means of knowing England, as he has begun a most interesting correspondence with the French journals which from his high standing in the republican party will carry weight. But of this hereafter as of much else which ought to be in common between us two.

Ever faithfully yours

J. S. MILL

2. The MS at King's ends here.

60. TO [WILLIAM BRIDGES ADAMS][1]

India House
20th October 1832

MY DEAR FRIEND

I should have returned the Preface[2] immediately after receiving your note; but I had it not at this house, & all yesterday I was too much engaged to be able to write to you. Now, however, I send the MS. with the very few pencil marks which you will find on it. I am glad that you want it, as I suppose I may conclude that the work itself is nearly or quite finished.

I am as desirous as you can possibly be, that we should meet & converse frequently at some length, and I had declined a very pressing & agreeable invitation for Friday[3] rather than put you off again—do not be angry with me—it was not from "punctilious ceremony" which I should never think of observing with a friend; but because I feared that you would think I was indifferent to your repeated invitation, & that I did not feel the value of friendship like yours. However the obstacle this time came from your side & I consequently was able to accept the other invitation, therefore do not regret that you happened to be engaged.

What you say respecting myself in your note I know you feel, and it is therefore very precious to me. We two possess what, next to community of purpose, is the greatest source of friendship between minds of any capacity; this is, not *equality*, for nothing can be so little interesting to a man as his own double; but, *reciprocal superiority*. Each of us knows many things which the other knows not, & can do many things which the other values but cannot himself do, or not so well. There is also just that difference of character between us which renders us highly valuable to

1. By permission of the Harvard College Library. The letter bears no identification of the recipient. The identification seems warranted, however, by internal evidence, even though Letter 67 seems to indicate that by Feb., 1833, JSM had still not met Adams.

William Bridges Adams (1797–1872), at this time under the pseudonym Junius Redivivus a prolific Radical writer and from 1832 to 1836 one of the chief contributors to W. J. Fox's *Monthly Repository*. (See Mineka, *The Dissidence of Dissent.*) His first wife was Elizabeth Place, daughter of Francis Place (see n. 7 below); his second, Sarah Flower, whom he married in 1834, was the ward of W. J. Fox and also a contributor to the *Repository*. In later life Adams was a successful inventor, known especially for the invention of the fish joint for railway rails.

2. A Preface to *The Producing Man's Companion; An Essay on the Present State of Society, Moral, Political, and Physical, in England*, published in 1833. This was a revised, second edition of *The Rights of Morality* [with same subtitle], 1832. JSM reviewed Junius Redivivus' writings in both *MR* (April, 1833), pp. 262–70, and *Tait's* (June, 1833), pp. 347–54.

3. Oct. 20, the date of this letter, fell on a Saturday.

each other in another way for *I* require to be warmed, *you* perhaps occasionally to be calmed. We are almost as much the natural complement of one another as man and woman are: we are far stronger together than separately, & whatever both of us agree in, has a very good chance, I think, of being true. We are therefore made to encourage and assist one another. Our intimacy is its own reward, & we have only to consider in what way it may be made most useful to both of us.

Never express any regret at taking up my time with any of your productions. I will not, (because I know you would not wish it) postpone to them, anything which is really of more immediate urgency: I say more *immediate*, because no employment of my time can be *in itself* better or more useful. I know of no one man now living who, take him for all in all, has a larger share of the qualifications (opportunity being included) for effecting unspeakable good, than you have; at the same time I feel that this good may be unboundedly increased by association & collision with other minds, & that for this advantage you are thrown principally on me, because your incognito[4] cuts you off from so many others from whom you might derive much of the same benefit. Although I agree with you in thinking that on the whole the reasons predominate in favor of your remaining unknown, I often regret that you are cut off by it from any certain knowledge how many more persons there are than you are aware of, who are qualified morally & intellectually to think, act, and feel with you. In your loathing of the very idea of being patronized I can fully sympathize—but you are in no danger of that; because you are not a littérateur who administers to people's amusement, but a thinker & writer whose doings affect their substantial interests, & who therefore when you are not valued & esteemed, will be disliked & feared, but at least always treated *de puissance en puissance*. Moore[5] or Campbell[6] might be patronized, but Place[7] or Cobbett never could, because nobody ever gives himself airs with persons who have *power* of their own, independent of, & for some purposes paramount to his.

Believe me

Yours ever faithfully

J. S. MILL

4. All his writings were signed Junius Redivivus.

5. Thomas Moore (1779–1852), the poet, and biographer of Byron.

6. Thomas Campbell (1777–1844), poet best known for his *The Pleasures of Hope* (1799) and *Gertrude of Wyoming* (1809).

7. Francis Place (1771–1854), London tailor, friend of Bentham and James Mill, was behind the scenes a very important leader in reform movements for at least a quarter of a century. For the best account of his activities see Graham Wallas, *The Life of Francis Place* (London, 1918).

61. TO THOMAS CARLYLE[1]

22d October 1832

MY DEAR CARLYLE

When I received your last,[2] I was on the point of writing to you, for the special purpose (in addition to all general ones) of giving you intimation of the existence of a person who is willing to undertake for the punctual transmission of the Examiner by Monday's post on the condition on which such things are frequently done, namely that he and you shall each pay half the subscription. You have therefore this resource in case of need, and though I have no experience by which to judge of the punctuality of the person in question, I will undertake to rebuke him for every breach of it which may be notified to me from you. As you surmise, I have written nothing in the Examiner lately, except a little article relating among other things to the trial of the St Simonians.[3] I write nothing regularly for the Examiner except the articles on French affairs: everything else is the exception, not the rule; and even of those little notices of France in the middle of the paper, there has been a suspension since July last, owing partly to my two absences from town, & partly to the uninteresting nature of all the passing events in that country. The same post however which brings you this letter, will bring an article of mine on the Doctrinaires & the new French Ministry,[4] & from this time you may expect to see these notices resumed. As for other newspaper-writing, it has been suspended by the more serious work mentioned in my last letter to you, which being over, other things will now have once more their turn.

What you say of Fonblanque is partly true,[5] or rather it is all true, but not the whole truth. It is only accident that makes him attach himself to Politics, but the bent & character of his mind renders war against the False his vocation instead of effort towards the True. He is essentially a com-

1. *Addressed*: Thos. Carlyle Esq / Craigenputtock / Dumfries. *Postmarks*: FREE / 23OC23 / 1832, and DUMFRIES / 2[?]OC1832. Franked by T. Hyde Villiers. MS at NLS. Carlyle's answer of Nov. 19 is in A. Carlyle, pp. 23–30.

2. Of Oct. 16. Published in A. Carlyle, pp. 16–23.

3. See Letter 58, n. 12. Of the Saint-Simonians, JSM remarks: "Of their doctrines we still think . . . that there is, out of all reckoning, more truth and substance in them than in any other of the numerous Utopian systems which are afloat. We agree in but few of their conclusions, yet we see an undeniable and permanent value in many of their premises. . . ."

4. Untitled article, *Examiner*, Oct. 21, 1832, pp. 680–81. MacMinn, *Bibliog.*, pp. 22–23, lists the succeeding notices of French affairs.

5. Of Fonblanque, editor of the *Examiner*, Carlyle had said in his previous letter (A. Carlyle, p. 18) that it was remarkable that "a man of his sharp faculties [and] keen genial nature" could bear to continue as editor of a political paper, and asked: "Is it your prediction that he will abide to the last by Politics?"

mentator on sophistry, hypocrisy, and folly. Under other circumstances he might have been a writer on manners or morals, not politics, but it would always have been in the same way: he used to write such things in the London Magazine & other periodicals formerly. He has no systematic or solid acquirements, & now unfortunately has no leisure to supply that want. To no one would it be more important to "have leave to sit wholly silent for some three years from this date, till he shall have got to the bottom of many things."[6] But, as you too truly say, *jacta est alea*; he must toil day and night to gain a subsistence by giving out what is in him, never stopping to take in more; even *that* problem is a hard enough one, determined as he is to have nothing to do with Lying in any form, and having other mouths to feed besides his own, with, I greatly fear, little prudence in pecuniary matters to keep his course which is impeded by so many unavoidable obstacles, clear of any avoidable ones.

I will immediately send you Thiers's History of the French Revolution[7] with perhaps some other French books, and some numbers of the Fox periodical.[8] What you say of Unitarians[9] is true of them as a class, but not of every individual among them. They seem to me to be a conceited sect, who think that God has given them a book for their guidance and that yet they are so wise that they can set the book itself right when it tells them anything different from what they could have found out of themselves. Fox, however, is not a half-man, but three quarters of a man at least: I do not know him sufficiently to be able to affirm more, but what I do know, makes me feel sure that a time will come when he will part company with Unitarianism and Unitarian preaching. I am satisfied that he would have done it long ago but that a Unitarian preacher may preach almost anything he pleases. It is the sort of necessity he is under of addressing himself to a set of Pharisaical formalists and word-mongers twice every Sunday when he could find fitter audience elsewhere, that will ultimately disgust him with his present ostensible calling. As for his political speeches, I only know them as you do by bad reports, very bad indeed, for they make the speeches feeble, when all who ever heard them concur in saying that they are very powerful & effective. But his politics are but a small part of himself, & few people so well qualified to have influence over others in that walk, overvalue its importance so little. Him among others you should know personally, &

6. A quotation from Carlyle's previous letter of his wish for himself (A. Carlyle, p. 22).

7. *Histoire de la Révolution française* (10 vols., Paris, 1823–27).

8. The *Monthly Repository*.

9. "I never could make much of Unitarians; from the great Channing downwards there is a certain mechanical metallic *deadness* at the heart of all of them; rhetorical clangour enough, but no fruit for me. Unluckily too they seem a sort of Half-men. . . ." (A. Carlyle, p. 20.)

the first time you are in London this among many other good works of the same sort do I reserve for myself to bring about. I do not think he writes much in his own Magazine. One paper "An Autumn in London"[10] I know to be his; it is very unlike his usual manner, but shews greater powers of a certain sort than I think he commonly evinces. The articles on Goethe are by Crabbe Robinson,[11] you therefore know all that is in them. A curious sort of man, Talfourd[12] the barrister, who wrote the paper on Hazlitt in the Examiner[13] (interesting but hollow & unsatisfactory) told me the other day that Goethe must be an impostor because Robinson praises him so highly. N.B. Talfourd admires Schiller exceedingly in Coleridge's translation.[14]

The Westminster Reviewer whom you are curious about is Lieutenant-Colonel T. Perronet Thompson, author of various pamphlets on Political Economy, part proprietor & now almost sole writer of the Westminster Review. He is a man of very extensive acquirements, besides having seen much of the world. Among other things he is a considerable mathematician, & has written what I believe to be the only good systematic book ever written on the physical principles of Music.[15] That book is the only work of his I ever saw which shews him to be capable of looking at more than one single aspect of each individual thing. He has an understanding like a pin, going very far into a thing, but never covering a larger portion of it than the area of a pin's point. He is a singular man, very clever in his way, & possessed of a rare faculty of familiarly illustrating & pushing into every corner of a large & complicated subject the one idea which is all he ever has thereon. From his writings you would judge him to be much of a coxcomb, from his conversation & demeanour one of the most modest of men. He is the most unalloyed of Radicals past, present, & to come, in every acceptation of that title whether among men or gods.

Tait, I am inclined to think, will succeed: narrow as it is, there is more heartiness and resolvedness about that magazine than about Bulwer's,[16] or any other so-called Liberal periodical now going. Then it is radical, which

10. *MR*, VI (1832), 660–67.

11. Henry Crabb Robinson (1775–1867), diarist and enthusiast for German literature, contributed a series of nine articles on Goethe to the *Monthly Repository* in 1832–33.

12. Thomas Noon Talfourd (1795–1854), later dramatist and biographer of Charles Lamb.

13. "The Late William Hazlitt," Oct. 14, pp. 661–62; Oct. 21, p. 678; and Nov. 2, pp. 708–9. The final instalment, not published at the time of this letter, was signed T.N.T.

14. *Wallenstein, A Drama in Two Parts* (London, 1800).

15. *Instructions to my Daughter for playing on the Enharmonic Guitar* (London, 1829). Thompson reviewed his own book in *WR*, XVI (April, 1832), 429–79. See L. G. Johnson, *General T. Perronet Thompson* (London, 1957), p. 158.

16. See Letter 58, n. 8.

the others are not, & so far better adapted to the inclinations of the mass. There is besides I think, a possibility of improvement in those writers: they have nothing or but little to give up, only to take in a wider range. I know none of them personally except one, that one however has written most of their best articles; he is an early & valued friend of mine, whom I once thought incurably *narrow*, but who has made such advances within the last eighteen months that I have the greatest hopes of him: Roebuck, who has lately made so much noise at Bath.[17] If No 3 of Tait, & the number for this month (October) should fall in your way, it may be interesting to you to run through his two articles on Rousseau.[18] Though you will desiderate much that is not there, yet if you know our Benthamic Utilitarians, you will acknowledge that it requires much vigour of intellect in one trained in that school, to be capable of writing those articles they are so unlike all that he can have learned from his instructors. I shall be much surprised if he do not turn out to be one of the very few *men* whom we have any chance of seeing in politics for an indefinite period. He has a strength of *will* which has had no parallel in that field since Napoleon. Would not a *Napoleon-idéologue* be an odd combination?

On the whole there are scarcely any left of the old narrow school of Utilitarians; what now distinguishes those who *were* so, (besides that as you say they were the reoriginators of *any* belief among us) is that they are decidedly *less* narrow than almost any other persons who aspire to the character of Thinkers in this country. The character of the school if such it could be termed, was to see *clearly* what they did see, though it was but little. This quality I have hopes that they will retain, as their views expand. You say that young minds do not end as they began; but besides this, the young minds have already far larger views than the old. Among those whom I know, the older a man is, the more of his belief is negative, & the less he thinks it worth while for him to throw his mind into that of any other man, or look at Truth from any other man's position. None however of them all has become so unlike what he once was as I myself, who originally was the narrowest of them all, having been brought up more exclusively under the influence of a peculiar kind of impressions than any other person ever was. Fortunately however I was not *crammed*; my own thinking faculties were called into strong though but partial play; & by their means I have been enabled to *remake* all my opinions.

Charles Buller is not only sure of Liskeard,[19] but is at this time one of the most popular and important men in the Eastern Division of Cornwall;

17. In his campaign to become MP for Bath; he was elected in Dec.

18. "Jean Jacques Rousseau," *Tait's*, I (June, 1832), 338–56, and II (Oct., 1832), 39–49.

19. Elected to Parliament for Liskeard that autumn, Buller held the seat until his death in 1848.

he speaks at all the meetings where the radical candidates face their constituents, & always makes the best speech of the day. Unhappily his health continues delicate & uncertain; & he has not acquired what was chiefly deficient in him, the power of continued & persevering application to business. I almost despair of his ever doing anything considerable, for want of this one quality. All the members for the Eastern Division of Cornwall, both county & towns, will be radicals, with perhaps one exception. It is a good genial kind of radicalism, that of the Cornish people, not mere hunger speaking out its cravings in maxims of politics. The rest of the Buller family are in their usual condition of mind, & body, & estate.

Austin was very ill for a time in Cornwall but recovered, & was completely set up in health & spirits by a little tour to the Land's End in which I accompanied him & Mrs Austin.[20] *Her* silence therefore cannot be occasioned by any untoward circumstance, but probably by her translation of Falk, about which she is very busy. I go there tonight to help resolve some doubts about a metaphysical chapter. I must resolve them in my own head first for it is a chapter which I was able to make nothing of when I tried it at Polvellen. I doubt not that she will speedily write; you & Mrs Carlyle are perpetually in her thoughts & frequently on her lips. I have not seen Glen since my return, but will very speedily call on him if he does not on me. I will also call on Fraser[21] whom I have not seen at all this summer.—Tell me when you go to Edinburgh, & where to address you there. We must as you say, see Edinburgh together one day, & (I will add) soon. If it be in summer, that will be a more convenient mode to me of passing a vacation in your company than visiting you at Craigenputtoch. There are several reasons for this.

Ever yours affectionately

J. S. MILL.

I understand from Napier's son that the books were sent, the neglect therefore is at Longman's & the remedy is in my own hands.—The St Simonians are not yet in prison, having appealed to the Court of Cassation: more of them hereafter. They have in the press (or by this time *out* of it) a full account of their trial: They will doubtless send it to me, & so will I to you. The article on them in the Westminster Review[22] is as you surmise by the man I told you of, Col. Thompson. I look forward with great interest to your paper on Diderot:[23] I have long wished for such a

20. Part of MS of JSM's "Journal of Cornwall Trip, Oct. 3–9, 1832" was in the possession of the late Isaac Foot, Pencrebar, Callington, Cornwall. A photostat of this and the rest of the MS are at LSE.
21. See Letter 51, n. 4.
22. See Letter 45, n. 8.
23. *FQR*, XI (April, 1833), 261–315.

paper from you. Buller has written a paper for the same review (it is out by this time) on the reign of Louis 18th.[24] I have not yet seen "The Tale."[25]

Assure Mrs Carlyle of my best regards.[26]

62. TO WILLIAM TAIT[1]

India House
7th November
1832

MY DEAR SIR

I am highly gratified by what you say of my paper on Currency,[2] and no less so at the notes you propose to add as from yourself, as I agree with you so decidedly and so warmly on both points that if we could have known each other's minds before I wrote the article, I would gladly have touched upon those collateral questions in the text.

As to the excellence of the Scottish system of banking I have no doubt of it, nor that the issue of notes down to £1, where the solvency of the issues is as well provided for as it is under that system, should be subject to no restriction except convertibility, into cash or into the notes of some Government Bank. I rejoice much at the view your Magazine has taken of this question, because many of our most enlightened radicals and political economists in this part of the world are of a contrary, and therefore in my view a wrong, opinion upon this point.

Then as to the National Debt, I agree with you and with Jefferson in thinking that no generation is entitled to mortgage the fruits of the labours of posterity: on us who have only our earnings (I mean myself for example) the National Debt is not, I admit, a sacred obligation: but it is so, on all who have inherited property from the generation which borrowed the money, for no one has a moral right to take his father's property and leave his father's debts unpaid. But we cannot distinguish between inherited and acquired property after so many years, and therefore, agreeing with you that it is a question of choice between one injustice and another, I hold

24. It did not appear until the Jan., 1833, *FQR*, XI, 89–127.

25. "The Tale" by Goethe (trans. and commentary by Carlyle), *Fraser's*, VI (Oct., 1832), 257–78.

This postscript is written at the top of the first page of the letter.

26. This sentence is written in the margin of the last page.

* * * *

1. *Addressed*: William Tait Esq. / Bookseller / Edinburgh. *Postmarks*: A / NO 7 / 1832, and NOV / ???9A / 1832. MS at LSE.

William Tait (1793–1864) had begun earlier that year the publication of the magazine bearing his name.

2. "The Currency Juggle," *Tait's*, II (Jan., 1833), 461–67, reprinted in *Dissertations*, I, 68–81.

that the least injustice would be done by paying off the debt at once by a tax on all actually acquired and accumulated property; viz. the funds themselves, the land, and all capital, but not laying any part of the burthen upon *income* not derived from property.

If [it][3] was possible to leave the debt unpaid and throw the interest of it upon property exclusively, I should consider that still better; but it would not do, since it would be a penalty on future accumulation, taxing those who save, and letting the prodigal go free.

I shall be happy to hear whether you agree with me in these opinions. At all events you have a right to add any notes you please, as from yourself. Believe me, my dear Sir

Very truly yours

J. S. MILL

I will write to Mr Nichol very soon;[4] in the mean while, accept my thanks for the introduction.[5]

63. TO WILLIAM TAIT[1]

India House
29th November 1832

MY DEAR SIR,

Finding it impossible to recast the article,[2] or find any place at which the matter you require could be inserted without breaking the thread of the argument, I have thrown the whole into a note, which may be annexed at the end, or may, if you prefer it, form a Supplement to the article. But on the whole, I think it should rather be a note, as that will excuse the very general and summary mode in which the questions are disposed of.

I think the hints I have thrown out respecting the National Debt will at least afford a subject of reflexion to thinking men—I should like much to learn from you what is thought of them by any of the persons whom you consider as authorities on this class of subjects.

I am much gratified by what you say of the success of the Magazine; which deserves it so well that I am not surprised it should obtain it.

Believe me
My dear Sir
Most truly yours

J. S. MILL.

3. Page torn. 4. See Letter 65.
5. This postscript appears at the top of the first page.

* * * *

1. MS in New York Public Library. 2. See preceding letter, n. 2.

64. TO THOMAS CARLYLE[1]

India House, 27th December 1832

MY DEAR CARLYLE

In your last letter,[2] received now upwards of a month, you said, "you will write soon again"—ill have I responded to this call; having been hindered therefrom by various occupations and thoughts, some of a pleasant, but more of a disagreeable kind, whereof the last alone are entitled to be received as any even the poorest excuse for this negligence. My conscience, however, now speaks to me in so reproachful a voice that I can no longer resist its commands.

During the interval you will have received my packet of books; of each and all of them save one I have spoken to you: that one is "The English in France"[3] a sketchy kind of book, composed of essays & tales, all intended to throw light upon France, painting it & all it contains *en beau*, a view of the matter which is entitled to be attended to, were it only because of its rarity: there is also much truth in the book, *though* not much depth, and on the whole it is as worth your reading as any other book in that parcel. A propos of writings about France, that article in the last number of the Foreign Quarterly was not Buller's; his was on the reign of Louis 18th & has not yet appeared, it will doubtless appear in the next number along with your Diderot[4] which I am very anxious to see. Cochrane[5] seems to me much what you describe him; a man he seems too who has a great love of fairness, and is above all an enemy of *extremes*—and who proves himself an impartial arbitrater between conflicting opinions by letting each in its turn speak through his pages, in as softened a voice as may be, whereby in truth his Review the better fulfils its mission, by representing the more correctly the attitude which English minds of all parties and sorts have taken up towards foreign nations. All reviews are hotch-potches with no definite object or presiding principle—but *this* kind of review can perhaps be so with less incongruity and absurdity than any of the others: so that if you & the Right Hon. T. P. Courtenay[6] appear side by side in it, we must not be shocked at the proximity.—As for myself, I have not written much

1. *Addressed*: Thos Carlyle Esq / care of Mess[rs] Bell & Bradfute / Edinburgh. *Postmarks*: FREE / 27 DEC 27 / 1832, and DEC / 29 / 1832. Franked by J. A. Roebuck. MS at NLS. Carlyle's answer of Jan. 12, 1833, is in A. Carlyle, pp. 30–36.

2. Dated Nov. 19. Published in A. Carlyle, pp. 23–30.

3. *The English in France*. By the Author of "The English in Italy" [C. H. Phipps, Marquis of Normanby] (London, 1828).

4. See Letter 61, n. 23, 24.

5. John George Cochrane (1781–1852), editor of the *Foreign Quarterly Review*, 1827–35.

6. Thomas Peregrine Courtenay (1782–1841), politician and pamphleteer. For identification of his contributions, see Eileen M. Curran, "The *Foreign Quarterly Review*, 1827–1846" (unpublished dissertation, Cornell University, 1958), p. 373.

since you last heard from me: except one or two articles in the Examiner, among which may be mentioned one on the French & English newspapers[7] & one last Sunday on Corn Laws & Tithes,[8] besides one not yet published, on Taxation:[9] also an article which will appear in Tait's January number, on Currency & the National Debt,[10] & a paper for Fox's January number.[11] This last attempts something much higher, and intrinsically more valuable, than all these writings on politics, but with far less success: it is not nearly so good of its kind, because I am not so well versed in the subject. It embodies some loose thoughts, which had long been floating in my mind, about Poetry and Art, but the result is not satisfactory to me and will probably be far less so to you—but you will tell me to what extent you think me wrong, or shallow. I wrote the paper from conviction (else it had never been written) but not from that strong conviction which *forces* to write: rather because I wished to write something for Fox, and thought there was a clearer field open for him in that direction than in the political one. This number of Fox shall be sent to you in the next parcel. The *periodicals* which I send you are *given*, you will recollect; not to be returned. I have also to send you, when I have done reading it, a printed copy which I have received of the trial of the St Simonians.[12] Of the speeches I have read Duveyrier's alone appears to me to have any other merit than that of a strong conviction. I have heard, but not from themselves, that Duveyrier and Eichthal have given up St Simonism. This as the newspapers say "needs confirmation," & if true, will excite in you as in me, great curiosity to know how it took place and *what* they are to be henceforth. I have been reading with considerable interest some numbers of the Revue Encyclopédique, which is conducted by a body of seceded St Simonians: I am on the whole much pleased with them: they have retained almost all the good which ever was in St Simonism, & are not become sceptics but rather prophets of a religion to come—they see that St Simon though a man far beyond his generation, was but a false Christ, and they appear to be expecting the true. Jules Lechevalier[13] and Abel Transon[14] have taken up with the system of M. Charles Fourier,[15] a man who has been writing for many years large and obscure books shewing how the

7. "French and English Journals," *Examiner*, Dec. 2, 1832, pp. 772–73.

8. "On the Necessity of Uniting the Question of Corn Laws with that of Tithes," *Examiner*, Dec. 23, 1832, pp. 817–18.

9. "Necessity of Revising the Present System of Taxation," *ibid.*, Jan. 13, 1833, pp. 19–20.

10. See Letter 62, n. 2.

11. "What is Poetry?" *MR*, VII (Jan., 1833), 60–70.

12. Probably *Le Procès en Cours d'Assises, 27 et 28 août 1832* (Paris, 1832).

13. Jules Lechevalier (1800–1850), economist and journalist.

14. Abel Louis Etienne Transon (1805–1876), engineer and a leading Saint-Simonian.

15. François Marie Charles Fourier (1772–1837), founder of the socialist system which bears his name.

world is to be saved. From an account of part of his system given by Transon in an article in the Revue Encyclopédique,[16] I gather that the moving force which is to change the world is to be "l'attraction passionée," mankind are to be made to Love *le travail* by various contrivances, which are to end in making them masters and controllers of physical nature: the sea I believe is ultimately to consist not of salt water but lemonade; I understand this is no joke, but the serious persuasion of M. Fourier.—Tell me if you have yet seen Dumont's *Mirabeau* or Babbage's books;[17] if not I will endeavour to put them also into the next parcel.—The books you sent were never received at Longman's; they *were* sent by Mr Napier to Black's: so that the fault lies either with the last-named bookseller or with the carriers of whatever description. Napier's son, who is here, has written to his father about it, & traced the matter thus far: if it can be traced further, it will be, so give yourself no trouble about it.

So the Elections are over. Almost all the candidates in whose success I took any personal interest, have succeeded. Among them are three men who, I expect, will *do* something: these are, Grote, Roebuck, & John Romilly: to these, if his inapplication will let him, we shall both be happy to add Charles Buller. All the rest will *talk*, & not *do*: nor will anything worth doing be really done for a while to come. One of the most likely *doers* among the young men, the only one among the official young men, has departed from us: poor Hyde Villiers.[18] He was an earnest workman, who would have plied his trade of politics honestly, and if not with first rate talents, yet with such as well used had been sufficient to do much. Take him for all in all we shall not soon find his equal among that class of men.—I suspect that I shall have to dip my pen in politics oftener and deeper than in proportion to the value I attach to it compared with other things; for it is the only subject to which, just at present, anybody will listen; and now that my friends have buckled to that work I must not desert them, but give such help as lies in me. Fonblanque still labours on, in his unsatisfactory, yet not wholly unprofitable vocation. You will have seen that he has gained an accession of power, that is of circulation, by the purchase of a rival radical paper.[19]—Austin is in tolerably good spirits, lecturing to a very small but really select class, and getting daily a clearer insight into his subject, as well as into other subjects still more important. But of him you will have heard at full length, for two days ago I saw at his

16. "Doctrine d'Association de M. Charles Fourier," *Revue encyclopédique*, LIII (Feb., 1832), 271–300. See Letter 91. JSM's later and better-informed opinion of Fourier (see *Principles of Political Economy*, II, i, 4) was much more favourable.

17. See Letter 58, n. 18.

18. JSM published a brief eulogy of him in the *Examiner*, Dec. 9, 1832, p. 792.

19. The *Ballot* was incorporated with the *Examiner*, beginning with the number of Dec. 2, 1832.

house a letter to Mrs Carlyle from Mrs Austin, ready folded up and sealed.—For various reasons I did not make use of your note to Leigh Hunt[20] as an introduction to him, though hereafter I shall be very happy to have another such opportunity: the note, however, went to him; the address (as I learnt at Moxon's)[21] was correct. Does the Examiner now reach you regularly? You will see in it very soon a paper of Charles Buller's on certain Election matters[22]—it will be either a letter or an article. His health I am sorry to say is still precarious—very slight causes are enough to derange it. I called on Glen a short time after my return from Cornwall, but found he had left his lodgings and gone into Scotland, where I suppose you have seen him. He must be back by this time, but whether to the same place I have not yet enquired, for which I have no excuse to make but the poor one I made for my delay in writing to you. I have seen, I believe, no one else in whom you take an interest. I shall send this letter to Messrs Bell & Bradfute,[23] as it is probable you will be at Edinburgh or on your way thither before this reaches you: do not punish my sins of omission by delaying to write to me, but write soon and at length. I trust you will soon hear from me again—I say *I trust* when if I really *trusted* in myself, I should say *I am sure.*

Yours ever faithfully

J. S. MILL

Kindest remembrances to Mrs Carlyle, who I hope still thinks of me sometimes.[24]

20. James Henry Leigh Hunt (1784–1859), essayist and poet, friend of Keats, Shelley, and Byron.

21. Edward Moxon (1801–1858), publisher of some of the greatest nineteenth-century poets, including Wordsworth, Tennyson, and Browning.

22. "The Working of the Reform Act," *Examiner*, Jan. 6, 1833, pp. 4–5.

23. Well-known Edinburgh firm of booksellers.

24. Written in the margin of the last page.

• • • 1833 • • •

65. TO JOHN PRINGLE NICHOL[1]

India House,
16th January, 1833.

MY DEAR SIR,

I had fully resolved that of us two, *you* should not be the first to write; and here have I allowed a fortnight to elapse since receiving your letter before I have ever acknowledged the reception of it. This you would I am sure excuse if I could tell you in what manner my time and thoughts have been engrossed. From the time when I first saw your papers[2] in *Tait's Magazine*, I have been ambitious of the honour of your acquaintance, and now that I am privileged to communicate with you I am not disposed to let the privilege *lapse* from disuse. It has often struck me that one of the many causes which prevent those who cultivate moral and political truth from occupying the place and possessing the influence which properly belong to them as the instructors and leaders of mankind, is that they never consider themselves as other labourers do, to constitute a *guild* or fraternity, combining their exertions for certain common ends, and freely communicating to each other everything they possess which can be used to promote these ends. As to the particular subject which has made us two known to each other—political economy—there are so many talkers about it, and so few (you will I am sure agree with me), even among professed economists, who study it scientifically, that all who do, ought to know each other.

[. . . .][3]

I long to see the article which it was my luck to anticipate—that we should agree on such a point was to be expected, as it is evident we look at these subjects from the same station or *Standpunkt*, as the Germans call it.

Is there any chance of your coming to town? I fear there is little of my soon visiting your part of the world—though my father's birthplace is

1. *Addressed*: Rev. J. P. Nichol, Academy, Montrose. Published in part in Knight. The originals of these letters have not been located.

John Pringle Nichol (1804–1859), astronomer, as a young man was deeply interested in political economy; in 1833 James Mill and Nassau Senior thought well enough of his work therein to recommend him for the chair of political economy vacated by the death of J. B. Say at the Collège de France, Paris. See Letter 71.

2. These cannot now be identified with certainty.

3. Presumably a deletion by Knight.

very near Montrose,[4] at the foot of the Grampians. I fear there are not many persons in your neighbourhood with whom you can profitably discuss these subjects, or who even take any interest in them. On selfish principles I ought to be glad of this, as it gives me a chance of oftener hearing from you. Pray write soon, if you have time, and believe me,

Most sincerely yours,

J. S. MILL.

66. TO WILLIAM TAIT[1]

[Jan. 23, 1833]

I shall probably send you, in time for your March number, a short review of an excellent book, the Producing Man's Companion, by Junius Redivivus[2]—whom I think the very best popular writer whom the enlightened radicals count in their ranks—though I like his *personal* articles in the Examiner less than the many admirable papers he has written in the True Sun, Mechanics Magazine & various other periodicals.

Believe me
Yours ever truly
J. S. MILL

67. TO THOMAS CARLYLE[1]

India House
2d February 1833

MY DEAR CARLYLE

First let me dispatch the matters of business. Cochrane is apprised of your present residence: That Holcroft[2] is so you will have learnt before this by receiving the Examiner direct. Holcroft's address is 13 Bartlett's

4. At Northwater Bridge, where James Mill's father was a shoemaker.

* * * *

1. *Addressed*: William Tait Esq / Bookseller / Edinburgh. Franked by G. Grote. *Postmarks*: [???], 23 JA 23, 1833 and JAN / 25 / 1833. MS at NLS. No salutation or date; perhaps a fragment.

2. JSM's review did not appear until the June number. See Letter 60, n. 2.

* * * *

1. *Addressed*: Thomas Carlyle Esq / Carlton Street / Stockbridge / Edinburgh. *Postmarks*: FREE / 4FE4 / 1833, and FEB / 6 / 1833. Franked by J. A. Roebuck. MS at NLS. In reply to Carlyle's letter of Jan. 12, 1833, A. Carlyle, pp. 30–36; answered by Carlyle, Feb. 22, *ibid*., pp. 37–41.

2. Carlyle had identified him as Thomas Holcroft, "A Son of the Dramatist [Thomas] Holcroft's, brother-in-law to a Mr. Badams a very old friend of mine." Thomas Holcroft, Jr. (d. 1852) was a London journalist (see *Gentleman's Magazine*, NS, XXXVII [April, 1852], 425).

Buildings, Holborn: as the people at the Adelphi, he says, well knew: Mr Badams's[3] address is 8, Old Church Street, Paddington. Holcroft writes, speaking of you "I am sure he must have given me up as a careless & negligent person & unworthy of having any thought bestowed upon him, for to my shame be it said that I have written but once to him since he left London. I earnestly respect & love him and could have wished for more frequent interchange of ideas, but I really dread to expose myself to his critical lash as an unauthorized correspondent. When you write, ask him if he will let me know under his own hand and seal how he and his wife are, and also whether I may venture to send him a frank."—I ought to have apprised you sooner of his address and Mr Badams's; however, you know them now—the fault is not *repaired* but it is *stopped.*—You shall very soon receive another packet of books. Let me hear from you first, however, whether you have access to the books I am going to mention. There exists a very voluminous collection of Memoirs of the French Revolution.[4] A considerable part of this I have, & among others two volumes of *Mémoires sur les Prisons,*[5] chiefly the "personal narratives" of people who were in confinement during the epoch of "Terror": I never have read those two volumes, strange as it may seem, & know not exactly the worth of the contents—but I should think they could not fail to be interesting, and to answer your purpose in some degree. If you have not access to these two volumes where you are, I will send them. Next—have you the means of getting the Memoirs of Levasseur?[6] He was one of the less noted members of the *montagne* party, & wrote his life or rather got it written very recently in order to justify that party—he is evidently a highly conscientious, well meaning man, with something of the spirit of an old Roman, and his book lets one into the aspect of that period as it presented itself to the honester minds among the actors, in a manner which has interested me deeply. Your friend Fraser lent it to me, and would, I am sure, allow me to forward it to you if you cannot get it at Edinburgh. You would learn more about Danton from this book than from any other I know—it is astonishing how little is known of such a man. Then, I have in the collection already mentioned the "Vieux Cordelier"[7] of Camille Desmoulins, which I think would interest you. The Memoirs of Mme

3. Dr. John Badams (d. 1833), a Birmingham manufacturer who had been trained as a doctor. Carlyle had met him through Edward Irving in 1824 and had spent six weeks at his home in Birmingham that summer.

4. St. A. Berville and J. F. Barrière, *Collection des mémoires relatifs à la révolution française* (68 vols., Paris, 1820–28).

5. Paris, 1823.

6. *Mémoires de René Levasseur (de la Sarthe) ex-conventionnel . . .* (4 vols., Paris, 1829–31).

7. *Le Vieux Cordelier, journal politique, rédigé en l'an II, par Camille Desmoulins* . . . 1825. In Berville-Barrière *Collection.*

Roland[8] you have, of course, read. I have several other memoirs of girondists but they are little more than long elegies.—Mirabeau, Danton, and Bonaparte are the only men who appear other than common in Thiers' pages:[9] but there were other remarkable men besides those three: Robespierre especially, who strangely enough, has been spoken of by all parties as a mediocre man, & Thiers thinks him so: it was always a puzzle to me how a mediocre man could remain master of the field among so many competitors, until I read some of his speeches and then saw that he was by far the most *skilful* of the combatants in every sense of the word.—On the whole, however, it is wonderful how little can be traced of the private and social life of that period. There is positively much more of it in Thiers than in any other of the innumerable books on the revolution which I have read. There is more of it (as is often the case) in their professed *fictions* than in their histories: a novel by Picard which I have, entitled "Le Gil Blas de la Revolution"[10] is worthy of some account in this respect, & I have been told that there are novels of Pigault Lebrun[11] which paint several periods of the revolution very vividly.—You have characterized Thiers' system of ethics most accurately.[12] I am afraid it is too just a specimen of the young French *littérateurs*, and that *this* is all they have made, ethically speaking, of their attempt to imitate the Germans in identifying themselves with the *past*. By dint of shifting their point of view to make it accord with that of whomsoever they are affecting to judge, coupled with their historical fatalism, they have arrived at the annihilation of all moral distinctions except *success* and *not success*.—The "Soirées de Neuilly"[13] mentioned by that "English in France" man,[14] I have, & admire it much as a literary work; it also paints, as I believe correctly, some of the aspects of French life under the restoration. But above all, to have a notion of French life as it is, you should get hold of the "Livre des cent et un".[15] It professes to be a description of Paris under all its aspects; & as all the French writers of the day who are deemed fit to write in it, do so, it must be instructive even if the 101 have painted nothing but the state of their own minds. Then I have various St Simonian docu-

8. An edition was included in the Berville-Barrière *Collection.*

9. See Letter 61, n. 7.

10. L. B. Picard, *Le Gil Blas de la révolution* (5 vols., Paris, 1824).

11. G. C. A. Pigault-Le Brun (1753–1835), novelist and playwright.

12. Carlyle had commented on Thiers' ethics: "He will prove to you that the power to have done a thing almost (if not altogether) gave you the right to do it: every hero of his turns out to be perfectly justified in doing whatsoever—he has succeeded in doing" (A. Carlyle, p. 34).

13. [H. A. Cavé and A. Dittmer], *Les Soirées de Neuilly, esquisses dramatiques et historiques, publiées par M. de Fongeray* (Paris, 1827).

14. See Letter 64, n. 3.

15. *Paris; ou le livre des cent-et-un* (15 vols., Paris, 1831–34).

ments to send to you. The society is broken up, & a large portion including Duveyrier and d'Eichthal is at Naples: Duveyrier and Stéphane [Flachat?][16] are now editing a daily paper. I will send you Duveyr[ier's][17] letter to me on the subject, which is a very odd one. He professes not to have changed a single opinion, and yet he admits that his whole line of conduct is changed. Those of the St Simonians who retain their connexion with the Pere Suprême and with each other, have made themselves *prolètaires* and gone off in a body to Lyons to work on the canals and railroads. Enfantin & Michel Chevalier are in prison. Bazard, I think I told you, is dead. The writers in the Revue Encyclopédique have retained all or nearly all that was good in the *doctrines* of the St Simonians, & now content themselves with *prophesying* a new religion. Latterly some of them seem to be looking out for it in a strange enough quarter—the East—they think that as the East only partially known, has given us something so good as the Bible, when we know it perfectly it will give us something infinitely better. This seems to me a stranger delusion than even Fourier's.—Do you know anything of the writings of somebody who writes everywhere & on all subjects and signs *Junius Redivivus*?[18] probably you only know what he has written in the Examiner, which are chiefly radical personalities and good for very little; but the man has great worth in him, & I should like to send to you various productions of his. He takes so much pains to conceal his name and properties, that he is probably some obscure person who thinks that the disclosure of his obscurity would diminish, not increase, the attention paid to his writings. You should know him however, as far as he can be known from his writings, for I am sure he would interest you more than most people would.—I know something of Miss Martineau[19] personally: her books, some of them at least, deserve I think all the praise they have received: I suspect all the good in her, comes out in them. She is about thirty, bred a "Socinian liberal," and I believe substantially so still: *narrow*, and *matter-of-fact* I should say, in the bad sense; the best about her, being indefatigable industry and a ravenous thirst for knowledge & *acquirement* of all kinds, at least all intellectual kinds. Brougham[20] has been taking pains to attach her to his car, and has paid so many attentions to her that for the present he has spoiled her: she will, however I think, end by finding him out. She has, I find, the faculty of making herself

16. Writing barely legible. Probably Stéphane Mony [until 1832, Mony-Flachat] (1810–1884), engineer and politician.

17. Covered by seal.

18. See Letter 60.

19. Harriet Martineau (1802–1876), had leaped into instant fame in Feb., 1832, with the publication of the first tale of her *Illustrations of Political Economy*.

20. Henry Brougham, Baron Brougham and Vaux (1778–1868), then Lord Chancellor.

personally disliked, by means it would seem of inattention to Christ's percept "judge not, that ye be not judged."

I hoped to have found your Diderot in the pre[sent][21] Foreign Quarterly, but was disappointed. I myself have written little, published nothing except some matters on a property tax, which you will have seen in the Examiner.[22] Meanwhile my time, though I can scarcely say it has been *employed*, has not been wasted; something either good or bad will come of it—let us hope the best.

I have not received those books yet—at all events the loss must be mine, not yours, as it could in no way have been averted by you—perhaps, though that is little to the purpose, it *might* by *me*, had I not delayed so long making any enquiry at Longman's. I have little news of anybody. The Austins are in their usual state—Austin lecturing to six or seven persons only, but those of a *kind* he likes. This strange Wittenagemote calling itself a reformed parliament is just meeting, & we are to see what it is to do: all that seems certain is, that it is to reform the Church—heaven bless the mark! where, I wonder, will they find a Church to reform. —Buller is by this time in town, but I have not seen him: did you recognize a letter of his in The Examiner respecting election petitions?[23] there will be another tomorrow on the private business of the House[24]—good symptoms —he *can* work if he chuses, *well*, & I will hope that he will.

Write again soon, in spite of the slackness of my correspondence—I do not want any of those books[25] and shall not, for a long time to come—keep them therefore as long as you like or till a convenient opportunity offers for sending them. Commend me to Mrs Carlyle, and believe me

Ever faithfully yours,

J. S. MILL

I have been reading Bourrienne[26]—it gives one a much more distinct idea of Napoleon than I had before: but I still cannot, with you, allow the one excellence strength of will, to outweigh the entire want of any virtuous purpose, and the willingness to employ any even the most paltry means.[27]

21. Page torn.
22. "Necessity of Revising the Present System of Taxation," *Examiner*, Jan. 13, 1833, pp. 19–20; and "Errors and Truths on a Property Tax," *ibid.*, Jan. 27, 1833, pp. 51–52.
23. See Letter 64, n. 22.
24. "Internal Reforms in the Commons," *Examiner*, Feb. 3, 1833, pp. 67–68.
25. See Letter 64, par. 2, and Carlyle's reply of Jan 12, 1833.
26. L. A. Fauvelet de Bourrienne, *Mémoire . . . sur Napoléon* (10 vols., Paris, 1829).
27. This paragraph is written at the side of the letter.

68. TO WILLIAM TAIT[1]

India House
28 February 1833

MY DEAR SIR

I send you a paper on Junius Redivivus,[2] for your Magazine, in case you think it worthy of insertion.

By the same opportunity I send a copy of a tract of mine on a topic of great immediate interest[3]—I add another copy which I will thank you to forward to Mr Nichol when you have an opportunity.

Many thanks for the trouble you took about the Professorship.[4] Nobody in this country has been heard of whose claims are at all equal to those of Mr Nichol. When I have anything definite to communicate—I will write to that gentleman direct.

Believe me
My dear Sir
Ever sincerely yours
J. S. MILL

69. TO WILLIAM JOHNSON FOX[1]

India House
Friday [March 1, 1833]

DEAR MR FOX

I *will* write a short paper for the next M.R. on Junius Redivivus.[2]

That article on Mehetabel Wesley[3] is very painful—as it ought to be—but beautiful and valuable, beyond anything that I have read either in the M.R. or elsewhere for many, many months. It is a good number, altogether, though the *first* article[4] is, I think, the weakest. You seem to me to over-

1. MS at LSE.
2. See Letter 60, n. 2.
3. His article, "Corporation and Church Property," *Jurist*, IV (Feb., 1833), 1–26, which was reprinted as a separate pamphlet by S. Sweet, Stevens and Son, and A. Maxwell, Oxford. A copy is in the library of Somerville College, Oxford.
4. See Letter 65, n. 1.

* * * *

1. *Addressed*: Rev. W. J. Fox / 1 Stamford Grove / Upper Clapton. *Postmarks*: [???]4 / MR 1 / 1833 /, and Leadenhall St. MS at King's. Excerpts published in Garnett, pp. 104 and 114.
2. "Writings of Junius Redivivus," *MR*, VII (April, 1833), 262–70.
3. [W. J. Fox], "A Victim" [John Wesley's sister], *MR*, VII (March, 1833), 164–77.
4. "On the Factory System," *MR*, VII (March, 1833), 145–53. Of uncertain authorship, but possibly by Fox.

praise Leigh Hunt[5]—I say *you*, that is, I assume that you are the writer, partly for that reason—I think you often overpraise, & the cause is, the keen sense of enjoyment which all things give you, that have *anything* of good or beautiful in them. *I* have fallen under the same accusation but for an opposite reason—the *best* gave me so little enjoyment compared with what it should give, that I could not afford *not* to like, even things which were very imperfect indeed.

That at least is over—I have grown excessively fastidious now.

I got home by one o'clock the other night—thanks to an accidental meeting with a cab at the beginning of Islington.

Ever yours faithfully

J. S. MILL.

70. TO THOMAS CARLYLE[1]

India House, 9th March 1833.

MY DEAR CARLYLE

I *ought* to write oftener; though not exactly for the reason you jocularly give. I ought; and I would, if my letters were, or could be, better worth having: yet, even such as they are, not being altogether valueless to you, they shall become more frequent. Truly I do not wonder that you should desiderate more "heartiness" in my letters,[2] and should complain of being told my thoughts only, not my feelings; especially when, as is evident from your last letter, you stand more than usually in need of the consolation and encouragement of sympathy. But alas! when I give my thoughts, I give the best I have. You wonder at "the boundless capacity Man has of loving"—boundless indeed it is in *some* natures, immeasurable and inexhaustible: but *I* also wonder, judging from myself, at the limitedness and even narrowness of that capacity in *others*. That seems to me the only really insuperable calamity in life; the only one which is not conquerable by the power of a strong will. It seems the eternal barrier between man and man; the natural and impassable limit both to the happiness and to the

5. [W. J. Fox], "The Poetical Works of Leigh Hunt," *MR*, VII (March, 1833), 178–84.

* * * *

1. *Addressed*: Thomas Carlyle Esq. / 18 Carlton Street / Stockbridge / Edinburgh. *Postmarks*: FREE / 11 [? ? ?] 11 / 183[3], and MAR / H 13 A / 1833. Franked by E. Strutt. MS at NLS. Published, with minor errors, in Elliot, I, 37–42. In reply to Carlyle's letter of Feb. 22, 1833, A. Carlyle, pp. 37–41; answered by Carlyle, March 21, 1833, A. Carlyle, pp. 42–45.

2. "Write to me, I pray you, with more and more heartiness; show me your feelings as well as your thoughts; and let us in all ways, while so much is permitted us, help one another as we can" (A. Carlyle, p. 37).

spiritual perfection of (I fear) a large majority of our race. But few, whose power of either giving or receiving good in any form through that channel, is so scanty as mine, are so painfully conscious of that scantiness as a *want* and an imperfection: and being thus conscious I am in a higher, though a less happy, state, than the self-satisfied *many* who have my wants without my power of appreciation. You speak of obstacles which exist for others, but not for me. There are many of Earth's noblest beings, with boundless capacity of love, whom the falseness and halfness which you speak of, have so hemmed round and so filled with distrust and fear that "they *dare* not love". But mine is a trustful nature, and I have an unshakeable faith in others though not in myself. So my case must be left to Nature, I fear: there is no mind-physician who can prescribe for me, not even you, who could help whosoever is helpable: I can do nothing for myself, and others can do nothing for me; all the advice which can be given, (and *that* is not easily *taken*) is, not to beat against the bars of my iron cage; it is hard to have no aspiration and no reverence but for an Ideal towards which *striving* is of no use: is there not something very pitiful in *idle* Hoping? but to be without Hope were worse?

You see it is cold comfort which I can give to any who need the greatest of comforts, sympathy in moments of dejection; I, who am so far from being in better mental health than yourself, that I need sympathy quite as much, with the added misfortune that if I had it, it could do me no good. When you knew me in London I was in circumstances favourable to your mistaking my character, and judging of it far too advantageously: it was a period of fallacious calm; grounded in an extravagant over-estimate of what I had succeeded in accomplishing for myself, and an unconscious self-flattery and self-worship. All *that* is at an end; which is a "progress" surely. I would not now take the greatest human felicity on such terms.

But this is enough for the present, in this strain; perhaps I may say more another time. Let me rather think of *you*, and what can be done to improve *your* environment. Your picture of Edinburgh is *triste* enough, and might serve, I fear, *a fortiori*, for all other provincial towns: there is an *odour* of literature and intellect about Edinburgh; at Glasgow, Liverpool, & the like, there is little else than the *stench* of Trade. London is better; far better; bad though even *it* be. There are here, in infinitesimal *proportion* indeed, but in absolute *number* more than a very few, actual *believers* some, whom I and even *you* could call *true* believers; to a very great extent, or entirely: among whom your thoughts would not fall like hand-grenades and put them to flight, but would at least be caught up and cherished, probably planted and reared into fruit. If you determine to leave Craigenputtock, there is surely no place so good as this; at least in the most important of all good things which locality can bring—kindred companionship. But you will have more things to consider, doubtless, than even that greatest of all, and you will not give *that* less than its proper weight.

I have no news to tell—the Reformed Parliament has not disappointed me any more than you; it is (as Miss Martineau, I understand, says of Brougham) so ridiculously like what I expected: but some of our Utilitarian Radicals are downcast enough, having deemed that the nation had in it more of wisdom and virtue than they now see it has, and that the vicious state of the representation kept this wisdom & virtue out of parliament. At least this good will come out of their disappointment, that they will no longer rely upon the infallibility of Constitution-mongering: they admit that we have as good a House of Commons as *any* mode of election would have given us, in the present state of cultivation of our people. They are digging a little nearer to the root of the evil now, though they have not got to the *tap*-root: read Roebuck's paper on National Education in Tait's last number;[3] while you have the number in your hand, look at the *first* article[4] in it, which is his also. He is narrow, still, but the other parliamentary radicals are narrower; all but our friend Charles [Buller], who has the finest understanding of the set, but wants strength of *will.* For myself, I have well-nigh ceased to feel interested in politics. The time is not yet come for renovation, and the work of destruction goes on of itself without the aid of hands. If any man of clear Insight were in parliament just now, I hardly know what he could hope or aim at, unless to sow in some few of the more impressible minds, the seeds of a renovation which will not be yet, nor soon. The Bad, God wot, is tumbling down quite as fast as is safe where there is nothing of Good ready to be put into its place: what need of help in rolling the ball down hill? I was wont to think that the benches of the House of Commons might be as a pulpit, from whence a voice might make itself heard further and more widely than even from *your* pulpit and mine, the Periodical Press. But what sort of a voice must it be which could be heard through all this din: what were a single nightingale amidst the cawing and chattering of 657 rooks and magpies and jackdaws? Truly if there were not in the world two or three persons who seem placed here only to shew that *all* is not hollow and empty and insufficient, one would despair utterly. It is only the knowledge that such persons have an actual existence on the sa[me globe][5] with us, which keeps alive any interest in anything besides oneself, or even could I but *believe* that the good I see in a few comes not from any peculiarity of nature, but from the more perfect developement of capacities and powers common

3. "National Education," *Tait's*, II (March, 1833), 755–65.
4. "The Reformed Parliament," *ibid.*, pp. 685–88.
5. Page torn. This is Elliot's reading.

to us all—and that the whole race were destined, at however remote a period either of individual or collective existence, to resemble the best specimen of it whom I have myself known—I verily believe, with that faith, I could be content to remain to eternity the solitary exception—

As for *work,* I have written perhaps of late not less than usual: but (except what has been already mentioned to you) nothing noteworthy that is likely to be soon published, except a notice[6] for Tait of that book of Junius Redivivus, which same book you will soon receive in a parcel through Fraser; along with two articles of mine which I have formerly written to you about; sundry Memoirs of the French Revolution; the Trial of the St Simonians; & two letters which contain all I know of their subsequent proceedings & present state. (Those former books which miscarried have been traced to this house, though I have not been able to recover them.) My parcel for you at present waits only for William Fraser's permission to send you his copy of Levasseur's Memoirs:[7] a permission too late applied for, & which has not yet reached me.—Junius Redivivus will interest you, were it only for this, that *he* too is evidently a believer: a *true* believer I think it may be said, so far as his faith has yet reached. There is vigour, & a capacity of Insight in him; & if we may judge from the quantity he writes (the quality being never positively bad, & often very good), an altogether indomitable power of work.—I have seen nothing of *your* writing for a long time: Cochrane, I see, has not yet printed your paper on Diderot; when shall we see it? deeply interesting it is sure to be.—You know something of Fraser's Magazine: do you know, or can you guess, the authorship of a recent paper on Byron?[8] it looks like the production of some half-fledged pupil of yours.

I have asked an instructed and clever Frenchman now here (one of the editors of the *National*) about the authenticity of those revolutionary portraits;[9] to which I also am no stranger. He tells me that the genuineness of many of them is very doubtful, and without any hint from me he at once instanced Danton; some of whose relations he knows, and has seen an authentic portrait. Danton he says was ugly, but not ignoble, either in mind or feature, and the portrait in the Collection wrongs him grievously.

As you conjectured, I have lost sight of poor Glen: only because I am

6. See Letters 60, n. 2, and 66, n. 2.

7. See Letter 67, n. 6.

8. "Critical Illustrations of Lord Byron's Poetry," *Fraser's*, VII (March, 1833), 303–17. Carlyle subsequently guessed that it was by John A. Heraud (1799–1887), poet and dramatist. Miriam M. H. Thrall in *Rebellious Fraser's* (New York, 1934), p. 267, attributes the article to Heraud and comments on its Carlylian tone and ideas.

9. Carlyle had written: "A series of Revolution Portraits (engravings) which I dug out lately, gave me great satisfaction: under each head stands, in a miniature compartment, the main scene he figured in: it is a valuable work, if genuine" (A. Carlyle, p. 40).

utterly ignorant of his place of abode: at his old lodgings they believe him to be still in Scotland, with his brother and such other relatives as he may have. I therefore know not what to do with your letter: poor fellow, it would have gladdened him to the very bottom of his soul to have received it, or but to have known that you had written to him: you probably have better means of discovering his whereabout in Scotland than I have.— Of our common friends or acquaintances I have little to tell. Austin is lecturing to fit audience though few, & will, I think, very probably go to live either at Berlin or at Bonn. He is still subject to his fits of illness, but they are I think less frequent. Mrs Austin is very much as usual: Falk is not yet through the press. The Bullers are all in London. I fear they have lost money by failures in India, not enough to impoverish them, but *any* loss falls heavily on people who live up to their income.

Yours ever faithfully,

J. S. MILL

I have heard nothing of Detrosier[10] for a long time: I believe he has returned to Manchester with the intention of setting up a school, or else of continuing to go about lecturing on physical subjects as he did formerly with some success.[11]

Make my best remembrances to Mrs Carlyle—I sometimes hear of her through Mrs. Austin. I do not say, "write soon" but I know you *will*.[12]

71. TO WILLIAM TAIT[1]

India House
30th March 1833

MY DEAR SIR

I will immediately write to Mr Nichol[2] myself. The appointment of the Professor[3] is still, I understand, quite undetermined—Mr Nichol's letter to you went to France, with the recommendation of my father and Mr Senior.[4] I think he should decidedly make himself known in any way to Talleyrand,[5] whose opinion would have very great weight.

10. Rowland Detrosier (1800?–1834), who had been secretary to the London Political Union, had been introduced to Carlyle by JSM the previous year.

11. This is written at the top of the first page.

12. Written in the margin of the last page.

* * * *

1. *Addressed*: William Tait Esq / Bookseller / Edinburgh. *Postmarks*: SUN / MR 31 / 1833, and FREE / A 2 / 1833. Franked by G. Grote. MS at NLS.

2. John Pringle Nichol.

3. See Letter 65. n. 1.

4. Nassau William Senior (1790–1864), economist.

5. Charles Maurice de Talleyrand-Périgord, Prince de Bénévent (1754–1838), French statesman, at this time ambassador to England.

With respect to the article on Junius Redivivus,[6] I myself have not made up my mind on the question whether the situation of the working classes is on the whole better or worse than it was: I worded the article so as if possible not to commit the Magazine to a decided opinion, but I thought the testimony of a writer who evidently knows much of the working people, an article of evidence very fit to be received, though not sufficient to decide the question. Could not you let the article stand as it is, and express your dissent from the opinion of J.R. in an editorial note? If not, I should like to see the article again before it is printed; not from any fear that you should "spoil" the article, but because when anything is to be *left out*, a writer almost always thinks it necessary that something else should be *put in*.

As to the matter of fact in dispute I feel convinced from the great diversity of opinion among equally good observers, & from the result of the enquiries of the Poor Law Commission, that the truth *varies* very much in different parts of the kingdom & among different classes of workmen.

Are there any other parts of the article which you object to?

I am so little master of my own time, and so little capable moreover of writing with spirit on any subject in which I do not happen to be feeling an interest at the moment, that I do not ven[ture][7] to *promise* to write at any given time on a given subject. As for Currency, I think it is blowing over—with regard to France I am so thoroughly *sick* of the wretched aspect of affairs there that I have written little about them in the Examiner for a long time.

Believe me
Most truly yours
J. S. MILL.

72. TO THOMAS CARLYLE[1]

India House 11th & 12th April 1833

MY DEAR CARLYLE

I write to you again a letter which I could wish were better worth having —*really* an apology for a letter: Your last, which you *called* so, deserved a better name. I would write, if it were only to thank you for having a better opinion of me than I have of myself. It is useless discussing which

6. See Letters 60, n. 2, and 66.

7. Page torn.

* * * *

1. *Addressed*: Thomas Carlyle Esq / 4 Great King St / Edinburgh. *Postmarks*: FREE / 13 AP 13 / 1833, and APR / C 15 A / 1833. Franked by G. Grote. MS at NLS. Published in part in Elliot, I, 42–46. In reply to Carlyle's letter of March 21, 1833, A. Carlyle, pp. 42–45; answered by Carlyle, April 18, 1833, A. Carlyle, pp. 45–52.

is right; time will disclose that; though I do not think that my nature is one of the many things into which you see "some ten years farther" than I do. At all events I will not if I can help it give way to gloom and morbid despondency, of which I have had a large share in my short life, and to which I have been indebted for all the most valuable of such insight as I have into the most important matters, neither will this return of it be without similar fruits, as I hope and almost believe; nevertheless I will and must, though it leaves me little enough of energy, master it, or it will surely master me. Whenever it has come to me it has always lasted many months, and has gone off in most cases very gradually.

I have allowed myself to be paralysed more than I should, during the last month or two by these gloomy feelings, though I have had intervals of comparative brightness but they were short. I have therefore a poor account to render of work done. Tait has not yet published that paper on Junius Redivivus, but in the meantime I have written another on the same subject for Fox, (a much better one as I think), which has appeared in the April number,[2] and should have been sent if I had got it in time for Fraser's parcel: you shall have it by the first opportunity. With this exception I have written little, and read less: but this shall have an end.

You will have received long before this time by Fraser, two tracts of mine, of very different kinds, a political or rather ethico-political one on Church & Corporation Property,[3] and the one I told you of, long ago, in Fox's periodical, on Poetry and Art.[4] That last you promised me a careful examination and criticism of: I need it much; for I have a growing feeling that I have not got quite into the heart of that mystery, and I want you to shew me how. If you do not teach me you will do what is better, put me in the way of finding out. But I begin to see a not very far distant boundary to all I am qualified to accomplish in *this* particular line of speculation. I have sent you fewer books than I thought I should have had to send: three volumes of Levasseur, the fourth I have read but Fraser has not yet got it: I shall put it into some future parcel. Of the proportion in which this book is the work of Levasseur himself, and the proportion in which it is got up by Achille Roche[5] the editor, one of the clever young political journalists of the day, I know no more than the book itself indicates, which does not seem to aim at concealing anything. The Soirées de Neuilly[6] I have lent to somebody and omitted to take the precaution of making a memorandum, so I have not been able to get it for this parcel. I have sent two volumes of Memoirs on the Prisons which

2. See Letter 60, n. 2.

3. See Letter 68, n. 3.

4. See Letter 64, n. 11.

5. Achille Roche (1801–1834), revolutionary journalist. Roche was fined and jailed in 1830 for writing Vol. II by himself. See Letter 67, n. 6.

6. This and the next two titles are identified in the notes to Letter 67.

I have not read; & another volume in which the only thing of value is the Vieux Cordelier by Camille Desmoulins. The account of Robespierre & the others by Villatte[7] is, I believe, worthy of no regard: he was one of the instruments of their tyranny, wrote this book after their fall in hopes of getting himself off, and I believe was guillotined after all. I have also sent the Trial of the St Simonians, a letter from d'Eichthal, & one from Duveyrier. I have lately heard again, both from, and *of*, the latter. He is now writing, in the Revue des deux Mondes, which he says is the first in France in the department of literature and art, & to which a number of their most celebrated writers, so far as any of their writers can be called celebrated, contribute. He writes to me "je me lance décidément dans le drame et le théâtre. Je fais une grande pièce, mais comme cela ne fait pas vivre pour le moment je cherche à gagner mon pain courrant par quelques articles de journaux. J'ai quelqu'espoir d'avoir à la revue des deux mondes où j'ai beaucoup d'amis, la fonction de rediger la chronique de quinzaine politique et théâtrale. En attendant je n'entends plus parler de d'Eichthal, qui est toujours en Italie." What I have heard of Duveyrier is, that being condemned to a year's imprisonment along with Enfantin & Chevalier, he applied through his relations for a pardon from the government, & obtained it, I suppose by declaring his intention of quitting the Father of Humanity. This I heard from a friend of his.—Such part of the St Simonians as remain faithful, or at least a large body of them headed by Barrault,[8] have as I find from the French newspapers, set out for the East (Constantinople I was told was their first destination) *pour chercher la femme libre*. This seems greater madness than I had imputed to them. It is among the inmates of a harem that they expect to find a woman capable of laying down or as they say *revealing* the new moral law which is to regulate the relations between the sexes! it will be lucky for them if the search is attended with no disagreeable personal consequences to them except only that of not finding. These St Simonians have done so much good, that one regrets they were not capable of doing more. One of the seceding members writes of them in the Revue Encyclopédique that the St Simonian society is the only spiritual fruit of the Revolution of 1830: it is literally so: the excessive avidity & barrenness of the French mind has never been so strikingly displayed: there are such numbers of talkers & writers so full of noise and fury, keeping it up for years and years, and not one new thought, new to *them* I mean, has been struck out by all the collision since I first began attending to these matters, except only those which the St Simonians have set afloat among them. It is no wonder that minds so little *productive*

7. [Joachim Vilate], *Causes secrètes de la révolution du 9 au 10 thermidor an II* . . . (Paris, [2 vols., 1795]). Also in Berville-Barrière *Collection*, in *Le Vieux Cordelier* volume.

8. Emile Barrault.

as the French should run wild with an interesting truth when they have had it impressed upon them. St Simon really for a Frenchman was a great man. Enfantin likewise *pourrait bien être aussi une espèce de grand homme* as Voltaire said: the others were probably mere redactors and amplifiers of *their* thoughts, a talent as common in France, as the power of original thinking seems to be rare.—If you can get hold of it at Edinburgh, read a novel called Arthur Coningsby,[9] by John Sterling: he is one of the men who would most interest you among those here; and his book will interest you; I should much like to know what it looks like when seen from your point of view.

Though I am sick of politics myself, I do not despair of improvement that way; *you* hear the cackle of the noisy geese who surround the building, *I* see a little of what is going on inside. I can perfectly sympathize in Bonaparte's contempt of the government of *bavards*: talking is one thing and *doing* another: but while every corner of the land has sent forth its noisy blockhead to talk, over head I am near enough to see the real men of *work*, and of head for work, who are quietly getting the working part of the machine into their hands, and will be masters of it as far as anybody can be with that meddling and ignorant assembly lawfully empowered to be *their* masters. After that let even *one* man come, who with honesty, & intellect to appreciate these *working* men, has the power of leading a mob, —no rare combination formerly, though a very rare one now; and there will be as good a government as there *can* be until there shall be a better people. It is a real satisfaction to me to know, & in some cases to have even been able somewhat to help on, several men who are now gaining by dint of real honesty & capacity a considerable and increasing influence though not an externally visible one, over the underworkings of our government. Some of them are as I am convinced, among the very fittest persons in the country to have that influence, fit or not as they may be in a greater or less degree for still higher purposes. *A chacun selon sa capacité* is far enough from being realised, to be sure, but the *real* deviation great as it is, falls far short of the *apparent*. It is much more in their apparent than in their real power that such men as Brougham and Althorp[10] are exalted above their proper station.

Fonblanque you see goes on hammering at the politics of the day, for better for worse: I have seen less than usual of him lately. The public mind is coming round to him: the popularity of the Reform Ministry will soon be at as low an ebb as that of the poor Patriot King. How long is this dreary work to last, before a *man* appears? Mrs. Austin is at present laid up with

9. Published anonymously (3 vols., London, 1833).

10. John Charles Spencer, Viscount Althorp and later third Earl Spencer (1782–1845), Whig political leader.

the prevalent influenza, a sort of cold accompanied with fever: she and her husband seem to have almost resolved to emigrate into Germany this autumn. The Bullers are here: Charles has gone the Western Circuit this spring, and got some briefs: I have increasing hopes of his steadiness and power of work. I have little to tell of any one else whom you know here. Is De Quincey still in Edinburgh? do you ever see him? and what do you think of him?[11] Your criticism on Miss Martineau is, I think, just: she reduces the *laissez faire* system to absurdity as far as the *principle* goes, by merely carrying it out to all its consequences. In the meantime that principle like other negative ones has work to do yet, work, namely, of a destroying kind, & I am glad to think it has strength left to finish that, after which it must soon expire: peace be with its ashes when it does expire, for I doubt much if it will reach the resurrection. I wish you could see something I have written lately about Bentham & Benthamism[12]—but you can't.

My best thanks to Mrs Carlyle for the few words of kindness she added to your last letter—I keep so little note of time that I know not whether I have redeemed my promise of writing after a less interval than usual—but you will write soon.—

Yours ever faithfully

J. S. MILL

I should have availed myself of the opportunity you afforded me to make acquaintance with Leigh Hunt, did I not find it absolutely necessary, if I mean either to *work* or to enjoy society, to restrict rather than to extend the number of my acquaintance. He is worth knowing, and a time may come for that among other things.—Have you seen Archibald Alison's History of the French Revolution?[13] If you have, just tell me whether it is worth reading, or reviewing—I suppose it is wrong, when one has taken the trouble to accumulate knowledge on a subject, not to work it up if one can into some shape useful to others—and if I am to write about the F.R. it may as well be while my recollections of the original authorities are fresh.[14]

J.S.M.

11. Thomas De Quincey (1785–1859), author of *The Confessions of an English Opium Eater*. In his reply of April 18 Carlyle described De Quincey as "bankrupt in purse, and as nearly as possible in mind. . . . one of the most irreclaimable Tories now extant" (in A. Carlyle, p. 48). Years later JSM reviewed favourably De Quincey's *Logic of Political Economy* in *WR*, XLIII (June, 1845), 318–31.

12. "Remarks on Bentham's Philosophy," published anonymously as an Appendix in E. L. Bulwer's *England and the English* (Paris, 1833), pp. 468–89. See Letter 82.

13. Sir Archibald Alison, *History of Europe during the French Revolution* (10 vols., Edinburgh, 1833–42). JSM criticized the first two volumes severely in *MR*, VII (July–Aug., 1833) 507–11, 513–16. The second instalment of the review he reprinted in *Dissertations*, I, 82–88.

14. This postscript is written at the top of the first page.

73. TO THOMAS CARLYLE[1]

India House 18th May 1833

MY DEAR CARLYLE

By this time you are again in your wilds,[2] and have had time to feel yourselves at home and settled there, and you are expecting a letter from me—and I have *two* to acknowledge and if so might be to repay. I have many things to say, too; at least they seem many before I begin to say them; they will seem few before I have done.—First, then, I have read your paper on Diderot.[3] Of the man, and of his works and of his cotemporaries, so far as I think at all, I think very much as you do: yet I have found more to differ from in that article of yours than in anything of *your* writing I commonly do. The subject seems to have carried you, and me as your reader, over a range of topics on which there has always been a considerable extent of undiscussed and unsifted divergence of opinion (pardon this *galimatias* of mixed metaphors) between us two; on some of which too I sometimes think that the distance has rather widened than narrowed of late. That may be *my* loss, and my fault; at all events it seems to me that there has been on my part something like a want of courage in avoiding, or touching only perfunctorily, with you, points on which I thought it likely that we should differ. That was a kind of reaction from the dogmatic disputatiousness of my former narrow and mechanical state. I have not any great notion of the advantage of what the "free discussion" men, call the "collision of opinions," it being my creed that Truth is *sown* and germinates in the mind itself, and is not to be struck *out* suddenly like fire from a flint by knocking another hard body against it: so I accustomed myself to *learn* by inducing others to deliver their thoughts, and to teach by scattering my own, and I eschewed occasions of controversy (except occasionally with some of my old Utilitarian associates). I still think I was right in the main, but I have carried both my doctrine and my practice much too far: and this I know by one of its consequences which I suppose would be an agreeable one to most men, viz. that most of those whom I at all esteem and respect, though they may know that I do not agree with them *wholly*, yet, I am afraid, think, each in their several ways, that I am considerably *nearer* to agreeing with them than I actually am. In short, I know that I

1. *Addressed*: Thomas Carlyle Esq / Craigenputtoch / Dumfries / N.B. *Postmarks*: FREE / 18 MY 18 / 1833, and DUMFRIES / 20 MAY 1833. Franked by G. Grote. MS at NLS. Published, with minor errors and omissions, in Elliot, I, 47–51. In reply to Carlyle's letters of April 18 and May 1, 1833, A. Carlyle, pp. 45–54; answered by Carlyle, June 13, 1833, A. Carlyle, 54–60.

2. The Carlyles had returned from Edinburgh to Craigenputtock in early May.

3. See Letter 61, n. 23.

have been wrong, by finding myself seated in the Gig[4] much more firmly than I have any business as an honest man to be. So you see, I am only *about* to have in all its fullness, that sincerity of speech for which you give me credit. I only had it thus far hitherto, that all I have ever spoken, by word of mouth or in writing, I have firmly *believed*, and have spoken it solely *because* it was my belief. Yet even that, in these days, was much, but not enough, seeing that it depends upon my own will to make it more. —The result of all which is that with you as well as with several others very unlike you, there will probably be a more frequent and free communication of *dissent* than has hitherto been, even though the consequence should be to be lowered in your opinion; *that* indeed if it were to be the result would be conclusive proof that I have been acting wrong hitherto, because it would shew that for being thought so highly of I had been partly indebted to not being thoroughly known—which I am sure is the case oftener than I like to think of.

You see there will be so much the more to talk over when we meet: and that will be this summer, unless, which is always possible, I should not be in a state of mind in which meeting with *any* one is profitable or delightful to me. I believe I am the least *helpable* of mortals—I have always found that when I am in any difficulty or perplexity of a spiritual kind I must struggle out of it by myself. I believe, if I could, whenever anything is spiritually wrong with me I should shut myself up from the human race, and not see face of man until I had got firm footing again on some solid basis of conviction, and could turn what comes into me from others into wholesome nutriment. I am often in a state almost of scepticism, and have no theory of Human Life at all, or seem to have conflicting theories, or a theory which does not amount to a Belief. This is only a *recent* state, and as I well know, a passing one, and my convictions will be firmer and the result of a larger experience when I emerge from this state, than before: but I have never found any advantage in communion with others while my own mind was unsettled at its foundations, and if I am not much mended when my vacation-time comes round, I will rather postpone a meeting with you until I am.

I have neither written nor read much since I last wrote to you, except one or two trifling things in the Examiner: including however one of a somewhat more weighty kind (though not much) which you will see in a week or two probably in that paper, under my old signature A.B.[5] I think I shall write more now, because I begin to see some things a little clearer, though many things which I once thought I understood—I now believe cannot be known with true Insight but by means of faculties which cannot

4. One of Carlyle's favourite symbols for conventional respectability. At the trial of John Thurtell in 1824 a witness testified that he had thought the accused murderer respectable because he kept a gig.

5. No such article seems to have appeared in the *Examiner* from May to July.

be acquired and which to me have not been given, save in most scanty measure. Alison's book which I asked you about, I have procured and read: the man is quite inconceivably stupid and twaddling, I think beyond anybody who has attempted to write elaborately on the subject. He has no research; the references with which he loads his margin are chiefly to compilations. I could write something about him or rather about his subject; but I could employ myself better unless there were some widely-circulated periodical that would publish it:[6] the Edinburgh Review perhaps would, were it not that I should wish to shew up Macaulay's ignorance of the subject and assumption of knowledge, as shewn in that very review.[7]

The long-missing parcel of books has at length turned up, and I have received intimation that the second is at Longman's. I did not mean you to return those Repositories, but they are not, to *you*, worth my sending back again. Keep all I send you henceforth. On learning that my parcel was not in time for Fraser's monthly packet, (which I thought I had taken care that it should be) I sent two more numbers of the Repository to be added to it, in one of which is the article I told you of, concerning Junius Redivivus. The passage you saw quoted about Books and Men, was from that; so there is not evidence therein of "another mystic"; so much the worse.[8] I was much interested by learning that *your* recent thoughts have been so nearly of the same kind; tell me what you have thought *since*, especially since you have thought of the question *practically*, as altering your own future choice of a mode of activity. The difficulty of comparing two magnitudes and distinguishing which is greatest, is as we all know, vastly enhanced when the magnitudes themselves are of almost infinitesimal smallness, and that unhappily seems to be the case at present with the portion of good, that one can see clearly a prospect of achieving in *any* course that one can chuse. Yet it seems to me that if one had a proper stage and proper tools, more is to be accomplished just now by the doer of the deed than by the sayer of the word—words are so little listened to now but when they are the prelude or the accompaniment to some deed; *my* word again is partly intelligible to many more persons than yours is, because mine is presented in the logical and mechanical form which partakes most of this age and country, yours in the artistical and poetical (at least in one sense of those words though not the sense I have been recently giving them) which finds *least* entrance into any minds now, except when it comes before them as mere dilettantism and pretends not to make any serious call upon them

6. See preceding letter, n. 13.

7. Macaulay's review of Dumont's *Recollections of Mirabeau* in *ER*, LV (July, 1832), 552–76.

8. Carlyle had written: "Yesterday in some newspaper I saw a sentence quoted from the *Monthly Repository* about Books and Men, which was curiously emblematic of my own late thoughts. If it was not you that wrote it (which I fear) then there must be another Mystic in England, whose acquaintance I should gladly make." (A. Carlyle, p. 53.)

to change their lives. But then, what career is open to the *doer*, if either in your position or in mine? write to me what has been passing in you on this matter, whether of a general kind or as affecting yourself individually.

I am sure I have twenty other things to say, but cannot think of them at this instant; I shall write again the sooner. Let me ask you this one question; Have you seen the book published by the Poor Law Commissioners?[9] If you have not, let me send it to you—often you have complained how little of the state of a people is to be learnt from books; *much* is to be learned of it from that book, both as to their physical and their spiritual state. The result is altogether appalling to the dilettanti, and the gigmen, and the ignorant and timid in high stations; to me it has been, & will be I think to you, rather consoling, because *we* knew the thing to be unspeakably bad, but this I think shews that it may be considerably mended with a considerably less amount of intellect, courage, and virtue in the higher classes, than had hitherto appeared to me to be necessary. Any way the book cannot fail to interest you, because *any* authentic *information* as to any human thing is interesting to you. I regard this enquiry with satisfaction under another aspect too; that it has been more honestly and more ably performed than anything which has been done under the authority of Govt. since I remember: and has, in consequence, been the means of getting some of the best men I know, for such purposes, put into other work of the same kind, and decidedly embarked in the same career. You will find among them my friend John Wilson whom you have seen; he is now Secretary to the Factory Commission. Chadwick also, the ablest of them all, may be said to be at the head of that Commission.

I know not of any news to tell. I have seen little of Fonblanque lately. The Austins are still bent upon going to live in Germany after the conclusion of his present course of Lectures. At the Literary Union I can learn no more of Glen than I knew before. Kindest remembrances to Mrs. Carlyle.[10]

Charles Buller is well, and in spirits, and increasingly disposed to work; he will not be lost, it were pity he should: his career will be politics I think, not the best career, far from that, but he will I now think, demean himself therein like a true man: his superiority to all those people is even *now*, little as he has yet done, beginning to be *felt*, and he is gaining influence which will enable him to utter such truth as is in him with some certainty of being listened to—he *is* pure-minded and not a self-seeker, I am sure of that.[11]

9. *Extracts from the Information Received by His Majesty's Commissioners as to the Administration and Operation of the Poor Laws* (London, 1833).

10. JSM's signature is not to be seen on this letter.

11. This paragraph is written at the top of the first page.

74. TO WILLIAM JOHNSON FOX[1]

India House
[18] May 1833

DEAR MR FOX

If there are any rumours that I was writing anything for the M.R. of this month, I am sorry I cannot confirm them. I have abundance of vague intentions of writing for you, but I have been very idle of late, and in fact never have been in a state more unfit for work; from various causes, the chief of which is, I think, a growing want of interest in all the subjects which I understand, and a growing sense of incapacity *ever* to have real knowledge of or insight into the subjects in which alone I shall ever again feel a strong interest. I have written nothing lately but a short article on that "Pauline",[2] which will not, I believe, be too long for the Examiner, and if so, will probably appear there.[3] *That* I have written chiefly because you wished it.[4] I fear there would scarcely be time to write anything which you would care for, now, this month, but if there is any subject within my range, on which you wish to have two or three pages only, tell me so and I will try what I can do.

I feel so unequal to any of the higher moral and aesthetic subjects, that because I would rather write something than nothing, I have had thoughts of offering you a few pages on a stupid book lately published by a man named Alison,[5] and pretending to be a history of the French Revolution. I am sick of that subject, but I could write something on it which perhaps would be of more use to the M.R. than something better would be—your having got over the "Unitarian storm"[6] with so little damage to the vessel is a real victory.

1. *Addressed*: Rev. W. J. Fox / 1 Stamford Grove / Upper Clapton. Dated 19 May but postmarked 7 NIGHT 7 / MY 18, and CORNHILL. MS at King's. Largely published in Garnett, pp. 103–4, 110.

2. [Robert Browning], *Pauline; a Fragment of a Confession* (London, 1833).

3. The *Examiner* would have none of it, and an enlarged version of it for *Tait's* was forestalled by a contemptuous brief notice (see Letter 83). JSM's liberally annotated review copy with a summary criticism written in the flyleaves, which Browning read on Oct. 30, 1833, is now in the Forster Collection of the Victoria and Albert Museum. Hayek, pp. 43–44, prints the criticism. It is commonly thought to have had crucial influence in turning Browning away from "confessional" to dramatic poetry. See W. C. DeVane, *A Browning Handbook* (2nd ed., New York, 1955), pp. 45–47.

4. Fox had become interested in Browning through his protégés Eliza and Sarah Flower, friends of the young poet from childhood. He reviewed both of Browning's first two publications enthusiastically. See Mineka, *The Dissidence of Dissent*, pp. 191–92, 308–13.

5. Archibald (later Sir Archibald) Alison (1792–1867), Tory historian. See Letters 72 and 73.

6. Evidently referring to the protest of orthodox Unitarians over the changes Fox was making in the *Monthly Repository*, until 1832 the official Unitarian organ. In

I knew not that you were to be in K.T.[7] on Wednesday, and I seldom go there without some special reasons on that day of the week, for as it cannot be right in present circumstances to be there *every* evening, none costs so little to give up as that in which there is a much shorter time and only in the presence of others. Had I known of your going I would have gone—as it is, I must take my compensation at Clapton—as I will very soon.

I *did* know the neighbourhood of Limpsfield—part of it at least—in my childhood, and have walked to it and about it since, but am not familiar with it. I do not know the particular walk you allude to, though your description enables me to conceive it almost as if I knew it. I mean to renew my acquaintance with Limpsfield, and cultivate it, and perfect it—that seems to me the only place on earth where it is possible to be happy—although it is you who have been there, and not I.—should I say *although*? and not rather *because*?

Does the Political Cyclopœdia[8] plan go on thrivingly? where in heaven and earth are you to find *writers*? It is very easy to find people who can write ill, but very difficult to collect together even one or two who can write well, especially when the purpose is didactic, not controversial.

Ever yours

J. S. Mill.

75. TO WILLIAM JOHNSON FOX[1]

India House
Monday
[May 20, 1833]

Dear Mr Fox

I am obliged to write in great haste, so I will only say this that I will write something on Alison[2] but *that* will be too late for this number—and that I will be with you at Clapton as soon as I am allowed by being off duty at

April, 1833, the Rev. Lant Carpenter of Bristol wrote to Fox protesting against the changes, but chiefly against the unorthodox views being advanced in the magazine on marriage and divorce. See Mineka, *The Dissidence of Dissent*, pp. 255–57.

7. Kent Terrace, home of Mrs. John Taylor, with whom by this time JSM was deeply involved.

8. No such work was published. This may have been a project of the unsuccessful Society for the Diffusion of Moral and Political Knowledge with which Fox was associated (see Letter 79, n. 7).

* * * *

1. *Addressed*: Rev. W. J. Fox / 1 Stamford Grove / Upper Clapton. *Postmark*: 7 NIGHT / MY 20 / 1833. MS at LSE.

2. See Letter 72, n. 13.

Kensington where my father whose sight is disabled for the present by inflammation, has need of me to read to him. He may have recovered by Wednesday, but at any rate I cannot *dine* with you for I shall not get away from this place early enough for that. *Au reste* I *will* come to you in a day or two whether he has recovered or not.

Yours ever

J. S. MILL

76. TO WILLIAM JOHNSON FOX[1]

I.H. [India House]
Wednesday
[June, 1833]

MY DEAR MR FOX

It is really not my fault that the French Revolution[2] is not yet completed; you shall have it, I think I may say, in two days at most. It will be a poor thing though—

As for *me*, I am going to K.T. [Kent Terrace] today, despite its being Wednesday. However meet we must, and soon too.

W.A.[3] *is* wrong, as Fonblanque was. I thought so from the first, & as soon as I found others thought differently, I made the matter sure by enquiry at the Colonial Office, from the highest authority (nearly) namely the head of the *West Indies* Department there.[4] He tells me (as I expected) that the slave is to pay *nothing* directly or indirectly towards his ransom. He is to be free ¼th now, & *entirely* in twelve years; & is not to be required to work for his master (or to work at all) during the ¼th nor is his master to be required to give him employment nor to pay him any rate of wages. So all commentary on the manifold absurdities & impossibilities of that part of the plan is useless now when it is abandoned.

I wrote a notice of "Pauline" for the Examiner which could not be inserted, & I am to alter & enlarge it for Tait.[5]

Yours faithfully

J. S. MILL.

1. *Addressed*: Rev. W. J. Fox / Upper Clapton. MS at King's. The date is established by the reference to JSM's review of Alison.

2. See Letter 72, n. 13.

3. Probably William Bridges Adams ("Junius Redivivus"), whose article "On the Ministerial Plan for the Abolition of Negro Slavery," appeared in *MR*, VII (July, 1833), 453–74.

4. Probably Henry Taylor (see Letter 51), though JSM also knew James Stephen, then counsel to the Colonial Office, later Under-Secretary for Colonies, who prepared the bill for abolishing the slave trade, 1833. See also Letter 80, n. 2.

5. See Letter 74, n. 2 and 3.

77. TO WILLIAM JOHNSON FOX[1]

India House
July 4, 1833

MY DEAR MR FOX

I am afraid I shall altogether forfeit all character with you for knowing my own mind or for telling it, by so constantly *talking* about going to see you, and never doing it. So I will not talk about it any more, but will do it all the sooner; & in the mean time I write to say how happy I shall be to bear my testimony to the Cause,[2] by maintaining it in the M.R. in the manner you propose, against the threatened attack. Of all propositions which could have been made to me for writing anything either in the M.R. or elsewhere, that is what I should like best—because it is the subject I am most interested in, and to be treated in the manner in which I think myself most equal to treating it. I have always done more justice to a subject when I have treated it controversially than when I have attempted a systematic exposition. I should not do for the pulpit, for I am always *cold* when I "have all the palaver to myself": and besides I always find most to say when I do not feel under an obligation to say all that *can* be said.

Pray let me know when I am to begin, that is, let me have the paper I am to reply to, as early as may be.

Yours ever faithfully

J. S. MILL

I think I have found out Pel Verjuice,[3] but I do not want to be told who he is—I like the new number of the M.R. very much, except the article on the education of women[4]—

1. *Addressed*: Rev. W. J. Fox / 1 Stamford Grove / Upper Clapton. *Postmarks*: 8 MORN [???] / JY [???], and 7 NIGHT 7 / JY [???] / 1833. MS at King's. Published in part in Garnett, pp. 104–5.

2. "Cause" against the existing system of taxation. An article, "Complaints & Proposals regarding Taxation," in the *Edinburgh Review*, complained of the gross injustice of having *progressive* house and window taxes. JSM rejected the claim of injustice in his "On the Defence of the House and Window Tax in the Edinburgh Review," *MR*, VII (Aug., 1833), 575–82.

3. The pseudonym of Charles Reece Pemberton (1790–1840), a frequent contributor to the *Monthly Repository*, which was at this time running serially his *Autobiography of Pel. Verjuice*. See Mineka, *The Dissidence of Dissent*, pp. 345–48, 420–21.

4. "On Female Education & Occupations," *MR*, VII (July, 1833), 489–98. The author has not been identified.

78. TO THOMAS CARLYLE[1]

[London,] 5th July 1833.

My dear Carlyle

I wrote a short letter to you intending to send it by your brother[2] when he went to Craigenputtoch; but he did not find time to call on me again and I having very foolishly mislaid his address, did not find out his place of abode till some hours after he had left town. As the letter was very short and had little in it, I cancelled it and determined to write a longer and better; which however I have not set about till now. In the meantime I have received your letter, which was welcome on many accounts: on none more than because it recognises in express words, what has always been tacitly recognised but seldom spoken or written about by either of us, the *negative* part of the relation between us—the fact that we *still* differ in many of our opinions, perhaps as you say (though of this I am not sure) throughout the range of a "half-universe." I certainly shall not hesitate to shew you "the length and breadth of my dissent." But the truth is, I had persuaded myself for a long time that the difference was next to nothing; was such as counted for little in *my* estimation at least, being rather in some few of our speculative premises than in any of our practical conclusions. When I came to *review* my opinions and ask myself after a considerable period of fresh thought and fresh experience, the deliberate question, which at some periods assumes a more serious and solemn aspect than at others, what I believed? what were my convictions? I found that they were, and for the present could not but be, more *materially* divergent from yours than I had for a time believed. As soon as I felt quite sure of this, I told you so; and though I wrote as if in a sceptical and unsettled state of mind, the very fact that I wrote at all about it proved that I had come into a more settled state. I think that I have obtained something like a firm footing, and additional rather than new light; I can hardly say that I have changed any of my opinions, but I seem to myself to *know* more, from increased observation of other people, and increased experience of my own feelings. All which is thus acquired *must* be clear gain; it is increased knowledge of the only valuable kind, knowledge of Realities; and it must be for want of intellect or for want of will if with additional ground to build upon, I cannot raise my edifice of Thought to a greater height and so look round and see more of Truth than I could see before. But of all these things we shall both write

1. *Addressed*: Thos. Carlyle Esq / Craigenputtoch / Dumfries. *Postmarks*: FREE / 6 JY 6 / 1833, and DUMFRIES / 8 JL 1833. Franked by G. Grote. MS at NLS. Published, with some omissions, in Elliot, I, 52–56. In reply to Carlyle's of June 13, 1833, A. Carlyle, pp. 54–60; answered by Carlyle, July 18, 1833, A. Carlyle, pp. 60–64.

2. Dr. John Carlyle.

and speak hereafter. Concerning my journey to Craigenputtoch all I can at present say is that if I go not thither I shall go nowhere else. However it will not, at all events be in August, for in that month my father will be absent, and it is inconvenient for both of us to be away from the India House at the same time. It cannot be till he return.—I had the pleasure of an hour's conversation with Dr. Carlyle on his passing through London, and was glad to learn that he is to be an inmate of Craigenputtoch all this summer and autumn.—My occupations for some time back have been rather internal than external; I have not been working much, but much has been working in me. I have written little, partly because I was better employed in obtaining whereof to write, than in writing, partly also because of press of business at the India House, and of certain temporary domestic occupations in my father's house. I have completed scarcely anything but a poor, flimsy, short paper on that book of Alison's, which I undertook in an evil hour, when the subject was as remote as possible from those which were occupying my thoughts and feelings at the time; and which I accordingly performed exceedingly ill, and was obliged to cancel the part which had cost me most labour. What is left, (it is not worth *your* perusal) will appear in the Monthly Repository: short as the whole is, it has been divided into two parts, of which one has appeared: it had been better to reserve the whole for another number. I shall in future never write on any subject which my mind is not full of when I begin to write; unless the occasion is such that it is better the thing were ill done than not at all, that being the alternative.—What you say of that paper of mine on Poetry and Art[3] is exactly what I think respecting it myself. I do not think it contains anything erroneous, but I feel that it is far from going to the bottom of the subject, or even very deep into it; I think I see somewhat further into it now, and shall perhaps understand it in time. I think I mentioned to you that I have carried the investigation (rightly or wrongly as it may be) one step farther in a paper (being a review of a new poem) which I wrote for the Examiner: it proved too long for Fonblanque, and it is to appear in Tait,[4] after such additions and alterations as I see it absolutely requires, and which I have not yet found time to give it. You say, you wish that you could help me in this matter; you *can*, and *do*, help me in all such matters, not by logical definition, which as I think I have said or written before, I agree with you in thinking not to be your peculiar walk of usefulness; but in *suggesting* deep and pregnant thoughts which might never have occurred to me, but which I am quite able when I have them to subject to all needful logical manipulation. This brings to my mind that I have never explained what I meant when writing once before in this strain I called you a Poet

3. See Letter 64, n. 11.
4. The ill-fated review of Browning's *Pauline*. See Letter 74.

and Artist. I conceive that most of the highest truths, are, to persons endowed by nature in certain ways which I think I could state, intuitive; that is, they need neither explanation nor proof, but if not known before, are assented to as soon as stated. Now it appears to me that the poet or artist is conversant chiefly with *such* truths and that his office in respect to truth is to declare *them*, and to make them *impressive*. This, however, supposes that the reader, hearer, or spectator is a person of the kind to whom those truths *are* intuitive. Such will of course receive them at once, and will lay them to heart in proportion to the impressiveness with which the artist delivers and embodies them. But the other and more numerous kind of people will consider them as nothing but dreaming or madness: and the more so, certainly, the more powerful the artist, *as* an artist: because the means which are good for rendering the truth impressive to those who know it, are not the same and are often absolutely incompatible with those which render it intelligible to those who know it not. Now this last I think is the proper office of the logician or I might say the metaphysician, in truth he must be both. The same person may be poet and logician, but he cannot be both in the same composition: and as heroes have been frustrated of glory "*carent quia vate sacro*," so I think the *vates* himself has often been misunderstood and successfully cried down for want of a Logician in Ordinary, to supply a logical commentary on his intuitive truths. The artist's is the highest part, for by him alone is real *knowledge* of such truths conveyed: but it is possible to convince him who never could *know* the intuitive truths, that they are not inconsistent with anything he *does* know; that they are even very *probable*, and that he may have faith in them when higher natures than his own affirm that they are truths. He may then build on them and act on them, or at least act nothing contradictory to them. Now this humbler part is, I think, that which is most suitable to my faculties, as a man of speculation. I am not in the least a poet, in any sense; but I can do homage to poetry. I can to a very considerable extent feel it and understand it, and can make others who are my inferiors understand it in proportion to the measure of their capacity. I believe that such a person is more wanted than even the poet himself; that there are more persons living who approximate to the latter character than to the former. I do not think myself at all fit for the one; I do for the other; your walk I conceive to be the higher. Now one thing not useless to do would be to exemplify this difference by enlarging in my logical fashion upon the difference itself: to make those who are not poets, understand that poetry is higher than Logic, and that the union of the two is Philosophy—I shall write out my thoughts more at length somewhere, and some*when*, probably soon. Yours faithfully,

J. S. MILL

I am so far from seeing any *intolerance* in your dislike of Speculation, unless it be either of the highest kind, or interesting for the sake of its interesting author, that I am exactly in the same case. I shall attend to this in making up my parcels for you hereafter. I have Madame Roland's memoirs and will send them with the Poor-Law book and what else of interesting I can get together.—What I said about "infinitesimal smallness" did not refer to the work itself but to the *effect*—no doubt in another sense, all who do all they can, do *equally*, and that *infinitely*. But when we are to chuse *what* we shall do, we must compare the *results*, and the difficulty is how to compare things infinitely small.[5] Tell me what you think about this, for it will perhaps lead to the root of some of the chief differences of opinion between us—[6]

79. TO JOHN PRINGLE NICHOL[1]

India House,
10th July, 1833.

My dear Sir,

Every letter I write to you begins with apologies for not writing sooner, and certainly not before they are due; though if "good intentions" might suffice (which they never can), I have been intending to write any time for the last four or five weeks. The first thing I have to say is that I fear there is no chance of the French Professorship.[2] Bowring has returned, I have seen him, and he says that the choice of a professor has been retarded by the impossibility of an agreement between the body who *chuse* and the ministry who *confirm*. "De Broglie and Guizot," he says in a note to me, "won't appoint Comte"[3] (he married one of Say's daughters, you may know him as the author of the *Censeur Européen* and a work on Legislation), "and the professors and members of the Institute won't appoint anybody else, and the matter rests there. Rossi"[4] (the friend of Dumont,[5] professor of *droit public* or something of the kind at Geneva) "has been sent for to Paris and is arrived; but it is doubtful whether he will be put forward by the Ministry. Comte seems determined not to give way." I do

5. See Letter 73 and Carlyle's reply (in A. Carlyle, p. 60).
6. This postscript is written at the top of the first page.

* * * *

1. Published by Knight, pp. 663–65. MS not located.
2. See Letter 65, n. 1.
3. Charles Comte.
4. Comte Pellegrino Rossi (1787–1848), economist and statesman. He was elected to the chair of political economy at the Collège de France in Aug., 1833.
5. Pierre Etienne Dumont (1759–1829), Swiss publicist and jurist, translator and editor of Bentham.

not think Comte the fit man—the most that can be said is that he will not do harm or discredit the science; but he is not profound in it. He is an excellent man, however, and the new Academy of Moral and Political Science in the Institute have recently shown some spirit by choosing him their perpetual secretary, contrary to the wishes of the Government, who oppose him because he is against them in politics. Their first idea of appointing an English economist was much better, but, perhaps, they would have found it difficult where the candidate had not established a high European reputation, to make out such a case as would justify in the eyes of Frenchmen the preference of a foreigner, however highly qualified, over "native talent," for it is not with us in political economy as it has long been with Italy in music—there is not a prejudice in our favour—therefore there must be a natural prejudice against us.

What you say in your last on the extreme desirableness of banding together the English Gironde is perfectly just and has been often thought of by almost all the leading philosophic reformers here, never more than lately; but it never was brought to any practical result nor, I fear, will it until the crisis becomes considerably more imminent than at present. The lamentable truth is that our Gironde, like the other Gironde, are a rope of sand; what our friend Tait (or rather the author of his first article for May)[6] said of them is not much, if at all, exaggerated. There are no leaders, and without leaders there can never be organization. There is no man or men of commanding talents among the Radicals in public life, or those whose position in respect of pecuniary independence enables them to put themselves forward personally. If there were but two or three men with *your* energy, what you propose might be done, and much else.

About a twelvemonth ago steps were actually taken for the formation of a Society for the Diffusion of Moral and Political Knowledge.[7] Hume had consented to be chairman, Warburton[8] vice-chairman, Grote treasurer, J. Romilly secretary, and there was a very creditable list of names for the Committee; they were to cause works to be written, and they were also to sanction others which were not written for them. No arrangements had been made, however, for the commencement of any work but one, which was only to be *sanctioned*, a Political Penny Magazine, of which Roebuck was to be the editor, and the appearance of which was to depend

6. "The Budget," *Tait's*, III (May, 1833), 137–40.

7. Francis Place, J. A. Roebuck, and Joseph Hume led the movement late in 1831 to establish such a society to publish tracts. A year later the plan was altered to project a "Penny Political and Moral Magazine," but the project collapsed when the ministry refused to repeal the stamp taxes on newspapers (see R. K. Webb, *The British Working Class Reader* [London, 1955], pp. 93–94). In 1834 Henry Brougham and Charles Knight (1791–1873) founded a short-lived Society for the Diffusion of Political Knowledge.

8. Henry Warburton (1784?–1858), radical MP 1826–41, 1843–57.

on alterations in the law, or on the chances of being able to evade it. The Ministry made private intimations to the parties concerned in this Penny Magazine Scheme, that the taxes on knowledge were to be taken off; fully believing this, they suspended their proceedings until that event. The Ministry broke faith with them, and in the meantime Roebuck got into Parliament, everybody's mind became otherwise occupied, and nothing was done.

I have little hope of any of the present race of parliamentary radicals. Some of them are full of crotchets, others fastidious and overloaded with petty scrupulosity; *none* have energy, except Roebuck and Buller; Roebuck has no judgment, Buller no patient persevering industry. Those two, however, will improve, and we shall hear more of them every year; all the others will remain, I think, very much the same men they are now. There is really more to be hoped from new converts like Clay[9] and Gisborne,[10] who are in the habit of uttering their sentiments boldly, than from the men who were Radicals in Tory times, and got the habit of *prudence* and *temporizing* which they cannot break themselves of even now.

What are we driving to? I do not expect a Revolution, because I think any unanimous demand of the people of this country will always be yielded to, as it was last year; but it is difficult to conjecture what acts of injustice they might, under circumstances of excitement, be provoked to demand. I expect a series of such Parliaments as this, with a step gained at every election. The cause of the evil is one which I foresaw and predicted long before—the anomaly of a democratic constitution in a plutocratically constituted society. Till changes take place which can only be remotely promoted by any Reform Bill, the people will continue from necessity to select their representatives from the same class as before, avoiding only those who are *committed* to principles which the people abhor. The consequence is they must take the *feebles.* All the marked and energetic men in the higher classes, a few excepted, were committed against Reform; that was the natural consequence of their education and the circumstances of *those* times. The people, therefore, threw them aside, and selected men from the second or third rank, who were not committed because it had never been thought worth while to ask their opinion, such men as would say they were for the Reform Bill, and the Whig Ministers. But further than this, they were not at all better than their class in opinions or feelings, and inferior to their predecessors in talent and judgment. They have acted as such men were sure to do: what will happen? There will be a fresh purgation; these being now disgraced will be thrown aside, and there will be a third levy from the self-same class, consisting of the same sort of men

9. Sir William Clay (1791–1869), liberal Whig MP 1832–57.

10. Thomas Gisborne (1794–1852), Whig MP 1830–31, 1832–37, 1839–41, 1843–52, vigorous supporter of free trade.

or still feebler ones, but who will say they are for the particular measure then most called for at the particular time by the people, and most recently resisted by the present house. That particular measure will then be carried, and all other things will go as badly as they do now. The same *next* time, and so on till the real waking minds of the country renounce money-getting, and till they are paid for devoting their time to legislation.

Have you considered the effect of the proposed Commutation of Tithe? The compulsory part of it is I perceive to be postponed till another year. As it will stop the increase of tithe at least in corn—as no new land, or new improvements will pay any tithe—it strikes me that the commuted tithe will continue wholly, or partially, a tax on the consumer, until the least productive land or capital shall, by the extension of cultivation and population, yield a rent equal to the commuted tithe, and *after* that it will become wholly a rent-charge. Do you think I am right? You continue I see to write with great spirit and excellent effect in Tait. I am much gratified by your favourable opinion of my tract on endowments.[11] You have, I dare say, recognized me in *The Examiner* on the Bank Question;[12] the article was superficial, and could not consistently with its purpose be otherwise. Nobody, except you and me, seems to *write* on that side of the question. My father quite agrees with us. Pray do not imitate my neglect in not writing soon, and believe me,

Yours very faithfully,

J. S. MILL.

You promised me a letter on the Property Tax—I never was more in need of it.[13]

80. TO JOHN STERLING[1]

12 July 1833

MY DEAR STERLING

I have been very long in writing to you and have only time to write a few words now—Taylor's answer to your question[2] is briefly this—"I have not heard of any plans of the Gov^t for the education of the negroes, nor do

11. See Letter 68, n. 3.

12. "The Ministerial Measure Respecting the Bank," *Examiner*, July 7, 1833, pp. 417–18.

13. See Letter 77.

* * * *

1. *Addressed*: Monsieur / M. John Sterling / chez Madame Barton / 4 Cölnthor / Bonn. MS at King's. Published in part in Elliot, I, 56–57.

2. Henry Taylor was in the Colonial Office. On June 10, 1833, Sterling wrote to JSM: "If you can learn anything as to the Gov^t. plans for the education of the slaves & will let me know you will do me a great service. I think I might be of some use in that matter & if you should see Taylor—whom I do not like to trouble with a letter on the subject—I wish you would ask him whether there is any probability of a

I expect to hear of any. Certainly if there were to be any Commission of enquiry on the subject, Sterling could not employ his time more serviceably to the ends which he has at heart than by getting himself placed upon it—nor would the Gov^{t} be likely to meet with any person half so well qualified to conduct such an enquiry." So much for these statesmen of ours—they always remind me of what Southey said to me at Keswick—pointing in a little Bible-book for children in size and shape an inch cube, to a wood-cut of Samson with a gate on his back about twenty times his own size, he said "that is like Lord John Russell[3] carrying away the British constitution" & sure enough that is about the proportion between the men & the work they have in hand.

I suppose you have by this time returned from your journey up the Rhine. I shall be much interested by the impression German literature and philosophy make upon you on a nearer acquaintance. That question between Schelling's view and Schleiermacher's is the one great question on the subject of religion. My own views as far as I have any fixed ones are much nearer to Schleiermacher's than to Schelling's and Coleridge's.[4] With *them* I do not at all see as my mind is at present constituted any chance of my ultimately agreeing. I think I am even further from them than I was. I suspect that your mind and mine have passed that point in their respective orbits where they approximate most—and that our premisses are now more nearly the same than our conclusions are likely to be. I think I am becoming *more* a Movement-man than I was, instead of less—I do not mean merely in politics, but in all things—& that you are becoming more and more inclined to look backward for good. However I am talking without book, for who in these times knows what he shall think rightest & best six months hence? Yours faithfully

J. S. MILL

Commission to enquire on the subject—& if he thinks I should stand any chance of being appointed to it—for if so I would certainly apply immediately. England seems to be going as an American would say 'all to immortal smash'." (Unpublished letter, MS at King's.)

3. Lord John Russell (1792–1878), one of the Whig leaders in the struggle for the Reform Bill.

4. Sterling had written from Bonn in his letter of June 10: "If circumstances permitted which they do not, I should like after reading Kant to spend some time at Munich near Schelling who since the death of Hegel of Berlin is I believe the only philosopher of marked & original genius in Germany. His views if I may rely on what I hear present a very remarkable conformity to those of Coleridge, for he too maintains that the Christian Mysteries are the highest Truths of Reason & that it is either necessary to assume or possible to prove every one of them a priori. Schleiermacher is I believe the head of a different school—& one I believe very popular among the learned here—They say he considers Philosophy and Religion altogether apart from each other & makes the latter an affair of sentiment and moral expediency. I incline strongly to Schelling's view—but unhappily he has published nothing important for many years & his earlier doctrines were very different from the present ones."

81. TO THOMAS CARLYLE[1]

[Late July, 1833]

MY DEAR CARLYLE

This note will be given to you by Mr. R. W. Emerson[2] of Boston (United States) who having been long a reader of your writings, is desirous to take the first opportunity of making your acquaintance. Mr. Emerson met with our friend Gustave d'Eichthal at Rome, and was by him referred to me as one who could give him the introduction to you which he wished for—I have great pleasure in doing so—Yours faithfully

J. S. MILL.

82. TO THOMAS CARLYLE[1]

India House, 2nd August 1833.

MY DEAR CARLYLE

This letter will be as you desire, extremely biographical: I was conscious myself of a deficiency in *that* department, in my last: which however was wholly *auto*biographic; for what is *my* life made up of, in the main, but my thoughts and feelings? I have no actions to relate except occasionally the promulgation of some thoughts and feelings. But I am now to speak of others rather than of myself. And first, of those in whom you are most interested. You have probably heard that the Austins do not quit England. The Chancellor is to appoint or has actually appointed a Commission to digest the Criminal Law and Austin is to be one of the members. This is work for him of the kind which he most likes, and for which he is best fitted: it is also a provision for him: he is to have £500 a year while it lasts, and it will doubtless lead to other employment in the same line. All his good fortune comes to him at the same time: the four Inns of Court, chiefly at the instigation of Bickersteth[2] (the most valuable man in the profession of the law—do you know about him?), have resolved to found

1. MS at NLS. Published in Elliot, I, 57.
2. JSM's first impressions of Ralph Waldo Emerson (1803–1882) were not especially favourable (see Letters 82 and 87). The introduction led to the lifelong friendship and correspondence of Emerson and Carlyle.

* * * *

1. No address, since included in Buller's letter. MS at NLS. Published, with minor errors and omissions, in Elliot, I, 57–62. In reply to Carlyle's of July 18, 1833, in A. Carlyle, pp. 60–64; answered by Carlyle, Sept. 10, 1833, A. Carlyle, pp. 65–68.
2. Henry Bickersteth, later Baron Langdale (1783–1851), Master of the Rolls; close friend of Bentham and James Mill.

two Lectureships, one of English Law, the other of Civil Law and Jurisprudence: this last it is not impossible that Austin may be appointed to: it is compatible with his other employment and will add £450 to his income. So he is likely to be placed in the best circumstances possible for *him*, whether we consider his usefulness or his own happiness. There are no fears now but for his health: I have always thought that anxiety was the chief cause of his frequent illnesses; they have been, however of late, considerably *more* frequent than formerly though less severe—he is ill now; as soon as he is fit to travel they are going out of town, probably to some place on the north coast of Devonshire, where they will remain till October, when he returns to commence his new duties. Mrs. Austin is now overloaded with proposals for translating; her fame as a translator has been, very deservedly, raised much higher by this "Falk."[3] As she will not now be at all dependent on the profits (McCulloch[4] would take me to task—I should say *wages*) of her literary undertakings, she will now be at liberty to consult only her own judgment of what will do most good: she will persevere, I have no doubt, and be useful.—You ask me about Grote: I happen to be able to tell you more about him than almost any one, having been intimate with him almost from my boyhood, though less so than formerly in proportion as I have diverged from his opinions: he is a Utilitarian; in one sense I am so too, but *he* is so in rather a narrow sense; has therefore a belief, a firm one, in *him* most deep and conscientious, for which chiefly he lives and for which he would die. He is a highly *instructed* man; an excellent scholar; has made great progress in writing a History of Greece,[5] some of the manuscript of which I have seen; it will be a work of great, though not of consummate merit: he was one of the first of his rank and station to proclaim strong Benthamic-Radical opinions; he published a pamphlet[6] of merit, in defence thereof against the Edinburgh Review, as long ago as 1820, when not so old as I am now, and another[7] two years ago just before the Reform Bill. He is a man of good, but not first-rate intellect: hard and mechanical; not at all quick; with less *subtlety* than any able and instructed man I ever knew: with much logical and but little aesthetic culture; *narrow* therefore; even narrower than most other Utilitarians of reading and education: more a disciple of my father than of any one else: industrious, brave, *not* very active or spirited; universally beloved for his extreme goodness, his simplicity, uprightness, and gentleness;

3. See Letter 58, n. 10.
4. John Ramsay McCulloch.
5. *A History of Greece* (12 vols., London, 1846–56).
6. *Statement of the Question of Parliamentary Reform: With a Reply to the Objections of the Edinburgh Review No. 61* (London, 1821).
7. *Essentials of Parliamentary Reform* (London, 1831).

resembling Ricardo in that particular, though a far inferior man to him in powers of intellect. He is by far the most *considered* of the radicals in the H. of C. [House of Commons] is more nearly their leader than any one else, & would be so altogether but that he has not the kind of talents which fit a man for a parliamentary leader; he has not sufficient readiness, decision, & presence of mind. After all I have said of him you will be surprised to learn that he reads German. He will be a man of considerable weight in politics soon. As I am on politics, I will ask you if you have seen, except in the abridgment which the Examiner will give,[8] Roebuck's speech on proposing a resolution for the establishment of a national education of the whole people: I should like you to see it, for it is a better exhibition of him than I think you have seen: it has raised him considerably, I think, in most people's estimation, which is seldom matter of praise but is really so in this instance. It was beginning to be supposed that he *could* do nothing: he has shewn now that he can; and we must add him to Grote and Buller to make up the only three among the radical members who have not disappointed the expectations of their friends. Of these three, and of all the rest, Buller is as you once said the only one who possesses any the smallest *genius*. But several of them may be and will be valuable as 'honest Artisans.' —I can tell you something of Detrosier.[9] He is again in London, and has some prospect of picking up a living as a lecturer on experimental physics: he is, it seems, accustomed to the craft, and qualified for it; he has made the attempt even here with success, and the only doubt about his having several profitable engagements arises from the freshness of his fame as Secretary to the Political Union. Assuredly Radicalism is not yet the road to wealth and honours, though its turn I think is coming. In the meantime Detrosier, poor fellow, with a foolish wife and two or three children, has some difficulty in making the two ends meet; however he has friends here, who will not let him be in want.—I had a short note from Gustave d'Eichthal the other day, dated from Rome, merely to introduce an American named Emerson, who had sought an introduction to me as a means of obtaining one to you: this I of course gave him;[10] he is going into Scotland and may possibly seek you out: he appears to be a reader and professes to be an admirer of your writings; therefore you might possibly do him some good: but from one or two conversations I have had with him, I do not think him a very hopeful subject. Of Fonblanque I have not seen very much lately; except (as you have) through the Examiner: in which I myself have written very little of late: almost the only paper I

8. Aug. 4, 1833, p. 488. Roebuck's speech had been delivered on July 30 in the House of Commons.

9. Rowland Detrosier.

10. Letter 81.

have sent to him for some time you will see in the next or the next but one:[11] I will let you find it out if you can; there is not much in it; it is all political. I have indeed written less of late than for a long time before; no longer for the reason I formerly mentioned, but literally from the pressure of comparatively trivial occupations, yet which in the particular circumstances were not such. The little remainder of my little paper on Alison's book[12] has just appeared: the two numbers of the M.R. containing it, shall reach you somehow soon. I have sent you no books this month, because I really could not get together enough to make it worth while: I had only the Poor Laws book. I have a promise of a copy of the Factory Commissioners Report:[13] when it comes, shall I send it? Madame Roland I had lent, and it did not return to me till a day or two too late. I have now a copy (borrowed) of one of Babbage's two books:[14] you once expressed a wish to see them: have you still that wish? or has it been satisfied! *Now* I have also (if you would care to see it) a book of Bulwer's, entitled "England & the English." I have not yet looked into it: but a Frenchman who is now in London said of it to Mrs. Austin, that though he had been here only a month that book did not tell him any one thing that was new to him: it must therefore be a very poor book. I told you in one of my letters[15] that I had been writing something about Bentham & his philosophy; it was for Bulwer, at his request, for the purposes of this book: contrary to my expectation at that time, he has printed part of this paper *ipsissimis verbis* as an appendix to his book: so you will see it; but I do not acknowledge it, nor mean to do so. I furnished him also at his request with a few yet rougher notes concerning my father, which he has not dealt so fairly by, but has cut and mangled and coxcombified the whole thing till its mother would not know it: there are a few sentences of mine in it, something like what they were when I wrote them; for the sake of artistic congruity I wish there were not. This I still less own, because it is not mine, in any sense. About my going to Craigenputtoch there will be some uncertainty till the very time, because the only contingency which would prevent it may happen at any time, and will remain possible to the very last. You will not hear positively that I am coming till the post immediately preceding my arrival—yes you will though, for I shall travel rather slowly. I am sorry that your brother's speedy return to Italy will prevent me from meeting him at Craigenputtoch: but I shall at all events see him on his passage through

11. "Municipal Institutions," *Examiner*, Aug. 11, 1833, pp. 497–98.

12. See Letter 72, n. 13.

13. Report of the Central Board of H.M. Commissioners Appointed to Collect Information as to the Employment of Children in Factories, *Parliamentary Papers*, 1833, XX.

14. See Letter 58, n. 18.

15. Letter 72, n. 12.

London?—I have read the first part of your Cagliostro;[16] not yet the second: I know not why you should call it "half mad"; it is merely like much of your writing, half ironical, half earnest; it may be of use to some people: If human beings would but do *thoroughly* all they do, I believe with you that Good would be much more forwarded than Evil: halfness is the great enemy of spiritual worth: whatever shames any human being out of *that*, is of unspeakable value. I have left little room for any of the many things I could willingly say on your last letter; neither is the letter before me, which however frequently happens to be the case when I am answering your letters. Do not mistake what I meant when I talked of *logic*; I did not mean it in the sense in which your answers to Sir William Hamilton[17] (who I suppose is the "schoolman" you allude to) would apply to it. Of logic, as the theory of the processes of intellect, I think not wholly as you, yet nearly: he who has legs can walk without knowledge of anatomy, yet you will allow that such knowledge may be made substantially *available* for the cure of *lameness*. By logic however I meant the antithesis of Poetry or Art: in which distinction I am learning to perceive a twofold contrast: the *literal* as opposed to the *symbolical*, and *reasoning* as opposed to *intuition*. Not the *theory* of reasoning but the *practice*. In reasoning I include all processes of thought which are *processes* at all, that is, which proceed by a series of steps or links. What I would say is that my vocation is, I think, chiefly for this last; a more extended & higher one than for any branch of mere "Philosophy of Mind" though far inferior to that of the artist.—We shall talk doubtless of these things, and also of many others, not excepting the one you mention, *Paris*—My notion of it is chiefly taken from its recent literature, which *is* exactly what Goethe called it, the literature of Despair—die Litteratur der Verzweiflung. You will not wonder at that—nor do I.

Buller who is about to write to you will put this letter under his cover—
Yours faithfully

J. S. MILL.

Thanks to Mrs. Carlyle for her two lines, and best remembrances to her and to Dr. Carlyle.

16. "Count Cagliostro," *Fraser's*, VIII (July-Aug., 1833), 19–28, 132–55.

17. Sir William Hamilton (1788–1856), philosopher, whose position JSM years later attacked in *An Examination of Sir W. Hamilton's Philosophy* (London, 1865). The reference is to Carlyle's letter of July 18 (A. Carlyle, p. 61); in reply, Carlyle says, Oct. 28: "Sir William was *not* the 'old schoolman' I once spoke of; that *Redivivus* was another considerably inferior character . . . *a ganz ausgestorbener Mann*. He lectured on Logic, and thought Logic was to be the salvation of the world." (A. Carlyle, p. 78.)

83. TO WILLIAM TAIT[1]

India House
6th August
1833

My dear Sir

You must have been a good deal surprised at hearing nothing from me respecting the literary article which was to be transferred from the Examiner to your Magazine.[2] The fact is that for some weeks past the pressure of other occupations had left me no time to take the article in hand and fit it for your use: and now at length when I had begun to rewrite it for you, I find that the work it is a review of (a poem named Pauline) has been disposed of in your last number by a passing notice,[3] in terms of contempt which though I think the poem was overpraised in the Monthly Repository, I cannot consider it to deserve. So I hope you will receive this as my apology for not fulfilling my engagement.

Believe me
Most truly yours
J. S. Mill

84. TO THOMAS CARLYLE[1]

India House, 5th September 1833.

My dear Carlyle

You have probably heard from Dr Carlyle before this reaches you, that I shall not, after all, see you this autumn. There were about twenty chances to one that I should, but it is the twenty-first which has taken effect in Reality. I was mistaken, too, when I said that if I went not to Craigenputtoch I should go nowhere: I am going to Paris: the same cause which I then thought, if it operated at all, would operate to keep me here, now sends me there.[2] It is a journey entirely of duty; nothing else, you will do me the justice to believe, would have kept me from Craigenputtoch after

1. *Addressed*: William Tait Esq. / care of Messrs Simpkin & Marshall. MS at NLS.
2. Review of Browning's *Pauline*. See Letter 74.
3. "Besides the above poems . . . we have *Paulina* [*sic*], *A Fragment of a Confession*; a piece of pure bewilderment" (*Tait's*, III [Aug., 1833], 668).

* * * *

1. *Addressed*: Thomas Carlyle Esq / Craigenputtoch / Dumfries / N.B. *Postmarks*: [???] / 5 SE / 1833, and [???] MFRIES / [???] SEP 1833. MS at NLS. Published in part in Elliot, I, 62–65. Carlyle's answer of Sept. 24, 1833, is in A. Carlyle, pp. 68–75.
2. The cause was the crisis that had been reached in the relationship of JSM with Mrs. John Taylor. Taylor agreed to an experimental separation for six months from his wife, who left for Paris in Sept. JSM followed on Oct. 10 and stayed until about Nov. 20. See Hayek, p. 49. See also Letter 89.

what I have said & written so often: it is duty, and duty connected with a person to whom of all persons alive I am under the greatest obligations. If I had not so short a vacation the two journeys would not be incompatible, but alas for him who must abide eleven months of the year at a desk in Leadenhall Street! All the compensation I can make to you will be to write often and fully, and tell you all I see and hear at Paris that will interest you. You said something in one of your letters about a projected residence of some time at Paris for yourself—it would not, I think, be pleasant to you, but extremely melancholy; *everywhere* however there is food enough for *that*—and I *do* believe that for observation of realities, at least human spiritual realities, there is no place in the world like Paris in the present age, for the reason you mentioned, that individualities of character are there *unchained*, not being kept down and fashioned to a model by a common overruling Belief—but again, nowhere in Europe, if I am not greatly mistaken, are there so *few* individualities of character as at Paris. I suspect Prussia is the only country *pleasant* to live in for one who loves mankind—but for that very reason not the fit place for one who is capable of being their spiritual benefactor in any however small a degree unless he was *born* there.

Dr Carlyle has been so good as to take charge of some books for you: viz. two Reports of the Factory Commission, full of the *biography* of history; the works of Madame Roland, the noblest character by far of the French Revolution, perhaps of France itself; though far from the most brilliant; & the two numbers of the Repository which contain my flimsy paper on Alison. That last was hardly worth sending; keep it however. I meant you to keep Junius Redivivus; I have other copies: it is not, however, worth sending back, to *you*. That and all the other books, came safe. What did you think of the *Vieux Cordelier*?[3] Villate's book,[4] which pretends to let one into the secrets of the *Terreur* I believe to be a mere tissue of lies and exaggerations: he was a *juré* of the revolutionary tribunal, deeply implicated in all the horrors of the time, and anxious by making great disclosures to save his own neck from *the reaction*, to which unless my memory fail me he nevertheless fell a sacrifice.—The Poor-Laws book, Dr Carlyle tells me you have: indeed I thought you would, for it has been very widely circulated: write me word what you think of it. Write to me also about your brother: he stays here so short a time that I shall not *know* him, only lay the foundation for future knowledge; but I have already seen enough to respect and like him and to hope for his future friendship.—I forgot to ask whether you have seen that "Arthur Coningsby"—it is scarcely worth sending,—though decidedly worth reading: perhaps it may go with other books:—also Bulwer's book.

3. See Letter 67, n. 7.

4. See Letter 72, n. 7.

I have read the latter half of Cagliostro with very great pleasure; greater than the first half: and I look forward to the appearance of Teufelsdreck[5] with great satisfaction: by the impression it makes upon me now, as compared with that which it made on the first reading, I shall have a kind of measure of the space which I have *franchi* (as the French say) in the interval; whether forwards, backwards, or to *one side*. I have certainly changed much since you knew me; in some things I have become, I think, more like yourself, in others more unlike; I am partly reconciled to not seeing you this year by the thought that next year I shall probably be firmer on my legs, spiritually speaking, and shall have a clearer and more fixed insight into what I am to be and to do, than I have at present, and that the relation between us will then be (much more than now) what you once called it, "a relation between two Somethings" and not between a Something & a Nothing.

—About that Cagliostro and that Teufelsdreck, by the way, it has frequently occurred to me of late to ask of myself and also of you, whether that mode of writing between sarcasm or irony and earnest, be really deserving of so much honour as you give to it by making use of it so frequently. I do not say that it is not good: all modes of writing, in the hands of a sincere man, are good, provided they are intelligible. But are there many things, worth saying, and capable of being said in that manner which cannot be as well or better said in a more direct way? The same doubt has occasionally occurred to me respecting much of your phraseology, which fails to bring home your meaning to the comprehension of most readers so well as would perhaps be done by commoner and more familiar phrases: however this last I say with the most perfect submission, because I am sure that every one speaks and writes best in his own mother tongue, the language in which he thinks.—I have just received a copy of some Evidence taken by the Poor Law Commissioners on the subject of Education, affording some striking instances of the good effect produced upon the very rabble of London by even such imperfect schooling as they now sometimes receive: shall I send it in my next parcel?

I am now reading, very sedulously, Voltaire's Correspondence: I have never read it before. It throws much light upon the spiritual character of that time, and especially of its literary men. How strangely Voltaire's own character has been mistaken; and how little does he seem to have been conscious of what he was about, to have had even any settled purpose in it. He certainly had no intention of being the Patriarch of any sect of Destructives, & if the priests would have let him alone, he would have let them

5. *Sartor Resartus*, which Carlyle, despairing of securing a publisher, had offered to James Fraser for serial publication. It appeared in *Fraser's Magazine* from Nov., 1833, to Aug., 1834. JSM had evidently read it in manuscript.

alone. In the greater part of his lifetime he seems to have been timid excessively, and would have abstained from almost anything in order to remain quiet at Paris. But after he had found the quiet he sought, at a distance, it was the revival of persecution as evinced by the suppression of the Encyclopédie, the condemnation of Helvetius's book, the speech of Le Franc de Pompignan at the Academy denouncing Voltaire himself personally, the success of Palissot's comedy of Les Philosophes, the abuse of the Philosophes by Fréron & others, &c., &c.[6] it was these things which erected Voltaire after the age of sixty-five into the leader of a crusade against Christianity; & it was then, too, that he seems to have found out that wit and ridicule were capable of being powerful weapons in his hands. He always seems to have despised the French, & thought them incapable of philosophy, or even of science; and he continually lamented that they insisted upon taking to speculation, which they were unfit for, and neglected the beaux-arts (what beaux-arts!) which had been the glory of the *siècle de Louis 14*.

I have no more room—mit Glück und Heil

J. S. MILL.

I shall remain here till the middle of October probably, so that your letters will reach me as usual. I cannot get a frank this time; all Parliament is out of town. My kindest remembrances to Mrs. Carlyle.[7]

85. TO WILLIAM JOHNSON FOX[1]

India House
Saturday [Sept. 7, 1833]

MY DEAR MR FOX

I am ashamed to say I can give no hope that Blakey[2] will be ready on Monday—though I think part of him will be. But I have nearly made up my mind to transfer to you the paper on Poetry[3] which I thought of putting

6. *Œuvres complètes de Voltaire* (66 vols., Paris, 1819–25), Vol. L, pp. 135, 141, 321, 337, 359, 362, 363, 389, 393, 533–38.
7. This postscript is written at the top of the first page.

* * * *

1. *Addressed*: Rev. W. J. Fox / 1 Stamford Grove / Upper Clapton. *Postmark*: T. P. / Cornhill; To be Delivere[d] by 10 Sund Mor / 7 NIGHT / SP. 7 / 1883. MS at King's. Excerpts published in Garnett, pp. 105, 106.
2. Robert Blakey, *History of Moral Science* (2 vols., London, 1833). JSM's review in *MR*, VII (Oct., 1833), 661–69.
3. "The Two Kinds of Poetry," *MR*, VII (Oct., 1833), 714–24, reprinted with his "What is Poetry?" (*MR*, VII [Jan., 1833], 60–70) in *Dissertations* under title "Thoughts on Poetry and its Varieties." JSM did not publish a review of Tennyson until nearly two years later, *London Review*, I (July, 1835), 402–24.

at the head of a review of Tennyson somewhere. I think I could make a better review of Tennyson, and with the same ideas too, in another way.

If you like the idea, and if you see *her*[4] before Monday, will you mention it to her—you know it is hers—if she approves, it shall be yours. I shall see her on Monday myself, and then I will speak of the matter to her. [Ye]s—she is like hers[elf]—if she is ever ou[t][5] of spirits it is always something amiss in *me* that is the cause—it is so now—it is because she sees that what ought to be so much easier to me than to her, is in reality more difficult—costs a harder struggle—to part company with the opinion of the world, and with my former modes of doing good in it; however, thank heaven, she does not doubt that I can do it—

Yes—I shall see you often, I hope, at Clapton when she is gone—[6]

yours ever

J. S. MILL

86. TO WILLIAM TAIT[1]

India House
24 September 1833

MY DEAR SIR

You have not heard from me as a contributor to your Magazine for some time past. I am now about to make up for my neglect by making a proposal to you which if accepted would furnish you with a "stock in hand" but which it is very probable may not suit you.

I have had by me for some time, five Political Economy essays,[2] ready for publication; four of them on particular points, containing views which I am desirous to submit to the judgment of the *scientific* students of the science,—in continuation and completion of Ricardo's doctrines. The fifth is a dissertation on the science itself,[3] and on the proper mode of studying

4. Mrs. Taylor.
5. Page torn where square brackets appear in this sentence.
6. She was soon to go to Paris to begin the trial separation from her husband. See preceding letter, n. 2.

* * * *

1. *Addressed*: W. Tait Esq. / Prince's Street / Edinbro'. *Postmarks*: FREE / SE 25 / 1833, and SEP / C 27A / 1833. Franked by J. A. Roebuck. MS at LSE.
2. These were eventually published in 1844 as *Essays on Some Unsettled Questions of Political Economy*. For the origin of these essays, see Letter 43, n. 14.
3. This essay was later published, *LWR*, XXVI (Oct., 1836), 1–29, under the title "On the Definition of Political Economy; and on the Method of Philosophical Investigation in that Science," and was later reprinted in the *Essays* cited above

it. The last may be considered as comparatively popular; the other four are, as from their nature and object they cannot but be, somewhat abstract; not more so however than De Quincey's "Templar's Dialogues" in the London Magazine.[4] There is no use in publishing these tracts as a separate voume, for few would read them and *nobody* would buy them. They must therefore remain in my desk unless they will suit you. In length they would average I think about the dimensions of an article on such subjects in the Edinburgh Review. They would not be attractive to the bulk of Magazine-readers, and the only chance of their suiting you lies in the extremely miscellaneous character of such a Magazine as yours, which should and does contain matter for almost all classes of readers. The high character which your work is establishing for itself in Political Economy would also make any elaborate paper on that subject less out of place in your pages than in those of any other periodical.

If you do not think the proposition quite inadmissible, be so good as to write to me, and I will send you one or two of them for your inspection —I should also be much obliged to our friend Mr Nichol if he would favour me with his remarks on them before anything is determined upon.

If you should finally resolve to publish them in the Magazine, I shall further request of you to have 100 copies of each, struck off for me & at my expense, to give away to the few persons who can be expected to take any considerable interest in such speculations.

I have not seen much in the Magazine lately which I could ascribe to Mr Nichol—nor have I heard from him—I hope he is not ill?

The French Professorship I fear is out of the question—the choice lies between Comte & Rossi.[5]

Most truly yours

J. S. MILL

I have not given up the idea of those "Essays on the Ambiguities of the Moral Sciences"[6] but for the present I see no chance of my having time for it—[7]

J.S.M.

---

with the title "On the Definition of Political Economy; and On the Method of Investigation Proper to It."

4. "Dialogues of Three Templars on Political Economy," *London Mag.*, IX (April–May, 1824), 341–55, 427–28, 547–66.

5. See Letter 79.

6. A never-completed project possibly arising from his review of George Cornewall Lewis' *Use and Abuse of Political Terms*; see Letter 51, n. 15.

7. This postscript is written at the top of the page.

87. TO THOMAS CARLYLE[1]

Mickleham, near Dorking, Surrey,
5th October 1833
(don't direct hither, though.)

MY DEAR CARLYLE

Two of your letters, both well deserving a better answer than this will be, have been waiting a long time for it: such as it is you shall have it now: You ask me to write with abandonment—it is pleasant in many ways to be asked *that*, and by you—doubt not but that I shall do so, more and more—I have not, and have never had, any voluntary or rather intentional *reserve* with any one whom I value, certainly not with you—but that is not enough—I am sensible in myself of a want of spontaneousness, a self-consciousness even in the act of *confiding*, which is perhaps natural enough in a *born metaphysician* as I am in the very worst sense, but which I dislike extremely both in myself and wherever else I see it, and which I believe I am getting rid of. There will I think be perfect spontaneous confidence, the *abandonment* you speak of, in the fullest sense, between us two, some time; I think as soon as we are completely intimate; I was going to say completely *know* each other, but that is an impossibility, as you well know. In the meantime it is very grateful to me to find that everything which brings me nearer to you, brings you also nearer to me, and that every approach to a closer intimacy is responded to as soon as made. Our friendship is a strong healthy young plant, which being in a good soil may be left to itself to grow. So no more of that at present—Now I will say that I am going to Paris probably at the end of this week. If I could have another letter from you before I go, well: if not, write when you are moved thereto, and a friend at the India House will forward your letter to Paris, for I do not wish to be five weeks without it. What you wish to be ascertained for you at Paris, shall be so; I shall be able to obtain the fullest and exactest information. Touching French dictionaries I am fully as ignorant as yourself: I learnt the language in the country itself, and acquired the colloquial part of it in greater perfection than most English do, so had never occasion for the sort of dictionary you want: I believe there is none good, none but such as you probably have; but I will inquire about that, too. Before I go I will send a parcel to Fraser's for you, containing Bulwer, Coningsby, and more French Memoirs if I can find any more worth sending. I am afraid you have already had the best of them.

1. *Addressed*: Thomas Carlyle Esq / Craigenputtock / Dumfries. *Postmarks*: FREE / 7 OC 7 / 1833, and DUMFRIES / 9 OCT 1833. Franked by G. Grote. MS at NLS. Published, with minor errors and omissions, in Elliot, I, pp. 65–71. Reply to Carlyle's of Sept. 10 and Sept. 24, 1833, A. Carlyle, pp. 65–75; answered by Carlyle, Oct. 28, 1833, A. Carlyle, 75–82.

With them shall go the October number of the Monthly Repository: containing *two* articles of mine: one, a review of a foolish book by a man named Blakey, of Morpeth, called a History of Moral Science;[2] for writing which he is utterly unfit, being a man who as you would say, has no eyes, only a pair of *glasses* and I will add, almost *opake* ones. The other article[3] is the little paper I told you I was writing in further prosecution of, or rather improvement on, the thoughts I published before on Poetry and Art. You will not find much in the first to please you; perhaps rather more in the second, but I fear you will think both of them too much infected by mechanical theories of the mind: yet you will probably in this as in many other cases be glad to see that out of my mechanical premisses I elicit *dynamical* conclusions—and I have a paragraph at the end of the article on Blakey's book by way of *manifesto*, to tell people that I don't care one straw about premisses except for the sake of conclusions. I have been very busy and active in writing lately; even on politics; did you detect me in those long-winded answers (in the Examiner) to the ministerial pamphlet?[4] but I tell it not to the profane. Your approval of the Alison paper was very gratifying; *I* also am conscious that I write with a greater appearance of *sureness* and strong belief than I did for a year or two before, in that period of *recovery* after the petrification of a narrow philosophy, in which one feels *quite sure* of scarcely anything respecting Truth, except that she is many-sided. Did you ever read Schleiermacher's paper on Socrates? I have been reading it in a number of Connop Thirlwall's "Philological Museum,"[5] a Cambridge classical periodical of merit: Schleiermacher's theory of Socrates is that besides knowing "that he knew nothing," he however knew also what knowledge *was*, and how it was to be come at: that was exactly my case and was the faith I also professed and taught for some years unconscious all the while that I had nothing else to teach: I have now got at some few things more: all of which, as they become clearer to myself, will be shewn to you either in what I publish, or in letters, or personal communication. You suggest to me, what I have many times thought of, the advisableness of my writing something more elaborate than I have yet written on the French Revolution: it is highly probable I shall do it sometime if you do not; but besides the difficulty of

2. See Letter 85, n. 2.
3. *Ibid.*, n. 3.
4. For titles and pagination of the seven articles in the series see MacMinn, *Bibliog.*, pp. 34–35.
5. Connop Thirlwall (1797–1875), historian and clergyman, published three papers in this volume on Schleiermacher and Socrates, all signed C.T.: "Schleiermacher on the Worth of Socrates as a Philosopher (From the Berlin Transactions of 1815)," *Philological Museum*, II (1833), 538–55; "Schleiermacher's Introduction to his Translation of Plato's Apology of Socrates," *ibid.*, pp. 556–61; and "Socrates, Schleiermacher and Delbrueck," *ibid.*, pp. 562–87.

doing it tolerably, there is a far greater difficulty of doing it so as to be read in England, until the time comes when one can speak of Christianity as it may be spoken of in France; as by far the greatest and best thing which has existed on this globe, but which is gone, never to return, only what was best in it to reappear in another and still higher form, some time (heaven knows when). One could not, *now*, say this openly in England, and be read—at least by the many; yet it is perhaps worth trying. Without *saying out* one's whole belief on that point, it is impossible to write about the French Revolution in any way professing to tell the *whole* truth. *A propos* I have been reading the New Testament; properly I can never be said to have *read* it before. I am the fitter to read it now; perhaps there is nobody within the four seas so utterly unprejudiced on the subject. I have *never* believed Christianity as a religion, consequently have no habitual associations of reverence, nor on the other hand any of *contempt* like so many who have become sceptics after having been taught to believe; nor have I, like so many, been bored or disgusted with it in my youth. As far as I know *your* impressions about Christ, *mine* from this reading are exactly the same. How strikingly just for instance is your contrast in your last letter, between the Christ of the Gospels, & the namby-pamby Christ of the poor modern Christians.[6] Many things have struck me in reading this book. One is that nearly all the good of the four Gospels is in St Matthew alone; & we could almost spare the other three. Mark and Luke however do no harm; but John has I think been the cause of almost all bad theology: the Christ of that Gospel also strikes me as quite unlike the Christ of the other three; a sort of Edward Irving, one might say. How clearly one can trace in all of them the *gradual* rise of his conviction that he was the Messiah: and how much loftier & more self-devoted a tone his whole language & conduct assumed as soon as he felt convinced of that. Reading his history has done me along with much other good, this in particular, that it has *completed* my hatred of the Gig: I can hardly feel easy now under the thought that I have one foot in it still: I shall probably dismount altogether from it in time.—It was more than I hoped for that your brother should form any favourable judgment of me from the very little he can have seen, and that not of the best kind. I am persuaded that I owe his good opinion chiefly to your testimony. He appeared to me very like you: though I cannot doubt but that there are differences enough: it was the likeness too of a scholar to his master.

6. Carlyle had written in his letter of Sept. 24, 1833: "How different, above all, is that honey-mouthed, tear-stained, soup-kitchen Jesus Christ of our poor shovel-hatted modern Christians from the stern-visaged Christ of the Gospels, proclaiming aloud in the market-place (with such a total contempt of the social respectabilities): '*Woe* unto you, Scribes and Pharisees, *hypocrites*!' Descend from your gigs, ye wretched scoundrels, for the hour is come!" (A. Carlyle, p. 70.)

Of your friends or acquaintance here I have little to relate: most of them are away from London & have not written to me. Only Rowland Detrosier is doing exceedingly well as a lecturer on physics—picking up also some money by writing—and he will do something and be of use: a man of clearer or quicker understanding I never saw: only he has had no help, and no materials for his understanding to work on: the most abstract truths when they are presented to him he seizes almost at a glance, & possesses himself of their spirit, not their letter merely. He will thrive best under *my* teaching just now; he is not yet ripe for yours. He is eager, ardent, and indefatigably laborious; and to the extent of his faculties, most *serious* in his purpose of knowing and teaching the Truth.—If I had known you as well when you were in London as I do now, how many more persons should I have brought to see you! I now know that *any* human being is interesting to you, all who have self-subsistence eminently so: now even of those I could have made you acquainted with not a few. Since you were so much pleased with Emerson[7] I feel encouraged to try you with almost any person whatever who has any sort of good in him: I should have thought *he* was about the last person who would have interested you so much as he seems to have done. But you, yourself, are doubtless in many things, changed, and as you have several times intimated, changing: I greatly desire to know in what, and how much; should be still *more* gratified if I could in any way aid you, paying back thereby some small part of the good, of that and so many other kinds, which I have received from you. I have done little for *you* yet; perhaps am incapable of doing much: but it was part of my former character, the character I am throwing off, that I seldom wished or ventured to *argue* with my *teachers*: I do not mean mere *logic-fence*, but that I was content to receive without giving, & rather avoided occasions for expressing difference of opinion. In that however as in much else "I will mend" as you said of something far less important—The Austins are at Boulogne—but I have not heard from them. *Falk* I am sorry to hear sells but indifferently. I find both from enquiry and observation that the puffing system has worn itself out, even more rapidly than seemed likely: & a united chorus of praise from all the press will scarcely now sell fifty copies of any work: Effingham Wilson[8] the bookseller is so sensible of this that he has resolved to cease advertising the praises of periodicals and to sell his wares by *samples*, advertising passages of the works themselves. Thus does all lying contain the seeds of its own destruction: when all human speech has ceased to

7. Emerson had presented JSM's letter of introduction on Aug. 25 and had stayed twenty-four hours at Craigenputtock. See Carlyle's letter of Sept. 10, A. Carlyle, p. 66.

8. Effingham Wilson (1783–1868), best known as the publisher of Tennyson's first volume and of Browning's *Paracelsus*.

be believed, it seems as if men must recommence speaking the truth: yet who knows? for how many centuries has the whole East persevered in lying, although the fact that "all men are liars" *there* forms part of all men's knowledge of the world. Bulwer's book[9] is considerably better than I expected; the "tenuity" does not amount to more than semitransparency. There was one thing in what you said of Madame Roland which I did not quite like—it was, that she was almost rather a man than a woman: I believe that I quite agree in all that you really meant, but *is* there really any distinction between the highest masculine & the highest feminine character? I do not mean the mechanical *acquirements*; those, of course, will very commonly be different. But the women, of all I have known, who possessed the highest measure of what are considered feminine qualities, have combined with them more of the highest *masculine* qualities than I have ever seen in any but one or two men, & those one or two men were also in many respects almost women. I suspect it is the second-rate people of the two sexes that are unlike—the first-rate are alike in both—except—no, I do not think I can except anything—but then, in this respect, my position has been and is, what you say every human being's is in many respects "a peculiar one."—

I shall write from Paris—probably more than once.

Yours faithfully,

J. S. Mill

Make my kindest respects to Mrs Carlyle and crave her forgiveness (though as it was a matter of moral necessity, not choice, that is hardly the right word) for the postponement of my visit.[10]

88. TO WILLIAM JOHNSON FOX[1]

I.H.
Friday
[Oct. 10, 1833]

Dear Mr Fox

I go off this evening & therefore shall not see you which I am sorry for.

Thanks for your kind offer of doing anything for me during my absence[2]—The only thing which occurs to me, that you could do, would be to

9. *England and the English.*
10. This postscript is written at the top of the first page.

* * * *

1. MS at King's. One excerpt is published in Garnett, p. 110, but dated June, 1833. The dating of Oct. 10 is drawn from the reference to the impending departure for Paris "probably at the end of this week" in his Oct. 5 letter to Carlyle (the preceding letter).
2. He remained in Paris until about Nov. 20.

send us a copy of the Repository for next month. You might send it to Dussard, whose address is 9 Great Castle Street Cavendish Square[;] he has opportunities for Paris once or twice a week.

I send "Pauline"[3] having done all I could—which was, to annotate copiously in the margin, and *sum up* on the flyleaf—on the whole the observations are not flattering to the author—perhaps too strong in the *expression* to be shewn to him.[4]

I also send three numbers of the Plato[5] for your inspection and judgment. They cannot in any case be *used* until I return for it is necessary they should be carefully looked over, some passages altered, and some preliminary matter written—Let us hope that the arrival of Elliott's drama[6] will relieve you from any difficulty in filling the present number—if not, you must write it all yourself—I do not think the remainder of those scraps will help you much. A propos I had them actually in my pocket at Clapton but neglected to give them to you—I am sorry your brother[7] has had the trouble of calling for them.

You shall hear from me very soon—as I hope I shall from you

Farewell—

J.S.M.

89. TO WILLIAM JOHNSON FOX[1]

[Paris, Nov. 5 or 6, 1833]

I could have filled a long letter to you with the occurrences and feelings and thoughts of any one day since I have been here—this fortnight seems an age in mere duration, and *is* an age in what it has done for us two.[2]

3. This is the copy now in the Forster Collection of the Victoria and Albert Museum.

4. But Browning did see the copy. See Letter 74, n. 3.

5. Eventually published in the *Monthly Repository* under the title "Notes on Some of the More Popular Dialogues of Plato": 1. "The Protagoras," VIII (1834), 89–99, 203–11; 2. "The Phaedrus," VIII, 404–20, 633–46; 3. "The Gorgias," VIII, 691–710, 802–15, 829–42; 4. "The Apology of Socrates," IX (1835), 112–21, 169–78. Reprinted in *Four Dialogues of Plato*, trans. JSM, ed. Ruth Borchardt (London, 1946). Never published were five further translations with notes (the Charmides, Euthyphron, Laches, Lysis, and Parmenides), the MSS of which are in the New York Public Library.

6. Ebenezer Elliott, the Corn Law Rhymer, did contribute to the *Monthly Repository*, but not any drama.

7. Charles Fox, publisher of the *Monthly Repository.*

* * * *

1. *Addressed*: Rev. W. J. Fox / 1 Stamford Grove / Upper Clapton / London / Angleterre. *Postmarks*: FPO / NO 7 / 1833, and 10.F. Noon [???] / NO 7 / 1833. MS at Yale. Published, with minor errors, in Hayek, pp. 49–54.

2. JSM and Mrs. Taylor. See Letter 84, n. 2.

It has brought years of experience to us—good and happy experience most of it. We never could have been so near, so perfectly intimate, in any former circumstances—we never could have been together as we have been in innumerable smaller relations and concerns—we never should have spoken of all things, and in all frames of mind, with so much freedom and unreserve. I am astonished when I think how much has been restrained, how much untold, unshewn, uncommunicated till now—how much which by the new fact of its being spoken, has disappeared—so many real unlikenesses, so many more false impressions of unlikeness, most of which have only been revealed to me since they have ceased to exist or these which still exist have ceased to be felt painfully. Not a day has passed without removing some real & serious obstacle to happiness. I never thought so humbly of myself compared with her, never thought or felt myself so little worthy of her, never more keenly regretted that I am not, in some things, very different, for her sake—yet it is much to know as I do now; that almost all which has ever caused her any misgivings with regard to our fitness for each other was mistaken in point of fact—that the mistakes no longer exist—& that she is now (as she is) quite convinced that we are perfectly suited to pass our lives together—better suited indeed for that perfect than for this imperfect companionship. There will never again I believe be any obstacle to our being together entirely, from the slightest doubt that the experiment would succeed with respect to ourselves—not, as she used to say, for a short time, but for our natural lives. And yet—all the other obstacles or rather the one obstacle being as great as ever—our futurity is still perfectly uncertain. She has decided nothing except what has always been decided—not to renounce the liberty of sight—and it does not seem likely that anything will be decided until the end of the six months, if even *then* finally. For me, I am certain that whatever she decides will be wisest and rightest, even if she decide what was so repugnant to me at first—to remain here alone—it is repugnant to me still—but I can now see that perhaps it will be best—the future will decide that.

When will you write again—she shewed me your letter—it is beautiful in *you* to write so to any one, but who could write otherwise to her?

I am happy, but not *so* happy as when the future appeared surer.

I had written thus far before receiving your letter, and I am glad of it. I have now taken a larger sheet and copied the above into it.

Your letter does indeed shew that you do not at all "understand her state" and never have understood it—this I have only lately begun to suspect, & never was quite sure of it till now—and I see that under the presumption that you were more aware than I perceive you are of the real state of her feelings, I myself have said & written things which have confirmed you in the wrong impression.

You seem to think that she *was* decided, and *is* now undecided—that the state of feeling which led to the separation has been as you say "interrupted" and is to be "recommenced." Now this is an incorrect and so far a lower idea of her than the true one—she *never* had decided upon anything except not to give up either the feeling, or the power of communication with me—unless she did so, it was *Mr. Taylor's* wish, and seemed to be necessary to his comfort that she should live apart from him. When the separation had actually taken place, the result did as you say seem certain—not because we had willed to make it so, but because it seemed the necessary consequence of the new circumstances if the feelings of all continued the same. This was the sole cause & I think cause enough for the hopefulness and happiness which I felt almost all that month and which must have made a false impression on you. I never felt sure of what was to be after the six months, but I felt an immense increase of the chances in my favour. When I came here, I *expected* to find her no more decided than she had always been about what would be best for all, but *not* to find her as for the first time I did, doubtful of what would be best for our *own* happiness—under the influence of that fact and of the painful feelings it excited, I wrote to you. *That* doubt, thank heaven, lasted but a short time—if I had delayed my letter two days longer I should never have sent it.

If Mr. Taylor feels as you believe he does, he has been very far from telling her "all he feels"; for his last letter to her, which came by the same post as this of yours (the first she ever shewed to me) is in quite another tone. He is most entirely mistaken in all the facts. Her affection for him, which originated in gratitude for his affection & kindness, instead of being weakened by this stronger feeling, has been greatly *strengthened*, by so many new proofs of *his* affection for *her*, & by the unexpected & (his nature considered) really admirable generosity & nobleness which he has shewn under so severe a trial. Instead of *reviving* in absence, her affection for him has been steady throughout; it is of quite another character from *this* feeling, & therefore does not in the least conflict with it *naturally*, & now when circumstances have thrown the two into opposition she can no more overcome, or wish to overcome the one, than the other. The difference is, that the one, being only *affection*, not *passion,* would be satisfied with knowing him to be happy though away from her—but if the choice were absolutely between giving up the stronger feeling, & making him (what he says he should be) durably wretched, I am quite convinced that either would be [more?][3] than she could bear. I know it is the common notion of passionate love that it sweeps away all other affections—but surely the *justification* of passion, & one of its greatest beauties & glories, is that in an otherwise fine character it weakens *no* feeling which deserves to subsist,

3. Page torn.

but would naturally strengthen them all. Because her letters to Mr. Taylor express the strong affection she has always felt, and he is no longer seeing, every day, proofs of her far stronger feeling for another, he thinks the affection has *come back*—he might have seen it quite as plainly before, only he refused to believe it. *I* have seen it, and felt its immense power over her, in moments of intense excitement with which I am sure he would believe it to be utterly incompatible.

Her affection for him, which has always been the principal, is now the sole obstacle to our being together—for the present there seems absolutely no prospect of that obstacle's being got over. She believes—& she knows him better than any of us can—that it would be the breaking-up of his whole future life—*that* she is determined never to be the cause of, & I am as determined never to urge her to it, as convinced that if I did I should fail. Nothing could justify it but "the most distinct perception" that it is not only "necessary to the happiness of both", but the only means of saving both or either from insupportable unhappiness. That can never be unless the alternative were entire giving up. I believe he is quite right in his impression that the worst for him which is to be expected at the end of the six months is her remaining permanently here. She will if it is in human power to do so, make him understand the exact state of her feelings, and will as at present minded, give *him* the choice of every possible arrangement except entire giving-up, with a strong wish that her remaining here may be his choice; with a full understanding however that the agreement whatever it be, is to be no longer binding than while it is found endurable. This seems but a poor result to come of so much suffering & so much effort, but for *us* even so the gain is great.

She has seen and approved all that precedes, therefore it is as much her letter as mine. So now you know the whole state of the case.

She is on the whole far happier than I have ever known her, and quite well physically though far from strong—I have many anxious *thoughts* of how she is to bear the being again alone with so little of hope to sustain her. I am so convinced of all I have written above, that if the final decision were already made (whatever it might be) I am certain that the fact of Mr. Taylor's being to be here so soon after I am gone would be a real & great good to her—but *now*, I am afraid unless she sees her way clearly to some tolerably satisfactory arrangement in the first few days of his visit she will only be made more unhappy by being made to feel still more keenly the impossibility of avoiding great unhappiness to him.

You know, perhaps, that her brother[4] has been here—nothing could have been better or sweeter than all he said & did—he was even *friendly*.

Can I do anything for you here—see any one, or bring over anything for you—I shall leave Paris probably Friday week.

4. Edward Hardy.

It is idle, almost, to *say* any thanks for all you are saying and doing for our good & for such part of the interest you feel in it, as regards me personally—I may be able some time or other to make some return to you for it all, more than by invoking as I do, all the blessings earth is heir to upon you and yours.

J.S.M.

90. TO WILLIAM JOHNSON FOX[1]

[Nov. 22, 1833]

In our conversation the other evening the more important matters of which we were thinking and talking made me forget to say that if you will send to me those Plato papers,[2] I will try to make them fit for the M.R.

You are I suppose provided for the next number—otherwise in a day or two I could finish one of those things.

I have the strongest wish, and some hope, that there will some day arrive a sketch of Paris, in the manner of some of your local sketches—if there does, it will be the most beautiful thing ever written—she has spoken quite enough to me at different times, to shew what it would be.

Have you seen Mr. Taylor? he has received a letter by this time, part of which she has sent to me, and which if he was still in the state in which you last saw him, will certainly put him completely out of it. Ed. Hardy[3] while he confirms all you told me of the impression her precious letter made upon him when it came, bringing back his old hopes and theories, affirms positively that all this had quite gone off before he received any other letter, & that his acquiescence in her return to him is *not* given under the influence of those hopes and theories but of a real intention of being with her as a *friend* and *companion*. His conduct & feelings *now*, will shew whether this is correct. I shall be anxious to know your impression when you shall have seen him in his present state.

It seems he had written to her *again* since I left Paris—she writes "I had yesterday one of those letters from Mr. Taylor which make us admire & love him. He says that this plan & my letters have given him delight—that he has been selfish—but in future will think more for others & less for himself—but still he talks of this plan being good *for all*, by which he means *me*, as he says he is sure it will 'prevent after misery' & again he wishes for complete confidence. I have written exactly what I think without reserve."

I have not time to write another word.

J.S.M.

1. *Addressed*: Rev. W. J. Fox / 1 Stamford Grove / Upper Clapton. *Postmark*: [???] / [???] 22[?] / 1833. MS at Yale. Published in part in Hayek, pp. 54–55.

2. See Letter 88, n. 5.

3. Brother of Mrs. Taylor.

91. TO THOMAS CARLYLE[1]

India House 25th November 1833

MY DEAR CARLYLE

As might have been anticipated I found no time while at Paris to write to you, and though I have now been in London a week, I have not been able till now to collect my thoughts for the sort of letter which my conscience tells me I ought to write. Let me dispose of business matters first. I have made the various inquiries you wanted made. First about the mode of living at Paris. M. Comte,[2] whom you may have heard of as a writer, & who is now Secretaire Perpetuel to the new Academy of Moral and Political Science, a man who has tried both countries & who lived in a very simple stile in both, who has lived in both as a man ever in narrow circumstances—married and having two or three children—*he* is my first witness, & he says that Paris & London are much on a par: that you may live luxuriously in Paris for less money than in London, but that for any stile of living *not* luxuriously, the expense is nearly the same in both cities, with perhaps a slight advantage in favour of Paris. Tanneguy Duchâtel,[3] who is an economist & statistician & I should think accurate in his facts, says that *un député* may if he chuse live at Paris during a six months session of the chamber for 300 francs (£12) a month if alone, for at most 500 francs (£20) if he have a wife and no children. The chief article of necessary consumption which is dearer at Paris than *en province* or in England, seems to be dress: *that,* if you stay only six months or so you can carry out a supply of for the whole time I suppose. You can have in the best quarters of Paris, lodgings which I think would perfectly suit you for 200 francs a month. This would include accommodation for a maid servant. Your food would be decidedly cheaper than in London. As to other matters, there is the most ample & ready access to many excellent libraries; some difficulty, but not I believe impossibility, in having permission to take books home with you. All persons of all sorts are accessible with the greatest ease to any one who had such introductions as you would have. A little way out of Paris the expenses are decidedly less, viz. houserent less, food of all sorts cheaper by the cost of conveyance and the very high *octroi.* In executing your smaller commissions at Paris I have had great assistance from Adolphe d'Eichthal who is much pleased

1. *Addressed*: Thos. Carlyle Esq / Craigenputtoch / Dumfries / N.B. *Postmarks*: 26NO26 / 1833, and DUMFRIES / 28 NOV 1833. Franked by Chas. Buller, Jr. MS at Carlyle House, London. Published, with errors and omissions, in Elliot, I, 71–81. In reply to Carlyle's of Oct. 28, 1833, A. Carlyle, pp. 75–82; answer by Carlyle, Dec. 17, 1833, A. Carlyle, pp. 82–88. On Aug. 8, 1837, JSM wrote Carlyle to ask for the return of this letter, for the purpose indicated below in n. 18.

2. Charles Comte.

3. Charles Tanneguy, comte Duchâtel.

at the prospect of your going there. The books which I ordered were not ready when I left Paris & I do not even know what the bookseller whom Adolphe employed had & had not been able to get. I fear there is no Dictionnaire Neologique but that appended to the Dict. de l'Academie. The Hénault[4] I expect to receive immediately, together with a map of the province "Ile de France" & I have hopes of several tracts on the *collier* affair.[5] Adolphe has sent your questions to several people whom he thought likely to be able to give you information, of whom one only has yet given him any answers; a certain Baron Darnay,[6] who was then (viz. during the *procès*) a *conseiller au parlement*: his responses, which do not give much information, I inclose. Apropos I find that the parcel I destined for you did not go, last month; the cause being that Fraser promised to send for it, and faithlessly neglected to do so. I have ordered no very great number of books, & of those I doubt whether many would interest you much: the works of Ballanche,[7] a sort of palingenesic philosopher now in some repute; Beranger's[8] poems; the Proverbes of Leclerc;[9] no memoirs except those of the Abbé Morellet[10] which I had read before, & know to contain several revolutionary scenes which would interest you. But it seems to me that the writing, buying, and reading of books has come to an end in France as well as here; in France it may perhaps revive sooner than here, having been extremely rife only five years ago & perhaps only temporarily interrupted by the débordement de la politique et des petits écrits. Here it has perished by a gradual decay, and the causes of its melancholy fate are I fear permanent.

But now to attempt to tell you anything about France and Paris! I cannot; one or two personal portraits I think I could give you, & that is the sum of all my personal knowledge—I can only say, go and look; look & you will certainly see: there is abundance to be seen, known, & judged of in six months or a year, little or nothing in one month, especially when the object of one's visit is not exclusively to *see*. Except of some few individuals, I have brought back no impressions but very general ones, & of these scarcely one of which I am quite certain, except *this* one that there is an infinity of things to see, & that it requires a less piercing eye-

4. C. J. F. Hénault, *Abrégé chronologique de l'histoire de France* (Paris, 1744; and many later editions).

5. The famous "affair of the diamond necklace"; Carlyle's article, "The Diamond Necklace," was not published until 1837.

6. Probably Baron Antoine Darnay (d. 1837), who had served under Prince Eugène Beauharnais in Italy and had been "directeur général du royaume d'Italie."

7. Pierre Simon Ballanche (1776–1847), mystical philosopher. His *Œuvres complètes* (6 vols., Paris, 1830–32).

8. Pierre Jean de Béranger (1780–1857).

9. Michel Théodore Leclercq, *Proverbes dramatiques* (4 vols., Paris, 1823–26, and various later editions).

10. *Mémoires inédites de l'Abbé Morellet . . .* (2 vols., Paris, 1821).

sight to see them, than here, because the natural signs and expressions of feeling & character are in a much less degree repressed by the ponderous dull atmosphere of custom & *respectability* which weighs upon them here. It really does seem to me that people care infinitely less in Paris about keeping in the *gig*: or what comes to the same thing when we are speaking of a *people*, the gig is lower, far nearer to the ground, does not so easily break down with you, & it is easy stepping *in* as well as *out*. It does appear to me that it needs little or no courage at Paris, to make the openest profession of any kind of opinions or feelings whatever. It is the very place which a speculative man should desire for promulgating his opinions, for you startle nobody, you are sure of an audience; sure of being supported, & what is perhaps still better, sure of being attacked. How different here. Littérateurs and artists there are I fancy next to none—those who pass for such I had not time to go amongst, but *you* easily might. I could, had I stayed longer. I suspect we have been too much impressed, you and I and others, by the Literature of Despair.[11] I was in hopes that *despair* was the necessary consequence of having no Belief, in a nation at least, though not always in an individual: but I fear that is only in the nobler spirits, or at least the *young* persons of strong feelings and artistical capabilities. In France I see every reason to believe that the mass of the well-to-do classes can make themselves comfortable without either God or Devil, either literal or *constructive*, and are well satisfied to eat their pudding in quiet—those I mean who have enough pudding to eat, which is an infinitely larger proportion than in this country. Most of the *educated* people have enough to make them comfortable, and there is very little of the artificial demand for *more money* which the striving & straining for respectability occasions here; respectability there does not depend upon money. All agree that any man who can dress decently may dine with or go to the soirées of anybody, & mix on terms of perfect equality with all whom he meets. Then the peasantry commonly have their bit of land, & consider themselves also as lords of the soil: except, therefore, the ambitious spirits & the working population of Paris and the great towns, people seem to be tolerably content with their lot. The government has for the last year or two made great efforts to fix the attention of the people on *les intérêts matériels*, on schemes of commercial improvement, railroads & the like; & they are half mad, many of them, about railroads, in mere unreasoning imitation of England & England's "prosperity." The *trades* of Paris, like the manufacturers of Lyons have formed unions & are all striking for wages, i.e. the skilled labourers, those who are highly paid already: & impartial people, such as Adolphe d'Eichthal, say that their object is not so much, more money, as to *elevate* their rank in society, since at present the gentlemen will not keep

11. See Letter 82.

company with them & they will not keep company with the common labourers. The revolutionary part of the republicans have opened a connexion with these Trade Societies, and attempt to turn them to purposes of revolution, with what success I know not: they themselves say "the greatest," the other republicans say "not so great," the non-republicans say "none at all," from all which I infer that nothing can be known about it. If I had stayed I should have managed to attend some of the meetings of these workmen: though it seems they are jealous of the presence of gentlemen, even gentlemen-republicans. On the whole, politics are for the present very much out of vogue: nor do I know what is *in* vogue, except railroads: not the theatres, for people are ceasing to go there: not literature, for nothing is written or read except the usual succession of novels which went on even during the Reign of Terror. The newspapers, even, are little read compared with two years ago; & even la propagande *républicaine* has taken refuge in little penny papers which are hawked every Sunday in the streets & on the boulevards. One must be at Paris to know how profoundly irreligious the French are: the higher kind of books and newspapers have got beyond the irreligious state and are mostly prophesying a religion or regretting the impossibility of one—or have at least learnt to recognise a historical value in the religions of the Past or at most think it an old joke, too stale to be revived now: but the little *feuilles* which one buys as one goes into a theatre, are the representatives of the Voltairian philosophy at present: the summits of the national intellect have emerged above it, and it has descended to envelop & overshroud the lower regions. Our friends the St. Simonians now St. Simonians no longer, have done much good, & are still doing some. The Père,[12] as you may have seen in the newspapers, having been let out of prison before his sentence was expired, has gone, with Fournel & some others of the set who were engineers, to persuade the Pacha of Egypt to let them cut a canal across the Isthmus of Suez—whereby the *deux mondes*, the *Orient* & the *Occident*, are still to be *réunis* by means of them. What has become of those who went to Constantinople in search of *la femme libre* I do not know. One or two, especially Jules Lechevalier & Abel Transon, have become disciples of Fourier, a sort of Robert Owen who is to accomplish all things by means of cooperation & of rendering *labour agreeable*, & under whose system man is to acquire absolute power over the laws of physical nature; among other happy results, the sea is to be changed into lemonade. Some have become Catholics; but among these are none of the considerable men of the set. The great majority have retained of St Simonianism about as much as is good and true, dropping the rest. The Bazard portion have mostly become republicans, the Enfantin portion, who were rich, strong partisans of *les moyens pacifiques*, have become

12. Prosper Enfantin.

juste milieu men in politics, endeavouring to work out improvement with the *existing* machinery. The government, acting I suppose on the judicious maxim that a Utopian *désenchanté* is very manageable, has restored to most of them who were engineers miners or the like, their rank in the service. Michel Chevalier was scarcely out of prison when they selected him to be sent to the United States to study their canals & railways. Flachat is now one of the three editors of the Constitutionnel, where he writes good articles on free trade & such like matters: he seems a sensible man, without much enthusiasm left in him; he stuck to them to the last, & had by his own account a *fièvre cérébrale* from the suffering & anxiety it caused him; after which he was very near becoming a Christian: now he seems to be left with a vague presentiment that there will be a religion some time or other. Leroux,[13] & Reynaud,[14] whom you remember as the protester against Enfantin, (both of whom I saw) go on prophesying a religion in the Revue Encyclopédique; their notions are somewhat singular, Reynaud's especially who thinks that the future religion will not be revealed, nor brought to light at once, but will be evolved gradually by le progrès de la raison publique, like a *science*. They have all sorts of vagaries too about the "Orient" & are grubbing into Sanscrit and Chinese literature in hopes of finding something which may help towards raising up this religion which is to be built up, brick after brick. I recollect in a number of the Revue Encyclopédique one of them says in express terms that since we know hardly anything of the East except the Bible, & since that is so good, doubtless if we knew more we should find something still better.—Among the individuals of another kind whom I saw & formed an acquaintance with, two made a particular impression upon me; two perfectly self-subsistent men in the best sense, or I am greatly mistaken in them; & in that, honorably distinguished from Frenchmen in general. Both these are republican leaders; leaders however of two very different sorts of republicans; or rather, not leaders, but men who follow no other person's lead, and whom every one is glad to follow. These are, Carrel,[15] the editor of the National, & Cavaignac,[16] whose speech when on trial for a conspiracy two years ago I translated & inserted in the *Examiner*,[17] where you may have seen it.[18] I knew Carrel as the most powerful journalist in France, sole

13. Pierre Leroux (1798–1871), philosopher, journalist, and politician.
14. Jean Reynaud (1806–1863), philosopher.
15. Armand Carrel (1800–1836), journalist.
16. Godefroi Cavaignac (1801–1845), politician.
17. In the column headed "Foreign Intelligence: France," *Examiner,* April 24, 1831, pp. 266–67. Not listed in JSM's bibliography of his writings.
18. Most of what follows was reproduced by JSM in his essay on Armand Carrel, *LWR*, XXVIII (Oct., 1837), 66–111, reprinted in *Dissertations,* I, 237–308. The article also includes a tribute to Cavaignac.

manager of a paper which while it keeps aloof from all *coterie* influence & from the actively revolutionary part of the republican body, has for some time been avowedly republican; & I knew that he was considered a vigorous, energetic *man of action*, who would always have courage & conduct in an emergency. Knowing thus much of him, I was ushered into the National office where I found six or seven of the innumerable *rédacteurs* who belong to a French paper, all dark-haired men with formidable *moustaches* (which many of the republicans have taken to wearing) & looking fiercely republican. Carrel was not there, & after waiting some time I was introduced to a slight elegant young man with extremely polished manners, no *moustaches* at all, and apparently fitter for a drawing-room than a camp; this was the commander-in-chief of those formidable looking champions. But it was impossible to be five minutes in his company without perceiving that he was accustomed to *ascendancy*, & so accustomed as not to feel it; instead of that eagerness & impetuosity which one finds in most Frenchmen, his manner is extremely deliberate; without any affectation he speaks in a sort of measured cadence, & in a manner of which your words "quiet emphasis" are more characteristic than of any man I know: there is the same quiet emphasis in his writings: a man singularly free, if we may trust appearances, from self-consciousness; simple, graceful, almost *infantinely* playful as they all say when he is among his intimates, & indeed I could see that myself; & combining perfect self-reliance with the most unaffected modesty; in opinions, & political position, the Fonblanque of France; like Fonblanque, too, standing quite alone (je n'aime pas, said he to me one day, à marcher en troupeau) occupying a midway position, facing one way towards the supporters of monarchy & an aristocratic limitation of the suffrage, with whom he will have no compromise, on the other towards the extreme republicans who have anti-property doctrines, and instead of his United-States republic, want a republic *de la façon de la Convention*, with something like a dictatorship in their own hands: he calls himself a Conservative Republican (*l'opinion républicaine conservatrice*); not but that he sees plainly that the present constitution of property admits of many improvements but he thinks they can only take place gradually or at least that philosophy has not yet matured them: & he would rather hold back than accelerate the revolution which he thinks inevitable, in order to leave time for ripening those great questions, chiefly affecting the constitution of property & the condition of the working classes, which would press for a solution if a revolution were to take place. As for himself he says that he is not *un homme spécial*, that his *métier de journaliste* engrosses him too much to enable him to study, and that he is profoundly ignorant of much upon which he would have to decide if he were in power; & could do nothing but bring together a body generally representative of the people, & assist in carrying into execution the dictates of their united wisdom. This is modest enough in the man who would certainly be President of the Republic if there were a republic within five years & the extreme party did not get the upper hand. He seems to know well what he does know: I have met with no such views of the French Revolution in any book, as those I have heard from him.—A very different man from Carrel is Cavaignac; he is president of the *Société des Droits de l'Homme*, who are the active stirring revolutionary party, who look up to *Robespierre*, and aim at *l'égalité absolue*: he is for taking the first opportunity for overthrowing the government by force, & thinks the opportunity must come in six months, or a year at farthest: a man whose name is energy; who cannot ask you the commonest question but in so decided a manner that he makes you start: a man who impresses you with a sense of irresistible power & indomitable will; you might fancy him an incarnation of Satan, if he were your enemy or the enemy of your party, & if you had not associated with him & seen how full of sweetness and amiableness & gentleness he is: intense in everything, he is the intensest of atheists, & says, "je n'aime pas ceux qui croient en Dieu" because "it is generally a reason for doing nothing for Man": but his notion of Duty is that of a Stoic; he conceives it as something quite infinite, & having nothing whatever to do with Happiness, something immeasurably above it: a kind of half Manichean in his views of the universe: according to him man's Life consists of one perennial & intense struggle against the principle of Evil, which but for that struggle would wholly overwhelm him: generation after generation carries on this battle, with little success as yet: he believes in perfectibility, & progressiveness, but thinks that hitherto *progress* has consisted only in removing some of the impediments to good, not in realising the good itself; that nevertheless the only satisfaction which man can realise for himself is in battling with this evil principle & overpowering it; that after evils have accumulated for centuries, there sometimes comes one great clearing-off on one day of reckoning called a revolution; that it is only on *such* rare occasions, very rarely indeed on any others, that good men get into power, & then they ought to seize the opportunity for doing all they can; that any government which is boldly attacked, by ever so small a minority, may be overthrown, & that is his hope with regard to the present government. His notion of *égalité absolue* is rather speculative than practical: he says he does not know whether it should be by an equal division of the *means* of production (land and capital) or by an equal division of the produce: when I stated to him the difficulties of both he felt & acknowledged them; all he had to propose were but a variety of measures *tending towards* an equalisation of property: & he seems to have a strange reliance on *events,* thinking that when the end is clearly conceived, the circumstances of the case would when power is in the right hands, suggest the most appropriate means. Cavaignac is the son of a Conventionalist and regicide. He is a much more accomplished man than most of the political men I saw there; has a wider range of ideas, converses on Art, & most subjects of general interest: always throwing all he has to say into a few brief energetic sentences, as if it was contrary to his nature to expend one superfluous word. Just as I was coming away he gave me the first two numbers of a periodical work[19] which a set of republicans have just set up. All of it seems to be rubbish except the introductory discourse, which is by Cavaignac, and which is an exposition of his philosophy, his idea of "the significance of man's life": it contains all that I have just written to you & much of the same sort, but my impressions were not derived from it, but from his conversation; and the essay appeared to me a complete *résumé* of the man: such as it is, it made no sensation whatever; it flew over the heads of Carrel & the rest, they all voted it vague, abstract, metaphysical, & the like: *you* will be struck with it; I send it in Fraser's parcel. I am to correspond with Cavaignac and Carrel & various others and shall know much more of them I hope: with Carrel I am to establish an exchange of articles; Carrel is to send some to the Examiner and I am to send some to the National, with liberty to publish them here. I could tell you much more of these men & other men, but this is enough for one letter—let me hear your remarks & questions, and they will remind me of a hundred things which I have omitted. I have other things to write, too, *not* about Paris: but they must wait. On the whole, I think you will go to Paris next summer, and *I* probably shall pay my visit to you there instead of Craigenputtoch. You will find several persons there eager to be friendly, among others, Cousin.[20] His name reminds me of a hundred things to tell you in my next.—Let me hear from you soon. My best remembrances to Mrs Carlyle.—Vale mei memor.

J. S. MILL

Read Buller on Mirabeau in the Cochrane Review[21]—did you detect me in the Ex^r reviewing Miss Martineau, & Col. Napier?[22]

19. *Paris révolutionnaire,* 4 vols., 1833–34 (reprinted, 1848). The introduction by Cavaignac was entitled "La Force révolutionnaire."

20. Victor Cousin (1792–1867), philosopher and educational reformer.

21. *FQR,* XII (Oct., 1833), 455–95.

22. Reviews of Harriet Martineau's *A Tale of the Tyne* in *Examiner,* Oct. 27, 1833, pp. 676–78; and of Col. Charles Napier's *The Colonies* in *ibid.,* Nov. 24, 1833, pp. 740–41.

This postscript is written at the top of the first page.

92. TO WILLIAM JOHNSON FOX[1]

26th November, 1833

Roebuck, Strutt,[2] Buller, and other radical members of Parliament have a scheme to start a radical review as their organ,[3] with individual signatures like J.R., in which we should all of us write—the thing looks possible, and everybody seems so eager about it that I really think it will come to pass.

If so, it will train up both readers and writers for *The Monthly Repository*, *The Examiner*, Tait, and all. Strength is multiplied by division when it is *growing* strength. [. . .]

The Examiner has hoisted a flag of distress. Fonblanque cannot go on, and the paper may stop any week. He can retrench so as to cover the weekly loss if he had £1000 in hand. This he proposes raising by inducing 100 persons to pay £10 each, for which they are to receive his paper for ten years, and for which (without counting on any increase of sale) he can carry it on on the chance of reduction of the stamp duties within that time. What think you of the scheme? And if you think well of it, would you—not subscribe yourself—but mention the proposition to any persons you know who would?

A much better plan *selon moi* would be that someone who has £1000 should put it down himself to become the proprietor, keeping Fonblanque as editor only, and the other persons interested remaining creditors of the paper. If I were not in the India House and were going to remain in England I would do so immediately, that is, I would propose it to Fonblanque, who I think must consent—and I would have him as political editor and take the literary and art department myself. But that it seems cannot be—and I fear nobody else will—though it would at worst be only an advance without interest, at best an extremely profitable investment.

93. TO VICTOR COUSIN[1]

India House, 30 novembre 1833

MON CHER MONSIEUR,

Parmi les documents que vous avez désiré avoir au sujet de ce qui ce fait ici sur l'éducation considérée comme affaire d'Etat, je n'ai pu encore me procurer que le discours de mon ami Roebuck,[2] qui m'a chargé de

1. Excerpts published in Garnett, pp. 151–52. MS not located.
2. Edward Strutt, later Baron Belper (1801–1880), then MP for Derby.
3. This was an early stage in the plans for the *London Review*, which was first published in 1835 with JSM as the real though not official editor.

* * * *

1. Published in J. Barthélemy-Saint-Hilaire, *M. Victor Cousin, Sa Vie et Sa Correspondance* (3 vols., Paris, 1895), I, 394–95. MS not located.
2. See Letter 82, n. 8. Roebuck frequently quoted Cousin in his speech.

vous en faire hommage en son nom. Vous verrez qu'il donne à l'élection populaire le choix des instituteurs primaires. Vous mettrez peut-être cela sur le compte du radicalisme; mais radicalisme ou non, je crois que, dans notre pays, où la centralisation n'est nullement dans les mœurs, c'est la le seul moyen de faire accepter par la nation l'éducation forcée.

Quant au commencement d'exécution que reçoit aujourd'hui ce principe introduit, pour ainsi dire, par supercherie, dans nos lois, mon ami Chadwick, qui en est l'auteur principal, m'a promis des renseignements que j'aurai l'honneur de vous faire parvenir par la première occasion. C'est alors que je prendrai la liberté de vous écrire plus au long.

Je n'ai pas encore vu Madame Austin, à qui cependant j'ai envoyé depuis longtemps les petits ouvrages que vous m'avez confiés pour elle. Un léger mal aux yeux qui m'a forcé de rester chez moi le soir, ne m'empêchera sans doute pas beaucoup plus longtemps d'aller la voir. Je ne sais pas si elle vous a écrit. Son adresse est, 5 Orme Square, Bayswater.

Agréez, mon cher Monsieur, l'hommage de mon profond respect.

J. S. MILL

Si vous vouliez me donner des nouvelles de votre santé, vous me feriez un très grand plaisir.

94. TO THOMAS CARLYLE[1]

Kensington
22d December 1833.

MY DEAR CARLYLE

Your letter had been hoped for and expected & in one sense waited for, a considerable time—for I *had* various matters of interest to write to you about, but as I hoped for a letter so soon I delayed writing till I could make my letter answer yours.

One of those matters is, the affair of the Examiner, of which you have heard somewhat from Hayward.[2] It *is* in difficulties, and those of so serious a kind, that if something had not been done or attempted *immediately* to save it, there was danger of its stopping altogether. The cause is melancholy enough, being less the circumstances of the paper, though it is not prosperous, than those of Fonblanque himself, who, like his father before him, has wanted firmness to restrain his expenses within his means. Since he

1. *Addressed*: Thomas Carlyle / Craigenputtoch / Dumfries / N.B. *Postmarks*: FREE / 24 DE 24 / 1833, and DUMFRIES / 26 DEC 1833. Franked by J. A. Roebuck. MS at NLS. Published, with omissions, in Elliot, I, 81–86. In reply to Carlyle's of Dec. 17, 1833, A. Carlyle, pp. 82–88; answered by Carlyle, Jan. 20, 1834, A. Carlyle, pp. 90–96.

2. Abraham Hayward (1801–1884), miscellaneous writer; strongly Tory in his views and in later life a bitter critic of JSM.

enlarged the paper in January 1831, it has yielded him little; it allows him nominally £500 a year; reckoning that in addition to its other expenses it has during these three years lost on the average £6 a week; which coming out of his £500 reduced it to below £200. He, meantime, has been living at a rate most needlessly expensive, and is at last so completely drained, & his credit I should think so completely exhausted, that he can go on no longer. Strange that a man who writes so feelingly and powerfully on this same weakness should so act—but not at all strange, only melancholy, that one who so acts, possessing intellect, should so write. If *his* difficulties do not ruin the paper, it is in no danger; for means of retrenchment present themselves to the extent of £8 or £9 a week, by discharging Chadwick,[3] whose work Fonblanque takes upon himself in addition to his own; and by cheaper arrangements for printing and paper; which however depend upon first paying off an arrear to his printer & stationer. £1000 would do all this, & start him fair with £500 a year & an improving property; for advertisements, the great source of profit to a paper, have as you must have observed with pleasure, multiplied exceedingly in the Ex^r since the reduction of the duty. The £1000 it were to be wished that some one person of the right disposition should have advanced, becoming thereby *proprietor*, in the place of F. whose personal circumstances would then have ceased to compromise the paper, & who would of course have been retained as editor. This I would myself have proposed to do, were not my position with regard to the India House, which hampers my freedom of action in a thousand ways but which shall not hamper it always, in this case an insuperable obstacle. What has been attempted is, to raise the money in subscriptions of £10 each from 100 persons, each of whom is to receive the paper gratis for ten years. Sixty promises have been obtained, the remaining forty are still to seek: as many as twenty more are I think as good as certain—but less than the whole hundred will not do, for the debts on the paper amount to £780 & money to the extent of the remainder will then be wanted to start it fair, or perhaps (for I know not) to keep poor Fonblanque out of the King's Bench. I am doing all I can to interest people in the matter—& should have written to you among the first, had I not known that you could do little (if anything) in the way either of subscribing or procuring subscriptions. I think we shall succeed, but it will require a vigorous effort.—The sale of the Examiner does not much exceed 3000 copies. This is as you say a scandalous symptom, yet there are many causes that contribute to it besides the scandalous ones that first suggest themselves. Of course it can only expect buyers (*readers* are quite another matter) from radicals: now of these the more vulgar sort find as much radicalism in other papers, of a more direct and palpable kind, with greater *breadth*, as the painters say: for Fonblanque's genius, fine as it is, goes all

3. Edwin Chadwick had been serving as sub-editor since 1830.

into the details—not into the general mode of treating a subject: he does not go straight to the main point, despising all little side views, dwell upon that & *make that* tell—like the Times, which with materials of no intrinsic value whatever writes *powerfully* for popular effect, as Fonblanque might do with *his powers*, though scarcely with his turn of mind. Then F.'s allusions, expressions, stile, all the *garb* of his thoughts is intelligible, or at least impressive, only to persons of literary, one might say almost *classical* education, & most of *them* are not radicals.—Not to mention that such as do not take a daily paper, require in a weekly one a better abstract of *news—that* I hope will now in some degree be mended. Then the more moderate radicals are revolted by the tone of hatred in which the paper is written. This feeling extends to many who would have no objection to, but would applaud, the utterance of the bitterest truths, but do not like a *perpetual* carping at little things, honestly indeed, yet often unfairly & making no personal allowances, sometimes misstating altogether the *kind* of blame which is deserved, & meting it out in unequal measures to different people, so as to give an appearance of spleen & personal antipathy to individuals—especially to some of the Ministers, & among them, most perhaps to some of those who deserve it rather *less* than the others. In all this there is much truth; on the other hand much also is to be said for Fonblanque, but on the whole not enough to acquit him entirely. So he has really no *partisans* at all, & loses by almost all his excellencies and by his faults too. At the very time when he was offending the moderate radicals by the nature of his attacks on the ministry, he was losing at the rate of 100 subscribers every week for some time by resisting the anti-police *furor*. Still, the position of the paper will be a good one if this money can be raised, & raised I hope it will be.

I have another piece of news to tell you: the principal radicals in parliament & many of those out of it have a scheme for starting a new quarterly review, & are exerting themselves so much for it that they will probably succeed in setting it going.[4] The first promoters of it were Roebuck, Buller, & I; & we shall probably be the surest & most regular contributors, though there will be abundance of others—All the educated radicals to whom the thing has been mentioned enter into it with a degree of warmth unusual with them & offer both pecuniary & literary assistance. There is but one exception—& that one I lament to say is Grote—who has gradually sunk into a state always too congenial to him, of thinking that no good is to be done & who therefore will certainly never do any—at most no harm, & scarcely that, for it *is* harm to discourage others. A bookseller is willing to take the risk for two years provided editorship & writers are found for that period—in order to do so, the rich radicals,

4. These discussions led to the founding of the *London Review* the following year. See Letters 96 and 104.

Strutt, Warburton, Sir. W. Molesworth,[5] the Marshalls[6] of Leeds, & others, are going to raise money of the necessary amount among themselves & their friends, in shares of £25 or £50 the same person being allowed to take any number. The plan (Roebuck's & mine, to which all have at once assented) is, to drop altogether every kind of lying; the lie of pretending that all the articles are *reviews*, when more than half of them are not; and the lie of pretending that all the articles proceed from a *corps*, who jointly entertain all the opinions expressed. There is to be no *we*; but each writer is to have a signature, which he may avow or not as he pleases, but which (unless there be special reasons to constitute an exception) is to be the *same* for *all* his articles, thus making him *individually* responsible & allowing his opinions to derive what light they can from one another. The editor answers only for adequate literary merit, & a general *tendency* not in contradiction to the objects of the publication. They would I believe make *me* editor if I would take it—but I cannot; hampered again! but this time it is of little consequence, for I hope they will have Mr. Fox, who will be quite as fit: if they will not have *him*, there *are* other candidates not *unfit* though not *so* fit. If this scheme goes on, I hope you will write *for* the review or at least *in* it. As an organ of utterance it will be at least more congenial to you than Fraser's Magazine. It is true the prejudices of our Utilitarians are at least as strong against some of your writings as those of any other persons whatever, & though the individual signature would smooth many difficulties, even *that* would hardly, with them, have covered your "Characteristics" or "Teufelsdröckh" (were you afraid of the word *Dreck*?) but such an article as that on Johnson they would have delighted in; that on Ebenezer Elliott & various others of yours would have suited them perfectly. In fact, I hardly know one of your *opinions*, as often as you do not feel yourself called upon to make a direct attack upon themselves, which they would have any difficulty in getting on with: and I expect no difficulty in getting a passport for any of *mine*, which except in mere metaphysics, are quite as unlike theirs as *yours* are: what revolts them is the combination of opinions new & often strange to them, with a *manner* (to them) equally new & still more strange, & which prevents them not only from understanding your meaning but from desiring to understand it. I have never found one of them who, after taking the trouble to read enough of your writings to understand any thing of your drift, did not recognise in them much more of what he deemed good than of what he deemed bad; it is true I have found few who would take that trouble, & some of those few

5. Sir William Molesworth (1810–1855), politician, who in the following year supplied the money to establish the *London Review*.

6. A wealthy mill-owning family of Leeds, active in Reform politics, including: John Marshall (b. 1765), MP for York 1826–30; John Marshall (1797–1836), MP for Leeds 1832–35; and William Marshall (1796–1872), MP for various constituencies 1826–68.

would not have done so if they had not had *faith* (derived from my testimony) that it was worth while. I tell you this, to let you know how the land lies. There is nothing in what I have said that needs be any obstacle to your writing for this review—it simply shews under what conditions either of subject or else of manner your writings will be acceptable to it. To *me* your manner being the natural clothing or rather *skin* of your thoughts, is (whenever I understand *those*) all that it should be: so however is Plato's: whom however I would not counsel to preach at St Paul's in good Attic Greek: of course I am exaggerating, for the purpose of illustration. Here is a letter neither *menschlich* nor *geistlich* but wholly *dinglich*: you will be I think not more than a week without another letter; there is so much of the two former kinds to be said. I have *not* answered your letter, as you see. As for *your* letters, they are never, I think, more *menschlich* than when they are *geistlich*, nor more *geistlich* than when menschlich. Yours affectionately

J. S. MILL

I long to see your *Collier*[7] book, yet could wish for the sake of it that you had received long since what you will receive soon, unless the diligence to which Adolphe d'Eichthal has entrusted it, prove unfaithful. This is, (if I rightly recollect, for I have not his letter by me) a collection, in two volumes 8vo, of all the *pièces du procès*; a book without *which, he* says, *everybody* says there is no getting any conception of what it was. This book is to come, along with the Hénault,[8] & shall go by Fraser's next, if it come in time. I know not why my parcel had not yet reached you. Do you still desire Babbage's book on Manufactures?[9] I have at length borrowed it, & can lend. The Roland *is* mine, and I do *not* want it: your books have never returned *after*, generally much *before* they were needed. Beaumarchais'[10] works since you have not read them will be of the greatest value & interest to you—they throw light on a great deal, had immense *effect* at the time, & are works of real genius. I have them not; but will endeavour to borrow them—it is quite a *new idea* to me that you have need of them.—Fraser's address is or *was* lately, 22 Wilton Crescent. I see little of him. my kind regards to Mrs Carlyle.[11]
Of the St Simonians next time; *vide* also a forthcoming Examiner.[12]
Roebuck, & much else, postponed.[13]

7. See Letter 91, n. 5. For Carlyle's description of the two volumes JSM refers to, see footnote to chap. II of "The Diamond Necklace."

8. See Letter 91, n. 4.

9. See Letter 58, n. 18.

10. P. A. C. de Beaumarchais (1732–1799), the celebrated dramatist.

11. This postscript is written at the top of the first page.

12. Probably JSM's review in *Examiner*, Feb. 2, 1834, pp. 68–69, of *St. Simonism in London* (London, 1833), by Fontana and Prati.

13. This second postscript is written (upside down) at the very top of the first page.

• • • 1834 • • •

95. TO THOMAS CARLYLE[1]

Kensington
12th January 1834.

MY DEAR CARLYLE

Your little note dated the 24th was evidently written before you received my letter written I forget when, but which I fear lost the first week's post. I am therefore still expecting an answer to that letter, but shall not wait for it, mindful that I still owe you an answer to your last long letter,[2]—and a fuller answer too than can be given in any moderate space. I feel that letter a kind of call upon me to a more complete unfolding to you of my opinions and ways of thinking than I have ever yet made; which however cannot be all accomplished at once, but must be gradual. In the very fact that there has not been that full explanation, and that I feel *moved* to it now, you may see that there has taken place a great change in my character and one of which you will wholly approve—a change, not from any kind of *in*sincerity, but *to* a far higher kind of sincerity than belonged to me before. This change has been progressive, and had barely *begun* to take place when you were in London two years ago. I was then, and had been for some years, in an intermediate state—a state of *reaction* from logical-utilitarian narrowness of the very narrowest kind, out of which after much unhappiness and inward struggling I had emerged, and had taken temporary refuge in its extreme opposite. My first state had been one of intense philosophic intolerance; not arising from the scornfulness of the heart but from the onesidedness of the understanding: seeing nothing myself but the distorted image, thrown back from many most oblique and twisted reflectors, of *one* side only of the truth. I felt towards all who saw any other side, not indeed a feeling of disdain, for that never was in my character but the very utmost excess of intellectual *vilipending*. At that time I was thought to *outrer* the doctrines of utilitarianism, even by those who

1. *Addressed*: Thos. Carlyle Esq. / Craigenputtoch / Dumfries. *Postmarks*: EX / 14 JA 14 / 1834; C+ / 14 JA 14 / 1834; and DUMFRIES / 16 JAN 1834. Franked by Charles Buller. MS at NLS. Published, with omissions, in Elliot, I, 87–93. In reply to Carlyle's of Dec. 17 and 24, 1833, A. Carlyle, pp. 82–90; answered by Carlyle, Jan. 20, 1834, A. Carlyle, pp. 90–96.

2. Of Dec. 17, 1833.

now consider me a lost sheep who has strayed from the flock and been laid hold of by the wolves. That was not wonderful; because even in the narrowest of my then associates, they being older men, their ratiocinative and nicely concatenated dreams were at some point or other, & in some degree or other, corrected and limited by their experience of actual realities, while I, a school-boy fresh from the logic-school, had never conversed with a reality; never seen one; knew not what manner of thing it was; had only spun, first other people's & then my own deductions from assumed premisses. Now when I had got out of this state, and saw that my premisses were mere generalizations of one of the innumerable aspects of Reality, & that far from being the most important one; and when I had tried to go *all round* every object which I surveyed, and to place myself at all points of view, so to have the best chance of seeing all sides; I think it is scarcely surprising that for a time I became catholic and tolerant in an extreme degree, & thought one-sidedness almost the one great evil in human affairs, seeing it was the evil which had been the bane of my own teachers, & was also that of those who were warring against my teachers. I never indeed was tolerant of aught but earnest Belief; but I saw, or seemed to see, so much of good & of truth in the positive part of the most opposite opinions & practices, could they but be divested of their exclusive pretensions, that I scarcely felt myself called upon to *deny* anything but Denial itself. I never made strongly prominent my *differences* with any sincere, truth-loving person; but held communion with him through our points of agreement, endeavoured in the first place to appropriate to myself whatever was positive in him, & if he gave me any encouragement, brought before *him* also whatever of positive might be in *me*, which he till then had not. A character most unlike yours; of a quite lower kind, & which if I had not outgrown, & speedily too, there could have been little worth in me.—Do you remember a paper I wrote in an early number of Tait,[3] reviewing a book by a Mr. Lewis (a man of considerable worth, of whom I shall have something more to say yet). That paper paints exactly the state of my mind & feelings at that time. It was the truest paper I had ever written, for it was the most completely an outgrowth of my own mind & character: not that what is there taught, was the best I even then had to teach; nor perhaps did I even think it so; but it contained what was *uppermost* in me at that time; and differed from most else that I knew in having *emanated from* me, not, with more or less perfect assimilation, merely *worked* itself *into* me.—Now from this my intellectual history, in relating which I have faith that I have not presumed too much upon your interest in me, you will easily see why it is that we two have so rarely canvassed together, or even mentioned to each other our differences. I never or rarely felt myself called upon to come into

3. See Letter 51, n. 15.

collision with any one, except those to whom I felt myself altogether superior, & with whom if I had any intellectual communion it was not for the sake of *learning* but of *teaching*. I have not, till lately, and very gradually, found out that this is not honest; that although I have not positively, I have negatively, done much to give to you and to others, a false opinion of me: though the deliberation with which you form your opinions, always waiting for sufficient grounds, has I think protected *you* from forming an actually false opinion of me, & I have only to accuse myself of not having afforded you sufficient means of forming the true. Whether if you knew me thoroughly I should stand higher, or lower, either in your esteem or in your affection, I know not; in some things you seem to think me *further* from you than I am, in others perhaps I am further from you than you know. On the whole I think if all were told I should stand lower; but there cannot fail, any way, to be much which we shall mutually not only respect but greatly prize in each other; and after all, this, as you & I both know, is altogether of secondary importance; the first being, that we, and all persons and all things, should be seen truly—and as they are.

Our differences are indeed of the first importance, and to you must appear of infinite importance; though for reasons which you will feel the force of, they do not, in my feeling, throw me to so great a distance from you as they perhaps will in yours. The first and principal of these differences is, that I have only, what appears to you much the same thing as, or even worse than, no God at all; namely, a merely probable God. By *probable* I do not mean as you sometimes do, in the sense of the Jesuits, "that which has weighty authorities in its favour". I mean that the existence of a Creator is not to me a matter of faith, or of intuition; & as a proposition to be proved by evidence, it is but a hypothesis, the proofs of which as you I know agree with me, do not amount to absolute certainty. As this is my condition in spite of the strongest wish to believe, I fear it is hopeless; the unspeakable good it would be to me to have a *faith* like yours, I mean as firm as yours, on that, to you, fundamental point, I *am* as strongly conscious of when life is a happiness to me, as when it is, what it *has* been for long periods now past by, a burthen. But I know that neither you nor any one else can be of any use to me in this, & I content myself with doing no ill, by never propagating my uncertainties. The reason why I think I shall never alter on this matter is, that none of the ordinary *difficulties* as they are called, as the origin of evil, & such like, are any serious obstacles to me; it is not that the logical understanding, invading the province of another faculty, will not *let* that other higher faculty do its office; there is wanting something positive in me, which exists in others; whether that something be, as sceptics say, an acquired association, or as you say, a natural faculty. So you see I am nearly as proper an object of your pity as Cavaignac; nevertheless I do not feel myself so, having, as I have, other supports, which the want of that one cannot take away. With respect to the immortality of the soul I see no reason to believe that it perishes; nor sufficient ground for complete assurance that it survives; but if it does, there is every reason to think that it continues in another state such as it has made itself here, & no further affected by the change than it would be by any equally great event during its sojourn on earth, were such possible. Consequently in all we do here we are working for our "hereafter" as well as our "now."—Now, were you aware that I was in such a state of uncertainty on these main points? I am almost sure that you were not much mistaken in the matter, but yet were not quite certain that you knew.

Another of our differences is, that I am still, & am likely to remain, a utilitarian; though not one of "the people called utilitarians"; indeed, having scarcely one of my secondary premisses in common with them; nor a utilitarian at all, unless in quite another sense from what perhaps any one except myself understands by the word. It would take a whole letter to make it quite clear to you what I mean; & I feel perfectly that I have stated the difference between us in a manner & in terms which give no just idea of what it really is, & that every explanation I shall hereafter make will show that difference to be less than the words I have used seem to import. One of the explanations I have to give, I partly indicate by saying, as I do most fully, that I entirely recognise with you the "infinite nature of Duty".[4] Yet by this too, if unexplained, I should convey an idea of as much *greater* an agreement with you than the truth warrants, as I do in the *other case* of a *less* agreement. This also must wait till another time for a fuller developement. You will see, partly, with what an immense number & variety of explanations my utilitarianism must be taken, & that those explanations affect its essence, not merely its accidental forms, when I tell you that on the very point on which you express your belief so kindly & with so much *ménagement* and appeal to my future self, & promise not to be angry if I differ from you "even with vehemence", I agree & have long agreed with you, even in the most decided and vehement manner. I have never, at least since I had any convictions of my own, belonged to the benevolentiary, soup-kitchen school. Though I hold the good of the species (or rather of its several units) to be the *ultimate* end, (which is the alpha & omega of my utilitarianism) I believe with the fullest Belief that this end can in no other way be forwarded but by the means you speak of, namely by each taking for his exclusive aim the developement of what is best in

4. From Carlyle's letter (see A. Carlyle, p. 84); cf. also *Sartor Resartus*, Bk. II, chap. 9.

himself.[5] I qualify or explain this doctrine no otherwise than as you yourself do, since you hold that every human creature has an appointed task to perform which task he is to know & find out for himself; this can only be by discovering in what manner such faculties as he possesses or can acquire may produce most good in the world: meaning by the world a larger or a smaller part of it as may happen. Thus *you* think it a part of your *duty*, of your *work*, to address yourself, through the press, to the "species" at large. Further than that I do not go; perhaps even less far. And when once I have written down my Belief & sent it forth in such manner as happens or seems to be the most effectual within my reach, I harass myself as little as you do with any thought about the consequences; being like yourself perfectly satisfied that what I have done, if done in the spirit of my own creed, will "prove in reality all & the utmost that I was capable of doing" for mankind.

And now do not "take it ill" if I say how much it surprised me that you should think it necessary to say you would not "take it ill" if I differed from you. I never for an instant suspected that you would take ill any difference of opinion while you continue fully assured that the dissentient is sincere, earnest, & truth-loving: and you never allow me to be under a moment's fear that you are unassured of that in my case. Grieved you might be at what you might deem my errors, but *that* feeling you could not mean to disavow; nor would it be any pleasure to me, but the contrary, if you could.—In your recent letters you have several times expressed *surprise* at opinions & feelings of mine which you did not expect, & which you have said proved to you how little you yet know me; & which in truth *did* shew, how small a part of my character I had yet shewn to you; so much smaller a part than I was aware of: truly I begin to think that instead of being as I once thought I was, the most self-conscious person living, I am much less self-conscious *now*, (whatever I was once) than almost anybody. But what most shews how little I had afforded you an insight into, is that the fact of *my* having recently read the New Testament, & what I wrote to you of the impressions it had made upon me,[6] should have formed as it seems to have done, an *era* in your opinion & feeling concerning me. In my own history it is no era; it has made no *new* impression, only strengthened the best of the old: I have for years had the very same idea of Christ, & the same unbounded reverence for him as now; it was because of this reverence that I sought a more perfect acquaintance with the

5. "The good of the species . . . I leave, with the most perfect trust, to God Almighty, the All-governing who does comprehend it; believing withal . . . that no good thing I can perform, or make myself capable of performing, *can* be lost to my Brothers, but will prove in reality all and the utmost that I was capable of doing for them." Carlyle's letter of Dec. 17, 1833, A. Carlyle, p. 85.

6. In Letter 87.

records of his life, that indeed gave new life to the reverence, which in any case was becoming or was closely allied with all that was becoming a living principle in my character.

Here is a very long letter; yet how little it says of all that is to be said! However you see that you are likely to know much more of me hereafter than you have known hitherto. I must expend this remaining space on matters of fact. The two volumes on the *collier*, together with Henault[7], came from Adolphe d'Eichthal & went off immediately, I hope in time to go by Fraser's last parcel. I wonder at your not having received the other books. The Examiner subscribers amount now to 80 of the required 100, & others are known to be coming.—The review proceeds hopefully, but assurance is needed of a greater number of acceptable writers. The paper on the Repository *was* mine, also that in last Examiner on the new number,[8] & I have recommenced my French articles. The paper on Miss Martineau[9] was really a paper on Impressment. D'Eichthal says you will find much on the *collier* in the history by the Abbé Montgaillard,[10] and in the Mémoires secrets de Bachaumont:[11] this last person wrote down the doings & talkings of every successive day. The 2 vols I have sent, contain the mémoires of the different parties in the cause. How find you the Goesman Memoires?[12] Make my kind remembrances to Mrs Carlyle and believe me Faithfully yours

J. S. MILL.

96. TO JOHN PRINGLE NICHOL[1]

Kensington,
17th January, [1834][2]

MY DEAR SIR,

Your letter gave me the pleasure your letters always do, and that is a constantly increasing pleasure, for every fresh communication discloses new points of agreement and sympathy. Whoever else may have difficulty

7. See Letter 91, n. 4 and 5.

8. "The Monthly Repository for December," *Examiner*, Dec. 15, 1833, pp. 788–89; "The Monthly Repository for January," *ibid.*, Jan. 12, 1834, p. 21.

9. See Letter 91, n. 22.

10. Abbé G. H. R. de Montgaillard, *Histoire de France* . . . (9 vols., Paris, 1827).

11. L. P. de Bachaumont, *Mémoires secrets* . . . (36 vols., London, 1777–89).

12. Since Carlyle had inquired (Dec. 17, 1833) whether JSM had "his [Beaumarchais'] *Mémoires*," probably a reference to the section of that work which deals with L. V. Goezman (1730–1794).

* * * *

1. Published by Knight, pp. 661–63. MS not located. The indicated deletion in the letter is by Knight.

2. Knight dates this letter as 1833, but internal evidence, notably the discussion of the projected Review, clearly points to 1834 as the correct year. See also n. 3.

in co-operating, we two shall find it easy; for wherever we turn our minds separately to the same subject, we seem always to arrive at the same, or at the lowest, perfectly harmonious conclusions. . . . About the *Review*—though I felt almost sure that you would approve of it, and enter into it with the warmth which I wish were as characteristic of all our friends as of you, it is no less a satisfaction to me to find that I was not mistaken. The project advances, and if we had a sufficient list of good writers on whom we could *rely* so as to be independent of chance contributions, we could start almost immediately; but, unhappily, "the harvest is great, and the labourers are few"—there are scarcely any first-rate minds forming—*indè origo mali*—we want such an organ quite as much to train up public instructors, to erect a Normal School of Literature as for any temporary or party purposes. Though I do not say so to any one whose zeal I am afraid of damping, I do not think we shall be ready before the 1st of January next year. We can do little till Parliament meets, and our friends come to town; and our arrangements will not be made in time to publish the first number before the end of the session, which is so bad a time for a new literary undertaking that it will be better to postpone, and employ the delay in accumulating a *stock* of good articles to start with. Meantime, we shall increase our *corps*, and shall ascertain the result of several experiments, especially Tait's reduction of price (Roebuck, who has just come from Bath, says the reduction will *tenfold* the sale in that city, but then Tait's magazine means Roebuck's magazine, at Bath, where his popularity is boundless. I say boundless, because he is able to get over everything though constantly meeting with rubs. Two public meetings have been necessary to obliterate the impression produced by his having, in Tait, termed Watts' hymns a "wretched farrago").[3] About an editor—the fittest who has presented himself, and also the least objected to hitherto, is Mr. Fox, whom you know probably most as a writer in *The Westminster Review*, and leader of the Political Union in London. His principles, opinions, talents, and attainments, render him, I think, eminently fit; the objection is his being a Unitarian minister, and that objection is only as to the *appearance*, not the fact, as you well know if you ever read *The Monthly Repository*, of which he is editor and proprietor, and has divested it of its sectarian character so completely as to have lost the support of almost all the Unitarians. His religion, of the most unobtrusive kind, is what the religion of all denominations would be, if we were in a healthy state—a religion of *spirit*, not of *dogma*, and catholic in the best sense. For writers, those we most rely on for regular support are my father, who, if he continues to be satisfied with the conduct of the *Review*, will, I have no

3. Roebuck's phrase did not specifically refer to Isaac Watts' hymns but to a work called "The Second Catechism, without Proofs," published by the Sunday School Union. See "Children's Books," *Tait's*, IV (Dec., 1833), 285–86.

doubt, write frequently; Roebuck, Buller, and myself (the originators of the scheme), Fonblanque, John Wilson, secretary to the Factory Commission, a most valuable man; Fox himself, to whom we have now the pleasure of adding you. Strutt and Hawkins[4] will write occasionally. Many others, some of them most valuable, have promised assistance, but we cannot count upon them to the same extent. With some of the very best it is on the cards whether they will be able to give us much of their time or none; for instance, Chadwick, the poor Law Commissioner, one of the most remarkable men of our time in the practical art of Government, Dr. Southwood Smith,[5] and a variety of others. Can you help us to swell the list? Since I have mentioned *The Monthly Repository*, I will exhort you if it falls in your way to read it, and I should be happy, if it does not, to send you a number now and then as I am anxious both for Mr. Fox's sake and for its merit, to spread it abroad in every way—it has an uphill fight for success, having lost almost all its old circulation and gained an entirely new one—and it has little or no bibliopolic support. It is highly gratifying to me to find my views on the definition and method of Political Economy[6] coinciding with those of so competent a judge as yourself—it is by the approbation of such persons as you (and how few they are) that the fate of such speculations must be decided—but I hope for more from you than simple approbation, you who will enter perfectly into the spirit of all I have written so far as it is true, will also be able to add much to it and to suggest all manner of further developments, clearer explanations and apter illustrations, and I most earnestly beg you to do so—as I am ambitious that the essay, even if for that end it should remain unpublished for twenty years, should become classical and of authority; and as I am persuaded that the *foundation* of the truth is here, I do not despair by the help of the very few whose help is worth having in such a case, of gradually perfecting the execution until it may deserve more than an ephemeral existence. I was prepared for our agreeing in the main, as I think we always shall on questions of philosophic method, because we always have hitherto, and because we have both of us laid the foundation in the study of physics. Though my acquaintance with either mathematical or experimental science is not profound as yours is, but extremely superficial, it is sufficient to have enabled me to lay hold of the *methods* and appropriate to myself fully as much as any metaphysician has ever done, the logic of physical science—yet I feel great imperfections still in that department, and look forward to soliciting much of your aid not only for little things like this but for a much more elaborate work on Logic which

4. Probably John Heywood Hawkins (1803–1877), MP for Newport, Isle of Wight, 1832–41.

5. Dr. Thomas Southwood Smith (1788–1861), sanitary reformer, active Benthamite and Unitarian.

6. See Letters 86 and 102.

I have made some progress in. I am extremely glad that you are writing for the F.Q.[7] an article which I have long wished written, and look forward to its perusal with great expectation both of pleasure and of valuable suggestions for the guidance of my own mind. It is a great honour to my MS. that you should wish to quote anything from it in your article; I most readily delegate to you absolute powers over it for that purpose; only the very flattering expressions which you are kind enough to apply to it in your letter induce me to request that if you mention my name (which I leave to your option) the quotation may be left to speak for itself. The passport of your recommendation is given by the fact of its insertion, and the public have seen so much of *coteries* of men puffing one another into a fictitious reputation that one is anxious to avoid any such appearance—but you do not need that I should say to you these things—though if *I* were writing of you perhaps I should. My habit and inclination is to simplicity in all things, and I can as little conceive that a man of any dignity of character can feel hurt by praise as by blame—but one is obliged to defer to appearances and avoid vulgarising oneself by being confounded with the herd of those who quack for a reputation. Tait has shown his usual want of delicacy (he has the least nicety of perception of all men I know) in laying praise with a trowel on his own contributors as he does—if I had not been past blushing I should have blushed the other day both for him and those of us whom he bedaubed in a recent number.[8]

Yours ever,

J. S. MILL.

97. TO WILLIAM TAIT[1]

India House
13th February
1834

MY DEAR SIR

A few weeks ago I cashed the accompanying draft for our friend Roebuck and I now send it, but am in no hurry for payment.

The first number of your new series is I think better than any of the old—and I like the getting up & the outward & inward appearance of the new much more than of the old.

7. No such article seems to have appeared in the *Foreign Quarterly Review*.
8. Probably a reference to this sentence: "We [*Tait's Magazine*] had the most gifted political writers of the day with us, and a publisher who, for activity and industry, has not been surpassed . . . " (*Tait's*, IV [Jan., 1834], 494).

* * * *

1. MS at LSE.

Is the "English Opium-Eater" the author of the clever gossiping paper on Hannah More?[2] and is it permitted to ask who he is? & also who is the writer on "the Decline & Fall of the Empire of Fashion"?[3]

The paper I like least is that on the "Streets of London."[4]

I shall expect with some anxiety the result of the experiment of lowering the price. Roebuck says that it will increase tenfold the sale at Bath—but Bath is not a fair specimen, for Tait to the Bath people means Roebuck, & all his party who can afford it are sure to buy it—

Ever yours

J. S. MILL.

98. TO WILLIAM JOHNSON FOX[1]

Friday [Feb. 14?, 1834]

I send the first of the notes[2]—I have two short ones besides, which I do not send yet, because something may occur in the remaining days of the month to change them.

You will tell me when I must close the series & send them to press?

On looking again at those two articles in the last M. R. I wonder how I could ever have said what I did say to their disadvantage—but I suppose first impressions, in a question of manner, are most likely to be right.

Thibaudeau[3] is so dilatory that I fear I shall scarcely have my French paper for this month.

I like the Coriolanus[4] better on a second reference to it.

I hope we shall meet oftener—we four or rather five[5]—as we did on Tuesday—I do not see half enough of you—and I do not, half enough,

2. [Thomas De Quincey], "Mrs. Hannah More," *Tait's*, IV (Dec., 1833), 293–321.
3. *Tait's*, NS I (Feb., 1834), 54–59. Author not identified.
4. "London Sights—The Streets," *Tait's*, pp. 38–44.

* * * *

1. MS at King's. Excerpt published by Hayek, pp. 92–93, but dated as of "about April 1834."
2. For his series, "Notes on the Newspapers," in *MR*, VIII, March-Sept., 1834. The first four of the notes are dated Feb. 5, 6, 7, and 12. For paging, see MacMinn, *Bibliog.*, p. 38.
3. Comte Adolphe Narcisse Thibaudeau (1795–1856), administrator, friend of Lafayette, Carrel, and Cavaignac, writer of English correspondence signed O. in the *National*.
4. [W. B. Adams], "Coriolanus No Aristocrat," *MR*, VIII (Jan.–April, 1834), 41–54, 129–39, 190–202, 292–99.
5. The group probably included Eliza and Sarah Flower, Mrs. Taylor, Fox, and JSM.

see *anybody* along with her[6]—*that* I think is chiefly what is wanting now—that, and other things like it—

J. S. M.

99. TO WILLIAM JOHNSON FOX[1]

Saturday [Feb. 22, 1834]

On second thoughts I do not find so much to say as I expected about tithes—a few lines will do their business.[2] If it would not be troublesome & expensive to add & subtract when the article is in type, we might see how much it prints to, & then judge. I go on at all events, writing the notes, so if it be found worth while to introduce a half sheet in the manner you mention, there is sure to be matter enough to fill it up.

On the subject of attendance[3] I agree with you, & will subjoin the sentence you suggest—respecting libel[4] I adhere to the full extent of my opinion, and should be glad if you differ from me to make the M.R. the scene of an amicable controversy on the subject. I think "tolerance, freedom, and sincerity" would not be generated; to suppose they would, is to suppose that the *revelations* in question would *ultimately* lead to this, that *true* statements would be believed & *false* ones disbelieved: now my whole argument rests upon this as its foundation that truth, in any rational sense of the term, cannot in such cases be *got at* by the public; that true charges *cannot* be distinguished from false ones by such a tribunal. I should expect one of two results; that the lives of all but the independent in fortune & brave in heart, would be thoroughly artificialized, by becoming one continued struggle to save appearances & escape misinterpretation, or else that freedom would work itself out by what seems to have taken place in America, calumny & scandal carried to such a length that nobody believes anything which appears in print, & as none can escape such imputations, nobody regards them.

J.S.M.

6. Mrs. Taylor.

* * * *

1. *Addressed*: Rev. W. J. Fox / 1 Stamford Grove / Upper Clapton. *Postmarks*: T. P / Leadenhall St, and 7 NIGHT 7 / FE. 22 / 1834. MS at King's. Published in part in Garnett, pp. 153–54.

2. The note on "The Ministerial Resolutions on the Irish Tithe," dated Feb. 21, did not appear in the March *Repository* but headed the "Notes on the Newspapers" in the April number (VIII, 233–34).

3. "Attendance in the House," *MR*, VIII (March, 1834), 167–69.

4. "Mr. O'Connell's Bill for the Liberty of the Press," *ibid.*, pp. 173–76. Daniel O'Connell (1775–1847), the famous Irish politician, had proposed that in cases of private libel, truth should be a justification. JSM saw "insuperable objections" to permitting the details of private conduct to be subjected to judicial investigation whenever any accuser wished. See Mineka, *The Dissidence of Dissent*, p. 274 n.

[*Postscript probably intended for Eliza Flower*]

The three beautiful children[5] shall have justice done them on the appearance of the third[6]—The birth of the eldest *was* announced,[7] and a good word spoken for the expected family—

February[8] *is* a beauty—but March[9] is grand—

I wish I could give him[10] half of my health and take half of some of his other endowments.

J.S.M.

Now I hope you will get this in time—

100. TO WILLIAM JOHNSON FOX[1]

[Feb. 24, 1834]

Let it be so by all means. You will have received today from her,[2] the note on Tithe.[3] As the subject will have got on into another stage by next month, this might if there be room & if it is worth while, be added at the end of the N°. as a separate short article.

I know all about the Saturday scheme, & in any way if it takes effect I hope to have a share in it. How *could* it give pain, or anything but extreme pleasure to me? but all the pros and cons have been discussed yestereven and she will have told you all that we think about it.

On the *truth* question she completely agrees with me.[4]

Health and peace and blessing and love to both—and continue to give some love to me as I do to you—

J.S.M.

It was sweet of you to write those last words.[5]

5. A feature of the *Repository* for 1834 was the publication each month of a "Song of the Month," music by Eliza Flower.

6. JSM praised the songs in his notice "Songs of the Months, Nos. I, II, III, IV," *Examiner*, April 20, 1834, p. 244.

7. In his notice, "The Monthly Repository for January," *Examiner*, Jan. 12, 1834, p. 21.

8. Charles Reece Pemberton's "St. Valentine's Day," *MR*, VIII (Feb., 1834), 99.

9. Sarah Flower's "Winds and Clouds," *MR* (March, 1834), 203.

10. Evidently Fox.

* * * *

1. *Addressed*: Rev. W. J. Fox / 1 Stamford Grove / Upper Clapton. *Postmarks*: T. P. / Leadenhall St. / 7 NIGHT 7 / FE 24 / 1834, and 8 MORN 8 / FE 25 / 1834. MS at King's. Published in part in Garnett, p. 154.

2. Mrs. Taylor.

3. See preceding letter, n. 2.

4. *Ibid.*, n. 4.

5. The postscript was probably intended for Eliza Flower.

101. TO THOMAS CARLYLE[1]

Kensington
2d March 1834

My dear Carlyle

This is going to be a strange miscellaneous kind of a letter. I have a long arrear of little things to bring up, and for the present few great ones to say—and am in a mood in which it is impossible for me to say them if I had, for nothing but the most dogged determination not to lose another post could induce me to overcome the extreme aversion which I feel to writing a letter this morning. I must take your two letters as an index of the subjects to be written about. First, to answer your questions as to the projected Periodical. On a rough classification of periodicals into Tory, Whig, & Radical, there are as you truly say, various radical reviews & magazines already; even radical-utilitarian ones; but the radical-utilitarians who promote this new project, do not recognise in any of the existing works what they want; they wish to throw the combined strength of the most thoughtful & fertile-minded of the radicals into one publication, of a more weighty & elaborate character than any magazine can be; allowing itself to treat subjects at greater length than the Repository, or Tait; excluding all things which compromise the radical cause by *platitude*, or mediocrity, or ignorance, or subservience to any popular delusion; & on the whole representing as favourably as the materials admit, the radical intellect, which certainly is not, & never has been, fairly represented. Tait and the Westminster give an altogether exaggerated notion of its poverty and bareness. The "philosophical radicals" are *narrow* enough, it is true, though few of them are so narrow as Col. Thompson, the presiding spirit of the Westminster Review. But many of them are far from being *empty*; and they are generally much offended by the emptiness of the radical publications. I have no doubt that this review if it be started, will be one with which it will be pleasant to be associated; one will have not only more freedom, but far better companionship than in any publication which has yet existed. I have no doubt of its being established, except that which arises from my abundant experience of the incapacity of the radicals to cooperate. Those of them who have money, & station, are mostly impracticably fastidious; men of small objections; men to whom small difficulties appear great ones. They mostly surprised me by taking up this

1. *Addressed*: Tho[s] Carlyle Esq / Craigenputtoch / Dumfries / N.B. *Postmarks*: FREE / 3 MR 3 / 1834; O / MR 3 / 1834; and DUMFRIES / 5 MAR 1834. Franked by Chas. Buller. MS at NLS. Published in part in Elliot, I, 93–97. In reply to Carlyle's of Jan. 20 and Feb. 22, 1834, A. Carlyle, pp. 90–99; answered by Carlyle, April 18, 1834, A. Carlyle, 99–102.

scheme with warmth.—Your papers on Knox, & on Authors,[2] would both, I think, be extremely suitable to such a work: suitable both in respect to the subjects, & to the light in which you are likely to place them—You have time before you however, for as it will not be possible to start the work until the dead time of the year, we think it better to wait for the beginning of the next. Before the time therefore when it will be necessary to set about one or other of your articles, you will have heard more; I hope, seen: for if you come to London you can judge for yourself.

I greatly commend your project of establishing yourself here; which I have long thought would, as far as all circumstances are concerned of which I could judge, be the best thing you could do. I have thought so, this much more than ever, lately, in proportion as I have seen that you are capable of deriving much pleasure & support from communion with persons who are even a *little* superior to the herd in any of the elements of spiritual worth. I can now promise you, what I had not ventured to promise a year ago, that you will *find* many more persons than you expect who will be more or less in sympathy with you, & interesting to you. Any way, you will find many more here than anywhere else. Meantime you may reckon upon my doing all I can to smooth the way to your coming, & when you are come, to your finding all that you do or may seek.

The parcel of books came through Tait, a considerable time before they were announced; & came safe, but, by what misadventure I know not, saturated with whiskey: from the odour of which it will require considerable airing to free them, so thoroughly are they impregnated. You have not told me whether you will have Babbage. I have not much else to send you, except Repositories. I would send Montgaillard & Bachaumont[3] if I had them or knew how to obtain them but by ordering them from a bookseller. Of the former I once read the first two volumes, & found much in them which at that time interested me; you will find the title in the review I wrote for the W.R. of Scott's Napoleon[4] if you still have the copy I gave you (if you have not I will send you another). Of Bachaumont, a work in innumerable volumes, I know nothing but what I may have read of it in the spurious Memoirs of Louis 18th,[5] which they say were almost wholly

2. Carlyle in his letter of Jan. 20, 1834, suggested that he might write for the proposed review two articles he had long had in mind, an "Essay on Authors" and another on John Knox. The first he seems never to have written, and one on Knox not until 1875. He did deal with Knox, however, in his lecture on "The Hero as Priest" (1840).

3. See Letter 95, n. 10 and 11.

4. "Scott's Life of Napoleon," *WR*, IX (April, 1828), 251–313. See Letters 19 and 22.

5. *Mémoires de Louis XVIII, recueillis et mis en ordre par M. le Duc de D**** [or rather, written by E. L. de La Mothe Houdancourt, pseudonym of Baron de La Mothe-Langon] (12 vols., Paris, 1832–33).

made up from it, & which were certainly most amusing & most *like* an authentic picture of what one may suppose to have been going on then. By the way, have you ever read the Memoirs of St Simon?[6] (the Duc de St Simon in the time of Louis 14th.) From what I read of it formerly (an abridged or rather mutilated edition) & from all I have heard of it since the complete edition appeared, I should think that no more complete *setting before one's eyes* of a set of human creatures, had ever been achieved: the creatures themselves it is true were as little worth it, as any who have really existed can well be. Adolphe has repeated his recommendation of Montgaillard & Bachaumont, which therefore I suppose would be of real & great use to you.

What of *work* I have been doing lately has been chiefly for the day, until something of a more durable kind ripen itself within me. You will have recognised in the Examiner the resumption of my papers on French politics.[7] Besides these I have written in the last Repository & mean to continue during the session "notes on the newspapers"[8] so as to present for once at least a picture of our "statesmen" & of their doings, taken from the point of view of a radical to whom yet radicalism in itself is but a small thing. This was worth doing I think, & I have not been capable of doing much else lately. The Repository is also publishing some notes of mine upon Plato,[9] mostly written long ago, which I thought might be of some interest & perhaps use, chiefly because they do not speculate and *talk about* Plato, but shew to the reader Plato himself. Copies of these I will speedily send to you through Simpkin & Marshall.—I am not at all "amazed" at your reading Homer, & should like very much to hear all you will have to say about him.—I entirely agree in what you say about Beaumarchais; of Morellet[10] I have no very accurate recollection.

I have scarcely heard at all from any of my acquaintances (*correspondents* I cannot call them) at Paris; except a note from Cousin asking me to do some things for him, & the least, or shortest word of salutation from Cavaignac. His preface to "Paris Revolutionnaire"[11] impressed me, much as it did you. It was to me, also, a *résumé* and piecing together of many scattered and fragmentitious notions gathered from his conversation. I have no doubt of the perfect sincerity of the paper; that is, of its containing the genuine views of life and human nature, which have possessed themselves of his convictions, & by which he steers his own course. He is

6. The complete edition referred to below was: *Mémoires complets et authentiques du Duc de Saint-Simon* (21 vols., Paris, 1829–30). Prior to this, from 1788 on, various incomplete editions had appeared.

7. The summary of French news in the *Examiner* each week from Dec. 29, 1833, to Feb. 16, 1834.

8. See Letter 98, n. 2.

9. See Letter 88, n. 5.

10. See Letter 91, n. 10.

11. See *ibid.*, n. 19.

accused however, of being much influenced by vanity, & the love of popularity: I should have thought, without ground, had not the most keen-sighted & penetrating discerner of character I ever knew, drawn from opportunities of observation at least equal to mine, that very inference.—I am not much surprised at not hearing from Carrel, as he is in such a state of persecution & harassing from the French government. This you will have learnt from the Examiner.

Fonblanque's business goes well. Thanks for your mention of it to Tait; who has subscribed, & promised to speak to others. There is no necessity however for any further exertions, as the money is now all obtained or as good as obtained.

I would say something in acknowledgment of your so kind answer to my letter of "revelations" but I really *cannot*, just now, say anything of what I would say. I would rather *ask* of you, to speak more & more freely to me on those subjects & unfold to me more & more your whole mind in regard to them. I will also ask one or two questions more: Is not the distinction between Mysticism, the mysticism which is of Truth, & mere dreaming, or the substitution of imaginations for realities, exactly this, that mysticism may be "translated into logic?" I mean in the only sense in which I ever endeavour so to translate it. You will understand what I mean. Logic proves nothing, yet points out clearly whether and how all things are proved. This being my creed, of course none of my mysticism, if mysticism it be, *rests* on logic as its basis; yet I require to see how it looks in the logical dialect before I feel sure of it. And if I have any *vocation* I think it is exactly this, to translate the mysticism of others into the language of Argument. Have not all things two aspects, an Artistic and a Scientific; to the former of which the language of mysticism is the most appropriate, to the latter that of Logic? The mechanical people, whether theorists or men of the world, find the former unintelligible, & despise it. Through the latter one has a chance of forcing them to respect even what they cannot understand—and that once done, they may be made to *believe* what to many of them must always be in the utmost extent of the term "things unseen." This is the service I should not despair of assisting to render, & I think it is even more needed now than works of art, because it is their most useful precursor, & one might, almost say, in these days their necessary condition.

Expand to me also more & more the meaning of "Humility" and "Entsagen."

I had almost forgotten to mention the cost of those books. The Mémoires Adolphe was obliged to pay 24 francs for; if they be not worth that to you, they will (when you have done with them) to me, who am a sort of collector of books on French history. The Hénault cost (I think) 12 francs.

There were I believe no others. Adolphe said he knew of no Dictionnaire Néologique, and we tried together to get a map of the "Ile de France" but could not find one. A map of the department of Seine et Oise might be got of course, & I expected that Adolphe would have sent it if he still found it impossible to procure the other. It can be got immediately if it would still be of use.

I am thinking of ordering from Paris a series which is in the course of publication & which from notices in the National I see to be very interesting, "Histoire parlementaire de la revolution française"[12] being by far the completest collection ever made of original documents; including debates in the Clubs, & so forth. There are likewise memoirs concerning & papers of Mirabeau,[13] published by a relation of his & undoubtedly authentic, but I fear having but little in them. These I shall attempt to borrow & look through before I buy them.

Thiers completely verifies the impression his history makes. Even among French ministers he *stands out*, conspicuously unprincipled.

Yours faithfully

J. S. MILL.

102. TO JOHN PRINGLE NICHOL[1]

India House,
15th April, 1834.

MY DEAR SIR,

The inclosed statement is all that I have been able to think of that can at all promote your purpose. It is taken from the annual statistical volume now published by the Board of Trade, and prepared by Mr. Porter,[2] of that department; a most valuable collection, which you ought to have, as it will not only save you hundreds of troublesome references, but also afford much information, the very existence of which you would not otherwise know of. This account, like many others in the volume, was prepared from returns furnished by the Inspector General of Exports and Imports

12. P. J. B. Buchez and P. C. Roux, *Histoire parlementaire de la révolution française* . . . (40 vols., Paris, 1833–38). Carlyle later reviewed the first twenty-three volumes for the *LWR*, V (April, 1837), 233–47.

13. *Mémoires biographiques, littéraires et politiques de Mirabeau, écrits par lui-même, par son père, son oncle et son fils adoptif* [ed. by the latter, J. M. N. Lucas de Motigny] (8 vols., Paris, 1834–35). The work was later reviewed unfavourably by Carlyle in *LWR*, IV (Jan., 1837), 382–439.

* * * *

1. Published by Knight, pp. 665–67. MS not located.

2. George R. Porter (1792–1852), statistician.

expressly for that work. The table of protections annexed to Sir Henry Parnell's book[3] is classified by himself; at least, he gives a separate list of those which he considers to be inoperative; and I, judging only by conjecture, am unable to correct it in any point. But for your purpose, which does not require minute accuracy, the enclosed paper may perhaps afford sufficient materials. I suppose you have Sir Henry's book.

I had been a letter in your debt for a most unreasonable time before I received your last, and I know not how to excuse myself for being so, for such a letter as yours was most assuredly deserved better treatment. Every letter I receive from you discovers, I will not say more and more points of agreement between us, for that would be little, but more and more traces of a general conformity in our views and in our methods; and this strikes me more whenever we travel on new ground. For instance, I was wondering whether you were a reader of Coleridge, and should certainly have asked you the question very soon, when you unexpectedly wrote to me about him exactly what I think of him myself—except, by the way, when you say, "as a politician he seems unprincipled." I think he is not *un*principled but *principled*—his views on politics are, I have reason to believe, systematic. Did you ever read his little work on Church and State?[4] If not, read it; if you have, tell me whether you agree with it in the main (I mean the Church part of it) as I do. Few persons have exercised more influence over my thoughts and character than Coleridge has; not much by personal knowledge of him, though I have seen and conversed with him several times, but by his works, and by the fact that several persons with whom I have been very intimate were completely trained in his school. Through them, too, I have had opportunities of reading various unpublished manuscripts of his; and, on the whole, I can trace through what I know of his works, pieced together by what I have otherwise learned of his opinions, a most distinct thread of connection. I consider him the most systematic thinker of our time, without excepting even Bentham, whose edifice is as well bound together, but is constructed on so much simpler a plan, and covers so much less ground. On the whole, there is more food for thought—and the best kind of thought—in Coleridge than in all other contemporary writers; and it is in many respects a great good that almost all the most accomplished and zealous of the rising defenders of the Church of England are pupils of his. They are mischievous only in this, that they will be effectual in keeping up, for a time, what they will not be effectual in shaping to their ideal of what it ought to be.

3. Sir Henry Brooke Parnell, later first Baron Congleton (1776–1842), liberal Whig politician and highly reputed political economist and writer on finance.
The "table of protections" is in App. III of *On Financial Reform* (3rd ed., London, 1831).

4. See Letter 43, n. 6.

I am expecting with great anticipations of pleasure, your paper[5] in the *Foreign Quarterly*—on a subject I have long wished to see treated as you will treat it—and also your tract on the Corn Law[6] controversy. You should have a Bread-eaters' Union to counteract the Bread-taxers' Union. That *Fife Herald*[7] interested me exceedingly; one so seldom has the pleasure of seeing a fallacy torn up by the roots, instead of being merely lopped, or at most levelled with the ground. What an immense superiority the *scientific* study of any detached point, by which I mean the habit of viewing it in its relations to all the rest of the field of which it forms a part, gives one over the mere dealers in εἰκότα και σημεῖα ![8] I was forcibly struck with this when, soon after reading your *Fife Herald*, I read Lord Milton's address to the landowners on the corn laws[9]—well meant, but as feeble and shallow as may be expected from those who, as Plato says, "study pottery in the pot itself;"[10] or, as Bacon says, "Naturam rei in *ipsâ re* perscrutantur."[11] It is a primitive fallacy to imagine that assurance of truth can be had by looking at the subject-matter in the *concrete*, without that process of analysis which men term abstraction. But that is the wise, practical way; and, for want of disciplined minds, you cannot make people understand that no conclusion obtained in that way ever rises above a more or less strong presumption, requiring to be philosophically verified—brought to the test of analytic investigation.

As for those Essays,[12] not only I do not want them but I beg you to keep them by you a while longer, and to annotate them copiously—they have much need of it. By-the-bye, I believe almost all that I have written in the fourth essay[13] concerning Interest is erroneous but it may lead you to think on the subject, if you have not already.

The Review scheme has been slumbering temporarily for want of assurance of a sufficient number of writers. O for ten men with your ardour

5. "Comparative Mortality of Different Populations," *FQR*, XIII (May, 1834), 272–82.

6. Unidentified.

7. Published in the town of Cupar. It was described in *Tait's* (NS III [March, 1836], 195) as "a Radical paper of distinguished ability, and extensively circulated among the numerous small towns of Fife, where reading and Radicalism are nearly universal." Nichol's contributions have not been identified.

8. "probabilities and signs."

9. Lord Milton's "Address to the Landowners of Great Britain on the Corn Laws," dated Feb., 1831, appeared in various editions, 1832–35.

10. JSM's own translation of Plato's *Gorgias*, 514E (see *Four Dialogues of Plato*, trans. JSM, ed. Ruth Borchardt [London, 1946]; p. 159), slightly alters the meaning of the passage, which might more literally be translated: "Isn't it foolish, as the proverb goes, to begin with the big jar when you're learning the potter's art?"

11. Adapted from Francis Bacon's *Novum Organum*, Aphorism LXX.

12. See Letters 86 and 96.

13. Early draft of "On Profits, and Interest," published in *Essays on Some Unsettled Questions of Political Economy*.

of character, and rectitude of intellect! I am not meaning it as praise, but as the expression of a lamentable fact that I know not any three except you, me, and Mr. Fox, who I feel sure will always be moving and could always move together—and I could name perhaps fifty who have every requisite except some *one*. There is always some fatal *want*. Now, by way of a beginning, will you say how much you think you could *undertake* to write regularly? I mean on the average, not to tie you to a particular *time*. We want sixteen sheets a quarter or thereabouts—if you will undertake for one sheet in every number, I will do the same, and I will see what others will do—but our poor Radicals! what a miserable figure they make in Parliament!

Yours ever faithfully,

J. S. MILL.

The "Philosophy of Taxation" is an excellent subject, and you will do it ample justice.

I have not yet sent the St. Simonians,[14] but I will send them almost immediately, and some numbers of the *Monthly Repository* with them.

J.S.M.

103. TO THOMAS CARLYLE[1]

India House
28th April 1834.

MY DEAR CARLYLE

I received, a week ago, your little note[2]—it had not escaped me that for an unusual length of time I had not heard from you—but I had ascribed it to the very cause you mention[3]—which is also the cause of *my* not having written for so long a period. The same reason will make this letter an empty one; nor should I write it did I not know that the most intrinsically worthless communication between us two is valuable to both. All that either cares about is so much better spoken than written of. You will find *me* too "altered & altering"; perhaps more so than you expect; more,

14. Perhaps "the earlier of the St. Simonian tracts," including Comte's *Système de politique positive*, the return of which Mill requested on Dec. 21, 1837. See Letter 228.

* * * *

1. *Addressed*: Thomas Carlyle Esq. / Craigenputtoch / Dumfries / N.B. *Postmarks*: L.S / 28 AP 28 / 1834, and DUMFRIES / AP 30 / 1834. MS at NLS. Published, with omissions, in Elliot, I, 97–99.
2. Of April 18, 1834, in A. Carlyle, pp. 99–102.
3. The Carlyles' impending move to London would make correspondence unnecessary; they arrived early in May and henceforth made their home there.

too, than will probably be quite intelligible to you, without my opening up to you many incidents in my spiritual history, which, on a principle which I have heard you also profess, I like not to speak fully and freely of, until I myself have a sufficiently clear perception of the meaning and bearing of them. But I too have what for a considerable time was quite suspended in me, the "feeling of growth." I feel myself much more *knowing*, more *seeing*, having a far greater experience, of *realities*, not abstractions, than ever before; nor do I doubt that this superior knowledge and insight will one day make itself available in the form of greater power, for accomplishing whatever work I may be called to, shall I say also for *chusing* the work which I may most worthily perform? Every increase of insight carries with it the uncomfortable feeling of being separated more & more widely from *almost* all other human beings; this one would the less care for, did it not also damp all those feelings which prompt one to exertion through the hope of *success*, I mean any other success than is constituted by the struggle itself. One feels more & more that one is drifting so far out of the course of other men's navigation as to be altogether below their horizon; not only they will not go with us, but they cannot see whither we are steering, & they believe if they ever catch a glimpse of us, that we are letting ourselves go blindly whither we may. However this must be, & may be, borne with, when one's own path is clear—and mine is always becoming clearer.—On every account which I can judge of, I am convinced that you do wisely in coming to London. Nowhere else, at least nowhere in this country are there so many realities to be known & communed with; whereof not a few in the shape of true-hearted men and women, who to the extent of their intellect or experience, believe aright & act according to their belief. There are very few of them in whom there is not wanting something of the very first importance, but still there is in many enough & more than enough of good to give you a stronger interest in them than merely that which you have in *all* Actualities. Some of these I shall have opportunities of making known to you, & you to them, to the mutual advantage and pleasure of both.—I should send to you various books, if you were not so soon to be here; among others several numbers of the Repository, with writings of mine in them: but a much more remarkable production than anything of mine is a novel which has lately appeared, entituled "Eustace Conway" written by a far superior man,[4] evidently, to the author of "Arthur Coningsby" but the tone of thinking is much the same. You will read it with great interest I am sure, though you will probably differ from many of the author's opinions as widely as I do—but you will perhaps agree in a greater number of them. I thought I had told you that the author of Arthur Coningsby is John Sterling, who at that

4. Frederick Denison Maurice.

time was in the ferment & effervescence of the process of forming his opinions & his character—now he has become as you say "compacted and adjusted" & like all Coleridge's disciples has become a sort of conservative & churchman—he is going into orders—but will not keep upon terms with any lie notwithstanding—he is able, which it is happy for him that he is, still to believe Christianity without doing violence to his understanding, and *that* therefore not being, to his mind, false in the smallest particle, he can & does denounce all which he recognises as false, in the speculation or practice of those among whom he is about to find himself.[5] I believe there are not a few such persons, & that many of the most earnest and most genially-natured of the youth of the English Universities are gone or going into the clerical profession with similar views. If the Church conformed to their ideal of what it should be, I could say to them, Ite fausto pede; but they will not regenerate it from within so soon as it will be pulled down from without.—I long to hear all you could say about Homer —I hope you will, some time, write & publish it. Mr Austin is better: Buller, poor fellow, is but indifferently in health. Have you yet seen Mrs Austin's Cousin?[6] Her preface is the truest & best piece of printed writing I have read for many months. Yours faithfully

J. S. MILL.

104. TO WILLIAM JOHNSON FOX[1]

[June 17, 1834]

I have some news for you. Molesworth, without any suggestion or solicitation, has spontaneously offered to establish, at his own expense, the review[2] we were talking of—making but one condition viz. that substantially it shall be under my direction—he knows that I cannot on account of my position in the India House, be myself the editor, or be ostensibly connected with the review in any way, except as an occasional writer—but he will appoint his editor under the complete understanding that he is to be guided altogether by me.

5. Sterling was ordained deacon in the Anglican Church on June 22, 1834, and for the next eight months served as curate at Herstmonceux. He resigned in Feb., 1835, partly because of ill health, but also because of religious difficulties. Though he continued his study of theological questions for some years, he never resumed clerical duties.

6. Her translation (London, 1834) of Victor Cousin's *Report on the State of Public Instruction in Prussia*, which JSM reviewed favourably in *MR*, VIII (July, 1834), 502–13.

* * * *

1. *Addressed*: Rev. W. J. Fox / 1 Stamford Grove / Upper Clapton. *Postmarks*: T. P / Leadenhall St; EVEN 4 / JU 17 / 1834. MS at King's. Published in Garnett, pp. 149–50.

2. The *London Review*.

This is a much more feasible scheme than the former one[3]—because there will be but one person to satisfy, and he a man of decided movement principles, docile, and who will certainly be pleased with the thing if it is such as will please us. At the same time we must not allow him to throw away his money—we must see our way clearly to being able to carry it on before we announce it—a failure would be disastrous to the cause.

I am anxious to talk over the matter with you and let us lay our heads together to see what can be done—a great part of the chance of success will depend upon the degree in which you can cooperate.

We can speak of it as Molesworth's review—none out of our own circle should be told that I have more to do with it that any of the rest of us.

Do think about it—& if you do not come to me in a day or two, we will come to you.

J.S.M.

105. TO WILLIAM JOHNSON FOX[1]

[June 26, 1834]

I have sent to P.R.[2] I think about as much matter as we agreed upon. I have no subjects remaining, except the Beer Bill,[3] on which I shall send (today) a single paragraph; the debate on education & crime; & the admission of Dissenters to the Universities:[4] on these last subjects I shall write something & send it, but if necessary it can stand over to next month, with an announcement to that effect.

I should like to have a proof—

The following are the titles:

Abolition of Patronage in the Church of Scotland
Mr Rawlinson & the man of no religion
Business of the House of Commons
The Tom-foolery at Oxford
Parliamentary Monstrosities
The Ministry.

3. See Letter 94.

* * * *

1. *Addressed*: Rev. W. J. Fox / 1 Stamford Grove / Upper Clapton. *Postmarks*: 4 / JU 26 / 1834 / EVEN / T P / Leadenhall St, and 2 EVEN 2 / JU 26 / 1834. MS at King's.

2. Paternoster Row, where the *Monthly Repository* was printed.

3. The paragraph on "The Beer Bill," dated June 20, concludes the "Notes on the Newspapers" in *MR*, VIII (July, 1834), 521–28. All but one ("Mr Rawlinson & the man of no religion") of the notes listed below appeared in the July issue.

4. Notes on "The Alleged Increase of Crime" and "Debate on the Universities Admission Bill" appeared in the Aug. number, pp. 589–90.

William Adams will like my notes this time—at least the first five. There is much of "the devil" in them.

How are you? do, one of you, write & let me know.

Our affairs have been gradually getting into a more & more unsatisfactory state—and are now in a state which, a very short time ago, would have made me quite miserab[le][5] but now I am altogether in a higher state than I was & better able to conquer evil & to bear it. I will tell you all about it some day—perhaps the first time we meet—but by that time perhaps the atmosphere will be clearer—adieu—

I have not spoken much to you about our affairs lately, as I did while she[6] was away; partly because I did not so much *need* to give confidence & ask support when she was with me, partly because I know you disapprove & cannot enter with the present relation between her & me & him.[7] but a time perhaps is coming when I shall need your kindness more than ever—if so, I know I shall always have it—[8]

106. TO HARRIET TAYLOR[1]

[Summer, 1834?]

I have been made most uncomfortable all day by your dear letter sweet & loving as it was dearest one—because of your having had that pain—& because of my having given you pain. You cannot imagine dearest how very much it grieves me now when even a small thing goes wrong now that thank heaven it does not often happen so, & therefore always happens unexpectedly. As for my saying "do not let us talk of that now" I have not the remotest recollection of my having said so, or what it was that I did not want to talk about—but I am sure that it was something which I considered to be settled & done with long ago, & therefore not worth talking any more about, a reason which you yourself so continually express for not explaining to me or telling me about impressions of yours, uncertainty about the nature of which is tormenting me—& I have latterly learnt sufficient selfsacrifice, sometimes to yield to that feeling, & leave off asking you questions which you tell me it is unpleasant to you to answer. But whatever it was that we were talking about on the common I am sure if I had thought that anything remained to be said about it, much more if I had thought that such a matter as whether we can or cannot be in complete sympathy, had

5. Page torn. 6. Mrs. Taylor. 7. John Taylor.
8. This postscript is written at the top of the verso.

* * * *

1. MS at Yale. No salutation or signature. Published, with minor variations, in Hayek, pp. 93–94, with facsimile of the original. At the end is written, in Mrs. Taylor's hand: "my *own adored* one!"

depended on what remained unsaid, I should have been a great deal more anxious to have everything said, than you would have been to say it. O my own love, if you were beginning to say something which you had been thinking of for days or weeks, why did you not tell me so? why did you not make me feel that you were saying what was important to you, & what had not been said or had not been exhausted before? I am writing you know in complete ignorance about what it was—but I am sure I have tormented you enough & long enough by refusing to acquiesce in your seemingly determined resolution that there *should be* radical differences of some sort in some of our feelings, and now having found, & convinced you, that there are none that need make us unhappy, I have learnt from you to be able to bear that there should be some—consisting chiefly in the want of some feelings in me which you have. But I thought we perfectly knew & understood what those were, & that neither of us saw any good in discussing them further—& when I ask you questions which you do not like to answer, it is only to know what is paining you at the time—not meaning to discuss feelings any more if it is feelings and not facts that are annoying you.

I know darling it is very doubtful if you will get this before I see you—but I cannot help writing it & perhaps I shall feel easier afterwards. at present I feel utterly unnerved & quite unfit for thinking or writing or any business—but I shall get better, & don't let it make you uncomfortable mine own—o you dear one.

107. TO WILLIAM JOHNSON FOX[1]

Monday
[July 14, 1834]

We had a great deal more discussion after we left you, and we all (three) most decidedly think that since the crisis in the congregation[2] appears to have been brought on principally by the belief[3] that a fact, which would be of the greatest importance in their eyes, though of none at all in yours,

1. *Addressed*: Rev. W. J. Fox / 1 Stamford Grove / Upper Clapton. *Postmarks*: T. P. / Leadenhall St /, and 4 EVEN 4 / JY. 14 / 1834. MS at King's. Published in part in Garnett, pp. 164–65.

2. The crisis in Fox's church, South Place Chapel, had arisen from his domestic difficulties. As early as 1832 because of his growing affection for his ward, Eliza Flower, Fox and his wife had agreed to consider themselves separated although they (and Eliza) continued to live under the same roof. In the summer of 1834 Mrs. Fox confided her troubles to some of her husband's congregation; the resultant scandal led to some demands that he resign. Fox had taken the position that he could not sacrifice his personal dignity by denying specific charges. On Aug. 15, he offered his resignation but in Sept. he was acquitted of the charges (in effect, of adultery) and was asked to withdraw his resignation. See Garnett, pp. 155–68, and Mineka, *The Dissidence of Dissent*, pp. 188–97.

3. Their belief that he and Eliza Flower had been lovers.

is true—it would be very foolish that you should not have the full advantage of its not being true. Even supposing that your separation from the chapel were inevitable in every case, the effect on your future prospects will entirely depend upon that fact being denied or not—& whether you feel it consistent, or not, with your personal dignity to deny it, we are quite convinced that we, and all your friends, ought. While that fact is denied and deniable, all who are otherwise favourably disposed to you will not be afraid to stand by you, & there will be at least a strong diversion in your favour against the tide which will set in against you. But if it were made impossible for any one to defend you except those who were willing to encounter the odium of justifying all which is now alleged against you, I am afraid you will be worse situated than if no defence were made at all, since people will make it a matter of conscience to discountenance what they consider the open profession & vindication of immorality.

This being the case, I should not, if I were in your situation, think myself bound to court attention to the fact that expediency only & not principle was the cause of your not having gone to the full length of what they assert. If they put that very question to you, no doubt you ought to say so —but I think not otherwise. It seems to me quite enough if you appeal to those articles in the Repos^y[4] as containing your principles on the subject. You might say that you have acted no otherwise than in consistency with those principles; and if they ask you whether the particular fact is true, you might deny altogether their concern with it or right to enquire into it, but nevertheless profess your willingness voluntarily to give the information sought, by denying the assertion. We all think it of great importance that every public mention of the charge should be accompanied by mention of your denying it—& also that the effect of this denial should not, unless it be absolutely necessary to your integrity, be injured by the public profession of the extent to which your principles go in that one matter. She[5] went to Walworth yesterday to endeavour to induce Mr Hardy[6] to move in the matter—I know not yet with what success. But it is of importance that the steps they take should be in a better spirit & taste than if the affair is left to its original promoters it probably would happen.

all quite well
let me hear from you

J.S.M.

4. Fox had expressed advanced views in the *Monthly Repository* on the emancipation of women and on divorce. See "The Dissenting Marriage Question," *MR*, VII (Feb., 1833), 136–42. For a discussion of his views, see Mineka, *The Dissidence of Dissent*, pp. 284–96.

5. Mrs. Taylor.

6. Dr. Thomas Hardy (*ca.* 1775–1849), father of Mrs. Taylor, and member of Fox's congregation.

108. TO [ADOLPHE NARCISSE THIBAUDEAU][1]

London
August 20, 1834.

I have great pleasure in introducing to you Mr Thomas Holcroft, whose father is doubtless known to you by his dramatic writings, if not by his other works, and whose mother was the daughter of Mercier,[2] your father's[3] colleague in the Convention.

Mr Holcroft is desirous of learning & observing as much as can be learned in a few weeks about French affairs, especially politics, and with your knowledge both of France & England he will learn more from you in two or three conversations than from any one else in as many months.

I am anxious to hear from you about the Globe. Did you receive my letter, and will the proposal suit you?

109. TO JOHN PRINGLE NICHOL[1]

India House,
30th August, 1834.

My dear Sir,

I need not say with how much pleasure I have read your letter, and how gladly I close with your proposal about a series of Political Economy papers for the Review.[2] I anticipate that you will have a far less formidable idea of the said Review by the time a number or two have appeared; I should think better of our times than I do if I thought it were possible to bring together a corps of writers who would contribute only articles of "a very exalted cast." If there are one or two such articles in every number my utmost hopes will be satisfied. However, there is no immediate necessity for an article on the state of the science generally, and we need not, therefore, discuss the sufficiency of the modest reason you give for not writing one. The article you offer for the first number is one I have long been desirous to see written, especially since (which is only lately) I became acquainted

1. Printed, without identification of recipient, in Morrison, 253. MS not located. The reference in the first paragraph to the recipient's father makes the identification highly probable.
2. Louis Sébastien Mercier (1740–1814), writer, member of the Convention during the Revolution.
3. Comte Antoine Claire Thibaudeau (1765–1854), politician and historian.

* * * *

1. Published by Knight, pp. 667–68. MS not located.
2. No such series appeared in the *London Review*.

with Chalmers's book,[3] which I have just finished a very careful perusal of. I have derived many new ideas from it, and it has even suggested an entirely new view of the order in which the truths of the science ought to be arranged. What he understands, he explains very clearly and forcibly. It is unfortunate that he is so profoundly ignorant of some branches of the subject.

About publishing my concluding essay[4] in the Review; I think with you, but am afraid it would take up too much room. The essay on gluts[5] must be entirely remodelled; there is much new speculation to be added to it. I think I shall, some time or other, write a Treatise on the whole Science. I am fearful that the Essay on Wages and Profits,[6] which you say you do not quite understand, is little better than elaborate trifling, and that the doctrine that profits depend on wages, though scientifically correct, does not present the more important aspect of the law of profits, perhaps not the ultimate law at all, and is, therefore, of little use in philosophy. The whole of the speculation on productive and unproductive[7] I must revise, or rather reconsider *ab initio*. I am impatient for your remarks on the commercial essay.[8] There is no hurry about the MSS. nor about the St. Simonian books.

Those scraps on Poetry in the *Repository*[9] I believe to be true as far as they go, but that is not far. There is much more ready to be written in the Review on that matter. I am much obliged to you for the little paper you sent me. I do not see any traces of the thoughtlessness or want of information you speak of, nor of presumption, unless you allude to the sarcastic sentence on Bentham. I think I agree in your view of the character of Hamlet, though you appear to go farther or to have gone farther at that time with the Coleridgian and German metaphysics than I do. But it is a great pleasure to meet you as I do in all regions of speculation. I believe, contrary to the vulgar opinion, that there never was a first-rate mind which was not universal, I mean in its studies, reflections, and feelings, although almost everyone must limit himself to a comparatively narrow sphere in his actual contributions to science, or art, or the business of life, for want of time to acquire the requisite practical skill in many different lines of activity.

3. Thomas Chalmers, *On Political Economy in Connexion with the Moral State and Moral Prospects of Society* (Glasgow, 1832). Chalmers (1780–1847), theologian, was professor of divinity at Edinburgh University for many years.

4. See Letters 86, 96, and 102.

5. Probably the early version of the essay "Of the Influence of Consumption on Production," which appeared as the second of his *Essays on Some Unsettled Questions of Political Economy*.

6. Probably the early version of "On Profits, and Interest," *ibid.*

7. "On the Words Productive and Unproductive," *ibid.*

8. "Of the Laws of Interchange between Nations; and the Distribution of the Gains of Commerce among the Countries of the Commercial World," *ibid.*

9. See Letter 85.

I have a strong wish, of a higher kind than curiosity, to see anything which you ever write on any subject. I should like particularly to see your paper for *The F.Q.* as soon as it is in a state in which you would like to let it out of your hands.

Your plan, in *The Fife Herald*, for the adjustment of the corn laws, is good, under certain conditions, but I doubt it will be with that question as with the Catholic—it will not be carried at all until it be carried *out and out.*

I will write to the Australian people[10] about your suggestion. They intend, I know, to have agents in various parts of the country; and Scotch labourers, both agriculturists and mechanics, are of the very kind they will most value. They will, I doubt not, grant free passage from the outset.

Brougham is only showing his true character, which is much public spirit and little honesty, with extreme excitability and a tongue ungovernable either by good feeling or discretion.[11] It is quite false, I believe, that he drinks, but there is madness in the family; and his flightiness is only the temperament of madness, without the actual disease.[12] Our friend *Tait* appears to sell well, but his writers are mostly naught. Let me hear from you soon again, and believe me,

Yours ever faithfully,

J. S. MILL.

110. TO VICTOR COUSIN[1]

India House, 4 septembre 1834

MON CHER MONSIEUR,

Il y a déjà bien longtemps que je me reproche tous les jours de n'avoir pas répondu à votre aimable lettre. Je ne veux pas retarder davantage ma réponse.

10. The South Australian Association, formed earlier in 1834, included among its directorate such friends of JSM as Buller, Grote, and Molesworth. The Association had succeeded earlier in Aug. in getting through Parliament the South Australian Act establishing a Crown colony. See Richard Garnett, *Edward Gibbon Wakefield* (New York, 1898), pp. 98–104.

11. For an account of Brougham's strange behaviour in the political crisis of the summer of 1834, see Arthur Aspinall, *Lord Brougham and the Whig Party* (Manchester, 1927), pp. 193–201.

12. Gossip was rife that Brougham was mad. *The Times*, which had now turned against him, on Aug. 19, 1834, p. 2, remarked: "For some months Lord Brougham has been under a morbid excitement, seldom evinced by those of His Majesty's subjects who are suffered to remain masters of their own actions" (quoted in Aspinall, *Lord Brougham and the Whig Party*, p. 209).

* * * *

1. Published by J. Barthélemy-Saint-Hilaire in *M. Victor Cousin, Sa Vie et Sa Correspondance* (3 vols., Paris, 1895), I, 396–98. MS not located.

Je savais que les séries des Rapports des deux Sociétés n'étaient pas complètes. Ceux qui manquaient aux envois, manquaient aux Sociétés elles-mêmes. J'ai pourtant renouvelé ma demande à l'une et à l'autre Société, en y ajoutant celle de vous envoyer tous les ans le rapport annuel. J'ai reçu de M. Dunn,[2] secrétaire de la British and Foreign School Society, une réponse des plus promptes, dans laquelle il disait qu'il tâcherait d'obtenir pour vous, de quelque membre de la Société, le Rapport de 1832, et qu'il se préparait de vous écrire incessamment. Le Secrétaire de la National Society, le Révérend J. C. Wigram,[3] ne m'a point répondu. Peut-être serait-il en correspondance avec vous. Si non, une lettre de vous pourrait bien avoir un meilleur résultat. L'adresse est Central national schools, Westminster.

Quant aux Poor Law Reports, Mme Austin n'est nullement coupable de leur non-arrivée. Permettez-moi d'écrire en mauvais français, quand je n'en ai pas de bon. Le fait est que mon ami Chadwick, qui vous envoya les Factory Reports, n'a pas envoyé ceux de l'Enquête des pauvres. Cependant, il m'a promis de vous envoyer incessamment le Rapport général; plus, un volume de rapports choisis des Assistant Commissioner; plus, son propre rapport en entier, dès qu'il en aura des exemplaires. C'est tout ce qui est en son pouvoir, bien qu'il soit nommé secrétaire du Bureau des pauvres, créé par la nouvelle loi.

Nous travaillons toujours à la cause de l'éducation. Cette année, Roebuck a prononcé un nouveau discours encore meilleur que le premier;[4] et il a obtenu un comité d'enquête, qui a fait du bien et qui annonce un renouvellement d'enquête dans la session prochaine. Le système coërcitif effraie surtout nos sectaires religieux, soit dans le sein de l'Eglise, soit hors d'elle. Le public l'a assez bien accueilli. En attendant, nous aurons, d'ici à la fin de l'année, un commencement d'écoles normales. En fait de fonds, les anciennes dotations suffisent, dès que le gouvernement les reprend d'entre les mains de mandataires infidèles, qui les gaspillent sans pitié. Je ne parle pas des Universités, mais des nombreuses Charity schools, et surtout des fondations, où des écoles devraient être et ne sont pas. Mais nos Universités, plus encores que nos Académies, ont besoin d'une réforme et même d'une réorganisation complète. L'Eglise seule s'y oppose, parce que les établissements d'Oxford et de Cambridge lui appartiennent; et s'ils ne forment pas de chrétiens, ils forment des churchmen.

2. Henry Dunn (1800–1878), religious and educational writer.

3. Joseph Cotton Wigram (1798–1867), religious and educational writer, secretary of the National Society for Promoting the Education of the Poor in the Principles of the Established Church; later, Bishop of Rochester.

4. Roebuck's second major speech on education had been made in the House of Commons on June 3, 1834, in support of his motion for a select committee to inquire into the means of establishing a system of national education. His first speech on the subject had been made on July 30, 1833.

Malgré le retard que j'ai mis à répondre à votre lettre, j'ose encore vous prier que vous me chargiez de toute autre commission que vous auriez à faire ici.

Veuillez agréer ma plus haute éstime.

J. S. MILL

111. TO JOHN PRINGLE NICHOL[1]

London, 14th October, 1834.

DEAR SIR,

When I received your first letter on the subject of the office, I happened to be in Buckinghamshire, thirty-five miles from London, taking advantage of the short holiday time which we are allowed at the India House. I wrote immediately to my father. When I received your second note it was Saturday, and, of course, writing again to hurry him would have done no good, the election coming on so soon as Tuesday. I found yesterday on my return that he had actually prepared a letter, which he expected to get Mr. Senior to sign along with him, but was prevented by a sudden attack of illness, from which he has only just recovered; and it would at all events have been too late. So you see it was not from any want of zeal on his part or on mine, but from cross-accidents, that the certificate did not reach you; a circumstance which I should extremely regret if it had any influence on the result of the election. We are both of us very sorry that the Edinburgh Bailies did not do themselves the honour of electing you; but the office after all was no very advantageous one, and one at least equally suitable to you can hardly fail to fall in your way. My father thinks that a professorship in a Scotch university[2] would suit you; and it may be in his power to be of some aid to you in obtaining one, if it were vacant. He thinks you would promote your success by writing in some work more known and talked of among the people on whom such things depend, than any you write in now; as, for instance, if you were to write something for that new society of the chancellor's for the diffusion of Political Knowledge.[3] For my part I feel certain, notwithstanding my father's name and Grote's, and those of several other Radicals,[4] that the society in question

1. Published by Knight, pp. 668–70. MS not located.
2. Nichol in 1836 was appointed Regius Professor of Astronomy at Glasgow University.
3. One of Brougham's purposes in founding the Society for the Diffusion of Political Knowledge was to combat "the violent and slanderous press." See Aspinall, *Lord Brougham and the Whig Party*, p. 208.
4. For a list of the original members of the Society, see *Companion to the Newspaper*, II (Aug., 1834), 168. The *Companion* was thereafter published under the auspices of the Society.

will be thoroughly Whig; but Political Economy, at least, is of no party. I am satisfied that my father will do everything he can to serve you, whenever he can find any opportunity.

Your long letter, received last month, interested me very much. I am glad that so competent a person as you are, has turned his attention to the philosophy of mathematics. I have thought, and even written on the subject, ever since I began to speculate on metaphysics at all; but with very imperfect success. I think, however, that my logical speculations have at length given me a clue to that subject also, and that I shall be able to get to the bottom of it in time; but I shall need all the help I can obtain from you, and from any other of the very few who have any capacity for such enquiries. One thing which I had already meditated, your letter has determined me to do; and that is, as you have found my Political Economy speculations not uninteresting to you, to request that you will allow me to send to you as much as is written of my book on *Logic*; if book it can be called, which is but the raw material out of which I shall some time or other make a book.[5] I anticipate the greatest pleasure and advantage from your remarks, whether they are in confirmation or contestation of my own ideas; and I see you are exactly in that stage of your enquiries, on this particular subject, in which what I have done may perhaps help you over some difficulties. You will then, I know, lend a hand to help me over mine.

For the present I am obliged to suspend this, which is my favourite pursuit, in order to stick to the Review. I am writing for it an attack upon Sedgwick's precious discourse,[6] which you perhaps know. I am not yet convinced of the possibility of using that Political Economy discourse[7] for the Review. The first part, on the definition, strikes me as being too technical; and the latter part, on the method of the science, though it may, as you suggest, admit of condensation, would I think, to produce any effect in a popular review, require amplification also, and illustration from the mistakes actually committed by individuals or schools of political economists. This might be done, though it scarcely suits my vocation, which is not for illustration or exemplification; I am always much too dry and abstract. But then I should be stirring up divisions among Political Econo-

5. Probably the MS in the Pierpont Morgan Library, which bears the following note on the first folio: "This copy of Mr Mill's Logic / being an early manuscript draft / was sent by the author to my Father / the late Professor J. P. Nichol. / J.N." The draft, not in JSM's handwriting, corresponds roughly to Books I to III, chap. 4, of the *System of Logic*.

6. The attack on Adam Sedgwick's *Discourse on the Studies of the University* (London, Cambridge, 1833) appeared in the first number of the *London Review*, I (April, 1835), 94–135; reprinted in *Dissertations*, I, 121–85.

7. Eventually published in *LWR*, XXVI (Oct., 1836), 1–29, and reprinted in *Some Unsettled Questions of Political Economy*.

mists, and giving a handle to the enemies of the science; which such men as Torrens[8] and Malthus and even Senior are constantly doing, and which I systematically avoid. I am even anxious that in your article on the theory of a "glut of capital," you should avoid the phrase "glut" or any other which will bring you into seeming collision (though not real) with my father's and Say's doctrine respecting a general glut. It may easily be shown that they were right; and yet that Chalmers and Wakefield[9] are not wrong. However, I need not say these things to you.

You were mistaken in ascribing the article on Bentham's Deontology[10] to me; it was written by the Rev. James Martineau,[11] brother of Harriet Martineau, and a Unitarian minister at Liverpool. He is a clever man, and has consented to be a frequent contributor to our Review. I think him one of the best metaphysicians of the day; as he has shown by a series of articles on Dr. Priestley, which appeared in *The Monthly Repository* early in 1833,[12] and which if you have not read them, are worth your reading. I agree in your high opinion of much of the article on that unfortunate book, which Bowring has made out of fragments of Bentham;[13] but I do not agree with him on all points. I dissent particularly from his adoption of what is called the selfish system, and which he has put under the same mantle as the utilitarian doctrine. I once wrote a brief statement of my views respecting Bentham's philosophy, and Bulwer printed it as an appendix to his *England and the English*,[14] where, perhaps, you have seen it. It is not, and must not be, known to be mine. You will observe, if it fall in your way, that my views differ from Mr. Martineau's both in going further and in not going so far. On the whole, the article disappointed me. There are few who can grapple with first principles on any subject. Of all views I have yet seen taken of the utilitarian scheme, I like Austin's best, in his book on *The Province of Jurisprudence*;[15] but even that falls very far short of what is wanted.

8. Robert Torrens (1780–1864), economist and advocate of Australian colonization.

JSM's first published letter to a newspaper had been a reply to an editorial by Torrens criticizing James Mill's views on the cost of production; see "Exchangeable Value," *Traveller*, Dec. 6, 1822, p. 3, and MacMinn, *Bibliog.*, p. 1.

9. Edward Wakefield (1774–1854), economist and father of the colonial statesman, Edward Gibbon Wakefield.

10. *MR*, VIII (1834), 612–24.

11. Rev. James Martineau (1805–1900), Unitarian divine and philosopher.

12. "On the Life, Character, and Works of Dr. Priestley," *MR*, VII (1833), 19–30, 84–88, 231–41; reprinted in Martineau's *Essays, Reviews and Addresses* (4 vols., London, 1890–91).

13. *Deontology or the Science of Morality* . . . (2 vols., London, 1834).

14. See Letter 72, n. 12.

15. John Austin, *The Province of Jurisprudence Determined* (London, 1832).

The few sketchy paragraphs which I added to the notes on the Phaedrus[16] do not give any just notion of my metaphysical creed, which is quite different from that of the Condillac school, and comes nearest to Hartley's and my father's. Have you ever read my father's metaphysical work?[17] If not, let me send you a copy. I think it explains completely the cause of our attaching the ideas of infinity and necessity to space and time. I know not that anyone can analyse or explain succession and co-existence, when reduced to their simplest forms. The theory of association presupposes them both, and divides associations into synchronous and successive. We must, I think, rank them as ultimate laws of our minds, or (what is the same thing in other words) of the phenomena of nature.

Believe me, yours ever faithfully

J. S. MILL.

112. TO JOHN PRINGLE NICHOL[1]

India House,
26th November, 1834.

MY DEAR SIR,

Your letter gave me all the pleasure such a letter from you must give. I feared I had made an unfavourable impression on you merely from consciousness of my own want of tact in expression, by which I continually give notions of my feelings and character different from the true ones.

I like your plan for the article on Chalmers exceedingly. I think, however, that the main point might be put in a more *trenchant* manner than you put it. . . . If you do not agree with me, write in your own way, which will probably in that case be the right one.

I should wish, if convenient to you, to have the articles on Tithes[2] *first*, and as soon as possible, because that is absolutely indispensable for the first number. The other, not being of temporary interest, we *may* be

16. "Notes on . . . Plato. No. 2. The Phaedrus," *MR*, VIII (1834), 404–20, 633–46.
17. *Analysis of the Phenomena of the Human Mind* (2 vols., London, 1829).

* * * *

1. Published by Knight, pp. 670–71. MS not located.
2. An article on "Tithes, and their Commutation," signed J.P.N., appeared in the first number of the *London Review*, I (April, 1835), 164–73. No article on Chalmers was published. The only other article signed J.P.N. published under JSM's editorship was "The State of Discovery and Speculation concerning the Nebulae," *LWR*, XXV (July, 1836), 390–409.

obliged to postpone till No. 2, in consequence of the superabundance of serious, and, to the many, dull articles. I am obliged myself, having now finished a very long article on that precious "Discourse" of Sedgwick's,[3] to turn to a literary subject,[4] though out of my proper line, merely to give relief to the number. The article on Sedgwick will, I am sure, interest you. I have said a number of things in it which I have never put into print before, and have represented the "utilitarian theory of morals," as he calls it, I think for the first time in its true colours. At all events, I have incidentally represented my own mode of looking at ethical questions; having never yet seen in print any statement of principles on the subject to which I could subscribe.

I will send the Logic[5] very soon. I anticipate the greatest help in it, both from your general powers of thought and from your peculiar acquaintance with the philosophy of algebra, in which I am myself far from profound, but yet have found the little I do know to be of the utmost possible use.

Well, here is the trial come at last,[6] and has already done more good than the Whigs would have done in a twelvemonth. The movement has advanced several years by this universal demonstration throughout the country, at once of hatred to the Tories, dissatisfaction with the Whigs, and conviction of the necessity not only of reforms, but of further *constitutional* reforms. We begin to think here that Peel will not accept office and that there will be no Tory ministry. At all events, whoever is in place, the march of Reform is wonderfully accelerated. How nobly and with what wisdom the people have acted. In the meantime our friends, as individuals, have gained vastly in importance and reputation. You have seen how this crisis has called Buller out, and made him what I always knew he was capable of being. If he improves his position, as I think he will, he will now be a very important man in Parliament. Roebuck also has raised himself greatly. We now see the importance of the rallying point which Lord Durham[7] has afforded. *Any* banner, placed so high that what is written upon it can be read by everybody, is all-important towards forming a party; but Lord Durham has really acted with consummate skill and in

3. See preceding letter, n. 6.
4. "Tennyson's Poems," which did not appear until the second number (July, 1835). See Letter 117.
5. See preceding letter, n. 5.
6. On Nov. 14, the King had suddenly dismissed the Whig ministry. This precipitate action took by surprise Tories as well as Whigs. Sir Robert Peel, who was to become the new Prime Minister, had to be summoned from Italy, where he was vacationing.
7. John George Lambton, first Earl of Durham (1792–1840), at this time emerging as a leader of the advanced Whigs. A few years later JSM became one of the staunchest defenders of Durham's Canadian policy (see Letter 228, n. 14).

the best possible spirit. Whether he is ever minister or not, we have a great prize in him.

I will not fail to send Malthus's book[8] as soon as I can get a copy of it.

Believe me, ever faithfully yours,

J. S. MILL.

113. TO ADOLPHE NARCISSE THIBAUDEAU[1]

India House
28th November
1834

MY DEAR THIBAUDEAU

I have not had a single line from you since you left London: however as I have myself been almost equally remiss, we will consider that account as balanced, & now I will proceed to business.

We are going to start our Review immediately. The first number will appear in two months unless we should think it necessary to postpone it till the public know who is to be minister, & are willing to read something besides newspapers. Now, it is of the utmost importance that we should have the best articles possible on France: & for this purpose we are anxious to keep up a regular communication with you & Carrel, or whichever of you has most leisure. It has occurred to me that the following arrangements might be made. 1. You, or Carrel, of both, might send articles, to be translated here, with liberty for us to make such alterations as are necessary to adapt them to the English public. In your articles, little alteration would probably be necessary, because you know England: in Carrel's, probably much more. 2dly. In other cases, some one here might write the articles, from materials furnished by you, the payment being equally divided. To give you an idea of what I mean: We want an article on Henry Bulwer's France.[2] Now what I should like would be that you, or if you have not time, Carrel, should take the trouble to read the book attentively, & write down every remark of importance which occurs to you on it, particularly in the way of correcting matters of fact. With such annotations before me, I could venture to review the book, & I am sure that I could make a very good article & one which would serve both countries extremely. But without such help I should not like to attempt it. Now tell me what you think of such an arrangement.

8. Possibly, in view of their concern with definitions in the study of political economy, Malthus' *Definitions in Political Economy* (London, 1827).

* * * *

1. MS in the Hollander Collection, University of Illinois Library.
2. The first two volumes of Henry Lytton Bulwer, *La France: sociale, politique et littéraire* (4 vols., Paris, 1834–36). See Letter 172, n. 2.

In the second place—if you would not object to send me the National in exchange for the Examiner, I beg you will send it by post, & I will pay the expenses, reduced as they now are.

In the third place, there is now at Paris a Mr. Priaulx,[3] a young man of a rich Guernsey family, who is a particular friend of Wilson,[4] of the Globe, & a clever & interesting person. He is authorized to communicate with you on all subjects relating to the Globe. Wilson has asked me to give Mr Priaulx a letter of introduction to you. Will you be so kind as to consider this an introduction.

On the state of our politics[5] you will learn as much from the English newspapers as I could tell you. The change of Ministry would have been a great evil if the people had remained quiet; but after the demonstration they have made, I think the effect will be very good. It is very probable that Peel will not chuse to accept office; if he does not, the whole thing is at an end. But if the Tories do come in, it must now be as Reformers, & even greater reformers than the poor Whigs were, otherwise they will be turned out on the very first day of the session. We might have waited whole years for such a unanimous declaration from the whole country in favour of the ballot, triennial parliaments & a further extension of the suffrage, as this has produced. We shall have no more now of the "final measure."[6] Be assured that the Movement has gained immensely by all this, & is gaining every day. In fact, it is impossible that anything which produces political excitement should not now do good. I am quite tranquil & easy about public affairs whichever way the present crisis terminates. We shall either have a Tory ministry granting large reforms, & a Whig & Radical opposition demanding larger; or we shall have the Whigs in again, & the two parties competing for the favour of the Radicals, who will evidently be the supreme power in the country; for all the present demonstrations are the work of the radicals; not a Whig stirs a finger even to bring the Whigs into place again.

Will you make my best regards to Carrel. I will write to him soon.—Pray write to me as soon as possible.

Yours ever

J. S. MILL

I send you the Examiners. I suppose it is to you & not to Carrel that they should now be sent.

3. Probably Osmond de Beauvoir Priaulx or De Preaux (1805–1891), barrister, author of *Outlines of a System of National Education* (London, 1834); of *National Education* (London, 1837); and of other works.

4. John Wilson. The London newspaper referred to should not be confused with the Saint-Simonian periodical, *Le Globe.*

5. See preceding letter, n. 6.

6. I.e., the position of the conservatives that the Reform Act of 1832 was a final constitutional change.

114. TO GUSTAVE D'EICHTHAL[1]

India House
29th November
1834

MY DEAR D'EICHTHAL

You would have a right to be greatly offended with me for having made no answer to two such letters as yours. I assure you my silence did not proceed from indifference; I was deeply interested in all the particulars you told me about Greece,[2] and highly gratified by the intelligence respecting yourself. I can only say that between my occupations, which have been unusually great, & my natural laziness, I always procrastinated, feeling that I ought not to write a short letter, & shrinking from the trouble of writing a long one: but I hope now that we shall correspond regularly. My present letter may be interesting to you, being written while we are in the midst of a political crisis. You have heard by this time of the dismissal of the Whig ministry & the reappointment of the Duke of Wellington, who however waits until Peel returns from Italy to form a Ministry. When this most unexpected event occurred, our friends were in some apprehension at first, because they knew how the lukewarmness, the temporizing, and general imbecility of the Whigs, had cooled the ardour of the people in their support, & it seemed not improbable that the people, thinking the Whigs no better than the Tories, might quietly look on. That was the hope of the Tories themselves. But the result has completely disappointed them. The conduct of the people has been noble. There has been one unanimous shout from the whole nation that they will not have the Tories on any terms; declaring at the same time that the Whigs have not satisfied them, & that they must have a ministry who will not only give them the consequences of the Reform Bill, but further organic reforms; the suffrage extended to all householders, triennial elections, & vote by ballot. Happily, Lord Durham had just before placed himself at the head of the radicals, first at the Edinburgh dinner to Lord Grey,[3] by taking up the gauntlet which Brougham had thrown down; next at the dinner given to himself

1. MS at Arsenal. Published, with omissions, in *Cosmopolis*, VI, 363–66, and in *D'Eichthal Corresp.*, pp. 164–71.

2. After the dispersal of the Saint-Simonians, D'Eichthal had gone to Greece and had become director of the "Bureau d'Economie politique," a kind of ministry of public works.

3. On Sept. 15, 1834. At the dinner, Brougham, already in trouble with the Grey faction of the party, counselled caution in the reform programme. Durham urged an immediate programme of sweeping reform. His speech was widely interpreted as a violent attack on Brougham; this was the beginning of the famous quarrel which led to the destruction of Brougham's political power. See C. W. New, *Lord Durham* (Oxford, 1929), pp. 244–79.

by the Glasgow Reformers,[4] where he publicly declared for the three constitutional changes which I have just mentioned. His words have gone forth & been reechoed by the whole people, & the Movement party now everywhere look to him. There have been already some addresses to the King to appoint him Minister. Nevertheless, he will not be minister yet, nor perhaps ever: he is too vain, too imperious, & too much the slave of mere temperament. But you need fear nothing for us; the Tories, at first elated, are already crestfallen: the growing opinion is, that Peel, when he sees the state of the country, will not accept office; & if he refuses, the Duke of Wellington will not go on. At all events, if they do take office, they will not survive the first day of the session except by outbidding the Whigs in popular measures. *Their own calculations* do not give them a majority in the elections if they dissolve parliament at present, & my belief is that they will not. At any rate, be assured that the Movement has advanced exceedingly by these events. You will be glad to hear that Buller & Roebuck have taken a most conspicuous part in this crisis, & have distinguished themselves exceedingly, Buller especially, who has headed the London reformers throughout, even from the first day. Roebuck at that time was out of town. They are sure to be important men in the history of their country before long. Roebuck during the last two sessions has risen in reputation & influence both in & out of Parliament, in a degree which would astonish you. The other radicals have all disappointed us: even Grote, who has been very inactive. Only one other man in the House, Clay, from whom we expected nothing, has distinguished himself on the popular side. I consider it certain that either the Whigs will come in again, with the Tories no longer resisting them in front & the people more than ever pressing them on from behind; or there will be a Tory ministry which will do more for the people than the Whigs have yet done, & a strong popular opposition consisting of the radicals joined by the best of the Whigs.

And now for our personal share in the Movement. One of the radical members, a friend of Buller's and mine, Sir William Molesworth, is about to establish a review at his private expense, & all our friends are to write in it, as well as all the Movement writers whom we have thought it worth while to ask; not one has refused. It will, unless I am much mistaken, be infinitely the best review ever yet published. You must not look in it for a *doctrine générale et unitaire*; you know as well as I do that English minds are not yet ripe for that; but whatever *vues d'avenir* there are in England, will be presented there in full detail. The object is, to rally the instructed radicals round a common standard, & induce the other radicals to follow them. And now I have a request to make. You have it in your power to serve us and our cause & to serve Greece at the same time, by chusing

4. On Oct. 29, 1834.

our review as a means of making known here, the present state of Greece. If you would send us, either as a review of Thiersch's book,[5] or in the form of an original essay, an article on the recent history, & present state & prospects of Greece, you will do us a great favour. We have no objection to publish the severest strictures on the conduct of our own Government or its functionaries, provided we are not committed to any *facts* which cannot be substantiated. We have the most perfect reliance on you, & should publish without hesitation any statement which came from you or recommended by you. The same article might be made a means of furthering your views of colonization, by giving publicity to the facilities & advantages the Greek Government affords to settlers, & by shewing the very favorable prospects which the state of Greece holds out to speculations of that kind. Our first number will be published in two months,[6] but I hope you will be able either to write, or get written for us, a paper which can appear in the second.

I suppose your plans of colonization are by this time in some degree matured. I have no doubt you are right in thinking it desirable that the first emigration should be of capitalists, & of mechanics and artizans. I have no doubt of your success. Numbers of both, are emigrating every year from this country, & if they feel any confidence in the security of person & property in Greece, they will emigrate thither as readily as to any other place. I can suggest no plan, except that of appointing some mercantile house in England the agent of the Greek Government for emigration, & making extensively known through them, the terms on which the Government will grant land, & the advantages of all other kinds which it will hold out. The main point is, to convince our capitalists that they & their property will be safe. This must be done by giving publicity, & *repeated, continual* publicity to all that the Government has done & goes on doing to restore order. I know no *one* thing so likely to have that effect, as the article I am proposing to you to write for our review, which we could get quoted & commented upon by the whole of the newspaper press, London & provincial. There are plenty of first-rate mechanics in Scotland who are ready to go, but they *must be taken out* by *capitalists* who will ensure them employment when there. The grand thing is to gain the confidence of capitalists. This depends wholly upon the impression you can make concerning the state of the country.

I am most truly glad that the Greek Government has had the good sense to place so important a department of its affairs in the hands of yourself, & of two such men as you describe your colleagues. If they chuse all their

5. Bernhard Thiersch, *Ueber das Zeitalter und Vaterland des Homer* (Halberstadt, 1832). No such review or article appeared in the *London Review*.

6. It did not appear until April, 1835.

other agents as well, I have no fear for the good administration of their country. The absence of a territorial aristocracy, & the deep root which popular municipal institutions seem to have in the country, are immense advantages. Have you seen Urquhart's book, "Turkey and its Resources"?[7] If so, is it to be depended upon?—Pray do not imitate my negligence, but write to me soon, & believe me

Ever faithfully & affectionately yours

J. S. MILL.

115. TO EDWIN CHADWICK[1]

I.H.
10 Dec. 1834

MY DEAR CHADWICK

Monsieur Guilbert,[2] one of the editors of the Bon Sens,[3] has come over here to learn all he can of the present condition & prospects of this country and its people. Your assistance would be of great use to him, by indicating documents & letting him know your own general views, & you will much oblige me by doing anything to aid him which your occupations allow.

Ever yours

J. S. MILL

116. TO FRANCIS PLACE[1]

[Dec., 1834?]

DEAR MR PLACE

M. Guilbert, one of the editors of the French newspaper, "Le Bon Sens," is desirous of the pleasure of your acquaintance. He is anxious to learn all he can about the state, moral, physical and intellectual of our working people, and nobody can tell him more on the subject than you can.

Yours faithfully

J. S. MILL

7. David Urquhart, *Turkey and Its Resources* (London, 1833).

* * * *

1. *Addressed*: Edwin Chadwick / 7 Trevor Square / Knightsbridge. MS at UCL.
2. Aristide Mathieu Guilbert (1804–1863), writer, who because of the exile of his father, had lived in London from 1815 to 1830. In the spring of 1835 he became Paris correspondent for the new *London Review* (see Letter 127).
3. *Le Bon Sens*, established as a Sunday paper shortly after the revolution of 1830 by members of the popular party, became a daily in April, 1834. The *Examiner*, Feb. 8, 1835, p. 82, praised it warmly.

* * * *

1. MS at Brit. Mus. Undated, but presumably written about the same time as the preceding letter to Edwin Chadwick.

117. TO JOHN PRINGLE NICHOL[1]

India House,
18th December, 1834.

MY DEAR SIR,

I am grieved to hear of your narrow escape, and most heartily congratulate you and myself that the danger is past. By all means keep yourself as quiet as possible, and do not even think of any intellectual exertion till you are completely recovered. I once lost a most valued friend, one of the most valued I ever had—though not to be compared with you in intellect—in consequence of a similar disease—the eldest son of Tooke, the political economist.[2] I believe he brought on the malady almost entirely by intense and unremitting study. I most earnestly entreat you, for the sake of us all, not to expose yourself to a similar danger. It is better that our first number should even appear without your article, than that your health should be exposed to the slightest risk. However, I hope that your health will be firmly re-established before we shall need your article. We do not think of publishing the first number while the crisis[3] lasts; and on the whole, if your paper reaches us by the end of January, I have no doubt that it will be in time. When I know whether a still longer delay will be compatible with its appearance in the first number, I will let you know.

On the whole, our prospects grow better and better—those of the Review, I mean, though I might add, those of the nation too. The Review is, and will be, principally deficient in articles on literary subjects. If you have leisure, may I hope that you will give some assistance in that department, as well as in your own peculiar one? I am obliged to do the same; and I find that we can in general trust none except our scientific writers with even our literary subjects. I shall have two in the first number; one on Sedgwick, and one on Tennyson's Poems[4]—the best poems, in my estimation, which have appeared since the best days of Coleridge.

Have you seen Peel's address to the electors of Tamworth?[5] Was there ever such empty mouthing? Nothing appears clearly in it but that he means to *halve* the reforms of even the poor Whigs. I hope they will dissolve Parliament. It will be a thousand pities now to lose the triumph which the elections will give us.

Yours in haste,

J. S. MILL.

1. Published by Knight, pp. 671–72. MS not located.
2. See Letter 29.
3. The political crisis brought on by the King's dismissal of the Whig ministry.
4. The article on Tennyson did not appear until the second number.
5. The famous Tamworth Manifesto, calling for a new Conservative programme of progressive reform, had just been published in *The Times*, p. 5, on the morning of this letter.

118. TO ALBANY FONBLANQUE[1]

Kensington
25 Dec. 1834

MY DEAR FONBLANQUE

Could you insert the enclosed[2] in your next paper?

You are fighting the good fight nobly—and you are the only writer (except Buller occasionally in the Globe) who are doing it with any spirit.

I send copies of the Prospectus of the new review. Some notice of it in your paper would be useful—but perhaps not during the present excitement. We shall send round our advertisements presently; & the Prospectus will appear in the January periodicals.

We do not think of publishing our first number till after the crisis:[3] & consequently not till after the meeting of Parliament, unless (which is most unlikely) the Tories should be so discouraged by the result of the elections as to retire.

Will you allow me to remind you of our hopes of an article from you for the first number? & to say that I am ready to work for the Examiner to any extent that could be needful while you are about it.

We have promises of support (as writers) from my father, Grote, John Austin, Bailey of Sheffield,[4] Peacock,[5] Fox, James Martineau of Liverpool, Nichol of Montrose, Cornewall Lewis, Buller, Roebuck, Wilson,[6] Strutt, Mrs. Austin—everybody in short whom we thought worth asking, except Bulwer, and he has *almost* promised. But without you we should be weak in some very important departments—& there would not be sufficient relief to our heaviness & dulness.

Yours faithfully
J. S. MILL

1. MS at LSE. Last two paragraphs published in *Life and Labours of Albany Fonblanque*, ed. E. B. de Fonblanque (London, 1874), p. 39.

2. Probably JSM's notice of Eliza Flower's *Songs of the Months. A Musical Garland*, in *Examiner*, Jan. 4, 1835, p. 4.

3. See Letters 112 and 114.

4. Samuel Bailey (1791–1870), philosophical writer greatly admired by James Mill. JSM reviewed favourably his *Rationale of Political Representation* in *London Rev.*, I (July, 1835), 341–71, but attacked his *Review of Berkeley's Theory of Vision*, *WR*, XXXVIII (Oct., 1842), 318–86, reprinted in *Dissertations*, II, 162–97. No contribution by Bailey to the *London Review* has been identified.

5. Thomas Love Peacock (1775–1866), novelist, long associated with the Mills in the employ of the East India Company. He contributed several essays to the *London Review*.

6. Probably John Wilson, secretary to the Factory Commission, and an editor of the *Globe* newspaper.

• • • 1835 • • •

119. TO JAMES MARTINEAU[1]

[1835]

The last two pages of the concluding paper[2] made an impression upon me which will never be effaced. In a subsequent paper of my own in the "Repository" headed "The Two Kinds of Poetry" (October, 1833) I attempted to carry out your speculation into some of those ulterior consequences which you had rather indicated than stated.

120. TO ARISTIDE GUILBERT[1]

India House
Saturday
[Jan. 17, 1835][2]

MY DEAR SIR

When I had the pleasure of seeing you today, I forgot to mention that I shall not be here on Monday, as I am going with my brother[3] (who is destined for the civil service in India) to the East India College near Hertford. We must therefore defer our next conversation till Tuesday.

Yours most truly

J. S. MILL.

1. Excerpt published in James Drummond and C. B. Upton, *Life and Letters of James Martineau* (2 vols., London, 1902), II, 276. MS not located. According to the editors the letter was to welcome Martineau as a contributor to the *London Review*.
2. "On the Life, Character, and Works of Dr. Priestley," *MR*, VII (1833), 19–30, 84–88, 231–41.

* * * *

1. *Addressed*: Monsieur Guilbert / 30 Red Cross Square. *Postmarks*: TP / CORNHILL /, and 183(?) . . . MS at King's. Published in Morrison, p. 253.
2. So dated in Morrison.
3. James Bentham Mill.

121. TO JOSEPH BLANCO WHITE[1]

India House
26th February
1835

MY DEAR SIR

I am truly delighted to hear that you are willing to cooperate in the new Review. There are few persons whose aid could be of so much, or nearly so much, importance to it, both with reference to its usefulness & to its success.

I do not know if you have yet seen the Prospectus. It has appeared on the cover of most of the reviews & magazines. The spirit of the review will be democratic, but with none of the exclusiveness and narrowness of the Westminster Review; & the plan adopted of individual signatures enables the various writers to indulge the liberty of individual opinion within considerably less narrow limits than are imposed by the plan of most reviews.

I will immediately send you some copies of the Prospectus under Sir William Molesworth's cover. I suppose Senior[2] told you that Sir William is the founder & proprietor of the review.

We hope to publish the first number by the end of March. I fear its fault will be, a deficiency of literary & other light matter & a superabundance of politics. At our first starting there is no way in which you could be of so much assistance to us as by writing some of those excellence pieces of literary criticism several of which you wrote for the former London Review;[3] such as that on Pollok's Course of Time,[4] for instance. I am afraid of trespassing on your kindness & "riding a willing horse to death" but yet I cannot help saying that if you could be prevailed upon to write something of this kind, even though short, for the first number, it would be of so much importance to the review that we would gladly keep the number open for it even till the last moment.

1. *Addressed*: Rev. J. Blanco White / 5 Chesterfield Street / Liverpool. *Postmark*: LS / 26FE26 / 1835. MS in the Liverpool University Library.

For JSM's earlier acquaintance with White, see Letter 45. After embracing Unitarian views, White in Jan. of this year had left Dublin, where he had lived in the home of his patron Archbishop Whately, and settled in Liverpool.

2. Nassau Senior.

3. A short-lived review, edited by White himself in 1829; only two numbers were published.

4. Robert Pollok, *The Course of Time: A Poem in Ten Books* (2 vols., Edinburgh, 1827), one of the most popular religious poems of the period; twenty-five editions were published by 1868. White's unfavourable criticism of it was published in his *London Review*, I (Feb., 1829), 233–51.

I have not read Tocqueville's book,[5] but from what Senior says of it, I have no doubt of the great value to us of such a review of it as you would make. For this we can give ample time, as it could not be printed before the second number.

The editor of the review is Thomas Falconer[6] Esq. 7 Gray's Inn Square, a friend of mine whom I think very highly of. As I am in continual communication both with him & with Sir W. Molesworth, any letter to me answers all purposes, and I should be proud to increase our acquaintance by corresponding with you on review matters.

Believe me
Most truly yours
J. S. MILL

122. TO JOSEPH BLANCO WHITE[1]

India House
2d March
1835

MY DEAR SIR,

The objection to "Pompeii"[2] is that Bulwer writes for the review; & it would be impossible to review it fairly without pointing out the gross blunders in scholarship & even in Latin grammar; now as no principle requires that we should point out errors of *this* kind in our friends, it is of no use wounding their *amour-propre* & depriving ourselves of their hearty cooperation.

But the other subject you mention, the works of Martinez de la Rosa,[3] would suit the review perfectly. The prose translations which you propose will be quite sufficient.

5. JSM's first mention of Alexis de Tocqueville's *De la démocratie en Amérique* (2 vols., Paris, 1835), which was to influence profoundly his political philosophy. Later in the spring he met Tocqueville during the latter's visit to England and a correspondence ensued (see Letter 137 and others). JSM eventually decided to review Tocqueville himself (see Letter 135) for the Oct., 1835, number of the *London Review*; upon the completion of the second part in 1840 he wrote another article for the Oct., 1840, *Edinburgh Review*.

6. Thomas Falconer (1805–1882), brother-in-law of J. A. Roebuck, barrister and later judge of county court circuits, though nominally editor was really sub-editor under JSM.

* * * *

1. MS at John Rylands Library, Manchester; bears no indication of recipient, but see n. 3.

2. A revised and corrected edition of *The Last Days of Pompeii*, originally published in 1834, appeared in 1835.

3. White's review of the works of Francisco Martínez de la Rosa (1787–1862), Spanish statesman and dramatist, appeared in the first number of the *London Review*, I (April, 1835), 76–93, under the title "Recent Spanish Literature."

Mr. Falconer will see this note, & if you receive it you may know that he agrees with it. I have no doubt that if he can suggest any other subject which would to him appear preferable, he will not omit to avail himself of the kind disposition which you manifest towards the review.

You have, I presume, received some copies of the Prospectus by this time

Believe me
Most truly yours
J. S. MILL

123. TO RICHARD BENTLEY[1]

India House
5th March
1835

MY DEAR SIR

I send M. Fiévée's memorandum on the nature of his work, and a note of my own stating what I know of M. Fiévée.[2] I should think the work might, if published in France, reckon upon a great sale in France itself, where the author does not wish to publish it himself, lest his work should be supposed to have some party object.

If Mr Bentley should wish for any further information I will give it, or obtain it from M. Fiévée, and if he thinks there would be any use in my meeting him I will (though it would be rather inconvenient) call upon him or should be glad to see him if he happened to be coming into the City.

Ever yours
J. S. MILL

[The enclosed note][3]

Monsieur Fiévée is one of the cleverest and liveliest French writers of the present age, as his "Correspondance politique et administrative"[4] published in the first few years after the restoration of the Bourbons sufficiently shews. His political opinions & the general character of his mind bear more resemblance to Burke than to any other English writer; though his great experience as a man of office & business, has supplied him with

1. MS in Bodleian Library.
Richard Bentley (1794–1871), publisher.

2. Joseph Fiévée (1767–1839). The memorandum has not been located. The work referred to was *Correspondance et Relations de J. Fiévée avec Bonaparte . . . (1802 à 1813)* (publié par l'auteur, Paris, 1836). See also Letter 146.

3. The MS of the note is in the Bentley Collection of the University of Illinois Library. The editor is indebted to Professor Jack Stillinger for supplying a copy of it.

4. *Correspondance politique et administrative, commencée au mois de mai 1814* . . . (3 vols., Paris, 1815–19).

much more practical knowledge of the affairs of the world than Burke had. He was much trusted by Napoleon, although Napoleon knew him to be in correspondence with the exiled family. It is well known that Napoleon's *conseil d'état* was composed of all the ablest administrators in France: M. Fiévée, besides being one of his *préfets*, was for a long time a member of this body. M. Fiévée enjoys a very high character in France & his statements may be depended upon. His sentiments and personal connexions were mostly royalist, but he gradually became alienated from that party as he found that they could not be induced to govern in a manner suited to the wants & circumstances of the age. He has never attached himself to Louis Philippe or his government.

124. TO ALBANY FONBLANQUE[1]

I.H.
Monday
[March(?), 1835]

MY DEAR FONBLANQUE

Thanks for the ticket. Thursday does quite as well. As you so kindly permit me I will some day soon ask for an order for Lestocq;[2] but I cannot yet say when.

I send a short paper on Swiss politics, which has been sent to me from (& is written by) Siebenpfeifer,[3] one of the leading German radicals, & now a Professor in the University of Berne. If it suits you it can be published & I shall be happy to translate it if necessary but I suppose your subeditor now renders you independent of such help.

Molesworth I know means to send you the sheets of the London Review. I suppose you guess the authorship of the Dialogue on the Ballot.[4] There are parts of it in which I do not wholly agree, but the speculations you allude to are not among them.

It is a great loss to the review not to have anything of yours in the first number—but if you could find time to write anything in the second, though I know how much you are occupied, your aid is too important not to be very urgently pressed for.

Ever faithfully

J. S. MILL

Bulwer will write for the 2[d] number & is zealously with us.

1. MS at LSE.
2. Auber's opera, first performed at Covent Garden on Feb. 21, 1835.
3. Philipp Jakob Siebenpfeiffer (1789–1845), political writer.
4. In *London Rev.*, I (April, 1835), 201–50; by James Mill.

125. TO THOMAS CARLYLE[1]

India House
7th March [1835].

MY DEAR CARLYLE—I will endeavour as you advise, to think as little as I can of this misfortune,[2] though I shall not be able to cease thinking of it until it is ascertained how far the loss is capable of being repaired—or rather reduced to a loss of time & labour only—There are hardly any means I would not joyfully take, if any existed by which I could myself be instrumental to remedying the mischief my carelessness has caused—That however depends not upon me. But there is one part of the evil—though I fear the least part—which I could repair—the loss to yourself of time & labour—that is of income. And I beg of you with an earnestness with which perhaps I may never again have need to ask anything as long as we live, that you will permit me to do this little as it is, towards remedying the consequences of my fault & lightening my self-reproach. It is what you would permit as a matter of course if I were a stranger to you—it is what is even *legally* due to you—and to have brought an evil upon a friend instead of a stranger is already a sufficient aggravation of one's regret, without the addition to it, of not being allowed to make even the poor amends one would make to a stranger.

1. MS at NLS. Published, with slight variations, in Elliot, I, 100–101. Carlyle's answer of March 9 in A. Carlyle, pp. 109–10.

2. On the preceding evening JSM in great distress had called upon the Carlyles and, after begging Mrs. Carlyle to go outside to speak to Mrs. Taylor, who was waiting in a cab, informed Carlyle that the manuscript of the first volume of his *French Revolution* had through carelessness been completely burned.

D. A. Wilson, *Carlyle to "The French Revolution" (1826–1837)* (London, 1924), Book X, chap. XVII, and others have accepted the legend (which must have originated with Carlyle) that the accident was really Mrs. Taylor's fault and that JSM gallantly accepted responsibility. Against too ready acceptance of this should be placed the evidence of Letter 126 and of a letter of JSM's sister Harriet to Carlyle shortly after (May 15, 1873) JSM's death when the *Daily Telegraph* in an obituary article attributed the by then famous literary accident to Mrs. Taylor: "As far as my recollection goes, the misfortune arose from my brother's own inadvertence, in having given your papers amongst waste paper for kitchen use. I can, perfectly well, remember our search, and my dear brother's extreme distress, and I fancy, though of this I do not feel so sure, that some pages were found." (MS 666, No. 109, at NLS.)

Carlyle in a gracious and touching reply to Miss Mill (May 17, 1873, MS 1778, NLS, hitherto unpublished) admitted that "in fact my impression really was, that night when your Brother came to us pale and agitated, as I have seldom seen any mortal, that Mrs. Taylor's house and some trifling neglect there, had been the cause of the catastrophe;—but in fact, to prevent him almost perishing with excess of misery, we had to forbear all questioning on the subject, which indeed was of no importance to either of us, and to bid him 'Be of Courage, never mind, Be certain I *can* write it again, and will'! . . . Your dear Brother's conduct to me in this matter, as indeed in all others, then and afterwards, was conspicuously noble, generous, and friend-like,—conduct of the First, almost only Friend I then had in London, one who would have made any sacrifice for me and what I then had most at heart."

If I could convince you what a relief this would be to me, & what an act of friendship—to say nothing of justice—it would be on your part I am sure you would not hesitate—Yours affectionately

J. S. MILL.

126. TO THOMAS CARLYLE[1]

India House
Tuesday
[March 10, 1835]

MY DEAR CARLYLE

Nothing which could have happened, could have been at this time so great a good to me as your note,[2] received this morning. I never thought it probable, & I wonder now how I could have thought it possible, that your answer would be different: it could not be so (gigmanity out of the question); but my anxiety made me exaggerate the chances against me.

Yes—when the thing is again done, & I have realised the feeling of certainty that another volume is there, as true & as beautiful as the former, all *will* be *wholer* than ever. I never before felt so fully the whole amount of the good of having somewhat more than one actually needs for urgent wants. That which can buy peace of conscience is precious.

You shall see or hear from me again almost immediately—but I will not take the *Fête des Piques*[3]—not that I believe such a thing could possibly happen again, but for the sake of retributive justice I would wear the badge of my untrustworthiness. If however you would give me the pleasure of reading it give it to Mrs. Taylor—in her custody no harm could come to it[4]—and I can read it aloud to her as I did much of the other—for it had not only the *one* reader you mentioned but a second as good. I can borrow De Stael's Considerations[5] easily—as my father has them. I did not think of them when I sent you other books—as there are very few facts in them—they are mostly speculations.[6]

1. MS at NLS. Published, with slight omissions, in Elliott, I, 101–2.

2. Of March 9, 1835, in A. Carlyle, pp. 109–10: "You shall do the thing you so earnestly entreat for [i.e., compensate Carlyle for the time lost by the burning of the manuscript]: it is not unreasonable; *ungigmanic* [i.e., unconventional] it may either be or not be."

3. Carlyle had offered to let JSM take the manuscript of this first book of Vol. II he was then completing—"provided you durst take it."

4. This would seem to exculpate Mrs. Taylor though D. A. Wilson cites this as only another instance of JSM's gallantry in defending her.

5. *Considérations sur les principaux événemens de la révolution française* (3 vols., London, 1818), by Anne Louise Germaine Necker, baronne de Staël-Holstein (1766–1817), writer and critic.

6. The letter is not signed.

127. TO ARISTIDE GUILBERT[1]

India House
19th March
1835

My dear Monsieur Guilbert

You have much reason to complain of me for not writing to you sooner. The fact is, I waited too long for an answer from the Globe, which I might have had sooner if I had taken a little more trouble. I got an answer the very day before I received your letter; & I have been so busy ever since, & have had to write so many letters that I was obliged to put off yours—knowing that you were already doing whatever was right, while others perhaps were not.—First, about the Review; I considered that from the first as certain. Molesworth, the very first time I mentioned it to him, agreed at once to your being our correspondent at Paris; & since receiving your letter he is very glad that he did consent. As for terms—you said, 150 or 200 francs per month; it will be either sum, according as you understood it. Your cooperation would be cheaply purchased at either price. Only, as our review is in some degree a doubtful speculation & our funds not unlimited, I have proposed to Molesworth & I now propose to you, to make the engagement at first for three months only. At the end of that time we shall know whether we can reckon upon sufficient assistance from French contributors to make it worth while retaining a French correspondent (though of this your letter leaves little doubt) & also, whether the success we can expect at first for our review, is such as renders it unnecessary for us to restrict our expenses to the utmost. If you agree, then, we will consider you as the correspondent of the review, from the 1st of this month (March) at 150, or 200 francs as you understand it. The payment will be made at the times & in the modes most convenient to you.

We are all much delighted with all you have done for the review, & with the prospects your letter holds out. The name of Carrel has done much for us already: his speech before the Chamber of Peers[2] has spread his fame in this country. The editor[3] of one of our best journals, the Spectator, advises strongly that we should request Carrel's permission to print his signature at full length. We shall be delighted to have an article on Courier[4] from him.

1. *Addressed*: Monsieur / M. Aristide Guilbert / Rue Joquelet /No 8 / à Paris. MS at Arsenal. Guilbert had been in England recently. See Letters 115 and 120.

2. In defence of M. Rouen, the responsible editor of the *National*, on Dec. 15, 1834, on a charge of impugning the dignity of the Chamber. See L. Blanc, *History of Ten Years* (London, 1845), II, 304–7. The *Examiner* on Dec. 21, 1834, pp. 808–9, printed excerpts of Carrel's speech.

3. Robert S. Rintoul (1787–1858), founder and editor of the *Spectator*.

4. Paul Louis Courier (1772–1825), soldier, Hellenist, and pamphleteer. No such essay appeared in the *London Review*. Carrel's *Essai sur la vie et les écrits de P. L. Courier* is published in the latter's *Œuvres complètes* (4 vols., Paris, 1829–30).

Half a page, of the most general kind, will be sufficient on the subject of Courier as a Hellenist; you have judged quite correctly that it is not in that point of view we wish for an appreciation of that great writer. The plan you have marked out for M. Nisard's first article,[5] seems very good. It is necessary to keep in mind that the English public are almost entirely ignorant that there *exists* a contemporary French literature; & their ideas of French writers are still those of the Voltaire period. The object therefore should be, *first*, in a general article, or more than one if necessary, to give a general view of the change which has taken place in French literature, & afterwards to follow this up by separate articles on separate writers. This, M. Nisard, from what I have seen of his writings, will I am convinced, do in the way best suited to us. I have seen a letter from him to his German friend, M. Garnier,[6] which shews him to be extremely well satisfied with my letter, & I am therefore well pleased at that *scène de comédie* which you recollect. He expresses a wish to remain anonymous, & says that you *agreed* in the expediency of it—I dare say you *suggested* it to him, though he thinks the suggestion came from himself.

The changes in French *philosophy* I think I shall myself treat in the review,[7] & shall be greatly indebted to you for all hints, & for suggesting to me all the books which I should read.

About placards, & advertisements, I will write to you again. There will be time, for the review will not appear for at least a fortnight. There will however be notices of it in some of the London papers before it appears.—We are anxious to have M. Nisard's first article in the second number, which will be published in June. Will you therefore beg him to set about it at his earliest convenience. The same request to Carrel; except that as his article is on a *special* subject, & not one of a series, we need not *press* him to have it ready by any given time, though of course the sooner the better. As both these articles will be very interesting, we will not limit them in point of space: say if necessary 30 to 40 pages of the review: & you know our pages are much larger than those of the French reviews.—We should like to exchange our review with any French reviews which may be willing, & which you may recommend. Carrel's offer of articles on the principal *men* of the Revolution is highly prized, & I will write to you again about it. We shall not want an article on the *Salon* this year at least; we must first *prendre notre place* as to Art in general. Cavaignac's writing

5. Désiré Nisard (1806–1888), literary historian and critic, was closely associated with Armand Carrel. His first contribution to the *London Review*, an essay on Victor Hugo, did not appear until Jan., 1836 (II, 389–417).

6. J. H. Garnier, a German refugee who supported himself by journalistic and translating work. JSM in the *Examiner* for Sept. 14, 1834 (p. 581), favourably reviewed Garnier's periodical, *Deutsches Leben, Kunst und Poesie.*

7. JSM seems not to have carried out this project.

I am afraid will not suit England; we will say nothing to him just yet, unless you have already spoken to him. Dussard[8] will be of considerable use to us, though at present I will not propose any article to him, as we already overflow with the sort of articles which he would write. The fact is, his line is also the line of most of *us*. We shall have an article on the Liberty of the Press very soon; & at all events we shall not fail to notice Carrel's admirable speeches. Tell us how many copies you would like to have of the *sheets* of the review & through what conveyance.

The *Globe*, it seems, is not inclined to have a regular correspondent at Paris—but would willingly insert, & pay for, occasional articles written in English. You know the kind of tone which suits the position of that journal.

As for politics, my dear friend, the game is up, as we say. The Tories will remain in place. The Opposition have spoiled all by their want of spirit & courage. The day after their victory in the choice of a Speaker, they could have done anything they pleased: the *prestige* of strength was wholly on their side. This instead of giving them courage, made them tremble lest their small majority should escape from them: & by conceding every point to the most timid among them, lest they should lose one or two votes, they have made such perpetual demonstrations of a belief in their own weakness that instead of one or two they have lost scores. The attempt to expel the ministry has been abandoned; they now only harrass them in detail. This reproach I address to our own friends as well as to others. Grote, Clay, and Warburton have spoiled all. Roebuck & Molesworth are the only ones among our friends (Hume I do not reckon such, though I esteem him much) who have a grain of spirit or energy. Those two are staunch, & if need be we shall unfurl the banner of our review against the radicals as well as the Whigs and Tories. They are giving us *du Maughin et Odilon Barrot*[9] over again. All parties are cowardly & torpid with us.

I am really grown so indifferent to all that these people do, that I cannot prevail upon myself to enter further into particulars; but you will see what we say in the review. The public mind, however, with us, is steadily progressive, & will force more & more improvements upon even a Tory ministry; for ministries, with us, always yield when they see that public opinion really requires it. We shall have either a Peel, or a Peel & Stanley[10] ministry, for years to come, I think.

8. Hippolyte Dussard. Years later he collaborated with J. G. Courcelle-Seneuil in translating JSM's *Political Economy*.

9. François Mauguin (1785–1854) and Odilon Barrot, leaders of the moderate opposition.

10. Edward George Geoffrey Smith Stanley (1799–1869), later fourteenth Earl of Derby, had broken with the Whig leadership in 1834, though he did not formally join Peel and the Tories until July 1, 1835.

We shall be glad to have Paul de Kock[11] from M. Barba,[12] on the terms you mention. If the proprietors of the Histoire Parlementaire will send it to us we will promise to make it the text of our first article on the French Revolution.[13] In general we shall be glad to receive any books which may be sent to us, though whether we can notice them will depend upon many various circumstances; but if not in the review, I can almost always, if they have any merit, get them favourably noticed *somewhere*. Will you thank all our friends for their kind interest in the review. The articles in the Bon Sens on England were true, & good: thanks for sending them. By the bye, do not write on the *out*side "for the Examiner."

Ever yours faithfully

J. S. MILL

128. TO THOMAS CARLYLE[1]

I.H.

Monday [March 23, 1835]

MY DEAR CARLYLE

Notwithstanding all which you said on Thursday night, I cannot feel that I have made you anything like compensation by placing you exactly in the same pecuniary state as when you began to write, the time which you have expended in writing being lost and gone, without result either to yourself or any one else, except the doubtful one of your making a better book the second time.

It would be not only more accordant with my conception of the justice of the case, but would be a much more complete relief to my conscience and in every way more pleasant to me, if you would consent to receive the sum I first mentioned[2] or at least something intermediate between that & the smaller one. This would be a gratification to me only inferior to that of being permitted to make compensation at all.

Ever affectionately yours

J. S. MILL

11. Charles Paul de Kock (1794–1871), novelist. See Letters 134 and 140.
12. Possibly Jean Nicolas Barba (1769–1846), author of *Vie et aventures de Pigault–Le Brun* (Paris, 1836).
13. Carlyle eventually reviewed it in *LWR* for April, 1837, pp. 233–47.

* * * *

1. MS at Huntington Library.
2. JSM tried to persuade Carlyle to accept £200 but finally had to yield to the latter's refusal to accept more than £100. See Carlyle's letters to his brother and his mother in *Letters of Thomas Carlyle, 1826–1836*, ed. C. E. Norton (London, 1889), pp. 506 and 510.

129. TO JOSEPH BLANCO WHITE[1]

India House
15th April
1835

MY DEAR SIR

I have learnt to my great surprise this morning, that owing to some inexplicable misunderstanding, Crabbe[2] has not yet been sent to you. You will, however, receive it immediately, along with your copy of the London Review and as we wish the second number to appear in June, we shall be very glad to have your article in the shortest time in which you can write it satisfactorily to yourself.[3]

Mr James Martineau, with whom I know you are in communication, has kindly offered to review for our next number, Bailey's excellent "Rationale of Representation".[4] Perhaps you would do us the favour to say to Mr Martineau that after a good deal of deliberation among the three or four persons who take most share in the conduct of the review, it has appeared to us that a subject involving so directly and comprehensively all the political principles of the review, should be retained in the hands of the conductors themselves, rather than placed in those of a contributor, however highly valued, who is not in direct and continual communication with them. But for this consideration, there is no writer for the review in whose hands we would rather see such a subject. The objections which Mr Martineau thought might be felt to his undertaking an article on Robert Hall,[5] we should not feel to be objections at all unless he himself felt them so, or unless he would feel bound to enter into a discussion of Hall's theological tenets, which probably he would not. In mentioning Hall, it was however, only intended to throw out a suggestion; & if Mr Martineau would either dislike that, or prefer any other subject, there is no wish to press it upon him. We are only anxious to have, at as early a period as may be convenient to him, *some* article from his pen. Anything similar or comparable to those admirable papers on Priestley in the Monthly Repository,[6] would be of the greatest value to us.

Would you and Mr Martineau have the kindness to mention any quarters —especially public institutions & the like—to which it would be advan-

1. MS in the Liverpool University Library. A portion of White's letter in reply is in Thom, II, 121–22.

2. *The Poetical Works of the Rev. George Crabbe; with his Letters and Journals, and his Life, by his Son* (8 vols., London, 1834).

3. White's article appeared in the second number, I (July, 1835), 316–41.

4. *The Rationale of Political Representation.* By the author of *Essays on the Formation of Opinions*, etc. [Samuel Bailey] (London, 1835). JSM himself reviewed the book in the second number (I, 341–71).

5. Robert Hall (1764–1831), popular Baptist preacher.

6. See Letter 119.

tageous to send copies of the review. Molesworth is disposed to distribute it pretty extensively—the first number at least—as the cheapest, and most useful, mode of advertising it.

I have begun to read Tocqueville. It seems an excellent book: uniting considerable graphic power, with the capacity of generalizing on the history of society, which distinguishes the best French philosophers of the present day, & above all, *bringing out* the peculiarities of American society, & making the whole stand before the reader as a powerful picture.—Did you ever read Guizot's Lectures?[7] If not, pray do.

Ever yours truly

J. S. MILL

130. TO ALBANY FONBLANQUE[1]

I.H.
Monday
[April 20(?), 1835][2]

DEAR FONBLANQUE

Thanks for your mention of the London Review.[3] I hope you will give us a formal article besides[4]—as we shall have but a poor chance of success unless our friends exert themselves for us—some of them are treating us as friends usually do.

We all greatly regret that the review was obliged to appear without anything of yours in it; & we hope exceedingly that you will write something in the second number. Nothing has occurred to any of us which we should like so much, as an article on the magisterial interferences with the people. But as you are so fully occupied, we should be too happy to have anything which you could do most easily & in least time.

If you give us something, we shall have an excellent bill of fare for No 2, twice as good as No 1.

Yours faithfully

J. S. MILL

7. *Cours d'Histoire moderne* . . . [consisting of] *Histoire générale de la civilisation en Europe depuis la chute de l'Empire romain jusqu'a la Révolution française* (Paris, 1828), [and] *Histoire de la civilisation en France depuis la chute de l'Empire romain jusqu'en 1789* (5 vols. Paris, 1829–32). White wrote the review of Guizot in the Jan., 1836, *London Rev.* (II, 306–36), but with cuts and additions by JSM (see Letters 135, 149, and 154).

* * * *

1. MS at LSE.

2. See the following letter.

3. A long excerpt from JSM's "Postscript" to the first number of the *London Rev.* (I, 254–56) was quoted in Fonblanque's leading article, "The Administration," *Examiner*, April 19, 1835, p. 241.

4. Fonblanque obliged with a leading article on the *Review* in the *Examiner,* May 10, 1835, pp. 289–90.

131. TO ALBANY FONBLANQUE[1]

[April 20, 1835]

How do you like the new Cabinet?[2] All things considered I am very well satisfied with it—but I hope you will *push* them to the ballot & a few other things—they can't stand without.

Ever yours

J.S.M.

132. TO THOMAS CARLYLE[1]

I.H.
Saturday
[?Spring or summer, 1835]

MY DEAR CARLYLE

If you have no objection to receive the Chronicle instead of the Globe, for the next fortnight or thereabouts, I find that to be the most convenient arrangement now when the whole household except my father & myself are in Surrey & my brother[2] still at the East India College.

If however you would rather have the Globe I can still contrive to supply you with it.

Ever yours faithfully

J. S. MILL

I shall probably be with you on Monday evening.

133. TO ARISTIDE GUILBERT[1]

India House
8th May
1835

MY DEAR MONSIEUR GUILBERT

I yesterday, by making a casual enquiry, learnt to my extreme astonishment, that no remittance had yet been made to you. I imagined I had

1. Probably a postscript to the foregoing. Written on the inside of a cover of a letter addressed: Albany Fonblanque Esq. / 5 Pine Apple Place / Kilburn Road. *Postmark*: 4 EVEN 4 / AP 20 / 1835. MS at LSE.

2. Of Lord Melbourne.

* * * *

1. MS at NLS. 2. James Bentham Mill.

* * * *

1. *Addressed*: M. Aristide Guilbert / Rue Joquelet / no 8, / à Paris / Parti rue

taken measures which had ensured its being done long ago. I have now set the matter to rights, & you will receive without delay 450 francs, for the months of March, April, & May. Pray let me know whether you have received copies of the review. They were sent, or at least orders were given for their being sent, through Black & Young, booksellers here. If you have received them I hope you have considered yourself at liberty to give them, in exchange or otherwise, whenever you thought it useful to the review to do so.

I have not written to you about the change of ministry[2] because I knew not what to write. I fear the whigs will do as little for the people as they possibly can: all their speeches & manifestoes indicate it, except Hobhouse's speech at Nottingham:[3] & you will see, that even Lord John Russell's defeat in Devonshire by the intimidation practised by the Tory squires & parsons will not make him an advocate of the ballot. Brougham, however, being excluded from office, is putting forth pamphlets & articles of very decided radicalism to the extreme annoyance of his former associates. You see how justly I described him to you.

At the late change it was well understood that the radicals as a body would not consent to take office. They thought, justly, that they had more power out of office than in it. To several members of the body (but to none of the leaders) offers were made of places, which they all refused, unless the leaders came in too. Brougham is reported to have said to a near relation of a cabinet minister "this *may* succeed, but it is the first time the attempt has been made to form a ministry excluding the able men of all parties." I don't believe this, but the *mot* is excellent.

Toqueville's book, "de la démocratie en amérique" is an admirable book. Can you tell me anything of Toqueville? What is his history? & in what estimation is he held in France?

We are anxious to receive the notice you promised respecting Paul de Kock. When & how is the copy of his works, to be paid for? We persist in our intention of bringing out our second number before the end of June.—Ever truly yours

J. S. MILL.

Joubert N°. 47. *Postmarks*: 196 / F 35; 19 / 35; and Calais / 10 MAI / 1835. MS at King's. Printed in Morrison, p. 253.

2. On April 8 Peel had resigned after a vain effort of six weeks to maintain a Tory administration. Melbourne then formed a straight Whig ministry which, though it did not include the Radicals, received their support.

3. On April 24 (see *The Times*, April 27, 1835). John Cam Hobhouse, later Baron Broughton de Gyfford (1786–1869), friend of Byron, Whig politician.

134. TO ARISTIDE GUILBERT[1]

India House
19th May
1835

MY DEAR GUILBERT

You may judge how much we have been annoyed by the neglect of the booksellers to send the copies of the review to Paris. It is one of numerous instances of such negligence which have occurred to us, proving the great difficulty of making a review succeed which is not the *property* of a bookseller. On receiving your letter I took immediate measures for having the omission supplied, & I hope it has been so. Pray apologize to our friends, & present copies to such of them, & of your editors & littérateurs generally, as you think ought to have it; obtaining for us in exchange, when you can, all your best periodicals.

You are aware that we do not want an *article* on Paul de Kock, but merely a short notice, to serve towards writing an article. The article itself is to be written by one of our English contributors, a man of great wit & learning.[2]

I have not received Carrel's letter. We attach great importance to having his article in our next number.[3] You do not say anything about his autograph. I have done nothing with it as yet.

I am much disappointed that M. Nisard has been obliged to renounce an undertaking for which he was so eminently qualified. We gladly accept his offer of separate articles on Victor Hugo, Lamartine &c. but it appears to us indispensable that they should be preceded by a general article on the new French literature generally. We do not wish for a detailed history of its origin—since that would cost M. Nisard so much research—but a general *character* of the old, & of the new literature, could cost neither much time nor labour to the author of those admirable papers in the Revue de Paris.

I said nothing about the article which M. de Cormenin[4] was so kind as to offer, because we should not have room for it for some time to come, & it is as well not to fix on a subject long beforehand. But his cooperation would be highly valuable to us.

As for politics—the grand struggle will be at the next registration. Peel's

1. *Addressed*: Monsieur / M. Aristide Guilbert / Rue Joubert / à Paris / No 47. *Postmark*: 210 / F 35. MS at King's. Printed in Morrison, p. 254.

2. Thomas Love Peacock. Although in both his article on "French Comic Romances," *London Rev.*, II (Oct., 1835), 69–84, and the one entitled "The Epicier," *ibid.*, II (Jan., 1836), 355–65, he promises to present an article on De Kock, none appeared.

3. No article by Carrel seems to have appeared.

4. Louis Marie de La Haye, vicomte de Cormenin (1788–1868), jurist and political writer.

speech at Merchant Tailors' Hall[5] speaks the voice of the whole party. The Tories will strain every nerve to get a majority in the Commons—but we shall beat them.

Yours ever

J. S. MILL.

The review is exciting great attention here, & already possesses very considerable political influence, which every number we publish will still further increase—J.S.M.

We will send you all the affiches we can spare.

135. TO JOSEPH BLANCO WHITE[1]

India House
19th May 1835

MY DEAR SIR

I should have written to you sooner, but I really could not make up my mind at once what to say about Tocqueville. I was quite ignorant of Falconer's intention to make such a proposition to you, & I am by no means confident that I can write such an article on the book as I wish to see written. It is not a subject requiring familiarity with the politics of the day, & I am far from being convinced that the Review will not be a loser by my writing the article instead of you. However if the subject is one on which you would *rather not* write, & it would be a *relief* to you to place it in other hands, that is decisive—& there are some disadvantages in having articles which involve the political principles of the review (though this does not involve them nearly so much as Bailey's book)[2] written at a distance from the conductors of the review & by contributors not in daily intercourse with them & with the details of whose opinions they are not conversant. I have therefore no objection to write the article if it be your wish & Falconer's also, for the third number.[3]

Many thanks for your remarks, which will be of great use to me.

Our second number is full—including your article on Crabbe, which I

5. On May 11. Peel urged Tories to seek control of the House of Commons in order to resist further constitutional reform. "We will not allow, if we can prevent it . . . such an infusion of democracy into the institutions of this country as shall essentially change their theory, and by slow degrees deprive us of the advantages we have so long enjoyed under our limited monarchy and ancient institutions" (*The Times*, May 12, 1835, p. 5).

* * * *

1. MS in the Liverpool University Library. White's reply of May 28, 1835, is in Thom, II, 126–27.
2. See Letter 129.
3. See Letter 121, n. 5.

hope the negligence of Willmer[4] will not prevent us from having the benefit of. We confidently reckon upon some paper of Mr Martineau for No. 3. Would he review the "Second Travels of an Irish Gentleman"?[5] It would be very important to make that book more known.

May we reckon upon your undertaking to give an account of Guizot's Lectures?[6]

I think our future numbers will far surpass our first—with which, though it was fully as good as I expected, on the whole I was far from being pleased.

Would you be kind enough to *suggest* to us any subjects on which we ought to have articles—& to Mr Martineau, any on which you think he might be induced to write.

Ever yours faithfully

J. S. MILL

136. TO JAMES MARTINEAU[1]

May 26, 1835.

In the opinions you express respecting a Church Establishment I entirely agree, and though some of the habitual contributors to the review still differ from us, the general tone of the review will, I have reason to hope, be that which you approve. A considerable change is, I think, taking place in the tone of thinking of the instructed Radicals on that point. Indeed, as they have (very generally) so far departed from Adam Smith's doctrines as not to admit the voluntary principle even with respect to secular education, it would be very strange if they admitted it with regard to religious. The mistake, I think, is in applying the *test* to the *doctrines* which the clergy shall teach, instead of applying it to their qualifications as teachers, and to the spirit in which they teach. When you give a man a diploma as a physician, you do not bind him to follow a prescribed method; you merely assure yourself of his being duly *acquainted* with what is known or believed on the subject, and of his having competent powers of mind. I would do the same with clergymen. . . . One of the most important objects which the review could be instrumental to, would be to discredit dogmatic

4. Bookseller who served as Liverpool agent for the *London Review*.

5. *Second Travels of an Irish Gentleman in Search of a Religion* (2 vols., Dublin, 1833). This was White's reply to Thomas Moore's *Travels of an Irish Gentleman in Search of a Religion* (2 vols., London, 1833). James Martineau discussed these in his article "Catholic and Protestant Claims to Infallibility," *LWR*, XXV (July, 1836), 425–49.

6. See Letter 129, n. 7.

* * * *

1. Excerpt published in J. Estlin Carpenter, *James Martineau* (London, 1905), pp. 165–66. MS not located.

religion and encourage the boldest spirit of rationalism. This too is the spirit which is spreading among the young and cultivated members of the English clergy. This I know from my acquaintance with some striking instances of it. There will shortly appear a posthumous work of Coleridge[2] (which I saw in manuscript before his death) altogether smashing the doctrine of plenary inspiration, and the notion that the Bible was *dictated* by the Almighty, or is to be exempt from the same canons of criticism which we apply to books of human origin.

137. TO ALEXIS DE TOCQUEVILLE[1]

11 Juin, 1835.

Vous me demandez, mon cher Monsieur, dans quelles limites doit s'exercer la collaboration que j'ai osé vous demander en faveur du *London Review*. C'est une question fort naturelle, mais qu'il n'appartient pas aux rédacteurs de la Revue de résoudre. La Revue n'a pas pour but la propagation d'un système donné, d'une doctrine générale et unitaire; je n'ai pas besoin de vous dire que jusqu'ici cette doctrine est encore à créer. En défaut d'une théorie complète, les fondateurs du *London Review* ont désiré que cet ouvrage périodique devînt un recueil des meilleures idées du siècle, notamment en fait de philosophie politique: et dans ce but ils voudraient obtenir la coopération des plus forts penseurs et des hommes les plus éclairés de notre temps, du moins parmi ceux qui sympathisent avec les tendances dominantes du siècle. Cette seule condition est de rigueur, attendu que pour pouvoir travailler utilement avec des amis du mouvement il faut l'être soi-même.

Dans une réunion de pareils hommes il ne vous appartient pas de jouer un role secondaire. Aussi ce que nous vous demandons n'est pas une collaboration en second ordre: nous ne vous invitons pas à mettre votre talent à notre disposition pour exposer ou pour discuter telle ou telle série d'idées ou de faits. Nous vous engageons à fixer, de concert avec nous, ce que sera la Revue elle-même; dans quel esprit, et sous l'influence de quelles idées, elle sera faite. La Revue a la prétention de représenter ce qu'il y a de plus avancé dans les doctrines démocratiques: c'est précisément ce que vous avez, vous-même, ou créé, ou fait ressortir avec une vigueur jusqu'ici inconnue, des faits ou des principes connus. Vous êtes donc fait pour dicter des conditions à la Revue, et non pour en recevoir d'elle. Notre vœu serait que vous vouliez bien vous joindre à nous, et vous servir de la Revue

2. This work of Coleridge's eventually appeared under the title *Confessions of an Inquiring Spirit*, ed. H. N. Coleridge (London, 1840).

* * * *

1. Published in Mayer, pp. 291–93. MS in the Tocqueville archives. Tocqueville's reply is in Mayer, pp. 293–95.

comme organe de vos opinions. Elle est déjà l'organe de ce qu'il y a de meilleur parmi nos hommes du mouvement; mais ces hommes, avec de grandes connaissances spéciales, sont, du moins la plupart d'entre eux, tellement au-dessous de votre niveau quant aux idées générales, que la direction que vous pourrez imprimer à la Revue par vos articles et par l'influence qu'exerceront ces articles sur les autres rédacteurs, décidera peut-être si ce journal servira à éclairer le public anglais sur les questions de haute politique, ou seulement à exciter l'esprit démocratique sans lui donner des principes capables de régler sa marche.

Quant aux moyens particuliers de présenter vos idées, aux questions particulières à traiter, etc., il ne nous appartient pas de vous les indiquer, encore moins d'y mettre des bornes. Un esprit comme le vôtre sait toujours ce qu'il peut et ce qu'il lui convient de faire, mieux que ne pourrait le lui indiquer même son plus intime ami. Tout ce que nous pourrons, c'est de vous dire de quoi nous avons le besoin le plus pressant. Il y a deux pays très importants à bien comprendre, ce sont la France et les Etats-Unis : nous ressentons un grand besoin d'expliquer ces pays à nos compatriotes; nous-même nous ne les connaissons pas assez pour cela et il n'y a peut-être que vous au monde qui soit capable de la faire. Ce serait déjà un cours de haute politique qu'une série d'articles de vous sur ces deux pays; vous avez assez fait vos preuves pour que nous ayons dans la justesse et dans la profondeur de vos vues, ainsi que dans leur impartialité, une confiance que nul autre écrivain ne saurait nous inspirer; vous êtes, enfin, précisément l'homme qu'il nous faut pour écrire sur ces deux pays, et s'il nous fallait désigner un sujet, c'est par là, et en premier lieu par la France, que nous vous prierions de commencer.

Veuillez, mon cher Monsieur, agréer l'hommage de mon éstime et de mon attachement.

J. S. Mill

India House.

138. TO JOSEPH BLANCO WHITE[1]

India House
23d June
1835

My dear Sir

Such a letter as your last might well have called forth an earlier acknowledgment than this. I assure you if I have delayed writing to you it was not for want of sympathizing in the warmest manner in all the

1. MS in Liverpool University Library. In reply to White's letter of June 10, 1835, in Thom, II, 134–36.

feelings which your letter expresses. I wish to heaven there were more persons capable of feeling & thinking in the same manner—& most earnestly do I hope that your sufferings bodily & mental may come to an end, & give you many years of tranquillity & activity at a time when such men are more than ever needed.

As for Guizot—there can be no objection whatever to making *two* articles provided each can be made in form independent of the other. English readers do not, I think, like articles which are *ostensibly* continued through several numbers of a periodical, but to the reality they do not object, only to the appearance. Therefore pray adjust it in the manner you find most convenient. I quite agree with you that only the most scanty justice can be done to the subject in one article.

I have not yet read Lord Brougham's Discourse[2] but the opinion of all competent judges with whom I have conversed accords with yours, which is besides in accordance with the character of his mind. He knows no subject well, having never seriously studied anything: he has more half knowledges than perhaps any man of our time, but I never could perceive that he had any complete knowledges at all, & I observe, all who really *know* any one of the subjects he writes about, think him a very wonderful man, but wonder why he is so unwise as to write on *that* particular subject.

Is there any literary subject which you would undertake for No. 3, in addition to Guizot? Forgive my encroaching upon you in this stile![3]

139. TO JOSEPH BLANCO WHITE[1]

India House
1st July
1835

My dear Sir

I write chiefly to inform you that I am about to set out for the Rhine next Saturday,[2] & shall not be back till the 10th of August, therefore till

2. Henry Brougham, *A Discourse of Natural Theology* (Brussels, 1835). White had written: "What do you intend to do with Lord Brougham? I have been sadly disappointed by his Discourse on Paley—so much so, that I almost fear I may be under some delusion. To find such a collection of crudities coming from a man of his talents and reading, is quite startling. . . . It appears to me that Lord Brougham has treated most branches of physical and metaphysical science, as *briefs* put into his hands, upon which he must say something plausible—just enough for the satisfaction of people not much above the juries he has addressed in the course of his life."

3. The end of the letter is missing.

* * * *

1. MS in Liverpool University Library. In reply to White's letter of June 27, 1835, published in part in Thom, II, 137–38.

2. A MS journal (82 pp., 2 vols., 4to, sewed) of this tour of the Rhine was sold in Sotheby's auction of March 27–29, 1922, as lot 716 (third day); its present location is unknown.

that time it will devolve upon Falconer to correspond with you respecting the review.

Lamb[3] will be immediately sent—before sending Anster's Faust[4] we are anxious to know in what way you think of treating it—for it would seem too difficult to make an article on one of the most celebrated of Goethe's works, without entering into a complete examination of Goethe himself, his writings & his influence—& that is so *great* a subject, that we must think of it, & discuss it among ourselves for a good while before we can safely embark upon it. Will you write to Falconer expressing your views & inclinations as to the matter?

The review will be published next Wednesday unless something unexpected should delay it. I am anxious to know what you think of the article "The Church & its Reform";[5] it is not such as you, or such as I would have written, & perhaps is too *brusque* in manner, but I think it will do us no discredit.

I should gladly write to you many more things but I am pressed for time. I shall read your work with great interest when I return.

Ever most truly yours

J. S. MILL

M. de Tocqueville will be at Liverpool in a few days. I suppose he has an introduction to you from Senior, but I will at all events write to him & ask him to call upon you.

140. TO ARISTIDE GUILBERT[1]

India House
14th August
1835

MY DEAR GUILBERT

I yesterday remitted to Monsr Delamarre Martin Didier, a banker of Paris, for you, the sum of 870 francs, which, with about five francs overpayment last time, will about make up,

3. Charles Lamb, *Specimens of English Dramatic Poets who lived about the time of Shakespeare* (new edition, 2 vols., London, 1835), which White reviewed in the *London Rev.*, II (Oct., 1835), 51–69.

4. Dr. John Anster's translation of *Faust* (London, 1835) was eventually reviewed in "Translations of Faust," *LWR*, XXV (July, 1836), 366–90, probably by J. H. Garnier.

5. The article (I, 257–95, signed P.Q.) was by James Mill.

* * * *

1. *Addressed*: Monsieur / M. Aristide Guilbert / Rue de Joubert / 47 / à Paris. *Postmarks*: F 35, and Paris / 16 AOUT / 1835. MS at King's. Printed in Morrison, pp. 254–55.

1. the 400 francs for Messrs Maurel & Blanchard[2]
2. the 300 francs due to yourself for the months of June & July, & 150 francs for the present month
3. the 25 francs due from myself to M. Faucher[3] for the notice on the subject of M. de Tocqueville.

When I asked you to procure notices of Paul de Kock, & Leclercq,[4] I did not contemplate their being so elaborate as those which you have furnished nor costing so much to the review. Both works are already in the hands of a distinguished English writer,[5] & of course we could not use, & did not wish to pay for, two criticisms of the same author: but as English reviewers are often ignorant of various things, necessary to be known in reviewing a French author, I was anxious that any particulars, the ignorance of which might expose our English reviewer to the commission of blunders, might be supplied to him from France. I do not say this by way of complaint; you did the best you could for the review, & the articles, that on Paul de Kock especially, are worth much more than we are to pay for them. I mention it only to account for your misunderstanding with Falconer. I never told him of the articles, but gave them at once to the gentleman who is reviewing Paul de Kock & Leclercq for us. The *review* will only pay for them when the articles are finished, & that was always my intention: but I always intended to advance whatever money might be needful from my own funds, being indemnified by the review hereafter; and this I have done by the remittance I have made to you. By applying to M. Didier you will be able to receive the money immediately.

How do you like our second number? It is *well* liked here, but has not yet acquired a large circulation, & its progress is so slow that we are obliged to economize our funds as much as possible. I consequently do not like to recommend to Sir William Molesworth to be at any further expense for a Paris correspondent. We originally hoped for some sale at Paris & for considerable aid from the Paris literary men of our own way of thinking: but we do not seem likely to have any sale at all, nor any literary assistance of much importance except from M. Nisard, even if we succeed in obtaining his. I feel myself very strictly accountable for the expenditure of funds which are not my own, & as Sir W. Molesworth is only willing to risk a limited sum on this experiment, I should regret much if that sum were not made to go as far as possible.

We have not yet received any French newspapers or reviews in exchange for our review: have you been able to effect any exchanges?

2. Unidentified. Morrison has "Manuel" instead of "Maurel."
3. Léon Faucher (1803–1854), economist and statesman.
4. Michel Théodore Leclercq (1777–1851), dramatist. No article on him appeared in the *London Review*.
5. Thomas Love Peacock.

Will these odious laws against the press pass?[6] & if they do, will any person of the least public spirit or love of freedom, consent to live in France under them?

Our Lords will pass the corporation bill,[7] with modifications, very bad in themselves, but leaving much good. They will not pass the Irish Church Bill. Have you taken notice of the numerous public meetings, & how the speeches & petitions almost always declare the House of Lords a nuisance.

Have you seen any of Roebuck's pamphlets?[8] They now sell 10,000.

Ever yours J. S. MILL

141. TO JOSEPH BLANCO WHITE[1]

India House
28th August
1835

MY DEAR SIR

I have now been about a fortnight returned from my continental excursion, but have been too much occupied in various ways to be able to write to you before: & I must now for the same reason cut this note very short.

I write in the first place to say how exceedingly pleased I have been with your pamphlet on Heresy & Orthodoxy.[2] It seems to me one of the most efficient protests which have been made in our time against the doctrine which has been the bane of Xianity, the doctrine that religious duty consists in the reception or adoption of a particular set of opinions, & not in the state of the affections & will.

In the next place, as we are obliged to think seriously now about our third number, we are anxious to know whether we can expect from you either the paper on Guizot,[3] or any literary article, which, as we are scant of such articles for this number, would be particularly precious.

6. A *projet* of sternly repressive laws against the press proposed early in Aug. in the Chamber of Deputies and finally adopted in Sept.

7. Royal assent to the Municipal Corporations bill was given on Sept. 9.

8. *Pamphlets for the People*, of which thirty-six weekly numbers appeared, began publication on June 11, 1835. In addition to Roebuck, its writers included Henry Chapman, Thomas Falconer, and Francis Place. See R. E. Leader, *Life and Letters of John Arthur Roebuck* (London, 1897), pp. 71, 75–78.

* * * *

1. MS in Liverpool University Library. An excerpt from White's reply, inexplicably dated Aug. 25, 1835, is in Thom, II, 143.

2. *Observations on Heresy and Orthodoxy* (London, 1835).

3. See Letter 129, n. 7.

You mentioned Lamb's Specimens of early English Dramatists as a subject—have you written anything upon it?

Believe me
Ever yours
J. S. MILL

Pray inform me particulars of the state of your health.

142. TO ALEXIS DE TOCQUEVILLE[1]

[Sept., 1835]

MY DEAR M. DE TOCQUEVILLE,

I write in English because it takes me so much more time to write in French. To you who understand English so perfectly I need not apologise.

Your letter[2] was most grateful to me on every account—for the expressions of personal friendship, which I hope I shall never deserve to forfeit—& which I trust I may some day have it in my power to prove to you how deeply I value. Next to that I was most delighted with the sure prospect your letter affords of our obtaining from you a cooperation which, while it would be of the greatest importance to the London Review would probably do more good in this country than the London Review itself; for, while a strong & general desire has of late years grown up here, to know something about France, there is as yet no source from which knowledge can be drawn. We have not so much as one readable history of the Revolution; & not our people merely, but our politicians & publicists, know about as much of France as they do of Timbuctoo. They do not even know the titles of the most celebrated books, or the names of the most celebrated men. Hardly any, even instructed Englishmen . . .[3] even looked . . . [at] Paul Louis Courier,[4] or Guizot's lectures,[5] or Thiers' history.[6] I do not think there are two hundred who if you spoke to them of these works would not be obliged to ask what they were. Therefore you see, my dear M. de Tocqueville, you need [not] be afraid of being tedious, or telling a twice told tale, if you write to the English about what France was before the Revolution. I should ask you to do so, even if it were *not* necessary as a preparation for

1. Published in Mayer, pp. 297–99. MS in Tocqueville archives.
2. Dated 12 7bre 1835, in Mayer, pp. 295–97.
3. Ellipsis points here and elsewhere indicate missing portions in the MS, which is torn.
4. See Letter 127, n. 4.
5. Lectures formed the basis of Guizot's *Histoire des origines du gouvernement représentatif* (1821–22), *Histoire générale de la civilisation en Europe* (1828), and *Histoire de la civilisation en France* (1829–32).
6. See Letter 61, n. 7.

understanding the France of the present day. *In itself* it is a matter most necessary to be set forth & interpreted to the English. And besides, if the mere facts, the mere *husk* of the ancien régime, were ever so stale to us, it would come fresh & with all the colours of youth out of your hands; for the oldest thing seems new when shewn as you shew it, in all kinds of previously unsuspected relations to all the other things which surround it.

Either the form of letters, or that of articles, would suit the plan of our review; perhaps that of letters, which you suggest, would be best, as leading the reader to *feel* that each paper is part of a series. Do not restrain yourself in space. We can afford you on an average between 30 & 40 pages of each number, & a page of the L.R. is equal to at least two of your book.

Almost everybody here thinks that the ministers, & the House of Commons, have shewn a deplorable want of energy & courage in the contest with the Lords.[7] It is not that. . . . However . . . the Lords & the Tories are the sufferers, in this instance. You can hardly conceive how the tone of the public about them is changed since I last saw you. Six months or a year ago, everybody would have been satisfied with a *fournée* of peers; now nobody mentions, or thinks of such a thing; everybody is full of the necessity of an absolute reorganization of the House: & by this time next year everybody will be for abolishing it, (at least as a hereditary & aristocratic body) altogether.

What you say of the probable effect of these . . . laws against the Press,[8] is encouraging, & in itself . . . highly probable. I know, too, that Carrel thinks . . . as you do on the subject—& him I conceive to be, next to you [the] best authority I know on the state of France. He has been desirous to moderate his tone, & this gives him an opportunity of doing so without loss of influence.

I have nearly finished a review of your book [for the] L.R.[9] The chief merit of it will be in the extracts: if I [have] succeeded in introducing them so as to excite attention to them I have done all I have aimed at. My article will be, as you [will] see, a shade or two more favourable to democracy than your book, although in the main I agree, so far as I am competent to judge, in the unfavourable part of your remarks, but without carrying them quite so far. The third number will appear in a fortnight & we shall endeavour to bring the fourth out in December, in which we hope to have your first article. Apropos, did M. de Beaumont. . . .

Ever, my dear M. de Tocqueville, yours faithfully,

J. S. MILL.

7. The House of Lords had succeeded in carrying certain amendments to the Corporation bill passed on Sept. 7. The Radicals maintained that the amendments nullified the reforms of the evils of the municipal corporations which the original bill was designed to eliminate (see *Annual Register for 1835*, pp. 242 ff. and 265–68).

8. See Letter 140, n. 6.

9. See Letter 121, n. 5.

Pray make my kindest remembrances to M. de Beaumont.[10] I will write to him very soon.

Is there a chance of your writing anything about Ireland for the French? It would be very instructive.

J.S.M.

143. TO THOMAS FALCONER[1]

I.H.
Saturday
3[d] Oct. [1835]

MY DEAR FALCONER

I write to report progress. *D'abord* I wish you would by the first post, write to Pringle,[2] to say that from the length to which some of our articles have gone, & the great quantity of matter not acceptable to light readers, which the number will contain, we are obliged to put off his article to No iv.[3] which is the less to be regretted as matter of the kind will be likely to be more read then than now. You may add (if you will venture to do so on my testimony) that the article is very good, & will be useful to us.—I want him to receive the first notice of the postponement from us, & not from the advertisement.

We shall be out next week. The only matter not sent to press is my Postscript[4] (which I think you will like) & the last half of Buller's article,[5] which he promised sh[d] have been here yesterday. What we have of it is very good, & pleasantly written. On the whole it is a good number. We shall rather exceed our 16 sheets, though we must omit the Nebulae.[6] By the bye, Nichol sent to me by post the first sheet of the Nebulae, saying that an accident had rendered his MS. illegible & that he was obliged to recopy it: & would send by every post one sheet, using thereafter alternately Grote's & Roebuck's frank: consequently I have received no more, both being out of town. But as we have not room for it, that is of no consequence.

10. Gustave de Beaumont de la Bonninière (1802–1866), politician and writer, associate of Tocqueville who accompanied him to America in 1831 and collaborated with him in publishing their *Du Système pénitentiaire aux Etats-Unis et de son application en France* (Paris, 1833).

* * * *

1. *Addressed*: T. Falconer Esq. MS in the possession of F. A. Hayek.
2. John Pringle Nichol.
3. "State of Discovery and Speculation concerning the Nebulae." It did not appear until July, 1836 (XXV, 390–409).
4. "Postscript.—The Close of the Session," *London Rev.*, II (Oct., 1835), 270–77.
5. "Journal by Frances Anne Butler," *ibid.*, pp. 194–227.
6. See n. 3 above.

Chapman[7] goes on very well.

Molesworth wants to write on Orangm.[8] & I should like him to do so, but as the *Atlas* man[9] wants the same thing, & as it may be good to have a friend in the Atlas—will you tell me how I can manage to get a sight of some numbers thereof, that I may see how he writes.

Nichol says his mode of treating the subject, being scientific & *a priori*, will not interfere with Wakefield's.[10]

We are to print 1000 of Law Reform[11] & sell it for 6[d]. That was Chapman's ultimate opinion. We must distribute it very largely. Could not you send some to the agents for the Political Pamphlet?[12]

I have set on foot a greater quantity of advertising than usual, as people complain of our not being advertised enough.

Ever yours

J. S. MILL

144. TO JOHN PRINGLE NICHOL[1]

India House
7th October, 1835.

MY DEAR NICHOL,

In consequence, I suppose, of Grote's and Roebuck's absence from town, I have received no part of your article on "Nebulae"[2] except the first sheet, which you sent to me direct. This, however, is of the less importance, as the unexpected length of some other articles would at all events have compelled us to omit it from this number. We will have it set up as soon as we receive it, and send you a proof—for we mean to bring out No. 4 in December. I hope your article on "Chalmers" will be ready by that time. The one on "Quetelet"[3] would in that case be better postponed.

7. Henry S. Chapman (1803–1881), journalist in Canada, 1823–34; closely associated with the *LWR* (see Letters 162 and 163); later, judge of Supreme Court of New Zealand.

8. Molesworth contributed two articles: "Orange Societies in Great Britain, Their Illegality and Criminality," *London Rev.*, II (Jan., 1836), 480–513, and "Orange Conspiracy," *LWR*, XXV (April, 1836) 181–201.

9. Possibly Robert Bell (1800–1867), editor of the *Atlas*, a weekly journal.

10. Probably Edward Gibbon Wakefield, but no article by him can be identified in the *London Review*.

11. A reprint of James Mill's article of that title, *London Rev.*, II (Oct., 1835), 1–51.

12. Roebuck's series, "Pamphlets for the People." See Letter 140, n. 8.

* * * *

1. Published by Knight, p. 672. MS not located.

2. See preceding letter, n. 3.

3. L. A. J. Quetelet (1796–1874), Belgian astronomer, meteorologist, and statistician. No article on either Chalmers or Quetelet appeared.

You will, I think, like No. 3; and No. 4 will be excellent. De Tocqueville has promised us a set of articles containing all that he knows and thinks about Maree.[4] Grote has promised one on "Greek History;"[5] and we have many other good articles, either ready or in prospect. But we are particularly anxious for the one on "Chalmers."

I shall read Combe's book[6] with a pleasure increased by receiving it from you. Phrenology, no doubt, may be to a certain extent reconciled with analytical psychology, that is, if it can be discovered that certain nervous peculiarities, affecting the kind or the intensity of our sensations, have to do with peculiar conformations of the brain. Thus, for instance, what they say about their "organ of amativeness" has some foundation, because we know that nymphomania can be traced to inflammation of the cerebellum. It is, I believe, ascertained that the nerves of external sense terminate mostly, if not wholly, in the cerebrum, those of internal in the cerebellum and spinal marrow. What or how much can be inferred from this I do not know. But the difficulty I feel *in limine* about phrenology is the insufficiency of the induction. I do not believe in anybody's judgments of the characters of individuals from anything the public ever know of their history. Besides, many of the skulls they argue from are not sufficiently authenticated as belonging to the persons to whom they ascribe them; e.g., the skull of Raphael—when his tomb was lately opened his real skull was found there.[7] I can easily imagine, however, that fine perceptions of sight may be connected with peculiarities of the optic nerve, probably continued into the adjacent parts of the brain, and so on. My opinion on the subject is not that of a competent judge, but I will read Combe without prejudice, and tell you my opinion of what he makes out.

Touching my outward man, which I wish much I could show you *in propriâ personâ*, if I can get any competent person to describe me to myself, I will give you the benefit. I do not know anybody that I am like, and am neither able to describe my own *physique* nor that of anybody else.

We print one thousand separate copies of an article of my father's on "Law Reform"[8]—the best popular paper ever written on the subject. We

4. Inexplicable as spelled here. If this is an error for *Marie*, JSM may be referring to the novel by Tocqueville's friend Gustave de Beaumont: *Marie, ou l'Esclavage aux Etats-Unis* (Paris, 1835). On the other hand, however, there is no reference to this work in the extant letters of Tocqueville to JSM. In his letter of 12 7bre 1835 (Mayer, pp. 295–97) Tocqueville proposed that he should write on the political and social condition of France before the Revolution, a proposal subsequently carried out (see Letters 142 and 169, n. 2). JSM included *Marie* in the books he reviewed in his "State of Society in America," *London Rev.*, II (Jan., 1836), 365–89.

5. No such article appeared.

6. George Combe (1788–1858), phrenologist. Which book of his on phrenology is referred to is uncertain.

7. See "Raphael's Remains," *Athenæum*, Nov. 16, 1833, p. 780.

8. The leading article in the *London Rev.*, Oct., 1835.

sell it for 6d. How many can you dispose of usefully by distribution? and do you think Mr. Tullis[9] can sell any?

I will write again soon.

Yours faithfully,

J. S. MILL.

145. TO AN UNIDENTIFIED CORRESPONDENT[1]

I.H.
13th October
1835

MY DEAR SIR

I have not had time before now, to fulfil my undertaking on the subject of the book I wrote to you about. Neither have I now time to write anything elaborate on the matter—but if a rather slight article would suit you, combining the trumpery book in question, with another called "Thoughts on the Ladies of the Aristocracy by Lydia Tomkins"[2] & made up, in considerable part, of extracts from the latter, I think I should now have time to undertake it.

Will you oblige me with a speedy answer & believe me

Ever yours truly

J. S. MILL

146. TO JOHN MURRAY[1]

India House
13th October, 1835

Mr. John Stuart Mill presents his compliments to Mr. Murray, & begs to inform him that he is authorized (through a common friend)[2] by the

9. Robert Tullis, publisher of the *Fife Herald,* and Nichol's father-in-law.

* * * *

1. MS in the possession of Professor Henry William Spiegel of the Catholic University of America, Washington, D.C. The person to whom JSM was writing may have been someone connected with the *Globe* newspaper, for which he wrote occasionally at this period. JSM apparently never wrote the proposed article.

2. This book evidently sought to capitalize on the popularity of Isaac Tomkins' (i.e., Henry Brougham's) *Thoughts upon the Aristocracy of England,* which reached at least eleven editions in the year of its publication, 1835. Lydia Tomkins' work appeared in at least three editions that year. Also published under the pseudonym of Isaac Tomkins in the same year was: *"We Can't Afford It!" Being Thoughts upon the Aristocracy of England. Part the second.* For a letter of James Mill to Brougham on Tomkins' works, see Bain, *James Mill,* pp. 380–81.

* * * *

1. MS in 1944 in possession of Sir John Murray, 50, Albemarle St., London, W.C.1.

John Murray (1778–1843), founder of the publishing business that bears his name.

2. Aristide Guilbert. See Letter 148.

well known French writer M. Fiévée, to propose to Mr. Murray the publication of a work[3] which he has prepared for the press containing the particulars of his conversations & confidential communications with Napoleon during a series of years.

M. Fiévée is doubtless well known to Mr. Murray, as not only one of the cleverest & most *spiritual* writers but one of the most experienced & most *practical* politicians in France. Although Napoleon knew him to be a decided royalist, & a correspondent of the exiled Bourbons, he made him not only a member of his *conseil d'état* (a body to which none but men of great & tried capacity were admitted) but also, as is well known, consulted him confidentially on many of the transactions of his reign. There is more to be learned of Napoleon's system of government from M. Fiévée's Correspondence politique et administrative[4] (published soon after the restoration) than from almost any other work; & the publication which he has now in contemplation must be still more valuable and interesting.

M. Fiévée's tone of thought & political opinions at the time when his Correspondence appeared, were very like those of Burke. He became more & more alienated from the royalists as they, having more & more chance of keeping in power, clung closer & closer to Napoleon's monstrous centralisation system of which M. Fiévée has always been a most decided and efficient enemy.

If Mr. Murray should be inclined to undertake the publication of the work, M. Fiévée will immediately send the manuscript, and place himself in direct communication with Mr. Murray.

147. TO THOMAS CARLYLE[1]

I.H.
17th October 1835

MY DEAR CARLYLE

If I had not promised to write to you I think I should hardly have written; for I have scarcely a simple fact to communicate, and as for sentiments and speculations one is not so desirous to communicate those by letter when one has and expects to have ample means of doing it by word of mouth. The only event in my history, of the slightest interest to you, which has occurred since you went away,[2] is the coming out of the 3[d]

3. See Letter 123, n. 2. 4. See *ibid.*, n. 4.

* * * *

1. *Addressed*: Thomas Carlyle Esq. / Scotsbrig / Ecclefechan / N.B. *Postmarks*: FREE / 17 OC 17 / 1835, and ES / 17 OC 17 / 1835. Franked by G. Grote. A MS copy is at NLS; the original of the latter half of the letter is at the Pierpont Morgan Library, New York. Carlyle's answer of Oct. 30, 1835, is in A. Carlyle, pp. 115–19.

2. On Sept. 21 Carlyle completed the rewriting of the burned manuscript of Vol. I of *The French Revolution*. Early in Oct. he went to Scotland to recuperate from the ordeal.

number of the London Review; whereby I have a little breathing time before I am obliged to busy myself about another. I cannot yet tell you either how the number is selling or how it is liked, but I expect a [. . .][3] that those who read it, who I fear will not be many, will like fully better than it deserves. I hope I shall soon write something for it myself, much better than anything I have written in this number.

Buller is now in town, on his way to the Exeter sessions, and is in capital health and spirits. I have no news to tell of anyone else—almost everybody is out of town, and of those who are here I have seen scarcely anything.

I suspect you must be nearly confined to indoor pleasures in Dumfriesshire now, for there can be little comfort in ranging the moors with such weather as we have had, of which you have probably had an enlarged edition. You have the good fortune at any rate to be free from newspapers: you have heard nothing about Don Carlo's [*sic*],[4] nor about O'Connell's dining with Lord Mulgrave,[5] nor the enormity of his calling the Duke of Cumberland a "mighty great liar,"[6] and you have remained a stranger to the infinite quantity of railroad projects which fill all that part of each day's newspaper which is not engrossed with the above topics. There has been nothing endurable but an article or two of Buller's in the Globe, and I fancy he will not write much more, in *that* newspaper at least.

Perhaps, by the bye, you did[7] not see, before you went away, the announcement that Bulwer is to publish a History of Athens[8]—what will this world come to! but I much wonder what it will be like.

Louis Philippe threatens to interdict even *English* papers which attack his government. I should much like to know what old Sieyes[9] thinks of the present state of France. That man's thoughts must be worth knowing. Austin's brother[10] who has been travelling in France says that all the people he conversed with at inns &c. though many of them disapproved

3. Two words illegible.

4. Don Carlos (1788–1855), after the death of his brother, King Ferdinand VII of Spain, provoked the first Carlist war (1833–39) by his efforts to gain the Spanish throne. Don Carlos had visited England in 1834.

5. On Oct. 7, 1835. Constantine Henry Phipps, second Earl of Mulgrave, later first Marquis of Normanby (1797–1863), had recently been appointed Lord Lieutenant of Ireland. His friendly meetings with Daniel O'Connell were being attacked at Protestant meetings and by *The Times* (see second editorial, p. 2, Oct. 10, 1835).

6. On Oct. 5 O'Connell, in an address to the Trades Political Union, said: "If they [the Orange faction] could, they would change the succession to the throne. They would do so, too, in favour of the white-whiskered Duke of Cumberland, because he is a bigot. Prince of the blood he is, to be sure, but, saving your presence, he is at the same time a mighty great liar" (reported in *The Times*, Oct. 10, 1835, p. 3).

7. The MS fragment at the Pierpont Morgan Library begins with this word.

8. *Athens: Its Rise and Fall* (London, 1837).

9. Comte Emmanuel Joseph Sieyès (1748–1836), journalist and statesman.

10. Charles Austin (1799–1874), lawyer.

of the conduct of the government, yet insisted on the necessity of standing by it, for fear of worse—he also says that the Gov^{t} people are trying to revive the anti-English feeling—& *that* one can see in their newspapers. They are adopting all Napoleon's maxims of internal policy—but one could see all this in Thiers' book.[11] What a curious page all this is in the history of the French revolution. France seems to be *désenchanté* for a long time to come—& as the natural consequence of political disenchantment—profoundly demoralized. All the educated youth are becoming mere venal commodities.

Grant[12] desires to be remembered to you. I have nothing else worth saying till we meet, which will be I suppose in a fortnight or so—.

Ever affectionately

J. S. MILL.

This letter would not be worth paying for so I have taken care to procure a frank.

148. TO ARISTIDE GUILBERT[1]

India House
19th October
1835

MY DEAR GUILBERT

I have delayed writing to you so long, hoping that I might be able to tell you by what means the Review will be sent to you—but unhappily I cannot yet tell you. As for Bennis,[2] I have tried him, & know that he cannot be relied on. A parcel which was delivered to him in Paris for me, did not reach London till three months after. However we will employ him if we find we can do nothing better.

I am well acquainted with M. Fiévée's writings & have a very high opinion of him. I have written to Mr Murray,[3] whom you know of course by name, proposing to him to publish M. Fiévée's work; & I expected to have had his answer before this; but it has not yet come.

11. Probably his *History of the French Revolution.*
12. Horace Grant.

* * * *

1. *Addressed*: Monsieur / M. Aristide Guilbert / 47 Rue de Joubert / à Paris. *Postmarks*: E / IH and 1835. MS at King's. Printed in Morrison, p. 255.
2. George G. Bennis (1790–1866), writer, and from 1830 to 1836 director of a *librairie des étrangers*, Paris.
3. Letter 146.

I send herewith, letters to M. de Cormenin, M. Garnier-Pagès,[4] & M. Nisard, as well as to another friend of mine, M. de Beaumont.[5] In the letters to the first three I tell them that you will give them copies as soon as they reach you: to M. Nisard the last number, & the present, to the others a complete set.

I will write to y[ou][6] again almost immediately.

Believe me
Yours faithfully
J. S. MILL.

149. TO JOSEPH BLANCO WHITE[1]

I.H.
21st October
1835

MY DEAR SIR

I have been thinking for some days past what subject I could propose to you for a literary article, but almost every thing lately published is so worthless that there is much difficulty in finding a *dignus vindice nodus.* I have been able to think of nothing better than the republication of Charles Lamb's *own* works. Is there not matter for some good & curious articles in *Spanish* literature? If you would give us specimens & criticisms of the principal Spanish authors, or articles on Spanish history, I think they would be interesting to the public and one is obliged to go abroad now for subjects for the literary critic.

Your article on Guizot is excellent as far as it goes but something seems still wanting to give a complete notion of the nature & value of Guizot's historical speculations. I will not ask you to take in hand again a subject of which I do not wonder that you should be tired, but if you would permit me, I should like much to add, mostly at the end of the article, a few more observations & specimens—especially that noble analysis of the feudal system in Lecture 4 of the first volume. The whole should then be submitted for your approval, either in MS. or in type.[2] If you consent to this do not trouble yourself to write only on purpose to say so as I shall consider silence as consent.

4. Probably Etienne Joseph Louis Garnier-Pagès (1801–1841), writer and politician, rather than his half-brother, Louis Antoine Garnier-Pagès (1803–1878), also a political figure.

5. Gustave de Beaumont.

6. Page torn by seal.

* * * *

1. MS in Liverpool University Library.

2. See Letter 154.

Your remarks in your last letter respecting the conduct of persons in the position of Bishop Coplestone[3] are profoundly true & admirably expressed.—I think you mention that you have not read the article which the Archbishop complained of—if you have time to read it, I should much like to know your opinion of it.

I hope you have duly received No. 3. If not, apply at once to Willmer for it, and make him send one to Mr Martineau likewise. You had better always apply to W. at once for books as we cannot depend on our publishers. They have too much to do.

Ever truly yours

J. S. MILL

150. TO ARISTIDE GUILBERT[1]

India House
30th October
1835

MY DEAR GUILBERT

I wrote to you a few days ago through M. Fillonneau,[2] sending at the same time letters to MM. de Cormenin, Garnier-Pagès, and Nisard. I had written a short letter to M. Nisard some time before.

I now write to say that 20 copies of No 3 & some copies of Nos 1 & 2 of the London Review have been sent to Galignani[3] in a packet addressed to you. I have made enquiry respecting the non-arrival of the copies of No 2, & I find that (while I was in Germany) they were sent, not to Baillière[4] but to Galignani, viz. 20 copies for sale, 8 addressed to you, a copy addressed to Carrel & another to M. Nisard. If you find any difficulty in getting the packets *with your name & address on them* from Galignani write to me directly. They *have* arrived at Paris or they *will* soon arrive. The parcel from Messrs Baldwin & Cradock booksellers, Paternoster Row.

When they reach you would it be too much to request the favour of you to give copies to those who ought to have them? in particular Carrel, Nisard, MM de Cormenin, Garnier-Pagès, Charles Comte, Odilon-Barrot, Alexis

3. Edward Copleston (1776–1849), Bishop of Llandaff.

* * * *

1. *Addressed*: Monsieur / M. Aristide Guilbert / Rue de Joubert / No 47 / à Paris. *Postmarks*: I NOV / 1835 / Angleterre / Par / Calais / and 297 / F / 35. MS at King's. Printed in Morrison, p. 255. Lacunae in the MS have been supplied from Morrison.
2. Unidentified.
3. Jean A. (1796–1873) and William G. Galignani (1798–1882), publishers.
4. J. B. M. Baillière (1797–1883), publisher.

de Tocqueville (Rue de Verneuil No 49) Gustave de Beaumont (rue du Bac, no 36 *bis*) Dussard (rue Richer No 22) & any other persons or periodical works whom you may select. I wish you would also give copies of all the three numbers to M. Gustave d'Eichthal, Rue Lepelletier No 14 & to M. Fiévée.

I mentioned in my letter that I had written to Mr Murray,[5] one of our leading booksellers, respecting M. Fiévée's work. I am much astonished at not having yet received an answer from him. If I do not speedily, I shall apply to another bookseller. The little essay which you sent by Madame Foulon,[6] is very good, it seems designed as an introduction to a set of Exercises: were the Exercises ever completed? If so, I think you should publish them here & I have little doubt of their success. For *separate* publication the essay would require some alterations, & would suit various other periodicals better than the London Review. But I could probably procure its insertion *somewhere*.

You said once that the proprietors of the "Histoire parlementaire de la révolution"[7] would be willing to send us that work if we would undertake to notice it. I already have it from the commencement to the close of the Constituent Assembly. If the proprietors would *promptly* send all the following volumes, & would continue to send the remainder, I will undertake that it shall be noticed, not only in the London Review but in other works. I say *promptly*, because if they do not send it I must buy it and then I shall not take any trouble to get it noticed.

Our third number is much more generally liked, I find, than our second.

Yours ever faithfully

J. S. MILL.

151. TO ARISTIDE GUILBERT[1]

India House
11th November
1835

MY DEAR GUILBERT

Mr Murray, the bookseller, is unluckily out of town, & the only answer I have been able to get from his son, is a recommendation to M. Fiévée to

5. Letter 146.
6. Unidentified. Morrison prints the name as *T*oulon.
7. See Letter 101, n. 12.

* * * *

1. *Addressed*: Monsieur / M. Aristide Guilbert / Rue de Joubert / No 47 / à Paris. *Postmarks*: Angleterre par Calais / 13 NOV / 1835 / and F 35 / 226. MS at King's. Printed in Morrison, p. 256.

send the manuscript for Mr Murray to see.[2] I think it would be advisable to send it, or at least part of it, as I am, myself, quite convinced that it will suit Mr Murray, but in case it should not, I could then apply *at once* to some other bookseller.

Have the copies of the London Review No 3, which were sent to you through Galignani, yet reached you? Pray enquire for them & let me know. I do not know exactly on what day Messrs Baldwin & Cradock sent them—but they were addressed to you, at your own residence, Rue de Joubert No 47.

M. Nisard has positively promised an article on Victor Hugo for the next number.[3] The letter he wrote to me on the subject amused me extremely—it quite corresponded with the character you gave him.

Our politics are in appearance sleeping—the ministry doing all they can to stop the discussion on the reform of the peerage—& they have succeeded, with respect to the daily newspapers—but not as to the weekly, or the country papers—& public opinion has in reality, fully decided the question, as you will see in a year or two.

Ever yours

J. S. MILL

152. TO ALEXIS DE TOCQUEVILLE[1]

19 novembre 1835.

Permettez-moi, mon cher M. de Tocqueville, de vous adresser les plus vives félicitations sur l'événement que M. de Beaumont m'a annoncé dans sa lettre du 8 de ce mois.[2] Puisse-t-il réaliser tous vos vœux et vous assurer le bonheur que vous méritez si bien et qui échappe si souvent à ceux qui, dans notre temps, et peut-être de tout temps, se sont occupés de faire quelque chose pour le bien de l'humanité.

Comme il se peut très bien, par la négligence des libraires, que vous n'ayez point encore reçu l'exemplaire qui vous était destiné du *London Review*, je vous en envoie un autre, accompagné d'un exemplaire de mon article sur la « Démocratie en Amérique »[3] que je soumets à votre bienveillante critique, en désirant vivement de votre amitié la communication

2. See Letter 146.
3. It appeared in the Jan., 1836, number (II, 389–417).

* * * *

1. Published in Mayer, pp. 301–2, as is also Tocqueville's answer of Dec. 3, pp. 302–4. MS in Tocqueville archives.
2. In Oct. he had married an English girl, Miss Mary Mottley.
3. "De Tocqueville on Democracy in America," *London Rev.*, II (Oct., 1835), 85–129.

de toutes les observations qui pourront naître dans votre esprit des doutes que j'ai exprimés sur une petite partie seulement de vos conclusions. Je suis loin d'avoir des idées fixes sur les questions dont il s'agit, et je suis avide de tous les renseignements qui pourraient m'aider à en former, et que personne autant que vous n'est dans le cas de me donner. Si je me trompe dans quelques-unes de mes observations, je le regrette d'autant moins que les lecteurs du *London Review* ne sont guère encore capables d'accueillir des opinions plus conformes aux vôtres que celles que j'ai exprimées, et je pourrai, avec le temps, rectifier mes erreurs.

Vous pensez bien que je ne veux pas, dans les circonstances présentes, vous importuner au sujet des articles que vous voulez bien destiner au *London Review*. Je vous dirai seulement que nous nous sommes décidés à ne faire paraître la 4e livraison que le 31 décembre, ce qui nous permettrait d'attendre plus longtemps un article dont il nous serait si avantageux d'enrichir cette livraison.

Croyez toujours, mon cher M. de Tocqueville, à ma haute estime et à mon amitié dévouée.

J. S. MILL.

India House.

153. TO HENRY S. CHAPMAN[1]

I.H.
Monday.
[Nov., 1835]

DEAR CHAPMAN,—

I send two articles which should be set up directly. One by J.R.[2] and another (the one on Guizot which I have, I think, with tolerable success) manufactured from a so-so article into a good one.[3] If they cannot print from the pencil I wish you would get somebody to put my alterations into ink.

Let me have proof as soon as possible of both these and of the "Aristocracy"[4] in which my father wishes to make some corrections.

I shall have an opportunity in a day or two for Mrs Austin, and I will send her one of my copies.

Yours ever,

J. S. MILL.

1. From copy in the possession of Professor J. M. McCrimmon, University of Illinois. Dated by reference to Guizot article in the next letter.

2. Probably John Robertson's article, "Lives of Bacon," *London Rev.*, II (Jan., 1836), 513–32. The article is signed "M.R.," a signature used by Robertson for other articles clearly identified as his.

3. See Letters 149 and 154.

4. [James Mill], "Aristocracy," *London Rev.*, II (Jan., 1836), 283–306, signed "P.Q."

154. TO JOSEPH BLANCO WHITE[1]

India House
24th November
1835

MY DEAR SIR

I have now the pleasure of sending you a proof of the article on Guizot,[2] in which I hope you will point out every, the smallest, thought or expression to which you in the slightest degree object, & will make any suggestions for the improvement of the article, which may occur to you. I think it will be very interesting & instructive & it is a kind of article which the review much wanted.

Perhaps the few remarks which I have inserted near the beginning of the article, respecting M. Guizot's political conduct, are not sufficiently in the tone & spirit of the rest of the article—if you think so, pray cancel them & substitute anything which you prefer—but it strikes me that something on that topic was wanted in that place.

I return, at the same time, a few pages of your MS. which I was obliged to omit in order to make room for what I added & to render the general character of the article less discursive.

Joanna Baillie[3] is just about to publish three more volumes of plays: would that not be a good opportunity for a review of her? She has never been properly reviewed. If you think so, I will undertake it, we will get them from the publisher & send them to you.

Ever yours truly

J. S. MILL

Let me hear from you soon respecting your health.

155. TO ARISTIDE GUILBERT[1]

India House
5th December
1835

MY DEAR GUILBERT

I think precisely as you do about M. Nisard's article.[2] We shall insert it, almost unaltered.

1. MS in Liverpool University Library. 2. See Letter 149.
3. Joanna Baillie (1762–1851), Scottish dramatist and poet, whose work JSM had admired since boyhood; he regarded her *Constantine Paleologus* as "one of the best dramas of the last two centuries" (*Autobiog.*, p. 11, n.). Her forthcoming publication was *Dramas* (3 vols., London, 1836). It was not reviewed in *LWR*.

* * * *

1. *Addressed*: Monsieur / M. Aristide Guilbert / Rue de Joubert / 47 / à Paris. MS at King's. Printed in Morrison, p. 256.
2. "Victor Hugo," *London Rev.*, II (Jan., 1836), 389–417.

We have also the promise (but do not mention this) of several articles on French society & civilization by M. de Tocqueville,[3] author of "La Démocratie en Amérique."

These articles & those of M. Nisard, are likely so much to increase the interest taken in the review in France, that we certainly ought to have a regular agency at Paris, & that of M. Paulin[4] is the one we should desire above all others. I do not however quite understand his conditions. Are the 600 francs you mention, 600 francs *per month*? If so, the expense is greater than we can afford; & we can hardly hope for advertisements enough to pay that expense when the *tax* on advertisements is deducted. And in regard to our "good offices for the books published by him" an English review which is more political & philosophical than literary, & does not notice, even English books unless they fall in its way while writing for some other purpose, could hardly, even with the best inclinations, *engage* to notice every book published by a particular house at Paris—neither could *we* undertake to notice any book *with praise* unless we thought the praise merited; but perhaps all that is meant is, to notice it in *the advertising sheet*—that we will readily do, though we shall have to pay taxes for all such notices as advertisements.

Let me hear from you again immediately on this subject.

I will get a written authority for your receiving the books from Galignani. I sent 20 copies of No 3. by M. Fillonneau.

I have not heard further from Mr Murray—I wait for M. Fiévée's *note descriptive*.

Ever yours truly

J. S. MILL

156. TO ARISTIDE GUILBERT[1]

India House
9th December
1835

MY DEAR GUILBERT

I suppose you have seen Falconer's brother & that he has told you all about Paulin. His name will appear as Agent on the cover of the forthcoming review, & I will thank you to conclude with him on the terms he proposes. It will be as well to have a written agreement merely as a memo-

3. Only one appeared that can be attributed to Tocqueville: "Political and Social Condition of France," *LWR*, XXV (April, 1836), 137–69, signed Δ.

4. J. B. A. Paulin (1796–1859), publisher.

* * * *

1. *Addressed*: Monsieur / Monsieur Aristide Guilbert / Rue de Joubert / 47 / à Paris. MS at King's. Printed in Morrison, p. 256.

randum for both parties. It will suit us best to pay the money four times a year, 250 francs on the publication of each number. Will you likewise request M. Paulin, as our agent, to expend a sum not exceeding 125 francs in advertising the present number. I will remit to you the money both for M. Paulin & for M. Nisard to any banker you may name, or we can remit it to M. Paulin that we may not give you trouble now when we have a paid Agent. Unless M. Paulin names some other banker—we will remit to M. Didier as before.

The fourth number is not yet out, owing to extreme misbehaviour on the part of our printer, which we shall not suffer to be repeated. Falconer has some arrangements in view at Dover & Calais by which we may ensure the rapid conveyance of our copies to Paris. We will send 30 copies to M. Paulin as soon as possible after the review appears. Should we send 30 copies only or 30 *for sale* in addition to, how many? for contributors, & exchanges.

M. Paulin is at liberty to sell them at any price (not lower than three francs) which he thinks most advisable, with a view as well to the reputation of the review as to its pecuniary profit.

Immediately on receiving M. Fiévée's paper, I forwarded a copy of it to Murray, from whom I have not yet received any answer. If one does not come soon, I will wit[hout] further delay, try an[other] bookseller.[2]

How goes on "le Progrès"?[3]

I suppose you hear sometimes of or from Mad. Foulon—I have done all I could for her, & I think Mrs Hume[4] or Mrs Grote will be of some use to her if she should not, as there is reason to hope, attain her object without them.

Ever truly yours

J. S. MILL.

157. TO ALEXIS DE TOCQUEVILLE[1]

11 Décembre, 1835.

MON CHER AMI,

Quand votre lettre est venue j'étais au lit et souffrent par une maladie dont je suis maintenant complètement rétabli. Votre lettre m'a causé la plus vive satisfaction. Rien ne pouvait m'être plus flatteur que l'appro-

2. Brackets indicate where page has been torn by seal.
3. Unidentified, but possibly the projected journal mentioned in Letter 157.
4. Wife of Joseph Hume, Radical MP.

* * * *

1. Published in Mayer, pp. 305–6, in reply to Tocqueville's of Dec. 3, *ibid.*, pp. 302–4. MS in Tocqueville archives.

bation que vous avez donnée à mon article.[2] Tout ce que j'ai dit, je l'ai senti, et j'aurais pu dire davantage sans dépasser l'admiration que je ressens pour votre ouvrage et pour son auteur. Quant à la discussion que j'ai ouverte avec vous sur plusieurs points, ne croyez pas que j'aie une conviction pleine et parfaite sur ces questions. Je les regarde certes comme très susceptibles d'une discussion ultérieure, et vous êtes, mon cher Tocqueville, un du très petit nombre de ceux avec une pareille discussion pourrait mener à quelque chose. J'en attends avec impatience l'occasion.

Je regarde avec vous la distinction entre *délégation* et *représentation* comme capitale. Ce n'est pas d'aujourd'hui que je tâche de la mettre en avant. Déjà en 1830 j'ai vivement soutenu dans l'*Examiner* la même opinion;[3] et en 1832, époque où l'on discutait beaucoup ici le mandat impératif, M. Fonblanque eut assez de patriotisme pour imprimer dans un journal deux longs articles de moi,[4] qui offensèrent beaucoup le public radical et lui fit perdre plusieurs de ses abonnés. Mon père, qui au reste est beaucoup plus démocrate que moi, partage très décidément la même opinion, seulement il pense avec une certitude que je suis loin de partager au même degré, que le peuple confondra rarement cette distinction.

Je n'ai senti aucun étonnement de ce que votre premier article ne nous soit pas encore parvenu. On ne peut pas faire vite, et faire aussi bien que vous faites; et ce sentiment consciencieux, qui vous empêche de faire les choses à demi, je l'éprouve moi-même; traiter un sujet moins bien que j'aurais pu le traiter, c'est une nécessité à laquelle je suis forcé quelquefois de me soumettre mais je la subis toujours avec une peine extrême. Si nous avions pu faire connaître publiquement votre nom, cela nous aurait été très utile, je crois même que cela aurait décidé le succès matériel de la revue, car vous êtes maintenant assez connu ici, et pas trop connu, pour que votre apparition dans une revue anglaise piquât vivement la curiosité publique par le double attrait du mérite reconnu et de la nouveauté. Cependant les raisons que vous me donnez sont trop fortes pour que je tâche de vaincre votre répugnance. Nous userons de votre permission en laissant percer votre nom. La prochaine livraison doit par des raisons d'affaires se publier le 31 de ce mois, par conséquent elle devra paraître sans votre

2. See Letter 152.

3. "Prospects of France," No. IV, *Examiner*, Oct. 10, 1830, pp. 642–44. "The true idea of a representative government is undoubtedly this, that the deputy is to legislate according to the best of his own judgment, and not according to the instructions of his constituents, or even to the opinion of the whole community" (*ibid.*, p. 642).

4. "Pledges," *Examiner*, July 1, 1832, pp. 417–18, and July 15, pp. 449–51. "The true idea of popular representation is not that the people govern in their own persons, but that they choose their governors. In a good government public questions are not referred to the suffrages of the people themselves, but to those of the most judicious person whom the people can find. The sovereignty of the people is essentially a delegated sovereignty." (*Ibid.*, p. 417.) See Letter 54, n. 12.

article à moins qu'il ne soit déjà fait. C'est une perte pour nous, mais nous sommes consolés un peu par la réflexion que notre marché avec le *Westminster Review* n'est pas terminé encore et le sera probablement avant la livraison d'Avril.[5] Votre article obtiendra par là dès le commencement une publicité plus étendue.

Rien ne me serait plus agréable que de faire un voyage à Paris et de vous y voir—Hélas! je suis lié pieds et mains pendant onze mois de l'année et il me faut attendre jusqu' à l'été prochain, alors je serai peut-être à Paris au moins plusieurs jours.

Tout à vous de cœur, mon cher ami, je vais signer ma lettre quoique vous n'ayez pas signé la votre.

J. S. MILL.

India House.

Mille amitiés à Beaumont. Je n'ai pas encore une réponse de M. Crawford.[6]

158. TO ARISTIDE GUILBERT[1]

India House
26th December
1835

MY DEAR GUILBERT

I was just writing to you when I received your note. I am most happy to hear of the journal you are about to establish[2] & of the excellent plan on which it is to be carried on. I am concerned that the popular party should now use *les intérêts matériels* as one of their main levers. "Il faut arriver à la république par les épiciers." You can with the more propriety announce yourself as a writer in our review, as your observations on *l'épicier* will appear in the present number as part of an article on that personage.[3]

5. See Letter 165, n. 2.

6. Probably William Sharman Crawford (1781–1861), Protestant liberal Irish politician, then MP for Dundalk; but possibly William Crawford (1788–1847), philanthropist, then inspector of prisons for the London and Midland districts, who shared with Beaumont and Tocqueville an interest in American prison practices. Beaumont was engaged at this time on a book on Ireland and may have sought information from W. S. Crawford.

* * * *

1. *Addressed*: Monsieur / M. Aristide Guilbert / Rue de Joubert / 47 / à Paris. *Postmarks*: F 35 / 243 and Angleterre / Par Calais / 28 DEC. MS at King's. Printed in Morrison, p. 257, but dated there Dec. 20, 1835.

2. Unidentified, but see Letter 156.

3. Guilbert's "observations" are presumably the section headed "Political Physiology of the Epicier," quoted (pp. 359–61) from a "French MS. communication," in Thomas Love Peacock's "The Epicier," *London Rev.*, II (Jan., 1836), 355–65.

I shall advise the proprietor of the review to accept M. Paulin's proposition. In the meantime write directly & tell me—considering the interest likely to be excited by M. Nisard's article—how many copies you would advise us to send—& what advertisements to insert in the Paris journals—& what you think would be the cost, & in what way the copies would get to Paris quickest & at what price you would advise that they should be sold.

Falconer would have sent the order upon Galignani, by his brother who has just gone to Paris, had he not set out in an unexpected hurry. Falconer told me some days ago that he would send it by letter to his brother at Paris, & I trust he has done so.

Was it 300 francs per sheet that you agreed were to be paid to M. Nisard? We will send the money either to him or to you, through any banker that you may prefer.

I have been waiting for M. Fiévée's paper—rather impatiently as our publishing season is approaching. There was no use in speaking again to Murray, or to any other bookseller, till the paper arrived. I am glad it is so soon coming.

Our forthcoming number will be far the best we have yet published, & will greatly eclipse all the other reviews. We have *three* articles on France: one on Guizot's Lectures, one on l'Epicier & the one on Victor Hugo.

I shall probably be able to send a positive answer to M. Paulin on Monday. In the meantime as we publish next Thursday *without fail*, pray write directly.

I shall write to M. Nisard on Monday—I have myself translated his article.

Ever truly yours my dear Guilbert

J. S. MILL.

· · · 1836 · · ·

159. TO [ADOLPHE NARCISSE?] THIBAUDEAU[1]

India House
Samedi
[1836?]

MON CHER THIBAUDEAU—

Ce serait une chose utile à la Revue de Londres si nous pouvions y insérer un bon et amusant article biographique et critique sur *Thiers.*[2] Ce n'est pas que ce petit fripon en vaille la peine, mais c'est que cela serait lu, chose très essentielle quand on écrit. C'est pourquoi je m'adresse à vous pour vous demander l'indication des renseignements nécessaires pour cela, et vos bons offices pour en obtenir. Ecrivez moi, je vous prie, un petit mot là-dessus, ou faites mieux, venez me voir, soit ici, soit à Kensington. J'irais vous chez vous si je le pouvais, mais il y a quinze jours que je le désire et que je ne le puis pas

tout à vous

J. S. MILL

160. TO SARAH AUSTIN[1]

India House
9th January
1836

I wrote to you, my dear Mütterlein, by Mr. Barry[2] but owing to his unexpectedly going away without seeing his brother to whom my letter was delivered he never received it, & it was brought back to me next day—so here goes to repair it.

Thanks for your kind note. I was only confined at home for a week, by a slight stomach attack, which as they tell me & I believe, has probably saved me from a much worse one—but I fancy I resumed my ordinary amount of bodily exercise too soon, & thereby retarded the recovery of

1. MS in the possession of Arthur Pforzheimer, Bookseller, 26 East 56th Street, New York City, in March, 1944.
2. No such article appeared.

* * * *

1. *Addressed*: Madame / Madame Austin / à Boulogne-sur-Mer. *Postmark*: Boulogne-sur-Mer / 10 / [. . . .] / 1836. MS at Yale.
2. Unidentified.

my strength, & I am still by no means completely reestablished.[3] My father has had no returns of unfavourable symptoms for many weeks now, but his recovery is very slow, & I do not expect that he will quite get rid of the cough before the warm weather. He does not feel the cold much, as while it lasts he does not stir out of a room which is kept of uniform temperature—& he does not suffer from the confinement nearly so much as I should have expected. He frequently enquires about you and Mr. Austin from every person whom he thinks likely to have heard from you.

I told Chadwick of the opportunity by Mr. Barry, & as I understand several parcels went to Boulogne with him I hope C. sent what you wanted. I did not send anything except my letter, literally because I knew nothing worth sending. The books & periodicals are even worse than they were before you went away. Even the Examiner has degenerated, & grown comparatively tame & dull. Fonblanque is using himself up by writing in the Chronicle,[4] the *euthanasia* of those who live at a greater expense than they can wisely afford—they kill themselves, or at least the best part of themselves, their minds, by demanding too much of them—"to this favour they must come" if they do no worse. The fourth number of the London Review, which is really a good number, would be better worth sending than anything else, but unluckily it was not, & is not even yet, out, thanks to the scurvy conduct of the printer. I will send it by the first opportunity I have, & if there is anything else in particular that you or Mr. Austin feel any curiosity about, tell me & I will be sure to send it.

What you say about my coming to see you is very kind of you my dear Mütterlein but I am not fit for travelling, nor yet unfit to be at the India House from which in my father's absence I could ill be spared.

I hope Von Raumer[5] is worth all the trouble you take about him—but heaven knows whether our stupid public will read or buy a book by a German *gelehrte* who is neither prince nor minister & whom they never heard of. My father suggested the other day that you should translate Thiers' history—it has never been translated, & would be sure to sell.

I grieve to hear that Mr. Austin is not well, though all I have heard of him since he was at Boulogne has been favourable as compared with his health anywhere else. What does he mean to do about the Examinership?[6]

3. This is the first indication in the extant letters of the onset of the serious illness that was to afflict him for much of the rest of the year and to leave him with permanently impaired health. In April his physician ordered him to Brighton to recuperate, and at the end of July the East India Company gave him a three months' leave of absence to seek health in travel on the Continent.

4. The *Morning Chronicle.*

5. Mrs. Austin's translation with H. E. Lloyd of Frederick L. G. von Raumer's *England in 1835* (3 vols.) was published in March, 1836.

6. Austin evidently declined the position, for later that year he accepted an appointment with Sir George Cornewall Lewis to investigate the government of Malta.

that is a sort of employment which probably would not knock him up, like writing—& the improvement in his circumstances with leisure & freedom from anxiety, might give him a better chance than he ever had before of being well in London.

I have nothing new to tell about Carlyle, Sterling, the Bullers, Grotes, &c.

My brother James has left Haileybury[7] with very great credit, & goes to India in about a month. The rest of the family are much as usual, except Jane, who is in indifferent health. Give my love to Lucy.[8] Farewell

Your Söhnchen

J. S. MILL

161. TO THOMAS FALCONER[1]

[Jan. 27, 1836]

DEAR FALCONER,—

A strange fatality attends our review. I do not believe there ever was any undertaking in which *every single* thing which ought to be done was so regularly left undone. We advertised the number as out when it was not out,[2] and to make amends (I suppose) I have not been able to find a single advertisement that made known the fact since it actually happened.[3] There was no advertisement in the "Examiner" on Monday,[4] nor in the "Chronicle" yesterday or to-day. It is true, as Peacock says, that "the London Review comes out surreptitiously." I also ascertained yesterday that at least two contributors, Bisset[5] and Garnier, had no copies sent to them. Bisset asked Chapman for one, and got it, and I shall give one to Garnier to-day, but for aught I know, not a single contributor has received a copy, except Peacock, who had one already. You have not answered my note enquiring whether Sterling and W. H. Smith[6] have had copies.

7. The East India College there.
8. Mrs. Austin's daughter, later Lady Lucy (or Lucie) Duff Gordon (1821–1869).

* * * *

1. From copy in the possession of Professor J. M. McCrimmon, University of Illinois. The dating is based on the remarks about the advertising of the *London Review* (see notes 2, 3, 4).
2. An advertisement in the *Examiner* for Dec. 27, 1835, p. 830, announced that the *Review* would be published on Dec. 31.
3. The *Examiner* for Jan. 17, 1836, p. 46, announced that the *Review* would be published on Jan. 18.
4. Really Sunday. The *Examiner* for Jan. 24 carried no advertisement of the *Review*, but the Jan. 31 number, p. 80, announced it as published.
5. Andrew Bisset (1803–?), barrister and historian.
6. William Henry Smith (1808–1872), philosopher and poet, writer for *Blackwood's Magazine*.

I wish you would get a copy of the Index of Vol. 2 for Peacock, as his copy being an early one, was destitute of that appendage.

Ever yours,

J. S. MILL.

We are the laughing stock of everybody who knows us, for our way of doing business.

162. TO HENRY S. CHAPMAN[1]

I.H.,
Tuesday.
[Feb. (?), 1836]

MY DEAR CHAPMAN,

I received your note only yesterday evening, at Kensington. I will endeavour to arrange matters with Falconer on the footing which you approve of. I quite agree with you as to what should be the limits of my own interference. The reading of proofs only devolved upon me because there were often alterations to be made after the article was already set up, and because time often pressed and it was desirable to make the alterations before sending the author his proof. We are now, however, so much in advance with our stock of articles that we need not hereafter be pressed for time as we have been hitherto.

As to any other interference on my part, it has been completely forced upon me against my will, and has been progressive with the necessity for it. When I began I counted upon Falconer's saving me the trouble either of *acting* or *thinking* as to business matters; and for a time I left him to himself. I presently found that nothing whatever was done by him unprompted. I therefore, to my great annoyance, had to suggest everything that occurred to me, but I now found that suggesting was not enough, for the suggestions though not objected to, were never acted upon. I supposed that this was for want of remembering them, and in this way I got the habit of reminding him continually, and asking him if the things were done or not. Finally, I found on asking, that in many cases they were not done even after numerous remindings, and thus has been brought about a relation between us so distasteful to me that I never will allow it to go on. At the same time I cannot sit calmly and see the thing go to the devil for want of doing a single thing that is necessary. Every person I know is continually complaining to me of the mismanagement; our utter incapacity is become a subject of general sarcasm and jokes, and at length our printers and publishers have such a contempt for us as men of business that they will not attend to a single one of our orders. If this is the case when I am

1. From a copy in the possession of Professor J. M. McCrimmon.

continually dunning Falconer, what would it be if I intrenched myself in my own department and let the thing go to ruin, saying it was his concern not mine? If Falconer had not been a friend, and of my own choice, and a person I like much and think very highly of, I should have spoken to Molesworth and said "find me another editor, or I give it up." The contrary being the case, I spoke to Falconer himself, and resolved to take upon myself the trouble he ought to have saved me, and if *even that* had produced any tolerable management I would have let the thing go on. But as even *that* will not, it must be changed.

Senior has some copies of his article,[2] but his publishers made such objections to the circulation of them here, that he has scarcely been able to give any away except to foreigners. He gave me one because I wanted to review it; if you like I will lend it to you.

I am still far from well—indeed rather worse than better, and I fear I shall be unable to write anything for No. 5,[3] and shall have to go into the country and give up for a time all work. I am the more anxious to have the editorship placed on a satisfactory footing that I may not feel anxious while I am away about the mode of its going on.

Will you oblige me by sending the enclosed to Liverpool.

Ever truly yours
J. S. MILL

163. TO HENRY S. CHAPMAN[1]

I.H.
Friday
[Feb., 1836]

DEAR CHAPMAN,

I have just written to Falconer to propose your being Sub-editor.[2] In the way I have put it, it cannot possibly hurt his feelings. In case he should not object what salary (disinterestedness apart, for Molesworth is anxious to give you the full value of your time and labour) should you consider adequate?

2. Nassau Senior, *An Outline of the Science of Political Economy*. This was first published as the article on political economy in the *Encyclopædia Metropolitana*, 1836, and a few copies were struck off for private circulation (see Marian Bowley, *Nassau Senior and Classical Economics* [London, 1937], p. 340). JSM seems not to have carried out his intention of reviewing Senior.

3. He did contribute, however, two articles to this number (April, 1836) of the *LWR*: "Civilization," pp. 1–28, and "The State of Politics in 1836," pp. 271–78.

* * * *

1. From copy in the possession of Professor J. M. McCrimmon.

2. The original bears a note by H. S. Chapman: "Memo: No communication ever received from Falconer."

So Pam.[3] is at an end,—it serves us with its dying breath. Is there to be a Sunday paper or not?[4]

Ever faithfully yours,

J. S. MILL.

We shall get the Westminster, Molesworth says—he has brought them almost to terms by giving them money in hand.[5]

164. TO SARAH AUSTIN[1]

I.H.
17th February
1836

MY DEAR MUTTERLEIN

Your letter is kind as you always are—& you know how great a pleasure it always is to me to be with you & Mr Austin. I am however so decidedly better within the last few days that I can perhaps do without going into the country at all, & certainly a few days in the country would quite reestablish me—against going so far there are therefore two reasons—the great inconvenience that even a week's absence is to my father while absent from the India House—& that the fatigue of the journey would do me more harm at present than a *very short* stay would do me good—the great thing I have to do is to avoid fatigue—there is nothing the matter with me but want of *tone* and strength. I certainly shall not allow myself to get into bad health, & I should [have][2] gone out of town before this if it had not been for the inconvenience to my father—& you may be sure he would not have allowed me to make that a reason, if I had been seriously ill.

Pray write again & give me more news of yourself & of Mr Austin. I seldom hear about you except in the most general terms.

3. Roebuck's series, *Pamphlets for the People*, ended with the number for Feb. 11, 1836. See Letter 140, n. 8.

4. Molesworth, Roebuck, and J. T. Leader were projecting a new radical paper on which Chapman was to be engaged. Professor McCrimmon possesses a copy of an unpublished letter from Molesworth to Chapman, dated March 3 [1836], which begins: "Roebuck has I presume informed you that we shall establish a paper—success to us—. Leader expects you on Saturday at two o'clock when all will be arranged." The plan apparently did not materialize at this time, but Molesworth, Leader, and others established a weekly newspaper *The Guide* in 1837 (see Letter 415, n. 2).

5. The merger of the *London Review* and the *Westminster Review* became effective with the April, 1836, number. See Letter 165, n. 2.

* * * *

1. *Addressed*: Madame / Madame Austin / à Boulogne sur Mer. *Postmarks*: ANGLETERRE / PAR / CALAIS; BOULOGNE-SUR-MER / 19 / F36 / 184; UR MER / 1836 / (61); BOULOGNE. MS at King's.

2. Page torn.

My father gets on very slowly—but he does get on. There is no news—as to public matters, the ministry are more popular & the radicals in better humour than at any time since the Reform Bill.

Your Söhnchen

J.S.M.

165. TO ALBANY FONBLANQUE[1]

I.H.
Friday
[Feb., 1836]

MY DEAR FONBLANQUE

Molesworth has just bought the Westminster Review to merge it in the London.[2] As the sole radical review we shall surely now have a good chance of success; but we have more need than ever of good articles, that the first number after the junction may be a striking one. You have now rather more leisure, I suppose, than you had during the last year—it would be of the very greatest importance to us if you would write something for the next number. Had you been able to write for us from the commencement it might have made a great difference to us. There are very few of the good radical writers who have not written for us—but you who for popular purposes are universally allowed to be the best, have not. I wish you would.

Yours ever faithfully

J. S. MILL

P.S. Was the article on the "Fudges in England" in the last West[r3] by Mr. Savage?[4] If so, I wish you would tell him that my father was greatly struck with it.

So they blackballed [Fellowes?] by 47 & [Hill?] by 67.[5] The radicals should blackball all Tories till they put down the conspiracy. I shall go there on purpose whenever I can & shall proclaim my intention.

1. Part published in *Life and Labours of Albany Fonblanque*, ed. E. B. de Fonblanque (London, 1874), pp. 39–40. MS at LSE. Bears pencil mark, 1834, but internal evidence establishes early 1836 as the proper date.

2. Molesworth paid the proprietor of the *Westminster* £1,000. The *Examiner* on March 20, 1836, p. 192, carried an advertisement announcing the merger. The first issue of the *London and Westminster Review* was that for April, 1836.

3. A review of *The Fudges in England* (London, 1835) by Thomas Brown *the Younger* (i.e., Tom Moore, the poet), *WR*, XXIV (Jan., 1836), 79–92.

4. Probably Marmion W. Savage (1803–1872), Irish journalist and novelist, editor of the *Examiner*, 1856–59.

5. The reference is to an election of members to the Athenæum, to which both JSM and James Mill, as well as Fonblanque, belonged (see T. Humphry Ward, *History of the Athenæum, 1824–1925* [London, 1926], pp. 41–42). The names are barely legible, but the conclusion seems warranted that the blackballed candidates were Robert Fellowes (1771–1847), philanthropist and liberal, and Matthew Davenport Hill, QC (1792–1872), reformer of criminal law.

166. TO WILLIAM JOHNSON FOX[1]

I.H.
Tuesday
[Feb. 23, 1836]

You know that Molesworth has bought the Westminster & that it is united with the London? That gives us a better chance of success—I should hope a very good one—but which depends entirely on our being able to make the combined review a striking one. I know that you do not like the London Review & I do not know how it is possible you should—still I hope you do not dislike it so much as to be unwilling to write in it—do not suppose that any article of yours would have the fate of Horne's.[2] There is nothing to induce one to put in his articles unless one completely agrees with them, but such articles as many of yours would be desirable for the review even if one differed from every word of them. I should differ from them occasionally, but not nearly so much as I differ in a contrary way from many which I am obliged to put in now—& I am the more desirous to throw something into the other scale.

You know I suppose that you are put upon the list of the Reform Club[3] as an original member.

How striking some of your Lectures must have been to hear. I admire them exceedingly. It is a pity the first two,[4] from the comparative triteness of the subject have less in them than the rest

[J?]S.M.

will you[5] give him this? & *will* you try to persuade him to do as it asks him *to*?

she[6] is well—that is as well as she ever is—I am still out of health—

J.S.M.

1. *But addressed*: Miss Flower / 5 Craven Hill / Bayswater. (Note postscript.) Eliza Flower lived in Fox's home. *Postmarks*: T. / Leadenhall, and 2 AM 2 / FE 23 / 1836. Published in Garnett, p. 183, except for postscript. MS at King's.

2. Richard Henry, or Hengist, Horne (1803–1884), miscellaneous writer and poet, took over the editorship of the *Monthly Repository* from Fox in July, 1836, and conducted it until July, 1837, when Leigh Hunt became editor.

3. Established in 1836 under the leadership of such reformers as Edward Ellice and Sir William Molesworth.

4. Fox's *Finsbury Lectures* were published separately from time to time between 1835 and 1840. The first two were: No. 1. "The Morality of Poverty"; No. 2. "Aristocratical and Political Morality." The *Examiner* for Jan. 3, 1836, p. 16, announces the sixth, "On the Morality of the Press," and lists the previous five.

5. Eliza Flower.

6. Mrs. Taylor.

167. TO ALBANY FONBLANQUE[1]

I.H.
Friday
[Feb. 27, 1836]

MY DEAR FONBLANQUE

I would have answered for Carlyle with the most perfect assurance on the points you mention, but as I anticipated, it does not suit him. He recommends Craik,[2] late of the Printing Machine[3]—of whom he says "he is a man limited, but honest, & singularly *healthy* & even robust, within his limits. He cannot be brilliant, but he can be decided, clear, & even emphatic. I should think him a believer with his whole heart in such policy as this present Russel-Melbourne & open to all manner of further light. The man is good tempered, courageous; can take a handsome lift of anything. If I mistake not, such an offer would be excellent news to him at present: I have not heard of him for months; which means, I fear, that he is in straits & uncertainty."

I am delighted to hear of the Selection from the Examiner[4]—many of your papers in it are too good to be let die. The selection will live as long as any such collection in our language. I am glad too for another reason—that we will have a swinging review of it in the "London & Westminster."

Pray let me know when the question you allude to is decided & in the meantime is there anything Mr. Savage[5] would write? He once offered to write for us & would have been asked to write on Orangeism then, if Molesworth had not wanted to do it himself.

I have given your message to my father & it was received as you would wish—but I think there was more need for him to send such a one to you—because you have seemed once or twice to think that when he attacked an opinion of yours, e.g. on the Pension List—he felt or thought with less estimation of you than I know he does. Now the fact I believe is that on that point of the P. List & on some others he had actually forgotten that you were of the opposite opinion—& being accustomed to find you on

1. MS at LSE. Dated by the passage quoted in first paragraph from Carlyle's letter, dated Thursday [Feb. 26, 1836], in A. Carlyle, pp. 120–21.

2. For what Carlyle in his letter calls "the Lichfield Editorship." George L. Craik (1798–1866), journalist and literary historian.

3. *The Printing Machine; or Companion to the Library and Register of Progressive Knowledge* (3 vols., London, 1834–35) had merged with *Leigh Hunt's London Journal* (2 vols., 1834–35) in 1835, but the combined *Leigh Hunt's London Journal and the Printing Machine* survived only until Dec., 1835.

4. Published by Fonblanque with the title *England under Seven Administrations* (3 vols., London, 1837). JSM reviewed it, *LWR*, XXVII (April, 1837), 65–98.

5. See Letter 165, n. 4.

what he thought the right side, he instinctively concluded you were so on these points. About the Pension list if he had anybody in view it was Grote, with whom he had previously had some personal discussion about it.

Ever yours

J. S. MILL

If you are at the Athenæum on Monday I wish you would vote for John Sterling[6]—& get anybody else you can to do so.

168. TO LORD WELLESLEY[1]

India House
31st March
1836

Mr John S. Mill is instructed by his Father, who has been for several months confined at home by illness, to express to Lord Wellesley his sense of the honour which his Lordship has conferred upon him by presenting him with a copy of his Dispatches,[2] and to say that he will do himself the honour of writing as soon as his health permits, to make his personal acknowledgments to Lord Wellesley.

169. TO ALEXIS DE TOCQUEVILLE[1]

2 avril 1836.

MON CHER TOCQUEVILLE,

Le *London and Westminster Review* N° 5 L 48 vient de paraître. Votre article[2] en est le principal ornement. J'ai moi-même surveillé la traduction que nous en avons fait faire, et j'espère que nous avons pu rendre vos idées avec fidélité et que nous n'avons pas absolument gâté le reste: nous avons au moins soigneusement suivi la clarté et la simplicité de votre style, que je regarde comme bien près de la perfection du style philosophique. Nous avons fait imprimer séparément quelques exemplaires de l'article, et

6. According to the secretary of the Athenæum, the name of Sterling was entered as a candidate for membership, but his name was subsequently withdrawn and not brought forward for election.

* * * *

1. MS in Brit. Mus.
Richard Colley Wellesley, Marquis Wellesley (1760–1842), Governor General of India, 1797–1805.

2. *The Dispatches, Minutes and Correspondence of the Marquess Wellesley During his Administration in India*, ed. M. Martin (5 vols., London, 1836–37).

* * * *

1. Published in Mayer, pp. 307–8. MS in Tocqueville archives.

2. "Political and Social Condition of France," *LWR*, XXV (April, 1836), 137–69. Reprinted in Mayer, II, 1.

nous nous permettons de vous en faire l'hommage; ils vous parviendront en même temps que la Revue elle-même, du moins je l'espère.

Nous sommes aussi vos débiteurs d'une somme de 600 francs que vous toucherez chez M. Delamarre, banquier. Ce n'est pas sans honte que je vous parle d'argent et surtout d'une si faible somme lorsqu'il s'agit d'un travail comme celui dont vous avez enrichi notre recueil.

Pourrons-nous espérer que la prochaine livraison offrira à notre public la suite de ce travail?[3]

Vous verrez que nous n'avons pas donné à l'article (comme nous avions pensé à le faire) la forme d'une lettre, puisqu'il n'y avait ni dans le style, ni dans le fond rien qui exigeât un changement dans la forme ordinaire de nos articles de la Revue.

J'apprends de M. Gustave de Beaumont qu'il s'occupe d'un ouvrage sur l'Irlande;[4] cette nouvelle m'a fait un plaisir extrême. Il me demande des renseignements; je me suis adressé à M. Cornewall Lewis pour en avoir, et j'ai appris qu'il avait déjà envoyé à M. de Beaumont tout ce qu'il jugeait utile, et notamment le livre qu'il vient de livrer au public et qui me paraît fort intéressant. Au reste j'écrirai très incessamment à M. de Beaumont.

C'est ici seulement un petit bout de lettre fait à la hâte; je vous en promets un meilleur en quelques jours.

Votre dévoué

J. S. MILL.

India House.

170. TO JOSEPH BLANCO WHITE[1]

India House
9th April
1836

MY DEAR SIR

I quite agree with you as to the desirableness of striking more directly than we have hitherto done against the prevailing tendencies of English religion.[2] Mr Martineau has at my request written an article on your two

3. The hope was unfulfilled. Tocqueville contributed no more to the *Review*; for the next four years he was too much occupied with the concluding volumes of his work on democracy.

4. Eventually published as *L'Irlande sociale, politique et religieuse* (2 vols., Paris, 1839).

* * * *

1. *Addressed*: Revd Blanco White, Upper Stanhope Street, Liverpool. Franked by Wm. Molesworth. *Postmark*: 9AP9 / 1836. MS in Liverpool University Library. In reply to White's letter of April 4, 1836, in Thom, II, 208–9.

2. White had written (Thom, II, 208): "It appears to me, that our Review avoids too much a direct collision with the mischievous system of religion, which the State supports. You—the leaders—are too much away from the mass of bigotry and superstition existing in the country, and, as it were, disdain the subject. . . . The Theologians should be routed: the evil they are doing is immense."

books, the "Second Travels" & the "Heresy & Orthodoxy" which breaks ground on the subject very well.[3] It could have been ready for the 4th number, but we were obliged to omit it even from the 5th, to make room for political or literary matter of a temporary kind. It will certainly be in the next, & I will suggest to him to append something on the Hampden controversy.[4] But I have long looked forward to having the same subject treated by yourself, whom from your published writings I cannot but regard as the best writer by far whom the country at present has on such topics. I hope you will think of it. We can, you see, afford you ample time, & you can yourself chuse the mode & the opportunity. It is only necessary to avoid directly expressing any opinion on points of faith or rather of dogma; that the review in attacking sectarianism may not get the character with the stupid part of the public, of being itself connected with any sect.

With regard to an article for our next number I have had some scruples about proposing anything to you so long as the article on Lamb remained *pending*. I never had more difficulty in making up my mind about any article than I have about that. It is an article which on many accounts it would be a great loss to the review not to insert—besides which it would be a thousand pities that all the trouble you have had about it should be lost. On the other hand I foresee that it will do us very serious injury with a large class of those who take most interest in literature & who as being friendly to the cause of *movement* are friendly to us—& will raise a storm about us which however ready to encounter when required by duty, I do not so much like to face on a matter on which even after all the modifications & explanations you have so good-naturedly given, I still find that my own views differ fundamentally from yours. I take it that in our estimation of the class of writers called *humourists* you & I should hardly ever agree[5]—

3. See Letter 135, n. 5.

4. Both Evangelicals and Tractarians joined in protesting Lord Melbourne's appointment in 1836 of Renn Dickson Hampden (1793–1868) as Regius Professor of Divinity at Oxford, because of the unorthodox views he had expressed in his Bampton Lectures of 1832. See R. W. Church, *The Oxford Movement, 1833–1845* (London, 1891), chap. IX.

5. JSM had apparently raised earlier questions of White's treatment of Charles Lamb's humour in an article proposed for the *Review*. On Feb. 7, 1836, White wrote (Thom, II, 183): "I certainly thought that the observations from which my disapprobation of Lamb's style of humour proceeds, were more generally received than your remarks imply. I ought, however, to have remembered that there is a set of very able men, writing constantly as critics, whose principal fund of humour arises from the *roystering*, (I use their own descriptive word,) carousing, eating, and drinking spirits, which they take a pleasure to bring out before the public. . . . Their humourous writing is a kind of *Row*. It is unquestionable that much of the *talk* which you find, especially in Blackwood, would be impertinent and coarse in refined company; how then can it be tolerable when addressed to the *public*? I cannot bear Fielding in many parts of his works, though I greatly admire his talent."

Though White promised to rewrite the article, he did not succeed in satisfying JSM and it was not published.

& that you dislike everything which has not a serious & truthful object. Do you not (I should think you did) prefer Schiller to Goethe? & do you like Falstaff & Poins—I should think not. I am obliged in these embarrassments to take a little more time for consideration.

As for any other subject, I can at present think of none but Joanna Baillie. What is your general notion of her merits? I ask this because you see we have broken ground at last on the subject of the greater poets of our age,[6] & it is therefore more necessary than heretofore that we should maintain in our future judgments, a consistency with what we have said in the literary articles of this number.

I believe Schmidt-Phiseldek is a very good view of Kant.[7]

I sympathize in your annoyance about your house.[8] How the vices of English law shew themselves in every relation of civil life.

I am slowly getting rid of my ailment. To accelerate the cure I am going for a short time to Brighton—probably on [Thurs]day.

What would you think of a historical subject? That is the kind of articles we now most want—for the first time we are at length able, though by no means desirous, to give you a holiday in pure literature. But there is a noble field open in European history which hardly any of our writers are able to tread.

I am delighted that you approve of my "Civilization."[9]

Ever yours

J. S. MILL

171. TO HENRY MILL[1]

[Brighton, April, 1836]

There seems to be a change considerably for the better in my bodily state within the last three days; whether it will last, I cannot yet tell; nor do I know whether the place has contributed towards it, as the more genial weather of yesterday and to-day is probably the chief cause. [He then says

6. In an article, "The Poets of our Age, Considered as to their Philosophic Tendencies," signed D., in the April number of *LWR*, pp. 60–71.

7. Conrad Friedrich von Schmidt-Phiseldek, *Philosophiæ criticæ secundum Kantium expositio systematica* (2 vols., Hafniae, Altonae, 1796–98).

8. White had written (Thom, II, 209): "I have had to learn experimentally the abominable state of the law in regard to landlord and tenant. . . . But I opened my eyes to the danger after I had put myself into the power of the landlord."

9. The leading article in the April, 1836, number of his *Review*, pp. 1–28.

* * * *

1. Excerpt published in Bain, *JSM*, p. 43. MS not located. The portion in brackets is Bain's summary. JSM had been sent to Brighton to recuperate from a severe illness (see Letter 160, n. 3).

Henry Mill (1820–1840), JSM's favourite younger brother.

that he will continue his stay if the improvement goes on, but is reluctant to be long absent, partly on account of his father's illness and partly on account of his tutoring "Mary and George". He trusts to Henry to keep him informed on the state of matters, and if he can be of any use to his father, he will forego the present advantages and trust to getting well as the summer advances.]

172. TO ALEXIS DE TOCQUEVILLE[1]

[Brighton]
27th April 1836.

MY DEAR TOCQUEVILLE,

You must be surprised that I did not immediately answer your letter— & so I would, if it had not found me ill & in bed—I have been in indifferent health all the winter & have lately had a short attack of rather a sharper kind. I now write to you from Brighton where I have come to try to get well—& I am just now too tired to write in French, but for that I need not apologize to you, though I ought for the shortness of this note.—As for the delay of your second article in the Review—I am less sorry for that than I am glad of the cause—I anticipate from the continuation of "La Démocratie" a more than ordinary share of the pleasure & instruction your writings always give me—I have more to learn of the influence of Democracy on private life & individual character than of its influence on political interests & you have taught me so much on the last that I hope you will teach me still more on the first.

Your article in the review though generally considered a little *abstract* (as the people here say of anything which is consecutive & methodical) has on the whole been very successful here; all who have read it admire it, & its successors are likely to have a still more numerous class of readers as they will relate to circumstances of more immediate & contemporaneous interest. Though we should have liked much to have had the second in our next number, we can very well wait for it till the number after, & should accept it most thankfully however long it might be delayed. The only thing that embarrasses us is—we want to review Bulwer's France[2] & cannot do it because we cannot interfere with a subject which we wish to have entirely in your hands. Could you—I will not ask you to suspend your labours even for a day—but could you persuade Beaumont or any other judicious friend, to send us a few cursory remarks on Bulwer's book which

1. Published in Mayer, pp. 310–11, in reply to Tocqueville's of April 10, *ibid.*, pp. 308–9. MS in Tocqueville archives.

2. See Letter 113, n. 2. The request for help from Beaumont proved unavailing, but eventually Tocqueville sent notes on Bulwer's book, which are printed in Mayer, pp. 318–24. No review of the book appeared in the *Westminster*, however.

we might work up into an article of our own—of course not entering philosophically into the subject, as that will be so much better done by you—we only wish to do justice to what is useful & meritorious in the book, & to correct any gross errors. Do not however give yourself any trouble or gêne about this, but I am sure your friendship will not feel itself taxed by my asking your advice how we may best treat Bulwer's book.

A letter which must have reached you immediately after writing your last will have explained to you about the 600 francs which were as much a debt as anything could be, though we were almost ashamed to offer you so mere a trifle—I will write again soon—I always say so, but this time you shall find me as good as my word.

Yours faithfully

J. S. MILL.

173. TO HENRY MILL[1]

[Brighton (May?), 1836]

[John was at Brighton for his own health during his father's last illness; but wrote assiduously to Henry, to know whether his hurrying back would be of any use.] As to my father, tell me as fully as you can how he is, both as to his illness itself, and as to spirits, and what you think would be pleasantest to him; not what he would wish or say out of kindness to me.

174. TO ALEXIS DE TOCQUEVILLE[1]

India House
15th June 1836.

MY DEAR TOCQUEVILLE,

Many thanks for your very kind note. I would not on any consideration be the cause of your interrupting for ever so short a time, meditations so important to the world as those must be which are to give rise to the second part of *La Démocratie en Amérique*. We have ample time before us, as it is already too late for the July number of the review, & perhaps Beaumont will be able to finish his article in time for the 30th of September. Will you oblige me by offering to him my best thanks for his kindness in having undertaken & commenced an article of so much importance to us & my warmest congratulations & wishes for his happiness.[2]

1. Excerpt published in Bain, *James Mill*, p. 409. MS not located. Bracketed portion is Bain's introduction to the excerpt.

* * * *

1. Published in Mayer, pp. 312–13, in reply to Tocqueville's of June 5, *ibid.*, pp. 311–12. MS in Tocqueville archives.
2. Beaumont was to marry Clémentine de Lafayette, grand-daughter of the General, on June 29.

There is not much happiness in our home at present. My father is sinking to his grave under a lingering pulmonary complaint—I fear there is no chance of his recovery. My own complaint does not cause me any uneasiness, it is slight, & not painful, & there is nothing serious in it but its obstinacy. It has hitherto resisted all remedies—if I should be obliged to travel, which I think not unlikely I must I fear go further off than Paris or any part of the north of France—not so much for climate as for a complete change of scene—.

I will write soon again at greater length.

Yours ever faithfully,

J. S. Mill.

175. TO SARAH AUSTIN[1]

Friday
[June 25, 1836]

There is nothing, that I am aware of, my dear Mütterlein, that requires the help you so kindly offer—we have been so long expecting this that most of the necessary arrangements were made, or ready to be made, at once. But you may be sure that if we do need anything which you can do for us there is no one we would more confidently apply to.

I am grieved that Mr. Austin is again ill—I thought him so well yesterday. He will receive an invitation to the funeral, but of course he will not come if he is ill or if it is inconvenient.

Your proposal about Derry[2] is very kind but quite impracticable—some time hence such a thing might be beneficial to him—but now I am sure he would dislike to leave us & his younger brothers & sisters would be made quite unhappy by his absence—he is their great friend, companion and teacher. We mean to send them all to Mickleham directly—where all, especially Derry, are anxious to go. If I should be obliged to travel for a longer time than a month or two I shall take the two boys with me for the whole or part of the time.[3]

Ever affectionately yours

J. S. Mill

1. MS in collection of autographs formed by Mrs. Richard Ford, sister of Sir William Molesworth. Collection in 1945 in possession of Sir John Molesworth-St. Aubyn, Pencarrow, Washaway, Bodmin, Cornwall. The letter is on black-edged notepaper, undated, but was apparently written very shortly after the death of James Mill on Wednesday, June 23, 1836.

2. The family's name for Henry Mill.

3. Ordered away for three months by his physician, JSM at the end of July took his two younger brothers Henry and George to the Continent.

176. TO THOMAS CARLYLE[1]

I.H.
Wednesday
[July 20(?), 1836]

MY DEAR CARLYLE My annotations, & proposed alterations in phraseology, amount as you will see, to but little; less than I expected—& you will probably think most of them trifling. My object has been to remove, when it can be done without sacrifice, anything *merely* quaint in the mode of expression—but I have very often not ventured to touch it for fear of spoiling something which I could not replace. The only general remark I have to make on the stile is that I think it would often *tell* better on the reader if what is said in an abrupt, exclamatory, & interjectional manner were said in the ordinary grammatical mode of nominative & verb—but on that as on everything else I ask nothing but that you will deal with it as you like, disregarding all my observations if you do not think them just—& in any case that you will not make the thing an annoyance to you. It is quite good enough & too good for us as it is. Ever faithfully yours

J. S. MILL

177. TO CLARA MILL[1]

Paris
3 August 1836

One having written to W[illie] & one to H[arriet] I must write to Clara —so here goes—We are all quite as well, perhaps rather better than was to be expected. George & Henry do not seem at all struck with Paris—they are I think too young to care much about it or to be impressed by it at all.

1. MS at NLS. Published in Elliot, I, 100, but dated as probably of 1835 and annotated as referring to the MS of the *French Revolution.* Carlyle's letter of Friday, July 22, 1836 (in A. Carlyle, pp. 133–35), however, is clearly an answer to this. The MS discussed is that of Carlyle's article on Mirabeau, which appeared in *LWR*, XXVI (Jan., 1837), 382–439. For Carlyle's scornful reception of the corrections, see *Thomas Carlyle: Letters to His Wife*, ed. Trudy Bliss (London, 1953), pp. 112–13.

* * * *

1. MS at LSE. *Addressed*: Mrs. Mill / Kensington / London / *Angleterre* /, but latter three lines have been crossed out and Mickleham / Surrey substituted. *Postmarks*: BIRFA . . . / 4 / A . . . / 183 . . .; LONDON / 6 / AUG / 1836; and 10FN10 / AUG / 1836. Published, with minor variations, in Hayek, pp. 101–2.

Accompanied by his younger brothers Henry and George, JSM had left England on July 30 to seek recovery of his health on the Continent. They met Mrs. Taylor and her children in Paris, evidently by prearrangement. To the letters which George and Henry wrote their sisters Wilhelmina and Harriet, JSM added this note to Clara.

Subsequently, leaving the children in Switzerland in the care of a nurse, JSM and Mrs. Taylor proceeded to the north of Italy, where they spent two months. At the end of Oct. they rejoined the children in Lausanne and returned to England (Nov. 12) by way of Paris (see next letter).

They seemed pleased with the country, & on the whole their excursion has been hitherto tolerably successful. But the only piece of thorough solid delight that George seemed to have was in meeting with a playfellow[2] about his own age whom he likes & who likes him very much. Nothing is settled yet about our travelling further—it is not finally settled whether we shall go alone or with our friends here, much less *when* we shall go & how—the places are all taken by the diligence for nearly a week to come, & posting so far is very expensive—but we shall see. One thing seems certain—that both Derry & I can stand travelling. We have not tried any night work to be sure yet. We will write you again from Geneva.

ever affectionately yours

J.S.M.

178. TO MRS. JAMES MILL[1]

[Paris]
[Nov. 4, 1836]

As we shall so soon be at Kensington there is not much to write. I have no doubt you did the best you could as to the house, & the sale;[2] & as the house is taken we will stay there till we can find another that we thoroughly like—& as we do not know how long it may be first, I shall have the bookshelves put up. You may as well do it before I come unless you have any doubt how I should like it to be done. I am much the same as to health—my head is often rather bad, otherwise I am as well almost as I ever was.

J.S.M.

179. TO ALEXIS DE TOCQUEVILLE[1]

Lundi.
[Nov. 9, 1836]

Après avoir été bien près de vous en Suisse, mon cher Tocqueville, sans vous rencontrer, j'arrive à Paris et vous êtes encore à la campagne, ainsi

2. Mrs. Taylor's son Herbert.

* * * *

1. MS at LSE. *Addressed*: Mrs. Mill / 18 Kensington Square / London / Angleterre. *Postmarks*: PARIS / 4 / NOV / 183 . . . and LONDON / 7 / NOV / 1836. Appended to a letter from Henry Mill to his sister Wilhelmina.

2. After the death of James Mill the family disposed of the house in Vicarage Place, Church Street, Kensington, in which they had lived since 1831, and moved to a smaller house in Kensington Square.

* * * *

1. Published in Mayer, pp. 299–301. There dated Nov. 9, 1835, but JSM was not in France in 1835 though he was in 1836. For other evidence that the date should be 1836, see notes below. Also, Tocqueville's letter of Nov. 19, 1836 (Mayer, pp. 313–16), appears to be a reply to this. MS in Tocqueville archives.

que Beaumont, et par là je me trouve privé du plaisir de voir, pendant le très peu de jours que je reste ici, presque les deux seules personnes que je tenais beaucoup à y trouver. Je regrette beaucoup de ne pas vous voir, et j'aurais voulu vous voir à Paris—nous ne nous sommes encore connus qu'en Angleterre, et cela aurait aidé à combler le vide que laisse pour moi à Paris la mort funeste de Carrel[2]—le seul homme en France, execpté vous, mon cher Tocqueville, pour qui je ressentais une véritable admiration—et cependant vous savez que j'aime les Français—la nation en général, et un grand nombre d'entre eux en particulier. J'ai à vous dire mille choses, mais avant tout j'ai à vous demander comment va la deuxième partie de la Démocratie. Je l'attends avec impatience, pour les lumières qu'elle répandra sur bien des questions dans mon propre esprit, pour le bien qu'elle fera à notre siècle et aux temps à venir, et pour l'intérêt que je porte à votre gloire. Je crains que votre voyage en Suisse, dont j'ai appris avec peine le motif n'ait dû retarder un peu la complétion de votre tâche. Moi-meme j'ai été forcé de suspendre mes travaux par des motifs de santé, et de faire un voyage en Suisse et en Italie, qui m'a fait du bien mais qui ne m'a pas guéri; mon mal pourtant n'a rien de très sérieux, c'est un dérangement local de la circulation du sang dans la partie droite de la tête; il a duré une année, c'est ma première maladie, mais elle se montre obstinée et il faut que je me résigne à la subir. Je m'y accoutume peu à peu et je crois que cela ne m'empêchera pas de travailler beaucoup cet hiver. Je suis assez content de la livraison de la revue qui a paru dans mon absence; je ne l'ai vue que chez Bennis,[3] depuis mon arrivée à Paris; mais comme, moi absent, on néglige tout, il s'est trouvé qu'on a négligé d'envoyer des exemplaires à nos amis d'ici et entre autres à Beaumont et à vous; je vais écrire à Londres pour mettre ordre à cela: dans huit jours vous aurez des exemplaires. Nous aurions bien besoin de votre secours pour le prochain numero; mais si votre grand travail n'est pas encore achevé, nous ne sommes pas assez peu modestes pour vous en demander. Seulement je vous engage beaucoup à faire usage de votre influence auprès de notre ami Beaumont pour tirer de lui un article ou au moins des notes sur la "France" de M. Henry Bulwer.[4] Tout en faisant de la haute philosophie historique sur la France au moyen de vos articles, nous voudrions en même temps nous trouver dans le cas de rectifier en passant les erreurs qu'on commet en écrivant sur la France, et rendre justice à ce qu'il y a de bon (et il y en a beaucoup) dans les idées de M. Bulwer. Nous ne pouvons pas faire cela sans la coopération de nos amis en France et j'ai une confiance dans les jugements de Beaumont que ne m'inspirerait nul autre à qui je pourrais m'adresser, confiance qui est due autant à son propre mérite

2. Carrel died on July 24, 1836, as the result of a duel with Emile de Girardin.
3. George G. Bennis.
4. See Letters 113, n. 2, and 172, n. 2.

qu'à l'étroite union qui existe entre lui et vous, union qui lui donne toujours l'occasion et l'habitude de comparer ses idées avec les vôtres. J'ai lu chez Bennis deux notices sur la Démocratie: l'une dans le Quarterly Review, qui est évidemment de Basil Hall;[5] tout ce qu'il a mis de lui est pitoyable, mais heureusement il y a mis beaucoup de vous, et il parle de vous et du livre comme il le doit. L'autre article est du North American Review;[6] j'attendais celui-là avec beaucoup d'intérêt pour savoir le parti que prendraient les écrivains américains sur le livre: j'ai été très content de voir que l'article est fait dans un esprit favorable; on y dit seulement que vous généralisez quelquefois un peu trop, et j'aurais voulu qu'on eût dit en quoi. A propos, j'observe que le American Quarterly Review, dans sa dernière livraison, s'élève très fortement contre le système des pledges:[7] cela m'a charmé, d'autant plus que cette revue passe (n'est-ce pas?) pour être démocrate, et pas fédéraliste comme le North American.

Ecrivez-moi vite, je vous prie: je serai ici pour deux ou trois jours. Parlez-moi de votre santé, de celle de Madame de Tocqueville, de vos travaux, de vos idées sur l'état de choses actuel et de sa durée probable; parlez-moi aussi de Beaumont et enfin de ce que vous ou lui pourrez faire pour la revue.

Avez-vous vu Senior en Suisse? Vous savez qu'il est Master in Chancery[8] et très content de l'être. Cela le rend plus riche et plus indépendant aussi.

Tout à vous mon cher Tocqueville.

J. S. MILL.

Hôtel Mirabeau, rue de la Paix.
(Compiègne November 9 1835.)[9]

180. TO ARISTIDE GUILBERT[1]

India House.
22^d^ Novr 1836

MY DEAR GUILBERT

I write to you in great haste, to say that I have this day directed Messrs Prescott & Grote & Co to remit to you £25. I presume it will be receivable at Delamarre's as usual.

5. *QR*, LVII (Sept., 1836), 132–62. Basil Hall (1788–1844), naval officer and writer of Tory views.

6. *North American Rev.*, XLIII (July, 1836), 178–206.

7. "The Rationale of Political Representation," *American Quar. Rev.*, XX (Sept., 1836), 174–216.

8. Senior had received the appointment on June 10, 1836.

9. *Sic*, but see n. 1 above.

* * * *

1. *Addressed*: Monsieur / M. Aristide Guilbert / 47 Rue de Joubert / à Paris. *Postmarks*: LONDO... / 22 NOV 1836 / and ANGLETERRE PAR CALAIS / 24 NOV 1836. MS at King's. Printed in Morrison, p. 257.

If your article[2] is to be inserted in the forthcoming number, we must not only have *the article itself* by the 15th of December, but we must have it soon enough to be *translated* before the 15th of December.

With many apologies for the brevity & abruptness of this note believe me my dear Guilbert

Ever yours faithfully

J. S. Mill.

181. TO EDWARD LYTTON BULWER[1]

India House
23[d] November
1836

My dear Sir

I have just returned from an absence of nearly four months on the Continent, rendered necessary by an obstinate though in no way alarming indisposition, which has lasted for more than a twelvemonth & which together with another far more melancholy circumstance[2] had obliged me during that period to put aside all occupations which could be dispensed with & among other things to leave my friend Molesworth's review[3] very much to shift for itself. Now, when I am sufficiently recovered to be able to revert to my former interests & pursuits, one of the things I am most concerned about is how the greatest value & efficiency may be given to that review—& I am sure that I speak the sentiments of all connected with it, when I say that nothing would conduce so much to either end as your hearty cooperation, if we could be so fortunate as to obtain it. I have, since my return, read your article on Sir Thomas Browne[4] with an admiration I have seldom felt for any English writings on such subjects—I did not know, at the time, that it was yours, & could not conceive what new accession had come to the Edinburgh Review. I first thought it might possibly be Macaulay's, but as I read on I felt it to be far too good for him—it has much of the same brilliancy, but not his affected and antithetical stile, & above all a perception of truth, which he never seems to have, & a genuine love of the True & the Beautiful, the absence of which in him,

2. The Jan., 1837, *LWR* contains no article that can be attributed to Guilbert.

* * * *

1. MS in the possession of Bulwer's great-grand-daughter, Lady Hermione Cobbold, Knebworth House, Knebworth, Herts. Collated by Dr. Eileen Curran, of Colby College. Published in Elliot, I, 102–5, and, with several omissions, in Earl of Lytton, *Life of Edward Bulwer, First Lord Lytton* (London, 1913).
2. The death of his father in June, 1836.
3. *LWR*.
4. *ER*, LXIV (Oct., 1836), 1–35.

is the reason why among his thousands of clever things & brilliant things there are so few *true* things—& hardly one which is the *whole* truth, & *nothing* but the truth. I could not help saying to myself, who would look for these qualities in the Edinburgh Review? how the readers of that review must be puzzled & bewildered by a writer who actually takes decided views, who is positively in earnest, & is capable of downright admiration & even enthusiasm! I am sure your writing must be lost upon them; they are not people who can recognise or care about truth; your beautiful things will be to them merely clever things & amusing things *comme tant d'autres*. Among us you would at least find both writers and readers who are in earnest. I grant that you, & such writing as yours, would be nearly as much out of place in our review *as it has been*, as in the Edinburgh: but not, as I hope it will hereafter be. As good may be drawn out of evil—the event which has deprived the world of the man of greatest philosophical genius it possessed[5] & the review (if such little interests may be spoken of by the side of great ones) of its most powerful writer, & the only one to whose opinions the editors were obliged to defer—that same event has made it far easier to do that, in the hope of which alone I allowed myself to become connected with the review—namely to soften the harder & sterner features of its radicalism and utilitarianism, both which in the form in which they originally appeared in the Westminster, were part of the inheritance of the 18th century. The Review ought to represent not radicalism but neoradicalism, a radicalism which is not democracy, not a bigotted adherence to any forms of government or to one kind of institutions, & which is only to be called radicalism inasmuch as it does not palter nor compromise with evils but cuts at their roots—& a utilitarianism which takes into account the whole of human nature not the ratiocinative faculty only—the utilitarianism which never makes any peculiar figure as such, nor would ever constitute its followers a sect or school—which fraternizes with all who hold the same *axiomata media* (as Bacon has it) whether their first principle is the same or not—& which holds in the highest reverence all which the vulgar notion of utilitarians represents them to despise—which holds Feeling at least as valuable as Thought, & Poetry not only on a par with, but the necessary condition of, any true & comprehensive Philosophy. I know I am writing very loosely & expressing myself very ill—but *you* will understand me—& as I have, through Molesworth's confidence in me, complete power over that review whenever I chuse to exercise it, I hope you will believe, that if the review has hitherto been too much in the old stile of radical-utilitarianism with which you cannot possibly sympathize very strongly (nor I either) it is because the only persons, who could be depended upon as writers, were those whose writings would not tend to give it any other tone.

5. James Mill.

My object will now be to draw together a body of writers resembling the old school of radicals only in being on the Movement side, in philosophy, morality, & art as well as in politics & socialities—& to keep the remnant of the old school (it is dying out) in their proper place, by letting them write only about the things which they understand. But this attempt must fail unless those who *could* assist it, *will*. Why should you not write, for us, a series of articles on the old English writers, similar to that on Browne? They would be quite invaluable to us: we have not among our habitual writers any who could be trusted to write on such subjects—those who would have enough of the requisite feelings & talents, have not the requisite reading. We have now, since the junction with the Westminster, readers enough to make it worth while; & readers who are in earnest, readers by whom what you write would be taken *au sérieux* & not as a mere play of intellect & fancy. Your writing for us need not hinder you from writing for the Edinburgh also if you like it—but I am sure you must often feel *that* not to be a fitting vehicle for anything not of a *stationary* character either in literature or politics—*passe encore* if you could hope by your writings to modify the character of the work itself—but that is hopeless. Now among us you could.

Do pray think of it & tell me the result of your thought. The time is evidently approaching when the radicals will once more be a distinct party & when people will look to the review as their organ—& much will depend upon its being an organ which represents the best part of them and not the narrowest & most repulsive.

Ever yours faithfully,

J. S. MILL.

182. TO EDWARD LYTTON BULWER[1]

I.H.
Tuesday
[Nov. 29, 1836]

MY DEAR BULWER—Accept my best thanks for the kind expressions in your letter. Nothing could be more gratifying to me than the whole tone of it & I could not be so unreasonable as to ask, under the circumstances you mention, for any greater degree of immediate cooperation than that which

1. *Addressed*: Edw. Lytton Bulwer Esq. M.P. / Reform Club / Pall Mall / to be forwarded. *Postmark*: 7NE[?]7 / NO 29 / 1836. MS in the possession of Lady Hermione Cobbold. Collated by Dr. Eileen Curran. Published in Elliot, I, 105–6.

you so kindly offer. I have been long looking for your work on Athens,[2] & rejoice in the prospect of its being out so soon. If it be not delayed longer than the time you mention we may perhaps hope for something from you for our April number? Everyone who writes criticism worthy the name, must write it as you say "slowly & with great labour" for it is precisely, of all things, that which it is most difficult to write well, & which is least supportable when slovenly—but a greater number & variety of important truths, (truths too with their application annexed) may be thrown into circulation in that way than in almost any other mode of writing. Though I shall in common with most people lose a great deal of pleasure when you leave off writing romances, it is still very good news that you are looking forward to an early time at which your powers will be devoted—I will not say to nobler, or more important objects, for Politics are not intrinsically nobler, & as usually pursued are far less noble than Art, but at least to objects of more pressing exigency, & where there is a wider field of usefulness open just at the present time. Nobody can doubt that whenever you do make politics & the things which are to be effected through politics, your principal object—& pursue that object with the energy & perseverance which you have so conspicuously shewn in the application of the same powers to other objects—there is a place reserved for you in the political history of this country which will not be a humble one.

If you do not find the atmosphere of the L. & W. Review more & more congenial to you it will not be my fault. Even at present when bad things are put in, it is not because they are liked, but for want of better—your aid, to whatever degree afforded, much more if (may I say, *when*) it may hereafter be habitually afforded, would of itself supersede, & displace much that it would be very desirable to see displaced. It would also conduce extremely to the success of the review, but the great thing is that it would conduce, more than any other literary assistance I can think of, to render the review what it is not now even in the slightest degree, an organ of real literary & social criticism.

What you say of the radi[cal]s[3] is too true—but I think they *are*, now, bestirring th[em]selves in all quarters—& as their jealousy is, I think, chiefly the natural carping of those who do nothing against all which is done, as they grow more active they may shake it off. The most active among them are the least capable of jealousy even now. I think they would all follow a good leader & would not be jealous of one whose power they felt & saw to be exerted in their behalf. They are really sincere men, & would value a man who worked vigorously in the cause.

Ever yours faithfully,

J. S. MILL.

2. See Letters 147, n. 8, and 206, n. 4.

3. Paper torn.

183. TO SIR WILLIAM MOLESWORTH[1]

I.H.
3rd December 1836

DEAR MOLESWORTH,

I send you some more of your article.[2] Do not be frightened at the number of pencil marks. This part bears the proof of being more hastily written than the preceding part. The ideas are not presented in so lucid an order. My suggestions will do something to do this: but you probably could do more.

You have, I believe, an article of Bisset's on the Universities: is it good for anything? would you send it for me to see?

I want your permission to propose you for the Political Economy Club. What think you of it?

Ever yours
J. S. MILL.

184. TO DAVID BARCLAY[1]

[1836]

The chief points are the time and place of his birth; who and what his parents were, and anything interesting that there may be to state about them: what places of education he went to: for what professions he was educated. I believe he went through a medical course, and also that for the Church, and I have heard that he was actually licensed as a preacher, but I never heard him say so himself, and never heard of it till after his death. I do not know whether it is true or not; perhaps you do. How long did he remain at the University, or prosecute his studies for the Church? The history of his connection with the late Sir John Stuart.[2]

184A. TO THOMAS CARLYLE (*see* page 743)

1. MS in 1945 in the possession of Sir John Molesworth–St. Aubyn.
2. Probably "Terms of Alliance between Radicals and Whigs," *LWR*, XXVI (Jan., 1837), 279–318.

* * * *

1. Excerpt published in Alexander Bain, *James Mill*, p. 11 n. MS not located.
David Barclay, an early friend of James Mill, occupied the farm upon which stood the cottage in which Mill had been born. Bain says that JSM, largely ignorant of his father's early life, wrote this letter to obtain information for Andrew Bisset, whom he had invited to write a biography of his father for the *Encyclopædia Britannica* (the seventh edition, published in parts between 1830 and 1842). The volume containing Bisset's biography of James Mill (with some passages by JSM) appeared in the summer of 1837. Bisset also contributed a biography to the volume of the *Penny Cyclopædia* published in 1839.
2. Sir John Stuart (originally Belsches), of Fettercairn (1753–1821), James Mill's early patron, for whom he named his eldest son. Two others of the Mill children were named for this family: for Lady Jane Stuart, and for her daughter, Wilhelmina, who became the wife of Sir William Forbes.

• • • 1837 • • •

185. TO ALEXIS DE TOCQUEVILLE[1]

7 Jan. 1837.

MY DEAR TOCQUEVILLE,

This is the first moment in which I have been able, with any comfort to myself, to take up my pen in order to write to you. And now, it is rather to ask for news of you than to say anything from myself. I am anxious to hear how you are getting on with the second part of La Démocratie—& when there is a likelihood of its appearance. I look forward with great eagerness to the pleasure first of reading it, & next of reviewing it. *A propos*, it would be of the greatest importance to the London & Westminster Review, to be the first English periodical that contained a notice of it, & if that notice could be given before the publication of the work, it would be a very great benefit to us indeed. Would this be possible? Could you send it to me in sheets? Or even by piecemeal, in order that I might be studying it & preparing myself to have an article ready at the first moment. One of the great secrets of success for a review in this country, is to have early notices of books that excite a general interest, & as often as possible to notice them before publication. Murray continually keeps back the books which he publishes, in order that the article in the Quarterly Review may precede the book it reviews.

The number of the review which has just appeared, & which if you have not yet received you soon shall, will I think interest you very much. The first article[2] in it is a *coup de parti*, a manifesto as we say of the radicals (or rather *for* the radicals) on the subject of the Whigs—intended to awaken the slumbering energy of the radical leaders, & to force the Whigs to take a decided part. It is written by Sir W. Molesworth, who has been making a considerable figure for the last few months—if you have seen English papers during that time. You will have marked the gradual development of the plan which he & several other of the radical members

1. Published in Mayer, pp. 316–18; in reply to Tocqueville's of Nov. 19, 1836, *ibid.*, pp. 313–16. MS in Tocqueville archives.
2. "Terms of Alliance between Radicals and Whigs," *LWR*, XXVI (Jan., 1837), 279–318.

have formed and are executing. I think them quite right. Whatever may be the appearances do not suppose that the mass of the middle & working classes are indifferent to the movement: they seem so, because, at elections & otherwise, everything they do for reform costs them immense sacrifices of their personal interests, sacrifices which they are ready to make for a great object but not for a small one. If any ministry would now bring forward the ballot, they would excite greater enthusiasm than even that which was excited for the Reform Bill. But as matters stand, the Whigs' majority is slipping away from them, & nothing will keep the Tories long out of power except either the adoption by the Whigs of a more radical policy, or the rise among the radicals themselves of able & energetic leaders, acting quite independently of the Whigs, as Molesworth, Roebuck, Leader & others are doing now. Of these two outlets from our false position, if we can but gain the last, we shall soon have the first two. You will soon see the ballot a cabinet measure, & then reform will have finally triumphed: the aristocratical principle will be completely annihilated, & we shall enter into a new era of government. The approaching session will be next to that of 1830/1831, the most important since 1688—& parties will stand quite differently at the commencement & at the close of it.

Did you see Buller when he was at Paris? I have seen him but once since his return, & forgot to ask him. He arrived at Paris, & at the very hotel where I was, the day after I had left it. He will I think play a very conspicuous part hereafter in our politics—he rose exceedingly in public estimation last year. At present his *rôle* is that of a mutual friend, or conciliator, between the Whigs & radicals—it is very desirable that there should be such a person, & he is well suited to the character. As for your politics—they seem to be still in the same torpid state.

I send today, to Beaumont, through the embassy, a very important pamphlet on Ireland, by the Secretary to the late Commission of Poor Law Enquiry.[3] I am not able to send a letter along with it, for I positively have not time. Pray make my excuses to him & tell him that it would be of the greatest use to the review if he (or you) would furnish at least *notes* for a review of Bulwer's book.[4]

Is there a chance of your coming here soon? I hope very much that we shall have Beaumont for a few months in the spring. Ever, my dear Tocqueville, yours faithfully

J. S. MILL.

India House.

3. John Revans, *Evils of the State of Ireland, their Causes and the Remedy—a Poor Law* (London, 1837).

4. See Letters 113, n. 2, and 172, n. 2.

186. TO EDWARD LYTTON BULWER[1]

18 Kensington Square
Saturday
[Jan., 1837]

MY DEAR SIR—Your note found me laid up with the influenza, which must be my excuse for not having immediately answered it. I had not previously contemplated a review of LaValliere,[2] for the same reason which has prevented our reviewing any former writing of yours: a critical estimate of you & your works was too serious a task to be lightly ventured upon, & your reputation had long passed the stage at which the cursory notice of a review could promote the success of any of your writings. However since an occasion has arisen on which you think that something we can do may be of service, the case is altered, & since I received your note I have been considering what would be the best way of having it done. I have good hopes, & I can promise that nothing shall prevent it, unless the very few persons who could do it as it ought to be done, should all fail me.[3]

There can be but one opinion as to the attacks in the Times;[4] those in the Spectator[5] I have not seen: but nobody can well doubt that if such a play as LaValliere had been written by anybody against whom there was no personal or political jealousy or hostility it would have obtained the loud encomiums of the whole press. You can however well afford to despise such attacks. Nobody whose judgment one cares for pays the least regard to the theatrical criticisms of newspapers—how they may affect the playgoing public I do not know.

I have been looking impatiently for some token of the appearance of "Athens"[6]—& did not like to say anything more to you about articles till I was sure that was off your hands but I have been thinking very much about subjects, & now when your most welcome announcement comes, I can suggest two, viz. Goldsmith, (Prior's Life)[7] & Cowper, *a propos* of the two new editions of him.[8] Either would be an excellent subject for an article of

1. MS in the possession of Lady Hermione Cobbold. Text provided by Dr. Eileen Curran.

2. *The Duchess de la Vallière*, published in 1836, but first produced, at Covent Garden, on Jan. 3, 1837.

3. He persuaded W. J. Fox to write the review. See Letters 187 and 200.

4. "It is in the worst taste of the worst school—the school of modern French romance" (*The Times*, Jan. 5, 1837, p. 3).

5. "We cannot pass uncensored the dramatist who calls upon us to sympathize with the woes of a discarded mistress and a disappointed voluptuary. It is the pathos of the stews." (*Spectator*, Jan. 7, 1837, p. 10.)

6. See Letter 147, n. 8.

7. James Prior, *The Life of Oliver Goldsmith* (2 vols., London, 1837).

8. Neither suggestion was adopted by Bulwer. The new editions of Cowper were those edited by Robert Southey in 15 vols. (1835–37) and by T. S. Grimshawe in 8 vols. (1835, 1836).

philosophical & imaginative criticism. But I have no preference for them, if you should like anything else better, especially any old writer.

Molesworth has not measured his words very scrupulously,[9] but the object was to act upon the radicals, who are people not easily moved. He wanted to give them a violent shake, in order to set them going. You will not find him at all intemperate *now*, or in the least desirous of turning out the ministry.

Ever yours faithfully

J. S. MILL.

I am concerned to see your note edged with black—whom have you lost?

187. TO WILLIAM JOHNSON FOX[1]

18 Kensington Square
[Jan., 1837]

I hope our Poor Law offences[2] have not made it hopeless to induce you to write for us a notice of Bulwer's play[3]—no one but you can do it in the only way in which it ought to be done, that of setting the stage in its proper position of worthiness, and encouraging the best writers to write for it. Bulwer wishes that we should notice it, because he is rather more sore than need be at the newspaper attacks, & thinks his play needs support against them—if it can *need* support against *such* attacks it should have it. You I believe think highly of the play—& if so there would be nothing to guard against, except that we should not seem to be paying him in puffs for an article of his which we shall probably have in the very same number—& that we should not seem to sanction as much as is merely conventional in the morality of that LaValliere story—but this is a point on which it is quite unnecessary to say anything to you—

You have no conception how much you would oblige me if you could manage to do it—though I know well what it is to ask more work from an overworked person—

I am here laid up by influenza, & have been so for some days.

J.S.M.

9. Probably a reference to his speech at a Reform Dinner at Bath on Jan. 5, 1837, but perhaps to his article in the Jan. *LWR*. See preceding letter, paragraph 2.

* * * *

1. Published, except for last sentence, in Garnett, pp. 183–84. MS at King's.
2. "Fallacies on Poor Laws," *LWR*, XXVI (Jan., 1837), 357–82, signed W. E. H[ickson].
3. See preceding letter, n. 2, and Letter 200, n. 2.

188. TO WILLIAM JOHNSON FOX[1]

18 Kensington Square
Friday
[Jan. 27, 1837]

I feel the position you are in with regard to Horne[2]—& all the rest of what you say on that subject. I feel it to my cost too. What to do I do not know. There is not a creature living who would do that for me, & whom I could trust to do it, unless it be you. Is there no remedy? could I in any way forward it? is there anything I could do for your paper[3] that would give you a few hours respite from it? or is there no hope?

I put "our" to the "poor law offences"[4] because it would be cowardly not, since I am as much responsible for them as any one can be. I hope you believe without my saying it, that I should not have put the article in, if it had appeared to me as it does to you, personally disrespectful to yourself—& this not because you are a contributor, but because you are *you*. The two between whom you are placed[5] may be "thieves"—I do not know them—& if so, it is natural you should feel offended—but I am persuaded the writer of the article does not think them such; in fact he compliments one of them, & I have reason to think, has a good opinion of at least the *intentions* of both. Neither did it seem to me that the T[rue] S[un] was spoken of disparagingly *on the whole*, though a difference of opinion was expressed with much warmth on a particular point.

I differ from you as entirely as the writer does, on the Poor Law question, & on a whole class of questions therewith connected. Nor have your articles in answer to the review, though I recognize in them your best & most effective stile of discussion, at all narrowed the difference between us, but rather widened it. But I hope there is no reason against letting this be an "open question" both among radicals & among London reviewers.

J.S.M.

I am not out yet—I mean not at the I.H. but I shall on Monday, I hope. she[6] is much better—how are you & yours?

1. Published, except for postscript, in Garnett, pp. 184–85. MS at King's.
2. R. H. Horne, with whose editorship of the *Monthly Repository* Fox was dissatisfied.
3. The *True Sun*. See Letter 200, n. 3.
4. See preceding letter.
5. The article had alluded to "the doctrines maintained, and the tone assumed by 'the London Dispatch,' 'The True Sun,' 'The Weekly Dispatch.'" Fox himself later wrote also for the *Weekly Dispatch*.
6. Mrs. Taylor.

189. TO SARAH AUSTIN[1]

18 Kensington Square
28th January 1837

MY DEAR MÜTTERLEIN—I could not send you the review last month, as I could not get a copy soon enough. If you ever see English newspapers, you will have seen that Molesworth's article[2] has been making considerable noise—as indeed it ought. His letters, speeches, & conduct in all respects for the last three months, have raised every one's opinion extremely of his talents & *caractère* & made him a sort of hero of the day—which however he is not intoxicated by, but as docile & modest as any one can well be.

You may wonder that I have been so long in writing to you—though after all, I write first: but you would not wonder if you knew the endless drudgery I have had upon my hands, with arrears of India house business, & private affairs, without counting review matters or any other writing. I came back with my general health & strength everything that could be wished for, though the complaint in my head, as a mere local affection, did not give way & is still nearly as troublesome as ever;[3] that is, *would* be troublesome if I had not learnt not to mind it. I saw Switzerland well, & Milan & the Italian lakes, & Piemont & the bay of Genoa thoroughly, but could not get further unless I had chosen to pass a fortnight in a lazaretto. Pray tell Mr Lewis[4] that I gave his present to M. Lacroix[5] at Nice whom I found a very obliging good natured old gentleman & liked very much: he spoke with much regard of Mr Lewis.

I have heard nothing of you, any of you, subsequent to your arrival at Malta—& wish very much to hear of everything which concerns you but especially about Mr Austin's health. I wish to ask his advice too about an inscription on a marble slab we are going to erect in the church where my father was buried. Nobody's opinion in such a matter would be of a tithe of the value of Mr Austin's, & I certainly will not do anything in the matter without his approbation. What has occurred to me is, to add after the usual particulars, these words—

"His life was one of consistent usefulness,
and history will appreciate its results.
His works are his best monument."

1. *Addressed*: Mrs. Austin. MS at King's. Mrs. Austin's unpublished letter in reply from Malta, March 3, 1837, is at LSE.
2. See Letter 185, n. 2.
3. His illness had produced a chronic facial twitch, an affliction from which he suffered the rest of his life.
4. George Cornewall Lewis. He and John Austin were then in Malta as commissioners to inquire into the administration of the island.
5. Unidentified.

If Mr Austin does not like this, or not so well as any other, perhaps he could in some interval of his laborious duties, find five minutes to think of something better—He perhaps alone of all persons living is as much interested in the matter as I am.

There is a review just started called the "Church of England review" the first number of which contains an attack on Lewis's last article[6]—pray tell him this. I have not seen it.

I can tell you little of any one in whom you are interested—for I see nobody but those who come to me. I have time to go to nobody. I must except Carlyle who has finished his book[7] & is in great joy thereat—not for any hope he may have of its success, but for having done with it.

I do hope I shall hear from you some time—though I am a bad correspondent I am always your Söhnchen

J.S.M.

190. TO JOHN PRINGLE NICHOL[1]

18, Kensington Square,
29th January, 1837.

MY DEAR NICHOL,

You must think me sadly neglectful of you, for I have not written to you a single line since that from Milan, although I knew how much you would wish to hear something about my health, at least. My excuse is, the quite oppressive weight of business I find resting on me. Till now I never knew what it was to be a thorough mechanical drudge. The accumulation of India House business from my long absence, and slack performance of duty for nearly a year previous, leaves me none of the occasional hours and days of respite I used to have there; above three hours a day are taken up by exercise; my occupations, pecuniary, preceptorial and other connected with my several trusts as executor, guardian, and so forth, take up much time; and I have not needed your caution against *writing* much for the Review, for the mere mechanical drudgery connected with editorship has so filled up the chinks of my time that I have hardly written a line since I returned. You saw the very little I wrote for the last number;[2] even that was all prepared last spring, though I had not put any of it on paper. And then you would hardly believe the quantity of letters I have to write—

6. "The London and Westminster Review for October 1836—The Voluntary Principle," *Church of England Quar. Rev.*, I (Jan., 1837), 121–40, was an attack upon Lewis' "Endowment and the Voluntary Principle: Separation of Church and State," *LWR*, XXVI (Oct., 1836), 244–77.

7. *The French Revolution.*

* * * *

1. Published by Knight, pp. 673–74. MS not located.
2. "Thoughts in the Cloister and the Crowd," *LWR*, XXVI (Jan., 1837), 348–57.

further, I am general referee, and chamber counsel to Molesworth and others of the active Radicals—whenever anything is to be done, I am to be asked whether it is right—whenever anybody is to be moved to do anything, I am to be moved first to move him—then I have to prepare myself for the Political Economy club every month—in short this will not do—and shall not. As for my health—I returned with my head no better,[3] but my general health and strength quite restored—nor has my head got at all worse since; indeed, no quantity of thinking or writing affects it at all; reading India House papers, beyond a certain number of hours, affects it, but on the whole I have to keep any tendency to increase (if there be any) completely under. I have not contrived, however, to keep off the influenza, which has run through our family as through most others, and has kept me in confinement here for the last fortnight, with cough, catarrh, sore throat, feverishness, and disordered stomach, the usual pleasures which accompany it. I have got quite rid of it now, or next thing to it, and shall go to the India House to-morrow to resume my drudgery.

And you—how are you? and what are you thinking of? Your class,[4] of course, in the first instance, but that can give you so little trouble that you cannot need to think of it much. What think you of the last number of the Review? What of the aspect of politics? What do people in your part of Scotland think of the Molesworth controversy?[5] Here there is a great outcry against Molesworth by all the Whigs and the timid Radicals, but for all that those very Radicals are making note of preparation for the active and unshackled line of conduct which Molesworth inculcates, and which they never would have felt themselves either prompted or compelled to if he, or some person of mark, had not taken a decided position, and so forced them to do the like. Whoever takes a step boldly in advance, risks much for himself, but is sure to do good to his cause. One thing is certain, Molesworth has greatly raised his character for judgment and tact—all those letters of his he wrote down in Cornwall with nobody near him to consult except Leader,[6] and yet how skilfully they were all worded—not a false step, except, indeed, that pettish letter to Fonblanque,[7]—and there he saw his error, and has since sent an ample apology, and they are now friends and will soon be allies. He is trying to form a party. I do not

3. See preceding letter, n. 3.

4. Nichol had become Regius Professor of Astronomy at the University of Glasgow the preceding year.

5. After announcing in Sept., 1836, that because of loss of support by old-line Whigs he would not again seek to represent East Cornwall in Parliament, Molesworth had become a candidate for Leeds. He was pursuing an intransigent Radical line, especially on the question of the ballot, which was threatening to destroy the uneasy alliance between the Whigs and the Radicals.

6. John Temple Leader (1810–1903), then MP for Westminster.

7. See *Examiner*, Dec. 25, 1836, p. 819. Molesworth had been irked by Fonblanque's criticism of him in the leader of Dec. 18 (*ibid.*, p. 801).

know what chance he has. Hume and Grote are with him, and Hume *will act* up to what he professes; whether Grote will, time only can show; Grote's was a good speech at the dinner.[8] You probably have not heard Molesworth's last move; he refused to go to the dinner at Leeds because the Radicals and Whigs jointly had sent resolutions to him pledging him to support ministers. He told them what kind of support alone he could give; thereupon they held a meeting, and the Radicals carried resolutions by an immense majority against the Whigs, concurring completely in his views, and sent a deputation to him to communicate them. This has broken the union of parties at Leeds, but he has the Whigs in his hands, for if he stands and does not turn out Beckett[9] he will turn out Baines,[10] therefore, the Whigs must end by coming to a decided coalition with him. I do think something will come out of the Radical party in this session, but I cannot foresee exactly what. I often wish I were among them; now would be the time for knitting together a powerful party, and nobody holds the scattered threads of it in his hands except me. But that cannot be while I am in the India House. I should not at all mind leaving it if I had £300 a year free from anxiety and literary labour, but I have at most £100. *Sed tempus veniet.* Write to me soon.

Yours affectionately,

J. S. Mill.

191. TO FRANCIS PLACE[1]

I.H.
Thursday.
[Feb. 9(?), 1837]

Dear Place

I do not above half like Roebuck's speech[2]—but friends, & radicals, should stand by one another—& therefore if it be decided to reprint the speech, there shall be no obstacle from the want of a pound from me.

8. At a great Reform Dinner at Drury Lane Theatre on Jan. 23, 1837. See *Examiner,* Jan. 29, 1837, pp. 71–73.

9. Sir John Beckett (1777–1847), the Tory candidate, head of the Leeds banking firm of Beckett & Co., was defeated in the General Election held in July. Molesworth and Baines were elected.

10. Edward Baines (1774–1848), journalist and MP for Leeds, 1834–41.

* * * *

1. MS at Brit. Mus.

2. At the opening of Parliament on Jan. 31, 1837, in the debate on the Address in Reply to the Speech from the Throne, Roebuck had sharply attacked the Whig ministry from the Radical, democratic point of view and had charged that there was a virtual alliance against further reform. Place greatly admired the speech; he at once wrote Roebuck a congratulatory note: "God bless you, my dear boy" (Brit. Mus. Add. MSS 35,150, f. 238).

I heartily wish that those who did such great things for the Stamp Question[3] would set about doing the same thing for the Ballot. It seems to me of *infinite* importance that Grote's motion[4] this year, should be preceded by a strong demonstration from the country in the form of public meetings & petitions. There are a hundred reasons for this, which to you, I need not state. Perhaps with the ballot might be joined repeal of the rate paying clauses—& if they were also to moot the question of a new schedule A for the small boroughs (where the ballot would have no effect)—either abolishing those boroughs, or throwing them (together with other unrepresented towns) into districts of boroughs, like the Scotch & Welsh—so much the better. I would not meddle with household suffrage at present. It raises enemies & does no good that would not be done by repealing the ratepaying clauses, though this *appears* so much smaller a change. Do not you think it was injudicious in Hume[5] to give notice of a motion for household suffrage?

Yours ever

J. S. Mill.

192. TO FRANCIS PLACE[1]

I. H.
Thursday
[Feb. 9(?), 1837]

My dear Place

I am very glad to hear of the Ballot meeting—there should be a Common Hall, *after* the West^r meeting.

If you lose that £10, or any part if it, I will ask permission to divide the loss with you.[2]

The meeting should not merely vote resolutions & a petition, but should name a deputation to go to Lord Melbourne & Lord John Russell & badger them on the subject. That is the way to bring them to terms—but I am speaking to you who know all these things far better than I do

ever yours

J. S. Mill.

3. On the repeal of the stamp tax on newspapers.

4. Grote had already announced his intention to present a bill for the election of members of Parliament by ballot. See *Examiner*, Feb. 5, 1837, p. 87. A similar motion had failed the preceding year.

5. Joseph Hume had announced his intention to introduce a bill to extend the elective franchise to householders in general.

* * * *

1. MS at Brit. Mus.

2. See the two following letters.

193. TO FRANCIS PLACE[1]

I.H.
Friday
[Feb. 10, 1837]

MY DEAR PLACE

It is disgraceful that those who rendered so great a service should be out of pocket.[2] Since there is a loss I must be allowed to bear my part of it to which purpose please to apply the enclosed.[3]

As for the ballot—there is nothing like *timing* the matter well. If £100 would suffice this time as well as last, I am convinced it might be raised in two days, for the radicals are feeling at last the necessity of doing something, & they *want* public meetings & petitions *now* to help them on.

As for Roebuck's speech[4]—it has greatly raised his character, & will do good—but in so far as it goes beyond Molesworth, I do not agree in it.

I think Fonblanque in the wrong,[5] but you need not I think regret having served him, for he is still as radical as ever & will be with us again soon, I am convinced.

Pray do not think of *hibernating*.[6] Radicalism seems to me to have a better chance just now than it has ever had before—the few who are active, having now determined to go on without the rest, which will soon oblige the others to follow.

Ever truly yours
J. S. MILL.

194. TO ALBANY FONBLANQUE[1]

I.H.
Monday
[Feb. 13(?), 1837]

DEAR FONBLANQUE—I called on you yesterday, (which I had not been able to do any evening last week) wishing to talk over a hundred things with

1. *Addressed*: Francis Place Esq. / 21 Brompton Square. *Postmarks*: 2 AN 2 / FE 10 / 1837, and TP / Cornhill. MS at Brit. Mus.

2. See Letters 192 and 194. 3. £5. See Letter 194. 4. See Letter 191, n. 2.

5. Fonblanque in the *Examiner*'s leading article for Feb. 5, 1837, had been critical of Roebuck for his attack on the Whig ministry.

6. Place retorted: "I have no present inclination to waste my time with men who are infirm of purpose, and worry myself to no useful purpose" (quoted in Graham Wallas, *Life of Francis Place* [London, 1898], pp. 351–52). The full draft of Place's letter is in Brit. Mus. Add. MSS 35,150, ff. 241–42.

* * * *

1. MS at LSE. Excerpts published in *Life and Labours of Albany Fonblanque*, ed. E. B. de Fonblanque (London, 1874), pp. 30–31.

you—but there is one thing which cannot wait, & which I *must* write to you about.

Unless you and a few others bestir themselves, & give the word to the people to meet & petition for the ballot during the next three weeks, Grote's motion[2] will go off as flatly as it did last year & if so, the consequences will be unspeakably mischievous. I reckon a Tory majority, & a Tory ministry almost certain at a very early period, unless we have a government which will propose the ballot. I know nobody at all acquainted with the constituencies who does not think the same. Buller for instance is half mad about it, & is for throwing overboard Reform of the Lords & everything else & pushing for the ballot & the ballot only. As for Ministers—I have advised Molesworth & shall advise every radical I know, to be guided in his tone & conduct about the ministry, mainly by the part they take on Grote's motion.

It is enough to drive one mad to see everybody thinking of everything except the precise thing which is of importance at the time, & so every opportunity lost.

I wrote to Place[3] to see if the Committee who managed all the correspondence & petitioning on the newspaper stamps for two sessions & only spent £110, would do the same for the ballot—he answered, that even those £110 they had not been able to raise & were £20 out of pocket! I had subscribed both years, that is £2, which was in proportion to my means, but I could not help sending him £5 now[4] for my share of the loss. In answer I received the enclosed which I shall keep as a memorial of the spiritless, heartless imbecility of the English radicals.[5] Pray read it & send it back to me, as I mean to fling it in the teeth of some of them.

I shall be surprised if after reading this you still think that it was not worth while risking something in order to awaken the people from their torpor.

Ever faithfully yours

J. S. MILL

I am delighted with the three volumes[6]—everything in them is quite fresh, & as good as new.

2. It was due to be presented on March 7.
3. Letter 191.
4. Letter 193.
5. *Ibid.*, n. 6.
6. Fonblanque's *England under Seven Administrations*, a three-volume collection of his political pieces in the *Examiner*. Published this month, the book was reviewed by JSM in *LWR*, XXVII (April, 1837), 65–98.

195. TO ALBANY FONBLANQUE[1]

I.H.
Thursday
[Feb. 16(?), 1837]

MY DEAR FONBLANQUE

Since I wrote to you I have heard again from Place, who says—but I had better enclose what he says. I do so that you may be *au courant* of what is doing as a word in the Examiner would be of great importance to the object.

Please return this & Place's other letter, which I want to shew to Molesworth & others.

It was a good debate on the qualification[2]—& a good division but Warburton, I think, played the fool[3]—& his bill must be watched. If they get the law merely relaxed, so as to include personal property, they will *enforce* it, & so make it practically worse than at present.

Ever yours
J. S. MILL

196. TO THOMAS CARLYLE[1]

[Feb. 23, 1837]

Mr Hunt's Article[2] will be in time if it be not later than the 12th of March: and whether it be printed or not in this N° (tho' I am anxious that it should) I undertake that he shall be paid for it.

1. MS at LSE.
2. In the House of Commons on Tuesday, Feb. 14, Molesworth had moved for leave to bring in a bill to abolish the property qualification of members of Parliament. The motion lost by a vote of 104 to 133.
3. Henry Warburton, who had previously given notice of a motion to amend the property qualification, supported Molesworth's motion, but suggested that in Committee some alteration of the qualification might be substituted for abolition of it.

* * * *

1. MS not located. An excerpt quoted in an unpublished letter by Carlyle to Leigh Hunt, dated Friday morning [Feb. 24, 1837], in Cornell University Library: "I have just received a letter from Mill; of which this is the first paragraph: [quoted paragraph] Hand to the work, therefore! And best speed to you! So says, / Yours always / T. Carlyle." JSM's letter was in answer to Carlyle's of Wednesday [Feb. 22, 1837], in A. Carlyle, pp. 147–48.
2. "Lady Mary Wortley Montagu," published in *LWR*, XXVII (April, 1837), 130–64.

197. TO GUSTAVE D'EICHTHAL[1]

India House
3d March
1837

MY DEAR D'EICHTHAL

I have indeed been very remiss in answering the letter which you wrote to me from Ems. But if you knew how completely my time has been occupied all this winter, I am sure you would pardon me. I was absent from the India House full five months last year & from England 3½ months in hopes of getting rid of a troublesome local affection of the head, which has not even yet left me. Since my return I have had arrears of all sorts of business to clear off, & have been obliged to put off everything which *could* be put off. I did not however postpone reading your book.[2] The copies you ordered to be sent to me I have never received, & I should not have known that the book existed, if I had not, in passing through Paris in November last, called upon your brother Adolphe, who gave me a copy. This I have read & read with very great interest indeed. It would be very difficult without going through the whole book chapter by chapter, to say exactly how much of the book I agree in—but in the main it appears to me very valuable: & your views respecting the difference between the Oriental & the European character, seem to me perfectly just. I quite agree with you that an infusion of the Oriental character into tha[t][3] of the nations of northern Europe would form a combination very much better than either separately. All the doubt I have, is, whether any considerable effect of that kind can be expected from the causes you contemplate—But doubtless whatever promotes friendly intercourse between these two varieties of mankind, & whatever teaches them to know & to like one another, must have a certain tendency of that sort.

In your little note from Vienna you do not tell me anything of your health—I am very anxious to hear whether it is completely reestablished.

I am forced to write to you very hastily & very briefly, as I am still so busy, I actually [do?] not know which way to [turn?]. You I suppose have more leisure, at least for the present, & I hope to hear from you soon at greater length.

I cannot close this note without saying how sincerely I lament the loss of your excellent Mother—

ever yours faithfully

J. S. MILL

1. *Addressed*: Monsieur / Monsieur Gustave d'Eichthal. MS at Arsenal.
2. Probably *Les Deux Mondes par M. Gustave d'Eichthal . . . , servant d'introduction à l'ouvrage de M. Urquhart "La Turquie et ses ressources,"* though the only copy located bears the imprint, Leipzig, 1837.
3. Brackets indicate where page is torn.

198. TO LEIGH HUNT[1]

India House
Monday
[March 13, 1837]

MY DEAR SIR

I regret much that I was from home when you took the trouble to call—but I hope to be indemnified another time & that our personal acquaintance thus begun will henceforth grow & prosper.

I am just about to send your MS.[2] to press with very great satisfaction at our having got it, & still more so at our having enlisted you as a contributor, I hope a frequent one. The remainder will be quite in time tomorrow there being no probability that there will be any points requiring discussion.

Ever truly yours

J. S. MILL

199. TO LEIGH HUNT[1]

India House
Wednesday
[March 15, 1837]

MY DEAR SIR

If my letter gave you pleasure I am sure yours gave as much to me independently of the very great value to us of the MS.[2] which accompanied it & which it was delightful to have to read among so many bad articles or (worse still) articles which required a world of trouble to make them good.

It is part of our plan to have signatures—what shall yours be? your sign manual?[3] ☞

In answer to your P.S.—I believe in the practice of most reviews, & certainly of ours, the book reviewed belongs to the reviewer, & we should never think of deducting its price from our payment.

Ever truly yours

J. S. MILL

1. *Addressed*: Leigh Hunt Esq. / 4 Upper Cheyne Row. MS at Brit. Mus. Carlyle, on Saturday, March 11, had urged Hunt to get his article to JSM that very night (see A. Carlyle, p. 149). On the outside of the letter is written: "I send you this back to read, because giving pleasure to others I knew it would give pleasure to yourself / L.H. [Leigh Hunt]"; and in pencil in yet another hand: "This moment arrived / ½ past 6. / T. C."

2. See Letter 196, n. 2.

* * * *

1. MS at Brit. Mus. MS dated in pencil in another hand: [?] circ 1840; the reference to Hunt's first contribution to the *London and Westminster Review* (see Letters 196 and 198), however, permits the inference of the date here assigned.

2. See Letter 196, n. 2.

3. Hunt continued to use this as his signature for other articles in the *Review*.

200. TO WILLIAM JOHNSON FOX[1]

Wed^y
[March 15, 1837]

Thanks—it[2] is beautifully done, & will illuminate our number. I would gladly, whenever possible, give a good many articles to T.S.[3] for such another.

Probably the Cromwell extracts[4] with such comment as they may need, may be added at the end without altering anything. At all events, the alteration can be made in the proof.

Thanks once more—I *feel* them—& the more because I have given you so little to thank *me* for—

J.S.M.

201. TO JOHN MACRONE[1]

Kensington
Thursday ev^g
[March 30 (?), 1837]

MY DEAR SIR

As you are acquainted with the nature of my connexion with the London & Westminster Review, & are also, I believe, aware that Mr Falconer is about to resign the editorship, I need not apologize for addressing myself to you instead of to Mr. Falconer, to save time. The review will, from a concurrence of very untoward circumstances, be delayed beyond the proper day.[2] Now it occurs to me that the best thing to be done in this case is to put a bold face upon it, & to tell all the booksellers that they need not wonder at not getting the review exactly to a day as it is intended hereafter

1. *Addressed*: Rev. W. J. Fox / 366 Strand. Marked: *private. Postmarks*: T. P. / Leadenhall, and 4 EG4 / MR 15 / 1837. MS at King's. Published in Garnett, p. 185.
2. "Bulwer's Tragedies," *LWR*, XXVII (April, 1837), 247–70. See Letters 186 and 187.
3. The *True Sun*. JSM made at least one contribution to this newspaper to free Fox to write the review; it was an unheaded article on the sale of public lands in the colonies, *True Sun*, Feb. 22, 1837, p. 3.
4. Fox's review contained generous extracts of Bulwer's tragedy *Cromwell*, which was not published until four years later in *The Dramatic Works of Sir Edward Lytton Bulwer* (London, 1841).

* * * *

1. MS at LSE.
John Macrone (*ca.* 1810–1837) best known as the early publisher of Charles Dickens, had published the *Westminster* and continued as publisher of the *London and Westminster* until his death in Sept. of this year.
2. Originally announced for publication on March 31, the April number did not appear until April 6. See *Examiner*, March 26, 1837, p. 208; April 2, p. 224; and April 9, p. 240.

not to publish on a fixed day, but to regulate the bringing out of the review with a view to the *timing* of the articles which it contains. This you may safely say; because it is the determination of the gentleman[3] who is to succeed Mr Falconer, that the review shall always be ready for publication by the *20th* of the month so that it may be brought out at whatever may appear the most advantageous moment between that & magazine-day.

I hope you will excuse my making this suggestion to you, but it seems to me of great importance & it is at the suggestion of the gentleman who is to be the future editor, that I make it. We are also, both of us, anxious that the country copies should not wait for the next monthly parcels, but should be sent off in separate parcels, the expense of which the review will of course pay.

I think you will have reason to be much pleased with the new editor. I am satisfied you will find him a most efficient man of business, & a man of infinite resource for the management of a review.

Believe me

very truly yours

J. S. MILL

John Macrone Esq.

202. TO LEIGH HUNT[1]

I.H.
Thursday
[April 6 (?), 1837]

MY DEAR SIR

Many thanks for all the kind & agreeable things in your note, which I have not had time to acknowledge sooner.

You will have perceived that I had only cancelled a single sentence,[2] & that for reasons which I think you will assent to, the first time I have an opportunity of stating them to you.

We have been thrown out this time by a concurrence of accident & I fear mismanagement. Some of our most important articles were thought of too late—others were accidentally delayed—& the holidays make printing establishments unusually inefficient.

3. John Robertson (d. 1875), a native of Aberdeen, who had been called to the bar at Lincoln's Inn and who had been working on the *Morning Chronicle*. He was to remain as nominal editor until JSM relinquished control of the *Review* in 1840.

* * * *

1. *Addressed*: Leigh Hunt Esq. / 3 Upper Cheyne Row / Chelsea. MS at Brit. Mus.
2. In Hunt's article, "Lady Mary Wortley Montagu." See Letter 196, n. 2.

We shall hereafter avoid I hope all such inconveniences—The present managing editor is about to retire & we have got a most efficient man, who understands the business in hand most perfectly, to supply his place.[3]

Ever yours truly

J. S. MILL

203. TO SARAH AUSTIN[1]

India House
26th April 1837

MY DEAR MUTTERLEIN

You may believe how glad I was to read your long letter & to learn all that it told me. Most of all I was delighted, & so were all to whom I have told it, that *something* has been already done,[2] & *that* a thing which, once done, is done for all countries & not only for poor little Malta. What you say of the feelings of the English to the Maltese[3] is all that one expected *in kind* but much worse in degree—it makes Canada quite intelligible to one—a subject on which our ministers have been dragging themselves & their supporters through the dirt, including Strutt & some other apostate radicals.

I send you the review—the last number to be brought out by Falconer[4]—he & I have all along differed completely as to the management & the difference at last came to a crisis & he resigned. It is now in the hands of a man[5] as efficient as he was inefficient, a man who seems made by nature to conduct the detail business of a review, & who (he is very young) promises, I think to be fit for much better things too. He is the author of the article on Shakespear's life,[6] in the October number. The present number has, I think, less intrinsic merit than most of the preceding, but is much more calculated for success. *A propos* of your remark on Carlyle's

3. See preceding letter, n. 3.

* * * *

1. *Addressed*: Mrs. Austin. MS at King's. Sent in parcel by Henry Reeve to Malta (see Letter 204). In reply to Mrs. Austin's unpublished letter of March 3 (MS at LSE).

2. Mrs. Austin had written: "With this packet they [John Austin and G. C. Lewis] send home their report on the Liberty of the Press & a draft of a Libel law which is entirely his [Austin's] & which Lewis says he believes to be the most perfect specimen of legislation in existence."

3. Mrs. Austin had written: "If I escape poisoning you may rejoice. . . . I am sorry to be an object of hostility to anybody, but civility to the Maltese is an inexpiable offence in the eyes of the English ladies, and I had no choice."

4. The April, 1837, number.

5. John Robertson.

6. "Shakspeare," *LWR*, XXVI (Oct., 1836), 30–57, signed M.R.

article Mirabeau:[7] I am not at all surprised that Mr Austin or that Lewis should dislike it, but it has been the most popular article we ever had in the review & I think has been extremely useful to us. Except Roebuck, Grote, & Senior, I have met with nobody here, of any account, who disliked it: & those three dislike everything, the *style* of which is not humdrum: for instance, Grote thinks the style of Henry Taylor's book[8] affected, & Senior thinks it execrable. Of course I do not mean that the same is the case with Mr Austin or with Lewis; I know the contrary; but I think, generally speaking, those who have disliked the article Mirabeau are those who cannot endure *any peculiarities* of style. On the other hand we have never had any article which has been so much admired by so many people. I do not think with you that Carlyle's usual peculiarities are exceeded in it, I think it falls greatly short of the average degree of them.

I have consulted Lord Langdale about the epitaph[9]—he thought mine a good one if there was to be any but on the whole preferred to have none—saying "I incline to think that a monumental inscription should contain no more than is required for the identification of the man. If the name does not live in history, we see what monumental inscriptions come to—if the name does live, as your father's will, the inscription however short which identifies it, excites the interest & awakens the recollections which are desired." This I think is an instance of his usual good sense & I have at length determined to abide by it. I do not however think that it is a fault in an epitaph to be pretentious (if I may coin such a word), provided it does not pretend to more than is thought just by friends & admirers. People expect that an epitaph shall contain what a man's admirers think of him—not what is thought by all the world.

The radicals as you will have seen have been unusual[ly] active, & Roebuck & Charles Buller are now in ver[y] high reputation everywhere—those two in particular, & th[e] party in general.[10] It is all owing to Molesworth, & to what he wrote & did during the three months previous to the opening of parliament. You say he is too fond of going to dinners—it may seem so at a distance, but to us who are here it is plain that he did not

7. "Memoirs of Mirabeau," *LWR*, XXVI (Jan., 1837), 382–439. Mrs. Austin had written: "Mr Lewis & my husband are clamorous against poor Carlyle's article & say you will ruin the review if you admit any more. I am afraid this is a very general opinion, though I grieve it should be so. I am anxious to see his book [*The French Revolution*] and yet I dread to see it. The article is certainly one of his most extravagant as to style."

8. *The Statesman* (London, 1836), reviewed by Grote (and in part by JSM) in the *LWR*, XXVII (April, 1837), 1–32.

9. For James Mill. See Letter 189. Mrs. Austin had written with reference to the proposed epitaph: "What does Lord Langdale say? He really knew & loved your father."

10. Brackets in this sentence indicate where page is torn.

go to one dinner too many—he went only when a demonstration *was* needed, & has produced an effect through the country which will be permanent. That, & its consequences, have altered the whole aspect of politics here, as you would feel if you could hear the things now said of radicalism & the radicals, by people not at all partial to them. I have been driving them these four years to what they have now at last done, & done most successfully.

I am quite well now except the merely local ailment in my head, & so are the boys & all the family. I have much more to say but have not time to say it.

Yours affect[y]

J. S. MILL

Henry Taylor & some other people have been arranging for Carlyle to give lectures on German literature[11] next month & with considerable prospects of success—there are about 100 tickets taken, many of them by people of note—

204. TO SARAH AUSTIN[1]

I.H.
28th April
1837

MY DEAR MÜTTERLEIN—I have written to you by Henry Reeve's[2] parcel, but I have something to say which induces me to write again.

Would Mr Austin like to be the Professor of Moral Philosophy at Glasgow? The chair is vacant, & it is worth £700 a year, but so long as old Mylne[3] lives (he is 83 years of age) it will only be worth £300. It is in the gift of the Professors, & one of them, my friend Nichol, who is an admirer of Mr Austin has written to me to ask if he would like it & to say that he could perhaps carry Mr Austin's election to the chair with such testimonials as it would be easy to get. If Mr Austin declines, he has nobody better than Bailey of Sheffield, & means to try for him.

Pray answer this as soon as you are able

YOUR SÖHNCHEN

11. This was the first of four series of public lectures Carlyle delivered annually, 1837–40. The first lecture was delivered on May 1, 1837.

* * * *

1. *Addressed*: Mrs. Austin / Malta. Franked by H. Taylor. MS in the possession of Mr. Gordon Waterfield.
2. Henry Reeve (1813–1895), man of letters, editor of the *Edinburgh Review*, 1855–95. He was a nephew of Mrs. Austin.
3. James Milne (1754–1839), who held the chair from 1797 until his death. He was succeeded by William Fleming (1791–1866).

205. TO HARRIET GROTE[1]

May, 1837

What you say of W.[2] accords with my expectations. I consider him, with his crotchettiness, and his fussiness, and his go-between inclinations, to be the evil genius of the Radical party. . . . He is "out of my books," as completely as Strutt and the rest of the pseudo-Radicals who voted for the extinction of popular government in Canada.[3]

206. TO EDWARD LYTTON BULWER[1]

I.H.
Wednesday
[May or June (?), 1837]

MY DEAR SIR

I have read your article[2] with great eagerness & delight—it is such as I expected from you & if we could have one such article in every number I should have no misgivings respecting our critical reputation.

I have hardly found a sentence in the article which has not my heartiest concurrence except perhaps some part of what you say of Shelley,[3] & *there* I am not sure that there is any difference—for all that you say to his disparagement, I allow to be true though not I think the whole truth—it seems to me that *much*, though not *most* of Shelley's poetry is full of the truest passion, & it seems to me hardly fair to put Shelley in the same *genus* as Gray when the imagery of the one however redundant & occasionally farfetched is always *true* to nature, that of the other as you say yourself drawn from books, & false—the one the exuberant outpouring of a seething fancy, the other elaborately studied & artificial.

But perhaps you think all this as well as I—if so, & only if so, would not some little addition or qualification give a truer impression?

1. Excerpt published in [Mrs. Harriet Grote], *The Philosophic Radicals of 1832* (London, 1866), p. 34. MS not located.
2. Probably Henry Warburton.
3. On March 6 Lord John Russell for the Whig ministry had presented to the House of Commons a set of ten resolutions dealing with the troubled affairs of Lower Canada and in effect declaring an intention to suspend representative government in the province. The House approved the resolutions by a large majority on March 8 despite the strenuous opposition of such Radicals as Roebuck, Hume, and Molesworth.

* * * *

1. Published in Elliot, I, 107. MS in the possession of Lady Hermione Cobbold. Collated by Dr. Eileen Curran.
2. "The Works of Thomas Gray," *LWR*, XXVII (July, 1837), 1–16.
3. *Ibid.*, pp. 14–15.

I had not time the other evening to tell you how much I am delighted with "Athens"[4]—the book is so good, that very few people will see how good.

Ever yours,

J. S. MILL

207. TO ARISTIDE GUILBERT[1]

India House
19th June 1837

MY DEAR GUILBERT

I have been so busy, such a mere mechanical drudge all the winter & spring, that I have neither had time nor energy to take pen in hand for any purpose which could possibly admit of postponement, & I was still in this condition when I received your letter of the 26th of last month. I have now, by seven months hard labour, acquired something of a respite & though I have been made rather unwell by this disagreeable, strange, irregular season, I have been able to find courage to write to you.—Do not vex yourself about any delay in your article on the Army;[2] even when we have it we may not be able to publish it immediately, for we must watch our opportunity & bring it out at the time when the public mind is turning to that class of subjects & when consequently it is most likely to be read. Of course the sooner we have it the better but I beg you by no means to put your health to any hazard for the sake of finishing it earlier—nor even to neglect any occupation which circumstances may render more pressing.

I cannot account for your not having received the Review. It has been regularly sent through M. Fillonneau, with the usual understanding that all who were on the list were to have copies. Perhaps M. Paulin can explain it. (Is he satisfied with the article on the Histoire Parlementaire?)[3] But at all events the matter shall be set right, for the review is now under a new editor; printer, publisher & everything else is changed, & it will not, I trust, be mismanaged in future. Whoever is our agent, you & all our other friends shall have written orders, on presenting which you will receive your copies.

Under the new management we have prospects of much greater pecuniary

4. *Athens, Its Rise and Fall* was published in May, 1837.

* * * *

1. *Addressed*: Monsieur / M. Aristide Guilbert / recommandé aux soins de / Monsieur Peschot / Propriétaire / 5 Rue Jadot / à Paris. *Postmarks*: E 21; 19 / JUNE / 1837 /; and Angleterre / Par Calais / 21 / JUIN / 1837. MS at King's. Printed in Morrison, p. 257, but dated June 29, 1837.
2. No such article appeared in *LWR*.
3. By Carlyle, *LWR*, XXVII (April, 1837), 233–47.

success than before—that is we may hope to pay our expenses, which we have never yet done.

The radicals, as you have seen, have been much more active this year than ever before, & have shewn, in parliament, much more talent. They are however much divided; some of them are for giving more, & others less, support to the ministry. As for me I am with the extreme party; though I would not always go so far as Roebuck, I entirely agree with those who say that the whole conduct of the Whigs tends to *amortir l'esprit public*, & that it would be a good thing for invigorati[ng][4] & consolidating the reform party if the Tories were to come in. But the country does not go with us in this & therefore it will not do for the radicals to aid in turning out the ministry; by doing so they would create so much hostility in their own party, that there would be no hope of a real united reform party with the country at its back, for many years. So we must linger on, each man doing for the present such good work as lies nearer to his hand—

ever yours my dear Guilbert

J. S. Mill.

208. TO JOHN ROBERTSON[1]

Kensington
Friday night
[June, 1837]

Dear Robertson

Pray read Clarkson's article[2] & say what you think of it. I am sure you will agree with me that it is, in its present state, totally inadmissible. I think it much worse on the whole than Atkinson's,[3] though better in some respects. I am anxious for your opinion as to whether it is possible by any omissions & alterations to make it tolerable. I am sure it will require many hours continued labour of a ready writer who knows a good deal about the subject himself. There is nothing good in the article that I can discover except an expression here & there, & the evidence he extracts from the Report.

4. Page torn.

* * * *

1. *Addressed*: J. Robertson Esq. MS at LSE. Dated by the references to the July, 1837, *LWR*.
2. Probably "The School of Design," *ibid*., pp. 116–39, signed E.C., which contained an analysis of a recent parliamentary inquiry and report on arts and manufactures.
3. Not identified.

There is the devil to pay on another score—the *new* printers have begun with page 1 instead of page 285—& if Bulwer's article is printed off, that error is so far irremediable.[4]

These said new printers are dreadfully inaccurate—so were Clowes's at times, but generally not. They will do better when they know the handwriting. Some of their blunders in my article were however very unaccountable to me.

My article I am sorry to say reads damned bad—not so the extracts, which are splendid.[5]

I have sent back one sheet, the only one I had, corrected, at nine this evening & shall call tomorrow morning for another.

I have an offer of twelve pages on the *immediately present* state of French politics, the marriage of the Duke of Orleans &c.[6] written republicanly by Thibaudeau one of the liveliest & wittiest writers now in France, & translated by Leader[7]—to be ready by Wednesday morning. I have not said yea or nay. Think of it & if you cannot come, send me word to the I.H. what you have thought.

Yours

J.S.M.

209. TO THOMAS CARLYLE[1]

India House
30th June 1837

MY DEAR CARLYLE

I send you the review. The article on your book[2] is I think producing a good effect, although the opinions which have reached me concerning the article either in print or orally are mostly unfavorable.

There has been a review of the book in Fraser,[3] evidently by Heraud. He labours a good deal to prove, that you are very like him, & therefore

4. Evidently it had been printed off, for Bulwer's "The Works of Thomas Gray" begins on page 1 of the July number.

5. JSM's review of Carlyle's *The French Revolution* (*LWR*, XXVII, 17–53) contains copious extracts.

6. No such article appeared.

7. John Temple Leader.

* * * *

1. *Addressed*: Thomas Carlyle Esq. MS at Brit. Mus. One passage published in William Foster, *The East India House* (London, 1924), p. 214. Carlyle's answer of July 18, 1837, in A. Carlyle, pp. 153–56.

2. See preceding letter, n. 5.

3. *Fraser's*, XVI (July, 1837), 85–104.

very good; but that you want something of being entirely like him, & therefore are not altogether perfect; & towards the end he prophecies for you & other writers in Fraser (apparently himself) present neglect & future undying fame. There is in Heraud a placid disregard of contemporary opinion, which would be greatness if he were not so *quite* sure of living for ever. But now he reminds one of the dying penitent's answer to his confessor who proposed to him, as a motive for patience, the example of Christ: "Ah, mon père, quand J.C. mourut le vendredi, il savait bien qu'il resusciterait le dimanche."

There are one or two good thoughts, well expressed, in the article too: but on the whole it will do the book little good: for instead of resting the justification of the unfamiliar, on familiar principles, he rests it on principles ten times more remote from common apprehension than the book itself, & has defended the book in an article ten times more unintelligible than it, with none of the beauty & not more than a tenth part of the truth.

Henry Taylor whom I met the other day has not read much of the book & has not made much of it, but he says it makes a very strong impression indeed upon some people, among whom he mentioned Frederic Elliot.[4] He says that Lockhart told him he found in every page something that offended him most exceedingly but yet he could not lay the book down. I hope Lockhart will review it himself & say so, though we thereby lose Croker.[5] Taylor did not know whether there would be a review or not. T. says that your lectures[6] have made a very favorable impression, except upon two or three people who did not attend after the first two lectures & had not sufficient common sense to see what ailed *those*.

Everybody is hurrying away to get reelected or elected. As for me I shall be here till the middle of September, though I have very little to do here at present. I have worked off my arrear of business at this office, & the work does not now come in nearly so fast as I can do it. It is the way of my work to go in that sort of manner—in fits—& I like that well enough, as it gives me intervals of leisure. I am using this interval to get on with my book —a book I have done little to since the review began, & which you will think very little worth doing—a treatise on Logic. I hope I do not overrate the value of anything I can do of that kind but it so happens that this, whatever be its value, is the only thing which I am sure I can do & do not believe can be so well done by anybody else whom I know of. In regard to all things which are not merely for the day, that seems to be the best rule for chusing one's work.—Further, I do it in order to deliver myself of various things which I have in my head on the subject. As for its being

4. Thomas Frederick Elliot.
5. John Wilson Croker. The *Quarterly* did not review the book.
6. See Letter 203, n. 11.

read, it will be so by fewer people than even yours, but it may be of use to some of those few.

Write soon & tell me how you enjoy your repose—

ever faithfully J. S. MILL.

too late for *S & M's*[7] parcel.

The Times says, your book "sometimes excites our admiration by its original eloquence & powerful thinking, sometimes offends us beyond endurance by its extravagant caprices of style & expression. The diction is sometimes almost monstrous."[8]

209A. TO HENRY MILL (*see* page 743)

210. TO LEIGH HUNT[1]

India House
7th July 1837

MY DEAR SIR

I fear you have not had your copy of the Review. We have adopted the plan of not sending copies to our contributors but letting them send for them—on the ground that it is less inconvenience to each of them to send to one place, than to us to send to many. But as the reason of the practice does not apply to contributors living so far off as you do, neither is it fit that the practice should, & I will therefore take upon myself individually to see you supplied.

I hope we shall have something from you in our next number[2]—does anything occur to you? & most sincerely do I now wish that you had written an article for us on Lamb, instead of Bulwer,[3] who has done it very little to my liking.

Believe me

Ever yours truly[4]

I wish all success to the old Repository in your hands.[5]

7. Simpkin and Marshall, Booksellers.

8. Not located. It is not from the long review (by W. M. Thackeray) in *The Times*, Aug. 3, 1837, p. 6.

This postscript is written on the outside, diagonally, above the address.

* * * *

1. MS at Brit. Mus.

2. It was to be over a year before another of Hunt's was to appear in the *LWR*. See Letter 240, n. 2.

3. "Letters of Charles Lamb," *LWR*, XXVII (July, 1837), 229–43.

4. The signature has been cut out.

5. Hunt had just taken over from R. H. Horne the proprietorship of the *Monthly Repository*. See Mineka, *The Dissidence of Dissent*, pp. 382–93.

211. TO JOHN ROBERTSON[1]

July 12, IH [India House], 1837.

DEAR ROBERTSON,

[. . .] I have had a letter from Tocqueville which shows that we can scarcely have his book[2] before our April number, and one from Nisard, alluding to a previous letter, which I never received, coming into our plans, and having no doubt of his being in time for this number. I send you a letter to him.

I do not think I can write anything worth having about Whewell[3] this time. Blackie's[4] I do not think will do, for an article on Menzel[5] is an article on Goethe, of whom Menzel is the great literary enemy. Moore,[6] if favorable, is not worth doing; if unfavorable, Peacock should do it, and it should not be in the same number as Southey[7] [. . . .]

If I had known you meant to write to Harriet Martineau, I should have wished for a consultation first, as the manner of doing it is of considerable interest to me personally. She and I are not upon terms, and I know her too well to make it likely that we ever shall be. I am therefore desirous, 1st, that she should not be identified with the Review more than its interest requires; 2d, that all communications with her should take place through another medium than mine; 3d, that nevertheless she should not think, as she is exactly the person to think, that her connection with the Review is in spite of me,—that I would prevent it if I could, but am unable.

If I knew exactly how you have written to her, I should know how to comport myself with a view to making the other impression. There is a letter for you from her at Hooper's:[8] have you left any instructions with Hooper about forwarding letters? I have read her book,[9] and like it less than I expected. I like all the feeling of it, but not the thought; but I should

1. Published by Towers, pp. 58–59. MS not located. Mrs. Towers says that it was addressed to Robertson at Boulogne, France, where he was vacationing. The bracketed ellipses indicate Mrs. Towers' deletions.

2. Tocqueville in his letter of June 24, 1837 (Mayer, p. 324), had expressed his hope that the second part of *Démocratie en Amérique* might be published by the spring of 1838; it did not appear, however, until 1840.

3. William Whewell (1794–1866), later Master of Trinity College, Cambridge, published his *History of the Inductive Sciences* this year.

4. John Stuart Blackie (1809–1895), Scottish professor and man of letters, who had published a verse translation of *Faust* in 1834.

5. Wolfgang Menzel (1798–1873), poet, critic, and historian, had published his *Die deutsche Literatur* in 1836.

6. Tom Moore.

7. No article on either Moore or Southey appeared in *LWR*.

8. Henry Hooper, bookseller, had recently become publisher of *LWR*.

9. Presumably her *Society in America*, published in May, 1837.

think an article by her on Miss Sedgwick's writings,[10] such as you suggest, would be interesting and useful to us.

Besides the letter to Nisard I send you one to Guilbert; if he is not in town he is at Saint-Germain, and you should go to him there. Those will be the most useful letters to you. Both Guilbert and Nisard speak English well; Guilbert excellently, and Nisard is married to an Englishwoman. I do not know anybody else who is likely to be in town except the d'Eichthals: Adolphe is too busy to be of any use to you, and Gustave you can always, if you like, call upon and use my name; he is the ex-St. Simonian author of a book on Greece[11] (and the East generally) which he wants reviewed, but which will scarcely do for *us*[. . . .] I advanced £25 to Bisset[12] on my own account, not for the Review. I do not wish to have anything more to do with the Review in that capacity[. . . .]

I saw Dickens yesterday; he reminds me of Carlyle's picture of Camille Desmoulins,[13] and his "face of dingy blackguardism irradiated with genius." Such a phenomenon does not often appear in a lady's drawing-room.

Yours ever,

J. S. MILL.

212. TO JOHN ROBERTSON[1]

July 28, 1837.

[. . . .][2] Guilbert's offer, however, promises fair, but I have never found that a Frenchman's promise to do anything punctually could be depended upon. They promise everything and do nothing. They are not men of business. Guilbert is better, being half an Englishman. Do you, however, decide.

The sheets of Mignet[3] will be a catch. Those of Hugo not, because he is exhausted and effete. Châles[4] is a humbug, whom I showed up in a letter

10. Miss Martineau's first contribution to *LWR*, "Miss Sedgwick's Works," appeared in the Oct., 1837, number, XXVIII, 42–65. Catherine Maria Sedgwick (1789–1867) was a popular American novelist.

11. *Les Deux Mondes* (Leipzig, 1837).

12. Andrew Bisset, a contributor to the *Review*.

13. In Bk. IV, chap. IV of *The French Revolution*. Dickens at this point was at the height of his early fame because of the extraordinary popularity of his nearly completed *Pickwick Papers*.

* * * *

1. Published by Towers, p. 59. MS not located.

2. Mrs. Towers summarizes the first part of the letter as saying that Guilbert has been vexed to have missed seeing Robertson, who has by this time left Paris.

3. F. A. M. Mignet (1796–1884), historian, associated with *Le National*. The work referred to cannot be identified.

4. Philarète E. Chasles (1798–1873), journalist, librarian, and later professor at the Collège de France.

intended for the National, but published in the Monthly Repository,[5] and the bare idea of his reviewing George Sand is enough to make one split. I would not give a farthing for the opinion of Galebert,[6] or anybody connected with his review, about writers, for they are mere milksops themselves; and Hugo's opinions, like most French literary men's opinions of one another, are affairs of coterie and puffery. *I* thought your Statistical Society article was for the January.[7] I of course defer to you about all questions of timing. But I differ from you about geology not being called for. I think the zoölogical speculations connected with geology are quite in season just now, and Nichol, I am sure, would do it with originality and well, judging from his articles for us, both of which were written when ill or in a hurry.[8] You may think him not a popular writer, but you will think quite differently when you read his Architecture of the Heavens.[9]

The falling off to be guarded against in substantial merit and originality does not arise from our having lost any of our writers, but in our *not using them.* I do not understand the false position you speak of, nor do I know what friends of ours we have attacked. Written, as you see, in a great hurry, and just as one chatters in walking *quick* from the India House to Hooper's.

Ever truly,

J. S. MILL.

213. TO JOHN ROBERTSON[1]

India House, Saturday,
August 6, 1837.

DEAR ROBERTSON,

I entirely approve your intention of remaining at Boulogne as long as possible, and I hope you will remain as long as what requires to be done here can be done by me, of which you are the most proper judge.

None of the three articles you expect are at Hooper's, nor any other article except one on Poland by a Pole,[2] which I have not looked at. There

5. "Letter from an Englishman to a Frenchman, on a Recent Apology in 'The Journal Des Débats,' for the Faults of the English National Character," *MR*, VIII (June, 1834), 385–95.

6. Probably Léon Galibert, editor of the *Révue britannique*.

7. "Transactions of the Statistical Society of London," signed R., did not appear in the *LWR* until April, 1838 (XXIX, 45–72).

8. In the numbers for April, 1835, and July, 1836.

9. *Views of the Architecture of the Heavens* (Edinburgh, 1837).

* * * *

1. Published by Towers, p. 60. MS not located.

2. No such article appeared in *LWR*.

are a few books, chiefly Spencer's Circassia[3] (from Colburn) and a translation of the King of Bavaria's Poems.[4] Hooper says he was mistaken about 1025 copies having been sold; it was only 925. That is only 25 since you went away. . . . Nichol says his article will be here next week. You do not know Nichol. He is one of the three or four persons living for whom I would answer that whatever they think and say they can do they *can.* He says: "I expect that the article will direct scientific attention to some few moot points in a mode not quite so limited as that of existing discussion regarding them. At all events, I shall show general readers at what geology has arrived." I will write to him immediately about connecting it with the geological transactions.[5]

As for me, I am so immersed in Logic and am getting on so triumphantly with it that I loathe the idea of leaving off to write articles. I do not think you are right about the elections. The Tories, where they have gained, have gained impartially from the Whigs and Radicals, and so where they have lost. The only exceptions are Middlesex and the City; in both of which many Tories chose to split with Whigs for the express purpose of turning out Hume and Grote.[6] Whenever the Tories choose to do this, of course the Radical candidates will, in the present state of parties, be in great danger. The Radicals *seem* to have lost most only because they have lost some of their most leading men, but those will come in again for some other place very soon; and a great number of the new members are very decided Radicals, though generally not intemperate ones. Neither are the Tories who are turned out the *extreme* Tories. They almost all belong to the hack official jobbing adventurer Tories, who are seldom ultras, as Twiss,[7] Bonham,[8] Ross,[9] and such like. On the whole, this election will so increase the already great difficulties of the Whigs that they must either propose the ballot and dissolve on it, or contrive to divide the Tory party, and make a compromise with one section of it. They stand much nearer to both goals than they ever did before, and have, I think, got clean up to the parting of the two roads. Either would be a decided improvement on the present aspect of affairs. For the present politics are wonderfully dull; and for the first time these ten years I have no wish to be in Parliament. If the offer

3. Edmund Spencer, *Travels in Circassia, Krim Tartary, etc.* (2 vols., London, 1837).

4. *A Selection from the Poems of Louis the First, King of Bavaria, Imitated in English Verse, by G. Everill* (London, 1837).

5. See Letter 228.

6. Joseph Hume was defeated for Middlesex, but was almost immediately returned for Kilkenny; George Grote barely escaped defeat for the City of London.

7. Horace Twiss (1787–1849), wit and politician, vehement opponent of reform, defeated for Nottingham.

8. Francis R. Bonham, defeated for Harwich.

9. Charles Ross (1799–1860), defeated for Northampton.

you speak of is made me, which I shall not think at all probable until it is done, I shall not accept it unless I find by inquiry here that I can hold it with my situation in this house. For an object of importance I should not mind sacrificing my own pleasures and comforts, and obliging all connected with me to alter their style of living and go (as the vulgar phrase is) down in the world; but I certainly would not do it in order to exchange the speculative pursuits which I like, and in which I can do great things, for the position of a Radical member of this coming Parliament.

Ever yours faithfully,

J. S. MILL.

I can do nothing about Hanover[10] without you. Châles *is* the man I mean.[11] He writes in the Journal des Débats and is a humbug; his reputation is, however, high.

214. TO THOMAS CARLYLE[1]

India House
8th August 1837

MY DEAR CARLYLE

The immediate object of my writing to you is to ask you whether you can manage to give me (if it be still in existence) a letter which I wrote to you in 1833[2] after my return from Paris, in which I said a great deal about Carrel. I have to write something about him for the review,[3] & it would be of great service to me were I able to refer back to what I wrote in the freshness of my impressions.

It is a great bore to me having to write anything just now, except my book,[4] which I am getting on with, fast & satisfactorily. But it cannot be helped.

The book I think will be a good book; which is more than I would venture to say of any other book which I could attempt to write just now. One good thing that it will do is, it will let you & me see whether we really differ, & if so, how far, without the fruitless attempt to become intelligible

10. Presumably the article, "History of Hanover," signed S.R.T., *LWR*, XXVIII (Oct., 1837), 198–216.

11. See preceding letter, n. 4.

* * * *

1. *Addressed*: Thomas Carlyle Esq. / Scotsbrig / Ecclefechan / N.B. *Postmark*: LS / 8 AU 8. MS at Pierpont Morgan Library, New York. Carlyle's reply of Aug. 10, 1837, is in A. Carlyle, pp. 157–59.

2. Letter 91.

3. "Armand Carrel," *LWR*, XXVIII (Oct., 1837), 66–111.

4. On logic.

to each other by spoken words on a subject so complicated & on which so many of the premisses have to be settled beforehand. Certainly we should, at present, differ much in our language, but I question whether our opinions are so widely apart as they may seem. You call Logic the art of telling others what you believe. I call it, the art, not certainly of knowing things, but of knowing whether you know them or not: not of finding out the truth, but of deciding whether it is the truth that you have found out. Of course I do not think that Logic suffices for this without any thing else. I believe in spectacles, but I think eyes necessary too. Neither do I mean by Logic, the Aristotelian way solely, or even mainly; nay, *that* I *do* consider to be only a way of stating a process of thought, not itself a process of thought at all. I do not think that I can explain myself any farther in fewer words than my book will consist of. Thanks for your promise of reading it, which I did not more than half expect, & did not at all think myself entitled to claim.

I suppose you saw the three columns of the Times[5] on your three volumes. Mr Sterling I suppose wrote it, & no doubt sent it to you—at least that is the belief I try to entertain whenever my conscience twits me that *I* did not. In case you have not seen it, I can give you in few words a summary of its contents: That the stile is *nearly* the worst possible, everything else nearly the best possible. The writer does not seem to be aware that this is something very like a contradiction in terms. But it is well meant, & cannot but give you many readers & Fraser some buyers who would not otherwise have been had.—However I fully sympathize in your wish to forget the book entirely—I promise you I shall forget mine, soon enough after it is published—nay probably before.

I am very glad you are resting yourself by doing nothing. I am resting myself by doing *something*—something which is not mere every day business, but allows me & requires me to exert my best (or some of my best) faculties. In truth I have not, for years before, had a mind free from occupation with pettinesses. That is the only true meaning of leisure—*choice* of work. It is not good for everybody, nor for anybody at all times: for me, just at present, it is good, & I am consequently happier than I have ever been since I had it last. I get a great deal into the country too, among trees & green fields, though with a very small share of rivulets & altogether without the Solway tide waves you speak of.

On the whole things go well with me, not the less so because I am as you say of yourself "sadder" than I have ever been—

Ever affectionately J. S. MILL

5. Of Aug. 3. JSM was mistaken as to Edward Sterling's authorship of the review; it was by W. M. Thackeray.

215. TO GUSTAVE D'EICHTHAL[1]

24 août 1837

Soyez persuadé mon cher ami que si je ne vous ai pas écrit c'était seulement par excès d'occupations: j'ai sur les mains l'India house, la revue, et un traité de Logique que j'avais commencé il y a longtemps, que j'ai repris dernièrement et qui s'avance rapidement vers sa fin. Par suite de cette préoccupation j'ai ajourné de jour en jour la réponse à vos lettres. Je les ai reçues, ainsi que trois exemplaires des Deux Mondes,[2] qui me sont parvenus successivement à de très courts intervalles. J'ai placé un exemplaire à la revue d'Edinbourg, un autre au British & Foreign Review. Pour en parler dans notre revue j'attends une occasion quelconque qui permette de la rattacher à quelque intérêt du moment: règle essentielle à observer chez nous, où les revues en général ne font pas bien leurs affaires et surtout essentielle pour nous, qui l'avons trop negligée et qui sommes forcés à présent de nous populariser autant que possible.

Avez vous reçu la dernière livraison de la revue? Sinon, demandez-en un exemplaire à M. Aristide Guilbert, Rue du Clos-Georgeot, No. 4. Si vous l'avez reçu vous aurez vu que Carlyle vient de publier un ouvrage fort remarquable sur la révolution française. Il se souvient toujours de vous avec plaisir. Il demeure 5 Cheyne Row Chelsea; Mme Carlyle y est à présent, son mari est pour le moment en Ecosse.

Je voudrais bien avoir le temps de vous écrire sur les questions générales, et encore plus de causer avec vous. Mais cela ne se peut pas pour le moment. Je dirai seulement que depuis bien des années je suis au même point que vous sur le *repos*: comme le sont en général tous ceux qui ont été formés à l'école poétique de Wordsworth et de Shelley. Mais j'avais ajourné cela comme n'étant pas de notre temps, et je ne sais pas si le commerce avec l'Orient nous y amenera—il me semble que nous n'y arriverons que par les changements sociaux qui peuvent progressivement arriver chez nous. Il y a des bornes très étroites à ce qu'un peuple ou même à ce qu'une personne peut apprendre des autres: Si nous pourrions apprendre cela en Orient, nous la pourrions en Italie—*le dolce far niente* n'est autre que le *Kilf*.[3] Je dis cela sans déroger à la valeur de votre ouvrage qui me semble un morceau de haute philosophie sociale, mais (chez nous au moins) en liant ces idées à la question d'Orient vous devez nécessairement nuire à leur succès.

1. MS at Arsenal. Letter bears no salutation or address.
2. See Letter 197, n. 2.
3. *Sic.* Professor Georg Iggers has pointed out that this is probably intended for *kief* (modern form *keyif*), a Turkish word defined by D'Eichthal as "cette heureuse disposition à jouer de ce qu'il y a de bon dans toutes les situations où l'on se trouve, sans trop s'inquiéter de ce qu'elles ont de mauvais" (*Les Deux Mondes*, p. 240).

Bien des amitiés à Adolphe—quand vous aurez un chemin de fer au Havre ou à Dieppe, et nous à Brighton, je viendrai quelquefois passer le dimanche avec vous—

J. S. MILL

216. TO ARISTIDE GUILBERT[1]

India House
29th August
1837

MY DEAR GUILBERT

It will be quite impossible to insert M. de Cormenin's article[2] in the next number, because we shall have an article on Carrel,[3] which will fill all the space we can devote to French politics. In the January number there will be room for it, & if M. de Cormenin will trust me with it I should like much to read it. You are aware how highly I think of M. de Cormenin as a thinker & as a political writer for France—but to say the truth I do not think his mode of treating his subject at all suitable to England. However since the article is already written, there is no occasion to judge upon presumptions. Ever yours my dear Guilbert—in great haste

J. S. MILL

Without hurrying you, we should like to have your article on the French army soon.[4]

217. TO JOHN ROBERTSON[1]

Leamington
Friday evening
[Sept. (?), 1837]

DEAR ROBERTSON

I agree with you in thinking the Sedgwick[2] quite unobjectionable, though there is less in it than I expected, & the extracts given do not inspire me with

1. *Addressed*: Monsieur / Aristide Guilbert / Rue de Clos Georgeot / à Paris. *Postmarks*: 29 / AUG / 1837 and 31 / AOUT / 1837. MS in the possession of Dr. James M. Osborn, Yale University.

2. Unidentified; no article by De Cormenin appears to have been published during JSM's editorship.

3. See Letter 214, n. 3.

4. See Letter 207, n. 2.

* * * *

1. Published, with omissions, by Towers, p. 61. MS at King's.

2. See Letter 211, n. 10.

any admiration for the books praised. I think your Theodore Hook[3] a much better article, though I have cancelled one or two portions of sentences positively (for various reasons too long to be mentioned here) & proposed to you to cancel or alter one or two more. There are one or two ideas which I think questionable, but with those I have not meddled, nor do I propose to do so. In reading the article this time it has struck me that there is a fault in some of your best sentences, which there used to be very often in mine, & perhaps is still, that of crowding too much into them, & in doing that, falling into a Latinism of construction, which in our non-inflected language, leaves it doubtful what substantives some of your adjectives are intended for. In *this* article there is also I think, (but not so often as I should have expected in an article written as you said this was, *invitâ Minervâ*) the fault of using three or four words which do not exactly fit, instead of one which does. In the few instances where this fault appeared to me to amount to a serious one I have tried to correct it, & I hope you will find, not at the sacrifice of any portion of your meaning. In other respects I like the article. The subject is I think viewed in the right light, & disposed of by making a few points & those the important ones, & treating them in a decided manner.

The Italian article[4] came to me I suppose in a proof from which corrections had already been made, but as I have made many more it will require to be carefully gone over. The translation, for instance, of the verses on Napoleon, required a great deal of correction. I doubt very much the expediency of the deviation from the old plan of keeping the same heading throughout a whole article: I think in our last number the headings puzzled & displeased people, & though the modification you now propose is not so objectionable, I think it is still rather so & I do not see any sufficient advantage to be gained by it—but if you wish decidedly to try the experiment I do not object, provided you will follow the old plan as to my own particular articles, for I don't like people not to see at once what they are about.

I hope exceedingly that you will be able to finish your other article[5] as it was begun, & for this number. If you cannot, it must lie over to the next, for the subject is not pressing & it is much better to have it later in time than inferior in quality in which case it will not do us the good we expect from it. I shall be much disappointed however if we are obliged to adopt either alternative & I will hope the contrary. Of course you have carte

3. "Works of Theodore Hook," *LWR*, XXVIII (Oct., 1837), 169–98. Theodore Edward Hook (1788–1841), novelist, wit, founder in 1820 of the *John Bull* newspaper, and editor of the *New Monthly Magazine*, 1836–41.

4. [Angelo Usiglio], "Italian Literature since 1830," *LWR*, XXVIII (Oct., 1837), 132–68.

5. Presumably "Congregational Dissenters," *ibid.*, pp. 217–60.

blanche about fill-up matter, as long as I see it at some stage or other. I would not be particular about going to the extent of our 16 sheets when we have a good number, & plenty of bills to make it look thick.

As to the order of the articles, I think Usiglio & Carrel[6] should not immediately follow one another, therefore if "Position of Parties"[7] goes first, Usiglio third, Carrel fifth, the only question is if Sedgwick should be second & Hook fourth, or the reverse. I should have been glad if Wheatstone[8] could have gone in either place & Sedgwick or Hook been left to follow Carrel: but I suppose that was not to be. You will make it all right I have no doubt & I sh[d] have said nothing about it if you had not asked me.

I have seen all there is to see at Leamington, & there being nothing that interests me in this dull part of England I am going to shift my quarters, & in doing so shall pass through town, of which opportunity I shall make all the use I can for the review. I expect to be at Kensington on Monday evening & will call at Hooper's some time in Tuesday forenoon where if I do not find you I hope I shall find a packet from you, & directions for finding you somewhere else.

I have written to Napier,[9] most likely his terms are per *article* & may not be higher than ours when the article is long which I hope this will be. You will see that I have attended to your suggestions about the political article & have altered, besides, some passages which were rather declamatory. Pray attend carefully to the revise—I tremble for it.

As we shall so soon meet I leave off—ever yours

J.S.M.

218. TO JOHN ROBERTSON[1]

Ross, 28 September, 1837

DEAR ROBERTSON,

I have read Harriet Martineau's article[2] with the greatest desire to do it justice, and the result is more unfavorable to it than ever before. I always thought the notion it presupposes of the Queen's position an incorrect one,

6. JSM's "Armand Carrel," *ibid.*, pp. 66–111.
7. JSM's "Parties and the Ministry," *ibid.*, pp. 1–26.
8. [Charles Wheatstone], "Willis on Reed Organ Sounds," *ibid.*, pp. 27–41. Charles (later Sir Charles) Wheatstone (1802–1875), scientist and inventor.
9. Sir William F. P. Napier contributed an article to the next number: "The Duke of Wellington," *LWR*, XXVIII (Jan., 1838), 367–436.

* * * *

1. Published by Towers, pp. 62–63. MS not located.
2. An article on the new Queen, which never appeared in *LWR*. Mrs. Towers prints (p. 62) part of a letter of Miss Martineau's, dated Aug. 26, 1837: "Here is my say about the Queen. It will appear to you very obvious, I fear, and perhaps too sermon-like; but indeed I think this strain of meditation much wanted to be uttered."

and I now think that even if that notion were correct she does not speak to the Queen in the right tone or give her the right advice. It seems to me that if we occupy ourselves with the Queen at all, we ought to make her believe that people feel interested about her just at present from mere curiosity, and not because they really believe she can do much; and that unless she has the qualities of Elizabeth she will be nothing, but that she should aspire to have these qualities, and that if she has she may be as great a ruler as Elizabeth.

Instead of that, H.M. says to her that Elizabeth in these days could do comparatively little for us, and that she must not aim at being like her; and why? Because she has many wills besides her own to consult—as if Elizabeth had not!—and a giant democracy to struggle with; yes, *to struggle with*! (is that what we should teach her?) as if Elizabeth had not Catholicism and Puritanism, and Philip and Catherine di Medici and Mary! I think this paper altogether contrary to the character which we are trying to give to the Review, namely, a character of dignity, and besides of *practicalness*. It is most completely unpractical; it is what a woman's view of practical affairs is supposed to be, and what the view of a person ignorant of life always is. She always treats the Queen like a young person. Now the Queen cannot be young, except in ignorance of the world, and kings and queens are that even at sixty. She always treats the Queen as *artless*. She cannot be artless, as a person full of anxieties, or who will be so, about doing her duty to her subjects. I am convinced she is just a lively, spirited young lady, thinking only of enjoying herself, and who never is nor ever will be conscious of any difficulties or responsibilities,—no more than Marie Antoinette, who was a much cleverer woman and had much more *will* and *character* than she is ever likely to have. She is conscious, I dare say, of good intentions, as every other young lady is; she is not conscious of wishing any harm to any one, unless they have offended her, nor of intending to break any one article of the Decalogue. That is the nature of the well-meanings of a person like her, and if we wish to give her any higher feelings or notions about her duties, we cannot go a worse way to work than H.M. does. If she reads us, she will not recognise any one of her own feelings in what the article says, and therefore will not mind us at all; besides, the article is a ready-made apology to her for being and for doing nothing.

This is a very small part indeed of what this last reading of the article has made me think to its disadvantage. It seems to me childish, and if we take away the prettiness and masculine structure of some of the sentences it is what people may forgive and like well enough in a woman, but not in a parcel of men. There is continual *trying hard* for philosophy in the article, and not an opinion or observation that you may not drive a coach and six through. I could not have believed how much this was the case till I examined it minutely, for I was imposed upon at first by the writing, which is in the style of a better kind of thought, and yet just the writing one would expect from Miss Mitford,[3] or any other woman who has written tragedies, and learnt to put good woman's feelings into men's words, and to make small things look like great ones. It is not like a person who knows what she is writing about, or who knows life in the world or the feelings produced by particular circumstances, and it will give us an air of *attempting* and not *attaining*, the sort of ignorance of courts which most excites the ridicule of those who know them, especially when exhibited in sententious, goody, small moralizing.

Altogether I cannot reconcile myself to its insertion in any shape, nor can I think of any note to prefix to it which would not in my view have a still worse effect, if possible, than inserting it just as it is, though even Dilke,[4] you see, thinks we ought to separate ourselves from it to a certain extent; and Dilke's opinion in favor of inserting it may be influenced by a wish to do her a good turn which might serve *his* turn in many ways, and this without any impeachment of his sincerity. I would not tell H.M. all I think of the article, but I would tell her what is true,—that I think it all very well from a woman to a woman, but not such as should be addressed by a body of men who aim at having authority *to* a woman and the public *of* that woman. We want *now* to give a *character* to the Review, as Carrel gave one to the National; and I am sure, if you attempt to scheme out to yourself the sort of article which with that view it would suit *us* to write to and of the Queen, you would arrive at an idea of one which this would not at all answer to. I dare not violate my instinct of suitableness, which we must the more strive to keep up the more we are exposed to swerve from it by our attempts to make the Review acceptable to the public. If you are not convinced by my reasons, consider it as a caprice which I cannot help. I hope you do not consider my putting a negative upon any article on such grounds as inconsistent with our conventions. . . .[5] I will write to you from Chepstow to tell you where next to write to me. I want to hear how you are getting on, and whether your foot is recovered.

Ever yours,

J. S. MILL.

I will try to send you my article[6] from Chepstow further improved.

3. Mary Russell Mitford (1787–1855), novelist and dramatist.
4. Charles Wentworth Dilke (1789–1864), editor of the *Athenæum*, 1830–46.
5. The omission is Mrs. Towers'.
6. Probably his political article for the Oct. number; see preceding letter, n. 7. The Oct. number was not published until Oct. 23.

219. TO JOHN ROBERTSON[1]

Brecon
Thursday
[Oct. 5, 1837]

DEAR ROBERTSON—

I sent off my article from Chepstow yesterday by the Pembroke & Milford Haven mail—& I hope it arrived safe. I got your letter the same morning. I detest that vile Queen thing[2] more than ever for being the cause of the first real difference we have ever had about the review. But I cannot see the force of what you say about our being committed. I am not committed, nor are you in any way which you cannot get rid of by throwing all upon me. You cannot be serious in what you say about Dilke: asking his opinion was not undertaking to be bound by it, & we never either of us looked upon it in that light: you will remember I am sure, that if we had, I should not have consented to his being asked, for I *said* over & over that I did not consider his opinion decisive, & that I expected him to take the same view with you. We never thought of taking his opinion but in conjunction with others. As for H.M. you have only to say to her that it is necessary for the review to *ménager* me, & that I have seen the article & decidedly object to it: you may say if it will assist you, that you tried to overcome my objection & thought you had succeeded, but were mistaken. This will relieve you entirely, at the price only of admitting yourself to be under the restraint of considerations of expediency from which no editor is or can be free. As for me, I am willing, as in this case I am bound, to take entirely upon myself the resentment of a very spiteful person, rather than admit the article. The truth is, I feel that I never can have stronger objections to any article, nor justified to myself by stronger reasons, & that to let them be overruled would be to give up all power whatever over the review, for a power which does not amount even to the right of excluding, in an extreme case, is no power at all. You completely misunderstood my meaning in what passed between us that evening: I never considered anything as settled, & I expressly said, two or three times, that I would take time to consider. I did think, towards the end of the evening, that you were assuming rather too confidently, that the compromise we proposed would be adopted, & I blame myself exceedingly that I led you into mistake by a foolish repugnance to put myself on the defensive, & weigh my words

1. *Addressed*: John Robertson Esq / 4 Grove Place / Brompton / London. *Postmarks*: TP / Rate 2^{d}; 10 FN 10 / OC 6 / 1837; and BRECON. Published with omissions by Towers, pp. 64–65. MS at King's.

2. See preceding letter.

when I was discussing confidentially with you. Until I had made up my mind to say *no* decidedly, it was unpleasant to be constantly pulling up & drawing in. We should never have been in this embarrassment if I had not been so extremely averse to bring a matter about which you had so strong an opinion, to a direct "collision" as they say in Parliament; one house throwing out a bill which the other has passed. I caught eagerly at every straw which offered in the shape of a compromise, & the one you suggested, of sending the article forth as H.M.'s, & not as our own, seemed to me the last chance of our settling the matter "without a division." But on reading the thing again I felt my objections to it so much strengthened, & my idea of its counterbalancing good qualities so much lowered, that nothing could reconcile me to its being inserted with any note which did not express *dissent* from it, with the reasons—& you must see how ridiculous that would make us. Putting it in an obscure place only adds a fresh ridicule to the rest—no place but a conspicuous one suits the subject—the first place or the last. I did not think that anything relating to the review could have given me the worry & annoyance this has, from first to last. It was in an evil hour we asked her to write. But it was *she* who proposed the subject, *I* only said it promised the best of several which she proposed. If it is but left out of this number, we will leave the question open for next number if you like. If we cannot settle it so I must come to town though that will be a great bore to me.

I wrote to you on Tuesday from Chepstow telling you that Aberystwith is the place to send to me. I shall wait there or thereabouts till I receive your answer to this letter

Ever yours

J.S.M.

220. TO JOHN ROBERTSON[1]

Farnborough
Sunday
[Oct. 29(?), 1837]

DEAR ROBERTSON

I do not think Garnier has any claim to be paid for the article on the Tyrol, unless we use it, which will depend upon your view of its suitable-

1. *Addressed*: John Robertson Esq. / care of Mr Hooper bookseller / 13 Pall Mall

ness to us.[2] I see no objection whatever, but no immediate demand. The article was not written in any way at our suggestion, but was brought to me ready written—I took it only for consideration, & gave him no reason direct or indirect to believe that it was accepted, unless our keeping it so long without returning it can be so considered—which it cannot, as it would have been returned to him & a positive answer given to him at any time if he had expressed any wish to that effect. So unless you think it will suit us he has I conceive no claim on the review—but if he thinks he has, & can make out any shadow of a case, pay him for it & charge it to me—& at any rate if he is going away for any length of time or for good, & you think he is in need of money, I shall be glad if you can find any pretext to make him take any sum he may require not exceeding £25 or £30, on my private account, though nominally it may be from the review.

As to the H.M. matter[3] I have no objection to discussing it in any way you think best, though if your feelings did not appear to be so much involved in it I should say the way you propose was making very much of a small matter. At all events I can say little about it until I know how & why you consider your honour implicated or your self respect endangered. To me these seem words greatly disproportioned to the occasion which appears to me a very simple one—a mere question of fact—Did I, or did I not, give you sufficient reason to think that I had waived my objection to the insertion of the article? I say I did not—you, I suppose, say I did—if so we have only for the future to take care to understand one another better, & to settle every thing finally & clearly between us two before we implicate ourselves with contributors—a caution which it would have been well if I had observed with Bisset as well as you with H.M. Unless indeed you understood our conventions to be such that while they lasted I could not exercise any veto. [But][4] if you understood that, then certainly [we] quite misunderstood each other: [I] not only [did] not, but could not, so long as I was carrying on the review for another person (who looked [to] me & not to you as responsible for its maintaining a certain character & a certain general spirit) give up all control over the contents. But it is of no use saying any more about it till I hear from you

Ever yours

J. S. MILL.

East. *Postmark*: [. . .] 8 / [. . .] 31 / 1837. Published in part by Towers, p. 65; there dated as of Oct. 31, but the nearest Sunday fell on Oct. 29. MS at King's.

2. No such article appeared in *LWR*.
3. See the two preceding letters.
4. Page torn. Words in brackets appear in Mrs. Towers' published version.

221. TO JOHN ROBERTSON[1]

Saturday
[Nov. 11, 1837][2]

DEAR ROBERTSON,

To my great satisfaction Carlyle consents to do at least the Scott,[3] and wishes to begin on Monday morning.

I should not like to baffle him in that, but in order to do it he wants Volume I of the Scott; so, pray, if you can buy, beg, or borrow it before that time, do. He has also a great wish to have the two books of and about Colonel Crockett,[4] and I think has a "month's mind" to write about them. So, pray, send those too, and if the Review does not find its account therein I will pay for them.

Yours in haste,

J. S. MILL.

222. TO WILLIAM TAIT[1]

India House
Saturday
[Nov. 18, 1837]

MY DEAR SIR

I write to you in greate haste just after receiving your letter—to say that before I can undertake what you propose, I must understand the circumstances better. I always fancied that a Life of Bentham by Bowring was to form part of the collected edition of his works:[2] was I mistaken? and next: This publication is in obedience to Mr Bentham's will, & by virtue of an engagement between you & his executors: how would they like my intermeddling? & on the other hand, neither do I like intermeddling

1. Published by Towers, p. 61. MS not located.

2. Mrs. Towers dates as probably of Sept., 1837, but Carlyle in a letter of Friday, Nov. 10 (in A. Carlyle, p. 162), alludes to JSM's talk with him on Nov. 9 about the review of Lockhart's *Life of Scott.*

3. Carlyle's review, "Lockhart's Life of Scott," appeared in the Jan., 1838, *LWR*, XXVII, 293–345.

4. David Crockett (1786–1836), American frontiersman. One of the books must have been *A Narrative of the Life of David Crockett, Written by Himself* (London, 1834), which was written to correct erroneous impressions created by an unknown writer's *Sketches and Eccentricities of Colonel David Crockett* (London, 1834).

* * * *

1. *Addressed*: William Tait Esq. / Bookseller / Edinburgh. *Postmarks*: LS / 18N018 / 1837; and NOV / C20F / 1837. MS at LSE.

2. John Bowring's *Memoirs of Jeremy Bentham* was eventually published in 1843 in vols. X and XI of *The Works of Jeremy Bentham* (Edinburgh and London, 1838–43).

with them, nor being in any way mixed up with their proceedings as I like to avoid getting into a hornet's nest.

Believe me
Yours ever

J. S. MILL

223. TO WILLIAM TAIT[1]

India House
Monday
[Nov. 20, 1837]

MY DEAR SIR

I wrote you a short & hurried note on Saturday, immediately after receiving your letter, in which I stated some difficulties about undertaking what you proposed to me. I have since considered the subject more fully & the result is that even independently of those difficulties, I am obliged to decline your proposition. I have several reasons for this, among which I will only mention, that the proper place for me to speak about Mr Bentham is the Review; that I intend, & have long intended, to write a very elaborate article, speaking my whole mind about him, on the occasion of the appearance of your edition of his works; & that I desire to reserve for that opportunity all I have to say.[2]

Regretting my inability to oblige you, believe me

Yours ever truly

J. S. MILL

224. TO LEIGH HUNT[1]

India House
Monday
[Nov. 20, 1837]

MY DEAR SIR

I observed in a recent number of the M.R.[2] a complaint made by you, in your usual gentle & kindly manner, of some reviewer who had lately

1. *Addressed*: William Tait Esq / Bookseller / Edinburgh. *Postmarks*: LS/21N021/ . . . / and NOV / 23 / 1837. MS at LSE.

2. This eventuated in his article "The Works of Jeremy Bentham," *LWR*, XXIX (Aug., 1838), 467–506.

* * * *

1. *Addressed*: Leigh Hunt Esq. / 3 Upper Cheyne Row / Chelsea. *Postmarks*: 4 EG 4 / NO 20 / 1837, and Leadenhall St. MS at Brit. Mus.

2. "Explanation and Retrospection—The Examiner Twenty Years Ago," *MR*, Enlarged Series I (Oct., 1837), 225–35.

spoken of M[r] Fonblanque as having *rescued the journalism of the* (radical) *party from contempt*, an expression which by whomsoever used would be grossly unjust to several writers & to yourself more than any, & which I will venture to say never could have been used by any one not grossly ignorant of the history of radical opinions. It did pass through my mind that the party complained of might be myself, but feeling sure that I had made no such misstatement, I dismissed the idea—however I have since been led to believe that I *was* the person meant & I have searched through my article[3] on Mr Fonblanque's late publication to ascertain what ground I had given for the mistake & how much I have to apologize for: but I have not found that I had anything to reproach myself with, beyond omitting an opportunity which I might fairly, & indeed ought to, have used for putting upon record my sense of your great merits as a political journalist, & of what you have done & suffered in the cause, in these very times the badness of which is dwelt upon in the article in question. I am sure if you will do me the justice to refer again to the article, you will not find it said, even by the most distant implication, that the *journalism* of the party, as such, was an object of contempt to anybody: what is said is, that radical *opinions* were an object of contempt to almost all persons of station & consideration; which I think you will allow they were, notwithstanding the exertions of a few persons, whose merits as *writers* even those same classes were constrained to allow: & it is no more than might have been said of Christianity after it had produced several generations of heroes & martyrs. It was not yourself only,[4] & Hazlitt, & Cobbett; Godwin, & Bentham, & my father, & various others, had laboured for radicalism with more or less of acceptance, & had gained or were gaining reputation to themselves individually, but the cause had not yet profited much by them: it has since, & we are now benefitting by what was then done—

Believe me with best wishes for yourself & the M.R.

ever truly yours

J. S. MILL

Have they sent your copy of this number of the Review?

3. "Fonblanque's England under Seven Administrations," *LWR*, XXVII (April, 1837), 65–98.

4. Hunt as the original editor of the *Examiner* had suffered various prosecutions and had been imprisoned for two years (1813–15) for a libel on the Prince Regent.

225. TO GEORGE CORNEWALL LEWIS[1]

India House
24th November
1837

My dear Lewis

I was out of town at the end of last month, otherwise I should have written to you in the packet containing Mrs. Austin's copy of the review.[2] I hope you liked the number. The political article[3] is I think in complete accordance with the views which you expressed in your little note to me which I wish had been a long letter. The article has had great success & the review is rising both in sale & in influence. A completely new tone must now however be taken, since the suicidal declaration of the Whigs against the reform of the reform bill.[4] I do not yet know what the radical members will do, though I know what they ought to do. They are in a great state of excitement. I hope it will not all end in a whiff of smoke.

I am chiefly desirous to speak to you of your article, on Authority in matters of Belief.[5] It is the first thorough & elaborate discussion of the subject that I have seen, & I think it admirable as an essay, nor is there I think one word in it that I do not concur in. But I see an insuperable difficulty in its appearing in our review. It seems to me suited only for students, & not for the public. Such articles however excellent are more than a dead weight, they are a positive injury to a popular periodical; our review must by this time have been abandoned if we had gone on publishing dissertations on abstract subjects, & on our present system, by which for the first time we are beginning to gain a footing with the public, neither my own article on Civilization nor that on Political Economy[6] would have been published. I am *now* convinced that this is a salutary necessity; doctrines make their way best with the public when they are introduced a propos of something in which the public is feeling an immediate interest; & we are forced upon the most effectual way of promoting

1. MS at Columbia University.
2. Both Lewis and the Austins were still in Malta.
3. See Letter 217, n. 7.
4. On Nov. 20, at the opening of the new Parliament, Wakley and Molesworth for the Radicals had attempted to amend the Address to the Throne by making it advocate extension of the franchise, vote by ballot, and shortening of the parliamentary term. Lord John Russell, for the Whig ministry, took a stand against further alteration of the Reform Act on the ground that "entering into this question of the construction of our representation so soon again would destroy the stability of our institutions" (*Examiner*, Nov. 6, 1837, pp. 757–58).
5. Not published at this time. Probably an early version of chap. IV ("On the Applicability of the Principle of Authority to Questions of Religion") of Lewis' *An Essay on the Influence of Authority in Matters of Opinion* (London, 1849).
6. In the *LWR* for April and Oct., 1836, respectively.

our ends, by the happy impossibility of attaining them at all in any other. If you will publish your paper in a volume of Essays, the review shall do all it can to attract notice to it—& the principles it inculcates are, as I have long thought, so extremely *needed* at the present day, that I am most eager to aid in promulgating them in any way which would give them a chance of being read by any considerable number of readers.

I have not time to write to Mrs. Austin this month, but I will not fail next month unless I have reason to suppose you are about to return. I hear good news of them from Henry Taylor.

ever yours

J. S. MILL

226. TO JOHN HILL BURTON[1]

India House
29th November 1837

SIR

If it is proposed to reprint, along with the Rationale of Evidence,[2] my preface & notes, I should like much to see the proofs, as there are various things in the notes which I regret having published. Otherwise I have nothing to suggest.

1. *Addressed*: J. H. Burton Esq. / 9 Warriston Crescent / Edinburgh. *Postmarks*: LS / 30 NO 30 / 1837, and DEC / C2F / 1837. Original in possession of Professor John Burton Cleland, of Adelaide, South Australia, the grandson of J. H. Burton. Copy supplied by Professor Cleland's son-in-law, Professor J. A. La Nauze of the Department of History, University of Melbourne.

John Hill Burton (1809–1881), Scottish historian, at the time of this letter was engaged in the editing of the collected edition of *The Works of Jeremy Bentham*, published under the superintendence of Bentham's executor, John Bowring.

2. Bentham's *Rationale of Judicial Evidence*, ed. JSM, 5 vols., 1827, was reprinted in the collected edition, vols. VI and VII. To the reprinted original Preface was added the following note, presumably by JSM: "At an interval of more than ten years from the first publication of this work, the original Editor feels that an apology is due from him for the air of confident dogmatism perceptible in some of his notes and additions, and for which he can only urge the palliation of their having been written in very early youth—a time of life at which such faults are more venial than at any other, because they generally arise, not so much from the writer's own self-conceit, as from confidence in the authority of his teachers. It is due, however, to himself to state, that the tone of some of the passages in question would have been felt by him, even then, to be unbecoming, as proceeding from himself individually: he wrote them in the character of an anonymous Editor of Mr. Bentham's work, who, in the trifling contributions which the author desired at his hands, considered (so far as mere manner was concerned) rather what would be accordant with the spirit of the work itself, and in Mr. Bentham admissible, than what would be decorous from a person of his years and his limited knowledge and experience. His name was subsequently affixed, contrary to his own strongly expressed wish, at the positive desire of the venerable author, who certainly had a right to require it." See also Letter 13.

I should rather have suggested putting the "Introduction"[3] after the Rationale itself—as being a sort of summary or résumé of it, a kind of Table Analytique, as I imagine it to be—& more dry & more abstruse than the work itself, consequently rather calculated to repel readers from it. But without having read the Introduction (except a small portion which was printed in Mr. B.'s lifetime) I cannot presume to judge.

With thanks for the attention shewn me by your troubling to write to me on the subject

believe me
your obed^{t} Servt
J. S. MILL

227. TO JOHN ROBERTSON[1]

Friday
evening
[Dec., 1837]

DEAR ROBERTSON

I have gone carefully over the Caricatures[2] & have cut out two or three sentences that struck me as feeble or superfluous & transposed a few more. On the whole I like it very much, though the *Grose* part[3] is a little in the way, as the matter explanatory of it is thrown into a note, where I could have wished that it also had been relegated. However I did not venture to do this without you, nor do I think it necessary to detain the MS from press, whither I shall tomorrow morning convey it, all except the last three or four pages which I keep to enable me to understand better what follows.

At present I think the article *might* stand first in the N°. but I wait to see it as a *whole*.

I return Chorley[4] with the first two pages cancelled & no other alteration except taking out a word here & there—The article improves upon

3. Bentham's *An Introductory View of the Rationale of Evidence* is placed at the beginning of vol. VI in the collected edition.

* * * *

1. *Addressed*: John Robertson Esq. MS at King's.
2. Robertson's article, "Caricatures," *LWR*, XXVIII (Jan., 1838), 261–93.
3. Discussion of the theory of caricature expounded by Francis Grose (1731?–1791), antiquarian and author of *Rules for Drawing Caricatures*, 1788.
4. The article was eventually published in the Aug., 1838, *LWR* (XXIX, 352–72). Bearing the title "England and Britany," it compared books on rural life by the French novelist Emile Souvestre (1806–1854) and the English miscellaneous writer William Howitt (1792–1879).

Henry Fothergill Chorley (1808–1872), miscellaneous writer and music critic for the *Athenæum*, 1830–68.

acquaintance. I hardly agree with him in the operatic & dressed out character he ascribes to Souvestre's writing, the passages from which seem to me to come from an article of quite a superior order to Howitt. I wish you would compare the two & tell me if you do not think so.

The Hoskins you sent is the wrong book: I want the Travels in Ethiopia, not the visit to the Oasis.[5] If you have not got it I will procure it somehow—

J.S.M.

228. TO JOHN PRINGLE NICHOL[1]

Kensington,
21st December, 1837.

MY DEAR NICHOL,

First as to the "great subject", I will read Peacock's Algebra.[2] Meanwhile, have you read a book termed *Cours de Philosophie Positive* by Auguste Comte,[3] the same Comte whose *Traité de Politique Positive* you have among the earlier of the St. Simonian tracts (by-the-bye, I should like soon to have these St. Simonian books[4] again, one is always wanting them)? This said book is, I think, one of the most profound books ever written on the philosophy of the sciences; and that of the higher branches of mathematics it appears to me to have *created*; the elementary and purely metaphysical parts it leaves nearly as it found them. I shall be much astonished if this book of Comte's does not strike you more than any logical speculations of our time. There are two enormous octavo volumes out, and two more to come.

Do by all means send both your articles, and the sooner the better: before the 1st of January if you can. If we are only able to take one this time, it will probably suit us best to take the Double Stars,[5] being a fresher subject. With regard to the Geological article, the present editor, Mr. Robertson—a countryman of yours, and a man who has a decided genius for managing a Review—says, "I would not insert an article by an angel on Geology, unless it reviewed and estimated the 'Geological Society' ";[6] as he has a project for successively stirring up all the learned Societies, by articles

5. G. A. Hoskins, *Travels in Ethiopia* (London, 1835); *Visit to the Great Oasis of the Libyan Desert* (London, 1837).

* * * *

1. Published by Knight, pp. 674–76. MS not located.
2. George Peacock, *A Treatise on Algebra* (Cambridge, 1830).
3. Two volumes of the eventual six had been published by this time: I. *Les Préliminaires généraux et la philosophie mathématique* (Paris, 1830); II. *La Philosophie astronomique et la philosophie de la physique* (Paris, 1835).
4. See Letter 102, postscript.
5. No such article appeared in *LWR*.
6. See Letter 213.

which would excite a personal as well as scientific interest among bodies of men whom our Review has scarcely yet reached, a thing which in his opinion would do very much for our sale. Will you meditate on this suggestion, and consider whether your article admits of being adapted to it? You can send the articles under cover to Buller, 1, Queen Square Place, Westminster; or Molesworth, 79, Eaton Square, with the words *Review* written somewhere conspicuously (not on the outside).

The Review is at present in a transition state. Molesworth is tired of spending money on it; and although there are hopes that this would not be necessary much longer, he does not like to be identified, now, with opinions which often differ from his. I do not choose to ask any new person to spend money on it, as I am going to try it myself. Our last number rose very decidedly in sale, and made a deep impression in many new quarters; it brought Robertson and me into communication both with the dissenters and the working-classes[7]—who are now courting us—and has made me a sort of *puissance* among the Radical members, which I was not before. Altogether it is a lever not to be let go, and I trust to vigour and energy in the prosecution of our improved plans of management to carry me through without sinking much money; especially if a few among those of our friends who can afford it will help us for a time with articles of the kind we want, to be paid for only in case of success, and at the convenience of the Review. Our plans are (1) in our literary articles to make freshness a primary object, never following on in the wake of other publications when the public curiosity is already sated; (2) always, if possible, to address a pre-existing curiosity; (3) in our serious articles to make our abstract speculations (except on purely scientific subjects) *grow* out of special occasions, and track the principle chiefly through the application; (4) to make all large bodies of people, of whatever kind, find something in our Review to interest *them in particular*; (5) to make ourselves a rallying-point for every section of the multifarious Radical party by thorough discussions, in a catholic spirit, of the particular questions most interesting to them. There are many other points, but it would be too long to enter into them, and it has taken us nearly a year to work the system into shape, and new points to be attended to are rising up every day.

You can be eminently useful to the Review by doing and by suggesting things in the spirit of this plan—among other things, by looking out for, and enabling us to give the earliest popular account of, the most interesting scientific novelties. If we could get the sort of scientific character which Playfair[8] gave *The Edinburgh* it would have a great effect on our sale.

7. Presumably Robertson's article, "Congregational Dissenters" in the Oct., 1837, *LWR*, had helped to bring this about.

8. John Playfair (1748–1819), mathematician and geologist.

The Radical members ought to have done at once, after Lord J.R.'s declaration,[9] what you say. I urged it upon them, and raved and stormed with no effect, but that of being thought an impracticable enthusiast. Molesworth, Leader,[10] Harvey[11] and Wakley[12] alone went with the things proposed. M.'s address to the Leeds people[13] was put forth on the failure of our attempt to obtain a collective demonstration. But the movement in the country has acted strongly upon them since, and I was yesterday at a meeting at Molesworth's of the above four, with Grote, Warburton and a few other Radical members, together with Roebuck, Rintoul, Fox and myself at which they showed a good deal of spirit, and resolved to form a party, and quitting the Ministerial benches, take up a separate position in the House. Grote in particular has got on wonderfully; and I think something will come of it.

There is much to be said about Ireland. I myself have always been for a good stout Despotism—for governing Ireland like India. But it cannot be done. The spirit of Democracy has got too much head there, too prematurely. I should much enjoy going there with you, but I have demands on my vacations (short as they are) which tie me up very much as to such journeys, and this year I believe I shall hardly get away for more than short periods of time, nor for any long distances.

I am delighted with what you are doing about Canada. I do not know what statistical materials there are, but Roebuck does. Talking to him by a third party is not enough; write to him using my name—he knows yours very well—tell him what you are about, and ask him to tell you what information would be of use to you and can be got. I do not myself think much information needful now; it has come to a fight, and right or wrong originally, the question now is, will this country give men and money to prevent a colony by force from separating when it has a mind to it?[14]

9. See Letter 225, n. 4.

10. John Temple Leader.

11. Daniel Whittle Harvey (1786–1863), then MP for Southwark.

12. Thomas Wakley (1795–1862), medical reformer, founder of the *Lancet*; MP, 1835–62.

13. "To the Electors of Leeds," in the advertising columns, *Spectator*, Dec. 3, 1837, p. 1149. Except for a few words at the beginning and end, it was written by JSM (see MacMinn, *Bibliog.*, p. 49).

14. Word had just been received in London that armed rebellion against the government had broken out in November in Lower Canada. The rebellion had actually been suppressed by Canadian forces by mid-December, but the news of its outbreak arriving on the eve of a parliamentary recess for Christmas led to much speculation whether the Whig ministry would resort to war. JSM earlier in the year had indicated his opposition to Whig policies on Canada (see Letter 205), and throughout 1838 he devoted much of his political activity and writing to the support of the Radicals' position and the work of Lord Durham, who on Jan. 15, 1838, accepted appointment as High Commissioner and Governor General of British North America (see Letters 231, 239, 248, 249, 250, and 252).

Tell me all that you would suggest about publishing arrangements for the Review. We have, on much consideration, abolished the system of agencies, i.e. of sending out copies for sale or return—but having lately received an application from Adam Black's[15] house to be our agents, we thought their name so valuable to us that we made an exception to our rule in their single instance. Tell me your opinion fully on the whole thing.

You are interested, I know, about Henry.[16] He is in excellent health, bringing up his mathematics by attending De Morgan[17] at University College. I have carried him through the Aristotelian logic this year, and he is now working at Hobbes.

Ever yours faithfully,

J. S. Mill.

15. Adam Black (1784–1874), Edinburgh publisher and politician.
16. JSM's brother.
17. Augustus De Morgan (1806–1871), professor of mathematics at University College, London, 1828–31 and 1836–66.

THE EARLIER LETTERS OF JOHN STUART MILL

1838–1848

132

India House
12th Oct 1843

My dear Sir
I have been a good deal surprised & even pained
by some passages relating to my father, in the
article on Bentham just published in the Edinburgh
Review. Several of the statements made on the
authority of Bowring are incorrect in point of fact, but
what I chiefly complain of is the insertion of some things
reported to have been said by Bentham, calculated to give
a most unfavorable, & as every one who really knew my
father must be aware, an utterly false impression of
the character & temper of his mind. Mr Bentham's
best friends well knew – I have heard some of
those who were most attached to him lament – his
entire incapacity to estimate the characters even
of those with whom he associated intimately. The
opinions he expressed of people depended very much

Letter 405, to Macvey Napier, from MS in the British Museum

• • • 1838 • • •

229. TO JOHN ROBERTSON[1]

Saturday
[Jan. (?), 1838]

DEAR ROBERTSON

I am going to have to fight a duel on your account. I have had a half hostile, half expostulatory letter from Hayward[2] on the subject of that passage, in the Martineau article,[3] in reply to which I have owned the proprietorship, disowned authorship & editorship, admitted having seen the article before it was printed off, & said that I did not consider the terms "blackguardising" & "lying" as applied to any one individually but to a *class* to which it was made matter of complaint against certain superior men that they allowed themselves to be assimilated. I of course did not tell him either who wrote the article or who edited it, and I told him that I had ordered any letter he might send to be forwarded to me. I have not yet received his answer & perhaps shall not till I leave town which will be today, so hold yourself prepared in case he should write a letter to you.

N.B. I told him that the writer had no malice against him, & I believed had never seen him.

ever yours

J. S. MILL

If you have anything to write, direct Post Office Southampton.[4]

1. MS at King's.
2. Abraham Hayward.
3. A review of Miss Martineau's *Retrospect of Western Travel*, *LWR*, XXVIII (Jan., 1838), 470–502. The offending passage (pp. 477–78) excoriated not only Hayward but also, among others, Lockhart, Wilson, Barnes, D'Israeli, and Theodore Hook for deserting their class to do "the base work of the aristocracy, fighting for them, writing for them, joking for them, blackguardizing for them, and . . . lying for them. . . ." The review was signed H.W.

A note was subsequently appended to Vol. XXIX of the *LWR* with reference to Hayward, stating "that neither against him nor against any of the other persons named was any distinct and personal charge made, because we were not in possession of proofs on which our charges could have been made distinct and personal."

4. This postscript is written at the top of the first page.

230. TO JOHN HILL BURTON[1]

India House
23^{d} January
1837 [*sic, recte* 1838]

MY DEAR SIR,

Pray excuse my not having sooner answered your letter, as my whole spare time and thoughts were occupied with poor Canada, about which what I have to say will be published in the L. & W. review on Saturday next.

With regard to the note or rather the passage which I propose should be appended to my preface,[2] on reperusal I should wish that after the words "accordant with the spirit of the work itself" you would be so kind as to add "and, in Mr. Bentham, admissible" and then proceed "than what would be decorous" &c. as before. Otherwise I shall have the appearance of censuring the tone of the work, which I am very far indeed from intending. I still wish to suppress any direct mention of my name, not to prevent it from being known to the reader if he chuses to enquire about it which I know cannot be done, but because its suppression is as it were, an act of disavowal as to any appropriateness in the notes and additions to my present frame of mind, and because I do not like to perk in the face of the world in general that the person known by my name has written things which he is ashamed of, when my name has never in any instance been put to writings I am not ashamed of.

I should think Sir John Campbell's Law Reform Acts, the orders of the 15 Judges promulgated a few years ago reforming the system of Pleading, and the Reports of the various Law Commissions, were the best authorities for the recent alterations in the law. Not being acquainted with many law books I cannot direct you to any other sources.

My notions of Mr. Bentham's intentions with respect to the "Introduction to the Rationale" (though I confess it is but an indistinct notion) has always been that he intended to put it forth as a kind of feeler, at a time when he did not contemplate finishing the work itself for publication at an early period. My opinion is entirely adverse to publishing the Introduction at all; & if that is decided upon, the later in the collection it comes the better. I would much rather it followed, than preceded, the Rationale.

1. *Addressed*: J. H. Burton Esq. / 9 Warriston Crescent / Edinburgh. *Postmarks*: LS / 23JA23 / 1838, and JAN / C 25+ / 1838. Original in possession of Professor John Burton Cleland, of Adelaide, South Australia; copy supplied by Professor J. A. La Nauze, Dept. of History, University of Melbourne.

2. See Letter 226, n. 2.

Mr. Smith's[3] proposal appears to me prepos[terous][4] & from all you mention I should not suppose him to be a man to whose judgment any more deference should be paid in constructing the Edition than is indispensable. I know nothing of Mr Smith whatever except that I think I remember hearing that a gentleman of that name had been the editor of the Rationale of Reward.

Believe me Dear Sir
Yours truly

J. S. MILL

231. TO ALBANY FONBLANQUE[1]

India House
30th Jany 1838

MY DEAR FONBLANQUE—I have not said or written one word to you in complaint of the extraordinary unfairness which you appear to me to have practised for some time against those radicals who oppose the present ministry—I know you never intend to be unfair, but you remember I always thought unfairness towards opponents to be one of your qualities even when you & I were on the same side in politics. It is especially in these late Canada discussions that I have thought your unfairness went beyond the bounds which in some degree confined it before. However I do not quarrel with you for this nor for your putting the last seal to your ministerialism by espousing the enmities of the ministry, & displaying personal hostility to old friends whom your new friends wish to hunt down. Perhaps if we chose to retaliate, we are not altogether without the power, but I at least never will, under whatever provocation, speak of you to the public in terms of disrespect, or even, if I can help it, of complaint. I will only, when the things you say touch me personally, point out to yourself the injustice of them, & my object in writing to you now is to do so in regard to what you say in your last number on the London Review.[2] You have entirely misstated facts. The London Review never bestowed the name

3. Richard Smith, identified only as "of the Stamps and Taxes Office." He had translated from the French and edited *The Rationale of Reward* (1825) and *The Rationale of Punishment* (1830). For a list of his contributions to the collected edition of Bentham's *Works*, see vol. X, p. 548.

4. MS torn.

* * * *

1. *Addressed*: Albany Fonblanque Esq. / 5 Pine Apple Place / Kilburn Road; *readdressed in another hand*: N 4 Up. Seymor St. West. *Postmarks*: 4 EB 4 / JA 30 / 1838, and 12 NN 12 / JA 31 / 1838. MS at LSE. Excerpt published in *Life and Labours of Albany Fonblanque*, ed. E. B. de Fonblanque (London, 1874), p. 32.

2. "Mr E. Bulwer and Mr Grote," *Examiner*, Jan. 28, 1838, p. 50: "The name of 'philosophical Radicals' was bestowed by themselves by the gentlemen whose opinions

philosophical radicals upon its own writers or upon the people whom Bulwer called so in his speech.[3] You knew at the time perfectly that it gave that name to the thinking radicals generally, to distinguish them from the demagogic radicals, such as Wakley,[4] & from the historical radicals of the Cartwright[5] school, & from the division of property radicals if there be any. You knew that if the London Review wished to be the review of this large body, we always considered the Examiner as the newspaper of it. You also knew that because this designation too often repeated gave a *coterie* air which it was felt to be objectionable, the phrase was varied, & phrases adopted to express merely those Reformers who were not professedly, Reformers only within the limits of the existing Constitution—such were the phrases thorough reformers, & so on—& yet for this very change of designation you blame the review & its writers just as the Chronicle yesterday[6] after founding a long attack solely upon identifying me with Roebuck or with Grote, concluded by reproaching me for differing from them.

I expected no better from the Chronicle but what is the meaning of *your* insisting upon identifying me with Grote or Roebuck or the rest? Do you in your conscience think that my opinions are at all like theirs? Have you forgotten, what I am sure you once knew, that my opinion of their philosophy is & has for years been *more* unfavourable by far than your own? & that my radicalism is of a school the most remote from theirs, at all points, which exists? *They* knew this as long ago as 1829, since which time the variance has been growing wider & wider. I never consented to have anything to do with the London Review but for the sake of getting together a body of writers who would represent radicalism more worthily than they did: you never could be induced to help me in this & until I could

---

are represented by the London Review. . . . To us it appeared better . . . that the world should find out that they were philosophical, than that they should proclaim it of themselves. But this is a matter of taste, and they are fond of calling themselves by good names, and, like ladies, seem glad to change them; so they have been 'philosophical Reformers,' and 'thorough Reformers,' and 'earnest Reformers,' and better still, 'entire Reformers.' "

3. In the House of Commons on Jan. 23, 1838.

4. Thomas Wakley.

5. Major John Cartwright (1740–1824), "the father of Parliamentary Reform."

6. An attack on JSM's article "Lord Durham and the Canadians" (*LWR*, XXVIII [Jan., 1838], 502–33): "It is by the writer of the political manifesto of the preceding number ["Parties and the Ministry," VI (Oct., 1837), 1–26] and is characterized by the same ability, the same absence of shrewd discernment in the adaptation of means to ends, and in the estimate taken of individuals, and the same tone of infallibility which were displayed in that production. The writer being thoroughly persuaded of the impossibility of himself and his friends being ever in the wrong, might take for his device '*nul n'a raison que nous et nos amis*', and possesses not a few of those qualities which in the days of the Inquisition would have made a good member of that tribunal." (*Morning Chronicle*, Jan. 29, 1838, p. 3.)

find persons who would, I could do little—but in proportion as I did find such persons I have been divesting the review of its sectarian character & have even gone this length that when Molesworth ceased to feel that the review represented his opinions I took it off his hands & am now myself the proprietor of it. In the face of this it is rather hard to be accused of ascribing all wisdom & infallibility to a set from whose opinions I differ more than from the Tories. But I cannot, because I differ from them, join like you in crying them down for sacrificing their own popularity in maintaining *my* opinions about Canada, & while I myself seek the radical party where it *is*, not where it is *not*, & endeavour to rest upon the general body of radical opinion in the country, I will not throw overboard the most honest men in public life for standing nobly in the breach on a great occasion. I will rather risk myself there with them even at the hazard of being accused by you of being exactly what it is my special object, my principle & also my interest to shew that I am *not*. And I should think much higher of your magnanimity if you did the same. Of your intentions & talents I have the same high opinion which I always had.

ever yours

J. S. MILL

232. TO JOHN ROBERTSON[1]

I.H. Tuesday
[Jan. 30 or early Feb., 1838]

DEAR ROBERTSON,

It seems to me that in any future communication we have with Bulwer, the points which it is our interest to make him feel, with the least possible appearance of intending to do so, are these: *First*, that we have the power, from our next number inclusive, either to begin preparing the radicals to support & even to call for their ministry, or to begin impressing them with the uselessness of their looking to any ministry for a long time to come: that we shall certainly take one line or the other; & it will depend upon the opinion we form of them, which: and *Secondly*, that our support of them will depend not only upon their embracing the policy which we think suitable to rally the body of moderate radicals round them, who are to be *our* party whoever is minister—but also upon our confidence in their *personnel*. That Ellice[2] & Stanley[3] (& we need not add, himself, but he will

1. Published by Towers, pp. 68–69. MS at LSE. Dated by Mrs. Towers as of "1837 during the Canada coercion and rebellion"; the last paragraph, however, apparently refers to the preceding letter, to Fonblanque.

2. Edward Ellice (1781–1863), Whig leader.

3. Edward John Stanley (1802–1869), then chief government whip and Secretary of the Treasury, who had been a disciple of Lord Durham.

see that *we* see through him, which always vastly increases such a man's respect for one) will make it their object to render the ministry a ministry of *intrigans*. That we need only call it that, and treat it as that, to damage it exceedingly, and that we *will* treat it as that if it *is* that. That we have no earthly objection to act *with* intrigans, but that we do not chuse to act *under* intrigans: that therefore if their ministry is *made up* of loose fish, & does not contain a due proportion of men who have a high character for private integrity and political earnestness, we will, even if we support their measures, attack & ridicule their persons, & then beware Messrs. Bulwer, Ellice, & even Lord Durham himself. The ways and times proper for insinuating such of these things as are to be insinuated & for stating such of them as are to be stated will present themselves to you as occasion arises.

I have written to Fonblanque[4] as I wrote to Black,[5] informing him of the same facts, telling him I think him excessively unfair towards us, but that no provocation shall induce me to attack him, & appealing to his love of truth not to mix us up with Roebuck, etc.

Ever yours,

J.S.M.

233. TO ALBANY FONBLANQUE[1]

India House
3[d] Feb. 1838

My dear Fonblanque—If my letter[2] gave you concern you have returned good for evil, since yours has given me great pleasure. The kind feelings you express to me personally are & have always been & I am as certain as I am about any such thing, always will be, completely reciprocated on my part. With regard to imputations which you say I have cast upon you in the eagerness of advocacy, I give you my word that I never intended to cast any: one single sentence in my political article of October last,[3] though it conveyed no imputation upon anybody, & did not allude to you in particular (while in that very article the Examiner was twice mentioned in an approving tone) was I admit, written under the provocation of an article of yours, one of those you wrote against the Spectator,[4] & which as it appeared to me

4. The preceding letter.
5. No such letter to John Black, editor of the *Morning Chronicle*, appears to be extant.

* * * *

1. *Addressed*: Albany Fonblanque Esq. / 48 Connaught Square. MS at LSE.
2. Letter 231.
3. See Letter 217, n. 7.
4. See especially "Tory Radical Consistency," *Examiner*, Sept. 3, 1837, p. 563, and "The *Spectator* and Ourselves," *ibid.*, Sept. 17, 1837, p. 595.

at the time *did* attempt to fasten imputations on an article in that paper on evidence which I thought altogether insufficient. I remember thinking at the time that if I had been personally unacquainted with you, I should have thought that article (what I am in general much slower to think of any one than people generally are) intentionally uncandid. As it was, the effect on me was to make me think that your alienation from those whom I will call the extreme radicals, had now reached the point, at which with the most complete intention on your part to be fair towards them, they could no longer expect justice from you. And this impression has been made upon me often since. If it has been made upon me, who have fought your battles so long & to say nothing of our long friendship, had to vindicate the correctness of my own judgment in thinking so highly of you as I do, it cannot be but that the same impression must have been made much more strongly upon all those, holding the opinions you attack, who are differently situated from me. This is a result which you cannot yourself wish for, & I have seen it with great pain.

In my article in the present number of the review[5] there is only one passage in which you might perhaps suppose you were pointed to, that in which "radical writers" are spoken of—but in this instance I not only did not refer to you, but if I had mentioned you, it would have been to *except* you from the imputations conveyed—& if anybody should suppose that you were among the persons meant, I shall owe you a reparation which I shall not be slow to make.

I did not complain of you for calling me *philosophical* in a spirit of sarcasm, but for imputing to Grote, Warburton &c the assumption of a name which as far as I know, *they* never used, though I did; & after fixing the name on them, then applying it to the London Review as being identified with them. I am so far from being that, that I am most anxious to distinguish myself from them—but I do not think the radical cause so strong as to sustain no injury from lowering the character of such men as those I have named—& I thought this time peculiarly one at which they had entitled themselves to be upheld. I felt much disappointed at your not taking this view along with me—but I hope I need not repeat that I am quite convinced that in this as in all other parts of your conduct you act with the most perfect persuasion of your being in the right.

The difference between us is, I suspect, as you suppose, partly in our estimation of men—& I should like very much to know better in what instances you think I err in my estimation of them. I should like this because I have been accustomed to the same charge from various people & from nobody so much as from those whom you probably think that I overestimate, & I have generally thought that the ground of this judgment

5. "Lord Durham and the Canadians," *LWR*, XXVIII (Jan., 1838), 502–33.

of me from most of those who formed it, was, that I saw much to be valued & admired in persons whom they disliked. If I err egregiously in my judgment of men I am not at present in a way to correct my error, for hitherto my experience has generally confirmed the judgments of men, which I had formed for myself, while it has often weakened those I had formed wholly or partially on the authority of others. But I should like to compare notes with you on men, & to see who are those respecting whom we differ.

As the state of opinion in the electoral body, I do not think you would find me so unacquainted with it as you suppose. I do not think the electoral body are favourable to my views on the points on which we differ; but rather the reverse. But I think they would by this time have been so, if the principal radicals & especially yourself had taken the tone which I think ought to have been taken. There is a great deal of passive radicalism in the electoral body, but very little active, & the grounds of my present practical views, whether right or wrong, are, that if this passive radicalism is not very soon transmitted into active, it will become impossible to do so, & that if the present ministry continue, with their present line of conduct, until the Tories turn them out without aid from their own supporters, Peel & [Well]ington[6] will come in without the Orangemen & *will be supported by O'Connell & 150 of the 200 ballot men in the House*. The only alternative is in my opinion, a Durham ministry within a year (or thereabouts)—or else the strongest Conservative Ministry we have had since Lord Liverpool's,[7] and the longer we wait for this last, the less chance there will be of making a strong Opposition. We are letting the cards slip out of our hands. This is the view by which I am guided, & I am driving for a Durham ministry. I may be wrong, but my object is to rest upon the whole body of radical opinion in the country & I grieve to find one part of it eating up another.

ever yours faithfully

J. S. MILL

234. TO ALBANY FONBLANQUE[1]

India House
6th Feby 1838

MY DEAR FONBLANQUE—I was a little inclined to reproach myself for having written to you (as I have since thought) rather unkindly—but you

6. Part covered by seal.

7. From 1812 to 1827.

* * * *

1. *Addressed*: Albany Fonblanque Esq. / 48 Connaught Square. *Postmark*: 2 AN 2 / FE 6 / 1838. MS at LSE.

are more than quits with me by your article last Sunday.[2] Of that article I do not very well know what to say, because it is a new position to me, to find any assertion which I make about myself & my concerns, treated exactly as if it had never been made. Could I expect after what I said in my letter to you, or even before it, that I should have been treated through three long columns, by one who has the friendly feelings to me that you profess, as being in the most complete manner identified with some half dozen men whom I have nothing to do with, & to whose opinions you are far more nearly allied than I am. You take me moreover at a very ungenerous disadvantage, because you know that I cannot chuse the time when people whom I respect are under a cloud, to proclaim to the world anything disparaging that I may happen to think of them: I cannot cry out on the housetops, like a mean truckling coward, "do not confound me with these men, I am not of them": nor is it my way at any time to do so: it *is* my *conduct* which must shew wherein I differ from them. You are moreover quite as unjust in making *them* accountable for the review as the review for them, since they do not recognise it as in any way their organ, & about that particular article not one of them was consulted, & I have no reason to believe that any one of them would approve of the course recommended in it. I shall remonstrate no further with you on the subject: if you continue henceforth to identify the review with them, you do it with your eyes open: but when I have made you, as I shall do, ashamed to go on any longer doing so, do not say *you are glad to see I am changed*: I shall not have changed; I shall only have spoken somewhat more of my mind than that very small portion of it which can be spoken on so small a subject as Lord John Russell, or so special a one as Canada.

You may believe me when I say that I do not in the least complain of your expressing yourself so strongly as you do on the subject of my article: that is all fair; & as, from considerations which you are not bound to share, I do not chuse to answer you publicly, I do privately. I only want however to mark two things, especially as I have not your article by me at present. One is, to shew you what I mean by saying that you are habitually unfair to opponents. You exemplify this in the very first sentence, when you describe me as proposing to turn out ministry after ministry till I get one *satisfactory* to some five or six members of parliament & to myself—& in this strain you continue always speaking of us as wanting to bring *ourselves*

2. The leading article in the *Examiner* for Feb. 4, 1838, p. 65, "Look Before You Leap," was a slashing attack on JSM's *LWR* article for Jan., "Lord Durham and the Canadians," in which, said Fonblanque, "is propounded the Bobadil [*sic*] plan for overthrowing Ministry after Ministry till a Government can be formed satisfactory to the extreme section of Reformers commonly called the Ultras, but whom we . . . should rather designate as the Detrimentals or Wrongheads. . . ." [The "Bobadil" plan for carrying a fortress—"twenty more, kill them too; twenty more, kill them too." See Ben Jonson, *Every Man in his Humour*, Act IV, sc. 5.]

in. Now would not any one suppose from this, that what I was dreaming of attaining was an extreme radical ministry? would any one suppose that I could have said that the mere exclusion from the present ministry of all who were pledged against the ballot, was all that should be aimed at? You must think me very easily satisfied if you describe the present ministry *minus* Lord John Russell as a ministry satisfactory to me. You may think this a small thing; but it amounts to no less than fastening on an opponent what *he* thinks would be presumptuous & ridiculous instead of what only *you* think so: & it appears to me that all the ridiculousness you attribute to my suggestion, entirely arises from putting this colour upon it.

The other thing I want to shew you is, how very little calm consideration you have given to my suggestion before pronouncing such a sentence of absurdity & self conceit upon it. You assume that after the proposed vote of want of confidence, the Whigs are to resign, & sit still till a Tory ministry is formed. They are not such fools. They would *not* resign, but would, the very next day, move, in some parliamentary form, that the House would have no confidence in any Tory ministry. There would be ways enough of wording it. Of course I am supposing that the Court is with them, & would not seek an excuse to turn them out. Nay, I have not the least doubt that the mere fact that forty or fifty radicals were known to be *ready* to vote for want of confidence, would effect the desired object without an actual vote, & without their losing ten of their supporters. By "the desired object" I mean, a modification of the *personnel* of the ministry; not even a Durham ministry, but a *Whig* ministry unfettered on the finality of the reform bill.

I have nothing further to say, except that for a person who complains of "imputations" you are very profuse of them.

ever yours truly

J. S. MILL

235. TO ALBANY FONBLANQUE[1]

I.H.
Wednesday
[Feb. 7, 1838]

MY DEAR FONBLANQUE

I am glad you are not angry & I am not conscious of being so—& it is some evidence of my not being angry, that I can bear to be called so, for I have generally observed that when any one is just hovering on the verge of anger, *calling* him angry invariably *makes* him so.

You are of course not to blame if you really think, & have thought all the

1. *Addressed*: Albany Fonblanque Esq. / 48 Connaught Square. *Postmark*: ???? / FE 7 / 1838. MS at LSE. One excerpt published in *Life and Labours of Albany Fonblanque*, ed. E. B. de Fonblanque, p. 31.

years you have known me, that I agree in my opinions with Grote or with any of those whom you allude to. I thought you had known me better: but if you did not, I certainly did not expect that your tone towards me would be altered merely by my writing to you a letter. What I will make you ashamed of is, having forgotten, or mistaken my opinions & feelings so long.

I cannot however admit your doctrine that one ought to treat any person or thing which one is opposed to, as it appears to the public, without regard to anything one may personally know, which places it in a different light. If I dealt in that way with you, I am sure you would have reason to complain of very gross injustice.

With regard to "the Grote conclave" there may be such a conclave, but I know nothing of it, for I have never been within the doors of Grote's house in Eccleston Street[2] & have been for the last few years completely estranged from that household. Surely there never was so surprising a proposition gravely advanced as that my saying that Roebuck (who was known to be the author of the former articles) was not privy to this, implied "that they were privy to it." If those are your rules of evidence I am not surprised at any false judgment you make.

How can you say the Review "countenances & agrees with" those people with the single exception of the suspension of the Canadian constitution, when it has been attacking them for inefficiency & for being unequal to their position for years, & most notably in the very last number? I tell them the same things to their faces whenever I see them. Immediately after Lord J.R.'s declaration[3] I tried to rouse them, & went to a meeting of most of the leading parliamentary radicals at Molesworth's[4] from which I went away *they* thinking me, I fancy, almost mad, & *I* thinking them craven. I do not except Grote, or Warburton, or Hume, all of whom were there. I except none but Molesworth & Leader, two raw boys. I assure you, when I told them in the review what I thought would be done by men of spirit & *real* practicalness of character I had perfect ground for feeling well assured that they would not do it. You have therefore no earthly reason for considering me "dangerous."

I am certain that in the concluding part of your article which you say refers "exclusively to the Grote conclave" there is no human creature who would not suppose that you were pointedly & determinedly & whether I would or not, including me—i.e. the review in general, & the writer of that article in particular.

ever yours truly

J. S. Mill

2. No. 3 Eccleston Street, to which Mr. and Mrs. Grote had moved in Oct., 1836. See Mrs. Grote, *The Personal Life of George Grote* (London, 1873), p. 108.

3. Lord John Russell's declaration of Nov. 20, 1837, as to the finality of the Reform Act of 1832. See Letter 225, n. 4.

4. See Letter 228.

236. TO THE SECRETARY OF UNIVERSITY COLLEGE[1]

India House.
13th Feby
1838

MY DEAR SIR

I do not know whether the appointment to the professorships of languages at the University College is referred by the Council to the consideration of the Professors, but if it is I hope you will excuse my saying a word to you in favour of a candidate for the Italian Professorship, Count Pepoli,[2] a member of the Provisional Government of Bologna. I know nothing of him personally, but I can vouch for his high literary reputation & acquirements on the authority of one of the most competent witnesses living, though not a very producible one perhaps, Mazzini,[3] the celebrated President of La Jeune Italie who appears to me one of the most accomplished & every way superior men among all the foreigners I have known, & profoundly versed in his country's literature. As you probably have not Mazzini's testimony before you, I have thought it but right to tell you what I have learned from him. I should consider his testimony sufficient by itself to warrant any such appointment.

Ever yours truly
J. S. MILL

237. TO GUSTAVE D'EICHTHAL[1]

27 February 1838

MY DEAR GUSTAVE

The presents constitution of our sinking fund is this: there is no fixed appropriation of annual revenue to it, but the *surplus* revenue, whatever it happens to be, is always paid over to the Commissioners of the Sinking

1. MS at UCL. Published in M. C. W. Wicks, *The Italian Exiles in London, 1816–1846* (Manchester, 1937), p. 288. Dr. Wicks reports (p. 176) that JSM's and other testimonials "were first sent to Carlyle and in his absence forwarded to the Secretary by Erasmus Darwin."
2. Count Carlo Pepoli (1796–1881), formerly professor of philosophy at the University of Bologna, at this time in exile in England. Pepoli received the appointment at University College and held it until 1847.
3. Giuseppe Mazzini (1805–1872), Italian patriot and revolutionary, was in exile in England from 1837 to 1848. He became a close friend of the Carlyles and contributed to the *LWR* as well as other English periodicals.

* * * *

1. *Addressed*: Monsieur / M. Gustave d'Eichthal / 14 Rue Lepelletier / à Paris. MS at Arsenal.

Fund (at the end of every quarter I belive) so ——[2] the amount continually varies— —— last quarter (1837) is the first in —— payment at all was ——? ——re happened to be n—— that quarter, Besides u—— deemed debt continues till ——mption of more. This ——ng fund was establish—— ministry, not long after —— into office: in 1831 or 1832 —— amount of redeemed d—— I do not know, but if you wish for the exact figures, I will procure them for you. The unredeemed debt on the 5th January 1831 was £757,486,997, besides exchequer bills £27,278,-400. At present the debt is rather greater, on account of the 20 millions compensation to the slave owners, which exceeds the amount of debt since redeemed. In 1816, when the debt was at its highest, the unredeemed debt, independently of exchequer bills, was £816,311——. so that there must have b—— re—— in the meanwhile, —— is there were redu—— me £90,538,701, to —— s, *per contra,* in —— 13,759 by funding [?] —— & by different operatio—— of conversion, reducing the interest but augmenting the capital

If these facts are not sufficient for your purpose, write to me immediately & I will get a complete & accurate statement. You may rely upon the correctness of all I have now stated.

If I were not so extremely busy I would write you a —— letter: I was very glad —— from you again & —— w that you wi——.[3]

ever yours fai——

J.S.M——

238. TO EDWARD LYTTON BULWER[1]

India House
3d March
1838

My dear Sir—I have read the Monthly Chronicle with deep interest & I hasten to make my acknowledgments to you for the feeling which prompted the very complimentary expressions with which you have accompanied your strictures on my article in the L. & W. R.[2]

2. Page torn. The double dashes throughout the remainder of the letter indicate missing portions.

3. What remains of the last line is crossed through, and illegible.

* * * *

1. *Addressed*: Edward Lytton Bulwer Esq. MP. / 8 Charles Street / Berkeley Square. *Postmark*: 6E6 / MR3 / 1838. MS in the possession of Lady Hermione Cobbold. Collated by Dr. Eileen Curran. Published in Elliot, I, 107–9.

2. Bulwer's leading article, "The Position and Prospects of the Government," *Monthly Chronicle,* I (March, 1838), 1–15, discusses JSM's "Lord Durham and the

I agree entirely in the greater part of the views set forth in the first article of the Monthly Chronicle, & especially in the general character you have given of the policy suited to the middle class. On the points in which I differ from you, or perhaps I should rather say, on which I would add to or qualify what you say, there would be much to be discussed between us at a suitable time & place. But I am much more desirous at present to express my great delight at the complete recognition which I find in that article, of its being advisable for the moderate radicals to form themselves openly & avowedly into a distinct body from the whigs—to shake off the character of a *tail*—& to act together as an independent body. My only quarrel with the parliamentary radicals has hitherto been, that they have not done this, nor seemed to see any advantage in doing it. But whenever I see any moderate radical who recognizes this as his principle of action, any differences which there can be between me & him cannot be fundamental, or permanent. We may differ as to our views of the conduct which would be most expedient at some particular crisis, but in the main principles of our political conduct we agree.

I have never had any other notion of practical policy, since the radicals were numerous enough to form a party, than that of resting on the *whole body* of radical opinion, from the whig-radicals at one extreme, to the more reasonable & practical of the working classes, & the Benthamites, on the other. I have been trying ever since the reform bill to stimulate, so far as I had an opportunity, all sections of the parliamentary radicals to organize such a union, & such a system of policy: not saying to them, Adopt my views, do as I bid you—but, Adopt *some* views, do *something*. Had I found them acting on any system, aiming at any particular end, I should not have stood upon any peculiar views of my own as to the best way of attaining the common object. The best course for promoting radicalism is the course which is pursued with most ability, energy, & concert, even if not the most politic, abstractedly considered, and for my own guidance individually, my rule is—whatever power I can bring in aid of the popular cause, to carry it where I see strength—that is, where I see, along with adequate ability & numbers, a definite purpose consistently pursued. Therefore if I find all that among you—& if I do not, I am quite aware that I shall find it nowhere else—you will find me quite ready to cooperate with you, if you

Canadians." "In the last number of the London and Westminster Review, we find the following advice: Turn out the Whigs, to bring in the Tories: turn out the Tories, in order to bring in the Radicals. With all due respect to the distinguished propounder of this doctrine [JSM], we must say that his device seems to have been pre-allegorized by Pope, in the Apologue to Sir Balaam:—

'Asleep and naked as an Indian lay,
An honest factor stole a gem away;
He pledged it to the knight—the knight had wit,
So kept the diamond—and the rogue was bit.' "

think my cooperation worth having. I am no "Impracticable," & perhaps the number of such is smaller than you think. As one of many, I am ready to merge my own views, whatever they may be, in the *average* views of any body of persons whom I may chuse to ally myself with: but not unless I have full opportunity of bringing my own views before the body, & giving to those views any degree of influence which their own intrinsic character may obtain for them, over its collective deliberations. You cannot wonder that having always been obliged to act alone, I act in my own way. As long as that is the case, I must struggle on, making mistakes & correcting them, doing the best I can under all the disadvantages of a person who has to shift for himself—& raising up allies to myself, where & how I can, as I have already done & am doing with a success that shows that I cannot be altogether in a wrong way. You have seen, in Robertson, no bad specimen, I think, of my *practicalness* in finding men suitable to my purpose. But enough of this.

Robertson requests me to put you in mind of his request to you, in which I most heartily join, on the subject of an article for our next number (*a propos* of Knighton,[3] the "Diary," &c.) on the social influence &c. of the Court. Such an article from you, would be a great treasure to us, & specially valuable in our next number as it is the best time of the year for such a subject.

Ever yours truly

J. S. MILL.

239. TO EDWARD LYTTON BULWER[1]

India House
5th March
1838

MY DEAR SIR

In answer to your question as to what I would be ready to do if my friends, as you call them, will not consent to what I think reasonable,—if a party can be formed, for the Durham policy, including such men as yourself & those whom you mention, & pursuing its objects by means which I think likely to be effectual, even though not exactly those I should myself

3. *Memoirs of Sir William Knighton*, ed. Dorothea Lady Knighton (2 vols., London, 1838). Knighton (1776–1836) was physician, private secretary, and keeper of the Privy Purse to George IV as Regent and King. Bulwer's review, "Courts of British Queens," appeared in the Aug. number of *LWR*, XXIX, 281–308.

* * * *

1. *Addressed*: Edward Lytton Bulwer Esq. M.P. / 8 Charles Street / Berkeley Square. Postmark illegible. MS in the possession of Lady Hermione Cobbold. Collated by Dr. Eileen Curran. Published in Elliot, I, 110–12.

have preferred—I am ready to give such a party all the aid I can, & as a necessary consequence, to throw off, so far as is implied in that, all who persevere in conduct either hostile to the party, or calculated to diminish its strength. But I do not think that any liberal party, out of office, can be strong enough to beat the Tories, without a degree of popular enthusiasm in its favour, which could not be had without the support of some of the men who, in the same proportion as they are thought impracticable, are thought honest. I have a personal knowledge of the men, far exceeding any which I believe you have, & from that knowledge I have no doubt that such a party as I am supposing could carry with it all of those men who are worth having, if in the first place real evidence is afforded them that popular objects, to the extent of those to which Lord Durham is pledged to are sincerely pursued, & if, secondly, their *amour propre* is not irritated by personal attacks—such for instance as that in the Chronicle[2] of this morning, or some recent ones in the Examiner. I think such attacks good policy in the Whigs, but in the moderate radicals as bad tactics almost as Thompson's insane conduct in Marylebone,[3] though I admit there are considerable palliations both for the one & the other. Both on public & private grounds I am not only precluded from joining in such attacks, but must defend them against any such, & I must do so all the more, in proportion as I separate myself from them in my political course. The October number of the review was the first in which I systematically advocated a moderate policy,[4] and it was consequently the first in which I personally complimented the extreme politicians. The Canada question then in an evil hour crossed the path of radicalism, & my difference of opinion from you on the course of conduct required by Lord John Russell's declarations made me again apparently one of them; which I regretted at the time, but could not help. But I have never swerved from my intention of detaching the review, and myself, from all coterie or sectarian connexion; & making the public see that the review has ceased to be Benthamite; & throwing myself upon the *mass* of radical opinion in the country. All this I determined to do when I had no hope of a radical party in parliament—& if such a party be formed I would of course prefer to ally myself with, rather than run a race against it for the moderate radicals. I could only enter into such a party as a representative, in it, of opinions more advanced in radicalism than the average opinions of the party—but, in my idea of the principles on which such a party ought to be constituted, it cannot do without the

2. A leading article attacking Molesworth, Leader, and the extreme Radicals, *Morning Chronicle*, March 5, 1838, p. 3. See also "The Position and Prospects of the Government," presumably by Bulwer, in his *Monthly Chronicle*, I (March, 1838), 1–17.

3. Col. T. Perronet Thompson on March 2 was badly defeated by the Tory Lord Teignmouth. For Thompson's behaviour, see *Spectator*, March 3, 1838, pp. 200–201.

4. In his article "Parties and the Ministry." See Letter 217, n. 7.

support of persons considered ultra in opinion, provided they are not impracticable in conduct.

With regard to Molesworth's motion,[5] we shall so soon know what comes of it, that there is little use in speculating about its probable effects, for the next two days I shall only say, that I neither counselled it nor knew of it till the notice was given; and when I first heard of it, disapproved of it. The position I have since taken about it is a sort of neutral one. I feel quite unable to foresee whether in the end its consequences will be good or bad. But one of those consequences, the division of the radical body, I feel all the evil of, & I regret much that such a union as we are discussing, earlier adopted, did not prevent such a division from arising. In the present state of matters, were I to urge Molesworth to turn back, I should only compromise my influence wi[th] him, without attaining the object. The division thus brought to a [cri]sis, some new state of things will arise, which we must work [to] the best ends we can.[6]

Thanks for your kind expressions about the Westminster. I need hardly say how much I value your assistance as a contributor & I shall be much disappointed if an article which would be of peculiar value to the review at present,[7] should, from the engagements you mention, be unavoidably lost to it.

I shall set about my political article for the next number[8] the moment I have made up my mind what the relations of the review are likely to be[9] to parties in parliament.

ever yours faithfully

J. S. MILL.

240. TO LEIGH HUNT[1]

India House
11th May
1838

MY DEAR SIR

Mr. Robertson, who goes out of town today for a few days, requests me to remind you of the proposition he made to you concerning an article on

5. On Feb. 20 Sir William Molesworth had fixed March 6 for his motion for an address to the Crown expressing no confidence in the Secretary of State for the Colonies, Lord Glenelg. Molesworth's speech on March 6 was a sharp attack on the government's colonial policy; his motion was defeated.

6. Brackets in this sentence indicate where page is torn.

7. See preceding letter, n. 3.

8. No political article appeared in the next (the April) number of *LWR*.

9. JSM originally wrote, "what my relations are likely to be," and then amended it as shown.

* * * *

1. MS at LSE.

the Tower of London[2]—which I hope it will not be inconsistent with your engagements to undertake. The subject is attractive, & treated by you, would be excellent for the light readers & would add to the sort of reputation we most want & are only beginning to acquire.

Robertson tells me you have a copy of Mr. Milnes' volume[3] of poems: if you are not needing it for a day or two, would it be too much to beg the favour of a sight of it? Something relating to the next number of the Review may depend upon the opinion we form of it—if left at Hooper's or sent by omnibus or parcel company to the I.H. I should receive it.

Ever yours truly

J. S. MILL

241. TO JOSEPH BLANCO WHITE[1]

India House
17th May 1838

MY DEAR SIR

I have been extremely concerned to hear from your friend Mr Thom[2] the form which your complaints have assumed & the increase of your infirmities. It grieves me to think that living alone as you do & at such a distance from most of your friends, they cannot know how you are attended, & have it little in their power to do anything that might promote your comfort. I do hope you will consider me as one of those whom it would most gratify to be of any use to you or to shew in any way my deep respect & regard for you. Pray do not hesitate a moment in letting me know of anything you need, & I should consider it a great favour if Mr Thom or some other friend would now & then write me word to tell me how you are.

It was hardly needful to ask permission of the review for the publication of the article which you were so kind as to write for us—we cannot of

2. Hunt contributed the article to the Aug., 1838, *LWR*, XXIX, 433–61.

3. Richard Monckton Milnes, *Poems of Many Years*, privately printed, 1838, reviewed by JSM in *LWR*, XXIX, 308–20.

* * * *

1. MS in Liverpool University Library. Excerpts published in J. H. Thom, "Archbishop Whately and the Life of Blanco White," *Theological Review*, IV (Jan., 1867), 112.

2. John Hamilton Thom (1808–1894), Unitarian minister, editor of the *Christian Teacher*, and editor of the life of White.

course derive anything but pleasure from seeing it in print & in the hands of every one who can be induced to read it, & I regret much that we could not with safety to the circulation of our review, make it the vehicle for sentiments so much bolder than any large class of readers can yet bear.

I have not yet thanked you for your notes on the Oxford Theology & on Sewell's article.[3] We have not yet been able to take up the subject, but we hope to do so in our October number,[4] & both those notes & those on Oxford itself will be of great assistance to us in treating those subjects which are of a kind that is more & more superseding in importance politics & everything else.

I assure you it is only my multiplied & multiplying occupations & cares that prevent me from being a much less infrequent correspondent of yours—they prevent me indeed from writing almost any letter without some special object—but to be of any use to you is an object for which I should easily find time.

Ever faithfully yours

J. S. MILL

242. TO JOHN ROBERTSON[1]

[June or July, 1838(?)]

DEAR ROBERTSON,

I cannot bestow upon Bulwer's article[2] any milder name than despicable, & nothing could reconcile me to inserting it in any shape but the absolute impossibility of finding any substitute for it in time. I have drawn my pen through some of the stupidest & most conceited things, and sent the rest to press—and God grant that nobody may read it, or that whoever does, will instantaneously forget every word of it.

Ever yours

J. S. MILL.

3. Probably the article "Memorials of Oxford," *QR*, LXI (Jan., 1838), 203–38, which has been identified as by the Rev. William Sewell (1804–1874), who was later to break with the Tractarians because of the Romanizing tendencies of their movement.

4. No such article appeared.

* * * *

1. Published by Towers, p. 65. MS at LSE.

2. Probably Bulwer's "Courts of British Queens," *LWR*, XXIX (Aug., 1838), 281–308.

243. TO JOHN ROBERTSON[1]

[July (?), 1838]

DEAR R.,—

I shall not be in town this evening, but will meet you at Hooper's to-morrow. I wish you would verify two queries of mine in the second sheet of Montaigne.[2] You will see them in a corrected proof which I have returned to Reynell's,[3] and from which, when that is done, it may be printed off. S[terling] has overlooked some bad mistakes.

I send the Arctic[4] with my corrections. They relate solely to small matters, but I do not think you are aware how often your sentences are not only unscholarlike, but absolutely unintelligible, from inattention to ambiguities of small words and of collocation. This article is a splendid instance of it.

Simpson[5] has made all his corrections in such a manner that the printers are sure not to attend to them, but I have left this to you to remedy when you have determined how far to adopt them.

J. S. MILL.

If we are *much* above our fourteen sheets, I think H.M.[6] ought to wait till October. It will do as well then, if not better, and I am very anxious to save expense of that kind.

244. TO HENRY COLE[1]

Kensington
Friday evg.
[July (?), 1838]

DEAR COLE,

It was provoking that they did not get the revise[2] ready for you, nor did I get mine till about six o'clock & I have been obliged to return it finally corrected for the press.

1. Published by Towers, p. 62. MS not located. Dated by Mrs. Towers as "Probably September, 1837," but the letter concerns the Aug., 1838, number of the *Review*.
2. John Sterling's "Montaigne and his Writings," *LWR*, XXIX (Aug., 1838), 321–52.
3. The printing office at 16 Little Pulteney St., Westminster, of Charles Reynell, printer of both the *LWR* and the *Examiner*.
4. "The Arctic Discoveries," signed S.R., *LWR*, XXIX (Aug., 1838), 373–92.
5. Sir George Simpson (1792–1860), administrator of the Hudson's Bay Company's territory. He had evidently been asked to check the accuracy of Robertson's article.
6. Harriet Martineau. Her article, "Domestic Service," did appear in the Aug. number, pp. 405–32.

* * * *

1. From copy supplied by Professor J. M. McCrimmon, University of Illinois, of the MS in his possession.
2. Cole's "Modern Wood Engraving," *LWR*, XXIX (Aug., 1838), 265–80.

We have said all that Jackson[3] wanted, in his note which I return herewith. We have also put in Branston's[4] name beside Vizetelly's[5] & have adopted several of your minor suggestions. I did not on consideration think it worth while to say anything more about [handbills?], when there was nothing to talk of but initial letters—nor to give a statement of the publications for which Orrin Smith[6] inquires, when our illustrations & the list annexed to them already do it sufficiently. Jackson's case was different, as he was passed rather slightly over. But Smith I am sure has nothing to complain of now.

I have put X (by itself) as the signature at the end.

Ever yours,

J. S. MILL.

245. TO AN UNIDENTIFIED CORRESPONDENT[1]

13 Pall Mall East
12th Septr 1838

MY DEAR SIR

According to Sterling's directions I send the proof of his very interesting article[2] to you—having first made two or three alterations which he desired me to make.[3] There is one further alteration which I asked him to consent to, but my letter did not reach Hastings till he had left it—& as he gave you full power to make alterations I venture to submit the expediency of doing so in this instance, to your judgment. The questionable point is, the intimation that Simonides may possibly have had some supernatural monition at the feast of Scopas.[4] I know all that may be said in favour of such a supposition—I know that Dr Johnson believed in ghosts, & Wesley said he could not positively refuse his belief to the *convulsionnaire* miracles at Paris. But these reasons do not at all convince me, & if it be necessary to stand up against the almost unanimous opinion both of the believing & unbelieving world, (who would agree in considering it impossible that a miracle should have been wrought in the name of false gods) I should like it to be on some occasion which required it & on which my own convictions went with it.

3. John Jackson (1801–1848), wood engraver.
4. Allen Robert Branston (1778–1827), wood engraver.
5. James Henry Vizetelly (d. 1838), publisher, father of Henry Vizetelly (1820–1894), pioneer of the illustrated press.
6. John Orrin Smith (1799–1843), wood engraver.

* * * *

1. MS at LSE. 2. "Simonides," *LWR*, XXXII (Dec., 1838), 99–136.
3. In a letter of Sept. 4, as yet unpublished; MS at King's.
4. See Sterling's article (cited in n. 2 above), p. 112.

I do not feel that I am at liberty to make any alteration myself, but you are, & to your discretion I refer it.

I shall be out of town for the next four weeks, during which time please direct to John Robertson Esq 13 Pall Mall East instead of me—& believe me

Most truly yours

J. S. MILL

246. TO SIR WILLIAM MOLESWORTH[1]

October, 1838.

[In a later letter from John Mill to Sir William, October 1838, there is a passage about a sum of £17 which Mill said was on "every account" Molesworth's and he adds:] If you get it, let Woolcombe[2] know that he may include it in the statement of your disbursements for the Review, which I am sorry to say it goes but a little way to liquidate.

247. TO JOHN ROBERTSON[1]

Axminster
2d October 1838

MY DEAR ROBERTSON

I duly received your letter, but I had so little to say in answer to it that I delayed from day to day until now in conscience I cannot delay any longer writing to tell you not to address any more letters to Torquay. I hope the one I received is the only one you have sent there, but as I left that neighbourhood two days ago I may perhaps have missed one. I am now going to Weymouth where I expect to stay about a week and shall be in town about the 15th as I intended.

I have been thinking very little about the review but a good deal about my Logic, of which I have, since I left town, completely planned the concluding portion & written a large piece of it which I hope I shall add to during my stay at Weymouth. I have also read the third (newly pub-

1. Excerpt published by Fawcett, p. 65. MS not located. The portion in brackets is Mrs. Fawcett's summary.

2. Thomas Woollcombe, Sir William's solicitor and friend. Molesworth, not wholly in agreement with JSM's political views and wearied of the financial burden of the *Review*, had yielded the proprietorship to JSM. See Letter 231.

* * * *

1. *Addressed*: John Robertson Esq. / 13 Pall Mall East / London. *Postmarks*: B / 4 OC 4 / 1838, and Axminster / 150. Published, with omissions, by Towers, pp. 66–67. MS at LSE.

lished) volume[2] of Comte's book, which is almost if not quite equal to the two former. This is much pleasanter work than planning the next number of the review—for which I have not a single idea beyond what we had when we last talked on the subject. Our not coming out in October is of no consequence at all,[3] for people will hardly say after our last brilliant number and our second edition,[4] that the review is dropped.

I have seen scarcely any newspapers, and none which contain reports of the Palace Yard meeting.[5] Those particulars about the arming are very ominous of important results at no long distance, but I cannot see in the menacing attitude of the working classes anything to prevent a Tory ministry and the middle classes are still very far indeed from the time when they will cry *Concede*—they will be much more likely to cry *Resist*!

Your idea about Mazzini's article seems to me good.[6] If Carlyle cannot take to either of the subjects we had in view for him we must be thankful for anything he can take to. I am sorry James Martineau has given up the Catholic subject. What answer have you given to Lucas?[7] As for the American Slavery article I think it a good subject for making the number interesting and saleable & as more likely to be well treated by H.M.[8] than [any] subject on which she has yet written for us, [but] it must be a condition that she shall not be sentimental, which she has more tendency to than any other writer we have.[9] You do not think of it for this number I believe. I cannot judge of the other two subjects you mention & as I said before I have not a single idea of my own—& am too glad at not having to think on the subject for a fortnight yet to come.

I am sorry you have been unwell—I have not been quite well myself, but am getting better. It was only a cold.

Ever yours,

J. S. MILL.

P.S. I think we are bound to give some answer to the Globe man,[10] driveler or not. I have no doubt he is a driveler or in the hands of drivelers on that subject.[11]

2. *La Philosophie chimique et la philosophie biologique* (Paris, 1838), Vol. III of his *Cours de Philosophie positive.*

3. The next number of the *LWR* is dated Dec., 1838.

4. The publication of a second edition of the Aug. number had permitted JSM to add his timely article, "Lord Durham and his Assailants," XXIX, 507–12.

5. A Chartist meeting on Sept. 17, 1838, addressed by, among others, William Lovett, Henry Hetherington, Ebenezer Elliott, and Feargus O'Connor.

6. Mazzini's article, "Prince Napoleon Louis Bonaparte," appeared in the Dec. *LWR* (XXXII, 85–98).

7. Probably Samuel Lucas (1811–1865), journalist and politician.

8. The leading article of the Dec. number was Harriet Martineau's "The Martyr Age of the United States."

9. Brackets in this sentence indicate where page is torn, but printed in Towers.

10. Not identified.

11. The postscript is written at the top of the first page.

248. TO SIR WILLIAM MOLESWORTH[1]

[Oct. 19, 1838]

The present turn in Canada affairs brings Lord Durham home, incensed to the utmost (as Buller writes to me)[2] with both Whigs and Tories—Whigs especially, and in the best possible mood for setting up for himself; and if so, the formation of an efficient party of moderate Radicals, of which our Review will be the organ, is certain—the Whigs will be kicked out never more to rise, and Lord D. will be head of the Liberal Party, and ultimately Prime Minister.

I am delighted with Buller; his letters to his father and mother and to me show him in a nobler character than he ever appeared in before, and he and Wakefield[3] appear to be acting completely as one man, speaking to Lord D. with the utmost plainness, giving him the most courageous and judicious advice, which he receives both generously and wisely. He is the man for us, and we shall have him and make a man of him yet. . . . There is a great game for you to play in the next session of Parliament. Buller has the best cards in the House of Commons, and I think he will play them well, but yours are the next best. As for me, this has awakened me out of a period of torpor about politics during which my Logic has been advancing rapidly. This winter, I think, will see me through the whole of it except the rewriting.

—Yours most truly,

J. S. MILL

249. TO SIR WILLIAM MOLESWORTH[1]

India House,
Nov. 14, 1838.

DEAR MOLESWORTH,—What think you of all this rumpus in Canada? I find all the Whigs and Moderates here blame Lord Durham for the Proclamation,[2] and he has already the greater part of the real Radicals

1. Published by Fawcett, pp. 203–4. MS not located.
2. Charles Buller had served as Chief Secretary to Lord Durham in Canada.
3. Edwin Gibbon Wakefield accompanied Durham to Canada as an unofficial adviser; he and Buller were responsible for much of Durham's famous Report.

* * * *

1. Published by Fawcett, p. 204. MS not located.
2. On learning that the government had disallowed his ordinance banishing to Bermuda some of the leaders of the Canadian revolt, Durham on Oct. 9 issued a proclamation of the act of indemnity passed by Parliament and of the disallowance of his ordinance. He further made the proclamation a defence of his policy in Canada.

against him for the Ordinance. But I think the Liberal party in the country generally is with him. I mean to stand by him, as my letters from Buller[3] and Rintoul's from Wakefield convince me that he was quite right in resigning, and that he comes home fully prepared (if the damned pseudo-Radicals do not get round him and talk him over) to set up for himself. For the purpose of acting at once upon him and upon the country in that *sens* I have written an elaborate defence of him, which will be published in the Review next week,[4] and will be in the newspapers before that. I hope exceedingly that you will approve of it, for if this man really tries to put himself at the head of the Liberals, your standing by him will do a world of good[. . . .] Write to me sometimes to say how you are[. . . .] Ever yours,

J. S. MILL

250. TO JOHN ROBERTSON[1]

13, Pall Mall, East, Monday.
[Nov., 1838]

DEAR ROBERTSON,

The inclosed is from Bulwer, and is exactly what we would expect from him. In the meantime Rintoul has shown me a letter from Wakefield, enthusiastic about Lord Durham, and full of the predictions respecting him which we most wish to see realized, though in general terms.

There is no concealing from ourselves that there is almost an equal chance of Lord D. acting either way,[2] and that his doing the one or the other will wholly depend upon whether Wakefield, we ourselves, and probably Buller and his own resentment, or Bulwer, Fonblanque, Edward Ellice, the herd of professing Liberals, and the indecision and cowardice indigenous to English noblemen, have the greatest influence in his councils.

3. A letter of Buller's to JSM, dated Quebec, Oct. 13, 1838, is published in the Dominion of Canada's *Report of the Public Archives for the Year 1928* (Ottawa, 1929), App. F, pp. 74–77. The MS of another, dated Oct. 19, is at LSE.

4. The *LWR* for Dec., containing JSM's "Lord Durham's Return" (XXXII, 241–60), was published Nov. 26, 1838.

* * * *

1. Published by Towers, p. 68. MS not located. Dated by Mrs. Towers as of "1837 during the Canada coercion and rebellion," but the reference to Wakefield's letter to Rintoul seems to establish approximately the same date as the preceding letter to Molesworth.

2. I.e., joining with the Radicals to form a new Liberal party or continuing with what JSM in the preceding letter called the "pseudo-Radicals" of the Whig party.

Give us access to him *early* and I will be d——d[3] if we do not make a hard fight for it.

Ever yours,

J. S. MILL.

251. TO MRS. JAMES MILL[1]

Paris
28th Dec[r] 1838

DEAR MAMMY

Please send the first page of this scrawl to Robertson[2]—it saves double postage.

I am about as well, I think, as when I left London. I had a wretched passage—for want of water the boat could not get into Boulogne till half past two in the morning—it set off at ½ past eight & spent the whole 18 hours in going as slowly as it could. My already disordered stomach stood the sickness very ill & I arrived very uncomfortable & was forced to start for Paris a very few hours afterwards. The first day I was uncomfortable enough, but as the effect of the sea went off I got better & arrived at Paris after 30 hours of the diligence much less unwell than I thought I possibly could. Unless I could have got to Marseilles by the 30th it was of no use getting there before the 9th so I do not start till Sunday morning & shall not travel any more at night, but post to Chalons (expensive as it is) & then go down the Saone & Rhone to Avignon. Letters put in the post on the 2nd directed to M. J.S. Mill Poste Restante à Marseille France, will be sure to reach me in time. After that direct Poste Restante à Pise, Italie.—I cannot tell if I shall have time to write to you from Marseille but I will endeavour. The weather has not got very cold yet & I dare say I shall get into the mild climate first.

They call England's a bad climate but the north and east of France have certainly a worse. What I most dread is the sea passage from Marseille to Leghorn—seasickness is so bad with me now. Love to all—

yours affectionately

J. S. MILL

3. It is improbable that JSM wrote the word thus.

* * * *

1. MS at LSE. *Addressed*: Mrs. Mill / 18 Kensington Square / Kensington / London / Angleterre. *Postmarks*: PARIS / 29 / DEC / 1838, and LONDON / 31 / DEC / 1838. Published, with minor variations, in Hayek, p. 106.

JSM had again been directed by his physician to take a medical leave of absence and go to the Continent for his health. Mrs. Taylor, who was also in poor health, arrived in Paris shortly ahead of JSM, but subsequently accompanied him to Italy. For an account of this period, see Packe, pp. 238–40.

2. See following letter.

252. TO JOHN ROBERTSON[1]

[Paris,] 28th December, 1838.

DEAR ROBERTSON,

The steamboat by which I shall go from Marseilles[2] does not leave till the *tenth*; therefore you may direct to me there as late as the 2d, or you may risk even the 3d, if there be any reason for it.

Use Browning's means of conveyance as much as you can, but if he sends Sordello we must not let him suppose that we can promise a review of it in the February number.[3]

I cannot, on looking forward to my movements, and the time it will take before I feel settled enough to write, feel it at all likely, if even *possible*, that I can do more than the organization in time to send you for publication in February. When we asked him for Sordello, it was in hopes of finishing it before I set out.

If it must be reviewed in the February number, somebody else must do it; and perhaps that is best, at any rate, for I *cannot* honestly give much praise either to Strafford or Paracelsus. Yet I do not know whom we could get to do it.

Is the account I have seen copied from the English papers of Lord D[urham]'s Canada plans authentic? They seem good mostly, but the notion of a separate colonial office for North America seems rather foolish in itself (as if, instead of curing the defects of the whole system, we were to try to get one set of colonies *excepted* from it) and quite unpractical to propose, because impossible to carry out, or even to make acceptable to anybody.

The idea of adding British America to the Queen's title is laughably pedantic and absurd, and the notion of giving the colonies representatives in the H. of C. cannot be entertained by anybody who has one grain of statesmanship in his head.

I do hope the report will contain no such nonsense, and if you think there is the slightest chance of it pray tell me, that I may write strongly to Buller[4] against it.

1. Published by Towers, pp. 69–70. MS not located. Presumably the first page of JSM's preceding letter of same date and place to his mother, which he asks her to detach and send to Robertson.

2. See preceding letter.

3. No review of Browning's *Sordello* appeared. The next number of the *LWR* was not published until April.

4. Charles Buller, as Lord Durham's secretary, played an important (some say the major) role in the composition of the famous Report, which was published early the next year: *Report on the Affairs of British North America from the Earl of Durham, Her Majesty's High Commissioner*. Ordered, by the House of Commons, to be printed (London, 1839).

I have inquired yesterday morning and this morning for letters, but found none. I doubt not I shall find some from you (if not from other people) at Marseilles.

Yours ever truly,

J. S. MILL.

Write fully to me on the reception Lord D.'s plans meet with, if these *be* his plans, and the sort of attacks made on them.

Write long letters and often,—you will have so much to write about. Your letters will be a great pleasure to me, as I expect from them the particulars of a game well played in which I have a deep stake.

J. S. MILL.

• • • 1839 • • •

253. TO AN UNIDENTIFIED CORRESPONDENT[1]

[Rome, March 11, 1839]

I have returned here after passing about three weeks very pleasantly in Naples, and the country about it. I did not for some time get any better, but I think I am now, though very slowly, improving, ever since I left off animal food, and took to living almost entirely on macaroni. I began this experiment about a fortnight ago, and it seems to succeed better than any of the other experiments I have tried. [The remainder of the letter describes Naples and the neighbourhood—"Pompeii, Baiæ, Pæstum, &c."]

254. TO AN UNIDENTIFIED CORRESPONDENT[1]

[March 21, 1839]

As for me I am going on well too—not that my health is at all better; but I have gradually got quite reconciled to the idea of returning in much the same state of health as when I left England; it is by care and regimen that I must hope to get well, and if I can only avoid getting worse, I shall have no great reason to complain, as hardly anybody continues after my age (33)[2] to have the same vigorous health they had in early youth. In the meantime it is something to have so good an opportunity of seeing Italy.

1. Excerpt published by Bain, *JSM*, p. 45. MS not located. Bracketed portion is Bain's summary.

* * * *

1. Excerpt published by Bain, *JSM*, p. 45. MS not located. Bain notes that the letter was written ten days after the preceding one.
2. The parenthesis is probably by Bain.

255. TO JOHN ROBERTSON[1]

[Italy, April (?), 1839]

Dear Robertson,

I have been very much annoyed by seeing announced in the advertisement of the Review the article[2] which, in a letter that must have reached you in time, I so very particularly requested you to omit; and my annoyance has not been diminished by the manner in which the announcement is made, which is fitter for the Satirist or the Age than for any periodical which lays claim either to a literary character or a gentlemanly one.

I certainly never contemplated making any work in which I was engaged a vehicle for either attacking or defending the reputation of women, and in whatever way it has been done, it must make the Review consummately ridiculous. However, it is of no use writing more about what is past mending.

256. TO JOHN ROBERTSON[1]

Rome, 6th April, 1839.

I have, as you see, taken plenty of time to consider about the manner in which what you told me about Lord Durham in your last letter affects the position of the Review and the question of continuing or not to carry it on.

The result is to strengthen very greatly the inclination I had before to get it off my hands. I shall form no sudden resolution, and above all shall wait till I see Lord Durham myself before I make up my mind finally. But if his purposes are such as he appears to have declared to you, I do not feel myself particularly called upon to tender him any other aid than that of my good wishes. He may be quite right, and there may be no better course to be taken than the one he means to take, but it cannot lead to the organization of a radical party, or the placing of the radicals at the head of

1. Published by Towers, p. 67. MS not located.

2. The April number (XXXII, 459–75) contained an article by Robertson, "Criticism on Women," a defence of women in general but in particular of women writers like Mrs. Norton, Lady Morgan, Miss Edgeworth, and Miss Martineau against the satirical, critical assaults which Robertson labels "Crokerism."

* * * *

1. Published by Towers, p. 70. MS not located.

the movement,—it leaves them as they are already, a mere appendage of the Whigs; and if there is to be no radical party there need be no Westminster Review, for there is no position for it to take, distinguishing it from the Edinburgh.

For my own part, I feel that if the time is come when a radical review should support the Whigs, the time is come when I should withdraw from politics. I can employ myself much better than in conducting a ministerial review, and should think my time and money ill spent in doing only what the Examiner and the Chronicle and all that class of publications can do and are doing much more effectually. In short, it is one thing to support Lord Durham in *forming* a party; another to follow him when he is only joining one, and that one which I have so long been crying out against.

If he shows any desire to cultivate my acquaintance I shall respond to it, shall give him my opinion freely whenever he asks it, and any help in a private way which he may think that he needs and that I can give; but as for the Review, even if he would bear the whole expense and leave me the entire control, I doubt *now* whether I should accept it. On the other hand, any chance of the Review's paying its expenses without being considered as his organ, or that of persons who are acting in concert with him, is still farther off than before.

I am sorry that my political article should have been inserted in any shape in a posture of affairs so unsuitable to it, and as I am sure it must have been very much altered to be put in at all, I do hope you have not put my signature to it.[2]

I do not feel clear about publishing even another number.[3] I have not put pen to paper except to write letters since I left Pisa, and I do not intend to do so: when I reach England I shall for some time be extremely busy; and to work hard for a thing one has almost determined to give up seems waste of labor. I shall be glad if you can avoid entering into any *positive* engagements about articles for the July number till I return and can look about me.

I have begun to improve in health (I think so, at least) since the weather grew hot,—it is now complete summer here,—and I expect much more benefit from the three months to come than I have derived from the three that are past. When will you write again?

Ever yours,

J. S. MILL.

2. "Reorganization of the Reform Party," *LWR*, XXXII (April, 1839), 475–508, bore JSM's usual signature, A.

3. Another number did not appear until Oct.; it carried no article by JSM.

257. TO MRS. JAMES MILL[1]

Venice
19th May 1839

MY DEAR MOTHER—I have been some days in this strange & fine old place, the most singular place in Italy—& I write to say that I am going to set out almost immediately on my return. I shall go by the Tyrol, & through Germany, slowly; if you write very soon, write to Mannheim; if not, to Brussels. As to how far the object of my journey has been attained, that is rather difficult to say, & I shall probably be able to say more about it after I have been for some time returned & have resumed my regular occupations. I certainly have not recovered my former health; at the same time I have no very troublesome complaint & no symptoms at all alarming & I have no doubt that by proper regimen & exercise I shall be able to have as good health as people generally have, though perhaps never again so good a digestion as formerly. In this however I shall be no worse off than three fourths of all the people I know. I am not the least liable to catch cold—I never was less so in my life, & all idea of the English climate being dangerous for me may be entirely dismissed from all your minds. I shall in time find out how to manage myself—indeed I think I have in a great measure found it out already.—I have found no letters at Venice except one old one from Robertson. I do not know if any have been written but I shall leave word to send them after me to Munich where at any rate I hope to find some. Will you shew this or tell the contents of it to Grant[2] & thank him warmly from me for his unwearied obligingness & kindness—& will you or the boys tell Mr. Robertson that his letter without date, but bearing I think the postmark 1st April, & directed to Rome, did not for some reason or other reach me there, but has followed me here, & is the last I have had from him & I am hoping for another with fresher news about himself & all other matters—also that I have not yet seen the review, for although they take it at the reading room in Florence, they had not yet got the last number. I have been unusually long without English news having neither had any letters nor seen any newspapers but of very old date. But I shall make it all up six weeks hence.—I have had a most pleasant stay in Italy & may say that I have seen it pretty thoroughly—I have left nothing out except Sicily, & a few stray things here & there. I have been last staying at the baths of Abano in the Euganean hills, not far from Padua—most lovely country, more of the English sort than Italy generally is—but the weather

1. MS at LSE. *Addressed*: Mrs Mill / 18 Kensington Square / Kensington / London / Inghilterra. *Postmarks*: VEN / . . . . / and LONDON / 29 / MAY / 1839. Published, with minor variations, in Hayek, pp. 108–9.

2. Horace Grant.

for a month past has been as bad as a wet English summer except that it has never been cold. Italy is a complete disappointment as to climate—not comparable as to brightness & dryness to the South of France, though I can easily believe that some parts of it are more beneficial to certain complaints. Among other fruits of my journey I have botanized much, & come back loaded with plants. By the bye among those I want Henry to dry for me, I forgot to mention the common elder. Italy is no disappointment as to beauty, it is the only country I have ever seen which is more beautiful than England—& I have not seen a mile of it that is not beautiful. I expect to enjoy the passage of the Alps exceedingly if the weather will let me, & there seems to-day some chance of its clearing—it is the first day without rain for a fortnight past.—Let me hear from some of you soon.

affectionately

J. S. MILL

258. TO JOHN ROBERTSON[1]

Munich, 31st May, 1839.

DEAR ROBERTSON,

On arriving here I found your letter of the 13th of May from Edinburgh. Another letter had followed me from Rome to Venice, though it must have reached Rome in time to have been given to me there.

I hope by this time you see your way through your troubles and annoyances, and are in better spirits and health.

About the state of politics and about the Review it is of no use writing much when we shall see each other so soon. I have seen no English papers since the turn-out and turn-in of the ministry,[2] and what I know of it is chiefly from letters, the latest and most explicit of which is from Buller.[3] But I expect no change whatever in the politics of the ministry as long as Melbourne is at their head; and when a change does come it will be so gradual and imperceptible that the Review will not profit much by it. I must get rid of the Review not only on account of the expense, but the time and exertion. I think myself, and still more everybody else, including the doctors and the India House people, will think, that I must not undertake so much work; especially when I first come back and have a long arrear of business at the I.H. It will be quite impossible for me to write *anything* for the Review, and the next number must certainly appear without anything of

1. Published by Towers, pp. 71–72. MS not located.

2. On May 7 the Melbourne ministry resigned but within forty-eight hours, after Sir Robert Peel's failure to form a government, was reinstated.

3. See Buller's letter of May 21 to Robertson, published by Towers, p. 71.

mine in it. I can better spare even money than time and labor for that number.

And I see no prospect of Lord Durham or anybody else taking it off my hands, as matters stand at present. I ought not to drop it without trying to preserve an organ for radicalism by offering it to any radical who would carry it on, on radical lines. Do you think Dilke[4] would now be willing to take it, and would you sound him on the subject? I have not yet seen the last number, for though the reading-room at Florence takes it, everything is so long in coming that they are always far behind. I shall probably see it at Brussels. Will you thank Buller for his letter, and say I would answer it if I were not likely to see him so soon?—but I am so little able to judge of the present state of the public mind in England that I cannot judge whether he or the ten radicals who voted against the ministry[5] were in the right. I think it likely that I should have done as he did, because the ministerial measure was probably right in itself, however absurdly defended; but if Grote and Molesworth thought the measure bad, I think they were right in voting against it. Buller's remarks on the general state of politics seem to me sensible and right; whether his practical views are right or not will depend very much on the conduct of the ministry, which I feel persuaded will entirely disappoint both him and you. The radicals will not insist on any conditions, and if they did the ministry would reject them.

I shall leave this place in a day or two for Mannheim and the Rhine, from whence I shall go to Brussels, where I hope to find a letter from you. I shall be in London at latest on the 30th of June. I am coming back not at all cured, but cured of caring much about cure. I have no doubt I shall in time get accustomed to dyspepsia, as Lafontaine hoped he should to the regions below.

Ever yours,

J. S. MILL.

259. TO AN UNIDENTIFIED CORRESPONDENT[1]

[Munich, May 31, 1839]

I am not at all cured, but I cease to care much about it. I am as fit for all my occupations as I was before, and as capable of bodily exertion as I have been of late years—only I have not quite so good a stomach.

4. Charles Wentworth Dilke.

5. The desertion of ten Radical members from the Whigs on the Jamaica bill division on May 6 led to the temporary dissolution of the Melbourne government.

* * * *

1. Excerpt published by Bain, *JSM*, p. 45. MS not located.

260. TO JOHN STERLING[1]

I.H.
24th July 1839

MY DEAR STERLING

I did not need the arrival of the second packet to know whether the article[2] would suit me or not—& if I could have had any doubts, that packet would have removed them—the contents of that same not being liable to even the minor objections which I might have raised to the first.

There are, as you surmised, (but confined almost entirely to the introductory part) many opinions stated in which speculatively I do not agree; but the time is long gone by when I considered such differences as those are, matters of first rate moment; & if I have a fault to find with your Introduction—it is a fault only with respect to *my* readers—viz. that it gives an account of the transcendental part (if I may so call it) of Carlyle's opinions in somewhat too transcendental a manner; & not interpreting his views in language intelligible to persons of opposite schools, will scarcely serve to recommend him to any (some of the religious excepted) who are not already capable of appreciating him in his own writings. But "I speak as to the wise—judge ye what I say."

In the passage on Superstition, I think you hardly do justice to Carlyle's meaning. When he called Voltaire the destroyer of European superstition,[3] I do not think he meant by superstition those fears & anxieties respecting the invisible world, which I understand you to mean that nothing but religion can save a meditative & sensitive character from—I think he meant by superstition, all such dogmatic religious belief as is not well grounded, & will not bear a close investigation, & especially, in his view, any religious belief resting on logic, or external evidences. If this be his meaning, what you say on the subject is scarcely in place—& the more commonplace meaning which I suppose him to have had, is perhaps maintainable, viz. that the first acute sceptic whose writings obtained European popularity, was thereby the destroyer for ever in the European mind of the absurdities which had entwined themselves with religion & the groundless arguments which were currently used in its support.

1. *Addressed*: Rev. John Sterling / Manor House / Clifton Place / Clifton / near Bristol. *Postmark*: LS / 24 JY 24 / 1839. MS at King's. Published in Elliot, I, 112–13. Sterling had moved his family from London to Clifton the preceding month.

2. Later note in JSM's hand: "The article on Carlyle ['Carlyle's Works,' *LWR*, XXXIII (Oct., 1839), 1–68], republished in Sterling's collected writings."

3. In his essay on Voltaire, first published in the *Foreign Review*, III (April, 1829), 419–75.

I have not a word more to say in the way of criticism—I am delighted with the article, & so I am persuaded will almost everybody be, whose good opinion is desirable—

ever truly yours

J. S. MILL.

261. TO EDWIN CHADWICK[1]

I.H.
Tuesday
[Aug. 6, 1839]

DEAR CHADWICK

I have not yet been able to manage a visit to you—& I do not like a flying visit, especially when it is also a *first* visit[2]—*shall* you be able to go down on Saturday? We all hope so very much.

Ever yours

J. S. MILL

262. TO JOHN ROBERTSON[1]

13 Pall Mall, East, Friday.
[Sept., 1839]

DEAR ROBERTSON,

Though I cannot find fault with you for not coming to town this week, it has happened unluckily, as I was waiting impatiently to talk with you about Horne's article and Mrs. Hall's.

The former I send. You will hardly believe that the fellow has not even *mentioned* any *one* of the plays he pretends to review. It is a mere dissertation (though for him tolerably well done) on his dreadful *ennuyeux* subject of the "precarious state of the drama," which nobody on earth cares for except playwriters by profession, and which he and a few others have made so dreadfully vulgar by their raving about it that the very sight of the words is disgusting to everybody of common good taste. Will you decide

1. *Addressed*: Edwin Chadwick Esq. / Poor Law Commission Office / Somerset House. *Postmarks*: TP / Leadenhall St. and 2 AN2 / AU6 / 1839. MS at UCL.
2. "*First* visit," i.e., to the newly established home of Chadwick, who had married Rachel Dawson Kennedy on July 23.

* * * *

1. Published by Towers, pp. 65–66. MS not located. Not dated by Mrs. Towers, but the reference to Mrs. Hall's article seems to establish the approximate date.

as to this article as you like, and write to Horne about it?[2] He has already been at the printer's, it seems.

As for Mrs. Hall's,[3] I have not yet dared to touch it. It is beyond all measure bad, and impossible to be made better. It has no one good point but a few of the stories towards the end, and those are told cleverly and with sprightliness, no doubt, but in the tone of a London shopkeeper's daughter.

If I have my way we shall reject it totally, but if you could possibly suggest to me any means of making it endurable I should be happy to try them.

One thing I am determined on: nothing shall go to Paris under my sanction and responsibility showing such ignorance and such cockney notions of France and French matters as this does.

J. S. M.

Leigh Hunt's article[4] is with the printers, and with some leaving out it does very well.

263. TO GUSTAVE D'EICHTHAL[1]

India House
14th September
1839

MY DEAR GUSTAVE

I am happy to hear from you again after so long an intermission of our correspondence.

I have received your little pamphlet[2] and have read it with the interest

2. The decision was evidently in the negative, for no such article appeared. R. H. Horne was apparently continuing on the theme of one of his earliest books, *The Exposition of the False Medium and Barriers Excluding Men of Genius from the Public* (London, 1833).

3. Anna Maria Hall (1800–1881), editor and novelist, wife of Samuel Carter Hall (1800–1889), editor and miscellaneous writer. Her one article published in *LWR* seems to have been the one referred to here: "Heads of the People," XXXIII (Oct., 1839), 162–81.

4. "New Translations of the Arabian Nights," *ibid.*, pp. 101–37.

* * * *

1. *Addressed*: Monsieur / M. Gustave d'Eichthal / 14 Rue Lepelletier / à Paris. *Postmarks*: LONDON / 14 / SEP / 1839 / F.B.O., and ANGL / 16 / SEPT / 39 / CALAIS. MS at Arsenal. Published in *Cosmopolis*, IX, 368–69, and in *D'Eichthal Corresp.*, pp. 171–73.

2. *Lettres sur la race noire et la race blanche* (Paris, 1839), in collaboration with Ismayl Urbain.

with which I always read anything of yours. I find in it, as I did in Les Deux Mondes,[3] a foundation of what seems to me important truth—I have long been convinced that not only the East as compared with the West, but the black race as compared with the European, is distinguished by characteristics something like those which you assign to them; that the improvement which may be looked for, from a more intimate & sympathetic familiarity between the two, will not be solely on their side, but greatly also on ours; that if our intelligence is more developed & our activity more intense, *they* possess exactly what is most needful to us as a qualifying counterpoise, in their love of repose & in the superior capacity of animal enjoyment & consequently of sympathetic sensibility, which is characteristic of the negro race.

I have even long thought that the same distinction holds, though in a less *prononcé* manner, between the nations of the north & south of Europe; that the north is destined to be the workshop, material & intellectual, of Europe; the south, its "stately pleasure-house"[4]—& that neither will fulfil its destination until it has made its peculiar function available for the benefit of both—until our *work* is done for their benefit, & until we, in the measure of our nature, are made susceptible of their luxury & sensuous enjoyment.

Thus you see I am very well prepared to give a favorable reception to your speculations & to join in your aspirations—& I am not less desirous than at any former period to keep up that sort of intellectual communion with you which I have already enjoyed. I do not find my enjoyment of speculation at all abated though I see less & less prospect of drawing together any body of persons to associate in the name & behalf of any set of fixed principles. Still, no good seed is lost: it takes root & springs up somewhere, & will help in time towards the general reconstruction of the opinions of the civilized world, for which ours is only a period of preparation, but towards which almost all the things & men of our time are working; though the *men*, for the most part, almost as unconsciously as the things. Therefore "cast ye your bread on the waters, & ye shall find it after many days."

I am much concerned to hear of your father's late illness & Adolphe's indisposition—pray assure them both, Adolphe especially, of my affectionate regards & tell me when you next write, very particularly, how they are.

ever truly yours,

J. S. MILL.

3. See Letter 197, n. 2.
4. Cf. Tennyson, "I built my soul a lordly pleasure-house" ("The Palace of Art").

264. TO JOHN STERLING[1]

India House
28 September 1839

MY DEAR STERLING

I have done by the separate copies[2] according to your directions, except that Carlyle having called on me the day I received your letter, I gave him the copy destined for him. He expressed great interest about it—& seemed to expect something much less favorable than he will probably find it. Putting together my idea of the man & of the thing, I cannot think but that he must be on the whole greatly pleased with it.

I would have written to you immediately after receiving your answer to my last if it had occurred to me that there could be any doubt about the satisfactoriness to me of that answer. I felt that you were quite right & I wrong about the way in which that part of the article would be taken by the majority of English religious people[3]—I though your corrections as far as they went diminished the force of my objections even in regard to the non-religious—& though I continued to think that there would have been a better way of stating Carlyle's creed, I felt quite unable to state what that better way would be, or to satisfy myself that it would be a better way from your point of view. Taking the article altogether, & notwithstanding that those of its thoughts to which I subscribe with a heartiness of assent & sympathy that I seldom feel in reading any speculations ancient or modern, are inseparably interwoven with views of the fundamentals of philosophy which I am unable rather than unwilling to adopt—I yet think there has been nothing published for many years so likely both to fix the attention of the best spirits & to be a source of light & warmth to them—& instead of thinking of it as you say you do with little pleasure, it will always be one of the most agreeable facts in my connexion with the review that this article appeared in it. I am even now not alone in thinking that it will be received by many as the appearance of a not insignificant new element in the present chaos of English opinion—& that many will look out eagerly for the future manifestations of the same.

If I carry on the review to another number it will be partly in order to publish in it an article on Coleridge[4] which I have always thought desirable as a counter-pole to the one on Bentham. I shall write the article whether

1. *Addressed*: Rev. John Sterling / Manor House / Clifton Place / Clifton / near Bristol. *Postmark*: LS / 28 SP 28 / 1839. MS at King's. Two paragraphs published in Elliot, I, 113–14.

2. Of Sterling's review of Carlyle in the Oct., 1839, *LWR*.

3. See Letter 260.

4. JSM did publish his article on Coleridge, in the last number of the *LWR* under his proprietorship, March, 1840, XXXIII, 257–302.

it appear in the review or elsewhere—& have begun a fresh study of Coleridge's writings for that purpose—but as there is so much of Coleridge which is not to be found except by implications in his published works, which are only one of the channels through which his influences have reached the age, I am fearful of understating both his merit & his importance—or rather of not producing sufficient detailed evidence to bear out my general estimate. I should have much preferred to see the subject treated by some one better versed in Coleridge, did it not seem essential to my purpose that the likeness should be taken from the same point of view as that of Bentham. It would be of most essential service to me to receive any suggestions or warnings from you, which may occur to you as needful, & especially such as would preserve me against overlooking any of the great thoughts, (whether general *philosophic* conceptions or single truths leading to important consequences) which he has contributed to the philosophy either explicit or implicit of the age, or which he has powerfully aided in deepening or diffusing. (I am ashamed of all this clumsy expression but you will understand what I mean). One essential part of my notice of him will be an attempt to enumerate & appreciate the principal of those thoughts, & perhaps that will be the only valuable part of the article. I hope therefore that I may be able to make it not absurdly incomplete.

I quite think with you that it is no part of my vocation to be a party leader, but at most to give occasional good advice to such as are fitted to be so. Whether I have any better vocation for being a philosopher, or whether you will think so when you see what I am capable of performing in that line, remains for the future to decide. I hope to give materials for the decision before long, as I can hardly fail I think to finish my Logic in the course of next year. I have endeavoured to keep clear so far as possible of the controversy respecting the perception of the highest Realities by direct intuition, confining Logic to the laws of the investigation of truth by means of extrinsic evidence whether ratiocinative or inductive. Still, I could not avoid conflict with some of the subordinate parts of the supersensual philosophy, which for aught I know may be as necessary to it as what may appear to me its fundamental principles & its only important results. I doubt therefore whether I can expect anything but opposition from the only school of metaphysical speculation which has any life or activity at present. But *nous verrons*. I have at all events made many things much clearer to myself than they were before—& that is something, even if I am destined to be my only disciple.

I am very far from agreeing, in all things, with the "Analysis,"[5] even on its own ground—though perhaps, from your greater distance, the interval between me & it may appear but trifling. But I can understand your need

5. James Mill's *Analysis of the Phenomena of the Human Mind* (1829).

of something beyond it & deeper than it, & I have often bad moods in which I would most gladly postulate like Kant a different ultimate foundation "subjectiver bedürfnisses willen" if I could.

I have left till the last what I have now barely room for—I consider myself your debtor not only in gratitude but pecuniarily for all that you have written in the review except the article on Montaigne[6]—that I as willingly accepted as you kindly offered. I hoped however that the profits of the review might some time or other enable it to pay its debt to you for that article too; but for the others you ought to be & must be paid now; gratuitous assistance to such an extent ought neither to be received nor given except where the giver is at least as well able to do without payment as the receiver is able to pay: what I have lost by the review is not so much as to be of importance to me, & this will not make any material addition to it. When I asked you to write I fully contemplated payment & would gladly have obtained cooperation like yours at any price I could afford. So when you next write pray tell me where & to whom I shall pay what is your due for this article & Simonides[7]—& now adieu—

Yours affectionately

J. S. Mill

265. TO JOHN STERLING[1]

India House
2d October
1839

My dear Sterling

I am very happy that you have put it in my power to acquit myself of a small part at least of the obligation I owe you. I know where I can get a copy of the Biographie Universelle at a very reasonable price—as well as Guizot's writings; & those you mention of my father's of course. But all these together are such a very small set off against two such articles as those, that you must really tell me of some other books that would be useful or pleasant to you, so that I might add them to the packet—& tell me where they should be sent.

6. See Letter 243, n. 2.

7. See Letter 245, n. 2.

* * * *

1. *Addressed*: Rev. John Sterling / Manor House / Clifton Place / Clifton / near Bristol. *Postmark*: LS / 2 OC 2 / 1839. MS at King's. Published in part in Elliot, I, 114–15.

I suppose you have got the review by this time—at least your father has, whom I saw yesterday & with whom I had some talk about your article[2]—he likes it very much but thinks you pass too lightly over Carlyle's faults—which as was to be expected, he exaggerates.—There is nothing of mine in the review except a few words of note at the end of your article. There is on the whole little in this number to interest you. The best thing is an article on Oliver Cromwell[3] by the editor, Robertson, which I should like you to read because I think it the first thing he has written which does anything like justice to his sentiments & capacity. Your very kind offer about reviewing Gladstone[4] I will think about. In reviewing Coleridge I cannot help going over much of the same ground, as his "Church & State" must of course be very prominent in any such view of him as I should take—this however is partly a reason *for*, as well as partly *against*, the treatment of the subject by you in the same number. I see no reason at all for your depreciating comments on the article on Carlyle—not that there are not things to be said against it, but I am convinced no competent judge except yourself, will see those things in as strong a light as you do—one naturally is a severe critic upon oneself. There *is*, no doubt, occasional looseness of expression—but also, frequently, great aptness & even condensation of it; & even something exceedingly like the stile of Coleridge himself, of whom I have been reading sentences which I could easily have mistaken for yours. I have come to this conclusion about your writing, that the more important & universal the subject, the better you treat it.

I have read through with great interest the little volume lately published by Pickering containing the Church & State & the Lay Sermons.[5] In the former I see more & more to admire, though I think, there & elsewhere, he runs riot with the great historical conception of a certain idea of the scope & fitting attributes of some social elements working in the minds of people from age to age without distinct consciousness on their part. This I am aware is the natural result of his system of metaphysics, but I who do not believe in pre-existent ideas see in as much as is true of this doctrine (& that much of it is true I contend as strongly as he) only the first confused view, suggested by our various instincts, of the various wants of society & of the mutual correlation of these.—On the particular doctrines of his political philosophy—it seems to me that he stands almost alone in having seen that the foundation of the philosophy of the subject is a perception what are those great interests (comprehending all others) each of which

2. "Carlyle's Works." See previous letter, and Letter 260.

3. *LWR*, XXXIII (Oct., 1839), 181–256.

4. W. E. Gladstone's *The State in its Relations with the Church* (London, 1838); no review of it appeared in *LWR*. See Letter 267.

5. *On the Constitution of Church and State* [3rd ed.], and *Lay Sermons* [2nd ed.], ed. H. N. Coleridge (London: William Pickering, 1839).

must have somebody bound & induced to stand up for it in particular, & between which a balance must be maintained—& I think with him that those great interests are two, *permanence* & *progression*. But he seems to me quite wrong in considering the land to be essentially identified with permanence & commercial wealth with progression. The land has something to do with permanence, but the antithesis, I think is rather between the contented classes & the aspiring—wealth & hopeful poverty—age & youth —hereditary importance & personal endowments.—As I think the Church & State the best, so the Lay Sermons seem to me the worst of Coleridge's writings yet known to me—though there are excellent passages in them.

I think exactly as you do about the doctrine which resolves the pleasure of music into association. I seem to myself to perceive clearly two elements in it, one dependent on association, the other not—& those elements combine in very varying proportions, as e.g. the former predominating in Gluck & Beethoven, the latter in Mozart.

I heard from Mr Sterling yesterday more than I liked to hear about the state of your health, though I trust not enough to inspire any serious apprehension. *Do* take care of yourself for you can ill be spared publicly or privately & by few (out of your own family) so ill as by

yours affectionately

J. S. Mill

As I finish this letter, behold a note from Carlyle.[6] He says "Sterling's is a splendid article: in spite of its enormous extravagance some will like it; many are sure to talk of it & on the whole to be instructed by it. No man in England has been better reviewed than I,—if also no one worse."—So far so good: & as for the "extravagance" I doubt not his modesty applies that appellation mainly to the praise.

The Moral Philosophy Chair at Glasgow is vacant, & my friend Nichol has written to me about finding some fit person to fill it—it is in the gift of the Professors & any good man would be sure of all that Nichol & Lushington[7] could do for him. Can you recommend any one? Alas that you are not in a condition to take it yourself.

It is worth, Nichol tells me, about £700 a year, & gives employment only for six months.[8]

6. In A. Carlyle, pp. 169–70, but dated Monday night [Oct. 7, 1839]; a more likely date for Carlyle's letter is Sept. 30, 1839. See also Carlyle's letter to Sterling, Sept. 29, 1839, in A. Carlyle, pp. 222–27.

7. Edmund L. Lushington (1811–1893), professor of Greek at Glasgow University; later the brother-in-law of Alfred Tennyson.

8. The last two paragraphs of the postscript are written at the top of the first page.

266. TO JOHN MITCHELL KEMBLE[1]

India House
14th October 1839

MY DEAR SIR,

There would be very great weight in the objections which you state to a junction of the two reviews[2] if the L. & W. really represented the sentiments of the great majority of those who buy it—but I do not believe this to be the case—I believe that the buyers of the L. & W. buy it only because it is the radical review & because they are radicals, i.e. people who wish to carry their changes beyond those which would be consented to by Whigs or Tories, & in particular who would widen the basis of the representative system. Provided these are the conclusions arrived at, I believe they will allow the writer to chuse his own premises. Among the points of principle which you enumerate, the Ballot is the only one which might threaten to set the readers of the L. & W. at variance with you, but I think rather because opposition to the ballot is interpreted as opposition to all radicalism. When the repudiation of the ballot is construed with a large declaration in favour of extension of the suffrage, yet on principles quite opposite to those of Chartism I do not think it would be found a very serious obstacle. The ballot though in my opinion necessary, & but little objectionable, is passing from a radical doctrine into a Whig one as will be seen the moment it is carried. It is essentially a juste milieu, middle class doctrine.

If I thought I could do better for my principles, different as they are in some important respects from yours, than by placing my review under your guidance, I would do so: but as in the present state of affairs in this country I know of no disposal I could make of it, without having to get over objections fully as strong and even stronger, I accept your offer of writing to Mr. Beaumont[3] on the subject although I can hardly expect that your unfavourable opinion, if it should continue, will not turn the scale against me. I do not utterly despair of your ultimately taking a more favourable view of the position, because I firmly believe that any set of writers promulgating extensive views of political & social improvement, freed from party trammels & exhibiting an example of superiority to the littlenesses of

1. From copy supplied by Professor Ney MacMinn of MS in his possession.
John Mitchell Kemble (1807–1857), philologist and historian; editor of the *British and Foreign Review*, 1835–44.

2. The *British and Foreign* and the *London and Westminster*. The merger was not effected.

3. Thomas Wentworth Beaumont (1792–1848), politician, and owner of the *British and Foreign Review*.

the age & of its notions of statesmanship, may obtain all the support which it possessed or can be hoped for by the L. & W. as at present conducted.

Yours very truly
J. S. Mill

267. TO JOHN STERLING[1]

India House
4th November
1839

My dear Sterling

I am truly sorry that you have found it necessary to renounce your project of reviewing Gladstone, but I cannot contest the reasons you assign for giving it up. I wish most heartily that there were any other channel through which you could conveniently do it, as I am sure it would do much good & for myself I feel a special desire to have your view of the matter in print. The British & Foreign Review has already had a tolerable article on Gladstone & Maurice[2]—otherwise that might have been a less exceptionable vehicle under the circumstances you mention, than, I feel, mine would be likely to be.

I imagine your books must have reached Clifton by this time—they are certainly on the way—at least they were all at Hooper's some days ago.

I have set to work upon an article on Coleridge, partly in consequence of the encouragement you gave me. It will not be a popular article; & perhaps not one person who reads it will like it; probably few will derive much benefit from it; but if I do what I have thoughts of doing, viz. to collect the few things I have printed which are worth preserving & republish them in a volume,[3] I shall be glad to have this among them because some of the others, without this, would give a false view of my general mode of thinking —& besides I sometimes think that if there is anything which I am under a special obligation to preach, it is the meaning & necessity of a catholic spirit in philosophy, & I have a better opportunity of shewing what this is, in writing about Coleridge, than I have ever had before.

Touching your question to me, whether I think that we know a sufficient number of Laws of particular Phenomena to be able to mount up to the Laws of the whole system of which they are a part—if you mean, to such laws as that which Coleridge ascribes to Heraclitus & Giordano Bruno, the

1. *Addressed*: Rev. John Sterling / Clifton / near Bristol. *Postmark*: LS / 4 NO 4 / 1839. Part published in Elliot, I, 116. MS at King's.

2. "The State and the Church," *BFR*, IX (Oct., 1839), 433–66.

3. This plan was eventually carried into execution with the publication of his *Dissertations and Discussions*, vols. I and II, 1859; vol. III, 1867; vol. IV, 1875.

essential polarity of all power[4]—I do not think that the time is come for such wide generalizations, though I do not consider the attainment of them hopeless at some future period. I am afraid that the only principles which I should at present recognize as laws of *all* Phenomena, are some of those which for that very reason are classed by Kant as laws of our perceptive faculty only—subjective, not objective—as for instance the subjection of all phenomena to the laws of Time & Space. But it would require a good deal of explanation before we could make ourselves understood by each other on this matter, & for my part I dare say I may have something to learn on this subject from the German philosophers when I have time to read them. You may think it presumptuous in a man to be finishing a treatise on logic & not to have made up his mind finally on these great matters. But mine professes to be a logic of *experience* only, & to throw no further light upon the existence of truths not experimental, than is thrown by shewing to what extent reasoning from experience will carry us. Above all mine is a logic of the indicative mood alone—the logic of the imperative, in which the major premiss says not *is* but *ought*—I do not meddle with.

My notion, a *vague* one enough, about the reason of Charles's consent to Strafford's death[5] is that he was frightened at the discovery of the "army-plot" just at that time—I have no recent familiarity with the details of the history, & Robertson is in the country.

ever yours faithfully

J. S. MILL

268. TO GUSTAVE D'EICHTHAL[1]

India House
12th Nov. 1839

MY DEAR GUSTAVE

I can answer your two questions. Buxton,[2] a rich brewer, is the head of the English Abolitionists—the principal supporter, & present successor, of Wilberforce:[3] & like him, a leader in what is called the religious world. He is, I believe, a very honest & well-meaning man. The object of the last bill relating to the Portuguese slave trade[4] (the legality of which on prin-

4. S. T. Coleridge, *The Friend* (1818), I, 155–56, footnote.
5. Sterling was working on his tragedy, *Strafford*, published in 1843.

* * * *

1. *Addressed*: Monsieur / Gustave d'Eichthal / 14 Rue Lepelletier / à Paris. *Postmark*: LONDON / 12 / Nov / 1839 / F.B.O. MS at Arsenal.
2. Sir Thomas Fowell Buxton (1786–1845), philanthropist.
3. William Wilberforce (1759–1833), the great Evangelical abolitionist.
4. A bill enacted Aug. 19, 1839, because of Portugal's failure to abolish the slave trade in accordance with treaties of 1810, 1815, and 1817. See *Annual Register*, LXXXI (1839), 242 ff.

ciples of international law is very doubtful) was to assume the right of search, capture, & condemnation of Portuguese vessels in our own Admiralty Courts, in all cases in which the same rights could be exercised over English vessels; including cases in which the only proof of a ship's being destined for the slave trade, is the appearance & fitting-up of the vessel itself. How far this bill will be executed time must shew. It goes much beyond anything warranted by existing treaties, & is justified only by the disregard which the Portuguese government has systematically shewn towards those treaties.

There is no later edition of my father's history[5] than the third, which I believe was that of 1826; & it is not often I think, to be met with under the full publishing price. But a bookseller, who has lately bought the copyright, has announced a new edition,[6] with a continuation; & this, no doubt, will bring down considerably the price of the old editions. Your friend therefore will be likely to have a better bargain by delaying his purchase for some months.

I have read with interest the two notices you sent me, of your little tract,[7] & I will not lose any opportunity of getting it noticed here; but I am not sanguine of doing any good by it. Our people are not ripe for any generalizations of so wide & ambitious a kind—for which even *you* have only been prepared by St Simonism. And you know very well that large ideas must be made to look like small ones *here*, or people will turn away from them. This is not a place for speculative men, except (at most) within the limits of ancient & traditional Christianity. The chief recent development of scientific speculation here is one of reaction, similar to that of De Maistre.[8] Have you heard of the new Oxford school?[9] If not, I shall have much to tell you when I have time to write you a long letter.

To whom, at the Ambassador, here, shall I address the letters which are to be under cover to M. Armand Lefebvre?[10]

ever yours

J. S. MILL

My kindest remembrances to your father & Adolphe.

5. *The History of British India,* first published in 1817.

6. The fourth edition, with notes and continuation by H. H. Wilson (9 vols., London, 1840–48).

7. Probably D'Eichthal's *Lettres sur la race noire et la race blanche.* See Letter 263, n. 2.

8. Joseph de Maistre (1754?–1821), leader of Neo-Catholic and anti-revolutionary movement in France.

9. See Letter 270 for JSM's description of the Oxford or Tractarian movement.

10. Armand E. Lefebvre (1800–1864), diplomatist and writer.

269. TO THOMAS CARLYLE[1]

[Early Dec., 1839]

It is a glorious piece of work,[2] & will be a blessed gospel to many, if they read it & lay it to heart.

I took a great piece of paper, to make notes upon, but found scarcely any to make. When I had done reading, the scrap which accompanies this[3] was all I had written. But I would strongly recommend the omission of much of the quotation from Sauerteig,[4] not because it is not true & good & beautiful in itself, but because much of it is not at all, or in a very inferior degree, pertinent to the subject. The historical view of the "eras" serves, I think, merely to interrupt the flow of the thoughts & feelings, & to make the conclusion comparatively flat. Yet what is said of the two tasks of England, & especially the *constitutional* task, must stand in some shape or other, though I think rather as your own than as Sauerteig's.

I incline to think that the condition of the working classes has not deteriorated; but all that you say on the matter, ought to be said by those who think it, & the far greater part of it, I think too. And the tone in which it is said, does not assume more certainty than the case admits of—while all the practical conclusions hold equally, howsoever the fact stands in that respect.

I should be very averse to disturb any other arrangement you may have made, or may wish to make—but it would delight me much to let this be the last dying speech of a Radical Review. I do not think a radical review *ought* to die without saying all this—& no one else could say it half as well. Any number of copies of it might be printed in pamphlet form from the same types.[5]

J.S.M.

1. MS at NLS. Part published as note to Carlyle's letter of Dec. 6, 1839, to JSM, in A. Carlyle, pp. 171–72.

2. Carlyle's *Chartism*, the MS of which he had sent JSM to read. Pencilled note on MS: "Enclosed in an ms of T. Carlyle marked 'Rejected fragments of Chartism.' (Ms. taken out long ago. A.C.)"

3. A copy of this letter, also at NLS, includes the following scraps of criticism: "page 9. Not just, I think, to the Poor Law. All this would be true of it if it only proceeded by refusing relief. But it gives relief, on terms which would hardly ever be refused, if ever, by the absolutely destitute. There cannot be more *absolute* destitution in the country, than the workhouses show.

"31. The relation between the higher & lower orders in the feudal times requires *more* developement and illustration."

4. Like Professor Teufelsdröckh in *Sartor Resartus*, Sauerteig, another mythical German professor. Carlyle disregarded JSM's advice; chap. VIII, "New Eras," of *Chartism* consists almost wholly of quotations from Sauerteig's supposed *History of the Teuton Kindred*. Sauerteig also appears in Carlyle's *Past and Present* (1843).

5. Carlyle rejected JSM's offer; the pamphlet was published before the end of Dec., 1839, by James Fraser. See also Carlyle's contemptuous remarks on the subject of JSM's offer, in J. A. Froude, *Thomas Carlyle: A History of His Life in London, 1834–1881* (2 vols., New York, 1884), I, 148.

270. TO GUSTAVE D'EICHTHAL[1]

18 Kensington Square
27th December 1839

MY DEAR GUSTAVE

I have been a long while without answering your last letter—which I should not have been if I could have given you any information worth sending on African affairs. I do not believe there has been any voyage on the Niger since Laird & Oldfield:[2] if there has, I am sure you will find references to it in Buxton's book.[3] It is said that there is to be another expedition soon to ascend the river in steamboats, but I do not know whether it is to be fitted out by Government or by individuals. I am very little conversant with the affairs of Western Africa or I could perhaps tell you more.

The continuation of my father's history[4] will come down to the last renewal of the Company's charter, in 1833. The whole, continuation & all, will be contained in eight volumes, which will cost 10s. 6d. or 12 shillings each, & will be published, it is hoped, monthly, beginning next February or March, so as to be completed within the year. But I think it very doubtful whether they will be able to complete it within so short a time.

You have not told me what information you wish for about Ireland, or our Asiatic affairs. As for the Oxford School, it is a new Catholic school without the Pope. It has revived & reasserted the *old* Anglican doctrine, that the English Church is the Catholic Church—that the Church of Rome since the Council of Trent is schismatic—& it claims in behalf of the Church, a real Spiritual Power, similar & almost equal to that which was exercised by the Catholic Church before the Reformation. The depositary of this Spiritual Power is, according to them, the body of *ordained* Clergy, that is, ordained by Bishops deriving their authority by apostolic succession from Jesus Christ. The principal peculiarity of this school is hostility to what they call ultra-Protestantism. They recognise tradition, & not the scriptures merely, as one of the sources of Christianity. They dislike the word Protestant altogether, as a word which denotes only negation and disunion. And they urge all the arguments of the 19th century against the 18th, of the St Simonians against the *école critique*, all these they urge against Protestantism of the common English kind. Some of them have even revived prayers for the dead, keeping saint's days, &c., & one of their

1. *Addressed*: Monsieur / Gustave d'Eichthal / Rue Lepelletier à Paris. Published, with omissions, in *Cosmopolis*, IX, 369–71, and in *D'Eichthal Corresp.*, pp. 174–77. MS at Arsenal.

2. See Macgregor Laird and R. A. K. Oldfield, *Narrative of an Expedition into the Interior of Africa, by the River Niger . . . in 1832, 3, 4* (2 vols., London, 1837).

3. Sir Thomas F. Buxton, *The African Slave Trade* (London, 1839).

4. See Letter 268.

leaders has published a book of Latin hymns,[5] including some to the Virgin. They reprobate the "right of private judgment" & consider *learning* rather than original thinking the proper attribut[ion][6] of a divine. They discourage the Methodistical view of religion which makes devotional feeling a state of strong *excitement*, & inculcate rather a spirit of humility & self-mortification. This is a very vague description of them but I have not studied them sufficiently yet to give a better. It is one of the forms, & the best form hitherto, of the *reaction* of Anglicanism against Methodism, incredulity & rationalism. They hold many of the opinions of Laud[7] & the semi-Catholic high-church divines of Charles the First's times, & their doctrine, which is spreading fast among the younger clergy, is giving great offence to the evangelical part of the Church (you know the Calvinistic part of it, who fraternize with the Dissenters, take that name) which had previously been increasing very much in numbers & influence. They are passive obedience men, & one of their chiefs preached a sermon on the 5th of November in which he said that we ought to beg forgiveness of God for the sin of our ancestors in turning out James the Second.[8] Among others of their proselytes it is said that Gladstone, the only rising man among the Tories, is one; the man who will probably succeed Peel as the Tory leader, unless this prevents him. The principal chiefs are Dr Pusey, an Oxford Professor, & Mr. Newman.

ever yours faithfully

J. S. MILL.

5. Probably Isaac Williams' *Hymns Translated from the Parisian Breviary* (1839).
6. Page torn.
7. William Laud (1573–1645), Archbishop of Canterbury.
8. Presumably the sermon by Edward Bouverie Pusey (1800–1882), Regius Professor of Hebrew at Oxford, *Patience and Confidence the Strength of the Church. A Sermon preached on the fifth of November before the University of Oxford, at St. Mary's . . .* (Oxford, 1837). The sermon was reprinted several times. It was attacked in *ER*, LXVI (Jan., 1838), 396–415. For a discussion of the sermon and the subsequent controversy, see Henry P. Liddon, *Life of Edward Bouverie Pusey* (4 vols., London, 1893–97), II, 16–20.

• • • 1840 • • •

271. TO LEIGH HUNT[1]

I.H.
Wed^y^
[Feb. 12, 1840]

My dear Sir

Many thanks for the letter which is very interesting & does great honor to the writer. As to the review however it will either cease or go out of my hands after the forthcoming number which will be out in a few days.

It must be some namesake of mine who sent the congratulations, unless it so happen that Robertson sent them in my name which he was well warranted in doing. Ill health & family distresses have come in aid of other causes which keep me away from the theatre but I read the announcement of your brilliant success[2] with no ordinary pleasure & I trust it is the commencement of a new era of prosperity for you. It is time that the world began to pay off its long arrear of debt for your services to it.

ever faithfully yours
J. S. Mill

272. TO CLARA MILL[1]

I.H.
Saturday
[Feb. 15, 1840]

My dear Clara

There is nothing new to tell you since my letter to Derry of yesterday.

1. *Addressed*: Leigh Hunt Esq. / 4 Upper Cheyne Row / Chelsea. *Postmark*: FE 12 / 18 . . . 0 /. MS in Brit. Mus.
2. Hunt's verse drama, *A Legend of Florence*, was first performed at Covent Garden on Feb. 7, 1840.

* * * *

1. MS at LSE. *Addressed*: Miss Mill / Post Office / Falmouth. *Postmark*: PAID / 15 FE 15 / 184?.
Earlier this year it had become evident that JSM's nineteen-year-old brother Henry

I understand from Oliver Grant[2] that you will still have to buy bedding, or at least mattresses & bolsters—he has undertaken to enquire whether they provide sheets & blankets or not. Whatever money you require at Falmouth Messrs Fox[3] will readily advance to you having been asked to do so in the letter from Capt. St Croix.[4] One advantage of your going by the Florence instead of the packet, will be, that as the Florence is not going any farther than Madeira, there will be no hurry about your landing—& you had better write from the vessel to Mr Innes,[5] that he may make the necessary arrangements—since he will have expected you by the packet & finding you not come by it, will not know when to expect you. We will probably have to provide a palankeen for Derry as well as to take lodgings or rooms at a hotel &c &c.

The Florence may be expected I presume at Falmouth by the end of the week. I am heartily glad we have been able to make so good an arrangement.

We have all written to James.[6] I hope some of you will write to give him the latest news of Derry.

I do not wonder that you find Falmouth beautiful. I wish there were a railroad that I might come down & see you for a day or so before you go.

I have been so busy I hardly knew which way to turn, & have not been well, besides—but I think I am getting better again. I shall write often while you remain at Falmouth.

Ever affectionately

J.S.M.

I have written to Sterling. As he was not to be at Madeira I am heartily glad for the sake of all of you that he was at Falmouth.[7]

("Derry") was in an advanced stage of consumption. A family decision was reached to try a warmer climate, and in the first week of Feb. Mrs. Mill, Clara, and Henry went to Falmouth, hoping to catch a mail packet to Madeira. They arrived too late for the packet, however, and at this point they were planning to go by the ship *Florence*. See *Pym*, I, 102–3, and Wilson Harris, *Caroline Fox* (London, 1944), p. 64 n.

2. Unidentified.
3. G. C. Fox and Co., shipping agents.
4. Unidentified.
5. Unidentified.
6. JSM's younger brother James had been in India since 1836.
7. Ever since 1836, when he first discovered that he had tuberculosis, Sterling had been obliged to spend winters in warmer climates: in southern France (1836–37), Madeira (1837–38), and Italy (1838–39). In the summer of 1839 he had moved his family from London to Clifton, near Bristol, hoping that its milder climate would permit him to remain in England, but by the end of the year he had to seek a still milder climate. In Jan., 1840, he went to Falmouth to embark for Madeira, but instead stayed on in Falmouth until spring.

273. TO HENRY COLE[1]

I.H.
Thursday
[Feb. (?), 1840]

DEAR COLE,

The review has been altogether so expensive an affair to me, & I am at present drained so dry by that, by my own journey,[2] by this new call upon me for Madeira,[3] etc., that I cannot incur the smallest extra expense on account of the next number of the review, and, all things considered, I would not recommend your doing so.

Unless the number sells more than 1,200, the article will do no good, as that has been for a long time the ordinary number sold—though I believe the *last* number sold rather fewer.

The conditional authority you mention I readily give—subject to the chance of Beaumont's[4] accepting.

Ever yours,

J. S. MILL

274. TO CLARA MILL[1]

I.H.
Wednesday
[Feb., 1840]

DEAR CLARA

We received your yesterday's letters. What may have been received at Kensington today I do not know.

After full consideration Harriet[2] prefers fatigue to the probability of seasickness & thinks that it will probably less unfit her for what she will have to do when she arrives. Her place has therefore been taken by the Falmouth mail for Thursday (tomorrow) & she anticipates being able to go right through at once & arrive on Saturday morning. You of course will know at what time the mail may be expected to come in & will do whatever is advisable.

1. MS in the possession of Professor J. M. McCrimmon, University of Illinois.
2. On the Continent for six months the previous year.
3. See preceding letter.
4. See Letter 266.

* * * *

1. MS at LSE. No address, postmark, or signature. Perhaps only a part of the letter.
2. JSM's sister, who was to join their mother and their sister Clara in Falmouth to help care for Henry. See Letter 272.

I shall send money by her sufficient for a present supply.

I will write tomorrow either to you or to poor dear Derry—& Harriet will of course know anything that I may have to say.

Arnott[3] has told both Harriet & me since you were at Falmouth that it was not a case in which a medical man would have recommended going to Madeira, & that the chief reason was that I so much wished it.[4] So far therefore he is not in fault—& he has shewn much real feeling through it all —but why was he not sincere with me sooner, so as to enable ourselves to judge? Why did he continue to do all he possibly could to persuade us that his not getting rid of the cough was quite an ordinary & not an alarming thing?

275. TO HENRY COLE[1]

Friday
[Feb. (?), 1840]

MY DEAR COLE,

Robertson tells me of a mode of carrying on the review with you and him combined which he says you are willing to agree to[2]—on which however it is quite impossible for me to decide unless I first see you. I waited till rather late at Kensington this morning thinking you might possibly come—& should then have gone to your house if I had thought I should find you there. This misadventure makes it impossible to terminate matters immediately, as I go out of town this afternoon & cannot return till Monday. But I think you may proceed with *your* arrangements on either supposition. I am more annoyed about Hickson,[3] who has reasons for wishing for a speedier decision.

Ever yours,

J. S. MILL

3. Neil Arnott (1788–1874), physician and philosopher; author of *Elements of Physics* (London, 1827–29). Arnott had been a close friend of James Mill in his latter years (see Bain, *James Mill*, pp. 338–39).

4. The proposed trip to Madeira for Henry Mill's health had had to be abandoned.

* * * *

1. MS in the possession of Professor J. M. McCrimmon.

2. This was probably the proposal described in an unpublished letter (n.d., owned by Professor McCrimmon) from Cole to JSM: "I had much talk with Hickson last night about the Review. He is most decidedly averse to Robertson's having the Editorship. . . . R. asked me whether I was willing to become the sole proprietor—he remaining the Editor under certain conditions to be agreed upon between us. . . . R. proposes to me. . . . that I should have the unconditional control of the Management or business part of the Review."

3. William Edward Hickson (1803–1870), educational writer, editor of the *Westminster Review*, 1840–52 (see Letter 278).

276. TO HENRY COLE[1]

India House
Saturday
[Feb. or March (?), 1840]

MY DEAR COLE,

I am afraid you will think me very changeable, but since I saw you last I have thought a good deal more about the proposed arrangement concerning the review, & have heard the opinion of one or two friends on the matter (I had consulted nobody before) & I find their opinion to be exceedingly strong that if the review goes on at all under the same name it will not be possible for me to destroy the connexion in people's minds between it and myself—& that it is much more to my credit that it should cease entirely than that it should be continued as anything else than the philosophical & political organ it was designed to be. I am not sure that after what has passed between us you have not a right to hold me to what was conditionally agreed upon but I hope you will not think it necessary to do so. Of course I hold myself responsible for the expense of the Postage article[2] & will pay for any work that you have entered into engagements for, & I hope that by laying all the blame, where alone it can justly fall, on me, you will be able to terminate the thing without any unpleasantness.

Ever yours truly,
J. S. MILL

277. TO HENRY COLE[1]

I.H.
Thursday
[Feb. or March (?), 1840]

MY DEAR COLE,

If you are willing to carry on the review under the name of *Westminster*, & with some slight alteration in the cover, I am willing to make it over to you, without requiring that it should be a new series or new numbering—unless before the present number comes out I receive some communication, at this eleventh hour, from Beaumont,[2] or from another quarter almost as improbable.

1. MS in the possession of Professor J. M. McCrimmon.
2. Cole's article, "The Postage Stamp," *LWR*, XXXIII (March, 1840), 491–505.

* * * *

1. MS in the possession of Professor J. M. McCrimmon.
2. See Letter 266.

It will give me still greater satisfaction to deliver it over to you & Hickson jointly, as he proposes, as it will both diminish your risk & aid you very much in the management.

Ever yours,

J. S. Mill

278. TO JOHN ROBERTSON[1]

[March (?), 1840]

I am exceedingly grieved by the consciousness that I must appear to you (what I never have been nor could be intentionally) unkind to you. The thought of this matter has been, ever since it was first mentioned by you in a letter last July, but especially of late, no small addition to the burthens of various sorts that have lain upon me.

I feel, however, that I have meant rightly to you and to every other interest concerned, and that I have acted to the best of my judgment; and though I feel painfully the impossibility of my convincing you that I am right, I am sure you will respect me more for acting upon my own conviction than for giving way, from feelings of friendship and confidence, without being convinced.

Cole repeatedly expressed his wish not to stand in the way of any arrangement more beneficial to you and independent of him; but we seemed to have already exhausted the possibilities of such, and as it was impossible to keep Hickson any longer without an answer, I have told Cole that I considered the Review as made over to them, although the formal transfer has not yet taken place.[2]

I am sure you have that in you which a disappointment in so poor a hope as this cannot unnerve or permanently discourage.

Ever yours,

J. S. Mill

279. TO JOHN ROBERTSON[1]

Kensington, Monday
[March, 1840?]

Dear Robertson,

Some points in your letter positively require from me a few words to set right a few matters in which you have quite misunderstood me,

1. Published by Towers, p. 72. MS not located.

2. See Letter 280.

* * * *

1. Published by Towers, pp. 72–73. MS not located.

and in which it would be very unpleasant to me that you should continue to do so.

First. I did not allude to that number of the Review for any purpose of disparagement. Why should I? It has fully less of the defects to which I alluded than I thought it would have. I referred to it *bona fide*, as I professed to do, namely, as evidence you could appeal to in contradiction to my opinion if I was wrong.

Second. When I spoke of unconciliativeness to contributors, I never meant that you were in the wrong in your disputes with them, but that you gave them unnecessary offense by matters of mere manner, and did not spare their vanity, which I am sure I have often said to you before; and also that I think you, in that particular, extremely unpractical, since no one can use others as instruments unless he makes them like his service.

Third. When I spoke of subserviency, I carefully explained that I was not speaking of your intentions or feelings, but of *their* expectations.

Fourth. I never said that *you* would get a character like Fonblanque's, but that the *Review* would. I have distinctly said to you several times that *you* personally would not suffer in any way, and I said it most distinctly in the very same sentence by saying I should be glad to aid you in a ministerial course by any other means than the Review.

Fifth. Finally, I *do* feel that I can and ought to support the ministry, but not connect myself with them (unless I had a voice in their councils); that is, I can neither take their money nor make over power which is in my hands and put it into theirs, though any power in my own hands I would, while I see as much cause as I now do, use in their support.

Having endeavored to put myself right in these points, I will now say that your readiness to give up a project, in my objections to which you do not at all concur, is a thing which, you may rely upon it, I shall not forget.

I think your letter to Lord N[ormanby][2] in perfectly good taste, as well as right feeling towards him.

Ever yours,

J. S. MILL.

2. Sir Constantine Henry Phipps, first Marquis of Normanby and second Earl of Mulgrave, prominent Whig leader.

Mrs. Towers (p. 72) explains that Robertson had hoped to get into Parliament, "and he would have used the Review, had he continued his editorship, to support the Whigs. . . . Lord Normanby had had one interview, if not more, with Robertson with reference to this subject."

280. TO HENRY COLE[1]

India House
12th March
1840

MY DEAR COLE,

I hereby make over to you & Mr William Hickson my whole interest in the London & Westminster Review—the work hereafter to be called the *Westminster Review* & the change of proprietorship to be announced in the next number.

Yours very truly
J. S. MILL

281. TO RICHARD MONCKTON MILNES[1]

India House
Saturday
[March, 1840]

MY DEAR SIR

My course on Monday morning next will be not anti-solar but at right angles to the sun's course, as I shall be on my way from Sussex. & even on other days I can seldom manage to stop on my way, as I do not like to arrive here much after ten. We keep earlier hours here both in the morning & in the afternoon, than the Government offices at the West End. Therefore I am obliged to renounce the pleasure, which would have been a great one, of breakfasting with you.

I cannot omit this opportunity of thanking you for the very interesting & valuable article you have contributed to this number of the London & Westminster,[2] & which I am very happy to have been the means of publishing before the termination of my connexion with the review.

Every truly yours
J. S. MILL

1. MS in the possession of Professor J. M. McCrimmon.

* * * *

1. MS at Trinity College Library, Cambridge.
Richard Monckton Milnes, later first Baron Houghton (1809–1885), writer and politician, author of *The Life, Letters, and Literary Remains of John Keats* (1848).
2. "American Philosophy.—Emerson's Works," signed R.M.M., *LWR*, XXXIII (March, 1840), pp. 345–72. This was the last number under JSM's proprietorship of the Review.

282. TO ROBERT BARCLAY FOX[1]

India House
16th April
1840

My dear friend (if you will allow me to adopt this "friendly" mode of address) your kind & sympathizing letter has given me great pleasure. There is no use in my saying more than has been said already about him who has gone before us where we must so soon follow—the thought of him is here & will remain here, & seldom has the memory of one who died so young, been such as to leave a deeper or a more beneficial impression on the survivors. Among the many serious feelings which such an event calls forth, there is always some one which impresses us most, some moral which each person extracts from it for his own more especial guidance—with me that moral is, "work while it is called today—the night cometh in which no man can work." One never seems to have adequately *felt* the truth & meaning of all that is tritely said about the shortness & precariousness of life till one loses some one whom one had hoped not only to carry with one as a companion through life, but to leave as a successor after it. Why he who had all his work to do has been taken, & I left who had done part of mine and in some measure as Carlyle would express it "delivered my message," passes our wisdom to surmise. But if there be a purpose in this, that purpose it would seem can only be fulfilled in so far as the remainder of my life can be made even more useful than the remainder of his would have been if it had been spared. At least we know this that on the day when we shall be as he is, the whole of life will appear but as a day, & the only question of any moment to us then will be, Has that day been wasted. Wasted it has not been by those who have been, for however short a time, a source of happiness & of moral good even to the narrowest circle. But there is only one plain rule of life eternally binding, & independent of all variations in creeds & in the interpretations of creeds & embracing equally the greatest moralities & the smallest—it is

1. *Addressed*: R. Barclay Fox Esq. / Neath Abbey / Glamorganshire. *Postmark*: B / 16 AP / 1840. Published in Pym, I, 173–79. MS in 1944 in the possession of Mr. W. H. Browning, of Eltham, Surrey.

Robert Barclay Fox (1817–1855), son of the scientific writer Robert Were Fox (1789–1877), and brother of Anna Maria Fox (1816–1897) and of Caroline Fox (1819–1871), diarist.

JSM on March 16 had joined his mother and his sisters Clara and Harriet in their attendance upon the last illness of Henry Mill (see Letters 272 and 274). After Henry's death on April 4, JSM had returned to London on April 10. During their stay in Falmouth the Mills had become intimately acquainted with the Foxes, a prominent Quaker family.

this—try thyself unweariedly till thou findest the highest thing thou art capable of doing, faculties & outward circumstances being both duly considered—and then DO IT—

You are very kind to say what you have said about those reviews[2]—the gift of unsold copies of an old periodical could under no circumstances have called for so warm an expression of thanks, & would have deserved an opposite feeling if I could not say, with the utmost sincerity, that I do not expect you to read much of it, or any of it unless you feel thereunto moved. My principal feeling in the matter was this—You are likely to hear of some of the writers, & judging of your feelings by what my own would be, I thought it might be sometimes agreeable to you to be able to turn to something they had written & imagine what manner of persons they might be. As far as my own articles were concerned there was also a more selfish pleasure in thinking that sometimes, however rarely, I might be conversing with my absent friends at 300 miles distance—We scribblers are apt to put not only our best thoughts but our best feelings into our writings, or at least if the things are *in* us they will not *come out of us* so well or so clearly through any other medium—& therefore when one really wishes to be *liked* (it is only when one is very young that one cares about being admired) it is often an advantage to us when our writings are better known than ourselves.

As for these particular writings of mine, all in them that has any pretension to permanent value will I hope during the time you are in London be made into two little volumes[3] which I shall offer to no one with greater pleasure than to you. The remainder is mostly politics—of little value to any one now—in which, with considerable expenditure of head & heart, an attempt was made to breathe a living soul into the Radical party—but in vain—there was no making those dry bones live. Among a multitude of failures I had only one instance of brilliant success—it is some satisfaction to me to know that, as far as such things can ever be said, I saved Lord Durham—as he himself, with much feeling, acknowledged to me, saying that he knew not to what to ascribe the reception he met with on his return from Canada, except to an article of mine[4] which came out immediately before. If you were to read that article now you would wonder

2. Caroline Fox noted in her journal on April 5 (Pym, I, 158): "A great parcel arrived in the evening with John Mill's kind regards, containing all the *London and Westminster Reviews* from their beginning, with notes in his own hand, and the names of the writers attached to the articles—a most valuable and interesting gift." Efforts to trace this set of volumes have thus far proved unavailing.

3. Not until 1859 were these articles republished, in the first two volumes of *Dissertations.* See Letter 267, n. 3.

4. "Lord Durham's Return." See Letter 249, n. 4.

what there was in it to bear out such a statement—but the *time* at which it appeared was everything—every one's hand seemed to be against him, no one dared speak a word for him, the very men who had been paying court & offering incense to him for years before (I never had) slunk away, or ventured only on a few tame & qualified phrases of excuse—not, I verily believe, from cowardice so much as because, not being accustomed to think about *principles* of politics, they were taken by surprise in a contingency which they had not looked for, and feared committing themselves to something they could not maintain—& if this had gone on, opinion would have decided against him so strongly that even that admirable Report of his & Buller's could hardly have turned the tide & unless some one who could give evidence of thought & knowledge of the subject, had thrown down the gauntlet at that critical moment, & determinedly claimed honour & glory for him instead of mere acquittal, & by doing this made a diversion in his favour & encouraged those who wished him well to speak out, & so kept people's minds *suspended* on the subject, he was in all probability a lost man, & if I had not been the man to do this nobody else would. And three or four months later the Report came out & then everybody said I had been right, & now it is being acted upon.

This is one of only three things, among all I attempted in my reviewing life, which I can be said to have succeeded in. The second was, to have greatly accelerated the success of Carlyle's French Revolution,[5] a book so strange & incomprehensible to the greater part of the public, that whether it should succeed or fail seemed to depend upon the turn of a die—but I got the first word, blew the trumpet before it at its first coming out & by claiming for it the honours of the highest genius frightened the small fry of critics from pronouncing a hasty condemnation, got fair play for it & then its success was sure.

My *third* success is that I have dinned into people's ears that Guizot is a great thinker & writer, till they are, though slowly, begining to read him—which I do not believe they would be doing, even yet, in this country but for me.

There, I think, is a full account of all the world has got by my editing and reviews.

Will you pardon the egotism of this letter? I really do not think I have talked so much about myself in the whole year previous as I have done in the few weeks of my intercourse with your family—but it is not a fault of mine generally, for I am considered reserved enough by most people—& I have made a very solemn resolution when I see you again to be more

5. By his review, "The French Revolution." See Letters 208, n. 5, and 209.

objective and less *subjective* in my conversation (as Calvert[6] says) than when I saw you last.

Ever yours faithfully,

J. S. Mill

It seems idle to send remembrances—they saw enough to know I am not likely to forget them.

283. TO JOHN STERLING[1]

I.H.
22d April
1840

My dear Sterling

Your letter should have been answered when I first received it, which was just before I left Falmouth. The bustle & turmoil of London when one comes back to it, & the accumulation of different sorts of business which I have had to dispose of, are very uncongenial to the mood in which such a letter is read or in which it should be responded to.

I rejoice greatly that we met at Falmouth; independently of the good, of many kinds, which your presence did, it is very much to me now, & more than I thought it would be, that my last recollections of Henry are shared with you. If he had lived he would certainly have been an additional bond between us, & now that he is dead his memory will be so—& perhaps as you say he is conscious of it. I do feel as you do that we have been more to each other lately than ever before, & I think on one side this is easily to be explained, for it is natural to you to feel more affectionately in proportion as you have shewn more kindness—that is one of the ways in which acts of love fructify & yield a large increase. On my own side less explanation is needed, for it seems to me that you have at all times been giving more & more to me—though there have been times when the contrary may have seemed to be the case—in consequence partly of constitutional or habitual defect of quickness of sensibility, but much more of the jarring elements both in my own character & in my outward circumstances which I have had to reconcile, as indeed is the case with most

6. John M. Calvert (1801–1842), physician. A fellow-victim of tuberculosis, Dr. Calvert had first met Sterling in Madeira in 1838. They had become close friends, and after giving up their plans to spend the winter again at Madeira they had stayed on together at Falmouth. Caroline Fox's journals recount numerous meetings with Calvert and Sterling.

* * * *

1. MS at Leeds. Published in Elliot, I, 116–18.

people, but I think both in an unusual degree and in an unusual manner with me—& which have made me describe an orbit very different from the direction of any one of the forces which urged me. And even now I am very far from appearing to you as I am—for though there is nothing that I do not desire to shew, there is much that I never do shew, & much that I think you cannot even guess.

My mother & sisters & George[2] have returned, & George is certainly better, not worse, for his journey. I have much anxious thought about him—to him the loss of Henry is a greater calamity than he can yet feel. As for me, I have begun to get ready my reprint—but I find some difficulty in finding enough for two volumes.[3] I have softened the asperity of the article on Sedgwick,[4] & cut out whatever seemed to take an unfair advantage against his opinions, of his deficiencies as an advocate of them.

ever affectionately

J. S. MILL.

284. TO MACVEY NAPIER[1]

India House
22^d April
1840

MY DEAR SIR

It is just possible you may have heard—though it is most likely you have not—that my connexion with the Westminster Review has terminated. The review has gone into other hands, & although I wish well to the new proprietors & think they will conduct it creditably & usefully, I do not feel myself in such a manner bound to them that I should wish to exclude myself from the power of addressing a larger auditory. This is also the feeling of several of the best of my late coadjutors in the Westminster, to whom, as well as to myself, it would be agreeable, if you give any encouragement to the proposition, to establish a connexion with the Edinburgh. I believe it is the feeling of nearly all Reformers that this is not

2. George Grote Mill (*ca.* 1825–1853), youngest of JSM's brothers, had been at Falmouth since April 2.
3. See Letter 267, n. 3.
4. "Professor Sedgwick's Discourse.—State of Philosophy in England," *London Rev.*, I (April, 1835), 94–135, eventually reprinted in *Dissertations* as "Professor Sedgwick's Discourse on the Studies of the University of Cambridge."

* * * *

1. MS in Brit. Mus. Published, except for last paragraph, in *Napier Corresp.*, pp. 325–26.
Macvey Napier, editor of the *Edinburgh Review*, 1829–47.

a time for keeping up a flag of disunion among them—& even I who have been for some years attempting it must be owned with very little success, to induce the Radicals to maintain an independent position, am compelled to acknowledge that there is not room for a fourth political party in this country—reckoning the Conservatives, the Whig-Radicals, & the Chartists as the other three. Of a clear view of this fact a natural consequence is, a different notion of what my own course ought to be—if I can hope to do any good it can only be by merging in one of the existing great bodies of opinion; by attempting to gain the ear of the liberal party generally, instead of addressing a mere section of it. There seems no longer any reason why my little rivulet should continue to flow separate, little as it can contribute to decide the colour or composition of that great stream.

Among those contributors to the Westminster who would like to become contributors of yours, those who I think would be of most use to you (besides Charles Buller with whom I believe you are already in communication) are Robertson, the late editor, & writer of many articles and George Fletcher,[2] the author of two very interesting papers, one in the number for December, 1838, on Heloisa & Abelard,[3] the other (in the last number) on Robin Hood.[4] If you have not seen these articles I am sure it would give you pleasure to read them especially the former.

Of Robertson's articles some were hastily got up under many disadvantages & he did himself scanty justice in them—but others I think are sufficient proof that he can do something considerable especially those on "Cromwell" "Caricatures" "Statistical Society" "Congregational Dissenters" & one or two others.

Ever yours truly

J. S. Mill

285. TO MACVEY NAPIER[1]

India House
April 27, 1840

My dear Sir,

Permit me in the first place to make my acknowledgments for the extremely kind & flattering manner in which you have received my propo-

2. Otherwise identified only as the author of *Studies in Shakespeare* (London, 1847), which contains essays contributed originally to the *Athenæum* in 1843–44 and to the *Westminster Review* in 1844–45. He also contributed to *Fraser's Magazine* in 1850.

3. *LWR*, XXXII, 146–219.

4. *LWR*, XXXIII (March, 1840), 424–91.

* * * *

1. MS in Brit. Mus. Published, except for last paragraph, in *Napier Corresp.*, pp. 326–27. (See preceding letter.)

sition for becoming a contributor to the Edinburgh. You have done me only justice in supposing that the idea of any compromise of the principles of the E. Review never entered into my mind—it did not occur to me even to disavow such a thought. Of course I did not expect to have the same range of subjects as I had in a review under my own exclusive control, nor to be allowed to commit the review to opinions which would be obnoxious to its other writers & its supporters. I look for no other latitude than that commonly allowed by periodical works to the individual modes of thinking of their various contributors. There will be no difficulty in our understanding one another, since the principles of the review are public property, & what I have written in the last year or two, or what I may now write will soon shew you what are the points if any, on which mine are irreconcileable with them. I am myself under an impression that there is very little of what I should now be inclined to say to the public in a review, which would be at all in contradiction to the established character & purposes of the Edinburgh.

As you conjecture, it is only occasionally that I should find time to write for you, especially at present, as I am desirous of finishing a book I have in hand. But the subject you suggest, my friend Tocqueville's book, is so very attractive to me that if the other arrangement you mention should not take effect, I would make an effort to get an article ready on Tocqueville for your October number.[2] With regard to other subjects, one thing which I should like very much, & on which I should not interfere with any of your existing contributors, would be to write occasionally on modern French history & historical literature, with which from peculiar causes I am more extensively acquainted than Englishmen usually are. If I had continued to carry on the London & W. review, I should have written more than one article on Michelet[3] a writer of great & original views, very little known among us. One article on his history of France, & another combining his Roman history with Arnold's,[4] might I think be made very interesting & useful. Even on Guizot[5] there may be something still to be written. I mention these things only that you may know the course my thoughts have taken in regard to future articles.

2. The review of Tocqueville's *Democracy in America* appeared, as here projected, in the Oct., 1840, number of *ER*, LXXII, 1–47; it was reprinted in *Dissertations*, II, 79–161.

3. Jules Michelet (1798–1874). JSM's review of the first five volumes of his *Histoire de France* (Paris, 1833–42) eventually appeared in *ER*, LXXIX (Jan., 1844), 1–39. It was reprinted in *Dissertations*, II, 198–259.

4. Michelet, *Histoire romaine: republique* (2nd ed., 3 vols., Paris, 1833). Thomas Arnold, *History of Rome* (3 vols., London, 1838–43).

5. JSM's review of "M. Guizot's Essays and Lectures on History" appeared in *ER*, LXXXII (Oct., 1845), 381–421; it was reprinted in *Dissertations*, II, 297–362.

I will immediately make known to Robertson & Fletcher your answer in respect to them & I have no doubt that you will find them valuable auxiliaries.

Ever my dear Sir
Truly yours,
J. S. MILL

286. TO GUSTAVE D'EICHTHAL[1]

India House
7th May
1840

MY DEAR GUSTAVE

I have been very long in answering your letters, having been absent from London for some weeks attending the deathbed of a brother, who was the pride & hope of our whole family & whose loss I shall have cause to regret as long as I live. This absence occasioned my losing the opportunity of seeing MM Stéphane Mony & Isaac Pereire,[2] both well known to me by their *antécédents* & the former personally. I have to thank you for a letter I have received from M. Michelet accompanying two volumes of his admirable history,[3] & which as I had not time to answer immediately I shall now defer answering until I have read the new volume. I was already intimately acquainted with the former volumes as well as with all his other works, & I beg of you to tell him that I have long felt the warmest admiration for them & have expressed it publicly on several occasions before the one which attracted your notice. I had long meditated reviewing his Roman history in the Westminster, & now that I am no longer connected with that review it is probable that I shall have the satisfaction of making both that, & his History of France still more widely known by means of the Edinburgh review in which I have engaged to write some articles on the new French historical school.[4] Would you oblige me with M. Michelet's address?[5]

1. *Addressed*: Monsieur / Gustave d'Eichthal. Published, with omissions, in *D'Eichthal Corresp.*, pp. 178–80. MS at Arsenal.
2. Isaac Péreire (1806–1880), French banker, earlier associated with the Saint-Simonians.
3. His *Histoire de France* in 17 volumes was published at intervals between 1833 and 1867. His letter of April 7 to JSM is at LSE.
4. See preceding letter.
5. Eugène d'Eichthal in *D'Eichthal Corresp.*, p. 179, appends as a note this part of a letter from Michelet to Gustave d'Eichthal:
"J'aurais voulu vous dire un mot de mon 5e volume qui va être attaqué de deux côtés opposés. J'espère pour le défendre (ce volume si peu favorable aux Anglais),

I have no doubt that the two books which you mention, Lyon's Voyage[6] & Crawfurd's History,[7] may be obtained here by watching an opportunity, at a tolerably cheap rate, but it is impossible to say how cheap, as it depends on accident. I would recommend to you for such commissions a bookseller named Edward Rainford, 86 High Holborn, & if you will communicate with him the first time through me you will have no difficulty with him afterwards. He is a most deserving person, & manages to get books exceedingly cheap.

I have not yet seen M. Guizot,[8] though I have been very near seeing him several times—& should have ventured to call on him if I were not so circumstanced as to hours, that it is impossible for me to call at any time of the day suitable to a civilized being.

Your opinion on the decisive character of the late triumph of parliamentary government[9] (ostensibly) & of democracy really, in France, is very interesting to me. It is a great event, & makes me recur to what I have so often thought, *les choses marchent vîte en France* (& in this age, altogether one may add)

ever yours

J. S. Mill

287. TO ALEXIS DE TOCQUEVILLE[1]

11th May, 1840

My dear Tocqueville,

I shall have the greatest pleasure in owing to your friendship a copy of the second part of your great work. I had already possessed myself of it

---

dans la haute impartialité d'un Anglais, de M. Mill, qui m'a écrit cette belle lettre que nous avons admirée ensemble. Vous avez trouvé, je pense, son exemplaire joint au vôtre?

. . . Si vous écrivez à M. Mill, veuillez lui faire considérer avec quelle méthode sévère, dans l'affaire de la Pucelle et dans bien d'autres j'ai écarté les *chroniques* pour m'en tenir aux *actes*. . . . Si M. Mill me fait l'honneur de parler de mon livre dans une revue anglaise, il m'obligera fort de faire remarquer combien cet historien qu'on traite trop aisément comme un homme d'*imagination*, a été dominé par la passion de la *vérité*."

6. Probably *The Private Journal of Captain G. F. Lyon During the Voyage of Discovery under Captain Parry* (London, 1824).

7. Probably John Crawfurd's *History of the Indian Archipelago* (London, 1820).

8. Guizot had been appointed ambassador to London the preceding February. JSM would have met Guizot on March 17 at the Grotes' had he not been detained at Falmouth by his brother Henry's illness. See Pym, I, 134. But see Letter 291.

9. The return of Thiers to power in March, 1840, as Premier was regarded as a triumph for the liberals.

* * * *

1. Published in Mayer, pp. 327–29. MS in Tocqueville archives.

& have now finished one careful perusal of it: several more will be required before I can master it, for although my own thoughts have been accustomed (especially since I read your First Part) to run very much in the same direction, you have so far outrun me that I am lost in the distance, & it will require much thought & study to appropriate your ideas so completely as to be qualified to say what portion of them I shall at last feel to be demonstrated & what, if any, may seem to require further confirmation. In any case you have accomplished a great achievement: you have changed the face of political philosophy, you have carried on the discussions respecting the tendencies of modern society, the causes of those tendencies, & the influences of particular forms of polity & social order, into a region both of height & of depth, which no one before you had entered, & all previous argumentation and speculation in such matters appears but child's play now. I do not think that anything more important than the publication of your book has happened even in this age of great events—& it is truly happy that it was produced in France & is therefore sure of being read by every thinking person both *in* France and *out* of it. Even in this stupid island where Guizot's Lectures[2] had scarcely penetrated until Guizot himself came here as ambassador—& when hardly anybody knows that there is a French philosophy subsequent to Voltaire—even here your book, *par exception*, is read, because luckily Sir R. Peel praised it,[3] & made the Tories fancy it was a Tory book: but I believe they have found out their error. It could only have been written in France or in England, & if written in England it would probably never have been known beyond a small circle.

Among so many ideas which are more or less new to me I have found (what I consider a very great compliment to the justness of my own views) that one of your great general conclusions is exactly that which I have been almost alone in standing up for here, and have not as far as I know made a single disciple—namely that the real danger in democracy, the real evil to be struggled against, and which all human resources employed while it is not yet too late are not more than sufficient to fence off—is not anarchy or love of change, but Chinese stagnation & immobility. Finding this view of the matter to have presented itself with the same strength of evidence to you, who are the highest living authority (& therefore the highest that has ever lived) on the subject, I shall henceforth regard it as the truth scientifically established, and shall defend it *envers et contre tous* with tenfold pertinacity.

2. The lectures printed in his *Cours d'Histoire moderne* (6 vols., Paris, 1829–32).

3. Peel had praised Tocqueville's book in his inaugural speech as Lord Rector of the University of Glasgow on Jan. 11, 1837, and again at the public dinner at Glasgow on Jan. 13, 1837 (see *A Correct Report of the Speeches by . . . Sir R. Peel . . . on January 11, 1837; and . . . January 13, 1837* (London, 1837).

When I last wrote to you I lamented that from having terminated my connection with the London & Westminster Review I should not have the opportunity of reviewing your book there, but I have now the pleasure of telling you that I am to have the reviewing of it in the Edinburgh Review which as you know is much more read, and which has never had a review of your First Part—I suppose none of the writers dared venture upon it, and I cannot blame them, for that review is the most perfect representative of the 18th century to be found in our day, & that is not the point of view for judging of your book. But I & some others who are going to write in the Ed. Review now, shall perhaps succeed in infusing some young blood into it. They have given me till October for this article.[4]

I received a long & most acceptable letter from Beaumont,[5] when I was 300 miles off, attending a very dear brother in his last illness. I owe him a long letter in return which shall be paid very shortly.

Though I am not a very regular correspondent you may believe me when I say that there is no living man in Europe whom I esteem more highly or of whose friendship I should be more proud than I am of yours. Unfortunately I have only one means of shewing it, but that I have used pretty freely, for your name somehow finds itself under my pen almost whenever I write—.

Ever affectionately yours

J. S. MILL.

India House.

288. TO ROBERT BARCLAY FOX[1]

I.H.

Friday [May 22, 1840][2]

Pray do not think of Saturday for the Museum if you have any other day disposable. My concern for your welfare bids me assure you that it is much pleasanter to go to such places when there is no crowd: besides which I have a secret reason which I do not mean to tell you, viz. that Saturday week is the only possible day on which I could not be there to welcome you, as I am inexorably bound to pass that Saturday and Sunday more than thirty miles from town. Woe is me—but the case is such that there is no help for it.

4. See Letter 285, n. 2. 5. Gustave Beaumont.

* * * *

1. MS in the possession of Mr. W. H. Browning.

2. The Fox family had come to London for a visit of several weeks, in part no doubt to attend the Yearly Meeting of the Society of Friends. The visit to the Museum at the India House, to which this and the following letter refer, took place on Thursday, May 28, 1840. See Pym, I, 197.

If however your ill fortune will have it that you are to see the Museum and Dulwich without my agreeable society, various topics of consolation suggest themselves, as for instance that it will be all the same thing a hundred years hence, that what can't be cured must be endured &c. &c. These & similar reflections I hope will enable you to bear your affliction with becoming fortitude & I will endeavour to support mine with antique heroism, that is to say as the antique heroes always did, by trying all they could to remove the cause of it. As a first step to which I send you an admission for Mondays & Thursdays that you may have no excuse for going on Saturday. Please to fill up the blank with some name or other before you go.

I am glad you are going to Carlyle's[3]—if your sisters can go you should ask leave to bring them.

J.S.M.

289. TO ROBERT WERE FOX[1]

India House
Tuesday
[May 26, 1840]

MY DEAR SIR

I will not take so ungenerous an advantage as not to tell you that Nichol[2] is *not* coming today & that he *is* coming on Thursday. If this should prevent you from coming this evening, the loss is ours—but at least I hope it will not unless you can come on Thursday instead, either to dinner or in the evening.

Mrs. Nichol & I hope Nichol also, will be of the party to the Museum here; & to Dulwich afterwards if what we are hardly allowed to think possible, should come to pass—but if it should not, & if Saturday is the most convenient day to your party, being also as convenient for my sisters as any other, I am not such a dog in the manger as not to protest in the most earnest manner against any consideration being had of me in the matter—especially as I am so much hampered as to hours.

Ever yours faithfully

J. S. MILL

3. Caroline Fox records that on May 19 while attending Carlyle's lecture on "The Hero as Man of Letters" with some of her family they had been introduced to Mrs. Carlyle by Harriet Mill, and had been invited to call. See *ibid.*, p. 182. JSM evidently did not know that Barclay Fox's sisters had already been invited when he wrote this letter. On June 3 both the Foxes and the Carlyles spent the evening at the Mills' home.

* * * *

1. *Addressed*: R. W. Fox Esq / London. MS at LSE.

2. John Pringle Nichol.

290. TO ROBERT BARCLAY FOX[1]

I.H.
Thursday
[June 4, 1840]

MY DEAR FRIEND As you say you reached home "this morning" I perceive you made no more haste than good speed—indeed to make the former compatible with the latter seemed, under the aspect of affairs last night, rather hopeless.[2] Let me congratulate you on the fact that the safe preservation of all of you was, under these somewhat inauspicious circumstances, achieved. As for us we have none of us experienced anything unpleasant except the remembrance of the shortness of your visit, & the uncertainty which as yet hangs over the next.

You might well doubt whether I had received your note, for such a note surely merited some acknowledgment—however not being able to respond to it in the only suitable manner viz. in verse, I left it without any response at all—feeling all the while a vast respect for you, for being able to write such good verses. But the feelings towards myself which they express require me to say once more how highly I value your friendship & how unexpectedly gratifying it is that in me, seen as you have seen me, you have found as much to like, as these verses seem to indicate. For you have not, nor have even those of your family whom I have been so fortunate as to see more of, as yet seen *me*, as I really & naturally am, but a *me* artificially made self-conscious, egotistical, & noisily demonstrative by having much feeling to shew & very little time to shew it in. If I had been looking forward to living peaceably within a stone's throw or even a few hours' walk or ride of you, I should have been very different. As it is, that poor little sentence of the poor Ashantee[3] really expresses the

1. *Addressed*: R. Barclay Fox Esq. / S. Gurney Esq. / Ham House / West Ham. *Postmark*: JU 4 1840. Published by Pym, II, 333–34, but dated "probably July 1842." MS in the possession of Mr. W. H. Browning.

2. This refers to an episode on the Foxes' return from a party at the Mills', described by Caroline Fox in her journal (Pym, I, 204), under June 3, 1840: "At last we were going, but our postillion was fast asleep on the coach-box. Barclay gave him an intimation of our presence, to which he languidly replied, 'All right,' but in a voice that showed clearly that it was all wrong. We asked for a hackney coach, but J. S. Mill was delightfully ignorant as to where such things grew, or where a likely hotel was to be found; and as our culprit was now a little sobered by fright and evening air, and passionately pleaded wife and children, we ventured forward, Barclay and J. Mill walking for a long way beside us."

3. Probably a reference to a remark of one of two young princes of Ashantee, William Quantamissa and John Ansah, who with their tutor, the Rev. T. Pyne, visited Falmouth in April, 1840 (see Pym, I, 168–72, and *The Times*, April 25, 1840, p. 5). In July the princes visited Wordsworth in the Lake Country (see Mrs. [Eliza] Fletcher, *Autobiography* [Edinburgh, 1875], 247–48).

spirit of all I have said & done with regard to any of your party, almost from the beginning until now, when one is to be but a remembrance, it is difficult to refrain from even awkward attempts to make the remembrance last for more than a few days or weeks.

And now till I have the opportunity of doing it myself, will you express for me, my warmest regards to your father & mother—& for your sisters & yourself, remember that you have not only as many additional "blessings in disguise" as there are sisters at Kensington, but also (unless it be peculiarly a feminine designation) one more, namely, yours affectionately

J. S. MILL

291. TO GUSTAVE D'EICHTHAL[1]

India House
17th June 1840

MY DEAR D'EICHTHAL

Your very interesting letter came in due course. As the prices of the books seemed to me reasonable, & quite as low as it was likely Mr Rainford[2] could procure them for without waiting, perhaps a considerable time, for an opportunity, I sent your note at once to Mr Russell Smith.[3] On receiving your subsequent note I called on Mr Smith who told me that the books were sent to Paris, in a parcel along with other books, on the 7th of this month, & that as soon as they arrived, you would receive a letter by the petite poste informing you where to send for them.

Since I received your letter I have written to M. Michelet. I addressed my letter *aux archives du royaume*. If you have an opportunity perhaps you would ask him whether it arrived properly. But it did not require nor did I expect any answer.

I dined last Saturday with M. Guizot whose conversation quite corresponds to the high idea I had formed of him from his writings. He was very kind & gave me a general invitation to call upon him. His having come here as ambassador is a real *événement*, for it makes our stupid incurious people read his books. You would be astonished how few here, even yet, know that there is such a thing as a philosophy of the 19th century in France, different from the 18th. We are certainly an ignorant nation, with all our self-conceit —& by reason of it. Still, we are improving—the best ideas of the age are

1. *Addressed*: Monsieur / Gustave d'Eichthal / 14 Rue Lepelletier / à Paris. *Postmarks*: G / JU 17 / 1840 and LONDON / 17. Published in part in *Cosmopolis*, IX, p. 372, and in *D'Eichthal Corresp.*, pp. 181–82. MS at Arsenal.
2. See Letter 286.
3. Probably R. Smith, bookseller at 25 Foley St., Portland Place, London.

in some degree insinuating themselves into our minds, though we in general are very little aware how or from whence they come to us.

You may measure the distance between France & England by that between Guizot & Peel, each the leader of the Conservative party in their respective countries. Happily though we are slow we are sure. We are the ballast of Europe, France its sail.

ever yours truly

J. S. MILL.

292. TO JOHN MITCHELL KEMBLE[1]

India House
26th June 1840

MY DEAR SIR

I know you will not consider it an intrusion on my part to ask you whether among the many persons of mental cultivation & attainments with whom you must necessarily be acquainted, who have the world still "before them where to choose"[2] & perhaps nothing very promising as yet offered for their choice, there be any one whom you could recommend as tutor to the eldest son (about twelve years old) of a person of very high rank[3] & of ideas & aspirations on the subject of education, considerably above what are common in any rank? I am not yet at liberty to say who the party is—it has only been told to me in confidence, because if it were to transpire there would be a troublesome quantity of applications & a corresponding number of disappointments. But there is, probably, no situation of the kind in England in respect to which more important consequences may depend on its being well filled.

Do you think your friend Mr. Edgeworth[4] would accept such a situation? & do you think him qualified for it? I only mention him because his writings prove him to be a man of considerable powers & accomplishments, & I think I have understood that he is not in such circumstances as would prevent his taking employment of this kind.

Ever truly yours

J. S. MILL

1. *Addressed*: J. M. Kemble, Esq. MS in the possession of Professor Ney MacMinn, Northwestern University.

2. Milton, *Paradise Lost*, Book XII, l. 646.

3. Unidentified.

4. Francis Beaufort Edgeworth (1809–1846), half-brother of the novelist Maria Edgeworth; he had been a student with Kemble and Sterling at Cambridge and had contributed to Kemble's *British and Foreign Review*. He had at one point set up a school at Eltham (see *Letters and Literary Remains of Edward Fitzgerald*, ed. W. A. Wright [London, 1889], I, 36). For a sketch of Edgeworth, see Thomas Carlyle, *Life of John Sterling* (London, 1851), Part II, chap. 4.

293. TO [JOHN MITCHELL KEMBLE?][1]

I.H.
Thursday
[July, 1840?]

My dear Sir

It would seem that Mr Edgeworth[2] is still at Edgeworthstown, but I know that he is, or was till lately, often in or near London. I wait for your further instructions before authorizing any communication to him.

From the little I know or have heard of the Mr Thompson[3] whom you speak of, I should think his recommendation a valuable one.

Ever yours truly
J. S. Mill

294. TO ROBERT BARCLAY FOX[1]

Kensington 3d August 1840

My dear friend Your letter came & was most welcome, & the same may be said of certain other missives[2] which I had the pleasure of despatching to Guildford. It was very pleasant to be able to figure to oneself your mode of existence at Penjerrick[3]—I often think one never knows one's friends or rather they are not properly one's friends until one has seen them in their home, & can figure to oneself some part at least of their daily existence. I am sure we all feel much nearer to all of you by having become so familiar with your local habitation or I may say habitations, & with so many of your haunts on that lovely coast—how often I fancy myself looking through the transparent spring air across the lovely blue bay to Pennance[4]—nor are reminiscences of Penjerrick either unfrequent or faint.

1. MS at LSE. No indication of person addressed. Paper bears watermark, 1838.
2. See preceding letter. 3. Unidentified.

* * * *

1. *Addressed*: R. Barclay Fox Esq. / Falmouth. *Postmark*: AUG 4 1840. Partly published by Pym, II, 313–15. MS in the possession of Mr. W. H. Browning.
2. Probably letters by Caroline and Anna Maria Fox to JSM's sisters, who were evidently spending part of the summer at Guildford, as they did in 1841 (see Letter 324).
3. The summer home of the Foxes, several miles from Falmouth.
4. *Sic.* Possibly *Penzance*, but Caroline Fox refers several times to walks to Pennance (see Pym, I, 109, 111, 119, 153).

It is curious that your letter about Tocqueville & Brown[5] found me also occupied with both of them—reviewing the one,[6] & reading the other once again after an interval of many years. I have not however yet got to his theory of the moral feelings, & though I remember that I did not like it, & took great pains, as I fancied quite successfully, to refute it, I cannot say I remember what it is—& so many of my philosophical opinions have changed since, that I can trust no judgment which dates from so far back in my history. My renewed acquaintance with Brown shews me that I was not mistaken in thinking he had made a number of oversights, but I also see that he has even more than I formerly thought of these characteristic merits which made me recommend him as the best *one* author in whom to study that great subject. I think you have described his book by the right epithets, & I would add to them that it seems to me the very book from which to learn both in theory & by example the true *method* of philosophising—the analysis in his early lectures of the true nature & amount of what we can learn of the phenomena of the world, seems to me perfect, & his mode of inquiry into the mind is strictly founded upon that analysis.

As for Tocqueville I do not wonder that you should find him difficult, for in the first place the philosophical writers of the present day have made almost a new French language, & in the next place he is really abstruse—by being so abstract, & not sufficiently (especially in the 2d part) *illustrating* his propositions. I find it tough work reviewing him, much tougher than I expected, especially as I was prevented from beginning so soon as I ought.

So you are now all or nearly all reassembled & we again see or fancy the family picture in its accustomed & original frame. That is much, although not so much as it would have been if we had not seen you in the opposite circumstances of London—I was going to say the *uncongenial* circumstances, but you are all so happily constituted that no circumstances are uncongenial to you—still some are more congenial than others & I can fancy for instance that if you were standing beside Sterling in one of Raphael's *stanze* in the Vatican you would find the situation very congenial *indeed*.

I cease to regret Sterling's sudden departure when I learnt that your party had had so much more of him & he of them in consequence of it.[7] What a pleasant winding up of their "mankind" tour.

5. Thomas Brown, author of *Observations on the Nature and Tendency of the Doctrine of Mr Hume concerning the relation of cause and effect* (Edinburgh, 1805), and *Lectures on the Philosophy of the Human Mind* (4 vols., Edinburgh, 1820).

6. See Letter 285, n. 2.

7. Sterling had returned to his family at Clifton, where the Foxes were visitors in July. See Pym, I, 206–15.

I return the old Michelet[8] with my prayer that your youngest sister whom I have hardly yet forgiven for not taking it & who must by this time be weary of the sight of it, will make haste to lay it up in some crypt of her autograph-cabinet & let the world see no more of it. I trust she is satisfied, for I have now kept it till another came—which proves to me by the extravagance of its compliments upon the letter I wrote to him, that if one gives a man exactly the sort of praise he wants to receive, one is sure of getting into his good graces.

The knowledge that an autograph of Guizot has probably reached you or will reach you from other quarters consoles me for not having one to offer—for his invitations to dinner are printed forms. I have dined with him again but one gets so little real conversation with any one who has to attend to his guests. The last time it was a most successfully made up party, I mean that fortune was most propitious to me in particular for of six guests three were persons I always like to meet & two of the other three were the two persons I most wished to meet—Thirlwall,[9] with whom I renewed an acquaintance of which the only event was a speech he made in reply to one of mine when I was a youth of nineteen—(it has remained impressed upon me ever since as the finest speech I ever heard)—& Gladstone whom I had never seen at all—and with both these I hope I have laid the foundation of a further knowledge especially as Thirlwall will now be in town in parliament time. How delighted Sterling must be at finding him a bishop—but hardly more so than I am.

Have you heard yet that Cunningham after all will only let us have *one* likeness of the present deponent[10]—so how my mother & Sterling are to settle it I do not know, as Mammy resolutely declines the equitable method of tossing up a halfpenny.

My sisters I dare say have written this very day. Pray tell us how your Aunt at Clifton[11] goes on & when your mother returns.

Your message to Carlyle shall be delivered—ever faithfully

J. S. MILL

8. Evidently an autograph of the French historian. JSM had contributed other autographs to Caroline Fox's collection.

9. Connop Thirlwall had recently been raised to the Bishopric of St. David's. His speech to the Co-operative Society in 1825 in reply to one of JSM's is also referred to in similar terms in the *Autobiog*., pp. 87–88.

10. JSM had his portrait painted while in Falmouth by a painter named Cunningham. Caroline Fox describes the portrait as "very beautiful; quite an ideal head, so expanded with patient thought, and a face of such exquisite refinement" (journal, April 10, 1840, in Pym, I, 168). Efforts to trace this portrait have not been successful.

11. Not identified.

295. TO MACVEY NAPIER[1]

India House
5th September
1840

My dear Sir

My article[2] has gone to Longman's this day. Whether it will answer your expectation I cannot venture to predict—but you will not find me, (as I have generally found those who have themselves conducted periodicals) an intractable contributor. If you were to bid me cancel the whole article & begin again, it would be no more than I have done before now with other articles of mine at the instigation of my own editor.

If the article suits you & it is not inconsistent with the practice of your Review, I should like to have half a dozen or at most a dozen separate copies chiefly to send abroad (of course I will readily pay the expense of them)—& I should also like to reserve the power of reprinting my articles & particularly this one, as I intend next spring to publish a collection of the few things I have written which either I or any one else thinks worth preserving, & I should like to include this in it as forming a sort of completion & winding up of the view which the publication will exhibit of my present opinions & modes of thinking.

With regard to alterations I repeat that you will not find me troublesome, but I should like, whenever time permits, to have the making of them myself. I do not mean that I object to your making any alteration in the first instance, since it often happens that the shortest & best way of making the nature of an objection intelligible is to suggest the *exact* change which would remove it.

Ever my dear Sir
Yours truly
J. S. Mill

296. TO MACVEY NAPIER[1]

India House
21st September
1840

My dear Sir

Allow me to thank you for your kind compliance, & more than compliance, with my wishes about the separate copies & the power of reprinting

1. MS in Brit. Mus.

2. On Tocqueville's *Democracy in America.*

* * * *

1. MS in Brit. Mus. Published, with one omission, in *Napier Corresp.*, pp. 327–29.

& to express the pleasure it gives me that you should have found reason to think favorably of my article.[2] Of course I cannot have the slightest objection to the omission of the sentence you mention, & am only glad that it is the only one upon which you feel it necessary to exercise your editorial scissors. I was prepared to find that there were parts of the article in which you could not agree, but on the points you mention I think a little explanation would remove most of the difference between us. I did not mean to class the power of combination as an element (except in a certain limited sense) of *fitness* for political power but only as one of the causes which actually *create* a political power whether the parties are fit for it or not. And my argument requires no more. My remarks also on Tocqueville's opinion that democracy does not bring to the helm the fittest persons for government, were only intended to moderate the strength with which he claims admission for that opinion, & to suggest grounds of hesitation & further examination; not to contradict the opinion itself for on the whole I to a great degree coincide in it, though not to the extent to which he carries it.

On the possibility of a mixed government it is probable that you & I & Tocqueville would on explanation agree. I agree & have long agreed in all you say on the point, but he would say that one of the three powers always *could* by constitutional means, carry any point it was in earnest about, if it chose to encounter the consequent odium & that the other two could *not* unless aided by the *one* or by a portion of it.

About future articles—those which I have chiefly thought about would require a good deal of reading & reflection, & considering that I have a book to finish I could hardly venture to name any particular time for their being ready. They are mostly historical—for instance one on the Romans & their history, a propos of Arnold's History and Michelet's—or, if you think the French Revolution not too stale a subject, I could write an article on Alison's book,[3] or on the Histoire Parlementaire[4] that would perhaps have still something of novelty in its views. But I should not like to undertake either of these if it were necessary to appoint any time within a year for their being ready—though they might *possibly* be finished much sooner. If I am to undertake anything soon it must be something requiring less time & research.

I have been much pressed to write on the Report (or rather Minutes of Evidence) of the Committee on Currency & Banks—especially by Mr. Tooke[5] with whom I agree on the subject more than with anybody else who has written on it—but I suppose you would look to McCulloch[6] on

2. See preceding letter, n. 2.
3. See Letter 72, n. 13.
4. See Letter 101, n. 12.
5. Thomas Tooke.
6. John Ramsay McCulloch.

that question, and even if he were not likely as I suppose he is, to write on it himself, you would probably hardly think it fair to him to put in an article which would contain what he would consider heresies. Mr. Tooke says he has no doubt the *Quarterly* would take it, & perhaps it would, but I think liberal writers ought to stick to liberal reviews, & my adhesion to the Edinburgh is in a certain sense political as well as literary.

Believe me, with much satisfaction at the new connexion which is now formed between us,

Yours ever faithfully

J. S. MILL

297. TO JOHN STERLING[1]

I.H.
1st Oct. 1840

MY DEAR STERLING

Döring's Life of Goethe[2] is a little book, about as long as one of the thicker volumes of the small edition of Goethe's works: therefore unless by a really first rate hand it is likely to be but meagre. The booksellers say it is thought well of but I can learn nothing specific about it. They know of no other Life. Nutt[3] says the price is six shs but offered me for four sh. the only copy he had, a worn one. A bookseller named Senior says the price is 4 s. but he had sold all his copies. Shall I order one from him? & shall it be sent to Knightsbridge?

I am to have a dozen separate copies of my review of Tocqueville & I will send you one. There is a review of him in Blackwood,[4] cleverish but hollow. What an antigallican tone in this whole number of Blackwood: & not a man among the writers who is not persuaded that he knows the whole French people, intus et in cute.[5] There is much more danger of war than people are aware of.[6] More than one credible testimony of Frenchmen now in Paris or lately there, assures me that the war feeling there is uni-

1. In reply to Sterling's letter from Clifton, Sept. 21, 1840 (MS at King's). MS at Leeds. Part published in Elliot, I, 118.

2. J. M. H. Döring, *J. W. v. Göthe's Leben* (Weimar, 1828), about which Sterling had inquired.

3. David Nutt (1810–1863), bookseller in Fleet Street, of whom Sterling had asked JSM to make inquiries.

4. *Blackwood's*, XLVIII (Oct., 1840), 463–78.

5. "inside and out." Cf. Persius, Satire III, 30.

6. In the autumn of 1840 there were widespread fears that Palmerston's policies with respect to intervention in the Levant to support Turkey against Mohammed Ali of Egypt might bring war between England and France. Thiers, the French Premier, who threatened war, was ousted in Oct. and succeeded by Guizot. By the end of the year Palmerston was widely credited with a great triumph. Liberals and Radicals in general, however, opposed him for aligning England with Russia, Prussia, and Austria. See also Letters 300 and 303.

versal, & has for the time silenced all others, that even those whose personal interests are opposed to it share the feeling, & that there is not now one voice against the fortifying of Paris which excited such clamour a few years ago. And that this is not from love of war, for they dislike it, but because they feel themselves *blessé* & humiliated as a nation. This is foolish, but who can wonder at it in a people whose country has within this generation been twice occupied by foreign armies? If that were our case we should have plenty of the same feeling. But it is melancholy to see the rapid revival of hatred on their side & jealous dislike on ours.

I am curious to see the review of Carlyle in the Quarterly.[7] From extracts I have no doubt it is by the author of the article on Socialism.[8] Merivale's article[9] has many sound criticisms, as much of appreciation as you can expect from an Edinburgh reviewer, & a few damnable heresies. Carlyle's dislike of it seems to me excessive, & nothing that he says surprises me more than that he should think Macaulay would have done it better. Macaulay would not have had half as much appreciation of him.

What you say about the absence of a disinterested & heroic pursuit of Art as the greatest want of England at present, has often struck me, but I suspect it will not be otherwise until our social struggles are over. Art needs earnest but quiet times—in ours I am afraid Art itself to be powerful must be polemical—Carlylean not Goethian—but "I speak as to the wise—judge ye what I say."—

Ever yours,

J. S. MILL

298. TO SIR WILLIAM MOLESWORTH[1]

19th November 1840

Your Leeds demonstration seems to me a very proper thing, done in the very best way, and I think that is the general impression about it. I cannot but think it has done, and will do, good both in France and here, and I am sure it has had a good effect in raising your public character.

7. "Carlyle's Works," *QR*, LXVI (Sept., 1840), 446–503. The review was by the Rev. William Sewell. See Francis Espinasse, *Literary Recollections* (London, 1893), p. 77 n.

8. "Socialism," *QR*, LXV (March, 1840), 484–527.

9. Herman Merivale (1806–1874), then professor of political economy at Oxford, later Under-Secretary for India. His article on Carlyle's *French Revolution* (2nd ed.) had appeared in *ER*, LXXI (July, 1840), 411–45.

* * * *

1. Excerpt published in Fawcett, p. 217. MS not located.

On Nov. 7, 1840, at the height of the war scare, Molesworth addressed a large audience of his constituents at Leeds, attacking Palmerston's policies and urging the maintenance of peace with France. The meeting, which passed a resolution heartily endorsing Molesworth's position, was reported in the *Examiner*, Nov. 15, 1840, p. 729.

299. TO MACVEY NAPIER[1]

India House
23[d] Nov[r] 1840

MY DEAR SIR

Many thanks for the very handsome payment which reached me this morning.

I have not yet seen Fletcher since I returned to town, but I am in daily expectation of doing so. He is unfortunately apt to be behind his time & though he was particularly anxious not to be so in this instance he was also particularly desirous to do his very best which may perhaps cause him to be behindhand—but I hope not.

I will keep Arnold in view[2] & set to work upon him as soon as I can. How soon that will be I do not precisely know: but it may very possibly be in time for your spring number. I feel much obliged for the latitude you give me.

Ever yours
in haste

J. S. MILL

300. TO ROBERT BARCLAY FOX[1]

I.H.
25 Nov. 1840

MY DEAR FRIEND It is very long since I either heard from you or wrote to you, but the correspondence between your sisters & mine, which is considerably more active than ours, has kept up a sort of communication between us, which though very agreeable I do not find entirely to supply the place of direct correspondence. I am not, I know, entitled to expect frequent letters while I shew myself so remiss in fulfilling my own part of the implied contract between absent friends. But we people whose whole life is passed in writing either to "Our Governor General of India in Council" or to everybody's governor general the English public, are I believe excusable if we like better to receive letters than to write them. I enclose a copy of a recent epistle of mine[2] to the latter of those great authorities. It will reappear as part of two little volumes which although you already have nearly all the contents of them, will some time or other in the course of next year appear before you as suppliants for a place on your shelf. About

1. MS in Brit. Mus.

2. See Letter 285, n. 4.

* * * *

1. *Addressed*: R. B. Fox Esq. Published with omissions by Pym, II, 316–17. MS in the possession of W. H. Browning.

2. Presumably his review of Tocqueville in the Oct., 1840, *ER*.

the same time I hope to have finished a big book[3] the first draft of which I put the last hand to a few weeks ago. I do not know whether the subject of it will interest you—but as you have been so much pleased with Brown,[4] many of whose views I have adopted, perhaps it may.

We have all of us been in great trepidation about the state of affairs in Europe. It would have been too bad if the two most lightheaded men in Europe, Palmerston[5] and Thiers, had been suffered to embroil the whole world[6] & do mischief which no one now living would have seen repaired. I do not know which of the two I feel most indignant with. The immediate danger is I hope over, but the evil already done is incalculable—the confidence which all Europe felt in the preservation of peace will not for many years be re-established & the bestial antipathies between nations & especially between France & England have been rekindled to a deplorable extent. All the hope is that founded on the French character which as it is excitable by small causes may also be calmed by slight things—& accordingly alternates between resentment against England and Anglomania.

You know of course that George[7] is at Torquay & also that Sterling is there, perhaps for the winter, perhaps only till he sets out for Italy. With kind regards to all, ever faithfully yours,

J. S. MILL.

301. TO GEORGE HENRY LEWES[1]

I.H.
Thursday
[probably late 1840]

MY DEAR SIR

I lost no time in setting about your paper on Shelley.[2] It abounds in true & important things & yet (for I know you want me to tell you exactly the impression it has made upon me) there is something about it which satisfies me less than is usually the case with your writings. It is easier however to say this, than to tell exactly what that *something* is, or to point out how the article could have been or could now be improved. After thinking a good deal about it I can get no nearer than this—that you do

3. The *Logic*, not published until 1843. 4. Thomas Brown. See Letter 294, n. 5.

5. Henry John Temple, third Viscount Palmerston (1784–1865), Secretary of State for Foreign Affairs (1830–41) and later Prime Minister.

6. See Letter 297, n. 6.

7. JSM's youngest brother. The reason for George's visit to Torquay can only be surmised; perhaps he was already manifesting symptoms of the family disease, tuberculosis, which was to lead to his early death, and the milder climate of Torquay had been recommended.

* * * *

1. Published in Kitchel, p. 28. MS at Columbia University.

George Henry Lewes (1817–1878), writer, later the husband of George Eliot.

2. The paper appeared in *WR*, XXXV (April, 1841), 303–44, signed G.H.L.

not seem to me to have laid down for yourself with sufficient definiteness, what precise impression you wished to produce, & upon what class of readers. It was particularly needful to have a distinct view of this sort when writing on a subject on which there are so many rocks & shoals to be kept clear of. For example I think you should have begun by determining whether you were writing for those who required a *vindication* of Shelley or for those who wanted a *criticism* of his poems or for those who wanted a biographic Carlylian *analysis* of him as a *man.* I doubt if it is possible to combine all these things, but I am sure at all events that the unity necessary in an essay of any kind as a work of art requires at least that one of these should be the predominant purpose & the others only incidental to it. If I can venture an opinion on so difficult & delicate a matter, I would say that the idea of a *vindication* should be abandoned. Shelley can only be usefully vindicated from a point of view nearer that occupied by those to whom a vindication of him is still needed. I have seen very useful and effective vindications of him by religious persons, & in a religious tone: but *we,* I think, should leave that to others, & should take for granted, boldly, all those premisses respecting freedom of thought & the morality of acting on one's own *credo,* which to anyone who admits them, carry Shelley's vindication with them. By descending into that other arena I think we only spoil what is already going on much better than anything we can do in that way can possibly mend.

I intended to say but a word now, & more when we meet, but I have run on to this length—I will add that there are several things in the article which Hickson could not, I am sure, with any common prudence print in his review.

You are certainly a conjurer, in finding out my old obscure articles. The only valuable thing in these two[3] is I think the distinction between poetry & oratory. The "Genius"[4] paper is no favorite with me, especially in its boyish stile. It was written in the height of my Carlylism, a vice of style which I have since carefully striven to correct & as I think you should do—there is too much of it in the Shelley. I think Carlyle's costume should be left to Carlyle whom alone it becomes & in whom it would soon become unpleasant if it were made common—& I have seen as you must have done, grievous symptoms of its being taken up by the lowest of the low.

As to my Logic, it has all to be rewritten yet.

ever yours,

J. S. Mill

come soon.

3. "What is Poetry?" (in which appears the distinction between poetry and oratory) and "The Two Kinds of Poetry" (which compares Wordsworth and Shelley), *MR,* VII (Jan. and Oct., 1833), 60–70, 714–24. See Letter 85, n. 3.
4. "On Genius," *MR,* VI (Oct., 1832), 649–59. See Letter 49, n. 2.

302. TO JOHN STERLING[1]

3rd December, 1840.

MY DEAR STERLING—I suppose this will reach you although directed only to the Torquay Post Office. I write only to keep up the thread of our correspondence, as I have nothing very particular to say.

When I advised you, if you go to Italy, to see Genoa and the Corniche, I forgot that you had not seen Venice and Munich. You certainly ought by no means to miss the pictures, of course, better than anything you would see there, though I cannot help thinking that the Venetian school is but the Flemish "with a difference"—that difference being chiefly the difference between Italian physique and Belgian or Dutch. But then again some of the sculptures at Munich are among the very first extant—and *you* will be interested in the modern German art; it is probably from knowing nothing of the subject, that what I saw of it appears to me a feeble, hot-house product. But *quære* whether anything so essentially objective as painting and sculpture can thrive in Germany—any more than Shakespeare or Beethoven could have been produced in Italy. This, however,[2] is *sus Minervam.*[3]

Have you any idea who that Fellow of St John's is, who publishes in the Monthly Chronicle his notes on Italy?[4] He has something in him but seems, as yet, very [low?] & inexperienced. Have you read either of Laing's books?[5] You should read his defence of them in the said Monthly Chronicle.[6]

I have been considering whether I ought to postpone revising my Logic in order to read the German books you mention. On the whole I think not,—their way of looking at such matters is so very different from mine, which is founded on the methods of physical science, & entirely *a posteriori.*—

Ever yours faithfully

J. S. MILL

I suppose George has seen you though we have not heard from him since—

1. *Addressed*: Rev. John Sterling / Post Office / Torquay. *Postmark*: PAID / DE 3 / 1840. In reply to Sterling's letter of Nov. 20, 1840 (MS at King's). Part of letter at LSE. Published with omissions in Elliot, I, 118–19.

2. The portion of the original letter which is at LSE begins with this word.

3. "A sow teaching the Goddess of Wisdom," a saying of ancient Greek origin (cf. Plutarch, *Demosthenes* 11, and Cicero, *De Oratore* 2.57.233 and *Academica* 1.5.18.

4. "Letters from the Continent," *Monthly Chronicle*, VI(July-Dec., 1840), 196–224, 289–315, 399–433, 505–31, and VII (1841), 11–37.

5. Samuel Laing (1780–1868), traveller and author of *A Journal of a Residence in Norway* (London, 1836); and *A Tour in Sweden* (London, 1839).

6. "Sweden and Norway," *Monthly Chronicle*, VI (Nov., 1840), 385–97.

303. TO JOHN STERLING[1]

I.H.
19th Decr
1840

MY DEAR STERLING

In consequence of what you wrote about Ritter's book[2] I have, after two unsuccessful attempts to get it in London, ordered it from Germany.

I think & feel very much as you do on the subject of the bad spirit manifested in France by so many politicians & writers & unhappily by some from whom better things were to be expected. But this does not appear to me to strengthen Palmerston's justification.[3] I do not believe that Thiers would have acted, in power, in a manner at all like his braggadocio afterwards when he knew that he had only the turbulent part of the population to throw himself upon, & no watchword to use but the old ones about making the Mediterranean a French lake, getting rid of the treaties of 1815, &c. I have no doubt that he would have attempted to make such an arrangement as should leave a powerful state at that end of the Mediterranean under French influence & I think he had a good right to attempt this, & we no right at all to hinder it if the arrangement was not objectionable on any other account. It appears to me very provoking treatment of France that England & Russia should be extending their influence every year till it embraces all Asia & that we should be so indignant at the bare supposition that France wishes to do a little of what we do on so much larger a scale. It is true we do it almost in spite of ourselves, & rather wish to keep others out than to get ourselves in; but we cannot expect France to think so, or to regard our professing it as anything but attempting to humbug them & not doing it well. I believe that no harm whatever to Europe would have resulted from French influence with Mehemet Ali,[4] & it would have been easy to *bind* France against any future occupation of the country for herself. We should then have avoided raising this mis-

1. In reply to Sterling's letter of Dec. 9, 1840 (MS at King's; part published in Tuell, *John Sterling*, pp. 72–74 and 131–32). MS at Leeds. Part published in Elliot, I, 119–20.

2. August Heinrich Ritter, *Vorlesungen zur Einleitung in die Logik* (Berlin, 1823). Sterling had also recommended books by Twesten, Schleiermacher, and Hegel.

3. See Letter 297, n. 6. Sterling on Dec. 9 had written: "Lord Palmerston went on much stronger grounds than I supposed in his bellicose policy. Thiers clearly meant himself and expected the support of the country in designing to frustrate any arrangement that would not leave Egypt strong & independent & Turkey nearly impotent—in order that France might at the first opportunity seize for herself the possessions that she thus would have detached even with an absolute certainty that Russia would in consequence obtain all the rest of Turkey." (Tuell, *John Sterling*, pp. 131–32.)

4. Mehemet (or Mohammed) Ali (1769–1849), Viceroy of Egypt.

chievous spirit in France—the least evil of which will be what Lord P.'s supporters no doubt think a great one, viz. that in another year France will be in strict alliance as to all Eastern matters with Russia as the only power who will give her anything for her support & moreover as her only means of retaliating upon England.

No one seems to me to have raised himself by this but Guizot, & he has done what perhaps no other man could have done & almost certainly none so well.

I am extremely grateful for your attentions to George & glad that you give so good an account of him. I wish you had been able to give a better one of the health of your own family. I have not seen either Carlyle or Mrs. Austin (I think) since I last wrote to you. Calvert I have heard nothing of for a long time except the rather indifferent news of him in your letter.

This is only an apology for a letter but for the present it must serve—

ever faithfully

J. S. MILL

304. TO ROBERT BARCLAY FOX[1]

Kensington
23d Decr 1840

MY DEAR FRIEND

I return with many thanks what I ought to have returned much sooner, the notes of the Welsh sermon. It is a really admirable specimen of popular eloquence, of a rude kind—it is well calculated to go to the very core of an untaught hearer—I believe there is much preaching of that character among the Methodists & more perhaps among their still wilder kindred the Ranters &c. Do you know Ebenezer Elliott's poem of *the Ranter?*[2] This might be such a man—I believe even this does good when it really penetrates the crust of a sensual & stupid boor who never thought or knew that he had a soul or concerned himself about his spiritual state. But in allowing that this may do good I am making a great concession, for I confess it is as revolting to me as it was to Coleridge[3] to find infinite justice represented as a sort of demoniacal rage that must be appeased by blood & anguish but provided it has that, cares not whether it be the blood &

1. Published, with omissions, in Pym, II, 317–21. MS in the possession of Mr. W. H. Browning.

2. In *The Splendid Village; Corn Law Rhymes; and Other Poems* (London, 1834), I, 141–56.

3. Cf. his *Aids to Reflection* in *The Complete Works of Samuel Taylor Coleridge*, ed. W.G. T. Shedd (New York, 1853), I, 277.

anguish of the guilty or the innocent. It seems to be but one step farther, & a step which in spirit at least is often taken, to say of God what the Druids said of their gods that the *only* acceptable sacrifice to them was a victim pure & without taint. I know not how dangerous may be the ground on which I am treading, or how far the view of the Atonement which is taken by this poor preacher may be recognised by your Society or by yourself; but surely a more christianlike interpretation of that mystery is that which—believing that Divine Wisdom punishes the sinner for the sinner's sake & not from an inherent necessity, more heathen than the heathen Nemesis—holds as Coleridge did[4] that the sufferings of the Redeemer were (in accordance with the eternal laws on which this system of things is built) an indispensable means of bringing about that change in the hearts of sinners, the want of which is the real & sole hindrance to the universal salvation of mankind.

I marvel greatly at the accuracy of memory which could enable Mrs Charles Fox[5] to write down from recollection so wonderfully vivid and evidently almost literally correct report of this sermon. I know that Friends cultivate that kind of talent but I should think few attain so high a degree of it.

The Testimony of the Yearly Meeting[6] I have read with great interest & though I had read several similar documents before I do not remember any in which the peculiarities of the Society in reference to the questions of Church Government &c which agitate the present day, are so pointedly stated & so vigorously enforced.

I am glad you have seen Molesworth. He is genuine, & *is perfectly* the thing he is; complete within his limited sphere. One ought to be satisfied with that; so few are as much & so very, very few are more. A man of Molesworth's sort of limitation has a natural tendency to be intolerant, because unappreciative of ideas & persons unlike him & his ideas—I knew how to excuse all that because I have been just like him myself & I believe knowing me keeps him out of much intolerance & prejudice because he sees that many things which are nothing to him are much to one whom he allows to be fully a match for him in the things in which his strength lies. I believe if I have done any good a large share of it lies in the example of a professed logician & political economist who believes there are other things besides logic & political economy. Molesworth in spite of his bluster, at least half believes it too, on trust from me. *Par exemple* one that will never be made to believe it at all, least in the sense I do, is one of the best of men & a highly instructed man too, Mr Grote—of whom Mrs Grote,

4. Cf. *ibid.*, pp. 303, 307. Punctuation has been supplied in this sentence.

5. Sarah Fox (née Hustler), wife of Charles Fox of Trebah (near Falmouth) and aunt of Robert Barclay, Caroline, and Anna Maria Fox.

6. Of the Society of Friends.

with more natural quickness & natural liveliness, is in point of opinions the caricature.

I am glad you like my article. I have just had a letter from Tocqueville[7] who is more delighted with it than I ventured to hope for. He touches on politics, mourning over the rupture of the Anglo-French alliance & as the part he took in debate has excited much surprise & disapproval here it is right to make known what he professes as his creed on the matter, viz. that if you wish to keep any people, especially so mobile a people as the French, in the disposition of mind which enables them to do great things you must by no means teach them to be reconciled to other people's making no account of them. They were treated, he thinks, with so great a degree of slight (to say the least) by our government that for their public men not to shew a feeling of *blessure* would have been to lower the standard of national pride which in the present state of the world he thinks almost the only elevated sentiment that remains in considerable strength. There is really a great deal in this although it does not justify & scarcely excuses the revival of the old national animosity or even the warlike demonstrations & preparations. A nation can shew itself offended without threatening a vengeance out of proportion to the affront & which would involve millions that never offended them with units that did, besides ruining themselves in the end, or rather in the beginning. And the tricky policy of Thiers, which is like the whole character of the man, is not in the least palliated by the offence given. But I do think it quite contemptible in England to treat the bare suspicion of France seeking for influence in the East as something too horrible to be thought of; England meanwhile progressively embracing the whole of Asia in her own grasp. Really to read our newspapers any one would fancy such a thing as a European nation acquiring territory & dependent allies in the East, were a thing never dreamt of till France perfidiously cast a covetous eye on the dominions of Mehemet Ali. I cannot find words to express my contempt of the whole conduct of our government or my admiration for the man who has conjured away as much as was possible of the evil done & has attained the noblest end, in a degree no one else could, by the noblest means. Of course, I mean Guizot who now stands before the world as immeasurably the greatest public man living. I cannot think without humiliation of some things I have written years ago of such a man as this, when I thought him a dishonest politician.[8] I confounded the prudence of a wise man who lets

7. Dated Dec. 18, 1840; in Mayer, pp. 329–31.

8. Despite his earlier distrust of Guizot as a politician (see Letter 35), JSM had at the same time expressed his admiration for Guizot as historian. Cf. the summary of French news in the *Examiner*, Oct. 21, 1832, p. 680, and the review (partly written by JSM), "Guizot's Lectures on European Civilization," *London Review*, II (1836), 306–36. For a later revision of JSM's view of Guizot as a politician, see Letter 501.

some of his maxims go to sleep while the time is unpropitious for asserting them, with the laxity of principle which resigns them for personal advancement. Thank God I did not wait to know him personally in order to do him justice, for in 1838 & 1839 I saw that he had reasserted all his old principles at the first time at which he could do so with success & without compromising what in his view were more important principles still. I ought to have known better than to have imputed dishonourable inconsistency to a man whom I now see to have been consistent beyond any statesman of our time & altogether a model of the consistency of a statesman as distinguished from that of a fanatic.

You have been a little premature in saying anything to a bookseller about my Logic for no bookseller is likely to hear anything about it from me for many months. I have it all to rewrite completely & now here is Sterling persuading me that I must read all manner of German Logic which though it goes much against the grain with me, I can in no sort gainsay. So you are not likely to see much of my writing for some time to come except such scribble as this—

All send love to all. Pray write soon—

Yours always—

J. S. MILL

305. TO GUSTAVE D'EICHTHAL[1]

Kensington
25th Decr 1840.

MY DEAR D'EICHTHAL

I did not write to you when I received the mournful & to me quite unexpected news of the loss of your father—not that I did not feel with you & for you, but I knew how little comfort words can give in such a case —& if they could, how many you have who are nearer & more efficacious consolers than I can be. There is certainly something in a father's death (quite independently of personal affection) more solemn & affecting than in any other loss. It closes the past, & as it were severs the connexion between oneself & one's youth. The only still worse loss is that which closes the future, as the death of a beloved wife or child, because *there* disappointed hopes are superadded. I had something like this to bear when I lost, less than a year ago, a brother only in his twentieth year who was likely if he had lived to be one of the most valuable men of our time as he was already one of the most loveable. But *allah akhbar* as your friends the Mussulmans say.

1. Published in *D'Eichthal Corresp.*, pp. 182–87, and in *Cosmopolis*, IX, 373–75. MS at Arsenal.

I received duly your letter to Sir T. Buxton[2] & forwarded it to him & I have since received the pamphlet[3] for which I thank you very much. What prospect is there of the appearance of the work itself? One of our principal papers, the Times I think, inserted the account which appeared in the Moniteur. There is every appearance that you have made out your case, & if you have it is a very important thing to have done. Islamism is a fortunate thing for the Africans & I sometimes think it is very unfortunate for the Indians of America that Mussulmans did not land there instead of Christians, as they would have been much more likely to adopt that type of religion & civilization than the other. You are very usefully employed in throwing light on these dark subjects—the whole subject of the races of man, their characteristics & the laws of their fusion is more important than it was ever considered till of late & it is now quite *a l'ordre du jour* & labour bestowed upon it is therefore not lost even for immediate practical ends.

I am out of heart about public affairs—as much as I ever suffer myself to be. I never thought that in our day one man had the power of doing so much mischief as that shallow & senseless coxcomb Palmerston has done.[4] Half the Liberal party, even many of the old Whigs, are against him, & it is most mortifying to think if the Tories had been in power & had done this (which they never would have dared) how gloriously we should have turned them out upon it & thereby cemented the friendship of France & England for generations to come. But the ten years of Whig administration have entirely demoralized our Liberal party. Lord Holland certainly died of it,[5] so old Rogers[6] says who you know is the familiar of the Whig houses & he adds that it will kill him too. The worst is that with all the good will in the world I can only palliate, not excuse the conduct of France & the spirit displayed by the French press & much of the French public. And this display you may believe me when I say it, has made numbers of our best & most thinking persons think Palmerston in the right who would otherwise have been grievously incensed against him. It is *that* which has done the mischief here. I fear the present generation of English will never again feel confidence in the French people. They are now convinced that the spirit of military & Bonapartist aggression & the bitterness of resentment against England are still alive—that France *cannot* be conciliated to England &

2. Sir Thomas Fowell Buxton.

3. Presumably an offprint of D'Eichthal's article, "Recherches sur l'histoire et l'origine des Foulahs ou Fellans," which appeared in the Nov., 1840, *Bulletin de la Société de géographie.* The "work" referred to in the next sentence was the longer treatise, *Histoire et origine des Foulahs ou Fellans,* published in the *Mémoires de la Société ethnologique* (Paris, 1841).

4. See Letters 297, 303, and 306.

5. Henry Richard Vassall Fox, third Baron Holland (1773–1840), prominent Whig leader, pro-French in his sympathies, had died on Oct. 22.

6. Samuel Rogers (1763–1855), poet, man of wealth, an intimate in the highest circles of the Whig party.

that the only chance for peace in Europe is in a strong conservative government which shall keep down the democracy & the public feeling for its own sake. I do assure you that until the French journalists & orators irritated & alarmed our public there was not a particle of feeling here against France or of interest one way or the other in the Egyptian question. The whole was a wretched freak of Palmerston for which God reward him instead of us—but *quicquid delirant Whigges plectuntur Achivi.*[7]

It is impossible not to love the French people & at the same time not to admit that they are children—whereas with us even children are care-hardened men of fifty. It is as I have long thought a clear case for the *croisement des races.*

It is really quite time that I should see & converse with you again, & with my dear & most valued friend Adolphe.[8] We are both of us much changed since we last met, you & I I mean, for Adolphe I should think is much the same as before. You probably have found out by experience as I have the meaning of growing "sadder & wiser" as one grows older & that too without growing at all unhappy but on the contrary happier. And you have felt as I have how one's course changes, as one gets experience but changes by *widening* & therefore still keeps the same direction as before only with a slower movement as attempting to hit more points at once. There is so much to say if one begins to let oneself go that I must not go on. Pray write soon & tell me among other things whether Guizot is likely to stand & what you now think of him. As for me I honour and venerate him, (it is but little to say) before all living statesmen though I differ from many of his opinions.

ever affectionately yours

J. S. Mill

306. TO ALEXIS DE TOCQUEVILLE[1]

30th December 1840.

My dear Tocqueville,

You may imagine how much pleasure it gave me to find that you were pleased with my review of your Second Part. I can very easily believe that many of those who had ventured to give an opinion upon your speculations had not taken so much pains or so conscientiously striven to understand & enter into the spirit of your speculations as I did, & many doubtless were

7. Cf. Horace (*Epistles* I.2.14): *Quicquid delirant reges, plectuntur Achivi* (Whatever folly the kings commit, the Achaeans pay the penalty).

8. Gustave d'Eichthal's brother.

* * * *

1. Published in Mayer, pp. 331–33; in reply to Tocqueville's of Dec. 18, *ibid.*, pp. 329–31. MS in Tocqueville archives.

not so well prepared for doing so by the previous direction of their thoughts and studies. And it is no more than natural to a mind like yours to be much more gratified by any evidence of your book's having worked in another mind & given birth to thought than by any amount of eulogy, or by a much more unqualified expression of concurrence, when not accompanied by such evidence.

It does not surprise me that this second part should be less popular than the first. The reason you assign, no doubt is partly the true one, but besides this, the thoughts in the second part are much more recondite, & whether one assents to them or not, are brought from a much greater depth in human nature itself, than those in your first publication. It constitutes still more than the other did, an era in science. I know how much thought it calls for from the reader when I remember how long it was before I could make up my mind about it, although few of my countrymen are so much accustomed to that kind of speculation and also I had previously thought that if there was any one of the leading intellects of this age to which I could flatter myself that my own had a kind of analogy it was probably yours. I therefore cannot wonder at the smaller extent of immediate popularity, especially as the most competent judges are exactly those who are not in a hurry to express any opinion on thoughts for the most part so entirely new.

Your observation that you do not believe in the errors of the public judgment as to literary works will be assented to by few Englishmen, and that such a thing should be said by a philosopher so much in advance of his countrymen is a high compliment to the French public which is certainly the cleverest public in the world, & as M. de Stendhal says, can understand everything, so far as intellect goes, even what they would have been quite incapable of originating. That is far from being the case with either the German or the English; who probably have more original genius than the French have hitherto manifested, but whose ideas seldom make much way in the world until France has recast them in her own mould & interpreted them to the rest of Europe & even sometimes to the very people from whom they first came. It is my belief however that in political & social philosophy the French are not only original but the *only* people who are original on a large scale & that as soon as they shall have appropriated, & fitted into their theories, the stricter & closer deductions of the English School in political economy & in some other matters of comparative detail they will give the law to the scientific world on these subjects. I do wish they would thoroughly master Ricardo & Bentham. Tanneguy Duchâtel did the former. They need not for that reason contract their telescopic view to our microscopic one, but they could and would combine the two & make them reconcilable.

I am very glad to have had from yourself your view of the unhappy embroilment between our two countries & I have shown that part of your letter to several people who had received a painful impression from your speech in the Chamber.[2] I agree with you in thinking our ministry very culpable, but our people are not to blame. You know that the English public think little & care little about foreign affairs & a ministry may commit them beyond redemption before they are aware. If the Tories had been in power they would have been suspected of anti-French predilections, they would have been watched, & would never have dared as these men have, or if they had, we should have gloriously turned them out on this question. But the ministry being liberal, and at a moment too when the liberal party has become entirely demoralised by seven years of a weak whig government, the public looked on in confidence that all was right, and that Palmerston knew more about the matter than they did, never dreaming that they had been brought to the brink of a war until it was revealed to them by the manifestations of feeling in France. Then, however, I firmly believe that the reaction you speak of in favour of the French alliance would have taken place, if there had not been such a lamentable want both of dignity & of common sense on the part of the journalists & public speakers in France. The whole of the feeling which has arisen since in this country, has arisen, you may believe me on such a subject, from the demonstrations since made in France—from the signs of rabid eagerness for war, the reckless hurling down of the gauntlet to all Europe, the explosion of Napoleonism and of hatred to England, together with the confession of Thiers & his party that they were playing a double game, a thing which no English statesman could have avowed without entire loss of caste as a politician. All this has made the most sober people here say openly that from the feeling which has shown itself in France, Palmerston must have had stronger grounds for his conduct than appear on the surface —never considering that Palmerston's conduct has revivified morbid feelings that were dying away. You know how repugnant to the English character is anything like bluster, & that instead of intimidating them, its effect when they do not treat it with calm contempt is to raise a dogged determination in them not to be bullied. All these feelings are decidedly beginning to abate since the peace party has had so strong a majority in the chamber of deputies, but the mischief is that the distrust will continue for a long time on our side as well as the resentment on yours. Palmerston supported by all the Tories and by half the Liberals will carry all before him in our Parliament but the opinion of most wise men here is that the Whig party have really destroyed themselves in the country by this. For

2. His speech, delivered on Nov. 30, 1840, was reported at length in *The Times* for Dec. 2 and 3, 1840, p. 5.

my part, I would walk twenty miles to see him hanged, especially if Thiers were to be strung up along with him. Do pray write to me again & at more length about this matter as I am most anxious to know your whole mind upon it—*en attendant* our meeting at Paris which I hope will be in the coming year.

Ever faithfully yours,

J. S. Mill.

India House.

• • • 1841 • • •

307. TO JANE WELSH CARLYLE[1]

India House
Saturday
[1841?]

DEAR MRS CARLYLE

I was prevented by want of time from writing to you yesterday as I said I would—but I believe it comes to the same thing.

Of all Balzac's things the Medecin de Campagne is the best, at least it is that which exhibits him in the best light: the Scenes Parisiennes are the very worst. But the Scenes de la *Vie Privée*, 5 vols. & Scenes de la Vie de Province, 4 vols. are a fair specimen of all he has done, & whoever has read them can judge of him. I would add to these, "Un grand homme de province à Paris" which is a continuation of a story in the Vie de Province, & "Le Lys dans la Vallée."

As for Sand I believe you know all she has wiitten: those I like best are Valentine, the Lettres d'un Voyageur & the new one "Le Compagnon du Tour de France."

so now goodbye & a pleasant journey to you.

J.S.M.

308. TO JOHN STERLING[1]

India House
5 Jan. 1841.

MY DEAR STERLING

Thanks for Twesten[2] which I will certainly read. I am now reading an older book, Lambert's Neues Organon,[3] of which Austin[4] speaks favorably

1. MS at the Pierpont Morgan Library, New York. The approximate date is established by the reference to George Sand's "new one," *Le Compagnon du Tour de France*, published late in 1840.

* * * *

1. Part published in Elliot, I, 120–21. MS at Leeds. In answer to unpublished letter of Jan. 4, 1841, by Sterling; MS at King's.

2. August D. C. Twesten, *Die Logik, insbesondere die Analytik* (Schleswig, 1825).

3. Johann Heinrich Lambert, *Neues Organon, oder Gedanken über die Erforschung und Bezeichnung des Wahren . . .* (Leipzig, 1764).

4. John Austin.

& which is certainly an able book though I do not know whether I shall find much in it that I had not found out myself or obtained from other sources.

I am glad you have been able to work, & glad you have left off working at least in the way which gave you a fever. I am glad too that it is a Tragedy. By the bye I never told you how very good I thought your lines in the Times on Acre & Napoleon.[5] I think I have seen nothing of yours yet, in a versified form at least, that seems to me equal to them.

About the war matters, I suspect we shall not make much of our discussion till we can carry it on by word of mouth. When I spoke of binding France,[6] I meant engaging her as a party in a general compact of European powers, which she could not afterwards have ventured to infringe. And the aggressions I meant are the proceedings by which we are gradually conquering all Asia, from Pekin to Herat—I did not mean that they were either aggressions in any bad sense, or provoking to France in themselves, but I do think it provoking that France should see England & Russia adding every year on a large scale to their territory & dependent alliances in the East & then crying out at the suspicion of her wishing to do something of the same kind as if it were an enormity never before heard of among the nations of Europe. But you must not think I defend France or would even excuse or palliate her conduct except so far as attacked by people themselves liable to the same accusations in all respects, except (so far as Thiers is concerned) that of duplicity.

I have had a letter from Tocqueville[7] which I put under this cover as you may like to see what he has to say for the part he has taken in this matter & how he connects it with his philosophic ideas. I have written to him a long letter[8] in reply to which I rather expect from him a long & controversial answer.[9] At all events I thought it right to try the chance of doing some good with him by speaking out with entire frankness, which his personally kind feelings towards me & his knowledge of my sentiments about France both in itself & in relation to England, gave me the power of doing without

5. "The Egyptian Vision," *The Times*, Dec. 9, 1840, p. 5.

6. In Letter 303. Sterling in his letter of Jan. 4 had disagreed with JSM: "Your argument on the Egyptian question I am sorry to say does not convince me. France had I think no right to insist on the independence of Egypt if that was likely to derange the actual relations of the European nations to each other & I do not perceive to what you allude when you say that we might bind France not to avail for her own advantage—the only way I can conceive of binding her or indeed any nation in such a matter is by making the intended step impossible which is what we have done. . . . What the aggressions are which you say naturally provoke France I do not know. We have done nothing at least since the peace at all resembling the conquest of Algiers & its occupation."

7. Of Dec. 18, 1840; in Mayer, pp. 329–31.

8. Letter 306.

9. Answer dated March 18, 1841; in Mayer, pp. 334–36.

offence. If he sends me an answer I will send that also to you. Please return this when you next write. You will see also how pleased he is with my review of him which considering how much of controversy there is in it, is an honour to him; & how complimentary he is upon it, which is an honour to me.

I need hardly say how earnestly I feel with you about the Corn Laws[10] & I therefore think the Anti Corn Law League right at Walsall.[11] To let in for a manufacturing town any man not an out & out opponent of the Corn Laws would I think have been a folly & something worse.

That you were able to bear this weather even at Torquay is very satisfactory &, no doubt, made it right for you to return to Clifton. Tell me how Mrs Sterling & your children are & give my kind remembrances to her.

ever yours faithfully

J. S. MILL

I had a long walk with Carlyle on Xmas day—he is as usual—Austin, I think, rather better than usual. I have not heard lately of Calvert.

309. TO GEORGE HENRY LEWES[1]

I.H.
Wed^{y}.
[Feb.?, 1841]

MY DEAR SIR,

Excuse my breaking in upon you at such a time as this,[2] but I think it best to write while the impression is fresh. Of course I do not expect any answer. I have read your MS. which I think very well done, & likely when finished & finally revised to be quite suitable to the Edinburgh.[3] You have not however yet convinced me that the line between poetry, & passionate writing of any kind, is best drawn where metre ends & prose begins. The

10. Sterling had written: "The iniquity of those Corn Laws & their widespread mischievousness made me rage. . . . Is there any chance of getting rid of them?"

11. At Walsall on Dec. 30, 1840, one Spencer Lyttleton, after refusing to pledge his support for immediate repeal of the Corn Laws, had withdrawn his candidacy for Parliament. The Anti-Corn-Law League sought pledges from parliamentary candidates. For details on the Walsall election, see Archibald Prentice, *History of the Anti-Corn-Law League* (2 vols., London, 1853), I, 176–84.

* * * *

1. Published in Kitchel, pp. 30–31. MS at Yale.

2. I.e., that of his marriage, on Feb. 18, 1841, to Agnes Jervis (1822–1902), daughter of Swinfen Jervis (1798–1867), MP for Bridport.

3. The article, "The Philosophy of Art: Hegel's Æsthetics," eventually appeared, not in the *Edinburgh*, but in the *BFR* for Oct., 1842 (XIII, 1–49).

distinction between the artistic expression of feeling for feeling's sake & the artistic expression of feeling for the sake of compassing an end, or as I have phrased it between poetry & eloquence, appears to me to run through all art; & I am averse to saying that nothing is poetry which is not in *words*, as well as to saying that all passionate writing in verse is poetry. At the same time I allow that there is a natural, not an arbitrary relation between metre & what *I* call poetry. This is one of the truths I had not arrived at when I wrote those papers in the Repository[4] but what afterwards occurred to me on the matter I put (in a very condensed form) into the concluding part of an article in the L. & W. on Alfred de Vigny.[5] I wish you would look at that same when you have time, (I will shew it to you) & tell me whether what I have said there exhausts the meaning of what you say about the *organic* character of metre, or whether there is still something further which I have to take into my theory.

I will carefully read your papers a second time and note down anything I have to remark, in the manner you suggested.

And now without any more on these rather untimely matters let me conclude by wishing you as I do most cordially all possible prosperity & happiness in your new condition, which all I have heard of the lady inclines me to regard as an enviable one.

ever yours

J. S. Mill

310. TO GUSTAVE D'EICHTHAL[1]

India House
23d February 1841

My dear d'Eichthal

I should not have delayed so long replying to your two letters if I had not been hoping every day that the pamphlets would arrive—but neither the two which you sent by the ambassador nor the six through the booksellers have reached me. I have always found that things sent through Paris booksellers were delayed for months & that it was of no use enquiring about them & that things sent by the ambassador generally came sooner or later without being enquired for & as it is very inconvenient to me to go or send to Manchester Square I have not hitherto done it, but if the packet does

4. See Letter 301, n. 3.
5. *LWR*, XXIX (April, 1838), 1–44, and reprinted in *Dissertations*, I, 312–54.

* * * *

1. Published in part in *D'Eichthal Corresp.*, pp. 188–90, and in *Cosmopolis*, IX, 375–76. MS at Arsenal.

not arrive I must do so. The Journal des Débats reached me & gave me great pleasure. The idea of your pamphlet[2] is so appropriate to the present time that it could not fail to excite attention. The Quarterly Review not long ago made a suggestion of a similar tendency for securing religious liberty &c at Jerusalem by placing it under the protection of *Austria*[3] (a not uninteresting *rapprochement* with your view of the mission of that power in "Les Deux Mondes.")[4] But the time is not yet come when the public mind can be drawn to the settlement of Syria nor will that time come until the apprehension of a European war is at an end, & that apprehension is now, in England, much more serious than it has ever yet been. The fortifications, & the arming, appear to most people here impossible to be accounted for except by aggressive designs on the part of France; it is in vain to say as those who know the state of the French mind do, that the purpose is merely defensive, because to every Englishman the idea that there is the least disposition anywhere to commit aggression against France appears so utterly senseless that no one can believe such an idea to be sincerely entertained in France. There is something exceedingly strange & lamentable in the utter incapacity of our two nations to understand or believe the real character & springs of action of each other. I am tempted to write a pamphlet or a review article on that very subject, but that I fear it would produce no effect. There will be much to discuss between you & me on that subject as well as on so many others when we meet.

Thanks my dear friend to you & Adolphe for your kind propositions respecting my visit to Paris. I have a very serious intention of going there, but there are things that may prevent me from doing so this next summer & if I do it will probably be under engagements which will prevent me from being able to make use of your kind & friendly offers to the extent I otherwise might—but neither those engagements nor anything else could or should prevent me if your & Adolphe's engagements do not, from seeing I hope very much of both of you & renewing our former intimate intercourse. I doubt not from what you say that you will by that time be married & though that is not likely to be the case with me I can yet very heartily congratulate you, more heartily than I generally can venture to congratulate an Englishman on a similar event which in nine cases out of ten changes a man of any superiority very much for the worse without making him happy. I do not believe that this is commonly the case in France & I would attempt to shew why, if the considerations entering into the question were not far

2. *De l'Unité européenne* (Paris, 1840, 35 pp.). See Letter 312. D'Eichthal had sent JSM a copy of the *Journal des Débats* for Jan. 18, 1841, which carried an article on the pamphlet.
3. In an article on "Foreign Policy," LXVII (Dec., 1840), 301.
4. See Letters 197, n. 2, and 215.

more complicated than most people have reflected upon. Excuse this poor letter—I will write again & I hope better when I have read your pamphlet.

yours affectionately
J. S. Mill

311. TO GEORGE HENRY LEWES[1]

18 Kensington Square
1st March 1841

My dear Lewes

I suspect the difference between us is a difference of classification chiefly. I accept all your inferences from my definition & am willing to stand by them. I do *not* think that epos *quâ* epos, that is, quâ narrative, is poetry, nor that the drama *quâ* drama is so. I think Homer & Aeschylus poets only by virtue of that in them which might as well be lyrical. At the same time you have just as much right to use the word Poetry in a different extension & as synonymous with "Art by the instrument of words" as music is Art by the instrument of rhythmic sounds, & painting, Art by the instrument of colours on canvas. Taking Poetry in this sense I admit that metre is of the essence of it or at least necessary to the higher kinds of it. In that case I claim the privilege of drawing within this large circle a smaller inner circle which shall represent poetry κατ' ἐξοχήν[2] or poet's poetry as opposed to everybody's poetry & of that I think mine the right definition. But "I speak as to the wise, judge ye what I say."

I return your Ms. with a good deal of pencil scratching at the back, for I have been, & intended to be, *hyper*critical. I have *studied* to find fault insomuch that you are to assume that I like & admire whatever I have not directly or by obvious implication objected to.

Your notion of the essentially religious nature of poetry seems to me to need a world of explanation. I think it will give entirely false ideas to English readers, & is only true in *any* degree if we, *more Germanico*, call every idea a religious idea which either grows out of or leads to, feelings of infinity & mysteriousness. If we do this, then religious ideas are the *most* poetical of all, an inmost circle within my inner circle; but surely not the *only* poetical, especially if your other definition of poetry be right.

I am afraid Mrs. Lewes will by this time find out that instead of being the *boree* on the subject of an unfinished article I have a strong vocation for being the bor*er* in respect of it. By the way, will you kindly make my

1. Published in Kitchel, pp. 31–32. MS at Yale.
2. *Par excellence.*

acknowledgements to her for an invitation I have been favoured with, & the *spirit* of which I most cordially accept (I never go to evening parties in the *flesh*) and believe me ever yours (and hers too)

J. S. MILL

312. TO GUSTAVE D'EICHTHAL[1]

India House
9th March
1841

MY DEAR GUSTAVE

I have received your letter of the 2d of March & also the *second* packet (but not the first) of two copies of "l'Unité Européenne" one of which I have sent to Carlyle. I will get the six copies from Messrs Belizard. Certainly the article in the Débats[2] could give no idea of the comprehensive & decided views taken in the pamphlet & altogether it does not seem to me, any more than the article in the Univers,[3] worthy of the subject. I am not surprised that such a paper as this should have given you *le caractère politique* for it is admirably suited to the moment & nothing could be better calculated to do good in France. It is much to be hoped & is in itself probable that the French Government will propose to itself as an object to reenter into the association of European nations & reassert its just influence in their deliberations by some such means as you suggest. The danger, I am sorry to say, is that *our* Government will not be prompt to seize this mode of reestablishing friendship & calming irritated susceptibilities. By most stupid & *grossier* mismanagement our Government has got itself committed to treating the affair of Syria as a mere question between a sovereign & a rebel governor, & has made all manner of unnecessary declarations, which will preclude it from entering, I fear into any proposition for superseding the authority of the Porte in what is absurdly called our territory. Wait a little & the Porte will get into such terrible embarrassments & will prove itself so utterly incapable of bringing the country into order and tranquillity that the necessity of a joint intervention of the European powers will become apparent to everybody, & then France will be able if she chuses to gain the well merited credit of intervening on a basis of enlightened philanthropy & enlarged views of futurity instead of leaving all to the other powers who would certainly continue to drag in the *ornières* of the old notions of government & international relations.

1. Published in *D'Eichthal Corresp.*, pp. 191–93, and in *Cosmopolis*, IX, 376–78. MS at Arsenal.
2. See Letter 310, n. 2.
3. Not located.

What you say on the character of the present state of feeling in France is most powerfully & vividly conceived & recommends itself to me as conformable to all that I in a more confused manner thought of it. But in this country everybody imagines that the French are far more warlike than they were in the time of M. Thiers, & it is of no use telling people the contrary. It must be left to time & events to correct the error. I have always thought that the events which have so deplorably resuscitated the old feelings of alienation between the two nations would produce an effect less sudden & violent on our people than on yours but more deeply rooted & more durable.

I have bought Salvador's last book & ordered the previous one.[4] I have not yet read either. I wish I had time to write to you a whole volume on the unheard of *travail d'esprit* which is pervading all branches of society & shades of opinion among us. We are in a curious time of the world.

ever yours

J. S. Mill

There is nothing recent about the Red Sea & the Euphrates.

313. TO ROBERT BARCLAY FOX[1]

India House
12th March
1841

My dear friend

I feel somewhat ashamed of having allowed two months to elapse since your last letter especially when I consider the inclosure which it contained, respecting which however I sent you a message by one of my sisters (a *verbal* message which she doubtless transmuted into a written one) which a little lightens the weight on my conscience. As there is a good side to everything bad (& not solely to the misfortunes of one's friends as La Rochefoucault would have it)[2] this tardiness on my part has had one good effect, viz. that on reading your little poem once more after a considerable

4. Joseph Salvador, *Jésus-Christ et sa doctrine. Histoire de la naissance de l'Eglise, de son organisation et de ses progrès pendant le premier siècle* (2 vols., Paris, 1838); and *l'Histoire des Institutions de Moïse et du peuple hébreu* (3 vols., Paris, 1828).

* * * *

1. *Addressed*: R. Barclay Fox Esq. / Falmouth. Published by Pym, II, 321–23. MS in the possession of Mr. W. H. Browning.

2. "Dans l'adversité de nos meilleurs amis, nous trouvons toujours quelque chose qui ne nous déplaît pas." *Reflexions, Sentences et Maximes morales de La Rochefoucauld* (Paris, 1853), p. 260.

interval I am able to say with greater deliberation than I could have said at the time, that I think your verses not only good, but so good, that it is no small credit to have done so well on so *extremely* hacknied a subject—the *great* simple elemental powers & constituents of the universe have however inexhaustible capabilities when any one is sufficiently fitted by nature & cultivation for poetry to have felt them as *realities*, that which a poet alone does habitually or frequently, which the majority of mankind never do at all & which we of the middle rank perhaps have the amazement of being able to do at some rare instants when all familiar things stand before us like spectres from another world—not however like phantoms but like the real things of which the phantoms alone are present to us or appear so in our common everyday state. That is truly a revelation of the seen, not of the unseen—& fills one with what Wordsworth must have been feeling when he wrote the line "filled with the joy of troubled thoughts."[3]

I cannot undertake to criticise your poem for I have no turn for that species of criticism, but there seems to me enough of melody in it, to justify your writing in verse, which I think nobody should do who has not music in his ear as well as "soul." Therefore if it were at all necessary I would add my exhortation to that which you have no doubt received from much more competent & equally friendly judges, Sterling for instance, to persevere. You have got over the mechanical difficulties which are the great hindrance to those who have feelings & ideas from writing good poetry—therefore go on & prosper.

I congratulate you on having Dr Calvert with you. Sterling you may or may not have for I had a letter from him yesterday dated at Clifton, on Thursday, & he had said if he went at all it would be on Wednesday. It would be a pleasure to us all to think of him as in the midst of you.

I have been doing nothing worth telling you for a long time for I cannot count among such things the rather tiresome business of reading German books of logic. It is true I have diversified that occupation by reading Euripides about whom there would be much to say if one had time & room. Have you ever read any of the great Athenian Dramatists? I had read but little of them before now & that little at long intervals so that I had no very just & nothing like a complete impression of them—yet nothing upon earth can be more interesting than to form to oneself a correct & living picture of the sentiments, the mode of taking life & of viewing it, of that most accomplished people. To me that is the chief interest of Greek poetic literature, for to suppose that any modern mind can be satisfied with it as a literature or that it can, in an equal degree with much inferior modern

3. Inaccurately quoted? Presumably, in view of the context, the reference is to the "Lines Composed a Few Miles Above Tintern Abbey": "And I have felt / A presence that disturbs me with the joy / Of elevated thoughts."

works of art (provided these be really genuine emanations from sincere minds), satisfy the requiremen[ts][4] of the more deeply feeling, more introspective, & (above even that) more genial character which Christianity & chivalry & many things in addition to these have impressed upon the nations of Europe, it is if I may judge from myself quite out of the question. Still, we have immeasurably much to win back as well as many hitherto undreamed of conquests to make & the twentieth & thirtieth centuries may be indebted for something to the third century before Christ as well as to the three immediately after him—

Here is a long letter full of nothing but the next shall be better. With kindest regards to your delightful circle—

yours ever,

J. S. MILL.

314. TO GEORGE HENRY LEWES[1]

I.H.
24 April 1841

MY DEAR LEWES

I have read the article[2] once but I should like to keep it, if you will permit me, long enough to read it again.

I see nothing fundamental in it that requires alteration though I would recommend a careful revision of the details, chiefly for the purpose of weeding out quaintnesses of expression, which find less favour in Edinburgh eyes than anywhere else—& perhaps I may add that the article strikes me, on a first reading, as being a little rambling. I do not know how the Edinburgh will like such severe diatribes against English criticism, which fall heavier on the Ed. itself than on anything else, but if it were my own case & I were sending such matter to the editor of the Edinburgh I should feel as if I were civilly giving him a thump on the face. In revising, it might be well to make it look as little German as possible—& I recommend, as you are so long in coming to Hegel & say so little about him, that you should stick a few titles of other books also at the beginning of the article.

You have come a little way to meet me, I see, & I believe I have come about as far, meanwhile, to meet you. As one hint among many towards a definition of poetry that has occurred to me, what do you think of this—

4. Page torn.

* * * *

1. Published in Kitchel, pp. 34–35. MS at Yale.
2. See Letter 309, n. 3.

"feeling expressing itself in the forms of thought." (That serves for *written* poetry, grammatical language being the form of *thought* not feeling) & it denotes that oh! & ah! are not poetry though Körner's[3] battle songs are. Then for the poetry of painting, sculpture &c. we have "feeling expressing itself in symbols" a definition which though often given for *all* poetry really serves very ill for the poetry of written or spoken language.

That article in the Edin. is not mine but Palgrave's,[4] & not the thing. I am too busy finishing my book to write articles. Anything I can do for you with Kemble I shall be glad of. Can you give me, that is him, any idea of the shape into which you will throw the subject?[5]

Ever yours

J.S.M.

Vive, vale, et *scribe*.

315. TO GEORGE HENRY LEWES[1]

[April, 1841?]

There need no more titles.[2] I had overlooked the fact that there were already several, but I would not call it an article on *Hegel*. I have marked quaintnesses with crosses, & made a few other remarks.

I like it better & better. But I fear the *Ed.* will find it too German. Still it ought to go there.

I did not give that phrase as a definition,[3] but as a contribution towards one. In turning over the thing to be defined, one feature after another turns up—& from the whole, a definition will one day or other emerge.

Should not your historical article[4] be on some *one* particular book? Editors are rather shy of such comprehensive plans of articles, especially with new contributors.

J.S.M.

3. Karl Theodor Körner (1791–1813), German poet, best known for his patriotic lyrics, *Leier und Schwert* (Berlin, 1814).

4. Sir Francis Palgrave (1788–1861), historian. The article referred to was "Progress of Historical Enquiry in France," *ER*, LXXIII (April, 1841), 84–120, reprinted in *The Collected Historical Works of Sir Francis Palgrave, K.H.*, ed. Sir R. H. Inglis Palgrave, F.R.S. (10 vols., Cambridge, 1919–22), X, 1–40.

5. See Letter 319.

* * * *

1. Undated fragment, but must refer to preceding letter. Published in Kitchel, p. 35. MS at Yale.

2. See last sentence of second paragraph of preceding letter.

3. See third paragraph of preceding letter.

4. Probably his article "Modern French Historians," a review of Augustin Thierry's *Récits des temps mérovingiens* (3 vols., Bruxelles, 1840), in *WR*, XXXVI (Oct., 1841), 273–308.

316. TO GUSTAVE D'EICHTHAL[1]

[Early May (?), 1841][2]

. . . to procure them for you.

I am truly glad that you & that M. Guizot expect from the fortifications a result so much the contrary of what everybody out of France expects from them. Englishmen of all parties, thinking it entirely frantic to suppose that any power whatever has, or is likely to have, a design of invading France, will be very long before they can be persuaded to look upon these measures of defence as proceeding from any other spirit than one of *offence.* I agree with you that the discussions[3] do honour to France, but I say so only because there were so many good speeches *against* a measure which had the popular cry in its favour. As to the speeches *for* it at least those of Thiers & his friends I only express the universal opinion here when I say that there has been no public exhibition for many years so discreditable to the country producing it.

As for us, we are entering into a new epoch: the proposition of our ministry respecting the tariff[4] & especially the corn laws, coming after many smaller measures of internal improvement, will rally the whole liberal party to the present ministry & will keep them in office for a long time to come.[5] Except our Chartists all the radicals will now be one with the Whigs, & I expect & believe that out of this crisis will arise a situation of things which will render the Whig Ministry what they have never been before, real mediators between the new & the old ideas & interests, and real preparers & softeners of the change to a new & better social organization. But I will write to you more at length about these matters soon. Meanwhile, adieu—With kind regards—

J. S. MILL.

I can tell you nothing certain yet about my own movements—

1. Published in *D'Eichthal Corresp.*, pp. 194–95, and in *Cosmopolis*, IX, 378–79. MS at Arsenal. The beginning of the letter has been lost.

2. Eugène d'Eichthal dates the letter 1841. The May date would seem to be justified by the reference in the second paragraph to the Melbourne government's espousal of a lowering of the duties imposed by the Corn Laws. Melbourne announced his change of policy on May 3, 1841.

3. The debate on the fortification of Paris took place in the Chamber of Deputies in Jan., 1841, and in the Chamber of Peers in March.

4. See n. 2 above.

5. JSM's prophecy proved false. On June 4 the Whig government lost on a vote of no confidence; in the ensuing election in the summer the Tories were returned to power under Sir Robert Peel.

317. TO EDWIN CHADWICK[1]

I.H.
Monday [May, 1841]

DEAR CHADWICK

Can you in any way help my cousin Harriet Burrow, a sister of Mr. Burrow who is a clerk in your office, to obtain the situation of matron to the Union Workhouse of Saffron Walden? It is a kind of thing which of course she would not seek if she had found it possible to do anything better for herself but for which she is more than qualified by experience & character, although only 25 years of age which I fear would be a presumption against her.

I inclose the advertisement.

Ever yours
J. S. MILL

318. TO ROBERT BARCLAY FOX[1]

India House
6th May 1841

MY DEAR FRIEND—I will be more prompt this time in contributing my part towards keeping the thread of our correspondence unbroken.

I am glad that you do not write *only* poetry—for in these days one composes in verse (I don't mean *I* do for I don't write verses at all) for oneself rather than for the public—as is generally the case in an age chiefly characterized by earnest practical endeavour. There is a deep rooted tendency almost everywhere, but above all in this England of ours, to fancy that what is written in verse is not meant in earnest, nor should be understood as serious at all (for really the common talk about being *moral* & so forth means only that poetry is to treat with respect whatever people are used to profess respect for, & amounts to no more than a parallel precept not to play at any indecent or irreverent *games.*) Prose is after all the language of *business*, & therefore is the language to do good by in an age when men's minds are forcibly drawn to external effort—when they feel called to what my friends the St Simonians not blasphemously call "continuing the work of Creation" i.e. cooperating as instruments of

1. Endorsed in another hand: "J. S. Mill / May / 41 / . Assistance of Mr. C. requested to obtain his cousin an appt as School Mistress of a W.H." MS at UCL.

* * * *

1. *Addressed*: R. Barclay Fox Esq. / Falmouth. *Postmark*: 6 MAY 1841. Published with omissions in Pym, II, 323–26. MS in the possession of Mr. W. H. Browning.

Providence in bringing order out of disorder. True, this is only a part of the mission of mankind & the time will come again when its due rank will be assigned to Contemplation, & the calm culture of reverence and love. Then Poetry will resume her equality with prose, an equality like every healthy equality, resolvable into reciprocal superiority. But that time is not yet, & the crowning glory of Wordsworth is that he has borne witness to it & kept alive its traditions in an age which but for him would have lost sight of it entirely & even poetical minds would with us have gone off into the heresy of the poetical critics of the present day in France who hold that poetry is above all & preeminently a *social* thing.

You ask my opinion on the punishment of death. I am afraid I cannot quite go with you as to the abstract right—for if your unqualified denial of that right were true, would it not be criminal to slay a human being even in the strictest self defence—if he were attempting to kill or subject to the most deadly outrages yourself or those dearest to you? I do not know whether the principles of your Society go this length: mine do not; & therefore I do hold that society has or rather that Man has a right to take away life when without doing so he cannot protect rights of his own as sacred as the "divine right to live." But I would confine the right of inflicting death to cases in which it was certain that no other punishment or means of prevention would have the effect of protecting the innocent against atrocious crimes, & I very much doubt whether any such cases exist. I have therefore always been favorable to the entire abolition of capital punishment though I confess I do not attach much importance to it in the case of the worst criminals of all, towards whom the nature of the punishment hardly ever operates on juries or prosecutors as a motive to forbearance.

Perhaps this view will afford you matter to confute in your essay—but indeed it is so trite that you have no doubt anticipated it.

There is nothing of mine in the Edinburgh this time—nor is it likely there will be till I have finished my book—the big book I mean, the Logic. I think I told you that the first draught was finished last autumn. I have now got to work on the rewriting & have just completed, tolerably to my own satisfaction, the first of the Six Books into which it will be divided. I don't suppose many people will read anything so scholastic, especially as I do not profess to upset the schools but to rebuild them—& unluckily everybody who cares about such subjects nowadays is of a different school from me. But that is the concern of a higher power than mine: my concern is to bring *out* of me what is *in* me, although the world should not find even after many days that what is cast on the waters is wholesome bread—nay even although (worst of all) it may happen to be, in reality, only bread made of sawdust.

So you are really to have Sterling always with you.[2] I congratulate you heartily—there is no place where I would rather wish him—except with me.—Carlyle is in the country roaming about, at least I have not heard of his being yet returned.[3] I quite agree with you as to his Lectures.[4] That little book contains almost all his best ideas in a particularly attractive shape, & with many explanations which he has not given elsewhere or has given only by way of allusion.

We have not heard from George for more than a fortnight—up to that time all was well with him & we shall soon have him with us again.[5]

Clara & Harriet will write soon—for aught I know they are writing to-day.

With kindest regards to Mr & Mrs Fox & your sisters & to all relations whom I have the good fortune to know (except those at Perran whom I trust soon to see), believe me, ever yours

(in no merely polite sense)

J. S. MILL.

319. TO JOHN MITCHELL KEMBLE[1]

India House
7th May 1841

MY DEAR SIR

A young friend of mine, by name Lewes, would like to write an article for your review[2] on the modern French Historians,[3] a propos of Buchez' Introduction à la science de l'histoire[4] or Michelet, Introduction à l'Histoire Universelle.[5] He is willing to take the risk of your not liking his article, but he is not willing to take, in addition, that of the subject's not suiting you. What say you?

He is rather a good writer, has ideas (even in the Coleridgian sense) &

2. Sterling moved his family from Clifton to Falmouth in June, 1841, where they lived until the spring of 1843.

3. He returned from Scotland on the day of this letter.

4. *On Heroes, Hero-Worship, and the Heroic in History*, delivered in 1840 (the Foxes had attended some of them), and published in 1841.

5. George Mill had probably spent the winter at Torquay for reasons of health. See Letter 300, n. 7.

* * * *

1. *Addressed*: J. M. Kemble Esq. MS in the possession of Professor Ney MacMinn.

2. The *British and Foreign Review*, of which Kemble was editor.

3. See Letter 315, n. 4.

4. P. J. B. Buchez, *Introduction à la science de l'histoire, ou science du développement de l'humanité* (Paris, 1833).

5. Jules Michelet, *Introduction à l'histoire universelle* (Paris, 1831).

much reading, & altogether I think he is a contributor worth having. You may have seen some papers of his in the Monthly Chronicle[6] & an article on the French Drama in the Westminster.[7]

Ever yours

J. S. MILL

320. TO JAMES MARTINEAU[1]

May 21, 1841

[When Dr. Martineau was in 1840 appointed Professor of Mental and Moral Philosophy and Political Economy in Manchester New College, he sent to Mr. Mill a copy of his Introductory Lecture and the Syllabus of his Course. On the 21st of May, 1841, Mill in acknowledging the volume, indulged "the happiest forebodings" of the work of the institution, from the soundness of its fundamental principles and the qualifications of its professors. He offered to ensure insertion in the "Westminster Review" for any article which Mr. Martineau might write in exposition and vindication of the principle of free teaching and free learning, of which Manchester New College was the unique representative.]

I had not been an uninterested observer of the affiliation of Manchester New College with the University of London; but I was not aware till I read your letter that the plan of instruction was founded upon the principle which I have always most earnestly contended for as the only one on which a University suitable to an age of unsettled creeds can stand, namely, that of leaving each Professor unfettered as to his premisses and conclusions, without regard to what may be taught by the rest. Besides all the other important recommendations of this principle, it is the only one which in our time allows such professorships to be filled by men of real superiority, whose speculations have the power of exciting interest in the subject. Such men can less and less endure to be told what they are to teach.

[After referring to the near approaching completion of his own important work on "Logic," Mr. Mill, in a passage which Dr. Martineau has in part reproduced in the preface to the "Types of Ethical Theory," ex-

6. Not identified.

7. *WR*, XXXIV (Sept., 1840), 287–324.

* * * *

1. Excerpts published by James Drummond and C. B. Upton, *Life and Letters of James Martineau* (2 vols., London, 1902), II, 276–77. MS not located. The passages in brackets are the editors' summaries of parts of the letter, I, 111–12, and II, 276–77.

presses his desire that his friend, if satisfied with the "Logic," would himself take up, systematically, some other part of the great subject of philosophy.]

As a Professor, you will, I know, take up the whole; but I do not want to have to wait for your Lectures, which, like Brown's,[2] will no doubt be published some day; but before that time I may very likely be studying them in another state of existence. I have been very much interested by your Introductory Lecture and Syllabus. I shall never forget the time when I was myself under that awful shadow[3] you speak of, nor how I got from under it, but it is all written down in my book.[4] Are not your general metaphysical opinions a shade or two more German than they used to be?

321. TO JOHN HAMILTON THOM?[1]

India House
21st May 1241

My dear Sir

Permit me to thank you for so promptly communicating to me the intelligence of our poor friend's death.[2] The accounts I had received of his condition from various friends during the last two or three years had led me to expect an earlier dissolution but I was not aware that his sufferings had been so severe.

Is there any prospect of a biography? It would be a most interesting life to write and most valuable to read—& so noble a spirit ought not to pass away from us & leave no record of what it was.

ever yours truly

J. S. Mill

2. Thomas Brown.

3. The editors point out that this refers to the following sentence in Martineau's Introductory Lecture: "It is probable that in the secret history of every noble and inquisitive mind there is a passage darkened by the awful shadow of the conception of Necessity; and it is certain that in the open conflict of debate, there is no question which has so long served to train and sharpen the weapons of dialectic skill."

4. Book VI, chap. 2 ("Of Liberty and Necessity"), *A System of Logic* (London, 1843).

* * * *

1. MS in Liverpool University Library. The MS bears no indication of the person addressed, but the ascription of it to Thom seems plausible since he had previously communicated with JSM about White (see Letter 241). Thom did publish a life of White.

2. Joseph Blanco White died on May 20, 1841.

322. TO ALBANY FONBLANQUE[1]

India House
Thursday
[June 17, 1841]

MY DEAR FONBLANQUE

I understand from Chadwick that he has said something to you about the probability of my being disposed to write on the free trade measures & that you were kind enough to say you should like to have an article from me on the subject. The fact however is that I am very hard at work finishing a book[2] of considerable labour and magnitude which unless I stick to it I cannot be sure of getting ready for the next publishing season, & it is therefore very inconvenient for me to allow any other subjects to divert me from that. Unless the call upon me were such as to make it worth while to throw aside every other pursuit & devote my whole thoughts & exertions to the cause for the next two or three months I should lose more than the cause would gain by any merely occasional assistance that I could give it: & I have not hitherto seen any necessity or opportunity for such a decided step. In the meantime I have been doing my part, like other people, in my own neighbourhood. The Kensington petition, printed in the Chronicle today,[3] is of my writing, & I had a great share in getting up the public meeting, which, though in a very unpromising neighbourhood, was a very striking demonstration.

As I am writing to you I will not omit, what I have never had a good opportunity of doing before, namely to express the great admiration I have felt for the writing and conduct of the Examiner during the last year & especially on the Eastern question on which it alone resisted an almost universal madness, & did so with an ability & in a spirit which seemed to me quite perfect.

I believe there is nothing of any importance in practical politics on which we now differ for I am quite as warm a supporter of the present government as you are. Except Lord Palmerston's Syrian folly,[4] I have seen nothing in their conduct since the last remodelling of the ministry two years

1. MS in 1961 in the possession of Major General E. B. de Fonblanque, The Cottage, Bank, Lyndhurst, Hants. Transcript supplied by Mr. William E. S. Thomas. Last paragraph published in *Life and Labours of Albany Fonblanque*, ed. E. B. de Fonblanque (London, 1874), p. 32.

2. The *Logic*.

3. *Morning Chronicle*, June 17, 1841, p. 6. The Kensington petition for free trade was adopted at a public meeting of the inhabitants of Kensington at the King's Arms on Tuesday, June 15. William Prescott presided.

4. See Letters 297, 298, 300, and 303–306.

ago, but what is highly meritorious; & now after this great act[5] a radical, unless he be a chartist, must be worse than mad if he does not go all lengths with them for men who are capable of doing what they have done on this occasion, & of supporting it moreover by speeches shewing so thorough a knowledge of the principles of the subject, will certainly bring forward any other great improvements which the time is or becomes ripe for. The moderate radical party, & moderate radical ministry, which I so much wished for & of which I wished that poor Lord Durham[6] would have made himself the leader, were merely a party & a ministry to do such things as they are doing, & in the same manner. They have conformed to my programme, they have come up to my terms, so it is no wonder that I am heart & soul with them.

ever yours

J. S. MILL.

323. TO MACVEY NAPIER[1]

India House
23d July 1841

MY DEAR SIR

A friend of mine who formerly wrote an article for your Supplement to the Encyclopedia, Mr. Weir,[2] is inclined to offer his services to you for the Edinburgh if they would be acceptable. He is an able & instructed man & a good writer, & could write valuable articles on many subjects but there are two kinds of subjects which he has chiefly in view: namely, the recent historical labours of the Germans, with which he is extensively & accurately acquainted; & Geography, of which he has made a systematic study, with a view to produce an elaborate work which from unforeseen circumstances it is probable will not be gone on with. You know how much of the reputation & popularity of the Quarterly has been owing to its articles of this sort & it strikes me as being a department which, in the Edin. is not systematically occupied. I think you would have every reason to be satisfied with what Mr. Weir would supply to you. If you are inclined to look favorably upon the project he would propose to furnish an article on Röppel's[3] Travels in Abyssinia, lately published in Germany & not at all

5. The Whig ministry's move in May, 1841, to lower the duties on grain. See Letter 316.
6. Lord Durham had died on July 28, 1840.

* * * *

1. MS in Brit. Mus.
2. William Weir (1802–1858), journalist, editor (1854–58) of the *Daily News*.
3. In Letter 326 JSM spells the name correctly as Rüppell.

known here. He says they are very interesting & important—& you might perhaps get the start of the Quarterly.

We are soundly thrashed in the Elections—but it is perhaps better so, for the ultimate interests of the party. It is the nature of Liberalism to require to be often reunited in opposition: liberalism always loses ground when in power, because in the first place it has to bear the brunt of that resistance to the pressure from without, the responsibility of which both when right & when wrong, should naturally fall upon Conservatism, & also because the impression of weakness is always given by the purely defensive position of a liberal government unable to carry its own liberal measures.

The 290 liberals in the new parliament, united as they have never been before, will be much more powerful, as well as more respectable, than a majority not exceeding 330 or 335.

ever yours truly

J. S. MILL

324. TO ROBERT BARCLAY FOX[1]

India House
24th July 1841

MY DEAR FRIEND

Have you not thought that I was dead, or gone mad, or had "left my home" like the "unfortunate gentlemen" who are advertised (or as Dickens expresses it, 'tized) in every day's newspaper—for none of my friends have heard of me for months past; not even Sterling, who of all men living had the strongest claim not to be so treated. But I meditate an ample reparation to him so far as a long letter can be so—& in the mean time I steal a moment to pay to you a small instalment of the debt which is due to you.

I suppose the most interesting subject to you as to most other people at this particular moment, is politics,—& in the first place I must say that your (or let me venture to say *our*) Falmouth is a noble little place for having turned out its Tory & elected two Liberals at the very time when it had received from the liberal government so severe a blow as the removal of the packets. If there had been many more such places the Tories would not have been, for another ten years, where they will be in half as many weeks. I cannot say however that the result of the elections has disappointed me. The remarkable thing is that the Corn Law question, *as such*, should have told for so little, either one way or the other. I expected that it would give us all the manufacturing places, instead of which we have *lost ground,*

1. Published with omissions in Pym, II, 326–28. MS in the possession of Mr. W. H. Browning.

even there! while it has not prevented us from turning out Tories from many small & purely agricultural towns. Now the only explanation which is possible of these facts, is one which reflects some light on the causes of the general result. The people of Leeds, Wigan, &c. cannot be indifferent to the Corn question; Tory or Liberal, it is a matter of life & death to them, & they know it. If they had thought that question depended on the result of the present elections, they *must* have returned Liberals. But their feeling was, that the Whigs cannot carry the Corn question, & that it will be as easily, if not more easily extorted from the Tories. And the agriculturists think the same[;] most likely we should have lost as many counties at the next general election even if the Corn question had not been stirred.

The truth is, & everybody I meet with who knows the country says so; the people had ceased to hope anything from the Whigs; & the general feeling among reformers was either indifference, or desire for a change. If they had not proposed, even at the last moment, these measures they would have been in a miserable minority in the new parliament. As it is, their conduct has to some extent reanimated radical feeling, which will now again resume its upward movement & the Whigs having put themselves really at the head of the popular party, will have an opportunity, which there seems considerable probability that they will use, of making themselves again popular. For my part they have quite converted me to them; not only by the courage & determination they have shewn (though somewhat too late) but by the thorough understanding they have shown of so great a subject. Their speeches in the great debates were really the speeches of philosophers.

I most entirely agree with you about the sugar question, & I was delighted to see that the anti slavery party in the country generally did not follow the aberrations of their parliamentary leaders. This part of the subject is admirably argued in an article in the Ed. Rev. just published.[2]

Have you yet resumed your speculations on capital punishment? As for me I have been quite absorbed in my Logic, which indeed it is necessary I should lose no time about, on pain of missing the next publishing season—when I hope to publish that & my reprint too.

With kindest regards to all your family (& apologies for so meagre a letter) believe me

yours ever

J. S. MILL.

My mother & sisters are at Guildford, some of them rather unwell with colds—George not being an exception.

2. "Grounds and Objects of the Budget" [by Nassau Senior], *ER*, LXXIII (July, 1841), 502–59. See F. W. Fetter, "The Authorship of Economic Articles in the *Edinburgh Review*, 1802–47," *Journal of Political Economy*, LXI (June, 1953), 257.

325. TO JOHN BLACK[1]

Kensington
Wed^y
[July 28 (?), 1841]

DEAR MR. BLACK

I have just been reading again that poem I told you of and I liked it so much that I could not help sitting down and scribbling off a hurried notice of it for you. Do with it as you please—I shall be glad to see either that or any other notice of the book in the Chronicle.[2]

Ever yours,
J. S. MILL

326. TO MACVEY NAPIER[1]

I.H.
Friday [July 30, 1841]

MY DEAR SIR

Mr Weir will immediately set about the article on Rüppell[2] (as I now find the name should be spelt) and send it to be disposed of at your pleasure & in your own time.

Though he has lived for some time in Germany a few years ago, neither his opinions nor his stile are at all of the Germanic order, & you need be under no apprehension of any unsuitableness on that score. I told him of your *caveat*, & he said there was perhaps more danger of a few Scotticisms.

Fletcher[3] is pretty well again & has been long busy on his article, which I think you will have before long—but he is so slow a workman that it is hazardous to make any promises in his behalf.

I think the present number of the Edinburgh the best you have published for some time, & altogether an admirable one—both solid & brilliant. The

1. *Addressed*: John Black. Esq. MS in the possession of Professor Jacob Viner, Princeton University.

2. JSM's review of Sterling's poem *The Election* appeared in the *Morning Chronicle* on July 29, 1841.

* * * *

1. In another hand on the verso: John S. Mills Esq / July 30th / 1841. MS in Brit. Mus.

2. Weir's review of Eduard Rüppell's *Reise in Abyssinien* (2 vols., Frankfurt am Main, 1838–40) appeared in *ER*, LXXIV (Jan., 1842), 307–28.

3. George Fletcher.

three articles by Stephen,[4] Mangles,[5] & Senior,[6] seem to me almost perfect, each in its way—& they are three men exactly suited to take a leading part in the literary & philosophical organ of the Liberal party being three of the most distinguished men of our time for an ardent spirit of improvement combined with good sense, & for the capacity of moulding philosophical truths into practical shapes. It is from such men that the party ought to take its tone & I am really proud of being enrolled in the same corps with them.

We are entering upon times in which the progress of liberal opinions will again, as formerly, depend upon what is *said* & *written*, & no longer upon what is *done*, by their avowed friends. Many things are often occurring to me which seem at the time, to be worth saying, respecting the modes in which a review like yours might, in the peculiar circumstances of the present time, forward this progress—but the thoughts generally die or remain dormant for want of an opportunity of discussing them. If I were living near you I dare say I should often teaze you with more suggestions than you have any need of. But at this distance I am obliged to keep my wisdom to myself, for like some kinds of wine it is not of quality to bear so long a journey.

ever yours truly

J. S. MILL

327. TO GEORGE HENRY LEWES[1]

I.H.
Wed^{y}
[Aug., 1841]

MY DEAR LEWES,

There is little use in detailed remarks on an unfinished article[2]—and in the absence of the extracts it is difficult to judge of the effect of the paper on the whole. There are a great number of good things in it, & I have no doubt of its ripening into a good article. Its deficiencies, as is usually the case with an *ébauche*, are chiefly in the introductory part. I think you should dwell much more, & in a more explanatory manner on the *idée mère* of

4. Sir James Stephen's "The Port-Royalists" was the leading article in the July, 1841, *ER*, LXXIII, 309–65.
5. Ross Donnelly Mangles (1801–1877), expert on Indian affairs; liberal MP for Guildford, 1841–58; chairman of the East India Company, 1857–58. His article in the July *ER*, LXXIII, 425–60, was on "Administration of Justice in India."
6. See Letter 324, n. 2.

* * * *

1. Published in Kitchel, pp. 37–38. MS at Columbia University.
2. This may have been an early version of "The State of Criticism in France," eventually published in the *BFR*, XVI (Dec., 1844), 327–62.

Nisard & of the article, the necessity of considering literature not as a thing per se, but as an emanation of the civilization of the period. The idea is one which it is of great importance to impress upon people. A writer in Blackwood this month,[3] on German literature, has said some things on the subject, not badly.

The concluding part, also, from the first mention of Lucan, seems too slight.

There is nothing Germanic in the style, but an occasional Gallicism or so.

The reviews generally give their extracts from foreign books translated—no doubt the editor would get that done, but woe betide the reviewer whose passages from a French or German xotbetic writer are translated by an English or Scotch hack.

ever yours

J.S.M.

328. TO GEORGE HENRY LEWES[1]

I.H.
Saturday
[Aug., 1841?]

My dear Lewes,

The differences of opinion I alluded to chiefly related to the character of the Romans. In the matter of "beauty, religion, form, or art" I objected to the assertion as too sweeping—you would not be understood if you said that there was no beauty in Lucan—& *beauty* altogether means with you only a *part* of poetic merit, while it would be understood as meaning the whole. Then the word *form* which in that sense is not English, & I think scarcely deserves to be so, would have suggested no idea to an editor but that of Germanism. But of all this, more another time.

I will make no more crusty tea for the incarnate solecism if she calls me a w—— but I will not write the atrocious word. No one is *that* but from consciousness of being hated by women & deserving to be so.

Ever yours

J.S.M.

3. "Traits and Tendencies of German Literature," *Blackwood's*, L (Aug., 1841), 143–60.

* * * *

1. Published in Kitchel, p. 38. MS at Yale.
The letter may refer to the article discussed in the preceding letter (see n. 2).

329. TO JOHN ROBERTSON[1]

September 7, 1841

I am doing and thinking of nothing but my Logic, which I shall soon have re-written the first half of, ready for press.

330. TO EDWIN CHADWICK[1]

I.H.
Friday
[Sept. 21, 1841]

DEAR CHADWICK—I go out of town this afternoon & do not return till Monday, when I will endeavour to call upon you on my way home, as I am very busy in the evenings on my Logic & do not like to interrupt it. However it is very possible I may be unable to call upon you on Monday, & if so I will try Tuesday.

Ever yours
J. S. MILL

331. TO SARAH AUSTIN[1]

India House
4th October 1841

DEAR MRS AUSTIN

I ought to have written to you & Mr Austin long ago, but I never felt myself so little inclined to write a single line that could possibly be put off, for ever since you left England every moment almost that I could spare for writing has been employed upon my Logic which I am determined to finish in time for next publishing season. I find the rewriting harder work still than I had anticipated. I knew that the whole business of arranging it & of making it readable was yet to come, but the thoughts themselves I find were much more crude & imperfect than I fancied, & those only who have tried to write a systematic treatise on anything, know what the difficulty is of keeping the whole of a subject before one at once. However I believe

1. Excerpt published in Alexander Bain, *Autobiography* (London, 1904), p. 111. MS not located.

* * * *

1. Endorsed in another hand: "J. S. Mill / Sept 21 / 41." MS at UCL.

* * * *

1. *Addressed*: A Madame / Madame Austin / Poste Restante / à Dresden. *Postmarks*: PAID / OC 4 / 1841 and POST / 11 OCT / U. MS at King's.

I have now broken the neck of the thing—about half of it, & the most difficult half, being finished, some parts of which I have had to rewrite three or four times.

I have watched constantly for American news but have seen nothing either good or bad worth writing about. You no doubt either saw or heard of what was stated by the American correspondent of one of the English papers in the very week you set out—that both the rival parties in Mississippi had put up candidates for the approaching election of Governor, who had voted for the measure which the present Governor refused to pass.[2] I have never had much apprehension about that matter ultimately going right. What do you mean by "this last blow"? Surely not anything still more recent than those which you told me of in London? And yet when I remember that you did not then think it impossible that you might return to England this winter—I am afraid.

As for politics, free trade & so forth, which you ask me about, things appear to me to be going on as well as can be expected. Peel gives every indication that his own inclinations are towards liberal measures both in commerce & in many other things, & next spring will most likely see him either bring forward some considerable improvement in the corn laws or quarrel with his party & resign, in which case the victory in a year or two will be still more complete, for the Peel Tories & the Liberals together can carry any thing. The serious part of the matter is that every year of delay does permanent mischief by its effect on the policy & feelings of other countries, & there is danger that free trade like Catholic emancipation & other Tory concessions will come too late for some of the good effects expected from it. The Tory writers here affect to think the ministry very strong but there is evidently a terrible storm brewing against them which they could, no doubt, succeed in weathering if they were not likely to fall to pieces in the attempt.

I have not taken any holidays this year, & do not intend. They are however, I hope, only postponed, not lost, as I shall claim a longer leave of absence some other year in consequence.

Mrs Taylor bids me tell you how one fine day (it was really not more than a week) she suddenly & with hardly any warning lost the use of her

2. JSM and the Austins, like many in England at this time, were concerned over the possible loss of their investments in American State bonds because of repudiation movements in some of the states. JSM's information about the situation in Mississippi was not wholly accurate, and his optimism proved unfounded. The retiring Governor, Alexander G. McNutt; the successful Democratic candidate, Tilghman M. Tucker; and the Whig candidate, David O. Shattuck, were all in favour of the repudiation of the Mississippi Union Bank bonds, and on Feb. 26, 1842, the bonds were finally repudiated by the State. See "Banking and Repudiation in Mississippi," *Bankers' Magazine* (N.Y.), XVIII NS (Aug., 1863), 89–109; and R. C. McGrane, *Foreign Bondholders and American State Debts* (New York, 1935), chap. x.

legs almost entirely—this was in June, & since, the little power of moving them that was left has become still less, in spite of all manner of remedies.[3] If the present system of treatment continued through the winter is ineffectual, she talks of trying Franzensbad (near Eger I think) next spring. Do you know anything of that place, or of the medical personages there?

I hope you will let me know immediately if there is anything I can do for you here which would not be better done by some of the many others who would be glad to make themselves of use, though few would be *so* glad as I should.

ever affectionately

J.S.M.

332. TO ALEXANDER BAIN[1]

[Autumn, 1841]

Have you ever looked into Comte's *Cours de Philosophie Positive*? He makes some mistakes, but on the whole, I think it very nearly the grandest work of this age.

333. TO GUSTAVE D'EICHTHAL[1]

India House
8th Novr 1841

MY DEAR D'EICHTHAL

I have long been a letter in your debt, & have remained so because I have not had a moment of leisure lately to think on the different matters on which I should wish to write to you. I do not think I have written once since I finished reading Salvador's two works,[2] & I certainly have not time to write at present the long letter which I felt a desire to write to you while I was reading them.

I cannot however longer delay telling you that I received the fifth volume

3. Mrs. Taylor eventually recovered from the paralysis, but her health thereafter was usually precarious.

* * * *

1. Excerpt published in Bain, *Autobiography*, p. 112. MS not located.

Alexander Bain (1818–1903), philosopher, first biographer of JSM. Bain had been encouraged by his friend John Robertson to begin a correspondence with JSM in Sept., 1841. They did not meet until the following spring, when Bain visited London.

* * * *

1. *Addressed*: Monsieur / M. Gustave d'Eichthal / 14 Rue Lepelletier / à Paris. *Postmark*: LONDON / [8?] NOV / 1841. MS at Arsenal.

2. See Letter 312, n. 4.

of M. Michelet's History of France & that it appears to me worthy of those which preceded it. Pray, when you see him, give him my very sincere thanks for it & say that as soon as I have finished a book which I have in hand & which is now very nearly ready for the press I will not only write *to* him but I will endeavour to write something to the public *concerning* him.[3]

I have not been in very good health lately, although my complaints are not serious—& the little time & thought that I had to spare from my occupations have been taken up by various cares. I hope my friends at Paris will consider these excuses sufficient for my apparent neglect of them. Next year I hope to be both in better health & with less work on my hands.

As for the state of public affairs here, I can make no prediction about it, except that I am fully satisfied it will go well. In what manner the good results will be brought about I cannot tell, but every contingency which can [occur?] appears to me to be the [bearer?] of good in some very important shape.[4] I rather think this is also the case with affairs in France & that you will agree with me. The only serious mischief which I am at all apprehensive of is foreign intervention in Spain & of that I trust there is very little chance.

With kind regards to Adolphe & all friends

ever yours affectionately

J. S. MILL.

334. TO AUGUSTE COMTE[1]

India House, London
8 Novembre 1841.

Je ne sais, Monsieur, s'il est permis à un homme qui vous est totalement inconnu, d'occuper quelques moments d'un temps aussi précieux que le vôtre en vous entretenant de lui et des grandes obligations intellectuelles dont il vous est redevable; mais encouragé par mon ami M. Marrast,[2] et pensant que peut-être au milieu de vos grands travaux philosophiques il ne

3. A promise eventually fulfilled in 1844 with the publication of his review of the first five volumes of Michelet's *Histoire de France*. See Letter 285, n. 3.

4. Brackets in this sentence indicate where page is torn.

* * * *

1. *Addressed*: Monsieur / M. Auguste Comte / à l'Ecole Polytechnique / à Paris. *Postmark*: LONDON / 8 NOV / 1841 / FBO. Published in Lévy-Bruhl, pp. 1–4; Comte's answer of Nov. 20, 1841, *ibid.*, pp. 4–11. All the MSS of JSM's letters to Comte are at Johns Hopkins.

2. Armand Marrast (1801–1852), journalist and politician; editor of the *Tribune* until 1834; when the paper was suppressed and he was imprisoned in 1835 he escaped and fled to England; upon return to France he became editor of the *National*; after the Revolution of 1848, he became President of the Assemblée Constituante.

vous serait pas complètement indifférent de recevoir d'un pays étranger des témoignages de sympathie et d'adhésion, j'ose espérer que vous ne trouverez pas déplacée ma démarche actuelle.

C'est dans l'année 1828,[3] Monsieur, que j'ai lu pour la première fois votre petit Traité de *Politique Positive*; et cette lecture a donné à toutes mes idées une forte secousse, qui avec d'autres causes mais beaucoup plus qu'elles, a déterminé ma sortie définitive de la section benthamiste de l'école révolutionnaire, dans laquelle je fus élevé, et même je puis presque dire dans laquelle je naquis. Quoique le Benthamisme soit resté, sans doute, très loin du véritable esprit de la méthode positive, cette doctrine me paraît encore à présent la meilleure préparation qui existe aujourd'hui à la vraie positivité, appliquée aux doctrines sociales: soit par sa logique serrée, et par le soin qu'elle a de toujours se comprendre elle même, soit surtout par son opposition systématique à toute tentative d'explication de phénomènes quelconques au moyen des ridicu[les][4] entités métaphysiques, dont elle m'a appris dès ma première jeunesse à sentir la nullité essentielle.

Depuis l'époque où j'ai pris connaissance de la première ébauche de vos idées sociologiques, je crois pouvoir dire que les semences jetées par cet opuscule ne sont pas restées stériles dans mon esprit. Ce n'est pourtant qu'en 1837[5] que j'ai connu les deux premiers volumes de votre Cours, à l'appréciation duquel j'étais heureusement assez bien préparé, n'étant resté totalement étranger à aucune des sciences fondamentales, dans chacune desquelles au reste j'avais toujours surtout recherché les idées de méthode qu'elle pouvait fournir. Depuis l'heureuse époque où ces deux volumes me sont connus, j'attends toujours chaque volume nouveau avec une vive impatience et je le lis et le relis avec une véritable passion intellectuelle. Je puis dire que j'étais déjà entré dans une voie assez voisine de la vôtre, surtout par l'impulsion que m'avait donnée votre ouvrage précédent; mais j'avais encore à apprendre de vous bien des choses de la première importance, et j'espère vous donner à quelque temps d'ici la preuve que je les ai bien apprises. Il reste quelques questions d'un ordre secondaire sur lesquelles mes opinions ne sont pas d'accord avec les vôtres; un jour peut être ce désaccord pourra disparaître: au moins je ne pense pas trop me flatter en croyant qu'il n'y a pas chez moi d'opinion mal fondée qui soit assiz enracinée pour résister à une discussion approfondie, telle qu'elle pourrait peut être se trouver dans le cas de subir si vous ne me refusez pas la permission de vous soumettre quelquefois mes idées et de vous demander des explications sur les vôtres.

Vous savez, Monsieur, que les opinions religieuses ont jusqu'ici plus de racine chez nous que dans les autres pays de l'Europe, quoiqu'elles aient

3. Actually it appears that he first read Comte in 1829. See Letters 26 and 27.
4. MS torn.
5. See Letter 228.

perdu depuis longtemps, ici comme ailleurs, leur ancienne valeur civilisatrice: et il est, je crois, à regretter pour nous que la philosophie révolutionnaire qui était encore en pleine activité il y a une douzaine d'années soit aujourd'hui tombée en décrépitude avant d'avoir fini sa tâche. Il est d'autant plus urgent pour nous de la remplacer en entrant à pleine voie dans la philosophie positive: et, c'est avec grand plaisir que je vous le dis, malgré l'esprit ouvertement anti-religieux de votre ouvrage, ce grand monument de la vraie philosophie moderne commence à se faire jour parmi nous, moins pourtant parmi les théoriciens politique que parmi les différentes classes de savants. Il se montre d'ailleurs depuis quelque temps, pour la premiére fois chez nous, dans les cultivateurs des sciences physiques, une tendance assez prononcée vers les généralités scientifiques, qui me paraît de très heureux augure, et qui porte à croire qu'il y a aujourd'hui pour nous plus à espérer de leur part que de la part des hommes politiques soit de spéculation soit d'action. Ceux-ci, en effet, sont tombés dans un affaissement pareil à celui qui s'est si fortement déclaré en France depuis 1830, et chacun voit qu'on ne pourra faire des choses nouvelles que par une doctrine nouvelle; seulement la plupart ne croient pas à l'avènement d'une telle doctrine et restent par conséquent dans un scepticisme de plus en plus énervant et décourageant.

Veuillez, Monsieur, me pardonner cette tentative un peu présomptueuse de me mettre en relation intellectuelle immédiate avec celui des grands esprits de notre temps que je regarde avec le plus d'estime et d'admiration —et croyez que la réalisation de ce vœu serait pour moi d'un prix immense.

J. S. MILL

335. TO JOHN MITCHELL KEMBLE[1]

India House
15th Nov.
1841

MY DEAR SIR

Mr. Weir, a friend of mine, of whom both as a man & as a thinker & writer I can speak very highly, has written me a note of which I inclose a portion. Would you be kind enough to send a line either to himself or to me, to say whether the article he proposes to undertake would suit you.

Ever yours

J. S. MILL

Mr. Weir has been for sometime engaged in extensive & accurate geographical researches.

1. MS owned by Professor Ney MacMinn.

336. TO AUGUSTE COMTE[1]

India House,
18 Décembre, 1841

MON CHER MONSIEUR COMTE—

Je suis vraiment honteux en me rappelant le temps qui s'est écoulé depuis que j'ai reçu la réponse, aussi bienveillante qu'honorable pour moi, que vous avez bien voulu faire à ma première lettre. Mais si j'ai paru montrer peu d'empressement à profiter d'une relation que j'ai si vivement désirée, cela n'a tenu qu'à des occupations urgentes, et dont la principale était précisément de nature à établir entre nous deux plus promptement que par toute autre voie, l'échange d'idées philosophiques dans lequel je compte trouver pour tout le reste de ma vie une si précieuse source soit d'instruction soit de stimulation intellectuelle. Je viens dans ces derniers jours d'achever un ouvrage assez volumineux qui va être livré à l'impression pour paraître, je crois, au printemps prochain. Si après sa publication vous daignez en prendre connaissance, ce que le prix que vous avez bien voulu mettre à la sympathie si fortement prononcée entre nos tendances intellectuelles, me permet seul d'espérer, l'exposition détaillée que j'y ai donnée d'un nombre assez considérable de mes idées vous indiquera jusqu'à un certain point les questions sur lesquelles il n'y a plus lieu à aucune discussion entre nous, et celles où je puis encore profiter de la maturité plus complette de vos conceptions philosophiques. Je vous soumettrai cet ouvrage avec d'autant plus de crainte, que le but même vous en sera certainement suspect, puisque c'est enfin un traité de logique, ou de méthode philosophique. Je suis certainement bien loin d'être insensible aux motifs qui vous ont porté à nier la possibilité, au moins dans la phase scientifique actuelle, d'une théorie de méthode, abstraction faite de la doctrine; même en se conformant à la condition à laquelle je me suis toujours fidèlement soumis de ne puiser la méthode que dans la doctrine même. Aussi je n'attribue nullement au travail que j'ai fait un caractère philosophique permanent, mais tout au plus une valeur transitoire, que je crois pourtant réelle, du moins pour l'Angleterre. Quant aux divergences partielles qui existent jusqu'ici entre ma manière de concevoir certaines questions philosophiques et la vôtre, je crains surtout que si vous en jugez par l'écrit en question vous ne soyez exposé à les croire plus grandes qu'elles ne sont, en ne faisant pas suffisamment la part des concessions que je me suis cru forcé de faire à l'esprit dominant de mon pays. Vous n'ignorez pas sans doute que chez nous l'écrivain qui avouerait hautement

1. *Addressed*: A Monsieur / M. Auguste Comte / 10 Rue Monneur le Prince / près l'Odéon / à Paris. *Postmark*: LONDON / 18 / DEC / 1841. MS at Johns Hopkins. Published in Lévy-Bruhl, pp. 11–15; in reply to Comte's letter of Nov. 20, 1841, *ibid*., pp. 4–11.

des opinions anti réligieuses, ou même anti-chétiennes, compromettrait non seulement sa position sociale, que je me crois capable de sacrifier à un but suffisamment élevé, mais aussi, ce qui serait plus grave, ses chances d'être lu. Je risque déjà beaucoup en mettant soigneusement de côté, dès le commencement, le point de vue religieuse, et en m'abstenant des éloges déclamatoires de la sagesse providentielle, généralement usités parmi les philosophes, même incrédules, de mon pays. Je fais rarement allusion à cet ordre d'idées, et, tout en tâchant de ne pas éveiller, chez le vulgaire des lecteurs, des antipathies religieuses, je crois avoir écrit de manière à ce que nul penseur, soit chrétien soit incrédule, ne puisse se méprendre sur le caractère véritable de mes opinions: me fiant un peu, je l'avoue, à la prudence mondaine, qui chez nous empêche en général les écrivains religieux de proclamer sans nécessité l'irréligion d'un esprit d'une valeur scientifique quelconque.

Un même motif, quoique moins fort, m'a fait quelquefois conserver (ce que je n'aurais probablement pas fait en France) certaines expressions d'origine métaphysique, en m'efforçant toujours d'y attacher un sens positif, et en éliminant autant que possible toutes les formules qui ne paraissent pas susceptibles aujourd'hui d'être envisagées seulement comme les noms abstraits des phénomènes. Je dois m'avouer, en même temps, suspect à vos yeux de tendances métaphysiques, en tant que je crois à la possibilité d'une psychologie positive, qui ne serait certainement ni celle de Condillac, ni celle de Cousin, ni même celle de l'école Ecossaise, et que je crois toute comprise dans cette analyse de nos facultés intellectuelles et affectives qui entre dans votre système comme destinée à servir de vérification à la physiologie phrénologique, et qui a pour but essentiel de séparer les facultés vraiment primordiales de celles qui ne sont que les conséquences nécessaires des autres, produites par voie de combinaison et d'action mutuelle.

Je vois que mon ami M. Marrast vous a donné sur mon compte quelques renseignements qui ne sont pas d'une exactitude complète. D'abord, je ne suis pas chargé des travaux statistiques de la Compagnie des Indes, mais bien d'une partie de l'administration politique de l'Inde, surtout en ce qui regarde les relations extérieures, y compris le contrôle général des nombreux rois ou roitelets indigènes qui sont dans notre dépendance, et dont la civilisation peu avancée nous donne souvent des embarras. Ensuite je dois vous dire que mon abstinence de la vie parlementaire ne peut pas être pour moi un titre de louanges, ayant toujours été nécessitée par l'incompatibilité de cette vie avec l'emploi dont je retire mes moyens de vie. Je puis d'autant moins vous laisser dans l'erreur à cet égard, que des occasions ont existé où si ma position personnelle ne m'avait pas interdit l'action politique directe, je crois que je m'y serais lais[sé][2] entraîner. Les

2. MS torn.

motifs auxquels j'aurais crû obéir eûssent été d'abord la difficulté, beaucoup plus grande ici qu'en France (vû la moindre activité spéculative de mes compatriotes) d'attirer l'attention même d'un public d'élite sur les idées théoriques d'un homme qui n'aurait pas fait ses preuves dans la vie active; et ensuite la considération, certainement bien fondée, que la véritable émancipation des spéculations sociologiques soit de l'empirisme, soit de la tutelle théologique ne saurait avoir lieu chez nous, tant que nous n'avons pas encore fait notre 1789, ce qu'il devient tous les jours plus difficile de faire au nom et par les moyens de la doctrine purement négative; et je crois même qu'une réaction durable ne tarderait pas à se déclarer en faveur des doctrines rétrogrades, sans l'influence des divers intérèts personnels qui se trouvent aujourd'hui froissés par les institutions que ces doctrines tendent à consacrer: intérêts qui pourtant seront bientôt frappés d'impuissance, même dans le sens subversif, s'ils ne trouvent quelques part, et même dans la vie politique, un point de ralliement spéculatif tel que les doctrines simplement révolutionnaires ne sont plus capable aujourd'hui d'offrir. Sentant au reste comme je le fais très sincèrement, jusqu'à quel point on est porté à se faire des illusions sur tout ce qui peut intéresser, même médiocrement la vanité personnelle, je dois probablement me féliciter de ce que la direction spéciale de mon activité a été principalement déterminée jusqu'ici par des causes indépendantes de ma propre sagesse.

J'attends avec impatience la publication du volume qui complètera votre grand ouvrage, et celle ensuite du traité spécial de politique qui doit le suivre, et où je compte trouver des éclaircissements sur bien des questions posées dans les 4me et 5me volumes et qui n'ont fait jusqu'ici qu'éveiller chez moi des besoins intellectuels sans y satisfaire complètement mais sur tout cela je compte à vous entretenir plus au long dans mes lettres à venir.

Votre bien dévoué

J. S. MILL.

337. TO JOHN MURRAY[1]

India House
20th Dec 1841

MY DEAR SIR

I have just finished preparing for the press a book of which I enclose the Preface and Table of Contents.[2] It will make two good-sized octavo

1. MS in the possession of Sir John Murray.

2. The *Logic*. JSM's friend John Sterling had written Murray on Dec. 16, 1841, reporting the completion of the book and describing it as "the labour of many years of a singularly subtle, patient, and comprehensive mind. It will be our chief speculative monument of this age." (Samuel Smiles, *A Publisher and His Friends* [2 vols., London, 1891], II, 499.)

volumes. I should like it to have the benefit of being published by you, but it does not suit me if I can do otherwise, to print it at my own risk, and I cannot tell whether it will suit you to do so at yours. I however request your consideration of the subject, and should be much obliged by an early determination, as I should wish at all events that it should be published in the approaching season.

Very truly yours

J. S. Mill

The whole or any part of the manuscript shall be sent for your inspection whenever you may require it, or at least as soon as I have finished reading it through and making the few final corrections.

• • • 1842 • • •

338. TO ALBANY FONBLANQUE[1]

India House
Saturday
[Jan. 1, 1842]

MY DEAR FONBLANQUE

Soon after the Copyright Bill was thrown out,[2] there appeared in the Examiner a very able article[3] in answer to Macaulay's speech[4] which appeared to many persons the best thing yet written on the subject & which as such has been inserted entire in an article of Lockhart,[5] published in the Quarterly this day.[6] Some of the supporters of Talfourd's Bill have thought that it would be useful to do with this question what is done with other questions by commercial and other bodies interested in them, namely to get a statement of the case drawn up by a competent person to be published & circulated as a pamphlet & I have been asked to ascertain whether the writer of that article in the Examiner would be willing to undertake this, being properly remunerated for which purpose a subscription is spoken of. I have not the least idea who the writer is, nor of course do I ask it, but if you would communicate with him, that is, if you would communicate *to* him what I have now written, & to me what he says about it, you will oblige the persons in question & perhaps do some considerable good to the cause.

ever yours truly

J. S. MILL

1. MS in the possession of Lady Hermione Cobbold. Collated by Dr. Eileen Curran.
2. Feb. 5, 1841.
3. "The Defeated Copyright Bill," *Examiner*, Feb. 28, 1841, pp. 130–31. Since this letter to Fonblanque is preserved in Bulwer's papers, the inference seems fair that the article was by Bulwer.
4. On Feb. 5, 1841. Reprinted in *Miscellaneous Works of Lord Macaulay*, ed. Lady Trevelyan (6 vols., New York, 1880), V, 228–43.
5. "The Copyright Question," *QR*, LXIX (Dec., 1841), 186–227. J. G. Lockhart was editor of the *Quarterly Review*, 1825–53.
6. The Dec., 1841, *QR* was published on Jan. 1, 1842. See *Spectator*, Jan. 1, 1842, p. 24.

339. TO GUSTAVE D'EICHTHAL[1]

I.H.
10th Jany 1842

MY DEAR GUSTAVE—I am really ashamed to see that your last letter, one of the most interesting I ever received from you, has remained more than six weeks unanswered. My only excuse is that I was & still am busy making the final revision of a book which is to be published this spring[2] & in which I have said all that I can find to say on Methods of Philosophic Investigation. I do not expect to find many readers for this book, but I had things to say on the subject, & it was part of my task on earth to say them & therefore having said them I feel a portion of my work to be done.

With regard to Salvador's two books,[3] the earliest made a very mixed impression upon me, the latest one wholly favourable: it seems to me that he has better understood the spirit of the times in which Christianity arose, & the nature of Christianity itself as a phenomenon in the history of the ancient world than anybody else, & that he is nearer the truth than even Strauss.[4] Altogether it is a grand book & I have instigated several people to read it. As for the first, it has also thrown much new light upon history & has made me think in a manner I never expected to do of the Hebrew people & polity, mais cela se ressent horriblement des quinze dernières années de la restauration—I could hardly help laughing at the manner in which he strains everything to recommend poor Moses to the Constitutional Opposition & to shew that the Jews were Liberals, political economists & Utilitarians, that they had properly speaking no religion, or next to none, & were altogether à la hauteur de l'époque, worthy sons of the 18th century. I would very strongly advise him to cancel the whole book & write it over again in a spirit worthy of his second work, written ten or twelve years later & for a public much more advanced. He is quite right for instance in saying that the liberty of prophesying was equivalent in the Jewish polity to the liberty of the press & the point is a new & striking one, but it really is not necessary to tell us that the prophets did not *pretend to be*, nor were supposed to be, specially accredited from God, that all the expressions implying them to be such are a mere façon de parler, meaning only that they were very clever fellows, & to fortify this by philological arguments from the usages & phrases of the Hebrew tongue. Why not say

1. *Addressed*: Monsieur / Gustave d'Eichthal / 14 Rue Lepelletier / à Paris. *Postmarks*: LONDON / 8 / JAN / 1842 and 10 / CALAIS. Published in *D'Eichthal Corresp.*, pp. 196–200, and in *Cosmopolis*, IX, 379–81. MS at Arsenal. The first postmark would seem to indicate that JSM had misdated his letter.

2. The *Logic* did not appear until 1843.

3. See Letter 312, n. 4.

4. D. F. Strauss (1808–1874), German rationalist theologian, author of *Das Leben Jesu* (2 vols., Tübingen, 1835), and *Christliche Glaubenslehre* . . . (2 vols., Tübingen, 1840–41).

at once that all persons of genius, inspired persons in the modern sense, poets & persons of imagination & eloquence who had great & wonderful powers not derived from teaching, were believed to derive these powers straight from God & were in consequence of that religious belief, permitted from religious motives to exercise that right of free speech & free censure of powerful persons, which certainly would not in that age have been conceded to any one who spoke merely as from himself?

I have been reading at odd times your old friend Leroux's book, De l'Humanité:[5] the historical part I like; those few pages on the schools & Greek philosophy are quite perfect; but when we come to his own theory, did ever mortal man write such intolerable nonsense! There are ideas in that too about Moses, but qui ne valent pas celles de Salvador.

I long to see your speculations on the subject but I would not advise your publishing a translation here, at least in the first instance: even Salvador has not been translated nor heard of, & nobody here is yet ripe for reading a serious philosophical discussion on the Bible. We are all either bigots or Voltairians. But we are improving. In ten years I think we shall have made some way, between our neo-Catholic school at [Oxf]ord[6] & the German Rationalists who are beginning to be *secretly* read here.

All you say on politics in your letter is extremely interesting & *evidently* true. You are the only person whose opinion on the political state & prospects of France I always feel that I can rely on. As for us, I believe that we are about to have a real *juste milieu* ministry & that things will go on tolerably smoothly till the grande question sociale des ouvriers becomes imminent, which it is rapidly becoming, perhaps more rapidly here than even with you. What will happen then, heaven knows. Il nous manque *un homme*, tout comme à vous.

Give my kindest regards to Adolphe & remembrances to all friends.

Ever yours,

J. S. MILL.

340. TO JOHN MURRAY[1]

India House

31st Jany 1842

MY DEAR SIR

I have now finished revising my Manuscript, and the remaining three Books shall be sent to you if you think fit. I believe I have already men-

5. Pierre Henri Leroux, *De l'Humanité, de son principe et de son avenir* . . . (2 vols., Paris, 1840).

6. Page torn. The Tractarian or "Puseyite" movement led by John Henry Newman.

* * * *

1. MS in the possession of Sir John Murray. See Letter 337.

tioned that they are of a rather more popular character than the three preceding.

You would oblige me very much, if you cannot give me an affirmative answer, by giving me a negative one as early as possible, since any other publisher to whom the MS. might be referred would probably also require some time for making up his mind and in that way the season might be lost.

Very truly yours

J. S. Mill

341. TO MACVEY NAPIER[1]

India House
8th Feby 1842

My dear Sir

Having now my hands clear of all other literary occupation, except in the matter of correcting proofs, I am at liberty to resume & strengthen my incipient connexion with the Ed. Rev. if it continues to be agreeable to you that I should do so. I have not at present any particular subjects in view, except those which we formerly spoke of[2] Michelet's Histories of Rome & France. If those subjects will still suit you I will begin preparing myself for them, but as this will necessarily require a good deal of reading & thought, indeed I might say a gradual crystallization of many thoughts at present held in a state of suspension, it may be some time before I am able to produce anything fit for you on these topics, while the process of preparation would not be interfered with by my writing something else for you in the meantime if you should have any subject in view on which I could write with less previous study. I am therefore open to any proposition you may be inclined to make.

I am glad to say that my friend Fletcher after a tedious & harrassing illness of a year in duration, is now tolerably recovered & at work vigorously on Cervantes—he says his article will soon be ready.[3]

ever yours

J. S. Mill

1. MS in Brit. Mus.
2. See Letter 285.
3. No such article appeared.

342. TO MACVEY NAPIER[1]

I.H.
18th Feby
1842

MY DEAR SIR

Your opinion & the prospects you hold out respecting Bain[2] & Lewes[3] are quite as favourable as I had any reason to expect. They are both very young men, the former in particular almost a youth, & they have the full measure of the defects natural in the one case to a young littérateur, in the other to a young metaphysician. I myself wrote a long letter to Bain about his article on Toys[4] pointing out some of the graver defects in it which he at once saw & admitted & neither he nor I ever supposed for a moment that that particular article would have been admissible into the Edinburgh. I only mentioned it to you or rather to your son in order to shew what the young man can already do & how much he has in him.

In one respect I think you judge both of them too severely. I do not think they are either of them coxcombs although Lewes at least is very likely to be thought so. But what gives him that air is precisely the buoyancy of spirit which you have observed in him, & he is so prompt & apparently presumptuous in undertaking anything for which he feels the slightest vocation, (however much it may be really beyond his strength) only because he does not care at all for failure, knowing & habitually feeling that he gets up stronger after every fall & believing as I do that the best way of improving one's faculties is to be continually trying what is above one's present strength. I should say he is confident but not at all conceited, for he will bear to be told anything however unflattering about what he writes—& when I say *bear*, I do not mean that he is so well fortified in self conceit as to bear with temper what he does not believe to be just—no, but to be convinced at the very first suggestion, that it *is* just & to betake himself without delay to correcting it. As for Bain, I can completely understand *him*, because I have been, long ago, very much the same sort of person, except that I had not half his real originality. I should have been thought quite as presumptuous if the things I wrote had found any body to publish them. When one is so young, & writes out one's thoughts exactly as they have grown up in one's own mind without reference to other people & without seizing the connexion between them & what others have previously written, one always seems to be laying the most unbounded &

1. MS in Brit. Mus.
2. Alexander Bain.
3. George Henry Lewes.
4. "On Toys," *WR*, XXXVII (Jan., 1842), 97–121.

groundless claims to discovery, when really one is not consciously making such claims to any extent at all, or not to any considerable extent.

I am very glad that I sent you the extract from Comte's letter.[5] I have no doubt he would be much gratified by a letter from Sir D. Brewster,[6] but I throw that out only as a suggestion.

ever yours truly

J. S. Mill.

343. TO JOHN MURRAY[1]

India House
24th Feb^y
1842

My dear Sir

Being prevented by official occupation from having the pleasure of calling upon you at any hour at which it is usually agreeable to discuss matters of business, I write to you again[2] to solicit an answer on the subject of my MS *on Logic*—not from any impatience but because the delay in signifying your intentions leads me to presume that you would rather not publish the book and therefore I am desirous of saying that although I should have been glad if you could have done so, I am not disappointed having never thought it very likely that you would. As however I should not like either to postpone the publication to another year or to hurry the printing, I should wish to try some other publisher as soon as possible and therefore if I have rightly conjectured your own feeling on the matter, I should be much obliged by your returning the MS.

very truly yours

J. S. Mill

5. Which letter has not been ascertained.
6. Sir David Brewster (1781–1868), Scottish scientist and educator.

* * * *

1. MS in the possession of Sir John Murray.
2. See Letters 337 and 340. Samuel Smiles in his memoir of John Murray, *A Publisher and His Friends* (2 vols., London, 1891), II, 499, notes that Murray was very ill at this time and could not give attention to the work.

344. TO AUGUSTE COMTE[1]

India House
25 février 1842

MON CHER MONSIEUR COMTE—

Je ne crois pas nécessaire de vous faire de nouvelles excuses sur le retard que je mets à répondre aux lettres si aimables et si instructives dont vous voulez bien m'honorer. Ce ne sont pas, cette fois-ci, des occupations qui m'ont empêché de vous écrire, mais plutôt des préoccupations. Je n'ai pas besoin de dire que des lettres telles que les vôtres ne doivent pas seulement être bien et mûrement pesées, mais aussi que pour y répondre dignement on a besoin de se trouver dans une disposition d'esprit tout à fait convenable.

Je dois commencer par vous témoigner la vive satisfaction avec laquelle j'ai appris la prochaine terminaison de l'ouvrage que j'ai si longtemps suivi avec une admiration toujours croissante. Ce travail est un exemple qui me confirme dans l'idée déjà ancienne chez moi, que les plus grandes choses sont faites le plus souvent par ceux qui ont le moins de loisir. Je sais trop ce que doivent être les pénibles travaux journaliers de votre état, pour ne pas m'étonner que vous ayez osé entreprendre et que vous soyez parvenu à accomplir une tâche si immense, et exigeant une si grande concentration d'esprit ainsi qu'une si rare dépense de forces intellectuelles. Je sais d'ailleurs combien au milieu de tout cela vous payez noblement votre tribut aux intérêts philanthropiques du moment, par le cours scientifique que vous faites chaque année aux ouvriers de Paris. C'est une manière de participation aux affaires du jour, bien plus féconde sans doute en résultats bienfaisants, que celle des stériles discussions de la presse périodique ou de la tribune parlementaire, au moins en France.

Quant à vos remarques sur l'incompatibilité, même en Angleterre, de l'action politique directe avec une influence réelle sur la rénovation philosophique qui seule aujourd'hui peut être d'une importance majeure, je ne suis déjà pas très éloigné de votre opinion, à laquelle je me rendrai peutêtre tout entier après la lecture, si vivement désirée, de votre 6me volume. Je puis du moins indiquer comme étant pour moi le résultat jusqu'ici le plus positif et le plus certain de l'étude du 5me volume, une conviction complète du grand principe que seul entre les philosophes contemporains vous avez énoncé, celui de la séparation définitive des deux pouvoirs, temporel et spirituel. Ces pouvoirs doivent incontestablement s'organiser d'une manière totalement distincte, ce qui au reste n'implique pas pour moi l'impossibilité

1. MS at Johns Hopkins. Published in Lévy-Bruhl, pp. 26–32. In answer to Comte's of Jan. 17, 1842, *ibid.*, pp. 16–25.

que le même individu puisse participer jusqu'à un certain point aux travaux de tous les deux. Je pense au contraire qu'une éducation partiellement active est nécessaire à la perfection de la capacité spéculative, ainsi qu'une éducation spéculative l'est, de l'aveu de tous les philosophes, à celle de la vie active. Je n'en suis pas moins radicalement guéri, et cela par votre ouvrage, de toute tendance vers les doctrines utopistes qui cherchent à remettre le gouvernement de la societé entre les mains des philosophes, ou même de le faire dépendre de la haute capacité intellectuelle, envisagée plus généralement. Comme la plupart des libres penseurs nourris dans les idées françaises du 19me [*sic*] siècle, je n'ai pas toujours complètement évité cette erreur irrationnelle; mais le sens commun et l'histoire en avaient jusqu'à un certain point fait justice chez moi, même avant la lecture des arguments irrésistibles par lesquels vous soutenez si victorieusement la doctrine contraire. Outre l'altération grave que la suprématie politique ne tarderait pas à produire dans les habitudes morales et intellectuelles de la classe spéculative, il me semble que cette domination ne serait nullement favorable au progrès intellectuel, en vue duquel, sans doute, elle a été surtout rêvée. Je trouve dans l'exemple de la Chine un grand appui à cette opinion. Dans ce pays-là, la constitution du gouvernement se rapproche autant peutêtre que cela se peut, du principe saint-simonien, et qu'est-ce qui en est résulté? le gouvernement le plus opposé de tous à toute sorte de progrès. La majorité d'une classe lettrée quelconque est peutêtre moins disposée que celle de toute autre classe, à se laisser mener par les intelligences les plus développées qui s'y rencontrent; et comme cette majorité ne pourrait, sans doute, se composer de grands penseurs, mais simplement d'érudits, ou de savans sans véritable originalité, il ne pourrait en résulter que ce qu'on voit dans la Chine, c'est à dire une pédantocratie.

Vous voyez donc que nous sommes tous deux en sympathie complète, quant à nos principes généraux sur ce sujet. Ce que je dois, là-dessus, à votre livre, c'est surtout d'avoir formulé dans le principe de la séparation des pouvoirs temporel et spirituel et de l'organisation de chacun sur les bases qui lui sont propres, une doctrine plus vague que j'avais moi-même tirée de l'histoire et que j'avais jetée dans les discussions du jour comme réponse décisive à tout système politique démocratique ou Benthamiste. Cette doctrine la voici: Que dans toutes les sociétés humaines où l'existence des véritables conditions du progrès continu a été prouvée *a posteriori* par l'ensemble de leur histoire, il y a eu, du moins virtuellement, un antagonisme organisé. Puisque dans nulle société le pouvoir dominant n'a pu résumer en soi tous les intérêts progressifs et toutes les tendances dont la réunion est nécessaire à la durabilité indéfinie de la marche ascendante, il a fallu partout aux intérêts et aux tendances plus ou moins antipathiques à ce pouvoir, un point de ralliement assez fortement constitué pour les protéger efficacement contre toute tentative soit réfléchie, soit seulement instinctive, de les comprimer; tentative dont le succès amènerait, après un temps ordinairement très court, soit la dissolution sociale, comme à Athènes, soit l'état stationnaire bien caractérisé de l'Egypte et de l'Asie. J'avais toujours ressenti une grande difficulté à concevoir la forme dans laquelle ce principe nécessaire au progrès devait trouver son application définitive à la politique moderne. Mais je vois dans la doctrine de la séparation des pouvoirs spirituel et temporel, une fois posée par vous, la solution de cette difficulté, puisque cette théorie réunit toutes les conditions de l'antagonisme indispensable, avec des recommandations qui lui sont propres et qui en font évidemment la forme théoriquement parfaite de l'application de ce principe.

Pour en revenir aux considérations personnelles; la question de participation au moins directe, au mouvement politique, se trouve pour moi à peu près décidée par ma position individuelle. Je remettrai à un autre temps l'exposition de mes vues sur les circonstances politiques de mon pays, qui malgré la force incontestable de vos objections, font encore à mes yeux de la tribune parlementaire la meilleure chaire d'enseignement public pour un philosophe sociologiste convenablement placé, et qui chercherait peut être à faire des ministères ou à les diriger dans sons sens, mais en s'abstenant d'en faire partie, sinon probablement dans des moments critiques que je ne crois pas, chez nous, très éloignés. Mais au lieu de parler de ces choses qui ne me regardent nullement, je m'autoriserai de votre sympathie bienveillante pour vous entretenir de celles qui me regardent, et je dirai que j'entre dans une époque de ma vie qui me mettra pour la première fois à même de savoir jusqu'à quel point l'activité purement philosophique, dirigée dans le sens de mes opinions et avec le dégré de capacité dont je puis disposer, est capable de donner dans notre pays une influence réelle sur la marche des idées, au moins chez les hommes les plus avancés. Jusqu'ici quoique plus connu qu'on ne l'est ordinairement lorsqu'on n'a jamais exercé aucune fonction publique évidente et qu'on n'a rien publié qu'anonymement, je suis totalement inconnu du public ordinaire et par conséquent je n'ai pas le moindre commencement d'autorité morale. Ceux d'ailleurs qui ne sont pas totalement étrangers à mes travaux ne me connaissent que comme une sorte d'homme politique, appartenant au parti révolutionnaire modéré, et qui a quelquefois écrit en philosophe sur les questions de la politique actuelle. Mais aujourd'hui je livre mon nom à la publicité, par un ouvrage purement philosophique et en même temps par la réimpression des meilleurs de mes écrits antérieurs dont pour la première fois je prends sur moi la responsabilité. Je ne me fais aucune illusion sur le dégré de succès dont l'une ou l'autre de ces publications est susceptible, mais quel qu'il puisse être il me donnera probablement une place quelconque parmi les supériorités intellectuelles reconnues, et me permettra jusqu'à un certain point d'apprécier le degré d'influence que je suis capable d'exercer sur le mouvement spirituel, ainsi que les meilleurs moyens de m'en servir.

Je regrette de vous avoir involontairement donné l'idée que l'ouvrage philosophique dont il est question avait pour but l'analyse de nos facultés mentales et de nos tendances morales. J'ai seulement entendu exprimer ma croyance à la possibilité et à la valeur scientifique d'une psychologie ainsi entendue; mais dans ma Logique, je ne m'occupe que de méthode, c'est à dire des actes intellectuels, en faisant autant que possible abstraction des facultés. Il n'est pourtant pas impossible que je m'occupe un jour de cette autre tâche, et afin d'y être mieux préparé je vous engage très fortement à m'indiquer les lectures les plus propres à me donner une véritable connaissance de la physiologie phrénologique. Chez nous la phrénologie n'a guère été cultivée que par des hommes d'une intelligence moins que médiocre, si j'en juge par ce que j'ai lu de leurs écrits, et je vous avouerai que j'ai longtemps regardée cette doctrine, au moins dans son état présent, comme indigne d'occuper l'attention d'un vrai penseur, idée dont je ne suis revenu qu'en apprenant par votre 3me volume que vous y adhériez au moins dans ses principales bases. Je suis donc resté fort arriére sur ce sujet important, ce à quoi je désire promptement remédier, et me faire le plus tôt possible, sur une question qui doit nécessairement exercer une grande influence sur mes spéculations à venir une opinion mûre, et aussi bien fondée qu'elle peut l'être.

Tout à vous de cœur

J. S. Mill,
(John Stuart)

345. TO MACVEY NAPIER[1]

I.H.
3^{d} March
1842

My dear Sir

I do not doubt that I could easily have an article on Michelet's Hist. of France ready for your October number, but as there will probably be another volume published before that time it is of no use setting about the article just yet, & as the book will extend to twelve volumes of which only five are yet published the subject will be good for a long time to come.[2]

I should have preferred if it had been possible to begin with the Romans

1. MS in Brit. Mus.
2. JSM's review did not appear in the *Edinburgh* until Jan., 1844.

because I think I can make a better, & certainly a more original article on them than on the middle ages, my acquaintance with which is not derived from the original authorities. The article on Michelet's France would be essentially an article on the middle ages, not on France & I may as well mention that my views of that portion of history are strongly Guelphic, that is I am almost always with the popes against the Kings. That is a view very seldom taken in this country, & I do not know how it would suit the Edinburgh Review. But the principles it involves lie at the heart of all my opinions on politics & history.

If there were any suitable peg on which to hang an article on the Romans, I should be much obliged by your suggesting it since Michelet's History is too old. I cannot help thinking that if you were fully aware of the importance of Michelet as a European thinker you would consider a book of his even if not quite recent (provided it is not previously much known in this country) as a better occasion for an article than a production of little value in itself even if fresh. I should have thought, too, that in regard to *foreign* books the question was not so much when they were published, as whether they are a fresh subject to the English reader. But you are the best judge of the principles & rules for conducting your review.

ever yours truly

J. S. Mill.

346. TO JOHN WILLIAM PARKER[1]

Kensington
Monday
[March, 1842]

My dear Sir

I send the portions of MS. which your friend[2] wishes to see—together with some other chapters or portions of chapters which from the manner in which the papers are stitched together, cannot conveniently be separated from them.

I fear some parts are by no means so legible as I could wish, owing to the number of interlineations & erasures. The portions moreover of the Third Book,[3] will scarcely perhaps be intelligible without the chapters which are intended to precede them. However they must take their chance

1. MS at LSE. No date [paper watermarked 1841].
John William Parker (1792–1870), publisher and printer.
2. Presumably the referee whom Parker had asked to see the manuscript of the *Logic*. See Letter 351, n. 2.
3. Book III of the *Logic*, "Of Induction."

& perhaps on the whole these fragments are as fair a specimen of the book as any others would be.

Ever yours truly

J. S. MILL

347. TO SARAH AUSTIN[1]

India House
11th March
1842

You must, both of you, have thought me very negligent or very indifferent, but it is not so. I have delayed writing from day to day in hopes that I might be able to tell you something or other about your own affairs, about America of course I mean. I watch very sedulously & interestedly, on your account, every indication of future events there, but without any result worth communicating. It seems to me however, as far as I have the means of observing, that the expectation *here* among people who attend to the matter, is that the debts, Mississippi included, will be *ultimately* recognised & paid.[2] It is certainly difficult to believe that prosperous & improving communities can go on long without feeling the inconvenience of not being trusted in pecuniary transactions.—Failing anything on this subject I was in hopes of being able to tell you something decisive about my own affairs, namely about my book—but all I have to tell is that I have only just succeeded in extorting a negative answer from Murray after a consideration or at least a delay which endured from the middle of December to last Tuesday. I am now in treaty with Parker, with whom Lewis[3] has placed me in communication but I know not yet what will be the result. I have not begun to print, as my object is if possible to induce somebody to take the risk—a thing I confess if I were myself a publisher I should hesitate to do. The book is all finished, however, revision and all, & has been so nearly two months & if Parker is tractable there will still be time to print it & bring it out this season. I am on the whole quite as well satisfied with the book as I ever thought I should be—perhaps more so. In any case it is the best I can do, & others must judge of it now, & make what they can of it, or leave it alone if it so pleases them.

I was very glad to hear from Stephen[4] the other day that an article is in preparation for the Edin. Rev. on a book[5] the nature of which I well

1. *Addressed*: Madame Austin / Poste Restante / Dresden. *Postmark*: LONDON / 11 / MAR / 1842. MS in Goldsmiths' Library, University of London.

2. Both JSM and the Austins suffered losses by the repudiation of the debts of some of the American states. See Letter 331, n. 2.

3. George Cornewall Lewis.

4. James Stephen.

5. Austin's review of Friedrich List's *Das nationale System der politischen Oekonomie* (Stuttgart and Tübingen, 1841), in *ER*, LXXV (July, 1842), 515–56.

remember though I have forgotten the author. Stephen took credit to himself for having instigated Mr. Austin to write & publish the things which he had already spoken to him (Stephen) on the subject & of which he appeared to have a most genuinely *sentie* admiration. I hardly know anything more likely to be of use here in making people think, & in putting the best views into the best minds, than that subject treated as Mr. Austin is sure to treat it—& the more nearly he writes as he would talk, the better in point of popular impressiveness it is sure to be. The only real danger is lest he should attempt to make it *too* good.

Politics here are going smoothly enough. Peel is making a considerable number of petty improvements, such however as would not have been thought petty formerly, while his corn law has at least the negative merit of doing so very little that it has no tendency to slacken the agitation. The most remarkable recent indication perhaps of the decay of prejudice is that a bill[6] has been brought into the H. of Lords to take away nearly all the disqualifications of witnesses, except that of the parties to the suit, & this is most strenuously supported by Lyndhurst[7] & all the Law Lords, old Wynford[8] being even eager to admit the parties too. At the present moment however nobody is thinking of anything but the Afghanistan disasters.[9] Everybody now condemns the folly of involving ourselves in that *galère* & nobody knows how we are now to get out of it. The thing will end in our exacting at immense cost some signal reparation for the treacherous menace & then evacuating the country, & that is the best end it can have. The feeling in France towards England seems as bad as ever and that in England towards France worse than ever. If the anti English feeling continues to grow in Germany also, things will be in a hopeful condition—

What are to be your movements this year? is there any chance of your coming here, even for ever so short a time? if not, how are you to be communicated with, & in particular how shall I send a copy of my Logic when it is printed? Whenever there is anything to be done for you here which cannot be done better by somebody else, do let me know & let me do it.

yours affectionately

J. S. MILL

6. The second reading of this bill for the improvement of the law of evidence was heard in the House of Lords on March 8, 1842.

7. John Singleton Copley, first Baron Lyndhurst, Lord Chancellor.

8. William Draper Best, first Baron Wynford (1767–1845), Deputy Speaker of the House of Lords.

9. An insurrection against the British in Afghanistan had arisen in Nov., 1841. In Jan. the British had been forced to evacuate Kabul and their forces were subsequently annihilated. News of the disaster at Kabul reached England early in March.

348. TO AUGUSTE COMTE[1]

India House
22 mars 1842

MON CHER MONSIEUR COMTE—

Je me félicite toujours de plus en plus des rapports de correspondance qui se sont si heureusement établis entre nous deux, en attendant, j'espère, des rapports personnels, qui me seraient encore plus précieux. Votre dernière lettre me fait sentir plus que jamais combien notre sympathie philosophique est déja intime, en montrant qu'elle ne se borne pas aux principes fondamentaux, mais qu'elle s'étend jusqu'aux questions secondaires de manière à indiquer que dans la suite elle se prononcera constamment de plus en plus. Non seulement les divergences qui semblaient d'abord exister dans notre manière d'envisager les relations mutuelles des deux puissances élémentaires, ont à peu près disparu par les explications que vous avez bien voulu me donner de votre opinion; non seulement vous avez donné votre sanction philosophique au principe de l'antagonisme continu comme condition de la progression humaine, principe qui faisait le terme le plus avancé du développement sociologique auquel j'étais parvenu par mes propres réflexions; mais aussi je retrouve chez vous une autre idée à laquelle j'ai toujours tenu beaucoup, et peutêtre seul parmi mes compatriotes. Je suis comme vous intimement persuadé que la combinaison de l'esprit français avec l'esprit anglais est un des besoins les plus essentiels de la réorganisation intellectuelle. L'esprit français est nécessaire afin que les conceptions soient générales, et l'esprit anglais pour les empêcher d'être vagues, défaut prédominant en France chez les intelligences secondaires, tandis que chez nous les généralisations quelconques ne trouvent guère d'accueil, en matière morale ou sociale, que de la part d'hommes très avancés. Je crois que c'est Voltaire qui a dit: "Quand un français et un anglais s'accordent, il faut qu'ils aient pleinement raison":[2] cela serait encourageant pour nous deux si nous en avions besoin, avec la conviction profonde que nous avons déjà. Il est au reste fort à regretter que les

1. *Addressed*: Monsieur / M. Auguste Comte / 10 Rue M. le Prince / près l'Odéon / à Paris. *Postmark*: LONDON / 22 / MAR / 1842. MS at Johns Hopkins. Published in Lévy-Bruhl, pp. 40–45. In answer to Comte's letter of March 4, 1842, *ibid.*, pp. 32–40.

2. JSM's quotation is not wholly accurate: "Quand un Français et un Anglais pensent de même, il faut bien qu'ils aient raison" (Lettre XXII, "Sur M. Pope et quelques autres poëtes fameux," *Lettres philosophiques*, in *Œuvres complètes de Voltaire*, ed. Louis Moland, XXII [Paris, 1879], 178).

penseurs de nos deux pays soient loin d'avoir les uns pour les autres l'estime qu'ils méritent. En mathématique, en physique, en chimie, en biologie même, les savants français et anglais se rendent justice mutuellement, et il en était ainsi même au plus chaud de la guerre révolutionnaire et napoléonienne. Il n'en est malheureusement pas de même en ce qui concerne les questions morales et sociales; et c'est ici l'angleterre qui est le plus en défaut. Le mouvement intellectuel français postérieur à la révolution est encore aujourd'hui pour la plupart des anglais même instruits, comme s'il n'avait pas existé. Vous me croirez à peine quand je dis que même les travaux de la nouvelle école historique sont à peine connus ici; que les écrits par exemple de M. Guizot ne commencent à être un peu lus que depuis qu'il a passé ici comme ambassadeur, et que ceux qui savaient devoir se rencontrer avec lui dans le monde ont trouvé convenable de connaitre au moins les noms de ses principaux écrits. Les anglais cherchent plus volontiers des idées nouvelles chez les allemands que chez les français et bien du monde a lu non seulement Kant, mais encore Schelling et Hegel sans même avoir lu Cousin, qui présente les mêmes idées ténébreuses avec une lucidité et un esprit de systématisation tout français. Dans cette inattention au mouvement philosophique de la france, il se rencontre toutefois de singulières exceptions. Je ne sais si je vous ai encore parlé d'une nouvelle école de philosophie théologique qui s'est élevée dans ces derniers temps à Oxford et qui me paraît destinée à remplir dans la régénération sociologique de l'Angleterre un rôle tout pareil à celui de l'école de De Maistre, dont elle partage essentiellement les doctrines. Comme cette école, elle juge la crise actuelle d'une manière à peu près vraie, se trompant seulement sur les remèdes; elle réhabilite le catholicisme et le moyen âge; elle s'appelle catholique, et prétend que l'église anglicane est toujours restée telle (à la vérité sans le pape, mais en transportant le pouvoir spirituel dans le corps des évêques) elle soutient le principe de l'autorité contre celui de la liberté illimitée de conscience, principe qui est encore plus fortement accrédité ici par les préjugés protestants qu'il ne l'a pu être en France par la philosophie de Voltaire et de Diderot, justement parce que sa victoire moins complète n'a pas permis qu'il se réduisît à l'absurde par le plein développement de ses conséquences antisociales. Cette école resemble aussi à l'école française catholique en ce qu'elle a été la première à fonder dans ce pays-ci une sorte de philosophie historique, tout à fait semblable, au reste, à celle de l'auteur du *Pape*,[3] que je doute pourtant si ces écrivains ont lu. Malgré cela ils ne laissent pas de jeter les yeux de temps en temps sur l'autre côté de la Manche, et il leur est arrivé une fois de prôner assez singulièrement la

3. Joseph de Maistre, *Du Pape* (2 vols., Lyon, 1819).

ridicule école de Buchez,[4] qui a parodié d'une manière si baroque les formes de la positivité, et dont les chefs se recommandent surtout à nos catholiques anglicans en ce que d'athées qu'ils étaient ils sont devenus catholiques romains.

J'attends avec un vif intérêt le jugement sur l'Angleterre qui se trouvera dans votre 6me volume. En tant que je connais votre opinion, elle s'accorde complètement avec la mienne, et je serais bien étonné d'une si grande justesse d'appréciation d'un pays ordinairement si mal connu en france si je n'y voyais pas un exemple de la grande puissance d'interprétation à l'égard des faits généraux et patents, qu'un esprit vraiment scientifique puise dans la connaissance approfondie des grandes lois sociologiques. Malgré la brièveté de la vie humaine, nous pouvons l'un et l'autre espérer de voir la position sociale et le caractère national de chaque portion importante du genre humain rattachés aux lois de la nature humaine et aux propriétés du milieu organique général ou particulier par une filiation aussi certaine sinon aussi complète que celle qui existe aujourd'hui dans les sciences les plus avancées. Je serais bien heureux si je me croyais capable de prendre une part vraiment importante, bien que secondaire, à ce grand travail.

Ce que vous me dites sur votre position personnelle, et sur la manière dont elle pourra être compromise par la liberté de discussion dont vous avez usé à l'égard du régime scientifique actuel, est de nature à ajouter une certaine inquiétude au plaisir avec lequel j'envisage la prochaine terminaison de votre mémorable travail. Il est certainement dans l'ordre que les philosophes soient aujourd'hui persécutés par les savants comme ils l'ont été autrefois par les prêtres, comme ils le seront probablement un jour par les industriels, et cela manquait peut être au cercle de l'enseignement sociologique à tirer de l'histoire des persécutions. Mais il est à espérer que vous au moins n'en serez pas la victime[5] et que lors même que vous éprouveriez de l'amour propre blessé d'un corps savant l'injustice infâme qui ne vous parait pas impossible, cela déterminerait de la part de toutes les personnes impartiales un sentiment contraire et qui pourrait exercer une influence plus qu'équivalents sur votre position même matérielle. Je crois avoir entendu

4. Philippe Joseph Benjamin Buchez (1796–1865), physician, politician, and writer. Originally, along with Comte, he had been associated with the Saint-Simonians. Comte had left them because they were too mystical; Buchez, because they were not spiritual enough. He subsequently developed a Neo-Catholic doctrine which attempted to reconcile Christianity and the ideals of the Revolution.

5. Comte in his letter of March 4 had predicted that the final volume of his great work might so offend the professional hierarchy as to cause him to lose his teaching position at the Ecole Polytechnique, an appointment that had to be renewed annually by vote of the professors. See Letter 377, n. 3.

dire à M. Marrast que vous aviez éprouvé aussi de la part du gouvernement de graves injustices; sans cela j'aurais cru que malgré la critique sévère que vous avez faite de l'ordre de choses actuel, le gouvernement d'aujourd'hui pourrait avoir été capable de vouloir utiliser votre capacité dans des fonctions d'enseignement supérieures à celles qui vous ont occupé jusqu'ici; d'autant plus que M. Guizot, avec qui pendant son séjour ici je me suis un peu entretenu de vous, s'est exprimé d'une manière honorable sur votre compte, et que, malgré les passions haineuses, dont on ne peut le disculper, il ne me parait pas dénué d'une certaine magnanimité.

Je vous remercie grandement des renseignements que vous avez eu la bonté de me donner sur les ouvrages phrénologiques à lire,[6] et je me propose de m'en occuper incessamment.

tout à vous

J. S. MILL.

349. TO ALBANY FONBLANQUE[1]

I.H.
5th April
1842

MY DEAR FONBLANQUE

I do not know whether the play[2] which accompanies this has been sent to your paper but in any case I send it to you because it is written by a friend of mine who is very highly deserving of notice & encouragement if you can honestly give him any. He has written very good things of other kinds, among others an excellent pamphlet on law reform[3] & one of the best extant defences of utilitarianism.[4] *I* like his tragedy also though I

6. Comte had recommended works by Spurzheim and Gall.

* * * *

1. MS at LSE.
2. *Athelwold; A Tragedy in Five Acts*, published in March, 1842, by William Henry Smith. The play was greatly admired by Mrs. Taylor. G. S. Merriam, *The Story of William and Lucy Smith* (Boston, 1899), p. 110, reports that JSM wrote to the author quoting the favourable opinion of Mrs. Taylor; no such letter has been found. The *Examiner*, which Fonblanque was editing, seems to have carried no review of *Athelwold*.
3. *Remarks on Law Reform* (London, 1840).
4. *A Discourse on Ethics of the School of Paley* (London, 1839).

can see faults in it, but of course I have not the impertinence to wish to impose my opinion upon you.

It has been rather scornfully cut up in the Spectator.[5]

ever yours

J. S. MILL

350. TO ROBERT BARCLAY FOX[1]

India House
5th April
1842

MY DEAR FRIEND

I am really ashamed to think of the time which has elapsed since I wrote to you or gave the smallest indication of remembrance of a family whom I have so much cause never to forget. I beg that you will all of you ascribe this omission on my part to any other cause than want of remembrance or of frequent thought of you—& I believe I could assign such causes as would go far towards palliating it. Now however I feel impelled to write to you by two feelings—one is the wish to condole with you on the loss which Sterling's going abroad[2] is to you & on the anxiety which after so much longer and more intimate knowledge of him than you had had when I last saw you, I am sure you must feel about a life and health so precious both to all who know him & to the world. It is a cruel thing that the hope of his being able to live even at Falmouth & be capable of work, without the periodical necessity for going abroad, should be thus blighted when it seemed to be so fortunately realised.[3] I fear not so much for his bodily state as for his spirits—it is so hard for an active mind like his to reconcile itself to comparative idleness & to what he considers as uselessness—only however from his inability to persuade himself of the whole amount of the good which his society, his correspondence, & the very existence of such a man diffuses through the world. It he did but know the moral & even intellectual influence which he exercises without writing or publishing any-

5. For March 5, 1842, p. 234.

* * * *

1. *Addressed*: R. Barclay Fox Esq. / Falmouth. *Postmark*: FALMOUTH / 6 APRIL 1842. Published with omissions in Pym, II, 329–31. MS in the possession of Mr. W. H. Browning.

2. Because of continuing slight haemorrhages, Sterling had been obliged to accept medical advice to take a trip to the Mediterranean.

3. The remainder of this paragraph was first published by Julius Hare in his memoir of Sterling in the latter's *Essays and Tales* (London, 1848), I, cxciii.

thing, he would think it quite worth living for, even if he were never to be capable of writing again.

Do, if you have a good opportunity, tell Mrs Sterling how truly I sympathise with her, although I do not intrude upon her with a direct expression of it.

My other prompting to write to you just now comes from the approach of spring, & the remembrance of what this *second* spring *ought* to bring, & I hope will.[4] Surely there is not any doubt of your all coming to London this year? There seemed some shadow of an uncertainty in one of the last letters which my sisters shewed me but I hope it has all cleared off.

Carlyle is in Scotland owing to the almost sudden death of Mrs Carlyle's mother. Mrs Carlyle was summoned too late to see her mother alive. She has returned & seems to have suffered much. Carlyle is still there, having many affairs to arrange. It is said & I believe truly that they will now be in much more comfortable circumstances than before. They heroically refused to receive anything from Mrs Welsh during her lifetime.

I have little to tell concerning myself. My book will not be published till next season for which I may thank Murray. He kept me two months waiting for the negative answer which I at last extorted from him, & which it is evident could as well have been given the very first day.[5] I could have accelerated the matter if I had chosen to dun him more, but I committed the mistake of treating him as a gentleman—& besides I really did not care enough about it. I am now in treaty with Parker & with considerable hope of success. Does it not amuse you to see how I stick to the high-church booksellers. Parker also publishes for Whewell with whom several chapters of my book are a controversy, but Parker very sensibly says he does not care about that. The book is now awaiting the verdict of a taster unknown to whom several chapters of his own choice have been communicated: & he gave so favourable a report on the table of contents, that one may hope he will not do worse by the book itself. If Parker publishes the book, he shall have my reprint too, if he will take it—but I am afraid he will not like anything so radical & anti-church as much of it is.[6]

Do, if you have time, write to me, & tell me your recent doings in the way of poetry or prose, together with as much of your thoughts & feelings respecting this little earth & this great universe as you are inclined to communicate—& in any case do not forget me.

ever yours

J. S. Mill

4. The Yearly Meeting of the Society of Friends in May, which the Foxes usually attended.

5. See Letter 343, n. 2.

6. See next letter, n. 3, and Letter 357, penultimate paragraph.

351. TO JOHN WILLIAM PARKER[1]

India House
6th April
1842

MY DEAR SIR

I am very much indebted to your referee[2] for so favorable an opinion, expressed in such complimentary terms, & am much gratified by the result. I will keep his observations in view in finally reading through the manuscript before it goes to press, but I fear I am nearly at the end of my stock of apt illustrations. I had to read a great deal for those I have given, & I believe that the chapters on Fallacies which preceded those that were submitted to your friend's judgment, are considerably richer than those he has seen, in examples selected as he recommends from eminent writers.

With respect to your very handsome offer of half profit, my feeling is that if I were to take advantage of your liberality in any manner, the shape in which I should most like to do so would be by a certain latitude in giving away copies—chiefly to foreigners or persons who would not be likely to buy the book although they would like to read it & who would therefore be more likely by making it known, to attract buyers to it than to interfere with its sale. I have not in view any alarming number, some 25 or 30 copies being as far as I can now judge, the extreme limit.

In reference to the contingency of a future edition, it is I think very unlikely that I should be inclined to change my publisher, especially when he is as I believe you to be, the most desirable one in England for the kind of book.

I have another publication in view which I should like to bring out about the same time with this book, as they might serve to advertise one another—a selection from a great number of articles, political literary & philosophical which I have published in different periodicals during the last eight or ten years, concluding with an article on Tocqueville's Democracy in America, in the Edinburgh Review for October 1840. It would be a sort of collection something like Carlyle's Miscellaneous essays, but extending only to two small volumes instead of five. I should be very glad if it suited you to publish this also,[3] but I have my doubts whether it would, as some of the opinions are likely to be considered ultra-liberal,

1. MS at King's.

2. The referee was William Cooke Taylor (1800–1849), miscellaneous writer and historian. Parker had sent the opinion in the referee's own handwriting but had withheld the name. "He forgot," said JSM, "that I had been an Editor, and knew the handwriting of nearly every literary man of the day" (Bain, *JSM*, p. 66 n.).

3. Parker declined. See Letter 357.

although (in the later papers especially) rather anti-democratic, so much so indeed as to have given great offence to many of the radicals. If you should be inclined to take this into consideration I should be happy to send you the collection.

yours very truly

J. S. MILL.

352. TO JOHN MITCHELL KEMBLE[1]

India House
13th April 1842

MY DEAR SIR

The accompanying paper is written by a clergyman of the Church of England, who has long quitted the Church on account of conscientious scruples. If his paper on Socrates should suit you he will be glad to follow it up by another on Plato & a third on Philo & the Platonisms of Christianity. He is a very sincere Christian & much respected by all who know him.

In case you should wish to communicate directly with him, his address is Rev. J. P. Potter[2] 8 Boyne Terrace Notting Hill.

Yours very truly

J. S. MILL

353. TO GEORGE CORNEWALL LEWIS[1]

I.H.
Wed^{y}
[April, 1842]

MY DEAR LEWIS

I am glad to tell you that Parker having received a very favourable answer from his referee has consented to publish an edition of 750 copies of the Logic at his own risk.

I have just received a long letter from Mrs. Austin.[2] She bids me give their love to you & say that M. de Lindenau[3] has your book[4] & that she shall see what he says of it—also to ask what you think of Otfried Müller's

1. MS in the possession of Professor Ney MacMinn.
2. Rev. John Philips Potter (1793–1861), who later published *Characteristics of the Greek Philosophers, Socrates and Plato* (London, 1845).

* * * *

1. MS at LSE.
2. The Austins were still in Germany.
3. Bernhard August von Lindenau (1779–1854), astronomer and statesman.
4. Probably *A History of the Literature of Ancient Greece; translated from the German Manuscript of Karl Otfried Müller* by G. C. Lewis (2 vols., London, 1840–42).

Nachlass[5] as a subject for translation. It seems to consist of three little books, on Rome, Naples & Venice. She says Mr Austin's article[6] is going on, but slowly & interruptedly & with terrible *anstrengung* & on the whole she writes in miserable spirits about him & about their present position.

How much I wish that any way could be found such as he would not reject, in which those here who are deeply interested in him might combine to make it possible for him to live in this country, at least during the uncertainty of American matters. Could nothing be thought of? I would cheerfully take upon myself a second income tax to aid towards such an object—& I should think there are quite enough of those who would gladly do so & who could without inconveniences.

ever yours

J. S. MILL

354. TO EDWIN CHADWICK[1]

Monday
[April, 1842]

MY DEAR CHADWICK,

I have read through your report[2] slowly & carefully. I do not find a single erroneous or questionable position in it, while there is the strength & largeness of practical views which are characteristic of all you do. In its present unrevised state it is as you are probably aware, utterly ineffective from the want of unity and of an apparent thread running through it and holding it together. I wish you would learn some of the forms of scientific exposition of which my friend Comte makes such superfluous use, & to *use* without *abusing* which is one of the principal lessons which practice & reflexion have to teach to people like you & me who have to make new trains of thought intelligible.

yours ever

J. S. MILL

5. The literary remains of the great German archaeologist, Karl Otfried Müller (1797–1840). Mrs. Austin appears not to have undertaken the translation.

6. See Letter 347, n. 5.

* * * *

1. MS at UCL. Endorsed in another hand: "John Mill Esq / on the Sanatory [*sic*] Report / April / 42."

2. Evidently a draft of *Report of the Poor Law Commissioners to the Secretary of State, on an inquiry into the sanitary condition of the labouring population of Great Britain*, 1842, XXVI (House of Lords).

355. TO VICTOR COUSIN[1]

India House, 27 avril 1842

MONSIEUR,

Je ne sais pas trop comment je trouve en moi-même, après une si longue interruption de notre correspondance, la hardiesse de vous adresser par mon jeune ami, M. G. H. Lewes, et en sa faveur, une lettre de recommandation. Mais vous savez que ceux de mes compatriotes qui s'occupent de haute philosophie sont malheureusement très peu nombreux; et comme M. Lewes est de ce petit nombre d'exceptions honorables, j'ai pensé que vous le verriez peut-être avec quelque plaisir. J'ai donc cru pouvoir me permettre de faire ce qui dépendait de moi pour lui procurer l'honneur et l'avantage de votre connaissance.

Ce n'est pas M. Cornewall Lewis, que vous connaissez probablement, et dont au moins vous avez entendu parler notre amie Mme Austin. Celui que je vous adresse est beaucoup plus jeune: mais il a des connaissances et une capacité qui donnent de grandes espérances, et il commence déjà à se faire connaître par ses écrits.

Moi-même, je viens de terminer un travail philosophique assez étendu, dont je compte vous faire l'hommage quand il sera imprimé. Je n'ose espérer de votre part, pour cet ouvrage, qu'une approbation très modérée, puisqu'il appartient plutôt a l'école de Locke qu'à la vôtre; mais je crois avoir profité, plus que ne l'a fait jusqu'ici cette ancienne école anglaise, des critiques et même des principes de la philosophie du XIXe siècle.

Veuillez agréer le témoignage de mes sentiments respectueux.

J. S. MILL

356. TO AUGUSTE COMTE[1]

India House
6 mai 1842

MON CHER MONSIEUR COMTE

D'après ce que vous m'avez indiqué dans une de vos lettres, ce qui restait à faire de votre dernier volume doit être aujourd'hui à peu près terminé. J'en attends la lecture avec une impatience que tout tend à accroître, et j'espère en retirer quelquavantage pour mon propre livre, dont l'impression, retardée par des délais de libraire, n'a pas encore commencé

1. Published in J. Barthélemy–Saint Hilaire, *M. Victor Cousin, Sa Vie et Sa Correspondance* (3 vols. Paris, 1895), II, 456–57. MS not located.

* * * *

1. MS at Johns Hopkins. Published in Lévy-Bruhl, pp. 53–57. In answer to Comte's letter of April 5, 1842, *ibid.*, pp. 45–53.

et qui ne paraîtra que sur la fin de l'année. Quels que puissent être à tout autre égard les résultats de cet ouvrage, je me flatte qu'il ne sera pas sans valeur comme œuvre de propagande et que les idées importantes que j'ai tirées de votre grand travail, en reconnaissant comme je le devais, la source d'où elles m'étaient venues, contribueront, avec la manière dont j'ai parlé de ce travail, y compris la partie sociologique, à attirer sur lui l'attention d'un certain nombre de lecteurs les mieux préparés et à provoquer leur adhésion au seul moyen d'étudier les phénomènes sociaux qui soit aujourd'hui au niveau de l'état intellectuel de l'humanité.

Vous devez sentir, du reste, sans aucune difficulté, que l'esprit anglais se trouve nécessairement moins préparé que celui des autres peuples avancés, à suivre et à perfectionner la science positive de l'histoire. La physique sociale devait certainement naître et grandir en france, et ne s'étendre que plus tard à ce pays ci, par la raison surtout que la civilisation française se rapproche de plus près que toute autre du type normal de l'évolution humaine, tandis que l'histoire anglaise s'écarte, comme vous l'avez si bien remarqué, très loin de la marche ordinaire. De ce caractère exceptionnel du développement anglais, ainsi que de la tendance éminemment insulaire que cette évolution anormale a imprimée à notre caractère national, il en est résulté chez nous une grande indifférence envers l'histoire européenne, dont nous avons l'habitude anti-scientifique de regarder la nôtre comme essentiellement séparée: et comme personne ne saurait parvenir à comprendre et à expliquer les anomalies sans avoir préalablement etudié le cas normal, les recherches qu'on a faites sur notre histoire nationale ne nous ont donné qu'un petit nombre d'érudits et pas un seul philosophe même du troisième ou quatrième ordre.

Quant à la tâche honorable que vous avez bien voulu me désigner, celle de rattacher la marche sociale de l'angleterre à la théorie sociologique fondamentale, je ne puis évidemment me dispenser de cette tentative, ne fût-ce que pour mieux affermir mes propres convictions sociales. Mais dans le cas même d'un succès complet, je crois que je ferais mieux de soumettre le résultat de mes travaux à vous-même et au public continental qu'à celui de mon pays, qui certainement ne saurait ni le juger ni en profiter convenablement, faute de connaître, je ne dis pas seulement les lois générales, mais les faits généraux eux-mêmes, sources des inductions dont ces lois sont tirées. Aujourd'hui même, ce que nous avons encore de mieux en fait de spéculation historique sur notre pays, c'est l'Essai de Guizot sur le système représentatif en angleterre,[2] et vous conviendrez que ce n'est pas là grand'chose.

Puisque je suis sur le chapitre de M. Guizot, je vous dirai que tout en

2. Presumably his lectures published in the *Journal des cours publics de jurisprudence, histoire et belles lettres* (2 vols., Paris, 1820–22), which were later revised

ayant toujours jugé comme vous ses spéculations politiques et sa métaphysique doctrinaire, j'ai éprouvé une impression pénible en apprenant l'idée désavantageuse que vous avez de son caractère[3] et qu'il ne mérite vraisemblablement que trop bien. On n'apprend pas sans peine qu'un homme en qui il faut reconnaître une véritable capacité scientifique, ait porté l'esprit de secte jusqu'à manquer de magnanimité envers un philosophe qui n'en a jamais manqué envers personne, et dont les écrits ont un charme particulier par l'admiration noble et profonde qu'il y témoigne à toute occasion pour tous ceux qui ont fait honneur à l'humanité, quelque éloignées qu'aient été leurs croyances des siennes propres. Il faut avoir le cœur bien petit pour ne pas trouver un attrait irrésistible dans cette noble sympathie avec tous les genres de grandeur morale et intellectuelle que je regarde au reste comme une des conditions essentielles de la vraie capacité philosophique, au moins de nos jours. Sans cela on ne peut être tout au plus que l'homme d'une spécialité, et les spécialités n'ont en sociologie, comme vous l'avez si bien établi, qu'une valeur provisoire. M. Guizot n'est certainement pas autre chose, quoique je croie que si vous aviez pris connaissance de son Cours d'Histoire,[4] vous y auriez reconnu, avec les mêmes intentions de positivité que dans son premier ouvrage, une capacité spéculative plus générale. Si mes compatriotes avaient une connaissance réelle de ce Cours, ils seraient beaucoup mieux préparés qu'ils ne le sont à la positivité sociologique.

J'ai commencé l'étude de Gall:[5] il me paraît un homme d'un esprit supérieur. Je le lis avec plaisir et j'espère aussi avec fruit. Dès que je serai à même de juger sa théorie, je vous écrirai ce qui m'en semble.

Je regrette d'autant plus vivement que les devoirs de votre position vous empêchent de faire un voyage, même court, dans ce pays-ci, attendu que moimême, par des circonstances particulières, je suis au moins pour cette année dans une situation à peu près pareille et que je serai probablement dans l'impossibilité de quitter Londres. La rélation personnelle que je désire si vivement établir avec vous se trouve par là ajournée, mais je ferai de mon mieux pour que ce retard dure le moins possible.

tout à vous

J. S. MILL.

for his *Histoire des origines du gouvernement représentatif en Europe* (2 vols., Paris, 1851).

3. In his letter of April 5 Comte had been bitterly critical of Guizot.

4. *Cours d'Histoire moderne* (6 vols., Paris, 1829–32).

5. Franz Joseph Gall, *Sur les fonctions du cerveau et sur celles de chacune de ses parties . . .* (6 vols., Paris, 1825). Gall (1758–1828), anatomist, physiologist, was the founder of phrenology. JSM had heard of Gall's theories as early as 1821 in a lecture at Montpellier (see *John Mill's Boyhood Visit to France*, ed. Anna Jean Mill [Toronto, 1960], pp. 110 ff.).

357. TO ROBERT BARCLAY FOX[1]

I. H.
10th May
1842

Many thanks my dear friend for your letter & its inclosures—& still more for the very agreeable intelligence that we may hope to see you all, & *expect* to see some of you very soon.

I have had much pleasure in reading both the prose & the verse which you sent me. I think I can honestly give downright straightforward praise to them both. The poetry has both thought & music in it, & the prose seems "to me much reflecting on these things" to contain the real pith of the matter, expressed "simply" & "perspicuously" & with the kind of force which so purely intellectual a subject required & admitted of.[2] If it were shewn to me as the production of a young writer whom I knew nothing of I should say at once that he was of the right school & likely to go far.

I have not time to enter upon metaphysics just now or I might perhaps discuss with you your curious speculation respecting a duality in the hyper-physical part of man's nature. Is not what you term the mind as distinguished from the spirit or soul, merely that spirit looking at things as through a glass darkly compelled in short by the conditions of its terrestrial existence to see & know by means of media, just as the mind uses the bodily organs, for to suppose that the eye is *necessary* to sight seems to me the notion of one immersed in matter. What we call our bodily sensations are all in the mind & would not necessarily or probably cease because the body perishes. As the eye is but the window *through* which, not the power *by* which, the mind sees, so probably the understanding is the bodily eye of the human spirit, which looks through that window, or rather which sees (as in Plato's cave) the camera-obscura images of things in this life while in another it may or might be capable of seeing the things themselves.

I do not give you this as my opinion but as a speculation, which you will take for what it is worth.

Thanks for your interest about my books. Parker has proved genuine & has behaved so well altogether that I feel twice as much interested as I ever did before in the success of the Logic for I should really be sorry if he were to lose money by it. He proposes to bring it out about Christmas. He will not publish the reprint as he makes a point of not publishing

1. *Addressed*: R. Barclay Fox Esq. / Falmouth. *Postmarks*: 10 MAY 1842 and FALMOUTH / 11 MAY 1842. Published, except for last paragraph, in Pym, II, 331–32. MS in the possession of Mr. W. H. Browning.

2. A lecture on modern British poets. See Pym, I, 292.

politics or polemics, so I shall print it myself in time for next season, & perhaps shall have a copy for you before that.

Give all kind remembrances from all to all—& to your sisters special ones from me for their kind wishes respecting my mental offspring. Please tell them also that I have lately seen for the first time their friend Henrietta Melvill[3] whose appreciation of & attachment to them were very pleasant to see.

ever yours

J. S. MILL.

358. TO SARAH AUSTIN[1]

India House
22d May 1842

You are most probably at Bonn & the agonies of the article for the Edinburgh[2] are over. I know what those agonies must have been but I think I also know what must be the relief from them & from that relief conjointly with the coming of a German summer, so much warmer than ours, dryer & less variable than ours, one may hope good results for his health: but above all from the consciousness of having *achieved* something, & he is sure to find by its reception that he has not toiled in vain, for he never wrote anything which did not satisfy all whom he would wish it to satisfy, except himself. I suppose there is something physical & organic in that incapacity of persuading himself that anything he does is done sufficiently well. Everybody who hears him talk on any subject in which he is interested would be quite satisfied if he would write the very words which he talks; almost any framework would serve to hold them together & that is exactly what Stephen expressed to me about the article now in question, he wished that the two lectures, as he called them, which he *heard* could be merely put on paper. By the bye I have no reason to believe that Mr Stephen was in any misapprehension about the subject of the article, although I was. About your own literary projects—I hope the article or articles for the Edin.[3] have come *zu Stande* as I think it is a kind of writing which suits you, & which is likely to be a better speculation than translating. For a translation to succeed, unless it be of something merely trumpery &

3. Henrietta Melvill (1816–1900), daughter of Sir James Cosmo Melvill (1792–1861), official of the East India Company.

* * * *

1. MS in the possession of Mr. Gordon Waterfield.
2. See Letter 347, n. 5.
3. Her next article in the *Edinburgh* appears to have been, "On the Changes of Social Life in Germany," LXXVII (Feb., 1843), 138–69.

gossiping there must be some peculiarly English interest involved in it, as in the case of Ranke[4] the interest of Protestantism. If those German selections[5] have done no more than pay their expenses I do not know what on the score of intrinsic merit could have any better chance. Of the books you mention I should think those on Rome, Naples & Venice[6] would have the best. Are they by Otfried Müller? His name is known here, which is seldom the case with any Germans not of the very first rank but I fancy I was wrong in concluding as I did at first from your letter that these books were by him. I know how much better suited the business of translating must often be to the state of your occupations & spirits than the more continuous exertion of even a review article & it is very desirable that you should have something of the kind in hand. You might finish Egmont[7] which would not take you very long & then *offer* it to Macready,[8] he is, from what I hear, exceedingly on the alert for any new theatrical speculation which has even a chance of *taking* & surely that would have a considerable chance. At any rate it might be published either alone or as part of a little volume of dramatic translations.—It is very dreary to think of you remaining in exile —the only thing which could make it *not* exiled would be your having friends near you, in the sense of real intimacy & that I thought it possible *you* & even *he* might have in Germany, but it seems not at Dresden: & although the German people are much more to your taste (as to mine) than the English, you seem to have fallen upon a time when all sorts of odious feelings are rife among them & besides as one grows older one is less & less capable of taking the species in general as an equivalent for the two or three whom one knows well enough to value them most in it. But I doubt if you would be better off in this respect anywhere in England, except London & its immediate neighbourhood, than in Germany. You ask me about the cheapness of living. The experience of all whom I am able to speak of, is that in such places as Dorking there is no advantage whatever in cheapness, over London, but rather a disadvantage. Of Selborne & such little places off the high roads I am unable to speak, but that would be a still more complete isolation than you are in at present. There *is* cheapness in remote parts as for example in Wales or Cornwall. The best place I know of the kind is Falmouth, because there are really interesting & superior

4. Mrs. Austin in 1840 had published her translation of Leopold von Ranke as *The Ecclesiastical and Political History of the Popes of Rome during the sixteenth and seventeenth centuries* (3 vols., London).

5. Her anthology of translations, *Fragments from German Prose Writers* (London, 1841).

6. See Letter 353, n. 5.

7. She had published her translation of two scenes from Goethe's *Egmont* in her *Fragments from German Prose Writers.*

8. William Charles Macready (1793–1873), actor, at this time manager of the Drury Lane Theatre.

people there, even without counting Sterling who is now fixed there. Whether this would be better or worse than the Continent you can best judge. I have very little to tell you about myself. The book is to be published by Parker who has in every respect behaved so well about it that I really begin to care a little about its chances of sale, as I should be sorry that he lost any money by the speculation. It is some encouragement to know that Deighton, the Cambridge bookseller (whom Parker very much consults) thinks that a book of the kind if competently executed *may* sell. I am sure I did not expect any such opinion from any publisher. Murray's procrastination lost the present season & Parker proposes to publish the book about Christmas & to begin printing it in July. You have I suppose more news of most of your friends here through other channels than I could give. The Grotes are just returned from Italy. Sterling was obliged to go there two months ago on account of a return of his usual spring symptoms but they went off before he reached Gibraltar & he will soon I suppose return. The black seal of my letter indicates no death that I care about. George has had to pass the winter at Clifton but his state has really improved—he has been with Dr. Carpenter[9] the physiologist, son of Dr. Lant Carpenter & a man whom I have a great esteem for, & I have no doubt he will have been much improved by it. Mrs Taylor is no better, but she means to try all remedies that are practicable here before going abroad.

Yours ever affectionately

J. S. MILL.

359. TO EDWIN CHADWICK[1]

I.H.
Thursday
[June 8, 1842]

DEAR CHADWICK

I should have written yesterday by post if you had not said you would send. I have read the whole report[2] carefully through again. The defects of arrangements are now corrected & I have nothing to suggest except that it be carefully revised by yourself or some other person to correct the

9. William Benjamin Carpenter (1813–1885), prominent physician and scientist (see Letter 386), son of Dr. Lant Carpenter (1780–1840), Unitarian minister.

* * * *

1. MS at UCL. Endorsed in another hand: "J. Mill Esqr / On the Sanatory [*sic*] Report / May [crossed out], June 8 / 42."
2. See Letter 354, n. 2.

numerous typographical errors & occasional ungrammatical sentences. I think it all excellent & shall be glad to write about it for any newspaper as you suggest.[3]

yours

J. S. MILL

360. TO AUGUSTE COMTE[1]

India House
9 juin 1842

MON CHER MONSIEUR COMTE—

Pour commencer par le sujet le plus spécial, bien que sans doute le moins important, de la lettre si honorable pour moi qui vous a été dictée par notre sympathie non seulement philosophique, mais j'ose le dire, personnelle; je vous donne, puisque votre délicatesse en a besoin, l'autorisation pleine et entière d'user à volonté du mot de pédantocratie[2] qui vous a tant souri, et même de tout autre mot et de toute idée que vous puissiez trouver chez moi. Je ne tiens pas assez au mérite aujourd'hui si répandu, d'une expression heureuse, la fût-elle beaucoup plus qu'elle ne l'est, pour penser que ceux qui la trouvent commode ne doivent pas s'en servir sans ma permission préalable, ou qu'ils doivent s'assujettir à l'obligation de me nommer. Toutefois c'est avec un plaisir véritable que je verrai mon nom associé au vôtre à l'occasion d'une doctrine fondamentale, que nous seuls peutêtre parmi les hommes de spéculation reconnaissons dans sa plénitude. L'assentiment fortement prononcé d'un second penseur peut effectivement comme vous l'avez senti, n'être pas inutile au progrès d'une opinion contraire aux idées régnantes, et naturellement repoussée par les propagateurs ordinaires de doctrines nouvelles. Il serait en même temps de votre prudence de ne pas vous servir à mon égard d'expressions trop flatteuses, et je le dis sans aucune affectation, par la seule considération que vous n'avez pas pû jusqu'ici suffisamment apprécier le degré de ma capacité réelle, pour vous en porter garant auprès du monde scientifique, et que la lecture de mon livre pourra rabaisser considérablement le jugement anticipé que vous voulez bien me témoigner si aimablement.

3. JSM kept his promise; he wrote the greater part of the article on Chadwick's Report in the *Examiner*, Aug. 20, 1842, pp. 530–31.

* * * *

1. MS at Johns Hopkins. Published in Lévy-Bruhl, pp. 64–69. In answer to Comte's of May 29, *ibid.*, pp. 57–64.

2. Comte had been much impressed with this coined word of JSM in his letter of Feb. 25, 1842 (Letter 344), and had asked permission to use it. Years later JSM again employed the word, in the penultimate paragraph of his *On Liberty*.

Je vous remercie infiniment des détails que vous m'avez donnés sur l'état actuel de la grande opération philosophique qui doit compléter votre immense travail. Chaque nouvelle indication des choses que ce volume contiendra, augmente encore l'impatience avec laquelle je l'attends et si malheureusement la publication se trouvait ajournée jusqu'au mois de décembre, j'éprouverais un regret que je n'ai nullement ressenti au délai de la publication de mon propre ouvrage. Il est d'ailleurs convenable que vous passiez le premier, afin que je puisse profiter pour mon travail de votre exposition finale des principes de la logique positive, exposition que je regrette de n'avoir pas eue sous les yeux dès le commencement d'une tentative semblable au fond quoique souvent différente par les formes.

J'ai lu les six volumes de Gall[3] avec une attention sérieuse, et je me trouve tout aussi embarrassé qu'auparavant pour bien juger sa théorie. Je suis à peu près persuadé qu'il y a quelque chose de vrai là-dedans, et que les penchans et les capacités élémentaires, quels qu'ils soient, se rattachent chacun à une portion particulière du cerveau. Mais j'éprouve de très grandes difficultés. D'abord, vous convenez de la prématurité de toute localisation spéciale, et en effet les preuves ne manquent pas pour montrer l'inexactitude de celles qu'on a tentées jusqu'ici. Je me citerai moi-même comme exemple. La seule chose que je sais avec certitude de mon développement craniologique, c'est que le prétendu organe de la constructivité est chez moi très prononcé. Un phrénologue très décidé s'est écrié au moment de me voir pour la première fois: *Que faites-vous de votre constructivité?* ("What do you do with your constructiveness?") Or je manque presque totalement de la faculté correspondante. Je suis dépourvu du sens da la mécanique, et mon inaptitude pour toute opération qui exige de la dextérité manuelle est vraiment prodigieuse. En accordant la futilité de la plupart des essais de localisation particulière, vous trouvez suffisamment établie la triple division du cerveau, correspond[ant][4] à la distinction des facultés animales, morales et intellectuelles. Je suis bien loin de prétendre que cela n'est pas; cependant à en juger par l'ouvrage de Gall, il me semble qu'il y aurait autant de preuves à donner pour un grand nombre des organes spéciaux que pour le résultat général. J'admets que la spécialisation des organes appropriés aux plus hautes facultés intellectuelles et morales doit par sa nature même, reposer sur une base inductive bien moins large que celle des organes que nous partageons avec les animaux inférieurs. Mais je ne vois pas très bien comment l'anatomie et la physiologie comparée puissent fournir une preuve concluante de la théorie générale sans en fournir pour une grande partie des détails. Gall me paraît avoir raison lorsqu'il dit que toute classification des animaux inférieurs, fondée sur le

3. See Letter 356, n. 5.
4. MS torn.

degré supposé de leur intelligence générale, est vague et anti-scientifique, vu que les espèces animales se distinguent entr'elles bien moins par l'étendue de leurs facultés mentales considérées dans leur ensemble, que par le degré très prononcé de telles ou telles capacités spéciales, dans lesquelles les différences d'intensité sont ordinairement si immenses que la plupart des cas sont réellement des cas extrêmes; en sorte qu'on devrait s'attendre à trouver plus facilement les conditions anatomiques par exemple de la constructivité chez le castor ou chez l'abeille, du sens local chez le chien ou chez les oiseaux voyageurs, que celles de l'intelligence en général. J'ajoute que si j'en juge par ma propre expérience, et par la comparaison que j'en ai faite avec celle d'autres observateurs meilleurs que moi et également dépourvus de toute préoccupation métaphysique ou théologique, la correspondance des facultés supérieures de l'homme avec le développement de la région frontale supérieure se trouve fort souvent en défaut. J'ai souvent vu une intelligence remarquable réunie à une petite tête ou à un front fuyant en arrière, tandis qu'on voit tous les jours des têtes énormes et des fronts bombés, avec une intelligence médiocre. Je ne donne certes pas ceci comme décisif, car je sais qu'il faut faire attention non seulement comme vous l'avez vous-même remarqué au degré d'activité de l'organe, mais aussi à l'ensemble de l'éducation, (envisagée dans la plus grande extension du mot) que l'individu a reçue, et à laquelle Gall n'a certainement pas fait une part suffisante. Les exagérations d'Helvétius[5] ont eu au moins l'avantage de donner une forte impulsion à la théorie difficile de l'éducation théorie qu'aujourd'hui on néglige à tel point d'approfondir, que la plupart des penseurs ignorent jusqu'où les circonstances extérieures combinées avec le degré de sensibilité nerveuse générale peuvent d'après les lois physiologiques mentales, non seulement modifier le caractère mais quelquefois même en déterminer le type. Des diversités de caractère individuel ou national, qui admettent une explication suffisante par les circonstances les mieux connues, se trouvent tous les jours résolues par la ressource facile d'une différence inconnue d'organisation physique, ou même, chez les métaphysiciens par des diversités primordiales de constitution psychique. Je pense au reste qu'on finira par rattacher tous les instincts fondamentaux, soit à la moelle épinière, soit à des ganglions cérébraux déterminés. Mais c'est encore pour moi un grand problème s'il existe peu ou beaucoup de ces instincts primitifs. Gall et Spurzheim[6] prononcent par exemple très décidément que le sentiment de la propriété est instinctif et primordial: mais de même que vous rejetez le sentiment de la justice du nombre des facultés spéciales, la fesant dériver de la bienveillance associée avec les diverses facultés intellectuelles,

5. Claude Adrien Helvétius (1715–1771), philosopher and psychologist.
6. Johann Caspar Spurzheim (1776–1832), a disciple of Gall in the development of phrenology.

de même ne devrait-on pas décider que le désir de s'approprier une chose susceptible de satisfaire à ses besoins quelconques, dérive naturellement et sans qu'il y ait lieu à une faculté spéciale, de l'ensemble de nos désirs, combinès avec l'intelligence, qui relie la conception du moyen à celle du but? Je n'ai pas besoin sans doute de vous dire que je vous soumets mes difficultés comme questions seulement, et non pas comme arguments.

Je vous sais beaucoup de gré de votre aimable bienveillance envers mon jeune ami Lewes, qui se réjouit très vivement de vous avoir vu. Je n'ai pas osé demander pour lui cet avantage parce que je savais qu'avec d'excellentes dispositions, et une certaine force d'esprit, il manque des bases essentielles d'une forte éducation positive. Je trouve très honorable à son caractère et à son intelligence la vive admiration qu'il éprouve pour vous, avec des moyens si imparfaits d'apprécier votre supériorité scientifique.

tout à vous

J. S. MILL.

361. TO JOHN AUSTIN[1]

India House
7th July 1842

DEAR MR AUSTIN

The book[2] you so kindly enquire about would have been in your hands by this time if I had decided to publish it this season. But the publisher, Parker, to whom by the advice of Lewis I had recourse on being rejected by Murray, & who has behaved so very well in the matter as to make me much more solicitous than I was before about the saleability of the book, thought it best to publish about Christmas next & to begin printing about this time: & I expect daily to hear that he is ready to commence. If you would like me to send you the sheets & Sir A. Gordon[3] would be so kind as to let me know when he has good opportunities I will do so.

I did not at all look forward to such good fortune as being reviewed by you, but I do not know of anything in the book to prevent it. It is true that the part relating to Induction is *not* "more occupied with the mental & social than with the mathematical & physical sciences" because it was more convenient to illustrate inductive methods from those subjects on which the conclusions elicited by them are undisputed. But I have chosen almost exclusively the simplest & best known cases, partly because my knowledge

1. In reply to letter by John Austin, June 27, 1842, at LSE. MS in Brit. Mus.
2. The *Logic*.
3. Sir Alexander Duff-Gordon (1811–1872), who had married Austin's only child, Lucie.

did not enable me to venture on any others without risk of making blunders, & partly because I did not wish to be unread by all who are not profoundly versed in physics. I do not think I have made much more use of mathematical & physical principles than Dugald Stewart & Brown.[4] I have, besides, endeavoured whenever I could, to make my examples carry their own explanation with them, & to give, as I went on, the knowledge necessary for understanding my meaning. The scientific examples are for those who have not already scientific habits of mind, but those who have, will be enabled by those habits, to understand the examples themselves.

If you do not review the book it will probably fall into the hands either as you suggest, of Sir W. Hamilton, or of Brewster.[5] The first would be hostile, but intelligent, the second, I believe, favourable, but shallow: neither, therefore, would exactly suit me. I have hopes of a review in the Quarterly, grounded on the fact that Herschel[6] writes in it, & his review of Whewell[7] contains so much that chimes with my comments on the same book that he would probably like to lend a helping hand to a writer on the same side with him. If so, such ample justice will be done to the book in so far as it is connected with physical or mathematical subjects, that it is much more important to have an article in the Edinburgh, strong on the other & more difficult parts of the investigation.

I have read the article on List[8] & find it as good as even I expected. I have had no opportunity yet of knowing what other people think of it as it is not yet in the hands of the general public—but I will watch the impression it makes & let you know. List seems to have as much confusion in his head as the advocates of prohibition[9] generally have, but the state of public feeling to which such a book recommends itself is a very serious consideration. What chance there is of a change of policy here, no one can foresee. But it seems to me that the more any person knows of the state of the country, both as to men's circumstances & their minds, the more doubtful he feels of the possibility of going on as we are. There is a speech of Lord Howick[10] in this very day's paper which dwells upon what is becoming

4. Thomas Brown.

5. Sir David Brewster.

6. Sir John Frederick William Herschel (1792–1871), astronomer.

7. The review of William Whewell's *History of the Inductive Sciences* (3 vols., London, 1837) and *The Philosophy of the Inductive Sciences* (2 vols., London, 1840) appeared in *QR*, LXVIII (June, 1841), 177–238.

8. See Letter 347, n. 5.

9. I.e., prohibitory tariffs.

10. Sir Henry George Grey, Viscount Howick, later third Earl Grey (1802–1894), statesman. The occasion of the speech was a parliamentary debate on the public distress. Much of his speech was devoted to the Corn Laws, but towards the close he remarked, as reported in *The Times* (July 7, 1842, p. 2), "he was induced to believe that a very different temper and spirit than had hitherto existed were fast springing up, that such a temper and spirit were no longer confined to the meetings of Chartists, but were rapidly gaining ground in the country."

daily more apparent, the spread of Chartism among the middle classes: & there is certainly alarm in the Tory camp: Lockhart the editor of the Quarterly said to Sterling a day or two ago "we do not know that we shall not have a French Revolution this very winter." Everybody thinks that the time is out of joint but nobody feels "born to set it right." Lockhart says the landlords are mad if they think they can go on as they do, but the only remedy he dreams about is "home colonization." He thinks if the parks were all cut up into square patches of arable & *let* (not given) to the labourers, things would go right, not seeing that it would be merely turning England into another Ireland. It makes one sick to see full grown men such babies—afraid to look the only real remedy in the face.

I may as well inclose you my table of contents[11] as it will shew you the arrangement of the topics.

ever yours

J. S. MILL

If the titles of my chapters should suggest to you any good examples, it is not too late for me to profit by them—

Do you know of any good German book on Roman history, subsequent to Niebuhr?[12] I have engaged to write something for the Ed. on the Romans & their place in history & in civilization.

362. TO AUGUSTE COMTE[1]

India House
le 11 juillet
1842

MON CHER MONSIEUR COMTE

Quand cette lettre vous parviendra, les doutes que vous aviez sur l'époque de la terminaison de votre grand travail seront déjà levées, et vous saurez si l'impatience de vos lecteurs doit se prolonger pendant quatre mois de plus. Il y avait pour moi une sorte de volupté intellectuelle dans l'idée de savourer ce dernier volume, comme il m'est arrivé a l'égard des autres, dans les beaux jours de l'été ou de l'automne, époque où l'on se trouve ordinairement plus susceptible à toute sorte de stimulations agréables, et où ma tête

11. The accompanying table of contents of the *Logic* has been omitted here.
12. The first two volumes of Barthold Georg Niebuhr's famous *Römische Geschichte* had been published in Berlin in 1812; the third volume in 1832.

* * * *

1. MS at Johns Hopkins. Published in Lévy-Bruhl, pp. 76–81; in answer to Comte's of June 19, *ibid.*, pp. 69–76.

travaille toujours, sinon mieux, au moins avec une conscience plus joyeuse de son activité. Mais si je dois renoncer à cette satisfaction luxurieuse [*sic*], et à celle beaucoup plus sérieuse de posséder et d'assimiler une portion si importante de vos idées philosophiques pendant que l'impression de mon propre ouvrage sera encore dans ses commencements; je ne m'en prends qu'à la déplorable imperfection de notre organisation sociale, dont le principal tort, à l'égard des hommes du premier ordre est bien moins de leur refuser la considération et la dignité sociale qui leur est dûe, que de les contraindre à user leurs forces et à dépenser la principale partie d'une vie déjà si courte, en cherchant par des travaux tout à fait subalternes les moyens même les plus modestes de vivre.

J'ai délibéré s'il ne conviendrait pas d'ajourner indéfiniment l'impression et la publication de mon livre pour le revoir en entier après la complétion du vôtre. Voici ce qui m'en a surtout détourné. Les bases générales de mon travail avaient été jetées et les deux tiers environ de l'ouvrage étaient faits, du moins en brouillon, avant que j'eusse connaissance de votre Cours. Si j'avais pû le connaître antérieurement, sourtout en entier, j'aurais peut être traduit cet ouvrage au lieu d'en faire un nouveau, ou si je l'avais fait, j'aurais vraisemblablement donné à l'exposition de mes idées, même sans intention nette à cet égard, une tournure un peu différente, et en quelques parties, moins métaphysique par les formes. Toutefois en y réfléchissant je trouve que la tournure quasi-métaphysique des premiers chapitres est peut-être mieux faite pour attirer les penseurs les plus avancés de mon pays, en me mettant en contact direct avec les questions qui les occupent déjà, et en rattachant mes idées logiques aux traditions de l'école de Hobbes et de Locke, école, comme vous savez, beaucoup plus près de la positivité que l'école allemande qui règne aujourd'hui, et maintenant foulée aux pieds par cette école à cause surtout de ce qu'elle a de mieux, sa répugnance intime aux vaines discussions ontologiques. Je ne crois pas être trompé par l'amour-propre en croyant que si mon ouvrage est lû et accueilli (ce qui me parait toujours très douteux) ce sera le premier coup un peu rude que l'école ontologique aura reçu en angleterre, au moins de nos jours, et que tôt ou tard ce coup lui sera mortel: or c'était là chose la plus importante à faire, puisque cette école seule est essentiellement théologique, et puisque sa doctrine se présente aujourd'hui chez nous comme l'appui national de l'ancien ordre social et des idées non seulement chrétiennes, mais même anglicanes. Au reste je crois avoir tout fait pour ce qu'ence qui depend de moi, la positivité seule profite de cette victoire, si toutefois elle est remportée. Or je crains que si je refondais mon travail pour le rendre tout à fait conforme aux dispositions actuelles de mon esprit, je ne lui ôtasse une partie de ce qui le rend propre à la situation philosophique de mon pays. Ce livre est l'expression de dix années de ma vie philosophique, et il sera bon pour ceux qui sont encore dans les conditions intellectuelles où j'étais alors, ce qui malheureusement suppose déjà un public fort choisi. J'aurai donc moins de regret en le laissant essentiellement comme il est, en comptant pourtant ne pas livrer à l'impression la dernière partie, qui seule a des rapports directs avec la sociologie, avant d'avoir lu avec l'attention et la délibération nécessaires votre sixième volume.

Vous me connaissez sans doute assez aujourd'hui pour croire à la sincérité de la sympathie que j'ai ressentie en apprenant que les dégoûts inséparables d'une position si peu convenable à vos goûts et à votre portée intellectuelle se sont maintenant compliqués de douleurs morales. Je n'ose pas encore me permettre de vous demander, à cet égard, plus de renseignements que vous ne m'en donnez spontanément. Plus tard peut être, j'aurais conquis le droit de chercher à partager vos souffrances: quant à les soulager, quand elles sont réelles, il y a ordinairement de la fatuité à se croire capable de cela.

Pour parler maintenant de Gall, je crains de vous avoir donné une idée exagérée de mon éloignement actuel de sa doctrine. Je suis bien loin de ne pas la trouver digne d'être prise, selon votre propre expression, en sérieuse considération; bien au contraire, je crois qu'elle a irrévocablement ouvert la voie à un ordre de recherches vraiment positives, et de la première importance. Si je n'ai pas paru autant frappé que vous avez pû vous y attendre, de la polémique de Gall contre les psychologues, cela ne tient peut-être qu'à ce qu'essentiellement elle n'était pas nouvelle pour moi qui avais tant de fois lu et tant médité les parties correspondantes de votre Cours. Malheureusement je ne puis pas me flatter d'arriver de bonne heure à des idées beaucoup plus arrêtées sur la partie affirmative de la doctrine de Gall, puisque si lui-même il n'a pas, selon vous, suffisamment connu la zoologie et l'anatomie comparée, je saurais encore moins, moi qui n'ai de ces sciences qu'une connaissance très superficielle, apprécier la force réelle des preuves qu'elles fournissent à l'appui des résultats généraux de la physiologie phrénologique, à moins que quelque savant ne les recueille et ne les mette devant moi comme devant tout le monde, en fesent le travail important dont vous indiquez dans votre lettre la nature et la nécessité. Espérons qu'il se rencontrera quelqu'un doué des connaissances nécessaires pour entreprendre cette tâche du point de vue sociologique. En attendant, et par des considérations tirées seulement de l'observation ordinaire, je trouve comme vous vraisemblable qu'il n'existe pas moins de dix forces fondamentales, soit intellectuelles, soit affectives, sauf à en faire le dénombrement exact et à trouver pour chacune d'elles son organe propre. Malgré la profonde irrationalité, à certains égards, de la classification faite par Gall des facultés humaines et animales, je lui rends la justice de reconnaître qu'elle est, au moins dans sa conception générale, très au-dessus de la classification banale des métaphysiciens. Gall a du moins conçu comme facultés distinctes, des capacités ou des penchans visiblement indépendants l'un de l'autre dans leur activité normale, sauf leurs nombreuses sympathies et synergies, au lieu que les prétendues facultés de l'attention, de la perception, du jugement, &c. ou celles de la joie, de la crainte, de l'espérance, &c. s'accompagnent normalement dans leurs actions, se suivent dans leurs variations, et ne ressemblent qu'aux diverses fonctions ou aux différents modes de sensibilité d'un même organe. Vous accorderez probablement que ce qu'il a de vraiment important dans la critique que Gall a faite des théories psychologiques se porte surtout sur ce point capital.

Votre devoué

J. S. Mill.

363. TO JOHN MITCHELL KEMBLE[1]

India House
16th July 1842

My dear Sir

Your note is a considerable disappointment to Mr. Potter,[2] as he had taken up the subject of his articles in no spirit of dilettantism but under the idea that it is specially applicable to the great questions of the present time & that "by cramming" as he writes "into the Religion of Socrates, the Mysticism of Plato, the Utilitarianism of Aristotle, & the Syncretism of Philo", all of which he regards as products of a social period in many respects similar to our own, he was likely to evolve principles eminently adapted to the solution of our present moral & social difficulties.

If you think the article does not sufficiently give evidence of this purpose you would, no doubt, be right in rejecting it. I fancied however when I read it that the object & spirit of the article would please you & suit your review though I could not judge whether the sentiments would.

Will you kindly inform me to what place I should send for the ms.?

Yours very truly

J. S. Mill

1. MS in the possession of Professor Ney MacMinn.
2. See Letter 352.

364. TO WILLIAM LOVETT[1]

India House,
27th July, 1842.

DEAR MR. LOVETT,

You will oblige me very much by letting me know when your Association[2] sets about the formation of the library which I had the pleasure of hearing mentioned in Mr. Hetherington's speech[3] as I may have it in my power to offer them a few books & should in particular be glad if they would accept from me one of the few sets which I have retained of the London review & the L & Westminster Review during the time of my connexion with those works, that is during the whole of the time they bore those names.

I have never yet met with any associated body of men whom I respect so much as I do your Association, or whom I am so desirous of aiding by every means & to every extent, consistent with my individual opinions. Those opinions, as you, at least, are aware, do not go with you to the full extent. The same horror which you yourself entertain of class legislation, makes me object, in the present state of civilization at least, if not on principle, to a legislature absolutely controlled by one class, even when that class numerically exceeds all others taken together. I would give you the choice of only a part, though a large & possibly progressively increasing part of the legislature but that part you should elect conformably to all the six points of the Charter[4] & I should object as much as any of you to surrendering one iota of any of them. For these reasons even if I were a public man, which I am not, I should not join either your movement or Sturge's,[5] while I would give any help I could to yours rather than to his,

1. MS in the Lovett Collection of the Municipal Reference Library, Birmingham. Copy supplied by Mr. Peter M. Jackson.
William Lovett (1800–1877), one of the most influential leaders of the Chartist movement.

2. The National Association for Promoting the Political and Social Improvement of the People, founded in 1841 by Lovett and his Chartist associates. On July 25, 1842, two days before this letter, the Association opened its National Hall at 242A, High Holborn (the renovated Gate Street Chapel), with a public festival devoted to public meetings, lectures, concerts, and classes. John Temple Leader, MP, presided at the opening ceremonies. JSM was a subscriber to the Association during 1842–43, along with such liberals as Joseph Hume, George Grote, and Charles Buller (see Julius West, *A History of the Chartist Movement* [Boston, 1920], pp. 159–61).

3. Henry Hetherington (1792–1849), veteran publisher of unstamped workingmen's papers, including *The Poor Man's Guardian* (1832–35), and a leader in the Chartist movement. He was the first secretary of the National Association. JSM no doubt heard him at one of the meetings referred to in the preceding note.

4. The demands of the Chartists, formulated as early as 1837, comprised: (1) manhood suffrage; (2) vote by ballot; (3) abolition of the property qualification for membership in Parliament; (4) payment of members; (5) equal electoral districts; (6) annual parliaments.

5. Joseph Sturge (1793–1859), philanthropist and reformer, had founded the National Complete Suffrage Union on April 9, 1842.

because yours has a more comprehensive range of objects & is a far more powerful instrument of good.

I do not obtrude these opinions upon you from any notion that their being my opinions makes them particularly worthy of attention, still less do I wish to convert you or your friends to them. Even if I could, I should not desire it. If you were not Chartists in the full force of the term, you would have far less power either of promoting the just claims of the numerical majority or of regulating their efforts and elevating their moral & intellectual state. But as I am really anxious to come among you, & to know you better, & to find out what means I have of aiding you, I think it useful & even honest to make all the explanations necessary for establishing a complete confidence, grounded on a full knowledge of each other's views & purposes. When you know exactly how far I differ from you, & exactly why, you will be able to judge when & in what I can make myself useful to you. It is but little that I can do: I have no connexion with any party & none now with any portion whatever of the press: but I have access to it, & am personally acquainted with many of the most intelligent people in the country, over whom one can always hope to exercise more or less influence. Therefore I may at least be useful in giving you a good name, or in counteracting those who attempt to give you a bad one. If either in this or in any other way anything which I can honestly do for you is worth your acceptance, it would probably be worth your while that we should meet occasionally & discuss & understand each other's principles & views. I have just now only an empty house to ask you to, but some few weeks hence if yourself & one or two of your friends—any of those who spoke on Monday who would think it worth their while—could spare me an evening & would not mind coming so far, we might make a good deal of progress.

Yours very sincerely,

J. S. MILL

365. TO HENRY COLE[1]

I.H.
6th Aug. 1842

MY DEAR COLE

I cannot remember any other interesting plants, beyond the bounds of Surrey, than the few I have here noted down. I have botanized very little in other counties, near London at least.

1. Text supplied by Professor J. M. McCrimmon from original owned in 1944 by Mr. Edward C. Ames, 2904 Goddard Road, Toledo, Ohio. Photostat copy now at LSE.

If you have done with my Surrey Flora I should be obliged by your returning it.

ever yours

J. S. MILL

Plants found in the neighbourhood of London but not in Surrey

---

Sisymbrium sophia, near Lower Halliford, Middlesex—also between Crayford & Erith in Kent.

The following in the neighbourhood of Hayes & Keston in Kent:
Lathroea squammaria—lane near Keston church
Narcissus pseudonarcissus—in a wood & adjoining thickets between Keston church & West Wickham
Narthecium ossifragum
Drosera rotundifolia
Hypericum elodes
Eriphorum angustifulium
} in marshy parts of Keston Heath
Hieracium sabaudum—Hayes common and neighbouring fields.
Potentille argentea—in dry gravelly parts of Keston Heath

Daphne laureola—in a wood near Chiselhurst
Hutchinsia petraea—wall of Eltham churchyard.

Sambucus ebulis, hedge between Loughton & Chigwell
Lactuca virosa, border of a field near Loughton on the east side of the high road.
Campanula hederacea—in different parts of the forest.

366. TO ALEXIS DE TOCQUEVILLE[1]

9th August 1842.

MY DEAR TOCQUEVILLE,

I am really ashamed of having allowed so long a time to elapse without writing to you. My excuses must be, a great deal to do, many letters to write which *could* not be postponed, & latterly (I mean during the last two months in which I have every day intended to write to you the day after)

1. Published in Mayer, pp. 336–38. MS in Tocqueville archives.

the languor of ill health. I am still far from well but I will not any longer defer writing to you. First, I have to thank you for your discourse to the Académie française[2] which I have read with great admiration, as to the most finished performance, both in point of style & in the elaboration of the ideas, which you have yet produced, at least to my knowledge, & sufficient in itself to justify your election to the body which represents or ought to represent the great writers of your country as you had already been deservedly placed in the still more illustrious body which represents its great thinkers.[3] I must at the same time add that I have read this stirring performance with an unusual share of the deep & melancholic interest with which I have long been affected by everything relating to the present state of France. I confess that the profound discouragement or at least the deeply rooted doubts & apprehensions respecting the destinies of France, which to me at least seemed to pervade the concluding portion of your discourse, have added greatly to the strength of the misgivings which I myself felt about that country, to which by tastes & predilections I am more attached than to my own, & on which the civilization of Continental Europe in so great a degree depends. I have often, of late, remembered the reason you gave in justification of the conduct of the liberal party in the late quarrel between England & France—that the feeling of orgueil national is the only feeling of a public-spirited & elevating kind which remains & that it ought not therefore to be permitted to go down. How true this is, every day makes painfully evident—one now sees that the love of liberty, of progress, even of material prosperity, are in France mere passing unsubstantial, superficial movements on the outside of the national mind & that the only appeal which really goes to the heart of France is one of defiance to l'étranger—& that whoever would offer to her satisfaction to that one want, would find the whole of her wealth, the blood of her citizens & every guarantee of liberty & social security flung down at his feet like worthless things. Most heartily do I agree with you that this one & only feeling of a public, & therefore, so far, of a disinterested character which remains in France must not be suffered to decay. The desire to shine in the eyes of foreigners & to be highly esteemed by them must be cultivated and encouraged in France, at all costs. But, in the name of France & civilization, posterity have a right to expect from such men as you, from the nobler & more enlightened spirits of the time, that you should teach to your countrymen better ideas of what it is which constitutes national glory & national importance, than the low & grovelling ones which they seem to have at present—lower & more

2. *Discours de M. de Tocqueville prononcé dans la séance publique du 21 avril 1842 en venant prendre séance à la place de M. Le Comte de Cessac* (Paris, 1842).

3. He had been elected a member of the Académie des Sciences Morales et Politiques in 1838.

grovelling than I believe exist in any country in Europe at present except perhaps Spain. Here, for instance, the most stupid & ignorant person knows perfectly well that the real importance of a country in the eyes of foreigners does not depend upon the loud & boisterous *assertion* of importance, the effect of which is an impression of angry weakness, not strength. It really depends upon the industry, instruction, morality, & good government of a country: by which alone it can make itself respected, or even feared, by its neighbours; & it is cruel to think & see as I do every day, to how sad an extent France has sunk in estimation on all these points (the three last at least) by the events of the last two or three years. Nothing can more destroy all impression of national strength, can more effectually prevent a nation from presenting an imposing aspect to its neighbours, than that determination neither to quarrel nor be friends—above all there is nothing which the English can less understand when they see France unwilling to come to an open breach & yet her ill humour breaking out on all petty second-rate occasions, the impression made upon them is one of simple puerility; it makes them feel the French to be a nation of sulky schoolboys. I myself make, I hope, all due allowances, certainly very great ones, for all this, but there are not, I fully believe, half a dozen other persons in England who do so, or in Germany either according to the best information I can obtain. If the French people did but know how much higher they would stand in the eyes of the world if they shewed only a great deal less solicitude about the *world's* opinion & less soreness about the consideration shewn them! for all the world knows that to be very uneasy about having one's importance recognized, shews that one has not much confidence in the grounds on which it rests.

I have not yet thanked you for your very kind reception of my young friend Lewes, who feels it as he ought to do & always speaks in the warmest manner of you and Madame de Tocqueville. He is very capable of appreciating the superiority of your philosophical ideas & was as much struck as it was natural he should be with the extreme rarity of impartiality such as yours: he found no other example of it among those he saw at Paris.

I hardly dare ask you to write to so bad a correspondent as I am, but a letter of yours has to me greater interest than that of a letter, it is like a new book, or a review article, giving materials for thought on great questions. I would rather have a monthly letter from you than read any monthly publication I ever knew—so pray think of me sometimes.

Yours ever affectionately

J. S. MILL.

India House.

367. TO AUGUSTE COMTE[1]

India House
le 12 août 1842

MON CHER MONSIEUR COMTE

Je commencerai ma lettre en répondant à la dernière partie de la vôtre du 22 juillet, à celle qui regarde la malheureuse famille dont vous me dépeignez d'une manière si intéressante la triste position.[2] Depuis que votre lettre m'est venue je n'ai pas cessé, et ne cesserai pas de faire pour le jeune homme dont il s'agit, la seule chose qui soit en mon pouvoir, c.à.d. de circuler parmi le petit nombre de banquiers et de négociants influents que je connais particulièrement et surtout parmi ceux qui connaissent votre nom, cette partie de votre lettre. La concurrence inouïe qui est le fléau de ce pays de mariages féconds, et l'engorgement perpétuel et en quelque sorte normal, de tous les canaux de l'industrie, rendent malheureusement fort incertain le succès de cette démarche, à laquelle du reste rien ne manquera de ma part. Quant à l'Inde il est inutile d'y penser. Vous avez très bien senti qu'on tient naturellement à ce que les places aux bureaux de la Compagnie soient remplies par des Anglais. Pour celles dans l'Inde, les plus considérables en sont destinées aux parens ou aux protégés des différents membres du corps dirigeant, et les emplois qu'on ne donne pas à des anglais sont réservés aux indigènes du pays. Restent les places au service des princes indiens. Mais d'abord on ne donne pas ces emplois en Europe: pour les avoir il faut aller les chercher dans le pays, et cela avec de très bonnes recommandations; encore a-t-on très peu de chances de les obtenir; sans compter que le gouvernement anglais, qui n'a pas perdu le souvenir des Bussy, des Deboigne et des Perron,[3] défendrait vraisemblablement aux princes qui sont dans leur dépendance, d'entretenir à leur service des étrangers Européens, et surtout peut être des français. Vous voyez ainsi combien peu je puis faire pour votre intéressant protégé. Au reste, la connaissance qu'il a des langues européennes me fait croire qu'il se trouverait mieux dans quelque maison de commerce où l'on aurait besoin de quelqu'un pour la correspondance étrangère. En fesant donc connaître sa position aux chefs de quelques maisons de commerce et de banque, je fais probablement pour lui ce qu'il y a de mieux à faire, au moins pour le moment.

Si le plaisir qu'une lettre a donné pouvait se reproduire tout entier dans la réponse, celle que je vous écris aujourd'hui serait certainement de toutes

1.MS at Johns Hopkins. Published in Lévy-Bruhl, pp. 90–94; in answer to Comte's of July 22, *ibid.*, pp. 81–90.

2. In his letter of July 22 Comte had asked JSM to help find a position for an unfortunate young friend of his.

3. Charles Joseph Patissier, marquis de Bussy-Castelnau (1718–1785); Benoît LeBorgne, comte de Boigne (1741–1830); Pierre Cuellier Perron (*ca.* 1755–1843); French military leaders in the Anglo-French wars in India.

les lettres que vous avez eues de moi jusqu'ici la plus agréable, car celle à laquelle je réponds a été pour moi une véritable fête: surtout par la nouvelle qu'elle m'annonçait de l'achèvement de votre 6me volume et de sa publication toute prochaine, choses dont vos dernières lettres m'avaient presque fait désespérer. Il me tarde d'avoir ce volume et de le lire, et je me sens peu disposé en attendant, à entamer avec vous des discussions philosophiques quelconques, que la lecture de la portion finale de votre système pourra rendre sitôt superflues. Cependant, j'ai toujours beaucoup désiré qu'une véritable et franche comparaison, en quelque sorte systématique, de nos idées soit philosophiques soit sociologiques pût s'établir entre nous deux; en sentant toutefois que cela exigeait nécessairement comme condition préparatoire que j'eusse une connaissance complète de votre grand travail philosophique dans son ensemble, et même que vous prissiez connaissance jusqu'à un certain point de ce que j'ai moi-même écrit, afin de pouvoir apprécier mon point de départ et l'ordre de mon développement intellectuel, ainsi que de suppléer à beaucoup d'explications et de faire porter la discussion, dès le commencement, sur les points réels et fondamentaux de divergence si toutefois il s'en trouve finalement, ce dont je ne puis pas décider. Je sais que je me suis toujours de plus en plus rapproché de vos doctrines à mesure que je les ai connues davantage et mieux comprises, mais vous savez bien, en qualité de géomètre qu'un décroissement continu n'est pas toujours un décroissement sans limite.

Je vous remercie on ne peut pas plus des détails que vous me donnez si aimablement sur votre position personnelle, ce que je ne compte pas comme la moindre des marques d'amitié véritable auxquelles vous m'accoutumez toujours de plus en plus. En apprenant à quel point, par suite de l'absurde modicité des traitements en france, un homme comme vous est mal rétribué de ses pénibles et fatigants travaux, je me sens presque honteux en avouant que je retire d'une seule place, importante il est vrai mais bien moins laborieuse que ce cumul d'enseignements mathématiques qui vous est imposé par le système des petits traitements, à peu près le triple de votre rétribution: ce qui du reste, eu égard à la cherté plus grande des choses de consommation ordinaire et aux dépenses de position proportionnellement plus grandes, n'équivaut probablement qu'au double. Il y a maintenant six ans que ce traitement m'est échu par suite de ce que nous nommons une *promotion* au bureau:[4] avant cela j'avais fait pendant treize ans essentiellement le même travail moyennant une rétribution, qui en s'accroissant annuellement ne dépassait guère la moitié de mon traitement d'aujourd'hui.

4. Two promotions in 1836 had brought him to rank only behind David Hill and Thomas Love Peacock in the Examiner's office. His salary was £1,200 a year. When Peacock and Hill retired in 1856, JSM was promoted to the Examinership at a salary of £2,000.

J'espère avoir encore une lettre de vous avant votre départ pour l'Ouest. Je vous remercie de m'avoir indiqué le moyen de vous faire parvenir des lettres pendant que vous serez en tournée. J'en ferai certainement usage, car après la lecture du 6me volume je ne pourrai assurément pas attendre votre retour à Paris, pour vous exprimer ce que cette lecture m'aura fait éprouver: Je suivrai votre conseil en laissant quelque port à payer, afin de stimuler l'activité de Mm. de la poste. Puisque je suis sur ce chapitre je vous dirai par parenthèse que la compagnie des Indes me fait l'honêteté de payer pour moi le port des lettres qui me sont adressées à leur bureau. Ainsi je vous engage à ne plus affranchir les vôtres comme vous l'avez fait jusqu'ici, car je ne vois aucun inconvénient à ce que les habitans de l'Inde supportent une partie des frais d'une correspondance philosophique dont on peut se permettre d'espérer que l'avenir de l'humanité, là comme ailleurs, pourra retirer quelque fruit.

Je suis bien aisé d'apprendre que vous êtes natif de Montpellier; c'est encore une source de sympathie, car j'ai moi-même passé dans cette ville les six mois les plus heureux de ma jeunesse, ceux de l'hiver 1820/21. C'est même là que j'ai pour la première fois trouvé un ami, c'est-à-dire un ami de mon propre choix, à la différence de ceux qui me furent donnés par des rélations de famille. Cet ami, je ne l'ai pas revu depuis; nous avons longtemps entretenu une correspondance qui enfin a cessé un peu par la faute de tous deux, et je ne sais pas même s'il est en vie; s'il l'est, il doit être pharmacien à Montpellier, et vous pouvez en avoir quelque connaissance. Il se nomme Balard;[5] c'est celui à qui la chimie est redevable de la découverte intéressante du brome: je ne sais pas si ensuite il a fait autre chose.

votre tout dévoué

J. S. MILL.

368. TO WILLIAM TAIT[1]

India House
17th August
1842

MY DEAR SIR

Although in the inclosed note my friend Sterling speaks of his name as unknown to you, I have no doubt of its being known, & known very well.

5. Antoine Jérôme Balard (1802–1876), chemist, known for his discovery of bromine. Comte in his reply of Aug. 24 reported that Balard was now professor of chemistry in Paris. Several of Balard's early letters to JSM are at LSE.

* * * *

1. MS at LSE.

I should think the connexion he proposes a most desirable one for your Magazine.

In case you chuse to write to him direct, his address is
Rev. John Sterling
Falmouth

Very truly yours
J. S. Mill

"The Election"[2] which he speaks of is one of the cleverest semi-satirical poems published since Beppo & Don Juan.

369. TO SARAH AUSTIN[1]

India House
22d August 1842

I write to you today without having much to say, in order to tell you what I have done or tried to do respecting your commissions. Senior[2] never received your note, as he had set off before it reached me. He could not therefore have taken anything to you. I could have sent through Mr. Klingemann[3] but I found that Laing's book[4] was out of print & a bookseller whom I employed was not able to procure me a copy. There is to be another edition soon, & when it comes out I will send it you if you think fit. But I would rather recommend your making Napier get it,[5] as he certainly ought to do. I have no doubt a copy was sent to him.—I could not send any sheets of my Logic because I have not yet begun to print it. The delay is not with me but with Parker who talked of beginning to print in July but has given no notice of being ready, & as the thing really does not press & he has behaved very well I do not chuse to urge him on the subject. It is very satisfactory that Napier has consented to take an article on the book from Mr Austin & I am particularly glad to hear of two articles on the stocks. It is a sign at least that Napier is not displeased with the reception of the former article,[6] & he is likely to hear

2. See Letter 325.

* * * *

1. MS in the possession of Mr. Gordon Waterfield.
2. Nassau Senior.
3. Unidentified.
4. Samuel Laing, *Notes of a Traveller on the social and political state of France, Prussia, Switzerland, Italy . . . during the present century* (London, 1842). The first edition was published in Jan.; a second, on Sept. 24, 1842.
5. Mrs. Austin was apparently planning to review the book for the *Edinburgh Review*.
6. See Letter 347, n. 5.

whatever complaints there are. As for dryness it is a fault belonging to the matter rather than the manner which was considerably more lively than I expected it to be though a little surcharged with classification in the first few pages. I *had* heard of that offer[7] & of Mr. Austin's refusal of it. Though I did not know the grounds of the refusal I felt that he was the best judge—& that no bystander can possibly judge for any person in such a case, especially for a person of his peculiarities & of his superiority of intellect. The expression of regret however at his determination, has been by no means confined to the persons whom you mention. I have not heard any *of them* speak of it but I have heard, & heard of several others of whose friendship for you & Mr Austin you have less doubt, & who expressed, not dissent, much less had they the presumption to express disapprobation, but rather seemed to feel discouragement, from an idea of its being very unlikely that anything should offer itself which would be liable to fewer objections than this Malta plan. Now however when I know his reasons I do not think so: & at all events if you are better as you are than with this, you are better as you are than with anything only as good as this.

I hope you will write other things like Steffens[8] both for Kemble & for Napier. I am sure they would be successful & profitable. I should have thought just the same of that article if it had been written by anybody else—it tells people with elegance & in an amusing garb & lively manner a number of the things which they most need to be told.

Thanks for your copious list of German books on Rome: I wish there was a chance of meeting with half of them, without buying *chat en poche*,—there are too many of them for such an experiment, nor is the occasion worth it. I shall read Wachsmuth[9] & one or two others if I can borrow them. I have already read to weariness about Rome for if one is particular about writing only what is true one has enough to do. I could have written a dashing article on the Romans such as Macaulay would write (though of course not so brilliantly) in a week, with the knowledge I had when I began to *read up* the subject. In the meantime I have been writing again for the old Westminster: Bailey of Sheffield has published a book to demolish Berkeley's theory of vision: & I have answered him,[10] feeling it

7. Austin had received an offer of an appointment to return to Malta. See letter of G. C. Lewis to George Grote, Sept. 6, 1842: "Austin had quite made up his mind as to the Malta project; his principal reason seemed to be that the salary was not sufficient to enable him to save anything, and he had enough to live upon in Germany. Moreover, he seemed quite uncertain about his health." (*Letters of Sir George Cornewall Lewis*, ed. Sir G. F. Lewis [London, 1870], p. 125.)

8. A review of the German philosopher Henrik Steffens' autobiography, *Was ich erlebte* (Breslau, 1840) in *BFR*, XIII (1842), 279–315.

9. Wilhelm Wachsmuth (1787–1866), German archaeologist and historian, author of *Die ältere Geschichte der Römer* . . . (Halle, 1819).

10. See Letter 373, n. 6.

my special vocation to stand up for the old orthodox faith of that school. I will send the article to Mr Austin for it will have a chance of interesting him, though few people else. It is the first fruits of my partial recovery from a three months illness, or rather out-of-health-ness, & it at least helps to pay my debt to Hickson who used to write for the review without pay when I had it.

It will be some comfort to get a real philosophical account of Prussia as the result of your winter in Berlin & I hope to hear from yourself somewhat more about the Berlinische Aufklärung from personal knowledge. From what you say I imagine it to be rather an un-German thing without the simplicity, cordiality, & above all the quietness, which are so agreeable in German life & ways to a person wearied with discontented, struggling (Benthamicè) devil-by-the-tail-pulling England. But my notion of it is quite vague & may be all wrong.

adieu

J. S. MILL.

370. TO ROBERT BARCLAY FOX[1]

India House
9th Sepr 1842

MY DEAR FRIEND

I can hardly justify myself for having left you so long without direct tidings of my existence, for I believe this is the first letter I write to you since we parted in London at the termination of your angel's visit. I was not very busy, either, in the earlier part of the time; but of late, that is from the beginning of July I have been both busy & unwell—the latter to a degree unusual with me, though without a vestige of danger. I am now so much better as to consider myself well, but am still busy, partly with revising my too big book, & making it still bigger by the introduction of additional examples & illustrations, partly by reading for an article on the Romans which I have promised to the Edinburgh. To this twofold drudgery, for it is really so I shall have to add presently the correcting of proofs, for part of the MS is already in the printer's hands.

I hardly know what subjects to write to you about unless I could know what are those about which you have been thinking: as for myself I have scarcely been thinking at all except on the two subjects I have just mentioned, Logic & the Romans. As for politics I have almost given up thinking on the subject. Passing events suggest no thoughts but what

1. *Addressed*: R. Barclay Fox Esq. / Falmouth. *Postmark*: FALMOUTH / SE 10 1842. Published in Pym, II, 334–36. MS in the possession of Mr. W. H. Browning.

they have been suggesting for many years past; & there is nothing for a person who is excluded from active participation in political life, to do, except to watch the signs which occur of real improvement in mankind's ideas on some of the smaller points, & the too slender indications of some approach to improvement in their feelings on the larger ones. I do believe that ever since the changes in the Constitution made by Catholic emancipation and the Reform Act,[2] a considerable portion of the ruling class in this country, especially of the younger men, have been having their minds gradually opened, & the progress of Chartism is I think creating an impression that rulers are bound both in duty & in prudence to take more charge, than they have lately been wont to do, of the interests both temporal & spiritual of the poor. This feeling one can see breaking out in all sort of stupid & frantic forms, as well as influencing silently the opinions & conduct of sensible people. But as to the means of curing or even alleviating great social evils people are as much at sea as they were before. All one can observe, and it is much, is a more solemn sense of their position, & a more conscientious consideration of the questions which come before them, but this is I fear as yet confined to a few. Still one need not feel discouraged. There never was a time when ideas went for more in human affairs than they do now—& one cannot help seeing that any one's honest endeavours must tell for something & may tell for very much, although, in comparison with the mountain of evil to be removed, I never felt disposed to estimate human capabilities at a lower rate than now.

On other subjects I have been doing very little except reading Maurice's "Kingdom of Christ"[3] &, for the second time, his "Moral Philosophy" in the Encyclopaedia Metropolitana.[4] The latter I like much the best, though both are productions of a very remarkable mind. In the former your Society has a special interest: did that or other considerations ever induce you to read it? He seems to me much more successful in showing that other people are wrong than that Churchmen or rather that an ideal Churchman is in the right. The Moral Philosophy is rather a history of ethical ideas. It is very interesting especially the analysis of Judaic life and society & of Plato & Aristotle & there seems to me much more truth in this book than in the other.

2. In 1829 and 1832 respectively.
3. Frederick Denison Maurice, *The Kingdom of Christ* (3 vols., London, 1837). A second, revised edition in 2 vols. appeared in 1842.
4. *Encyclopædia Metropolitana*, ed. Edward Smedley, Hugh James Rose, and Henry J. Rose, published in 59 parts (London, 1817–45). Maurice's article, published in 1840, was the basis of his later treatises on the history of philosophy which were eventually combined in his *Moral and Metaphysical Philosophy* (2 vols., London, 1871–72).

Our people[5] have been at Paris and are just returned. I suppose their or rather our friends will soon hear of them. They are full of the subject of what they have seen & enjoyed & altogether the thing has answered perfectly. Certainly however pleasant home may be there is great pleasure in occasionally leaving it. I wish some of *you* thought so and that *we* lived in some place where you wanted very much to come.—

Yours faithfully
J. S. MILL.

371. TO AUGUSTE COMTE[1]

India House
le 10 Septembre 1842

MON CHER MONSIEUR COMTE—

Vous me croirez à peine quand je vous dirai que même aujourd'hui je n'ai pas encore votre 6me volume. Personne ici ne l'a. Vous ne pouvez pas, sans en avoir fait l'expérience personnelle, vous faire une idée convenable des lenteurs et de l'indifférence de ce petit nombre de libraires qui entretiennent chez nous le commerce des livres entre la france et l'angleterre. Moi-même je ne croyais pas que ces lenteurs pussent se prolonger à tel point, d'autant moins que je n'en avais pas eu connaissance à l'occasion des autres volumes, n'ayant appris leur publication à Paris que par leur apparition ici. Aujourd'hui même pas un de ces libraires ne me donne une espérance certaine pour un jour donné. Si j'avais prévu de si longs retards, j'aurais fait venir l'ouvrage de Paris directement, au moyen de quelques personnes de ma famille qui s'y trouvaient alors: mais comme elles ne devaient revenir qu'au bout de quinze jours, je ne voulais pas attendre leur arrivée. Maintenant elles sont ici depuis huit jours, et moi, malgré ma faim, je suis encore à jeûn de votre livre. Jamais je n'ai trouvé plus difficile l'exercice de l'attribut essentiellement philosophique de la patience. Cependant c'est le seul remède, car je sais, par expérience, que si je m'adressais à quelqu'une des maisons de Paris qui font des expéditions à l'Angleterre, il faudrait peut-être attendre encore trois mois. On voit très bien que l'industrie n'est pas, au moins jusqu'à présent, du ressort des Français, car, bienque si éveillés à tant d'autres égards, ils font les affaires du commerce quasi en dormant. Leur défaut total de ce que nous

5. JSM's family.

* * * *

1. MS at Johns Hopkins. Published in Lévy-Bruhl, pp. 106–10; in reply to Comte's of Aug. 24, *ibid.*, pp. 95–105.

appelons ici ponctualité me paraît expliquer leur infériorité industrielle par rapport à plusieurs autres nations qui n'ont certainement sur eux aucune supériorité naturelle.

Aujourd'hui donc je n'ai à vous entretenir que d'affaires personnelles. Pour en commencer par celle de votre intéressant protégé,[2] je vous dis avec regret que par suite de l'immense concurrence dont l'accroissement progressif est à peine compensé par toutes les améliorations industrielles des temps modernes, mes efforts pour lui ont été jusqu'ici infructueux. Je vous envoie la réponse du banquier le plus important de Londres, homme recommandable à tous égards, et très distingué par son intelligence. C'est la plus favorable de celles qui j'ai reçues, et la seule qui donne une lueur d'espérance: vous verrez comme cette lueur est faible. Toutefois je ne relâcherai pas mes efforts, et si la chose est possible j'espère que j'y parviendrai.

Vous pouvez vous figurer, beaucoup mieux que je ne saurais l'exprimer, combien je dois sentir profondément l'honneur et la douceur de la preuve d'amitié réelle que vous me donnez en vous ouvrant à moi avec une si touchante confiance sur les chagrins de votre situation personnelle. Quant à l'événement important de la rupture probablement finale de vos liens domestiques,[3] je trouve très naturelles les souffrances morales qui ont accompagné chez vous cette crise de votre existence affective, mais en résultat je pense comme vous que cette séparation doit probablement exercer, sur votre avenir, une influence favorable. Lorsqu'une personne douée de l'élévation morale et intellectuelle qu'avec la noble impartialité qui vous distingue, vous accordez à Mme Comte—lorsque, dis-je, une personne pareille, et un homme de votre superiorité à tous égards se trouvent fatalement condamnés à ne pouvoir vivre ensemble qu'en état de lutte continué, je pense qu'ils doivent, dans l'intérêt bien entendu de l'un et de l'autre, surtout s'ils n'ont pas d'enfans, se résigner à vivre séparément. De pareilles incompatibilités, qui souvent existent sans aucun tort vraiment grave de l'une ou de l'autre part, ont rendu pour moi, jusqu'ici, la question du divorce une question indécise, comme plusieurs autres questions de morale particulière, depuis longtemps jugées et decidées pour vous. Je suis loin d'avoir sur ces matières, une opinion contraire à la vôtre; je n'ai pas, à vrai dire, une opinion arrêtée, et je suis même assez porté à croire[4] . . . car pour en décider irrévocablement il faudrait attendre une con-

2. See Letter 367, n. 2.

3. Comte had written in his letter of Aug. 24 (Lévy-Bruhl, pp. 102–4) of the "voluntary, and probably irrevocable, departure" on Aug. 2 of his wife, to whom he had been married for seventeen years. She had left him and been taken back several times before, but this time he refused. She continued to hope for a reunion and they corresponded for a number of years.

4. Here some words are missing in the MS.

naissance plus profonde de la nature humaine, soit en général, soit dans ses variétés. Peut être ma conversion, à cet égard, serait une œuvre réservée à votre Traité de Politique. En tout cas je sens profondément ce qu'il y a d'amer dans la position d'un homme fait comme vous pour le bonheur domestique, et dont les efforts pour y atteindre se terminent, après tant d'années, par un si triste dénouement. Cet isolement doit être surtout pénible à un homme qui par goût et par habitude se tient retiré du monde ordinaire et ne cherche que chez lui la satisfaction de ses besoins d'affection. Du moins ceux à qui vous faites l'honneur d'admettre en leur faveur des exceptions à votre règle ordinaire de vie, ne peuvent qu'éprouver le désir le plus vif de vous offrir des consolations sympathiques quelconques, tout en sentant l'insuffisance profonde de toute compensation pareille. Quant aux conditions accessoires de la séparation, vous avez agi dignement, et d'une manière convenable à l'élévation de votre caractère.

Je suis très sensible à votre désir, si honorable pour moi, d'employer les prémices du loisir comparatif dont vous allez jouir, à vous informer de mes divers écrits. Mais je serai charmé si Marrast n'a pas pu vous donner les renseignements que vous vous proposiez de lui demander à ce sujet. La plupart des articles que j'ai insérés dans des revues sont si intimement mêlés à des choses du moment, et presque tous se caractérisent, à plusieurs égards, par une si grande immaturité d'idées, que vous feriez mieux de vous borner, en ce qui les regarde, à la lecture d'un petit nombre d'entre eux, que je me propose de réimprimer avec des suppressions et des émendations considérables. Quand j'ai parlé de la lecture de ce que j'avais déjà écrit comme devant faciliter de votre côté la confrontation de nos idées philosophiques, j'avais principalement en vue l'ouvrage systématique dont l'impression vient de commencer, et qui avec toutes les imperfections que je lui reconnais, et toutes celles que je n'y reconnais pas, dépasse pourtant de beaucoup tout ce que j'avais fait antérieurement. Non seulement j'y ai traité des questions plus profondes, et en les approfondissant davantage, mais aussi les concessions que je suis forcé de faire aux opinions régnantes y sont bien moins étendues, en raison du public plus choisi auquel l'ouvrage est destiné.

Il ne me reste plus, pour le moment, qu'à vous faire les remerciements les plus sincères des renseignements si satisfaisants que vous m'avez donnés sur mon ancien ami M. Balard, que je croyais ne plus revoir. J'accepte avec reconnaissance votre proposition obligeante de me servir d'intermédiaire pour renouer mes relations avec lui, pourvu toutefois que cette aimable infraction en ma faveur d'une de vos régles d'hygiène mentale ne vous coûte réellement pas.

votre devoué

J. S. MILL.

372. TO ROBERT BARCLAY FOX[1]

I.H.
20 Sept. 1842

MY DEAR FRIEND

I write this line in haste to ask of you & your family an act of kindness for a destitute person, namely the little girl whose card, as a candidate for the Orphan Asylum, is enclosed. You know how these things are decided—by the majority of votes of an enormous number of subscribers: but the list, like all similar ones, swarms with the names of your friends the Friends & your interest with them would be equivalent to many promises of votes. I know nothing of the girl or her family personally, but one of the men I most respect is warmly interested for them, Joseph Mazzini, whom you have heard of (but whom I would not mention to everybody as his name, with some, would do more harm than good). Mrs Carlyle is also exerting herself for them.

I will send to you or cause to be sent as many cards as you can make use of, in case your interest is not preengaged for other candidates to the full number.

I am quite well again & everybody here is well, otherwise we have no particular news. Carlyle has been making a Cromwellian tour to Huntingdon, St. Ives, Hinchinbrook, &c. He will really, I think, write a Cromwellian book.[2]

ever yours,

J. S. MILL

373. TO MACVEY NAPIER[1]

India House
3d October
1842

MY DEAR SIR

I have been reading very much on the subject of the Romans, much more indeed than has turned out to be necessary or useful for the article I

1. *Addressed*: R. B. Fox, Esq. / Falmouth. *Postmarks*: B / PAID / SE 20 1842 and SE 21 / 1842. MS in the possession of Mr. W. H. Browning. Published by Pym, II, 337.

2. Carlyle's three-day "Cromwellian tour" had been made in the first week of Sept. See his letter to John Carlyle in J. A. Froude, *Thomas Carlyle: A History of His Life in London, 1834–1881* (2 vols., New York, 1884), I, 235. His "Cromwellian book" was published three years later: *Oliver Cromwell's Letters and Speeches* (2 vols., London, 1845).

* * * *

1. MS in Brit. Mus.

proposed to write. I am quite prepared to set about it if we could determine on what hook to suspend it. The following occur to me:

1. Michelet's Roman History which I mentioned to you formerly.[2]

2. Walter's excellent History of the Roman Constitution & Laws, published at Bonn in 1840.[3]

3. The Roman History in the Library of Useful Knowledge[4] the objection to which however is its being unfinished.

4. Arnold's Roman History.[5] Since reading this book again from the beginning it seems to me much more appropriate for my purpose than it did before. But as a posthumous third volume is expected this seems so far a reason for waiting until it comes out which I suppose will not be till the spring.

If this therefore be the book we determine upon, I cannot write my article just yet—& in the mean time if there is anything else which I could do for you I should like very much to do it. I would rather not write my review of Michelet's Hist. of France at present because another historical subject would be apt to drive my Roman history out of my head.

As I mentioned to your son, there is a metaphysical article of mine in the Westminster review just now published:[6] would that have suited the Edinburgh? I ask the question because it is convenient to know what sort of articles you would be willing to receive from me.

ever yours truly

J. S. MILL

374. TO ALEXANDER BAIN[1]

Oct. 3, 1842

I am quite well and strong, and now walk the whole way to and from Kensington[2] without the self-indulgence of omni*bi.*

2. See Letters 285, n. 3, and 296.

3. Ferdinand Walter, *Geschichte des römischen Rechts bis auf Justinian.*

4. *The History of Rome* published by the Society for the Diffusion of Useful Knowledge was in three parts: Division I [to 390 B.C.] by Henry Malden (London, 1830); Division II [390 B.C. to A.D. 31] by William Bodham Donne (London, 1841); *The History of Rome under the Emperors* by Charles Merivale (London, 1841–43).

5. Thomas Arnold, *History of Rome* (3 vols., London, 1838–43). The third volume, ed. J. C. Hare, appeared in 1843.

6. "Bailey on Berkeley's Theory of Vision," *WR*, XXXVIII (Oct., 1842), 318–36. A review of Samuel Bailey's *A Review of Berkeley's Theory of Vision* (London, 1842). Reprinted in *Dissertations*, II, 162–97.

* * * *

1. Excerpt published in Bain, *JSM*, p. 77. MS not located.

2. Where his home then was.

375. TO J[AMES?] WHITING[1]

India House
15th October 1842

SIR

I feel it highly complimentary to a person so little known to the public as myself, to have been thought of by you and recommended by the distinguished men whose names you mention, for so honorable an office as that of assisting to decide on the merits of remedies for the evils of the present social and economical condition of the country. After giving, however, my best consideration to the nature of the task to which I am solicited by your flattering invitation, I do not feel that I could undertake it with any prospect of a result satisfactory to you or to myself.

You have in view, if I understand your object rightly, something more than a mere dissertation upon the causes of commercial vicissitudes: No Essay would fulfil your intentions which did not include the whole subject of the condition of the labouring classes, and the means which might or should be adopted to alleviate the evils and improve the advantages incident to that condition. Now I will state to you candidly that I see little chance of the production of any essay which would appear to me adequate to so great a subject. It contains matter not for one essay, however able or comprehensive, but for many essays. The causes of existing evils, it seems to me, lie too deep, to be within reach of any one remedy, or set of remedies; nor would any remedial measure, which is at present practicable, amount to more than a slight palliative for those evils: their removal, I conceive, can only be accomplished by slow degrees, and through many successive efforts, each having its own particular end in view, and so various in their nature that a dissertation which attempted to embrace them all must be so general as to be very little available for the practical guidance of any. Although, then, I think it probable that many useful remarks and suggestions may be called forth by the competition which you propose to institute and shall watch its results with great interest, I have little expectation of its leading to the production of any paper to which, with the views I have stated, I could with any satisfaction join in awarding the prize, nor can I think that any person holding such views is one upon whom it would be agreeable to the competitors that the fate of their Essays should in any degree depend.

I have the honor to be
Sir
Your obedient Servant

J. Whiting Esq. J. S. MILL

1. MS owned by Frederick B. Adams, Jr., of New York.

The recipient has not been identified with certainty. He may have been James Whiting (*ca.* 1777–1871), founder of the *Atlas* newspaper in 1826 and a writer on social and economic questions.

376. TO MACVEY NAPIER[1]

India House
15th October
1842

MY DEAR SIR

Your letter received this morning is extremely satisfactory as to the article on the Romans & I shall probably make Michelet & Walter the text of it.[2] I could scarcely be ready by the January number, as when once one begins to read German books on historical subjects, the more one reads, the more one wants to read. I am rather glad that the Ed. Rev. should pay the tribute due from us all to the memory of Arnold,[3] before I have occasion to speak of his History. And if an early publication of the posthumous volume should be announced, I could still wait for it.

I do not know whether your approval of the article in the Westr,[4] especially as to the composition, may not have a bad effect upon me by encouraging me to write hastily as the article was written in three days & was never meant to be a thing of any pretension. I should hardly have thought it worthy of the Ed. but I should probably have given you the refusal of it, if I had not been committed to the Westr before I contemplated anything more than one of the small-print notices which that review usually contains. I should never send there anything which you would take, if I were not under a sort of personal obligation to the present proprietor,[5] not only for saving me the mortification of letting the review drop while in my hands, but as one of my principal contributors (& a gratuitous one) while I managed it. My reason for asking whether you would have taken this particular article, was that I might know what subjects suit your review & are not preengaged. The historical articles which I have been thinking of for you are things of great labour & require a long time for the preparation, but there are many things which I could write offhand, & should often do so if I knew that they would suit you. I could easily have something ready for the January number without detriment to my progress with the Romans, if we could hit upon any subject which suited us both.

You have touched up Alison very well[6] & it was time. My fingers have often itched to be at him. The undeserved reputation into which that book

1. MS in Brit. Mus.
2. See Letter 373.
3. The tribute (written by Herman Merivale) appeared in the Jan., 1843, *Edinburgh*, "The Late Dr. Arnold," LXXVI, 357–81.
4. See Letter 373, n. 6.
5. W. E. Hickson.
6. Review of Archibald Alison, *History of Europe, from the Commencement of the French Revolution in 1789, to . . . 1815* (10 vols., Edinburgh and London, 1833–42) in *ER*, LXXVI (Oct., 1842), 1–60.

is getting, merely because it is the Tory history, & the only connected one of that important time, is very provoking.

Yours very truly
J. S. MILL.

377. TO AUGUSTE COMTE[1]

India House
le 23 octobre 1842.

MON CHER MONSIEUR COMTE—

Les incroyables retards que j'ai éprouvés à l'égard de votre 6me volume,[2] et ensuite son ampleur extraordinaire et l'abondance de ses matières, ne m'ont permis d'en achever la première lecture que la veille même du jour ou j'écris cette lettre. Ce volume a dignement complété un ouvrage nécessairement unique dans le développement de l'humanité, car en supposant même que vous n'eussiez pas posé les premières bases fondamentales de la doctrine sociologique positive, vous n'en resteriez pas moins le fondateur de la vraie méthode sociologique, dans tout ce qu'elle a de vraiment caractéristique et par suite celui de la systématisation définitive des connaissances humaines. Quant aux doctrines spéciales de ce précieux volume, j'étais, j'ose le dire, suffisamment préparé par l'ensemble des volumes précédents et par notre correspondance, pour ne sembler trouver même dans les parties les plus remarquables de cette élaboration finale, que la confirmation et le développement d'idées que je possédais déjà, sauf quelques dissidences d'opinion d'importance mineure, dont je m'étais déjà aperçu et que la lecture de ce volume a notablement diminuées. Une seule fois j'y ai ressenti cette sorte de secousse que vos travaux m'ont souvent fait éprouver, et qui résulte de la subite appréhension d'une grande idée lumineuse et nouvelle. C'est dans l'endroit où vous parlez des hautes qualités sociales qu'on finira par trouver dans la vie industrielle, malgré le mobile essentiellement égoïste qui la dirige presque exclusivement aujourd'hui. A ce sujet vous apprendrez peut être avec intérêt un rapprochement caractéristique qui a lieu entre vos idées et celles d'un de nos écrivains les plus remarquables, dont le nom ne vous est pas probablement resté inconnu, M. Carlyle, qui bien que doué de facultés plutôt esthétiques que scientifiques, et procédant par intuition beaucoup plus que par raisonnement, a souvent des éclairs de génie qui en font en quelque sort un prophète et précurseur du progrès social. Cet

1. MS at Johns Hopkins. Published in Lévy-Bruhl, pp. 119–24; in reply to Comte's of Sept. 30, *ibid.*, pp. 110–18.

2. *Cours de philosophie positive: Complément de la philosophie sociale, et conclusions générales* (Paris, 1842), Vol. 6.

homme recommandable avec qui je suis lié depuis onze ans, me disait dernièrement qu'il ne fallait pas désespérer de l'idéalisation poétique de l'industrie; car, disait-il, voyez quelle grande poésie on a su tirer de la vie militaire, quoiqu'il n'y ait rien de plus naturellement laid que l'acte de tuer, accompagné des diverses circonstances physiques qui s'y rapportent; mais cependant en fesant convenablement ressortir ce que cette opération brutale comportait ou suscitait de dignité et de noblesse morale, on est parvenu à trouver là dedans tout un monde de poésie et d'art. Cette réflexion m'a vivement frappé, mais je n'ai pas d'abord reconnu, pas plus que M. Carlyle, ce que vous avez si admirablement établi, c.à.d. que les éminentes qualités sociales de la vie militaire dérivent toutes entières de son organisation, et de son caractère de fonction sociale, l'instinct guerrier en lui-même étant un de nos plus ignobles penchants, tandis que la discipline intellectuelle et surtout morale qui a résulté de l'association d'hommes plus ou moins civilisés pour faire la guerre, même offensive, a été un moyen fécond, et dans une certaine époque le seule moyen possible, de développer la sociabilité humaine. Une fois donc qu'on sera parvenu à effectuer une véritable organisation de l'industrie, on lui imprimera par là même les qualités sociales qui lui ont semblé jusqu'ici les plus antipathiques, et dont la décroissance apparente dans notre époque de transition a motivé tant de craintes exagérées, que j'ai moi-même partagées, sur les tendances morales du type moderne de civilisation industrielle. Vous m'avez rendu le service immense de dissiper irrévocablement, en ce qui me concerne toute crainte pareille, et cette grande idée a eu tout de suite pour moi, comme il en arrive souvent à pareille occasion, un caractère d'évidence qui fait qu'on s'étonne de ne l'avoir pas rencontrée plus tôt et sans suggestion extérieure.

J'apprécie convenablement la sage réserve dont vous avez usé en écartant comme prématurée toute discussion immédiate sur la plupart des institutions politiques proprement dites, au moins dans l'ordre temporel. Vous avez très bien fait sentir que la régénération sociale dépend maintenant de l'essor spirituel, ce qui devient au reste de plus en plus évident aux esprits éclairés par l'impuissance aujourd'hui constatée de toutes les tentatives théoriques et pratiques qu'on fait depuis bientôt cent ans pour renouveler l'état de l'humanité par les seules institutions. Je crois même cette heureuse révolution spéculative plus avancée dans ce pays-ci que partout ailleurs, désenchantés comme nous sommes des institutions soi-disant libres à raison d'une plus intime familiarité pratique. Chez nous aujourd'hui les prolétaires croient presque seuls à l'efficacité réformative [*sic*] des institutions démocratiques, encore les chefs les plus considérés du mouvement politique prolétaire, parmi lesquels il y en a de très recommandables, mènent aujourd'hui habituellement de front avec leurs projets politiques, des idées de moralisation et de culture intellectuelle pour les masses populaires, dirigées à la vérité jusqu'ici, comme il n'en pouvait être autrement, par une philosophie métaphysique et négative. Vous avez donc très judicieusement employé vos efforts surtout à caractériser le nouveau pouvoir spirituel, dont la naissance même, et à plus forte raison son incorporation dans le système social, suffirait déjà, dans un gouvernement temporel quelconque, à dissiper en grande partie le désordre, même matériel, soit en rectifiant et en élargissant les idées des classes dirigeantes, soit en leur imposant, de gré ou de force, une moralité meilleure. Vous vous êtes donc sagement borné, quant à l'ordre temporel, à poser le principe incontestable, que la direction en doit désormais appartenir aux chefs industriels, en laissant indécises bien des questions, destinées à être progressivement résolues par les sociologistes positifs, et sur lesquelles je désirerais bien entamer déjà avec vous une discussion philosophique. Telles sont, par exemple, celle des moyens à prendre pour atténuer l'influence inévitable jusqu'à un certain point mais si exagérée aujourd'hui, que le hasard, celui de la naissance surtout, exerce en désidant du personnel de la haute industrie, indépendamment des conditions de la capacité industrielle. Vient ensuite la question de la part d'influence qu'il pourrait être convenable de réserver, dans l'ordre politique, aux classes industrielles inférieures, question qui renferme l'avenir des institutions représentatives, quant aux deux seules fonctions qu'on pourrait concevoir comme leur appartenant dans l'avenir, d'abord comme moyen d'enseignement politique pour les masses, et ensuite comme organe régulier pour constater ou refuser l'adhésion populaire aux réglemens généraux émanés des chefs.

Je me propose maintenant, après un court intervalle, de reprendre la lecture de votre élaboration sociologique depuis son commencement au 4^m^ volume, afin d'en mieux saisir l'ensemble et de m'en rendre en même temps plus familiers les principaux détails.

Je me suis réservé peu de place pour vous parler dans cette lettre, soit de la grande série de travaux futurs que vous annoncez à la fin du volume, soit de votre préface et de l'indigne conduite de votre éditeur et de son patron M. Arago.[3] Quant à ce dernier je me réjouis vraiment qu'il se soit

3. In his "Preface Personnelle" to the sixth volume Comte blamed his failure to secure tenure and an adequate compensation at the Ecole Polytechnique upon the antipathy of his colleagues to the positive philosophy. He singled out for particular attack Professor François Arago (1786–1853), one of the most distinguished scientists of the time. M. Bachelier, Comte's publisher, who was under obligations to Arago, demanded that Comte delete the attack on Arago. When Comte refused, Bachelier without permission printed before the Preface an "Avis de l'Editeur" in which he disavowed the attack on Arago. Comte later that year successfully brought suit against Bachelier in the Tribunal de Commerce, and the publisher was required to suppress the "Avis" in all the unsold copies.

For an account of the controversy which led to Comte's losing his position in 1844, see Emile Littré, *Auguste Comte et la philosophie positive* (2nd ed., Paris, 1864), chap. VII of Part II.

emporté tellement au delà des bornes que la prudence aurait imposées à tout homme moins aveuglé par la vanité et par l'instinct de la domination. S'il s'était contenté de dire qu'il reconnaissait à M. Sturm[4] des titres mathématiques supérieurs aux vôtres, on aurait pu croire à sa bonne foi, et sa réputation scientifique aurait donné à son opinion, ainsi exprimée, quelque poids auprès de la partie du public qui ne pouvait juger par lui-même. Heureusement il a manqué de cette prudence vulgaire et a donné à tous ceux qui ont lu même partiellement vos deux premiers volumes, ainsi qu'à une génération entière d'élèves polytechniques, le droit de lui dire avec pleine conviction qu'il en a menti: ce qui sera certes, beaucoup plus nuisible à la considération publique et européenne dont il se glorifie, que son mensonge ne le saurait être à la vôtre. Quant à votre préface, j'avoue qu'avant d'avoir lu le volume lui même je craignais que le défi ainsi jeté à ceux dont dépendaient vos moyens actuels de vie ne fût de nature à aggraver le danger qu'il signalait, mais dès que j'ai vu les dures vérités qu'avec votre franchise ordinaire vous avez dites dans le 57me chapitre sur l'incapacité et la bassesse morale de la plupart des savans actuels, j'ai trouvé profondément convenable une préface qui au fond ne contient rien de plus offensant pour eux que le livre lui même et qui en désignant personnellement les plus coupables est de nature à inspirer aux autres une salutaire crainte.

Votre dévoué

J. S. MILL.

378. TO JOHN STERLING[1]

I.H.
Saturday
[November 1842][2]

MY DEAR STERLING

I have at last got the enclosed paper for you from Henry Cole.

I have been reading your review of Tennyson[3] for the second time, after an interval of several weeks. I have found more difference than I expected in our judgments of particular poems, & I will not pretend that I think yours the more likely to be right, for I have faith in my own *feelings* of Art, but I have read & reflected so little on the subject compared with you, that I

4. Charles Sturm (1803–1855), French mathematician.

* * * *

1. All but first sentence published in Elliot, I, 121–22. MS at Leeds.
2. In pencil in another hand.
3. "Poems by Alfred Tennyson," *QR*, LXX (Sept., 1842), 385–416.

have no doubt you could give many more reasons for your opinions than I should be fully competent to appreciate. Still, I think I could justify my own feelings on grounds of my own, if I took time enough to meditate—but I doubt its being worth while—the thing is not in my *fach*.

The preliminary remarks are very delightful reading, & I think they do as much as can be done to render this age, what Carlyle says no age is, romantic to itself. But I think Tennyson, having taken up the same theory, has miserably misunderstood it. Because mechanical things may generate grand results he thinks that there is grandeur in the naked statement of their most mechanical details. Ebenezer Elliott has written a most fiery ode on the Press,[4] which is a mechanical thing like a railroad, but the mechanicality is kept studiously out of sight. Tennyson obtrudes it.

ever yours

J. S. MILL

379. TO JOHN STERLING[1]

I.H.
Wed^y
[Nov. 1842]

MY DEAR STERLING,

I am very glad indeed to hear that you are writing the sort of paper you mention. As to Tennyson, you were right in getting so much praise of him into the Quarterly[2] by no greater sacrifice than leaving some of the best of the earlier poems unmentioned. I do not differ from your principle that the highest forms of poetry cannot be built upon obsolete beliefs—although what you say of the Ancient Mariner & Christabel seems to me true of the Lady of Shalott, and the objection does not seem to me to lie strongly against the Lotos eaters or Œnone. But neither is the idyl one of the *highest* forms of poetry—neither Spenser, Tasso, nor Ovid could have been what they were by means of *that*. And greatly as I admire Michael & its compeers, that is not the crowning glory of Wordsworth. And how poor surely is Dora compared with some dozen of Wordsworth's poems of that kind.

4. "The Press; Written for the Printers of Sheffield on the Passing of the Reform Bill," in *The Splendid Village . . . and Other Poems* (3 vols., London, 1833–35), I, 121–22.

* * * *

1. Published in Elliot, I, 122–23. MS at Leeds.
2. See preceding letter.

My remark on mechanical details does not apply to Burleigh, which seems to me Tennyson's best in that stile—not much, if at all, to the Gardener's Daughter, a good deal to Dora which I do not like—a little to some parts of Locksley Hall: but in a most intense degree to such things as Audley Court, Walking to the Mail, the introduction to Morte d'Arthur; & the *type* of what I object to is the three lines of introduction to Godiva, which he has stuck in, as it were in defiance. But, mind, I do not give my opinion as worth anything, to you especially—& my feeling is only to be reckoned as that of one person, competent in so far as capable of almost any degree of *exalté* feeling from poetry.

Have you seen Macaulay's old-Roman ballads?[3] If you have not, do not judge of them from extracts, which give you the best passages without the previous preparation. They are in every way better, & nearer to what one might fancy Campbell[4] would have made them, than I thought Macaulay capable of. He has it not in him to be a great poet; there is no real genius in the thing, no revelation from the depths either of thought or feeling—but that being allowed for, there is real *verve*, & much more of the simplicity of ballad poetry than one would at all expect. The latter part of the Battle of the Lake Regillus, & the whole of Virginia, seem to me admirable.—

Yours ever,

J. S. MILL

380. TO GEORGE HENRY LEWES[1]

I.H.
Friday
[Nov. (25?) 1842]

MY DEAR LEWES,

I return Sand's letter which it was very pleasant to have an opportunity of reading. I have no right or claim to send any message to her but I should be very willing she should know that there [are] other warm admirers of her writings & of herself even in this canting land—among whom I am neither the only nor the best.

I think your article on Göthe[2] decidedly your highest flight, as yet.

3. *Lays of Ancient Rome* had been published on Oct. 27, 1842. JSM reviewed it favourably in *WR*, XXXIX (Feb., 1843), 105–13.

4. Thomas Campbell.

* * * *

1. Published in Kitchel, pp. 27 and 38. MS at Yale.

2. "Character and Works of Göthe," *BFR*, XIV (March, 1843), 78–135.

Without being the *dernièr mot* on such a man, it recommends itself to my knowledge of him as *truer* than any other writing on the subject which I have met with. There are also some striking thoughts in it & although there is considerable Carlylism in the opening pages, & something of the tranchant manner which makes people call you by various uncomplimentary names indicative of self-conceit, both these defects disappear as you go on & full two thirds of the article seem to me to be in a stile infinitely nearer to excellence than any of your other writings known to me: for being perfectly simple & apparently unconscious, it shews its good points to the best advantage and wherever feeling is shewn, it is, consequently, really eloquent. All that seemed to me unsuccessful in the beginning of the Spinosa,[3] because it looked artificial & studied, is here, for the contrary reason, completely successful.

Please to observe here that I am by no means biassed in favour of the article by its compliments to myself,[4] which rather tell the other way for I have a dislike to seeing my own ugly name in print.

Tell the lady, with my best wishes, that I am getting very hungry.[5]

Yours (in the dual number)

J. S. Mill

After receiving your tart note I reopen this to add my warmest congratulations.[6]

381. TO ALEXANDER BAIN[1]

Dec. 5, 1842

I have not been very well, but am a little better.

3. "Spinoza's Life and Works," *WR*, XXXIX (May, 1843), 372–407.

4. Lewes in the article on Goethe quoted a long passage from JSM's essay on Bentham (see *BFR*, XIV [March, 1843], 131: the passage beginning, "Every human action has three aspects,—its *moral* aspect, or that of its *right* and *wrong*; its *aesthetic* aspect, or that of its *beauty*; its *sympathetic* aspect or that of its *lovableness*," and ending "the error of moralists in general, and of Bentham, is to sink the two latter entirely," may be found in *Dissertations*, I, pp. 412–13).

5. In the original a line is drawn through the sentence, probably because of the postscript.

6. "The congratulations were, no doubt, on the birth of Lewes's eldest son, Charles Lee Lewes, born Nov. 24, 1842" (Kitchel, p. 39).

* * * *

1. Excerpt published by Bain, *JSM*, p. 77. MS not located.

382. TO GEORGE HENRY LEWES[1]

I.H.
Wedy
[Dec. 7, 1842]

MY DEAR LEWES,

I think your preface[2] excellent & likely to be of extremely great use. You have hit off the characteristics of the different authors admirably, & the style is uniformly good & quite free from any of the defects which have been complained of. I intend reading it again & making a remark or two but they are really of little importance.

Did you see the letter in the Times today in answer to your article on anonymous writing.[3]

Commend me to the respectable mère de famille.[4]

Yours

J. S. MILL

383. TO AUGUSTE COMTE[1]

India House
le 15 décembre
1842

MON CHER MONSIEUR COMTE

Depuis la venue de votre lettre du 5 novembre jusqu'à la réponse que j'y fais maintenant, il s'est écoulé un intervalle d'une longueur qui, je l'espère bien, se répétera rarement dans notre correspondance. Ce laps de temps a été fort rempli chez moi par des devoirs indispensables et par une santé momentanément dérangée, mais surtout par une lecture lente et approfondie de votre élaboration sociologique dans sa totalité, lecture dont le commencement a été retardé, bien malgré moi, et que j'ai voulu terminer avant de vous rien écrire, résolution dont je crois avoir à me féliciter.

1. Published in Kitchel, pp. 39–40, but undated. Now dated by reference in paragraph 2. MS at Yale.

2. Professor Kitchel thinks that this refers to an early draft of the Preface to his *Biographical History of Philosophy*, which was not published, however, until 1845.

3. A letter signed Z (*The Times*, Wednesday, Dec. 7, 1842, p. 5) objects to Lewes' attack (in "The Errors and Abuses of English Criticism," *WR*, XXXVIII [Oct., 1842], 466–86) on anonymous criticism. Z. calls Lewes a radical and takes issue with his contention that anonymous criticism harmed Keats, Shelley, Byron, and Coleridge.

4. See Letter 380, n. 6.

* * * *

1. MS at Johns Hopkins. Published in Lévy-Bruhl, pp. 134–40; in reply to Comte's of Nov. 5, *ibid.*, pp. 124–33.

Vous avez très bien senti qu'un travail comme celui de vos trois derniers volumes ne pouvait être pleinement jugeable que dans son ensemble, et même après une lecture plusieurs fois renouvelée. J'en ai fait moi-même l'épreuve la plus décisive. D'abord je n'avais jamais, malgré plusieurs lectures très attentives, convenablement senti la haute valeur scientifique du 4me volume, faute d'en avoir pu suffisamment assimiler les doctrines avant de les avoir vu compléter par vos derniers travaux: jusque-là je n'y voyais surtout que la préparation indispensable de l'élaboration historique du 5me volume, en sentant toutefois dignement la portée de votre grande conception de la statique sociale. Quant au 5me volume, je lui avais toujours rendu pleine justice, mais il me restait de m'en pénétrer encore plus profondément. En ce qui se rapporte spécialement au 6me volume, vous avez dû d'après ma lettre précédente, me croire moins capable que je ne l'étais réellement d'en apprécier la grandeur, qui dépasse peut-être à mes yeux, tout ce que vous aviez fait antérieurement. En effet, par un privilège réservé aux esprits pleinement systématiques et *compréhensifs*, (mot anglais dont je ne connais pas d'exact équivalent en français) vous aviez jeté dans les volumes précédents de si féconds germes de toutes les principales conceptions du volume final, que les choses les plus merveilleuses que j'y lisais me faisaient l'effet de les avoir toujours connues. C'est en relisant successivement, et à loisir, toutes les parties de l'élaboration, que j'ai éprouvé une impression finale et décisive, non seulement plus forte mais essentiellement nouvelle, en tant que celle-ci est surtout morale. Je crois que ce qui se passe à présent en moi est une première vérification spéciale de la grande conclusion générale de votre Traité, l'aptitude de la philosophie positive, une fois organisée dans son ensemble, à prendre pleine possession des hautes attributions sociales jusqu'ici très imparfaitement remplies par les seules religions. Ayant eu la destinée, très rare dans mon pays, de n'avoir jamais cru en Dieu, même dans mon enfance j'ai toujours vu dans la création d'une vraie philosophie sociale le seul fondement possible d'une régénération générale de la moralité humaine, et dans l'idée de l'Humanité la seule qui pût remplacer celle de Dieu. Mais il y a loin de cette croyance spéculative au sentiment que j'éprouve aujourd'hui de la pleine efficacité ainsi que de l'avènement prochain de cette inévitable substitution. Quelque bien préparé qu'on puisse être, comparativement à la plupart des esprits, à subir les conséquences mentales de cette conviction, il est impossible qu'elle ne détermine pas une sorte de crise dans l'existence de tout homme dont la nature morale n'est pas trop au dessous des devoirs qu'elle impose; soit en démontrant clairement que le travail direct de la régénération politique et surtout morale qu'on a toujours rêvée pour un avenir indéfini, est réellement devenu possible de nos jours et que le temps est venu où les dévouemens individuels peuvent vraiment réaliser un fruit appréciable pour une si grande cause, soit en déterminant, par une réaction nécessaire, un sentiment amer des diverses imperfections particulières qui tendent à nous rendre plus ou moins indignes d'une telle destinée. Il n'y a du reste, aucune raison de croire que cette crise doive se terminer chez moi autrement que d'une manière favorable soit à mon bonheur individuel, soit à l'utilité de mon action sociale.

Quant au désir si honorable pour moi, que vous me témoignez de savoir si, après une mûre appréciation, je regarde vos derniers chapitres et surtout le premier des trois comme propres à déterminer la constitution finale d'une nouvelle philosophie générale, c.à d. d'une pleine systématisation durable de l'ensemble de nos conceptions réelles vous devez sans doute sentir déjà, d'après tout ce que je viens de dire que je ressens très profondément cette conviction, et que j'adhère entièrement aux conclusions générales de votre ouvrage, sauf quelques notions secondaires qui ne me semblent pas suffisamment éclaircies, et qui en supposant même qu'elles ne le fussent jamais, n'altéreraient en rien le caractère essentiellement satisfaisant de cette immense systématisation. A cela j'ajoute que bien que j'aie longtemps pensé qu'un esprit pleinement conséquent ne peut exister que sous l'ascendant complet de la philosophie positive, je n'avais jamais cru qu'il pût exister déjà, et dès le premier pas, une réalisation si complète de cette éminente propriété de l'esprit positif. Vous me faites peur par l'unité et le complet de vos convictions, qui semblent par là ne pouvoir jamais avoir besoin de confirmation de la part d'aucune autre intelligence, et je sens que cette précieuse sympathie que vous me témoignez à un degré très au dessus de mon mérite réel et que vous avez proclamée avec une si noble confiance à tous les esprits philosophiques de l'Europe dans la note que vous m'avez consacrée, m'est bien nécessaire aujourd'hui pour ne pas trembler devant vous.

Avec cela il y a toujours des questions plus ou moins secondaires sur lesquelles je conserve encore, soit une opinion différente de la vôtre, soit des difficultés non encore résolues. Quoique les unes et les autres tendent problement à disparaître, je ne dois pas chercher à atténuer ce qu'il peut exister entre nous de différence réelle, d'autant moins que je sens aujourd'hui, à l'égard de toute opinion que vous avez sanctionnée, la nécessité de me défendre contre l'entraînement, toujours plus à craindre dans ma nature particulière qu'un esprit critique exagéré. J'ajourne toute indication plus précise de ces différences, jusqu'à l'époque très prochaine de la publication de mon livre, qui vous en indiquera, soit directement, soit plus souvent indirectement, quelques-unes. Je vous dirai, à propos de ce livre, dont les trois quarts sont maintenant imprimés, qu'il me paraît toujours, même dans les parties qui ont l'air le plus métaphysique, très propre à faciliter, pour mon pays la transition de l'esprit métaphysique à l'esprit positif. Quant à la valeur propre des conceptions positives qui s'y trouvent, je ne puis avoir là dessus d'opinion définitive que lorsqu'elles auront été connues et jugées par vous, jusqu'ici seul juge compétent à ce sujet.

J'ai appris, avec le plus vif intérêt tout ce que vous m'avez dit dans votre dernière lettre sur les choses qui vous sont personnelles, d'abord, l'effet favorable de votre préface, que j'ai besoin au reste de savoir confirmé par le résultat de la réélection annuelle; ensuite l'éclatante punition que vous vous disposez à faire subir à vos indignes ennemis, et finalement, le programme des travaux que vous destinez à votre année de *repos*, qui serait certes une année de très forte contention intellectuelle pour tout autre que vous. Je crois que votre volume sur la géométrie analytique[2] pourra avoir un grand succès ici, ainsi que le traité de philosophie mathématique que vous annoncez pour un temps plus éloigné. Il y a certainement aujourd'hui chez nos jeunes géomètres un commencement de tendances à chercher la régéneration scientifique des conceptions mathématiques, tendances dont la métaphysique allemande qui domine maintenant ici, commence à s'emparer, à sa manière, à peu près comme la métaphysique française a tâché de le faire par l'organe de Condillac. Je crois au reste d'après l'accueil que plusieurs de nos savans ont fait à vos deux premiers volumes, qu'ils sont réellement mieux préparés que les savans français à sentir la portée de vos grandes conceptions de philosophie mathématique qui même aussi peu développées qu'elles le sont dans le 1er volume ont été dès lors pour moi la première preuve décisive de la force et de la fécondité de votre génie philosophique.

Le M. Carlyle dont je vous parlai est tout autre que le célèbre athée (Carl*i*le)[3] qui n'avait réellement d'autre mérite éminent que celui de son courage et qui a fini, je crois, par une sorte de conversion christiano-déiste. M. Carlyle est un homme très supérieur a celui-là, quoique moins complètement émancipé. Il est connu par plusieurs ouvrages, entr'autres par une Histoire de la Révolution française, prise d'un point de vue imparfait mais progressif pour ce pays-ci, et remarquable par un véritable génie épique, autant que ce génie peut se développer sans autre doctrine générale que ce qu'on peut appeler la critique de la critique. Cet ouvrage représente l'esprit organique dans l'état vague, ou plutôt l'esprit du besoin d'organisation, et comme c'est là l'esprit qui règne ici dans la partie la plus avancée du public, l'ouvrage a eu, malgré le style le plus excentrique, un grand retentissement.

Je ne négligerai aucune occasion de m'informer plus particulièrement sur les deux traductions allemandes de votre Cours. Je crois les penseurs allemands très préparés à abandonner, dès qu'on leur donnera quelque chose de mieux, leur ténébreuse métaphysique, essentiellement épuisée

2. *Traité élémentaire de Géométrie analytiqe à deux et à trois dimensions* (Paris, 1843).

3. Richard Carlile (1790–1843), printer and author of freethought papers.

aujourd'hui dans son pays natal. Je vous suis toujours très obligé de vos démarches amicales auprès de M. Balard, et bien heureux qu'on se souvienne encore de moi à Montpellier. Je serais bien aise de savoir les noms de ceux de vos amis qui me font l'honneur inattendu de ne m'avoir pas oublié![4]

tout à vous et pour toujours

J. S. MILL.

384. TO ROBERT BARCLAY FOX[1]

I.H.
19th Dec^{r}
1842

MY DEAR FRIEND

Do not think because I did not answer your last most interesting letter, that I either failed to sympathise with you with all in it that demanded sympathy or to appreciate the friendship and confidence shewn by your writing on such things to me. But it is little that can be done by words of consolation in such cases, & that little, few perhaps are less qualified to do than I, while you have those near you who are more than sufficient to do all that can be done. I do not feel the less but the more for your disappointment from the proof which the verses you sent me gave of your determination to be one of those to rise stronger & nobler from such trials.

There are abundance of subjects on which I should like a little mental communion with you if I could get my thoughts together for the purpose. First, there is in public affairs, much in the wind. Your prediction about the Corn Laws seems in a way to be verified sooner than we either of us expected, & that is sure to lead to great changes in the condition & character of our rural population & above all in the relation of landlords & tenants which on its present footing is essentially an unwholesome relation & *cannot* last. Things have certainly come to a strange pass when the manufacturing majority must starve in order that the agricultural minority may —starve also. But these things, important as they are, do not occupy so much of my thoughts as they once did; it is becoming more & more clearly evident to me that the mental regeneration of Europe must precede its social regeneration & also that none of the ways in which that mental regeneration is sought, Bible Societies, Tract Societies, Puseyism, Socialism, Chartism, Benthamism &c. will *do*, though doubtless they have all some

4. See Letter 386.

* * * *

1. *Addressed*: R. Barclay Fox Esq. / Perran Cottage / near Truro. *Postmark*: 19 DE 1842. Except first paragraph, published in Pym, II, 338–39. MS in the possession of Mr. W. H. Browning.

elements of truth & good in them. I find quite enough to do in trying to make up my own mind as to the course which must be taken by the present great transitional movement of opinion & society. The little which I can dimly see, this country even less than several other European nations is as yet ripe for promulgating.

In the meantime I do not know that there was anything better for me to do than to write the book I have been writing, destined to do its little part towards straightening & strengthening the intellects which have this great work to do. The said book is printed as far as p. 160, vol 2, & will be published when Providence & the publisher see fit. I heard of you the other day from Philip Melvill[2] who I believe brought the first intelligence which had reached the India House of such a thing being on the anvil. A propos, there was some time ago a very pretty, but very unnecessary—what shall I call it? deprecation from your sister Caroline relative to this book & to something which occurred near the tombs of the old Templars.[3] I do not recollect any more of what passed than that she accused herself of having impliedly instigated a very natural announcement which I made, *certainly* not for the *first* time then, touching the superfluousness of her troubling any bookseller respecting the two volumes in question, since I should as soon have thought of my own brother *buying* any book of mine as of any of your family doing so. You will certainly receive in due time what has been from the first destined for you—I mean you in the plural number, for I never separate you in fact or in thought—& the one who reads most of it may keep it, if the others chuse.

George is quite well and vigorous, & promises much. I think he will do credit to his bringing up. My other pupil Mary[4] is doing well too. As for the others you know them & they can answer for themselves. We are thankful for the exertions of you all about the little orphan.[5] What her chances are I do not know. Such elections by universal suffrage are as you truly say a monstrous thing.

ever affectionately

J. S. Mill

2. Philip Melvill (1817–1854), in the East India service, became Secretary to the Chief Commissioner for Affairs in the Punjab, 1853.

3. Caroline Fox in her journal (Pym, I, 316) records that on June 16, 1842, the Mills joined the Foxes in a tour of the old Church of the Templars. "John Mill talked about his book on Logic, which he is going to give us; but he declares it will be more intelligible than interesting—how intelligible he will find out in two years. He forbids my reading it, though, except some chapters which he will point out. 'It would be like my reading a book on mining because you [the Foxes] live in Cornwall—it would be making Friendship a burden.' "

4. His sister, Mary Elizabeth Mill (1822–1913), later (1847) Mrs. Charles Frederick Colman.

5. See Letter 372.

• • • 1843 • • •

385. TO HENRY COLE[1]

I.H.
Friday
[Jan. 6, 1843]

DEAR COLE,

I should like very much to make acquaintance both with the Michael Angelos & with Mr. Dilke,[2] but if the weather & a bad cold permit me to go out I am supposed to go early & walk with Carlyle.

Yours ever,
J. S. MILL.

386. TO AUGUSTE COMTE[1]

India House
28 janvier 184[3]

MON CHER MONSIEUR COMTE

Votre dernière lettre, que j'avais bien vivement désirée, m'a fait grand plaisir sous tous les rapports. D'abord elle m'a appris l'heureux résultat de votre procès avec Bachelier,[2] résultat qui fait honneur au tribunal de commerce et qui donnera sans doute une idée juste de l'affaire à ceux qui n'en ayant aucune vraie connaissance, auraient pu n'y voir qu'une question d'amour-propre entre vous et Arago. Quant à ce qui s'est passé dans la

1. From a copy in the possession of Professor J. M. McCrimmon. A note on the verso in a hand other than JSM's dates this letter Jan 7—43, but this is probably the date of receipt of the letter, since Friday of this week fell on Jan. 6.
2. Probably Charles Wentworth Dilke.

* * * *

1. MS at Johns Hopkins. Published in Lévy-Bruhl, pp. 150–55; in reply to Comte's of Dec. 30, 1842, *ibid.*, pp. 140–50.
2. The case had been tried on Dec. 15. See Letter 377, n. 3.

première audience, je le savais déjà par la Gazette des Tribunaux, qui en a rendu un compte sommaire, mais à peu près exact puisqu'il s'accordait essentiellement avec celui que vous m'avez donné. Il me manquait seulement de savoir quel effet cette discussion avait fait sur votre esprit, et si les indignes menaces qu'on avait osé vous adresser à l'égard de votre réélection pouvaient offrir un danger réel. J'ai appris avec joie, par votre lettre que ce danger n'est pas fort à craindre, et que les charlatans qui pour conserver leur propre considération croient avoir besoin de rabaisser la vôtre, nuiront probablement moins à vous qu'à eux-mêmes.

J'ai appris aussi avec beaucoup d'intérêt que l'insurrection des biologistes contre la domination oppressive et aujourd'hui irrationnelle des géomètres, commence déjà à se prononcer. Votre dernier volume ne peut manquer de donner une forte impulsion à cette tendance salutaire, qui à son tour doit beaucoup favoriser l'avènement de la nouvelle philosophie à laquelle les biologistes sont nécessairement mieux préparés que toute autre classe de savans, au moins en france. Je dis en france, car je crains que si nos géomètres valent mieux à certains égards que les vôtres, il n'en est pas de même quant à nos biologistes. Cela tient à plusieurs causes. D'abord, malgré les défauts de l'éducation scientifique en france, je la crois au fond beaucoup meilleure que chez nous. Soit par les tendances trop exclusivement pratiques de notre caractère national, soit par le fractionnement encore plus exagéré qu'ailleurs des diverses études positives, le véritable esprit scientifique est très rare chez nous, et si quelques-uns le possèdent jusqu'à un certain point, ils l'ont, le plus souvent, puisé dans les livres français; sauf peut-être les écossais, chez qui l'éducation publique a un caractère plus français qu'anglais, ce qui explique le mérite éminent des penseurs écossais depuis Kaimes[3] et Ferguson[4] jusqu'à mon père qui mort en 1836, fut le dernier survivant de cette grande école. Quant à la biologie, elle reste encore chez nous, plus que chez vous, dans cet état provisoire si bien caractérisé par vous et même par Bacon, celui dans lequel la science n'est pas encore séparée de l'art correspondent. Sauf l'histoire naturelle concrète, qui a pris ici depuis douze à quinze années un élan très vigoureux, les connaissances biologiques ne sont guère cultivées que par des médecins ou chirurgiens, qui, s'ils ont de la capacité, sont bientôt absorbés dans les travaux accablants d'un métier ici surtout terrible. Sans doute la séparation

3. Henry Home, Lord Kames (1696–1782), Scottish judge and writer. His *Essays on the Principles of Morality and Natural Religion* (Edinburgh, 1751), written to combat the doctrines of David Hume, resulted in his own orthodoxy being questioned; he was tried but acquitted by the Presbytery of Edinburgh.

4. Adam Ferguson (1723–1816), professor of pneumatics and moral philosophy at Edinburgh University.

des recherches biologiques d'avec l'art médical serait aujourd'hui pleinement opportune; elle est très bien préparée par l'état général du public scientifique, mais chez nous les prévisions sociales ne sont pas encore allées jusqu'à doter cette classe de savans du moyen de vivre comme tels, soit par la cultivation de leur science, soit par sa propagation. Cela est tellement vrai qu'un jeune biologiste de mes amis, le Dr Carpenter,[5] que je crois être sans contredit le plus philosophe de tous ceux qui chez nous étudient les lois des corps vivans, qui a écrit les meilleurs traités de physiologie générale et humaine que nous possédons dans notre langue, et qui s'il était français obtiendrait sans peine une des meilleures chaires de vos écoles de médecine, est encore à chercher ici le moyen de gagner la subsistance même la plus modeste en se consacrant à la science. Ajoutez à ceci que nos biologistes sont en général bien loin d'être émancipés sous le rapport réligieux, quoiqu'ils soient peut-être plus près de cette émancipation que les autres savans et vous verrez qu'il n'y a pas de quoi s'encourager beaucoup pour le progrès rapide de la nouvelle philosophie.

A tout prendre, le public anglais ne me paraît assez bien préparé qu'à la réception de vos principes de philosophie générale, en y superposant toutefois, par une transaction profondément irrationnelle, l'idée d'une providence agissant par des lois générales; notion préparée et même beaucoup travaillée par les demi-philosophes timides qui ont rempli chez nous pendant le 18me siècle la place de l'énergique école négative française. Mais je ne trouve pas à beaucoup près chez notre public le même degré de préparation à l'égard de votre philosophie sociale, attendu que l'un des fondements principaux de cette philosophie est la loi naturelle du décroissement spontané de l'esprit réligieux, doctrine qui effraie encore presque tous les esprits en Angleterre, au point que si moi-même je la proclamais ouvertement on n'oserait pas me lire. Je risque déjà quelque chose en déclarant hautement, partout dans mon livre, l'admiration que je ressens pour votre grand ouvrage, sans faire la moindre réserve théologique, qu'à ma place tout autre anglais, je crois, n'aurait pas manqué de faire.

La publication de mon livre, aujourd'hui très prochaine, a été un peu retardée par le remaniement complet que j'ai cru devoir faire à la dernière partie pour la mettre plus en harmonie avec ma manière actuelle de penser, depuis la lecture de votre 6me volume et l'étude plus approfondie que j'ai faite des deux volumes précédens. J'y ai fait maintenant beaucoup plus de place à la nouvelle doctrine, tout en la prenant du point de vue de mon propre travail, et je crois que, sous ce rapport, mon livre est maintenant

5. William Benjamin Carpenter, best known for his *Principles of General and Comparative Physiology* (London, 1839), the second edition of which JSM had reviewed briefly in *WR*, XXXVII (Jan., 1842), 254.

le plus avancé que mon pays soit encore susceptible de recevoir. J'ai d'ailleurs l'espoir bien fondé que tout ce qui chez nous est capable de comprendre votre ouvrage viendra apprendre chez moi où trouver quelque chose de mieux que moi.

Je vous demande pardon de n'avoir jusqu'ici rien dit en réponse au désir que vous avez plus d'une fois si aimablement témoigné de resserrer notre amitié par une entrevue personnelle prochaine. M. Lewes m'avait mal compris: malheureusement j'ai toujours eu la presque certitude que des circonstances qui tiennent à mes relations personnelles les plus intimes, me retiendraient cet hiver à Londres, mais dans le cas où ces circonstances se prolongeraient beaucoup plus longtemps je suis très décidé à courir à Paris, ne fût-ce que pour deux ou trois jours, et dans l'unique intention de vous voir.

Je suis bien aise de savoir les noms de ceux de vos amis à Montpellier qui conservent encore quelque souvenir de mon séjour dans cette ville[6] que je ne cesserai jamais d'aimer. Cela ne m'étonne pas beaucoup de la part de l'aimable Roméo Pouzin,[7] avec qui j'ai été plus lié qu'avec toute autre personne de Montpellier, à l'exception de Balard et de la famille Bérard.[8] Quant à M. Emile Guillaume,[9] il me fait un honneur qui me flatte d'autant plus que je dois l'avoir très peu connu, puisque j'ai oublié jusqu'a son nom.

J'attends avec un vif intérêt le résultat de la sorte d'expérience sociale que vous allez faire à l'ouverture de votre cours annuel d'astronomie et qui aura comme vous le sentez une grande importance par rapport à la propagation libre de la philosophie pleinement positive. Heureux si je croyais qu'on en vînt jusque-là dans ce pays-ci, de mon vivant! Cette liberté de discussion dont on jouit en france est la compensation de bien des misères. Nous en sommes bien loin encore, mais qui sait? dans un temps de transition morale les choses marchent plus vite qu'elles n'en ont l'air.

Votre tout dévoué

J. S. MILL

6. In the winter of 1820–21.

7. Comte had reported that Dr. Roméo Pouzin was now a professor in the school of pharmacy.

8. The family of Etienne Bérard, prominent chemist of Montpellier. His son, Jacques Etienne Bérard (1789–1869), achieved an even greater reputation as a chemist (see *John Mill's Boyhood Visit to France*, ed. Anna Jean Mill [Toronto, 1960], p. 38).

9. Not identified. Perhaps the M. Guillaume referred to in JSM's Notebook of 1820 (see *ibid.*, p. 76, n. 140 and 141).

387. TO ROBERT BARCLAY FOX[1]

India House
14 Feb. 1843

MY DEAR FRIEND—In a few days you will receive two ponderous volumes,[2] concerning which you have shewn an interest that I desire very much they may justify. I have not defaced them with any marks because after going finally through the whole as it passed through the press I have come to the conclusion that it will not bear to be read in any way except straight through, & it is probably worth *your* reading it that way, while I am certain it is not worth it to your sisters being a kind of book so entirely abstract that I am sure they would never think of reading it if it did not happen to be written by one whom they know—& to make that a reason for reading a book out of one's line, is to make friendship a burden. If I could fix on any part as capable of being read with any interest apart from the rest, it would be the fifth book, on Fallacies, & especially the chapter in the sixth book on Liberty & Necessity, which is short & in my judgment the best chapter in the two volumes. However as Sterling will have a copy and will certainly read it through, he will be able to tell your sisters if there is any part which he thinks would interest them—in case they require any opinion besides yours. You will not suspect me of the stupid coxcombry of thinking that they could not understand it, which would be my own condemnation, for if they could not, the book would be a failure. I only mean that whatever be the value of the book, it is (like a book of mathematics) *pure* & not *mixed* science, & never can be liked by any but *students* & I do not want them to spoil themselves by becoming that, on my account —They know that when I write anything on philosophy in the *concrete*, on politics or morals or religion or education or in short anything directly practical or in which feeling & character are concerned I desire very much to be read by them because *there* I can hope really to interest them—but any interest they could feel in this would be only like what I might feel in a treatise on mining.

The last news I have heard about Sterling was not quite so satisfactory as before in respect to rapidity of recovery: will you write a line to me on the matter? Does he think of going away this spring?

Our little girl did not carry her election,[3] but the proxies were not lost,

1. *Envelope addressed*: R. Barclay Fox Esq. / Perran Cottage / Truro. *Postmark*: LS 14 / FE 1843. MS in the possession of Mr. W. H. Browning. Published in Pym, II, 340–41.

2. JSM'S *Logic*.

3. See Letter 372.

but bartered for an equivalent number next June, when Mazzini tells me she is sure of success, that is (I suppose) if those who gave their proxies this time will be kind enough to do so again.

yours ever,

J. S. MILL.

388. TO ALEXIS DE TOCQUEVILLE[1]

le 20 février 1843.

Je vous envoie, mon cher Tocqueville, une letter que j'ai insérée dans le *Morning Chronicle*[2] à votre intention. Je ne sais pas si on la lira, mais je sais qu'elle était bien nécessaire, car ici on donne raison à Lord Brougham contre vous. Les passions en sont aujourd'hui au point où l'on ne regarde plus assez près pour faire des catégories parmi ses adversaires, et l'on fait peser sur les plus modérés la responsabilité des choses les plus folles qu'on croit avoir été faites ou dites par les plus écervelés. Il en est souvent ainsi entre deux partis, à plus forte raison entre deux nations, qui arrivent plus difficilement à s'entendre par des explications mutuelles, et dont chacune lit encore plus exclusivement les organes de son opinion. J'ai souffert de voir la manière dont on envisage ici votre conduite sur ces malheureuses questions de politique extérieure. On ne veut rien voir sinon que vous vous êtes rangé du côté du "war party", et comme on s'attendait à autre chose de votre part, on se venge sur vous de sa propre incapacité de comprendre les idées et les principes qui vous ont inspiré. Cela ne m'étonne point; il est très naturel que les Anglais ne comprennent pas la France, pas plus que les Français ne comprennent l'Angleterre. Vous même n'avez vous pas dit, dans le discours en question, que les Anglais ont trouvé le moyen de chasser la France de l'Espagne? Ne dirait-on pas que comme la plupart de vos compatriotes vous croyez les Anglais tout occupés d'étendre leur territoire et leur importance au dehors? Je vous jure qu'il n'y a pas deux Anglais qui se soient assez occupés de l'Espagne pour avoir un seul instant eu l'idée d'y rivaliser d'influence avec la France. Tout ce que vous voyez à ce sujet dans nos journaux est une affaire d'amour-propre entre Palmerston et Peel, à quoi le public

1. Published in Mayer, pp. 340–41; in reply to Tocqueville's of Feb. 9, *ibid.*, pp. 339–40. MS in Tocqueville archives. Tocqueville protested vigorously against an attack made upon him in the House of Lords on Feb. 2 in a debate on the right of search. Brougham centred his attack on a speech made by Tocqueville in the Chamber of Deputies on Jan. 28, reprinted from the *Moniteur* in his *Œuvres*, ed. Gustave Beaumont (9 vols., Paris, 1864–66), IX, 389–406. Tocqueville's letter to Brougham is in Mayer, pp. 341–42.

2. "Lord Brougham and M. de Tocqueville," Feb. 20, 1843, p. 3.

hausse les épaules. Heureusement notre public ne s'occupe jamais d'affaires étrangères. Sans cela l'Europe serait toujours en feu: voyez ce qui est advenu de ce que nous avons eu, un seul instant, un homme à caractère français à notre Foreign Office. Vous savez que j'aime la France, mais j'avoue qu'il en est assez d'une seule en Europe. Vous voyez que je vous dis franchement ce que je pense, sans craindre de vous offenser et je vous dirai avec la même sincérité que je trouve votre discours admirable et que je ne suis pas éloigné de votre opinion sur la question elle-même. Je crois que si le gouvernement français avait pris dans le commencement le ton que vous lui conseillez, cela aurait pu réussir, mais aujourd'hui ce serait impossible. L'Angleterre ne voudrait pas céder aux provocations et aux menaces des forcenés de la Chambre et du journalisme, soit libéral soit conservateur, la Presse ou le National. Je voudrais qu'on crucifiât le premier homme qui osât dire à la tribune d'un peuple des injures contre un autre peuple. Il faut des générations entières pour guérir le mal que cela peut faire dans un jour. Cela est bien méprisable dans un siècle qui a tant besoin du concours des hommes enérgiques et éclairés de tous les pays avancés pour l'œuvre difficile de réorganiser la société européenne.

Je suis charmé que vous soyez content de M. Hickson:[3] sans être un homme de génie, il est d'un mérite rare et très précieux dans son genre, et je connais peu d'hommes d'un patriotisme et d'une philanthropie plus active et plus éclairée. On le retrouve dans tout ce qui se fait de plus avancé chez nous.

Votre devoué

J. S. MILL.

India House.

389. TO SARAH AUSTIN[1]

India House
28th Feb.
1843

DEAR MRS AUSTIN

I should have answered your letter much sooner, if only on account of the proposal to Parker, but that he told me he would himself write & no doubt you have long since received an answer from him, more explicit as to

3. William Hickson, for whom he had provided a letter of introduction to Tocqueville.

* * * *

1. MS in the possession of Mr. Gordon Waterfield.

details than the answer he gave *me*. The History of the Reformation[2] he thought would not suit him, but the other book you mentioned, he thought would, & was quite willing to close with the project, but did not seem confident as to the sufficiency of such pecuniary terms as the state of the market in his opinion allowed him to offer. And as your doing the thing at all would of course depend upon his making it worth your while, it is for him to make his proposition. *Au reste*, everything I have seen of him is in his favour: pretending to no character but that of a tradesman, he has in every respect in which I have had to do with him acted like a gentleman, while Murray who sets up for a gentleman & a patron of letters seems to be in reality a mere tradesman & not a good one. I believe however this is not the same with the Oxford Parker,[3] so that there may be a chance there if this fails. This one[4] is bookseller to the University of Cambridge.—In the meanwhile I am glad you are going on writing for the Edinburgh which I suspect is more lucrative work than even *your* translating & which you are so well qualified for. I liked your article on Mad. Schopenhauer[5] very much, both as pleasant reading & for the tone of its remarks, which are of a kind very much wanted here, & *now* likely as far as I can judge to be well received, for the eyes of a great number of English people are decidedly opening to much of what is wrong in their own country & comparatively right elsewhere. I hear your article underwent much excision from Napier, & that he wants more painting of manners & less general reflection. I think him wrong, &, as he always is, *arrière*, for the Edinburgh review & the Holland-house set[6] who preside over it are the last refuge of the ideas & tastes of a generation ago; but I suppose his mandates must be complied with, & he has left quite as much of valuable remark in this article as it needed *& more* than is in all the other articles taken together which he published along with it in his exceedingly poor extra number.

What you tell me about Grote does not surprise me though I am sorry for it both on his account & yours. As for Mrs Grote, you know her, & would not expect either good feeling or good taste from her. But Grote has always seemed rather a sensitive person—however he is a disappointed man, & has come to the time of life at which people generally fold their wings & take to their *comforts*. At that stage very few men, in my experience, retain their sympathies at all strongly towards those with whom they are

2. Mrs. Austin's translation of Leopold von Ranke's *History of the Reformation in Germany* was published by Longman in 1844.

3. John Henry Parker (1806–1884), bookseller and writer on architecture.

4. John William Parker, JSM's publisher.

5. See Letter 358, n. 3. The article was a review of books by two German novelists, Johanna Schopenhauer and Caroline Pichler.

6. Holland House, the London home of Henry Fox, Lord Holland, was for forty years the most famous of the Whig salons. For an account of the visitors who came there, see Princess Marie Liechtenstein, *Holland House* (London, 1875), chap. IV.

not in habits of daily intercourse. Perhaps too, half of the evil in Grote is shyness; & not knowing how to *express* sympathy: especially being perhaps in some degree concious of having already shewn less of it than you had reason to expect.—As to the calamity itself,[7] I could have told you months before, all that he *can* have had to tell, but I thought you would know it quite soon enough. The concern has declared itself insolvent & is in the hands of trustees, but from what I hear I do not believe it to be hopeless that something may be saved for the shareholders, though in any such case the probabilities are of course against it. Grote, as you know, habitually looks at the gloomiest side of things. The Mississippi matter[8] however is of much more importance really, as you were deriving no income from the money in the company before, so that in regard to *present* exigencies & interests the loss of the principal is only nominal. The Mississippi bonds I feel satisfied *must* ultimately be paid though I fear not quite so soon as I once thought. In the mean time I cannot help reverting to the idea I once threw out in a letter to you & which you promised to take into consideration at a proper time, & there seems none so proper as now. I really believe something might be done, though it is not very easy to hit upon the exact shape which would be best.

I have sent the remaining sheets of my book, addressed to Mr Austin, in the parcel from Asher's correspondent here (Nutt of Fleet Street) which was made up yesterday. The book is to be published tomorrow. But do not let Mr Austin suppose because the sheets are sent that he is under any engagement to make the use of them which he so kindly proposed. I should of course have sent the book to him in any case & though he would be the best of all reviewers for it he must not plague himself about it. It must take its chance.

I inclose a line from my sister Clara. I have neither encouraged nor opposed her project,[9] of the feasibility of which nobody can so well judge as you. If it be otherwise feasible of course the "cannot" in her note is not to be taken literally, as long as there are others who "can".

Yours affectionately

J. S. MILL.

7. The bankruptcy of an unidentified company in which both the Austins and the Grotes had investments must have been a much harder blow for the Austins than for the Grotes, who were comparatively well to do. The portion of George Grote's letter of Feb., 1843, to John Austin published in Janet Ross, *Three Generations of Englishwomen* (London, 1892), p. 191, throws no light on the matter. Even the Grotes, however, found their losses serious enough as to oblige them to make some retrenchments; Mrs. Grote in a letter to her sister in June, 1843, reported that they had lost £11,000 "by American failures" (see *The Lewin Letters*, ed. T. H. Lewin [2 vols., London, 1909], II, 24).

8. See Letter 331, no. 2.

9. To go to Germany (see Letter 408, postscript).

390. TO AUGUSTE COMTE[1]

India House
le 13 mars 1843

MON CHER MONSIEUR COMTE

Avant de recevoir cette lettre vous aurez sans doute reçu de ma part un exemplaire du livre en faveur duquel vous voulez bien admettre une exception à votre régime cérébral habituel.[2] Je souhaite qu'il mérite une distinction si honorable, et je me félicite toujours davantage de notre heureux rapprochement personnel, sans lequel je n'eusse pas pû espérer d'obtenir, sur mes spéculations philosophiques le seul jugement qui ait pour moi une importance réelle. C'est encore une bonne fortune pour moi que mon livre soit tombé précisément dans ce que vous nommez votre année de repos, et que vous puissiez en prendre connaissance sans déranger aucunement le cours de vos travaux. En sollicitant pour cet ouvrage toute votre indulgence j'ai besoin de vous indiquer que le premier livre date essentiellement de 1829, que le deuxième est un simple *rifaccimento* d'un travail fait en 1832, sauf la polémique contre le représentant de la métaphysique allemande, qui seule est récente; et que le troisième lui-même, où j'entre enfin franchement dans la méthode positive, a été fait, dans tout ce qu'il a de plus essentiel, avant que j'eusse pris connaissance de votre grand travail, même quant à ses premiers volumes. C'est peut-être une chose favorable à l'originalité de mon point de vue philosophique que d'avoir si tard connu ce qui devait exercer sur mon esprit une si grande influence, mais il est bien certain que mon livre en vaut moins, quoique peutêtre il n'en devienne que mieux convenable aux lecteurs qu'il aura. Quant à ses chances de succès vous apprendrez avec plaisir qu'elles se déclarent déjà d'une manière pleinement satisfaisante, en égard à l'apathie spéculative de notre public et à l'opposition tranchée qui existe entre l'esprit de ce livre et celui de la philosophie à la mode. Je commence à espérer que ce livre pourra devenir un vrai point de ralliement philosophique pour cette partie de la jeunesse scientifique anglaise qui ne tient pas beaucoup aux idées religieuses; et je crois cette émancipation essentielle moins rare, même chez nous, qu'elle ne le paraît. Surtout ce livre me semble propre à servir de digne pour arrêter le dangereux progrès de la philosophie allemande. Jusqu'ici cette philosophie nous a été plus utile que nuisible; elle a déterminé chez nous une véritable tendance aux généralités scientifiques et à la systématisation de l'ensemble des connaissances humaines; cela nous manquait presque entièrement, et ne pouvait guère nous arriver par une autre route:

1. MS at Johns Hopkins. Published in Lévy-Bruhl, pp. 165–70; in reply to Comte's of Feb. 27, *ibid.*, pp. 155–65.
2. Comte's practice of not reading other writers' books.

Mais socialement parlant cette philosophie est aujourd'hui chez nous pleinement rétrograde, quelle que soit la tendance sceptique qu'on lui ait reproché d'exercer dans son pays natal, où en effet elle a rempli puissamment une fonction dissolvante envers les anciennes croyances, tandis qu'ici on s'en sert pour retremper philosophiquement ces croyances, contradiction qui ne répugne en rien au caractère vague et arbitraire des prémisses logiques d'une pareille philosophie. Depuis la chute irrévocable de la métaphysique négative, cette philosophie allemande a pû se vanter d'offrir seule à l'esprit humain une coordination systématique de la pensée; elle se prétend supérieure à ses prédécesseurs surtout en ce qu'elle constate tous les phénomènes de la sensibilité et de l'activité humaine, et qu'elle en rend compte à sa manière, tandis que les autres systémes nient tout ce qu'il ne savent pas expliquer selon leurs principes propres: et jusqu'ici, personne n'est venu se planter en face de cet ennemi, en remplissant convenablement les mêmes conditions. Désormais on pourra choisir; on ne sera plus rejeté vers le camp allemand faute de trouver ailleurs un système philosophique nettement formulé. Chez nous aussi le positivisme a déployé son drapeau.

J'attends maintenant avec un vif intérêt les discussions philosophiques qui s'engageront probablement avant peu entre nous deux et qui auront une grande influence sur mes travaux à venir. Il est vrai que très souvent dans mon livre je n'ai fait qu'effleurer les questions où ma manière de penser ne se recontrait pas encore précisément avec la vôtre, et il y en a même que la nature du livre ne m'a pas permis d'aborder. Cependant ce livre vous donnera le moyen de pénétrer assez à fond dans mon esprit, pour que les discussions partielles deviennent beaucoup plus faciles et plus commodes. J'ajourne jusqu'après ces discussions tout projet sérieux de travail nouveau. L'essentiel pour moi, quant à présent, c'est de continuer ma propre éducation philosophique, et je n'écrirai probablement, d'ici à quelque temps, rien de plus important que quelques études historiques d'un ordre secondaire. J'espère du reste recueillir de vos conseils amicaux un grand avantage en ce qui tien à la direction de mon activité intellectuelle, surtout lorsque vous serez mieux en état de juger mon genre de capacité caractéristique. Cette espérance donne un nouvel attrait à mon projet d'aller passer quelques jours auprès de vous, et il ne tiendra pas à moi que ce projet ne s'accomplisse avant la fin du printemps. En ce cas, votre aimable proposition de me recevoir chez vous serait trop agréable pour pouvoir être refusée, d'autant plus que ce serait le moyen de ne perdre, pour le but presque unique de mon voyage, que le moins possible d'un temps nécessairement très raccourci.

Je vous félicite bien cordialement de la terminaison de votre travail classique, qui devait être effectivement pour vous d'autant plus ennuyeux qu'il a été moins fatigant; et je me réjouis avec vous de la reprise de vos promenades habituelles, dont j'apprécie la douceur par ma propre expérience. Comme vous j'ai toujours eu l'habitude de beaucoup marcher, et je prépare toujours les méditations un peu difficiles en me promenant: je trouve cet acte physique tellement favorable à la pensée que même dans mon bureau je marche toujours, ne restant assis que strictement le temps qu'il faut pour écrire des choses déjà préparées debout. Votre traité de géométrie analytique me sera encore plus précieux parce que je le tiendrai de vous-même. Ce trait est vivement attendu non seulement par moi mais encore par un jeune frère[3] dont l'éducation m'a été léguée par mon père et qui par les dispositions scientifiques qu'il montre, jointes à un heureux caractère, m'aide à supporter la perte irréparable d'un autre frère[4] plus âgé, mort en 1840 avant l'âge de vingt ans, noble jeune homme qui a fait le charme des dernières années de mon père et sur l'amitié duquel je comptais pour ma vie tout entière.

Je suis bien sensible à l'honneur que vous me faites en demandant mon avis sur votre project de prendre une connaissance spéciale de la philosophie allemande. Je ne suis pas peutêtre en droit de donner là-dessus une opinion très décidée, n'ayant moi-même lu ni Kant ni Hegel ni aucun autre des chefs de cette école, que je n'ai d'abord connue que par ses interprètes anglais et français. Cette philosophie m'a été, à moi, fort utile; elle a corrigé ce qu'il y avait de trop exclusivement analytique dans mon esprit nourri par Bentham et par les philosophes français du 18me siècle: ajoutez à cela sa critique de l'école négative, et surtout un sens réel quoique trop incomplet des lois historiques et de la filiation des divers états de l'homme et de la société, sens qui est, je crois, le plus développé chez Hegel. Moi j'avais encore besoin de tout cela, et vous ne l'avez pas. Plus tard lorsque j'ai essayé de lire quelques ouvrages philosophiques allemands, il s'est trouvé que je possédais déjà tout ce qu'ils avaient d'utile pour moi, et le reste m'a été fastidieux au point de ne pouvoir pas en continuer la lecture. En me mettant donc à votre place, je doute si cette étude peut vous offrir un avantage suffisant pour décider en sa faveur une infraction à votre hygiène cérébrale, et je ne sache pas qu'une connaissance plus exacte des points de rapport entre cette doctrine et la vôtre puisse vous servir de grand chose dans vos travaux. Je crois que pour être lu et goûté en Allemagne, ce qu'il faut est surtout l'esprit systématique; cet esprit vous le possédez au suprême degré: et votre véritable point de contact avec les philosophes allemands est dans les faits concrets que vous expliquez bien tandis qu'ils les expliquent mal. Cependant j'approuve beaucoup votre dessein d'apprendre la langue allemande afin de lire les grands poètes de ce peuple. Les poésies lyriques de Goethe surtout me semblent dignes des plus beaux temps de l'antiquité

3. George Mill.
4. Henry Mill.

par la perfection de la forme, et souvent bien supérieures par le fond, comme la matière esthétique moderne l'est à l'ancienne.

Je n'ai pas besoin de dire que je verrai avec grand plaisir Mazhar Effendi,[5] et que tout ce que je puis faire pour lui pendant son séjour ici lui est d'avance assuré.

tout à vous

J. S. MILL

391. TO GEORGE BENTHAM[1]

India House
14th March
1843

DEAR MR BENTHAM

I was very glad to see your handwriting again, though the mere fact of sending my book[2] did not require or merit any acknowledgment from you. My object in writing to you now is to ask whether you are making or likely to make an *English* herbarium or whether you care about having English specimens because if you do I am likely to be thinking a little of botany this year & being in a different part of England from that in which you are now fixed,[3] I should be much pleased by being permitted to collect specimens for you. Any that I already have I need hardly say I should be most happy to send but they amount to so little compared with what I should like & might hope to do that I hardly like to offer them. If however you would give me what lawyers call a roving commission, I would do my best.

You probably have abundance of the Edinburgh Catalogues. However I enclose one in case you should be willing to take the trouble of returning it to me after marking any plants of which you might wish to have other *English* specimens from the south east parts of England. I could also send you a catalogue of Surrey plants & their habitats, tolerably large though very incomplete, being derived solely from my own individual observations —it would shew you what the plants are that I could most readily procure from this neighbourhood.

ever truly yours

J. S. MILL

5. Comte in his letter of Feb. 27 bespoke JSM's help for him as a former pupil who has become an official in charge of public works in Egypt and who plans to visit England to gain technical information.

* * * *

1. MS at Kew.

2. The *Logic*.

3. George Bentham in 1841 had moved to Pontrilas House, Hereford. Previously, from 1834, he had lived in the house in Queen Square which he had inherited from his uncle Jeremy.

392. TO GEORGE BENTHAM[1]

India House
24th March
1843

DEAR MR BENTHAM—I am sorry you troubled yourself to send back the Catalogue, not having marked it. I will keep on the lookout for the rare Orchidiae &c. I fear none of those I have from Surrey &c. are decidedly rare ones. I collected a few rather rare species in Italy, the orchis romana, papilionacea provincalis, & a few other plants almost peculiar to the Roman Campagna—the rarest, I believe, being the Vicia tricolor. Nothing but the persuasion that you must certainly have all these has prevented me from long since offering you them or any others I have. If any of the two or three I have mentioned would be of the least value to you I should feel really obliged by your saying so, as I should try anything else however trifling which you would put it in my power to do for you or yours.

I am very glad you are occupied in aiding the completion of the Prodromus as you have already done so essentially by your settlement of the Labiatae & Scrophulariacea.[2] I am always to be seen or heard of here at 18 Kensington Square & though I am not often at the Athenaeum without some special cause, your being to be met with there would be cause sufficient.

ever truly yours

J. S. MILL

393. TO SIR EDWARD LYTTON BULWER[1]

India House
27th March
1843

MY DEAR SIR LYTTON

You very much overpraise my rather ambitious attempt, but I am very glad that you find enough in the book[2] to repay the trouble of reading and I shall be amply satisfied if it is found to deserve half the good you say of it. I hope you may have time to give me the benefit of the doubts & suggestions you speak of. I can say quite sincerely & I believe from sufficient

1. MS at Kew.
2. In his *Labiatarum Genera et Species* . . . (London, 1832–36) and other publications. See the bibliography of his scientific publications in B. Daydon Jackson, *George Bentham* (London, 1906), pp. 269–84.

* * * *

1. MS in the possession of Lady Hermione Cobbold. Collated by Dr. Eileen Curran. Published in Elliot, I, 123–24.
2. The *Logic*.

self-knowledge that I value the pointing out of an error more highly than any amount of praise.

I am afraid the proposition that Morality is an Art, not a Science, will hardly be found on closer examination to have so much in it as you seem to have thought was intended. It follows as a necessary corollary from my particular mode of using the word Art, but at bottom I fancy it is merely what everybody thinks, expressed in new language.

You would find Comte exceedingly well worth your better knowledge. I do not always agree in his opinions but so far as I know he seems to me by far the first speculative thinker of the age.

Yours very truly

J.S. MILL

394. TO JOHN AUSTIN[1]

I.H.
Saturday
[Spring, 1843?]

MY DEAR AUSTIN

Your opinion of my Logic is very gratifying to me.

I have read the little tract which you sent me from Mr Ramsay.[2] There is much good in it; evidence of many right opinions & feelings & of some sound knowledge. The chief fault seems to me that of entire unpracticalness.

I cannot surmise from it of what character Mr Ramsay's ethical book[3] may be, but if it falls in my way I will certainly make myself acquainted with it.

Yours ever truly

J. S. MILL

395. TO AUGUSTE COMTE[1]

India House
le 20 avril 1843.

MON CHER MONSIEUR COMTE

Aussitôt que j'ai appris par votre lettre du 25 mars que mon livre ne vous était pas encore parvenu, j'ai pris des informations chez l'éditeur, et j'ai trouvé que par un retard du libraire Dulau qui s'en était chargé, le paquet ne

1. MS at LSE.

2. Probably George (later Sir George) Ramsay (1800–1871), philosophical writer. The tract in question has not been identified.

3. *An Enquiry into the Principles of Human Happiness and Human Duty* (London, 1843).

* * * *

1. MS at Johns Hopkins. Published in Lévy-Bruhl, pp. 178–83; in reply to Comte's of March 25, *ibid.*, pp. 171–78.

devait partir que le 30. Je me suis depuis assuré qu'en effet il est parti ce jour-là, et j'espère que l'exemplaire est entre vos mains depuis 15 jours. Dans le cas contraire c'est Bossange, du quai Voltaire, qui vous en répondra. Ces sortes de délais, auxquelles je suis fort habitué, indiquent, ainsi que le port monstrueux qu'on vous a demandé, un état de véritable barbarie dans l'organisation matérielle du commerce intellectuel entre nos deux pays. Quant aux difficultés fiscales je crois que la faute est du côté de notre gouvernement, qui, suivant l'esprit national, n'a jamais vu dans la propagation de la pensée autre chose qu'une industrie particulière, et n'a pas plus songé à faciliter l'envoi des livres par la poste, que celui des draps; pas plus dans l'intérieur qu'avec l'étranger. Toutefois, puisque nous sommes entrés depuis quelques ans dans la voie des réformes postales, je crois que nous adopterons bientôt dans cette matière spéciale un régime plus civilisé. La disposition d'esprit qui permet de pareilles mesquineries change tous les jours: nous sommes à cet égard en plein progrès; et la préoccupation absolue des intérêts industriels que naguère on pouvait encore regarder comme nationale, est déjà très généralement flétrie comme indice d'un esprit étroit et d'une éducation inférieure. La génération actuelle vaut mieux, à mille égards, que celle qui l'a précédée. On respire un air bien plus libre et plus pur que dans ma première jeunesse.

Je vous remercie mille fois de l'envoie de votre ouvrage classique.[2] J'aurais volontiers commencé, selon vos conseils, par une première lecture très rapide, mais je n'avais pas d'abord assez de loisir continu pour cela, et je tenais à commencer sans délai; ensuite, j'ai perdu depuis si longtemps l'habitude des lectures mathématiques ou du moins algébriques, que j'eusse craint de ne pas saisir réellement l'esprit du livre si je ne m'attachais pas à y suivre, avec connaissance de cause, tous les calculs. Ainsi que beaucoup de ceux qui s'occupent habituellement de méditations générales, j'ai la mémoire très mauvaise pour toute sorte de détails, même scientifiques; et quoique je retrouve toujours avec une grande facilité tout ce que j'ai une fois appris, je ne puis jamais présumer avec sûreté de la suffisance de mes connaissances actuelles d'un sujet quelconque lorsqu'elles ne sont pas d'acquisition récente. Je me suis donc mis à travailler comme un écolier à votre ouvrage, et je me flatte que je serai bientôt capable de subir passablement un examen assez approfondi à son sujet. Malgré la lenteur inévitable de cette manière de lire, je n'ai pas manqué d'apercevoir dans l'ouvrage cette sorte de symétrie qui fait d'un traité scientifique parfait, en quelque façon un ouvrage d'art, et je ne doute point d'éprouver encore davantage ce sentiment à une seconde lecture exclusivement dirigée à l'appréciation de l'ensemble. Sous le rapport logique, je connaissais assez votre merveilleuse puissance de généralisation philosophique pour ne m'étonner nulle-

2. See Letter 383, n. 2.

ment à trouver dans votre manière de traiter ce sujet spécial un vrai modèle de ce que sera un jour l'enseignement mathématique comme moyen d'éducation des facultés spéculatives de l'homme. Mais j'avoue que malgré la profonde impression faite sur moi par le premier volume de votre grand ouvrage, je n'avais pas senti aussi profondément que je la sens maintenant, l'aptitude éminent de l'analyse mathématique, convenablement étudiée, pour développer l'esprit scientifique. Il est bien fâcheux que jusqu'ici cette heureuse qualité soit non seulement neutralisée mais vraiment tournée en sens contraire par la routine irrationnelle qui préside partout à l'éducation mathématique. Votre ouvrage aura ici un lecture diligent dans la personne de Sir William Molesworth, que vous connaissez peutêtre de nom comme ayant fait les frais intellectuels et pécuniaires de la belle édition des œuvres de Hobbes,[3] dont vous avez fait une mention honorable dans une note de votre 5me volume. Sir William Molesworth, d'ailleurs admirateur éclairé de votre grand ouvrage, a fait de fortes études scientifiques. Il s'occupe beaucoup à présent de philosophie mathématique, et comme il a une véritable capacité scientifique, malgré une certaine raideur intellectuelle qui gêne un peu la marche de son intelligence, je m'efforce de le décider à faire un livre à ce sujet, en attendant celui que vous avez annoncé et que vous avez dû ajourner à un avenir un peu lointain. J'espère qu'il se trouvera bientôt parmi la jeunesse scientifique française des penseurs capable de régénérer, sous l'inspiration de vos ouvrages et de votre conversation, les diverses branches de l'enseignement mathématique, travail si important que bien qu'il ne puisse pas vous appartenir, voué comme vous l'êtes à des travaux encore plus élevés, le temps que vous avez consacré à en fournir un premier exemple décisif n'est certainement pas mal employé. Votre projet primitif d'écrire votre cours populaire d'astronomie offrait une utilité analogue, et j'aurais regretté que ce projet fût abandonné si je ne craignais, pour une santé si précieuse l'effet d'un nouveau travail sédentaire pendant l'année naturellement destinée à raffermir vos forces physiques pour la noble tâche qui vous attend. Ne se pourrait-il pas que, dans l'impossibilité où vous vous trouvez d'écrire vos divers cours, quelqu'un de ceux qui ont l'avantage de les suivre le fit à votre place, comme on l'a fait quelquefois pour d'autres professeurs? Une simple révision par vous-même pourrait alors suffire, et le succès pécuniaire ne manquerait guère de récompenser suffisamment le travail du rédacteur.

Je trouve que vous avez sagement fait en renonçant à votre velléité passagère de vous occuper de la philosophie des allemands et en vous bornant

3. *The English Works of Thomas Hobbes of Malmesbury*, ed. Sir William Molesworth (11 vols., London, 1839–45). Also, *Thomae Hobbes Malmesburiensis Opera philosophica quae Latine scripsit omnia . . .* , ed. Sir William Molesworth (5 vols., London, 1839–45).

à leur poésie, dans laquelle Goethe est comme vous le sentez déjà, sans rival. Je crois pourtant que le jugement sévère que vous portez sur Schiller[4] n'est pleinement mérité que pour la première moitié de ses écrits, très hautement condamnés par lui-même à un âge plus mûr. Vous trouveriez peut être dans son Wallenstein, dans sa Jeanne d'Arc, dans son Guillaume Tell, et dans ses poésies lyriques une capacité poétique réele quoique de second ordre, et une ombre même du génie créateur de Goethe, avec une élévation morale que généralement on ne reconnaît pas dans ce dernier, ou qui du moins est loin d'y être aussi saillante. Il y a de très belles choses dans Richter,[5] dans Tieck,[6] etc. mais le plus souvent sous la forme du roman en prose. Les romans de Goethe sont au contraire, à mon avis, ce qu'il a fait de moins bon, soit par la forme, soit même par le fond, quoiqu'il y ait semé une foule de pensées justes et profondes et qu'on y trouve un grand nombre de tableaux d'une poésie admirable.

Je me promets d'écrire incessamment à M. Balard que j'espère aussi voir si, comme je le désire, ma visite domiciliaire chez vous s'accomplit avant la fin du printemps. Il se peut toutefois que je sois forcé de l'ajourner jusqu'au mois d'octobre, aussitôt après la terminaison de votre tournée officielle. Dans ce cas-là je crains que M. Balard ne soit plus à Paris quand j'y serai.

Je n'ai pas encore vu Mazhar Effendi, qui probablement n'est pas arrivé. Je l'attends avec un grand intérêt.

Votre dévoué

J. S. MILL.

J'allais oublier de vous dire qu'en lisant votre ouvrage j'ai trouvé dans les formules un assez grand nombre d'erreurs typographiques dont je vous donnerai si vous voulez la liste.

396. TO JOHN STERLING[1]

I.H.
26 April [1843]

I do not write to you, my dear Sterling, with any such vain notion as of attempting to offer you any comfort under the double blow[2] which has

4. Comte in his letter of March 23, 1843 (Lévy-Bruhl, p. 175), had written: "le fameux Schiller ne m'a jamais paru, d'après les traductions, qu'une sorte de gauche imitateur du grand Shakespeare, bien plutôt qu'un vrai poète; sa niaise sentimentalité métaphysique, réchauffée par l'influence de Rousseau, m'est d'ailleurs insupportable."
5. Johann Paul Friedrich Richter (1763–1825), German novelist and humorist.
6. Johann Ludwig Tieck (1773–1853), German poet, dramatist, and novelist.

* * * *

1. MS at Leeds. Published in Elliot, I, 124–25. The year has been pencilled in in another hand.
2. Sterling's mother had died on April 16; his wife, two days later.

fallen upon you—the first so hard, the last so much harder—though I hardly know among possible things any which I would not do or which it would not be the truest joy to me to do if it could help to lighten your burden either of grief or of care. But it is a kind of mockery to talk of the great things one will never have the power of doing—it is only little things one has the opportunity to be useful in, & little enough in *them.* Heaven knows there are few things which we, here, can do for you, & we have little claim to be preferred to others in regard to even those few; but I know how oppressive small cares are when they come on the back of great sufferings, & if any here could assist in relieving you from even the smallest of those, I do not believe you know, or can know, how pleasant it would be to do and how pleasant to think of when done. And with so many young creatures in your charge and your own health requiring so much care, even we might sometimes and in some ways be able to give useful help without intruding into the place of any who might be equally desirous & more capable. If it should be so, it will be real friendship & kindness in you to give us the opportunity. Do not think of writing in answer to this unless it be to tell us of something that can be done—but by & by, when you are better able, we shall wish very much to hear what your plans are both for yourself & the children & if possible, to be in some, if even the smallest degree, included in them.

Ever most affectionately,

J. S. MILL.

397. TO SIR JOHN F. W. HERSCHEL[1]

India House,
1st May 1843

MY DEAR SIR,

Permit me to acknowledge with much pleasure your kind note, which deserves much more of thanks than my sending you the book, since that was due to the very great help I derived from your speculations in writing it. You will find that the most important chapter of the book,[2] that on the four Experimental Methods, is little more than an expansion & a more scientific statement of what you had previously stated in the more popular manner suited to the purpose of your "Introduction."[3] Besides, you were,

1. MS in the possession of the Royal Society and published with its permission.
2. The *Logic.*
3. Herschel's *A Preliminary Discourse on the Study of Natural Philosophy* (London, 1831), which constituted "The Introduction or Preface to the Cabinet of Natural Philosophy" in Dionysius Lardner's *Cabinet Cyclopædia* (133 vols., London, 1830–49). JSM had reviewed it favourably in the *Examiner,* March 20, 1831, pp. 179–80.

perhaps, of all living Englishmen, the one by whom I was most desirous that my book should be judged, since most of those who would be competent judges of the metaphysical part are not thoroughly competent in the physical, and conversely.

Mr. Beneke's book[4] I have heard of & intend to read. I feel little doubt of your finding Comte's book worthy your better knowledge. It is a book very likely to be undervalued on a partial inspection, especially as those of his opinions which are most objectionable to most Englishmen (& now I believe even to Frenchmen) lie on the surface.

I am so conscious of superficiality in many of the departments of knowledge from which I have been forced to gather materials for attempting to methodize the process of investigating truth, that I should be very grateful if you could, without encroaching on time which is more valuably employed, note down some of the many errors I must have committed as well as of the important ideas I must have missed. It is very uncertain if I shall ever have an opportunity of improving the book by any such memoranda but for my own instruction I should value them much and could make them useful in other ways.

Believe me
Yours with great respect
J. S. MILL.

398. TO AUGUSTE COMTE[1]

India House
le 15 juin 1843

MON CHER MONSIEUR COMTE—

Je me reproche un peu d'avoir tant retardé ma réponse à vos deux lettres si pleines d'intérêt, lettres qui avaient droit à la réponse la plus prompte, et qui l'auraient sans doute obtenue de moi dans l'état normal de mes facultés mentales; mais j'éprouve, pour toute communication avec vous, le besoin, ou du moins le désir, de me sentir dans la plénitude de mes forces, et je suis tombé au contraire depuis quelque temps dans une sorte de langueur intellectuelle, pour ne pas dire morale, qui tient, à ce que je crois, surtout à des causes physiques. Sans aucune maladie bien définie, j'éprouve une faiblesse nerveuse et une affection quasi-fébrile chronique

4. Probably Friedrich Eduard Beneke's *System der Logik als Kunstlehre des Denkens* (2 vols., Berlin, 1842).

* * * *

1. *Addressed*: Monsieur / Auguste Comte / 10 Rue M. le Prince / près l'Odéon / à Paris. *Postmark*: 15 JU 15 / 1843. MS at Johns Hopkins. Published in Lévy-Bruhl, pp. 204–10; in reply to Comte's of May 16 and May 28, *ibid.*, pp. 183–204.

que j'ai, du reste, ressentie à diverses époques antérieures de ma vie, et que je connais assez familièrement pour savoir qu'elle ne durera pas longtemps. Le meilleur moyen de me rétablir entièrement serait, je crois, un voyage de quelques mois, mais à dèfaut d'un pareil remède, qui en effet me serait à peu près impossible, je suis sûr de retrouver peu à peu ma santé ordinaire si rien ne m'arrive de nature à l'affaiblir davantage. Les médecins me conseillent en attendant de ne travailler que le moins possible, mais je ne suivrai leur conseil qu'autant que ma propre expérience peut m'en faire reconnaître la nécessité, la médecine ne me paraissant pas être parvenue à un état de positivité assez parfaite pour que la liberté de conscience ait encore cessé dans cet ordre d'idées.

Pour en venir à des choses plus importantes, je vous remercie bien vivement de m'avoir donné de si amples détails sur un sujet que vous avez cru avec raison devoir être pour moi du plus vif intérêt, celui de la lutte que vous avez eu à subir lors de votre réélection.[2] Dans l'intervalle de vos deux lettres j'ai beaucoup réfléchi sur l'issue possible de cette lutte et sur la manière dont il y aurait lieu d'organiser la transition que peutêtre il vous faudra opérer de votre position présente à une autre qui ne serait plus pénible qu'en ce qu'elle serait d'abord plus précaire. L'heureuse terminaison, au moins momentanée, de cette crise, me dispense de vous entretenir aujourd'hui des diverses choses qui me sont passées par la tête, au sujet surtout de la conduite à tenir par vos amis dans le cas où l'affaire aurait tourné autrement. J'ai besoin pourtant de vous dire une chose qui est de celles qu'on peut dire hardiment lorsqu'on s'adresse à un caractère aussi supérieur à toute fausse délicatesse qu'incapable de manquer à la vraie: C'est que, quelque avenir qui vous soit réservé, toute pensée de détresse matérielle réelle vous est interdite, aussi longtemps que je vivrai et que j'aurai un sou à partager avec vous. Je crois même qu'après votre première lettre j'aurais osé vous faire en ce sens une proposition spéciale, sans certains éventualités personnelles, qui seront sans doute décidées avant l'époque de la réélection de l'an prochain et dont l'issue influera nécessairement beaucoup sur la proposition à faire. Comme ces éventualités se décideront probablement en peu de temps j'aime mieux en ajourner l'explication jusqu'à ce que je puisse vous en annoncer en même temps le résultat, qui au reste ne saurait, quel qu'il soit, m'ôter la faculté de servir d'abri temporaire, s'il y a lieu, à celui qui de tous les hommes vivants, honorerait le plus une pareille offre en l'acceptant.

Quant à ce qui dans votre lettre me regarde personnellement, il est presque superflu de vous dire avec quelle satisfaction profonde j'ai appris l'accueil que vous avez donné à mon travail philosophique, et la haute approbation que vous en témoignez, approbation propre à remplir mes

2. The renewal of his annual appointment at the Ecole Polytechnique.

désirs les plus ambitieux, et qui dépasse de beaucoup mes espérances. Vous devez bien sentir que votre opinion, sur la valeur de cet écrit, est la seule qui pouvait notablement influer sur la mienne propre, tandis que celle-ci n'était, et ne pouvait être que provisoire, tant que la partie vraiement positive et dogmatique de l'ouvrage n'avait pas reçu la sanction du juge le plus compétent, et même jusqu'ici le seul compétent, dans les questions quelconques de méthodologie systématique. Maintenant que cette sanction si précieuse lui est acquise, il m'est permis de me féliciter de l'assurance désormais inébranlable que je possède, d'être pour quelque chose non seulement dans la propagation initiale mais même dans la fondation de la philosophie finale, quelque modeste que soit la part qui m'appartienne dans cette noble œuvre. Nous pouvons aussi nous réjouir ensemble de l'heureux augure à retirer pour cette philosophie d'un tel accord spontané entre deux esprits qui seuls jusqu'ici se sont sérieusement occupés d'organiser la méthode positive, aprés une préparation convenable ou même passable, et qui partant de points très éloignés l'un de l'autre et ne se réunissant qu'à deux tiers du chemin, se trouvent pourtant en harmonie sur tous les points essentiels. Un pareil accord serait à lui seul une preuve presque suffisante de la vérité et même de l'opportunité de la nouvelle philosophie, en fesant juger qu'elle est propre à déterminer de vraies convictions dans tout esprit qui réunira les conditions nécessaires de connaissances positives et de capacité intellectuelle primitive.

Rassuré dorénavant quant aux questions de méthode, où je ne crains plus aucune divergence sérieuse, soit sur la théorie générale de la positivité, soit sur son application spéciale aux études sociales, je n'ai plus qu'à souhaiter un accord également parfait à l'égard des doctrines sociales. Jusqu'ici cet accord existe surtout par rapport à la partie de vos doctrines qui plus que toute autre vous appartient en propre. Je parle des lois générales de la dynamique sociale et du développement historique de l'humanité, en y comprenant les corollaires pratiques si importants qui en dérivent, et dont le plus essentiel est à mes yeux le grand principe de la séparation des deux pouvoirs. A l'égard des doctrines de la sociologie statique, que vous n'avez pas inventées mais bien acceptées des anciennes théories sociales, quoique vous les ayez soutenues avec votre énergie accoutumée de conviction philosophique, il y a encore entre nous des dissentiments réels. Ces dissentiments ne tiennent, sans doute, à plusieurs égards, qu'à ce que je n'ai pas encore atteint un état de conviction complette sur des choses qui sont à vos yeux démontrées. Tout en reconnaissant pleinement, par exemple, la nécessité sociale des institutions fondamentales de la propriété et du mariage, et en n'admettant aucune utopie sur l'un ou sur l'autre sujet, je suis cependant très porté à croire que ces deux institutions peuvent être destinées à subir de plus graves modifications que vous ne le semblez penser, bien que je me sente totalement inhabile à prévoir ce qu'elles seront.

Je vous ai déjà dit que la question du divorce est pour moi indécise, malgré la puissante argumentation de votre 4me volume, et je suis atteint d'une hérésie plus fondamentale encore, puisque je n'admets pas en principe la subordination nécessaire d'un sexe à l'autre. Vous voyez qu'il nous reste encore des questions d'importance majeure à discuter entre nous, discussion qu'il serait au reste fort oiseux d'entamer à la fin d'une lettre. Ces matières tombent précisément dans la partie de votre grande entreprise philosophique qui va vous occuper le plus prochainement, et dans laquelle cet ordre de questions obtiendra naturellement une discussion plus approfondie que dans votre grand ouvrage.

Je suis bien heureux que mon livre vous paraisse capable d'être utile aussi en France, pourvu qu'il soit convenablement traduit en français, et je suis forcé à croire que je pourrais moi-même exécuter cette traduction, puisque vous ne m'en jugez pas incapable. Ce serait cependant pour moi un travail très pénible et très ennuyeux, car si j'écris passablement la langue française, je suis loin de l'écrire avec facilité: j'ai d'ailleurs lieu de croire que la chose sera faite sans que je m'en mêle. Avant l'impression du livre, notre ami Marrast a exprimé, avec une persistance amicale à laquelle j'a dû céder, le désir de le traduire en français, et quoique, suivant ma prévision, il n'a pas trouvé le loisir nécessaire pour une pareille occupation, il vient de me mander que le livre est entre les mains d'un des professeurs de Paris les plus distingués "qui," dit-il, "profitera de ses premiers loisirs pour le traduire." M. Marrast ne m'a pas encore dit le nom de ce professeur, mais il vous le dira sans doute, et l'intérêt que vous voulez bien porter à cette entreprise aura peut-être sur son exécution une heureuse influence.[3]

Veuillez dire à M. de Blainville[4] combien je me sens flatté de l'attention dont cet illustre savant veut bien honorer mon ouvrage. Quel que puisse être son jugement éventuel sur ce livre, je mettrai toujours un grand prix à avoir été lu par un homme que j'ai appris de vous à estimer si profondément. Je me réjouis avec vous de l'honorable conduite de M. Poinsot[5] dans la crise que vous avez subie. J'ai rempli votre commission auprès de Sir William Molesworth qui aura, j'espère, un jour l'avantage de vous connaître plus directement.

Votre dévoué

J. S. MILL.

3. Comte replied that he now saw little of Marrast and did not know who the professor was; he further warned JSM against blindly entrusting the translation of the *Logic* to someone who might be hostile to positivism (Lévy-Bruhl, p. 215). On Dec. 23 Comte reported that the professor in question was a M. Mallet, professor of philosophy at the Collège de Saint-Louis (*ibid.*, p. 293) [Charles Auguste Mallet (1807–1876)]. Mallet did not translate the *Logic*.

4. Henri Marie Ducrotay de Blainville (1777–1850), eminent naturalist.

5. Louis Poinsot (1777–1859), mathematician, secretary of the Academy of Science.

399. TO ROBERT BARCLAY FOX[1]

I.H.
Thursday
[Probably June or July 1843][2]

MY DEAR BARCLAY—

Could you not manage on your way to Cornwall (which will be I suppose by the Great Western Railway) to halt for a day & see my sisters, who are at Marlow, only 5 or 6 miles from the Maidenhead Station? It would be a great pleasure to them & would not detain you long.

I wish we could prevail on Mr & Mrs Charles Fox[3] to do the same—& I wish I could see them. How long do they remain in town?

ever yours
J. S. MILL.

400. TO AUGUSTE COMTE[1]

India House
le 13 juillet 1843

MON CHER MONSIEUR COMTE—

J'espère que cette lettre vous atteindra avant le commencement de votre tournée officielle, qui du reste ne suspendra pas sans doute notre correspondance, et je ne doute pas qu'à quelque temps d'ici je serai plus en état de vous écrire convenablement. Le dérangement passager que je vous ai annoncé dans ma dernière lettre, de ma santé morale et physique, ne s'est pas encore terminé, tandis que le remède que vous jugez avec raison être le mieux assorti à cette situation, celui d'un voyage de quelques mois, me semble plus éloigné que jamais. Il ne s'ensuit point cependant que je ne puisse pas me permettre une absence de quelques jours, et si mes espérances, à cet égard, ne sont pas trompées, je compte toujours passer auprès de vous un court intervale vers la fin d'octobre. Quant au conseil amical que vous me donnez, de me distraire autant que possible, ce conseil est un peu difficile à suivre, par la raison que j'ai le malheur, si c'en est un, d'être très peu amusable. Je ne suis guère capable de goûter

1. MS in the possession of Mr. W. H. Browning.
2. The only evidence for dating this letter is that in his letter of Oct. 23 (Letter 408) JSM refers to a visit of Barclay Fox to London earlier in the year, and that Barclay appears to have been absent from Falmouth in June and July.
3. Barclay Fox's uncle and aunt, of Trebah, near Falmouth.

* * * *

1. MS at Johns Hopkins. Published in Lèvy-Bruhl, pp. 219–25; in reply to Comte's of June 29, *ibid.*, pp. 210–19.

longtemps aucun délassement, à moins qu'il ne se rattache, et même assez directement, à un grave intérêt quelconque, et surtout à l'ensemble de mes occupations sérieuses: j'ajouterai même que le demi-travail intellectuel qui a toujours été mon principal amusement, n'a le pouvoir de m'intéresser longtemps qu'à la condition d'une alternation rapide avec le travail complet. Dans un état de faiblesse chronique qui m'empêche de sérieusement travailler, ma nature et mes habitudes ne comportent guère d'autre remède efficace qu'un voyage, et celui-là n'est pas à ma portée. Cependant il n'y a pas là de quoi vous inquiéter sur ma santé à venir car dans le cas où ce mal chronique viendrait à s'empirer beaucoup, les obstacles cesseraient probablement, et je pourrais m'éloigner pour un temps plus ou moins prolongé. A présent même, tout irait mieux si je me trouvais dans l'état normal de mes occupations intellectuelles, c.à.d. occupé à suivre un travail commencé, ou même une série de travaux homogènes; mais je ne me sens pas momentanément la vigueur d'esprit et de volonté nécessaire pour entrer dans un nouvel ordre quelconque de travaux.

Cette même raison me défend aussi d'entamer dès à présent, comme je l'aurais désiré, la discussion sérieuse des graves questions sociales sur lesquelles nos opinions ne s'accordent pas encore. La confiance que vous m'exprimez que cette divergence d'opinion ne sera que passagère est pour moi un nouveau témoignage de la haute estime que j'ai eu le bonheur d'obtenir de vous et dont il me serait très pénible de voir la moindre diminution. En effet, nous qui sommes si pleinement d'accord sur l'ensemble de la méthode scientifique et qui sommes, j'ose le dire, également émancipés à l'égard des préjugés quelconques, soit révolutionnaires, soit conservateurs; si nous ne devions pas nous accorder finalement sur les questions dont il s'agit, notre dissentiment serait presque une preuve que les principes biologiques dont dépend en dernier ressort la solution de ces questions, ne sont pas encore suffisamment mûris, ce qui assurément ne serait pas fort étonnant, vû la positivité si récente et si imparfaite des hautes études biologiques. Je crains pourtant que notre dissidence n'ait des racines plus profondes que celles que vous me signalez dans votre lettre. Je partage complètement votre manière de penser sur la tendance de notre époque à régler par les lois ce qui ne devrait dépendre que des mœurs, aberration fort naturelle dans une époque de transition sociale, où l'on respecte si peu les institutions qu'on les crée ou les détruit avec la même légèreté, tandis que le défaut de croyances communes prive l'opinion générale de sa force normale de répression morale. Je ne crois pas être atteint, dans le cas dont il s'agit, de cette tendance irrationnelle, et je ne prétends nullement à décider quelles devraient être les lois sur l'association domestique, ni que ces lois doivent être autres qu'elles ne sont. Ce que nous aurions à vider entre nous serait précisément la question de mœurs: si nous pouvions nous accorder là dessus, je crois que nous nous rencontrerions bien facilement à l'égard des institutions. En attendant, ce que j'aurais à dire à l'appui de mon hérésie principale serait tiré tout entier de principes biologiques, très imparfaits sans doute, ce qui peut tenir à l'insuffisance de mes connaissances en biologie, mais peut être aussi à l'insuffisance actuelle de la théorie biologique elle même, dans sa partie la plus directement applicable aux spéculations sociologiques. Il se peut même que je mérite d'être rangé parmi ceux que vous avez caractérisés par une phrase de votre lettre, celle où vous parlez de ceux dont le cœur est complice des déviations intellectuelles. Quant à cela, vous en jugerez; toujours est-il que, tout en repoussant, de toutes les forces de mon esprit, l'anarchique doctrine des temps révolutionnaires, hautement contradictoire à l'ensemble de l'expérience humaine, que l'attachement, même passionné, exige l'absence d'autorité, et croyant comme je le crois fermement que dans l'état normal des relations humaines une sympathie réelle et réciproque peut et doit exister entre le protecteur et le protégé, et peut exister même entre l'esclave et le maître, je ne trouve pourtant pas que toutes les sympathies doivent être d'inégalité: je ne crois pas que ce soit là leur dernier mot et je crois qu'il y a place aussi pour l'égalité dans les affections humaines. Je ne la crois incompatible avec l'harmonie que chez les natures inférieures, les plus livrées aux penchants égoïstes, ou au moins lorsque l'une des deux natures est de cette espèce. Sans aucune vaine sentimentalité, je trouve que l'affection qu'une personne d'une nature un peu élevée peut éprouver pour un être réellement subordonné à son autorité, a toujours quelque chose d'imparfait, dont on ne se contente qu'à désespoir de pouvoir placer ailleurs une sympathie plus complète. Il est très possible qu'en ceci je juge trop la nature humaine d'après la mienne propre, qui, à plusieurs égards, est peut-être exceptionnelle. Mais voici en quoi je ne crois pas que je puisse me tromper: c'est que pour décider cet ordre de questions la philosophie a besoin de l'expérience des femmes autant que de celle des hommes, et cette expérience elle ne l'a pas encore. Ce n'est guère que d'avant-hier que les femmes pensent, ce n'est que d'hier qu'elles disent leurs pensées, et, ce qui est plus important encore, leur expérience de la vie: le plupart de celles qui écrivent, écrivent pour les hommes, ou du moins ont peur de leur désapprobation, et on ne peut pas plus se fier au témoignage de celles-là qu'à celui du très petit nombre de celles qui sont en état de rébellion ouverte. Or il me semble que l'influence sur la vie intime et morale, d'une relation quelconque de dépendance ne peut pas se décider uniquement sur les idées et sur l'expérience des supérieurs. Ceci ressemble, je le sais, à une idée émise par les saint-simoniens, à qui, en effet, je reproche surtout qu'après avoir proclamé leur propre incompétence à décider les grandes questions sociales qu'ils ont soulevées, ils ont eu la folie ou la charlatanerie d'en offrir une prétendue solution, dont ils avaient ainsi eux mêmes reconnu d'avance l'absurdité. Je n'avais pas, en commençant cette lettre, l'intention d'y tant dire sur ce sujet, mais je compte vous soumettre petit à petit tout ce que je trouve à dire là dessus, comme à mon frère aîné, pour ne rien dire de plus, en philosophie.

Je me félicite de la manière fraternelle dont vous avez accueilli une offre qui ne méritait pas la qualification que vous lui avez donnée de généreuse, puisque je me serais senti avili à mes propres yeux en ne la fesant point. En effet, pensant ce que je pense de vous, et du rôle que vous remplissez dans notre époque et même en ne comptant pour rien notre amitié, si je vous savais dans la détresse ou même en danger d'y tomber, et qu'ayant les moyens de vous en retirer je n'en usais point pour quel usage les réserverais-je? Je sens comme vous que ce devoir appartiendrait normalement à d'autres que moi, et je ne prétends pas à leur dérober l'honneur de son accomplissement, mais il m'importait beaucoup d'avoir l'assurance que si, le cas arrivant, ceux-là ne vous tendaient pas la main, vous accepteriez la mienne, pendant la durée du besoin que vous en auriez.

Quant au projet de traduction de mon livre, j'aurai les yeux là dessus, et si ce projet s'exécute, je tâcherai d'empêcher toute suppression importante, surtout si elle était de nature à atténuer les expressions destinées à vous rendre une justice philosophique que je tiens encore plus à vous rendre en france qu'en angleterre. Si malgré mes efforts le traducteur se permettait un pareil acte d'infidélité, je n'hésiterais certes pas à le dénoncer en France par une réclamation publique.

Mon jeune ami Lewes, qui se range de plus en plus à notre doctrine commune, vient d'insérer dans une revue anglaise, le *British & Foreign Review*, un article sur les diverses écoles philosophiques,[2] ou prétendues telles qui existent actuellement en France, dans lequel après une critique assez sévère de toutes les autres, il finit par une appréciation sommaire et assez intelligente de votre système, dont il fait un éloge franc et vigoureux, accompagné de la haute expression d'admiration de votre éminente supériorité intellectuelle. Je compte que cet article fera aussi sa part pour attirer sur votre grand ouvrage l'attention des lecteurs anglais.

Je ne manquerai pas de faire un emploi convenable des exemplaires que vous m'avez addressés de l'arrêt du tribunal de commerce, qui me semble aussi satisfaisant dans ses termes que dans ses conclusions.

votre tout dévoué

J. S. MILL

2. "The Modern Metaphysics and Moral Philosophy of France," *BFR*, XV (1843), 353–406.

401. TO AUGUSTE COMTE[1]

India House
le 30 août 1843

Mon cher Monsieur Comte

Au moment d'écrire cette lettre, c.à d. après en avoir fait le brouillon, travail indispensable chez moi lorsque j'écris en français quelque chose d'un peu important, je reçois la lettre que vous a inspirée votre aimable inquiétude sur ma santé. Je suis heureux de pouvoir dissiper cette sollicitude. Si mon état physique ne s'est pas beaucoup amélioré, il n'a certainement pas empiré, et je commence à rentrer, sous le rapport moral, dans mon état ordinaire. Je me promets bien de répondre dorénavant à vos lettres avec plus de promptitude et je me reproche les alarmes que mon silence a fait naître chez vous. Ce retard inusité tient effectivement un peu à Mazhar Effendi, mais non pas de la manière que vous pensiez. Je désirais seulement pouvoir vous parler un peu de lui. Il est venu à mon bureau avec le Docteur Bowring,[2] et m'a donné votre lettre peu de jours après sa date: depuis cela il n'est plus revenu, et comme il n'a pas non plus répondu à un billet que je lui ai écrit, je crois qu'il doit être parti pour l'intérieur du pays, où en effet il trouverait, en fait d'établissements industriels et de travaux publics, des choses bien plus intéressantes qu'à Londres. Dans cc cas-là j'espère le voir davantage lorsqu'il sera de retour, d'autant plus que la première fois il n'est pas resté assez longtemps pour que j'aie pu faire vraiment connaissance avec lui. Lorsqu'il est venu, ma famille était à la campagne et ma maison encombrée d'ouvriers, mais à son retour j'aurai la faculté de lui donner un accueil plus satisfaisant.

Pour reprendre notre importante discussion sociologique, je crois comprendre ce que vous voulez dire en comparant la constitution organique du sexe féminin à un état d'enfance prolongée. Je n'ignore pas ce qu'ont dit à ce sujet beaucoup de physiologistes, et je sais que non seulement par les systèmes musculaire et cellulaire mais encore par le système nerveux, et très probablement par la structure cérébrale, les femmes sont moins éloignées que ne le sont les hommes, du caractère organique des enfants. Cela pourtant est bien loin d'être décisif pour moi. Afin qu'il le fût, il faudrait prouver que l'infériorité des enfants par rapport aux hommes dépendît de la différence anatomique de leur cerveau, tandis qu'elle dépend évidemment en majeure partie, sinon entièrement, au seul défaut d'exercice. Si l'on pouvait garder toujours son cerveau d'enfant, pendant qu'on en dévelop-

1. MS at Johns Hopkins. Published in Lévy-Bruhl, pp. 236–42; in reply to Comte's of July 16 and Aug. 28, *ibid.*, pp. 225–35.
2. John Bowring.

perait les fonctions par l'éducation et par un exercice soigné et réglé, on ne resterait certainement pas enfant, on serait homme, et on pourrait devenir homme très supérieur, tout en offrant, sans doute, des déviations notables du type ordinaire de l'humanité. De même je ne nie pas que le type moral féminin ne présente, en terms moyen, des divergences considérables du type masculin. Je ne prétends pas définir au juste en quoi consistent ces divergences naturelles et je ne sais pas si le temps est encore venu pour cela, mais je sais que des physiologistes très éminents prétendent que le cerveau des femmes est moins grand, moins fort par conséquent, mais plus actif que celui des hommes. D'après cela les femmes devraient être moins capable de travail intellectuel continu et prolongé, mais propres à plus faire en peu de temps que les hommes, et à faire mieux qu'eux tout ce qui exige une grande promptitude d'esprit. Elles seraient donc moins propres à la science, et plus propres au moins par leur organisation, à la poésie et à la vie pratique. Ceci me semble s'accorder assez bien avec ce qui s'observe dans la vie. Cependant on risquerait d'exagérer beaucoup le degré de diversité réelle, si on ne tenait pas compte de la différence d'éducation et de position sociale: car, que les femmes soient ou ne soient pas naturellement inférieures en capacité d'effort intellectuel prolongé, il n'est pas douteux que rien dans leur éducation n'est arrangé de manière à développer en elles cette capacité, tandis que chez les hommes l'étude des sciences, et même celle des langues mortes, a certainement cette tendance. D'ailleurs chez un grand nombre d'hommes, surtout dans les classes supérieures des travailleurs, leurs occupations journalières exigent, ou du moins permettent, un travail suivi de la pensée, tandis que chez la grande majorité des femmes l'obsession perpétuelle des soins minutieux de la vie domestique, chose qui distrait l'esprit sans l'occuper, ne permet aucun travail intellectuel qui ait besoin soit d'isolement physique, soit même d'attention suivie. Parmi les hommes eux-mêmes on ne reconnaît certainement pas une grande aptitude pour le travail de l'intelligence chez ceux dont l'enfance a été étrangère à toute étude tandis que les nécessités de leur vie postérieure n'ont pas remplacé à cet égard ce qui avait manqué à leur éducation primitive. Je trouve aussi que dans les choses ordinaires de la vie, sur lesquelles l'intelligence des femmes s'exerce autant ou plus que celle des hommes, les femmes, même médiocres, montrent ordinairement plus de capacité que les hommes médiocres. Un homme ordinaire n'a guère d'intelligence, que dans sa spécialité propre, au lieu qu'une femme en a pour des intérêts plus généraux. Vous me direz que la vie affective prédomine plus chez les femmes sur la vie intellectuelle: mais vous avouerez vous-même que ceci ne doit s'entendre que de la vie sympathique: l'égoïsme pur prédomine beaucoup plus chez les hommes: et si la sympathie devient le plus souvent chez les femmes un égoïsme à plusieurs personnes, elle le devient de même chez tous les hommes, sauf ceux qui une éducation, justqu'ici très rare, a développé à un haut degré le point de vue d'ensemble et l'habitude d'envisager les effets les plus généraux d'une conduite quelconque. Vous savez que c'est là précisément ce qui manque plus que tout le reste à l'éducation des femmes, au point qu'on ne compte même pas comme vertu à leur sexe de donner la préférence à l'intérêt général sur celui de leur famille ou de leurs amis. Je ne veux pas pour cela nier que les femmes, comme tous ceux dont l'excitabilité nerveuse dépasse le degré ordinaire, ne doivent naturellement ressembler plus pour le caractère aux hommes jeunes qu'aux hommes âgés, ni qu'elles n'aient naturellement plus de difficulté que les hommes du premier ordre à faire abstraction des intérêts présents et individuels; mais je crois que ce défaut-là trouve une compensation spontanée dans l'absence d'un autre défaut particulier aux philosophes, qui souvent font abstraction non pas seulement d'intérêts immédiats mais de tout intérêt réel; au lieu que les femmes, toujours placées au point de vue pratique deviennent très rarement des rêveurs spéculatifs, et n'oublient guère qu'il s'agit d'êtres réels, de leur bonheur ou de leurs souffrances. N'oublions pas qu'il n'est nullement question de faire gouverner la société par les femmes mais bien de savoir si elle ne serait pas mieux gouvernée par les hommes et par les femmes que par les hommes seuls. Au reste il est peutêtre très naturel qu'à cet égard vous et moi soyons d'opinion différente. Vous êtes français, et l'on a remarqué de tout temps que le caractère français tient déjà un peu des défauts, ainsi que des qualités, propres aux jeunes gens et aux femmes; vous pouvez donc penser qu'en fesant aux femmes une part plus large, on donnerait plus de force à ce qui déjà en a trop; au lieu que les défauts du caractère anglais sont plutôt en sens contraire. Sans entrer plus loin dans cette discussion subordonnée, je vous ferai observer cette seule circonstance qu'on a toujours reconnu dans les français, jusqu'à un certain point, l'organisation qu'on regarde comme féminine, et cependant quel peuple a produit de plus grands philosophes et des hommes d'Etat plus distingués?

En voilà assez pour le moment sur cette grande question biologique et sociologique. Je vous dirai maintenant une bonne nouvelle. Nous avons fait pour notre philosophie commune une conquête de premier ordre: c'est celui [*sic*] du jeune Bain, dont j'ai fait une mention honorable dans mon livre, que je lui avais communiqué avant sa publication, et qu'il a enrichi de beaucoup d'exemples et même de quelques idées utiles. Quoique âgé seulement de 26 ans il occupe depuis deux ans provisoirement en Ecosse une chaire de philosophie morale qu'il espère obtenir définitivement. C'est de tous les hommes de sa génération à moi connus, celui qui a posé le plus solidement les bases de l'éducation positive, par l'étude approfondie des cinq premières sciences fondamentales dans leur ordre hiérarchique: il a ensuite étudié mon livre, et cet été, le jugeant assez bien préparé, je lui ai fait lire le vôtre, qu'il a tout de suite compris et apprécié, et auquel il vient de consacrer trois mois d'étude vigoureuse. Il avait reçu de son éducation écossaise de fortes impressions religieuses, qui bien que déjà un peu affaiblies, n'ont réellement cédé qu'à l'influence directe de vos spéculations. Par une exception rare de nos jours, il ne s'était pas beaucoup occupé de politique et de questions sociales: il avait vaguement l'esprit progressif de notre siècle, et voilà tout. Sous l'influence de la méthode positive qu'il a parfaitement comprise et dont ses antécédents intellectuels lui avaient donné l'habitude, l'esprit de généralisation scientifique qu'il possède à un haut degré ne risque pas de s'égarer dans le vague. C'est un penseur véritable, qui devait entrer sans effort dans la bonne voie dès qu'elle lui serait indiquée, et qui, soit par l'universalité, soit par l'originalité de son esprit, doit servir non seulement à répandre puissamment mais aussi à perfectionner la sociologie positive. Sa position dans l'enseignement public lui donne sous le premier rapport de grands avantages, d'autant plus que je luis crois un talent didactique très supérieur.

Je vous félicite cordialement de l'accomplissement de votre pénible corvée de l'hôtel de ville. Vous me ferez grand plaisir en disant à M. Roméo Pouzin combien je suis sensible au souvenir si durable qu'il a gardé de relations si courtes, souvenir aussi doux que flatteur pour moi. Je voudrais qu'il dépendit de moi d'aller le revoir avec vous à Montpellier, où j'espère bien retourner un jour. Si vous voyez M. Balard à Montpellier, je serai charmé d'avoir de ses nouvelles. Je lui ai écrit il y a, je crois trois mois. A moins de quelque chose d'imprévu, je ne doute pas de l'accomplissement de la visite fraternelle que j'ai si longtemps désirée. Au revoir donc dans les derniers jours d'octobre.

Votre tout dévoué

J. S. MILL.

402. TO ALEXANDER BAIN[1]

[Sept., 1843]

I am now vigorously at work reviewing Michelet's *History of France* for the *Edinburgh*. I hope to *do* Napier, and get him to insert it before he finds out what a fatal thing he is doing.

1. Excerpt published in Bain, *JSM*, p. 78. MS not located.

403. TO JULES MICHELET[1]

India House
le 12 septembre
1843

MONSIEUR

Il y a longtemps que notre correspondance est suspendue, et en effet j'ai eu honte de vous écrire à cause de la longue interruption de mon projet de donner dans la revue d'Edinbourg une analyse de vos principaux ouvrages. Une santé faible et des occupations encore plus urgentes ont causé ce délai inattendu, mais aujourd'hui je m'occupe sérieusement d'un article sur votre Histoire de France, où j'ai fait déjà beaucoup de progrès, et je prends la liberté de vous écrire pour vous demander s'il y a des explications quelconques que vous désireriez qu'on donnât au public anglais et dont la revue d'edinbourg serait susceptible de servir d'organe.

Vous savez probablement qu'une revue anglaise, le *British and Foreign Review*, a fait, l'année passée, une assez vive sortie contre vous au sujet de Boniface VIII.[2] Le critique prétend que vous avez fait un récit fort peu exact de la vie de ce pape. Cette revue vous a fait depuis reparation jusqu'à un certain point en citant et en louant votre ouvrage,[3] mais comme l'attaque peut avoir laissé des traces dans quelques esprits, je serais bien aise de faire dire quelque chose là dessus dans l'Edinburgh review si vous m'en fournissez les moyens.

Agréez, Monsieur, l'assurance de ma plus haute estime.

J. S. MILL.

1. *Addressed*: Monsieur / le Professeur Michelet / aux archives du royaume / à Paris. *Postmarks*: LONDON / 12 / SEP / 1843 and [...] ANGL. / 14 / SEPT / 43. MS at Bibliothèque Historique de la Ville de Paris, rue de Sevigné, Paris. Transcript provided by Professor Cecil Lang.

2. "Boniface VIII," *BFR*, XIII (1842), 415–41. Michelet was attacked for misstatements, inadequate use of sources, groundless assertions, important omissions, and "stupid" mistakes.

3. In "Histories of the Reformation" (a review of works by Leopold Ranke and J. H. Merle d'Aubigné), *BFR*, XV (1843), 101–51. At one point, after citing Michelet, this reviewer, in a footnote (p. 119), remarks: "We must not pass by this opportunity of noticing this most singular and original writer; the most attractive of recent historians, with all his faults, of which the vulgar Anti-Anglicism of his last volumes seems to us not the least."

404. TO AUGUSTE COMTE[1]

India House
le 13 octobre
1843

MON CHER MONSIEUR COMTE

Je vous écris à la hâte pour vous annoncer que notre entrevue si longtemps attendue est destinée, cette fois encore, à subir un empêchement. Des circonstances, dont j'ai entrevu la possibilité mais que depuis quelque temps j'avais cessé de croire probables, ont fini par devenir un obstacle décisif à mon voyage.[2] Je suis, par plusieurs raisons, très peu à même de pouvoir faire d'avance avec certitude des projets d'absence, ce qui fait que j'évite toujours soigneusement de faire à cet égard des engagements absolus. Toutefois je croyais, presqu'avec assurance, que celui-ci s'accomplirait. Je regrette beaucoup que je n'aie pas pu vous avertir plustôt, mais les circonstances ne se sont décidées qu'hier au soir après l'heure de la poste. Je désire infiniment que ceci vous parvienne avant le jour fixé pour votre départ de Montpellier.

En répondant à la lettre que vous m'avez écrite de Bordeaux, je reprendrai la discussion sociologique que nous avons entamée et que je regarde avec vous comme une des plus graves que la science puisse comporter. Mais je ne veux pas tarder à vous exprimer dès à présent la félicitation la plus cordiale sur la perspective d'une amélioration important dans votre position à l'école polytechnique.

L'influence naturelle de ce changement, non seulement sur votre propre bonheur, si essentiellement lié à la sécurité de votre avenir matériel, mais encore sur votre autorité intellectuelle et même à certains égards sur la liberté de vos travaux, doit faire accueillir par vos amis toute espérance semblable avec la plus vive satisfaction.

votre dévoué

J. S. MILL.

1. *Addressed*: A Monsieur / Auguste Comte / Examinateur pour l'Ecole Polytechnique / en tournée à / Montpellier / département de l'Hérault. *Postmark*: LONDON / 13 / OCT / 1843. MS at Johns Hopkins. Published in Lévy-Bruhl, pp. 254–55; in reply to Comte's of Oct. 5; *ibid.*, pp. 242–53.

2. The probable reasons were the very poor health of Mrs. Taylor at this time and the financial losses he had suffered in the repudiation of some American bonds.

405. TO MACVEY NAPIER[1]

India House
14th Oct. 1843

MY DEAR SIR

I have been a good deal surprised & even pained by some passages relating to my father, in the article on Bentham just published in the Edinburgh Review.[2] Several of the statements made on the authority of Bowring are incorrect in point of fact, but what I chiefly complain of is the insertion of some things reported to have been said by Bentham, calculated to give a most unfavorable, & as every one who really knew my father must be aware, an utterly false impression of the character & temper of his mind. Mr Bentham's best friends well knew—I have heard some of those who were most attached to him lament—his entire incapacity to estimate the characters even of those with whom he associated intimately. The opinions he expressed of people depended very much upon their personal relations to himself: & as in the last few years of his life there was some coolness on his part towards my father, it is not unlikely that he may at times have said unpleasant things of him; but it is surely very blamable in a biographer to publish to the world every casual expression which such a man, or indeed any man, may have let fall to the disparagement of others. The additional publicity which your reviewer has given to the reflection on my father, was entirely unnecessary & uncalled for, in the place where it is introduced, (unless, indeed, lowering my father's character was his express object): & you will, I know, excuse me for saying that I should not have expected, from so old a friend of my father & one who respected him so much as yourself, that you would have been a party to the needless publication of an attack upon him of the most personal kind, from a quarter so suspicious, & yet from the connexion of the reporter with Bentham (which is not commonly known to have been confined to the period of his extreme old age) so likely to be generally credited & circulated.

I feel that something on my part to counteract the impression has now become indispensable. While the mischief was confined to the readers of Bowring's book, I thought it better to take no notice, but publication in the Edinburgh review is another matter. The silence of my father's friends, & of his natural representative, would now amount to acquiescence, & an illhumoured remark, very probably misreported by Bowring, would go down to posterity as a true judgment of my father's character—On such wretched trifles depends the remembrance that mankind retain of those

1. MS in Brit. Mus. Published, with one omission, in *Napier Corresp.*, pp. 441–42.
2. A review [by William Empson] of John Bowring's *Memoirs of Jeremy Bentham* (Edinburgh, 1843) in *ER*, LXXVIII (Oct., 1843), 460–516.

whose whole lives have been devoted to their service. I know I am asking an unusual thing, & though not I believe an unprecedented one, yet one with which I can hardly hope for your compliance—but would it be quite impossible for you to print, with the next number of the review, a short letter from me, containing my protest on the subject?[3] If such a thing is ever admissible, I think this case gives a claim to it, & you are aware how difficult it will otherwise be to find a channel for communicating the truth as extensively & as efficaciously as your review will circulate the calumny.

Believe me my dear Sir
yours very truly
J. S. MILL

406. TO AUGUSTE COMTE[1]

India House
le 17 octobre 1843

MON CHER MONSIEUR COMTE

Je désire vivement que vous ayez reçu, avant de quitter Montpellier, une lettre que je me suis trouvé dans la fâcheuse nécessité de vous écrire pour vous avertir que notre projet d'entrevue avait de nouveau échoué. Quoique je susse toujours que dans certaines éventualités, cette visit amicale pouvait devenir impossible, de manière à me défendre nécessairement toute promesse absolue, cependant depuis quelque temps je croyais ces éventualités assez peu probables pour ne conserver plus aucun doute sérieux sur la réalisation de notre projet. Cette attente a été trompée et j'ai, de plus, le regret de n'avoir pû vous annoncer cette nouvelle que, pour ainsi dire, au dernier moment.

Je ne vous écris aujourd'hui qu'à cause de l'incertitude si ma lettre antérieure vous est parvenue. Je me réserve de répondre, au premier jour de loisir, à votre discussion sur l'importante question sociologique qui nous divise. Je n'ai dans ce moment-ci que le temps d'écrire quelques mots de plus, et je les emploierai à vous parler d'un ancien ami de mon père et de moi-même, M. Austin,[2] qui va passer l'hiver actuel à Paris et qui m'a témoigné un vif désir de vous connaître. C'est un homme d'une haute intelligence et d'une grande élévation de caractère, et je ne pourrais vous

3. The request was granted. See Letter 407.

* * * *

1. *Addressed*: Monsieur / M. Auguste Comte / 10 Rue M. le Prince / près l'Odéon / à Paris. *Postmark*: 17 OCT 17 / 1843. MS at Johns Hopkins. Published in Lévy-Bruhl, pp. 255–56.
2. John Austin.

citer aucun homme dont l'amitié me soit plus précieuse. Par suite d'une mauvaise santé et de son peu de goût pour la société ordinaire, il évite, comme vous, plutôt qu'il ne recherche, toute liaison personnelle nouvelle. Cependant, malgré la superficialité de ses connaissances mathématiques, et nonobstant plusieurs graves dissentimens d'opinion d'avec vos théories sociales, votre ouvrage l'a tellement frappé qu'il regretterait beaucoup de demeurer à Paris sans vous connaître personnellement. Sa femme,[3] beaucoup plus connue que lui, a une certaine réputation de femme supérieure, réputation méritée à quelques égards; elle a d'ailleurs une sociabilité presque française. Je crois vraiment que vous auriez quelque plaisir à les connaître tous deux.

tout à vous

J. S. MILL.

407. TO MACVEY NAPIER[1]

I.H.
21st October 1843

MY DEAR SIR

I am truly sorry that what seems to me a most natural feeling on the subject of the reflections on my father[2] should appear to you unreasonable, & I am proportionally obliged to you for your friendly compliance with a request which you think uncalled for.[3] I shall adhere to your conditions, as indeed I should have done if you had said nothing about them. No review can be expected to insert a controversy with itself—I have no claim upon you for more than an opportunity of correcting false statements or false impressions of fact.

After the most honest self examination I cannot charge myself with any oversusceptibility in the matter. If I had been really chargeable with any, I should have found much more to complain of than I did; for there are other things in the article quite as injurious to my father as the passage which I wrote to you about. There are misstatements of fact, as well as true facts presented in a false light, respecting my father's connexion with Bentham, sufficient to make any one believe that Bentham had conferred upon my father the most sacred obligations, for which he had shewn himself ungrateful. To this however I did not feel that I had any right to object since the

3. Sarah Austin.

* * * *

1. MS in Brit. Mus. Published, with omissions, in *Napier Corresp.*, pp. 442–44.
2. See Letter 405.
3. JSM's vindication of his father appeared under the title, "Letter from John S. Mill, Esq., to the Editor" in *ER*, LXXIX (Jan., 1844), 267–71.

statements were taken from Bowring's book, & had not, as you truly say, been contradicted—indeed I did not know of their existence till I read them in the review. But I did feel hurt, when instead of reprobating the practice of publishing the idle words which one man may say of another in a moment of ill humour, your reviewer repeated & circulated, on no better foundation, general imputations against my father of a selfish, malignant disposition, which I thought you could have told him, from your own knowledge, were grossly unfounded. If he did not give his direct sanction to them, the impression on every reader must be nearly if not quite the same as if he had. Besides, in such a case not to defend is to attack, & the attack was more painful as coming from a friendly quarter.

Neither can I agree with you that the needlessness of the citation is not a thing to be considered. Everybody must judge for himself whether it was needless or not, but whoever judges that it was, will draw his presumptions accordingly respecting the animus of the writer.

The reason why I took no notice of Bowring's book was literally that I had not read it. I never attached sufficient value to anything Bowring could say about Bentham, to feel any curiosity on the subject. I was not then aware that the book contained any misstatement respecting my father's private affairs. This particular passage I certainly was aware of, & intended to notice when I had again occasion to write anything either about Bentham or my father. But my experience of the literary estimation in which Bowring is held, & of his reputation for judgment & accuracy, was not such as to make me believe that the loose talk of Bentham, reported by him, would excite general attention, or pass for more than it is worth. The case is very much altered when that loose talk has received the imprimatur of the Edinburgh Review.

I feel sure that you acted as you thought right, & that you did not know my father sufficiently to feel, in the way I thought you would, the injustice of the accusation. This is no small disappointment to me, but I cannot justly blame you for it, & I can sincerely say that I shall not retain, respecting yourself, any feeling of soreness whatever.

Believe me
my dear Sir
very truly yours
J. S. MILL

My review of Michelet[4] is finished, & I shall probably send it in next week's parcel from Longmans'. I am keeping it a few days for revision.

4. See Letters 285, n. 3, and 333.

408. TO ROBERT BARCLAY FOX[1]

India House
23d October 1843

MY DEAR FRIEND

I am ashamed when I think that I have not once written to you since you called upon me in your way home—but you would excuse me if you knew in how many ways my time and thoughts have been occupied. It is not, however, so much my work, in the proper sense, as by other things, for I have written little or nothing, extraofficially, except an article on the recent French historians, & especially on Michelet's History of France,[2] which I have just finished & which has brought my hand in again for work. You will see it in the Edin. Review unless Napier takes fright at some of the very heterodox things, in the eyes of an Edinburgh reviewer, still at the point of view of the 18th century, which the article contains. There is in particular some arrant Hildebrandism[3] which I suspect will shock him especially after the Scotch kirk controversy.[4]

By the by you will perhaps see in the same number another communication[5] from me, with my name signed to it, occasioned by a shabby, trumpery article on Bentham which has just appeared in the review. The writer's object seems to be to bring down as much as he can the character both of Bentham and of every one whose name has ever been connected with his—& he states facts & opinions respecting my father against which I have thought it imperative on me to protest publicly & have asked Napier to let me do it by a letter in his review, which he has consented to. I am sure if you have seen the article you will say it was high time.

I went down for a day to Sterling at Ventnor[6] a few weeks ago, & found him as cheerful & as well as could be hoped for after what he has gone through. He had got into his house, & what remained to be done by work-

1. *Addressed*: R. Barclay Fox / Perran Cottage / near Truro. *Postmark*: TRURO / OC 24 / 1843. MS in the possession of Mr. W. H. Browning. Published in part in Pym, II, 341–42.

2. See preceding letter, n. 4.

3. In the review JSM praised the mediaeval Catholic Church as "the authorized champion of intelligence and self-control" and as at that time "the great improver and civilizer of Europe" (*Dissertations*, II, 231). He also praised Hildebrand, Pope Gregory VII (*ca.* 1025–1085), for strengthening the power of the papacy against the state and for his reforms within the church itself (*ibid.*, pp. 236–37).

4. Earlier in 1843 a long-threatened schism in the Church of Scotland on the question of its Assembly's power over local presbyteries had resulted in the withdrawal of about one-third of its ministers and members to form the Free Church of Scotland.

5. See preceding letter, n. 3.

6. After the death of his mother and his wife in April, Sterling had bought a house at Ventnor, Isle of Wight, and moved his family there in June, 1843.

people would soon be finished. Ventnor is a little cocknified place which has grown up on the site of a very small country village, but Sterling's is the most desirable situation in it, being the *highest*—it looks over the village to the sea, & itself abuts upon the almost precipitous side of a walk down where the sheep bells tinkle close to his windows. Moreover there are just trees enough about the house to cover it up when you look at it from below. He is much pleased at the thought of having at last a fixed home & it is much in favour of his health & spirits that he is now, for the first time quite free from all anxiety about pecuniary matters. But here have I been describing the place to you as if you had not seen it. I have probably, indeed, a stronger *impression* about it than you, as I have *lived in* the house for 24 hours.—Sterling is now in town, on business, for a few days. I have seen him—he continues well. His father though still appearing much broken, certainly seems a good deal better.

Thanks for the votes which *your* (*plural*) persevering kindness has got for the little girl.[7] With regards & remembrances to all

Yours

J. S. MILL.

Clara continues well & prosperous—she is still at Frankfort.

409. TO CAROLINE AND ANNA MARIA FOX[1]

[Oct. 23, 1843][2]

I just slip in this little bit of paper for the sake of remembrance & to say—no, to say that I do not know what to say to such a flaming panegyric as that bestowed on my unworthiness by a young lady who has done me the honour to learn fallacies under my tuition. In spite of so much encouragement I cannot in conscience take off my injunction against reading the remainder of the book (which however is, I assure you, quite as clever) so whoever does read any of it must know that she does it at her own risk & responsibility.

The only as lofty panegyric that I have yet met with is from the Puseyite review the British Critic,[3] which almost exhausts language in admiration of me & my book, & then adds that notwithstanding I shall certainly go

7. See Letter 387.

* * * *

1. MS in the possession of Mr. W. H. Browning.
2. As the article referred to in the body of the letter appeared in Oct., this letter is probably of the same date as the preceding one to R. B. Fox, with which it was presumably enclosed.
3. *British Critic,* XXXIV (Oct., 1843), 349–427, by W. G. Ward.

to ——. I trust there was no such mental reservation in the praise of my other eulogist.

I wish heartily I could walk to Falmouth (or Rome) one of these fine mornings. I want extremely to look upon the blue Cornish sea or the Mediterranean for one half hour, not to speak of the Ariadne in the Vatican, & the two young Cornish women whose names you will find somewhere on the envelope.

J.S.M.

410. TO AUGUSTE COMTE[1]

India House
le 30 octobre 1843

MON CHER MONSIEUR COMTE,

Notre dissidence sur la question que vous caractérisez avec raison comme la plus fondamentale que puissent présenter les spéculations sociales ne doit certainement faire naître aucune inquiétude sur la possibilité finale d'une suffisante convergence d'opinion parmi les gens instruits, sur des bases purement rationnelles. Mais cette dissidence, et la manière de penser que la discussion dévoile de part et d'autre, me confirme dans l'opinion que les bases intellectuelles de la sociologie statique ne sont pas encore suffisamment préparées. Les fondements de la dynamique sociale sont aujourd'hui, à mon gré, pleinement constitués: mais, quant à la statique, l'histoire n'y tenant plus la première place, et n'y pouvant servir qu'à titre d'éclaircissement en quelque sorte accessoire, quoique je ne me dissimule pas l'importance de ce rôle secondaire; le passage de la statique sociale à l'état vraiment positif exige par conséquent, comparativement à la dynamique, une bien plus grande perfection de la science de l'homme individuel. Il suppose surtout un état très avancé de la science secondaire que j'ai nommée Ethologie,[2] c.à.d. de la théorie de l'influence des diverses circonstances extérieures, soit individuelles, soit sociales, sur la formation du caractère moral et intellectuel. Cette théorie, base nécessaire de l'éducation rationnelle, me paraît aujourd'hui la moins avancée de toutes les spéculations scientifiques un peu importantes. Une certaine connaissance réelle, même empirique, de cet ordre de rapports naturels, me semble on ne peut plus rare, et les saines observations ne le sont pas moins, soit par la difficulté du

1. *Addressed*: Monsieur / Auguste Comte / 10 Rue M. le Prince / près l'Odéon / à Paris. *Postmark*: 30 OCT 30 / 1843. MS at Johns Hopkins. Published in Lévy-Bruhl, pp. 259–72; in reply to Comte's of Oct. 5 and 22, *ibid.*, pp. 242–53, 257–59.

2. JSM's projected book on ethology, the science of the formation of character, had been outlined in Book VI, chap. 5 of the *Logic*, but it was never completed. See also Letters 416, 417, and 482.

sujet, soit par la tendance qui prévaut le plus souvent dans cet ordre de recherches, à regarder comme inexplicable tout ce qu'on n'est point parvenu à expliquer. Le genre d'étude biologique commencé, quoique avec une grande exagération, par Helvétius, n'a trouvé personne pour le poursuivre; et je ne puis pas m'empêcher de croire que la réaction du 19me siècle contre la philosophie du 18me a déterminé aujourd'hui une exagération en sens contraire, tendant à faire aux diversités primitives une part trop large, et à dissimuler, sous plusieurs rapports, leur vrai caractère. Je trouve très naturel que vous expliquiez chez moi cette opinion par mon insuffisante connaissance de la théorie physique de la vie animale, et surtout de la physiologie cérébrale. Je fais, et je continuerai à faire mon possible pour faire disparaître toute objection semblable. J'ai fait des études consciencieuses sur ce sujet; j'ai même lu avec une attention scrupuleuse les six volumes de Gall. J'ai trouvé fort juste une grande partie de sa polémique contre la psychologie de ses devanciers, dont au reste j'avais dès longtemps dépassé le point de vue: mais vous savez déjà que les principes généraux qui seuls selon vous sont jusqu'ici constatés dans la science phrénologique, ne me paraissent nullement prouvés par son livre, qui, au contraire, s'il prouvait quelque chose, tendrait plutôt, il me semble, conformément à l'intention de l'auteur, à déterminer l'organe cérébral de certains instincts spéciaux, soit animaux, soit particulièrement mentaux. J'admets la nécessité de prendre en sérieuse considération tous les rapports qu'on peut espérer d'établir entre la structure anatomique et les fonctions intellectuelles ou morales: je saisirai avec empressement tout moyen de m'éclairer davantage sur ce sujet; si vous m'indiquez dans ce but quelques nouvelles lectures à faire, je les ferai: mais tout ce que j'ai lu ou pensé jusqu'ici me porte à croire que rien n'est vraiment établi—que tout est encore vague et incertain dans cet ordre de spéculations. Il me semble même très difficile qu'elles sortent de cet état, tant que l'analyse éthologique de l'influence des circonstances extérieures, même générales, est aussi peu avancée qu'elle l'est; les diversités anatomiques ne devant répondre qu'à des *résidus* (pour me servir ici de ma terminologie logique),[3] après qu'on a soustrait du phénomène total, tout ce qui comporte une autre explication quelconque. Si, dans notre discussion sur les tendances caractéristiques des deux sexes, j'ai cité une opinion que je savais être celle de plusieurs physiologistes éminens, et qui ferait croire les femmes moins propres que les hommes aux travaux cérébraux de longue haleine, partant aux sciences et à la philosophie, ce n'est pas que ce soit là mon opinion propre; je la donnais comme la seule parmi les théories de ce genre qui ne me semblait pas en contradiction flagrante avec les faits: encore si on l'admettait, elle n'indiquerait de la part des

3. See his discussion of the method of residues in his *Logic*, Book III, chap. VIII, sec. 5.

femmes, aucune inaptitude pour la science, mais seulement une moindre vocation spéciale pour elle. Maintenant, que cette théorie physiologique soit vraie ou non, c'est ce que je ne prétends pas décider; les progrès scientifiques le décideront probablement un jour. J'écarterai donc, dans la suite de notre discussion, les considérations anatomiques en me tenant disposé à accueillir tout renseignement nouveau que vous puissiez m'indiquer ou qui se présente de toute autre part. Vous pensez d'ailleurs qu'indépendamment de ces considérations, une analyse exacte de l'expérience générale, tant usuelle qu'historique, suffit pour établir vos conclusions.

Quant à l'expérience usuelle, j'avoue que la mienne ne s'accorde pas, en ce qui est en question, avec la vôtre. Ne croyez pas que je me flatte aucunement de bien connaître les femmes; il est très difficile de connaître intimement qui que ce soit; et la difficulté pour tout être mâle de connaître réellement, je ne dis pas les femmes, mais une femme quelconque, est le plus souvent insupérable [*sic*]. Celui qui les connaît le mieux à certains égards, ne les connaît pas du tout à d'autres. Cependant je crois le milieu anglais plus favorable, à tout prendre, pour les connaître, que le français. D'après tout ce que j'ai pu apprendre, soit par les livres, soit par ma propre observation ou par celle des autres, l'éducation des jeunes filles est beaucoup plus sexuelle, pour ainsi dire, en france, qu'elle ne l'est en angleterre. Je ne dis pas ceci dans le sens physique, quoique à cet égard aussi ce soit vrai: je veux dire que l'effet à produire sur l'autre sexe leur est habituellement présent, pour ne pas dire habituellement proposé, comme but principal de leur conduite, et même dès l'enfance. Cela est beaucoup moins vrai ici, cela n'est même pas vrai du tout, en thèse générale, et cette différence a des résultats immenses, non seulement sur le développement propre de leurs facultés mais sur la possibilité aux hommes de les bien connaître, puisqu'en france elles sont constitutées en état permanent de simulation: ici, au contraire, il y a seulement, en général, de la dissimulation, effet de la compression sociale, encore celle-là même est essentiellement involontaire, les femmes, le plus souvent, n'en ayant, elles-mêmes presque pas conscience. Elles se regardent certainement chez nous, et les hommes les regardent aussi, moins comme femmes, et beaucoup plus comme des êtres humains en général. Leur éducation leur impose bien, en leur qualité de femmes, quelques règles spéciales de bienséance, mais comme préceptes généraux, et sans qu'elles les rapportent à leur position envers les hommes, ou envers un homme quelconque. Leur dépendance sociale gêne beaucoup leur développement mais ne l'altère pas autant qu'en france.

Quoi qu'il en soit de cela, mes propres observations ne m'indiquent rien qui puisse justifier le jugement absolu que vous portez sur les femmes, d'incapacité pour toute direction des affaires quelconques. D'abord à l'égard du gouvernement domestique, il est, je crois, généralement reconnu que les ménages sont mieux gouvernés en angleterre que partout ailleurs, du moins en ce qui regarde la discipline et l'obéissance, tant à l'égard des enfants qu'à celui des domestiques. Ces derniers ont en général (si on excepte l'Ecosse) moins d'intelligence qu'en France ou en Italie, mais ils font leur tâche avec beaucoup plus d'exactitude et de perfection matérielle, qui pourtant ne s'obtiennent qu'au prix d'une surveillance intelligente et continue. Or le gouvernement domestique appartient ici exclusivement à la femme: le mari se croirait ridicule s'il s'en mêlait: il est très souvent d'une ignorance et d'une incapacité souveraine dans tout ce genre de détails. Pour la direction industrielle, les femmes ne l'ont jamais exercée jusqu'ici qu'en des établissements d'une étendue très modérée, où pourtant on n'a pas remarqué quelles s'en soient plus mal acquittées que les hommes, ni que l'esprit de suite leur ait manqué: effectivement quand on veut s'entendre sur le sens des mots, je ne trouve pas que ce soit du tout ce qui leur manque. L'esprit de suite qui vous paraît avec raison la principale condition du succès prolongé dans les entreprises industrielles de premier ordre, ne peut pas être la capacité de soutenir une forte contention intellectuelle pendant huit ou dix heures par jour: s'il en était ainsi, fort peu d'hommes s'en tireraient avec succès. Ce qui fait l'esprit de suite, c'est sans doute la persévérance dans un dessein arrêté ou dans un plan donné, jusqu'à ce que l'essai en soit suffisamment fait. Or je ne crois pas qu'on puisse contester cela aux femmes, comparativement aux hommes. Je ne crois pas que le caprice, que la mobilité, dont on les accuse (quoiqu'on soit bien loin de les en accuser en angleterre) s'exercent dans les choses qui regardent leurs intérêts permanents; je crois qu'on ne trouve nulle part, dans les desseins importants, plus de patience et de longanimité que chez elles: d'ailleurs je trouve leur caprice, même dans les cas les plus caractérisés, beaucoup plus apparent que réel, quoiqu'elles sachent quelquefois très bien s'en servir comme moyen d'agir sur ceux parmi les hommes qui les envisagent, pour citer vos paroles, comme de charmans jouets. Vous les jugez moins aptes que les hommes à la prépondérance de la raison sur la passion, c'est-à-dire, plus portées à suivre l'impulsion présente de tout désir énergique. Je pourrais dire au contraire qu'elles le sont beaucoup moins, si je voulais juger cette question d'après l'expérience journalière; car le renoncement aux choses qu'elles désirent est chez elles l'ordre usuel de la vie, au lieu que chez les chefs de famille mâles ces sacrifices n'arrivent guère que dans les grandes occasions, et que ces chefs se montrent ordinairement très peu patients à les supporter dans les choses où ils ne s'en sont pas fait une habitude. Mais je ne veux rien fonder là dessus, parce que je reconnais dans la patience des femmes ainsi que dans l'impatience des hommes en ce qui froisse leurs inclinations, l'effet naturel de la puissance d'une part et de la dépendance de l'autre. Il faut donc décider cette question par des considérations *à priori*. Or il me semble que la prépondérance de la raison sur l'inclination est proportionnée à l'habitude qu'on a de s'examiner soi-même, et de se rendre compte de son caractère et de ses défauts. Celui qui n'est point parvenu à avoir la conscience exacte de son propre caractère, ne saura pas diriger sa conduite d'après sa raison. Il continuera d'obéir à ses habitudes, soit d'action, soit de sentiment ou de pensée. Je crois que cet examen de soi-même, malheureusement trop rare partout, l'est pour le moins autant chez le sexe mâle que chez les femmes. Une conscience intime de soi-même, et l'empire sur soi qui en résulte, sont des faits très exceptionnels chez les uns et les autres: mais si vous demandiez à la plupart des anglais leur jugement sur ce point, vous trouverez chez eux, quelle que soit d'ailleurs leur opinion sur le compte des femmes, un préjugé tout contraire à la doctrine que vous soutenez; beaucoup d'entre eux seraient portés à croire les mâles incapables d'exercer sur eux-mêmes une force de répression morale égale à celle qu'ils regardent comme le propre des femmes. Sans partager cette idée exagérée, je l'admets au moins comme indice que le témoignage de l'expérience n'est pas exclusivement de l'autre côté. D'ailleurs, l'opinion générale accorde aux femmes une conscience ordinairement plus scrupuleuse que celle des hommes: or qu'est-ce que la conscience, si ce n'est pas la soumission des passions à la raison?

Je viens maintenant à l'argument fondé sur la persistance, jusqu'à notre temps, de la subalternité sociale des femmes, comparée à l'émancipation graduelle des classes inférieures dans les nations les plus avancées, quoique ces classes aient partout commencé par être esclaves. Cette différence historique ne vous paraît explicable que par une infériorité organique de la part des femmes. Je crois pourtant voir à cet argument une réponse suffisante. Il est vrai que les esclaves sont parvenus, dans les populations d'élite, à s'élever jusqu'à la liberté, et même quelquefois à l'égalite sociale. Mais je ne crois pas que cela ait jamais eu lieu à l'égard des esclaves domestiques. Ceux-là ne se sont, je crois, jamais émancipés eux-mêmes: ils y sont parvenus à la suite des autres esclaves, sans y avoir contribué par leurs propres efforts. C'est qu'il y a dans la dépendance continue, dans celle de tous les instants, quelque chose qui énerve l'âme, et qui arrête dès le commencement tout essor vers l'indépendance. Le serf est dans une tout autre position: il a des devoirs plus ou moins fixes à remplir envers son maître; ces devoirs remplis, il est à peu près libre: il a de la propriété à lui; il est forcé à la prévoyance; il ne reçoit pas le pain d'autrui, il est chargé du soin de sa propre subsistence: il a même du pouvoir sur les autres; il est maître chez lui; il a femme et enfants, il est responsable pour eux, il s'exerce dans le commandement, il apprend à se croire quelque chose. Tout cela était déjà vrai, jusqu'à un certain point, chez les esclaves agricoles des anciens; et pourtant, le premier pas dans leur émancipation, celui de leur transformation en serfs, n'a pas, je crois, résulté de leurs propres efforts, mais de l'intérêt des maîtres, secondés par l'autorité morale de l'église. C'est seulement depuis l'état de servage que leur élévation sociale a été essentiellement duê à eux-mêmes. Or il faut reconnaître que la position spéciale des femmes, quoique sans doute très supérieure en Europe à ce que furent jamais les serfs, est dépourvue de cette demi-indépendance, de cette habitude de diriger, entre certaines limites, leurs propres intérêts, sans aucune intervention supérieure, qui a toujours appartenu aux serfs, et qui a été, ce me semble, la principale source de l'essor par lequel ils se sont peu à peu élevés à la liberté. La servitude des femmes, quoique bien plus douce, est une servitude sans intermission, et qui s'étend à tous les actes, et qui les décharge, bien plus complètement que les serfs de toute haute prévoyance et de toute vraie direction de leur propre conduite, soit envers la societé, soit même dans le sens de l'intérêt individuel. Cela étant, la douceur comparative de cette servitude est une raison de plus pour qu'elle se prolonge. Je ne crois pas qu'il y ait un homme sur cent mille, qui, n'ayant jamais joui de la liberté, soit capable de la préférer à l'état d'esclave caressé, état si conforme à la paresse qui est universelle et à la lâcheté qui est très générale dans notre espèce. Jamais d'ailleurs des esclaves quelconques n'ont été si soigneusement élevés, dès la première enfance, dans la ferme croyance qu'ils doivent toujours être assujettis à d'autres hommes, et que les affaires réelles de la vie ne sont pas du tout de leur ressort, que le sont et l'ont toujours été les femmes. Tous les ressorts sympathiques de leur nature particulière sont employés à leur faire chercher le bonheur non pas dans leur vie propre, mais exclusivement dans la faveur et dans l'affection de l'autre sexe, ce qui ne leur est accordé qu'à condition de dépendance: peu importe alors qu'un grand nombre d'entr'elles vivent et meurent sans se lier à aucun homme, puisque la direction exclusive de leur esprit et de leur ambition dans ce sens pendant leur jeunesse doit empêcher plus tard, si ce n'est dans des cas tout à fait exceptionnels, tout élan réel dans une autre direction, même en supposant une suffisante indépendance pécuniaire, et le milieu social le plus favorable. Il est inutile de vous parler de l'influence que doit exercer l'intimité toute particulière de cette classe de dépendants avec leurs maîtres, intimité si au-delà de celle qui peut exister dans tout autre cas; je ne parle pas non plus de l'influence morale de l'infériorité en force physique, qui, même en ne supposant, du côté des mâles, aucun abus direct de leur puissance musculaire, doit nécessairement amener un certain respect involontaire, et une certaine habitude de dépendance, qui finit même souvent par s'établir entre deux mâles dont l'un est plus faible que l'autre, s'ils sont très liés ensemble.

Ces considérations me paraissent plus que suffisantes pour expliquer un retard presqu'indéfini de l'émancipation sociale des femmes, sans qu'on puisse induire delà qu'elle ne doive jamais arriver. Au moins vous avouerez qu'elle ne pouvait avoir lieu que longtemps après celle des serfs, qui n'est pas elle-même un fait très ancien. Il me semble, au reste, que l'élévation des femmes est déjà aussi avancée, et qu'elle s'avance aussi vite, qu'on pourrait s'y attendre, d'après la théorie de l'égalité naturelle. Elles ne peuvent pas faire comme les serfs, qui ne se sont affranchis qu'en formant des sociétés à part, c'est-à-dire les villes, où même, le plus souvent, ils ont eu à soutenir une longue lutte militaire avec leurs seigneurs: lutte dans laquelle leur supériorité en nombre, accompagnée d'égalité en forces physiques, fut une compensation puissante de leur infériorité en éducation militaire. Les femmes, au contraire, ne pouvaient s'élever socialement qu'en prouvant de plus en plus, par des efforts individuels, dans toutes les carrières qui ne leur sont pas interdites, qu'elles sont capables de plus grandes choses qu'on ne leur accordait auparavant. Il me semble qu'à cet égard elles font de rapides progrès, et que par ce moyen, le seul possible, leur affranchissement s'opérera par elles-mêmes. Depuis un siècle chaque génération a dépasse la précédente quant au nombre et au mérite de leurs écrits: ce mouvement progressif est surtout devenu très accéléré en France et en Angleterre depuis 50 ans. Plusieurs femmes se sont même élevées, dans leurs écrits, jusqu'au génie créateur; quoique les facultés qui le constituent ne dussent servir le plus souvent, chez le sexe qui ne fait pas d'ordinaire des études sérieuses et qui n'a pas à vivre de son travail, qu'à titre d'ornement, ou tout au plus au bonheur de la vie intérieure. Ce qui leur a principalement manqué jusqu'ici en littérature comme dans les beaux-arts, c'est une forte originalité; mais il est très naturel que cela manque, surtout dans les commencemens, à ceux qui viennent les derniers: ce sont les romains qui viennent après les grecs. La littérature féminine a nécessairement commencé par imiter la masculine; elle s'est conformée aux types et aux idées reçues, et ce n'est que d'aujourd'hui qu'on voit des femmes qui écrivent comme femmes, avec leurs sentimens et leur expérience féminine. Elles feront cela, je crois, de plus en plus, et je ne doute pas qu'alors on ne voie cesser le reproche qu'on leur a fait de n'avoir rien su créer de premier ordre, car toute grande création suppose nécessairement une conception originale.

Je ne dirai qu'une chose de plus. Dans la haute direction des affaires humaines, le rôle de reine est le seul qui ne soit pas fermé aux femmes. Ce rôle seul, par une anomalie accidentelle que vous qualifiez de ridicule, et qui l'est en effet par son contraste bizarre avec l'ensemble de leur position sociale, leur est resté ouvert dans la plupart des pays européens. Or, à partir du tems où la royauté a cessé d'exiger surtout la capacité militaire, jusqu'à celle [*sic*] où elle a commencé à ne plus exiger, ni même en quelque sorte comporter, aucune capacité quelconque; dans cet intervalle d'à peu près deux siècles, les reines n'ont-elles pas honorablement rempli leur fonction sociale? et l'histoire ne montre-t-elle pas dans ce temps tout autant de grandes reines, proportion gardée, que de grands rois? Je le crois du moins, et cette expérience, faite en des circonstances qui sont très loin d'être favorables, ne doit pas avoir peu de poids, à ce qui m'en semble, dans la question de leur capacité gouvernementale. Je vous envoie, comme vous voyez, mon cher Monsieur Comte, un traité au lieu d'une lettre.[4] Je ne m'en excuse pas, car sans doute vous pensez comme moi qu'une question si fondamentale mérite qu'on la retourne de tous les côtés, et qu'on ne perd pas son temps à la discuter longuement. Je tiens d'ailleurs beaucoup à ce que vous ne croyiez pas que ce soit ici de ma part une idée légèrement adoptée: il y a peu de questions que j'aie plus méditées, et bien qu'en général je sois connu pour ne pas tenir à des opinions une fois admises, dès qu'on me prouve qu'elles sont mal fondées, celle-ci a résisté chez moi à tout ce qu'on lui a opposé jusqu'ici. Comme vous avez aussi de votre part une opinion très arrêtée, il n'est guère probable qu'une discussion épistolaire, ou même orale, fasse disparaître notre dissentiment, mais elle peut, sans cela, nous être, de plus d'une manière, très utile.

Il me reste peu de place pour vous parler d'autre chose. J'ai fait part à M. Austin de votre aimable intention de faire en sa faveur une exception à votre règle d'éviter les nouvelles connaissances. Il y est très sensible et se propose d'aller vous voir. Je pense que vous vous en trouverez bien: c'est un homme très digne de votre sympathie, et dont la conversation est pleine d'idées justes et profondes. Je ne connais personne qui juge plus sainement l'angleterre, et aussi, autant que je puis prononcer là dessus, l'allemagne, où il a longtemps séjourné.

Mon jeune ami Bain est digne de tout votre intérêt, et tout annonce qu'il ne trompera pas nos espérances. Il m'écrit souvent de l'Ecosse des lettres admirables de bon sens et de profondeur. Il trouve les esprits, même dans ce pays si religieux en apparence, merveilleusement bien préparés pour l'avènement final du positivisme. "At a distance," dit-il, "one can hardly believe, how very few points of every day human life are touched by theologic views. Theology is descending rapidly to the mere Esthetic & to a bond of social agglomeration, the desire of which last is its greatest hold."

votre dévoué

J. S. MILL.

4. JSM's discussion here of the role and education of women should be compared with his final treatment of the topic in *The Subjection of Women* (London, 1869).

411. TO ALEXANDER BAIN[1]

Nov. 3, 1843

My review of Michelet is in Napier's hands. If he prints it, he will make some of his readers stare.

412. TO ALEXIS DE TOCQUEVILLE[1]

Le 3 novembre 1843.

Vous savez, mon cher Tocqueville, combien tout ce qui vient de vous m'est agréable et vous ne pouvez douter du plaisir que m'a donné l'opinion si flatteuse que vous venez de me témoigner à l'égard de ma *Logique*, et qui est d'autant plus précieuse qu'elle vient d'une lecture lente et consciencieuse. C'est un grand bonheur d'écrire pour des intelligences et pour des caractères comme la vôtre, quand on est assez heureux pour obtenir leur approbation. Je vous suis d'ailleurs redevable de tant d'instruction et de plaisir intellectuel que j'ai toujours très vivement désiré de pouvoir un jour payer *in kind*, comme nous disons, et de mériter auprès de vous l'honneur d'être regardé comme un collaborateur réel dans la cause du progrès intellectuel et social. J'éprouve un grand plaisir en apprenant que vous partagez mes idées sur la méthode propre à perfectionner la science sociale: les suffrages qu'on doit le plus ambitionner en pareille matière sont ceux du très petit nombre des penseurs qui, comme vous, ont rendu des services vraiment importants à cette science. Votre approbation du point de vue d'où j'ai envisagé la question de la liberté humaine m'est aussi très précieuse. Je regarde moi-même ce chapitre-là[2] comme le plus important du livre : il est l'expression fidèle des idées où j'étais arrivé depuis bientôt quinze ans, que je n'avais jamais écrites, mais dans lesquelles je puis dire que j'avais trouvé la paix, puisqu'elles seules avaient satisfait pleinement chez moi au besoin de mettre en harmonie l'intelligence et la conscience, en posant sur des bases intellectuelles solides le sentiment de la responsabilité humaine. Je ne crois pas qu'aucun penseur un peu sérieux puisse jouir d'une vraie tranquillité d'esprit et d'âme, jusqu'à ce qu'il ait accompli quelque solution satisfaisante de ce grand problème. Je ne desire pas imposer ma propre solution à ceux qui sont satisfaits de la leur, mais je crois qu'il y a beaucoup d'hommes pour qui elle sera, comme elle a été pour moi, une véritable ancre de salut.

Je compte bien, suivant vos aimables conseils, ne pas en rester à ce

1. Excerpt published in Bain, *JSM*, p. 78. MS not located.

* * * *

1. Published in Mayer, pp. 346–47; in reply to Tocqueville's of Oct. 27, *ibid.*, pp. 344–46. MS in Tocqueville archives.
2. Book VI, chap. 2, "Of Liberty and Necessity."

seul ouvrage, quoique je ne me trouve pas de force à traiter systématiquement une science aussi difficile et aussi peu avancée que celle de la politique. J'ai l'espoir d'y contribuer quelque chose par des travaux partiels quoique je n'aie pas encore décidé ce qu'ils seront. En attendant je m'occupe un peu de faire connaître en Angleterre les bons écrivains français: je viens de faire un article sur les historiens et notamment sur Michelet.[3] Et vous, que ferez-vous? Vous consacrerez-vous maintenant uniquement à la politique? Je le regretterais beaucoup, car tout en appréciant très hautement la valeur de la chaire politique (si cette expression est permise), je crois qu'il y a plus d'hommes capables de faire le peu qu'on puisse faire à présent dans la vie publique qu'il y en a qui peuvent écrire des livres tels que vous pourriez les faire. Ne traiterez-vous jamais la France comme vous avez traité l'Amérique? Vous l'avez bien commencé dans ce petit écrit dont vous parlez dans votre lettre et qui déjà jette une lumière importante sur plusieurs questions sociales et historiques généralement très mal comprises.

Merci mille et mille fois de votre invitation amicale. Il n'y en a point à laquelle je me rendrais avec plus de plaisir mais je n'ose rien promettre, à cause de la rareté et de la courte durée de mes vacances qui, par conséquent, sont presque toujours remplies par des obligations indispensables.

Ne viendrez-vous jamais ici?

Votre tout dévoué

J. S. MILL.

India House.

413. TO ALEXANDER BAIN[1]

[Autumn, 1843]

There is no chance, for Social Statics[2] at least, until the laws of human character are better treated.

414. TO HENRY COLE[1]

I. H. Tuesday
[Nov. 14, 1843]

MY DEAR COLE

A year or two ago when you said something to me about paying the £100 which I had the pleasure of accommodating you with formerly, I

3. See Letters 285, n. 3, and 333.

* * * *

1. Excerpt published in Bain, *JSM*, p. 78. MS not located.
2. See Letters 410 and 416.

* * * *

1. MS in the possession of the Rt. Rev. Charles Larrabee Street, as is also Cole's reply of Nov. 15, 1843.

said to you "pay me *last*". Now however I have certain reasons for wishing to call in all money due to me[2] & I therefore write to retract what I then said.

I have always considered the help I then gave you as a just & proper support to the honorable & public spirited course you took at that time.[3] If you had been thrown out of office and emolument permanently by your conduct at that time I should never have asked you for payment nor regretted the loss. Nor have I ever said a word to you about it until now. Now however I should really be very glad if you would make the earliest arrangements for the payment, either at once or by instalments, as would not interfere with you & your family's comfort & convenience, and I only mention this because, though I always knew you would pay me if you lived & had the means, you might suppose that the time of payment still continued to be altogether unimportant to me, which however is no longer the case.

Very truly yours,

J. S. Mill

415. TO HENRY COLE[1]

I.H. Thursday
[Nov. 16, 1843]

My dear Cole

Your letter is all that is right & honorable, & kind also. No explanation was requisite of your not having paid the money, as I always ascribed it to the causes you mention—except that I did not know how you had acted about the Guide,[2] which does you great honour.

The reasons which induce me to wish for the money are not so urgent

2. JSM and his family had lost heavily by the repudiation of debts by some of the American states. See Letter 331, n. 2.

3. Cole had been employed by a newly established Record Commission in 1831, under the secretaryship of Charles Purton Cooper (1793–1873). In 1836, at the risk of losing his position, Cole had memorialized the Record Commission about the arbitrary conduct of Cooper. Cole's appeal to his friend Charles Buller led to Buller's bringing the subject of the mismanagement of the Record Commission before the House of Commons on Feb. 18, 1836. A subsequent investigation led to the vindication of Cole and the establishment of the Public Record Office in 1838, at which time Cole was appointed one of the four senior assistant-keepers (see Sir Henry Cole, *Fifty Years of Public Work* [2 vols., London, 1884], I, 1–33).

* * * *

1. MS in the possession of the Rt. Rev. Charles Larrabee Street. Endorsed in another hand: "J. Mill 1843. Agreeing to proposed time of payment of loan—H.C."

2. The *Guide* was a weekly newspaper established by Molesworth, J. T. Leader, Cole and others, with Cole as editor; it ran from April 22, 1837, to April 1, 1838. Cole, in his answer to JSM's letter of Nov. 14, 1843, explained that he had discharged debts of the *Guide* of £150 more than need to have been ascribed to him.

as to time, as to require that you should put yourself at all out of the way to pay me in a shorter time than that you mention. Nor even, if it should prove more inconvenient than you expect, would I have you make a point of doing it even in that time unless my need of it should grow stronger than I can at present foresee. All I intended to ask of you was exactly what you say—that it should be put in train as among the first things to be settled.

Ever yours
with sincere regard
J. S. MILL

416. TO AUGUSTE COMTE[1]

India House
le 8 décembre 1843

MON CHER MONSIEUR COMTE,

Puisque vous jugez que la discussion qui a tenu dernièrement une si grande place dans notre correspondance, est maintenant parvenue au point au delà duquel elle ne peut plus être portée avec avantage, je m'abstiendrai de la prolonger en y ajoutant des observations quelconques sur votre dernière lettre. Cette lettre n'a nullement ébranlé ma conviction, comme, en effet, elle n'y était pas destinée, mais seulement à mieux constater les points de divergence entre nos deux manières de penser. Je dois dire pourtant que plus je médite cette question, et plus je me raffermis dans mon opinion, qui, de très ancienne date chez moi, ne s'est pas trouvée démentie mais certainement confirmée par les faits qui se sont présentés à mon observation dans la vie; en quoi elle diffère de beaucoup d'autres opinions que j'avais seulement acceptées de la philosophie négative de mon temps et que j'ai depuis modifiées ou abandonnées. Permettez-moi de dire aussi que notre discussion, par cela même qu'elle n'a pas changé mon opinion, a nécessairement tendu à la fortifier; car malgré l'élaboration plus complette que vous vous proposez de donner à cette question dans le Traité dont vous allez commencer la préparation, je suis bien persuadé que vous possédez parfaitement tout ce qu'on peut dire de mieux à l'appui d'une doctrine à laquelle vous tenez si fortement, et je crois que ce qui vous reste à dire ne pourra plus être que le commentaire, en quelque sorte, de ce que vous m'avez déjà indiqué.

Cette discussion a laissé chez moi, à d'autres égards, des traces permanentes, et je pense qu'elle aura un certain effet sur la direction de mes travaux à venir. Je vois de plus en plus que c'est la statique sociale qui maintenant appelle surtout les esprits convenablement préparés. Vous avez

1. MS at Johns Hopkins. Published in Lévy-Bruhl, pp. 283–87; in reply to Comte's of Nov. 14, *ibid.*, pp. 273–83.

fondé définitivement la sociologie dynamique, et nul esprit émancipé, suffisamment pourvu de connaissances positives, ne peut manquer à reconnaître dans votre grande loi du développement humain et dans ses divers corollaires, une explication vraie de l'ensemble du passé social, et la prophétie d'un avenir indéfini. Il importe à présent que la statique sociale soit maintenue au niveau de la dynamique, qui sans elle, ne peut pas être, comme vous le dites très bien, suffisamment rationnelle, ni surtout servir nullement à contrôler l'anarchie actuelle des doctrines sociales. Pour cela je crois qu'il faut surtout travailler à perfectionner, ou plutôt, on peut presque dire, à créer l'Ethologie; en appréciant convenablement la nature et le degré des effets éthologiques produits soit par l'organisation, soit par les diverses circonstances extérieures. Je conviens avec vous que dans ces spéculations, où la méthode des résidus doit nécessairement devenir d'un usage très étendu, l'ordre des soustractions partielles n'est rien moins qu'indifférent. On doit, ce me semble, commencer par soustraire les influences dont l'effet comporte, avec le plus de facilité et de précision, l'appréciation directe: ce seront, le plus souvent, celles qui ont le plus d'importance réelle; mais peut étre pas toujours. Au reste, on devra probablement procéder tantôt du dehors en dedans, tantôt en sens inverse, suivant les moyens qu'on a d'apprécier directement les effets dûs soit à une position extérieure quelconque, soit à un type quelconque d'organisation. Je me promets, à ce propos, de lire le cours de M. de Blainville, ou du moins la partie qu'il en a livrée au public: je regrette beaucoup que ce travail ne soit pas publié intégralement. J'ai commencé à lire les œuvres anglaises de M. Spurzheim, et je ne négligerai pas les ouvrages que vous m'avez indiqués de cet auteur. Je voudrais essayer de me rendre propre à faire quelque chose pour l'Ethologie, qui sera probablement, quoique je ne sache pas encore sous quelle forme, le sujet du premier livre que j'écrirai.

Je compte sur la lecture très prochaine de votre petite brochure sur l'école polytechnique, qui, d'après votre indication, doit être à peu près terminée, et qui, si elle n'influe pas immédiatement sur la constitution à donner à cette importante école, attirera du moins, sans doute, l'attention publique par l'opportunité de sa publication. Je désire vivement que les mutations à faire dans le personnel polytechnique s'opèrent de manière à vous rendre enfin la justice qu'on vous refusa si indignement à la dernière occasion, et j'attends avec impatience le dénouement de cette sorte de crise.

Quant à mon traducteur, dont Marrast ne m'a jamais dit le nom, je ne sais rien à son égard, que ce que je vous ai déjà annoncé. J'écrivis à Marrast, il y a plusieurs mois, une lettre un peu chaleureuse pour le déterminer à veiller sur la fidélité de la traduction, notamment en ce qui regarde le juste hommage que j'ai rendu à votre ouvrage et à vous-même.

Je n'ai pas reçu de réponse, ce qui tient peut-être de la part de Marrast, à son étourdissante occupation de journaliste, qui lui permet rarement de m'écrire. Au reste je ne compte pas beaucoup sur cette traduction, et je ne serai nullement étonné si elle n'a jamais lieu, ce qui vaudrait beaucoup mieux que des suppressions quelconques.

Je suis bien flatté de l'honneur que M. de Blainville a rendu à mon livre par une lecture soigneuse et par la haute approbation qu'un esprit si supérieur a bien voulu lui témoigner. Dans mon propre pays cet ouvrage a un succès bien au-delà de ce que j'avais espéré: la plupart des esprits compétents soit à juger, soit seulement à profiter de ce genre de spéculations, ont pris, ou se préparent à prendre, connaissance de ce livre, et les opinions qu'ils expriment lui sont jusqu'ici très favorables. Ce qui vous étonnera peut être, l'école Anglo-Catholique, sur laquelle je vous donnai autrefois quelques renseignements et qui a pris une importance très considérable, quoique seulement passagère dans notre public spéculatif, a trouvé bon d'afficher une haute protection de mon ouvrage: leurs divers organes lui ont consacré des articles[2] quelquefois assez remarquables, et on me dit qu'à Oxford où ils sont très puissants, tout le monde me lit. C'est à peu près comme si De Maistre préconisait votre grande ouvrage. Vous comptez bien qu'ils font ceci avec de nombreuses réserves, surtout sous le rapport religieux, mais cela vaut mieux à tous égards que s'ils me louaient sans restriction. D'un autre côté, on me lit à Cambridge pour se préparer aux examens de l'université, car M. Whewell y interroge les élèves sur son propre ouvrage, et comme on pense qu'il dirigera volontiers des questions dans le sens des doctrines que j'ai combattues, on lit mon livre afin de savoir ce qu'elles sont.

Je n'ai pas revu Mazhar Effendi. Je suis parvenu à savoir qu'il a quitté Londres, où probablement il n'est pas encore revenu. Quand il sera de retour il trouvera mon dernier billet, et j'aurai fait à son égard tout ce qui dépendait de moi.

Votre dévoué,

J. S. MILL

417. TO ALEXANDER BAIN[1]

[Late 1843]

I do not know when I shall be ripe for beginning "Ethology".[2] The scheme has not assumed any definite shape with me yet.

2. The most notable was W. G. Ward's in the *British Critic* (see Letter 409, n. 3).

* * * *

1. Excerpt published in Bain, *JSM*, p. 78. MS not located.
2. See Letters 410 and 416.

• • • 1844 • • •

418. TO ALEXANDER BAIN[1]

Jan. 8, 1844

I am reading a German professor's book on Logic—Beneke[2] is his name—which he has sent to me after reading mine, and which had previously been recommended to me by Austin and by Herschel as in accordance with the spirit of my doctrines. It is so in some degree, though far more psychological than entered into my plans. Though I think much of his psychology unsound for want of his having properly grasped the principle of association (he comes very close to it now and then), there is much of it of a suggestive kind.

419. TO MACVEY NAPIER[1]

India House
10th Jany
1844

My dear Sir

Your note of the 6th arrived safe, & permit me to thank you for the very handsome remittance inclosed in it.

I do not feel *confident* of having the Guizot[2] ready for your next number, even if you should have room for it. When I can speak more positively on the subject I will inform you.

The insertion of the words "my father" required no apology. I should very willingly have inserted them myself, if you had asked me: although *of* myself I should not have used them—the ground on which I begged you to insert my letter[3] not being filial feeling but the desire to correct an injustice. However, considerations which affect only manner, are always, in my eyes, of quite subordinate importance to matter.

1. Excerpt published in Bain, *JSM*, p. 79. MS not located.
2. See Letter 397, n. 4.

* * * *

1. MS in Brit. Mus.
2. "M. Guizot's Essays and Lectures on History," *ER*, LXXXII (Oct., 1845), 381–421; reprinted in *Dissertations*, II, 297–362.
3. See Letters 405 and 407.

Senior's article[4] is full of excellent matter, though I think he is too hard upon O'Connell & the Repealers.

With cordial return of your kind wishes on the occasion of the new year, believe me

yours very truly,

J. S. Mill

420. TO AUGUSTE COMTE[1]

India House
le 17 Janvier 1844

Mon cher Monsieur Comte

Je suis comme vous voyez un peu en retard pour ma réponse à votre dernière lettre, ce qui tient surtout à un nouveau dérangement chronique de ma santé qui gêne considérablement ma faculté de penser. Je crains que ma lettre actuelle ne se ressente un peu de cet affaiblissement, d'autant plus que la paresse d'esprit qui en est la suite, me décide pour la première fois depuis le commencement de notre correspondance à vous écrire sans faire de brouillon. Je vous préviendrai à ce propos, que malgré mon habitude à cet égard je ne suis pas, par rapport à la conservation de notre correspondance, en meilleur état que vous: je garde soigneusement toutes vos lettres, mais je n'ai pas conservé les miennes, pas même en brouillon, excepté toutefois les parties qui se rapportent à notre grande discussion récente que j'ai transcrite en entier sur vos lettres et sur les miennes et recueillie dans un livre.

Il est fort peu probable que je me trouve naturellement amené à imprimer quelque chose d'un peu important sur la question dont il s'agit, avant d'avoir eu l'occasion de lire votre traité de sociologie, malgré le retard nécessairement produit par votre intention de ne le faire paraître qu'intégralement. Quant à cette résolution elle-même, bien que j'en doive nécessairement retirer un vrai désappointement, en ne lisant pendant plusieurs années rien de vous et en ne pouvant suivre comme je l'ai fait jusqu'ici le progrès de votre grande entreprise philosophique, je dois pourtant applaudir à votre décision. Cette élaboration, en effet, ne me paraît pas susceptible d'être appréciée ou même étudiée avec fruit, si ce n'est dans

4. [Nassau Senior], "Ireland," *ER*, LXXIX (Jan., 1844), 189–266.

* * * *

1. MS at Johns Hopkins. Published in Lévy-Bruhl, pp. 295–98; in reply to Comte's of Dec. 23, 1843, *ibid.*, pp. 288–95.

son ensemble. Vous avez déjà donné toutes les idées de philosophie sociologique qui soient à mon sens, vraiment propres à être accueillies à titre de préparation: il reste à présent à établir systématiquement, dans leur connexité, les principales doctrines de la science sociale; et une publication partielle serait aussi peu propre à remplir ce but-là, qu'elle l'eût été dans le cas par exemple, de mon propre livre.

Je croyais avoir donné dans l'avant-dernier chapitre de mon ouvrage,[2] une adhésion publique complette à votre loi fondamentale de l'évolution humaine. J'en avais certainement l'intention bien arrêtée. Je n'ai pas le moindre doute, ni sur la vérité et l'universalité de cette grande loi, ni sur sa susceptibilité de servir de fondement à l'explication des principaux faits secondaires du développement humain ce que je n'aurais jamais cru possible, à un degré si complette, avant les preuves nombreuses que vous en avez données dans votre grand ouvrage, en réalisant, à tant d'égards importans, cette explication. C'est parce que le travail dynamique se trouve par là dans un état déjà assez avancé que je regarde l'établissement des principes de la statique comme devant occuper la place la plus importante dans la phase prochaine de notre entreprise.

Je serai vraiment heureux si la traduction de mon libre vient enfin à dépendre du jeune Bernard[3] que je préférais de beaucoup à un professeur quelconque ignoré, non seulement par ce que vous m'en dites, mais encore plus parce que vous exerceriez naturellement sur lui une autorité morale qui empêcherait toute atteinte grave à l'exactitude soigneuse qu'exige une pareille tâche.

Je suis très content de l'impression qu'ont faite sur vous M. et Mme Austin.[4] Le premier mérite bien tout ce que vous dites à sa louange, soit sous le rapport de son intelligence, soit par élévation de son caractère et par la noblesse de ses sentimens. C'est d'ailleurs l'homme le plus dénué de préjugés, conservatoires [*sic*] ou révolutionnaires, religieux ou anti-réligieux, qu'on puisse trouver peut-être dans toute l'angleterre. Sa femme est non seulement très aimable mais vraiment supérieure, quoique je connaisse des femmes qui la dépassent infiniment. C'est par le bon sens

2. The *Logic* (first edition) Book VI, chap. x, "Of the Inverse Deductive, or Historical Method." Professor John M. Robson has called to the editor's attention the fact that late editions have twelve chapters; chap. xi was added in the fifth edition.

3. Otherwise unidentified than as Comte's unfortunate protégé (see Lévy-Bruhl, p. 293), for whom Comte had sought JSM's help (see Letter 367, and Comte's letter of July 22, 1842, Lévy-Bruhl, p. 88). Apparently nothing ever came of the proposal to have Bernard translate the *Logic.* A translation was eventually published by Louis Peisse: *Système de logique déductive et inductive, exposé des principes de la preuve et des méthodes de recherche scientifique, par John Stuart Mill. Traduit sur la 6e edition anglaise* . . . (2 vols., Paris, 1866).

4. See Comte's letter of Dec. 23, 1843, Lévy-Bruhl, p. 294.

des idées et par la clarté et l'élégance de l'expression qu'elle excelle le plus, soit dans la conversation, soit dans le peu qu'elle a écrit. Quant à la tendance *blue* je crois qu'elle s'en défendrait très vigoureusement: Son genre de vanité me semble tout autre, c'est du reste, un reproche qui atteint tout naturellement toute femme qui se mêle de littérature.

Mon ami Bain me mande qu'à sa recommandation un libraire d'Aberdeen y a fait venir deux exemplaires de votre grand ouvrage. Il ajoute: "The Bookseller who ordered them found it impossible to procure them in London, which he ascribed, I know not with what truth, to a great and sudden demand for the book through the country." Il est certain que votre nom se rencontre aujourd'hui beaucoup plus souvent dans les feuilles périodiques. Je ne vois pas encore beaucoup de citations une peu considérables, si ce n'est dans les articles de notre ami Lewes.[5]

Les tentatives des meneurs jésuitiques auprès de vous m'amusent beaucoup. Je crois nos chefs anglo-catholiques beaucoup plus consciencieux. Il y a meme parmi eux quelques esprits supérieurs.

tout à vous

J. S. MILL

421. TO WILLIAM TAIT[1]

I.H.
5th Feb.
1844

MY DEAR SIR

It will not be in my power at present for reasons connected with my other engagements & with my health, to furnish you with the paper you wish for, nor am I sure that if I could furnish one, it would be of the kind you wish— so much new light having been thrown on banking questions by the discussions of the last few years that my former opinions require much reconsideration.

I should be glad to hear anything you can tell me about Professor Nichol, as he has written to me very seldom of late years.

Very truly yours

J. S. MILL.

5. See Letter 400, n. 2.

* * * *

1. MS at LSE.

422. TO SARAH AUSTIN[1]

India House
26th February
1844

DEAR MRS. AUSTIN—I had heard a favourable account of Mr Austin from Lewis[2] before I received your letter, & I am very glad to have it confirmed—the experiment of whether Paris agrees with his health & whether he likes it as a place to live in, which is one great element of health, was well worth trying & I congratulate him on its having succeeded thus far. I hope he is well enough to go on with what he had begun to write. It seems to me of more importance than ever that the public should have his account of Prussia & the Prussian government since I have read Laing's.[3] I want to see *his* view of *that* view of Prussian affairs. There is a real faculty of observation & original remark about Laing which is likely to give his book considerable influence here, whenever his prejudices coincide with the common English ones, which in spite of many appearances to the contrary, they generally do. It is strange to find a man recognizing as he does that the Norwegian, & German, & French state of society are much better for the happiness of all concerned than the struggling, go-ahead English & American state, & yet always measuring the merit of all things by their tendency to increase the number of steam engines, & to make human beings as good machines & therefore as mere machines as those. His attacks on the peculiarities of the German governments are likely to have the more influence because they are in all probability exaggerations of truths.

Comte's taking to you is what I should have expected. I do not find that his profession of avoiding society stands good at all towards those who seek, or whom he thinks likely to value, him. He is at war with most of his cotemporaries, & is disposed to like those who give him the appreciation he thinks unjustly withheld by others: reste à savoir whether his liking would hold unless kept up by homage or services to himself.

Thanks for your invitation—but there is nothing in the state of my health to require change, that being much the same as it was when I saw you last—& I do not wish to leave London or apply for any holiday at present. I am looking forward to a real holiday in summer which will set me up for some time—

yours ever

J. S. MILL

1. MS at King's.
2. George Cornewall Lewis.
3. Samuel Laing, *Notes of a Traveller on the Social and Political State of France, Prussia, Switzerland, Italy, and other parts of Europe, during the present century* (London, 1842).

423. TO ROBERT BARCLAY FOX[1]

India House
22d March
1844

MY DEAR FRIEND

Many thanks for your writing to tell me of your present & prospective happiness.[2] I had heard of it through your sisters & mine, but it was pleasant to receive the intelligence from yourself.

If this important event in your life turns out as favourably as you have apparently the best reasons to expect, there are as I often think, few persons whose lot in life is more favourable than yours or who have more reason to look forward to a happy existence. In any case you have my sympathy & good wishes in the fullest measure.

I am sorry for what you tell me about Sterling. I had not heard of or from him for some time, nor indeed had I written to him lately, having been rather unsocial & neglectful of such duties for the last few months. I have the most agreeable remembrance of a visit to him last October.[3] The brightness of that sea & air have often "flashed upon the inward eye" between that time & this.

yours most truly

J. S. MILL

424. TO WILLIAM TAIT[1]

India House
22[d] March
1844

MY DEAR SIR

The opinion you expressed the other day that those Pol. Economy papers[2] of mine if printed would have a good chance of selling enough to pay their expenses, induces me to ask you whether you would be inclined, on that chance, to take the risk of publishing them. I have never hitherto offered them to any publisher, but if you were really inclined to it I should think

1. MS in the possession of Mr. W. H. Browning.
2. His engagement to Miss Jane Backhouse of Darlington had been announced.
3. See Letter 408.

* * * *

1. MS at LSE. Page 3 of letter bears note in another hand [Tait's]: "Agreed to this, by letter 25 March 1844."
2. Later that year published by J. W. Parker: *Essays on Some Unsettled Questions of Political Economy* (London, 1844). See Letter 43, n. 14.

seriously of the matter. I should probably think it right to offer them first to Parker, but I have no idea that he would publish them.

Yours very truly

W. Tait Esq. J. S. MILL.

425. TO JOHN WILLIAM PARKER[1]

India House
30th March
1844

MY DEAR SIR

I have been urged by various people to publish certain Political Economy essays[2] which I wrote some years ago & have kept by me in manuscript, in which form several of my friends have read them. They are of too abstract a character for popularity, but the most important of them has a direct bearing upon the question of Reciprocity which has been raised by Col. Torrens in his "Budget"[3] & so much discussed of late & therefore, among political economists, they would doubtless excite some attention though not, I am afraid, among the general public.

I should not have thought of proposing to any publisher to take the risk of printing them, if I had not lately had an offer to that effect—but having had such an offer I should at once close with it if I did not wish first to ascertain whether you would undertake the publication. I should prefer you as publisher to any one else, though I do not feel at all confident that it will suit you.

The Essays will I think make an octavo volume of some 250 pages.

Very truly yours,

J. S. MILL

426. TO AUGUSTE COMTE[1]

India House
le 3 avril 1844

MON CHER MONSIEUR COMTE

Depuis plusieurs jours deux exemplaires de votre Discours[2] me sont parvenus par l'intermédiaire de Madame Austin, qui m'en promet encore

1. MS at Goldsmiths' Library, University of London. 2. See preceding letter.

3. Robert Torrens, *The Budget. On Commercial and Colonial Policy, with an introduction, in which the deductive method, as presented in Mr. Mill's System of Logic is applied to the solution of some controverted questions in political economy* (London, 1844).

* * * *

1. MS at Johns Hopkins. Published in Lévy-Bruhl, pp. 306–9; in reply to Comte's of Feb. 6, *ibid.*, pp. 299–305.

2. *Discours sur l'Esprit positif* (Paris, 1844). See Lévy-Bruhl, p. 301.

trois par la première occasion et je viens d'en recevoir cinq directement. Je commence à les placer le plus convenablement que je le puis, en évitant d'en donner à ceux sur qui on peut compter pour en acheter et qui le peuvent sans aucun inconvénient. Ce petit sommaire m'est parvenu au moment où je faisais une nouvelle lecture sérieuse de votre sixième volume, qui en raison de sa publication plus récente, et aussi parce que je l'avais laissé emporter en Ecosse par mon ami Bain, était celui de tous que j'avais lu le moins souvent. J'ai trouvé dans le Discours un résumé admirable des conclusions générales de votre Système, avec quelques éclaircissements accessoires. Mais plus j'y réfléchis, plus il me semble merveilleux que vos artisans parisiens puissent comprendre cela. Sans doute puisqu'ils y portent un intérêt soutenu ils doivent en recueillir un certain fruit, et je suis bien persuadé que ce qu'ils en retirent doit nécessairement leur profiter beaucoup. Mais il me semble très difficile, même pour les intelligences très cultivées, de se placer au point de vue philosophique de ce petit Traité sans s'y être élevé graduellement par la préparation des six volumes de votre grand Traité. Je trouve, de même, qu'il ne pourrait résulter qu'un avantage très problématique de la traduction actuelle de votre Discours en anglais. Les principes logiques énoncés dans ce Discours dans une forme nécessairement abstraite feraient ici peu d'effet, sans avoir été précédés de l'exposition concrète; ceux même à qui ces principes ne répugneraient pas n'en sentiraient probablement pas assez la valeur et la portée, tandis que des lecteurs mal préparés, qui craignent le travail lent et fatigant d'une étude suivie de votre Cours, se croiraient le droit de juger définitivement votre philosophie d'après une appréciation rapide d'un petit écrit qui leur semblerait à tort destiné à en présenter les titres, ainsi que les principaux résultats. Le seul attribut caractéristique de la nouvelle philosophie, dont on aurait par cet écrit une suffisante connaissance réelle, ce serait son incompatibilité radicale avec toute théologie quelconque, et c'est précisément ce qu'il importe beaucoup qu'on ne reconnaisse pas encore, parce que cette idée, généralement répandue, détournerait de cette étude un grand nombre d'esprits, surtout jeunes, qui, si on ne les effrayait pas dans le commencement, finiraient par s'accoutumer à toutes les conséquences, même anti-religieuses, du positivisme. Le temps n'est pas venu où sans compromettre notre cause, nous pourrons en angleterre diriger des attaques ouvertes contre la théologie, même chrétienne. Nous pouvons seulement l'éluder, en l'éliminant tranquillement de toutes les discussions philosophiques et sociales et en passant à l'ordre du jour sur toutes les questions qui lui sont propres. Par conséquent il me paraît que le propagandisme que vos ouvrages ne manqueront pas d'exercer en angleterre comme ailleurs, aura lieu par leur lecture directe. Ceux qui ajoutent une certaine culture scientifique à une émancipation ou même à une demi-émancipation religieuse, sont presque toujours capables de lire votre livre en français et la traduction ne leur en serait d'aucune utilité.

J'attends avec beaucoup d'intérêt votre Cours populaire d'astronomie. Je désire vivement apprendre la manière dont vous présentez cette science à des esprits sans aucune préparation mathématique sérieuse. Nous avons chez nous des traités populaires d'astronomie, assez bien faits au reste, mais qui se contentent, comme à l'ordinaire, d'en faire connaître empiriquement les résultats, sans donner, comme vous avez dû le faire, une idée nette et juste, quoique générale, de la méthode par laquelle la raison humaine est parvenue à découvrir et à démontrer les lois des phénomènes soustraits en apparence à ses principaux moyens d'exploration.

J'ai reçu dernièrement une nouvelle preuve de l'impression générale produite par le succès de ma Logique. Un libraire m'a fait la proposition d'imprimer un petit recueil de discussions en économie politique,[3] que j'ai écrites il y a longtemps et que ce même libraire avait autrefois refusé de publier. Il y a là des choses qui peuvent encore être utiles et je me suis décidé d'accepter la proposition en ajoutant à ce petit livre la réimpression d'un article de revue[4] dans lequel j'avais autrefois expliqué, à propos de l'économie politique, les principes de la méthode déductive. J'ai même encore l'idée, puisque mes méditations éthologiques ne seront pas mûres de longtemps, de faire en attendant ce qui ne serait pour moi qu'un travail de quelques mois, c'est-à-dire un traité spécial d'économie politique,[5] analogue à celui d'Adam Smith qui n'est certainement plus au niveau de ce temps-ci, tandis que sa place n'est pas encore convenablement remplie. Je sais ce que vous pensez de l'économie politique actuelle: j'en ai une meilleure opinion que vous, mais si j'écris quelque chose là dessus ce sera en ne perdant jamais de vue le caractère purement provisoire de toutes ses conclusions concrètes, et je m'attacherais surtout à séparer les lois générales de la production, nécessairement communes à toutes les sociétés industrielles, des principes de la distribution et de l'échange des richesses, principes qui supposent nécessairement un état de société déterminé, sans préjuger que cet état doive ou même qu'il puisse durer indéfiniment, quoiqu'en revanche il soit impossible de juger les divers états de la société sans prendre en considération les lois économiques qui leur sont propres. Je crois qu'un pareil traité peut avoir, surtout ici, une grande utilité provisoire et qu'il servira puissamment à faire pénétrer l'esprit positif dans les discussions politiques.

tout à vous

J. S. Mill

3. See next letter.
4. See Letter 43, n. 14.
5. Eventually published as *Principles of Political Economy, with Some of their Applications to Social Philosophy* (2 vols., London, 1848).

427. TO WILLIAM TAIT[1]

India House
8th April
1844

MY DEAR SIR

After receiving your note I determined to publish the Essays & accordingly made a tender of them in the first instance, as I felt bound to do, to Parker, who after a few days consideration contrary to my expectation consented to publish them.

I am therefore precluded from closing, as I should otherwise have done, with your proposition. But I consider you as completely the primary cause of their being published, as I should not probably have thought of offering them to any publisher if you had not mentioned the subject to me.

You certainly do not lose much profit by not being the publisher.

Very truly yours
J. S. MILL

428. TO JOHN MITCHELL KEMBLE[1]

I.H.
Saturday [May (?) 1844]

MY DEAR SIR

I have commenced an article on Duveyrier's Lettres Politiques[2] & expect to have finished it in a fortnight or three weeks when if you are inclined to take such an article I will send it to you.

Very truly yours
J. S. MILL

429. TO JOHN WILLIAM PARKER[1]

India House
10 May
1844

MY DEAR SIR

This will introduce to you my friend Mr. G. H. Lewes who wishes to converse with you on the subject of a literary work projected by him.[2]

1. MS at LSE.

* * * *

1. MS in 1944 in the possession of Dr. Adrian Ver Brugghen, Evanston, Ill. See Letter 433.

2. Eventually published as "Duveyrier's Political Views of French Affairs," *ER*, LXXXIII (April, 1846), 453–74.

* * * *

1. *Addressed*: J. W. Parker Esq. / West Strand. MS at LSE.

2. Presumably Lewes' *A Biographical History of Philosophy*, which Parker published in four volumes, 1845–46.

Of course I cannot judge how far such a work would suit you as a publisher but I have a very high opinion of Mr Lewes' qualifications for undertaking it.

Very truly yours
J. S. MILL

430. TO JOHN MITCHELL KEMBLE[1]

India House
28th May 1844

MY DEAR SIR

My friend Mr David Masson,[2] of Aberdeen, has requested me to give him a line of introduction to accompany an article on Wallace[3] which he proposes offering to your review. I think you will find that he has treated the subject in a way by no means commonplace or trite & I consider him likely to be a valuable contributor to any review. If I were still an editor myself I should certainly print the article.

Believe me
very truly yours
J. S. MILL

431. TO JOHN STERLING[1]

India House
29th May 1844

MY DEAR STERLING

For some time after I heard of your last dreadful attack I was afraid to write to you, your father having given me what seemed strong reasons against doing so—but as these do not seem any longer to exist, I venture to write. I do most earnestly hope that you will not give way to discouragement about your state, although I know by painful experience how natural it is to do so & what mere idle words everything must appear that can be said to you by persons who have so much less means of judging than yourself. But there is a surprising elasticity in your constitution which has

1. MS in the possession of Professor Ney MacMinn.
2. David Masson (1822–1907), Scottish man of letters, best known for his *The Life of John Milton* (6 vols., Cambridge and London, 1858–80). Bain had introduced him to JSM in the summer of 1843 (see David Masson, *Memories of London in the "forties"* [Edinburgh, 1908]).
3. No such article appeared in the *BFR*.

* * * *

1. Published in Elliot, I, 125–27. MS at Leeds.

carried you through shocks which would have been fatal to many a stronger person, & that is what we have to rest hope upon. And there is one thing which cannot be said to you too often, because I have seen before that there was real need of saying it. If there should be but little chance of your recovering anything like solid or perfect health, or even of your possessing permanently & safely such a degree of it as you have sometimes had for considerable periods together, in the last few years, I am afraid you will think that anything short of this is not worth having or worth wishing for—that you will be useless & helpless & that it is better to be dead. I enter most perfectly into such a feeling & should very likely feel the very same if I were as I have several times thought I might be, in your circumstances—but I cannot conceive anything more completely mistaken than in your case such a feeling would be. If you were never able to go through any active exertion, or to write a single line, except an occasional letter, or to exercise any influence over mankind except the influence of your thoughts & feelings upon your children & upon those by whom you are personally known and valued, you would still be, I sincerely think, the most useful man I know. It is very little that any of us can do, except doing good to those nearest to us—& of what we *can* do the smallest part, in general, is that which we calculate upon & to which we can attach our name. There are certainly few persons living who are capable of doing so much good by their indirect & unconscious influence as you are & I do not believe you have ever had an adequate conception of the extent of influence you possess & the quantity of good which you produce by it. Even by your mere existence you do more good than many by their laborious exertions. I do not speak of what the loss of you would be, or the blank it would make in life even to those who like me have except for short periods had little of you except the knowledge of your existence & of your affection. None of us could hope in our lives to meet with your like again—& if we did, it would be no compensation. And when I think how many of the best people living are at this moment feeling this, I am sure that you have much to live for.

All connected with me whom you know are feeling deeply interested about you, including Clara,[2] who has repeatedly written most anxiously wishing to know all that can be known about your health & intentions. She is now at Dresden & has been much interested & excited by the change of scene & manner of life; her ἀποδημια[3] has been a completely successful experiment & she does not seem at all disposed to return soon. George is now working under me in the India House to which he has been appointed by the Directors in a way very kind & agreeable to me. He is learning his business very successfully & is in other respects of great promise. I myself

2. JSM's sister.
3. "being away from home."

have been writing several review articles, one on Guizot's essays[4] & lectures, at the request of Napier though I do not know when he will print it, & one on the Currency,[5] which is just coming out in the *Westminster*. I have also been able to get published some Political Economy essays,[6] written fourteen years ago. This is one effect of the success of the Logic. I think my next book will be a systematic treatise on Political Economy, for none of the existing ones are at all up to the present state of speculation.

Ever my dear Sterling yours most affectionately

J. S. MILL

432. TO AUGUSTE COMTE[1]

India House
le 6 juin 1844

MON CHER MONSIEUR COMTE

Vous devez recevoir bientôt, si vous ne l'avez pas encore reçu, un exemplaire d'un petit volume de moi[2] que je vous ai fait adresser par l'éditeur, quoique je ne puisse pas espérer qu'il vous intéresse beaucoup ni que fous fassiez en sa faveur une nouvelle exception à votre règle d'hygiène cérébrale, à laquelle vous avez dérogé d'une manière si honorable pour moi, en faveur d'un ouvrage plus important. Je ne le vous ai envoyé que pour mémoire, et parce que je ne voudrais pas qu'il parût quelque chose en mon nom, sans que vous en eussiez connaissance. Je n'y mets pas au reste beaucoup d'importance; c'est un recueil de discussions d'économie politique, écrites il y a 14 ou 15 ans et restées depuis lors en manuscrit, à l'exception d'une seule qui se rapportant principalement à la méthode, comportait un intérêt plus général et qui a paru dans une revue en 1836.[3] Puisque je les avais écrites et qu'on m'a proposé de les publier j'ai cru qu'elles valaient la peine de les imprimer mais non celle de les refaire, sauf des corrections verbales et quelques suppressions motivées par le progrès postérieur de mes conceptions logiques, progrès essentiellement dû à votre grand ouvrage.

Je me félicite de l'approbation que vous voulez bien donner à mon projet de faire sur l'économie industrielle des sociétés un traité un peu plus systématique. Je ne me sentais pas auparavant suffisamment assuré de votre adhésion à ce projet, qui pouvait vous paraître essentiellement anti-scienti-

4. See Letter 419, n. 2.
5. "The Currency Question," *WR*, XLI (June, 1844), 579–98.
6. See Letter 427.

* * * *

1. MS at Johns Hopkins. Published in Lévy-Bruhl, pp. 321–25; in answer to Comte's of May 1, *ibid.*, pp. 310–20.
2. *Essays on Some Unsettled Questions of Political Economy.*
3. See Letter 86, n. 3.

fique, et qui le serait en effet si je n'avais le plus grand soin de bien établir le caractère purement provisoire de toute doctrine sur les phénomènes industriels qui fasse abstraction du mouvement général de l'humanité. Je crois que ce dessein, s'il pouvait être convenablement exécuté, aurait l'avantage de préparer l'éducation positive de beaucoup d'esprits qui s'occupent plus ou moins sérieusement des questions sociales, et il me semble aussi qu'en prenant pour modèle général le grand et le beau travail d'Adam Smith, j'aurais des occasions importants de répandre directement quelques-uns des principes de la nouvelle philosophie, comme Adam Smith a fait pour la plupart de ceux de la métaphysique négative dans ses applications sociales sans éveiller les défiances ombrageuses en déployant aucun drapeau. Je crois d'ailleurs qu'un tel ouvrage a aujourd'hui des chances favorables pour s'emparer de son terrain spécial, en écartant les traités existants, tous essentiellement surannés même par rapport à l'état actuel de l'opinion publique, qui si elle ne trouve pas bientôt quelque chose d'un peu mieux, se détournerait certainement de cet ordre d'études, sans que ce dégoût puisse encore profiter à autre chose qu'à l'empirisme systématique qui nie toute doctrine générale en matière sociologique.

Je vous remercie vivement de vos remarques philosophiques sur la discussion pendante en France sur la liberté d'enseignement. Sans avoir suivi les différentes phases de cette discussion j'avais saisi ce qu'il y a d'anormal et de contradictoire dans les positions respectives des théologiens et des métaphysiciens à l'égard de cette lutte, où leurs rôles sont comme vous l'avez si bien dit, essentiellement renversés: ce qui du reste a lieu aujourd'hui dans presque toutes les grandes discussions politiques, non seulement en france mais même ici, où les situations, malgré des différences superficielles, sont les mêmes au fond. Le parti des anciennes idées a cessé, ici comme ailleurs, de gouverner: quel que soit le parti dominant, il n'y a des différences réelles de doctrine que chez ceux qui suivent: les chefs se conduisent toujours dans des intentions de juste milieu; ils n'ont que les prémisses convenues de leur parti politique, en renonçant à toutes les conséquences. C'est seulement depuis quelques ans, et surtout depuis le dernier avènement du parti tory,[4] que cette situation commence à être généralement comprise; et c'est surtout aujourd'hui qu'elle se dessine très fortement par les attaques systématiques qu'une partie des Torys,[5] dirigée par quelques jeunes gens assez remarquables, a entreprisés au nom des anciens principes, contre la politique actuelle du parti conservateur. C'est là encore une phase indispensable de notre mouvement social et intellectuel. Les doctrines négatives étant tombées en discrédit avant d'avoir accompli leur œuvre, il est indispensable que les anciennes doctrines sociales reprennent un peu de leur

4. In 1841.
5. The Young England party, which included Benjamin Disraeli.

influence antérieure afin qu'elles aussi puissent de nouveau démontrer expérimentalement leur impuissance actuelle. C'est ce qu'elles ne tarderont pas à faire. En attendant tout cela sert à ranimer les spéculations sociales. Dans les temps modernes la pensée n'est jamais, au fond, ennemie de la pensée: tous les penseurs sont tellement en danger d'être opprimés par les médiocrités de leur propre parti que leur sympathie mutuelle est à peu près assurée, sauf des rivalités personnelles directes.

Je regrette beaucoup, quoique je n'en sois nullement surpris, que vous ayez éprouvé un dérangement physique auquel il est très difficile d'échapper quand on travaille comme vous, à peu près sans intermission. La cessation totale de travail cérébral soutenu, pendant quelques mois, que vous me recommandez avec un intérêt si amical, vous serait probablement encore plus avantageux qu'à moi. Je ne manquerais pas de profiter de votre conseil si une pareille relâche me devenait réellement importante, et dans ce cas-là je n'aurais aucune difficulté à obtenir un congé de la longueur suffisante. Il n'y a lieu aujourd'hui à aucune démarche pareille, puisque je me porte mieux que je ne me suis porté depuis deux ans, et je me sens aussi propre qu'à l'ordinaire à toute espèce de travail intellectuel. J'espère m'y livrer beaucoup cette année.

Ne vous mettez pas en peine à l'égard de la traduction de mon livre; il en sera comme il pourra. Si, comme je l'espère, le professeur de Marrast ne la fait pas, il sera toujours libre au jeune Bernard[6] de l'entreprendre, pourvu toutefois qu'il y ait un éditeur qui veuille s'en charger, ce qui peut-être ne se trouvera pas, par des raisons que vous sentirez très facilement, car les doctrines de mon livre sont tout aussi opposées à celles de toutes les écoles régnantes en France, que celles du vôtre, et si de mon côté je n'ai attaqué personne, au moins je vous ai loué, en m'abstenant de louer aucun chef de coterie. Si par ces raisons le livre n'est pas traduit, nous l'avons bien merité.

tout à vous

J. S. Mill

433. TO JOHN MITCHELL KEMBLE[1]

I.H.
6th June 1844

My dear Sir

I have been disappointed by not finding time to finish my article on Duveyrier.[2] Part of it is completed & the first draught made of the rest but I have been so taken off by things of more immediate emergency &

6. See Letter 420, n. 3.

* * * *

1. MS in the possession of Professor Ney MacMinn.
2. See Letter 428, n. 2.

especially by official work that I have not been able to get it completed & now I am about to go out of town for some weeks during which it must be suspended. I have no doubt however of being able to let you have it before the end of August, which I suppose will be in time for your autumn number.

Very truly yours

J. S. MILL

434. TO AUGUSTE COMTE[1]

India House
le 12 août
1844

Il fallait, mon cher Monsieur Comte, que la première de vos lettres qui ne me fût pas venue promptement fût précisément celle dont la prompte arrivée importait le plus. J'arrive aujourd'hui d'un congé court et dont la destination était depuis longtemps rigoureusement fixée et je viens seulement de lire cette lettre et d'apprendre tout ce qu'elle contient. Vous me connaissez, j'espère, assez pour croire que je m'associe on ne peut pas plus à votre indignation et que je me réjouis cordialement que les indignes menées de ceux que vous avez avec votre franchise philosophique si justement dénoncés vous aient moins nui qu'il n'y avait d'abord lieu de craindre. Quoique le rétard de ma réponse vous ait probablement décidé à vous adresser directement à M. Grote, je n'ai pas perdu un moment à lui faire part de votre lettre; il est à la campagne et je n'ai pas pu encore avoir de réponse. Je connais assez son caractère et je suis assez sûr de l'estime profonde qu'il a pour vous pour que je n'eusse pas hésité, même si vous n'y aviez pas pensé, à demander ses conseils dans un pareil cas, en lui offrant l'occasion de participer par lui-même et de provoquer la participation de ses amis riches à une œuvre qui ne peut manquer de faire honneur à ceux qui y prennent part. Comme vous le désirez, par des raisons dont je reconnais la justesse, je réserverai mes propres ressources pour le cas où leur emploi serait indispensable ce dont je pourrai mieux juger en quelques jours d'ici. Je vous écris, mon cher ami, au milieu des embarras de toutes sortes dont on est entouré quand on arrive. Je vous écrirai au long le plustôt possible.

tout à vous

J. S. MILL

1. MS at Johns Hopkins. Published in Lévy-Bruhl, pp. 340–41; in reply to Comte's of July 22, *ibid.*, 325–39.

Comte had written that in May his enemies had defeated him for re-election to his examinership at the Ecole Polytechnique, thereby depriving him of much of his income. He asked JSM to help raise 6,000 francs among his English friends for his support. Grote and Molesworth subsequently provided the money (see Letters 435, 438, and 439).

435. TO AUGUSTE COMTE[1]

India House
14 août 1844

MON CHER AMI

M. Grote prend sur lui la moitié de la somme nécessaire. Demain j'espère pouvoir vous dire définitivement d'où viendra l'autre moitié. En tout cas les six mille francs sont assurés.

votre devoué

J. S. MILL

436. TO JOHN MITCHELL KEMBLE[1]

I.H.
14th Aug. 1844

MY DEAR SIR

How much time can you give me to finish Duveyrier[2] for your next number. I have just returned & find myself loaded with occupation.

Very truly yours

J. S. MILL

437. TO JOHN STERLING[1]

I.H.
16 Aug. 1844

MY DEAR STERLING—The trifling thing you ask might have been done without asking—& if there is anything in which I can ever be useful or

1. MS at Johns Hopkins. Published in Lévy-Bruhl, p. 341.

* * * *

1. MS in the possession of Professor Ney MacMinn.
2. See Letters 428 and 433.

* * * *

1. Published in Elliot, I, 127. MS at Leeds. In reply to a letter from Sterling reporting that he was at the point of death. He died Sept. 18, 1844.

Sterling's last letter to JSM, dated Hillside, Sept. 8, 1844, is at Yale University:

My dear Mill—We neither of us can need assurances of what we are to each other but your letters have a tone in them that I would fain reply to fittingly if I could. But I am so weak that I dare not in the least give way to any strong feeling or it leaves me completely broken & helpless. I have been looking at old letters of my own (yours you shall have again) & how much I find if that were wanted to put me in mind of you. How many many scores of times have I been thinking how we sat together on the Baths of Caligula. Let us hope to meet upon some other height with a still nobler prospect. Heaven bless you. Always & entirely yours

JOHN STERLING

On the verso in JSM's hand:

"Sterling
8 September 1844
nine days before his death"

helpful to you or yours, you cannot do me a greater kindness than by telling me of it.

I have never so much wished for another life as I do for the sake of meeting you in it. The chief reason for desiring it has always seemed to me to be that the curtain may not drop altogether on those one loves & honours. Every analogy which favours the idea of a future life leads one to expect that if such a life there be, death will no further change our character than as it is liable to be changed by any other important event in our existence—and I feel most acutely what it would be to have a firm faith that the world to which one is in progress was enriching itself with those by the loss of whom this world is impoverished.

If we lose you, the remembrance of your friendship will be a precious possession to me as long as I remain here, & the thought of you will be often an incitement to me when in time of need & sometimes a restraint. I shall never think of you but as one of the noblest, & quite the most loveable of all men I have known or ever look to know.

J.S.M.

438. TO AUGUSTE COMTE[1]

India House
le 20 août
1844

MON CHER AMI

Nous tenons une partie de la seconde moitié du déficit, et je suis assuré d'obtenir le reste sans recourir à mes propres fonds. La chose a traîné un peu, seulement à cause de l'absence de tous ceux à qui on devait s'adresser de préférence et qui ne sont pas à Londres dans ce tems-ci. D'un jour à l'autre je puis être à même de vous annoncer le résultat définitif de mes démarches.

Je ne tarderai pas à faire parvenir à M. Whewell de votre part un exemplaire de votre Discours.[2] Il m'en reste encore, puisque je ne le donne qu'à ceux que je juge capables d'en profiter, et pas assez riches pour devoir l'acheter. Comme mon libraire-éditeur est aussi celui de M. Whewell, il m'est facile de me servir de son intermédiaire dans le cas dont il s'agit.

Je désire beaucoup savoir de vous la nature de cette nouvelle crise polytechnique. Il me semble qu'elle offre à l'autorité un puissant moyen de changer tout ce qu'il y a de nuisible dans le règlement de l'école.

tout à vous

J. S. MILL

1. MS at Johns Hopkins. Published in Lévy-Bruhl, pp. 344–45; in reply to Comte's of Aug. 15, *ibid.*, pp. 342–44.
2. *Discours sur l'Esprit positif*, which Comte had asked JSM to send.

439. TO AUGUSTE COMTE[1]

India House
le 23 août
1844

MON CHER AMI

Il est ouvert en votre faveur chez MM. Delamarre Martin Didier et Co banquiers, Rue des Jeuneurs, à Paris un crédit de 3000 francs et le 1er février prochain une autre somme pareille sera à votre disposition chez les mêmes banquiers. La somme provient tout entière de M. Grote et de sir William Molesworth, M. Grote s'étant opposé formellement à ce qu'on essayât d'y associer d'autres. Il a trouvé plus convenable de ne s'adresser qu'à des esprits complètement émancipés sous le rapport religieux, jugeant que nul autre n'était capable de vous apprécier suffisamment. Sans cela je n'eusse pas craint de m'adresser à deux d'entre les chefs de banque les plus distingués, qui admirent beaucoup vos ouvrages: chez l'un d'eux surtout j'ai pu m'assurer personnellement qu'il avait pour vous une admiration *sentie*, malgré ses opinions religieuses assez prononcées. Cependant je trouve avec M. Grote que la chose est mieux comme elle est. Lui et Sir William Molesworth sont tous deux assez riches pour que vous ne puissiez pas vous croire obligé en conscience de les rembourser jamais, et je sais que vous leur feriez plus de plaisir en ne les remboursant pas. Ainsi tout est arrangé pour le mieux, et vous pourrez ainsi jouir sans inquiétude de votre loisir inaccoutumé, et vous occuper en tems opportun du commencement de votre second grand ouvrage.

votre dévoué

J. S. MILL

440. TO AUGUSTE COMTE[1]

India House
le 5 october 1844

MON CHER MONSIEUR COMTE

Mon absence de Londres, quoique courte, a laissé aux affaires du bureau le temps de s'accumuler de manière à m'avoir laissé jusqu'ici peu de loisir pour m'occuper d'autre chose que de mes devoirs officiels et d'affaires domestiques. Après deux mois de travail et de préoccupation qui ne m'ont

1. MS at Johns Hopkins. Published in Lévy-Bruhl, pp. 345–46.

* * * *

1. MS at Johns Hopkins. Published in Lévy-Bruhl, pp. 354–59; in reply to Comte's of Aug. 23 and 28, *ibid.*, pp. 347–53.

permis ni aucune étude ni le très peu de distractions dont j'ai l'habitude, ce n'est vraiment que depuis hier que je me suis trouvé assez libre d'occupation et de pensée pour pouvoir songer à vous écrire. Je n'ai, par conséquent, rien de bien intéressant à vous apprendre sur mon propre compte, sauf l'état de ma santé, qui sans être forte, est maintenant à peu près bonne et capable de supporter tout ce que je serai probablement en lieu d'exiger d'elle. A cet égard le congé que j'ai obtenu m'a rendu un service véritable. Puisse le loisir inusité qui vous est échu cette année vous avoir pareillement servi, en dissipant le dérangement exceptionnel que votre santé semblait avoir subi sur les commencemens de l'année, que la crise que vous avez traversée était de nature à empirer, mais qui était apparemment de la sorte de dérangement qui lorsqu'ils ne sont pas de trop longue date, n'ont guère besoin pour la guérison, que d'un changement suffisant d'habitudes, et surtout d'une intermission de travail. Si, en outre, cette intermission vous a permis de commencer votre seconde grande élaboration philosophique, je n'ai assurément pas besoin de vous dire que je m'en réjouirai profondément. Plus on s'avance dans la vie, et mieux on sent le prix du temps. J'ai souvent besoin de me rappeler avec une émotion pénible, combien l'incertitude de la vie fait un devoir à chacun de mettre le plutôt possible à l'abri de tout hasard les choses utiles qu'il peut faire mieux que les autres ou que les autres ne peuvent ou ne veulent pas faire. Peu d'années s'écoulent sans que cette réflexion soit douloureusement fortifiée par quelque perte irréparable. Je viens d'en subir une, par la mort prématurée d'un du très petit nombre de ceux pour qui j'éprouvais une amitié vive et une estime parfaite.[2] Il réunissait à l'un des plus nobles caractères qui puissent exister, une profondeur de sympathie qui tient de l'idéal féminin et qu'on ne trouve que fort rarement en angleterre si ce n'est dans les femmes et encore très exceptionnellement. Avec une grande étendue de connaissances et une forte intelligence, il n'avait pas le véritable esprit positif; il était pourtant très au delà de nos écoles métaphysiques les plus avancées. Ecclésiastique anglican, il avait depuis longtemps cessé d'appartenir par ses opinions à une église quelconque, et à en juger par ce qu'il avait fait et par les progrès de son intelligence pendant dix ans d'une santé faible et fragile, il eût rendu de très grands services au progrès moral et intellectuel par l'influence qu'il aurait exercée sur des esprits auxquels le positivisme pur ne peut pas encore avoir accès. Il est mort de phtisie pulmonaire à l'âge de 38 ans. M. et Mme Austin l'ont connu et aimé, sans avoir été, je crois, autant que moi en état d'apprécier sa valeur.

Je trouve toujours que le positivisme marche ici, mais il y a encore très peu d'hommes qui par la force primitive de leur esprit et par le degré

2. John Sterling. See Letter 437, n. 1.

de leur préparation, soient capables de s'approprier complètement la méthode et de faire faire des progrès à la doctrine. Je ne vois que Bain en qui, si je mourais demain, je serais sûr de laisser un successeur. Vous avez pu juger notre digne ami M. Grote. Il a bien dépassé son Benthamisme primitif, mais la métaphysique négative fait toujours le fond de sa culture intellectuelle. Molesworth, avec les mêmes tendances générales, a l'esprit plus libre; il est, aussi plus jeune mais son intelligence est plus déductive qu'inductive; sa nature est géomètre: il est par nature ce que j'étais il y a quinze ans par mon éducation. Austin s'est élevé très lentement et très péniblement au-dessus de ce niveau, mais sa déplorable santé, l'imperfection de son éducation scientifique, et son incapacité maladive de rien terminer, empêchent malheureusement de pouvoir compter sur lui pour des choses du premier ordre, qu'il est, à tout autre égard, fait pour dignement accomplir. Restent donc les jeunes gens, et parmi ceux de ma connaissance je ne vois que chez Bain l'étoffe d'un esprit du premier ordre, avec des habitudes intellectuelles parfaitement bonnes. Et nous pouvons nous vanter, vous et moi, d'avoir décidé de sa direction. S'il vit, et il a heureusement une organisation forte, il fera de grandes choses, et il soutiendra dignement la cause du positivisme chez nous. Je compte sur lui pour former beaucoup d'élèves à Aberdeen, où il enseigne publiquement avec un succès remarquable. Je crois d'ailleurs que la philosophie positive trouvera plus d'apôtres actuels en écosse qu'en angleterre, non seulement à cause de l'influence des antécédents philosophiques de ce pays, qui sont, comme vous savez plus voisins de l'esprit positif, mais encore par plusieurs autres raisons. D'abord, l'instruction supérieure y est beaucoup plus répandue qu'ici: les écoles supérieures et les universités sont de nature à mettre cette instruction à portée de la classe moyenne, et même de quelques fils de paysans, classe qui a fourni noblement son contingent à la gloire intellectuelle de l'Ecosse. Ensuite cette instruction elle même est moins exclusivement littéraire et plus scientifique qu'en angleterre. En troisième lieu, bien que les croyances religieuses soient restées plus fortes chez le peuple écossais, l'influence ecclésiastique y est beaucoup plus faible, ce qui est aujourd'hui plus qu'équivalent. Enfin, je trouve qu'il y a une analogie réelle dans la tournure de l'esprit écossais et de l'esprit français. Vous n'avez certainement pu méconnaître à quel point les Hume, les Ferguson, les Adam Smith, les Millar,[3] les Brown, les Reid,[4] même les Chalmers ressemblent intellectuellement à des français, tandis que nos philosophes anglais, en exceptant peut

3. John Millar (1735–1801), professor of law at Glasgow, author of *Observations concerning the distinctions of Ranks in Society* (London, 1771) and *An Historical View of the English Government* . . . (London, 1787, and later enlarged editions), works which James Mill had greatly admired.

4. Thomas Reid (1710–1796), exponent of the "common sense" school of philosophy.

être Hobbes, appartiennent à une type différent: chez Locke, chez Berkeley, chez Hartley, chez Coleridge, ches Bentham même, c'est un ordre d'idées et de tendances intellectuelles profondément disparates, et je pense qu'un esprit vraiment anglais, sorti de notre éducation publique, et étranger à toute culture continentale, est, à beaucoup d'égards, plus éloigné du véritable esprit positif qu'aucun autre homme instruit. Vous vous plaignez avec raison de l'état du public français, dont l'incapacité positive tient aujourd'hui, ce me semble, à des causes plutôt morales qu'intellectuelles. Ici nous avons encore beaucoup de chemin à faire pour nous placer au niveau intellectuel de Guizot, et ce sont déjà des hommes très supérieurs au vulgaire qui ont accompli ce progrès, quelque minime qu'il doive paraître au point de vue de la vraie positivité.

Je ne sais si je vous ai dit que j'avais exécuté votre commission auprès de M. Whewell, en lui faisant parvenir un exemplaire de votre Discours. J'avais, comme vous, reçu son petit opuscule.[5] Je conçois que ne connaissant probablement pas ses autres ouvrages, vous ayez vu avec une juste indulgence ce qu'il y avait de bon dans cette brochure. Pour moi je l'ai trouvée très faible: tout ce qu'il a dit, il l'avait beaucoup mieux dit ailleurs, et ce qui m'y a le plus frappé c'est qu'en reproduisant, très imparfaitement, les objections de son critique, il en a montré si peu d'intelligence qu'il oppose à ses objections les mêmes choses qu'il avait dites auparavant sans tenir aucun compte des réponses. Le critique auquel il répond, et que moi-même j'ai cité dans l'avant-dernier chapitre de mon 2me livre, est l'illustre physicien sir John Herschel, que je trouve très supérieur à M. Whewell. Je ne sais (par parenthèse) si je vous ai dit qu'il m'a mandé que mon livre l'avait décidé à étudier le vôtre: je ne sais s'il l'a fait avec fruit. On me dit que M. Whewell se propose de me réfuter aussi, dans le premier ouvrage qu'il publiera.[6] J'ai toujours comté un peu sur son goût polémique, pour engager une discussion utile. D'ailleurs il mérite toute notre reconnaissance par les améliorations importantes qu'il a faites dans le système d'enseignement de Cambridge et par l'attention qu'il a attirée sur les grandes questions philosophiques. Il a trouvé l'esprit philosophique assoupi: il est un de ceux qui ont le plus fait pour le réveiller.

tout à vous

J. S. MILL

5. Whewell had printed and circulated privately a reply to Sir John Herschel's review of his *History of the Inductive Sciences* and his *Philosophy of the Inductive Sciences* in the *QR* for June, 1841. Whewell subsequently published the reply in the second edition of *The Philosophy of the Inductive Sciences* (London, 1847), II, 669–79.

6. *Of Induction, with especial reference to Mr. J. Stuart Mill's System of Logic* (Cambridge, 1849). Professor J. M. Robson has pointed out that JSM took note of Whewell's arguments in the third (1851) edition of the *Logic*.

441. TO WILLIAM TAIT[1]

India House
4th November
1844

MY DEAR SIR

Are you provided with an article on Johnstone's [*sic*] "Travels in Southern Abyssinia"?[2] & if you are not, should you be disposed to insert one in the Magazine if on seeing it you find it suitable?

Very truly yours
J. S. MILL

442. TO HENRY S. CHAPMAN[1]

India House
8th November, 1844

MY DEAR CHAPMAN,

I am afraid you must by this time think that I have forgotten my promise to write to you, but I have never ceased to bear it in mind, although in the matter of letter writing there is usually a long interval with me, between purpose and performance. I have not much personal news to tell you. My own life goes on just as it did, and I see very few people, Roebuck, Graham, and our other friends, as seldom as anybody else.

You will rather, I suppose, expect to hear from me about public matters; but even these I have scarcely anything prominent or prononcé to relate, in the way of events. It is rather the state of the public mind which is curious and interesting. There is a prodigious current setting in every day more strongly, of superficial philanthropy. English benevolence can no longer be accused of confining itself to niggers and other distant folks; on the contrary everybody is all agog to do something for the poor. A great many things have conduced to this, some good, some bad. The anti-poor-law cry; the state of the houses of the poor, and their sanitary condition, as made

1. MS at LSE.
2. Charles Johnston, *Travels in Southern Abyssinia* (2 vols., London, 1844).

* * * *

1. MS in the possession of Mrs. W. Rosenberg, Wellington, N.Z. Copy supplied by Professor J. M. McCrimmon. Copy bears date of 8th November, 1846, but internal evidence (see notes 5 and 9, below) clearly indicates 1844 as the correct date.

Henry S. Chapman had left England in June, 1843, for New Zealand to take up his duties as the newly appointed Judge of the Supreme Court for the Southern Division.

known by Chadwick's official investigations; the conditions of large masses of people as shown by the enquiries of Commissions about factories, mines, etc., then in another way the speculations of Carlyle,[2] the Puseyites,[3] and others, about the impossibility of any social stability or security if there is not a habitual bond of good offices and sympathy between the ruling classes and the ruled, especially the poor—which speculations would have had no effect whatever if there were no chartism and socialism to frighten the rich. One sees plainly that while the noise is made up by a few sincere people, the bulk of the following has for its motive the desire of preventing revolution, and perhaps still more, the desire of taking the popularis aura out of the sails of the Anti-Corn-law league.[4] In both these things they will fail. The Corn Law *must* go, and very soon,[5] and as for revolution, there has been nothing in our day so calculated to produce it as the talk now in vogue, none of which is lost upon the working class, who do not thank them for it one jot, but whom it greatly strengthens in the faith that it is other people's business to take care of them, that all of the rich have more than they is a wrong to them, and that the rich themselves are partly ashamed of this wrong, and partly afraid of its consequences and desiring to buy them off at the expense of those who are better off, is always asserted; and I never remember a time when any suggestion of anti-population doctrine[6] or of forethought and self-command on the part of the poor was so contemptuously scouted as it is now. The "Times" is at the head of this movement, and has contributed very much to set it going. Strange to say, I believe it is sincere. There has been a great change of late years in the "Times", owing it is said, to young Walter,[7] who is a sort of Puseyite, and the "Times" falls in with everything which Puseyism has set going. There is a great appearance of honesty now about all it does. You are not to suppose, however, that all is bad and stupid about this philanthropy-movement—on the contrary there is very much good in it, and it will lead to many very good things being done. Among other things I have no doubt it will lead in time to a considerable move in favour of colonization, and to shew what other things it leads to, the "Times" already talks occasionally

2. Notably in his *Past and Present* (1843).

3. See Letter 270 and JSM's letters, "Puseyism," in the *Morning Chronicle* for Jan. 1, 1842 (p. 1) and Jan. 13, 1842 (p. 3) for his views on the Oxford Movement.

4. The League, which had been founded in 1839, led the agitation for the repeal of the Corn Laws.

5. The repeal did not take place until June, 1846.

6. Doctrine based on the theories of T. R. Malthus.

7. John Walter III (1818–1894), soon (1847) to become the third bearer of the name to be proprietor of *The Times*. The younger Walter's adherence to the Oxford Movement was a source of serious friction with his father and led to estrangement between them (see *The History of the Times, 1841–1884* [New York, 1939], pp. 10–11).

of the great benefits of the labourers being proprietors of land! Things never seemed to tend so rapidly to a complete bouleversement of our social system, though whether peaceably or violently, none can tell. I am thinking of saying out my say on all these things in a treatise on political economy, not in the abstract manner of Ricardo and my father, but in the practical and popular manner of Adam Smith. The whole science requires extremely to be recast, incorporating, of course, Wakefield's and all the other new doctrines and shewing how they do not contradict but *fit into* the others, and such a book if one were able to do it well would at once supersede all the existing treatises, which are, one and all, effete and useless except as matter of history, and would give a right direction to the revived interest which begins to be felt in the study, and which languishes for want of a book at once free from gross error and teaching the applications along with the principles, which it is the beauty of Adam Smith's book that he did. A propos, I published, last spring, the political economy essays which you know of. The success of my Logic brought an offer from Tait to publish them,[8] whereupon I made an offer of them to my own publisher, Parker,[9] which he accepted, and to my surprise the trade subscription was nearly 100. I have not heard anything about the sale; I should fear it is but small. However, Parker has no reason to complain, as it was his own choice, and he has made money by me. On the 25th March we had already divided profit on the Logic, and I expect it will soon be out of print. It has had a degree of success I never expected, and has got into the hands of almost everybody who could be supposed to read such a book.

There is no probability of any change of Ministry here; the Whigs are in as much discredit as ever, Peel is much greater than ever, but nobody wants him turned out, because his hinges are so well oiled and he yields to pressure. I fully expect every session to shew concessions to liberalism, and every year certainly helps to disorganise all the old order. I only wish for personal changes, because I wish that ill-conditioned fellow Stanley[10] to be out of his post of mischief. The Governor[11] he has sent you seems to be hardly better than the last, although so much better was expected from him.

I hope to hear from you soon, as I am very much interested both in the

8. See Letter 424.

9. Letters 425 and 427.

10. Edward George Geoffrey Smith Stanley, then Lord Stanley of Bickerstaffe, later the fourteenth Earl of Derby, at this time Colonial Secretary. For an account of Stanley's conduct of New Zealand affairs, see W. D. Jones, *Lord Derby and Victorian Conservatism* (Oxford, 1956), pp. 94–101.

11. Robert Fitzroy (1805–1865), from 1843 to Nov., 1845, Governor of New Zealand. He had commanded the *Beagle* during Charles Darwin's famous voyage. As Governor he was in frequent conflict with the New Zealand Company and was accused of favouring the natives over the white settlers.

prospects of the Colony and in your own. I fancy that I can figure to myself the position of a New Zealand settler better than I can that of most distant objects, sufficiently well to make it really interesting to me. I hear a little about Nelson[12] by means of Bell's circulars,[13] but I am more curious about Wellington, though I have no land there. Give my kind regards to Revans,[14] and will you kindly ask him if he was out of pocket in any way by my rascal of a relation John Burrow.[15] His draft of £10 was paid. If there is anything more I will repay it.

Ever yours truly,

J. S. MILL.

443. TO MACVEY NAPIER[1]

India House
9th November
1844

MY DEAR SIR

I have been feeling lately a very great inclination to write something on the doctrines & projects which are so rife just at present on the fashionable subject of the "Claims of Labour"[2]—& the little book so called, would furnish an appropriate text, if you are inclined to the subject, & would not prefer seeing it in other hands. It appears to me that along with much of good intention, & something even of sound doctrine, the speculations now afloat are sadly deficient, on the whole, in sobriety & wisdom—forgetful, in general, of the lessons of universal experience, & of some of those fundamental principles which one did think had been put for ever out of the reach of controversy by Adam Smith, Malthus, & others. The general tendency is to rivet firmly in the minds of the labouring people the persuasion that it is the business of others to take care of their condition, with-

12. The towns of Nelson and Wellington were both in the Southern Division over which Chapman had jurisdiction as Judge.

13. Probably information circulated by the New Zealand Company which it had obtained from Francis (later Sir Francis) Dillon Bell (1821–1898), a relative of E. G. Wakefield. Bell, who had been in the service of the Company in London since 1838, had gone to New Zealand in 1843 to select lands on behalf of the Company.

14. Samuel Revans (1808–1888) in the 1830's had founded with Chapman the *Daily Advertiser* in Montreal. He left Canada in 1837 and joined Wakefield in the New Zealand colonization; he published the first newspaper there, the *New Zealand Gazette*.

15. Presumably a cousin of JSM on his mother's side.

* * * *

1. Published in *Napier Corresp.*, pp. 477–78. MS in Brit. Mus.

2. JSM's review of Arthur Helps' *The Claims of Labour: an Essay on the Duties of the Employers to the Employed* (London, 1844) appeared in *ER*, LXXXI (April, 1845), 498–525.

out any self control on their own part—& that whatever is possessed by other people, more than they possess, is a wrong to them, or at least a kind of stewardship, of which an account is to be rendered to them. I am sure you will agree with me in thinking it very necessary to make a stand against this sort of spirit while it is at the same time highly necessary as well as right, to shew sympathy in all that is good of the new tendencies, & to avoid the hard, abstract mode of treating such questions which has brought discredit upon political economists & has enabled those who are in the wrong to claim, & generally to receive, exclusive credit for high & benevolent feeling.

I do not know of anything so important at the present time as to attempt to place these subjects in their right position before the public—& it can nowhere be done so well as in the Edinburgh review—where I hope it will be done even if it should not suit you that I should do it—although I know no reason for thinking that the manner in which I should treat the subject would be unsuitable to you.

Very truly yours

J. S. Mill

444. TO WILLIAM TAIT[1]

India House
12th Novr 1844

My dear Sir

I send you the article on Johnston,[2] which as you will see, is not mine. It is a light amusing article, chiefly of extracts, & I think it will be pleasant reading for the readers of the Magazine. The few words said about Harris's book[3] are, I should hope, not sufficient to come into unpleasant collision with anything you have said before. Johnstone [*sic*] & his book are, I think, worthy of better treatment than they have received—the book seems to me both more amusing & more interesting than Harris's.

I have ordered a copy of the Essays[4] to be sent to you. I ought to have done so before, as you had certainly a good claim to a copy. I have given away scarcely any. As for Parker it is not his way to give copies, either to the press or to any one else. But I ought myself to have looked to your receiving one.

Very truly yours

J. S. Mill

W. Tait Esq.

1. MS at LSE.
2. See Letter 441, n. 2. The article seems not to have been published.
3. Sir William Cornwallis Harris, *The Highlands of Æthiopia* (3 vols., London, 1844). It had been reviewed in *Tait's* in March and April, 1844.
4. *Essays on Some Unsettled Questions of Political Economy*. See Letter 427.

445. TO MACVEY NAPIER[1]

India House
20th Novr 1844

MY DEAR SIR

The article[2] which I have in view would, according to my present conception of it, be rather one of principles than of details; & would, so far, admit the more easily of being brought within the space to which you consider it necessary to confine it. My object would be to examine & controvert what appears to me an erroneous theory of the condition of the labouring classes. The practical consequences of the theory break out in all sorts of propositions of things to be done for the poor either by the Government, the millowners, the landowners, or the rich in general; some of which propositions have more or less of utility & good sense in them, others are quite chimerical & absurd, but *all* are absurd when looked to as things of great or permanent efficacy. The discussion of the theory will naturally involve a consideration of the real nature of the duties both of Government & of the various classes of society towards the poor; tending mainly to the conclusion, that the greater part of the good they can do is indirect, & consists in stimulating & guiding the energy & prudence of the people themselves: in all which I should wish to use details copiously for purposes of example & illustration, but without laying any particular stress upon them, & still less undertaking to specify with any minuteness what particular things either the Government, or the employers of labour, ought to do or attempt.

According to this idea of what the article would be, it does not seem to be of any special importance that it should precede in its appearance any particular discussion in the House of Commons; but of very considerable importance that it should appear soon: the question being, as you justly remark, the greatest of the day, & moreover most emphatically the question of *the* day: & although the interest of it with thinkers is not likely to abate, anything written on the subject would both be more useful, & much more successful, if it appeared before the subject has been overlaid by the wearisome longwinded discussions of all the periodicals & all the speakers in parliament.

The Times gives us little else from day to day—& the other newspapers are beginning to be full of it. For a time, this works in favour of the interest of the subject—but after a time it will work the contrary way, by exhausting the freshness of the ideas.

We seem quite to agree in our general view of the subject & if you think favorably of the sketch I have now given you of the mode in which

1. Published in *Napier Corresp.*, pp. 478–79. MS in Brit. Mus.
2. See Letter 443.

it should be treated, I will set about it & write the article while my mind is full of the subject.

ever yours truly

J. S. Mill

Guizot of course can wait indefinitely.[3]

446. TO AUGUSTE COMTE[1]

India House
le 25 novembre 1844

Mon cher Monsieur Comte

Vous ne vous trompiez pas en jugeant que votre volume astronomique[2] ne m'était pas encore parvenue lorsque j'écrivais ma dernière lettre. Il ne m'est arrivé, comme de coutume, que très tard, ce qui a depuis longtemps cessé de me surprendre. C'est seulement depuis une huitaine de jours que j'ai pu achever la lecture de ce travail intéressant, dont la valeur a dépassé mes espérances. Il est vraiment heureux que vous vous soyez décidé à écrire ce Traité: quoique d'une importance secondaire en rapport à votre grande entreprise philosophique, il n'en est pas moins fait pour exercer une notable influence en hâtant la formation d'une véritable école positive, et il me semble que vous même vous n'appréciez pas encore suffisamment sa valeur à cet égard. Nous reconnaissons l'un et l'autre de plus en plus combien on doit peu compter pour la cause du positivisme sur ceux qui en possèdent déjà les bases scientifiques. Il importe donc infiniment, sous tous les rapports de mettre le plus tôt possible à la portée des intelligences convenables, non fournies d'instruction scientifique spéciale, ce qu'il faut de connaissances positives pour s'approprier les idées fondamentales de la méthode scientifique, sans les assujettir préalablement à de longues et pénibles études techniques, qui leur répugneraient le plus souvent au point d'empêcher tout développement ultérieur de leur capacité scientifique, attendu que pour sentir réellement l'importance de cette préparation positive, il faudrait posséder déjà l'esprit positif. Pour sortir donc de ce cercle vicieux, il n'y a rien de plus urgent que d'avoir un Cours de *science* positive, préliminaire naturel de votre Cours de philosophie positive. Or ce petit ouvrage en remplit admirablement les conditions, autant que le comportent son étendue et son caractère de spécialité. Depuis quelque temps les traités scientifiques à l'usage du public paraissent chez nous en grande abondance;

3. See Letter 419, n. 2.

* * * *

1. MS at Johns Hopkins. Published in Lévy-Bruhl, pp. 369–73; in reply to Comte's of Oct. 21, *ibid.*, pp. 359–69.
2. *Traité philosophique d'astronomie populaire* (Paris, 1844).

il y en a d'assez bien faits; J. Herschel lui-même a fait un traité populaire d'astronomie.[3] Mais dans ces traités on n'essaie pas même de faire servir de si mémorables conquêtes de l'intelligence humaine à constater la manière dont elle doit procéder pour en faire de nouvelles. Il est même, je crois, heureux que ces écrivains n'aient pas tenté d'enseigner la méthode, mais seulement la doctrine, vu l'insuffisance de leurs propres notions logiques; insuffisance tellement prononcée qu'il n'y a presque pas un seul traité de science positive, soit classique, soit populaire, qui ne tende sous quelques égards notables à fausser le véritable esprit de la marche scientifique. Or il me paraît que vous avez comblé, d'une manière admirable, cette déplorable lacune. Je ne croyais guère qu'il fût possible de donner à des lecteurs à qui on supposaerit si peu de préparation mathématique une connaissance si pleinement satisfaisante du vrai caractère de la science astronomique, et des procédés scientifiques qui l'ont créée. Après un pareil exemple, nous pouvons nous flatter de voir prochainement des ouvrages au moins passables du même genre, par rapport aux autres sciences fondamentales. Ce sera je crois le fruit que nous recueillerons de la première extension notable de la philosophie positive parmi les intelligences du second ordre. Aujourd'hui même je sens que les difficultés du propagandisme positif commencent à s'aplanir par suite de ce que vous avez fait. Le défaut d'instruction scientifique préalable n'est plus un obstacle pour faire comprendre ce que c'est que le positivisme à ceux qu'on pourrait décider à lire votre petit Traité. On peut même dire qu'après cette seule lecture une intelligence bien organisée se trouverait mieux préparée aux spéculations sociales que la presque totalité des savans actuels, sans parler des métaphysiciens.

J'ai appris avec une joie véritable que la méprisable taciturnité de la presse française à votre égard allait enfin être rompue, et je suis bien aise que ce soit par M. Littré,[4] à qui depuis longtemps j'ai voué une haute estime. Je le connais très bien de réputation; je l'ai même vu, en 1836, à Paris, où sa figure de savant solitaire et son maintien calme et modeste m'on beaucoup frappé. Probablement, il ne se souvient guère de notre entrevue. Je ne savais pas qu'il fût en sympathie avec la nouvelle philosophie, et je m'en réjouis vivement: son accession, quelqu'incomplète qu'elle puisse être, est du plus heureux augure, et j'attends avec impatience son appréciation de votre grand ouvrage. Si cette publication s'effectue dans le National, ou même dans un journal quelconque, elle attirera sur la philosophie positive l'attention de beaucoup de lecteurs qui n'en tenaient

3. Herschel's treatise on astronomy published in Lardner's *Cabinet Cyclopædia* in 1833 and translated into French by M. Peyrot in 1834 was the basis of his much expanded *Outlines of Astronomy* (London, 1849, and later editions).

4. Emile Littré (1801–1881), scholar, philosopher, and lexicographer; one of Comte's most ardent disciples, though he rejected Comte's later theories; author of *Auguste Comte et la philosophie positive* (Paris, 1863).

auparavant aucun compte, qui n'en avaient peut-être pas même entendu le nom, et parmi eux il doit s'en trouver de bien préparés pour sa réception complète. Si vous pouviez m'envoyer les numéros du journal qui contiendront ces articles ce serait me faire un très grand plaisir: ceux-là on peut les confier à la poste. Dans tout cas je compte sur vous pour m'en indiquer les dates.

J'espère que vous êtes depuis longtemps parfaitement rétabli des suites du trouble physique que vous avez subi le mois dernier. Une maladie éruptive par suite d'une surexcitation nerveuse est certainement un exemple très remarquable, quoique d'un genre aujourd'hui très familier, du *consensus* biologique, et surtout de cette complication des phénomènes de la vie animale avec ceux de la vie organique qui a rendu si difficile et si tardive leur séparation logique, sans laquelle pourtant la biologie ne pouvait nullement devenir positive. J'ai appris avec un vif intérêt le résultat de vos observations spontanées sur les effets intellectuels du jeûne, et je vous félicite d'avoir surmonté la plus sérieuse difficulté de votre nouvelle élaboration philosophique. Je juge essentiellement comme vous le genre d'esprit de M. Herschel, et je ne fonde aucun espoir sérieux sur sa lecture de votre Cours, qui, je crois, aura peu d'influence, ici comme ailleurs, sur les hommes dont la réputation est faite. Je trouve toutefois dans la critique qu'il a faite de la philosophie de Whewell, des marques d'une certaine capacité philosophique: au moins il a échappé aux influences germaniques, ce qui chez nous n'est pas peu de chose. Je n'ai jamais lu Vico[5] mais autant que j'en puis juger je crois votre opinion de lui très bien fondée.

Tout à vous,

J. S. MILL

447. TO ADOLPHE D'EICHTHAL[1]

India House
10th December
1844

MY DEAR ADOLPHE

I was truly disappointed the other day when I found that you had been here & that I had missed you. Wednesday is a day on which I am usually

5. Giovanni Battista Vico (1668–1744), Italian jurist and philosopher, often regarded as the founder of the philosophy of history, and mentioned by JSM in the *Logic*, Book VI, chap. x, sec. 3.

* * * *

1. MS at Arsenal.

engaged with the Court of Directors, as it is the day of their meeting. I should have enjoyed greatly seeing you once again & comparing notes with you (as we say) on a great many subjects.

I have read with very great interest the papers you sent me, the report on the *caisse de retraite,* & the four numbers of the Moniteur Grec.[2] The first is very important, & all the views & propositions seem to me extremely well-considered & reasonable: what is the probability of their being adopted? The Greek paper is well written & seems candid. I have always been inclined to think well of Coletti[3] because I knew him to be a friend of yours & of your brother's & I knew Gustave's high opinion of him, & I was not inclined to think the worse of him for being attacked by our newspapers with which I am as thoroughly disgusted as I am with yours. But I do not know how to get over the gross illegalities which his party seem to be committing in the exclusion of the partisans of the former ministry from the chamber on any or on no pretext—a thing which the Moniteur Grec in its fourth number seems to admit, or at least to be unable to deny. It is impossible for me to think otherwise than ill of any minister to whom a constitution & laws are a dead letter which they think nothing of violating—& the infamous conduct of your government in the affairs of Spain inclines every one here to put the worst construction on whatever is done in any constitutional country by the party which is supposed to have the support of the French diplomatic agent.—I doubt if I could induce any English newspaper of influence to insert the correspondence which you propose—but I could perhaps succeed either with the Times or the Morning Chronicle, both of which however would probably combat in their leading articles the views of their correspondent. Still, if you think it worth while, I will try—& I should for my own part have much pleasure in doing so.

I owe a letter to Gustave in return for one he wrote to me communicating the interesting fact of the birth of his son, on which I beg you to offer to him my sincere congratulations. Although I have not been a very frequent correspondent lately, either with him or my other friends at Paris, I have not lost any of my regard for them & there is no one I shall be more glad to see again than him.

ever & most truly yours

J. S. MILL

2. *Moniteur grec,* a tri-monthly ministerial journal in French sponsored by M. Coletti; it began publication in Athens in Oct., 1844 (see *Moniteur universel,* Oct. 30, 1844, p. 2809, and Nov. 11, 1844, p. 2857).

3. John Kolettis [Jean Coletti] (1788–1847), Greek general and statesman, ambassador to France, 1835–44.

448. TO AUGUSTE COMTE[1]

India House
le 31 décembre
1844

MON CHER MONSIEUR COMTE

C'est avec une peine extrême que j'ai appris le déplorable résultat, en ce qui vous regarde, de cette tentative avortée de réorganisation dans l'école polytechnique,[2] qui devait au contraire, suivant toute apparence, consolider votre position de manière à vous mettre à l'abri de toute attaque future de la part de ceux que votre franchise philosophique a soulevés contre vous. Malheureusement il y a lieu de s'attendre à une inimitié plus forcenée de leur part, en raison directe de l'importance croissante de la nouvelle école. On peut croire que les savans, ainsi que les prêtres, auraient pu se soumettre à vous laisser tranquille dans la position modeste qui vous était échue, s'ils avaient pu compter que par un silence calculé ils pourraient vous ensevelir dans l'obscurité: mais, lorsqu'ils s'aperçoivent que votre nom commence à percer, et que partout où l'on vous fait une place quelconque, on vous en fait une très élevée, dès lors, ce n'est plus seulement la vanité blessée qui est en jeu, c'est toute l'importance sociale d'une classe puissante qui se trouverait compromise si on ne parvenait à étouffer une voix qu'on sait bien ne pouvoir réduire au silence qu'en vous ôtant tout moyen de vivre ou du moins de loisir. Vous aurez donc des ennemis de plus en plus acharnés, et plus ils vous auront nui, plus ils chercheront à vous nuire. Il est certes bien digne de vous, de voir dans cet ensemble de circonstances, si fâcheuses en ce qui vous regarde personnellement, des motifs de consolation fondés sur le retentissement social auquel ce duel à mort doit donner lieu et qui sans doute, comme vous en faites l'observation, serait resté dans des proportions minimes si nulle existence sociale ne se trouvait compromise dans la lutte. Il faut espérer du moins que si vous subissez les peines du martyre vous en aurez aussi les honneurs, et que l'humanité en recueillera le fruit. Il n'y a d'esperi réel que dans l'opinion, et ce sera une importante expérience sociologique qui décidera si aujourd'hui une classe sociale peut persécuter un philosophe isolé sans avoir même le concours du gouvernement. Il est très malheureux que la fermeté du maréchal Soult[3] ne se soutienne pas: je craindrais bien que l'influence

1. MS at Johns Hopkins. Published in Lévy-Bruhl, pp. 384–87; in reply to Comte's of Dec. 25, *ibid.*, pp. 373–83.

2. A reorganization of the council of the Ecole Polytechnique, which Comte had hoped would lead to a vote favourable to his reinstatement as examiner, had proved disappointing; by a vote of ten to nine the new council had confirmed the action of the former council in displacing Comte (see his letter of Dec. 25).

3. Nicolas Jean de Dieu Soult, Duke of Dalmatia (1769–1851), Marshal of France, at this time Minister of War. The administration of the Ecole Polytechnique lay within the jurisdiction of his department.

auguste dont on vous a parlé n'y soit pour quelque chose. Le devoir du gouvernement serait, s'il répugne à casser l'arrêt du nouveau conseil polytechnique sitôt après l'avoir organisé, de vous enlever à cette carrière, en vous en faisant une autre, plus importante, en vous nommant, par exemple, à quelque chaire du premier ordre, qui conviendrait à quelque partie du cercle immense de vos connaissances scientifiques et historiques. Ce serait pour M. Guizot une belle occasion de montrer de la magnanimité, s'il en a, suivant le noble exemple de M. Poinsot, et j'ai appris avec un vrai plaisir que dans la question immédiate au moins, un homme de sa capacité, auquel je n'ai jamais pu refuser une certaine estime, s'est montré disposé à bien agir. Il est fâcheux que cette affaire doit probablement traîner en longueur, et que vous ne pouvez pas savoir au plus tôt, à quoi vous en tenir. Si malheureusement vous êtes réduit de nouveau à la ressource de l'enseignement privé, comptez sur tous mes efforts et sur ceux de tous mes amis qui vous connaissent ou sur lesquels je puis exercer quelque influence. Je ne connais actuellement aucun anglais riche qui habite Paris, mais il doit sans doute y en avoir que je pourrais mettre en mouvement, du moins indirectement. Vous m'indiquerez le moment où il conviendrait de commencer cette tentative, si malheureusement il y a lieu.

Les articles de Littré[4] sont excellents. Je ne m'attendais nullement à une si pleine adhésion, et je la trouve du plus heureux augure. Quel que soit le génie de l'auteur d'une théorie quelconque le public n'y prend pas beaucoup d'intérêt tant qu'il reste seul de son avis, trouvant fort naturel qu'un homme tienne à ses propres idées: mais dès que ces idées sont solennellement adoptées par un second penseur d'une supériorité reconnue, la bataille est presque gagnée; les esprits supérieurs ne tardent plus à y affluer en foule. C'est une véritable époque dans la nouvelle crise sociale, que cette importante adhésion, qui me rappelle celle de Berthollet aux doctrines de Lavoisier.[5] La mienne n'était pas, à beaucoup près, aussi importante, ne pouvant guère agir sur la France, seul pays vraiment préparé aujourd'hui pour la régénération philosophique. Je voudrais bien savoir quelle réception l'Allemagne donne à votre grand ouvrage. J'ai lieu de croire que le mien y est mieux accueilli que je ne pouvais m'y attendre, si je puis me fier aux rapports d'un allemand que je vis il y a huit jours et qui me raconta entr'autres choses qu'il avait lu un article très favorable à ce sujet dans un journal publié dans la petite ville de Hohenzollern——quelque chose (j'ai oublié le reste du mot) ce qui équivaudrait au plus à un simple chef lieu de département au centre de la France et qu'on y disait que c'était le

4. On Comte and positivism, in the *National.*

5. Antoine Laurent Lavoisier (1743–1794), chemist famous for overthrowing the hypothesis of phlogiston and thereby reorganizing the science of chemistry. Claude Louis Berthollet (1748–1822) readily accepted and extended Lavoisier's theories.

meilleur ouvrage philosophique que l'angleterre a produit de nos jours, en y ajoutant que ce n'était certainement pas de la philosophie allemande. Je pense qu'il y a en allemagne un commencement très décidé de réaction contre la philosophie qu'on appelle allemande et que la méthode positive y trouvera de l'appui plus tôt qu'on ne pouvait le croire. Il doit y avoir parmi les physiciens et physiologistes et même parmi la jeunesse active qui désire s'occuper de politique, une sincère aversion, d'un côté pour le vague et d'un autre côté pour les tendances quiétistes de la métaphysique de Schelling et de Hegel.

Tout à vous

J. S. Mill

• • • 1845 • • •

449. TO SARAH AUSTIN[1]

India House
January 18, 1845

. . . About poor Comte's affairs, he has himself written to me very fully,[2] and informed me of the final close of the whole matter, so far as his restoration to the examinership is concerned. I am glad on every account that you interested yourself with Guizot for him, and that you mentioned my name in the manner you did,[3] although it would hardly have been warrantable in me to take any direct measure of the same kind, as my acquaintance with Guizot is so very slight. It may be useful to Comte on future occasions to have given evidence to Guizot of our interest in him. He himself seems to bear up bravely against his misfortune. I perceive he has considerable hope that when a vacancy occurs in any one of the several other Polytechnic offices, the opportunity may be taken of repairing the injustice done him; and I hope the occasion may occur soon, as I have much doubt about the success of his other plans. The private lessons in mathematics may answer, notwithstanding their high price, but not, I fear, if he relies at all upon the rich English. What do you think of his Review project?[4] To me it seems a very doubtful one; and I fear, too, he will be disappointed by the very little help I shall be able to give him in writing for it, although I will do all I can. About Comte himself I have formed very much the same opinion that you have,[5] both as to his good and bad points

1. Published in Janet Ross, *Three Generations of English Women* (revised ed., London, 1893), pp. 208–10. MS not located. Though addressed to Sarah Austin this is also an answer to an as yet unpublished letter (MS at Yale) by John Austin, dated Dec. 25, 1844.

2. Comte's letters of Dec. 25, 1834, and Jan. 10, 1845, Lévy-Bruhl, pp. 373–83 and 388–400.

3. Austin had reported in his letter of Dec. 25 that he had called on Guizot on Dec. 23 and told him that if he could help Comte he would thereby "confer a great personal favour upon Mr. John Mill & myself."

4. In his letter of Jan. 10, 1845, Comte outlined at length a proposal initiated by Emile Littré for the establishment of a Positive Review. See also JSM's letter of Jan. 27, 1845 (the next letter).

5. Austin had written: "I fear, from what M. Dunoyer told me, that there is a good deal of prejudice against Comte, as being a mere man of speculation, more intent upon impressing his own theories upon the students, than upon exactly performing the duties of his office. It is probable, too, that the fit of insanity under which he has

of character. He is evidently (either from character or the tendencies of a solitary thinker, little appreciated by the world), most obstinately bent upon following his own course, regardless not only of giving offence (which might be a virtue), but of compromising his means of livelihood.[6] He piques himself exceedingly upon being the only Frenchman who speaks out his opinions without any compromises or reserves, and he has gone so far in that course that I think he would do himself more harm than good now by swerving from it. At all events, I am certain he will not abate one jot of his "franchise philosophique," and therefore there is not much use in advising him to do so. He is a man one can only serve in his own way.

What you say about Guizot and his family interests me exceedingly.[7] A man in such a position as his, acts under so many difficulties, and is mixed up in so many questionable transactions that one's favourable opinion is continually liable to receive shocks, and I have for many years been oscillating in Guizot's case between great esteem and considerable misgivings. Nothing I ever heard of him tells so much in his favour as the feeling you express about him after familiar intercourse. If he was an angel he would be sure to be misunderstood in the place he is in. I do not know whether to wish or to deprecate his being thrown out of it, which seems now so likely to happen.

I have been chiefly occupied lately in writing an article for the *Edinburgh Review* on the "claims of labour."[8] I never knew a time when so much nonsense, and mischievous nonsense, too, was afloat on that subject, and

---

suffered, coupled with the hostility of the men of science whom he has provoked, may have led to a general belief that he is half mad. . . .

"From all that I have seen of Comte, I believe that he is a man of great sincerity and uprightness (which appears, indeed, to be generally admitted); and (what, perhaps, you would not think) that he is a man of a generous and affectionate temper. But of all the men I ever saw (excepting Mr. Bentham) he is the most confident in his own capacity and views, and the least inclined to attend to the suggestions of others. It is, therefore, nearly impossible to get him to act with ordinary prudence.

"I have rarely seen a man so interesting, and who so well supported, on personal acquaintance, the favourable impression made by him at a distance. . . ."

6. Austin had written: "I wish you could persuade Comte to be more reserved about religion. He sets it aside with a cool contempt, which even in impious France, does harm to his worldly condition; not to mention, that his peremptory rejection of that, and of all philosophy concerned with the insoluble and transcendent, raises a presumption against his scientific capacities in many of the best minds not acquainted with his book. But, like Mr. Bentham (of whom he constantly reminds me), he is so wedded to his own devices and so full of presumptuous contempt for all which has been done by others, that I fear he would not be moved even by your insinuations."

7. "Nothing can exceed the kindness of M. Guizot, and of his noble-hearted mother, to Mrs. Austin and myself. Though his talents are great, various & imposing, I am far more struck by the elevated moral character which seems to break out spontaneously in his conversation & manners. . . . Neither he nor his children (so far as I can see) are at all spoiled by his extraordinary rise in the world. . . ."

8. See Letters 443 and 445.

I thought it a most useful thing to enter a protest against the intolerable mass of pseudo-philanthropy now getting into vogue, and to commit the *Edinburgh Review* at the same time (if possible) to strong things in favour of good popular education and just laws. I am afraid, however, that some of the strong things I have said on both sides will frighten so timid a man as Napier, and that he will not dare to print them unmodified. He always, of himself, seems to like my articles, and evidently always hears so much said against them afterwards, by the octogenarian clique, Rogers,[9] Sidney Smith,[10] etc., whom he looks up to, that he has now, I think, a constant terror lest I should get him into a scrape.

Is there any chance of the article on Prussia soon, or of a book rather than an article, or of a reprint of your husband's former book,[11] with the second volume which he projected? I feel certain that a book with his name would be read by numbers of people to whom it would do good, and nothing but books seems to do good now. The time for writing books seems to have come again, though unhappily not for living by doing it.

Ever affectionately yours,

J. S. Mill

450. TO AUGUSTE COMTE[1]

India House
le 27 janvier 1845

Mon cher Monsieur Comte

Comme vous me l'avez demandé dans votre dernière lettre, j'ai mûrement réfléchi sur le projet de revue qui vous a été proposé par M. Littré, et j'ai consulté ceux de mes amis les plus compétens en pareille matière, qui se trouvaient à portée de communication. Avant de vous en donner le résultat général, je dois m'expliquer pleinement en ce qui regarde ma coopération personnelle. Je trouve des obstacles insurmontables à ce qu'elle soit aussi étendue que vous le désirez, ou même assez étendue pour que vous puissiez beaucoup compter là-dessus. Le degré de coopération que vous me demandez me prendrait à peu près tout le temps dont je puis habituellement disposer pour écrire, même en renonçant à toute publication ultérieure en mon propre nom. Ensuite quand cette difficulté n'existerait

9. Samuel Rogers.

10. Sydney Smith (1771–1845), canon of St. Paul's, writer and wit; one of the founders of the *Edinburgh Review*.

11. *The Province of Jurisprudence Determined* (London, 1832).

* * * *

1. MS at Johns Hopkins. Published in Lévy-Bruhl, pp. 400–404; in reply to Comte's of Jan. 10, *ibid.*, pp. 388–400.

pas, je ne comprends pas assez ce que serait la revue, ni même ce qu'elle pourrait être, pour que je puisse aujourd'hui prendre un engagement absolu de collaboration. Tant qu'il s'agit de méthodes philosophiques, de doctrines historiques, des lois du développement social passé et présent, je sais à quoi m'en tenir: je ne crois pas qu'il y ait entre nous deux aucune divergence d'opinion très sérieuse. Mais en fondant une revue, et surtout en la fondant au nom d'un système de philosophie, on prend l'engagement de se jeter dans toutes les questions, d'une certaine importance, qui se discutent aujourd'hui: et sur ce terrain-là il n'y a pas à présumer qu'il y aurait une harmonie suffisante dans nos opinions. Je pense que si vous étiez appelé à vous prononcer sur toutes les questions et à dire toutes vos idées, nous nous trouverions en désaccord plus souvent et plus sérieusement que vous ne semblez le croire, et que moi-même je ne l'avais d'abord espéré. Ce n'est qu'après avoir vu au moins un ou deux numéros de la revue que je pourrais décider avec connaissance de cause jusqu'à quel point je pourrais utilement y prendre part.

En m'expliquant ainsi sur ce qui me regarde, je vous indique déjà les doutes que j'éprouve sur l'opportunité du projet en lui-même. En effet, le positivisme ne me paraît pas encore bien en état de se produire avec avantage comme école. Pour en faire une aux yeux du public il faudrait un corps commun de doctrine, et il n'y a encore qu'une méthode et quelques principes très généraux, qui même ne sont pas encore reconnus par la majorité de ceux qui acceptent le principe essentiel du positivisme, celui de rejeter absolument toute spéculation sur les causes premières, en se bornant à la recherche des lois effectives des phénomènes. Dans l'intérêt donc du développement spéculatif, cet essai de propagande me paraîtrait prématuré: voilà du moins quel serait mon avis, si l'on pouvait faire abstraction de la légitime influence des circonstances personnelles. Sous ce dernier rapport, tout dépend des chances du succès, dont je ne suis pas, comme observateur éloigné, en position de juger; mais l'opinion d'un homme tel que Littré, fortifiée par celle de M. de Blainville et des autres amis que vous m'indiquez, doit avoir un grand poids. Quant à l'Angleterre, tout m'avertit qu'il y a peu à espérer. Je vous dirai ce que me mande, à ce sujet, M. Grote. Il dit qu'il ne connaît, outre lui-même, que deux individus qui probablement s'abonneraient à la revue. Ce sont Molesworth et le docteur Arnott,[2] médecin très estimé, auteur d'un traité de physique populaire, et qui a connu même avant moi les premiers volumes de votre Cours. Il peut tout au plus se trouver, selon M. Grote, quelques savans qui liraient la revue avec plaisir pour y recueillir des idées philosophiques sur les sciences physiques: encore serait-ce de rares exceptions, vu la tendance aujourd'hui si prononcée à transiger avec la théologie par des concessions générales, en se réservant la liberté tacite des détails, qui seuls importent à des esprits

2. Neil Arnott.

emprisonnés pour la plupart dans leur étroite spécialité. Comme le dit M. Grote, nous sommes à présent dans un temps où le philosophe se prosterne avec affectation devant le prêtre. Je serais plein d'espoir si je croyais l'époque venue où l'on pourrait, avec succès, arborer un drapeau franchement positif, en secouant ouvertement tout lambeau des doctrines du passé (sauf leur valeur historique) et refusant toute concession, même tacite, envers les théories surnaturelles. Je ne crois pas cette époque aussi éloignée qu'elle paraît à bien d'autres: il n'y faudrait peut être qu'un peu de hardiesse, et je ne serais pas très éloigné d'en faire moi-même l'essai. Mais alors ce serait dans un livre. Comme en toute révolution spéculative, il faut que les livres précèdent les revues. Je pense bien que votre grand ouvrage fait du chemin ici; on en parle peu, mais on y fait de tems en tems des allusions, et Bain, qui fréquente plus que moi le monde savant, me dit qu'il en voit des preuves croissantes. Quoique je craigne que ceci ne regarde principalement les premiers volumes, ces volumes mêmes doivent tendre à accoutumer ceux qui les lisent à l'élimination totale de l'élément théologique, comme ils l'ont décidée chez Bain lui-même. Mais cette action sur les penseurs isolés serait plus gênée que hâtée par une tentative quelconque de constituer publiquement une école anti-religieuse, qui en effrayant le public et en entamant des discussions prématurées du moins en angleterre, donnerait probablement ici une nouvelle force à la réaction religieuse. Au reste M. Grote m'a témoigné son intention de se faire inscrire comme actionnaire. De mon côté je vous engage à m'inscrire pour cinq actions et à m'indiquer l'époque où j'aurai à verser la première souscription. Si je fais des articles on pourra me les compter jusqu'à concurrence des versements ultérieurs, mais je ne veux pas accepter d'autre rétribution pécuniaire.

Quant à l'avis que vous me demandez sur le choix d'un titre, l'un ou l'autre de ceux que vous me désignez me semble admissible mais il me paraîtrait plus simple de dire tout court, *revue positive*, en vous désignant ensuite comme directeur. Quant aux autres questions, nous avons le temps d'y songer.

tout à vous

J. S. MILL

451. TO DR. WILLIAM BENJAMIN CARPENTER[1]

31 Jan. 1845

I had heard the "Vestiges"[2] several times attributed to you, but I have always said I was certain you were not the author.

1. Excerpt published in Maggs Bros. Catalogue No. 641, 1937, item 144. MS not located.

2. [Robert Chambers], *Vestiges of the Natural History of Creation* (London, 1844).

I do not think I ever told you that I heard from Comte that M. Littré, the very distinguished editor & translator of Hippocrates,[3] values very highly your "General Physiology"[4] & that Comte saw the book at Littré's house & from a hasty inspection of it thought very favourably both of the plan & execution.

452. TO HENRY COLE[1]

I.H.
5 Feb. 1845

MY DEAR COLE

Many thanks for the cheque, which I did not expect to receive so soon.[2] I hope your sending it is a good sign of the success of the Hist. Register.[3] Above all I hope you have not sent it at any inconvenience. If you have, pray tell me so & I will refund it. The remaining £45 can wait your perfect convenience.

Most truly yours
J. S. MILL

453. TO HENRY C. CAREY[1]

East India House
London
15th February 1845

SIR—I have to acknowledge, with thanks, the letter which you did me the honour to address to me on the occasion of my sending you a small volume of Political Economy Essays. I have also to repair my omission to acknowledge the receipt of the systematic Treatise[2] which you were so good as to send to me some time before.

3. Hippocrate, *Œuvres complètes* . . . ed. Emile Littré (10 vols., Paris, 1839–61).
4. See Letter 386, n. 5.

* * * *

1. MS in the possession of Professor J. M. McCrimmon.
2. See Letters 414, 415.
3. *Historical Register, with the sanction and assistance of various government departments.* This short-lived paper (Jan. 10–Mar. 8, 1845—10 nos.) was described as "a stamped newspaper and register of family events, national and private biography, life and health."

* * * *

1. *Addressed*: Henry C. Carey Esq. / care of Messrs Carey, Lea, and Blanchard / Philadelphia / United States. *Postmarks*: 1 / PAID / 15FE15 / 1845 and L/FE 16. MS in Princeton University Library.
Henry Charles Carey (1793–1879), publisher and economist.
2. *Principles of Political Economy* (3 vols., Philadelphia, 1837–40).

I was fully prepared to find that you would differ widely from many of the opinions I had expressed, as I do from many of those contained in your more elaborate work. Those differences do not surprise me, on a subject so imperfectly understood, a subject too, which independently of all defects in the manner of studying it, is, I cannot but think, in its own nature much more complicated than you appear to believe. It is fortunate that political economists do not differ so radically in their conclusions, as the diversity of their premisses might lead any one to expect, & that your doctrines point as directly as those of any follower of Adam Smith or Ricardo, to the gradual abandonment of the restrictive, or as it is improperly called, the protective policy—to which I am not the less rootedly hostile because I differ from you in thinking that in certain exceptional cases, the conditional maintenance of some part of the system may be justified or even required by self-protection.

I thank you very sincerely for having taken the trouble to express your sentiments so fully & freely on those parts of my little book which you disagree with. I could give what would appear to me sufficient answers to your objections, but it will perhaps be preferable to state in few words what I conceive to be the principal difference between your scheme of Political Economy, as very clearly set forth in your book, & my own. Most of what appears to me erroneous in your opinions, flows by direct consequence from your refusing to admit (as of any influence in practice) any other source of exchangeable value than labour.

In the case of all useful articles which admit of indefinite increase by means of labour, the labour required for producing them is, no doubt, the regulator & measure of their value; & I look upon it as one of the chief merits of Ricardo to have established in its full generality this law, which is still far from being admitted by the common herd of political economists. It therefore gave me pleasure to see so fundamental a principle thoroughly recognized & enforced by an American political economist; but it seems to me that you overlook half the truth when you deny that a different law governs all cases of either natural or artificial monopoly, & that cases partaking more or less of that character are so far from being exceptions, that they constitute a full half of all the cases which arise; land & its produce being the most conspicuous, but very far from the sole, example.

In the case of land, this principle of value would indeed be of no practical importance if you were right in your doctrine that the effect of an increase of capital & population is to enable the increased agricultural produce thereby required, to be obtained at a smaller instead of a greater cost. This is true up to the point of density in population, which is indispensable to the use of costly machinery & to the adequate combination & division of labour. The limit cannot be fixed precisely. But, that there is a limit, it is hardly possible, I think, for any one living in an old country, to doubt; & that when this point is attained, the natural law by which (in any given state of knowledge) a double expenditure on land yields less than a double return, prevails, on the average, over the antagonist influence of new inventions & discoveries. I cannot help attributing the contrary opinion which you entertain on this subject, to your living in a country where population does not yet press upon the productive powers of the soil, & where, consequently, the value of land does not yet much exceed a compensation for the capital expended in clearing & bringing it into cultivation.

The nature & tendencies of our difference of opinion need not be further explained to one who has shewn so correct a comprehension as you have, of the doctrines which he contends against; & I need only further add my congratulations upon the increasing cultivation of these speculations in so important a portion of the civilized world as the United States, & my unfeigned acknowledgment of the spirit of complete fairness, so rare in controversial writers, with which you have throughout treated the opinions & writers that you controvert.

Believe me with sincere respect
yours

J. S. Mill

454. TO MACVEY NAPIER[1]

India House
17th Feby 1845

My dear Sir

I did not know, or had forgotten, that the review was or considered itself committed on Wakefield's[2] principle & on small holdings, otherwise I should not have written on them as I have, nor have written on them at all without communicating with you. I am sorry that the great power of the Edinburgh Review is engaged on what appears to me the wrong side of two of the most important questions which political economists or statesmen have to do with, & I am sorry too on account of the article, which will suffer very much by the excision of those two discussions—I cannot consider them excursions from the subject of the article,[3] which I take to be, not solely the things which cannot, but also those which can, be done for the labouring classes. The grand defect of the subject, both in itself & with a view to effect, was, that almost everything to be said was negative—that there was so little positive to propose—& even of that little the article now loses the

1. MS in Brit. Mus.
2. Edward Gibbon Wakefield, the colonizer.
3. "The Claims of Labour," *ER*, LXXXI (April, 1845), 498–525.

greater part, & that to which I chiefly trusted for gratifying the disagreeableness & unpopularity of the other branch of the argument & shewing that the doctrines called Malthusian do not as is vulgarly supposed, imply that in one's opinions on social arrangements one looks only to amount of production & not to the producers. However since it is as you tell me, there is no more to be said. I have struck out all that I had written on colonization, expressly reserving that question to be discussed separately, & merely expressing an opinion that something *is* to be done in that way—from which opinion I hope the review does not dissent. I cannot think it even *possible* to pass over the subject of allotments.[4] If that were left out, in addition to colonization & the short time question, it would be leaving out not the part of Hamlet merely, but all the principal characters, those three being the only projects now afloat, for improving the condition of the poor, to which any one really attaches any serious importance. In treating of this I have attempted, without expressing my opinion in favour of small holdings, to retain, for the sake of the general argument, as much of what I originally said on that subject, as may serve to shew that the allotment question as it now presents itself is quite independent of that larger question, & that one may be in favour of small holdings, under some institutions & in some circumstances, & yet disapprove of allotments. This is quite necessary to the strength of our case against allotments & unless it can be managed I do not see how I could make a satisfactory thing of the article.

Since the whole is actually in type as I originally wrote it, I should be very much obliged if you would have struck off for me one copy (two or three would be still better) before the alterations in the last half sheet are made; that in case of the republication which I meditate, my opinions may be represented fairly,[5] which in the present case unfortunately they cannot be in the review. In the hope that you will thus oblige me I have corrected the printing of the passages which are to be cancelled.

In the various minor matters you will see that I have endeavoured as far as possible to comply with your wishes—except in one instance, that of the word *ideas* in page 7, which I cannot admit to be not English as there used; it is used in the ordinary sense in which we speak of "men of ideas" or of a book as being "wanting in ideas" or say that a writer's "ideas are better than his mode of expressing them" &c &c. I should not wish to retain the word if I could find any other that would replace it, but I have tried every cognate word that I could think of, & for different reasons all are objectionable. If that were altered the whole of the first part of the paragraph must

4. The practice of allotting garden plots to labourers. In the article JSM expressed approval of the practice when it was adopted to increase the happiness of workers but not when it was designed simply to supplement low wages.

5. The article was reprinted in *Dissertations*, II, 260–96, with omissions but without substantial additions.

be recast & I am sure I could not express the meaning as well in any totally different arrangement & phraseology.

As for a heading, would there be any objection to "The Claims of Labour"? It gives at once a complete notion of what the article is about, & as it happens also to be the title of the book reviewed, the review will be relieved from the responsibility of any little tinge of affectation that there may appear to be in the phrase.

I have made a few alterations of my own in different parts of the article, all tending towards curtailment.

Very truly yours,

J. S. MILL.

455. TO ALEXANDER BAIN[1]

[March, 1845]

Have you seen Ward's book, *The Ideal, &c.?*[2] It is a remarkable book in every way, and not the least so because it quotes and puffs me in every chapter, and Comte occasionally, though with deep lamentations over our irreligion.

456. TO MACVEY NAPIER[1]

India House
21 April
1845

MY DEAR SIR

I have this morning received your remittance, which, as on former occasions, is extremely liberal in its amount.

I hope you will be much benefitted by quiet & country air & that the next accounts will report a great improvement in your health.

It could scarcely be expected that the review would be much noticed by the press in the thick of the Maynooth discussions,[2] but the effect of the Ed. Rev. is not dependent on newspaper notices.

1. Excerpt published in Bain, *JSM*, p. 80. MS not located.
2. William George Ward, *The Ideal of a Christian Church Considered in Comparison with Existing Practice* (London, 1844).

* * * *

1. MS in Brit. Mus.
2. Sir Robert Peel, Prime Minister, had proposed on April 3 a measure increasing from £9,000 to £26,000 the parliamentary grant to Maynooth College in Ireland. Since Maynooth educated Roman Catholic priests, Protestant fury in both England and Ireland rose to extravagant heights. The Maynooth grant became the great political controversy of the year. The measure finally became law on June 16.

The great majority[3] makes the victory over religious bigotry a most valuable triumph. Since so much opposition to a reasonable Irish policy still exists we may rejoice that it has collected itself in such force to be so completely beaten. Peel's & Graham's speeches[4] are of most favourable augury, though one is glad that they received personally their deserts from Macaulay[5] & others.

yours ever truly

J. S. MILL

457. TO AUGUSTE COMTE[1]

India House
le 26 avril 1845

MON CHER MONSIEUR COMTE

Depuis le jour où j'appris que la crise polytechnique s'était terminée, au moins pour le moment, à votre désavantage, je n'ai perdu aucune des occasions, malheureusement assez rares, qui se sont présentées pour faire connaître votre nouvelle position à ceux qui pourraient avoir des relations quelconques avec des anglais riches demeurant à Paris. Je ne sais pas si ce que j'ai pû faire produira quelque fruit, mais jusqu'ici ce fruit ne s'est pas encore montré. Je crains qu'il n'y ait besoin d'une grande persévérance pour en obtenir. Les riches anglais, même lorsqu'ils ne demeurent pas en angleterre ont l'habitude bien établie d'envoyer leurs fils à Oxford ou à Cambridge. Pour être admis à ces établissemens-là on exige à peine les premiers éléments de la géometrie et de l'algèbre; et l'on désire si peu chez nous les connaissances mathématiques en elles-mêmes, que naguère encore il ne se trouvait presque pas un seul bon professeur ou maître de mathématiques à Londres. Il n'y en avait guére qu'à Cambridge. Aujourd'hui cet état de choses s'est un peu amélioré. Toutefois on peut encore dire que ce qu'il a de goût pour les études mathématiques chez nous s'est concentré à Cambridge, et que le peu d'hommes riches, qui désirent que leurs fils s'en occupent, les y envoient, le plus souvent sans aucun enseignement préparatoire digne du nom. Il est donc fort douteux s'il se trouve à Paris un seul anglais qui serait disposé à profiter de vos leçons quand

3. For the bill on its second reading in the Commons.

4. Peel spoke on April 18; Sir John Graham (1792–1861), Home Secretary at the time, on April 17.

5. Macaulay in his speech on April 14, though he supported the Maynooth grant, castigated the Tories for their inconsistencies on Irish policy.

* * * *

1. MS at Johns Hopkins. Published in Lévy-Bruhl, pp. 412–16; in reply to Comte's of Feb. 28, *ibid.*, 404-12.

même on serait parvenu à lui faire croire sur parole votre éminente capacité scientifique que certainement très peu de mes compatriotes sont en état d'apprécier directement. Voilà les difficultés qu'on m'a faites, et dont je reconnais la gravité. M. Grote s'accorde là dessus avec moi, et comme moi il s'efforce de les vaincre. De mon côté je ne me découragerai pas et peutêtre le hasard nous favorisera.

Je m'occupe à présent principalement de lectures préparatoires au traité populaire d'économie politique dont je vous entretenais dernièrement. Entre autres livres plus ou moins intéressans je n'ai pas manqué de lire celui de M. Dunoyer,[2] dont le nom ne m'était déjà pas inconnu: je l'avais même vu autrefois chez J. B. Say et ses travaux dans le Censeur avec votre homonyme,[3] m'étaient connus depuis longtemps. Son ouvrage actuel me paraît, à plusieurs égards, très digne d'éloge. Il est certainement beaucoup trop absolu dans ses idées négatives: cependant, on ne peut guère regretter une opposition, même exagérée, à la tendance qui porte à faire par les lois ce qui ne devrait dépendre que des mœurs. Je lui reproche davantage de n'avoir pas même entrevu la nécessité, si prononcée pourtant dans son système, d'un pouvoir spirituel. Il est bien étonnant aujourd'hui qu'un homme éclairé puisse faire un système social, dans lequel nécessairement il suppose la réception générale de ses propres opinions morales et politiques, sans cependant s'occuper le moins du monde des conditions que suppose essentiellement l'existence d'un système d'opinions communes faisant autorité. Il est vraiment trop naïf de croire aujourd'hui que la simple liberté de discussion suffise pour cela. Cependant, puisque dans votre avis la négation totale de toute organisation spirituelle est préférable à la mauvaise ébauche d'organisation qui existe à présent, il serait probablement à désirer qu'on essayât d'appliquer les idées de M. Dunoyer dans leur simple nudité. Ce serait une grande expérience sociologique. Je sais beaucoup de gré à M. Dunoyer pour la mention honorable qu'il a faite de votre Cours, tout en se reconnaissant incompétent pour le juger définitivement.

A propos de cela, nous avons obtenu, vous et moi, les honneurs d'une publicité assez éclatante par l'intermédaire d'une des chefs de l'école anglo-catholique, M. Ward, qui fit paraître, il y a une année ou davantage, un assez gros volume[4] dans lequel il peignit en de très noires couleurs l'état actuel de l'église anglicane, et de la société anglaise, se déclara très nettement contre la réformation de Luther et appela l'église anglicane à

2. Charles Barthélemy Dunoyer (1786–1862), economist and statesman. Comte had recommended to JSM a new book by Dunoyer: *De la liberté du travail* (3 vols., Paris, 1845).

3. Dunoyer had edited with Charles Comte, son-in-law of J. B. Say the economist, the journal *Le Censeur* from 1820 to 1825, to which Auguste Comte had also contributed.

4. See Letter 455.

rentrer dans le giron du catholicisme romain. Cet ouvrage fit grand scandale ici, et l'Université d'Oxford vient de priver l'auteur de ses grades universitaires comme ne faisant plus partie, au moins en droit, de l'église anglicane. Ce n'est que dernièrement que j'ai lu son ouvrage, bien que j'eusse entendu qu'il y était question de moi. Je m'y suis trouvé cité dans chaque chapitre et plus souvent encore, avec d'immenses éloges, entremêlés de plaintes sur mon incrédulité et sur la tendance athéistique de mes écrits: il disait, de plus, avoir lu la plus grande partie de votre Cours, sur la foi de ce que j'en disais; il va sans dire qu'il vous tance encore plus vertement que moi sur votre irréligion; cependant il cite plusieurs passages, il fait l'éloge de votre capacité, et même de vos intentions; il dit que vous reconnaissez avoir pris bien des choses chez de Maistre, mais qu'il vous trouve très supérieur en profondeur à ce penseur. Suivant lui, il faut en venir à notre irréligion à nous, si on ne revient pas à la philosophie catholique car il prône la philosophie du catholicisme tout autant que la foi. C'est une chose assez amusante que nous trouvions un appui si décidé dans ce camp-là et que M. Ward soit accusé par ses adversaires dans la Quarterly Review,[5] d'avoir tiré plus d'enseignements de mon école que de celle des théologiens anglicans.

Mon ami Bain vient de se servir de votre traité d'astronomie pour son enseignement universitaire. Il a fait cette année-ci un cours de physique, au lieu du cours de philosophie morale qu'il avait fait trois années de suite. Il n'était malheureusement que suppléant, dans la dépendance absolue du professeur,[6] vieux radoteur qui ne voulait plus de lui cette année, malgré le vœu général de ses collègues. Bain a été recommandé au gouvernement par six professeurs pour la chaire de physique, mais on y a nommé un autre, très inférieur probablement à lui. Il n'y a été nommé que par interim. Je ne sais par conséquent ce qu'il fera dorénavant.[7] Il est décidé à se présenter comme candidat à la chaire de philosophie morale quand elle viendra à vaquer, ce qui probablement aura lieu bientôt, mais n'ayant que son mérite et l'appui des professeurs, il peut se voir de nouveau mis de côté. Il dit sur votre cours d'astronomie "I never saw a finer specimen of philosophical or scientific arrangement. There is almost a startling propriety in the places alloted to each point. Herschel's book is a mere chaos in comparison."

tout à vous

J. S. MILL.

5. "Ward's *Ideal of a Christian Church*," *QR*, LXXV (Dec., 1844), 149–200.

6. The Rev. George Glennie (d. Nov. 9, 1845), professor of moral philosophy at Marischal College.

7. Later that year Bain was appointed professor of mathematics and natural philosophy in the Andersonian University of Glasgow, a position which he resigned after one year.

458. TO JOHN HAMILTON THOM[1]

India House
9th May 1845

MY DEAR SIR,

I have purposely delayed thanking you for your present of the Memoirs and Portrait of our friend Mr Blanco White, until I had time to read the book regularly through. It is a book of very solemn and painful interest. If, as Carlyle says, there is the fifth act of a tragedy in every peasant's death-bed,[2] we may say that the tragedy of Mr Blanco White's life is both of a deeply pathetic and of a truly heroic character.

I feel something almost amounting to remorse when I consider that, having had the privilege of knowing such a man, I have so few of the recollections which I so envy you the possession of—recollections of having contributed by sympathy and service to soothe the sufferings of his last few years. But though I always respected him highly, I never knew a tenth part either of his nobleness or of his sufferings, and still less that yearning for sympathy which seems to have been his characteristic through life, and which so greatly enhances the honour due to his repeated sacrifices of all earthly ties and friendship to the love of truth and of duty. It is always so. Men's worth is only known when they are dead and we can do nothing more for them.

But, to change from the elegiac to the epic—the third volume appears to me of great intrinsic worth, and likely to serve the cause for which he suffered so much in an eminent degree, by the clear, strong, earnest manner in which it declares things which when spoken are almost too obvious not to be admitted, but which hardly any one dares to speak.

Believe me, with great respect, yours sincerely,

J. S. MILL

459. TO AUGUSTE COMTE[1]

India House
le 21 juin 1845

MON CHER MONSIEUR COMTE

C'est avec bien de la peine que j'ai appris l'insuccès des démarches que vous aviez prises jusqu'à la date de votre dernière lettre, pour reprendre l'enseignement privé. M. Grote a vivement partagé mon regret, et mal-

1. Published by J. H. Thom in "Archbishop Whately and the Life of Blanco White," *Theological Review*, IV (Jan., 1867), 112–13. MS not located.
2. In his essay on Burns, *ER*, XLVIII (Dec., 1828), 278.

* * * *

1. MS at Johns Hopkins. Published in Lévy-Bruhl, pp. 426–29; in reply to Comte's of May 15, *ibid.*, 417–26.

heureusement nous n'avons eu ni l'un ni l'autre un meilleur succès dans tout ce que nous avons tenté ici en votre faveur. Il y a parmi les anglais en général une indifférence profonde envers l'éducation scientifique. On regarde la science comme une spécialité qui n'est l'affaire que des savans par état, ou qui touche tout au plus certaines fonctions industrielles, comme celle d'ingénieur, encore dans ce métier même on se contente presque toujours de connaissances empiriques. Nous sommes à cet égard très en arrière de la France, malgré le fâcheux effet qui résulte à certains égards chez vous, de l'organisation prématurée d'une classe savante qui n'est pas au niveau de sa destinée à venir. En France le cas qu'on fait de la science est prouvé par l'abus même que les savans peuvent faire de leur influence, et dont vous avez été malheureusement mais très naturellement la victime, précisément parce que la grande réforme que vous vous efforcez d'accomplir dans les choses humaines s'annonce comme devant commencer par la classe savante elle-même.

En retournant dans ma pensée votre position actuelle et les moyens d'y remédier, j'ai eu l'idée de vous proposer de faire l'essai de notre milieu anglais d'une nouvelle manière. Quoique, dans mon opinion, le temps ne soit pas venu où une revue franchement positive aurait ainsi la moindre chance de succès, il n'en est pas de même lorsqu'il ne s'agit que de faire pénétrer l'esprit positif dans l'intelligence publique d'une manière plus graduelle, au moyen des revues existantes. L'accueil qu'on a fait ici à ma Logique est une preuve entre plusieurs qu'il existe chez nous un public capable de goûter des discussions, même très élevées, dans l'ordre positif, sauf quelques réserves indispensables mais faciles: ces discussions serviraient même à donner de la réputation à la revue qui les ferait paraître, quoique ne pouvant pas en faire le fond. A cet égard, l'Angleterre est peutêtre en ce moment-ci mieux préparée que la France. Je conçois très bien que même en ne supposant pas les obstacles qu'y opposerait l'esprit de coterie de la presse française, il pourrait vous répugner d'entrer en relation avec des ouvrages périodiques quelconques en France: mais il me semble que la chose serait plus practicable ici, d'autant plus que les rapports pourraient n'être qu'indirects, par mon intermédiaire. Je vous engage donc à réfléchir s'il n'y a pas telle ou telle question secondaire que vous pourriez traiter, ou tel ou tel travail scientifique ou historique par exemple, dont vous pourriez faire la critique, d'une manière qui conviendrait à quelque revue anglaise. Je ferais moi-même la traduction, ou la ferais faire sous mes yeux, et d'ailleurs à mon défaut il n'est pas douteux que Bain ou Lewes tiendraient à honneur de la faire. Il est vrai que cette sorte de travail accessoire dérangerait nécessairement jusqu'à un certain point votre régime cérébral habituel; mais à tout prendre, le pénible métier de l'enseignement privé exigerait peut être des frais d'énergie cérébale encore plus considérable, sans laisser espérer une aussi grande utilité secondaire. Ce dont je vous parle, je l'ai toujours fait moi-même. Pendant l'élaboration de mon ouvrage scientifique, et même quelquefois depuis, j'ai publié dans des revues de petits opuscules que je pouvais faire avec facilité, mais que je savais bien n'avoir qu'une valeur transitoire ou même momentanée, et qui n'étaient guère pour moi, en effet, qu'une sorte de délassement intellectuel. Cela n'a pas laissé d'être utile au succès de mes travaux plus sérieux; j'y dois très probablement la majorité de mes lecteurs, sans compter que je leur fais un peu, par ce moyen, une sorte d'éducation préparatoire. Je crois qu'il y a sous ce rapport, quelque chose à faire, que cela pourrait être utile aussi bien que lucratif, et si ce projet vous semble exécutable je vous offre tout ce que je puis faire pour en surmonter les diverses difficultés.

Bain est très flatté de ce que son jugement favorable de votre traité astronomique vous a fait plaisir, et il dit "His remarks of sympathy with my disappointment and difficult position, I received with sincere delight." Il est ici depuis quelques jours. En ce moment-ci il est sans position, et sans aucune perspective certaine d'en avoir; mais il a plusieurs chances plus ou moins prochaines: il est jeune et d'heureux caractère, et il ne manquera pas d'obtenir tôt ou tard une digne réparation. Au reste ses tribulations sont bien loin d'être aussi graves ni aussi injustes que les vôtres. Il est maltraité parce que sa supériorité n'est pas encore assez connue, et non pas à cause de sa supériorité même.

votre tout dévoué

J. S. MILL

460. TO AUGUSTE COMTE[1]

India House
le 24 juin
1845

MON CHER MONSIEUR COMTE

Depuis samedi, jour où je vous écrivis ma dernière lettre, voici ce qui est arrivé. Je viens de voir un anglais ou plutôt un écossais de ma connaissance nommé Williamson[2] dont le fils,[3] âgé d'à peu près 21 ans, s'est beaucoup occupé d'études positives. Il désire placer son fils en pension à Paris chez quelque professeur ou savant, pendant l'hiver prochain, et peut être plus longtemps encore, pour y profiter des avantages scientifiques de cette capitale du monde savant. J'ai pensé que cela pourrait vous con-

1. *Addressed*: Monsieur / Auguste Comte / Rue M. le Prince / près l'Odeon / à Paris. *Postmark*: PAID / 24 JU 24 / 1845 / and BOULOGNE. MS as Johns Hopkins. Published in Lévy-Bruhl, pp. 429–31.

2. Alexander Williamson, long a clerk at the East India Co., in 1830 had moved to Wright's Lane, Kensington, near the home of his fellow employee, James Mill.

3. Alexander William Williamson (1824–1904), later professor of chemistry at the University of London. JSM's recommendation led to his studying for three years with Comte.

venir. Je ne connais le fils que par ce que m'en dit le père. D'après celui-ci, le jeune homme a fait de bonnes études mathématiques et biologiques mais il s'est appliqué encore davantage à la chimie et à l'électrologie. Il a étudié à Giessen en Hesse sous le célèbre Liebig,[4] qui en a, selon le père, la plus haute opinion, et qui en parle comme d'un homme destiné à faire des choses importantes dans la chimie. Il paraît s'être attaché avec zèle aux recherches originales et au perfectionnement des généralites scientifiques. Le père désirerait en faire un professeur. Le père, ex-employé de la compagnie des Indes, n'est pas, je crois, un homme très intelligent, mais il a longtemps demeuré en France et en allemagne, il s'est désappris de tout préjugé insulaire, il aime beaucoup les Français, et, chose importante, il n'a, pas plus que son fils, aucune croyance religieuse, au contraire, il y répugne profondément. C'est au reste un homme d'un caractère irréprochable. Sans être riche il jouit d'une certaine aisance. Je lui ai parlé de vous, en lui disant que je ne savais pas s'il vous conviendrait de prendre son fils en pension, mais que je vous en parlerais. Il aurait préféré à quelques égards, pour son fils, une vie de famille, mais, d'après ce que je lui ai dit de vous, il ne regarde pas votre vie de célibataire[5] comme un obstacle insurmontable; et je crois que vous pourriez vous entendre avec lui, soit pour des leçons spéciales de haute science, soit pour la direction générale des études scientifiques du jeune homme, même dans le cas où il ne vous conviendrait pas de le prendre en pension, ou ne vous conviendrait qu'à des conditions que le père regarderait comme inacceptables. En attendant j'ai conseillé au père de faire lire au fils votre grand ouvrage, et j'ai pris sur moi de dire que vous lui donneriez volontiers des conseils d'ami, si même vous ne pouviez pas accueillir l'affaire d'une autre manière. Le père part en quelques jours pour la Saxe, par conséquent si la chose vous semble digne de considération ce ne serait pas mal de me le faire savoir au plus tôt.

tout à vous,

J. S. MILL

461. TO AUGUSTE COMTE[1]

[June, 1845]

MON CHER MONSIEUR COMTE

Ce petit mot est destiné à servir d'introduction auprès de vous pour MM. Williamson, père et fils, qui vous sont déjà assez connus par mes

4. Baron Justus von Liebig (1803–1873), German chemist.
5. Comte's wife had left him in 1842; see Letter 371, n. 3.

* * * *

1. MS at Johns Hopkins. Published in Lévy-Bruhl, pp. 450–51. Undated, but JSM in his letter of July 8, 1845 (Letter 463), mentions having written this note of introduction.

lettres. Je n'ai pas besoin de les recommander de nouveau aux bons offices et conseils que vous m'avez déjà permis de leur promettre en votre nom.

Votre tout dévoué

J. S. MILL

462. TO THOMAS CARLYLE[1]

I.H.
Monday
[July 7, 1845]

MY DEAR CARLYLE

I have no pretium affectionis nor any other kind of pretium attached to the Whitelocke[2] & I should think it money wasted on your part to provide me with another, for which I shall probably never have any use. "The tools to him who can use them" & it would be a real pleasure to me if you will keep the Whitelocke, with your annotations & come to me some evening *without*, instead of *with*, another to replace it.

Yours ever

J. S. MILL

463. TO AUGUSTE COMTE[1]

India House
le 8 juillet 1845

MON CHER MONSIEUR COMTE

Votre lettre à Mme de V.[2] est sans doute fort propre à adoucir les préventions de ceux ou de celles qui, déjà à moitié détachés des anciennes

1. *Postmark*: 7 JULY 1845. MS at NLS.

2. Probably Sir Bulstrode Whitelocke's *Memorials of the English Affairs . . . from the Beginning of the Reign of King Charles the First, to King Charles the Second his happy restauration*, first published in London, 1682. Carlyle had no doubt borrowed the book in preparing his edition of *Oliver Cromwell's Letters and Speeches* (2 vols., London, 1845).

* * * *

1. MS at Johns Hopkins. Published in Lévy-Bruhl, pp. 447–50; in reply to Comte's of June 27 and 30, *ibid.*, pp. 431–46.

2. In his letter of June 30 Comte had asked JSM's advice about publishing in an English periodical a letter he had written to Mme de Vaux (Clotilde de Vaux, sister of one of his students, whom he had met that year and for whom he developed a passionate devotion that survived her death in 1846). In his letter of July 14 to JSM, Comte refers to the composition as *Sainte Clotilde*.

idées, tiennent fortement par l'imagination et par les affections à la satisfaction que l'ancien système, en tant que système organique, offrait et devrait offrir à la partie morale et sympathique de notre nature. Par ces raisons mêmes je la crois impropre au public anglais. Poser le positivisme en contradiction ouverte avec toute religion quelconque est peut être la seule manière de le présenter dont il serait à mon avis très inopportun de faire usage aujourd'hui en angleterre. Un temps viendra où ce sera peut être très utile de donner ici de la publicité à cet opuscule: ce sera le temps, peut être prochain, où vous serez publiquement attaqué et dénoncé ici comme athée. Alors il conviendra peut être de faire voir et comprendre au public l'intervalle immense qui sépare votre athéisme de celui, seul connu ici, de l'école de Diderot et d'Holbach.[3] Aujourd'hui je pense qu'il faudrait, en écrivant pour l'angleterre, se taire absolument sur la question religieuse, sauf à porter indirectement aux croyances religieuses tel coup qu'on voudra. Cette réserve serait surtout nécessaire de la part d'un écrivain déjà connu pour avoir professé ouvertement des opinions anti-religieuses parce que les directeurs des revues y regarderont de plus près que dans tout autre cas. C'est au reste la seule réserve dont vous auriez besoin. A tout autre égard il n'y a rien dans vos écrits qui puisse servir d'obstacle à ce qu'on les accueille ici. Je conçois au reste l'impossibilité de laisser à côté la question religieuse dans un ouvrage systématique, ou même en traitant une seule question sociale du premier ordre: mais, tant qu'il ne s'agit que de critique ou des questions secondaires, on pourrait, ce me semble, se contenter de traiter le sujet comme si la religion n'existait pas. Mais aujourd'hui la publication, en anglais, d'un opuscule en votre nom, où toute croyance religieuse serait ouvertement repoussée, vous fermerait très probablement toutes les revues de ce pays-ci. On craint et on repousse ici les *mots* anti-religieux bien plus que la chose.

Je trouve au contraire très convenable à l'Angleterre votre idée d'écrire sur la situation des sciences et des savans en france et en angleterre: seulement je conseillerais que ce ne fût pas en forme de lettres: les revues chez nous ne voudraient pas de cette forme, et les magazines, outre qu'ils rétribuent moins leurs collaborateurs, ont beaucoup moins d'importance intellectuelle et sociale. Je conseillerais d'écrire, en tête de l'article, le nom de quelque ouvrage récent, ayant un rapport plus ou moins direct au sujet traité: sauf à n'en dire que deux mots, si l'ouvrage ne mérite pas davantage: vous pourrez, après cela, n'en plus tenir compte.

Quant à la question pécuniaire immédiate, je compte, de manière ou d'autre, à entamer auprès de M. Grote la question d'un subside supplémentaire, de façon à sonder sa disposition à y coopérer: malheureusement

3. The French *philosophes* and Encyclopedists, Denis Diderot (1713–1784) and Paul Henri Dietrich, baron d'Holbach (1723–1789).

le jour même où je devais le voir, et où je comptais discuter avec lui votre proposition, il s'est trouvé dans la nécessité de partir subitement pour les eaux de Kissingen à cause de la santé de Mme Grote. Il compte être de retour avant le milieu d'août. Quant à Molesworth, une plus grande délicatesse m'est commandée par diverses raisons. D'abord j'ai été, en partie, la cause pour lui d'une perte pécuniaire considérable par une revue qu'il fonda sous ma direction;[4] ensuite, il n'y a pas un an qu'il s'est marié, et qu'il a fait plusieurs dépenses considérables qui l'ont empêché de fournir au subside de l'année passée une aussi forte part qu'il en avait je crois, très sincèrement le désir. Je l'ai peu vu depuis son mariage, et c'est surtout M. Grote qui est intervenu auprès de lui et s'il s'agissait d'une seconde intervention je crois qu'elle se ferait le plus avantageusement par le même moyen. Je ne sais pas si M. Grote vous a averti dans le temps (je pense que c'était surtout à lui de le faire) que par suite de gêne momentanée de Molesworth, il (M. Grote) avait admis contrairement à son intention première, et pour la somme de 50 livres sterling, un troisième coadjuteur, M. Raikes Currie, banquier et député.[5] Au reste, voici probablement ce que se diraient ces messieurs. S'ils croyaient certain que, dans un temps défini et pas trop prolongé, vous obtiendriez soit une réparation officielle, soit d'autres ressources équivalentes, je ne doute nullement que ceux qui vous ont aidé jusqu'ici, seraient disposés à prolonger leur secours, pour vous épargner soit la nécessité de déranger vos habitudes permanentes par un motif temporaire, soit l'ennui et la perte de temps qui résulteraient d'une tentative pour obtenir des ressources auxiliaires dont bientôt vous n'auriez plus besoin. C'est la question de temps, et de l'indéfini, qui seule pourrait les faire hésiter. Je trouve donc qu'il serait utile que sans faire aucune démarche auprès d'eux vous m'adressiez une lettre destinée à leur être montrée, où vous exposeriez simplement, et comme avertissement général à vos amis d'ici, ce que vous pensez sur votre avenir pécuniaire en France. Par suite de l'absence de Mr. Grote, on ne pourra rien faire qu'à une époque qui approchera très près du terme fatal du 1er septembre, mais s'il vous arrive par là quelque inconvénient, vous savez qu'en cas d'urgence je suis là.

M. Williamson[6] est reparti pour la Saxe. Je lui ai donné pour lui et pour son fils, une lettre d'introduction adressée à vous. Il sera à Paris en octobre et c'est alors qu'il pourra être question de leçons à donner au jeune homme.

votre dévoué

J. S. MILL

4. The *London Review* in 1835.
5. Raikes Currie (1801–1881), banker; MP for Northampton, 1837–57.
6. See Letter 460.

464. TO SIR JOHN F. W. HERSCHEL[1]

India House
9th July 1845.

MY DEAR SIR

The correspondence which took place between us, two years ago,[2] must be my warrant, if the object I have in view requires any, for taking the liberty of writing to you respecting a passage in the Address which you delivered to the British Association for the Advancement of Science at its first evening meeting on the 19th of last month.[3]

In that discourse you spoke of a recent publication of mine in so handsome a manner as would have more than satisfied a much greater degree of vanity than I possess. But my purpose in writing to you is not to make acknowledgments for your politeness nor to express my gratification at your favourable opinion, but to call your attention to an act of injustice which you have, I am sure unintentionally, committed against the scientific reputation of a distinguished man. You have publicly imputed to M. Auguste Comte, not only a gross blunder in reasoning, but one inconsistent with the most elementary knowledge of the principles of astronomical dynamics. If M. Comte had been capable of such a blunder, he would have been quite incapable of writing any one chapter of the Cours de Philosophie Positive, & I am sure nothing is necessary but a more careful reference to that work, to convince you that he never was guilty of it.

You say that for the purpose of giving a numerical verification to the hypothesis of the nebular origin of the solar system, M. Comte computes the time of rotation which the sun must have had about its axis so that a planet situated on its surface should not press upon that surface. That as the basis of this calculation M. Comte employs "the elementary Huyghenian theorems for the evaluation of centrifugal forces, in combination with the law of gravitation—a combination which, I need not explain to those who have read the first book of Newton, leads direct to Kepler's law," and then you accuse him of "gravely turning round upon us and addressing the coincidence of the resulting periods compared with the distances of the planets with this law of Kepler, as *being* the numerical verification in question." Well may you add "where is there a student to be found who has graduated as a Senior Optime in this University, who will not at once lay his finger on the fallacy of such an argument, & declare it a vicious circle." But, that Mr. Comte has fallen into this vicious circle is a statement

1. MS in the possession of the Royal Society, as is also Herschel's reply of July 10. A further letter of Herschel's of July 13 is at Yale.

2. See Letter 397.

3. Herschel's presidential address at the fifteenth meeting of the Association, at Cambridge, published in the *Athenæum* for June 21, 1845, pp. 612–17.

only to be accounted for by supposing that you have not read the astronomical portion of M. Comte's work, but only referred, & that cursorily, to a single passage of it.

It would be difficult for even the shallowest person to have attempted to give a philosophical outline of astronomy without being aware that the evidence by which Newton proved the law of gravitation was the fact of its leading demonstratively to Kepler's laws; & that Kepler's law of the relation between the distances & the periodic times, was deduced from the law of gravitation combined with the Huyghenian measure of the centrifugal force. Accordingly if you refer to an earlier chapter in the same volume of M. Comte, being that in which he unfolds the evidence of the law of gravitation, you will find (pp. 227–231) that all which you so contemptuously bring forward in condemnation of M. Comte, is brought forward *by* him. You will find the same exposition repeated in the corresponding chapter of his very striking "Traité Philosophique d'Astronomie Populaire." It was impossible that the accordance of Kepler's law with the premises from which he knew & said that it demonstratively followed, could appear to him to be a "numerical verification," not of those premisses, but of something quite unconnected with them, viz. the nebular hypothesis.

And if you only refer again to the very passage, to which I venture to think that your former reference must have been a very hasty one, I am confident that you will see how completely you have mistaken its import. It was not the coincidence of the resulting periods of the planets "with this law of Kepler" that M. Comte considered as a numerical verification of their nebulous origin; it was the coincidence (within certain limits of error) between the periods, as resulting from the calculation, & *the actual periodic times of the planets, as known by observation.* The reference to Kepler's law is only incidental, & the sole use made of it is to dispense with the necessity of performing the calculation separately for each planet, since, when it has been made for any one, Kepler's law gives the correlative result for every other.

I speak without any knowledge of the Memoir or Memoirs on the subject, which M. Comte read before the Academy of Science, and with which you appear to be equally unacquainted. A reference to them would doubtless shew both "the steps" & "the data of his calculations," which could not have been given with any propriety in the Cours. I also write without communication with M. Comte, who is probably quite unaware of the attack made upon him. But on the face of the Cours itself & of the very passage from which you quote, it is evident to me that the attack has been made under a misapprehension, & I cannot doubt that your love of justice will induce you to reexamine the subject.

A judgment from you, delivered with preparation, & on an occasion of so much publicity, must have a serious effect upon the scientific reputation of any author: and you cannot be unaware how little chance anyone, who may dispute its justice, would have of obtaining, from the scientific or from the general public of this country, even a hearing, against your authority. So great a power involves a proportional responsibility; and when it has been inadvertently exercised to the injury of anyone, I cannot doubt your being most desirous that the error should be pointed out.

I remain,
Yours very truly
J. S. MILL

Sir J. F. W. Herschel, Bart.

465. TO SIR JOHN F. W. HERSCHEL[1]

India House
14th July
1845

MY DEAR SIR

I beg to acknowledge your letters of the 10th & 13th. If you will permit me I should like to send the Athenaeum[2] to M. Comte as from yourself, *with a copy of your last note*,[3] which I think would be more agreeable to him, or to any man, than the direct communication of your animadversions could be disagreeable.

The question raised by your criticism of M. Comte appears to me, I confess, to be one which a mere reference to his book would decide. In saying (as he does) that a theorem compounded of Huyghens and Newton's laws leads directly to the law of Kepler, does he represent *this* as a verification of the nebular hypothesis? In your address you say he does. I continue to think, that if you refer again to his book, you will see that he does not; & moreover that he does, elsewhere, represent that same logical sequence as a verification not of the nebular hypothesis, but of the law of gravitation.

1. *Addressed*: Sir J. F. W. Herschel Bart. / Collingwood / Hawkhurst / Kent. *Postmarks*: W / PAID / 14 JY 14 / 1845, and STA . . . HURST / JY 15 / 1845. MS in the possession of the Royal Society, as is also Herschel's reply of July 16.

2. See preceding letter, n. 3.

3. Of July 13, in which Herschel had asked JSM to avoid mentioning his name in sending the *Athenæum* to Comte: "In all such cases I consider it highly unjust to remark on the writings of an author unfavorably without putting him in possession of the *ipsissima verba* of the remarks, but then it should be so done as to give no unnecessary offence of a personal nature."

What may be the value of what he *does* bring forward as a numerical verification I cannot pretend to say; I am not acquainted with what he has written expressly on the subject; & if I were, it would become me to express myself much more modestly on *that* question. The verification would of course consist in the agreement of the periodic time of each planet, with what would be the period of the sun's revolution if it were suddenly expanded so as to touch the planet. For computing that period the elements would be, the present period of the sun's rotation, the sun's equatorial radius, the mean distance of the planet from the sun, and—Kepler's law. I therefore presume that M. Comte *must* either prove or assume (as stated in your letter) that Kepler's law applies to the successive states of the sun itself, & not merely to the planets when detached from it. On what grounds he does so, his own dissertation must shew.

Admitting, however, the impossibility of proving the proposition stated in your letter, still it cannot be considered a mere arbitrary assumption; & if it can be shewn that the present rotation of the sun takes place in the same time in which it ought to take place supposing that proposition & the nebular hypothesis to be true, would not that be of considerable weight as an additional argument in favour of the nebular hypothesis? A proof, it would not be; but M. Comte, you will observe, distinctly disclaims the pretension of having *proved* the hypothesis.

And now, without troubling you further on this subject, permit me to say, that I thankfully accept your offer[4] with respect to my own book. I am well aware that any one, not a mathematician by profession, is likely in going over such a field as I have done, to have committed many such errors as those you propose pointing out; & for myself, though I formerly went quite through the usual course of mathematics & its applications & have occasionally revived my recollection by recurring to parts of it, I do not pretend to have retained any accurate memory of more than the outline. I have therefore always hoped that if my book had any success, some of those who possess the requisite knowledge would take the trouble to free it from errors of this description, & I shall endeavour to profit to the utmost by every indication you may give.

I remain
Very truly yours
J. S. MILL.

4. In his letter of July 10 Herschel in speaking of JSM's *Logic* noted "the general high opinion I have formed and expressed of it in a philosophical point of view" but thought "the least felicitous portions of it, those in which points of physical science and mathematics are touched upon. I should have no objection if you desired it, to specify some particular instances which have occurred to me inter legendum to which this remark applies. . . ."

466. TO SIR JOHN F. W. HERSCHEL[1]

India House
17th July 1845

MY DEAR SIR,

I have now nothing more to do than to thank you for the fullness and explicitness of your letter[2] received this morning, & to say that I will immediately send a copy of it to M. Comte.[3]

Very truly yours
J. S. MILL.

467. TO AUGUSTE COMTE[1]

18 juillet 1845

MON CHER MONSIEUR COMTE—

Dans une lettre très récente vous vous êtes félicité du ton bienveillant et amical dont vous aviez été traité jusque là par vos critiques anglais. Il était impossible que cela durât très longtemps, et déjà cela ne dure plus. Comme, par la nature de votre grand ouvrage il ne devait guère être connu encore que des savans, c'est de leur part qu'est venue la première attaque, et elle porte sur une question isolée, celle de votre vérification numérique de l'hypothèse cosmogonique de Laplace. A la réunion annuelle des savans anglais qui eut lieu cette année à Cambridge, sir John Herschel a prononcé un discours d'ouverture dont vous trouverez dans le journal *The Athenæum*[2] une copie corrigée par l'auteur, que je vous envoie de sa part. Quoique je fusse nommé avec éloge dans ce discours, je n'en ai pas eu une connaissance immédiate. L'ayant enfin lu, je me sentis blessé de l'injustice qu'il me semblait montrer à votre égard, et encore plus par le ton de supériorité qu'il s'était permis envers vous et je lui adressai la première lettre de la correspondance ci-jointe. Les lettres suivantes[3] s'expliquent toutes seules. J'y ajoute (numéro 6) une autre attaque d'une main différente, qui a paru dans la revue d'Edimbourg.[4] L'année passée un ouvrage anonyme a paru

1. MS in the possession of the Royal Society, as is also Herschel's reply of July 18.
2. Herschel's letter of July 16 criticizing in detail Comte's astronomical theories.
3. In his note of July 18 Herschel expressed some reluctance to JSM's sending a copy to Comte.

* * * *

1. MS at Johns Hopkins. Published in Lévy-Bruhl, pp. 465–68; in reply to Comte's two letters of July 14, *ibid.*, pp. 451–65.
2. See Letter 464.
3. Letters 464, 465, and copies of Herschel's replies.
4. [Adam Sedgwick], "The Vestiges of the Natural History of Creation," *ER*, LXXXII (July, 1845), 1–85.

ici, ouvrage très superficiel, mais dont l'auteur inconnu mérite, au moins par ses intentions, beaucoup d'éloges. Sous le titre de "Vestiges of the Natural History of Creation" il tâche de *deviner* une sorte de cosmogonie positive, en y ajoutant, sous une forme différente et moins absurde, l'hypothèse de Lamarck sur la transformation des espèces, &c. &c. Quoique d'une valeur purement négative, cet ouvrage n'a pas laissé de faire ici une sensation assez prononcée, et je crois qu'il tend à préparer un peu les esprits pour le positivisme. Son succès a été un grand scandale pour les gens religieux et pour beaucoup de savans, et la revue d'Edimbourg vient de publier un long article plein de rancunes savantes et sacerdotales, que je sais de bonne part être d'un nommé Sedgwick, professeur de géologie à Cambridge, avec lequel j'eus des démêlés autrefois.[5] Or, l'auteur des "Vestiges" cita votre vérification de l'hypothèse de Laplace. C'est, je crois, ce qui détermina l'attaque de Herschel, et Sedgwick vous attaque de même dans le passage ci-joint. Vous verrez que celui-ci parle un peu plus en connaissance de cause, puisqu'il paraît avoir lu votre mémoire original, tandis que Herschel ne parle que d'après le Cours de Ph. Positive. Vous verrez que j'ai pris bien garde de ne pas vous compromettre dans ce que j'ai osé dire, de ma propre part, en votre défense. C'est maintenant à vous de juger s'il vous convient ou non de repousser ces attaques, d'une manière publique ou privée.

J'ai appris avec le plus grand intérêt ce que vous me mandez sur la maladie nerveuse dont vous venez de sortir, et dont vous avez si heureusement profité pour déterminer par des méditations décisives, le caractère distinctif de vos travaux sociologiques à venir. J'ai envoyé de suite votre billet à M. Raikes Currie. Je tombe d'accord sur l'ineptitude de notre usage de donner à tous les articles de revue la forme d'un compte rendu: malheureusement, cela est de rigueur dans toutes nos grandes revues, qui outre leur importance plus grande, sont aussi les seules qui rétribuent convenablement leurs rédacteurs. Mais cette obligation n'est que de forme; vous pouvez y mettre le titre de l'édition la plus récente de quelque ouvrage bien connu: il arrive quelquefois que, sauf le titre mis à l'article, il n'y est pas une seule fois question de l'écrit dont on prétend rendre compte.

Ayant obtenu un congé, beaucoup plus court pourtant que celui de l'année passée, je vais partir pour une tournée dans laquelle mon adresse sera trop incertaine pour qu'on puisse m'envoyer des lettres. Ce temps ne sera pourtant pas perdu pour vos affaires. Comme M. Grote sera peut être de retour avant moi, je lui adresserai la lettre que vous m'avez écrite à ma demande,[6] et je l'accompagnerai des observations qui me paraîtront con-

5. JSM's "Professor Sedgwick's Discourse [*On the Studies of the University*]—State of Philosophy in England," *London Review*, I (April, 1835), 94–135. Reprinted in *Dissertations*, I, 121–85.

6. Comte's second letter of July 14, Lévy Bruhl, pp. 460–65. See Letter 463.

venables, de manière à ce qu'il les reçoive dès son arrivée. Il en arrivera alors ce qu'il pourra. Le succès me paraît le résultat le plus probable.

tout à vous

J. S. MILL

468. TO GEORGE GROTE[1]

[July, 1845]

DEAR MR. GROTE,—A short time ago Comte, finding that his attempts to replace by private teaching the deficit in his income did not promise any immediate success, asked my opinion as to the possibility of a prolongation, for a short time, of the aid so generously afforded to him last year. I thereupon advised him to write me a letter[2] containing an exact statement of the grounds of his expectations of a change for the better in his position, after which I would have a consultation with you on the subject. This letter, as you will probably be in London again before I shall, I enclose.

In Comte's position I think my conduct would have been different: in the first place, I should have endeavoured by saving to provide a fund for such emergencies, and if this failed I should have preferred living as I could upon my reduced income so long as it was physically possible. But it is to be said for him, on the first point, that he had every reason to believe his income a permanent one, and on the second, that it is harder to be advised to break up all his arrangements and to alter his confirmed habits from a cause which he firmly believes to be not only temporary, but of very short duration. If, therefore, you think that it would be possible and advisable to raise another subscription for him I should be happy, in case of need, to contribute my part towards it. At the same time, as he certainly does not mean to be understood as asking for such a favour, so, if the answer be negative, it need not have the character of a refusal.

469. TO AUGUSTE COMTE[1]

India House
le 22 septembre
1845

MON CHER MONSIEUR COMTE

Je suis de retour ici depuis longtemps, mais M. Grote ne l'est que depuis quelques jours, et votre lettre est restée chez lui pendant son absence.

1. Published in Elliot, I, 139–40. MS not located. Dated by Elliot as of Dec. 22, 1848, but evidence from this and from the Mill-Comte correspondence indicates that it should be dated as of the summer of 1845.

2. See preceding letter, n. 6.

* * * *

1. MS at Johns Hopkins. Published in Lévy-Bruhl, pp. 475–76; in reply to Comte's of Aug. 8, *ibid.*, pp. 468–74.

Aussitôt après son retour nous nous sommes vus, et nous avons causé sur votre position. Il a dû lui-même vous annoncer le résultat, qui ne paraît pas devoir être de nature à remédier à vos embarras.

Quant à Molesworth, dont je n'ai eu que plus tard la réponse, tout en témoignant un regret sincère que la gêne de vos affaires se soit encore prolongée il ne paraît nullement disposé à renouveler son subside à moins d'une nécessité absolue qu'il ne juge pas être arrivée.

Je ne connais aucune autre personne à laquelle je puisse convenablement m'adresser dans un cas pareil.

Je ne veux pas mêler des causeries ordinaires à l'annonce d'une chose sérieuse, et je me bornerai par conséquent à vous dire que je n'ai cru devoir mettre aucune suite à ma correspondance avec Herschel. Si je lui avais dit que vous n'aviez pas l'intention de lui répondre, il n'aurait certainement pas apprécié les raisons que vous avez pour cela: il n'y aurait vu qu'un aveu indirect de l'irréfutabilité de son raisonnement, surtout si de mon côté je m'abstenais également de le réfuter; ce que je ne pourrais certainement faire sans avoir connaissance de votre mémoire en manuscrit, à moins de recevoir de vous-même des renseignements équivalents.

Mandez-moi bientôt ce que vous comptez faire.

tout à vous

J. S. MILL

470. TO HENRY REEVE[1]

India House
23rd Sept. 1845

MY DEAR SIR,

You can hardly feel more interested in preventing the removal of Captain Meadows Taylor from Shorapur[2] than I do myself, because (to say nothing of personal considerations), I have a very high opinion of the merits of his administration of Shorapur. I may say, indeed, that his being at Shorapur now is owing to me, for some expressions of approval and praise in a dispatch written by me was what induced the Indian Government to suspend their intention of replacing him by a civil servant of the company, and to refer the matter home. I have endeavoured to induce the Court of

1. Excerpt published in the Preface by Henry Reeve to Meadows Taylor's *The Story of My Life* (Edinburgh, 1877). New edition, with Introduction and Notes by Henry Bruce (London, 1920). MS not located.

2. Philip Meadows Taylor (1808–1876), military officer in India and novelist; carried out the pacification of the State of Shorapore in 1841 and remained there as resident until 1853. Early in 1845 a move had been made to supplant Captain Taylor with a civil servant of the East India Co. (see *The Story of My Life* [1920 ed.], pp. 204–9). Taylor was a second cousin of Reeve.

Directors to negative the proposition. I do not, however, expect to obtain anything so decided, as they do not think it right to fetter the Indian Government in its choice of instruments. But as the Court will certainly give no encouragement to the project, I think it will blow over, and Captain Taylor will remain.[3]—Very truly yours,

J. S. MILL

471. TO HENRY REEVE[1]

[Late Sept., 1845]

Whatever may be the cause that is working against Captain Taylor, I am convinced that Fraser[2] has nothing to do with it. Fraser, as far as I know, has always written to Government very much in his favour. Captain Taylor is quite in error if he supposes that the Nazarana[3] business has done him any harm. Fraser did not agree with him on the subject, but the home authorities and Sir H. Hardinge[4] did, and do most strenuously.

472. TO AUGUSTE COMTE[1]

India House
le 3 octobre 1845

MON CHER MONSIEUR COMTE

J'espère que vous ne trouverez pas mauvais que je regarde toute nouvelle intervention auprès de sir W. Molesworth comme peu convenable de ma part. Pour l'autoriser il faudrait être beaucoup plus lié que je ne le suis avec lui. Il n'y a jamais eu d'intimité entre nous; et depuis longtemps nous ne nous voyons presque pas, si ce n'est une ou deux fois par an peut être, chose assez fréquente à Londres, comme vous savez sans doute, même entre de très anciennes connaissances. Il y a plusieurs ans que je ne suis pas entré une seule fois dans sa maison. Vous voyez donc que je ne suis guère en droit de faire un appel quelconque, surtout réitéré, à sa liberalité, lorsqu'il n'y a pas lieu de compter d'avance sur un accueil favorable. Ensuite, quant

3. JSM's prediction was fulfilled.

* * * *

1. Excerpt published, like the preceding letter, in Henry Reeve's Preface to Meadows Taylor's *The Story of My Life*. MS not located.
2. General James Stuart Fraser (1783–1869), the Resident in Hyderabad.
3. Occasional dues exacted from the State of Shorapore by the ruler of Hyderabad. Taylor had sought to lessen the tribute levied on the weaker State, Shorapore.
4. Sir Henry Hardinge, later first Viscount Hardinge of Lahore (1785–1856), Governor General of India, 1844–47.

* * * *

1. MS at Johns Hopkins. Published in Lévy-Bruhl, pp. 480–82; in reply to Comte's of Sept. 24, *ibid.*, pp. 476–79.

à la sorte de communication indiquée dans votre lettre, vous me pardonnerez, j'espère, si je ne trouve pas que dans le cas actuel, elle soit justifiée par sa réponse antérieure. Il n'y a, en effet, rien de nouveau à lui annoncer. Il sait déjà quelle est votre position, ou à peu près. Je conçois bien combien il est dur de se voir privé de la moitié d'un revenu qu'on croyait assuré, et sur lequel on avait réglé ses habitudes; je sens combien est minime, pour un homme comme vous, la rétribution de cinq mille francs qui vous reste. Mais enfin, puisque vous avez encore cette somme, Sir W. Molesworth a sans doute jugé que votre gêne, quelque regrettable qu'elle soit, ne fait pas un cas de nécessité absolue. Voilà les raisons qui me détourneraient personnellement de faire auprès de lui une nouvelle démarche quelconque. Mais ces raisons, vous êtes vous-même en état d'en juger; et si vous êtes disposé à lui écrire directement en votre nom, son adresse est Sir William Molesworth Bart, M.P. I Lowndes Square, Knightsbridge, London.

Je regrette vivement que ce que je puis avoir dit sur les chances d'un nouveau subside vous ait donné une confiance que j'étais loin de vouloir vous inspirer, et qui a abouti à un désappointement. Quelles que puissent être ces chances, j'ai pensé et même dit qu'elles devaient dépendre de l'opinion qu'auraient MM. Grote et Molesworth sur l'extrême probabilité d'une prompte terminaison de votre crise actuelle: or c'est apparemment cette opinion qui s'est trouvée en défaut: la perspective qu'offrait votre lettre leur aura paru trop indéfinie, et ils auront pensé qu'un secours modique ne farait que retarder le moment de sacrifices pénibles sans remédier à leur nécessité.

Il est heureux que les mutations déterminées par le choix qu'on fera au poste de directeur des études vont fournir un moyen de voir plus clair dans les chances d'une réintégration officielle. Si les nominations à faire dépendent, comme celle d'examinateur, du conseil polytechnique, vous aurez probablement lieu de juger, par l'allure que prendra le conseil à l'occasion de votre candidature, s'il est vraiment disposé à changer de conduite envers vous. Si, d'un autre côté, les nominations dépendent du gouvernement, vous pourrez également juger de sa bonne volonté. Je désire beaucoup que de manière ou d'autre, l'occasion puisse amener, sinon une réparation, au moins l'indication sûre d'une disposition à l'accorder prochainement.

Je n'ai pas encore commencé, sauf quelques lectures préliminaires, le travail d'économie politique qui doit m'occuper pendant l'hiver. Le plan de l'ouvrage est tout fait, et je suis assez familiarisé avec la plupart des matériaux pour pouvoir espérer que lorsque j'aurai commencé à écrire, j'avancerai vite, et que le livre sera terminé avant l'été.

tout à vous

J. S. MILL.

473. TO MACVEY NAPIER[1]

India House
20th October
1845

My dear Sir

Your liberal remittance reached me duly, & I thank you for it, and also for the separate copies which you were so considerate as to think of although I neglected to ask for them at the proper time.

The omission of the concluding paragraph[2] I do not regret: it could be well spared, & though I am fully convinced of the truth of all it contained, I was not satisfied with the manner in which it was expressed. You are of course quite right in not printing what you think would expose you to attack, when you do not yourself agree in it. At the same time, I do not know how a public writer can be more usefully employed than in telling his countrymen their faults, & if that is considered anti-national I am not at all desirous to avoid the charge. Neither do I think that the English, with all their national self-conceit, are now much inclined to resent having their faults pointed out—they will bear a good deal in that respect.

I am glad you find the reception of the article satisfactory. I am not acquainted with Gilbert Stuart's writings:[3] those of Millar[4] I have long known, & there is as you say, a considerable similarity between some of his historical speculations & Guizot's.

With regard to a review of the Logic, I am not disappointed by your having had to give up the attempt. As far as the compliment is concerned, the wish is equivalent to the deed—& for the interests of the book itself, which is the main point, the notice of the Ed. Rev. might have been of essential importance to it, but as things have luckily turned out the book has reached nearly everybody who could be expected to buy or read a book of the kind. By the bye, it has narrowly missed being reviewed in the Quarterly by Herschel but he also has abandoned the intention.[5] Believe me

Very truly yours

J. S. Mill

1. Published in *Napier Corresp.*, pp. 510–11. MS in Brit. Mus.
2. Of his review of Guizot (see Letter 419, n. 2).
3. Gilbert Stuart (1742–1786), historian and reviewer; Napier may have referred to Stuart's *A View of Society in Europe* (Edinburgh, 1778), a study of the early and mediaeval period influenced by the principles of Montesquieu.
4. John Millar. See Letter 440, n. 3.
5. Herschel had so informed JSM in his letter of July 10, 1845.

474. TO MACVEY NAPIER[1]

India House
27th October
1845

MY DEAR SIR

I have just finished an article which I am desirous of offering to the Edin. Rev. It is a review[2] of a book which I had occasion to mention in a note to the article on the "Claims of Labour," Duveyrier's Lettres Politiques. But as the title of the book gives little or no indication of the contents of the article, I have taken the liberty of sending it at once through Longman. It is the last I mean to write, for the present on any French topic—& its subject is, not French history or literature, but present French politics, introducing, however, remarks & speculations of a more general character. I cannot of course judge whether it will suit you, but I have put nothing into it which seemed inconsistent with its admission into the Edin. Rev. If you take it, pray let it wait your own time for insertion—& the more so, as it may be some little time before I have leisure to write another article on any subject.

Whewell's book,[3] which you kindly suggest, I have not yet read, but from turning over the pages I do not think it is a book on which I should be at all desirous of writing.

Believe me
yours ever truly
J. S. MILL

475. TO HENRY S. CHAPMAN[1]

India House
12th November, 1845.

MY DEAR CHAPMAN,—

Thank you exceedingly for your long and interesting letter. Since it was written the troubles of the Colony are, I hope, nearly blown over, the fool Fitzroy[2] being recalled, and matters made up between the Company and the Government. As the revenue cannot get up again immediately, and as there

1. MS in Brit. Mus.
2. See Letter 428, n. 2.
3. Presumably William Whewell's *The Elements of Morality, including Polity* (2 vols., London, 1845). JSM eventually wrote on "Whewell's Moral Philosophy" in *WR*, LVIII (Oct., 1852), 349–85 (reprinted in *Dissertations*, III, 132–92).

* * * *

1. MS in the possession of Mrs. W. Rosenberg. Copy supplied by Professor J. M. McCrimmon.
2. See Letter 442, n. 11. Lord Stanley had dismissed Governor Fitzroy in a dispatch dated April 30, 1845, which reached New Zealand in Nov.

has been so much extra expense I suppose they will not be able to pay your arrears at once, but doubtless you will succeed in getting put upon the Parliamentary vote in April. You have been very ill-treated, but that is what may be said of everybody in New Zealand, and indeed of many in almost all the other colonies, in the hands of Stanley, a man who has no conscience, and has I believe, not the ordinary feelings of honour—only pettishness and petulant self-will. It is fortunate you have been able to live with what they have paid you, and with the produce of your land—your account of which has very much interested me. I lost no time in asking Dr. Royle[3] for the Himalayan seeds, and he says there is no use in sending them from England when they can so easily go direct. He will write immediately to Dr. Jameson,[4] Superintendent of the E.I. Company's botanical garden at Saharunpore (at the foot of the Himalayas) asking him to send you seeds of any useful plants that are likely to suit your climate, and you can at once place yourself in communication with Dr. Jameson, and send him New Zealand seeds for trial in India. Many thanks for thinking of ferns for me. If you have anybody there who can name them it would be useful, as there are probably no books here on the botany of New Zealand; but if not, I will find someone to name and describe them here, as in any case there are likely to be new ones among them. Any other plants would be interesting as well as ferns,—all is fish that comes to my net, and there may be among plants picked up indiscriminately in a new country, as many and as interesting nondescripts as there were in Graham's Mexican collection.[5]

We have had but two subjects of much public interest in England this year; the one is railways, for which there has been a perfect frenzy. On the return of prosperity after the depression of the last few years, all the speculation which usually arises at such times, has taken that one direction, and not only a railway, or four or five rival railways are planned between almost every two towns of the smallest importance in the Kingdom, but all Europe, India, and the Colonies are to have railways made for them by English capital. If the thing had gone on a month longer I am convinced someone would have brought out "the Great New Zealand, Auckland and Wellington Junction railway company." However, there has just been a collapse, numbers having, under the allurement of premiums, taken many more shares than they could pay calls or even deposits on, intending to sell

3. John Forbes Royle (1799–1858), surgeon and naturalist, from 1838 in the employ of the India House in charge of correspondence relating to vegetable productions. He had been superintendent of gardens and in medical charge of the station at Saharunpore from 1823 to 1831.

4. Dr. William Jameson (1815–1882), botanist, pioneer of tea planting in India.

5. George John Graham, close friend of JSM in the 1820's, had travelled in Mexico, 1827–29, and collected some 400 specimens of Mexican plants. These are mentioned by George Bentham in the preface to his *Plantæ Hartwegianæ* (London, 1839).

all or part of it in case the market at last began to fall and money to get scarce, as people wanted to borrow that they might not be obliged to sell immediately. The rate of interest rose, and at last the Bank raised its rate of discount; this gave the alarm, and being followed by some thundering articles in the "Times", in which all the schemes or most of them were scouted as fraudulent bubbles, the long-eared public changed from ignorant and mad confidence to equally senseless distrust. Down came shares, and some of the very most promising schemes could not be proceeded with, because of those who had asked for shares and obtained them not one third would or could pay even the deposits. While the thing lasted there were enormous gains made, many people made large fortunes, and there must be corresponding losses to those who bought at high premiums, unless they are able and have courage to hold on, in which case the greater part will lose little.

The second subject which is occupying the public is the potato disease. It is certain that a very large proportion, nobody knows how large, of the potato crop is destroyed or in course of destruction, by this disease, not only in Ireland and Great Britain but in Belgium and Germany. It is also just discovered that the wheat crop is very deficient, a thing I expected from the prevalence of wind and rain at the blooming time. This also is general throughout Europe. In Russia there are already meal mobs, and exportation has been, I believe, prohibited. The deficiency is very great in North Germany, Holland and Belgium have suspended their corn laws; France and the South of Europe have little or no corn to spare, and we have only America to look to. The best quality of wheat is already at 74 sh. here, but the bad quality of the crop, which was very badly got in, keeps down the averages; and everybody feels that the sliding scale is an entire failure, bonded corn actually leaving this country to go elsewhere. Of course everybody thinks and says that the corn laws must go this winter, and the question only is whether any, even the smallest duty shall be suffered to remain. There have been four Cabinet Councils in almost successive days, and a general belief or hope existed that an Order in Council would be issued opening the ports, but the Ministers have separated and gone to the country without doing anything. It is rumoured that they are divided, Peel being on the side of remission; but I do not believe the rumour to be founded on anything except its abstract a priori probability. Peel always misses the moment; but it is so universally seen and admitted by friends and enemies that the corn laws are doomed, that they can hardly escape their fate. I think there will be such a demonstration on the subject before Parliament meets as will finish them, and most happy will that be, for that odious question stands in the way of all others. If it is given up in the coming session we shall certainly see free trade victorious in America too, for J. K. Polk[6] and the party who brought him in are avowed friends of a tariff for revenue only, and the repeal of the corn laws by giving them the Western States would make them irresistible. As for Europe, at least France and Germany, any approach to free-trade there has now become hopeless. They are receding further from it every day as their industrial interests grow stronger and require more power in the State; and in Germany the rising feeling of nationality all tends in that mischievous direction. It is not a matter of calculation now, but of passion, and I sincerely believe that there is in the public eye both of France and of Germany a strenuous desire to bring down the wealth and power of England, if they can. They wish to get wealth and power themselves by imitating England, that is, by having manufacture and an import trade, and besides that they are jealous of England, dislike the English ascendancy, and would have pleasure in weakening it though they were to get nothing by it. I believe this feeling to have been greatly heightened if not created by the meddling, mischievous Palmerston policy in 1841,[7] which besides irritating France, excited intense disgust in Germany. There is, however, a considerable and rising school of sound political economy in France now; the "Revue des Economistes," a monthly publication in which Dunoyer, Passy,[8] Horace Say, and a number of other rational men write, and which is edited by Dussard (did you know him when he was in England? He then learnt the English political economy very well) has a very tolerable sale, which I am sure no such book would have in England. Dunoyer's book "De la liberté du travail," is one of the books best worth reading which have come out lately. I have now actually begun the book I meditated, and hope to complete it by the end of winter. I shall profit by your remarks on Wakefield's plan, which seems perfectly just, especially as to the lottery system.[9] Absenteeism is an evil in a new settlement, and might have been a much greater one. Wakefield by the way has very uncertain health now and is very much unfitted for work or activity. Whenever he gets at all excited, and you know his excitability, he is threatened with apoplexy.

The New Zealand Company have done very wisely in allowing the holders of the land at Nelson to exchange it on favourable terms for the earlier numbers which, by a measure I always thought very questionable, had been withheld from them. I mean to use the option with regard to my town and rural allotments; the accommodation land has answered very well. You, I remember, had land at Nelson too, but yours were better numbers.

6. James Knox Polk (1795–1849), as President of the United States, 1845–49, fought for and obtained tariff reductions.

7. See Letters 303 to 305, and 308.

8. Hippolyte Philibert Passy (1793–1880), economist and politician.

9. In administering sales of land through the New Zealand Co., Edward Gibbon Wakefield awarded priorities in choice of lands by a lottery system.

However, I daresay you will be able to exchange some of them to advantage.

I had not heard of Revans'[10] failure, which I infer from your speaking of his "execution creditor." I am very sorry for it, but in a place like Wellington I suppose he will soon re-establish himself.

Pray write sometimes; I will not wait for your next, but will write again in three or four months if I find anything interesting to relate.

With kind regards to your family,

Yours ever faithfully,

J. S. MILL

476. TO SIR JOHN F. W. HERSCHEL[1]

India House
19th December
1845

MY DEAR SIR

Some time ago, you did me the favour to intimate that you would have no objection to communicate to me some of your remarks on my "System of Logic,"[2] particularly those parts of it in which physical and mathematical subjects were adverted to. I have so little claim to ask you to take this trouble, that I am almost ashamed to remind you of your intention—but as I am informed by the publisher that he is about to prepare for a second edition, the advantage which I hope to derive from your criticisms would be peculiarly valuable if it could be afforded in time for that purpose.

I remain
Very truly yours
J. S. MILL

477. TO SIR JOHN F. W. HERSCHEL[1]

India House
29th Decr 1845

MY DEAR SIR,

Pray receive my thankful acknowledgments for your letter. I had already been convinced by other criticisms, that the chapter on which you comment

10. Samuel Revans. See Letter 442, n. 14.

* * * *

1. MS in the possession of the Royal Society.
2. In Herschel's unpublished letter of July 10, 1845. See Letter 465, n. 4.

* * * *

1. MS in the possession of the Royal Society. In reply to Herschel's letter of Dec. 22, also in the Royal Society Library.

required to be seriously reconsidered & that Laplace was not so far wrong as I had ventured to think him.[2] The other point however,[3] on which I differed from him, is one on which I have not hitherto been shaken, but I have not the smallest reluctance to acknowledge myself wrong on this also if it turns out that I am so.

With many thanks, & sincere hopes for the termination of your indisposition

believe me
Very truly yours
J. S. MILL

2. Herschel's chief criticism of the *Logic* in his long letter of Dec. 22 concerned "your objections against Laplace's statement of the theory of Probabilities in p. 70 etc. of your 2nd Vol.—and against his conclusions in the case specified in page 195 of that volume.

"With these objections I can no ways agree and I will not conceal from you that I read them with great concern and an earnest wish that you would give them a full reconsideration."

3. Herschel, *ibid.*, "I have not left myself space to enter into the other question agitated [?] by you in p. 195 about the credibility of the witnesses in Laplace's case. . . . I feel quite satisfied myself and hope to make it clear to you that Laplace is perfectly right."

• • • 1846 • • •

478. TO GEORGE GROTE[1]

1st January, 1846

MY DEAR MR. GROTE,—Since our last conversation on Comte's affairs, I have had two letters from him,[2] a short and a long one, both of which I enclose. The latter of them is so little creditable to his delicacy or gratitude, or, rather, shews an inordinate self-importance overriding both, that I should have been ashamed to send it to you if it had not seemed to be his intention that I should.

The shorter letter was written when he first heard from me that Molesworth was not disposed to renew his subscription. In answer[3] to it I declined applying further to Molesworth, saying that he would not, probably, consider the case one of necessity while Comte had still 200£ a year. Two months after, I received the long letter.

As you will see that he then expressed himself as if I had led him to count upon the success of an application for a second subscription, I must say to you, what I said to him, that I did not intentionally give him any confidence, for I felt none myself. His sanguine disposition ran away with him in this, as in other cases. I said to him (as I once told you) that very likely he might receive further help if it were only wanted for a short, and definite, but not for an indefinite time. I do not remember saying anything else, except that "the letter he sent to me, and which I sent to you, seemed to me well suited for its object:" that I said, because he referred it to my judgement.

Ever yours truly,

J. S. MILL

P.S.—I hope the first two volumes of the History[4] will soon be out; I long to see them.

1. Printed in *Posthumous Papers* (of George Grote), ed. Mrs. Grote (privately printed, London, 1874), p. 94. MS not located.

2. Comte's letters of Sept. 24, 1845, and Dec. 18, 1845.

3. Letter 472.

4. JSM reviewed the first two volumes of *A History of Greece*, in the *Spectator*, April 4, 1846, pp. 327–28, and in the *ER*, LXXXIV (Oct., 1846), 343–77. The latter review is reprinted in *Dissertations*, II, 363–415.

479. TO AUGUSTE COMTE[1]

India House
le 12 janvier 1846

MON CHER MONSIEUR COMTE

Votre lettre du 18 décembre exige de moi une réponse sérieuse, et qui aurait été immédiate, si je n'eusse été forcé d'attendre un moment où je pourrais le faire à loisir, et avec la reflexion convenable.

Votre appréciation de la conduite tenue envers vous en Angleterre me paraît reposer sur une erreur de fait. La sévère condamnation morale que vous portez sur ceux qui ont cessé de vous accorder l'appui pécuniaire qu'ils vous avaient donné temporairement, se pourrait tout au plus concevoir, en leur supposant des opinions, des sentiments, et, à tous égards, une position morale envers vous, qui n'existent pas, et dont ils n'ont certainement jamais fait profession. S'ils vous avaient accepté comme leur chef spirituel, s'ils vous regardaient comme le représentant de leurs convictions, comme l'apôtre d'un système de doctrines et de sentimens auquel ils adhéraient essentiellement; je ne sais pas s'ils se seraient crus moralement obligés de prolonger leurs subsides, mais je suis persuadé qu'ils l'auraient fait, et je les estimerais peu si je pensais qu'en pareil cas ils croiraient avoir assez fait déjà. Mais de la sympathie partielle qu'ils éprouvent pour vos opinions, et de l'admiration très réelle qu'ils ressentent envers vos talents, il y a loin à cette intime solidarité d'opinions et de sentimens. C'est leur prêter, sans fondement, vos propres convicitions, que de dire qu'ils se sont crus "moralement obligés" à faire pour vous ce qu'ils ont fait. Je ne vois dans leur procédé autre chose qu'un sentiment de philanthropie envers un philosophe éminent, pris au dépourvu par une persécution inattendue. Sans doute ils ont tous les trois une haute admiration pour votre grand ouvrage; ils le regardent comme une traité philosophique du premier ordre; ils reconnaissent en avoir beaucoup appris; et Grote, dont je parle le plus parce que je le connais le mieux, avoue qu'il y doit des modifications dans plusieurs de ses opinions. Grote, et probablement Molesworth, acceptent encore aussi pleinement que vous-même l'idée mère de vos travaux, c. à d. la substitution du point de vue scientifique au point de vue religieux, et l'application aux études sociales de la méthode philosophique qui préside aujourd'hui irrévocablement à toutes les autres études. Ils pensent encore, je puis à peu près l'assurer, du moins quant à Grote, que vous avez, le premier, conçu la méthode positive d'une manière qui la rend propre à

1. MS at Johns Hopkins. Published in Lévy-Bruhl, pp. 499–505; in reply to Comte's of Dec. 18, 1845, *ibid.*, pp. 482–98.

cette dernière extension. Il y a bien là de quoi motiver une haute estime philosophique. Mais quant à votre manière particulière de concevoir la sociologie dogmatique, ils sont si loin de la partager, que pour me borner à Grote, qui en est encore probablement le moins éloigné des trois, je crois savoir que sauf la question religieuse, la plupart des doctrines sociales que vous professez sont très en désaccord avec ses opinions et bien que cette dissidence ne l'empêche pas de rendre justice à votre haute valeur philosophique, elle importe beaucoup à l'obligation que vous lui supposez de concourir à la propagation active d'opinions sociales dont beaucoup ne lui semblent ni vraies ni utiles à propager.

Il n'y a donc pas lieu d'accuser, en ce cas, la faiblesse des convictions actuelles. Ce n'est pas un cas de demi-conviction ni de demi-volunté; c'est un cas de conviction très arrêtée d'un désaccord essentiel d'opinion. Vous vous trompez davantage encore en pensant qu'un sentiment étroit de nationalité y soit pour quelque chose. Contrairement à l'opinion générale du continent, je suis d'avis qu'il y a moins de nationalité chez les anglais que chez tout autre peuple civilisé. Ils ont aujourd'hui beaucoup moins de préjugés et de préventions nationales que les peuples du continent; on peut seulement, à cet égard, les accuser d'indifférence; ils font peu d'attention aux autres peuples, et ignorent en général ce qui s'y fait; mais ceux parmi eux, qui ne partagent pas cette ignorance, ceux qui connaissent assez le continent pour en juger, soit par leurs études, soit par leurs voyages, ceux-là sont cosmopolites au delà de ce que vous pouvez vous imaginer; et s'il y a des hommes dont cela est surtout et particulièrement vrai, ce sont précisément ceux à qui vous avez eu à faire.

Quant au projet de revue, et à la manière dont il fut accueilli, vos reproches retombent surtout sur moi: les autres n'ont eu dans cette affaire qu'un rôle passif. Je n'ai même parlé là dessus qu'avec Grote, et sans le consulter, pas plus que Molesworth, sur la réponse à vous faire. Je lui a demandé son avis sur la probabilité de pouvoir placer des actions et trouver des abonnés en angleterre, parce que ma propre opinion, quelque décidée qu'elle fût, ne pouvait pas vous suffire. Je ne lui ai pas seulement demandé s'il y prendrait part. Lui seul pouvait juger jusqu'à quel point cela lui convenait, tant personnellement qu'en égard à ses opinions. Sous ce dernier rapport j'aurais espéré que la franche explication que je vous donnai sur la question de ma propre coopération, aurait suffi, et peut être à plus forte raison à l'égard des autres. Mon hésitation fut expréssement motivée sur le défaut d'un accord suffisant d'opinion. Je pense comme alors que l'acceptation commune du principe positif, et même un accord essentiel d'idées sur la méthode, ne sont pas une base suffisante pour une entreprise commune de propagation sociologique; sans toutefois rien prescrire à l'égard de ceux dont les opinions sociales, en tant qu'arrêtées, sont d'accord. Cette harmonie initiale est bien loin d'exister entre nous deux, pour ne rien dire des autres: sans cela, aurais-je accueilli la proposition comme je l'ai fait? et la tentative que nous avons faite pour vider notre différence d'opinion sur une seule question fondamentale, n'a pas été assez heureuse pour nous encourager à en entamer d'autres, ou pour faire croire que le positivisme puisse bientôt offrir au monde un système social capable de réunir tous ceux qui acceptent sa méthode. Plus j'y réfléchis et moins je crois à la proximité d'un résultat semblable, qui me paraît exiger plusieurs progrès antérieurs, non suffisamment effectués, et surtout un notable perfectionnement de la science positive de l'homme. Les dissidences qui existent en matière sociale entre deux penseurs consciencieux, qui se ressemblent d'aussi près que vous et moi dans leurs principes logiques, doivent tenir à ce que l'un ou l'autre n'entend pas assez bien les lois de la nature humaine. Une connaissance plus approfondie de ces lois me paraît une condition nécessaire d'une théorie sociologique rationnelle. Personne aujourd'hui ne s'occupe convenablement de lever cet obstacle, et je crois de plus en plus que c'est là le genre de tentative philosophique par lequel un penseur bien préparé pourrait aujourd'hui rendre le plus de service, tant à la théorie qu'à la pratique sociale.

Je dois encore décharger MM Grote et Molesworth de la responsabilité de l'allusion que j'ai faite à leurs sentimens présumés sur ce qui constituerait à votre égard le cas de nécessité. Ils ne m'avaient pas articulé un seul mot, à ce sujet, et je suis seul responsable d'une explication qui, je le vois avec peine, vous a blessé. Cependant je ne doute pas, non plus qu'alors, que j'ai exprimé leurs véritables sentimens. Je pense, certes, comme vous, qu'il serait très déplacé de la part de qui que ce soit, de prétendre vous imposer des règles de conduite dans vos dépenses privées, et que vous êtes pleinement en droit de n'y avoir égard qu'à votre opinion propre. Cela est même presque superflu à dire. S'ils ont pris ce sujet en considération, ce n'est pas pour régler votre conduite, mais la leur. Votre jugement est définitif pour vous, le leur l'est également pour eux. Quant à leur droit de se faire une opinion là dessus, il me semble découler nécessairement du fait même de l'intervention pécuniaire, et je trouve très simple qu'on ne se croie pas tenu à faire pour l'aisance d'un philosophe ce qu'on ferait volontiers pour sa subsistence. Vous jugez très sévèrement ceux qui "du sein de leur opulence" émettraient un tel avis. Sans doute, tant qu'il y aura des riches, et qu'un homme possédera plus qu'un autre sans avoir plus de mérite personnel, il y aura toujours quelque couleur de justice à de pareilles plaintes. Pour moi je ne les trouve nullement bien fondées. Je conçois qu'on ne compte pas avec ses amis personnels les plus chers, ou avec celui qu'on regarderait comme son chef spirituel et maître réveré, ou même peut-être avec celui pour le jugement duquel, dans toute question de conduite, on aurait, d'après une intime connaissance personnelle, un respect et une déférence telle, qu'on se reposerait aveuglément sur lui, en se dispensant de se faire une opinion propre. Mais partout où ces conditions n'existent pas, il me semble permis qu'on ait égard à la possibilité d'une économie sur les dépenses de celui qu'on veut aider, et je ne pense pas que, pour cela, on mérite l'accusation de s'immiscer à tort dans les affaires d'autrui.

Vous voyez, mon cher Monsieur Comte, qu'en donnant mon avis, avec une pleine franchise, sur votre lettre, je ne la juge pas d'après des considérations de délicatesse arbitraire et de convention, dont je crois qu'un homme sérieux, dans un cas important, peut se dispenser. C'est le fond même de la question que nous n'envisageons pas de la même manière. Mais nous sommes d'accord sur votre droit incontestable de travailler désormais pour votre aisance privée, dussiez-vous par là retarder la suite de vos travaux spéculatifs. Vous avez bien assez fait pour n'avoir pas besoin de justification, quelque parti que vous preniez à cet égard.

J'ai fait part de votre lettre à Grote et à Molesworth, mais ils n'ont aucune participation directe ou indirecte à ma réponse, que je ne leur ai pas même communiquée.

Vous me demandez des nouvelles de M. et Mme Austin. Je les ai vus tous deux à Londres, où ils ont passé après leur retour d'Allemagne. Ils se portaient alors assez bien. Ils doivent être maintenant à Paris, où vraisemblablement vous avez eu de leurs nouvelles.

Tout à vous

J. S. MILL

480. TO SIR JOHN F. W. HERSCHEL[1]

India House
20th February 1846

MY DEAR SIR

With many apologies for troubling you so much on the subject of my Logic—will you permit me to ask whether there is anything in the *first* volume on which I may hope for any remarks from you?

1. MS in the possession of the Royal Society.

I ask this because I am much urged by the publisher to send the volume to press for a second edition.

Believe me
Very truly yours
J. S. MILL

481. TO SIR JOHN F. W. HERSCHEL[1]

India House
28th Feby 1846

MY DEAR SIR,

Many thanks for your remarks, all of which shall be attended to.

As to the first—I was quite aware that the tendency of the moon to the earth was not known to be as $1/D^2$ before Newton, but as Newton's name is not mentioned in that passage which only traces the successive order of the discoveries as an illustration of method, I had not thought it necessary to guard the phraseology on that collateral point. I shall now do so.[2]

On the 2nd point—I knew that the shock of a comet could only alter the ellipse to some other *conic section* & to avoid the apparent ignorance I will change the wording.[3]

What you say on the difference between the evidence of a medium in the cases of light & of gravity, ought, in justice to the advocates of a medium, to be brought in somewhere, & I will take care to do so.[4]

I will omit the reference to M. Comte on the subject of pathological phenomena.[5] I have never read Dr. Holland's book,[6] & I got the remark from Comte.[7]

Nothing has happened to make your observations on the other proposition of Laplace of less importance to me.

Very truly yours
J. S. MILL

1. MS in the possession of the Royal Society.

2. JSM made only a slight change in wording; cf. Book III, chap. 12 ("Of the Explanation of Laws of Nature"), sec. 5, ¶ 1, with the corresponding passage in the second edition of the *Logic* (London, 1846). The first American edition (New York, 1846) and subsequent American so-called editions do not contain JSM's revisions.

3. Cf. Book III, chap. 14 ("Of the Limits to the Explanation of Laws of Nature; and of Hypotheses"), sec. 6, ¶1, with the corresponding paragraph in the second edition.

4. Cf. *ibid.*, ¶2 with ¶3 and footnote in the second edition.

5. In Book III, chap. 11 ("Of the Deductive Method"), sec. 1, ¶8, the reference to Comte is removed in the second edition.

6. Probably Dr. (later Sir) Henry Holland (1788–1873), physician and writer on medical subjects, rather than Dr. George Calvert Holland (1801–1865), also a writer on medical and scientific topics. The book has not been identified.

7. See *Cours de Philosophie positive, Tome troisième, contenant la philosophie chimique et la philosophie biologique* (Paris, 1838), pp. 331 ff.

482. TO AUGUSTE COMTE[1]

India House
le 26 mars 1846

MON CHER MONSIEUR COMTE

Je n'ai pas jugé nécessaire de répondre promptement à votre lettre du 23 janvier. Il m'a semblé inutile de prolonger la discussion sur le sujet spécial de votre lettre. Nous avons suffisamment fait connaître l'un a l'autre notre façon de penser. Cette communication n'a nullement diminué la divergence qui existait d'abord, et qui concerne, comme vous avez reconnu, les sentiments autant que les idées et les principes. Je bornerai donc ma réponse à quelques explications sur ce qui, dans votre lettre, me regarde personnellement, sans quoi vous pourriez croire que j'accepte vos observations comme fondées, ou que je les repousse sans raison aucune, ne pouvant y répondre.

D'abord, il est certain qu'il n'y a pas eu, comme vous semblez le croire, de malentendu sur la nature de la coopération pécuniaire que vous espériez obtenir en Angleterre pour le projet de revue. Vous avez alors très clairement expliqué la nature du projet, et indiqué les ressources pécuniaires nécessaires pour le mettre en exécution. Votre lettre a été soumise à MM. Grote et Molesworth. Ils ont dû croire et ils ont certainement cru en effet, que cela équivalait à leur faire la proposition de fournir eux mêmes les fonds en tout ou en partie. J'ai ensuite demandé spécialement à M. Grote son avis sur la possibilité d'obtenir ces fonds, et c'était l'inviter, autant que je trouvais convenable de le faire, à se prononcer sur sa coopération personnelle. Il s'en est abstenu en pleine connaissance de cause.

En second lieu, je ne dois pas passer sous silence quelques unes de vos observations sur l'intensité particulière que vous attribuez aux préjugés nationaux en Angleterre. Votre opinion à cet égard, loin d'être aucunement affaible, vous conduit à ne voir dans ma persuasion contraire qu'un nouvel exemple du fait que vous croyez signaler, puisque, dites-vous, une prévention nationale sur l'excellence du caractère propre à la nation anglaise, vous paraît seule pouvoir en faire ainsi méconnaître le principal défaut actuel. Vous me pardonnerez si je dis que la supposition que vous faites à mon égard est propre à faire sourire tous ceux qui connaissent un peu la tournure habituelle de mes idées et de mes sentiments. Je suis depuis longtemps dans une espèce d'opposition ouverte contre le caractère national anglais, qui, à plusieurs égards, m'est antipathique et à qui je préfère, à tout prendre, le caractère français, allemand, ou italien. Vos propres expressions témoignent assez combien je sens plus profondément que vous les défauts du caractère anglais, puisque vous regardez comme le plus

1. MS at Johns Hopkins. Published in Lévy-Bruhl, pp. 520–24; in reply to Comte's of Jan. 23, *ibid.*, pp. 505–19.

grand de ses défauts les préjugés nationaux, tandis que moi je lui en trouve d'autres plus graves, plus fondamentaux, et surtout plus difficiles à corriger. Je crois au reste que sans devenir suspect de prévention nationale, on peut faire beaucoup moins de cas que vous ne faites de l'opinion générale du continent en pareille matière. Il est fort naturel que les étrangers se trompent sur le caractère d'un peuple: le nôtre, très peu expansif, offre moins de prises à l'observation qu'un autre; et comme les peuples continentaux se ressemblent beaucoup plus entr'eux qu'ils ne ressemblent aux anglais, ils doivent se comprendre mieux et se juger mutuellement avec moins d'inexactitude qu'ils ne jugent l'Angleterre. Pour moi qui depuis ma première jeunesse, me suis occupé d'étudier le caractère anglais, j'aurais peine à vous dire combien les observations faites là dessus par les étrangers les plus éclairés, même quand elles sont justes, me semblent superficielles, et jusqu'à quel point, même lorsqu'il y a lieu à des critiques sévères, toutes celles que je lis me paraissent manquer le but, en donnant une interprétation française ou allemande à des phénomènes anglais. On donne aux anglais également des défauts et des qualités qu'ils n'ont pas; souvent ceux qu'on leur donne sont l'exact contraire de ceux qu'ils ont réellement.

Pour en venir maintenant à l'explication que vous donnez de nos différences d'opinion sur la seule question biologique et sociale que nous avons expressément discutée en sens contraire, celle de la prétendue infériorité intellectuelle des femmes. Vous vous rendez raison de ce dissentiment par l'insuffisance de mes études et de mes méditations biologiques. Je pense qu'il y a, sous ce rapport, quelque malentendu. Je ne crois pas avoir moins étudié la biologie que toutes les autres sciences fondamentales. Je crois la connaître à peu près aussi bien. Je connais assez bien la méthode, et les principales généralités de toutes, y compris la biologie. Peut être même je me tiens plus au courant des derniers progrès de cette science que de ceux des autres. Quant aux méditations, c'est surtout, chez moi, sur les questions biologiques qu'elles portent. Mais enfin, que mes connaissances anatomiques et physiologiques répondent ou non à l'idée que vous vous en faites de votre point de vue, il m'est également, du mien, permis de croire que j'ai plus étudié, et mieux apprécié, à certains égards, la théorie des phénomènes intellectuels et moraux que vous n'avez dû le faire, vû le mépris que vous professez pour la psychologie, dans laquelle vous comprenez toute étude directe des phénomènes mentaux, en fesant abstraction de leurs conditions organiques. Donc, en supposant de votre part et de la mienne, une chance égale d'insuffisante compétence, je croyais avoir fait la part, sans prévention aucune, de nos points de vue respectifs. Je pense que j'aurais pu réclamer pour moimême la supériorité de chances, à aussi bon droit que vous la réclamez pour vous; et même à meilleur droit peut être, puisque, de mon côté, je ne méprise pas vos avantages comme vous méprisez les miens; je m'occupe, au contraire, de me les donner à moi-même, en augmentant, autant que possible mes connaissances biologiques, ce qui, je le remarque par parenthèse, au lieu d'affaiblir mes convictions antécédentes n'a tendu jus'qu'ici qu'à les fortifier. Quant à l'appui que vous croyez tirer de la concordance entre vos conclusions philosophiques et l'opinion vulgaire, il me semble que l'existence d'une opinion ne peut en faire présumer la vérité que dans le cas où l'on ne pourrait donner d'autre explication raisonnable, de son existence; comme vous le reconnaissez vous même par rapport aux opinions religieuses, et dans bien d'autres cas encore.

Quoi qu'il en soit, je tends de plus en plus à faire de l'étude des fonctions intellectuelles et morales ma principale occupation philosophique, en la menant toutefois, comme vous le conseillez, de pair avec les spéculations sociales, car je reconnais pleinement qu'on ne peut pas connaître l'homme individuel en fesant définitivement abstraction de la société, dont il est indispensable de savoir apprécier philosophiquement les diverses influences. Toutefois je persiste à croire que la sociologie, comme science, ne peut plus faire aucun progrès capital sans s'appuyer sur une théorie plus approfondie de la nature humaine. La force des circonstances peut amener des améliorations pratiques importantes, mais la théorie sociologique ne me paraît comporter actuellement que des progrès secondaires, tant qu'on ne s'occupe pas en même temps de perfectionner la théorie intellectuelle et morale de l'homme. Je tâche de payer mon tribut à ces progrès secondaires par le traité d'économie politique dont je m'occupe et qui s'avance rapidement. Après cela je destine mes principaux efforts à cette autre grande tentative,[2] et je me propose bien de ne négliger aucun genre d'études qui puisse me rendre plus propre à la poursuivre.

L'élection annuelle d'examinateur doit avoir eu lieu: quel en a été la résultat? Aurait-on réparé l'injustice commise envers vous? ou est-ce un parti pris que d'y persévérer?

tout à vous

J. S. Mill

483. TO SIR JOHN F. W. HERSCHEL[1]

India House
30th March 1846

My dear Sir

The printers have come to an end with reprinting the first volume of my Logic & I am pleased to send them what is ready of the second.

2. See Letter 410, n. 2.

* * * *

1. MS in the possession of the Royal Society.

I attach great importance to being right on the point of difference with Laplace, which occurs in the last chapter of Book *III*,[2] on which, too, even if the views I at present entertain are right, they evidently require to be stated more clearly & at greater length. Should I not, therefore, be favoured with any remarks from you before the printers reach that chapter (which at their present rate of progress will be very soon) I shall make them halt at that point, as long as I find in any way compatible with the interests & wishes of the publisher.

Very truly yours

J. S. MILL

484. TO HARRIET GROTE[1]

India House
1st April, 1846

DEAR MRS. GROTE,—McV. Napier has now, some days since, accepted my offer to review your History[2] (for the "Edinburgh Review").[3] He wishes that it should not be later than the October number, and by that time I expect to have it ready.

The article for the "Spectator" is in Rintoul's[4] hands. It is rather long, but its length does not seem to frighten him.

I have taken my extracts from the 2nd vol., which has not yet been quoted, I believe, people not having had time to master it. You will see by the article that I like it very much. I was excessively sorry when I got to the end of it, and am impatient for the next volume.

Yours ever,

J. S. MILL

Napier says that Lewis[5] had offered to review the book for the editor, so that I have prevented an article from him. It would have been such a very good one that I hope he will write it and print it somewhere else.

2. Chap. 25, "Of the Grounds of Disbelief," sec. 5 of the first edition, sec. 6 in later editions.

* * * *

1. Published in *Posthumous Papers* (of George Grote), p. 98. MS not located.
2. See Letter 478, n. 4.
3. Although in parentheses, this should probably be in brackets as Mrs. Grote's interpolation.
4. Robert S. Rintoul.
5. George Cornewall Lewis.

485. TO SIR JOHN F. W. HERSCHEL[1]

India House
8th April 1846

MY DEAR SIR

Your second letter has, as you anticipated, convinced me. An analysis of the cases, such as you have given, is the last appeal when there is any doubt, & if I had resorted to it (which would have been more in conformity with my usual mode of working) I could not have fallen into the error which I committed, & which I am greatly indebted to you for causing me to rectify.

I have written a new conclusion to the chapter,[2] in which I hope I have presented Laplace's principle in a light which will prevent others from falling into my error.

I do not, however, think that Laplace's example is a fair type of the universal character of what are called Coincidences. But what I have to say on this point does not at all infringe upon the logical soundness of Laplace's principles.[3]

I had already entirely rewritten the chapter on the general Doctrine of Chances,[4] on which subject I now entirely agree with Laplace. I have there too, as knowing by experience where the shoe pinched, been able, I think, to ease it a little.

Having benefitted so much by your criticisms I need hardly say how glad I should be of any others.

Very truly yours
J. S. MILL

486. TO MACVEY NAPIER[1]

India House
1st May 1846

MY DEAR SIR

Before I received your letter, I had already acknowledged to Edinburgh, your remittance which was larger than I expected & for which I now renew my thanks.

1. MS in the possession of the Royal Society; in reply to Herschel's letters of April 2 and 3, also in the Library of the Royal Society.
2. The revised sec. 5 of Book III, chap. 25, "Of the Grounds of Disbelief," is numbered sec. 6 in later editions.
3. JSM in the second edition added a new sec. 5 to Book III, chap. 25, to discuss coincidences.
4. Book III, chap 18, "Of the Calculation of Chances."

* * * *

1. Part published in *Napier Corresp.*, pp. 526–27. MS in Brit. Mus.

I cannot complain of your having left out the passage[2] controverting the warlike propensity of the French, though I should have been glad if it had been consistent with your judgment to have retained it. The opinion is a very old & firm one with me, founded on a good deal of personal observation & I do not think you will find that Englishmen or other foreigners *who have lived long in France* & mixed in French society, are, so generally as you seem to think, of a different opinion. I have certainly heard, from such persons, the same opinion which I have expressed, & quite as strongly. And I am sure you will admit that national importance, & consideration among other nations, may be very strongly desired & sought by people who would rather have it in any other way than by war. I venture to say thus much because I think the Edin. has lately been sometimes very unjust to the French—I allude to Senior's otherwise excellent articles[3] which he & I have sometimes had disputes about.

Touching Whately's Rhetoric[4]—I have read it twice, first when it came out, & again within the last few years, & I think of it as of all his other books, that it is full of ideas, & would make a good article in itself, but still more so if the occasion were taken—(which would be worth while as I think the Ed. has never done it)—for a general estimate of the man & of his writings. Senior is as you know a personal intimate & his admiration of Whately is probably much less qualified than mine is—but W. is certainly a very remarkable & even eminent man, & one whose merits & faults are both very important to be pointed out.

Your son has given me a reference to Merivale's[5] article which I shall lose no time in reading.

I forget whether I remembered to mention that I should like half a dozen copies of the article in the Edin. though I know you were kind enough to ask me the question. If I omitted to say so perhaps you could still procure me *two* copies from the waste

Believe me ever

yours truly

J. S. MILL

2. In his "Duveyrier's *Political Views of French Affairs*," *ER*, LXXXIII (April, 1846), 453–74.

3. A bibliography of Senior's contributions to periodicals, including the *Edinburgh Review*, for which he wrote frequently after 1840, may be found in S. Leon Levy, *Nassau W. Senior: The Prophet of Modern Capitalism* (Boston, 1943), pp. 415–16.

4. Richard Whately, *Elements of Rhetoric* (London, 1828); 7th ed., revised, 1846.

5. Herman Merivale, a frequent contributor to the *Edinburgh*. A partial list of Merivale's contributions to periodicals is included in the brief memoir of him by Charles Merivale in the *Transactions of the Devonshire Association*, 1884.

487. TO WILLIAM TAIT[1]

India House,
4th June,
1846.

MY DEAR SIR,

My friend Mr. Alexander Bain, wishing to be a contributor to your magazine, has asked me to give him an introduction to you, which I do with great pleasure. I have said incidentally in my Logic the very high opinion I have of Mr. Bain and the great use he was of to me in making the book fit to present to the public and I need only say that I think he would be a most valuable contributor to any liberal periodical.

Very truly yours,
J. S. MILL

488. TO AUGUSTE COMTE[1]

East India House
le 13 août 1846.

MON CHER MONSIEUR COMTE

Votre petit billet du 10 m'est parvenu la veille même du jour que j'avais fixé définitivement pour rompre un silence effectivement très prolongé. La cause du retard n'a pas été une perturbation quelconque de ma santé, qui est restée à peu près comme à l'ordinaire. Ce fut d'abord une de ces absences occasionnelles[2] (quoique non strictement périodiques) auxquelles vous faites allusion: ensuite après mon retour je me suis trouvé accablé d'occupations qui m'ont fait différer de jour en jour la lettre qui vous était dûe. Ces occupations pressantes ne se sont terminées qu'hier, et je vais maintenant pouvoir reprendre mon travail d'économie politique, suspendu depuis deux mois, et que j'espère désormais pouvoir continuer sans intermission jusqu'à sa complétion définitive.

Votre lettre du 6 mai contenait en effet des choses graves, auxquelles je n'aurais pas manqué de répondre promptement, si j'avais cru pouvoir par là donner quelque soulagement sympathique à une juste et profonde

1. MS in the Mitchell Library, Sydney, New South Wales.

* * * *

1. MS at Johns Hopkins. Published in Lévy-Bruhl, pp. 538–40; in reply to Comte's of May 6 and Aug. 10, *ibid.*, pp. 525–37.
2. JSM had had a vacation of two months this year, during which he had taken with Mrs. Taylor a tour of about six weeks to the Rhine and northern France.

douleur.[3] Je sais ce que doit être, pour tout homme capable d'une affection profonde, un événement tel que celui que vous m'avez annoncé. Mais de pareils malheurs, quand ils sont réels et fondés, ne me paraissent comporter d'autre soulagement que le triste affaiblissement spontané qui suit du temps et de la réflexion. La perte d'une unique sympathie personnelle, est toujours au-dessus ou au-dessous de toute consolation. C'est une blessure dont la gravité ne saurait être appréciée que par celui qui la subit.

Quant au reste du contenu de votre lettre, je trouve dans la publication hollandaise que vous m'indiquez, et dans la lettre dont vous m'avez envoyé copie, une nouvelle preuve du progrès des idées positives en europe. On s'attendrait peutêtre moins qu'ailleurs à un tel témoignage dans un pays comme la Hollande, qui semblait ne plus s'intéresser aux questions spéculatives et dont le développement philosophique a sans contredit beaucoup perdu à l'isolation littéraire où elle se trouve à cause de sa langue particulière, depuis que les penseurs ont renoncé à se servir d'une langue européenne. Ce signe de vie, et même d'une activité mentale assez avancée, est d'autant plus intéressant qu'il est plus inattendu. Tout indique au reste que les principes de votre grand ouvrage ont pris irrévocablement leur place dans la discussion européenne, et que rien désormais ne pourra les étouffer. Dès que ce point a été atteint, tout est fait. C'est tout ce que les penseurs peuvent accomplir, ou sont tenus à accomplir pour leurs idées. Dès qu'elles sont écoutées; dès que les partisans des doctrines contraires sont forcés de les connaître et d'en tenir compte, la cause est gagnée; elles deviennent dès lors une force sociale réelle, et plus ou moins puissante, en raison de la portion de vérite et d'importance réelle qui leur appartient. La critique systématique que vous m'annoncez devoir être faite de votre ouvrage par un des principaux organes de l'école métaphysique, indique encore plus décidément, que vous en êtes venu là. Je crois que ce temps va bientôt arriver aussi pour moi, quoique je n'aie encore éprouvé que des attaques très faibles. Je m'efforce au reste d'en hâter le moment par l'écrit dont je m'occupe actuellement, écrit plus en rapport que le premier avec l'esprit pratique et politique de l'angleterre, et où je m'abstiendrai encore moins que dans l'autre, de heurter les opinions reçues. Je crois le temps très favorable pour toute doctrine nouvelle capable de soutenir une discussion approfondie. Toutes les anciennes idées sont depuis peu très visiblement déchues, aux yeux mêmes de tout le monde, et l'on demande à grands cris des principes nouveaux. S'il y avait ici seulement deux ou trois hommes généralement considérés, qui fussent moralement et intellectuellement au niveau des besoins de l'époque, nous pourrions espérer de conquérir bientôt la liberté dont la France jouit heureusement, celle de tout dire: c'est surtout

3. Comte had reported the death on April 5 of his beloved friend Mme Clotilde de Vaux.

ce qui nous manque à présent, car les seules questions qui ne font point aujourd'hui de progrès sont celles dont l'opinion interdit toute véritable discussion.

tout à vous

J. S. MILL

489. TO ALEXANDER BAIN[1]

September 1846

I have just corrected the proof of my review of Grote,[2] in which I have introduced no little of the Comtean philosophy of religion. Altogether I like the thing, though I wrote it in exactly four days, and re-wrote it in three more, but I had to read and think a good deal for it first. . . . [I have] got on well with the *Pol. Ec.* I am on the point of finishing the third book.[3]

490. TO HENRY COLE[1]

India House,
7th September, 1846.

MY DEAR COLE,

Having been out of town I have only just received your note and its enclosure. I am truly glad of the improvement in your circumstances, and should have regretted much if you had paid me before it was perfectly convenient.

I have the pleasure of remembering that I have rendered you a service at a time when you needed it, and needed it on account of conduct for which you merited reward instead of loss.[2]

Very truly yours,

J. S. MILL

491. TO MACVEY NAPIER[1]

India House
22nd October
1846

MY DEAR SIR

Your very liberal remittance arrived safely, & I return you my best thanks for it.

1. Excerpt published in Bain, *JSM*, pp. 85–86. MS not located.
2. For the *Edinburgh Review*, Oct., 1846.
3. "Exchange."

* * * *

1. MS in the possession of Professor J. M. McCrimmon.
2. See Letters 414, 415.

* * * *

1. MS in Brit. Mus.

I have no other subject at present in view & shall probably be otherwise occupied for some months.

The new number of the review[2] seems to me a very good one.

yours ever

J. S. Mill

492. TO JAMES BENTHAM MILL[1]

Nov. 2, 1846

[. . . a letter to his brother James (2nd Nov.) shows that he was labouring under illness:] had been ill, now better, but still a bad cold.

493. TO ALEXANDER BAIN?[1]

Mid-November 1846

[In the middle of November, he wrote that the articles[2]] have excited a good deal of notice, and have quite snatched the initiative out of the *Times*. [He adds—] It is a capital thing to have the power of writing leaders in the *Chronicle* whenever I like, which I can always do. The paper has tried for years to get me to write to it, but it has not suited me to do it before, except once in six months or so.

494. TO ALEXANDER BAIN?[1]

28 December 1846

I continue to carry on the *Pol. Econ.* as well as I can with the articles in the *Chronicle*.[2] These last I may a little slacken now, having in a great measure, as far as may be judged by appearances, carried my point, *viz.*, to have the waste lands reclaimed and parcelled out in small properties among the best of the peasantry.

2. *ER*, Oct., 1846.

* * * *

1. Excerpt published in Bain, *JSM*, p. 86. MS not located. The bracketed portion is Bain's introduction to the excerpt.

* * * *

1. Excerpts published in Bain, *JSM*, p. 86–87. MS not located. The bracketed portions are Bain's introduction to the excerpts.
2. Between Oct. 5, 1846, and Jan. 7, 1847, JSM contributed forty-three leading articles on Irish affairs to the *Morning Chronicle* (see MacMinn, *Bibliog.*, pp. 60–67).

* * * *

1. Excerpt published in Bain, *JSM*, p. 87. MS not located.
2. See preceding letter, n. 2.

• • • 1847 • • •

495. TO RICHARD MONCKTON MILNES[1]

I.H.
Wedy [1847?]

My dear Milnes

It would be very agreeable to me to breakfast with you on Saturday, but I cannot venture to play truant from my office to the extent which that would require.

Yours ever

J. S. Mill

496. TO SIR ALEXANDER DUFF-GORDON[1]

India House
Jan. 27, 1847

My dear Sir Alexander,

I regret to hear that Mr. Austin is again suffering from illness, which has, perhaps, been brought on by the application required in writing his admirable article in the "Edinburgh",[2] and by the very natural and intelligible reaction after it was finished. In his bad health he must at least have the consolation of feeling himself useful, for the article is exactly one of those things which he can do so well, and which so few are capable of doing at all—a *thorough* discussion of the subject it treats of, going down to the roots and fundamentals of a matter never treated in that way before—eminently calculated not only to give clear ideas and to correct vague feelings and confused notions on that particular subject, but also to educate the minds of those who wish to *study* such subjects—a class that would probably be much more numerous if there were not so lamentable a paucity of such helps to them. One of the persons of greatest intellect that I have known said, after reading the article, "What a pity the same man does not, in the

1. MS in Trinity College Library, Cambridge. Undated, but MS has pencilled: 1847?

* * * *

1. Published in *Letters of the Rt. Hon. Sir G. C. Lewis, Bart.*, ed. G. F. Lewis (London, 1870), pp. 153–54. MS not located.
2. "Centralization," *ER*, LXXXV (Jan., 1847), 221–58.

same manner, *precisionize* other and even more important questions of political morals;" and I do hope that he will now be encouraged to do so. There is really some hope of this now that he has actually *finished* something; for his inability to satisfy *himself* is the only thing except ill health which has ever seemed to me to stand in the way.

Very truly yours,

J. S. MILL

497. TO ALEXANDER BAIN[1]

27 January 1847

You will have seen by this time how far the ministry are from having adopted any of my conclusions about Ireland,[2] though Lord J. Russell[3] subscribes openly to almost all the premises. I have little hope left. The tendency of their measures seems to me such that it can only bring about good to Ireland by excess of evil. . . . I have so indoctrinated the *Chronicle* writers with my ideas on Ireland, that they are now going on very well and spiritedly without me, which enables me to work much at the *Political Economy*, to my own satisfaction. The last thing I did for the *Chronicle* was a thorough refutation, in three long articles, of Croker's article on the Division of Property in France.[4]

498. TO GEORGE JACOB HOLYOAKE[1]

[February 22, 1847][2]

Of practical conclusions there are also several from which I should decidedly differ, particularly Communism.

1. Excerpts published in Bain, *JSM*, p. 87. MS not located.
2. In his leading articles in the *Morning Chronicle* (see Letter 493).
3. Lord John Russell, later first Earl Russell, was at this time Prime Minister.
4. [J. W. Croker], "Agriculture in France—Division of Property," *QR*, LXXIX (Dec., 1846), 202–38. JSM published four, not three, articles: on Jan. 9, 11, 13, and 16 (see MacMinn, *Bibliog.*, p. 67, and Letter 514).

* * * *

1. MS fragment in the possession of Co-operative Union Ltd., Holyoake House, Manchester. Published in Joseph McCabe, *Life and Letters of George Jacob Holyoake* (2 vols., London, 1908), II, p. 65.

Holyoake (1817–1906), self-styled "secularist," bookseller, publisher of the *Reasoner* and other journals, and a leader in the development of the co-operative movement. In 1842 he had been imprisoned for blasphemy.

2. The MS is so dated in another hand. In view of Mrs. Taylor's discussion of Holyoake, the *Reasoner*, and morality in her letter to JSM of July 25, 1848 (Hayek, pp. 124–27), it has been suggested by Professor J. M. Robson that the date should be 1848.

The use made of the word "morality" is likely to give an idea of much greater agreement with the ordinary moral notions, emanating from and grounded on religion, than I should suppose you intend. Most people do not understand by morality a subject as open to discussion as any other, and on which persons have different opinions, but think it a name for the set of opinions they have been accustomed to.

499. TO HENRY S. CHAPMAN[1]

India House
9th March, 1847.

MY DEAR CHAPMAN,—

My conscience has been reproaching me for months with not having yet redeemed my promise of writing to you again, especially after having received your interesting letter of April last. But you must, I am sure, know by experience how difficult it is to keep engagements of that sort when one's mind and time are much occupied, and when the distance of one's correspondent and the long time requisite for an interchange of letters prevents communication from being habitual and in a manner spontaneous. To give you an idea of some of my hindrances I will just tell you what my occupations are. In the first place, a great increase of my India House business, both from the general and progressive growth of the correspondence, and also from my having the charge of a second department in addition to my own, being responsible for a branch of the correspondence which is now carried on by my brother George. In the next place I have had a book to write which will be as large a one when printed as the Logic, and which I have now (within the last week) completed, sauf the revising, or rather rewriting, which is an indispensable part of anything of importance which I write. This book is the one you had had some incorrect information about, as you thought it was to be an edition of Adam Smith, whereas it is a book to replace Adam Smith, that is, to attempt to do for political economy what A.S. did at the time when he wrote, to make a book which, while embodying all the abstract science in the completest form yet attained, incorporating all important improvements, should at the same time be essentially a book of applications exhibiting the principles of the science in the concrete. I was the more prompted to do this inasmuch as it would enable me to bring in, or rather to bring out, a great number of opinions on incidental matters, moral and social, for which one has not often so good an opportunity, and I have used this privilege as freely as Adam Smith did, and I fully expect to offend and scandalize ten times as many people as I shall please, but

1. MS in the possession of Mrs. W. Rosenberg. Copy supplied by Professor J. M. McCrimmon.

that is "all in a day's work," and I always intended to make that use of any standing I might get among publicists. I have got a certain capital of that sort by the Logic, and I now cannot too soon use it up in useful investments. That then, has been my second occupation. My third has been to write a good deal this autumn and winter on the questions of the day, especially the Irish question,[2] on which people seem to me to be running mad, each more than the other. No one idea that has been started for using this opportunity to effect anything for the permanent good of Ireland has met with any favourable reception; the whole English people are rushing frantically to expend any number of millions upon the present exigency, without much caring how, and taking their revenge on the Irish gentry by the infliction of a lavish poor law which if it passes will as it seems to me render the evils of Ireland incurable except by an universal seizure of the land and expulsion of the proprietors; and almost all the men on whom one counted for resisting any such monstrosity, have thrown themselves headlong into the very midst of the stream. Roebuck, of all men in the world, is quite an active leader in the movement, and as for the first time in his public life he is enlisting his talents in support of the madness of the movement, he has suddenly made himself a person of much more importance than he ever was before, and is continually flattered by the Times, which is the real author and leader of this movement and the substantial ruler of the country. Molesworth, except that he has only made one speech[3] instead of fifty, is just as bad. Lord J. Russell and Lord Lansdowne[4] six weeks before the meeting of Parliament, expressed in private the strongest opinions against any such measure as the one they have now introduced. I find nobody but Senior and Grote who are true to their colours. The English Poor Law, with the strongest profession of adherence to its principle, is in fact to be thrown overboard by abolishing the Central Board and substituting a functionary who is to sit in Parliament and to be virtually a member of the Ministry. Of course every little workhouse squabble will become a Parliamentary affair, and to avoid a debate in Parliament everything will be given up. Have not these people just ordered "a day of fasting and humiliation"[5] merely to escape a debate on a motion by Mr. Plumptre,[6] the man

2. See Letter 493, n. 2.

3. On Feb. 15, 1847.

4. Sir Henry Petty-Fitzmaurice, third Marquis of Lansdowne (1780–1863), then President of the Council under Lord John Russell, led the debate on the Irish Relief Bill on Feb. 15, 1847.

5. March 24, 1847, was so appointed by proclamation that prayers might be made "for the removal of those heavy judgments which our manifold sins and provocations have most justly deserved, and with which Almighty God is pleased to visit the iniquities of this land, by a grievous scarcity and dearth of divers articles of sustenance and necessaries of life . . ." (*Annual Register for 1847*, "Chronicle," p. 40).

6. John Pemberton Plumptre (1807–1864), MP for East Kent, on Jan. 20, 1847, in the debate on the Address from the Throne, proposed the appointment of a general fast.

who thinks that the potato failure is a punishment from Heaven for the grant to Maynooth?[7] Besides this new officer will go out with every Ministry, and besides, he will never be able to get elected without giving pledges inconsistent with a faithful discharge of his duties. I have never felt so thoroughly disgusted with the state of public affairs. The only good I see likely to arise out of all these things is that I think they are sure to give a great stimulus to colonization, for Ireland will be in a state next year that will make the landlords sell the clothes off their backs to get rid of the people. But it will be a colonization wholly of Irish, and of the very worst sort; and with an outdoor relief poor law they will just set about peopling again, and will replace even two millions in half a generation. The only propitious circumstances is the great progress of free trade. Our repeal of the Corn laws is working wonders; first the great relaxation of the American tariff, next the triumphal progress of Cobden[8] through Europe. Think of the French Government authorising a League (Societe des Libres Exchangite)[9] and permitting public meetings and speeches. I have great sympathy too with the fine old Pope.[10] I hope he has many years to live; he is much younger than Popes usually are, but unhappily they say he has had epileptic fits when a child, and has had a return of them lately. The priests will poison him if they can, as the Jesuits are said to have poisoned Ganganelli.[11] O'Connell is done up,[12] and probably dying, killed, I should think, by the death of O'Connellism.

Yours most truly,

J. S. MILL

500. TO ALEXANDER BAIN[1]

March 27, 1847

The people are all mad, and nothing will bring them to their senses but the terrible consequences they are certain to bring on themselves, as shown

7. See Letter 456, n. 2.

8. Richard Cobden (1804–1865), leader of the agitation for the repeal of the Corn Laws achieved in 1846. From Aug. 5, 1846, to Oct. 11, 1847, Cobden travelled in Europe, preaching everywhere the gospel of free trade.

9. Presumably the "Association pour la liberté des échanges," founded in 1846, and supported by a number of JSM's friends and acquaintances, including Michel Chevalier, Charles Dunoyer, and Horace Say (see *Journal des Economistes*, Sept.–Dec., 1846 and Jan., 1847).

10. Giovanni Maria Mastai-Ferretti (1792–1878), became Pope Pius IX in 1846.

11. Giovanni Vincenzo (or Lorenzo) Ganganelli (1705–1774), Pope Clement XIV from 1769 to 1774, dissolved the Jesuit order in 1773; the story that he was poisoned by the Jesuits has been generally discredited.

12. Daniel O'Connell had made his last speech in the House of Commons in Feb. and had gone to the Continent for his health; he died on May 15, 1847.

* * * *

1. Published in Bain, *JSM*, p. 87. MS not located. Dated by reference to Whately's speech.

in Whately's speech yesterday[2] in the House of Lords—the only sensible speech yet made in either House on the question. Fontenelle said that mankind must pass through all forms of error before arriving at truth.[3] The form of error we are now possessed by is that of making *all* take care of *each*, instead of stimulating and helping each to take care of himself; and now this is going to be put to a terrible trial, which will bring it to a crisis and a termination sooner than could otherwise have been hoped for.

501. TO JOHN AUSTIN[1]

13th April 1847.

DEAR MR. AUSTIN,—There is no occasion to send anything you may write to me by any circuitous channel. If I did pay postage I should not grudge it for your letters, but in fact I do not. The I.H. pays all my letters except penny post letters which everybody pays before sending.

The notice in the *Chronicle*,[2] to which I am indebted for your letter, was, as you supposed, mine. It is really a pity that all the trouble you must have taken with the article on Centralisation should have produced nothing more than a review article.

I am very glad that you should write anything whatever; but I hope especially now when your pecuniary affairs are settled in the manner you desire, that you will rather write books than reviews. An entirely unknown person, whose books no one would read, must begin by reviews, but you have written a book which, for the kind of book, has been very successful, and what you write is more likely to be read with your name than without it. A book gives much more scope than a review for your peculiar forte, the analysis of a subject down to its ultimate scientific elements. A review is not a slight thing to you; you take the same pains with it as you would with a scientific treatise, which in fact it is; & all who can be benefited by it at all would prefer to have it in a permanent form. It seems to me that reviews

2. On March 26, 1847, in opposition to a motion for a select committee on Irish Poor Laws; the substance of it was published as App. D in his *Introductory Lectures on Political Economy* (4th ed., London, 1855).

3. "Telle est notre condition, qu'il ne nous est point permis d'arriver tout d'un coup à rien de raisonnable sur quelque matière que ce soit; il faut avant cela que nous nous égarions long-temps, et que nous passions par diverses sortes d'erreurs et par divers degrés d'impertinences" ("Digression sur Les Anciens et Les Modernes" in *Œuvres de Fontenelle* [Paris, 1790], V, 287).

* * * *

1. Published with errors and omissions in Elliot, I, 128–33. MS draft is in the possession of Dr. James M. Osborn of Yale University; a MS fragment of the draft is at LSE (see n. 8, 10, below).

2. An unheaded leading article on Austin's article "Centralization" (see Letter 496, n. 2) in *Morning Chronicle*, Feb. 6, 1847, pp. 4–5.

have had their day, & that nothing is now worth much except the two extremes, newspapers for diffusion & books for accurate thought. Every thinker should make a point of either publishing in his life if possible, or at any rate leaving behind him the most complete expression he can produce of his best thoughts, those which he has no chance of getting into any review. There are two books I have heard you speak of as projects: a continuation of "The Province of Jurisprudence" that is in fact a publication & completion of your lectures: this would be the easiest to you, so much of it being already done: the other which would be more important is a systematic treatise on morals. This last may wait long for any one with the intellect & the courage to do it as it should be done. And until it is done we cannot expect much improvement in the common standard of moral judgments & sentiments.

Of the two subjects you mention in your letter, the "province of government" is no doubt important in itself, & peculiarly a question of the present time. I have necessarily thought a good deal about it lately for the purposes of a practical treatise on Pol. Economy & I have felt the same difficulty which you feel about the *axiomata media.* I suspect there are none which do not vary with time, place, & circumstance. I doubt if much more can be done in a scientific treatment of the question than to point out a certain number of *pro's* and a certain number of *con's* of a more or less general application, & with some attempt at an estimation of the comparative importance of each, leaving the balance to be struck in each particular case as it arises. But that subject is I think tolerably safe as far as theory is concerned, for the thinking minds of the Continent & of England have fairly thought up to it & it is sure to be amply discussed & meditated upon for the next ten or twenty years. It is hardly a subject for any one who is capable of things much in advance of the time.

On the other subject, The "antecedents of the Revolution," I much doubt if what you propose to write will do any good to those whom you hope to influence by it. I think with you that the English higher classes (of the German I know nothing) mean well, "what little they do mean" as my father said of some person. They have grown good even to goodiness, as they shew every year more & more. But also every year shews more & more their *pitoyable* absence of even that very moderate degree of intellect, & that very moderate amount of will & character which are scattered through the other classes but of which they have certainly much less than the average share, owing to the total absence of the habit of exerting their minds for any purpose whatever. I used to hope, as my father did (with all his democratic predilections), that when their political monopoly was taken away they would be induced to exert themselves in order to keep ahead of their competitors, but I have quite ceased to think so. If there is anything of which experience convinces me more & more it is that (beyond a certain point) facilities, as they are called, are hindrances, & that the more the path to any meritorious attainment is made smooth to an individual or a class, from their early youth, the less chance there is of their realising it. Never to have had any difficulties to overcome seems fatal to mental vigour. The doctrine of averting revolutions by wise concessions to the people does not need to be preached to the English aristocracy. They have long acted on it to the best of their capacity, & the fruits it produces are soup-kitchen and ten hours bills.

As far as I see, the influence of democracy on the aristocracy does not operate by giving them any of the strength of the people but by taking away that which was their own; making them bend with a willing submission to the yoke of bourgeois opinion in all private things, and be the slaves, in public matters, of the newspapers which they dislike & fear. I confess I look less & less to that quarter for anything good. Whatever is valuable in the traditions of gentlemanhood is a *fait acquis* to mankind; as it is really grounded on the combination of good feeling with correct intellectual perceptions, it will always be kept alive by really cultivated persons; the most complete *parvenus* now in this country have as much of it as people of family, & for its diffusion must not our real reliance be on the extension & improvement of education? I have even ceased to think that a leisured class, in the ordinary sense of the term, is an essential constituent of the best form of society. What does seem to me essential is that society at large should not be overworked, nor over-anxious about the means of subsistence, for which we must look to the grand source of improvement, repression of population, combined with laws or customs of inheritance which shall favour the diffusion of property instead of its accumulation in masses.

It is, I dare say, very natural, that living in France, you should be much impressed with the unfavourable side of a country that has passed through a series of revolutions. The inordinate impulse given to vulgar ambition, down to even a low class, & the general spirit of adventurership are I have no doubt disgusting enough, but may not much of them be ascribed to the mere accident of the brilliant fortune of a "certain lieutenant of artillery" (as Stendhal says), & much to the habitual over-governing by which power & importance are too exclusively concentrated upon the Government & its functionaries. In England on the contrary I often think that a violent revolution is very much needed, in order to give that general shake-up to the torpid mind of the nation which the French Revolution gave to Continental Europe. England has never had any general break-up of old associations & hence the extreme difficulty of getting any ideas into its stupid head. After all, what country in Europe can be compared with France in the adaptation of its social state to the benefit of the great mass of its people, freed as they are from any tyranny which comes home to the greater number, with justice easily accessible, & the strongest inducements to personal prudence & forethought. And would this have been the case without the great changes in the state of property which even supposing good intentions in the Government could hardly have been produced by anything less than a Revolution?

I judge M. Guizot's conduct in the Spanish affair[3] as you do: he is evidently not above low tricks & equivocations, which seem to be quite excused to every Frenchman by their being for the supposed honour & glory of France.[4] Guizot I wished to think better of, but after all this only brings me back, and that not altogether, to my first opinion of him, which some parts of his public conduct from 1839 downwards had modified.[5]

Your impression of Comte's delinquencies is a fine instance of the growth of rumour: your informants must be either ill-informed or such exaggerators that I wonder you should have believed them. In the first place, Comte (to whom *I* did *not* give money, but Grote and Molesworth did) never wrote to *Grote* anything but what was perfectly convenable. He wrote a letter to *me* which he authorised me to shew to G. & M. if I thought fit, & I did think fit; but it contained nothing like reproaches.[6] It contained a theory that, in default of the government, it is the duty of rich individuals to subscribe their money to enable philosophers to live and carry on their speculations. I do not agree in his theory.[7] I thought it an instance of "the importance of a man to himself" but even with the addition of his not having economised the money previously given to him this is a totally different thing from what you have been told.

The judgment to be passed on this incident would involve the wide subject of how the degree in which a person should be judged by his own deliberate principles should be combined with one's judgment on the

3. Guizot had broken faith with the British in the affair of the Spanish marriages; by intrigue Queen Isabella II and her sister were induced to marry in 1846 descendants of the French Bourbons.

4. At this point the following passage has been deleted from the draft: "English politicians have generally low objects, & reserve any conscience & dignity they may have, for the choice of means, while Frenchmen I think have oftener aims that one can call elevated but are much more unscrupulous in their expedients, a combination made quite intelligible on a grander scale, by Machiavelli & the Italian [patriots ?] of the Middle Ages."

5. See Letter 304, n. 8.

6. Comte's letter of Dec. 18, 1845 (Lévy-Bruhl, pp. 482–98). JSM's memory here seems not to have been very accurate; most readers would regard Comte's letter as one long reproach (cf. especially Lévy-Bruhl, p. 495).

7. The remainder of the sentence has been deleted: "& still less in his attempt to impose its obligations on persons who do not admit it, who were in no respect his disciples nor in any other intellectual relation to him than to any other thinker of any eminence with some of whose opinions they agreed."

principles themselves, and one's opinion of the causes which made him adopt them.[8]

You ask what I think of the Irish measures. I expect nothing from them but mischief, or if any good, only through excess of evil. If you were here you would, I believe, think as I do. The Government & the public seem both alike to have quite parted company with experience & common sense. There is not one man in the H of C [House of Commons], & only two or three in the H of L [House of Lords] (Whately being one) who seem to have a single sound or rational idea on the whole subject: those from whom one had most right to expect better are just as bad as the rest. I doubt if outdoor relief would do for Ireland under any mode of administration, but as it is they are holding out to the people the most unbounded expectations, & if the poor law is to be worked without fulfilling them, the life of no guardian & no relieving officer will be worth a week's purchase, & the country will be ungovernable except by military occupation of every village. The only good I expect is that the result *must* produce a strong reaction in the public mind against the present wild notions about the mode of being good to the poor.[9]

I expect to be in Paris shortly with the friends with whom I always endeavour to pass my holidays but it is uncertain if they will remain long enough to admit of my going to see anyone; if I do I will certainly call on you.[10]

Ever sincerely yours,

J. S. MILL

502. TO ALEXANDER BAIN[1]

5th May 1847

[Before arriving in London this year, I had another letter (5th May). He delays to commence rewriting his book till he sees the upshot of the Irish business.] The conduct of the ministers is wretched beyond measure upon all subjects; nothing but the meanest truckling at a time when a man with a decided opinion could carry almost anything triumphantly.

8. This paragraph in the draft fragment at LSE is labelled: (A).

9. At this point the following sentences have been deleted in the draft: "But it is discouraging to see how short a time any such impression lasts. In 1834 much ground seems to have been gained [by the adoption of the Poor Law of that year] but how quickly it has all been lost."

10. This paragraph, not included by Elliot, is labelled (B) in the draft fragment at LSE and crossed through with a red line (Elliot's usual method of indicating a deletion in a MS). The paragraph was written to replace the deleted sentences quoted in n. 9.

* * * *

1. Excerpt published in Bain, *JSM*, p. 88. MS not located. Bracketed portion is Bain's introduction to the excerpt.

503. TO WILLIAM E. HICKSON[1]

India House
Saturday
[May 8, 1847]

MY DEAR HICKSON

It would not be convenient to me at present to write an article on currency. Neither could I write the article wanted just now, without a much greater knowledge than I possess or could easily acquire respecting the facts of the money market. My opinions on the general subject "with the latest additions & corrections" will come out next winter in my book.

I believe I agree with most of what you say in your note.

yours ever
J. S. MILL

504. TO AUGUSTE COMTE[1]

India House
le 17 mai 1847

MON CHER MONSIEUR COMTE

Je pense qu'il pourrait vous être intéressant d'avoir quelques renseignements sur les choses qui se passent actuellement en angleterre et en Irlande, d'autant plus qu'elles me semblent caractériser, d'une manière frappante, une sorte de crise sociale.

Vous savez que le siècle où nous sommes est celui des transactions, et surtout de la grande transaction qui se renouvelle sans cesse à des conditions variables, entre les pouvoirs anciens et les idées modernes. Vous savez aussi que l'Angleterre est le pays des transactions par excellence. Ce que, peut-être vous ne savez pas, c'est la forme particulière que revêtit aujourd'hui chez nous la grande transaction européenne. Nous sommes entrés à plein voile dans le système du gouvernement charitable. Il y a longtemps qu'on prêche aux classes supérieures qu'elles ne remplissent plus leur mission, qu'elles sont tenues à faire quelque chose pour ceux dont le travail les nourrit, qu'elles n'ont le droit de gouverner qu'à condition d'être moralement responsables du bien-être de la société, et notamment de la classe pauvre, etc. Or, comme cette remontrance amicale leur est venue

1. MS at the Huntington Library.

* * * *

1. *Addressed*: A Monsieur / M. Auguste Comte / Rue M. le Prince / près l'Odéon / à Paris. MS at Johns Hopkins. Published in Lévy-Bruhl, pp. 548–53.

d'un côté tandis que le chartisme et le socialisme apparaissaient de l'autre, elles ont dû, quelle que fût leur insouciance, y obtempérer quelque peu, et petit à petit elles sont venues jusqu'à prendre au sérieux ces doctrines de responsabilité gouvernementale, qui, au fond, ne laissaient pas d'être passablement flatteuses à leur amour-propre d'aristocratie. Seulement, elles ont entendu cette obligation de la manière dont elles le pouvaient, c. à d. de la manière la plus facile et la plus ignoble, en la réduisant aux proportions de l'aumône. Aujourd'hui il n'est question que de donner aux pauvres; non seulement de l'argent, mais aussi, il est juste de le dire tout ce qu'on croit leur être utile, comme le raccourcissement des heures de travail, une meilleure police sanitaire, de l'éducation même, chrétienne et protestante surtout, mais sans exclusion de quelques connaissances terrestres. Il s'agit enfin de les gouvernor paternellement, et la cour, les nobles, les riches s'y disposent tout tranquillement, sans jamais se douter qu'il faille pour cela autre chose que de la bonne volonté, et en concevant le but selon la mesure de leur propre capacité intellectuelle et morale, c. à d. d'abord en fesant abstraction complète de la dignité morale de la classe pauvre. Cela est très naturel, attendu qu'ils n'ont que faire de ce sentiment pour eux-mêmes, n'ayant plus la dignité morale du passé, et n'ayant pas encore celle de l'avenir; d'ailleurs s'ils en avaient, ils ne la croiraient pas faite pour des gens pauvres, pour des ouvriers. Ensuite ils oublient complètement, ou plutôt ils n'ont jamais su, que le bien-être ne s'accomplit pas par les seules qualités passives, et qu'en général ce qu'on fait pour les personnes ne leur est utile qu'à condition de seconder seulement ce qu'elles font pour elles-mêmes. Ils se flattent que le bonheur des prolétaires dépend des riches, et ne se doutent pas qu'en définitif il dépend de l'énergie, du bon sens et de la prévoyance des prolétaires eux-mêmes; que le philanthrope le plus haut placé n'y peut rien, qu'en éclairant et en renforçant ces précieuses qualités chez les pauvres et que si au contraire il y porte attente, s'il tâche de mettre l'intervention sociale à la place de ces vertus individuelles, il devient nécessairement nuisible au lieu d'utile. Mais de cela nos philanthropes comme il faut n'ont pas la moindre idée, dénués qu'ils sont de toute connaissance approfondie et pétris de suffisance aristocratique.

La tendance que je viens de caractériser, et qui se signale depuis plusieurs ans d'une manière croissante, arrive aujourd'hui à une expérience décisive, amenée par la disette irlandaise. Cette île malheureuse, victime si longtemps de la tyrannie et de l'intolérance anglaises, dont maintenant elle n'a plus à se plaindre, semble destinée à être victime encore une fois de notre philanthropie. Vous connaissez le déplorable état industrial de ce pays, partagé entre une multitude démesurée de paysans paresseux et affamés, et un petit nombre de grands propriétaires insouciants et la plupart endettés, qui tirent du sol tout ce qu'il peut rendre, en rançonnant les paysans non pas par la force brutale mais par la concurrence effrénée de ces malheureux, toujours prêts à promettre plus que la terre ne produit. Depuis longtemps ce fléau est signalé à l'opinion publique: les Anglais reconnaissent le mal, ils désirent y remédier, mais ils y ont toujours échoué devant leur propre incapacité politique et sociale; n'ayant d'autre idée d'amélioration générale que celle de faire entrer tous les pays dans le système anglais, tant politique qu'industriel, tandis que ce système est tout à fait impropre à l'Irlande. C'est un grand malheur pour l'Irlande que de se trouver sous la domination d'un pays tout exceptionnel, et dont les principes ne sont en toute chose que la généralisation de l'exception, tandis qu'elle appartient, elle, au type normal européen, et que ce sont des idées continentales qu'il lui faut. Pour tout autre penseur qu'un anglais, le remède est clair, c'est le système de la petite propriété convenablement modifiée. Il faudrait assurer aux propriétaires actuels, en rente fixe, le revenu net de leurs terres, en laissant la terre elle même à la disposition absolue des cultivateurs. Avec cela on aurait probablement en peu de temps, une production triple ou quadruple de celle d'aujourd'hui, et une population aussi laborieuse, aussi prévoyante, et aussi indépendant que les paysans français. Or, les anglais ne comprennent rien à ce système; ceux qui croient en savoir quelque chose, et c'est le plus petit nombre, sont remplis des idées les plus fausses. Ils n'ont jamais pu concevoir d'autre amélioration en Irlande que d'en faire une autre angleterre, c. à d. un pays à grande culture, avec une population de laboureurs salariés. Or, sans rien préjuger sur l'avenir lointain de l'humanité, il est certain qu'aujourd'hui en Irlande ce système-là ne vaut rien. En le supposant même possible avec le caractère Irlandais, il entraînerait la suppression de la presque moitié de la population ouvrière actuelle. Ne pouvant donc pas réaliser cette heureuse idée, que fait-on? On jette à l'Irlande une loi des pauvres. On décrète que la population ouvrière tout entière vivra d'aumône. On lui promet au moins que tous les indigens auront de l'aumône autant qu'il leur en faut, et les indigens c'est toute la population agricole.

Pour moi je ne vois de cette loi d'autre résultat probable pour l'Irlande que celui de réduire tout le monde au niveau de la misère générale, après quoi je m'attends à une dissolution sociale complète. Lorsqu'on aura passé par d'affreux malheurs, il faudra procéder à la reconstitution de la société, du sein d'une désorganisation totale, sans une idée constructive quelconque, et après avoir fait prendre au peuple des mœurs essentiellement anarchiques, car je ne connais pas de gouvernement possible là où la majorité a pris l'habitude de demander à grands cris la subsistance et le bonheur aux autres au lieu de les chercher par elle-même. Certes, on n'a pas eu de pareilles idées en 1793, et on n'a aujourd'hui chez les communistes rien d'aussi profondément anti-social. Ce qui en sortira, impossible de prévoir.

J'y vois pour seule consolation, une réaction certaine contre le système du gouvernement charitable. On aura une grande preuve expérimentale de cette vérité qu'on ne peut pas traiter l'ouvrier comme on traite le bétail, c. à d. le faire travailler pour les autres en lui donnant une bonne nourriture et un bon gîte. Cela n'était possible que lorsqu'on y ajoutait le fouet. On ne peut pas plus en industrie qu'en autre chose, faire marcher l'ancien système en lui ôtant l'un après l'autre tous ses moyens d'action.

tout à vous

J. S. Mill

505. TO WILLIAM E. HICKSON[1]

India House
16th June 1847

My dear Hickson

I send you a short review of a political economy treatise—written by my youngest sister,[2] who is a student in political economy and who wishes to take the chance of your thinking the paper fit for insertion. It is the first attempt of a beginner in writing for the press & you will not therefore expect anything very brilliant. I am able to countersign the political economy of the article. In other respects & indeed in all respects you will of course exercise your own judgement. The writer has no such great opinion of her own performance as to be astonished at a decision in the negative, but I do not think the paper will do you any discredit, or I would not have undertaken to propose it to you.

ever your truly,

J. S. Mill

506. TO EDWIN CHADWICK[1]

India House
Wed^{y}
[June? 1847]

My dear Chadwick

After much consideration I have come to the decision that my best course will be to sell the certificates if I can get 20 per cent for them. But

1. MS at the Huntington Library. 2. Mary Elizabeth Mill.

* * * *

1. MS at UCL. Paper bears watermark 1847. The financial transaction discussed here probably concerned the sale of some of JSM's and his sisters' holdings in devalued bonds of some American State governments (see Letter 508).

I do not know how to effect this unless you will kindly manage it for me. If you would have no objection to ask your correspondent to dispose of £6000 more of the certificates, if it can be done on the same terms as yours, you would confer an obligation on me & I would in that case send you the certificates in time to be sent over by the packet on the 4th.

I have found the printed Case & I will give it my best attention.

ever truly yours

J. S. MILL

507. TO EDWIN CHADWICK[1]

I.H.
Friday
[June? 1847]

MY DEAR CHADWICK

I have read this letter[2] carefully through twice & I have nothing to suggest for the improvement of it except the correction of numerous clerical errors —these I have either corrected in pencil, or made a mark opposite to them when I was unable to supply the correction.

I should have returned it sooner, but not having had a pencil with me when I first read it, I waited till I had time to read it again.

ever truly yours

J. S. MILL

Such a letter ought to satisfy any *statesman* of his good fortune in having the writer of it at his disposal—but whether any of these men have sufficient brains to appreciate brains in another, remains questionable.

1. MS at UCL. Endorsed in another hand: "Poor Law Correspondence on matters of E. C." Paper watermarked, 1847.

2. Probably one of the several *Vindicating Letters* which Chadwick submitted to the ministry in June of 1847 defending his record as Secretary of the Poor Law Commission against the charges of the commissioners. For the full story of the Andover "scandal," of 1846 and the parliamentary struggle over the revision of the Poor Law Amendment Bill of June, 1847, see S. E. Finer, *The Life and Times of Sir Edwin Chadwick* (London, 1952), pp. 243–91. Chadwick lost his position but was immediately given an appointment in charge of a Royal Commission of Inquiry into London sanitation.

508. TO EDWIN CHADWICK[1]

Kensington
Saturday
[June 19, 1847]

MY DEAR CHADWICK

You have a most powerful case in your own defence & against the Commissioners—reinforced with great effect by Tufnell's letter.[2] There are only two things which I can suggest: first, that you should dwell more on the point which Lord J. R. the other day laid almost exclusive stress upon as an accusation against you. viz. your telling the Ass^{t} Com^{rs} that their representations of abuses would be far from welcome[3] (N.B. I have no doubt you told them in that respect the exact truth) & *secondly* a careful revision of the composition. The long paper[4] in particular is full of unfinished & ill constructed (sometimes ungrammatical) sentences—this is evidently owing in many cases, but not always, to incorrect copying.

I am extremely obliged both to you & to Mrs Chadwick's relation for your kindness about the certificates.[5] With regard to the power of attorney, as some of the certificates belong not to me but to my sisters, do you suppose they must all give powers of attorney (which would be difficult, they are so scattered, & some of them out of England) or is it sufficient that I, being empowered though not formally, by them to dispose of their certificates, should give a single power of attorney for the whole lot?

As I suppose you went through the same formalities in your own case, you can also tell me in what manner the Lord Mayor is to attest the power. The letter you sent me is worded as if the Lord Mayor had personally to appear before the Consul.

yours ever truly

J. S. MILL

1. MS at UCL Endorsed in another hand: "1847? on E.C. Evidence before Andover Committee," but internal evidence (see n. 3 below) indicates the period of the June, 1847, debate on the Poor Law Amendment Bill (see preceding letter, n. 2).

2. Edward Carleton Tufnell (1806–1886), Assistant Commissioner of Poor Laws (1835–74). Tufnell on May 28, 1847, had written Chadwick a letter supporting the latter's charges against the Poor Law commissioners (see Finer, *Life and Times of Sir Edwin Chadwick*, p. 245). Chadwick circulated the letter widely.

3. In the debate on the Poor Law Amendment Bill on June 17 Lord John Russell criticized Chadwick sharply: "I say that [his] practice of telling assistant commissioners that if they made complaints they would be regarded with displeasure, I do call that undermining the Commissioners appointed to carry out the Poor Law Act" (*The Times*, Friday, June 18, 1847, p. 3).

4. Probably Chadwick's major *Vindicating Letter*, described by Finer, *Life and Times of Sir Edwin Chadwick* (p. 290) as "a massive manuscript dossier of some sixty pages, together with six documentary appendices."

5. See Letter 506.

509. TO EDWIN CHADWICK[1]

I.H.
Friday
[June or July?, 1847]

MY DEAR CHADWICK

Many thanks. I will do as you direct.

I have received the Settlement Evidence[2] & have read a great part of yours with pleasure & admiration. It will be of much use to me. I differ from you as yet only on one (not fundamental) point.

Yours
J. S. MILL

510. TO EDWIN CHADWICK[1]

Kensington
Monday evg.
[Aug. 20, 1847]

MY DEAR CHADWICK—The enclosed speaks for itself & I have written it on a separate paper that it may more conveniently be sent to Mr. Stuart[2] if you see no objection. I should have spoken to you about it when I saw you, as well as renewed my thanks to you & Mrs Chadwick, if I had found you alone—but you will easily understand that I did not wish to admit any other persons to unnecessary confidences on my money affairs or those of my relations.

ever your most obliged
J. S. MILL.

1. MS at UCL. Endorsed in another hand: 1847 / On reading Settlement Evidence.
2. See *Parliamentary Papers*, 1847, XI, The Select Committee on Settlement and Removal, which contains evidence given by Chadwick in March, 1847. The settlement laws dealt with changes of residence by paupers as affecting their eligibility for relief.

* * * *

1. MS at UCL. *Addressed*: Edwin Chadwick Esq / Gwydyr House / Whitehall / and marked *private*. *Postmark*: AU 20 18?7.
Presumably refers to the financial transactions discussed in Letters 506, 508, and 515.
2. Identified only as William Stuart of Liverpool, evidently an agent in the financial transactions.

511. TO JOHN WILLIAM PARKER[1]

[Summer?, 1847]

MY DEAR SIR

I write this note to introduce to you Miss Hall,[2] who being unacquainted with the name of the present editor of Fraser's Magazine but understanding that you are now the publisher, is desirous of addressing herself to you on the subject of a contribution to the Magazine. I was well acquainted with her mother, the late Mrs. Hall, for whom I had a great respect & who had contributed several things to Fraser's Magazine in the time of Dr. Maginn.

Very truly yours
J. S. MILL

512. TO JOHN WILLIAM PARKER[1]

India House
27th October
1847

MY DEAR SIR

When I wrote to you hastily the other day about the Political Economy proposing that the conditions of our agreement should be the same as for the Logic, I had not referred to the agreement itself, & I did not know what I find to be the fact, that our engagement for the Logic was for *all future* editions. In the present case I do not wish to bind myself for the future, but to engage only for one edition, leaving the question entirely open as to future editions in case they should be wanted. This is the more reasonable, as there cannot this time be any considerable risk of loss, since the present book being on a popular subject is pretty sure to sell as many copies as will pay its expenses. It would probably be much more to my advantage to publish the Political Economy on my own account, which

1. MS at Pierpont Morgan Library. Parker's name does not appear on the letter; he had been JSM's publisher since 1843. Parker took over the publication of *Fraser's* beginning with Vol. XXXVI (July to Dec., 1847) from G. W. Nickisson, who published it from Jan., 1842 to June, 1847. The letter is undated, but the paper is watermarked 1847.

2. Not otherwise identified than as the daughter of Robert Hall, MD (1763–1824), explorer and writer on scientific subjects, and Agnes C. Hall (1777–1846), translator, novelist, and contributor to various periodicals, including *Fraser's*.

* * * *

1. MS in the Cornell University Library.

I am quite ready & disposed to do, if the publication of a single edition at half profit should not be agreeable to you.

Believe me
Very truly yours
J. S. MILL

513. TO WILLIAM E. HICKSON[1]

India House
15 Nov. 1847

MY DEAR HICKSON

To enable me to make up my mind decidedly on the question of resuming the Westminster or not, it would be necessary for me to know exactly the position & circumstances of the review. & in particular 1st the Average N° of copies sold. 2nd the annual expenses 3rd what replies per number it affords on the average for the payment of contributors.

If I had this information I could very speedily give you an answer.

Yours ever truly
J. S. MILL

514. TO EDWIN CHADWICK[1]

India House
19 Nov. 1847

MY DEAR CHADWICK

It would be great injustice to this article[2] to compare it with the review of the same book by Croker in the Quarterly,[3] but I am still more sorry to read it because its evident honesty and carefulness will make it a great deal more mischievous.

What I thought about Rubichon's book I have said in the Morning Chronicle of the 9th, 11th, 13th & 16th of last January.[4] It is I think right that the author of the article should see those papers, & should be aware of the facts & books there cited.

He will easily detect one error in the second article of the Chronicle, into which the Quarterly reviewer misled me. But it does not touch the main question.

I have acquired some additional facts of importance since that time: among others the last Census of the French population. I strongly recommend to the writer of the article M. Legoyt's paper on the Census, in the

1. MS in the possession of Miss D. Hickson, Claremont, Hove, Sussex, in 1944.

* * * *

1. MS at UCL. 2. Unidentified. 3. See Letter 497, n. 4.
4. *Ibid.* The book reviewed by Croker was *De l'Agriculture en France. . . .* Par M. L. Mounier avec des Remarques par M. [Maurice] Rubichon (2 vols., Paris, 1846).

Journal des Economistes for March & May last.[5] He will there find among other things that for the last quarter of a century the number of births has been stationary, & that the population is regularly though slowly increasing *solely* by diminution of the number of deaths, which is *less* in each quinquennial period. I ask any one whether that *could* be the case if M. Rubichon's representation of the state & tendency of things in France were true.

Ever truly yours

J. S. MILL.

515. TO EDWIN CHADWICK[1]

[Dec.?, 1847]

MY DEAR CHADWICK

I have mislaid Mr Stuart's[2] address & as I do not know if a letter addressed simply "Liverpool" would reach him, will you kindly fill up the address of the inclosed & send it to the post with your own letters. It is to inform him that the bill he remitted has been duly paid

I congratulate you on the *immediate* success of your first recommendation to the Govt.[3] It looks promising & like people in earnest

most truly yours

J. S. MILL

516. TO ROBERT BARCLAY FOX[1]

India House

6th Decr 1847

MY DEAR BARCLAY

I could almost reproach you for having thought it necessary to ask me whether I agree in the sentiments expressed in your letter. They are to me

5. Alfred Legoyt, "Recensement de la population de la France en 1846 . . ." *Journal des Economistes*, XVI (March, 1847), 337–46, and XVII (May, 1847), 169–94.

* * * *

1. MS at UCL. Note in another hand: "John Mill / 1847?" Dated by reference in second paragraph.

2. There is in the Chadwick papers at UCL the following receipt dated Oct. 29, 1847, and signed by JSM: "Received from Edwin Chadwick Esq. the three bills of exchange mentioned in a letter from William Stuart Esq. Liverpool, dated 28th October 1847."

3. Probably refers to the government's acceptance of the recommendation made by the Royal Commission of Inquiry into London sanitation to which Chadwick had been appointed in Aug. On Nov. 30, 1847, coincidental with the publication of the first report of the Commission, six of the London commissions of sewers were superseded and a new, central Metropolitan Commission of Sewers was established (see *The Times* for Dec. 2 (p. 4) and 3 (p. 6), 1847, and Finer, *Life and Times of Sir Edwin Chadwick*, pp. 316–17).

* * * *

1. MS in the possession of Mr. W. H. Browning.

part of my daily bread, & I have expressed them in the book you allude to (which is on the point of going to press) not as things in any way disputable, or requiring to be asserted, but as things undeniable by anybody who has the smallest capacity for speculating on the future. Such people however are miserably few, or we should not see the wretched attempts of newspaper writers at this very moment to persuade the English people that London will be sacked by the French if they don't protect it by a militia of 180,000 men & batteries all along the coast.[2] Such things are enough to drive one mad.

I am very happy that you still think of me sometimes. Pray give my kindest regards & Clara's to our friends at Falmouth. My other sisters are all away. *Ferraboschi*[3] is Jane's name. It is an Italian name, not a Slavonic.

Have you heard of the forthcoming reprint of some of Sterling's writings?[4] It is coming out with a kindly & graceful biographical introduction by Archdeacon Hare,[5] full of interesting extracts from his letters—doing justice to Sterling & mildly commenting on his heterodoxy—

Yours affectionately

J. S. Mill

517. TO WILLIAM E. HICKSON[1]

India House
Monday
[Dec. 6, 1847]

My dear Hickson

I have just received some slips of your article[2] which I will read carefully. I do not know anywhere of any full discussion of the difference between the rate of interest & the value of the circulating medium. Writers have generally supposed that it may be sufficient to *point out* the ambiguity

2. A furore had arisen over the state of the nation's defences, partly because of the publication on Nov. 29 in the *Morning Chronicle* of part of a letter of Jan. 9, 1847, by the Duke of Wellington to Sir John Burgoyne, sharply critical of the coastal defences. The *Examiner* later printed the whole letter (Jan. 8, 1848, p. 25). See also Sir Herbert Maxwell, *The Life of Wellington* (2 vols., London, 1899), II, 361–64.

3. Jane Stuart Mill had married Marcus Paul Ferraboschi on Sept. 28, 1847.

4. John Sterling, *Essays and Tales*, collected and edited, with a Memoir of his Life, by J. C. Hare (2 vols., London, 1848).

5. Julius Charles Hare (1795–1855), archdeacon of Lewes; Sterling had been his curate at Hurstmonceaux, 1834–35.

* * * *

1. MS at the Huntington Library.

2. Presumably the article "History and Exposition of the Currency Question," *WR*, XLVIII (Jan., 1848), 448–82.

& have noticed it as Tooke does in chap. 13 of his "Inquiry into the Currency Principle."[3] I have gone a little more into it in my forthcoming book.[4]

yours ever

J. S. MILL

518. TO J. F. MOLLETT[1]

[Dec., 1847]

SIR—I have much pleasure in enclosing a subscription towards the testimonial to Mr. Lovett,[2] whom I respect as the chief among that portion of the Chartists who make the improvement of the working classes as much an object as their emancipation, & who are free from the reproach commonly made against democrats of desiring to bring political franchises down to their own level but no further. By including the political equality of women among their principles they shew that their object is the general good & not merely their own.

In expressing however my concurrence in the purpose[3] [*interlined*] of the circular you have addressed to me, may I be allowed to declare my dissent from that portion of it in which a refusal to serve in the militia is put forward as a claim to admiration,[4] as I regard such a refusal as one

3. Thomas Tooke, *An Inquiry into the Currency Principle* (London, 1844).
4. *Principles of Political Economy*, Book III, chaps. VIII and XXIII.

* * * *

1. *Addressed*: J. F. Mollett / 27 Nelson Terrace / Stoke Newington. MS draft on folio 32v of the MS of JSM's *Political Economy* (the press copy of the first [1848] edition), at the Pierpont Morgan Library. This draft is written over another, pencilled draft of the same letter. The existence of this and the following letter was called to the attention of the editor by Professor J. M. Robson.

J. F. Mollett, identified only as a friend and associate of the Chartist leader William Lovett (see his *Life and Struggles of William Lovett* [London, 1876], p. 333). Letter 520 is clearly in reply to Mollett's answer to this letter.

2. Early in the following year Lovett was presented with a public testimonial at the National Hall along with a silver tea-service and a purse of 140 sovereigns (see Lovett, *Life*).
3. Substituted for *object*.
4. Lovett had long been an opponent of compulsory military service. In 1831 upon his refusal to serve or provide a substitute some of his household goods had been confiscated (see Lovett, *Life*, pp. 65–67).

of the mistakes of youthful enthusiasm, & the mention of it as a blunder.[5] I am Sir

yr obedient servant

JSM

I have handed the circular to such of my acquaintance as I thought likely to feel interested in the[6] subscription.

519. TO WILLIAM ELLIS[1]

[Dec., 1847]

DEAR ELLIS. Have you seen the inclosed Circular? it may perhaps not have been sent to you, and has only been sent to me within the last few days.[2] They do not seem to be taking any effectual means of making it known[3]

520. TO J. F. MOLLETT[1]

30th December 1847

SIR,—Your note of the 30th places Mr. Lovett's refusal to serve in the militia[2] in a different light from that in which I had considered it. Knowing nothing of the fact except from your circular, I had surmised that it might have been founded on such principles as those professed by the Peace Society,[3] principles with which I wholly disagree, as, though I think it an

5. This paragraph is a revision of a preceding paragraph of the draft, which reads as follows: If I may be allowed to remark on the contents of the circular you have addressed to me I sh^{d}. say that I sh^{d} be sorry to [see my name following *cancelled*] give any countenance which my name might afford to [the *cancelled*] a refus.

6. The following words, "purpose of it," have been cancelled.

* * * *

1. MS draft on folio 33V of the MS of JSM's *Political Economy* (see preceding letter, n. 1) at the Pierpont Morgan Library. From its position in the MS of the *Political Economy* and from its content, the inference seems valid that it refers to the subscription for William Lovett.

William Ellis (1800–1881), economist, insurance executive, and educational reformer and philanthropist. He had been a member of JSM's Utilitarian Society, 1823–26.

2. This sentence replaces the following cancelled words: As it has only been sent to me within the last few days.

3. The draft bears no signature.

* * * *

1. Published in Elliot, I, 133–34. MS at Leeds. Evidently a reply to Mollett's answer to Letter 518.

2. See Letter 518, n. 4.

3. The Society for the Promotion of Permanent and Universal Peace, usually known as the London Peace Society, founded in 1816 by William Allen (1770–1843), friend of James Mill (see Christina Phelps, *The Anglo-American Peace Movement in the Mid-Nineteenth Century* [New York, 1930], pp. 37, 43–44).

effect of the progress of improvement to put an end to war, I regard war as an infinitely less evil than systematic submission to injustice.

With the principles on which it appears that Mr. Lovett really acted I have much more sympathy, though I do not think, to use your words, that "he would have been false to the principles he professed had he acted otherwise," any more than I think him bound by those principles to refuse the payment of taxes. To resist a social system which one thinks wrong by disobeying the laws in detail must, I think, depend for its justification in each particular case on the circumstances and motives which dictated it; but if adopted and acted upon as a principle it would render government impossible under any institutions yet devised, since, in a democracy, minorities might claim and exercise the right of obstructing the execution of all laws which they disapproved.

• • • 1848 • • •

521. TO AUBREY DE VERE[1]

India House
February 3, 1848

MY DEAR SIR,—I am ashamed not to have sooner acknowledged your kind present of your book on Ireland,[2] especially as I read it immediately on receiving it. Anything you write on Ireland must be well worth attending to, as no one can doubt who has read your Evidence before Lord Monteagle's Committee[3]—to say nothing of anything else. No one can sympathise more than I do in the feeling which pervades your book, that England is not entitled to throw the first stone at Ireland, being, so far as that expression can be used of a nation, guilty of all the guilt as well as of all the suffering and folly of Ireland. I have always strenuously urged the same doctrine in all I have ever written or said about Irish affairs, which is not a little in quantity at least. I agree too in most of the opinions you express, except that I look much more than you do to reclamation of waste lands and alteration of landed tenures, and less to emigration as a remedy. Perhaps also I should not let off the generality of Irish landlords quite so easily as you do, though there are among them not a few of the most meritorious landlords (probably) upon earth.

Very truly yours,
J. S. MILL

522. TO JOHN AUSTIN[1]

India House
22^d Feb. 1848

MY DEAR AUSTIN

The enclosed pages, of which I beg your acceptance, contain the only alterations *in opinion* in the 2^d edition of the Logic. Whatever other alterations were made, are little more than verbal.

1. Published in Wilfrid Ward, *Aubrey de Vere, a Memoir* (London, 1904), p. 132. MS not located.
Aubrey de Vere (1814–1902), Irish poet.
2. *English Misrule and Irish Misdeeds* (London, 1848).
3. Thomas Spring-Rice, first Baron Monteagle of Brandon (1790–1866), Whig leader. See *Report from the Lords select committee on colonization from Ireland*. H.C. 1847 (737), vi; (737 II), vi.

* * * *

1. MS at LSE.

I do not suppose the Pol. Economy will call upon *you* for any changes of opinion, as I imagine you agree with me in sticking pretty closely to Ricardo on the points which he touched. I doubt if there will be a single opinion (on pure political economy) in the book, which may not be exhibited as a corollary from his doctrines.

Your approbation of the Logic is of great value to me.

Yours ever truly
J. S. MILL

523. TO HENRY S. CHAPMAN[1]

India House.
29 February, 1848.

MY DEAR CHAPMAN,—

I have owed you a letter for a long time, and I am now very glad that I put off writing, as it enables me to be one of the first to tell you of the extraordinary events of the last week at Paris, a second "three days" ending in the proclamation of a French Republic.[2] I am hardly yet out of breath from reading and thinking about it. Nothing can possibly exceed the importance of it to the world or the immensity of the interests which are at stake on its success. I need not go through the course of the events, as you will learn all that from the newspapers, and I hardly know at what end to begin in commenting upon it. The republicans have succeeded because *at last* they had the good sense to raise the standard not of a republic but of something in which the middle classes could join, viz., electoral reform—then the madness of Louis Philippe and Guizot in forbidding, at the last moment, the reform banquet at Paris, stirred up the people, and after three days very like the former three, in each of which some great concession was made just too late, ending with Louis Philippe's abdication and flight, the republicans remained masters of Paris and France, and formed a Provisional Government in which the two most powerful men are Marrast, editor of the "National," and, who would ever have thought it—Lamartine![3] In my meditations and feelings on the whole matter, every second thought has been of Carrel—he who perhaps alone in Europe was qualified to direct

1. MS in the possession of Mrs. W. Rosenberg. From copy supplied by Professor J. M. McCrimmon.

2. The Revolution of 1848 had broken out on Feb. 23, Louis Philippe had abdicated on the 24th, and Lamartine on behalf of a provisional government had proclaimed a republic.

3. Alphonse de Lamartine (1792–1869), poet, historian, and statesman.

such a movement, to have perished uselessly, and the very man who killed him, now a prominent reformer[4]—the man who went to Louis Philippe and told him that he must abdicate! Without Carrel, or, I fear, any one comparable to him, the futurity of France and of Europe is most doubtful. Hitherto, however, nothing can be more admirable than the conduct both of the Provisional Government and of the people. It makes even base English journalists enthusiastic. The whole thing also is very well taken here. Nobody seems the least uneasy or terrified at the idea of a French republic. Indeed they do not seem half as much alarmed as there is reason to be. The dangers are, first of war: an article in the "National" to-day is, however, very rassurant, shewing so exactly the right feeling and opinions on the subject that one could not wish to alter a word. Still, the state of Italy and the certainty of an immediate rising all over Lombardy which I cannot believe that the other nations would look on and see put down, will make it hardly possible to hold back the French people from interfering. Secondly, Communism has now for the first time a deep root, and has spread widely in France, and a large part of the effective republican strength is more or less imbued with it. The Provisional Government is obliged to coquet with this, and to virtually promise work and good wages to the whole labouring class: how are they to keep their promise, and what will be the consequences of not keeping it? Meantime a National Assembly is to be called, elected no doubt by universal suffrage, in which all the sense and all the nonsense of France will be represented, and in which there is pretty sure to be at once a schism between the bourgeois and the operatives—a Gironde and a Montagne, though probably without any guillotine. What an anxious time it will be. If France succeeds in establishing a republic and reasonable republican government, all the rest of Europe, except England and Russia, will be republicanised in ten years, and England itself probably before we die. There never was a time when so great a drama was being played out in one generation. I pity those who, like you, hear of these things from the Antipodes.

But I can tell you nothing worth hearing that you will not learn from the journals. I really *know* nothing myself, for though I know several of the marked men I do not know whether they have in them ideas and knowledge and vigour for such a task as they have before them. In a month or two I shall be able to give you a better opinion about probabilities.

Thanks for the information you sent me about New Zealand affairs, and thanks for your beautiful set of ferns which arrived safe, in perfect condition, and gave me great pleasure. I shall wish much to hear how the

4. Emile de Girardin (1806–1881), journalist and politician, had killed Carrel in a duel in 1836.

colonists like the suspension of their Constitution,[5] and what you in particular think of it. I have no inclination to write about any minor or personal matters at such a time as this.

I saw John Revans yesterday, who had come over on sundry matters, but in particular to push a scheme of his for a general Tax on Expenditure on which he published a very clever pamphlet.[6]

Yours always,
J. S. MILL

524. TO SARAH AUSTIN[1]

India House
7th March
1848

DEAR MRS. AUSTIN—I suppose by this time you are quite convinced that the English at Paris are not in the smallest danger,[2] & that there is no likelihood of any manifestations by the English Government or press which can give umbrage to the French people. I presume the roads are now open, & passports may be had by those who desire them. It was very natural that the Provisional Gov[t] should exert its temporary dictatorship to prevent a precipitate flight of foreigners *en masse*, not only because a panic always tends to spread, but because a sudden diminution of employment for the population of Paris would have been a great element of disorder. Next to the admirable conduct of the people & of the new authorities, the most striking thing in these memorable events is the evidence afforded of the complete change of times—The instantaneous & unanimous acquiescence of all France in a republic—while in this country as far as I can perceive, there is not a particle of the dread & uneasiness which there would have been a few years ago at the idea of a French republic. There is a strong, & a very friendly interest felt in the position of France, & in the new & difficult questions which the republican government will have to solve—especially those relating to labour & wages. For my part I feel the strongest confidence that what will be done or attempted on that subject will end in

5. Royal assent was given to the New Zealand Government Bill on March 7, 1848, suspending the constitution granted in 1846.

6. John Revans, *A Per-Centage Tax on Domestic Expenditures to Supply the Whole of the Public Revenue* . . . (London, 1847). Revans was a brother of Samuel Revans, a fellow colonist of Chapman.

* * * *

1. Published in Elliot, I, 134–35, but dated Feb. 27. MS in the Royal Library, Copenhagen, Denmark.

2. See preceding letter.

good. There will be doubtless a good deal of experimental legislation, some of it not very prudent, but there cannot be a better place to try such experiments in than France. I suppose that regulation of industry in behalf of the labourers must go through its various phases of abortive experiment, just as regulation of industry in behalf of the capitalist has done, before it is abandoned, or its proper limits ascertained.

Who can it be that takes Mr Austin's name in the Times,[3] & attempts to imitate his style? I am afraid the letter signed "John Austin" must have been seen by many who never saw the disavowal of it, in an obscure corner of the paper: & there were several things in it which it is very disagreeable that Mr Austin should be supposed to have written—especially the flattery of the Times, the meanest, most malicious & most hypocritical among our very low newspaper press.

Very truly yours,

J. S. Mill

525. TO SARAH AUSTIN[1]

March [?], 1848.

Dear Mrs. Austin,—I return to you Mr. Austin's letter. I never thought I should have differed from him so widely in feeling on any public event as it appears I do on this. But I cannot think myself unfeeling because I do not attach all the importance which (no doubt from his and your personal relations with some of those concerned) he seems to attach to the effect of the Revolution on individual interests. The monetary crisis in London last October produced quite as much suffering to individuals as has arisen, or, as far as I can see, is likely to arise, from an event which has broken the fetters of all Europe.[2] If it had done no more than emancipate some millions of serfs in Hungary,[3] that, in my eyes, would have been a hundredfold compensation. As for future prospects, nobody, I suppose, is so foolish as not to see that there are many unfavourable chances. But to suppose that the unfavourable chances preponderate seems to me, I confess, as much a "dream" as the contrary expectation appears to you. And my hopes rise instead of sinking as the state of things in France unfolds itself.

3. A letter from Paris, dated Jan. 12, signed John Austin, on the feelings of the French towards the English, *The Times*, Jan. 14, 1848, p. 4.

* * * *

1. Published in Elliot, I, 135–36. MS not located.
2. The success of the Feb. revolution in France set off revolutions in a number of countries.
3. In March a revolution had led to the abolition of serfdom by the Diet of Hungary.

526. TO ARMAND MARRAST[1]

[May?], 1848

MON CHER M. MARRAST,—Je vous ai adressé un exemplaire d'un traité d'économie politique que je viens de publier,[2] et dans lequel je discute quelques unes des grandes questions sociales dont le gouvernement républicain et l'assemblée nationale auront à s'occuper. Je ne puis espérer qu'au milieu des graves occupations qui vous obsèdent,[3] vous ayez du temps disponible pour la lecture d'un ouvrage théorique. Mais, comme je crois pouvoir affirmer que l'esprit de ce livre est propre à lui assurer votre sympathie, je vous l'offre, afin que si vous ne le lisez pas, vous puissiez, au moins, si vous le jugez à propos, le faire lire à d'autres.

J'ai encore un autre but en vous écrivant. Je ne veux pas m'étendre en phrases générales sur la sympathie profonde que j'éprouve et dois éprouver pour l'œuvre de régénération sociale qui se poursuit maintenant en France. Il faudrait n'avoir aucun sentiment de l'avenir de l'humanité pour ne pas reconnaître que, grâce à la noble initiative prise par la France, ce qui se débat aujourd'hui sur son terrain est l'affaire du genre humain tout entier. Je voudrais ne pas me borner à une stérile admiration, je désirerais apporter à cette grande œuvre mon contingent d'idées et tout ce que j'ai d'utile dans l'intelligence, du moins, jusqu'à ce que mon propre pays, si arriéré à beaucoup d'égards comparé au vôtre, en ait besoin. Je sais que vous ne dirigez plus le *National*, mais votre influence y doit encore dominer; je vous demande, donc, s'il pourrait convenir à ce journal d'accepter de moi quelques articles que je ferais de temps en temps, soit sur l'état de choses en Angleterre, soit portant sur les questions de politique, générale et sociale. J'essaierais de faire en sorte qu'on pût se dispenser d'un traducteur si vous trouvez mon français assez supportable pour qu'après une révision préalable il puisse passer. Il me semble qu'en designant cette correspondance par une épigraphe particulière, comme par exemple, "Lettres d'un Anglais,"[4] on mettrait suffisamment à couvert la responsibilité du journal tant à l'égard du style qu'à celui des opinions. Au reste, la correspondance serait complètement dans le sens du *National*, en tant qu'il s'est prononcé, jusqu'ici; je ne puis donner trop d'éloges au bon sens dont le journal a fait preuve en toute occasion depuis février. En tout cas, que mes idées se trouvassent en unisson ou en désaccord avec celles du journal, la rédaction resterait seul

1. Published in Elliot, I, 136–37. MS not located, except for fragment at LSE. Approximately dated by the first sentence.
2. His *Principles of Political Economy* was published on April 25, 1848.
3. Marrast was then a member of the Provisional Government of France, serving as Mayor of Paris.
4. Nothing seems to have come of this offer.

juge de leur opportunité. Si l'on accepte ma proposition, il va sans dire que cette collaboration sera gratuite, en ce que concerne la rétribution pécuniare.—Votre dévoué,

J. S. MILL

527. TO EUGÈNE SUE[1]

[May?], 1848.

MONSIEUR,—J'ai pris la liberté de vous adresser un exemplaire d'un traité que je viens de publier sur l'économie politique et sur quelques unes de ses applications à la science sociale.

Ne vous effrayez pas du nom de cet ouvrage. Je vous l'offre pour deux motifs principaux, dont l'un me regarde plus particulièrement moi-même, tandis que l'autre se rapporte à mes sentiments envers vous.

Quant au premier, j'avoue que j'ai eu envie de vous prouver qu'on peut être économiste, et même professer un grand nombre des opinions de Malthus et de Ricardo, sans être pour cela un Duriveau,[2] ou un flatteur des Duriveau. Je vous dirai en outre comme fait, que quant aux Duriveau de mon pays si toutefois il y en a, ceux qui se font tous instruments, non seulement, ne professent pas les opinions de ces économistes, mais en général les puent et les conspuent, presqu'autant que vous.

Mon second motif c'est le désir de vous témoigner la vive sympathie que j'éprouve pour le noble esprit de justice et de progrès dont vos derniers romans sont pénétrés, et pour quelques idées capables dont vous vous y êtes fait l'organe. Mon livre vous prouvera que sur la grande question de l'héritage je suis absolument de l'avis du docteur Just;[3] tandis que sur le mariage et sur l'entière égalité de droits entre les hommes et les femmes les opinions de l'auteur de "Martin" et du "Juif Errant"[4] sont non seulement les miennes mais j'ai la conviction profonde que la liberté, la démocratie, la fraternité, ne sont nulle part si ce n'est dans ces opinions, et que l'avenir du progrès social et moral ne se trouve que là.

1. Published in Elliot, I, p. 137–38. MS not located.

Eugène Sue (1804–1857), voluminous and sensational novelist. JSM had published in the *Examiner* (Dec. 11, 1847, p. 787) a letter remonstrating against an attack on Sue's novel *Martin l'enfant trouvé* (12 vols., Paris, 1846–47) and maintaining that the work did inculcate sound principles.

2. Count Duriveau is the evil master of the foundling Martin in the novel referred to above.

3. Dr. Just Clément, another character in the novel.

4. *Juif errant* (10 vols., Paris, 1844–45).

528. TO EDWARD GIBBON WAKEFIELD[1]

India House
Thursday
[1848]

MY DEAR WAKEFIELD,

I am very glad that you think the public statement in my book,[2] of what is so justly due to you both as a colonizer & as a political economist, likely to be of use at this particular time. I am still more glad to hear that you are writing the book you speak of.[3] I have long regretted that there does not exist a systematic treatise, in a permanent form, from your hand and with your name, in which the whole subject of Colonization is treated, as the express subject of the book—so as to become at once the authoritative book on the subject. At present people have to *pick up* your doctrines, both theoretical & practical. I cannot help urging you to complete the book, with as much expedition as is consistent with the care due to your health, which your life is too valuable to permit any relaxation of.

ever truly yours,
J. S. MILL

529. TO WILLIAM E. HICKSON[1]

India House
18th August 1848

MY DEAR HICKSON

M. Desainteville[2] whom you perhaps remember, has written to me to say that he wrote, as long ago as 1840, an article on the Polytechnic School[3] which he offered to you, through me; which was accepted, & for which he was to have £10, & did receive £5 on account, but has never since heard anything of the other £5 or of the article. I remember something passed about an article on the Polytechnic School by Desainteville, but not what it was. You may perhaps have a more precise recollection. He says that £5

1. Published in Richard Garnett, *Edward Gibbon Wakefield* (London, 1897), pp. xvi, xvii. MS in Brit. Mus.
2. *Political Economy*, Book II, chap. XIII, sec. 4, and the last chapter.
3. *A View of the Art of Colonization* . . . (London, 1849).

* * * *

1. MS at the Huntington Library.
2. JSM and Mrs. Taylor had known B. E. Desainteville, a Frenchman living in London, as early as 1830 (see Hayek, p. 37).
3. D., "The Polytechnic School of Paris," *WR*, XXXVI (Oct., 1841), 331–58.

would be of consequence to him just now. He says also that if the article is not to be made use of he much wishes that it could be found & returned to him.

Very truly yours
J. S. MILL

530. TO WILLIAM E. HICKSON[1]

I.H.
Monday [Aug. 21 (?), 1848]

DEAR HICKSON

My best plan is to send you Desainteville's letter which contains all the information I have. From my own recollection I am unable to say anything on the subject.

D. seems to be unaware of the article's having ever appeared in the review.[2]

Very truly yours
J. S. MILL

I sent the Pol. Ec. to the Journal des Economistes *as I thought*, i.e. I sent it to Dussard as editor. I must however inquire about it.

531. TO JOHN PRINGLE NICHOL[1]

India House,
30th September, 1848.

MY DEAR NICHOL,

You may well call Comte's a strange book.[2] I agree with you too that it is well calculated to stir the mind and create a ferment of thought, chiefly, I think, because it is the first book which has given a coherent picture of a supposed future of humanity with a look of possibility about it, and with enough of *feature* for the reason and imagination to lay hold of it by. To me the chief worth of the book seems to consist in, first, the systematic and earnest inculcation of the purely *subordinate* role of the intellect as the minister of the higher sentiments. Second, in making much clearer, than to me they ever were before, the grounds for believing that the *culte de*

1. MS at the Huntington Library. 2. See preceding letter.

* * * *

1. Published by Knight, pp. 676–77. MS not located.
2. *Discours sur l'ensemble du Positivisme* (Paris, July, 1848).

l'humanité is capable of fully supplying the place of a religion, or rather (to say the truth) of *being* a religion—and this he has done, notwithstanding the ridiculousness which everybody must feel in his premature attempts to define in detail the *practices* of this *culte*. In most of the other doctrines of the book I wholly dissent from him. With all his science he is characteristically and resolutely ignorant of the laws of the formation of character; and he assumes the differences which he sees between women and men, philosophers and men of action, rich people and proletarians (or rather between the limited specimens of each class which come within the scanty means of knowledge of a recluse, whose knowledge even of books is purposely restricted)—all these differences he assumes as ultimate, or at least necessary facts, and he grounds universal principles of sociology on them. These principles too, when reduced to practice, would be the most contrary to human liberty of any now taught or professed; for it seems to me that he would make everybody's way of life (or at all events after one choice) as inexorably closed against all change of destination or purpose, as he would make the marriage-contract. In all this, and most emphatically in all his doctrines about women, I think and have always thought him in a radically wrong road, and likely to go farther and farther wrong, and I think his political writings (apart from his admirable historical views) likely to be mischievous rather than useful; except *quâ* socialist, that is, calling for an entire renovation of social institutions and doctrines, in which respect I am entirely at one with him.

It is wretched to see the cause of *legitimate* Socialism thrown so far back by the spirit of reaction against that most unhappy outbreak at Paris in June.[3] Still it makes one better pleased with Humanity in its present state than I ever hoped to be, to see that there are, at least in France, so many men in conspicuous station who have sincerely every noble feeling and purpose with respect to mankind, which one thought was confined to perhaps a dozen people in Europe. I believe that the principal members of the Provisional Government, and many of the party who adhere to them, most purely and disinterestedly desired (and still seek to realize) all of "liberty, equality and fraternity," which is capable of being realized now, and to prepare the way for all which can be realized hereafter. I feel an entireness of sympathy with them which I never expected to have with any political party.

If you have not read it, read Lamartine's beautiful *Histoire des Girondins*.[4] I think his whole conception of the great socialist questions, so far as there stated, and especially of the question of Property, as summed up in

3. Extremists of the left had attempted to overthrow the new government, and much blood was shed before order was restored.

4. Alphonse de Lamartine, *Histoire des Girondins* (8 vols., Paris, 1847).

his criticism on the measures of the Convention at the end of the fifth volume, everything that can be desired; and the whole book (which I have never read till now, indeed I have not yet finished it) exactly such as I should have expected from his consistently noble conduct since February. I also sympathise very strongly with such socialists as Louis,[5] who seems to be sincere, enthusiastic, straightforward, and with a great foundation of good sense and feeling, though precipitate and *raw* in his practical views. He has been abominably treated about the insurrectionary movements, of which I believe him to be as innocent as you or me. Our newspaper writers, and especially those of *The Times*, ought to be flogged at a cart's tail for their disgusting misrepresentations and calumnies of such men, directly in the face of the evidence they pretended to found their assertions upon; and I would very willingly help to apply the *cat* to any one of them.

Thanks for the pamphlet of which I have only yet read the title-page, but *that* proves to me that the author is in the right road.

Ever most truly yours,

J. S. MILL

532. TO JOHN JAY[1]

[Nov., 1848]

DEAR SIR,—Permit me to return you my best thanks for your handsome present of the American edition of my "Political Economy."[2] . . .

I am obliged to you also for the *North American Review* containing an article on my book.[3] The article is laudatory enough to satisfy an appetite for praise much stronger than mine. But the writer is one whose tone of thinking and feeling is extremely repugnant to me. He gives a totally false idea of the book and of its author when he makes me a participant in the derision with which he speaks of Socialists of all kinds and degrees. I have expressed temperately and argumentatively my objections to the particular plans proposed by Socialists for dispensing with private property; but on

5. Louis Blanc (1811?–1882), historian and socialist politician. After the defeat of the workers in the Paris revolt of June, 1848, he was forced into an exile which lasted until 1871. He had recently arrived in England. As noted later in this letter, *The Times* had been especially savage in its criticism of him (see *The Times*, Sept. 7, 1848, p. 4, and Sept. 12, 1848, p. 4). *The Times* on the latter date also printed a long letter from Blanc defending his conduct.

* * * *

1. Published in Elliot, I, 138–39. MS not located.
John Jay (1817–1894), American lawyer, author, and diplomat.

2. The American edition had been published in Boston by C. C. Little and J. Brown. The ellipsis following this sentence is Elliot's.

3. Vol. LXVII (Oct., 1848), 370–419. The article also reviewed J. R. McCulloch's *A Treatise on the Succession to Property Vacant by Death* (London, 1848).

many other important points I agree with them, and on none do I feel towards them anything but respect, thinking, on the contrary, that they are the greatest element of improvement in the present state of mankind. If the chapter in which I mention them had been written after instead of before the late revolutions on the Continent I should have entered more fully into my opinions on Socialism and have done it much more justice.

On the population question my difference with the reviewer is fundamental, and in the incidental reference which he makes to my assertion of equality of political rights and of social position in behalf of women, the tone assumed by him is really below contempt. But I fear that a country where institutions profess to be founded on equality, and which yet maintains the slavery of black men and of all women, will be one of the last to relinquish that other servitude.

533. TO GEORGE JACOB HOLYOAKE[1]

India House
7th Decr 1848

SIR,—What in your note of the 22nd you ask me to do, would be to write a dissertation on morality, which at present I have not time for. But the root of my difference with you is that you appear to accept the present constitution of the family & the whole of the priestly morality founded on & connected with it—which morality in my opinion thorough deserves the epithets of "intolerant, slavish & selfish".

It was quite unnecessary to return my notes,[2] as it is a matter of complete indifference to me whom they are seen by.

Yours truly,
J. S. MILL

534. TO ÉMILE LITTRÉ[1]

22nd December 1848

MONSIEUR,—J'ai eu l'honneur de recevoir votre circulaire au sujet de M. Comte. Je vous envoie ci-joint un billet de 250 francs comme contribution mais non comme cotisation annuelle. Je vous prie de vouloir bien m'en accuser réception. Je regrette d'apprendre que la position pécuniaire de

1. MS in the possession of Co-operative Union Ltd., Holyoake House, Manchester. Quoted in part by Joseph McCabe, *Life and Letters of George Jacob Holyoake* (2 vols., London, 1908), I, p. 339, and II, pp. 64–65.

2. For information on these see *ibid.*, II, 64, and G. J. Holyoake, *John Stuart Mill as Some of the Working Classes Knew Him* (London, 1873), p. 26.

* * * *

1. Published in Elliot, I, 139. MS not located.

M. Comte vient d'être encore empirée.[2] J'ai une très haute estime pour ses travaux en ce qui regarde la théorie de la méthode positive, mais je suis très éloigné de sa manière d'appliquer cette méthode aux questions sociales. La plupart de ses opinions sociologiques sont diamétralement opposées aux miennes.

Additional Letters

23A. TO THOMAS COATES[1]

1 Queen Square Westminster
23^d January 1829

SIR,

I have the honor to request that you will submit to the Committee of the Society for the Diffusion of Useful Knowledge, the accompanying Treatise, which if thought worthy of a place in the Library of U.K. [Useful Knowledge], I beg may be considered as a gratuitous contribution to that work.

Some expressions will be found in this tract, implying the previous publication of a Treatise on Wages, which has already been submitted to the Committee by Mr Edward Strutt. Should that Treatise fail of being accepted by the Committee, it will be necessary that the present one should be materially altered, or perhaps entirely withdrawn.[2]

I have the honor to be
Sir
Your obed^t Servt
J. S. MILL.

Thomas Coates Esq.

2. When his salary had been further reduced, Littré with others published an appeal for subscriptions. Comte henceforth until his death in 1857 subsisted on such gifts.

* * * *

1. *Addressed*: Thomas Coates Esq. / Secretary to the Society for the Diffusion / of Useful Knowledge. *Bears note*: 23^d. Jany. 1829. M^r. J S. Mill / w^h. M.S. Pol. Econ^y. / (ans^d. TKC [?]). MS at UCL.

Thomas Coates, solicitor, associate of William Tooke, served as secretary of the S.D.U.K. from its inception in 1826. From 1832 to 1835 he was the first secretary to the Council of the University of London.

2. Neither treatise was published. This appears to be the only mention in extant papers of JSM's having written such a treatise. It antedated by about two years the essays on political economy planned and partly written by him and George John Graham (see Letter 43, n. 14).

184A. TO THOMAS CARLYLE[1]

I.H.
Friday
[Dec. 9, 1836]

MY DEAR CARLYLE

Let it be Wortley[2] by all means, & I will immediately get the book.

209A. TO HENRY MILL[1]

[July 6, 1837]

Ιωαννης Δερικῳ χαιρειν. Επειδη, ὠ δερικε, εμε τῃ Φρι ἡμερᾳ, και μη τῃ Κρονου ἡμερᾳ, προς ὑμας ἡκειν δει· τουτου ἑνεκα ὑμας, ὠ φιλοι, ἁμαξαν τινα ἡ Φαεθοντα μισθοῦσθαι χρη, ὁπως Κρονου ἡμερᾳ ἑις Ἡλιου δυοντος κωμην, και Θεου λιθον, πορευωμεν.

Εν τοις ὑγροις, ὠ δερικε, της Ποταμου πηγης, μεγα φυτον ἑωρακα, και επιθυμῶ ἑχειν· αλλ' ἰσως ἑυρηκας ἀυτο, ἡ εν ποταμου πηγῃ, ἡ εν τῳ Ὀυιλδῳ. Χαιρε.

Ινδικου ὀικου.

1. MS fragment in the Luther Brewer Collection of the University of Iowa. Evidently an answer to Carlyle's letter of Dec. 8, 1836 (in A. Carlyle, pp. 141–42). Presumably Carlyle tore off the top of the letter and sent it on to Leigh Hunt, since it bears the following note in Carlyle's hand: "My dear Sir, / Here is Mill's answer about the *Wortley*: I suppose the Book will come one of these days. / T.C."

2. Lady Mary Wortley Montagu, *Letters and Works*, ed. Lord Wharncliffe (3 vols., London, 1837), which Leigh Hunt was proposing to review. See Letters 196, 198, 199, and 202.

* * * *

1. *Addressed*: Mr. Henry Mill / Park Place / Sevenoaks / Kent. *Postmark*: PAID / LS / 6 JY 6 / 1837. MS at LSE. Henry ("Derry") was presumably spending his vacation in Kent, probably with his family, who ordinarily spent a good part of the summer away from London.

The editor is greatly indebted to Mr. C. G. Allen of the Library of the London School of Economics and to Mr. C. E. Hubbard of the staff of the Royal Botanic Gardens, Kew, for help in identifying the placenames and providing the following translation.

"John sends greeting to Derry. Since I must come to you on Friday and not on Saturday, you, my dears, must therefore hire a carriage or phaeton so that on Saturday we can go to the village of setting Sun [Westerham] and to stone of God [Godstone].

"In the wet parts of the source of River [Riverhead] I have seen a large plant and want to have it. But perhaps you have found it either in [Riverhead] or in [the Weald?]. / India House."

Mr. C. E. Hubbard writes: "*The* Weald, rather than the village of Weald, certainly seems indicated for 'en to Ouildo'. But we are quite at a loss to suggest a possible identity for the 'large plant'. So far as we know, the Riverhead region is not noted for any specially interesting or uncommon plant that might answer to this description. One could think, for example, of *Rumex hydrolapathum* L. or *Archangelica officinalis* Hoffm. as large marsh plants that might attract the eye of a schoolboy, but these would be only shots in the dark."

Indexes

GENERAL INDEX

THE TEXT of the notes as well as of the letters has been analysed in the preparation of this index. Included are titles of books and articles mentioned or alluded to by JSM, but titles of works cited as references in the notes have been excluded. Listed under the heading "Mill, John Stuart," are a small number of subheadings (plus an alphabetical list of his writings mentioned in the text) which it seemed more appropriate to group thus rather than distribute throughout the Index. Page numbers in bold-face type indicate the location of notes identifying recipients of letters and persons mentioned in them. Place names have not been listed unless they appeared to have some significance.

INDEX OF CORRESPONDENTS

THIS INDEX includes only letters written by JSM. Excerpts quoted from letters written *to* JSM are listed in the general index under the respective names of the writers. In the following list, previously unpublished letters are indicated by an asterisk. Letters that contain previously unpublished passages are indicated by a dagger.

www.ingramcontent.com/pod-product-compliance
Lightning Source LLC
LaVergne TN
LVHW080402090826
844660LV00054B/1252

* 9 7 8 1 4 4 2 6 3 1 4 8 9 *